# BUSINESS MATH

## Eighth Edition

## CHERYL CLEAVES
Southwest Tennessee Community College

## MARGIE HOBBS
The University of Mississippi

PEARSON
Prentice Hall

Upper Saddle River, New Jersey
Columbus, Ohio

**Library of Congress Control Number:** 2007936418

**Editor in Chief:** Vernon R. Anthony
**Senior Acquisitions Editor:** Gary Bauer
**Editorial Assistant:** Kathleen Rowland
**Development Editor:** Ohlinger Publishing Services
**Production Editor:** Louise N. Sette
**Design Coordinator:** Diane Ernsberger
**AV Project Manager:** Janet Portisch
**Cover Designer:** Wanda Espana
**Senior Operations Supervisor:** Patricia Tonneman
**Director of Marketing:** David Gesell
**Marketing Manager:** Leigh Ann Sims
**Marketing Coordinator:** Alicia Dysert

This book was set in Times Roman by Aptara, Inc. It was printed and bound by R.R. Donnelley & Sons Company. The cover was printed by Phoenix Color Corp.

Pearson Education Ltd.
Pearson Education Singapore Pte. Ltd.
Pearson Education Canada, Ltd.
Pearson Education—Japan

Pearson Education Australia Pty. Limited
Pearson Education North Asia Ltd.
Pearson Educación de Mexico, S.A. de C.V.
Pearson Education Malaysia Pte. Ltd.

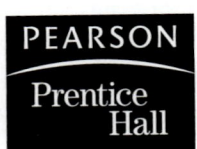

10 9 8 7 6 5 4 3 2 1
ISBN 13: 978-0-13-159121-9
ISBN 10:    0-13-159121-5

# FROM THE AUTHORS

## About the 8th Edition of Business Math

The focus of the 8th edition of *Business Math* is to provide you with the tools you will need to solve mathematical problems you will encounter in both your personal and business lives. We present math in familiar contexts: math needed for everyday business transactions, math needed to make important personal finance decisions, and math needed to start or run a small business.

To carry out these themes, we strengthened the content and added new topics where appropriate. We expanded coverage of the math needed for everyday business transactions by providing additional exercises and examples of realistic business transactions. We sharpened the focus of math needed to manage personal finances by providing examples, exercises, and concept analysis questions that require you to think about your personal financial plans so you learn how to manage your money and make more intelligent transaction and investment decisions. Many of you are interested in entrepreneurship and small business, so we also cover the math needed to establish and run a small business.

To better connect the math with relevant real-world problems, this edition features 21 new chapter-opening cases that highlight how the math topic to be discussed is applied in a real-world context. We also added over 40 new end-of-chapter problem-solving cases on topics of interest to students and retained the 10 Video Cases from the 7th Edition in a new appendix.

Expanded coverage and new topics were added to several chapters based on comments from reviewers. We added coverage of formulas to find the future value and compound interest; to find the present value of an investment; to find the future value of an ordinary annuity or an annuity due; and to find a sinking fund payment or the present value of an annuity. We expanded the coverage for online banking in Chapter 4 and added to Chapter 7 coverage on relative frequency distributions, the mean of grouped data, and comparative and component bar graphs. In Chapter 11 we added learning outcomes on making partial payments before the maturity date and on finding the true or effective interest rate of a simple discount note. In Chapter 15 we added the formula for finding the principal and interest payment of a mortgage, and we added the topic of calculating the principal, interest, taxes, and insurance (PITI) payment on a home mortgage and calculating mortgage qualifying rates. The lower-of-cost-or-market (LCM) rule was added to Chapter 17 and to Chapter 18 we added coverage on insurance for multiple carriers. In general, more calculator steps were added and the number of Microsoft Excel exercises increased.

The teaching package has also been heavily upgraded for this edition. We are most excited about the addition of **MyMathLab®** for *Business Math*. MyMathLab is a powerful classroom management, homework, tutorial, and assessment tool that can be packaged with this textbook.

## Reading Your Math Textbook

In developing an effective study plan it is important to use all your available resources to their maximum advantage. The most accessible of these resources is your textbook. Incorporate an effective strategy for reading your textbook into your study plan.

### Beginning a Chapter

1. Examine the chapter opening pages. Read the Chapter Title, Section Titles, and Learning Outcomes to determine what will be covered in the chapter. Read the case to get a sense of the business topics covered in the chapter.
2. Read the Summary that is near the end of the chapter. The Summary lists each learning outcome of the chapter with some tips on what to remember and at least one example. Use the summary as a checklist to rate your initial knowledge of the chapter's learning outcomes.

This rating can be a numerical one. For example, 0 means that you know nothing about this topic; 1 means that you know a little about this topic; 2 means that you know quite a bit, but there may be a few gaps in your understanding; and 3 means that you know this topic very well.

Another possible rating strategy can be a minus/check/plus system. Minus means you need to work on this topic, check means you know the topic moderately well, and plus means you know the topic very well.

## Beginning a Section

1. Read the section title and the learning outcomes for the section.
2. Read the introductory paragraph.
3. Locate the Section Exercises at the end of the section. Read the directions for each "clump" of exercises. This will give you an idea of the type of problems you will be working and what to look for as you read the section.
4. Begin reading the section. Make notes on concepts that you do not understand or examples for which you are not able to follow the explanation. This will be the basis for questions to ask in class.

## Continuing Through the Chapter

1. Work on one learning outcome at a time. After reading and studying one learning outcome, work the Stop and Check exercises for that outcome. Always check your answers with the text or ReviewMaster CD and ask questions as appropriate. Assess your understanding of each outcome and practice or get help as you think necessary. Be realistic in your self-assessment!
2. Continue outcome by outcome, section by section, checking your understanding as you go.
3. Work the section or end-of-chapter exercises as assigned by your instructor.

## Reviewing the Chapter

1. After finishing a chapter, thumb through the entire chapter and read the Tip Boxes and How To sections.
2. Read the Summary again and rate your understanding of each outcome again. Review or get assistance as necessary.
3. Use the key terms in the margin as a checklist for your understanding of the new terminology used in the chapter.
4. Work the Practice Test at the end of the chapter and check your answers. Review or get assistance as necessary.

## Finishing the Chapter

1. Prepare for the test on the chapter. Ask your instructor which outcomes require mastery for testing purposes. Some outcomes may not require mastery, and others may even be optional.
2. Read the chapter-ending cases to gain some insight about where these concepts are used in real life.

## General Tips

1. Practice an outcome until you feel comfortable that you understand the concept. Abundant practice material is available to you that is specifically geared to your text (Section Exercises, Exercise Sets A & B, and Companion Website). Other practice is available through generic mathematics software and other texts. Only you know when you have practiced enough. Be realistic in the self-assessment of your understanding. Practice helps you retain the information for a longer period of time, but don't wear yourself out! Finding that appropriate balance is your goal.
2. Use the Critical Thinking questions to help you check your conceptual understanding.
3. Don't forget the Glossary/Index as you move through the text so that you can remember definitions and concepts. Perhaps you are not starting your study at the beginning of the text and need to review a few concepts from chapters you did not cover. Examining the Glossary/Index should be your first step in accomplishing your review.

We wish you much success in your study of mathematics. Many of the features in this book were suggestions made by students such as yourself. If you have suggestions for improving the presentation, please give them to your instructor or email the authors at ccleaves@bellsouth.net or at margiehobbs@bellsouth.net

Good luck in your study of business mathematics.

# TIME-TESTED PEDAGOGY AIDS STUDENT LEARNING

## LEARNING OUTCOMES

**7-1 Measures of Central Tendency**
1. Find the mean.
2. Find the median.
3. Find the mode.
4. Make and interpret a frequency distribution.
5. Find the mean of grouped data.

**7-3 Measures of Dispersion**
1. Find the range.
2. Find the standard deviation.

**LEARNING OUTCOMES** outlined at the beginning of each chapter, repeated throughout the chapter, and reviewed in the summary keep students focused on important concepts.

## HOW TO — Find the mean of grouped data

1. Make a frequency distribution.
2. Find the products of the midpoint of the interval and the frequency for each interval for all intervals.

**HOW TO** sections take students through the steps to solve different business applications.

---

**Net price rate:** the complement of the trade discount rate.

Since the complement is a percent, it is a rate. The complement of the trade discount rate is the **net price rate**. The single trade discount rate is used to calculate the amount the retailer *does not* pay: the trade discount. The net price rate is used to calculate the amount the retailer *does* pay: the net price.

**KEY TERMS** are highlighted in bold in the text and called out in the margin with their definitions.

---

### ✅ STOP AND CHECK

1. Find the net price of the PC software SystemWorks that lists for $70 and has a discount rate of 12%.
2. The InFocus LP 120 projector lists for $3,200 and has a trade discount rate of 15%. Find the net price.
3. Canon has a fancy new digital camera that lists for $1,299 and has a trade discount of 18%. What is the net price?
4. Find the net price of 100 sheets of display board that list for $3.99 each, 40 pairs of scissors that list for $1.89 each, and 20 boxes of push pins that list for $3.99 if a 22% trade discount is allowed.

**STOP AND CHECK** exercises give students practice so they can master every outcome. Solutions are in an appendix at the end of the text.

---

### TIP

**Who Pays and When**
The chart summarizes the most common shipping terms.

| Term | Who Pays | When | Who Doesn't Pay |
|---|---|---|---|
| FOB-shipping | Buyer | On receipt | Seller |
| Freight collect | Buyer | On receipt | Seller |

**TIP BOXES** give students alternate strategies for solving problems, point out common mistakes to avoid, and give instruction on using calculators.

---

### EXAMPLE 1

Calculate the cash discount and the net amount paid for an $800 order of business forms with sales terms of 3/10, 1/15, n/30 if the cost of shipping was $40 (which is included in the $800). The invoice was dated June 13, marked *freight prepay and add*, and paid June 24.

Net price of merchandise        Apply the cash discount rate *only* to the net amount of

**EXAMPLES** show all the steps and use annotations and color to highlight the concepts.

---

## 11-2 SECTION EXERCISES

### SKILL BUILDERS

1. Find the exact interest on a loan of $32,400 at 8% annually for 30 days.
2. Find the exact interest on a loan of $12,500 at 7.75% annually for 45 days.

**SKILL BUILDERS AND APPLICATIONS** are two types of exercises within section exercises that help students first master basic concepts and then apply them.

---

| What You Know | What You Are Looking For | Solution Plan |
|---|---|---|
| Houses sold during the period: 9<br>Prices of these houses: $270,000, $250,000, $150,000, $150,000, $150,000, $150,000, $149,000, $145,000, and $125,000 | Which statistic gives the most realistic picture of how much a home in Tyreville is likely to cost?<br>Find the mean, median, and mode. | Mean = sum of values ÷ number of values<br>Median = middle value when values are arranged in order<br>Mode = most frequent value |

**Solution**

Mean = sum of values ÷ number of values

**FIVE-STEP PROBLEM-SOLVING STRATEGY** gives students an efficient and effective way to approach problem solving and gives them a strategy for good decision making.

---

## SUMMARY — CHAPTER 7

**Learning Outcomes      What to Remember with Examples**

## EXERCISES SET A — CHAPTER 7

*Find the range, mean, median, and mode for the following. Round to the nearest hundredth if necessary.*

## PRACTICE TEST — CHAPTER 7

1. Use the data to find the statistical measures.
   42  86  92  15  32  67  48  19  87  63

## CRITICAL THINKING — CHAPTER 7

1. What type of information does a circle graph show?
2. Give a situation in which it would be appropriate to organize the data in a circle graph.

- **SUMMARY** at the end of each chapter functions as a mini study–review with learning outcomes and step-by-step instructions and examples.
- **TWO PROBLEM SETS (A AND B)** are provided on perforated pages for easy removal. Ample room for students' work is provided, so these can be assigned as hand-in homework.
- **PRACTICE TEST** gives students a chance to gauge their knowledge of the chapter material and see where they need to review.
- **CRITICAL THINKING** questions ask students to apply their knowledge to more complex questions and build their decision-making skills.

# ACKNOWLEDGMENTS

We especially thank the students and faculty who used the seventh edition for their thoughtful suggestions for improving this book. We also appreciate and thank the long list of reviewers who have contributed their ideas for improving the text.

Colleagues who reviewed the seventh edition and provided ideas and suggestions for improving the eighth edition are:

Dawn Addington, Albuquerque TVI
Mildred Battle, Marshall Community and Technical
Susan Bennet, Wake Technical Community College
Kathleen DiNisco, Erie Community College
Beverly Hallmon, Suffolk Community College
Jenna Johannpeter, Southwestern II College
Jean McArthur, Joliet JC
Karen S. Mozingo, Pitt Community College
Lisa Rombes, Washtenaw Community
Barbara Schlachter, Baker College, Auburn Hills
Kimberly D. Smith, County College of Morris
Thomas Watkins, Solano Community College
Joe Westfall, Carl Albert State College
Andrea Williams, Shasta College

Some of the reviewers of earlier editions include:

Benjamin W. Bean, Utah Valley State College
Anne L. Cremarosa, Reedley College
Marsha T. Faircloth, Southwest Georgia Technical College
Amy Fowler, Cleveland State Community College
John Lehnen, Heald College
Dyan Pease, Sacramento City College
Susan Peterson, Northwest Technical College–Moorhead
Sally P. Proffitt, Tarrant County College–Northeast Campus
Keith Purrington, Irvin Valley College
Don R. Stanley, Heald College
Margene E. Sunderland, Fayetteville Technical Community College
Joyce G. Walsh-Portillo, Broward Community College
Nancy Wellerp, Grand Rapids Community College (retired)

The Pearson Education team has been outstanding. The key players are listed on the copyright page and we want to thank all of them for the role they played in this project. Our team leader, Gary Bauer, Senior Acquisitions Editor, had the vision, expertise, and perseverance to bring the vision to reality. Louise Sette played a vital role in making sure the project progressed in a timely manner and taking care of every minute detail to ensure a quality product. We thank you, Louise. Monica Ohlinger and Diane Durkee of Ohlinger Publishing Services did an excellent job of coordinating aspects of the manuscript production. We thank you both. David Drewrey read and worked every example and exercise to ensure the business and mathematics were on target. Any errors found in the text are the direct responsibility of the authors. Rob Farinelli updated the test bank by adding exercises for new sections and accuracy checking the entire test bank.

Jeffrey Noble brought a fresh perspective to the eighth edition by writing exciting and interesting chapter opening features for all chapters and by writing many of the case studies found at the end of each chapter. Jeffrey also revised the PowerPoint presentation and scripted and recorded video tapes for each of the many learning outcomes in the text. Students will learn from his work while enjoying his presentations.

We also thank Tamra Davis, Tulsa Community College; Sally Proffitt, Tarrant County College; Cheryl Fetterman, Cape Fear Community College; Joyce Walsh-Portillo, Broward Community College; Blane Franckowiak, Tarrant County College; Anne Cremarosa, Reedley College; Alton Evans, Tarrant County College; and Beverly Vance, Southwest Tennessee Community College who contributed to various aspects of the seventh edition and Rod Starns of Running Pony Productions, Memphis, TN, who produced the *Business Math in the Real World* videos and the learning outcome videos.

As the manuscript for this edition was developed, we consulted with numerous business professionals so that we could reflect current business practices in the examples and exercises. We thank all of our consults for so graciously sharing their expertise.

We also thank the friendly employees at our favorite FedEx Kinkos on Poplar Avenue in Memphis, Tennessee. They always greeted us with a smile and made sure that our packages were delivered on time and often ahead of schedule.

Our families have always been supportive in all our projects; but in this project we especially thank Shirley Riddle for her tireless sorting, researching, and organizing inventory throughout the process of selling The 7th Inning inventory and Allen Hobbs, who willingly made many trips to Memphis or to Batesville, MS, to make sure our mailings were sent in a timely manner.

**CHERYL CLEAVES AND MARGIE HOBBS**

# PHOTO CREDITS

# BRIEF CONTENTS

# CONTENTS

**CHAPTER 3**     **DECIMALS**    **72**

**CHAPTER 4**     **BANKING**    **100**

## CHAPTER 16    DEPRECIATION    548

## CHAPTER 17    INVENTORY    582

# BUSINESS MATH

# How Much Is Your Degree Worth?

With revenues approaching $2 billion annually, on-line gaming has become more popular than ever. In fact, today in the United States, nearly 83,000,000 people play simple on-line games such as checkers, bridge, or mahjong. A typical Friday afternoon may find more than 36,000 people playing pool on Yahoo!. The incredible numbers of on-line gamers have led to soaring revenues, making on-line advertising one of the fastest growing business sectors in the world today. Yahoo!, for example, saw total revenues skyrocket in 2005 to over $5,000,000,000 ($5 billion)—Google to over $6 billion (yes, that's nine 0s!).

But while checkers or pool may be popular with more people, committed gamers have a number of alternatives to choose from. One of the most popular is EverQuest, a role-playing game that has been around since the mid-1990s. The virtual world inside EverQuest is called Norrath, and it took 6 years and $28 million to create. To date, more than 500,000 people have subscribed to the virtual world, and at any given time there are about 60,000 people from over 120 countries playing simultaneously. EverQuest represents an entire world with its own diverse species, economic systems, alliances, and politics. There are more than 40,000 unique items for players to discover, create, or buy within the game.

But what does playing EverQuest have to do with whole numbers, or with studying math in general? Research by U.S. economist, Edward Castronova, showed that EverQuest players earned an average of over $3 for every hour spent playing the game by trading skills and possessions with other players. But does studying math (or any other subject) have an economic value, as well? The answer, of course, is yes. The average college student will spend approximately 150 hours per subject studying or attending class, or 3,000 hours total for an associate's degree. Increased earnings for graduates with associate's degrees will total nearly $120,000 over a career, as compared to high school graduates. For every hour you spend studying or attending class, you will get $40 back! So before you get started gaming, make sure your math homework is finished!

## LEARNING OUTCOMES

### 1-1 Place Value and Our Number System

1. Read whole numbers.
2. Write whole numbers.
3. Round whole numbers.

### 1-2 Operations with Whole Numbers

1. Add whole numbers.
2. Subtract whole numbers.
3. Multiply whole numbers.
4. Divide whole numbers.

This text will prepare you to enter the business world with mathematical tools for a variety of career paths. The chapters on business topics build on your knowledge of mathematics, so it is important to begin the course with a review of the mathematics and problem-solving skills you will need in the chapters to come.

In most businesses, arithmetic computations are done on a calculator or computer. Even so, every businessperson needs a thorough understanding of mathematical concepts and a basic number sense in order to make the best use of a calculator. A machine will do only what you tell it to do. Pressing a wrong key or performing the wrong operations on a calculator will result in a rapid but incorrect answer. If you understand the mathematics and know how to make reasonable estimates, you can catch and correct many errors.

## 1-1 PLACE VALUE AND OUR NUMBER SYSTEM

### LEARNING OUTCOMES

1 Read whole numbers.
2 Write whole numbers.
3 Round whole numbers.

**Digit:** one of the ten symbols used in the decimal-number system: 0, 1, 2, 3, 4, 5, 6, 7, 8, 9.

**Whole number:** a number from the set of numbers including zero and the counting or natural numbers: 0, 1, 2, 3, 4, . . . .

**Mathematical operations:** calculations with numbers. The four operations that are often called basic operations are addition, subtraction, multiplication, and division.

Our system of numbers, the decimal-number system, uses ten symbols called **digits:** 0, 1, 2, 3, 4, 5, 6, 7, 8, 9. Numbers in the decimal system can have one or more digits. Each digit in a number that contains two or more digits must be arranged in a specific order to have the value we intend for the number to have. One set of numbers in the decimal system is the set of **whole numbers:** 0, 1, 2, 3, 4, . . . .

Most business calculations involving whole numbers include one or more of four basic **mathematical operations:** addition, subtraction, multiplication, and division.

## 1 Read whole numbers.

What business situations require that we read and write whole numbers? Communication is one of the most important skills of successful businesspersons. Both the giver and the receiver of communications must have the same interpretation for the communication to be effective. That is why understanding terminology and the meanings of symbolic representations is an important skill.

**Period:** a group of three place values in the decimal-number system.

Beginning with the ones place on the right, the place values are grouped in groups of three places. Each group of three place values is called a **period.** Each period has a name and a ones place, a tens place, and a hundreds place. In a number, the first period from the left may have less than three digits. In many cultures the periods are separated with commas.

**Place-value system:** a number system that determines the value of a digit by its position in a number.

Reading numbers is based on an understanding of the **place-value system** that is part of our decimal number system. The chart in Figure 1-1 shows that system applied to the number 381,345,287,369,021.

To apply the place-value chart to any number, follow the steps given in the HOW TO feature. You'll find this feature, and examples illustrating its use, throughout this text.

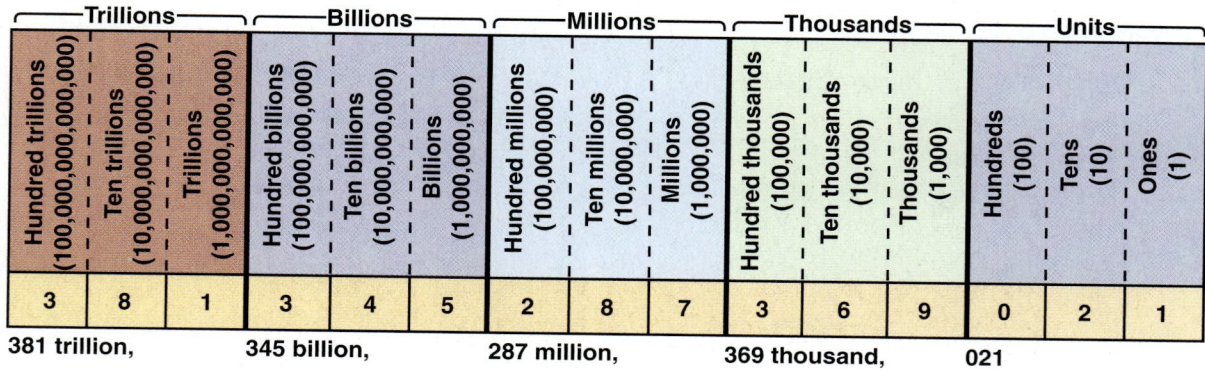

| Trillions | | | Billions | | | Millions | | | Thousands | | | Units | | |
|---|---|---|---|---|---|---|---|---|---|---|---|---|---|---|
| Hundred trillions (100,000,000,000,000) | Ten trillions (10,000,000,000,000) | Trillions (1,000,000,000,000) | Hundred billions (100,000,000,000) | Ten billions (10,000,000,000) | Billions (1,000,000,000) | Hundred millions (100,000,000) | Ten millions (10,000,000) | Millions (1,000,000) | Hundred thousands (100,000) | Ten thousands (10,000) | Thousands (1,000) | Hundreds (100) | Tens (10) | Ones (1) |
| 3 | 8 | 1 | 3 | 4 | 5 | 2 | 8 | 7 | 3 | 6 | 9 | 0 | 2 | 1 |
| 381 trillion, | | | 345 billion, | | | 287 million, | | | 369 thousand, | | | 021 | | |

**FIGURE 1-1**
**Place-Value Chart for Whole Numbers**

## HOW TO — Read a whole number

|  |  |
|---|---|
|  | Read the number<br>4,693,107 |
| 1. Separate the number into periods beginning with the rightmost digit and moving to the left. |  |
| 2. Identify the period name of the leftmost period. | 4 million |
| 3. For each period, beginning with the leftmost period:<br>  (a) Read the three-digit number from left to right.<br>  (b) Name the period. | 4,693,107 four *million*, six hundred ninety-three *thousand*, one hundred seven |
| 4. Note these exceptions:<br>  (a) Do not read or name a period that is all zeros.<br>  (b) Do not name the units period. |  |

---

### EXAMPLE 1  Read the number 3,007,047,203.

3 007 047 203

3 billion, 007 million, 047 thousand, 203

Identify each period name.

Read the words for the numbers in each period. Name each period except the units period.

**Three billion, seven million, forty-seven thousand, two hundred three.**

---

### TIP

**Points to Remember in Reading Whole Numbers**

1. Commas separating periods are inserted from right to left between groups of three numbers. The leftmost period may have fewer than three digits.
2. The period name will be read at each comma.
3. Period names are read in the singular: *million* instead of *millions,* for example.
4. Since no comma follows the units period, that will serve as your reminder that the period name *units* is not read.
5. *Hundreds* is NOT a period name.
6. Every period has a ones, tens, and hundreds *place*.
7. The word *and* is NOT used when reading whole numbers.
8. Commas ordinarily do not appear in calculator displays.
9. If a number has more than four digits, but no commas, such as you see on a calculator display, insert commas when you write the number. The comma is optional in numbers with four digits.

---

 **STOP AND CHECK**

*Write the words used to read the number.*

**1.** 7,352,496

**2.** 4,023,508

**3.** 62,805,000,927

**4.** 587,000,000,912

## 2 Write whole numbers.

Suppose you are in a sales meeting and the marketing manager presents a report of the sales for the previous quarter, the projected sales for the current quarter, and the projected sales for the entire year. How would you record these figures in the notes you are taking for the meeting? You will need to have a mental picture of the place-value structure of our numbering system.

> **HOW TO** Write a whole number
>
> 1. Begin recording digits from left to right.
> 2. Insert a comma at each period name.
> 3. Every period after the first period must have three digits. Insert zeros as necessary.

### EXAMPLE 1  Write the number, given its word name.

(a) Fifteen million, three hundred sixty-two thousand, five hundred thirty-eight

(b) Five hundred forty-two billion, five hundred thousand, twenty-nine

(a) 15, __ __ __,__ __ __
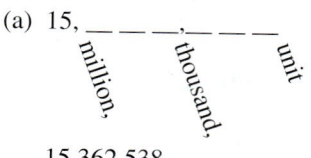

15,362,538

**The number is 15,362,538.**

Record the first digits followed by a comma when the period name *million* is heard (or read). Then anticipate the periods to follow (thousand and unit).

Fill in each remaining period as the digits and period names are heard (or read).

(b) 542,__ __ __,__ __ __,__ __ __
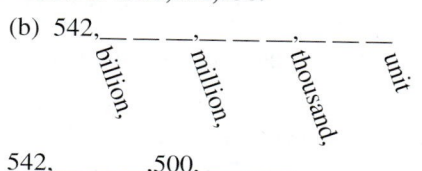

542,__ __ __,500,__ __ __

542,000,500,029

Record the first period and anticipate the periods to follow (million, thousand, and unit).

The next period name you hear (or read) is *thousand,* so you place the 500 in the thousand period, saving space to place three zeros in the million period.

Place three zeros in the *million* period and listen for (read) the last three digits. You hear (read) *twenty-nine,* which is a two-digit number. Thus, a 0 is placed in the hundreds place.

**The number is 542,000,500,029.**

## ✔ STOP AND CHECK

1. Write the number for eighteen billion, seventy-eight million, three hundred ninety-seven thousand, two hundred three.

2. Write the number for thirty-six thousand, seventeen.

3. Krispy Kreme had profits of nine hundred thirty-two thousand, eight hundred six dollars. Write the profit in numbers.

4. Jet Blue, one of the nation's most profitable airlines, sold fifty-two thousand, eight hundred ninety-six tickets. Write the number.

## 3 Round whole numbers.

**Rounded number:** an approximate number that is obtained from rounding an exact amount.

**Approximate number:** a rounded amount.

Exact numbers are not always necessary or desirable. For example, the board of directors does not want to know to the penny how much was spent on office supplies (though the accounting staff should know). Approximate or rounded numbers are often used. A **rounded number** does not represent an exact amount. It is instead an **approximate number.** You round a number to a specified place, which may be the first digit from the left in a number.

### HOW TO — Round a whole number to a specified place

Round 2,748 to the nearest hundred.

1. Find the digit in the specified place.     2,748
2. Look at the next digit to the right.     2,748
   (a) If this digit is less than 5, replace it     2,700
       and all digits to its right with zeros.
   (b) If this digit is 5 or more, add 1 to the
       digit in the specified place, and replace
       all digits to the right of the specified
       place with zeros.

### EXAMPLE 1 — Round to the indicated place.

(a) 52,647 to the nearest hundred
(b) 16,982 to the nearest hundred

(a) 52,647     The hundreds digit is 6.
    52,647     The digit to the right is 4.
    **52,600**     4 is less than 5; leave 6 and replace all digits to the right with zeros.
(b) 16,982     The hundreds digit is 9.
    16,982     The digit to the right is 8.
    **17,000**     8 is 5 or more, so add 1 to 9 to get 10. Carry 1 (from 10) to 6 to get 7. Record 7 and replace all digits to the right with zeros.

### EXAMPLE 2 — Round 2,748 to the first digit.

The specified place is the place of the first digit.

2,748     The first digit is 2.
    The digit to the right of 2 is 7.
2,748     7 is 5 or more, so step 2b applies: Add 1 to 2 to get 3, and
3,000     replace all digits to its right with zeros.

**2,748 rounded to the first digit is 3,000.**

## ✓ STOP AND CHECK

1. Round 3,784,921 to the nearest thousand.

2. Round 6,098 to the nearest ten.

3. Round 52,973 to the nearest hundred.

4. Round 17,439 to the first digit.

5. Southwest Airlines, one of the largest in the United States, sold 584,917 tickets. Write this as a number rounded to the first digit.

6. The two-year-average median household income for Maryland in a recent year was $57,265. Round to the nearest thousand dollars.

### SKILL BUILDERS

*Write the words used to read the number.*

1. 22,356,027

2. 106,357,291,582

3. 730,531,968

4. 21,000,017

5. 523,800,007,190

6. 713,205,538

*Write as numbers.*

7. Fourteen thousand, nine hundred eighty-five.

8. Thirty-two million, nine hundred forty-three thousand, six hundred eight.

9. Seventeen billion, eight hundred three thousand, seventy-five.

10. Fifty million, six hundred twelve thousand, seventy-eight.

11. Three hundred six thousand, five hundred forty-one.

12. Three hundred million, seven hundred sixty thousand, five hundred twelve.

13. Round 483 to tens.

14. Round 3,762 to hundreds.

15. Round 298,596 to ten-thousands.

16. Round 57,802 to the first digit.

### APPLICATIONS

17. Cisco, the world's largest Internet equipment maker, recorded earnings of about $3,585,000,000. Write the words used to read Cisco's earnings.

18. Net income at Levi Strauss, the world's biggest maker of branded clothing, was expected to be twenty-five million, nine hundred seventy-two thousand, eight hundred dollars. Write as a number.

19. McDonald's produced 86,347,582 Big Macs. How many Big Macs were produced to the nearest million?

20. Oslo, Hong Kong, Tokyo, and New York City are the four most expensive cities in the world, according to one source. Workers in Oslo work 1,582 hours per year on average. Round the number of hours to the first digit.

# 1-2 OPERATIONS WITH WHOLE NUMBERS

### LEARNING OUTCOMES

1 Add whole numbers.
2 Subtract whole numbers.
3 Multiply whole numbers.
4 Divide whole numbers.

The operation of addition is used to find the total of two or more quantities. At Dollar General you purchase two toys, three bottles of cleaning products, and four types of cosmetic products. We use addition to find the total number of items purchased.

## 1 Add whole numbers.

If you purchase more than one item, you do not ordinarily pay for each item separately. Instead, the prices of all items are added together and you pay the total amount.

Numbers being added are called **addends.** The answer, or result, of addition is called the **sum** or **total.**

**Addends:** numbers being added.

**Sum or total:** the answer or result of addition.

$$
\begin{array}{ll}
\text{addends} & \begin{array}{r} 2 \\ 3 \\ +4 \\ \hline 9 \end{array} \quad \begin{array}{l} 2 + 3 = 5 \\[1em] 5 + 4 = 9 \end{array} \\
\text{sum or total} &
\end{array}
$$

Only two numbers are added at a time. These two numbers can be added in either order without changing the sum. This property is called the **commutative property of addition.** It is casually referred to as the *order property of addition.*

**Commutative property of addition:** two numbers can be added in either order without changing the sum.

When more than two numbers are added, two are grouped and added first. Then, the sum of these two numbers is added to another number. The addends can be grouped two at a time in any way. This property is called the **associative property of addition** and is casually referred to as the *grouping property of addition.*

**Associative property of addition:** when more than two numbers are added, the addends can be grouped two at a time in any way.

---

### HOW TO — Add whole numbers

1. Write the numbers in a vertical column, aligning digits according to their places.
2. For each *place* in turn, beginning with the ones place:
   (a) Add the *place* digits.
   (b) Write the units digit of this sum directly below the *place* digit of the last addend.
   (c) Write the remaining digits of the sum directly above the *next place* digit of the first addend.

---

### EXAMPLE 1  Add $472 + 83 + 3,255$.

Write the numbers in a vertical column, aligning digits by place value.

$$
\begin{array}{r}
^{2\,1} \\
472 \\
83 \\
3,255 \\
\hline
3,810
\end{array}
$$

Add the ones place digits, carrying 1 to the tens place. Add the tens place digits, carrying 2 to the hundreds place. Add the hundreds place digits. Finally, add the thousands place digits.

**The sum is 3,810.**

---

There are several ways to improve your accuracy in calculations. One is to recalculate. A second way is to recalculate using a calculator. A third way is to **estimate** the result before or after you calculate.

**Estimate:** to find a reasonable approximate answer for a calculation.

A quick and often-used way to estimate a sum is to round each addend to its first digit and add the rounded addends.

Estimate $472 + 83 + 3{,}255$.

1. Estimate the sum by rounding each addend.
2. Add the rounded amounts, mentally if possible.
3. Check addition by adding the numbers again. The second time the numbers can be added in a different order or by using a different method.

|  |  |
|---|---|
| 472 | 500 |
| 83 | 80 |
| + 3,255 | + 3,000 |
| 3,810 | 3,580 |

Check:

|  |
|---|
| 3,255 |
| 472 |
| + 83 |
| 3,810 |

**EXAMPLE 2**  Estimate the sum by rounding each addend to its first digit. Compare the estimate to the exact sum.

Estimate:

| 885 | rounds to | 900 |
| 569 | rounds to | 600 |
| 343 | rounds to | 300 |
| 231 | rounds to | 200 |
| + 562 | rounds to | + 600 |
|  |  | 2,600 |

The rounded numbers have all zeros in the tens and ones places. Mentally add the digits in the hundreds place and affix the two zeros.

Exact sum:

$$\overset{2\ \ 2\,2}{885}$$
569
343
231
+ 562
2,590

**The estimate is 2,600; the exact sum is 2,590.**

When we perform calculations with a calculator or computer software, it is important to estimate and to check the reasonableness of our answer. There are many different types of calculators, and each type may operate slightly differently. You can teach yourself how to use your calculator using some helpful learning strategies.

***Five-Step Problem-Solving Strategy***  Decision making or problem solving is an important skill for the successful businessperson. The decision-making process can be applied by either individuals or action teams. Many strategies have been developed to enable individuals and teams to *organize* the information given and to *develop* a plan for finding the information needed to make effective business decisions or to solve business-related problems.

The plan we use is a five-step process. This feature will be highlighted throughout the text. The key words to identify each of the five steps are:

| What You Know | What You Are Looking For | Solution Plan |
|---|---|---|
| What relevant facts are known or given? | What amounts do you need to find? | How are the known and unknown facts related? What formulas or definitions are used to establish a model? In what sequence should the operations be performed? |

**Solution**

Perform the operations identified in the solution plan.

**Conclusion**

**What does the solution represent within the context of the problem?**

**EXAMPLE 3**   Holly Hobbs supervises the shipping department at AH Transportation and must schedule her employees to handle all shipping requests within a specified time frame while keeping the payroll amount within the amount budgeted. Complete the payroll report (Table 1-1) for the first quarter and decide if Holly has kept the payroll within the quarterly department payroll budget of $25,000.

**TABLE 1-1**
**Quarterly Payroll Report for the Shipping Department**

| Employee | Quarterly Payroll |
|---|---|
| Doroshonko, Nataliya | $ 5,389 |
| Campbell, Karen | 5,781 |
| Linebarger, Lydia | 6,463 |
| Ores, Vincent | 5,389 |
| **Department Total** | $23,022 |

| What You Know | What You Are Looking For | Solution Plan |
|---|---|---|
| Quarterly pay for each employee (in table)<br><br>Quarterly department budget: $25,000 | Quarterly department payroll<br><br>Is the payroll within budget? | Quarterly department payroll = sum of quarterly pay for each employee<br><br>Compare the quarterly department payroll to the quarterly department budget |

**Solution**

Find the quarterly department payroll.

Using a calculator:

$5389 \boxed{+} 5781 \boxed{+} 6463 \boxed{+} 5389 \boxed{=} \Rightarrow 23022$

The quarterly department payroll is $23,022, which is less than the budgeted amount of $25,000.

**Conclusion**

**Holly's department payroll for the quarter *is* within the amount budgeted for the department.**

##  STOP AND CHECK

*Mentally estimate the sum by rounding to the first digit. Compare the estimate with the exact sum.*

**1.** $372 + 583 + 697$

**2.** $9,823 + 7,516 + 8,205$

**3.** $\$618 + \$736 + \$107$

**4.** $\$1,809 + \$3,521$

**5.** Hales Shipping Company is projecting revenue of $1,200,000. At the end of the year Hales had revenue of $789,000 from its ten largest clients and $342,000 from its other clients. Did the company reach its projection?

**6.** Marie's Costume Shop projected annual revenue of $2,500,000. Revenue for each quarter was $492,568; $648,942; $703,840; and $683,491. Did the shop achieve its revenue goal?

## 2  Subtract whole numbers.

Subtraction is the opposite of addition. We use subtraction to find a *part* when we know a total amount and one of two *parts*. We may need to know the amount of change when a price has increased to a higher price. If we do not have enough material to complete a job, we may need to know how much more material is needed.

When subtracting one number from another, the number subtracted from is called the **minuend.** The number being subtracted is called the **subtrahend.** The result of subtraction is called the **difference.**

**Minuend:** the beginning amount or the number that a second number is subtracted from.

**Subtrahend:** the number being subtracted.

**Difference:** the answer or the result of subtraction.

$$
\begin{array}{rcl}
135 & \rightarrow & \text{minuend} \\
- \ 72 & \rightarrow & \text{subtrahend} \\
\hline
63 & \rightarrow & \text{difference}
\end{array}
$$

The order of the numbers in a subtraction problem *is* important. That is, subtraction is *not* commutative. For example, $5 - 3 = 2$, but $3 - 5$ does not equal 2.

Grouping in subtraction *is* important. That is, subtraction is *not* associative. For example, $(8 - 3) - 1 = 5 - 1 = 4$, but $8 - (3 - 1) = 8 - 2 = 6$.

> **HOW TO**  Subtract and check whole numbers
>
> 1. Write the numbers in a vertical column, the subtrahend below the minuend, aligning digits according to their places.
> 2. For each *place* in turn, beginning with the ones place:
>    (a) If the *place* digit of the minuend is less than the *place* digit of the subtrahend, **regroup** by subtracting 1 from the *next place* digit to the left. Add 10 to the *place* digit of the minuend.
>    (b) Subtract the *place* digits.
>    (c) Write this difference directly below the *place* digit of the subtrahend.
> 3. Check the difference by adding the subtrahend and the difference. Their sum should be the same as the minuend.

**Regroup:** regroup digits in the minuend by borrowing 1 from the digit to the left of a specified place and adding 10 to the digit in the specified place. This is also called *borrowing.*

## EXAMPLE 1  Subtract 27 from 64.

$$\begin{array}{r} 64 \\ -27 \end{array}$$

Arrange the numbers so that the places align.

$$\begin{array}{r} 5 \ 14 \\ 6 \ 4 \\ -2 \ 7 \\ \hline 3 \ 7 \end{array}$$

4 is smaller than 7, so regroup by subtracting 1 from the tens place (thus 6 becomes 5) and add 10 to the ones place.
Subtract ones-place digits; then subtract tens-place digits.

Using a calculator:

$64 \ \boxed{-} \ 27 \ \boxed{=} \Rightarrow 37$

*Check:*

$$\begin{array}{r} 27 \\ +37 \\ \hline 64 \end{array}$$

The sum of the subtrahend and difference equals the minuend.
The difference is correct.

**The difference of 64 and 27 is 37.**

### TIP

**Estimating Subtraction**

To estimate subtraction, round each value and subtract the rounded amounts. In the example, an estimate would be $60 - 30 = 30$.

---

## ✔ STOP AND CHECK

*For each subtraction, mentally estimate by rounding to the first digit; then find the exact difference.*

1. Subtract 96 from 138.

2. Subtract: $1,352 - 787$

3. Subtract: $\$3,807 - \$2,689$

4. Subtract 5,897 from 10,523.

5. Jet Blue sold 2,196,512 tickets and Southwest Airlines sold 1,993,813 tickets. How many more tickets did Jet Blue sell?

6. According to the Bureau of Labor Statistics, the number of U.S. firms with 1 to 4 employees was 2,734,133 and the number of firms with 5 to 9 employees was 1,025,497. How many more firms had 1 to 4 employees?

---

## 3  Multiply whole numbers.

Multiplication is a shortcut for repeated addition.

The new Krispy Kreme donut store at London-based Harrods sends 3 dozen (36) donuts each to 75 neighboring merchants to celebrate the grand opening of its first European location. We can multiply to get the total number of Krispy Kreme donuts sampled.

When multiplying one number by another, the number being multiplied is called the **multiplicand.** The number we multiply by is called the **multiplier.** Each number can also be called a **factor.** The result of multiplication is called the **product.** Numbers can be multiplied in any order without changing the product. When the multiplier has more than one digit, the product of each digit and the multiplicand is called a **partial product.**

**Multiplicand:** the number being multiplied.

**Multiplier:** the number multiplied by.

**Factor:** each number involved in multiplication.

**Product:** the answer or result of multiplication.

**Partial product:** the product of one digit of the multiplier and the entire multiplicand.

$$\begin{array}{r} 75 \quad \leftarrow \text{multiplicand} \\ \times \ 36 \quad \leftarrow \text{multiplier} \\ \hline 450 \\ 2 \ 25 \\ \hline 2,700 \quad \leftarrow \text{product} \end{array}$$

$\leftarrow$ factors

$\leftarrow$ partial products

1. Write the numbers in a vertical column, aligning digits according to their places.
2. For each *place* of the multiplier in turn, beginning with the ones place:
   (a) Multiply the multiplicand by the *place* digit of the multiplier.
   (b) Write the partial product directly below the multiplier (or the last partial product), aligning the ones digit of the partial product with the *place* digit of the multiplier (and aligning all other digits to the left accordingly).
3. Add the partial products.

## EXAMPLE 1 — Multiply 127 by 53.

$$
\begin{array}{r}
127 \\
\times \quad 53 \\
\hline
381 \\
6\ 35 \\
\hline
6{,}731
\end{array}
$$

127 ← multiplicand
53 ← multiplier
381 ← first partial product: $3 \times 127 = 381$; 1 in 381 aligns with 3 in 53.
6 35 ← second partial product: $5 \times 127 = 635$; 5 in 635 aligns with 5 in 53.
6,731 ← product: add the partial products.

**The product of 127 and 53 is 6,731.**

## TIP

**Placing Partial Products Properly**

When you multiply numbers that contain two or more digits, it is crucial to *place the partial products* properly. A common mistake in multiplying is to forget to "indent" the partial products that follow the first partial product.

$$
\begin{array}{r}
265 \\
\times \quad 23 \\
\hline
795 \\
5\ 30 \\
\hline
6{,}095
\end{array}
$$

We get the second partial product, 530, by multiplying $265 \times 2$. Therefore, the 0 in 530 should be directly below the 2 in 23.

**CORRECT**

$$
\begin{array}{r}
265 \\
\times \quad 23 \\
\hline
795 \\
530 \\
\hline
1{,}325
\end{array}
$$

**INCORRECT**

As in addition, you can improve your multiplication accuracy by recalculating manually, by recalculating using a calculator, and by estimating the product.

Zeros are used in many helpful shortcuts to multiplying. Pay careful attention to the position of zeros in partial products. When one of the numbers being multiplied has ending zeros, you can use a shortcut to find the product.

## HOW TO — Multiply when numbers end in zero

1. Mentally eliminate zeros from the end of each number.
2. Multiply the new numbers.
3. Attach to the end of the product the total number of zeros mentally eliminated in step 1.

## EXAMPLE 2 — Multiply 20,700 by 860.

$$
\begin{array}{r}
20{,}7\ 00 \\
\times \quad 86\ 0 \\
\hline
1\ 242 \\
16\ 56 \\
\hline
17{,}802{,}000
\end{array}
$$

Mentally eliminate three zeros from the ends of 20,700 and 860.
Multiply 207 by 86, aligning digits and finding partial products.

Attach the three zeros that were mentally eliminated in step 1.

**The product of 20,700 and 860 is 17,802,000.**

**EXAMPLE 3** Max Wertheimer works at the Wendy's warehouse and is processing store orders totaling 45,000 sixteen-ounce cups. He found 303 packages of sixteen-ounce cups. Each package contains a gross of cups. Does Max need to order more cups from the manufacturer to fill the store orders if one gross is 144 items?

| What You Know | What You Are Looking For | Solution Plan |
|---|---|---|
| Store orders: 45,000 cups | Total quantity of cups on hand | Total quantity of cups on hand = packages of cups on hand × cups per package |
| Packages of cups on hand: 303 | Should more cups be ordered? | |
| Cups per package: 1 gross, or 144 | | Compare the total quantity of cups on hand with 45,000 cups. |

**Solution**

Using a calculator:

303 ⊠ 144 ▭ ⟹ 43632

**Conclusion**

There are 43,632 cups in the warehouse, but store orders total 45,000. **Max needs to order more cups from the manufacturer to fill all the store orders.**

## STOP AND CHECK

*Mentally estimate the product by rounding to the first digit. Find the exact product.*

**1.** 317 × 52

**2.** 6,723 × 87

**3.** 4,600 × 70

**4.** 538,000 × 420

**5.** A plastic film machine can produce 75 rolls of plastic in an hour. How many rolls of plastic can be produced by the machine in a 24-hour period? Arcaro Plastics has 15 of these machines. How many rolls of plastic can be produced if all 15 machines operate for 24 hours?

**6.** Malina Kodama creates 48 pottery coffee cups and 72 pottery bowls in a day. How many can be produced in a 22-day month? If 809 coffee cups and 1,242 bowls were sold in the same 22-day month, how many of each item remained in inventory?

## 4 Divide whole numbers.

**Dividend:** the number being divided or the total quantity.

**Divisor:** the number divided by.

**Quotient:** the answer or result of division.

**Whole-number part of quotient:** the quotient without regard to the remainder.

**Remainder of quotient:** a number that is smaller than the divisor that remains after the division is complete.

**Partial dividend:** the part of the dividend that is being considered at a given step of the process.

**Partial quotient:** the quotient of the partial dividend and the divisor.

Christine Shott received a price quote by fax for a limited quantity of discontinued telephone answering machines. The fax copy was not completely readable, but Christine could read that the total bill, including shipping, was $905 and each answering machine costs $35. How many answering machines were available and how much was the shipping cost? Division is used to find the number of equal parts a total quantity can be separated into.

When dividing one number by another, the number being divided (total quantity) is called the **dividend.** The number divided by is called the **divisor.** The result of division is called the **quotient.** When the quotient is not a whole number, the quotient has a **whole-number part** and a **remainder.** When a dividend has more digits than a divisor, parts of the dividend are called **partial dividends,** and the quotient of a partial dividend and the divisor is called a **partial quotient.**

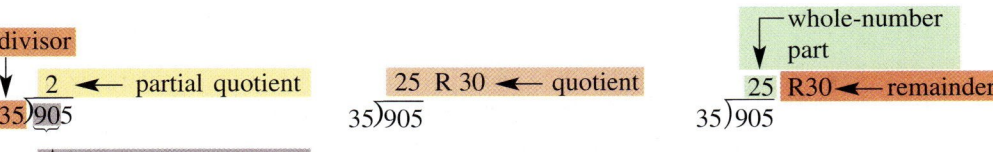

Christine now knows that 25 answering machines are available. What does the remainder represent? The dividend, $905, is in dollars, so the remainder also represents dollars. The remainder of $30 is the shipping cost.

## HOW TO — Divide whole numbers

1. Beginning with its leftmost digit, identify the first group of digits of the dividend that is larger than or equal to the divisor. This group of digits is the first *partial dividend*.
2. For each partial dividend in turn, beginning with the first:
   (a) Divide the partial dividend by the divisor. Write this partial quotient above the rightmost digit of the partial dividend.
   (b) Multiply the partial quotient by the divisor. Write the product below the partial dividend, aligning places.
   (c) Subtract the product from the partial dividend. Write the difference below the product, aligning places. The difference must be less than the divisor.
   (d) Next to the ones place of the difference, write the next digit of the dividend. This is the new partial dividend.
3. When all the digits of the dividend have been used, write the final difference in step 2c as the remainder (unless the remainder is 0). The whole-number part of the quotient is the number written above the dividend.
4. To check, multiply the quotient by the divisor and add the remainder to the product. This sum equals the dividend.

$$905 \div 35$$

$$35\overline{)905}$$

$$\begin{array}{r} 25 \\ 35\overline{)905} \\ 70 \\ \hline 205 \\ 175 \\ \hline 30 \end{array}$$

*Check:*

$$\begin{array}{r} 25 \\ \times\ 35 \\ \hline 125 \\ 75 \\ \hline 875 \end{array} \qquad \begin{array}{r} 875 \\ +\ 30 \\ \hline 905 \end{array}$$

## TIP

**What Types of Situations Require Division?**

Two types of common business situations require division. Both types involve distributing items equally into groups.

1. Distribute a specified total quantity of items so that each group gets a specific equal share. Division determines the number of groups.

   For example, you need to ship 78 crystal vases. With appropriate packaging to avoid breakage, only 5 vases fit in each box. How many boxes are required? You divide the total quantity of vases by the quantity of vases that will fit into one box to determine how many boxes are required.
2. Distribute a specified total quantity so that we have a specific number of groups. Division determines each group's equal share.

   For example, how many ounces will each of four cups contain if a carafe of coffee containing 32 ounces is poured equally into the cups? The capacity of the carafe is divided by the number of coffee cups: 32 ounces ÷ 4 coffee cups = 8 ounces. Eight ounces of coffee are contained in each of the four cups.

## EXAMPLE 1

Tuesday Morning Discount Store needs to ship 78 crystal vases. With standard packing to avoid damage, 5 vases fit in each available box. How many boxes will be needed to ship the 78 vases? Does the Tuesday Morning shipping clerk need to arrange for extra packing or will each box contain exactly 5 vases?

| What You Know | What You Are Looking For | Solution Plan |
|---|---|---|
| Total quantity of vases to be shipped: 78 | How many boxes are required to ship the vases? | Quantity of boxes needed = total quantity of vases ÷ quantity of vases per box |
| Quantity of vases per box without the extra packing: 5 | Is extra packing required? | Quantity of boxes needed = 78 ÷ 5 |

$$\begin{array}{r} 15 \text{ R3} \\ 5\overline{)78} \\ \underline{5} \\ 28 \\ \underline{25} \\ 3 \end{array}$$
Divide 78 by 5. The whole-number part of the quotient is 15; the remainder is 3.

*Check:*

Multiply the whole-number part of the quotient, 15, by the divisor, 5. Then add the remainder. The sum should equal the dividend, 78.

$$\begin{array}{r} 15 \\ \times\ 5 \\ \hline 75 \end{array} \qquad \begin{array}{r} 75 \\ +\ 3 \\ \hline 78 \end{array}$$
The result checks.

The quantity of boxes needed is 15 boxes containing 5 vases and 1 box containing 3 vases.

Fifteen boxes will have 5 vases each, needing no extra packing. One additional box is required to ship the remaining 3 vases for a total of **16 boxes needed. Extra packing is needed to fill the additional box.**

## TIP

**Using Guess and Check to Solve Problems**

An effective strategy for solving problems involves guessing. Make a guess that you think might be reasonable and check to see if the answer is correct. If your guess is not correct, decide if it is too high or too low. Make another guess based on what you learned from your first guess. Continue until you find the correct answer.

Let's try guessing in the previous example. Estimating we find that we can pack 70 vases in 14 boxes ($14 \times 5 = 70$). Since we need to pack 78 vases, how many vases can we pack with 15 boxes? $15 \times 5 = 75$. Still not enough. Therefore, we will need 16 boxes, but the last box will not be full.

## TIP

**Carefully Align Partial Dividends and Partial Quotients**

Be careful in aligning the numbers in a division problem and in entering zeros in the quotient.

$$\begin{array}{r} 507 \\ 5\overline{)2,535} \\ \underline{2\ 5} \\ 3 \\ \underline{0} \\ 35 \\ \underline{35} \\ 0 \end{array}$$

5 will not divide into 3. Place a zero in the quotient before bringing down the next digit.

$$\begin{array}{r} 570 \\ 5\overline{)2,535} \\ \underline{2\ 5} \\ 35 \\ \underline{35} \\ 0 \end{array}$$

**CORRECT**                   **INCORRECT**

As with multiplication, ending zeros in division can lead to a shortcut.

## HOW TO   Divide numbers ending in zero by place-value numbers like 10, 100, 1,000.

1. Mentally eliminate the same number of ending zeros from both the divisor and the dividend.
2. Divide the new numbers.

EXAMPLE 2

Divide the following: (a) 531,000 ÷ 300   (b) 63,500,000 ÷ 1,000

(a) 531,000 ÷ 300                    Eliminate two ending zeros from both numbers.

5,310 ÷ 3                            Divide.

$$\begin{array}{r} 1,770 \\ 3)\overline{5,310} \end{array}$$

531,000 ÷ 300 = 1,770

(b) 63,500,000 ÷ 1,000               Eliminate three ending zeros from both numbers.

63,500 ÷ 1 = 63,500                  Divide.

##  STOP AND CHECK

*Divide.*

**1.** 2,772 ÷ 6

**2.** 6,744 ÷ 24

**3.** 14,335 ÷ 47

**4.** 1,263 ÷ 15

**5.** The Gap purchases 5,184 pairs of blue jeans to be distributed evenly among 324 stores. How many pairs should be sent to each store?

**6.** Auto Zone purchases 26,560 cans of car wax on a special manufacturer's offer. It distributes a case of 64 cans to each store. How many stores can get the special offer?

## 1-2 SECTION EXERCISES

### SKILL BUILDERS

*Mentally estimate the sum by rounding to the first digit.*

**1.**
```
  328
  583
+ 726
```

**2.**
```
  671
  982
+  57
```

**3.** Add: 791 + 1,000 + 52

*Subtract and check the difference.*

**4.**
```
  5 5
- 3 6
```

**5.**
```
  3 0 8
- 2 7 5
```

**6.** 5,409 − 2,176

*Multiply and check the product.*

**7.**
```
    730
×    60
```

**8.**
```
    904
×    24
```

**9.** 1,005 by 89

*Divide and check the quotient.*

**10.** $96 \div 6$

**11.** $13,838 \div 34$

**12.** $17\overline{)4,420}$

## APPLICATIONS

**13.** The menswear department of the Gap has a sales goal of $1,384,000 for its Spring sale. Complete the worksheet (Table 1-2) for the sales totals by region and by day. Decide if the goal was reached. What is the difference between the goal and the actual total sales amount?

### TABLE 1-2

| Region | W | Th | F | S | Su | Region Totals |
|---|---|---|---|---|---|---|
| Eastern | $ 72,492 | $ 81,948 | $ 32,307 | $ 24,301 | $ 32,589 | |
| Southern | 81,897 | 59,421 | 48,598 | 61,025 | 21,897 | |
| Central | 71,708 | 22,096 | 23,222 | 21,507 | 42,801 | |
| Western | 61,723 | 71,687 | 52,196 | 41,737 | 22,186 | |
| Daily Sales Total | | | | | | |

**14.** Atkinson's Candy Company manufactures seven types of hard candy for its Family Favorites mixed candy. The bulk candy is repackaged from 84 containers that each contain 25 pounds of candy. The bulk candy is bagged in 3-pound bags and then packed in boxes for shipping. Each box contains 12 bags of mixed candy. Wilma Jackson-Randle reports that she currently has 1,000 3-pound bags on hand and 100 boxes of the size that will be used to ship the candy. Decide if enough materials are in inventory to complete the mixing and packaging process.

**15.** University Trailer Sales Company sold 352 utility trailers during a recent year. If the gross annual sales for the company was $324,800, what was the average selling price for each trailer?

**16.** An acre of ground is a square piece of land that is 210 feet on each of the four equal sides. Fencing can be purchased in 50-foot rolls for $49 per roll. You are giving a bid to install the fencing at a cost of $1 per foot of fencing plus the cost of materials. If the customer has bids of $1,700, $2,500, and $2,340 in addition to your bid, decide if your bid is the low bid for the job to determine if you will likely get the business.

**17.** If you are paying three employees $7 per hour and the fence installation in Exercise 16 requires 21 hours when all three employees are working, determine how much you will be required to pay in wages. What will be your gross profit on the job?

**18.** The 7th Inning buys baseball cards from eight vendors. In the month of November the company purchased 8,832 boxes of cards. If an equal number of boxes were purchased from each vendor, how many boxes of cards were supplied by each vendor?

**19.** If you have 348 packages of holiday candy to rebox for shipment to a discount store and you can pack 12 packages in each box, how many boxes will you need?

**20.** Bio Fach, Germany's biggest ecologically sound consumer goods trade fair, had 21,960 visitors. This figure was up from 18,090 the previous year and 16,300 two years earlier. What is the increase in visitors to Bio Fach from two years earlier to the present?

**21.** The "communication revolution" has given us prepaid phone calling cards. These cards are used to make long-distance phone calls from any phone. In a recent year the industry posted sales of $500,000. Three years later the sales figure had risen to $200,000,000. What is the increase in sales over the three-year period?

**22.** Strategic Telecomm Systems, Inc. (STS), in Knoxville, Tennessee, made one of the largest single purchases of long-distance telephone time in history. STS purchased 42 million minutes. If STS paid 2 cents per minute, how much did they pay for the purchase? To convert cents to dollars, divide by 100.

**23.** If STS resells the phone time at an average of 6 cents per minute, how much profit will it make on the purchase?

**24.** American Communications Network (ACN) of Troy, Michigan, also markets prepaid phone cards, which it refers to as "equity calling cards." If ACN employs 214,302 persons in 32 locations, on the average, how many employees work at each location?

## Section Outcome

## What to Remember with Examples

### Section 1-1

**1** Read whole numbers. (p. 4)

1. Separate the number into periods beginning with the rightmost digit and moving to the left.
2. Identify the period name of the leftmost period.
3. For each period, beginning with the leftmost period:
   (a) Read the three-digit number from left to right.
   (b) Name the period.
4. Note these exceptions:
   (a) Do not read or name a period that is all zeros.
   (b) Do not name the units period.
   (c) The word *and* is never part of the word name for a whole number.

> 574 is read *five hundred seventy-four.*
> 3,804,321 is read *three million, eight hundred four thousand, three hundred twenty-one.*

**2** Write whole numbers. (p. 6)

1. Begin recording digits from left to right.
2. Insert a comma at each period name.
3. Every period after the first period must have three digits. Insert zeros as necessary.

> Write the number: twenty billion, fifteen million, two hundred four.
>
>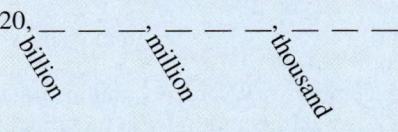
>
> Record the first digits and anticipate the periods to follow.
>
> 20, __ 15,__ __ __, 204     Fill in the remaining periods, using zeros as necessary.
>
> 20,015,000,204

**3** Round whole numbers. (p. 7)

1. Find the digit in the specified place.
2. Look at the next digit to the right.
   (a) If this digit is less than 5, replace it and all digits to its right with zeros.
   (b) If this digit is 5 or more, add 1 to the digit in the specified place, and replace all digits to the right of the specified place with zeros.

> 4,860 rounded to the nearest hundred is 4,900.
> 7,439 rounded to the nearest thousand is 7,000.
> 4,095 rounded to the first digit is 4,000.

### Section 1-2

**1** Add whole numbers. (p. 9)

1. Write the numbers in a vertical column, aligning digits according to their places.
2. For each *place* in turn, beginning with the ones place:
   (a) Add the *place* digits.
   (b) Write the units digit of this sum directly below the *place* digit of the last addend.
   (c) Write the remaining digits of the sum directly above the *next place* digit of the first addend.

> Add:   364
>     + 473
>      837
>
> Add: 2,074 + 485 + 12,592
>
>    2,074
>      485
>  + 12,592
>   15,151

**Estimate and check addition.**

1. Estimate the sum by rounding each addend.
2. Add the rounded amounts, mentally if possible.
3. Check addition by adding the numbers again. The second time the numbers can be added in a different order or by using a different method.

Estimate and check the first sum in the previous example.

|  | Estimate | Check |
|---|---|---|
| 364 | 400 | 473 |
| + 473 | + 500 | + 364 |
| 837 | 900 | 837 |

**2** Subtract whole numbers. (p. 12)

1. Write the numbers in a vertical column, the subtrahend below the minuend, aligning digits according to their places.
2. For each *place* in turn, beginning with the ones place:
   (a) If the *place* digit of the minuend is less than the *place* digit of the subtrahend, add 10 to the *place* digit of the minuend and subtract 1 from the *next place* digit of the minuend.
   (b) Subtract the *place* digits.
   (c) Write this difference directly below the *place* digit of the subtrahend.
3. Check the difference by adding the subtrahend and the difference. Their sum should be the same as the minuend.

| 754 | 807 | 9,000 | 1079 | 10,000 |
|---|---|---|---|---|
| − 329 | − 321 | − 3,521 | − 298 | − 999 |
| 425 | 486 | 5,479 | 781 | 9,001 |

**3** Multiply whole numbers. (p. 13)

1. Write the numbers in a vertical column, aligning digits according to their places.
2. For each *place* of the multiplier in turn, beginning with the ones place:
   (a) Multiply the multiplicand by the *place* digit of the multiplier.
   (b) Write this partial product directly below the multiplier (or the last partial product), aligning the ones digit of the partial product with the *place* digit of the multiplier (and aligning all other digits to the left accordingly).
3. Add the partial products.

| 543 | 509 |
|---|---|
| × 32 | × 87 |
| 1 086 | 3 563 |
| 16 29 | 40 72 |
| 17,376 | 44,283 |

**Multiply when numbers end in zero.**

1. Mentally eliminate zeros from the end of each number.
2. Multiply the new numbers.
3. Attach to the end of the product the total number of zeros mentally eliminated in step 1.

| 8,1⎪00 | $18 \times 10 = 180$ |
|---|---|
| × 3⎪00 | $18 \times 100 = 1,800$ |
| 2,4 3⎪0, 000 | $18 \times 1,000 = 18,000$ |

**4** Divide whole numbers. (p. 15)

1. Beginning with its leftmost digit, identify the first group of digits of the dividend that is larger than or equal to the divisor. This group of digits is the first *partial dividend.*
2. For each partial dividend in turn, beginning with the first:
   (a) *Divide* the partial dividend by the divisor. Write this partial quotient above the rightmost digit of the partial dividend.

**(b)** *Multiply* the partial quotient by the divisor. Write the product below the partial dividend, aligning places.

**(c)** *Subtract* the product from the partial dividend. Write the difference below the product, aligning places. The difference must be less than the divisor.

**(d)** Next to the ones place of the difference, *write* the next digit of the dividend. This is the new partial dividend.

**3.** When all the digits of the dividend have been used, *write* the final difference in step 2c as the remainder (unless the remainder is 0). The whole-number part of the quotient is the number written above the dividend.

**4.** To check, multiply the quotient by the divisor and add the remainder to the product. This sum will equal the dividend.

$$
\begin{array}{r}
287 \text{ R1} \\
3\overline{)862} \\
6 \\
\hline
26 \\
24 \\
\hline
22 \\
21 \\
\hline
1
\end{array}
\qquad
\begin{array}{r}
804 \\
56\overline{)45{,}024} \\
44\ 8 \\
\hline
22 \\
0 \\
\hline
224 \\
224
\end{array}
\qquad
\begin{array}{l}
21{,}000 \div 10 = 2{,}100 \\
21{,}000 \div 100 = 210 \\
21{,}000 \div 1{,}000 = 21
\end{array}
$$

**Divide numbers ending in zero by place-value numbers such as 10, 100, 1,000.**

**1.** Mentally eliminate the same number of ending zeros from both the divisor and the dividend.

**2.** Divide the new numbers.

Divide $483{,}000 \div 200$

$483{,}000 \div 200$       Eliminate two ending zeros from both numbers.

$4830 \div 2$       Divide.

$$
\begin{array}{r}
2415 \\
2\overline{)4830}
\end{array}
$$

$483{,}000 \div 200 = 2{,}415$

# EXERCISES SET A

*Write the word name for the number.*

1. 4,209

*Write the word name for the number.*

2. 301,000,009

3. According to Toyota, the company has invested more than $7 billion in manufacturing, research, and design. Write this number as an ordinary number.

4. Toyota claims to be the fourth-largest vehicle manufacturer in America. It also claims to create more than twenty thousand direct jobs. Write this number as an ordinary number.

*Round Exercises 5 through 7 to the specified place.*

5. 378 (nearest hundred)

6. 9,374 (nearest thousand)

7. 834 (nearest ten)

8. A color video surveillance system with eight cameras is priced at $3,899. Round this price to the nearest thousand dollars.

9. Fiber-optic cable capacity for communications such as telephones grew from 265,472 miles to 6,316,436 miles in a six-year period. Round each of these numbers of miles to the nearest hundred thousand.

*Round to the first digit.*

10. 3,784,809

*Round to the first digit.*

11. 5,178

*Add.*

12. 47 + 385 + 87 + 439 + 874

*Add.*

13. 32,948 + 6,804 + 15,695 + 415 + 7,739

*Mentally estimate the sum by rounding each number to the first digit. Then find the exact sum.*

14.
```
   74,374
   82,849
   72,494
+  89,219
```

15.
```
   3,748
   9,409
   3,577
+  4,601
```

*Mentally estimate the sum in Exercise 16 by rounding each number to the nearest hundred. Then find the exact sum.*

16.
```
   747
   854
   324
+  687
```

17. Mary Luciana bought 48 pencils, 96 pens, 36 diskettes, and 50 bottles of correction fluid. How many items did she buy?

18. Kiesha had the following test scores: 92, 87, 96, 85, 72, 84, 57, 98. What is the student's total number of points?

*Estimate the difference by rounding each number to the first digit in Exercises 19 through 21. Then find the exact difference.*

**19.**  9,748
−5,676

**20.**  83,748,194
−27,209,104

**21.**  84,378
−28,746

**22.** Sam Andrews has 42 packages of hamburger buns on hand but expects to use 130 packages. How many must he order?

**23.** An inventory shows 596 fan belts on hand. If the normal in-stock count is 840, how many should be ordered?

*Multiply and check the product.*

**24.**  5,931
×  835

**25.**  1,987
×  394

**26.** 33 × 500

**27.** 7,870 × 6,000

*Mentally estimate the product in Exercise 28 by rounding each number to the first digit. Then find the exact product.*

**28.**  7,489
×   34

*Mentally estimate the product in Exercise 29 by rounding each number to the nearest hundred. Then find the exact product.*

**29.**  3,128
×   478

**30.** A day-care center has 28 children. If each child eats one piece of fruit each day, how many pieces of fruit are required for a week (five days)?

**31.** Industrialized nations have 2,017 radios per thousand people. This is six times the number of radios per thousand people as there are in the underdeveloped nations. What is the number of radios per thousand people for the underdeveloped nations?

*Divide and check the quotient.*

**32.** 1,232 ÷ 16

*Estimate the quotient in Exercise 33 by rounding each number. Then find the exact quotient.*

**33.** $85\overline{)748{,}431}$

**34.** A parts dealer has 2,988 washers. The washers are packaged with 12 in each package. How many packages can be made?

**35.** If 127 employees earn $1,524 in one hour, what is the average hourly wage per employee?

# EXERCISES SET B

*Write the word name for the number.*

**1.** 97,168

*Write the word name for the number.*

**2.** 5,200,000

**3.** Local people build Toyota vehicles in twenty-six countries around the world. Write this number as an ordinary number.

**4.** By its own claim, HFS, Inc., is the world's largest hotel franchising organization. It claims to have five thousand, four hundred hotels with four hundred ninety-five thousand rooms in over seventy countries, and more than twenty percent of the franchises are minority-owned. Write each of the numbers as an ordinary number.

*Round Exercises 5 through 7 to the specified place.*

**5.** 8,248 (nearest hundred)

**6.** 348,218 (nearest ten-thousand)

**7.** 29,712 (nearest thousand)

**8.** A black-and-white video surveillance system with eight cameras is priced at $2,499. What is the price to the nearest hundred dollars?

**9.** The industrialized nations of the world have six times the number of radios per thousand people as the underdeveloped nations. The industrialized nations have 2,017 radios per thousand people. Round the number of radios to the nearest hundred.

*Round to the first digit.*

**10.** 2,063,948

*Round to the first digit.*

**11.** 17,295,183,109

*Add.*

**12.** 72 + 385 + 29 + 523 + 816

*Add.*

**13.** 46,867 + 7,083 + 723 + 5,209

*Mentally estimate the sum by rounding each number to the first digit. Then find the exact sum.*

**14.**
```
    374
    847
    521
    873
  + 482
```

**15.**
```
   3,470
     843
   3,872
  +  574
```

*Mentally estimate the sum in Exercise 16 by rounding each number to the nearest hundred. Then find the exact sum.*

**16.**
```
   4,274
     643
   1,274
  +   97
```

**17.** Jorge Englade has 57 baseball cards from 1978, 43 cards from 1979, 104 cards from 1980, 210 cards from 1983, and 309 cards from 1987. How many cards does he have in all?

**18.** A furniture manufacturing plant had the following labor-hours in one week: Monday, 483; Tuesday, 472; Wednesday, 497; Thursday, 486; Friday, 464; Saturday, 146; Sunday, 87. Find the total labor-hours worked during the week.

*Mentally estimate the difference by rounding each number to the first digit in Exercises 19 through 21. Then find the exact difference.*

**19.**  370,408
  −187,506

**20.**  12,748
  −  5,438

**21.**  109,849
  −  35,464

**22.** Frieda Salla had 148 tickets to sell for a baseball show. If she has sold 75 tickets, how many does she still have to sell?

**23.** Veronica McCulley weighed 132 pounds before she began a weight-loss program. After eight weeks, she weighed 119 pounds. How many pounds did she lose?

*Multiply and check the product.*

**24.**  5,565
  ×  839

**25.**  78,626
  ×  87

**26.** 283 × 3,000

**27.** 405 × 400

*Mentally estimate the product in Exercise 28 by rounding each number to the first digit. Then find the exact product.*

**28.**  378
  ×  72

*Mentally estimate the product in Exercise 29 by rounding each number to the nearest hundred. Then find the exact product.*

**29.**  378
  ×  546

**30.** Auto Zone has a special on fuel filters. Normally, the price of one filter is $15, but with this sale, you can purchase two filters for only $27. How much can you save by purchasing two filters at the sale price?

**31.** Industrialized nations have 793 TV sets per thousand people. If this is nine times as many TVs per thousand people as there are in the underdeveloped nations, what is the number of TVs per thousand people in the underdeveloped nations?

*Divide and check the quotient.*

**32.** 4,020 ÷ 12

*Estimate the quotient in Exercise 33 by rounding each number. Then find the exact quotient.*

**33.** 346)174,891

**34.** A stack of countertops measures 238 inches. If each countertop is 2 inches thick, how many are in the stack?

**35.** Sequoia Brown has 15 New Zealand coins, 32 Canadian coins, 18 British coins, and 12 Australian coins in her British Commonwealth collection. How many coins does she have in this collection?

# PRACTICE TEST

*Write the word name for the number.*

**1.** 503

**2.** 12,056,039

*Round to the specified place.*

**3.** 84,321 (nearest hundred)

**4.** 58,967 (nearest thousand)

**5.** 80,235 (first digit)

**6.** 587,213 (first digit)

*Write the number.*

**7.** Five billion, seventeen million, one hundred thirty-five thousand, six hundred thirty-two.

**8.** Seventeen million, five hundred thousand, six hundred eight.

*Estimate by rounding to hundreds. Then find the exact result.*

**9.** $863 + 983 + 271$

**10.** $987 - 346$

*Estimate by rounding to the first digit. Then find the exact result.*

**11.** $892 \times 46$

**12.** $53\overline{)4{,}021}$

**13.** An inventory clerk counted the following items: 438 rings, 72 watches, and 643 pen-and-pencil sets. How many items were counted?

**14.** A warehouse is 31 feet high. Boxes that are each two feet high are to be stacked in the warehouse. How many boxes can be stacked one on top of the other?

**15.** A parts dealer has 2,988 washers. The washers are packaged with 12 in each package. How many packages can be made?

**16.** Baker's Department Store sold 23 pairs of ladies' leather shoes. If the store's original inventory was 43 pairs of the shoes, how many pairs remain in inventory?

**17.** Galina makes $680 a week. If she works 40 hours a week, what is her hourly pay rate?

**18.** A day-care center has 28 children. If each child eats two pieces of fruit each day, how many pieces of fruit are required for a week (five days)?

**19.** An oral communication textbook contains three pages of review at the end of each of its 16 chapters. What is the total number of pages devoted to review?

**20.** John Chang ordered 48 paperback novels for his bookstore. When he received the shipment, he learned that 11 were on back order. How many novels did he receive?

1. Addition and subtraction are inverse operations. Write the following addition problem as a subtraction problem and find the value of the letter $n$.

   $12 + n = 17$

2. Multiplication and division are inverse operations. Write the following multiplication problem as a division problem and find the value of the letter $n$.

   $5 \times n = 45$

3. Give an example illustrating that the associative property does NOT apply to subtraction.

4. Give an example illustrating that the commutative property does NOT apply to division.

5. Describe a problem you have encountered that required you to add whole numbers.

6. Describe a problem you have encountered that required you to multiply whole numbers.

7. What operation is a shortcut for repeated addition? Give an example to illustrate your answer.

8. If you know a total amount and all the parts but one, explain what operations you would use to find the missing part.

9. What operation enables you to find the cost per item if you know the total cost of a certain number of items and you know each item has the same price?

10. Find and explain the mistake in the following. Rework the problem correctly.

$$
\begin{array}{r}
59 \\
12\overline{)6{,}108} \\
6\,0\phantom{00} \\
\hline
108 \\
108 \\
\hline
\end{array}
$$

## Challenge Problem

**Sales Quotas.** A sales quota establishes a minimum amount of sales expected during a given period for a salesperson in some businesses, such as selling cars or houses. In setting sales quotas, sales managers take certain factors into consideration, such as the nature of the sales representative's territory and the experience of the salesperson. Such sales quotas enable a company to forecast the sales and future growth of the company for budget and profit purposes.

Try the following quota problem:

A sales representative for a time-sharing company has a monthly sales quota of 500 units. The representative sold 120 units during the first week, 135 units during the second week, and 165 units during the third week of the month. How many units must be sold before the end of the month if the salesperson is to meet the quota?

## 1.1 Take the Limo Liner

At Graphic Express, Inc., Bob is planning to take three managers to a weekly meeting in New York. Traveling from Boston to New York for meetings has been part of the normal course of doing business at Graphics Express for several years, and the travel expenses and wasted time represent a considerable cost to the company. Normally, Bob's managers set up travel arrangements individually and get a reimbursement from the company. Desiring to cut costs and increase productivity, Bob decides to investigate alternative modes of making this weekly trip. He discovered that Amtrak Acela Express costs $178 for the round trip from Boston to New York. A taxi from the train station to the meeting costs about $40. The managers live in different parts of Boston, so carpooling in one car has not worked well; however, if two of the managers drive the 440-mile round trip drive and each takes one of the other managers, the process might be manageable, and the cost is only the mileage reimbursement of $167 plus $25 parking for each car. A round trip airline ticket is about $265 if purchased in advance. Though the flight is only about one hour in duration, the total travel time when flying from home to the New York office is about the same as when driving—the trip takes between three and four hours depending on traffic. The taxi from the airport to the meeting costs about $40. A new service called Limo Liner, a sort of bus with upgrades, advertises that round-trip cost is about $40 less than an Amtrak ticket, and they offer extra services including a kitchen, TVs, restrooms, and a conference table that can be reserved. A taxi from the Limo Liner terminal to the meeting will cost around $20. In the past, most of the managers have flown to the meeting—citing the ability to work en route as a productivity advantage. The idea of using the Limo Liner intrigues Bob. He likes the idea that he and his managers could work together while they travel but wonders if this feature is worth the expense.

1. What is the cost of Bob and his three managers traveling by each method: by Amtrak with two taxi fares in New York, in individual cars including parking, carpooling in two cars including parking, by airplane with two taxi fares in New York, and by Limo Liner with two taxi fares in New York?

2. In the past, costs for the trip have totaled around $1,140 per trip for the group of four people using different methods of traveling to New York. Bob thinks he and his managers should probably drive in two cars to save the most money, but he is still intrigued by the possibility of conducting a meeting on the Limo Liner while traveling to New York. How much will the company save with either of these options? Which method of travel might yield the most productivity increase?

Though the savings are greater if they carpool, taking the Limo Liner would allow the managers to work en route for three hours, either as a group or individually, for a cost of $208 over carpooling. Additionally, traveling by Limo Liner should also decrease the fatigue factor for 2 people having to drive for 3–4 hours. The Limo Liner seems like an idea worth trying.

3. Each year Bob and his managers attend 40 weekly meetings in New York. How much will the cost savings be in a year over past average cost if the group travels regularly by Limo Liner?

## 1.2 Two Degrees Better Than One

Vicki attends Cape Fear Community College, where she will graduate at the end of the current semester. She has thought about continuing her education to get another degree. Tuition for one semester for 16 or more credit hours is $568, or she can pay $35 per credit hour if she takes fewer than 16 credit hours. Student fees are $6 per credit hour, and there is a technology fee of $1 per credit hour. Vicki will be finishing a business administration degree and she will need to take 13 more 3-credit-hour courses to complete an E-commerce degree. Vicki hopes to use the combined degrees to get a job with a firm doing business on the Internet. The courses that she needs are offered on a planned schedule, so Vicki figures that she needs to stay in school for 3 more consecutive semesters to complete the E-commerce degree. Vicki has noticed that there is a customer service certificate program that would require her to take only 2 extra courses (Business Ethics and Customer Service) once she has finished her business administration degree. She could count Customer Service as an elective course toward her E-commerce degree, so it will serve two purposes. She figures that if she takes 14 courses in 3 semesters, she will have two business degrees and the customer service certificate, which would greatly improve her prospects of landing the job that she wants.

1. Vicki has determined that she will need to take five courses during her first two semesters in the E-commerce program and four courses during the third semester. How much will each semester cost?

2. Vicki needs to determine how much money she will need to borrow if she works 15 hours a week at a local plant nursery. Her take-home pay will be $7 per hour, and she figures that she can work 50 weeks in a year. Her rent would be free because her Aunt Rosalyn has a spare room for her. Her share of the groceries will be $100 a month; a cell phone will cost $20 under her father's plan. Car insurance, clothes, and other expenses will come to about $300 per month. How much will she need to borrow to complete her school plan?

3. If Vicki works 20 hours a week and all other assumptions remain the same, can she avoid having to take out a loan?

## 1.3 The Cost of Giving

United Way comprises more than 1,300 local chapters that raise resources and mobilize care units for communities in need. According to their web site, the United Way raised $3.98 billion during their 2005–2006 fund drive. A substantial portion of those funds was raised through annual campaigns and corporate sponsorships. Alaina has been asked to coordinate her company's United Way fund drive. Because she has seen some of the projects United Way has supported in her own community, Alaina is excited to help her company try to reach its goal of raising $100,000 this year. Alaina will be distributing pledge cards to each of the company's employees to request donations. There are 150 people working on the first shift, 75 people working on the second shift, and a crew of 25 people working on the third shift.

1. If each person were to make a one-time donation, how much would each person need to donate for the company to reach its goal of raising $100,000?

2. Alaina feels that very few people can contribute this amount in one lump sum, so she is offering to divide this amount over 10 months. If the employees agree to this arrangement, how much will be deducted from each person's monthly paycheck?

3. Two weeks have passed and Alaina has collected the pledge cards from each of the employees with the following results:

   - First Shift: 100 employees agreed to have $40 a month deducted for 10 months; 25 employees agreed to make a one-time contribution of $100; 15 employees agreed to make a one-time contribution of $50. The remaining employees agreed to have $20 withheld for the next 10 months.
   - Second Shift: 25 people agreed to a one-time contribution of $150; 25 people agreed to have $40 a month deducted for 10 months; and the remaining employees agreed to a one-time contribution that averaged about $35 each.
   - Third Shift: All 25 people agreed to double the $40 contribution and have it deducted over the next 10 months.

   How much was pledged or contributed on each shift?

4. Has Alaina met the company's goal of raising $100,000 for the year? By how much is she over or short?

5. If Alaina's company were to match the employee's contributions with $2 for every $1 the employees contributed, how much would the company contribute? What would be the total contribution to the United Way?

Source: Cape Fear Community College website, North Carolina, http://cfcc.net.

## Extreme Makeover: Home Edition

One of ABC's top rated television series is *Extreme Makeover: Home Edition*. The hour-long episodes are devoted to providing a deserving family with a home makeover. In just seven days, a team of designers and workers attempts to renovate an entire house including the exterior, interior, and landscaping, while the family is sent on vacation. The majority of episodes are one hour; however, in some instances (mainly if there are complications) the episode will be aired in two parts, with half airing each week.

Most shows begin with a shot of the host in the design team's bus saying "I'm Ty Pennington, and the renovation starts right now." While a typical residential construction project may last three months, the builders and designers must accomplish their task in just one week, $\frac{1}{12}$ of the normal time! For the next seven days, the workers use fractions as they plan, measure, cut, and replace. For example, fractions are used to measure the length of 2 by 4s, roof trusses, shingles, siding, flooring, cabinets, appliances, countertops, and so on. Even the designers must use fractions to ensure that everything fits within the given space when they add the finishing touches such as furniture and appliances. All of this is important, because errors of $\frac{1}{8}$ or $\frac{1}{16}$ of an inch can have disastrous results!

Of course, plans don't always work out as expected. It's day five, and one of the local contractors has discovered a major problem in the kitchen. The countertop has been measured incorrectly by $3\frac{3}{4}$ inches. This means that none of the refrigerators on the market will fit the space. The team has the following choices: 1) order a custom refrigerator; 2) cut the countertop to the appropriate length; or 3) tear out a completed wall that has already been dry-walled, plastered, and painted. A custom refrigerator would cost $2,500 or $\frac{2}{3}$ more than a standard one, but with just two days remaining, would it arrive on time? The countertop could be cut, but the custom cabinets have already arrived and they can't be changed. Tearing out an existing wall is a hassle, but it would likely cost less than $500. If you were project manager, what would you do?

Finally, at the end of seven days and with all construction problems resolved, the family returns home. When Ty and the family give the order "Bus driver, move that bus!" the family sees the result of the team's efforts. The end result is a very happy and appreciative family who received a home makeover completed in just a fraction of the time it would normally take.

## LEARNING OUTCOMES

### 2-1 Fractions

1. Identify types of fractions.
2. Convert an improper fraction to a whole or mixed number.
3. Convert a whole or mixed number to an improper fraction.
4. Reduce a fraction to lowest terms.
5. Raise a fraction to higher terms.

### 2-2 Adding and Subtracting Fractions

1. Add fractions with like (common) denominators.
2. Find the least common denominator for two or more fractions.
3. Add fractions and mixed numbers.
4. Subtract fractions and mixed numbers.

### 2-3 Multiplying and Dividing Fractions

1. Multiply fractions and mixed numbers.
2. Divide fractions and mixed numbers.

 A corresponding Business Math Case Video for this chapter, *Introduction to the 7th Inning Business and Personnel*, can be found in Appendix A.

# 2-1 FRACTIONS

## LEARNING OUTCOMES

1 Identify types of fractions.
2 Convert an improper fraction to a whole or mixed number.
3 Convert a whole or mixed number to an improper fraction.
4 Reduce a fraction to lowest terms.
5 Raise a fraction to higher terms.

**Fraction:** a part of a whole amount. It is also a notation for showing division.

**Fractions** are used to represent parts of whole items. Often fractions are implied in the narrative portion of reports and news articles. For example, a news article may claim that three out of four voters are in favor of a proposed change in a city ordinance.

## 1 Identify types of fractions.

We use fractions as a way to represent parts of whole numbers. The fraction is also used to represent two relationships between numbers. The first relationship is the relationship between a part and a whole. If one whole quantity has four equal parts, then one of the four parts is represented by the fraction $\frac{1}{4}$ (Figure 2-1).

**Denominator:** the number of a fraction that shows how many parts one whole quantity is divided into. It is also the divisor of the indicated division.

**Numerator:** the number of a fraction that shows how many parts are considered. It is also the dividend of the indicated division.

**Fraction line:** the line that separates the numerator and denominator. It is also the division symbol.

**Proper fraction:** a fraction with a value that is less than 1. The numerator is smaller than the denominator.

**Improper fraction:** a fraction with a value that is equal to or greater than 1. The numerator is the same as or greater than the denominator.

**FIGURE 2-1**
**One part out of four parts is $\frac{1}{4}$ of the whole.**

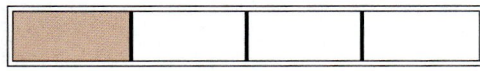

Another relationship represented by fractions is the relationship of division. The fraction $\frac{1}{4}$ can be interpreted as 1 divided by 4 or $1 \div 4$.

In the fraction $\frac{1}{4}$, 4 represents the number of parts contained in one whole quantity and is called the **denominator**. When the fraction is interpreted as division, the denominator is the divisor. The 1 in the fraction $\frac{1}{4}$ represents the number of parts under consideration and is called the **numerator**. When the fraction is interpreted as division, the numerator is the dividend.

The line separating the numerator and denominator may be written as a horizontal line (—) or as a slash (/) and is called the **fraction line**. When the fraction is interpreted as division, the fraction line is interpreted as the division symbol.

A fraction that has a value less than 1 is called a **proper fraction**. A fraction that has a value equal to or greater than 1 is called an **improper fraction**.

> **EXAMPLE 1** Visualize the fraction to identify whether it is a proper fraction. Describe the relationship between the numerator and denominator of proper fractions.
>
> (a) $\frac{2}{5}$ (b) $\frac{3}{2}$ (c) $\frac{4}{4}$
>
> (a) Figure 2-2 represents $\frac{2}{5}$ or two parts out of five equal parts.
>
> **FIGURE 2-2**
>
> **The fraction $\frac{2}{5}$ is a proper fraction, since it is less than one whole quantity. The numerator is smaller than the denominator.**
>
> (b) Figure 2-3 represents $\frac{3}{2}$ or three parts when the one whole quantity contains two equal parts.
>
> **FIGURE 2-3**
>
> **The fraction $\frac{3}{2}$ is more than one whole quantity. It is an improper fraction.**
>
> (c) Figure 2-4 represents $\frac{4}{4}$ or four parts when the one whole quantity contains four equal parts.
>
> **FIGURE 2-4**
>
> **The fraction $\frac{4}{4}$ represents one whole quantity. It is an improper fraction.**

**EXAMPLE 2**    Which fractions in Example 1 are improper fractions? Describe the relationship between the numerator and denominator of improper fractions.

**The fractions $\frac{3}{2}$ and $\frac{4}{4}$ are improper fractions. In an improper fraction, the numerator is equal to or greater than the denominator.**

---

 **STOP AND CHECK**

*Write the fraction that is illustrated. Indicate if the fraction is proper or improper.*

1.
2.

*Identify the fractions as proper or improper.*

3. $\dfrac{3}{7}$      4. $\dfrac{12}{5}$      5. $\dfrac{16}{16}$      6. $\dfrac{5}{9}$

---

## 2    Convert an improper fraction to a whole or mixed number.

In Figure 2-3, the fraction $\frac{3}{2}$ was shown as one whole quantity and $\frac{1}{2}$ of a second whole quantity. This amount, $\frac{3}{2}$, can also be written as $1\frac{1}{2}$. An amount written as a combination of a whole number and a fraction is called a **mixed number**. Every mixed number can also be written as an improper fraction.

**Mixed number:** an amount that is a combination of a whole number and a fraction.

    To interpret the meaning of an improper fraction, we use its whole number or mixed number form. Thus, it is important to be able to convert between improper fractions and mixed numbers.

---

**HOW TO**    Write an improper fraction as a whole or mixed number

Write $\frac{12}{3}$ and $\frac{13}{3}$ as whole or mixed numbers.

$$3\overline{)12}\;\;\overset{4}{\phantom{)}} \qquad 3\overline{)13}\;\;\overset{4\,R1}{\phantom{)}}$$

1. Divide the numerator of the improper fraction by the denominator.
2. Examine the remainder.
   (a) If the remainder is 0, the quotient is a whole number: The improper fraction is equivalent to this whole number.

$$\frac{12}{3} = 4$$

   (b) If the remainder is not 0, the quotient is not a whole number: The improper fraction is equivalent to a mixed number. The whole-number part of this mixed number is the whole-number part of the quotient. The fraction part of the mixed number has a numerator and a denominator. The numerator is the remainder; the denominator is the divisor (the denominator of the improper fraction).

$$\frac{13}{3} = 4\frac{1}{3}$$

---

**EXAMPLE 1**    Write $\frac{139}{8}$ as a whole or mixed number.

$$8\overline{)139}\;\;\overset{17\,R3,\ \text{or }17\frac{3}{8}}{\phantom{)}}$$

Divide 139 by 8. The quotient is 17 R3, which equals $17\frac{3}{8}$.

$$\begin{array}{r} 8 \\ \hline 59 \\ 56 \\ \hline 3 \end{array}$$

$$\frac{139}{8} = 17\frac{3}{8}$$

## 3   Convert a whole or mixed number to an improper fraction.

A mixed number can be written as an improper fraction by "reversing" the steps you use to write an improper fraction as a mixed number. This process is similar to the process for checking a division problem. In the division of an improper fraction with a result of $3\frac{1}{5}$, the divisor is 5, the quotient is 3, and the remainder is 1. To check division, multiply the divisor by the quotient and add the remainder. Examine the similarities in changing a mixed number to an improper fraction. Figure 2-5 illustrates this process.

In words, five times three plus one written over five.

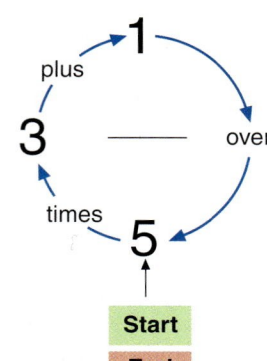

In symbols,

$$3\frac{1}{5} = \frac{5 \times 3 + 1}{5} = \frac{16}{5}$$

**FIGURE 2-5**
$3\frac{1}{5}$ written as an improper fraction.

| **HOW TO** | Write a mixed number or whole number as an improper fraction |
|---|---|
| **Mixed number:** | Write $1\frac{2}{5}$ and 9 as improper fractions. |
| 1. Find the numerator of the improper fraction. | $(5 \times 1) + 2 = 7$ |
|   (a) Multiply the denominator of the mixed number by the whole-number part. | |
|   (b) Add the product from step 1a to the numerator of the mixed number. | |
| 2. For the denominator of the improper fraction use the denominator of the mixed number. | $\dfrac{7}{5}$ |
| **Whole number:** | |
| 1. Write the whole number as the numerator. | $\dfrac{9}{9}$ |
| 2. Write 1 as the denominator. | $\dfrac{9}{1}$ |

**EXAMPLE 1**   Write $2\frac{3}{4}$ and 8 as improper fractions.

$$2\frac{3}{4} = \frac{(4 \times 2) + 3}{4} = \frac{11}{4}$$

For the numerator, multiply 4 times 2 and add 3.

$$8 = \frac{8}{1}$$

Write the whole number as the numerator and 1 as the denominator.

$$2\frac{3}{4} = \frac{11}{4} \text{ and } 8 = \frac{8}{1}.$$

## 4 Reduce a fraction to lowest terms.

**Equivalent fractions:** fractions that indicate the same portion of the whole amount.

**Lowest terms:** the form of a fraction when its numerator and denominator cannot be evenly divided by any whole number except 1.

Many fractions represent the same portion of a whole. Such fractions are called **equivalent fractions**. For example, $\frac{1}{2}$, $\frac{2}{4}$, and $\frac{4}{8}$ are equivalent fractions (Figure 2-6).

To be able to recognize equivalent fractions, we often reduce fractions to lowest terms. A fraction in **lowest terms** has a numerator and denominator that cannot be evenly divided by any whole number except 1.

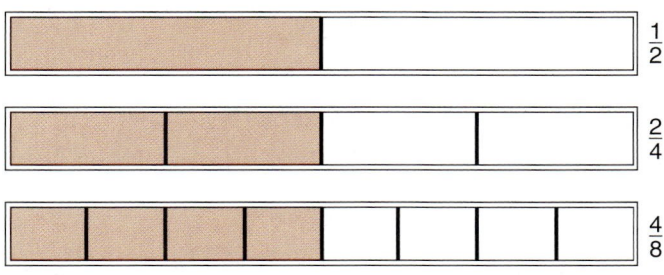

**FIGURE 2-6**
**Equivalent fractions**

**HOW TO**   Reduce a fraction to lowest terms

1. Inspect the numerator and denominator to find any whole number that both can be evenly divided by.
2. Divide both the numerator and the denominator by that number and inspect the new fraction to find any other number that the numerator and denominator can be evenly divided by.
3. Repeat steps 1 and 2 until 1 is the only number that the numerator and denominator can be evenly divided by.

Reduce $\frac{8}{10}$ to lowest terms.

8 and 10 are divisible by 2.

$$\frac{8 \div 2}{10 \div 2} = \frac{4}{5}$$

**EXAMPLE 1**   Reduce $\frac{30}{36}$ to lowest terms by inspection.

$$\frac{30}{36} = \frac{30 \div 2}{36 \div 2} = \frac{15}{18}$$

Both the numerator and the denominator can be evenly divided by 2.

$$\frac{15}{18} = \frac{15 \div 3}{18 \div 3} = \frac{5}{6}$$

Both the numerator and the denominator of the new fraction can be evenly divided by 3.

$\frac{30}{36}$ **is reduced to $\frac{5}{6}$.**

Now 1 is the only number that both the numerator and the denominator can be evenly divided by. The fraction is now in lowest terms.

**Greatest common divisor (GCD):** the greatest number by which both parts of a fraction can be evenly divided.

**By inspection:** using your number sense to mentally perform a mathematical process.

The most direct way to reduce a fraction to lowest terms is to divide the numerator and denominator by the **greatest common divisor (GCD)**. The GCD is the greatest number by which both parts of a fraction can be evenly divided. The GCD often can be found **by inspection**. Otherwise, a systematic process can be used.

## HOW TO    Find the greatest common divisor of two numbers

1. Use the numerator as the original divisor and the denominator as the dividend.
2. Divide.
3. Divide the original divisor from step 2 by the remainder from step 2.
4. Divide the divisor from step 3 by the remainder from step 3.
5. Continue this division process until the remainder is 0. The last divisor is the greatest common divisor.

## EXAMPLE 2    Find the GCD for $\frac{30}{36}$; then write the fraction in lowest terms.

$$\begin{array}{r} 1\,R6 \\ 30\overline{)36} \end{array}$$    Use the numerator as the original divisor and the denominator as the dividend.

$$\begin{array}{r} 5\,R0 \\ 6\overline{)30} \end{array}$$    Divide the original divisor by the original remainder.

**GCD = 6.**    When the remainder is 0, the last divisor is the GCD.

Reduce using the GCD.

$$\frac{30}{36} = \frac{30 \div 6}{36 \div 6} = \frac{5}{6}$$    Divide the numerator and denominator by the GCD.

$\frac{30}{36}$ **reduced to lowest terms is $\frac{5}{6}$.**

## STOP AND CHECK

1. Reduce $\frac{18}{24}$ to lowest terms by inspection.

2. Reduce $\frac{12}{36}$ to lowest terms by inspection.

3. Find the GCD for $\frac{16}{24}$; reduce the fraction to lowest terms.

4. Find the GCD for $\frac{39}{51}$; reduce the fraction to lowest terms.

5. Find the GCD for $\frac{12}{28}$; reduce the fraction to lowest terms.

6. Find the GCD for $\frac{18}{24}$; reduce the fraction to lowest terms.

## 5   Raise a fraction to higher terms.

Just as you can reduce a fraction to lowest terms by dividing the numerator and denominator by the same number, you can write a fraction in *higher* terms by *multiplying* the numerator and denominator by the same number. This process is used in addition and subtraction of fractions.

## HOW TO    Write a fraction in higher terms given the new denominator

Change $\frac{1}{2}$ to eighths, or $\frac{1}{2} = \frac{?}{8}$.

1. Divide the *new* denominator by the *old* denominator.

$$\begin{array}{r} 4 \\ 2\overline{)8} \end{array}$$

2. Multiply *both* the old numerator and the old denominator by the quotient from step 1.

$$\frac{1}{2} = \frac{1 \times 4}{2 \times 4} = \frac{4}{8}$$

**EXAMPLE 1** Rewrite $\frac{5}{8}$ as a fraction with a denominator of 72.

$$\frac{5}{8} = \frac{?}{72}$$

Write the problem symbolically.

$$8\overline{)72}^{\,9}$$

Divide the new denominator (72) by the old denominator (8) to find the number by which the old numerator and the old denominator must be multiplied. That number is 9.

$$\frac{5}{8} = \frac{5 \times 9}{8 \times 9} = \frac{45}{72}$$

Multiply the numerator and denominator by 9 to get the new fraction with a denominator of 72.

$$\frac{5}{8} = \frac{45}{72}$$

## ✔ STOP AND CHECK

1. Write $\frac{7}{12}$ as a fraction with a denominator of 36.

2. Write $\frac{3}{4}$ as a fraction with a denominator of 32.

*Change the fraction to an equivalent fraction with the given denominator.*

3. $\frac{1}{2}, \frac{}{18}$

4. $\frac{3}{5}, \frac{}{25}$

5. $\frac{5}{12}, \frac{}{36}$

6. $\frac{7}{8}, \frac{}{24}$

## 2-1 SECTION EXERCISES

### SKILL BUILDERS

*Classify the fractions as proper or improper.*

1. $\frac{5}{9}$

2. $\frac{12}{7}$

3. $\frac{7}{7}$

4. $\frac{1}{12}$

5. $\frac{12}{15}$

6. $\frac{21}{20}$

*Write the fraction as a whole or mixed number.*

7. $\frac{12}{7}$

8. $\frac{21}{20}$

9. $\frac{18}{18}$

10. $\frac{17}{7}$

11. $\frac{16}{8}$

12. $\frac{387}{16}$

*Write the whole or mixed number as an improper fraction.*

13. $6\frac{1}{4}$

14. $27\frac{2}{5}$

15. $2\frac{1}{3}$

16. $3\frac{4}{5}$

17. $1\frac{5}{8}$

18. $6\frac{2}{3}$

*Reduce to lowest terms.*

**19.** $\dfrac{12}{15}$

**20.** $\dfrac{12}{20}$

**21.** $\dfrac{18}{24}$

**22.** $\dfrac{18}{36}$

**23.** $\dfrac{24}{36}$

**24.** $\dfrac{13}{39}$

*Change the fraction to an equivalent fraction with the given denominator.*

**25.** $\dfrac{3}{8}, \dfrac{}{16}$

**26.** $\dfrac{4}{5}, \dfrac{}{20}$

**27.** $\dfrac{3}{8}, \dfrac{}{32}$

**28.** $\dfrac{5}{9}, \dfrac{}{27}$

**29.** $\dfrac{1}{3}, \dfrac{}{15}$

**30.** $\dfrac{3}{5}, \dfrac{}{15}$

# 2-2 ADDING AND SUBTRACTING FRACTIONS

## LEARNING OUTCOMES

1 Add fractions with like (common) denominators.
2 Find the least common denominator for two or more fractions.
3 Add fractions and mixed numbers.
4 Subtract fractions and mixed numbers.

## 1 Add fractions with like (common) denominators.

The statement that three calculators plus four fax machines is the same as seven calculators is not true. The reason this is not true is that calculators and fax machines are *unlike* items, and we can only add *like* terms. It is true that three calculators plus four fax machines are the same as seven office machines. What we have done is to *rename* calculators and fax machines using a like term. Calculators and fax machines are both office machines. In the same way, to add fractions that have different denominators, we must rename the fractions using a like, or common, denominator. When fractions have like denominators, we can write their sum as a single fraction.

### HOW TO  Add fractions with like (common) denominators

Add $\dfrac{2}{9} + \dfrac{1}{9}$.

1. Find the numerator of the sum: Add the numerators of the addends.

$$2 + 1 = 3$$

2. Find the denominator of the sum: Use the like denominator of the addends.

$$\dfrac{2}{9} + \dfrac{1}{9} = \dfrac{3}{9}$$

3. Reduce the sum to lowest terms and/or write as a whole or mixed number.

$$\dfrac{3}{9} = \dfrac{3 \div 3}{9 \div 3} = \dfrac{1}{3}$$

### EXAMPLE 1  Find the sum: $\dfrac{1}{4} + \dfrac{3}{4} + \dfrac{3}{4}$.

$$\dfrac{1}{4} + \dfrac{3}{4} + \dfrac{3}{4} = \dfrac{1 + 3 + 3}{4} = \dfrac{7}{4}$$

The sum of the numerators is the numerator of the sum. The original like (common) denominator is the denominator of the sum.

$$\dfrac{7}{4} = 1\dfrac{3}{4}$$

Convert the improper fraction to a whole or mixed number.

**The sum is $1\dfrac{3}{4}$.**

*Add. Reduce or write as a whole or mixed number if appropriate.*

1. $\dfrac{3}{4} + \dfrac{1}{4} + \dfrac{1}{4}$

2. $\dfrac{3}{8} + \dfrac{7}{8} + \dfrac{1}{8}$

3. $\dfrac{1}{5} + \dfrac{2}{5} + \dfrac{2}{5}$

4. $\dfrac{5}{8} + \dfrac{3}{8} + \dfrac{1}{8}$

5. $\dfrac{5}{12} + \dfrac{7}{12} + \dfrac{11}{12}$

## 2 Find the least common denominator for two or more fractions.

**Least common denominator (LCD):** the smallest number that can be divided evenly by each original denominator.

To add fractions with different denominators, the fractions must first be changed to equivalent fractions with a common denominator. It is desirable to use the **least common denominator (LCD)**—the smallest number that can be evenly divided by each original denominator.

The common denominator can sometimes be found by inspection—that is, mentally selecting a number that can be evenly divided by each denominator. However, there are several systematic processes for finding the least common denominator. One way to find the least common denominator is to use prime numbers.

**Prime number:** a number greater than 1 that can be divided evenly only by itself and 1.

A **prime number** is a number greater than 1 that can be evenly divided only by itself and 1. The first ten prime numbers are 2, 3, 5, 7, 11, 13, 17, 19, 23, and 29.

### HOW TO  Find the least common denominator for two or more fractions

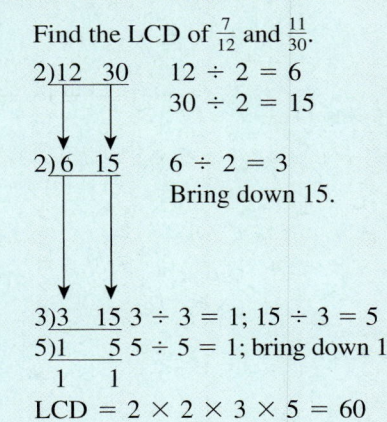

Find the LCD of $\dfrac{7}{12}$ and $\dfrac{11}{30}$.

1. Write the denominators in a row and divide each one by the smallest prime number that any of the numbers can be evenly divided by.
2. Write a new row of numbers using the quotients from step 1 and any numbers in the first row that cannot be evenly divided by the first prime number. Divide by the smallest prime that any of the numbers can be evenly divided by.
3. Continue this process until you have a row of 1s.

$$2)\underline{12\quad 30} \qquad 12 \div 2 = 6$$
$$30 \div 2 = 15$$

$$2)\underline{6\quad 15} \qquad 6 \div 2 = 3$$
$$\text{Bring down 15.}$$

$$3)\underline{3\quad 15} \qquad 3 \div 3 = 1; 15 \div 3 = 5$$
$$5)\underline{1\quad 5} \qquad 5 \div 5 = 1; \text{bring down 1.}$$
$$\quad 1\quad 1$$

4. Multiply all the prime numbers you used to divide the denominators. The product is the least common denominator.

$$\text{LCD} = 2 \times 2 \times 3 \times 5 = 60$$

### EXAMPLE 1  Find the least common denominator (LCD) of $\dfrac{5}{6}$, $\dfrac{5}{8}$, and $\dfrac{1}{12}$.

$2)\underline{6\quad 8\quad 12}$     Write the denominators in a row and divide by 2, the smallest prime divisor.
$6 \div 2 = 3; 8 \div 2 = 4; 12 \div 2 = 6$

$2)\underline{3\quad 4\quad 6}$     Divide by 2 again.
Bring down 3. $4 \div 2 = 2; 6 \div 2 = 3$.

$2)\underline{3\quad 2\quad 3}$     Divide by 2 again. Bring down both 3s.
$2 \div 2 = 1$.

$3)\underline{3\quad 1\quad 3}$     Divide by 3.
$\quad 1\quad 1\quad 1$     $3 \div 3 = 1$. Bring down 1.
$2 \times 2 \times 2 \times 3 = 24$     The LCD is the product of all the divisors.

**The LCD is 24.**

✔ **STOP AND CHECK**

*Find the least common denominator.*

1. $\dfrac{1}{6}, \dfrac{5}{12}$    2. $\dfrac{15}{24}, \dfrac{37}{48}$    3. $\dfrac{1}{2}, \dfrac{5}{8}$    4. $\dfrac{8}{11}, \dfrac{3}{7}$    5. $\dfrac{5}{42}, \dfrac{7}{30}, \dfrac{9}{35}$

## 3  Add fractions and mixed numbers.

We can use the procedure for finding a least common denominator to add fractions with different denominators.

---

**HOW TO**  Add fractions with different denominators

Add $\dfrac{2}{3} + \dfrac{3}{4}$.

1. Find the least common denominator.

$\text{LCD} = 12$ by inspection

2. Change each fraction to an equivalent fraction using the least common denominator.

$\dfrac{2}{3} = \dfrac{2 \times 4}{3 \times 4} = \dfrac{8}{12}$

$\dfrac{3}{4} = \dfrac{3 \times 3}{4 \times 3} = \dfrac{9}{12}$

3. Add the new fractions with like (common) denominators.

$\dfrac{8}{12} + \dfrac{9}{12} = \dfrac{17}{12}$

4. Reduce to lowest terms and/or write as a whole or mixed number.

$\dfrac{17}{12} = 1\dfrac{5}{12}$

---

**EXAMPLE 1**  Find the sum of $\dfrac{5}{6}, \dfrac{5}{8}$, and $\dfrac{1}{12}$.

$\text{LCD} = 24$                From Example 1 in Learning Outcome 2.

$\dfrac{5}{6} = \dfrac{5 \times 4}{6 \times 4} = \dfrac{20}{24}$        Change each fraction to an equivalent fraction.

$\dfrac{5}{8} = \dfrac{5 \times 3}{8 \times 3} = \dfrac{15}{24}$

$\dfrac{1}{12} = \dfrac{1 \times 2}{12 \times 2} = \dfrac{2}{24}$        Add the numerators and use the common denominator.

$\dfrac{37}{24} = 1\dfrac{13}{24}$        Write the improper fraction as a mixed number.

**The sum is $1\dfrac{13}{24}$.**

---

**HOW TO**  Add mixed numbers

1. Add the whole-number parts.
2. Add the fraction parts and reduce to lowest terms.
3. Change improper fractions to whole or mixed numbers.
4. Add the whole-number parts.

## EXAMPLE 2

Add $3\frac{2}{5} + 10\frac{3}{10} + 4\frac{7}{15}$.

Find the LCD.

$2)\underline{5\quad 10\quad 15}$

Divide by 2. $10 \div 2 = 5$.
Bring down 5 and 15.

$3)\underline{5\quad 5\quad 15}$

Divide by 3. $15 \div 3 = 5$.
Bring down both 5s.

$5)\underline{5\quad 5\quad 5}$
$\quad 1\quad 1\quad 1$

Divide by 5. $5 \div 5 = 1$.

$2 \times 3 \times 5 = 30$

LCD

$$3\frac{2}{5} = 3\frac{2 \times 6}{5 \times 6} = 3\frac{12}{30}$$

Change fraction parts to equivalent fractions with LCD.

$$10\frac{3}{10} = 10\frac{3 \times 3}{10 \times 3} = 10\frac{9}{30}$$

Add whole numbers. Add fractions.

$$4\frac{7}{15} = 4\frac{7 \times 2}{15 \times 2} = 4\frac{14}{30}$$

$$17\frac{35}{30}$$

Reduce fraction and change improper fraction to mixed number.

$$\frac{35}{30} = \frac{7}{6} = 1\frac{1}{6}$$

$$17 + 1 + \frac{1}{6} = 18\frac{1}{6}$$

Add whole numbers.

**The sum is $18\frac{1}{6}$.**

---

## TIP

**Estimate Sum of Mixed Numbers**

A quick way to estimate the sum of mixed numbers is to add only the whole number parts. This estimate is smaller than the exact sum of the mixed numbers. To find an estimate that is larger than the exact sum, add 1 to the low estimate for each mixed number addend. Do not add 1 for whole number addends. Apply this estimation process to the example.

$3 + 10 + 4 = 17$ low estimate
$17 + 1 + 1 + 1 = 20$ high estimate

The exact sum is between 17 and 20. Refer to the example to see the exact sum is $18\frac{1}{6}$, which is in the interval of the estimate.

---

## EXAMPLE 3

If an employee works the following overtime hours each day, find his total overtime for the week: $1\frac{3}{4}$ hours on Monday, $2\frac{1}{2}$ hours on Tuesday, $1\frac{1}{4}$ hours on Wednesday, $2\frac{1}{4}$ hours on Thursday, and $1\frac{3}{4}$ hours on Friday.

$$1\frac{3}{4} = 1\frac{3}{4}$$

LCD is 4.

$$2\frac{1}{2} = 2\frac{2}{4}$$

Change $2\frac{1}{2}$ to $2\frac{2}{4}$.

$$1\frac{1}{4} = 1\frac{1}{4}$$

Add fractions.

$$2\frac{1}{4} = 2\frac{1}{4}$$

Add whole numbers.

$$1\frac{3}{4} = 1\frac{3}{4}$$

$$= 7\frac{10}{4}$$

$$\frac{10}{4} = \frac{5}{2} = 2\frac{1}{2}$$

$$= 9\frac{1}{2}$$

$$7 + 2\frac{1}{2} = 9\frac{1}{2}$$

**The total overtime is $9\frac{1}{2}$ hours.**

## 4 Subtract fractions and mixed numbers.

In subtracting fractions, just as in adding fractions, you need to find a common denominator.

### HOW TO    Subtract fractions

**With like denominators**

1. Find the numerator of the difference: Subtract the numerators of the fractions.
2. Find the denominator of the difference: Use the like denominator of the fractions.
3. Reduce to lowest terms.

Subtract $\frac{5}{12} - \frac{1}{12}$.

$5 - 1 = 4$

$\frac{5}{12} - \frac{1}{12} = \frac{4}{12}$

$\frac{4}{12} = \frac{1}{3}$

**With different denominators**

1. Find the least common denominator.
2. Change each fraction to an equivalent fraction using the least common denominator.
3. Subtract the new fractions with like (common) denominators.
4. Reduce to lowest terms.

Subtract $\frac{5}{12} - \frac{1}{3}$.

LCD = 12

$\frac{1}{3} = \frac{1 \times 4}{3 \times 4} = \frac{4}{12}$

$\frac{5}{12} - \frac{4}{12} = \frac{1}{12}$

### EXAMPLE 1    Subtract: $\frac{5}{12} - \frac{4}{15}$.

Find the LCD.

| | |
|---|---|
| 2)12  15 | Divide by 2. $12 \div 2 = 6$. Bring down 15. |
| 2) 6  15 | Divide by 2. $6 \div 2 = 3$. Bring down 15. |
| 3) 3  15 | Divide by 3. $3 \div 3 = 1$; $15 \div 3 = 5$. |
| 5) 1   5 | Divide by 5. $5 \div 5 = 1$. Bring down 1. |
|     1   1 | |
| $2 \times 2 \times 3 \times 5 = 60$ | LCD = 60 |

$$\frac{5}{12} = \frac{5 \times 5}{12 \times 5} = \frac{25}{60}$$  Change to equivalent fractions.

$$-\frac{4}{15} = -\frac{4 \times 4}{15 \times 4} = -\frac{16}{60}$$  Subtract fractions.

$$\frac{9}{60} = \frac{3}{20}$$  Reduce.

**The difference is $\frac{3}{20}$.**

---

**HOW TO**  **Subtract mixed numbers**

Subtract $2\frac{1}{3} - 1\frac{1}{2}$.

1. If the fractions have different denominators, find the LCD and change the fractions to equivalent fractions using the LCD.
2. If necessary, regroup by subtracting 1 from the whole number in the minuend and add 1 (in the form of LCD/LCD) to the fraction in the minuend.
3. Subtract the fractions and the whole numbers.
4. Reduce to lowest terms.

$$2\frac{1}{3} = 2\frac{2}{6} = 1 + \frac{6}{6} + \frac{2}{6} = 1\frac{8}{6}$$
$$-1\frac{1}{2} = -1\frac{3}{6} \qquad\qquad = -1\frac{3}{6}$$
$$\qquad\qquad\qquad\qquad\qquad\qquad \frac{5}{6}$$

---

**EXAMPLE 2**  Subtract $10\frac{1}{3} - 7\frac{3}{5}$.

$$10\frac{1}{3} = 10\frac{5}{15} = 9 + \frac{15}{15} + \frac{5}{15} = 9\frac{20}{15}$$  Change fractions to equivalent fractions with the same LCD. Regroup in the minuend.

$$-7\frac{3}{5} \qquad\qquad\qquad\qquad = -7\frac{9}{15}$$  Subtract fractions. Subtract whole numbers.

$$\qquad\qquad\qquad\qquad\qquad 2\frac{11}{15}$$  The fraction is already in lowest terms, so you do not have to reduce it.

**The difference is $2\frac{11}{15}$.**

---

**TIP**

**Regroup or Borrow**

Regrouping is also referred to as borrowing. The original form of the number has the same value as the new form of the number. Reexamine the previous example.

$$10\frac{5}{15} = 10 - 1 + 1 + \frac{5}{15} = 9 + 1 + \frac{5}{15}$$
$$= 9 + \frac{15}{15} + \frac{5}{15}$$
$$= 9\frac{20}{15}$$

---

**EXAMPLE 3**  An interior designer had 65 yards of fabric wall covering on hand and used $35\frac{3}{8}$ yards for a client's sunroom. How many yards of fabric remain?

$$65 = 64\frac{8}{8}$$  Regroup by subtracting 1 from 65.  $1 = \frac{8}{8}$

$$-35\frac{3}{8} = -35\frac{3}{8}$$  Subtract: $\frac{8}{8} - \frac{3}{8} = \frac{5}{8}$. Then subtract $64 - 35 = 29$.

$$29\frac{5}{8}$$

**$29\frac{5}{8}$ yards of fabric remain.**

*Subtract.*

**1.** $\dfrac{7}{8} - \dfrac{3}{8}$

**2.** $\dfrac{5}{8} - \dfrac{1}{12}$

**3.** $12\dfrac{5}{8} - 3\dfrac{7}{8}$

**4.** $15\dfrac{11}{12} - 7\dfrac{5}{18}$

**5.** $32 - 14\dfrac{5}{12}$

**6.** $27\dfrac{4}{15} - 14\dfrac{7}{12}$

**7.** Marcus Johnson, a real estate broker, owns 100 acres of land. During the year he purchased additional tracts of $12\dfrac{3}{4}$ acres, $23\dfrac{2}{3}$ acres, and $5\dfrac{1}{8}$ acres. If he sold a total of $65\dfrac{2}{3}$ acres during the year, how many acres does he still own?

**8.** To make a picture frame two pieces $10\dfrac{3}{4}$ inches and two pieces $12\dfrac{5}{8}$ inches are cut from 60 inches of frame material. How much frame material remains?

## 2-2 SECTION EXERCISES

### SKILL BUILDERS

*Perform the indicated operation. Write the sum as a fraction, whole number, or mixed number in lowest terms.*

**1.** $\dfrac{1}{9} + \dfrac{2}{9} + \dfrac{5}{9}$

**2.** $\dfrac{7}{8} + \dfrac{5}{8}$

**3.** $\dfrac{5}{6} + \dfrac{7}{15}$

**4.** $\dfrac{5}{8} + \dfrac{7}{12}$

**5.** $4\dfrac{5}{6} + 7\dfrac{1}{2}$

**6.** $23\dfrac{5}{12} + 48\dfrac{7}{16}$

**7.** $51\dfrac{5}{18} + 86\dfrac{9}{24}$

**8.** $5\dfrac{7}{12} + 3\dfrac{1}{4} + 2\dfrac{2}{3}$

**9.** $\dfrac{7}{8} + 2\dfrac{3}{24} + 6\dfrac{1}{6}$

**10.** $3\dfrac{5}{9} + 5\dfrac{1}{12} + 2\dfrac{2}{3}$

*Find the difference. Write the difference in lowest terms.*

**11.** $\dfrac{7}{8} - \dfrac{3}{8}$

**12.** $\dfrac{8}{9} - \dfrac{2}{9}$

**13.** $\dfrac{3}{4} - \dfrac{5}{7}$

**14.** $9\dfrac{2}{3} - 6\dfrac{1}{2}$

**15.** $15 - 12\dfrac{7}{9}$

**16.** $21\dfrac{3}{5} - 12\dfrac{7}{10}$

**17.** $15\dfrac{8}{15} - 7\dfrac{5}{12}$

**18.** $23\dfrac{1}{8} - \dfrac{7}{12}$

**19.** $8\dfrac{1}{3} - 5$

**20.** $12\dfrac{1}{5} - 7\dfrac{4}{5}$

## APPLICATIONS

**21.** Loretta McBride is determining the amount of fabric required for window treatments. A single window requires $11\dfrac{3}{4}$ yards and a double window requires $18\dfrac{5}{8}$ yards of fabric. If she has two single windows and one double window, how much fabric is required?

**22.** Marveen McCready, a commercial space designer, has taken these measurements for an office in which she plans to install a wallpaper border around the ceiling: $42\dfrac{3}{8}$ feet, $37\dfrac{5}{8}$ feet, $12\dfrac{3}{8}$ feet, and $23\dfrac{3}{4}$ feet. How much paper does she need for the job?

**23.** Rob Farinelli is building a gazebo and plans to use for the floor two boards that are $10\dfrac{3}{4}$ feet, four boards that are $12\dfrac{5}{8}$ feet, and two boards that are $8\dfrac{1}{2}$ feet. Find the total number of feet in all the boards.

**24.** Tenisha Gist cuts brass plates for an engraving job. From a sheet of brass, three pieces $4\dfrac{4}{5}$ inches wide and two pieces $7\dfrac{3}{8}$ inches wide are cut. What is the smallest piece of brass required to cut all five plates?

**25.** The fabric Loretta McBride has selected for the window treatment in Exercise 21 has only 45 yards on the only roll available. Will she be able to use the fabric or must she make an alternate selection?

**26.** Rob Farinelli purchased two boards that are 12 feet and will cut them to make $10\frac{3}{4}$-foot boards for the gazebo he is building. How much must be removed from each board?

**27.** Rob Farinelli purchased four boards that are each 14 feet to make $12\frac{5}{8}$ foot boards for his gazebo. Upon measuring, he finds they are $13\frac{15}{16}$ feet, $14\frac{1}{8}$ feet, 14 feet, and $13\frac{13}{16}$ feet. How much must be removed from each board to get $12\frac{5}{8}$-foot boards?

**28.** Charlie Carr has a sheet of brass that is 36 inches wide and cuts two pieces that are each $8\frac{3}{4}$ inches wide. What is the width of the leftover brass?

## 2-3 MULTIPLYING AND DIVIDING FRACTIONS

### LEARNING OUTCOMES

1 Multiply fractions and mixed numbers.
2 Divide fractions and mixed numbers.

### 1 Multiply fractions and mixed numbers.

Alexa May has three Pizza Hut stores. Her distributor shipped only $\frac{3}{4}$ of a cheese order that Alexa had expected to distribute equally among her three stores. What fractional part of the original order will each store receive?

Each store will receive $\frac{1}{3}$ of the *shipment,* but the shipment is only $\frac{3}{4}$ of the *original order.* Each store, then, will receive only $\frac{1}{3}$ of $\frac{3}{4}$ of the original order. Finding $\frac{1}{3}$ of $\frac{3}{4}$ illustrates the use of multiplying fractions just as "2 boxes **of** 3 cans each" amounts to $2 \times 3$, or 6 cans. Similarly, $\frac{1}{3}$ **of** $\frac{3}{4}$ amounts to $\frac{1}{3} \times \frac{3}{4}$.

We can visualize $\frac{1}{3} \times \frac{3}{4}$, or $\frac{1}{3}$ **of** $\frac{3}{4}$, by first visualizing $\frac{3}{4}$ of a whole (Figure 2-7).

**FIGURE 2-7**
3 parts out of 4 parts $= \frac{3}{4}$ of a whole.

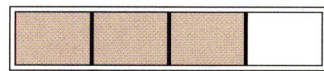

Now visualize $\frac{1}{3}$ of $\frac{3}{4}$ of a whole (Figure 2-8).

**FIGURE 2-8**
1 part out of 3 parts in $\frac{3}{4}$ of a whole $=$

1 part out of 4 parts or $\frac{1}{4}$ of a whole.

$$\frac{1}{3} \quad \text{of} \quad \frac{3}{4} \quad \text{is} \quad \frac{1}{4}$$
$$\frac{1}{3} \quad \times \quad \frac{3}{4} \quad = \quad \frac{1}{4}$$

## HOW TO — Multiply fractions

Multiply $\frac{1}{2} \times \frac{7}{8}$.

1. Find the numerator of the product:
   Multiply the numerators of the fractions.

   $1 \times 7 = 7$

2. Find the denominator of the product:
   Multiply the denominators of the fractions.

   $2 \times 8 = 16$

3. Reduce to lowest terms.

   $$\frac{1}{2} \times \frac{7}{8} = \frac{7}{16}$$

---

## EXAMPLE 1

What fraction of the original cheese order will each of Alexa's three stores receive equally if $\frac{9}{10}$ of the original order is shipped?

| What You Know | What You Are Looking For | Solution Plan |
|---|---|---|
| Fraction of shipment each store can receive: $\frac{1}{3}$ Fraction of original order received for all the stores: $\frac{9}{10}$ | Fraction of original order that each store will receive equally | Fraction of original order that each store will receive = fraction of shipment each store can receive $\times$ fraction of original order received. |

### Solution

$$\frac{1}{3} \times \frac{9}{10} = \frac{1 \times 9}{3 \times 10} = \frac{9}{30}$$   Multiply numerators; multiply denominators.

$$\frac{9}{30} = \frac{3}{10}$$   Reduce to lowest terms.

### Conclusion

**Each store will receive $\frac{3}{10}$ of the original order.**

---

## TIP

**Reduce Before Multiplying**

When you multiply fractions, you save time by reducing fractions *before* you multiply. If *any* numerator and *any* denominator can be divided evenly by the same number, divide both the numerator and the denominator by that number. You can then multiply the reduced numbers with greater accuracy than you could multiply the larger numbers.

$$\frac{1}{\overset{\scriptstyle }{\underset{1}{3}}} \times \frac{\overset{1}{3}}{4} = \frac{1}{4} \qquad \frac{1}{\underset{1}{3}} \times \frac{\overset{3}{9}}{10} = \frac{3}{10}$$   A numerator and a denominator can be divided evenly by 3 in both examples.

---

## HOW TO — Multiply mixed numbers and whole numbers

1. Write the mixed numbers and whole numbers as improper fractions.
2. Reduce numerators and denominators as appropriate.
3. Multiply the fractions.
4. Reduce to lowest terms and/or write as a whole or mixed number.

**EXAMPLE 2**

Multiply $2\frac{1}{3} \times 3\frac{3}{4}$.

$$2\frac{1}{3} \times 3\frac{3}{4} = \frac{(3 \times 2) + 1}{3} \times \frac{(4 \times 3) + 3}{4}$$

Write the mixed numbers as improper fractions.

$$= \frac{7}{\overset{}{\underset{1}{3}}} \times \frac{\overset{5}{15}}{4}$$

Divide both 3 and 15 by 3, reducing to 1 and 5. Multiply the numerators and denominators.

$$= \frac{35}{4} = 8\frac{3}{4}$$

Write as a mixed number.

**The product is $8\frac{3}{4}$.**

---

## TIP

**Are Products Always Larger Than Their Factors?**

A product is not always greater than the factors being multiplied.

When the *multiplier* is a proper fraction, the product is *less than* the original number. This is true whether the *multiplicand* is a whole number, fraction, or mixed number.

$5 \times \dfrac{3}{5} = 3$              Product 3 is less than factor 5.

$\dfrac{3}{4} \times \dfrac{4}{9} = \dfrac{1}{3}$              Product $\frac{1}{3}$ is less than factor $\frac{3}{4}$.

$2\dfrac{1}{2} \times \dfrac{1}{2} = \dfrac{5}{2} \times \dfrac{1}{2} = \dfrac{5}{4} = 1\dfrac{1}{4}$              Product $1\frac{1}{4}$ is less than factor $2\frac{1}{2}$.

---

 **STOP AND CHECK**

*Multiply. Write products as proper fractions or mixed numbers in lowest terms.*

**1.** $\dfrac{3}{7} \times \dfrac{5}{8}$     **2.** $\dfrac{4}{9} \times \dfrac{3}{8}$     **3.** $3\dfrac{1}{4} \times \dfrac{5}{13}$     **4.** $1\dfrac{1}{9} \times 3$     **5.** $2\dfrac{2}{5} \times \dfrac{15}{21}$

**6.** The outside width of a boxed cooktop is $2\frac{3}{8}$ feet, and a shipment of boxed cooktops is placed in a 45-foot trailer. How many feet will 16 cooktop boxes require?

**7.** Computer boxes are $2\frac{1}{3}$ feet high. How high is a stack of 14 computer boxes?

---

## 2  Divide fractions and mixed numbers.

Division of fractions is related to multiplication.

*Total amount = number of units of a specified size times ($\times$) the specified size.* If you know the total amount and the number of equal units, you can find the size of each unit by dividing the total amount by the number of equal units. If you know the total amount and the specified size, you can find the number of equal units by dividing the total amount by the specified size.

Home Depot has a stack of plywood that is 32 inches high. If each sheet of plywood is $\frac{1}{2}$ inch, how many sheets of plywood are in the stack? How many equal units of plywood are contained in the total stack? Divide the height of the stack (total amount) by the thickness of each sheet (specified size).

$32 \div \dfrac{1}{2}$   Total thickness divided by thickness of one sheet of plywood

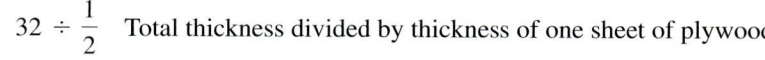

Another way of approaching the problem is to think of the number of sheets of plywood in 1 inch of height. If each sheet of plywood is $\frac{1}{2}$ inch, then two sheets of plywood are 1 inch thick. If there are two sheets of plywood for each inch, there will be 64 pieces of plywood in the 32-inch stack.

$$32 \div \frac{1}{2} = 32 \times \frac{2}{1} = 64$$

**Reciprocals:** two numbers are reciprocals if their product is 1. $\frac{4}{5}$ and $\frac{5}{4}$ are reciprocals.

The relationship between multiplying and dividing fractions involves a concept called **reciprocals**. Two numbers are reciprocals if their product is 1. Thus, $\frac{2}{3}$ and $\frac{3}{2}$ are reciprocals ($\frac{2}{3} \times \frac{3}{2} = 1$) and $\frac{7}{8}$ and $\frac{8}{7}$ are reciprocals ($\frac{7}{8} \times \frac{8}{7} = 1$).

## HOW TO    Find the reciprocal of a number

Write the reciprocal of 3.

1. Write the number as a fraction.

$$\frac{3}{1}$$

2. Interchange the numerator and denominator.

$$\frac{1}{3}$$

## EXAMPLE 1    Find the reciprocal of (a) $\frac{7}{9}$; (b) 5; (c) $4\frac{1}{2}$.

(a) The reciprocal of $\frac{7}{9}$ is $\frac{9}{7}$.    The reciprocal can be stated as $1\frac{2}{7}$.

(b) The reciprocal of $\frac{5}{1}$ is $\frac{1}{5}$.    Write 5 as the fraction $\frac{5}{1}$.

(c) The reciprocal of $4\frac{1}{2}$ is $\frac{2}{9}$.    Write $4\frac{1}{2}$ as the fraction $\frac{9}{2}$.

In the Home Depot discussion, we reasoned that $32 \div \frac{1}{2}$ is the same as $32 \times 2$. So, to divide by a fraction, we *multiply* by the *reciprocal* of the divisor.

## HOW TO    Divide fractions or mixed numbers

Divide $\frac{3}{4}$ by 5.

1. Write numbers as fractions.
2. Find the reciprocal of the divisor.

$$\frac{3}{4} \div \frac{5}{1}$$

3. Multiply the dividend by the reciprocal of the divisor.

$$\frac{3}{4} \times \frac{1}{5} = \frac{3}{20}$$

4. Reduce to lowest terms and/or write as a whole or mixed number.

$$\frac{3}{20} \text{ (lowest terms)}$$

## EXAMPLE 2    Madison Duke makes appliqués from brocade fabric. A customer has ordered five appliqués. Can Madison fill the order without buying more fabric? She has $\frac{3}{4}$ yard of fabric and each appliqué requires $\frac{1}{6}$ of a yard.

| What You Know | What You Are Looking For | Solution Plan |
|---|---|---|
| Total length of fabric: $\frac{3}{4}$ yard | The number of appliqués that can be made from the fabric | Number of appliqués that can be made = total length of fabric ÷ length of fabric needed for each appliqué |
| Length of fabric needed for each appliqué: $\frac{1}{6}$ yard | Can Madison fill the order? | |

| Number of appliqués $= \dfrac{3}{4} \div \dfrac{1}{6}$ | Total fabric $\div$ fabric in 1 appliqué |
| | Multiply by the reciprocal of the divisor. |

$$= \dfrac{3}{\overset{}{\underset{2}{\cancel{4}}}} \times \dfrac{\overset{3}{\cancel{6}}}{1}$$  Reduce and multiply.

$$= \dfrac{9}{2} = 4\dfrac{1}{2}$$  Change improper fraction to mixed number.

**Conclusion**

Madison can make four appliqués from the $\frac{3}{4}$ yard of fabric.

**Since the order is five appliqués, Madison cannot fill the order without buying more fabric.**

## EXAMPLE 3

Find the quotient: $5\frac{1}{2} \div 7\frac{1}{3}$.

$$5\dfrac{1}{2} \div 7\dfrac{1}{3} =$$  Write the numbers as improper fractions.

$$\dfrac{11}{2} \div \dfrac{22}{3} =$$  Multiply $\frac{11}{2}$ by the reciprocal of the divisor, $\frac{3}{22}$.

$$\dfrac{\overset{1}{\cancel{11}}}{2} \times \dfrac{3}{\underset{2}{\cancel{22}}} = \dfrac{1 \times 3}{2 \times 2} = \dfrac{3}{4}$$  Reduce and multiply.

**The quotient is $\frac{3}{4}$.**

##  STOP AND CHECK

*Find the reciprocal.*

**1.** $\dfrac{5}{12}$

**2.** 32

**3.** $7\dfrac{1}{8}$

*Divide. Write the quotient as a proper fraction or mixed number in lowest terms.*

**4.** $\dfrac{7}{8} \div \dfrac{3}{4}$

**5.** $2\dfrac{2}{5} \div 2\dfrac{1}{10}$

**6.** $3\dfrac{3}{8} \div 9$

**7.** Kisha stacks lumber in a storage bin that is 72 inches in height. If she stores $\frac{3}{4}$-inch-thick plywood in the bin, how many sheets can she expect to fit in the bin?

## SKILL BUILDERS

*Find the product.*

**1.** $\dfrac{3}{8} \times \dfrac{4}{5}$

**2.** $\dfrac{5}{7} \times \dfrac{1}{6}$

**3.** $5\dfrac{3}{4} \times 3\dfrac{8}{9}$

**4.** $\dfrac{3}{8} \times 24$

*Find the reciprocal.*

**5.** $\dfrac{7}{12}$

**6.** $\dfrac{3}{5}$

**7.** $9$

**8.** $12$

**9.** $5\dfrac{4}{7}$

**10.** $3\dfrac{3}{8}$

*Find the quotient.*

**11.** $\dfrac{5}{8} \div \dfrac{3}{4}$

**12.** $\dfrac{3}{5} \div \dfrac{9}{10}$

**13.** $2\dfrac{2}{5} \div 1\dfrac{1}{7}$

**14.** $5\dfrac{1}{4} \div 2\dfrac{2}{3}$

## APPLICATIONS

**15.** Pierre Hugo is handling the estate of a prominent business-woman. The will states that the surviving spouse is to receive $\frac{1}{4}$ of the estate and the remaining $\frac{3}{4}$ of the estate will be divided equally among five surviving children. What fraction of the estate does each child receive?

**16.** Marvin Jones needs to estimate the number of sheets of plywood in a stack that is 75 inches tall. If each sheet of plywood is $1\frac{1}{8}$ inch thick, how many sheets should he expect?

**17.** A roll of carpet that contains 200 yards of carpet will cover how many rooms if each room requires $9\frac{3}{4}$ yards of carpet?

**18.** A box of kitty litter is $8\frac{3}{4}$ inches tall. How many boxes of kitty litter can be stored on a warehouse shelf that can accommodate boxes up to a height of 40 inches?

**19.** Carl Heinrich has lateral filing cabinets that need to be placed on one wall of a storage closet. The filing cabinets are each $3\frac{1}{2}$ feet wide and the wall is 21 feet long. Decide how many cabinets can be placed on the wall.

**20.** Each of the four walls of a room measures $18\frac{5}{8}$ feet. How much chair rail must be purchased to install the chair rail on all four walls? Disregard any openings.

**21.** Four office desks that are $4\frac{1}{8}$ feet long are to be placed together on a wall that is $16\frac{5}{8}$ feet long. Will they fit on the wall?

**22.** Ariana Pope is making 28 trophies and each requires a brass plate that is $3\frac{1}{4}$ inches long and 1 inch wide. What size sheet of brass is required to make the plates if the plates are aligned with two plates per horizontal line?

## Learning Outcomes

## What to Remember with Examples

### Section 2-1

**1** Identify types of fractions. (p. 36)

The denominator of a fraction shows how many parts make up one whole quantity. The numerator shows how many parts are being considered. A proper fraction has a value less than 1. An improper fraction has a value equal to or greater than 1.

Write the fraction illustrated by the shaded parts.

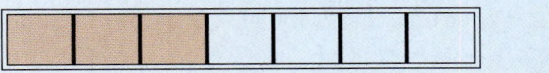
$\dfrac{3}{7}$

Identify the fraction as proper or improper.

$\dfrac{5}{8}$ proper        less than 1

$\dfrac{8}{8}$ improper       equal to 1

$\dfrac{11}{8}$ improper      greater than 1

**2** Convert an improper fraction to a whole or mixed number. (p. 37)

1. Divide the numerator of the improper fraction by the denominator.
2. Examine the remainder.
   (a) If the remainder is 0, the quotient is a whole number: The improper fraction is equivalent to this whole number.
   (b) If the remainder is not 0, the quotient is not a whole number: The improper fraction is equivalent to a mixed number. The whole-number part of this mixed number is the whole-number part of the quotient. The fraction part of the mixed number has a numerator and a denominator. The numerator is the remainder; the denominator is the divisor (the denominator of the improper fraction).

$$\dfrac{150}{3} \qquad 3\overline{)150}\;\;50\,\text{R0} \qquad \dfrac{150}{3} = 50; \qquad \dfrac{152}{3} \qquad 3\overline{)152}\;\;50\,\text{R2} \qquad \dfrac{152}{3} = 50\dfrac{2}{3}$$

**3** Convert a whole or mixed number to an improper fraction. (p. 38)

1. Find the numerator of the improper fraction.
   (a) Multiply the denominator of the mixed number by the whole-number part.
   (b) Add the product from step 1a to the numerator of the mixed number.
2. For the denominator of the improper fraction use the denominator of the mixed number.
3. For a whole number write the whole number as the numerator and 1 as the denominator.

$$5\dfrac{5}{8} = \dfrac{(8 \times 5) + 5}{8} = \dfrac{40 + 5}{8} = \dfrac{45}{8} \quad \text{Mixed number as improper fraction}$$

$$7 = \dfrac{7}{1} \quad \text{Whole number as improper fraction}$$

**4** Reduce a fraction to lowest terms. (p. 39)

1. Inspect the numerator and denominator to find any whole number that both can be evenly divided by.
2. Divide both the numerator and the denominator by that number and inspect the new fraction to find any other number that the numerator and denominator can be evenly divided by.
3. Repeat steps 1 and 2 until 1 is the only number that the numerator and denominator can be evenly divided by.

$$\frac{12}{36} = \frac{12}{36} \div \frac{2}{2} = \frac{6}{18} \quad \text{or} \quad \frac{12}{36} \div \frac{12}{12} = \frac{1}{3}; \quad \frac{100}{250} = \frac{100}{250} \div \frac{50}{50} = \frac{2}{5}$$

$$= \frac{6}{18} \div \frac{2}{2} = \frac{3}{9}$$

$$= \frac{3}{9} \div \frac{3}{3} = \frac{1}{3}$$

**Find the greatest common divisor of two numbers.**

1. Use the numerator as the original divisor and the denominator as the dividend.
2. Divide.
3. Divide the original divisor from step 2 by the remainder from step 2.
4. Divide the divisor from step 3 by the remainder from step 3.
5. Continue this division process until the remainder is 0. The last divisor is the greatest common divisor.

---

Find the GCD of 27 and 36.

$$\begin{array}{r} 1\ R9 \\ 27\overline{)36} \\ 27 \\ \hline 9 \end{array} \qquad \begin{array}{r} 3 \\ 9\overline{)27} \\ 27 \\ \hline 0 \end{array}$$

The GCD is 9.

---

Find the GCD of 28 and 15.

$$\begin{array}{r} 1\ R13 \\ 15\overline{)28} \\ 15 \\ \hline 13 \end{array} \qquad \begin{array}{r} 1\ R2 \\ 13\overline{)15} \\ 13 \\ \hline 2 \end{array} \qquad \begin{array}{r} 6\ R1 \\ 2\overline{)13} \\ 12 \\ \hline 1 \end{array} \qquad \begin{array}{r} 2 \\ 1\overline{)2} \\ 2 \\ \hline 0 \end{array}$$

The GCD is 1.

---

**5** Raise a fraction to higher terms. (p. 40)

1. Divide the *new* denominator by the *old* denominator.
2. Multiply both the old numerator and the old denominator by the quotient from step 1.

$$\frac{3}{4} = \frac{?}{20} \qquad\qquad \frac{2}{3} = \frac{?}{60}$$

$$\begin{array}{r} 5 \\ 4\overline{)20} \end{array} \qquad\qquad \begin{array}{r} 20 \\ 3\overline{)60} \end{array}$$

$$\frac{3}{4} = \frac{3}{4} \times \frac{5}{5} = \frac{15}{20} \qquad \frac{2}{3} \times \frac{20}{20} = \frac{40}{60}$$

---

## Section 2-2

**1** Add fractions with like (common) denominators. (p. 42)

1. Find the numerator of the sum: Add the numerators of the addends.
2. Find the denominator of the sum: Use the like denominator of the addends.
3. Reduce to lowest terms and/or write as a whole or mixed number.

$$\frac{3}{5} + \frac{7}{5} + \frac{5}{5} = \frac{15}{5} = 3 \qquad\qquad \frac{82}{109} + \frac{13}{109} = \frac{95}{109}$$

---

**2** Find the least common denominator for two or more fractions. (p. 43)

1. Write the denominators in a row and divide each one by the smallest prime number that any of the numbers can be evenly divided by.
2. Write a new row of numbers using the quotients from step 1 and any numbers in the first row that cannot be evenly divided by the first prime number.
3. Continue this process until you have a row of 1s.
4. Multiply all the prime numbers you used to divide by. The product is the least common denominator (LCD).

Find the least common denominator of $\frac{5}{6}, \frac{6}{15}$, and $\frac{7}{20}$.

$$2)\underline{6 \quad 15 \quad 20}$$
$$2)\underline{3 \quad 15 \quad 10}$$
$$3)\underline{3 \quad 15 \quad 5}$$
$$5)\underline{1 \quad 5 \quad 5}$$
$$\phantom{5)}1 \quad 1 \quad 1$$

LCD $= 2 \times 2 \times 3 \times 5 = 60$

Find the least common denominator of $\frac{4}{5}, \frac{3}{10}$, and $\frac{1}{6}$.

$$2)\underline{5 \quad 10 \quad 6}$$
$$3)\underline{5 \quad \phantom{0}5 \quad 3}$$
$$5)\underline{5 \quad \phantom{0}5 \quad 1}$$
$$\phantom{5)}1 \quad \phantom{0}1 \quad 1$$

LCD $= 2 \times 3 \times 5 = 30$

**3** Add fractions and mixed numbers. (p. 44)

**Add fractions with different denominators.**

1. Find the least common denominator.
2. Change each fraction to an equivalent fraction using the least common denominator.
3. Add the new fractions with like (common) denominators.
4. Reduce to lowest terms and/or write as a whole or mixed number.

Add $\frac{5}{6} + \frac{6}{15} + \frac{7}{20}$.

The LCD is 60.

$$\frac{5}{6} = \frac{5}{6} \times \frac{10}{10} = \frac{50}{60}$$

$$\frac{6}{15} = \frac{6}{15} \times \frac{4}{4} = \frac{24}{60}$$

$$\frac{7}{20} = \frac{7}{20} \times \frac{3}{3} = \frac{21}{60}$$

$$\frac{5}{6} + \frac{6}{15} + \frac{7}{20} = \frac{50}{60} + \frac{24}{60} + \frac{21}{60} =$$

$$\frac{95}{60} = \frac{19}{12} = 1\frac{7}{12}$$

Add $\frac{4}{5} + \frac{3}{10} + \frac{1}{6}$.

The LCD is 30.

$$\frac{4}{5} \times \frac{6}{6} = \frac{24}{30}$$

$$\frac{3}{10} \times \frac{3}{3} = \frac{9}{30}$$

$$\frac{1}{6} \times \frac{5}{5} = \frac{5}{30}$$

$$\frac{4}{5} + \frac{3}{10} + \frac{1}{6} = \frac{24}{30} + \frac{9}{30} + \frac{5}{30} =$$

$$\frac{38}{30} = \frac{19}{15} = 1\frac{4}{15}$$

**Add mixed numbers.**

1. Add the whole-number parts.
2. Add the fraction parts and reduce to lowest terms.
3. Change improper fractions to whole or mixed numbers.
4. Add the whole-number parts.

Add $2\frac{1}{2} + 5\frac{2}{3} + 4$.

The LCD is 6.

$$2\frac{1}{2} = 2\frac{3}{6}$$
$$5\frac{2}{3} = 5\frac{4}{6}$$
$$\underline{4 \phantom{\frac{1}{2}} = 4\phantom{\frac{4}{6}}}$$
$$11\frac{7}{6} \qquad \frac{7}{6} = 1\frac{1}{6}$$

$$11 + 1\frac{1}{6} = 12\frac{1}{6}$$

**4** Subtract fractions and mixed numbers. (p. 46)

**Subtract fractions with like denominators.**

1. Find the numerator of the difference: Subtract the numerators of the fractions.
2. Find the denominator of the difference: Use the like denominator of the fractions.
3. Reduce to lowest terms.

**Subtract fractions with different denominators.**

1. Find the least common denominator.
2. Change each fraction to an equivalent fraction using the least common denominator.
3. Subtract the new fractions with like (common) denominators.
4. Reduce to lowest terms.

$$\frac{10}{81} - \frac{7}{81} = \frac{3}{81} = \frac{1}{27} \qquad \frac{7}{8} - \frac{1}{3} = \frac{21}{24} - \frac{8}{24} = \frac{13}{24}$$

**Subtract mixed numbers.**

1. If the fractions have different denominators, find the LCD and change the fractions to equivalent fractions using the LCD.
2. If necessary, regroup by subtracting 1 from the whole number in the minuend and add 1 (in the form of LCD/LCD) to the fraction in the minuend.
3. Subtract the fractions and the whole numbers.
4. Reduce to lowest terms.

$$24\frac{1}{2} = 24\frac{2}{4} = 23\frac{6}{4} \qquad\qquad 53 = 53\frac{0}{5} = 52\frac{5}{5}$$
$$-11\frac{3}{4} = -11\frac{3}{4} = -11\frac{3}{4} \qquad -37\frac{4}{5} = -37\frac{4}{5} = -37\frac{4}{5}$$
$$12\frac{3}{4} \qquad\qquad\qquad 15\frac{1}{5}$$

**Section 2-3**

**1** Multiply fractions and mixed numbers. (p. 50)

**Multiply fractions.**

1. Find the numerator of the product: Multiply the numerators of the fractions.
2. Find the denominator of the product: Multiply the denominators of the fractions.
3. Reduce to lowest terms.

$$\frac{3}{2} \times \frac{12}{17} = \frac{36}{34} = 1\frac{2}{34} = 1\frac{1}{17}; \qquad \frac{7}{9} \times \frac{15}{28} = \frac{5}{12}$$

or

$$\frac{3}{2} \times \frac{12}{17} = \frac{18}{17} = 1\frac{1}{17}$$

**Multiply mixed numbers and whole numbers.**

1. Write the mixed numbers and whole numbers as improper fractions.
2. Reduce numerators and denominators as appropriate.
3. Multiply the fractions.
4. Reduce to lowest terms and/or write as a whole or mixed number.

$$3\frac{3}{4} \times 3\frac{2}{3} = \frac{15}{4} \times \frac{11}{3} = \frac{165}{12} = \frac{55}{4} = 13\frac{3}{4}; \qquad 5\frac{7}{8} \times 3 = \frac{47}{8} \times \frac{3}{1} = \frac{141}{8} = 17\frac{5}{8}$$

or

$$\frac{15}{4} \times \frac{11}{3} = \frac{55}{4} = 13\frac{3}{4}$$

**2** Divide fractions and mixed numbers. (p. 52)

**Find the reciprocal of a number.**

1. Write the number as a fraction.
2. Interchange the numerator and denominator.

The reciprocal of $\frac{2}{3}$ is $\frac{3}{2}$ or $1\frac{1}{2}$.

The reciprocal of 6 is $\frac{1}{6}$. $\qquad 6 = \frac{6}{1}$.

The reciprocal of $1\frac{1}{2}$ is $\frac{2}{3}$. $\qquad 1\frac{1}{2} = \frac{3}{2}$.

**Divide fractions or mixed numbers.**

1. Write the numbers as fractions.
2. Find the reciprocal of the divisor.
3. Multiply the dividend by the reciprocal of the divisor.
4. Reduce to lowest terms and/or write as a whole or mixed number.

$$\frac{55}{68} \div \frac{11}{17} = \frac{\cancel{55}}{\cancel{68}} \times \frac{\cancel{17}}{\cancel{11}} = \frac{5}{4} = 1\frac{1}{4};$$

$$3\frac{1}{4} \div 1\frac{1}{2} = \frac{13}{4} \div \frac{3}{2}$$

$$= \frac{13}{4} \times \frac{2}{3} = \frac{13}{6} = 2\frac{1}{6}$$

**NAME** _____    **DATE** _____

## EXERCISES SET A

1. Give five examples of fractions whose value is less than 1. What are these fractions called?

2. Give five examples of fractions whose value is greater than or equal to 1. What are these fractions called?

*Write the improper fraction as a whole or mixed number.*

3. $\dfrac{124}{6}$

4. $\dfrac{84}{12}$

5. $\dfrac{17}{2}$

*Write the mixed number as an improper fraction.*

6. $5\dfrac{5}{6}$

7. $4\dfrac{1}{3}$

8. $33\dfrac{1}{3}$

*Reduce to lowest terms. Try to use the greatest common divisor.*

9. $\dfrac{15}{18}$

10. $\dfrac{20}{30}$

11. $\dfrac{30}{48}$

*Rewrite as a fraction with the indicated denominator.*

12. $\dfrac{5}{6} = \dfrac{}{12}$

13. $\dfrac{5}{8} = \dfrac{}{32}$

14. $\dfrac{9}{11} = \dfrac{}{143}$

15. A company employed 105 people. If 15 of the employees left the company in a three-month period, what fractional part of the employees left?

*Find the least common denominator for these fractions.*

16. $\dfrac{1}{4}, \dfrac{1}{12}, \dfrac{11}{16}$

17. $\dfrac{5}{56}, \dfrac{7}{24}, \dfrac{7}{12}, \dfrac{5}{42}$

18. $\dfrac{2}{1}, \dfrac{1}{5}, \dfrac{1}{10}, \dfrac{5}{6}$

*Add. Reduce to lowest terms and/or write as whole or mixed numbers.*

**19.** $\dfrac{3}{5} + \dfrac{4}{5}$

**20.** $\dfrac{2}{5} + \dfrac{2}{3}$

**21.** $7\dfrac{1}{2} + 4\dfrac{3}{8}$

**22.** $11\dfrac{5}{6} + 8\dfrac{2}{3}$

**23.** Two types of fabric are needed for curtains. The lining requires $12\dfrac{3}{8}$ yards and the curtain fabric needed is $16\dfrac{5}{8}$ yards. How many yards of fabric are needed?

*Subtract. Borrow when necessary. Reduce the difference to lowest terms.*

**24.** $\dfrac{5}{12} - \dfrac{1}{4}$

**25.** $7\dfrac{4}{5} - 4\dfrac{1}{2}$

**26.** $5 - 3\dfrac{2}{5}$

**27.** $4\dfrac{5}{6} - 3\dfrac{1}{3}$

**28.** A board $3\dfrac{5}{8}$ feet long must be sawed from a 6-foot board. How long is the remaining piece?

*Multiply. Reduce to lowest terms and/or write as whole or mixed numbers.*

**29.** $\dfrac{5}{6} \times \dfrac{1}{3}$

**30.** $5 \times \dfrac{2}{3}$

**31.** $6\dfrac{2}{9} \times 4\dfrac{1}{2}$

*Find the reciprocal of the numbers.*

**32.** $\dfrac{5}{8}$

**33.** $\dfrac{1}{4}$

**34.** $3\dfrac{1}{4}$

*Divide. Reduce to lowest terms and/or write as whole or mixed numbers.*

**35.** $\dfrac{3}{4} \div \dfrac{1}{4}$

**36.** $7\dfrac{1}{2} \div 2$

**37.** $3\dfrac{1}{7} \div 5\dfrac{1}{2}$

**38.** A board 244 inches long is cut into pieces that are each $7\dfrac{5}{8}$ inches long. How many pieces can be cut?

**39.** Bill New placed a piece of $\dfrac{5}{8}$-inch plywood and a piece of $\dfrac{3}{4}$-inch plywood on top of one another to create a spacer between two two-by-fours, but the spacer was $\dfrac{1}{8}$ inch too thick. How thick should the spacer be?

**40.** Certain financial aid students must pass $\dfrac{2}{3}$ of their courses each term in order to continue their aid. If a student is taking 18 hours, how many hours must be passed?

**41.** Sol's Hardware and Appliance Store is selling electric clothes dryers for $\dfrac{1}{3}$ off the regular price of $288. What is the sale price of the dryer?

## EXERCISES SET B

*Write the improper fraction as a whole or mixed number.*

**1.** $\dfrac{52}{15}$  **2.** $\dfrac{83}{4}$  **3.** $\dfrac{77}{11}$  **4.** $\dfrac{19}{10}$

*Write the mixed number as an improper fraction.*

**5.** $7\dfrac{3}{8}$  **6.** $10\dfrac{1}{5}$

*Reduce to lowest terms. Try to use the greatest common divisor.*

**7.** $\dfrac{18}{20}$  **8.** $\dfrac{27}{36}$  **9.** $\dfrac{18}{63}$  **10.** $\dfrac{78}{96}$

*Rewrite as a fraction with the indicated denominator.*

**11.** $\dfrac{7}{9} = \dfrac{}{81}$  **12.** $\dfrac{4}{7} = \dfrac{}{49}$

**13.** If 8 students in a class of 30 earned grades of A, what fractional part of the class earned A's?

*Find the least common denominator for these fractions.*

**14.** $\dfrac{7}{8}, \dfrac{1}{20}, \dfrac{13}{16}$  **15.** $\dfrac{1}{8}, \dfrac{5}{9}, \dfrac{7}{12}, \dfrac{9}{24}$  **16.** $\dfrac{5}{12}, \dfrac{3}{15}$

*Add. Reduce to lowest terms and/or write as whole or mixed numbers.*

**17.** $\dfrac{7}{8} + \dfrac{1}{8}$  **18.** $\dfrac{1}{4} + \dfrac{11}{12} + \dfrac{7}{16}$  **19.** $3\dfrac{1}{4} + 2\dfrac{1}{3} + 3\dfrac{5}{6}$

**20.** Three pieces of lumber measure $5\dfrac{3}{8}$ feet, $7\dfrac{1}{2}$ feet, and $9\dfrac{3}{4}$ feet. What is the total length of the lumber?

*Subtract. Borrow when necessary. Reduce the difference to lowest terms.*

**21.** $\dfrac{6}{7} - \dfrac{5}{14}$

**22.** $4\dfrac{1}{2} - 3\dfrac{6}{7}$

**23.** $12 - 4\dfrac{1}{8}$

**24.** $4\dfrac{1}{5} - 2\dfrac{3}{10}$

**25.** George Mackie worked the following hours during a week: $7\dfrac{3}{4}, 5\dfrac{1}{2}, 6\dfrac{1}{4}, 9\dfrac{1}{4}$, and $8\dfrac{3}{4}$. Maxine Ford worked 40 hours. Who worked the most hours? How many more?

*Multiply. Reduce to lowest terms and/or write as whole or mixed numbers.*

**26.** $\dfrac{9}{10} \times \dfrac{3}{4}$

**27.** $\dfrac{3}{7} \times 8$

**28.** $\dfrac{9}{10} \times \dfrac{2}{5} \times \dfrac{5}{9} \times \dfrac{3}{7}$

**29.** $10\dfrac{1}{2} \times 1\dfrac{5}{7}$

**30.** After a family reunion, $10\dfrac{2}{3}$ cakes were left. If Shirley McCool took $\dfrac{3}{8}$ of these cakes, how many did she take?

*Find the reciprocal of the numbers.*

**31.** $\dfrac{2}{3}$

**32.** $8$

**33.** $2\dfrac{3}{8}$

**34.** $5\dfrac{1}{12}$

*Divide. Reduce to lowest terms and/or write as whole or mixed numbers.*

**35.** $\dfrac{5}{6} \div \dfrac{1}{8}$

**36.** $15 \div \dfrac{3}{4}$

**37.** $7\dfrac{1}{2} \div 1\dfrac{2}{3}$

**38.** A stack of $1\dfrac{5}{8}$-inch plywood measures 91 inches. How many pieces of plywood are in the stack?

**39.** Sue Parsons has three lengths of $\dfrac{3}{4}$-inch PVC pipe: $1\dfrac{1}{5}$ feet, $2\dfrac{3}{4}$ feet, and $1\dfrac{1}{2}$ feet. What is the total length of pipe?

**40.** Brienne Smith must trim $2\dfrac{3}{16}$ feet from a board 8 feet long. How long will the board be after it is cut?

**41.** Eight boxes that are each $1\dfrac{5}{8}$ feet high are stacked. Find the height of the stack.

## PRACTICE TEST

*Write the reciprocal.*

**1.** 5

**2.** $\dfrac{3}{5}$

**3.** $1\dfrac{3}{5}$

*Reduce.*

**4.** $\dfrac{12}{15}$

**5.** $\dfrac{15}{35}$

**6.** $\dfrac{21}{51}$

*Write as an improper fraction.*

**7.** $2\dfrac{5}{8}$

**8.** $3\dfrac{1}{12}$

*Write as a mixed number or whole number.*

**9.** $\dfrac{21}{9}$

**10.** $\dfrac{56}{13}$

*Perform the indicated operation. Reduce results to lowest terms and/or write as whole or mixed numbers.*

**11.** $\dfrac{5}{6} - \dfrac{4}{6}$

**12.** $\dfrac{5}{8} + \dfrac{9}{10}$

**13.** $\dfrac{5}{8} \times \dfrac{7}{10}$

**14.** $\dfrac{5}{6} \div \dfrac{3}{4}$

**15.** $10\frac{1}{2} \div 5\frac{3}{4}$

**16.** $56 \times 32\frac{6}{7}$

**17.** $2\frac{1}{2} + 3\frac{1}{3}$

**18.** $137 - 89\frac{4}{5}$

**19.** Dale Burton ordered $\frac{3}{4}$ truckload of merchandise. If approximately $\frac{1}{3}$ of the $\frac{3}{4}$ truckload of merchandise has been unloaded, how much remains to be unloaded?

**20.** A company that employs 580 people expects to lay off 87 workers. What fractional part of the workers are expected to be laid off?

**21.** Wallboard measuring $\frac{5}{8}$ inch thick makes a stack $62\frac{1}{2}$ inches high. How many sheets of wallboard are there?

**22.** If city sales tax is $5\frac{1}{2}\%$ and state sales tax is $2\frac{1}{4}\%$, what is the total sales tax rate for purchases made in the city?

1. What two operations require a common denominator?

2. What number can be written as any fraction that has the same numerator and denominator? Give an example of a fraction that equals the number.

3. What is the product of any number and its reciprocal? Give an example to illustrate your answer.

4. What operation requires the use of the reciprocal of a fraction? Write an example of this operation and perform the operation.

5. What operations must be used to solve an applied problem if all of the parts but one are given and the total of all the parts is given? Write an example.

6. What steps must be followed to find the reciprocal of a mixed number? Give an example of a mixed number and its reciprocal.

7. Under what conditions are two fractions equal? Give an example to illustrate your answer.

8. Write three examples of dividing a whole number by a proper fraction.

9. Explain why the quotient of a whole number and a proper fraction is *more* than the whole number.

10. Explain the difference between a proper fraction and an improper fraction.

## Challenge Problem

A room is $25\frac{1}{2}$ feet by $32\frac{3}{4}$ feet. How much will it cost to cover the floor with carpet costing $12 a square yard (9 square feet), if 4 extra square yards are needed for matching? If a portion of a square yard is needed, an entire square yard must be purchased.

## 2.1 Bitsie's Pastry Sensations

It was the grand opening of Elizabeth's pastry business, and she wanted to make something extra special. As a tribute to her Grandma Gertrude—who had helped pay for culinary school (and incidentally nicknamed her Bitsie), she had decided to make her grandmother's favorite recipe, apple crisp. Although she thought she remembered the recipe by heart, she decided she had better write it down just to make sure.

### Apple Crisp

4 cups tart apples — Peel, core, and slice.

$\frac{1}{2}$ cup brown sugar

$\frac{1}{2}$ tsp ground cinnamon — Add to apples and mix.

$\frac{1}{4}$ tsp ground nutmeg — Pour into a buttered $9 \times 13$-inch

$\frac{1}{4}$ tsp ground cloves — glass baking dish.

2 tsp lemon juice

$\frac{2}{3}$ cup granulated sugar

$\frac{1}{8}$ tsp salt — Blend until crumbly.

$\frac{3}{4}$ cup unbleached white flour

$\frac{1}{3}$ cup butter

$\frac{1}{4}$ cup chopped walnuts, pecans, or raisins — Add to the sugar/flour mixture and sprinkle over apples.

Heat oven to 375°F. Bake until topping is golden brown and apples are tender, approximately 30 minutes.

1. Elizabeth planned to make 6 pans of apple crisp for the day, using extra tart granny smith apples—just like her grandmother had. But after peeling, coring, and slicing she had a major problem: she only had 10 cups of apple slices. It was getting late and she needed to get some pans of apple crisp into the oven. She knew that 10 cups of apples was $2\frac{1}{2}$ times as much as the 4 cups she needed, so she decided to use multiplication to figure out $2\frac{1}{2}$ batches. Based on her hasty decision, how much of each ingredient will she need?

2. After looking at her math, Elizabeth realized her mistake. She didn't have a pan that she could use for half a batch, and her math seemed too complicated anyway. She decided she would just make a double batch for now, because then she wouldn't need to multiply. Using addition, how much of each ingredient would she need for a double batch?

3. The two pans of apple crisp were just starting to brown when Elizabeth returned from the store with more apples. But instead of tart apples, the store had only honey crisp, a much sweeter variety. After preparing 14 more cups of apples, she could make 3 batches using the honey crisp (12 cups) and the fourth and final batch using both kinds of apples. Her concern, though, was the sweetness of the apples. For the batches using the honey crisp only, if the brown sugar and granulated sugar were reduced by $\frac{1}{2}$, how much sugar should she use for each batch? How much for all 3 batches?

# 2.2 Atlantic Candy Company

Tom always loved the salt water taffy his parents bought while on summer vacations at the beach. His fond memories probably had something to do with his accepting a job with the Atlantic Candy Company as a marketing manager. Among other things, his new job involves assessing the mix of flavors in a box of taffy. He remembers saving the orange and green with red pieces for last because they were his favorites; however, the company has recent market research that shows that his favorite flavors are not the most popular flavors with most other people. Milk chocolate, dark chocolate, and chocolate mint are the most popular flavors, followed by peppermint and licorice. Tom knows that most 1-lb boxes of Atlantic Candy Company taffy containing 64 pieces include 4 green with red pieces, 3 white with red peppermint pieces, 3 white with green peppermint pieces, 3 milk chocolate pieces with white and pink bull's-eye centers, 2 milk chocolate with green peppermint pieces, 7 white pieces, 12 dark chocolate pieces, 9 orange pieces, 15 milk chocolate pieces, and 6 licorice pieces.

1. What fraction of the pieces of taffy have chocolate in them? What fraction of the pieces are Tom's favorite orange and green with red?

2. Does the Atlantic Candy Company assortment need to be adjusted to match the most people's taste preference better if the top five choices are considered? What fraction of the pieces in the Atlantic Candy Company 1-lb box are chocolate, peppermint, and licorice? Hint: If a piece falls in two categories, count it only once.

3. Based on the market research, Tom thinks it would be profitable to sell an assortment box that has double-size pieces of taffy in chocolate and peppermint in a special holiday gift box. If they use a $\frac{1}{2}$-lb box how many pieces should they include? (1 lb = 64 regular-size pieces)

4. If they produce another $\frac{1}{2}$-lb. box containing an equal number of double-size milk chocolate taffy, chocolate-mint taffy, and peppermint taffy, how many pieces of each flavor will there be in this special gift box?

# Decimals

# Shaun White: Snowboarding

Shaun White scored 46.8 out of 50 to win the gold medal in the men's halfpipe in the 2006 Winter Olympics. Halfpipe is an aerial thrill show where snowboarders launch themselves more than 20 feet into the air, and spin, twist, and turn in ways that don't seem possible. The success of snowboarding is due largely to the success of skateboarding, which started with no rules and no judges. Now one of the hottest winter sports, it is scored by a point system and has required moves and degrees of difficulty. In the 2006 Games, there were five judges for overall impressions, and runs were scored according to the execution of tricks, variety of tricks, difficulty, pipe use, and amplitude (height). A 50 is a perfect score, and as little as 0.1 could keep competitors off the medal stand.

White has also participated in the Winter X Games, where he has medaled every year since 2002. Including all Winter X Games through 2007, his medal count stands at 10 (6 gold, 3 silver, 1 bronze). White is 5' 8.5" (1.73 m) tall, and weighs 140 lb (63.5 kg). He is also known as "The Flying Tomato" because of his mop of red hair.

Success hasn't always come easily to Shaun. He missed qualifying for the 2002 Olympics by only three-tenths of a point (0.3), and then had to watch as the Americans swept the halfpipe event. White made the 2006 U.S. Olympic snowboard team, but on his first of two qualifying runs, he fell during a landing, scoring just 37.7. The maximum deduction for a fall was 20% of the total score. So how much did Shaun's fall cost him? Only the judges knew for sure, but what decimal would you use to calculate the maximum deduction? Would you multiply, or would it be easier to divide?

One thing was certain, Shaun was in seventh place, 1.7 points behind the nearest competitor, and only the top six would advance to the finals. On his second (and final) qualifying run, White had to go big or go home. White soared, nailing his second qualifier and scoring 45.3 out of a possible 50 points, the best score in the field. The rest, of course, is history.

## LEARNING OUTCOMES

### 3-1 Decimals and the Place-Value System

1. Read and write decimals.
2. Round decimals.

### 3-2 Operations with Decimals

1. Add and subtract decimals.
2. Multiply decimals.
3. Divide decimals.

### 3-3 Decimal and Fraction Conversions

1. Convert a decimal to a fraction.
2. Convert a fraction to a decimal.

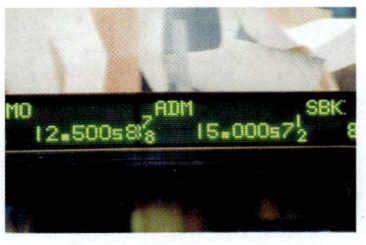

# 3-1 DECIMALS AND THE PLACE-VALUE SYSTEM

### LEARNING OUTCOMES

1 Read and write decimals.
2 Round decimals.

Decimals are another way to write fractions. We use decimals in some form or another every day—even our money system is based on decimals. Calculators use decimals, and decimals are the basis of percentages, interest, markups, and markdowns.

## 1 Read and write decimals.

**Decimal system:** a place-value number system based on 10.

Our money system, which is based on the dollar, uses the **decimal system**. In the decimal system, as you move right to left from one digit to the next, the place value of the digit increases by 10 times (multiply by 10). As you move left to right from one digit to the next, the place value of the digit gets 10 times smaller (divide by 10). The place value of the digit to the right of the ones place is 1 divided by 10.

There are several ways of indicating 1 divided by 10. In the decimal system, we write 1 divided by 10 as 0.1.

**FIGURE 3-1**

1 whole divided into 10 parts. The shaded part is 0.1.

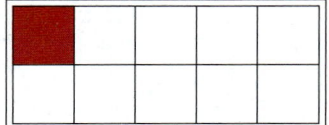

**Decimal point:** the notation that separates the whole-number part of a number from the decimal part.

**Whole-number part:** the digits to the left of the decimal point.

**Decimal part:** the digits to the right of the decimal point.

How much is 0.1? How much is 1 divided by 10? It is one part of a 10-part whole (Figure 3-1). We read 0.1 as one-tenth. Using decimal notation, we can extend our place-value chart to the right of the ones place and express quantities that are not whole numbers. When extending to the right of the ones place, a period called a **decimal point** separates the **whole-number part** from the **decimal part**.

The names of the places to the right of the decimal are tenths, hundredths, thousandths, and so on. These place names are similar to the place names for whole numbers, but they all end in *ths*. In Figure 3-2, we show the place names for the digits in the number 2,315.627432.

| Millions | | | Thousands | | | Units | | | | | | | | | | | | | |
|---|---|---|---|---|---|---|---|---|---|---|---|---|---|---|---|---|---|---|---|
| Hundred millions (100,000,000) | Ten millions (10,000,000) | Millions (1,000,000) | Hundred thousands (100,000) | Ten thousands (10,000) | Thousands (1,000) | Hundreds (100) | Tens (10) | Ones (1) | Decimal point | Tenths 0.1 | Hundredths 0.01 | Thousandths 0.001 | Ten-thousandths 0.0001 | Hundred-thousandths 0.00001 | Millionths 0.000001 | Ten-millionths 0.0000001 | Hundred-millionths 0.00000001 | | |
| | | | | | 2 | 3 | 1 | 5 | . | 6 | 2 | 7 | 4 | 3 | 2 | | | | |

**FIGURE 3-2**
**Place-Value Chart for Decimals**

| HOW TO | Read or write a decimal | |
|---|---|---|
| | | Read 3.12. |
| 1. Read or write the whole-number part (to the left of the decimal point) as you would read or write a whole number. | | Three |
| 2. Use the word *and* for the decimal point. | | and |
| 3. Read or write the decimal part (to the right of the decimal point) as you would read or write a whole number. | | twelve |
| 4. Read or write the place name of the rightmost digit. | | hundredths |

**EXAMPLE 1** Write the word name for these decimals: (a) 3.6, (b) 0.209, (c) $234.93.

(a) three and six-tenths
(b) two hundred nine thousandths
(c) two hundred thirty-four dollars and ninety-three cents

3 is the whole-number part. 6 is the decimal part.
The whole-number part, 0, is not written.
The whole-number part is dollars. The decimal part is cents.

---

**TIP**

**Informal Use of the Word *Point***

Informally, the decimal point is sometimes read as *point*. Thus, 3.6 is read *three point six*. The decimal 0.209 can be read as *zero point two zero nine*. This informal process is often used in communication to ensure that numbers are not miscommunicated. However, without hearing the place value, it is more difficult to get a sense of the size of the number.

---

**TIP**

**Reading Decimals as Money Amounts**

When reading decimal numbers that represent money amounts:

Read whole numbers as *dollars*.
Decimal amounts are read as *cents*. In the number $234.93, the decimal part is read ninety-three *cents* rather than ninety-three *hundredths of a dollar*. Since 1 cent is one hundredth of a dollar, the words *cent* and *hundredth* have the same meaning.

---

## ✓ STOP AND CHECK

1. Write 5.8 in words.

2. Write 0.721 in words.

3. Write $38.15 in words.

4. Write four hundred thirty-four and seventy-six hundredths as a number.

5. Write three thousand five hundred forty-eight ten-thousandths as a number.

6. Write four dollars and eighty-seven cents as a number.

---

## 2  Round decimals.

As with whole numbers, we often need only an approximate amount. The process for rounding decimals is similar to rounding whole numbers.

**HOW TO**  Round to a specified decimal place

| | Round to hundredths: |
|---|---|
| | 17.3754 |
| 1. Find the digit in the specified place. | 17.3754 |
| 2. Look at the next digit to the right. | 17.3754 |
|    (a) If this digit is less than 5, eliminate it and all digits to its right. | |
|    (b) If this digit is 5 or more, add 1 to the digit in the specified place, and eliminate all digits to its right. | 17.38 |

**EXAMPLE 1**    Round the number to the specified place: (a) $193.48 to the nearest dollar, (b) $28.465 to the nearest cent.

(a) $193.48    Rounding to the nearest dollar means rounding to the ones place. The digit in the ones place is 3.

    $193.48    The digit to the right of 3 is 4. Since 4 is less than 5, step 2a applies; eliminate 4 and all digits to its right.

    $193

**$193.48 rounded to the nearest dollar is $193.**

(b) $28.465    Rounding to the nearest cent means rounding to the nearest hundredth. The digit in the hundredths place is 6.

    $28.465    The digit to the right of 6 is 5. Since 5 is 5 or more, step 2b applies.

    $28.47

**$28.465 rounded to the nearest cent is $28.47.**

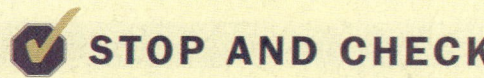

## STOP AND CHECK

**1.** Round 14.342 to the nearest tenth.

**2.** Round 48.7965 to the nearest hundredth.

**3.** Round $768.57 to the nearest dollar.

**4.** Round $54.834 to the nearest cent.

## 3-1 SECTION EXERCISES

### SKILL BUILDERS

*Write the word name for the decimal.*

**1.** 0.582      **2.** 0.21      **3.** 1.0009      **4.** 2.83      **5.** 782.07

*Write the number that represents the decimal.*

**6.** Thirty-five hundredths      **7.** Three hundred twelve thousandths      **8.** Sixty and twenty-eight thousandths      **9.** Five and three hundredths

*Round to the nearest dollar.*

**10.** $493.91      **11.** $785.03      **12.** $19.80

*Round to the nearest cent.*

**13.** $0.5239      **14.** $21.09734      **15.** $32,048.87219

*Round to the nearest tenth.*

**16.** 42.3784      **17.** 17.03752      **18.** 4.293

## APPLICATIONS

**19.** Tel-Sales, Inc., a prepaid phone card company in Oklahoma City, sells phone cards for $19.89. Write the card cost in words.

**20.** Destiny Telecom of Oakland, California introduced a Braille prepaid phone card that costs fourteen dollars and seventy cents. Write the digits to show Destiny's sales figure.

## 3-2 OPERATIONS WITH DECIMALS

### LEARNING OUTCOMES

1. Add and subtract decimals.
2. Multiply decimals.
3. Divide decimals.

### 1 Add and subtract decimals.

Some math skills are used more often than others. Adding and subtracting decimal numbers are regularly used in transactions involving money. To increase your awareness of the use of decimals, refer to your paycheck stub, grocery store receipt, fast-food ticket, odometer on your car, bills you receive each month, and checking account statement balance.

---

### HOW TO   Add or subtract decimals

Add $32 + 2.55 + 8.85 + 0.625$.

1. Write the numbers in a vertical column, aligning digits according to their places.
2. Attach extra zeros to the right end of each number so that each number has the same quantity of digits to the right of the decimal point. It is also acceptable to assume blank places to be zero.
3. Add or subtract as though the numbers are whole numbers.
4. Place the decimal point in the sum or difference to align with the decimal point in the addends or subtrahend and minuend.

```
  32
   2.55
   8.85
   0.625
 44.025
```

---

### TIP

**Unwritten Decimals**

When we write whole numbers using numerals, we usually omit the decimal point; the decimal point is understood to be at the end of the whole number. Therefore, any whole number, such as 32, can be written without a decimal (32) or with a decimal (32.).

---

### TIP

**Aligning Decimals in Addition or Subtraction**

A common mistake in adding decimals is to misalign the digits or decimal points.

| | | | |
|---|---|---|---|
| 32 | All digits and decimal | 32 | ← not aligned correctly |
| 2.55 | points are aligned | 2.55 | |
| 8.85 | correctly. | 8.85 | |
| 0.625 | | 0.625 | ← not aligned correctly |
| 44.025 | | 1.797 | |

**CORRECT**  **INCORRECT**

## EXAMPLE 1

Subtract 26.3 − 15.84.

$$
\begin{array}{r}
\scriptstyle 5\ 12\ 10 \\
26.3\ 0 \\
-\ 15.8\ 4 \\
\hline
10.4\ 6
\end{array}
$$

Write the numbers so that the digits align according to their places. Subtract the numbers, regrouping as you would in whole-number subtraction.

**The difference of 26.3 and 15.84 is 10.46.**

## ✔ STOP AND CHECK

1. Add: 67 + 4.38 + 0.291

2. Add: 57.5 + 13.4 + 5.238

3. Subtract: 17.53 − 12.17

4. Subtract: 542.83 − 219.593

5. Garza Humada purchased a shirt for $18.97 and paid with a $20 bill. What was his change?

6. The stock of FedEx Corporation had a high for the day of $120.01, a low of $95.79, and it closed at $117.58. By how much did the stock price change during the day?

## 2  Multiply decimals.

Suppose you want to calculate the amount of tip to add to a restaurant bill. A typical tip in the United States is 20 cents per dollar, which is 0.20 or 0.2 per dollar. To calculate the tip on a bill of $28.73 we multiply 28.73 × 0.2.

We multiply decimals as though they are whole numbers. Then we place the decimal point according to the quantity of digits in the decimal parts of the factors.

### HOW TO    Multiply decimals

1. Multiply the decimal numbers as though they are whole numbers.
2. Count the digits in the decimal parts of both decimal numbers.
3. Place the decimal point in the product so that there are as many digits in its decimal part as there are digits you counted in step 2. If necessary, attach zeros on the left end of the product so that you can place the decimal point accurately.

Multiply 3.5 × 0.3

$$
\begin{array}{r}
3.5 \quad \text{one place} \\
\times\ 0.3 \quad \text{one place} \\
\hline
1.0\ 5 \quad \text{two places}
\end{array}
$$

## EXAMPLE 1

Multiply 2.35 × 0.015.

$$
\begin{array}{r}
2.35 \quad \text{two decimal places} \\
\times\ 0.015 \quad \text{three decimal places} \\
\hline
1175 \\
235 \\
\hline
0.03525 \quad \text{five decimal places.}
\end{array}
$$

One 0 is attached on the left to accurately place the decimal point.

**The product of 2.35 and 0.015 is 0.03525.**

## HOW TO   Multiply by place-value numbers such as 10, 100, and 1,000.

1. Determine the number of zeros in the multiplier.
2. Move the decimal in the multiplicand to the right the same number of places as there are zeros in the multiplier. Insert zeros as necessary.

## EXAMPLE 2   Multiply 36.56 by (a) 10, (b) 100, and (c) 1,000.

(a)  $36.56(10) = 365.6$         Move the decimal one place to the right.

(b)  $36.56(100) = 3,656$        Move the decimal two places to the right.

(c)  $36.56(1,000) = 36,560$     Move the decimal three places to the right. Insert a zero to have enough places.

## EXAMPLE 3   Find the amount of tip you would pay on a restaurant bill of $28.73 if you tip 20 cents on the dollar (0.20, or 0.2) for the bill.

| What You Know | What You Are Looking For | Solution Plan |
|---|---|---|
| Restaurant bill: $28.73<br>Rate of tip: 0.2 (20 cents on the dollar) of the bill | Amount of tip | Amount of tip = restaurant bill $\times$ rate of tip<br>Amount of tip = 28.73 $\times$ 0.2 |

### Solution

$28.73 \boxed{\times} .2 \boxed{=} \Rightarrow 5.746$     Round to the nearest cent.

### Conclusion

**The tip is $5.75 when rounded to the nearest cent.**

 # STOP AND CHECK

*Multiply.*

**1.** $4.35 \times 0.27$

**2.** $7.03 \times 0.035$

**3.** $5.32 \times 15$

**4.** $8.31 \times 4$

**5.** A dinner for 500 guests costs $27.42 per person. What is the total cost of the dinner?

**6.** Tromane Mohaned purchased 1,000 shares of IBM stock at a price of $94.05. How much did the stock cost?

## 3   Divide decimals.

Division of decimals has many uses in the business world. A common use is to determine how much one item costs if the cost of several items is known. Also, to compare the best buy of similar products that are packaged differently, we find the cost per common unit. A 12-ounce package and a 1-pound package of bacon can be compared by finding the cost per ounce of each package.

### HOW TO   Divide a decimal by a whole number

Divide 95.2 by 14.

$$14\overline{)95.2}$$

1. Place a decimal point for the quotient directly above the decimal point in the dividend.
2. Divide as though the decimal numbers are whole numbers.
3. If the division does not come out evenly, attach zeros as necessary and carry the division one place past the desired place of the quotient.
4. Round to the desired place.

$$
\begin{array}{r}
6.8 \\
14\overline{)95.2} \\
84 \\
\hline
11\;2 \\
11\;2 \\
\hline
\end{array}
$$

### EXAMPLE 1   Divide 5.95 by 17.

$$
\begin{array}{r}
0.35 \\
17\overline{)5.95} \\
5\;1 \\
\hline
85 \\
85 \\
\hline
\end{array}
$$

Place a decimal point for the quotient directly above the decimal point in the dividend.

**The quotient of 5.95 and 17 is 0.35.**

### EXAMPLE 2   Find the quotient of 37.4 ÷ 24 to the nearest hundredth.

$$
\begin{array}{r}
1.558 \\
24\overline{)37.400} \\
24 \\
\hline
13\;4 \\
12\;0 \\
\hline
1\;40 \\
1\;20 \\
\hline
200 \\
192 \\
\hline
8 \\
\end{array}
$$
rounds to 1.56

Carry the division to the thousandths place, and then round to hundredths. Attach two zeros to the right of 4.

**The quotient is 1.56 to the nearest hundredth.**

### HOW TO   Divide by place-value numbers such as 10, 100, and 1,000.

1. Determine the number of zeros in the divisor.
2. Move the decimal in the dividend to the left the same number of places as there are zeros in the divisor. Insert zeros as necessary.

### EXAMPLE 3   Divide 23.71 by (a) 10, (b) 100, and (c) 1,000.

(a) $23.71 \div 10 = 2.371$     Move the decimal one place to the left.

(b) $23.71 \div 100 = 0.2371$     Move the decimal two places to the left. It is preferred to write a zero in front of the decimal point.

(c) $23.71 \div 1,000 = 0.02371$     Move the decimal three places to the left. Insert zeros to have enough places.

If the divisor is a decimal rather than a whole number, we make use of an important fact: Multiplying both the divisor and the dividend by the same factor does not change the quotient. We can see this by writing a division as a fraction.

$$10 \div 5 = \frac{10}{5} = 2$$

$$\frac{10}{5} \times \frac{10}{10} = \frac{100}{50} = 2$$

$$\frac{100}{50} \times \frac{10}{10} = \frac{1,000}{500} = 2$$

We've multiplied both the divisor and the dividend by a factor of 10, and then by a factor of 10 again. The quotient is always 2.

## HOW TO    Divide by a decimal

Divide 3.4776 by 0.72.

$$0.72_\wedge \overline{)3.4776}$$

1. Change the divisor to a whole number by moving the decimal point to the right, counting the places as you go. Use a caret ($\wedge$) to show the new position of the decimal point.
2. Move the decimal point in the dividend to the right as many places as you moved the decimal point in the divisor.

$$0.72_\wedge \overline{)3.47_\wedge 76}$$

3. Place the decimal point for the quotient directly above the *new* decimal point in the dividend.

$$0.72_\wedge \overline{)3.47_\wedge 76}$$

4. Divide as you would divide by a whole number.

$$\begin{array}{r} 4.83 \\ 0.72_\wedge \overline{)3.47_\wedge 76} \\ \underline{2\,88} \\ 59\ 7 \\ \underline{57\ 6} \\ 2\ 16 \\ \underline{2\ 16} \end{array}$$

## EXAMPLE 4    Find the quotient of 59.9 ÷ 0.39 to the nearest hundredth.

$$0.39\overline{)59.90} \qquad 39_\wedge \overline{)5,990_\wedge}$$

Move the decimal point two places to the right in both the divisor and the dividend.

$$39\overline{)5,990_\wedge}$$

Place the decimal point for the quotient directly above the new decimal point in the dividend.

$$\begin{array}{r} 153.589 \approx 153.59 \text{ (rounded)} \\ 39\overline{)5,990.000} \\ \underline{39} \\ 2\ 09 \\ \underline{1\ 95} \\ 140 \\ \underline{117} \\ 23\ 0 \\ \underline{19\ 5} \\ 3\ 50 \\ \underline{3\ 12} \\ 380 \\ \underline{351} \\ 29 \end{array}$$

Divide, carrying out the division to the thousandths place. Add three zeros to the right of the decimal point.

**The quotient is 153.59 to the nearest hundredth.**

## TIP

**Symbol for Approximate Number**

When numbers are rounded they become approximate numbers. A symbol that is often used to show approximate numbers is $\approx$.

## EXAMPLE 5

Alicia Toliver is comparing the price of bacon to find the better buy. A 12-oz package costs $2.49 and a 16-oz package costs $2.99. Which package has the cheapest cost per ounce (often called **unit price**)?

| What You Know | What You Are Looking For | Solution Plan |
|---|---|---|
| Price for 12-oz package = $2.49 | Cost per ounce for each package | Price per ounce = $\dfrac{\text{Cost of 12-oz package}}{12}$ |
| Price for 16-oz package = $2.99 | Which package has the cheaper price per ounce? | Price per ounce = $\dfrac{\text{Cost of 16-oz package}}{16}$<br>Compare the prices per ounce |

### Solution

Price per ounce = 2.49 ÷ 12 = ⟹ 0.2075     12-oz package

Price per ounce = 2.99 ÷ 16 = ⟹ 0.186875    16-oz package

Rounding to the nearest cent, $0.2075 rounds to $0.21 and $0.186875 rounds to $0.19.

$0.19 is less than $0.21.

### Conclusion

**The 16-oz package of bacon has the cheaper unit price.**

## ✓ STOP AND CHECK

*Divide.*

**1.** 100.80 ÷ 15

**2.** 358.26 ÷ 21

**3.** Round to tenths: 12.97 ÷ 3.8

**4.** Round to hundredths: 103.07 ÷ 5.9

**5.** Gwen Hilton's gross weekly pay is $716.32 and her hourly pay is $19.36. How many hours did she work in the week?

**6.** *The Denver Post* reported that Wal-Mart would sell 42-inch Hitachi plasma televisions in a 4-day online special for $1,198 each. If Wal-Mart had paid $648,000,000 for a million units, how much did each unit cost Wal-Mart?

## 3-2 SECTION EXERCISES

### SKILL BUILDERS

*Add.*

**1.** 6.005 + 0.03 + 924 + 3.9

**2.** 82 + 5,000.1 + 101.703

**3.** $21.13 + $42.78 + $16.39

**4.** $203.87 + $1,986.65 + $3,047.38

*Subtract.*

**5.** $407.96 - 298.39$

**6.** 500.7 from 8,097.125

**7.** $468.39 - $223.54

**8.** $21.65 - $15.96

**9.** $52,982.97 - $45,712.49

**10.** $38,517 - $21,837.46

*Multiply.*

**11.** $\begin{array}{r} 19.7 \\ \times\ \ 4 \\ \hline \end{array}$

**12.** $0.0321 \times 10$

**13.** $73.7 \times 0.02$

**14.** $43.7 \times 1.23$

**15.** $5.03 \times 0.073$

**16.** $642 \times $12.98$

*Divide and round to the nearest hundredth if necessary.*

**17.** $123.72 \div 12$

**18.** $35\overline{)589.06}$

**19.** $0.35\overline{)0.0084}$

**20.** $1,482.97 \div 1.7$

## APPLICATIONS

**21.** Kathy Mowers purchased items costing $14.97, $28.14, $19.52, and $23.18. How much do her purchases total?

**22.** Jim Roznowski submitted a travel claim for meals, $138.42; hotel, $549.78; and airfare, $381.50. Total his expenses.

**23.** Joe Gallegos purchased a calculator for $12.48 and paid with a $20 bill. How much change did he get?

**24.** Martisha Jones purchased a jacket for $49.95 and a shirt for $18.50. She paid with a $100 bill. How much change did she receive?

**25.** Laura Voight earns $8.43 per hour as a telemarketing employee. One week she worked 28 hours. What was her gross pay before any deductions?

**26.** Cassie James works a 26-hour week at a part-time job while attending classes at Southwest Tennessee Community College. Her weekly gross pay is $213.46. What is her hourly rate of pay?

**27.** Calculate the cost of 1,000 gallons of gasoline if it costs $1.47 per gallon.

**28.** A buyer purchased 2,000 umbrellas for $4.62 each. What is the total cost?

**29.** All the employees in your department are splitting the cost of a celebratory lunch, catered at a cost of $142.14. If your department has 23 employees, will each employee be able to pay an equal share? How should the catering cost be divided?

**30.** BP Oil offers a prepaid phone card for $5. The card provides 20 minutes of long-distance phone service. Find the cost per minute.

## 3-3 DECIMAL AND FRACTION CONVERSIONS

### LEARNING OUTCOMES

1 Convert a decimal to a fraction.
2 Convert a fraction to a decimal.

### 1 Convert a decimal to a fraction.

Decimals represent parts of a whole, just as fractions can. We can write a decimal as a fraction, or a fraction as a decimal.

| HOW TO | Convert a decimal to a fraction |
|---|---|
| | Write 0.8 as a fraction. |
| 1. Find the denominator: Write 1 followed by as many zeros as there are places to the right of the decimal point. | Denominator = 10 |
| 2. Find the numerator: Use the digits without the decimal point. | $\dfrac{8}{10}$ |
| 3. Reduce to lowest terms and/or write as a whole or mixed number. | $\dfrac{4}{5}$ |

**EXAMPLE 1** Change 0.38 to a fraction.

$$0.38 = \frac{38}{100}$$

$$\frac{38}{100} = \frac{19}{50}$$

The digits without the decimal point form the numerator.

There are two places to the right of the decimal point, so the denominator is 1 followed by two zeros.

Reduce the fraction to lowest terms.

**0.38 written as a fraction is $\frac{19}{50}$.**

EXAMPLE 2 Change 2.43 to a mixed number.

$$2.43 = 2\frac{43}{100}$$

The whole-number part of the decimal stays as the whole-number part of the mixed number.

**2.43 is $2\frac{43}{100}$ as a mixed number.**

---

## TIP

**Relate the Number of Decimal Places and the Zeros in the Denominator to the Place Value**

The number of places after the decimal point indicates the number of zeros in the denominator of the power of 10.

$$0.8 = \frac{8}{10} \qquad 0.38 = \frac{38}{100} \qquad 2.43 = 2\frac{43}{100}$$

Note that the number after the decimal point indicates the numerator of the fraction.

---

## ✓ STOP AND CHECK

*Write as a fraction or mixed number, and write in simplest form.*

**1.** 0.7 **2.** 0.32 **3.** 2.087 **4.** 23.41 **5.** 0.07

---

## 2  Convert a fraction to a decimal.

Fractions indicate division. Therefore, to write a fraction as a decimal, divide the numerator by the denominator, as you would divide decimals.

---

### HOW TO  Write a fraction as a decimal

1. Write the numerator as the dividend and the denominator as the divisor.
2. Divide the numerator by the denominator. Carry the division as many decimal places as necessary or desirable.
3. For repeating decimals:
   (a) Write the remainder as the numerator of a fraction and the divisor as the denominator.
   or
   (b) Carry the division one place past the desired place and round.

---

EXAMPLE 1 Change $\frac{1}{4}$ to a decimal number.

$$\begin{array}{r} 0.25 \\ 4\overline{)1.00} \\ \underline{8}\phantom{0} \\ 20 \\ \underline{20} \end{array}$$

Divide the numerator by the denominator, adding zeros to the right of the decimal point as needed.

**The decimal equivalent of $\frac{1}{4}$ is 0.25.**

**Divide by Which Number?**

An aid to help remember which number in the fraction is the divisor: Divide by the bottom number. Both *by* and *bottom* start with the letter *b*.

In the preceding example, $\frac{1}{4}$ was converted to a decimal by dividing by 4.

**Terminating decimal:** a quotient that has no remainder.

**Nonterminating or repeating decimal:** a quotient that never comes out evenly. The digits will eventually start to repeat.

When the division comes out even (there is no remainder), we say the division terminates, and the quotient is called a **terminating decimal**. If, however, the division *never* comes out even (there is always a remainder), we call the number a **nonterminating** or **repeating decimal**. If the quotient is a repeating decimal, either write the remainder as a fraction or round to a specified place.

**EXAMPLE 2** Write $\frac{2}{3}$ as a decimal number in hundredths (a) with the remainder expressed as a fraction and (b) with the decimal rounded to hundredths.

(a)
$$\begin{array}{r} 0.66\frac{2}{3} \\ 3\overline{)2.00} \\ \underline{1\ 8} \\ 20 \\ \underline{18} \\ 2 \end{array}$$

(b)
$$\begin{array}{r} 0.666 \approx 0.67 \\ 3\overline{)2.000} \\ \underline{1\ 8} \\ 20 \\ \underline{18} \\ 20 \\ \underline{18} \\ 2 \end{array}$$

$\frac{2}{3} = 0.66\frac{2}{3}$ **or** $\frac{2}{3} \approx 0.67$.

**EXAMPLE 3** Write $3\frac{1}{4}$ as a decimal.

$$3\frac{1}{4} = 3.25$$

The whole-number part of the mixed number stays as the whole-number part of the decimal number.

$3\frac{1}{4}$ **is 3.25 as a decimal number.**

 **STOP AND CHECK**

*Change to decimal numbers. Round to hundredths if necessary.*

1. $\frac{3}{5}$
2. $\frac{7}{8}$
3. $\frac{5}{12}$
4. $7\frac{4}{5}$
5. $8\frac{4}{7}$

## 3-3 SECTION EXERCISES

### SKILL BUILDERS

*Write as a fraction or mixed number and write in simplest form.*

1. 0.6
2. 0.58
3. 0.625
4. 0.1875
5. 7.3125
6. 28.875

*Change to a decimal. Round to hundredths if necessary.*

**7.** $\dfrac{7}{10}$

**8.** $\dfrac{3}{8}$

**9.** $\dfrac{7}{12}$

**10.** $\dfrac{7}{16}$

**11.** $2\dfrac{1}{8}$

**12.** $21\dfrac{11}{12}$

## Learning Outcomes

### Section 3-1

**1** Read and write decimals. (p. 74)

## What to Remember with Examples

**Read or write a decimal.**

1. Read or write the whole number part (to the left of the decimal point) as you would read or write a whole number.
2. Use the word *and* for the decimal point.
3. Read or write the decimal part (to the right of the decimal point) as you would read or write a whole number.
4. Name the place of the rightmost digit.

> 0.3869 is read *three thousand, eight-hundred sixty-nine ten-thousandths.*

**2** Round decimals. (p. 75)

**Round to a specified decimal place.**

1. Find the digit in the specified place.
2. Look at the next digit to the right.
   (a) If this digit is less than 5, eliminate it and all digits to its right.
   (b) If this digit is 5 or more, add 1 to the digit in the specified place, and eliminate all digits to its right.

> 37.357 rounded to the nearest tenth is 37.4.
> 3.4819 rounded to the first digit is 3.

### Section 3-2

**1** Add and subtract decimals. (p. 77)

1. Write the numbers in a vertical column, aligning digits according to their places.
2. Attach extra zeros to the right end of each decimal number so that each number has the same quantity of digits to the right of the decimal point (optional).
3. Add or subtract as though the numbers are whole numbers.
4. Place the decimal point in the sum or difference to align with the decimal point in the addends or subtrahend and minuend.

> Add: $32.68 + 3.31 + 49$
>
> $$\begin{array}{r} 32.68 \\ 3.31 \\ +\ 49. \\ \hline 84.99 \end{array}$$
>
> Subtract: $24.7 - 18.25$
>
> $$\begin{array}{r} 24.70 \\ -18.25 \\ \hline 6.45 \end{array}$$

**2** Multiply decimals. (p. 78)

**Multiply decimals.**

1. Multiply the decimal numbers as though they are whole numbers.
2. Count the digits in the decimal parts of both decimal numbers.
3. Place the decimal point in the product so that there are as many digits in its decimal part as there are digits you counted in step 2. If necessary, attach zeros on the left end of the product so that you can place the decimal point accurately.

> Multiply: $36.48 \times 2.52$
>
> $$\begin{array}{r} 36.48 \\ \times\ 2.52 \\ \hline 72\,96 \\ 18\,24\,0 \\ 72\,96 \\ \hline 91.92\,96 \end{array}$$
>
> Multiply: $2.03 \times 0.036$
>
> $$\begin{array}{r} 2.03 \\ \times\ 0.0\,36 \\ \hline 1\,2\,18 \\ 6\,0\,9 \\ \hline 0.07\,3\,08 \end{array}$$

**Multiply by place-value numbers such as 10, 100, and 1,000.**

1. Determine the number of zeros in the multiplier.
2. Move the decimal in the multiplicand to the right the same number of places as there are zeros in the multiplier.

Multiply: 4.52(1,000)

4.52(1,000) = 4,520 — Move the decimal three places to the right. Insert a zero to have enough places.

3 Divide decimals. (p. 80)

**Divide a decimal by a whole number.**

1. Place a decimal point for the quotient directly above the decimal point in the dividend.
2. Divide as though the decimal numbers are whole numbers.
3. If the division does not come out even, attach zeros as necessary and carry the division one place past the desired place of the quotient.
4. Round to the desired place.

Divide: 58.5 ÷ 45

$$\begin{array}{r} 1.3 \\ 45\overline{)58.5} \\ \underline{45} \\ 13\ 5 \\ \underline{13\ 5} \end{array}$$

**Divide by place-value numbers such as 10, 100, and 1,000.**

1. Determine the number of zeros in the divisor.
2. Move the decimal in the dividend to the left the same number of places as there are zeros in the divisor. Insert zeros as necessary.

Divide: 4.52 ÷ 100

4.52 ÷ 100 = 0.0452 — Move the decimal two places to the left. Insert a zero to have enough places. It is preferred to write a zero in front of the decimal.

**Divide by a decimal.**

1. Change the divisor to a whole number by moving the decimal point to the right, counting the places as you go. Use a caret (∧) to show the new position of the decimal point.
2. Move the decimal point in the dividend to the right as many places as you moved the decimal point in the divisor.
3. Place the decimal point for the quotient directly above the *new* decimal point in the dividend.
4. Divide as you would divide by a whole number.

Divide: 0.770 ÷ 3.5

$$\begin{array}{r} 0.22 \\ 3.5_\wedge\overline{)0.7_\wedge70} \\ \underline{7\ 0} \\ 70 \\ \underline{70} \end{array}$$

Divide: 0.485 ÷ 0.24
Round to the nearest tenth.

$$\begin{array}{r} 2.02 \quad = 2.0\ \text{rounded} \\ 0.24_\wedge\overline{)0.48_\wedge50} \\ \underline{48} \\ 50 \\ \underline{48} \\ 2 \end{array}$$

## Section 3-3

**1** Convert a decimal to a fraction. (p. 84)

1. Find the denominator: Write 1 followed by as many zeros as there are places to the right of the decimal point.
2. Find the numerator: Use the digits without the decimal point.
3. Reduce to lowest terms and/or write as a whole or mixed number.

$$0.05 = \frac{5}{100} \div \frac{5}{5} = \frac{1}{20} \qquad 0.584 = \frac{584}{1,000} \div \frac{8}{8} = \frac{73}{125}$$

**2** Convert a fraction to a decimal. (p. 85)

1. Write the numerator as the dividend and the denominator as the divisor.
2. Divide the numerator by the denominator, taking the division out as many decimal places as necessary or desirable.
3. For repeating decimals:
   (a) Write the remainder as the numerator of a fraction and the divisor as the denominator.
   or
   (b) Carry the division one place past the desired place and round.

$$\frac{5}{8} = 8\overline{)5.000} \qquad \frac{1}{6} = 6\overline{)1.000}$$

$$
\begin{array}{r}
0.625 \\
8\overline{)5.000} \\
4\,8 \\
\hline
20 \\
16 \\
\hline
40 \\
40 \\
\hline
\end{array}
\qquad
\begin{array}{r}
0.166 \approx 0.17 \\
6\overline{)1.000} \\
6 \\
\hline
40 \\
36 \\
\hline
40 \\
36 \\
\hline
4
\end{array}
$$

## EXERCISES SET A

*Write the word name for the decimal.*

**1.** 0.5      **2.** 0.108      **3.** 0.00275      **4.** 17.8

**5.** 128.23      **6.** 500.0007

*Round to the specified place.*

**7.** 0.1345 (nearest thousandth)      **8.** 384.73 (nearest ten)      **9.** 1,745.376 (nearest hundred)      **10.** $175.24 (nearest dollar)

*Add.*

**11.** $0.3 + 0.05 + 0.266 + 0.63$      **12.** $78.87 + 54 + 32.9569 + 0.0043$

**13.** $\$5.13 + \$8.96 + \$14.73$      **14.** $\$283.17 + \$58.73 + \$96.92$

*Subtract.*

**15.** $500.05 - 123.31$      **16.** $125.35 - 67.8975$      **17.** $423 - 287.4$      **18.** $482.073 - 62.97$

*Multiply.*

**19.**
$$\begin{array}{r} 27.63 \\ \times \quad 7 \\ \hline \end{array}$$

**20.**
$$\begin{array}{r} 6.42 \\ \times 7.8 \\ \hline \end{array}$$

**21.**
$$\begin{array}{r} 75.84 \\ \times 0.28 \\ \hline \end{array}$$

**22.** $27.58 \times 10$

*Divide. Round to hundredths if necessary.*

**23.** $34\overline{)291.48}$  **24.** $2.8\overline{)94.546}$  **25.** $296.36 \div 0.19$  **26.** $41{,}285 \div 0.68$

*Write as fractions or mixed numbers in simplest form.*

**27.** 0.55  **28.** 191.82

*Write as decimals. Round to hundredths if necessary.*

**29.** $\dfrac{17}{20}$  **30.** $\dfrac{13}{16}$

**31.** A shopper purchased a cake pan for \$8.95, a bath mat for \$9.59, and a bottle of shampoo for \$2.39. Find the total cost of the purchases.

**32.** Leon Treadwell's checking account had a balance of \$196.82 before he wrote checks for \$21.75 and \$82.46. What was his balance after he wrote the checks?

**33.** Four tires that retailed for \$486.95 are on sale for \$397.99. By how much are the tires reduced?

**34.** If 100 gallons of gasoline cost \$142.90, what is the cost per gallon?

**35.** What is the cost of 5.5 pounds of chicken breasts if they cost \$3.49 per pound?

**36.** A.G. Edwards is purchasing 100 cell phones for \$189.95. How much is the total purchase?

## EXERCISES SET B

*Write the word name for the decimal.*

**1.** 0.27

**2.** 0.013

**3.** 0.120704

**4.** 3.04

**5.** 3,000.003

**6.** 184.271

*Round to the specified place.*

**7.** 384.72 (nearest tenth)

**8.** 1,745.376 (nearest hundredth)

**9.** 32.57 (nearest whole number)

**10.** $5.333 (nearest cent)

*Add.*

**11.** 31.005 + 5.36 + 0.708 + 4.16

**12.** 9.004 + 0.07 + 723 + 8.7

**13.** $7.19 + $5.78 + $21.96

**14.** $596.16 + $47.35 + $72.58

*Subtract.*

**15.** 815.01 − 335.6

**16.** 404.04 − 135.8716

**17.** 807.38 − 529.79

**18.** 5,003.02 − 689.23

*Multiply.*

**19.**  3 84
   ×3.51

**20.**  0.0015
   ×6.003

**21.** 73.41
   ×  15

**22.** 1.394 × 100

*Divide. Round to the nearest hundredth if division does not terminate.*

**23.** $27\overline{)365.04}$    **24.** $74\overline{)85.486}$    **25.** $923.19 \div 0.541$    **26.** $363.45 \div 2.5$

*Write as fractions or mixed numbers in simplest form.*

**27.** 0.75    **28.** 17.5

*Write as decimals. Round to hundredths if necessary.*

**29.** $\dfrac{1}{20}$    **30.** $3\dfrac{7}{20}$

**31.** Rob McNab ordered 18.3 square meters of carpet for his halls, 123.5 square meters for the bedrooms, 28.7 square meters for the family room, and 12.9 square meters for the playroom. Find the total amount of carpet he ordered.

**32.** Janet Morris weighed 149.3 pounds before she began a weight-loss program. After eight weeks she weighed 129.7 pounds. How much did she lose?

**33.** Ernie Jones worked 37.5 hours at the rate of $14.80 per hour. Calculate his earnings.

**34.** If sugar costs $2.87 for 80 ounces, what is the cost per ounce, rounded to the nearest cent?

**35.** If two lengths of metal sheeting measuring 12.5 inches and 15.36 inches are cut from a roll of metal measuring 240 inches, how much remains on the roll?

**36.** If 1,000 gallons of gasoline cost $1,589, what is the cost of 45 gallons?

## PRACTICE TEST

**1.** Round 42.876 to tenths.

**2.** Round 30.5375 to one nonzero digit.

**3.** Write the word name for 24.1007.

**4.** Write the number for three and twenty-eight thousandths.

*Perform the indicated operation.*

**5.** $39.17 - 15.078$

**6.** $27.418 \times 100$

**7.** $0.387 + 3.17 + 17 + 204.3$

**8.** $28.34 \div 50$ (nearest hundredth)

**9.** $\begin{array}{r} 324 \\ \times\, 1.38 \\ \hline \end{array}$

**10.** $0.138 \div 10$

**11.** $128 - 38.18$

**12.** $\begin{array}{r} 17.75 \\ \times\; 0.325 \\ \hline \end{array}$

**13.** $2.347 + 0.178 + 3.5 + 28.341$

**14.** $91.25 \div 12.5$

**15.** $317.24 - 138$

**16.** $374.17 \times 100$

**17.** A patient's chart showed a temperature reading of 101.2 degrees Fahrenheit at 3 P.M. and 99.5 degrees Fahrenheit at 10 P.M. What was the drop in temperature?

**18.** Eastman Kodak's stock changed from $26.14 a share to $22.15 a share. Peter Carp owned 2,000 shares of stock. By how much did his stock decrease?

**19.** Stephen Lewis owns 100 shares of PepsiCo at $47.40; 50 shares of Alcoa at $27.19; and 200 shares of McDonald's at $24.72. What is the total stock value?

**20.** What is the average price per share of the 350 shares of stock held by Stephen Lewis if the total value is $11,043.50?

1. Explain why numbers are aligned on the decimal point when they are added or subtracted.

2. Describe the process for placing the decimal point in the product of two decimal numbers.

3. Explain the process of changing a fraction to a decimal number.

4. Explain the process of changing a decimal number to a fraction.

*Identify the error and describe what caused the error. Then work the example correctly.*

5. Change $\dfrac{5}{12}$ to a decimal number.

$$\begin{array}{r} 2.4 \\ 5)\overline{12.0} \\ \underline{10} \\ 2\,0 \end{array} \qquad \dfrac{5}{12} = 2.4$$

6. Add: 3.72 + 6 + 12.5 + 82.63

$$\begin{array}{r} 3.72 \\ 6 \\ 12.5 \\ \underline{82.63} \\ 87.66 \end{array}$$

7. Multiply: $4.37 \times 2.1$

$$\begin{array}{r} 4.37 \\ \times\ 2.1 \\ \hline 4\,37 \\ \underline{87\,4} \\ 91.77 \end{array}$$

8. Divide: $18.27 \div 54$. Round to tenths.

$$\begin{array}{r} 2.95 \approx 3.0 \\ 18.27\,)\overline{54.00\ 00} \\ \underline{36\ 54} \\ 17\ 460 \\ \underline{16\ 443} \\ 1\ 0170 \\ \underline{9135} \\ 1035 \end{array}$$

## Challenge Problem

Net income for Hershey Foods for the third quarter is $143,600,000 or $1.09 a share. This is compared with net income of $123,100,000 or $0.89 a share for the same quarter a year ago. What was the increase or decrease in shares of stock?

## 3.1 Pricing Stock Shares

Shantell recognized the stationery, and looked forward to another of her Aunt Mildred's letters. Inside, though, were a number of documents along with a short note. The note read: "Shantell, your Uncle William and I are so proud of you. You are the first female college graduate in our family. Your parents would have been so proud as well. Please accept these stocks as a gift towards the fulfillment of starting your new business. Cash them in or keep them for later, it's up to you! With love, Aunt Millie." Shantell didn't know how to react. Finishing college had been very difficult for her financially. Having to work two jobs meant little time for studying, and a nonexistent social life. But she never expected pecans, or raisins. With dreams of opening her own floral shop, any money would be a godsend. She opened each certificate and found the following information: Alcoa—35 shares at 15 3/8; Coca Cola—150 shares at 24 5/8; IBM—80 shares at 40 11/16; and AT&T—50 shares at 35 1/8.

1. Shantell knew the certificates were old, because stocks do not trade using fractions anymore. What would the stock prices be for each company if they were converted from fractions to decimals?

2. Using your answers with decimals from number 1, find the total value of each company's stock. What is the total value from all four companies?

3. Shantell couldn't believe her eyes. The total she came up with was over $9,000! Suddenly, though, she realized that the amounts she used could not possibly be the current stock prices. After 30 minutes online, she was confident she had the current prices: Alcoa: 35 shares at $34.19; Coca Cola: 150 shares at $48.05; IBM: 80 shares at $95.03; and AT&T: 50 shares at $38.88. Using the current prices, what would be the total value of each company's stock? What would be the total value for all of the stocks? Given the answer, would you cash the stocks in now or hold on to them to see if they increased in value?

## 3.2 JK Manufacturing Demographics

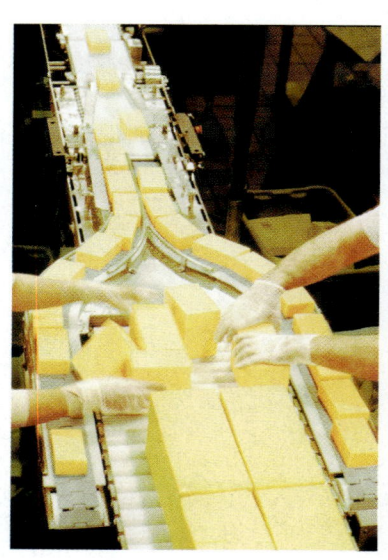

Carl has just started his new job as a human resource management assistant for JK Manufacturing. His first project is to gather demographic information on the personnel at their three locations in El Paso, San Diego, and Chicago. Carl studied some of the demographics collected by the Bureau of Labor Statistics (www.stats.bls.gov) in one of his human resource classes and decided to collect similar data. Primarily, he wants to know the gender, level of education, and ethnic/racial backgrounds of JK Manufacturing's workforce. He designs a survey using categories he found at the Bureau of Labor Statistics web site.

Employees at each of the locations completed Carl's survey, and reported the following information:

**El Paso:** 140 women, 310 men; 95 had a bachelor's degree or higher; 124 had some college or an associate's degree; 200 were high school graduates, and the rest had less than a high school diploma; 200 employees were white non-Hispanic, 200 were Hispanic or Latino, 20 were black or African American, 15 were Asian, and the rest were "other."

**San Diego:** 525 women, 375 men; 150 had a bachelor's degree or higher, 95 had some college or an associate's degree, 500 were high school graduates, and the rest had less than a high school diploma; 600 employees were Hispanic or Latino, 200 were black or African American, 50 were white non-Hispanic, 25 were Asian, and the rest were "other."

**Chicago:** 75 women, 100 men; 20 had a bachelor's degree or higher, 75 had some college or an associate's degree, 75 were high school graduates, and the rest had less than a high school diploma; 100 employees were white non-Hispanic, 50 were black or African American, 25 were Hispanic or Latino, there were no Asians or "other" at the facility.

1. Carl's supervisor asked him to summarize the information and convert the raw data to a decimal part of the total. Carl designed the following chart to organize the data. To complete the chart, write a fraction with the number of employees in each category as the numerator and the total number of employees in each city as the denominator. Then convert the fraction to a decimal rounded to the nearest hundredth. Enter the decimal in the chart. To check your calculations, the total of the decimal equivalents for each city should equal 1 or close to 1 due to roarding discrepancies.

| Gender | El Paso | | San Diego | | Chicago | |
|---|---|---|---|---|---|---|
| Men | 310 | | 375 | | 100 | |
| Women | 140 | | 525 | | 75 | |
| **Total** | 450 | | 900 | | 175 | |

| Education | El Paso | | San Diego | | Chicago | |
|---|---|---|---|---|---|---|
| Bachelor's degree or higher | 95 | | 150 | | 20 | |
| Some college or an Associate's degree | 124 | | 95 | | 75 | |
| HS graduate | 200 | | 500 | | 75 | |
| Less than a HS diploma | 31 | | 155 | | 5 | |
| **Total** | 450 | | 900 | | 175 | |

| Race/Ethnicity | El Paso | | San Diego | | Chicago | |
|---|---|---|---|---|---|---|
| White/non-Hispanic | 200 | | 50 | | 100 | |
| Black/African American | 20 | | 200 | | 50 | |
| Hispanic/Latino | 200 | | 600 | | 25 | |
| Asian | 15 | | 25 | | | |
| Other | 15 | | 25 | | | |
| **Total** | 450 | | 900 | | 175 | |

# CHAPTER 4 | Banking

# Record Keeping: Identity Theft

Last year, the Federal Trade Commission logged 635,000 consumer complaints for fraud and identity theft, with 61% for fraud and 39% for identity theft.

In response, the Federal Reserve, in cooperation with other regulatory agencies, issued rules that require banks to adopt a risk-based response program to address incidents of unauthorized access to the customer information they electronically hold. Banks must notify customers "as soon as possible" by e-mail or written letter of "an incident of unauthorized access to sensitive customer information," defined as Social Security numbers, account numbers, and other details.

To reduce or minimize the risk of becoming a victim of identity theft or fraud, you can take these basic steps:

- Keep a list of all your credit accounts and bank accounts in a secure place, so you can quickly call the issuers to inform them about missing or stolen cards. Include account numbers, expiration dates, and telephone numbers of customer service and fraud departments.
- Shred and destroy unwanted documents that contain personal information including credit, debit, and ATM card receipts and preapproved credit offers.
- Never permit your credit card number to be written onto your checks.
- Take credit card receipts with you. Never toss them into a public trash container.

- Do not carry extra credit cards, Social Security card, birth certificate, or passport in your wallet or purse except when necessary.
- Order your credit report at least once a year. If you are a victim of identity theft, your credit report will contain the telltale signs of activity.
- Ask your financial institutions to add extra security protection to your account.
- Install virus and spyware detection software and a firewall on your computer and keep them updated.
- Deposit mail in U.S. Postal Service collection boxes. Do not leave mail in your mailbox overnight or on weekends.

If you think you are a victim of identity theft, follow these guidelines:

- Contact the fraud departments of each one of the three consumer reporting companies to place a fraud alert on your credit report. A fraud alert tells creditors to follow certain procedures before opening any new accounts.
- Close the accounts that you know or believe have been tampered with or opened fraudulently.
- File a complaint with the FTC. You may print a copy of your complaint to provide important standardized information for your police report.
- File a report with your local police or police in the community where the identity theft took place.

## LEARNING OUTCOMES

### 4-1 Checking Account Transactions
1. Make account transactions.
2. Record account transactions.

### 4-2 Bank Statements
1. Reconcile a bank statement with an account register.

 A corresponding Business Math Case Video for this chapter, *Which Bank Account is Best?*, can be found in Appendix A.

Most businesses and many individuals use computer software and online banking for making, recording, and reconciling transactions for a bank account. All of the processes discussed in this chapter are similar to the processes used with a computer. It is important to use banking forms correctly, to keep accurate records, and to track financial transactions carefully.

## 4-1 CHECKING ACCOUNT TRANSACTIONS

### LEARNING OUTCOMES

1 Make account transactions.
2 Record account transactions.

Financial institutions such as banks and credit unions provide a variety of services for both individual and business customers. One of these services is a **checking account**. This account holds your money and disburses it according to the policies and procedures of the bank and to your instructions. Various checking account forms or records are needed to maintain a checking account for your personal or business financial matters. The bank must be able to account for all funds that flow into and out of your account, and written evidence of changes in your account is necessary.

### 1 Make account transactions.

Any activity that changes the amount of money in a bank account is called a **transaction**.

When money is put into a checking account, the transaction is called a **deposit**. The bank refers to this transaction as a **credit**. A deposit or credit *increases* the amount of the account. One bank record for deposits made by the account holder is called the **deposit ticket**. Figure 4-1 shows a sample deposit ticket for a personal account. Figure 4-2 shows a sample deposit ticket for a business account. Deposit tickets are available to the person opening an account along with a set of preprinted checks. The bank's account number and the customer's account number are written at the bottom of the ticket in magnetic ink using specially designed characters and symbols to facilitate machine processing. The bank also has generic forms that can be used for deposits by writing in the account information.

> **Checking account:** a bank account for managing the flow of money into and out of the account.

> **Transaction:** a banking activity that changes the amount of money in a bank account.

> **Deposit:** a transaction that increases an account balance; this transaction is also called a credit.

> **Credit:** a transaction that increases an account balance.

> **Deposit ticket:** a banking form for recording the details of a deposit.

### HOW TO  Make an account deposit on the appropriate deposit form

1. Record the date.
2. Enter the amount of currency or coins being deposited.
3. List the amount of each check to be deposited. Include an identifying name or company.
4. Add the amounts of currency, coins, and checks.
5. If the deposit is to a personal account and you want to receive some of the money in cash, enter the amount on the line "less cash received" and sign on the appropriate line.
6. Subtract the amount of cash received from the total for the net deposit.

### EXAMPLE 1
Complete a deposit slip for Lee Wilson. The deposit on May 29, 2008, will include $392 in currency, $0.90 in coins, a $373.73 check from Nichols, and a tax refund check from the IRS for $438.25. Lee wants to get $100 in cash from the transaction.

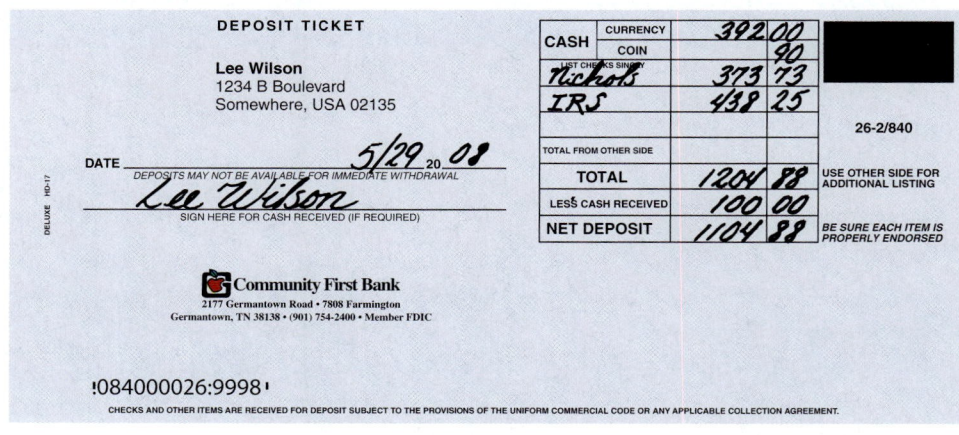

**FIGURE 4-1**
**Deposit Ticket for a Personal Account**

Businesses generally will have several checks to deposit for each transaction. A different type of deposit ticket allows more checks to be entered on one side of the deposit ticket, and a copy of the ticket is kept by the business. When depositing to a business account, you do not have the option of receiving a portion of the deposit in cash.

**EXAMPLE 2** Macon Florist makes a deposit on August 19, 2008, that includes the checks shown in Table 4-1. Complete the deposit ticket (Figure 4-2).

### TABLE 4-1
#### Checks to be deposited

| Name | Amount | Name | Amount |
|------|--------|------|--------|
| Carlisle | 72.21 | Shotwell | 38.75 |
| Smith | 26.32 | Yu | 31.15 |
| Mason | 42.86 | Collier | 23.96 |
| Malena | 41.13 | Taylor | 46.12 |
| Mays | 18.97 | Ores | 32.84 |
| James | 17.85 | Fly | 28.15 |
| Johnson | 28.73 | Jinkins | 61.36 |
| Miller | 16.15 | Young | 37.52 |

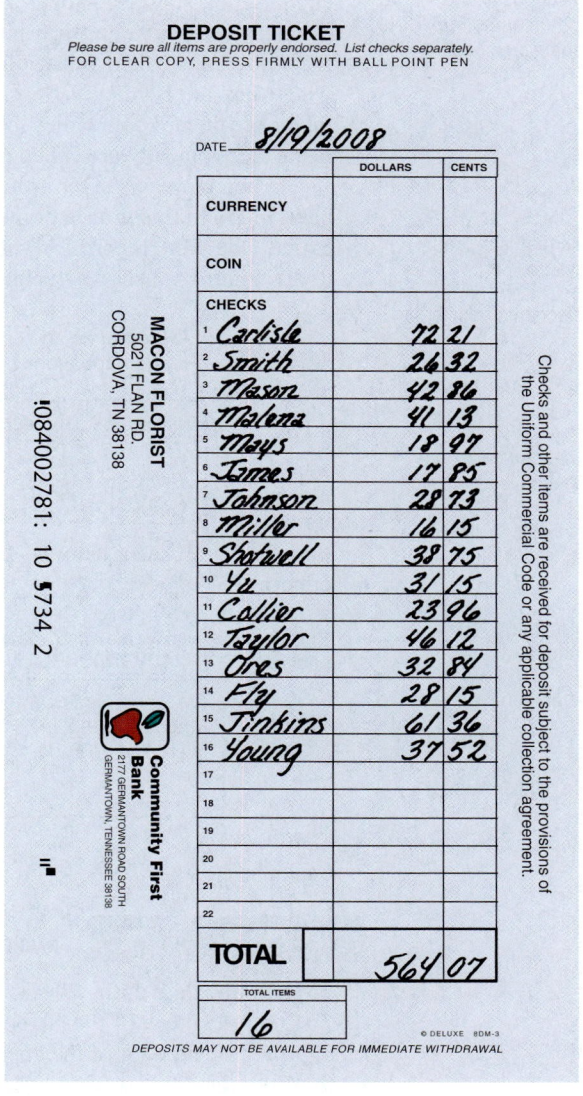

FIGURE 4-2

Complete Deposit Ticket for Macon Florist

**Bank memo:** a notification of a transaction error.

**Credit memo:** a notification of an error that increases the account balance.

**Debit memo:** a notification of an error that decreases the account balance.

**Automatic teller machine (ATM):** an electronic banking station that accepts deposits and disburses cash when you use an authorized ATM card, a debit card, or some credit cards.

If the bank discovers an error in the deposit transaction, it will notify you of the correction through a **bank memo**. If the error correction increases your balance, the bank memo is called a **credit memo**. If the error correction decreases your balance, the bank memo is called a **debit memo**.

Deposits to bank accounts can be made electronically. Individuals or businesses may make deposits using a debit card or an **automatic teller machine (ATM)** card. Individuals may also request their employer to deposit their paychecks directly to their bank account by completing a form that gives the banking information, including the account number. Government agencies encourage recipients of Social Security and other government funds to have these funds **electronically deposited**. Businesses that permit customers to use credit cards to charge merchandise or subscribe to an automatic check processing service ordinarily receive payment through electronic deposit from the credit card or check processing company. These transactions are sometimes called **point-of-sale transactions**, since the money is transferred electronically when the sale is made. VISA, MasterCard, American Express, and Discover are examples of major credit card companies that electronically transmit funds to business accounts. Transactions made electronically are called **electronic funds transfers (EFTs)**.

When money is taken from a checking account, this transaction is called a **withdrawal**. The bank refers to this transaction as a **debit**. A withdrawal or debit *decreases* the amount of the account. One bank record for withdrawals made by the account holder is called a **check** or **bank draft**. Figure 4-3 shows the basic features of a check.

**Electronic deposit:** a deposit that is made by an electronic transfer of funds.

**Point-of-sale transaction:** electronic transfer of funds when a sale is made.

**Electronic funds transfer (EFT):** a transaction that transfers funds electronically.

**Withdrawal:** a transaction that decreases an account balance; this transaction is also called a debit.

**Debit:** a transaction that decreases an account balance.

**Check or bank draft:** a banking form for recording the details of a withdrawal.

**Payee:** the one to whom the amount of money written on a check is paid.

**Payor:** the bank or institution that pays the amount of the check to the payee.

**Maker:** the one who is authorizing the payment of the check.

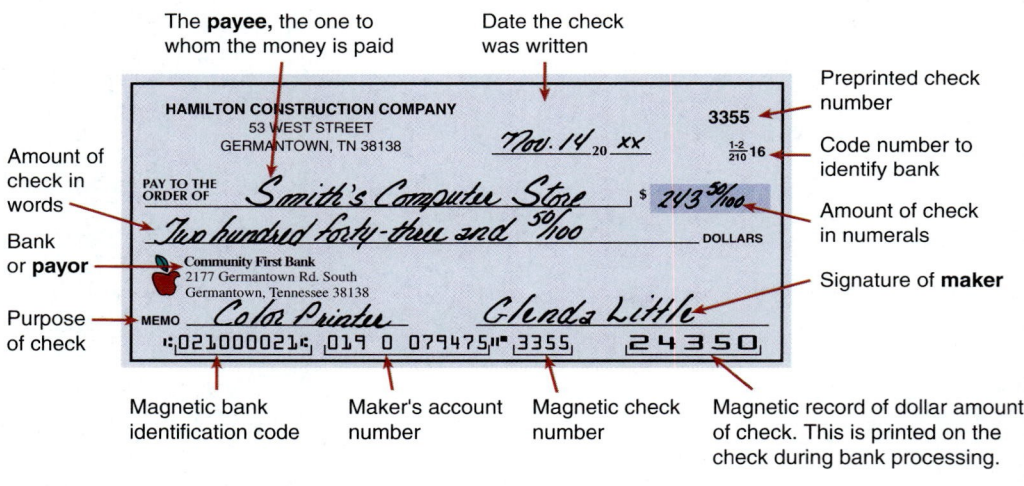

**FIGURE 4-3**
**Bank Check**

**HOW TO**   Make a withdrawal using a check

1. Enter the date of the check.
2. Enter the name of the payee.
3. Enter the amount of the check in numerals.
4. Write the amount of the check in words. Cents can be written as a fraction of a dollar or by using decimal notation.
5. Explain the purpose of the check.
6. Sign the check.

**EXAMPLE 3** Write a check dated April 8, 20XX, to Disk-O-Mania in the amount of $84.97 for CDs.

Enter the date: 4/8/20XX.
Write the name of the payee: Disk-O-Mania.
Enter the amount of the check in numerals: 84.97.
Enter the amount of the check in words. Note the fraction $\frac{97}{100}$ showing cents, or hundredths of a dollar: eighty-four and $\frac{97}{100}$.
Write the purpose of the check on the memo line: CDs.
Sign your name.
The completed check is shown in Figure 4-4.

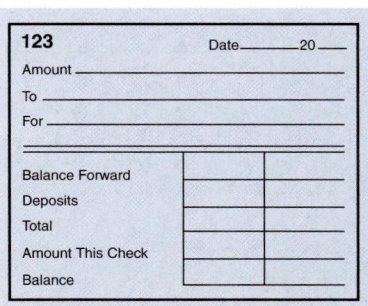 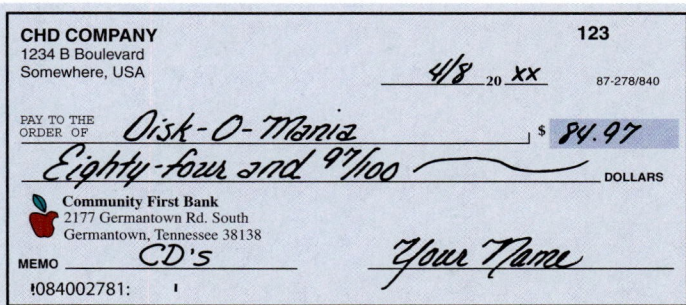

**FIGURE 4-4**
**Completed Check**

**Signature card:** a document that a bank keeps on file to verify the signatures of persons authorized to write checks on an account.

When a checking account is opened, those persons authorized to write checks on the account must sign a **signature card**, which is kept on file at the bank. Whenever a question arises regarding whether a person is authorized to write checks on an account, the bank refers to the signature card to resolve the question.

**Automatic drafts:** periodic withdrawals that the owner of an account authorizes to be made electronically.

**Online banking services:** a variety of services and transaction options that can be made through Internet banking.

Withdrawals from personal and business bank accounts can also be made electronically. Many persons elect to have regular monthly bills, such as their house note, rent, utilities, and insurance, paid electronically through **automatic drafts** from their bank account. The amount of the debit is shown on the bank statement. One time electronic checks can be authorized when a company accepts an electronic check over the telephone. When this service is used, the bank routing number, your bank account number, and the amount of the check are given over the phone. Generally the customer is given a confirmation number to use if there is any dispute over the transaction. **Online banking services** are becoming more and more popular. These services allow you to pay bills and manage your account using the Internet. Accounts are accessible 24 hours a day, seven days a week. Bank statements are posted on line and account holders can file them electronically or print paper copies.

**Debit card:** a card that can be used like a credit card but the amount of debit (purchase or withdrawal) is deducted immediately from the checking account.

**Personal identification number (PIN):** a private code that is used to authorize a transaction on a debit card or ATM card.

Individuals may also use a **debit card** to pay for services and goods. A debit card looks very similar to a credit card and often even includes a credit card name and logo such as Visa. The debit card works just like a check except the transaction is handled electronically at the time the transaction is made. Debit card transactions generally require a **personal identification number (PIN)** to authorize the transaction. ATM/debit cards can be used to make deposits to checking or savings accounts, get cash withdrawals from checking or savings accounts, transfer funds between checking and savings accounts, make payments on bank loan accounts, and to get checking and savings account information. Debit cards can be used to make purchases in person, by phone, or by computer. Debit cards can also be used to get cash from merchants who permit it.

*Don't toss those ATM or debit card receipts!* Customers are issued receipts when they deposit or withdraw money from an automatic teller machine. Use these receipts to update your account register and to verify against your next bank statement. When you are certain the transaction has been properly posted by your bank, dispose of the receipts by shredding or by some other means to maintain the security of your banking record.

## TIP

**Know the Services Offered by Your Bank and the Related Fees**

Banks and other financial institutions are offering more and more services to customers. Get to know what services are offered and what fees are charged for these services. Some services are free, while others are not.

## STOP AND CHECK

1. Complete the deposit ticket for Harrington's Pharmacy (Figure 4-5). The deposit includes $987 in cash, $41.93 in coins, and three checks in the amounts of $48.17, $153.92, and $105.18. The deposit was made on July 5.

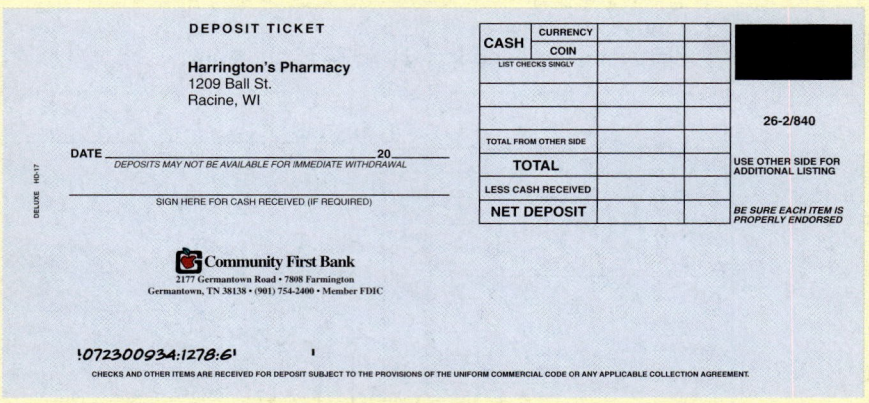

**FIGURE 4-5**
**Deposit Ticket**

2. Complete the deposit ticket for SellIt.com (Figure 4-6). The deposit is made on April 11, 20XX, and includes the following items: cash: $821; and checks: Olson, $18.15; Drewrey, $38.15; Tinkler, $82.15; Brannon, $17.19; McCready, $38.57; Mowers, $132.86; Lee, $15.21; and Wang, $38.00.

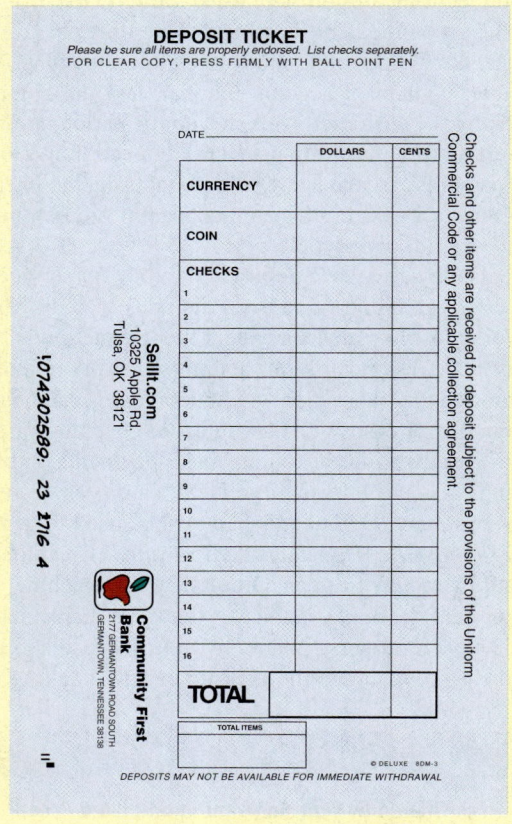

**FIGURE 4-6**
**Deposit Ticket**

**3.** Write a check (Figure 4-7) dated October 18, 20XX, to Frances Johnson in the amount of $583.17 for a tool chest. Albert Adkins is the maker.

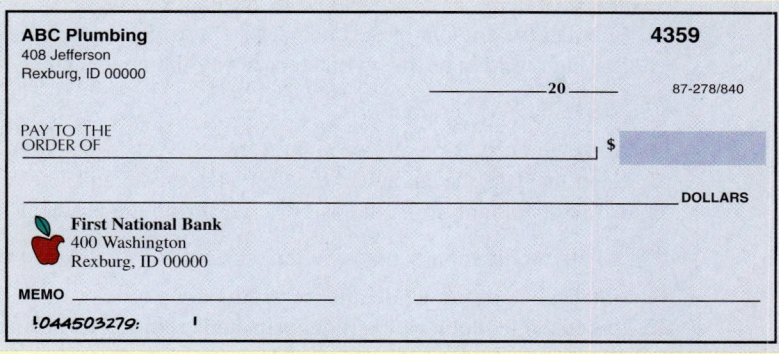

**FIGURE 4-7**
**Check Number 4359**

**4.** Max Murphy wrote a check dated August 18, 20XX, to Harley Davidson, Inc., for motorcycle parts. The amount of the check is $2,872.15. Complete the check in Figure 4-8 to show this transaction.

**5.** Describe some advantages of online banking.

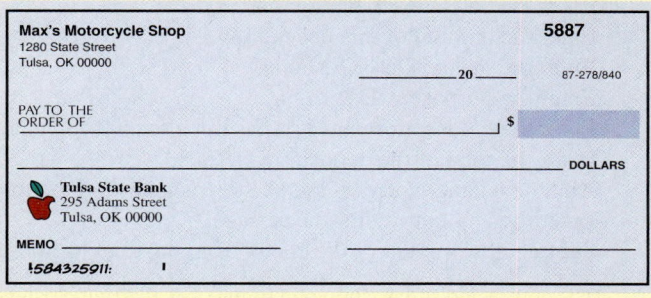

**FIGURE 4-8**
**Check Number 5887**

---

## TIP

**Keep Accurate, Up-to-Date Account Records**
The key to maintaining control of your banking account balance is to record and track every transaction. In today's busy world, it is easy to use a debit card or online banking to make many charges in a short time. Recording every transaction *when it is made* will help you keep track of your balance.

## 2 Record account transactions.

Businesses and individuals who have banking accounts must record all transactions made to the account.

Check writing supplies are available for handwritten, typed, or computer-generated checks. One type of checkbook has a **check stub** for each check. The check stub is used to record account transactions; computer-generated checks also produce a check stub. Another form for recording transactions is an **account register**. The account register is separate from the check but includes the same information as a check stub. Electronic money management systems generally produce a check stub and keep an account register automatically from the information entered on the check.

**Check stub:** a form attached to a check for recording checking account transactions that shows the account balance.

**Account register:** a separate form for recording all checking account transactions. It also shows the account balance.

For checks and other debits:

1. Make an entry for every account transaction.
2. Enter the date, the amount of the check or debit, the person or company that will receive the check or debit, and the purpose of the check or debit.
3. Subtract the amount of the check or debit from the previous balance to obtain the new balance.
4. For handwritten checks with stubs, carry the new balance forward to the next stub.

For deposits or other credits:

1. Make an entry for every account transaction.
2. Enter the date, the amount of the deposit or credit, and a brief explanation of the deposit or credit.
3. Add the amount of the deposit or credit from the previous balance to obtain the new balance.

On an electronic money management system:

1. Enter the appropriate details for producing a check.
2. Record other debits and all deposits and credits. The account register is maintained by the system automatically.
3. For business accounts or personal accounts that are used for tracking expenses, record the type of expense or budget account number.

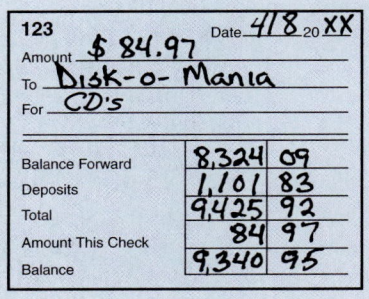

**FIGURE 4-9**
**Completed Stub**

## EXAMPLE 1

Complete the stub (Figure 4-9) for the check written in the preceding example. The balance forward is $8,324.09. Deposits of $325, $694.30, and $82.53 were made after the previous check was written.

The check number, 123, is preprinted in this case.
Enter the date: 4/8/20XX.
Enter the amount of this check: $84.97.
Enter the payee: Disk-O-Mania.
Enter the purpose: CDs.
Enter the balance forward if it has not already been entered: $8,324.09
Enter the total of the deposits: $1,101.83.
Add the balance forward and the deposits to find the total: $9,425.92.
Enter the amount of this check: $84.97.
Subtract the amount of the check from the total to find the balance: $9,340.95.

The completed stub is shown in Figure 4-9. Carry the balance to the next stub as the Balance Forward.

Account registers for individual account holders are generally supplied with an order of personalized checks. Most banks also supply an account register upon request. Figure 4-10 shows a sample of a standard account register page.

### RECORD ALL TRANSACTIONS THAT AFFECT YOUR ACCOUNT

| NUMBER | DATE | DESCRIPTION OF TRANSACTION | DEBIT (−) | √T | FEE (IF ANY) (−) | CREDIT (+) | BALANCE |  |
|--------|------|----------------------------|-----------|----|-----------------|------------|---------|--|
|        |      |                            |           |    |                 |            | 8,324 | 09 |
|        | 3/31 | Deposit                    |           |    |                 | 325 00     | +325 | 00 |
|        |      | tax refund                 |           |    |                 |            | 8,649 | 09 |
|        | 4/3  | Deposit                    |           |    |                 | 694 30     | +694 | 30 |
|        |      | paycheck                   |           |    |                 |            | 9,343 | 39 |
|        | 4/5  | Deposit                    |           |    |                 | 82 53      | +82 | 53 |
|        |      | travel reimbursement       |           |    |                 |            | 9,425 | 92 |
| 123    | 4/8  | Disk-O-Mania               | 84 97     |    |                 |            | −84 | 97 |
|        |      | computer diskettes         |           |    |                 |            | 9,340 | 95 |
|        |      |                            |           |    |                 |            |      |   |
|        |      |                            |           |    |                 |            |      |   |
|        |      |                            |           |    |                 |            |      |   |

**FIGURE 4-10**
**Check Register**

As banking becomes increasingly complex and more electronic and the penalty for overdrawing bank accounts escalates, it becomes more important to carefully maintain an account register of all transactions. Debit cards are very common as a substitute for checks. With the increased use of electronic transactions, it becomes more important to keep systematic records of all account transactions. Thus, the account register can be used to record transactions made while away from your computer. Then the computer can be used to calculate balances as new transactions are entered.

**Endorsement:** a signature, stamp, or electronic imprint on the back of a check that authorizes payment in cash or directs payment to a third party or account.

Before a check can be cashed, it must be **endorsed**. That is, the payee must sign or stamp the check on the back. There are several ways to endorse a check. The simplest way is for the payee to sign the back of the check exactly as the payee's name is written on the front of the check. Banks generally cash checks drawn on their own bank or checks presented by payees who are account holders. A bank cashing checks drawn on its own bank normally requires the payees to present appropriate identification if they are not account holders at that bank. Banks will cash checks drawn on a different bank for payees who are account holders and require the payee's account number to be written below the signature. The payee's account will be debited if the check is returned unpaid.

Appropriate identification is required for receiving cash from an account or for cashing a check. This identification is also required for opening an account. The Patriot Act of 2001 now requires financial institutions to follow specific identification procedures. Most banks require two forms of identification (ID), with at least one being a primary form of identification. An acceptable primary ID must include a photo and be issued by a government agency. Some examples are a state driver's license or ID, a military ID, or a passport or visa. Some secondary forms of identification are a credit card, utility bill, property tax bill, or employer ID.

**Restricted endorsement:** a type of endorsement that reassigns the check to a different payee or directs the check to be deposited to a specified account.

While banking procedures are designed to prevent misuse of checks, it is a good idea to use a **restricted endorsement** for signing checks. One type of restricted endorsement changes the payee of the check. The original payee writes "pay to the order of," lists the name of the new payee, and then signs the check. This choice would be used when you want to assign the check to someone else. Another type of restricted endorsement is used for depositing the check into the payee's bank account. The payee writes "for deposit only," lists the account number, and then endorses the check. Most banking practices only allow checks to be deposited to a business account if they have a business listed as the payee. That is, they do not allow cash to be received for a check made out to a business. For greater security most businesses endorse checks as soon as they are received. Many businesses imprint the endorsement on checks using an electronic cash register or an ink stamp.

The Federal Reserve Board regulates the way endorsements can be placed on checks. As Figure 4-11 shows, the endorsement must be placed within $1\frac{1}{2}$ inches of the left edge of the

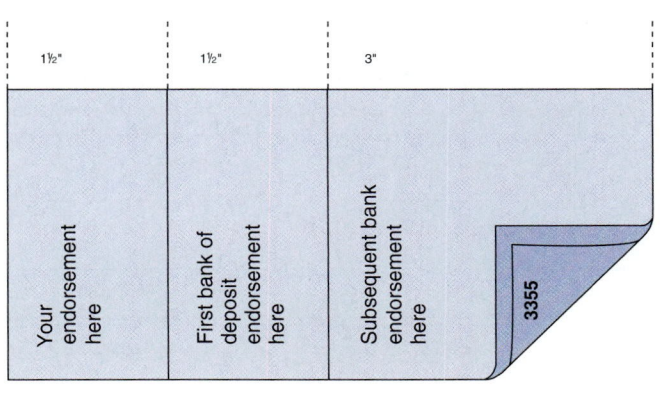

**FIGURE 4-11**

**The Back of a Check Showing Areas for Endorsements**

check. The rest of the back of the check is reserved for bank endorsements. Many check-printing companies now mark this space and provide lines for endorsements.

Electronic checks do not require the same type of endorsement. Personal identification numbers (PINs) and knowledge of bank routing numbers and account numbers are used to maintain security with electronic transactions.

## STOP AND CHECK

1. Examine the check stub in Figure 4-12 to answer these questions.
   a. How much is check 1492 written for?

   b. What was the account balance from the previous transaction?

   c. What is the new balance?

**FIGURE 4-12**
**Check Stub Number 1492**

| 1492 | Date Mar 15 20 XX |
|---|---|
| Amount $152.87 | |
| To Brown's Shoes | |
| For Shoes | |

| | | |
|---|---|---|
| Balance Forward | 2,896 | 15 |
| Deposits | +800 | 00 |
| Total | 3,696 | 15 |
| Amount This Check | −152 | 87 |
| Balance | 3,543 | 28 |

2. Complete the check stub for check 4359 (Figure 4-13) written to Frances Johnson on October 18, 20XX, in the amount of $583.17 for a tool chest.

**FIGURE 4-13**
**Check Stub Number 4359**

| 4359 | Date 20 |
|---|---|
| Amount | |
| To | |
| For | |

| | | |
|---|---|---|
| Balance Forward | 5,902 | 08 |
| Deposits | | |
| Total | | |
| Amount This Check | | |
| Balance | | |

3. Complete the account register in Figure 4-14 to record check 5887 written on August 18, 20XX, to Harley Davidson, Inc., for motorcycle parts that cost $2,872.15. Also record a debit card entry of $498.31 made on August 20, 20XX, to Remmie Raynor for pool services.

### RECORD ALL TRANSACTIONS THAT AFFECT YOUR ACCOUNT

| NUMBER | DATE | DESCRIPTION OF TRANSACTION | DEBIT (−) | √ T | FEE (IF ANY) (−) | CREDIT (+) | BALANCE | |
|---|---|---|---|---|---|---|---|---|
| | | | | | | | | |
| | | | | | | | | |
| | | | | | | | | |
| | | | | | | | | |

**FIGURE 4-14**
**Account Register**

4. Complete the account register in Figure 4-15 to show the purchase of a tool chest using check number 4359 written to Frances Johnson on October 8, 20XX. Also record an ATM withdrawal of $250 on October 8, 20XX.

### RECORD ALL TRANSACTIONS THAT AFFECT YOUR ACCOUNT

| NUMBER | DATE | DESCRIPTION OF TRANSACTION | DEBIT (−) | √ T | FEE (IF ANY) (−) | CREDIT (+) | BALANCE | |
|--------|------|----------------------------|-----------|-----|------------------|------------|---------|---|
| | | | | | | | 5,108 | 31 |
| 4358 | 10/6 | Quesha Blunt | 49 80 | | | | −49 | 80 |
| | | Cleaning Service | | | | | 5,058 | 51 |
| Dep | 10/6 | Deposit | | | | 843 57 | +843 | 57 |
| | | travel reimb. | | | | | 5,902 | 08 |
| | | | | | | | | |
| | | | | | | | | |
| | | | | | | | | |

**FIGURE 4-15**
**Account Register**

## 4-1  SECTION EXERCISES

## SKILL BUILDERS

1. On April 29, 20XX, Mr. Yan Yu made a deposit to the account for Park's Oriental Shop. He deposited $850.00 in cash, $8.63 in coins, and two checks, one in the amount of $157.38, the other in the amount of $32.49. Fill out Mr. Yu's deposit ticket for April 29, 20XX (Figure 4-16).

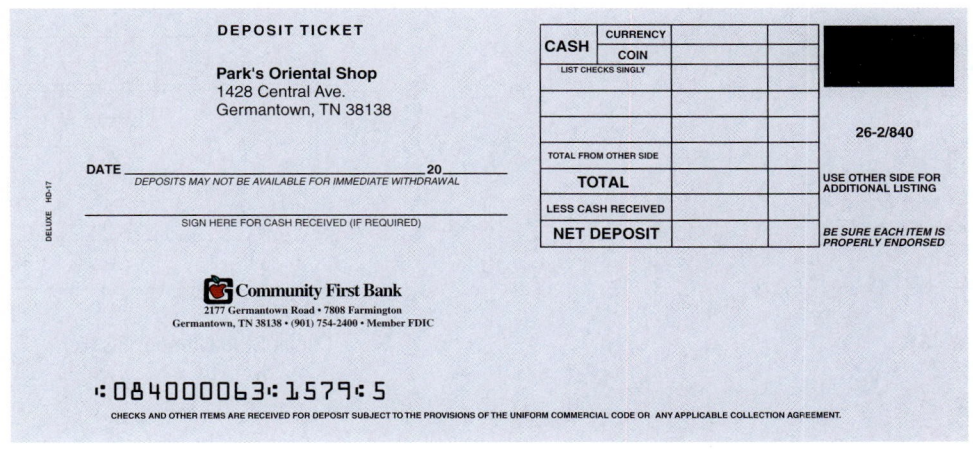

**FIGURE 4-16**
**Deposit Ticket for Park's Oriental Shop**

2. Complete the deposit ticket for Delectables Candies in Figure 4-17. The deposit is made on March 31, 20XX, and includes the following items: cash: $196.00; and checks: Cavanaugh, $14.72; Bryan, $31.18; Wossum, $16.97; Wright, $28.46; Howell, $17.21; Coe, $32.17; Beulke, $17.84; Palinchak, $31.96; and Paszel, $19.16.

DEPOSIT TICKET

Please be sure all items are properly endorsed. List checks separately.
FOR CLEAR COPY, PRESS FIRMLY WITH BALL POINT PEN

DATE

| | DOLLARS | CENTS |
|---|---|---|
| CURRENCY | | |
| COIN | | |
| CHECKS | | |
| 1 | | |
| 2 | | |
| 3 | | |
| 4 | | |
| 5 | | |
| 6 | | |
| 7 | | |
| 8 | | |
| 9 | | |
| 10 | | |
| 11 | | |
| 12 | | |
| 13 | | |
| 14 | | |
| 15 | | |
| 16 | | |
| 17 | | |
| 18 | | |
| 19 | | |
| 20 | | |
| TOTAL | | |

TOTAL ITEMS

Checks and other items are received for deposit subject to the provisions of the Uniform Commercial Code or any applicable collection agreement.

DELECTABLES CANDIES
5981 POPLAR AVE.
MEMPHIS, TN. 38121

87-278/840

Community First Bank
2177 GERMANTOWN ROAD SOUTH
GERMANTOWN, TENNESSEE 38138

⑆084002781⑆ 11 2118 3

© DELUXE 8DM-3

DEPOSITS MAY NOT BE AVAILABLE FOR IMMEDIATE WITHDRAWAL

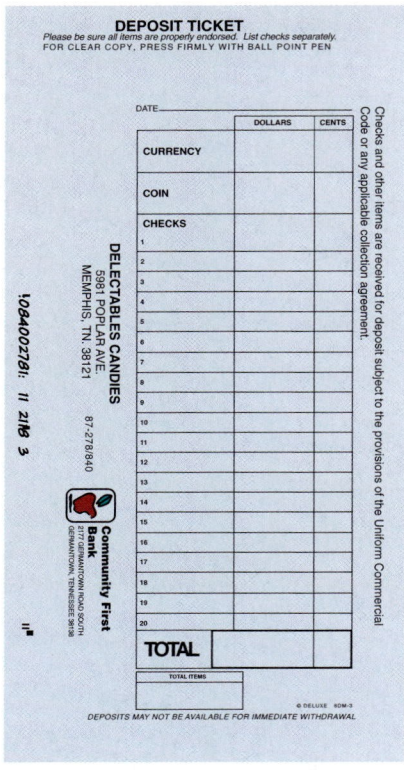

FIGURE 4-17
**Deposit Ticket for Delectables Candies**

3. On April 29, 20XX, after Mr. Yu made his deposit (see Exercise 1), he wrote a check to Green Harvest in the amount of $155.30 for fresh vegetables. Write a check (Figure 4-18) as Mr. Yu wrote it.

Park's Oriental Shop
1428 Central Ave.
Germantown, TN 38138

456

_______ 20 _____ 87-278/840

PAY TO THE ORDER OF ______________________

______________________ DOLLARS

Community First Bank
2177 Germantown Rd. South
Germantown, Tennessee 38138

MEMO ______________ ______________

⑆084002781⑆ ⑈

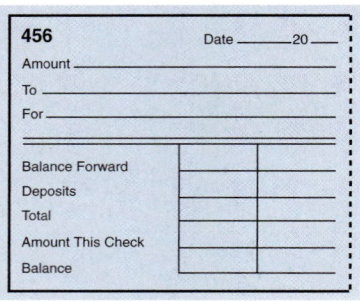

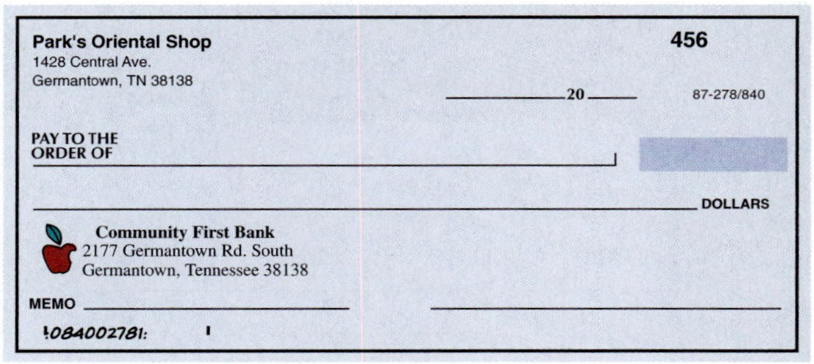

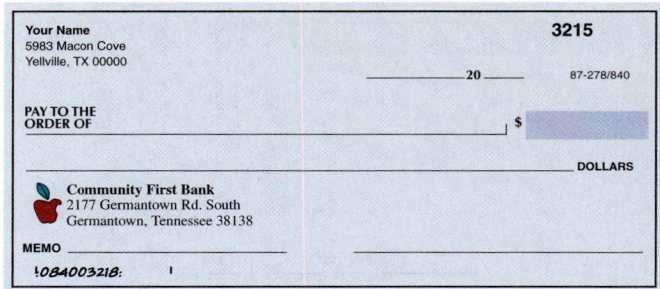

FIGURE 4-18
**Check Number 456**

4. Write a check dated June 20, 20XX, to Ronald H. Cox Realty in the amount of $596.13 for house repairs (Figure 4-19).

Your Name
5983 Macon Cove
Yellville, TX 00000

3215

_______ 20 _____ 87-278/840

PAY TO THE ORDER OF ______________________ $

______________________ DOLLARS

Community First Bank
2177 Germantown Rd. South
Germantown, Tennessee 38138

MEMO ______________ ______________

⑆084003218⑆ ⑈

FIGURE 4-19
**Check Number 3215**

5. Before Mr. Yu made his deposit (see Exercise 1), the balance in the account was $7,869.40. Complete the check stub for the check you wrote in Exercise 3 (Figure 4-20).

456 Date _______ 20 ___

Amount ____________

To ____________

For ____________

| | | |
|---|---|---|
| Balance Forward | | |
| Deposits | | |
| Total | | |
| Amount This Check | | |
| Balance | | |

FIGURE 4-20
**Check Stub Number 456**

6. Complete the check stub for the check you wrote in Exercise 4 if the balance brought forward is $2,213.56 (Figure 4-21).

3215 Date _______ 20 ___

Amount ____________

To ____________

For ____________

| | | |
|---|---|---|
| Balance Forward | | |
| Deposits | | |
| Total | | |
| Amount This Check | | |
| Balance | | |

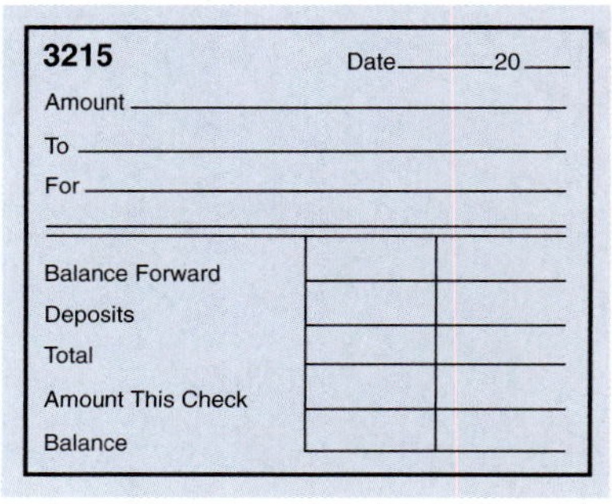

FIGURE 4-21
**Check Stub Number 3215**

**7.** Enter in the account register in Figure 4-22 all the transactions described in Exercises 1, 3, and 5, and find the ending balance.

| | | RECORD ALL TRANSACTIONS THAT AFFECT YOUR ACCOUNT | | | | | BALANCE | |
|---|---|---|---|---|---|---|---|---|
| NUMBER | DATE | DESCRIPTION OF TRANSACTION | DEBIT | √ | FEE | CREDIT | 7,869 | 40 |
| Dep | 4/29 | Deposit Payroll | $ | | | $1,048 50 | +1,048 | 50 |
| | | | | | | | 8,917 | 90 |
| 456 | 4/29 | Green Harvest | 155 30 | | | | −155 | 30 |
| | | | | | | | 8,762 | 60 |

**FIGURE 4-22**
Account Register

**8.** On September 30 you deposited your payroll check of $932.15. You then wrote the following checks on the same day:

| Check Number | Payee | Amount |
|---|---|---|
| 3176 | Electric Co-op. | $107.13 |
| 3177 | BP Oil | $47.15 |
| 3178 | Visa | $97.00 |

You made a deposit of $280 at your bank's ATM on October 3. Show these transactions in your account register in Figure 4-23, and show the ending balance if your beginning balance was $435.97.

| | | RECORD ALL TRANSACTIONS THAT AFFECT YOUR ACCOUNT | | | FEE | | BALANCE | |
|---|---|---|---|---|---|---|---|---|
| NUMBER | DATE | DESCRIPTION OF TRANSACTION | DEBIT (−) | √ T | (IF ANY) (−) | CREDIT (+) | 435 | 97 |
| Dep. | 9/30 | Payroll Direct Deposit | | | | 932 15 | +932 | 15 |
| | | | | | | | 1,368 | 12 |
| 3176 | 9/30 | Electric Co-op | 107 13 | | | | −107 | 13 |
| | | | | | | | 1,260 | 99 |
| 3177 | 9/30 | BP Oil | 47 15 | | | | −47 | 15 |
| | | | | | | | 1,213 | 84 |
| 3178 | 9/30 | Visa | 97 00 | | | | −97 | 00 |
| | | | | | | | 1,116 | 84 |
| ATM | 10/3 | Deposit (Refund Check) | | | | 280 00 | +280 | 00 |
| | | | | | | | 1,396 | 84 |

**FIGURE 4-23**
Account Register

**9.** Describe how the check in Exercise 4 would be endorsed for deposit to account number 26-8224021. What type of endorsement is this called?

**10.** If you were the owner of Green Harvest (Exercise 3), would you be able to exchange this check for cash? If so, describe how you would endorse the check. If not, explain how you could handle the check.

**11.** List three banking transactions that can be made with an ATM/debit card.

**12.** How can you use a debit card to make purchase of goods?

### LEARNING OUTCOME

**1** Reconcile a bank statement with an account register.

Financial institutions provide account statements to their checking account customers to enable account holders to reconcile any differences between that statement and the customer's own account register. These statements are either mailed or provided online.

## 1    Reconcile a bank statement with an account register.

**Bank statement:** an account record periodically provided by the bank for matching your records with the bank's records.

**Service charge:** a fee the bank charges for maintaining the checking account or for other banking services.

**Returned check:** a deposited check that was returned because the maker's account did not have sufficient funds.

**Returned check fee:** a fee the bank charges the depositor for returned checks.

**Nonsufficient funds (NSF) fee:** a fee charged to the account holder when a check is written for which there are not sufficient funds.

**Automatic teller machine (ATM):** an electronic banking station that accepts deposits and disburses cash when you use an authorized ATM card, a debit card, and some credit cards.

**Outstanding checks:** checks that have been written and given to the payee but have not been processed at the bank.

**Outstanding deposits:** deposits that have been made but have not yet been posted to the maker's account.

**Bank reconciliation:** the process of making the account register agree with the bank statement.

The primary tool for reconciling an account is the **bank statement**, a listing of all transactions that take place in the customer's account. It includes checks and other debits and deposits and other credits.

Most bank statements explain the various letter codes and symbols contained in the statement. One of the first steps to take when you receive a bank statement is to check this explanatory section for any terms that you do not understand in the statement.

One of the items that may appear on a bank statement is a **service charge**. This is a fee the bank charges for maintaining the checking account; it may be a standard monthly fee, a charge for each check or transaction, or some combination.

Another type of bank charge appearing on a bank statement is for checks that "bounce" (are not backed by sufficient funds). Suppose Joe writes you a check and you cash the check or deposit it. Later your bank is notified that Joe does not have enough money in his bank account to cover the check. So Joe's bank returns the check to your bank. Such a check is called a **returned check**. Your bank will deduct the amount of the returned check from your account. Your bank may also deduct a **returned check fee** from your account to cover the cost of handling this transaction. If you write a check for which you do not have sufficient funds in your account, your bank will charge you a **nonsufficient funds (NSF) fee**. The bank notifies you through a debit memo of the decrease in your account balance.

Your bank statement also reflects electronic funds transfers such as withdrawals and deposits made using an **automatic teller machine (ATM),** debit cards, wire transfers, online transfers, and authorized electronic withdrawals and deposits.

What does *not* appear on the bank statement is the amount of any check you wrote or deposit you made that reaches the bank *after* the statement is printed. Such transactions may be called **outstanding checks** or **deposits**. This is one reason your bank statement and your account register may not agree initially.

When a bank statement and an account register do not agree initially, you need to take steps to make them agree. The process of making the bank statement agree with the account register is called reconciling a bank statement or **bank reconciliation**.

The first thing to do when you receive a bank statement is to go over it and compare its contents with your account register. You can check off all the checks and deposits listed on the statement by using the ✓ column in the account register (refer to Figure 4-10) or by marking the check stub.

There are several methods for reconciling your banking records. We will use a method that uses an account reconciliation form. Figure 4-24 shows a sample bank statement reconciliation

**FIGURE 4-24**
**Account Reconciliation Form**

form. A reconciliation form is often printed on the back of the bank statement. The bank's form leads you through a reconciliation process that may be slightly different from the one given in this book, but the result is the same: a reconciled statement.

## HOW TO — Reconcile a bank statement

1. Check off all matching transactions appearing on both the bank statement and the account register.
2. Enter into the register the transactions appearing on the bank statement that have not been checked off. Check off these transactions in the register as they are entered. Update the register balance accordingly. This is the adjusted register balance.
3. Make a list of all the checks and other debits appearing in the register that have not been checked off. Add the amounts on the list to find the *total outstanding debits*. Use Figure 4-24 as a guide.
4. Make a list of all the deposits and other credits appearing in the register that have not been checked off in step 1. Add the amounts on the list to find the *total outstanding credits*. Use Figure 4-24 as a guide.
5. Calculate the *adjusted statement balance* by adding the statement balance and the total outstanding deposits and other credits, and then subtracting the total outstanding checks and other debits: Adjusted statement balance = statement balance + total outstanding credits − total outstanding debits.
6. Compare the adjusted statement balance with the adjusted register balance. These amounts should be equal.
7. If the adjusted statement balance does not equal the register balance, locate the cause of the discrepancy and correct the register or notify the bank accordingly.
8. Write *statement reconciled* on the next blank line in the account register and record the statement date.

## TIP

**Finding Discrepancies**

When your adjusted statement balance does not equal your account register balance, you need to locate the cause of the discrepancy and correct the register accordingly.

To do so, first be sure you have calculated the adjusted statement balance accurately. Double-check, for instance, that the list of outstanding debits is complete and their sum is accurate. Double-check the list of outstanding credits, too. Double-check that you correctly added the total outstanding credits and subtracted the total outstanding debits from the statement balance. If you are sure you have carried out all the reconciliation steps correctly, the discrepancy may be due to an error that you made in the account register or to an error made by the bank. Here are some common errors and strategies to locate them.

**Error:** You entered a transaction in the register, but you did not update the account register balance.
**Strategy:** To locate the transaction, calculate the difference of the adjusted statement balance and the register balance (subtract one from the other). Compare this difference with each transaction amount in the register to see if this difference matches a transaction amount exactly.
**Error:** You transposed digits—for instance, 39 was entered as 93—when entering the amount in the register or when listing outstanding items from the statement.
**Strategy:** Divide the difference between the adjusted statement balance and the adjusted register balance by 9. If the quotient has no remainder, check the entries to find the transposed digits.
**Error:** You entered the check number as the amount of the check.
**Strategy:** Check the amount of each check as you check off the correct amount.
**Error:** You entered a transaction in the register, but to update the register balance, you added the transaction amount when you should have subtracted, or vice versa.
**Strategy:** To locate the transaction, calculate the difference of the adjusted statement balance and the adjusted register balance (subtract one from the other.) Divide the difference by 2. Compare this result with each transaction in the register to see if it matches a transaction amount exactly.
**Error:** You entered a transaction in the register, but to update the register balance, you added (or subtracted) the transaction amount incorrectly.
**Strategy:** To locate the transaction, begin with the first transaction in the register following the previous reconciliation. From this point on, redo your addition (or subtraction) for each transaction to see if you originally added (or subtracted) the transaction amount correctly.

When using software programs to keep banking records, the user enters transaction amounts into the computer, and the program updates the register balance. At reconciliation time, the user enters information from the bank statement into the computer, and the program reconciles the bank statement with the account register.

These programs can also be useful for budgeting and tax purposes. Transactions can be categorized and tracked according to the user's specifications. Monthly and yearly budgets can be prepared accordingly, for both individuals and businesses. At tax time, these programs may even be used to generate tax forms.

## EXAMPLE 1

Pope Animal Clinic regularly transfers money from its checking account to a special account used for one-time expenditures such as equipment. The decision to transfer is made each month when the bank statement is reconciled. Money is transferred only if the adjusted statement balance exceeds $2,500; all the excess is transferred. The bank statement is shown in Figure 4-26, and the register is shown in Figure 4-27. Should money be transferred? If so, how much?

| What You Know | What You Are Looking For | Solution Plan |
|---|---|---|
| Bank statement transactions (Figure 4-26) and register transactions (Figure 4-27) | The adjusted statement balance and the adjusted checkbook balance. | Adjusted statement balance = statement balance + total outstanding credits − total outstanding debits (Figure 4-25). |
| Balance in excess of $2,500 is transferred. | Should money be transferred? If so, how much? | Transfer any amount that is more than $2,500. |

### Solution

Check off all matching transactions appearing on both the statement and the register (Figures 4-26 and 4-27).

Now enter into the register the transactions appearing on the bank statement that have not been checked off. The service fee is the only transaction not checked off. As you enter it into the register, check it off the bank statement and the register. Now use the account reconciliation form (Figure 4-25) to list the outstanding credits and debits: transactions appearing on the register that have not been checked off.

### Conclusion

The adjusted statement balance is more than $2,500.
**Money should be transferred.** Since the excess over $2,500 should be transferred, **the amount to be transferred is** $3,167.85 − $2,500, or **$667.85**.

| $ | | BALANCE AS SHOWN ON BANK STATEMENT | | BALANCE AS SHOWN IN YOUR CHECKBOOK | $ | |
|---|---|---|---|---|---|---|
| 3,177 | 82 | | | | 3,172 | 85 |
| 200 | 00 | ADD DEPOSITS NOT SHOWN ON STATEMENT | | SUBTRACT AMOUNT OF SERVICE CHARGE | 5 | 00 |
| 3,377 | 82 | NEW TOTAL | | NEW TOTAL | 3,167 | 85 |
| 209 | 97 | SUBTRACT TOTAL OF OUTSTANDING CHECKS | | ADJUSTMENTS IF ANY | 0 | |
| 3,167 | 85 | YOUR ADJUSTED STATEMENT BALANCE | SHOULD EQUAL | YOUR ADJUSTED CHECKBOOK BALANCE | 3,167 | 85 |

| Outstanding Deposits (Credits) | | |
|---|---|---|
| Date | Amount | |
| 5/25 | $ | 200 00 |
| | | |
| | | |
| | | |
| | | |
| Total | $ | 200 00 |

| Outstanding Checks (Debits) | | |
|---|---|---|
| Check Number | Date | Amount |
| 239 | | $ 117 28 |
| 240 | | 92 69 |
| | | |
| | | |
| | | |
| Total | | $ 209 97 |

**FIGURE 4-25**
**Account Reconciliation Form**

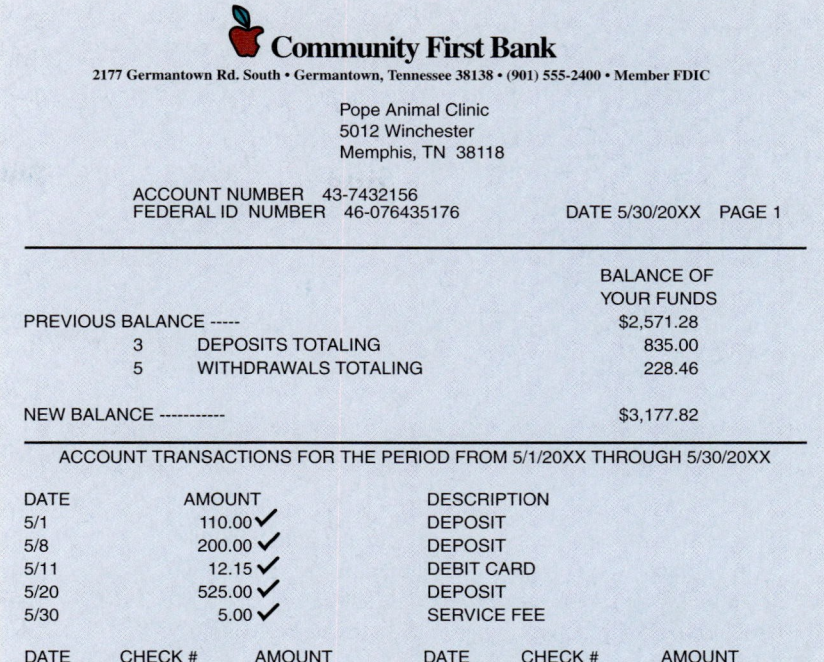

**FIGURE 4-26**
Matching Transactions Checked Off the Bank Statement

### Community First Bank

2177 Germantown Rd. South • Germantown, Tennessee 38138 • (901) 555-2400 • Member FDIC

Pope Animal Clinic
5012 Winchester
Memphis, TN 38118

ACCOUNT NUMBER 43-7432156
FEDERAL ID NUMBER 46-076435176          DATE 5/30/20XX   PAGE 1

|  |  | BALANCE OF YOUR FUNDS |
|---|---|---|
| PREVIOUS BALANCE ----- |  | $2,571.28 |
| 3 | DEPOSITS TOTALING | 835.00 |
| 5 | WITHDRAWALS TOTALING | 228.46 |
| NEW BALANCE ----------- |  | $3,177.82 |

ACCOUNT TRANSACTIONS FOR THE PERIOD FROM 5/1/20XX THROUGH 5/30/20XX

| DATE | AMOUNT |  | DESCRIPTION |
|---|---|---|---|
| 5/1 | 110.00 ✓ |  | DEPOSIT |
| 5/8 | 200.00 ✓ |  | DEPOSIT |
| 5/11 | 12.15 ✓ |  | DEBIT CARD |
| 5/20 | 525.00 ✓ |  | DEPOSIT |
| 5/30 | 5.00 ✓ |  | SERVICE FEE |

| DATE | CHECK # | AMOUNT | DATE | CHECK # | AMOUNT |
|---|---|---|---|---|---|
| 5/1 | 235 | 42.95 ✓ | 5/15 | 237 | 95.73 ✓ |
| 5/7 | 236 | 72.63 ✓ |  |  |  |

CHECKING DAILY BALANCE SUMMARY

| DATE | BALANCE OF YOUR FUNDS | DATE | BALANCE OF YOUR FUNDS |
|---|---|---|---|
| 5/1 | 2,638.33 | 5/15 | 2,657.82 |
| 5/3 | 2,626.18 | 5/20 | 3,182.82 |
| 5/7 | 2,553.55 | 5/30 | 3,177.82 |
| 5/8 | 2,753.55 |  |  |

---

RECORD ALL TRANSACTIONS THAT AFFECT YOUR ACCOUNT

| NUMBER | DATE | DESCRIPTION OF TRANSACTION | DEBIT (−) | | √T | FEE (IF ANY) (−) | CREDIT (+) | | BALANCE | |
|---|---|---|---|---|---|---|---|---|---|---|
|  |  |  |  |  |  |  |  |  | 2,571 | 28 |
| 235 | 4/20 | Pet Supply Company | 42 | 95 | ✓ |  |  |  | −42 | 95 |
|  |  |  |  |  |  |  |  |  | 2,528 | 33 |
| Deposit | 5/1 | Customer Receipts |  |  | ✓ |  | 110 | 00 | +110 | 00 |
|  |  |  |  |  |  |  |  |  | 2,638 | 33 |
| Debit | 5/1 | K-mart | 12 | 15 | ✓ |  |  |  | −12 | 15 |
|  |  |  |  |  |  |  |  |  | 2,626 | 18 |
| 236 | 5/1 | Telephone Company | 72 | 63 | ✓ |  |  |  | −72 | 63 |
|  |  |  |  |  |  |  |  |  | 2553 | 55 |
| Deposit | 5/8 | Customer Receipts |  |  | ✓ |  | 200 | 00 | +200 | 00 |
|  |  |  |  |  |  |  |  |  | 2,753 | 55 |
| 237 | 5/10 | Chickasaw Electric Co. | 95 | 73 | ✓ |  |  |  | −95 | 73 |
|  |  |  |  |  |  |  |  |  | 2,657 | 82 |
| 238 | 5/15 | Protein Technologies Dog food | 117 | 28 |  |  |  |  | −117 | 28 |
|  |  |  |  |  |  |  |  |  | 2,540 | 54 |
| 239 | 5/15 | Rand M Drug Co. | 92 | 69 |  |  |  |  | −92 | 69 |
|  |  |  |  |  |  |  |  |  | 2,447 | 85 |
| Deposit | 5/20 | Customer Receipts |  |  | ✓ |  | 525 | 00 | +525 | 00 |
|  |  |  |  |  |  |  |  |  | 2,972 | 85 |
| Deposit | 5/25 | Customer Receipts |  |  |  |  | 200 | 00 | 200 | 00 |
|  |  |  |  |  |  |  |  |  | 3,172 | 85 |
|  | 5/30 | Service Fee | 5 | 00 | ✓ |  |  |  | 5 | 00 |
|  |  |  |  |  |  |  |  |  | 3,167 | 85 |
|  | 5/30 | Statement reconciled |  |  |  |  |  |  |  |  |

REMEMBER TO RECORD AUTOMATIC PAYMENTS/DEPOSITS ON DATE AUTHORIZED.

**FIGURE 4-27**
Reconciled Account Register

*The bank statement for Katherine Adam's Apparel Shop is shown in Figure 4-28.*

1. How many deposits were made during the month?

2. What amount of interest was earned?

3. How much were the total deposits?

4. How many checks appear on the bank statement?

5. What is the balance at the beginning of the statement period?

6. What is the balance at the end of the statement period?

7. What is the amount of check 8214?

8. On what date did check 8219 clear the bank?

9. Kroger Stores permit customers to get cash with a debit card. Lindy Rascoe has an ATM/debit card from her bank in Illinois. Can she use the card to get $200 cash at the Kroger checkout counter in her college town of Fresno, CA?

10. The account register for Katherine Adam's Apparel Shop is shown in Figure 4-29. Update the register and reconcile the bank statement (see Figure 4-28) with the account register using the account reconciliation form in Figure 4-30.

### 🍎 Community First Bank

2177 Germantown Rd. South • Germantown, Tennessee 38138 • (901) 555-2400 • Member FDIC

KATHERINE ADAM'S APPAREL SHOP
1396 MALL OF AMERICA
MINNEAPOLIS, MN

ACCOUNT NUMBER   12-324134523
FEDERAL ID  NUMBER   33-35462445          DATE 6/30/20XX   PAGE 1

|  |  | BALANCE OF YOUR FUNDS |
|---|---|---|
| PREVIOUS BALANCE ----- |  | 700.81 |
| 4 | DEPOSITS TOTALING | 8,218.00 |
| 5 | WITHDRAWALS TOTALING | 5,433.08 |
| NEW BALANCE ----------- |  | 3,485.73 |

ACCOUNT TRANSACTIONS FOR THE PERIOD FROM 6/1/20XX THROUGH 6/30/20XX

| DATE | AMOUNT | DESCRIPTION |
|---|---|---|
| 6/1 | 1,830.00 | DEPOSIT |
| 6/5 | 2,583.00 | DEPOSIT |
| 6/15 | 3,800.00 | DEPOSIT |
| 6/30 | 5.00 | INTEREST EARNED |

| DATE | CHECK # | AMOUNT | DATE | CHECK # | AMOUNT |
|---|---|---|---|---|---|
| 6/2 | 8213 | 647.93 | 6/12 | 8217* | 416.83 |
| 6/3 | 8214 | 490.00 | 6/20 | 8219* | 3,150.00 |
| 6/5 | 8215 | 728.32 |  |  |  |

CHECKING DAILY BALANCE SUMMARY

| DATE | BALANCE OF YOUR FUNDS | DATE | BALANCE OF YOUR FUNDS |
|---|---|---|---|
| 6/1 | 2,530.81 | 6/12 | 2,830.73 |
| 6/2 | 1,882.88 | 6/15 | 6,630.73 |
| 6/3 | 1,392.88 | 6/20 | 3,480.73 |
| 6/5 | 3,247.56 | 6/30 | 3,485.73 |

**FIGURE 4-28**

**Bank Statement for Katherine Adam's Apparel Shop**

RECORD ALL TRANSACTIONS THAT AFFECT YOUR ACCOUNT

| NUMBER | DATE | DESCRIPTION OF TRANSACTION | DEBIT (−) | √T | FEE (IF ANY) (−) | CREDIT (+) | BALANCE 700 | 81 |
|---|---|---|---|---|---|---|---|---|
| 8213 | 5/28 | Lands End | 647 93 | | | | −647 | 93 |
| | | | | | | | 52 | 88 |
| Deposit | 6/1 | Receipts | | | | 1,830 00 | +1,830 | 00 |
| | | | | | | | 1,882 | 88 |
| 8214 | 6/1 | Collier Management Co. | 490 00 | | | | −490 | 00 |
| | | | | | | | 1,392 | 88 |
| 8215 | 6/3 | Jinkins Wholesale | 728 32 | | | | −728 | 32 |
| | | | | | | | 664 | 56 |
| Deposit | 6/5 | Receipts | | | | 2,583 00 | +2,583 | 00 |
| | | | | | | | 3,247 | 56 |
| 8216 | 6/5 | Minneapolis Utility Co. | 257 13 | | | | −257 | 13 |
| | | | | | | | 2,990 | 43 |
| 8217 | 6/10 | State of MN | 416 83 | | | | −416 | 83 |
| | | | | | | | 2573 | 60 |
| Deposit | 6/15 | Receipts | | | | 3,800 00 | +3,800 | 00 |
| | | | | | | | 6,373 | 60 |
| 8218 | 6/15 | Tracie Burke salary | 2,000 00 | | | | −2,000 | 00 |
| | | | | | | | 4,373 | 60 |
| 8219 | 6/20 | Brown's Wholesale | 3,150 00 | | | | −3,150 | 00 |
| | | | | | | | 1,223 | 60 |
| Deposit | 7/2 | Receipts | | | | 1,720 00 | +1,720 | 00 |
| | | | | | | | 2943 | 60 |

**FIGURE 4-29**
Account Register for Katherine Adam's Apparel Shop

| $ | | BALANCE AS SHOWN ON BANK STATEMENT | | | BALANCE AS SHOWN IN YOUR REGISTER | $ | |
|---|---|---|---|---|---|---|---|
| | | TOTAL OF OUTSTANDING DEPOSITS | | | SUBTRACT AMOUNT OF SERVICE CHARGE | | |
| | | NEW TOTAL | | | NEW TOTAL | | |
| | | SUBTRACT TOTAL OF OUTSTANDING CHECKS | | | ADJUSTMENTS IF ANY   Interest | | |
| | | YOUR ADJUSTED STATEMENT BALANCE | SHOULD ← EQUAL | | YOUR ADJUSTED REGISTER BALANCE | | |

| Outstanding Deposits (Credits) | | | | Outstanding Checks (Debits) | | |
|---|---|---|---|---|---|---|
| Date | Amount | | | Check Number | Date | Amount |
| | $ | | | | | $ |
| | | | | | | |
| | | | | | | |
| | | | | | | |
| | | | | | | |
| | | | | | | |
| Total | $ | | | | Total | $ |

**FIGURE 4-30**
Account Reconciliation Form

# 4-2 SECTION EXERCISES

## SKILL BUILDERS

*Use Tom Deskin's bank statement (Figure 4-31) for Exercises 1–3.*

1. Does Tom pay bills through electronic funds transfer? If so, which ones?

2. Did Tom use the automatic teller machine during the month? If so, what transactions were made and for what amounts?

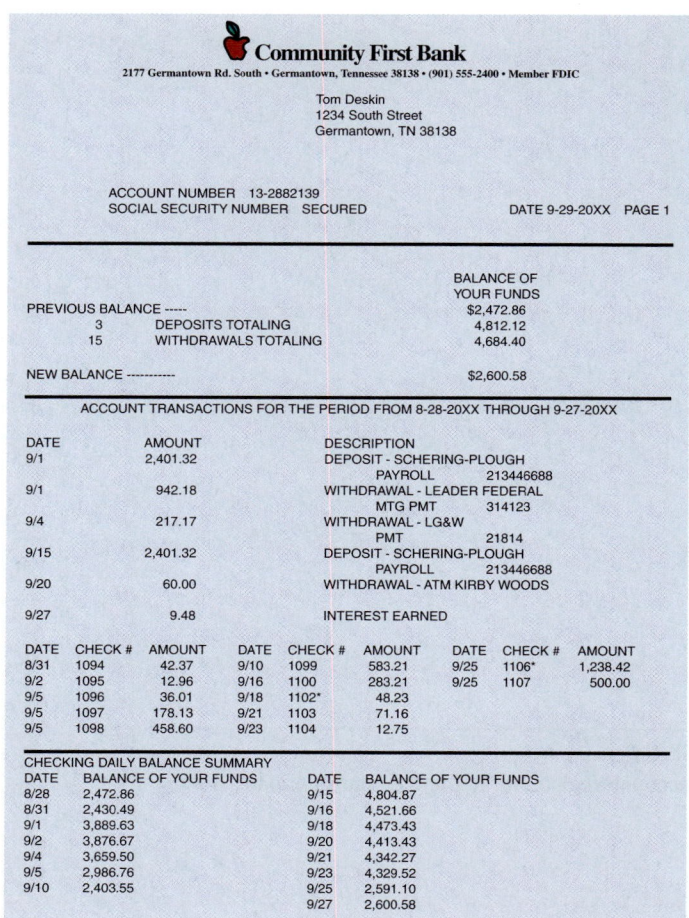

**Community First Bank**

2177 Germantown Rd. South • Germantown, Tennessee 38138 • (901) 555-2400 • Member FDIC

Tom Deskin
1234 South Street
Germantown, TN 38138

ACCOUNT NUMBER   13-2882139
SOCIAL SECURITY NUMBER   SECURED                      DATE 9-29-20XX   PAGE 1

|  |  | BALANCE OF YOUR FUNDS |
|---|---|---|
| PREVIOUS BALANCE ----- |  | $2,472.86 |
| 3 | DEPOSITS TOTALING | 4,812.12 |
| 15 | WITHDRAWALS TOTALING | 4,684.40 |
| NEW BALANCE ----------- |  | $2,600.58 |

ACCOUNT TRANSACTIONS FOR THE PERIOD FROM 8-28-20XX THROUGH 9-27-20XX

| DATE | AMOUNT | DESCRIPTION |
|---|---|---|
| 9/1 | 2,401.32 | DEPOSIT - SCHERING-PLOUGH PAYROLL   213446688 |
| 9/1 | 942.18 | WITHDRAWAL - LEADER FEDERAL MTG PMT   314123 |
| 9/4 | 217.17 | WITHDRAWAL - LG&W PMT   21814 |
| 9/15 | 2,401.32 | DEPOSIT - SCHERING-PLOUGH PAYROLL   213446688 |
| 9/20 | 60.00 | WITHDRAWAL - ATM KIRBY WOODS |
| 9/27 | 9.48 | INTEREST EARNED |

| DATE | CHECK # | AMOUNT | DATE | CHECK # | AMOUNT | DATE | CHECK # | AMOUNT |
|---|---|---|---|---|---|---|---|---|
| 8/31 | 1094 | 42.37 | 9/10 | 1099 | 583.21 | 9/25 | 1106* | 1,238.42 |
| 9/2 | 1095 | 12.96 | 9/16 | 1100 | 283.21 | 9/25 | 1107 | 500.00 |
| 9/5 | 1096 | 36.01 | 9/18 | 1102* | 48.23 |  |  |  |
| 9/5 | 1097 | 178.13 | 9/21 | 1103 | 71.16 |  |  |  |
| 9/5 | 1098 | 458.60 | 9/23 | 1104 | 12.75 |  |  |  |

CHECKING DAILY BALANCE SUMMARY

| DATE | BALANCE OF YOUR FUNDS | DATE | BALANCE OF YOUR FUNDS |
|---|---|---|---|
| 8/28 | 2,472.86 | 9/15 | 4,804.87 |
| 8/31 | 2,430.49 | 9/16 | 4,521.66 |
| 9/1 | 3,889.63 | 9/18 | 4,473.43 |
| 9/2 | 3,876.67 | 9/20 | 4,413.43 |
| 9/4 | 3,659.50 | 9/21 | 4,342.27 |
| 9/5 | 2,986.76 | 9/23 | 4,329.52 |
| 9/10 | 2,403.55 | 9/25 | 2,591.10 |
|  |  | 9/27 | 2,600.58 |

**FIGURE 4-31**
**Tom Deskin's Bank Statement**

3. What were the lowest and highest daily bank balances for the month?

5. Tom Deskin's account register is shown in Figure 4-32. Use one of the account reconciliation forms in Figure 4-33 to reconcile the bank statement in Figure 4-31 with the account register.

4. A bank statement shows a balance of $12.32. The service charge for the month was $2.95. The account register shows deposits of $300, $100, and $250 that do not appear on the statement. Outstanding checks are in the amount of $36.52, $205.16, $18.92, $25.93, and $200. The register balance is $178.74. Find the adjusted statement balance and the adjusted register balance. Use one of the account reconciliation forms in Figure 4-33.

RECORD ALL TRANSACTIONS THAT AFFECT YOUR ACCOUNT

| NUMBER | DATE | DESCRIPTION OF TRANSACTION | DEBIT (−) | √T | FEE (IF ANY) (−) | CREDIT (+) | BALANCE |
|---|---|---|---|---|---|---|---|
|  |  |  |  |  |  |  | 2472 86 |
| 1094 | 8/28 | K-mart | 42 37 |  |  |  | − 42 37 |
|  |  |  |  |  |  |  | 2430 49 |
| 1095 | 8/28 | Walgreen's | 12 96 |  |  |  | − 12 96 |
|  |  |  |  |  |  |  | 2417 53 |
| Deposit | 9/1 | Payroll Schering-Plough |  |  |  | 2,401 32 | +2,401 32 |
|  |  |  |  |  |  |  | 4,818 85 |
| AW | 9/1 | Leader Federal | 942 18 |  |  |  | − 942 18 |
|  |  |  |  |  |  |  | 3,876 67 |
| AW | 9/1 | LG & W | 217 17 |  |  |  | − 217 17 |
|  |  |  |  |  |  |  | 3,659 50 |
| 1096 | 9/1 | Kroger | 36 01 |  |  |  | − 36 01 |
|  |  |  |  |  |  |  | 3,623 49 |
| 1097 | 9/1 | Texaco | 178 13 |  |  |  | −178 13 |
|  |  |  |  |  |  |  | 3445 36 |
| 1098 | 9/1 | Univ. of Memphis | 458 60 |  |  |  | −458 60 |
|  |  |  |  |  |  |  | 2986 76 |
| 1099 | 9/15 | GMAC Credit Corp | 583 21 |  |  |  | −583 21 |
|  |  |  |  |  |  |  | 2403 55 |
| 1100 | 9/18 | Visa | 283 21 |  |  |  | −283 21 |
|  |  |  |  |  |  |  | 2,120 34 |
| 1101 | 9/10 | Radio Shack | 189 37 |  |  |  | − 189 37 |
|  |  |  |  |  |  |  | 1,930 97 |
| 1102 | 9/10 | Auto Zone | 48 23 |  |  |  | − 48 23 |
|  |  |  |  |  |  |  | 1,882 74 |
| Deposit | 9/15 | Payroll-Schering Plough |  |  |  | 2401 32 | +2,401 32 |
|  |  |  |  |  |  |  | 4,284 06 |

REMEMBER TO RECORD AUTOMATIC PAYMENTS/DEPOSITS ON DATE AUTHORIZED.

RECORD ALL TRANSACTIONS THAT AFFECT YOUR ACCOUNT

| NUMBER | DATE | DESCRIPTION OF TRANSACTION | DEBIT (−) | √T | FEE (IF ANY) (−) | CREDIT (+) | BALANCE |
|---|---|---|---|---|---|---|---|
|  |  |  |  |  |  |  | 4284 06 |
| 1103 | 9/15 | Geoffrey Beane | 71 16 |  |  |  | −71 16 |
|  |  |  |  |  |  |  | 4212 90 |
| 1104 | 9/14 | Heaven Scent Flowers | 12 75 |  |  |  | −12 75 |
|  |  |  |  |  |  |  | 4200 15 |
| 1105 | 9/20 | Kroger | 87 75 |  |  |  | −87 75 |
|  |  |  |  |  |  |  | 4,112 40 |
| ATM | 9/20 | Kirby Woods | 60 00 |  |  |  | −60 00 |
|  |  |  |  |  |  |  | 4052 40 |
| 1106 | 9/21 | Traveler's Insurance | 1,238 42 |  |  |  | −1,238 42 |
|  |  |  |  |  |  |  | 2813 98 |
| 1107 | 9/23 | Nation's Bank-Savings | 500 00 |  |  |  | −500 00 |
|  |  |  |  |  |  |  | 2,313 98 |

**FIGURE 4-32**
**Tom Deskin's Account Register**

| | | | | |
|---|---|---|---|---|
| $ | BALANCE AS SHOWN ON BANK STATEMENT | | BALANCE AS SHOWN IN YOUR REGISTER | $ |
| | TOTAL OF OUTSTANDING DEPOSITS | | SUBTRACT AMOUNT OF SERVICE CHARGE | |
| | NEW TOTAL | | NEW TOTAL | |
| | SUBTRACT TOTAL OF OUTSTANDING CHECKS | | ADJUSTMENTS IF ANY Interest | |
| | YOUR ADJUSTED STATEMENT BALANCE | = | YOUR ADJUSTED REGISTER BALANCE | |

| Outstanding Deposits (Credits) | |
|---|---|
| Date | Amount |
| | $ |
| | |
| | |
| | |
| | |
| | |
| Total | $ |

| Outstanding Checks (Debits) | | |
|---|---|---|
| Check Number | Date | Amount |
| | | $ |
| | | |
| | | |
| | | |
| | | |
| | | |
| | Total | $ |

| | | | | |
|---|---|---|---|---|
| $ | BALANCE AS SHOWN ON BANK STATEMENT | | BALANCE AS SHOWN IN YOUR REGISTER | $ |
| | TOTAL OF OUTSTANDING DEPOSITS | | SUBTRACT AMOUNT OF SERVICE CHARGE | |
| | NEW TOTAL | | NEW TOTAL | |
| | SUBTRACT TOTAL OF OUTSTANDING CHECKS | | ADJUSTMENTS IF ANY Interest | |
| | YOUR ADJUSTED STATEMENT BALANCE | = | YOUR ADJUSTED REGISTER BALANCE | |

| Outstanding Deposits (Credits) | |
|---|---|
| Date | Amount |
| | $ |
| | |
| | |
| | |
| | |
| | |
| Total | $ |

| Outstanding Checks (Debits) | | |
|---|---|---|
| Check Number | Date | Amount |
| | | $ |
| | | |
| | | |
| | | |
| | | |
| | | |
| | Total | $ |

**FIGURE 4-33**
**Reconciliation Form**

## Learning Outcomes

### Section 4-1

**1** Make account transactions. (p. 102)

## What to Remember with Examples

*To make account deposits, on the appropriate deposit form (Figures 4-34 and 4-35):*

1. Record the date.
2. Enter the amount of currency or coins being deposited.
3. List the amount of each check to be deposited, including an identifying name or company.
4. Add the amounts of currency, coins, and checks.
5. If the deposit is to a personal account and you want to receive some of the money in cash, enter the amount on the line "less cash received" and sign on the appropriate line.
6. Subtract any cash received from the total for the net deposit.

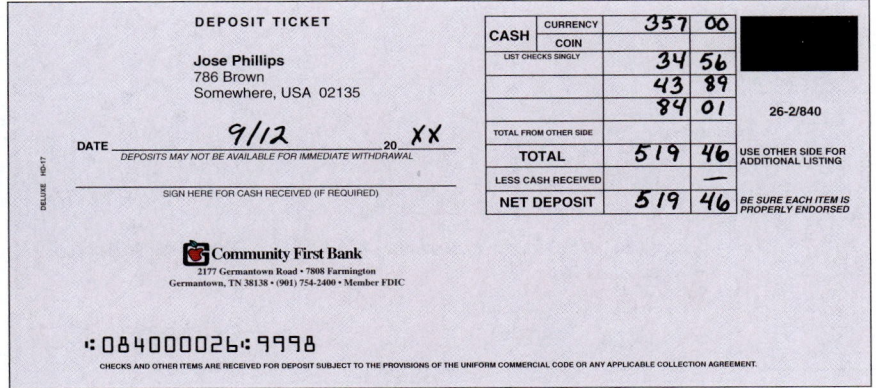

**FIGURE 4-34**
Deposit Ticket

**FIGURE 4-35**
Deposit Ticket

*To make a withdrawal using a check:*

1. Enter the date of the check.
2. Enter the name of the payee.
3. Enter the amount of the check in numerals.
4. Write the amount of the check in words. Cents can be written as a fraction of a dollar or by using decimal notation.
5. Explain the purpose of the check.
6. Sign the check.

**2** Record account transactions. (p. 107)

*On a check stub or an account register (Figures 4-36 and 4-37):*

*For checks and other debits:*

1. Make an entry for every account transaction.
2. Enter the date, the amount of the check or debit, the person or company that will receive the check or debit, and the purpose of the check or debit.
3. Subtract the amount of the check or debit from the previous balance to obtain the new balance.
4. For handwritten checks with stubs, carry the new balance forward to the next stub.

*For deposits or other credits:*

1. Make an entry for every account transaction.
2. Enter the date, the amount of the deposit or credit, and a brief explanation of the deposit or credit.
3. Add the amount of the deposit or credit from the previous balance to obtain the new balance.

*On an electronic money management system:*

1. Enter the appropriate details for producing a check.
2. Record other debits and all deposits and credits. The account register is maintained by the system automatically.
3. For business accounts or personal accounts that are used for tracking expenses, record the type of expense or budget account number.

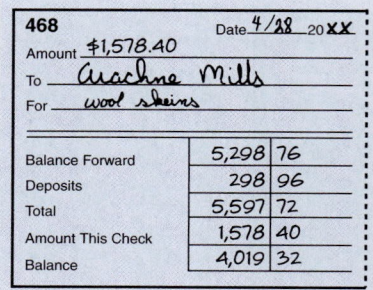

**FIGURE 4-36**
**Business Check and Stub**

**FIGURE 4-37**
**Account Register**

| | RECORD ALL TRANSACTIONS THAT AFFECT YOUR ACCOUNT | | | | | | | |
|---|---|---|---|---|---|---|---|---|
| NUMBER | DATE | DESCRIPTION OF TRANSACTION | DEBIT | √ | FEE | CREDIT | BALANCE | |
| | | | | | | | 5,298 | 76 |
| | 4/21 | Deposit | | | | 298 96 | +298 | 96 |
| | | | | | | | 5,597 | 72 |
| 468 | 4/28 | Arachne Mills | 1,578 40 | | | | -1,578 | 40 |
| | | | | | | | 4,019 | 32 |

## Section 4-2

**1** Reconcile a bank statement with an account register. (p. 114)

1. Check off all matching transactions appearing on both the bank statement and the account register.
2. Enter into the register the transactions appearing on the bank statement that have not been checked off. Check off these transactions in the register as they are entered. Update the register balance accordingly.
3. Make a list of all the checks and other debits appearing in the register that have not been checked off. Add the amounts on the list to find the *total outstanding debits.*
4. Make a list of all the deposits and other credits appearing in the register that have not been checked off in step 1. Add the amounts on the list to find the *total outstanding credits.*
5. Calculate the *adjusted statement balance* by adding the statement balance and the total outstanding credits, and then subtracting the total outstanding debits: Adjusted statement balance = statement balance + total outstanding credits − total outstanding debits (Figure 4-39).
6. Compare the adjusted statement balance with the register balance. These amounts should be equal.

7. If the adjusted statement balance does not equal the register balance, locate the cause of the discrepancy and correct the register accordingly.
8. Write *statement reconciled* on the next blank line in the account register and record the statement date.

Figure 4-38 shows the bank statement for Eiland's Information Services. Steps 1 and 2 of the reconciliation process have been carried out: matching transactions have been checked off and all transactions appearing on the bank statement have been entered in the register and checked off including the service charge of $0.72 and interest earned of $14.32. The updated register balance is $18,020.36.

Now we complete the account reconciliation form in Figure 4-39 by recording the total outstanding debits and the total outstanding credits, transactions in the register that do not appear on the bank statement.

The adjusted statement balance does not equal the register balance. To locate the error, first find the difference of the two amounts: $19,304.72 - 18,020.36 = 1,284.36$. This amount does not match any transaction exactly. So, divide the difference by 2: $1,284.36 \div 2 = 642.18$. This amount matches a deposit made on 6/15. The deposit was subtracted from the balance when it should have been added. Make an entry in the account register to offset the error: deposit $1,284.36, which is the amount that was subtracted in error plus the amount of the 6/15 deposit. Figure 4-40 shows the reconciled register. Notice the entry "statement reconciled" dated 7/2.

## Community First Bank

2177 Germantown Rd. South • Germantown, Tennessee 38138 • (901) 555-2400 • Member FDIC

EILAND'S INFORMATION SERVICES
314 ROSAMOND ST
DRUMMONDS, TN 38072

ACCOUNT NUMBER   21-4658321
FEDERAL ID NUMBER   13-8467214

DATE 7/2/20XX   PAGE 1

|  |  | BALANCE OF YOUR FUNDS |
| --- | --- | --- |
| PREVIOUS BALANCE ----- |  | $3,472.16 |
| 3 | DEPOSITS TOTALING | 2,498.50 |
| 7 | WITHDRAWALS TOTALING | 1,647.55 |
| NEW BALANCE ----------- |  | $4,323.11 |

ACCOUNT TRANSACTIONS FOR THE PERIOD FROM 6/3/20XX THROUGH 7/2/20XX

| DATE | AMOUNT | DESCRIPTION |
| --- | --- | --- |
| 6/15 | 642.18 ✓ | DEPOSIT |
| 6/20 | 1,842.00 ✓ | DEPOSIT |
| 7/2 | .72 ✓ | SERVICE CHARGE |
| 7/2 | 14.32 ✓ | INTEREST EARNED |

| DATE | CHECK # | AMOUNT | DATE | CHECK # | AMOUNT |
| --- | --- | --- | --- | --- | --- |
| 6/15 | 5832 | 200.00 ✓ | 6/17 | 5835 | 82.37 ✓ |
| 6/16 | 5833 | 225.00 ✓ | 7/2 | 5837* | 175.00 ✓ |
| 6/17 | 5834 | 72.00 ✓ | 7/2 | 5839* | 892.46 ✓ |

CHECKING DAILY BALANCE SUMMARY

| DATE | BALANCE OF YOUR FUNDS | DATE | BALANCE OF YOUR FUNDS |
| --- | --- | --- | --- |
| 6/3 | 3,472.16 | 6/17 | 3,534.97 |
| 6/15 | 3,914.34 | 6/20 | 5,376.97 |
| 6/16 | 3,689.34 | 7/2 | 4,323.11 |

FIGURE 4-38
Bank Statement

| | | | | |
|---|---|---|---|---|
| $ 4,323 11 | BALANCE AS SHOWN ON BANK STATEMENT | | BALANCE AS SHOWN IN YOUR REGISTER | $ 18,006 76 |
| 20,000 00 | TOTAL OF OUTSTANDING DEPOSITS | | SUBTRACT AMOUNT OF SERVICE CHARGE | − 72 |
| 24,323 11 | NEW TOTAL | | NEW TOTAL | 18,006 04 |
| 5,018 39 | SUBTRACT TOTAL OF OUTSTANDING CHECKS | | ADJUSTMENTS IF ANY | +14 32<br>+ 1,284 36 |
| $19,304 72 | YOUR ADJUSTED STATEMENT BALANCE | ← SHOULD EQUAL → | YOUR ADJUSTED REGISTER BALANCE | $19,304 72 |

| Outstanding Deposits (Credits) | |
|---|---|
| Date | Amount |
| 6/25 | $ 20,000 00 |
| | |
| | |
| | |
| | |
| Total | $ 20,000 00 |

| Outstanding Checks (Debits) | | |
|---|---|---|
| Check Number | Date | Amount |
| 5836 | | $ 42 18 |
| 5838 | | 4,976 21 |
| | | |
| | | |
| | | |
| | | |
| | Total | $ 5,018 39 |

FIGURE 4-39

Account Reconciliation Form

RECORD ALL TRANSACTIONS THAT AFFECT YOUR ACCOUNT

| NUMBER | DATE | DESCRIPTION OF TRANSACTION | DEBIT (−) | √ T | FEE (IF ANY) (−) | CREDIT (+) | BALANCE |
|---|---|---|---|---|---|---|---|
| | | | | | | | 3472 16 |
| 5832 | 6/13 | City of Chicago | 200 00 | ✓ | | | −200 00 |
| | | | | | | | 3,272 16 |
| 5833 | 6/13 | City of Phoenix | 225 00 | ✓ | | | −225 00 |
| | | | | | | | 3,047 16 |
| 5834 | 6/14 | City of Fresno | 72 00 | ✓ | | | −72 00 |
| | | | | | | | 2,975 16 |
| 5835 | 6/15 | Hardware house | 82 37 | ✓ | | | −82 37 |
| | | | | | | | 2,892 79 |
| Deposit | 6/15 | Can Com, Inc. * | 642 18 | ✓ | | | −642 18 |
| | | | | | | | 2,250 61 |
| 5836 | 6/18 | Office Max | 42 18 | | | | −42 18 |
| | | copies | | | | | 2,208 43 |
| 5837 | 6/20 | City of New Orleans | 175 00 | ✓ | | | −175 00 |
| | | | | | | | 2,033 43 |
| Deposit | 6/20 | List Purchases | | ✓ | | 1842 00 | +1842 00 |
| | | | | | | | 3,875 43 |
| Deposit | 6/25 | Federal Credit Union | | | | 20,000 00 | +20,000 00 |
| | | Small business loan | | | | | 23,875 43 |
| 5838 | 6/30 | Hardware house | 4976 21 | | | | −4976 21 |
| | | computer | | | | | 18,899 22 |
| 5839 | 6/30 | Wade office Furniture | 892 46 | ✓ | | | −892 46 |
| | | Desk chair, file Cabinet | | | | | 18006 76 |
| | 7/2 | Service Charge | | ✓ | 72 | | −72 |
| | | | | | | | 18,006 04 |
| | 7/2 | Interest earned | | ✓ | | 14 32 | +14 32 |
| | | | | | | | 18,020 36 |

REMEMBER TO RECORD AUTOMATIC PAYMENTS/DEPOSITS ON DATE AUTHORIZED.

* Posting error (should be in deposit column)

RECORD ALL TRANSACTIONS THAT AFFECT YOUR ACCOUNT

| NUMBER | DATE | DESCRIPTION OF TRANSACTION | DEBIT (−) | √ T | FEE (IF ANY) (−) | CREDIT (+) | BALANCE |
|---|---|---|---|---|---|---|---|
| | | | | | | | 18,020 36 |
| | 7/4 | Correction to deposit on 6/15 | | ✓ | | 1,284 36 | +1,284 36 |
| | | | | | | | 19,304 72 |
| | 7/2 | Statement Reconciled | | ✓ | | | ——— |
| | | | | | | | |

FIGURE 4-40

Account Register

**1.** Write a check (Figure 4-41) dated June 13, 20XX, to Byron Johnson in the amount of $296.83 for a washing machine. Complete the check stub.

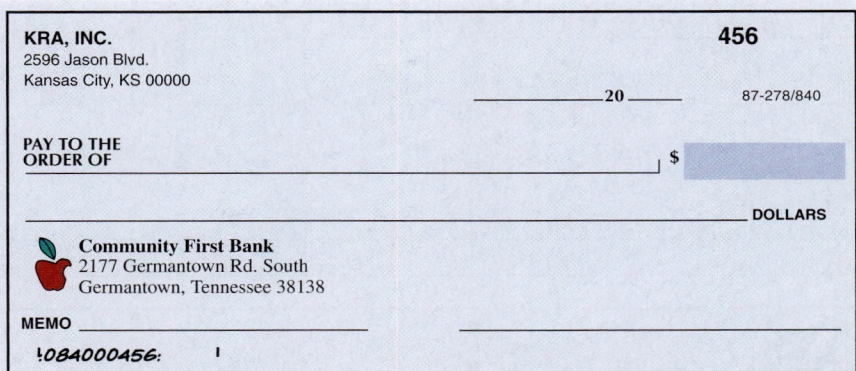

**FIGURE 4-41**
**Check Number 456**

**2.** Write a check (Figure 4-42) dated June 12, 20XX, to Alpine Industries in the amount of $85.50 for building supplies. Complete the check stub.

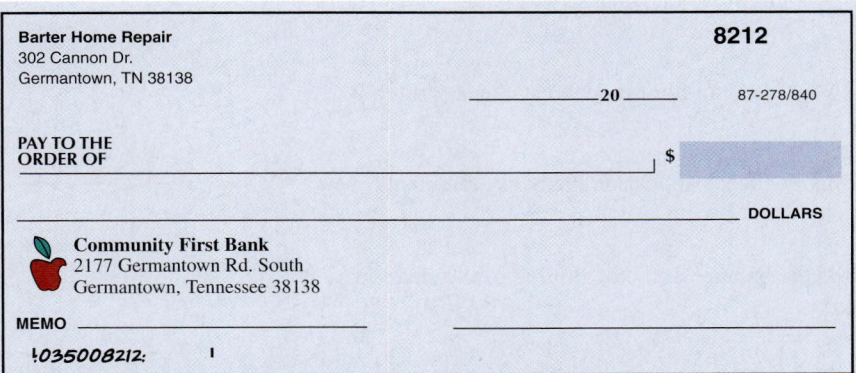

**FIGURE 4-42**
**Check Number 8212**

**3.** Complete a deposit slip (Figure 4-43) to deposit checks in the amounts of $136.00 and $278.96, and $480 cash on May 8, 20XX.

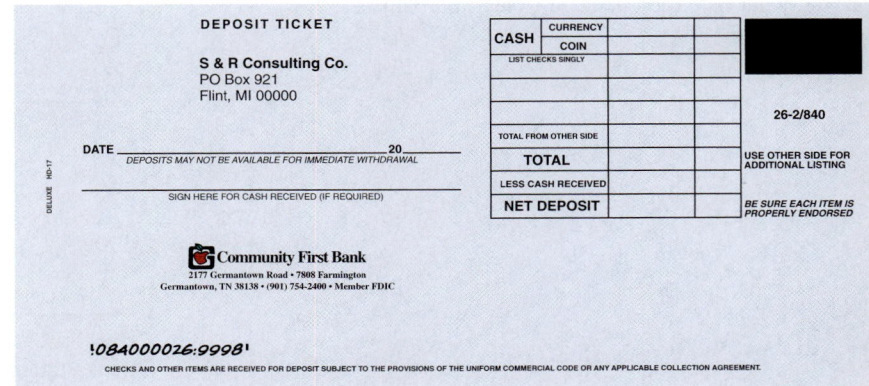

**FIGURE 4-43**
**Deposit Ticket for S & R Consulting Co.**

**4.** Enter the following information and transactions in the check register for Happy Center Day Care (Figure 4-44). On July 10, 20XX, with an account balance of $983.47, the account debit card was used at Linens, Inc., for $220 for laundry services, and check 1214 was written to Bugs Away for $65 for extermination services. On July 11, $80 was withdrawn from an automatic teller machine, and on July 12, checks in the amounts of $123.86, $123.86, and $67.52 were deposited. Show the balance after these transactions.

| | | RECORD ALL TRANSACTIONS THAT AFFECT YOUR ACCOUNT | | | | | |
|---|---|---|---|---|---|---|---|
| NUMBER | DATE | DESCRIPTION OF TRANSACTION | DEBIT (−) | √T | FEE (IF ANY) (−) | CREDIT (+) | BALANCE |
| | | | | | | | |
| | | | | | | | |
| | | | | | | | |
| | | | | | | | |
| | | | | | | | |
| | | | | | | | |

**FIGURE 4-44**
**Check Register**

*Tree Top Landscape Service's bank statement is shown in Figure 4-45.*

**5.** How many deposits were cleared during the month?

**6.** What amount of service charge was paid?

**7.** What was the amount of the largest check written?

**8.** How many checks appear on the bank statement?

**9.** What is the balance at the beginning of the statement period?

**10.** What is the balance at the end of the statement period?

**11.** What is the amount of check 718?

**12.** On what date did check 717 clear the bank?

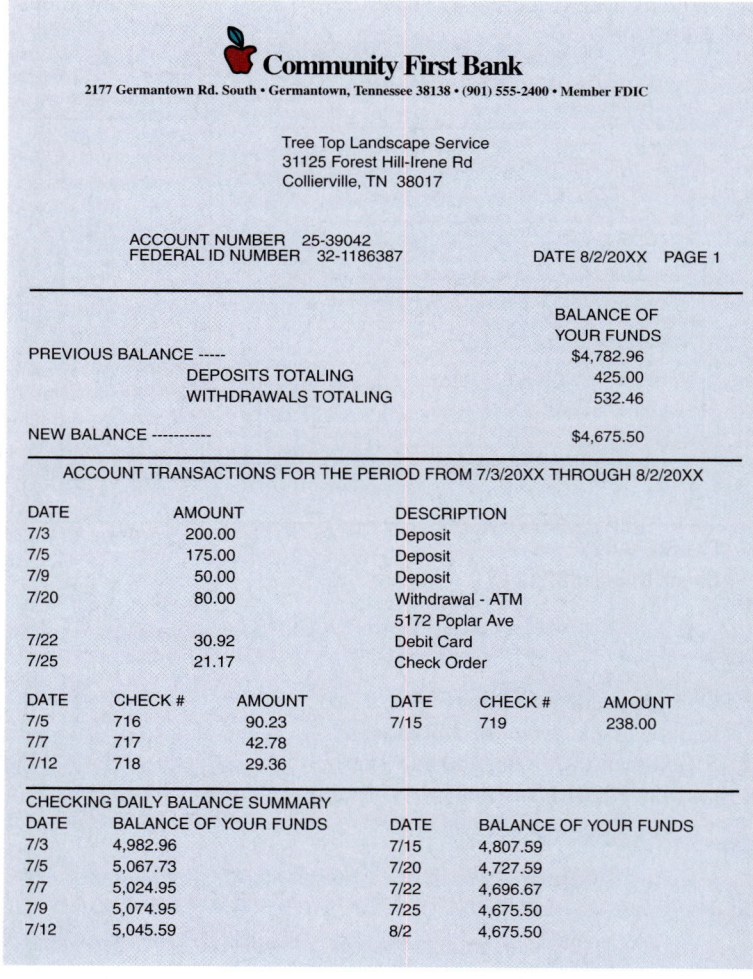

**Community First Bank**
2177 Germantown Rd. South • Germantown, Tennessee 38138 • (901) 555-2400 • Member FDIC

Tree Top Landscape Service
31125 Forest Hill-Irene Rd
Collierville, TN 38017

ACCOUNT NUMBER 25-39042
FEDERAL ID NUMBER 32-1186387
DATE 8/2/20XX PAGE 1

| | BALANCE OF YOUR FUNDS |
|---|---|
| PREVIOUS BALANCE ----- | $4,782.96 |
| DEPOSITS TOTALING | 425.00 |
| WITHDRAWALS TOTALING | 532.46 |
| NEW BALANCE ----------- | $4,675.50 |

ACCOUNT TRANSACTIONS FOR THE PERIOD FROM 7/3/20XX THROUGH 8/2/20XX

| DATE | AMOUNT | DESCRIPTION |
|---|---|---|
| 7/3 | 200.00 | Deposit |
| 7/5 | 175.00 | Deposit |
| 7/9 | 50.00 | Deposit |
| 7/20 | 80.00 | Withdrawal - ATM 5172 Poplar Ave |
| 7/22 | 30.92 | Debit Card |
| 7/25 | 21.17 | Check Order |

| DATE | CHECK # | AMOUNT | DATE | CHECK # | AMOUNT |
|---|---|---|---|---|---|
| 7/5 | 716 | 90.23 | 7/15 | 719 | 238.00 |
| 7/7 | 717 | 42.78 | | | |
| 7/12 | 718 | 29.36 | | | |

CHECKING DAILY BALANCE SUMMARY

| DATE | BALANCE OF YOUR FUNDS | DATE | BALANCE OF YOUR FUNDS |
|---|---|---|---|
| 7/3 | 4,982.96 | 7/15 | 4,807.59 |
| 7/5 | 5,067.73 | 7/20 | 4,727.59 |
| 7/7 | 5,024.95 | 7/22 | 4,696.67 |
| 7/9 | 5,074.95 | 7/25 | 4,675.50 |
| 7/12 | 5,045.59 | 8/2 | 4,675.50 |

**FIGURE 4-45**
**Bank Statement for Tree Top Landscape Service**

13. Tree Top Landscape Service's account register is shown in Figure 4-46 and its bank statement in Figure 4-45. Update the account register and use the reconciliation form in Figure 4-47 to reconcile the bank statement with the account register.

RECORD ALL TRANSACTIONS THAT AFFECT YOUR ACCOUNT

| NUMBER | DATE | DESCRIPTION OF TRANSACTION | DEBIT (−) | √ T | FEE (IF ANY) (−) | CREDIT (+) | BALANCE 4,782 96 |
|---|---|---|---|---|---|---|---|
| 716 | 7/1 | Dabney Nursery | 90 23 | | | | 4,692 73 |
| 717 | 7/1 | Office Max | 42 78 | | | | 4,649 95 |
| Deposit | 7/3 | Louis Lechleiter | | | | 200 00 | 4,849 95 |
| Deposit | 7/5 | Tony Trim | | | | 175 00 | 5,024 95 |
| Deposit | 7/9 | Dale Crosby | | | | 50 00 | 5,074 95 |
| 718 | 7/10 | Texaco Gas | 29 36 | | | | 5,045 59 |
| 719 | 7/10 | Nation's Bank | 238 00 | | | | 4,807 59 |
| Deposit | 7/15 | Bobby Cornelius | | | | 300 00 | 5,107 59 |
| ATM | 7/20 | Withdrawl Branch | 80 00 | | | | 5,027 59 |
| Debit card | 7/20 | AT&T | 30 92 | | | | 4,996 67 |
| 720 | 7/20 | Visa | 172 83 | | | | 4,823 84 |
| | | | | | | | |
| | | | | | | | |
| | | | | | | | |

REMEMBER TO RECORD AUTOMATIC PAYMENTS/DEPOSITS ON DATE AUTHORIZED.

FIGURE 4-46
Account Register for Tree Top Landscape Service

| $ | BALANCE AS SHOWN ON BANK STATEMENT | | BALANCE AS SHOWN IN YOUR REGISTER | $ |
|---|---|---|---|---|
| | TOTAL OF OUTSTANDING DEPOSITS | | SUBTRACT AMOUNT OF SERVICE CHARGE | |
| | NEW TOTAL | | NEW TOTAL | |
| | SUBTRACT TOTAL OF OUTSTANDING CHECKS | | ADJUSTMENTS IF ANY Check Order | |
| | YOUR ADJUSTED STATEMENT BALANCE | ←SHOULD EQUAL→ | YOUR ADJUSTED REGISTER BALANCE | |

| Outstanding Deposits (Credits) | | | Outstanding Checks (Debits) | | |
|---|---|---|---|---|---|
| Date | Amount | | Check Number | Date | Amount |
| | $ | | | | $ |
| | | | | | |
| | | | | | |
| | | | | | |
| | | | | | |
| Total | $ | | | Total | $ |

FIGURE 4-47
Account Reconciliation Form

**14.** The July bank statement for A & H Iron Works shows a balance of $37.94 and a service charge of $8.00. The account register shows deposits of $650 and $375.56 that do not appear on the statement. Checks in the amounts of $217.45, $57.82, $17.45, and $58.62 are outstanding. The register balance before reconciliation is $720.16. Reconcile the bank statement with the account register using the form in Figure 4-48.

EXCEL

| $ | | BALANCE AS SHOWN ON BANK STATEMENT | | BALANCE AS SHOWN IN YOUR REGISTER | $ |
| | | TOTAL OF OUTSTANDING DEPOSITS | | SUBTRACT AMOUNT OF SERVICE CHARGE | |
| | | NEW TOTAL | | NEW TOTAL | |
| | | SUBTRACT TOTAL OF OUTSTANDING CHECKS | | ADJUSTMENTS IF ANY | |
| | | YOUR ADJUSTED STATEMENT BALANCE | SHOULD → ← EQUAL | YOUR ADJUSTED REGISTER BALANCE | |

| Outstanding Deposits (Credits) | | | Outstanding Checks (Debits) | | |
|---|---|---|---|---|---|
| Date | Amount | | Check Number | Date | Amount |
| | $ | | | | $ |
| | | | | | |
| | | | | | |
| | | | | | |
| | | | | | |
| Total | $ | | | Total | $ |

**FIGURE 4-48**
**Account Reconciliation Form**

**15.** The September bank statement for Dixon Fence Company shows a balance of $275.25 and a service charge of $7.50. The account register shows deposits of $120.43 and $625.56 that do not appear on the statement. Checks in the amounts of $144.24, $154.48, $24.17, and $18.22 are outstanding. A $100 ATM withdrawal does not appear on the statement. The register balance before reconciliation is $587.63. Reconcile the bank statement with the account register using the form in Figure 4-49.

| $ | | BALANCE AS SHOWN ON BANK STATEMENT | | BALANCE AS SHOWN IN YOUR REGISTER | $ |
| | | TOTAL OF OUTSTANDING DEPOSITS | | SUBTRACT AMOUNT OF SERVICE CHARGE | |
| | | NEW TOTAL | | NEW TOTAL | |
| | | SUBTRACT TOTAL OF OUTSTANDING CHECKS | | ADJUSTMENTS IF ANY | |
| | | YOUR ADJUSTED STATEMENT BALANCE | SHOULD → ← EQUAL | YOUR ADJUSTED REGISTER BALANCE | |

| Outstanding Deposits (Credits) | | | Outstanding Checks (Debits) | | |
|---|---|---|---|---|---|
| Date | Amount | | Check Number | Date | Amount |
| | $ | | | | $ |
| | | | | | |
| | | | | | |
| | | | | | |
| | | | | | |
| | | | | | |
| Total | $ | | | Total | $ |

**FIGURE 4-49**
**Account Reconciliation Form**

# EXERCISES SET B

## CHAPTER 4

1. Write a check dated August 18, 20XX (Figure 4-50), to Valley Electric Co-op in the amount of $189.32 for utilities. Complete the check stub in Figure 4-50.

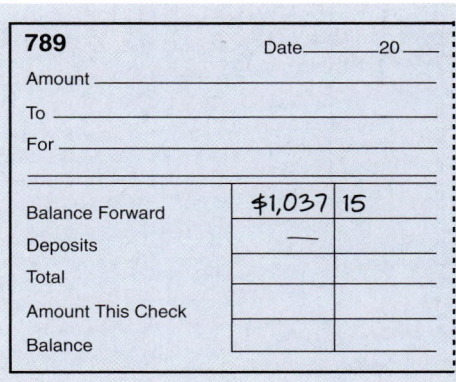

**FIGURE 4-50**
Check Number 789

2. Write a check dated December 28, 20XX (Figure 4-51), to Lundy Daniel in the amount of $450.00 for legal services. James Ludwig is the maker. Complete the check stub.

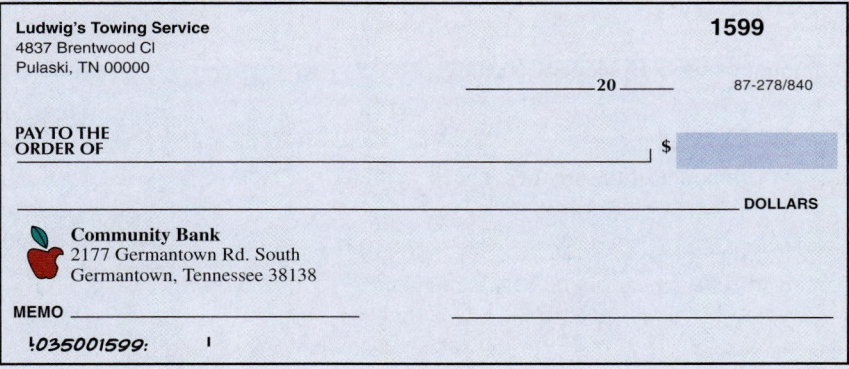

**FIGURE 4-51**
Check Number 1599

3. Complete a deposit slip on November 11, 20XX (Figure 4-52), to show the deposit of $100 in cash, checks in the amounts of $87.83, $42.97, and $106.32, with a $472.13 total from the other side of the deposit slip.

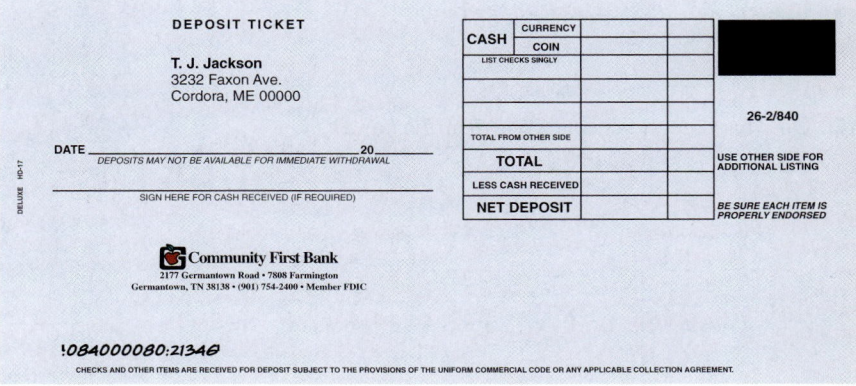

**FIGURE 4-52**
Deposit Ticket for T. J. Jackson

**4.** Enter the following information and transactions in the check register for Sloan's Tree Service (Figure 4-53). On May 3, 20XX, with an account balance of $876.54, check 234 was written to Organic Materials for $175 for fertilizer and check 235 was written to Klean Kuts in the amount of $524.82 for a chain saw. On May 5, checks in the amounts of $147.63 and $324.76 were deposited at the bank ATM. Show the balance after these transactions.

| | | RECORD ALL TRANSACTIONS THAT AFFECT YOUR ACCOUNT | | | | | |
|---|---|---|---|---|---|---|---|
| NUMBER | DATE | DESCRIPTION OF TRANSACTION | DEBIT (–) | √ T | FEE (IF ANY) (–) | CREDIT (+) | BALANCE |
| | | | | | | | |
| | | | | | | | |
| | | | | | | | |
| | | | | | | | |
| | | | | | | | |
| | | | | | | | |

**FIGURE 4-53**
**Account Register**

*Enrique Anglade's bank statement is shown in Figure 4-54.*

**5.** How many deposits were made during the month?

**6.** What amount of service charge was paid?

**7.** What was the amount of the smallest check written?

**8.** How many checks appear on the bank statement?

**9.** What is the balance at the beginning of the statement period?

**10.** What is the balance at the end of the statement period?

**11.** What is the amount of check 5375?

**12.** On what date did check 5376 clear the bank?

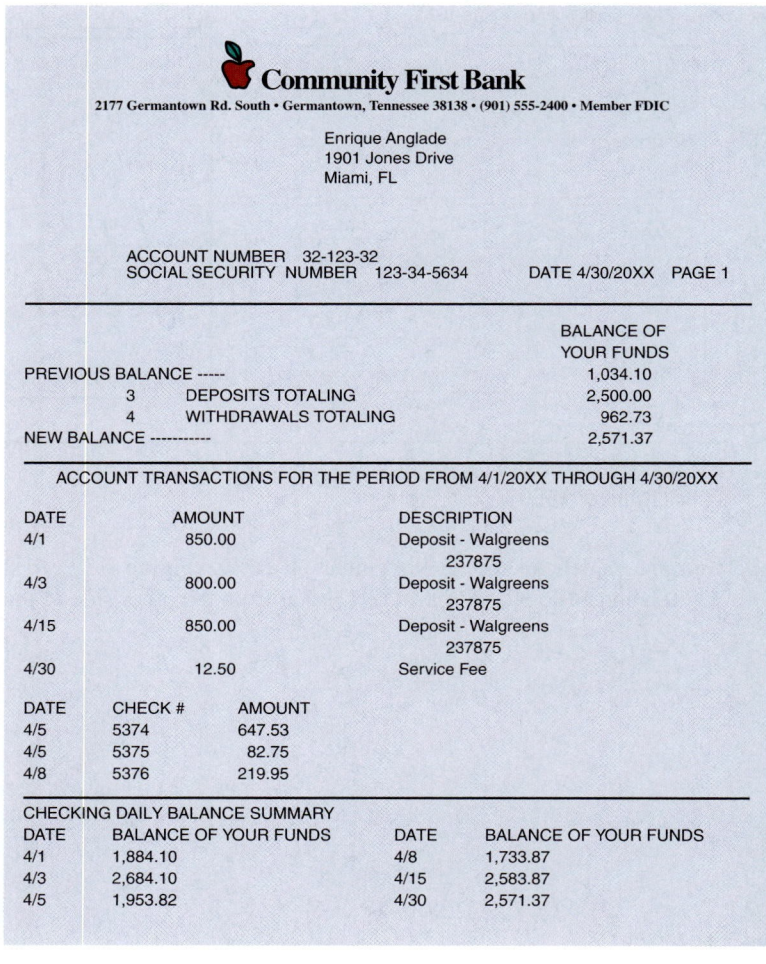

**FIGURE 4-54**
**Bank Statement for Enrique Anglade**

**13.** Enrique Anglade's account register is shown in Figure 4-55. Update the account register and reconcile the bank statement (see Figure 4-54) with the account register by using the reconciliation form in Figure 4-56.

RECORD ALL TRANSACTIONS THAT AFFECT YOUR ACCOUNT

| NUMBER | DATE | DESCRIPTION OF TRANSACTION | DEBIT (−) | √ T | FEE (IF ANY) (−) | CREDIT (+) | BALANCE |  |
|---|---|---|---|---|---|---|---|---|
| | | | | | | | 1,034 | 10 |
| Deposit | 4/1 | Payroll | | | | 850 00 | +850 | 00 |
| | | | | | | | 1,884 | 10 |
| Deposit | 4/3 | Payroll − Bonus | | | | 800 00 | +800 | 00 |
| | | | | | | | 2,684 | 10 |
| 5374 | 4/3 | First Union Mortgage Co. | 647 53 | | | | −647 | 53 |
| | | | | | | | 2,036 | 57 |
| 5375 | 4/3 | South Florida Utility | 82 75 | | | | −82 | 75 |
| | | | | | | | 1,953 | 82 |
| 5376 | 4/5 | First Federal Credit Union | 219 95 | | | | −219 | 95 |
| | | | | | | | 1,733 | 87 |
| 5377 | 4/15 | Banc Boston | 510 48 | | | | −510 | 48 |
| | | | | | | | 1,223 | 39 |
| Deposit | 4/15 | Payroll | | | | 850 00 | +850 | 00 |
| | | | | | | | 2,073 | 39 |
| 5378 | 4/20 | Northwest Airlines | 403 21 | | | | −403 | 21 |
| | | | | | | | 1,670 | 18 |
| 5379 | 4/26 | Auto Zone | 18 97 | | | | −18 | 97 |
| | | | | | | | 1,651 | 21 |
| ATM | 5/4 | Cordova Branch | 100 00 | | | | −100 | 00 |
| | | | | | | | 1,551 | 21 |

REMEMBER TO RECORD AUTOMATIC PAYMENTS/DEPOSITS ON DATE AUTHORIZED.

**FIGURE 4-55**
**Account Register for Enrique Anglade**

| $ | | BALANCE AS SHOWN ON BANK STATEMENT | | BALANCE AS SHOWN IN YOUR REGISTER | $ | |
|---|---|---|---|---|---|---|
| | | TOTAL OF OUTSTANDING DEPOSITS | | SUBTRACT AMOUNT OF SERVICE CHARGE | | |
| | | NEW TOTAL | | NEW TOTAL | | |
| | | SUBTRACT TOTAL OF OUTSTANDING CHECKS | | ADJUSTMENTS IF ANY | | |
| | | YOUR ADJUSTED STATEMENT BALANCE | SHOULD EQUAL | YOUR ADJUSTED REGISTER BALANCE | | |

| Outstanding Deposits (Credits) | | | Outstanding Checks (Debits) | | |
|---|---|---|---|---|---|
| Date | Amount | | Check Number | Date | Amount |
| | $ | | | | $ |
| | | | | | |
| | | | | | |
| | | | | | |
| | | | | | |
| Total | $ | | | Total | $ |

**FIGURE 4-56**
**Account Reconciliation Form**

**14.** Taylor Flowers' bank statement shows a balance of $135.42 and a service charge of $8.00. The account register shows deposits of $112.88 and $235.45 that do not appear on the statement. The register shows outstanding checks in the amounts of $17.42 and $67.90 and two cleared checks recorded in the account register as $145.69 and $18.22. The two cleared checks actually were written for and are shown on the statement as $145.96 and $18.22. The register balance before reconciliation is $406.70. Reconcile the bank statement with the account register using the form in Figure 4-57.

| $ | BALANCE AS SHOWN ON BANK STATEMENT | | BALANCE AS SHOWN IN YOUR REGISTER | $ |
|---|---|---|---|---|
| | TOTAL OF OUTSTANDING DEPOSITS | | SUBTRACT AMOUNT OF SERVICE CHARGE | |
| | NEW TOTAL | | NEW TOTAL | |
| | SUBTRACT TOTAL OF OUTSTANDING CHECKS | | ADJUSTMENTS IF ANY | |
| | YOUR ADJUSTED STATEMENT BALANCE | SHOULD EQUAL | YOUR ADJUSTED REGISTER BALANCE | |

| Outstanding Deposits (Credits) | | Outstanding Checks (Debits) | | |
|---|---|---|---|---|
| Date | Amount | Check Number | Date | Amount |
| | $ | | | $ |
| | | | | |
| | | | | |
| | | | | |
| | | | | |
| Total | $ | | Total | $ |

**15.** The bank statement for Randazzo's Market shows a balance of $1,102.35 and a service charge of $6.50. The account register shows a deposit of $265.49 that does not appear on the statement. The account register shows outstanding checks in the amounts of $617.23 and $456.60 and two cleared checks recorded as $45.71 and $348.70. The two cleared checks actually were written for $45.71 and $384.70. The register balance before reconciliation is $336.51. Reconcile the bank statement with the account register using the form in Figure 4-58.

| $ | BALANCE AS SHOWN ON BANK STATEMENT | | BALANCE AS SHOWN IN YOUR REGISTER | $ |
|---|---|---|---|---|
| | TOTAL OF OUTSTANDING DEPOSITS | | SUBTRACT AMOUNT OF SERVICE CHARGE | |
| | NEW TOTAL | | NEW TOTAL | |
| | SUBTRACT TOTAL OF OUTSTANDING CHECKS | | ADJUSTMENTS IF ANY | |
| | YOUR ADJUSTED STATEMENT BALANCE | SHOULD EQUAL | YOUR ADJUSTED REGISTER BALANCE | |

| Outstanding Deposits (Credits) | | Outstanding Checks (Debits) | | |
|---|---|---|---|---|
| Date | Amount | Check Number | Date | Amount |
| | $ | | | $ |
| | | | | |
| | | | | |
| | | | | |
| | | | | |
| Total | $ | | Total | $ |

## PRACTICE TEST

### CHAPTER 4

1.  Write the check and fill out the check stub provided in Figure 4-59. The balance brought forward is $2,301.42, deposits were made for $200 on May 12 and $83.17 on May 20, and check 195 was written on May 25 to Lon Associates for $152.50 for supplies. The check was signed by Lonny Branch.

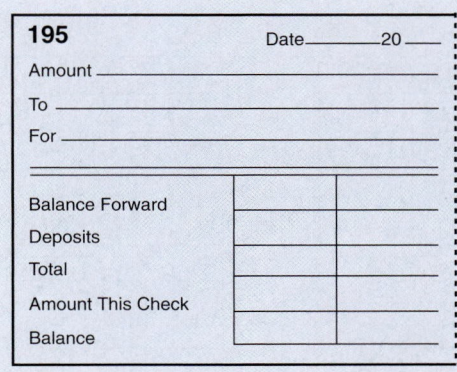
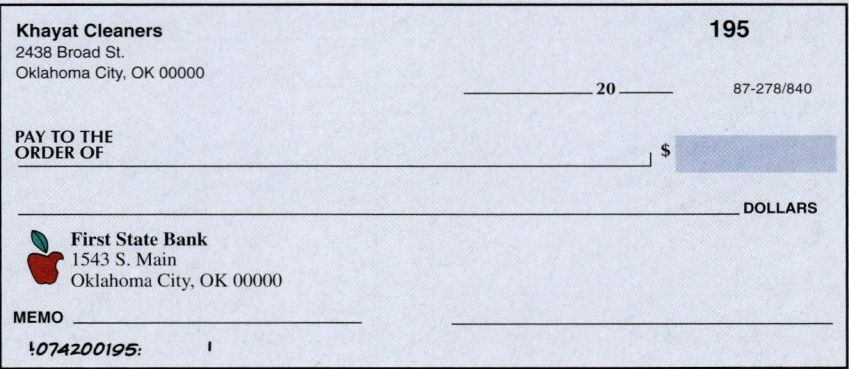

**FIGURE 4-59**
**Check Number 195**

*D.G. Hernandez Equipment's bank statement is shown in Figure 4-60.*

2.  What is the balance at the beginning of the statement period?

3.  How many checks cleared the bank during the statement period?

4.  What was the service charge for the statement period?

5.  Check 3786 was written for what amount?

6.  On what date did check 3788 clear the account?

7.  What was the total of the deposits?

8.  What was the balance at the end of the statement period?

9.  What was the total amount for all checks written during the period?

### Community First Bank

2177 Germantown Rd. South • Germantown, Tennessee 38138 • (901) 555-2400 • Member FDIC

D. G. Hernandez Equipment
25 Santa Rosa Dr.
Piperton, TN  38027

ACCOUNT NUMBER  8-523145
FEDERAL ID NUMBER  46-28345135          DATE 3/31/20XX   PAGE 1

| | | BALANCE OF YOUR FUNDS |
|---|---|---|
| PREVIOUS BALANCE ----- | | 5,283.17 |
| 2 | DEPOSITS TOTALING | 3,600.00 |
| 6 | WITHDRAWALS TOTALING | 1,900.49 |
| NEW BALANCE ---------- | | 6,982.68 |

ACCOUNT TRANSACTIONS FOR THE PERIOD FROM 3/1/20xx THROUGH 3/31/20xx

| DATE | AMOUNT | DESCRIPTION |
|---|---|---|
| 3/15 | 1,600.00 | Deposit |
| 3/17 | 19.00 | Returned Check Charge |
| 3/31 | 2,000.00 | Deposit |

| DATE | CHECK # | AMOUNT | DATE | CHECK # | AMOUNT |
|---|---|---|---|---|---|
| 3/2 | 3784 | 96.03 | 3/15 | 3788 | 973.12 |
| 3/7 | 3786* | 142.38 | 3/31 | 3792* | 182.03 |
| 3/12 | 3787 | 487.93 | | | |

CHECKING DAILY BALANCE SUMMARY

| DATE | BALANCE OF YOUR FUNDS | DATE | BALANCE OF YOUR FUNDS |
|---|---|---|---|
| 3/2 | 5,187.14 | 3/15 | 5,183.71 |
| 3/7 | 5,044.76 | 3/17 | 5,164.71 |
| 3/12 | 4,556.83 | 3/31 | 6,982.68 |

**FIGURE 4-60**
**Bank Statement for D. G. Hernandez Equipment**

10. D. G. Hernandez Equipment's account register is shown in Figure 4-61. Reconcile the bank statement in Figure 4-60 with the account register in Figure 4-61. Use the account reconciliation form in Figure 4-62.

RECORD ALL TRANSACTIONS THAT AFFECT YOUR ACCOUNT

| NUMBER | DATE | DESCRIPTION OF TRANSACTION | DEBIT (-) | √T | FEE (IF ANY) (-) | CREDIT (+) | BALANCE 5,283 17 |
|---|---|---|---|---|---|---|---|
| 3784 | 2/27 | | 96 03 | | | | −96 03 |
| | | | | | | | 5,187 14 |
| 3785 | 3/5 | | 346 18 | | | | −346 18 |
| | | | | | | | 4,840 96 |
| 3786 | 3/5 | | 142 38 | | | | −142 38 |
| | | | | | | | 4,698 58 |
| 3787 | 3/11 | | 487 93 | | | | −487 93 |
| | | | | | | | 4,210 65 |
| 3788 | 3/11 | | 973 12 | | | | −973 12 |
| | | | | | | | 3,237 53 |
| 3789 | 3/15 | | 72 83 | | | | −72 83 |
| | | | | | | | 3,164 70 |
| Dep. | 3/15 | | | | | 1,600 00 | +1,600 00 |
| | | | | | | | 4,764 70 |
| 3790 | 3/17 | | 146 17 | | | | −146 17 |
| | | | | | | | 4,618 53 |
| 3791 | 3/20 | | 152 03 | | | | −152 03 |
| | | | | | | | 4,466 50 |
| 3792 | 3/31 | | ★ 182 08 | | | | −182 08 |
| | | | | | | | 4,284 42 |
| Deposit | 3/31 | | | | | 2000 00 | +2,000 00 |
| | | | | | | | 6,284 42 |

REMEMBER TO RECORD AUTOMATIC PAYMENTS/DEPOSITS ON DATE AUTHORIZED.

**FIGURE 4-61**
**Account Register**

| $ | BALANCE AS SHOWN ON BANK STATEMENT | | BALANCE AS SHOWN IN YOUR REGISTER | $ |
|---|---|---|---|---|
| | TOTAL OF OUTSTANDING DEPOSITS | | SUBTRACT AMOUNT OF SERVICE CHARGE | |
| | NEW TOTAL | | NEW TOTAL | |
| | SUBTRACT TOTAL OF OUTSTANDING CHECKS | | ADJUSTMENTS IF ANY | |
| | YOUR ADJUSTED STATEMENT BALANCE | SHOULD EQUAL | YOUR ADJUSTED REGISTER BALANCE | |

| Outstanding Deposits (Credits) | | | Outstanding Checks (Debits) | | |
|---|---|---|---|---|---|
| Date | Amount | | Check Number | Date | Amount |
| | $ | | | | $ |
| | | | | | |
| | | | | | |
| | | | | | |
| | | | | | |
| Total | $ | | | Total | $ |

**FIGURE 4-62**
**Account Reconciliation Form**

11. Before reconciliation, an account register balance is $1,817.93. The bank statement balance is $860.21. A service fee of $15 and one returned item of $213.83 were charged against the account. Deposits in the amounts of $800 and $412.13 are outstanding. Checks written for $243.17, $167.18, $13.97, $42.12, and $16.80 are outstanding. Complete the account reconciliation form in Figure 4-63 to reconcile the bank statement with the account register.

| $ | BALANCE AS SHOWN ON BANK STATEMENT | | BALANCE AS SHOWN IN YOUR REGISTER | $ |
|---|---|---|---|---|
| | TOTAL OF OUTSTANDING DEPOSITS | | SUBTRACT AMOUNT OF SERVICE CHARGE | |
| | NEW TOTAL | | NEW TOTAL | |
| | SUBTRACT TOTAL OF OUTSTANDING CHECKS | | ADJUSTMENTS IF ANY | |
| | YOUR ADJUSTED STATEMENT BALANCE | SHOULD EQUAL | YOUR ADJUSTED REGISTER BALANCE | |

| Outstanding Deposits (Credits) | | | Outstanding Checks (Debits) | | |
|---|---|---|---|---|---|
| Date | Amount | | Check Number | Date | Amount |
| | $ | | | | $ |
| | | | | | |
| | | | | | |
| | | | | | |
| | | | | | |
| Total | $ | | | Total | $ |

**FIGURE 4-63**
**Account Reconciliation Form**

1. If adjacent digits of an account register entry have been transposed, the error will produce a difference that is divisible by 9. Give an example of a two-digit number and the number formed by transposing the digits, and show that the difference is divisible by 9.

2. Give an example of a three-digit number and the number formed by transposing two adjacent digits. Show that the difference is divisible by 9.

3. Give an example of a four-digit number and a number formed by transposing any two adjacent digits. Show that the difference is divisible by 9.

4. Will the difference be divisible by 9 if two digits that are *not* adjacent are interchanged to form a new number? Illustrate your answer.

5. What if more than two digits are interchanged? Will the difference still be divisible by 9? Illustrate your answer.

6. When you receive your bank statement, you should first identify any items on the statement that are not listed in your account register. Discuss some items you may find on a bank statement and explain what should be done with them.

7. Explain the various types of endorsements for checks.

8. Explain why you would not want to use a deposit ticket that had someone else's name printed on it to make a deposit for your account even if you cross out the account number and name and enter your own.

9. Describe the process for reconciling a bank statement with the account register.

10. Discuss at least three advantages for a business to have a checking account.

# Challenge Problem

Terry Kelly talked with her investment counselor. She was advised to calculate her current net worth and to project her 2008 net worth to determine if her 2008 projections would accomplish her objective of increasing her net worth. She listed the following assets and liabilities for 2007. To calculate her net worth, she found the difference between total assets and total liabilities.

ASSETS:

| | | |
|---|---|---|
| Checking account | 2,099 | |
| Savings account | 2,821 | |
| Auto | 10,500 | |
| Home and furnishings | 65,000 | |
| Stocks and bonds | 4,017 | |
| Other personal property | 3,200 | |
| Total assets | | |

LIABILITIES:

| | | |
|---|---|---|
| Car loan | 8,752 | 6,652 |
| Home mortgage | 54,879 | 53,992 |
| Personal loan | 1,791 | 0 |
| Total liabilities | | |

Terry's home appreciated (increased) in value by 0.04 times the 2007 value while her car depreciated (decreased) in value by 0.125 times the 2007 value. Her car loan decreased by $2,100 while her home mortgage balance decreased by $887. Terry plans to pay her personal loan in full by the end of 2008. Of her $2,000 planned investment, she will place $1,000 in savings and $1,000 in stocks and bonds. She also plans to reinvest the interest income of $141 (in savings) and the dividend income of $364 (in stocks and bonds) earned in 2007. She projects her checking account balance will be $1,500 at year-end for 2008.

Calculate Terry's total assets and total liabilities for 2007. Then calculate her net worth for 2007. Use the information given to project Terry's assets and liabilities for 2008. Then project her 2008 net worth. How much does Terry expect her net worth to increase (or decrease) from 2007 to 2008?

## 4.1 Mark's First Checking Account

During his first year in college, Mark Sutherland opened a checking account at the First National Bank of Westerly, Nebraska. His account does not have a minimum balance requirement, but he does pay a monthly service charge of $3.00. Mark has just received his first monthly bank statement and notices that the end-of-month balance on the statement is quite different from the end-of-month balance he shows in his check record. The bank statement and Mark's check record are summarized below.

| ACCOUNT: Mark J. Sutherland ACCOUNT # 43967 | | | | PERIOD: January 3, 2008 through January 31, 2008 |
|---|---|---|---|---|
| **Bank Statement of Activity This Month** | | | | |
| **Beginning Balance** | | **Deposits and Other Credits to Your Account** | **Checks and Other Charges to Your Account** | **Ending Balance** |
| | | 300.00 | 206.25 | 93.75 |
| 03 | Deposit | 300.00 | | |
| 05 | 100 | | 16.50 | |
| 07 | 101 | | 20.00 | |
| 09 | Debit card transaction | | 17.45 | |
| 12 | 103 | | 42.96 | |
| 14 | 104 | | 16.87 | |
| 17 | 105 | | 5.00 | |
| 17 | 106 | | 11.43 | |
| 17 | ATM withdrawal | | 25.00 | |
| 19 | 107 | | 25.00 | |
| 24 | 108 | | 14.04 | |
| 28 | 109 | | 9.00 | |
| 31 | Service Charge | | 3.00 | |

| Mark's Check Record | | | | | |
|---|---|---|---|---|---|
| Date | No. | Payee | For | Amount | Balance |
| 1/3 | | Deposit | | 300.00 | 300.00 |
| 1/3 | 100 | Harmon Foods | Food | 16.50 | 283.50 |
| 1/4 | 101 | Cash | | 20.00 | 263.50 |
| 1/5 | 102 | VOID | | | |
| 1/7 | 103 | Mel's Sporting Goods | Gym shoes | 42.96 | 220.54 |
| 1/10 | 104 | Valley Cleaners | Dry cleaning | 18.67 | 201.87 |
| 1/13 | 105 | Sharon Mackey | Birthday present | 5.00 | 196.87 |
| 1/14 | 106 | University Bookstore | Supplies | 11.43 | 190.44 |
| 1/14 | 107 | Cash | | 25.00 | 175.44 |
| 1/19 | 108 | Harmon Foods | Food | 14.04 | 161.40 |
| 1/24 | 109 | Mom | Repay loan | 9.00 | 152.40 |
| 1/25 | 110 | Poindexter's Café | Sharon's birthday party | 20.00 | 132.40 |
| 1/26 | | Deposit | | 50.00 | 182.40 |
| 1/28 | 111 | Exxon | Monthly statement | 12.96 | 169.44 |

1. What are the steps Mark needs to include when reconciling his account record with the bank's statement?

2. Reconcile Mark's record with the bank statement using the steps listed in the previous answer.

3. Why are there differences between Mark's records and the bank's statement? What could Mark do during the next month to make the month-end reconciliation easier?

4. Suppose Mark finds a $100 deposit in his bank statement that he knows he did not make. What should he do?

# 4.2 Expressions Dance Studio

It was the end of a very long first month in her sole proprietorship, and Kara Noble was exhausted. Between moving into a new apartment and teaching dance classes five nights a week, there was not much downtime. Consequently, the mail had started to pile up. After sorting through a few bills and way too much junk mail, Kara spotted her first bank statement from U.S. Bank. The format was different from what she was used to, and she was startled to see the ending balance of only $506.18, less than the balance she thought she had. Kara went to find her business check book, which along with the bank statement is summarized below:

Source: Winger and Frasca, *Personal Finance: An Integrated Planning Approach,* 6th edition (Upper Saddle River, NJ: Prentice Hall, 2002).

| | | FINANCIAL SUMMARY: 08/25/07 to 09/25/07 | | | |
|---|---|---|---|---|---|
| **ACCOUNT: Expressions Dance** <br> **ACCOUNT #: 1007508279** | | | **ENDING BALANCE: $506.18** | | |
| **Date** | **Activity** | **Deposits/Other Additions** | **Withdrawals/Other Deductions** | | **Ending Balance** |
| 9/1/2007 | Deposit | 2,475.00 | | | 2,475.00 |
| 9/7/2007 | 1001 | | 110.00 | | 2,365.00 |
| 9/7/2007 | 1000 | | 900.00 | | 1,465.00 |
| 9/14/2007 | 1003 | | 156.00 | | 1,309.00 |
| 9/14/2007 | 1002 | | 29.49 | | 1,279.51 |
| 9/20/2007 | Deposit | 336.19 | | | 1,615.70 |
| 9/24/2007 | Debit | | 93.50 | | 1,522.20 |
| 9/24/2007 | Debit | | 25.75 | | 1,496.45 |
| 9/24/2007 | Debit | | 4.79 | | 1,491.66 |
| 9/25/2007 | 1005 | | 900.00 | | 591.66 |
| 9/25/2007 | Service charge | | 3.00 | | 588.66 |
| 9/25/2007 | Check printing | | 82.48 | | 506.18 |

| **Check #** | **Date** | **Pay to** | **Memo** | **Amount** | **Balance** |
|---|---|---|---|---|---|
| Deposit | 9/1/2007 | Deposit | Business Loan | $2,475.00 | $2,475.00 |
| 1000 | 9/1/2007 | Stephens Properties | Sept. Studio Rent | $900.00 | $1,575.00 |
| 1001 | 9/5/2007 | Renae Peterson | Refund | $110.00 | $1,685.00 |
| 1002 | 9/10/2007 | Gannett Newspapers | Ad Bill | $29.49 | $1,655.51 |
| 1003 | 9/12/2007 | Liturgical Publications | Ad Bill | $156.00 | $1,499.51 |
| Deposit | 9/20/2007 | Deposit | Students | $336.19 | $1,835.70 |
| 1004 | 9/21/2007 | Wisconsin Dance | Owed money to Kari | $133.62 | $1,702.08 |
| 1005 | 9/22/2007 | Stephens Properties | Oct. Studio Rent | $900.00 | $802.08 |
| Debit card | 9/23/2007 | Pom Express | Poms | $39.50 | $762.58 |
| Debit card | 9/23/2007 | Gas | Gas | $25.75 | $736.83 |
| Deposit | 9/27/2007 | Deposit | Students | $319.71 | $1,056.45 |
| Deposit | 9/29/2007 | Deposit | Studio rental fee | $200.00 | $1,256.54 |
| 1006 | 9/30/2007 | VOID | Mistake | $ | $1,256.54 |
| 1007 | 9/30/2007 | Cintas Fire Protection | Extinguisher Replace | $36.93 | $1,219.61 |
| 1008 | 9/30/2007 | Besberg Realty | October Apt. Rent | $570.00 | $649.61 |

**1.** What steps should Kara take to reconcile her bank statement? (Hint: they are listed in your text.)

**2.** Reconcile Kara's checkbook for Expressions Dance with the bank statement following the steps you provided in your answer to question 1.

**3.** What are some ways that Kara can avoid discrepancies in the future?

**4.** The last entry in Kara's Expressions Dance checkbook register is for check #1008 written to Besberg Realty for her personal apartment rent. Is it legal to write checks for personal expenses out of a business account? Even if it is legal, is it a good idea?

# Equations

# Bungee Jumping: How High Should You Go?

Bungee jumping, like many extreme sports, has become increasingly popular in recent years. Few things are quite as exhilarating as seeing the ground come rushing at you—only to be yanked back skyward in the nick of time. But did you know that bungee jumping safety is based on applied math equations?

Tim does, and he is opening a new business, Extreme Bungee Jumping. His primary concern, of course, is with the safety of the jumpers. One mistake and the results could be catastrophic! He has been reviewing the math equation used in the computer program that came with the bungee jump cord he purchased, and realizes there are five variables: the height of the platform, the length of the cord, the elasticity or spring of the cord, the weight of the individual, and an appropriate safety margin. Tim learns that a safety margin of 2 m is acceptable. He knows the length and spring of the cord, as stated by the manufacturer.

Tim wants to try out his new bungee jumping equipment, but is unsure how tall the tower must be to ensure a safe jump. For Tim to complete the calculations, he must know his weight, which is 165 lb or 75 kg. He uses 75 kg, and gets the following results:

height $= 47.285 + 2$ meters (added for safety) $= 49.285$ m
(based on solving the quadratic equation: $h^2 - 755h + 100 = 0$)

The tower must be at least 49.285 m tall to accommodate jumpers who are 165 lb or less. Tim was glad that the computer did the calculations for him. But the good news was that he could now bungee jump safely. Luckily for you, the equations in this chapter are much easier to follow. So, it is time to jump in!

## LEARNING OUTCOMES

### 5-1 Equations

1. Solve equations using multiplication or division.
2. Solve equations using addition or subtraction.
3. Solve equations using more than one operation.
4. Solve equations containing multiple unknown terms.
5. Solve equations containing parentheses.
6. Solve equations that are proportions.

### 5-2 Using Equations to Solve Problems

1. Use the problem-solving approach to analyze and solve word problems.

### 5-3 Formulas

1. Evaluate a formula.
2. Find a variation of a formula by rearranging the formula.

# 5-1 EQUATIONS

## LEARNING OUTCOMES

1 Solve equations using multiplication or division.
2 Solve equations using addition or subtraction.
3 Solve equations using more than one operation.
4 Solve equations containing multiple unknown terms.
5 Solve equations containing parentheses.
6 Solve equations that are proportions.

**Equation:** a mathematical statement in which two quantities are equal.

**Unknown** or **variable:** the missing amount or amounts that are represented as letters in an equation.

**Known** or **given amount:** the known amounts or numbers in an equation.

**Solve:** find the value of the unknown or variable that makes the equation true.

**Isolate:** perform systematic operations to both sides of the equation so that the unknown or variable is alone on one side of the equation. Its value is identified on the other side of the equation.

An **equation** is a mathematical statement in which two quantities are equal. Equations are represented by mathematical shorthand that uses numbers, letters, and operational symbols. The letters represent unknown amounts and are called **unknowns** or **variables**. The numbers are called **known** or **given amounts**. The numbers, letters, and mathematical symbols show how the knowns and unknowns are related. *Solving an equation* like $10 = 2 \times B$ means finding the value of $B$ so that 2 times this value is the same as 10. We accomplish this by performing systematic operations so that the unknown value is **isolated**. That is, the letter representing the unknown or variable stands alone on one side of the equation.

## 1  Solve equations using multiplication or division.

To begin our examination of equations, we look at equations that involve multiplication or division and one unknown value.

---

### HOW TO  Solve an equation with multiplication or division

Solve the equation
$5N = 20$

1. Isolate the unknown value:
   (a) If the equation contains the *product* of the unknown factor and a known factor, then *divide* both sides of the equation by the known factor.

   $$\frac{5N}{5} = \frac{20}{5}$$

   (b) If the equation contains the *quotient* of the unknown value and the divisor, then *multiply* both sides of the equation by the divisor.
2. Identify the solution: The solution is the number on the side opposite the isolated unknown-value letter.

   $N = 4$

3. Check the solution: In the original equation, replace the unknown-value letter with the solution; perform the indicated operations; and verify that both sides of the equation are the same number.

   $5(4) \stackrel{?}{=} 20$
   $20 = 20$

---

**TIP**

**Multiplication Notation**

If there is no sign of operation between a number and a letter, a number and a parenthesis, or two letters, it means multiplication. So $2A$ means $2 \times A$, $2(9)$ means $2 \times 9$, and $AB$ means $A \times B$. In equations, multiplication is usually indicated without the $\times$ sign.

**TIP**

**What Does $\stackrel{?}{=}$ Mean?**

The symbol $\stackrel{?}{=}$ is used when checking a solution until the solution is verified.
$2(9) \stackrel{?}{=} 18$ can be read as *Does 2 times 9 equal 18?*

### EXAMPLE 1  Solve the equation $2A = 18$. (A number multiplied by 2 is 18.)

$2A = 18$     The product and one factor are known.

$\dfrac{2A}{2} = \dfrac{18}{2}$     Divide by the known factor on both sides of the equation.

$A = 9$     The solution is 9.

*Check:*

$2A = 18$     Replace $A$ with the solution 9 and see if both sides are equal.
$2(9) \stackrel{?}{=} 18$
$18 = 18$

**The solution of the equation is 9.**

## EXAMPLE 2

Find the value of $A$ if $\dfrac{A}{4} = 5$. (A number divided by 4 is 5.)

$\dfrac{A}{4} = 5$     The quotient and divisor are known. The dividend is unknown.

$4\left(\dfrac{A}{4}\right) = 5(4)$     Multiply both sides of the equation by the divisor, 4.

$A = \boxed{20}$     The solution is 20.

*Check:*

$\dfrac{A}{4} = 5$     Replace $A$ with the solution 20 and see if both sides are equal.

$\dfrac{20}{4} \stackrel{?}{=} 5$

$5 = 5$

**The solution of the equation is 20.**

---

## TIP

**Why Divide or Multiply Both Sides?**

In Examples 1 and 2, both sides of the equation were divided or multiplied by the known factor. This applies an important property of equality. *If you perform an operation on one side, you must perform the same operation on the other side.*

---

 **STOP AND CHECK**

**1.** Solve for $A$: $3A = 24$

**2.** Solve for $N$: $5N = 30$

**3.** Solve for $B$: $8 = \dfrac{B}{6}$

**4.** Solve for $M$: $\dfrac{M}{5} = 7$

**5.** Solve for $K$: $\dfrac{K}{2} = 3$

**6.** Solve for $A$: $7 = \dfrac{A}{3}$

---

## 2 Solve equations using addition or subtraction.

Suppose 15 of the 25 people who work at Carton Manufacturers work on the day shift. How many people work there in the evening? You know that 15 people work there during the day, that 25 people work there in all, and that some unknown quantity work there in the evening. Assign the letter $N$ to the unknown number of night-shift workers. The information from the problem can then be written in words as "the night-shift workers plus the day-shift workers equal 25" and in symbols: $N + 15 = 25$. This equation is one that can be solved with subtraction.

### HOW TO    Solve an equation with addition or subtraction

Solve the equation
$B + 2 = 8$

1. Isolate the unknown value:
   (a) If the equation contains the *sum* of an unknown value and a known value, then *subtract* the known value from both sides of the equation.

$$\begin{array}{r} B + 2 = 8 \\ -2 \quad -2 \end{array}$$

   (b) If the equation contains the *difference* of an unknown value and a known value, then *add* the known value to both sides of the equation.
2. Identify the solution: The solution is the number on the side opposite the isolated unknown-value letter.

$B = 6$

3. Check the solution: In the original equation, replace the unknown-value letter with the solution, perform the indicated operations, and verify that both sides of the equation are the same number.

$6 + 2 \stackrel{?}{=} 8$
$8 = 8$

$$N + 15 = 25$$

The sum and one value are known.

$$\underline{\phantom{N} - 15 \qquad -15}$$

Subtract the known value, 15, from both sides.

$$N \phantom{+15} = \phantom{0} 10$$

$$N = 10$$

The solution is 10.

*Check:*

$$N + 15 = 25$$

Replace $N$ with the solution, 10, and see if both sides are equal.

$$10 + 15 \stackrel{?}{=} 25$$

$$25 = 25$$

**The solution is 10.**

$$A - 5 = \phantom{0}8$$

The difference and the number being subtracted, 5, are known.

$$\phantom{A} + 5 \qquad + 5$$

Add 5 to both sides.

$$A \phantom{- 5} = \phantom{0} 13$$

The solution is 13.

*Check:*

$$A - 5 = 8$$

Replace $A$ with the solution, 13, and see if both sides are equal.

$$13 - 5 \stackrel{?}{=} 8$$

$$8 = 8$$

**The solution is 13.**

---

## TIP

**Solve by Undoing**

In general, unknowns are isolated in an equation by "undoing" all operations associated with the unknown.

- Use addition to undo subtraction.
- Use subtraction to undo addition.
- Use multiplication to undo division.
- Use division to undo multiplication.

To keep the equation in balance, we perform the same operation on both sides of the equation.

---

 **STOP AND CHECK**

*Solve for the missing number.*

**1.** $A + 12 = 20$     **2.** $A + 5 = 28$     **3.** $N - 7 = 10$

**4.** $N - 5 = 11$     **5.** $15 = A + 3$     **6.** $28 = M - 5$

---

## 3   Solve equations using more than one operation.

Many business equations contain more than one operation. To solve such equations, we undo each operation in turn. We first undo all additions or subtractions and then undo all multiplications or divisions. Our goal is still to isolate the unknown.

Solve the equation
$$3N - 1 = 14$$

1. Isolate the unknown value:

   (a) Add or subtract as necessary *first*.

   $$
   \begin{array}{rcr}
   3N - 1 & = & 14 \\
   + 1 & & + 1 \\
   \hline
   3N & = & 15
   \end{array}
   $$

   (b) Multiply or divide as necessary *second*.

   $$\frac{3N}{3} = \frac{15}{3}$$

   $$N = 5$$

2. Identify the solution: The solution is the number on the side opposite the isolated unknown-value letter.

3. Check the solution: In the original equation, replace the unknown-value letter with the solution and perform the indicated operations.

   $$3(5) - 1 \overset{?}{=} 14$$
   $$15 - 1 \overset{?}{=} 14$$
   $$14 = 14$$

---

**Order of Operations:** the specific order in which calculations must be performed to evaluate a series of calculations.

**TIP**

**Order of Operations**

When two or more calculations are written symbolically, the operations are performed in a specified order.

1. Perform multiplication and division as they appear from left to right.
2. Perform addition and subtraction as they appear from left to right.

To solve an equation, we *undo* the operations, so we work in reverse order.

1. Undo addition or subtraction.
2. Undo multiplication or division.

In the example in the preceding How To box, examine the sequence of steps.

To solve:     Undo subtraction.
               Undo multiplication.

To check:     Multiply first.
               Subtract.

---

**EXAMPLE 1**     Find $A$ if $2A + 1 = 15$. (Two times a number increased by 1 is 15.) The equation contains both addition and multiplication. Undo addition first, and then undo multiplication.

$$
\begin{array}{rcr}
2A + 1 & = & 15 \\
- 1 & & - 1 \\
\hline
2A & = & 14
\end{array}
$$
    Undo addition.

$$2A = 14$$     Undo multiplication.

$$\frac{2A}{2} = \frac{14}{2}$$

$$A = \boxed{7}$$     Solution.

*Check:*

$$2A + 1 = 15$$     Replace A with 7 in the original equation and see if both sides are equal.

$$2(7) + 1 \overset{?}{=} 15$$     Multiply first.

$$14 + 1 \overset{?}{=} 15$$     Add.

$$15 = 15$$

**The solution is 7.**

**EXAMPLE 2** Solve the equation $\dfrac{A}{5} - 3 = 1$. (A number divided by 5 and decreased by 3 is 1.)

The equation contains both subtraction and division: Undo subtraction first, and then undo division.

$$\dfrac{A}{5} - 3 = 1 \qquad \text{Undo subtraction.}$$

$$\underline{\phantom{\dfrac{A}{5}} + 3 \qquad +3}$$

$$\dfrac{A}{5} = 4 \qquad \text{Undo division.}$$

$$5\left(\dfrac{A}{5}\right) = 4(5)$$

$$A = 20 \qquad \text{Solution.}$$

*Check:*

$$\dfrac{A}{5} - 3 = 1 \qquad \text{Replace } A \text{ with 20 in the original equation and see if both sides are equal.}$$

$$\dfrac{20}{5} - 3 \overset{?}{=} 1 \qquad \text{Divide first.}$$

$$4 - 3 \overset{?}{=} 1 \qquad \text{Subtract.}$$

$$1 = 1$$

**The solution is 20.**

---

 **STOP AND CHECK**

*Solve.*

**1.** $3N + 4 = 16$

**2.** $5N - 7 = 13$

**3.** $\dfrac{B}{8} - 2 = 2$

**4.** $\dfrac{M}{3} + 2 = 5$

**5.** $\dfrac{S}{6} - 3 = 4$

**6.** $12 = \dfrac{A}{5} - 8$

---

## 4 Solve equations containing multiple unknown terms.

In some equations, the unknown value may occur more than once. The simplest instance is when the unknown value occurs in two addends. We solve such equations by first combining these addends. Remember that $5A$, for instance, means 5 times $A$, or $A + A + A + A + A$. To combine $2A + 3A$, we add 2 and 3, to get 5, and then multiply 5 by $A$, to get $5A$. Thus, $2A + 3A$ is the same as $5A$.

---

**HOW TO** Solve an equation when the unknown value occurs in two addends

Find $A$ if $2A + 3A = 10$

1. Combine the unknown-value addends that are on the same side of the equation:
   (a) Add the numbers in each addend.
   (b) Represent the multiplication of their sum by the unknown value.
2. Solve the resulting equation.

$$(2 + 3)A = 10$$
$$5A = 10$$

$$\dfrac{5A}{5} = \dfrac{10}{5}$$
$$A = 2$$

## EXAMPLE 1

Find $A$ if $A + 3A - 2 = 14$.

| | |
|---|---|
| $A + 3A - 2 = 14$ | First, combine the unknown-value addends. Note that $A$ is the same as $1A$, so $A + 3A = (1 + 3)A = 4A$. |

$$4A - 2 = 14 \qquad \text{Undo subtraction.}$$
$$\underline{+\,2 \qquad +\,2}$$
$$4A \quad = \quad 16$$

$$\frac{4A}{4} = \frac{16}{4} \qquad \text{Undo multiplication.}$$

$$A = 4 \qquad \text{Solution.}$$

*Check:*

$$A + 3A - 2 = 14 \qquad \text{Replace } A \text{ with 4 and see if both sides are the same.}$$
$$4 + 3(4) - 2 \stackrel{?}{=} 14 \qquad \text{Multiply first.}$$
$$4 + 12 - 2 \stackrel{?}{=} 14 \qquad \text{Add.}$$
$$16 - 2 \stackrel{?}{=} 14 \qquad \text{Subtract.}$$
$$14 = 14$$

**The solution is 4.**

---

## TIP

**Adding Unknown Values**

$A$ is the same as $1A$. When combining unknown-value addends, and one of the addends is $A$, it may help you to write $A$ as $1A$ first.

$$A + 3A = 1A + 3A = 4A$$

---

 **STOP AND CHECK**

*Solve.*

**1.** $B + 3B - 5 = 19$

**2.** $4B - 7 = 13$

**3.** $7 + 3B + 2B = 17$

**4.** $5A - 3 + 2A = 18.$

**5.** $3C - C = 16$

**6.** $12 = 8C - 5C$

---

## 5  Solve equations containing parentheses.

To solve an equation containing parentheses, we first write the equation in a form that contains no parentheses.

---

### HOW TO  Solve an equation containing parentheses

Find $A$ if $2(3A + 1) = 14$

1. Eliminate the parentheses:
   (a) Multiply the number just outside the parentheses by each addend inside the parentheses.
   (b) Show the resulting products as addition or subtraction as indicated.
2. Solve the resulting equation.

$$2(3A + 1) = 14$$

$$6A + 2 = 14$$

$$6A + 2 = 14$$
$$\underline{-\,2 \qquad -\,2}$$
$$6A \quad = \quad 12$$

$$\frac{6A}{6} = \frac{12}{6}$$

$$A = 2$$

## EXAMPLE 1

Solve the equation $5(A + 3) = 25$.

$$5(A + 3) = 25$$
$$5A + 15 = 25$$

First eliminate the parentheses. Multiply 5 by $A$, multiply 5 by 3, and then show the products as addition.

$$5A + 15 = 25$$
$$\quad\; -15 \quad\; -15$$
$$\overline{5A \quad = \quad 10}$$

Undo addition.

Undo multiplication.

$$\frac{5A}{5} = \frac{10}{5}$$

$$A = 2$$

Solution

*Check:*

$$5(A + 3) = 25$$

Replace $A$ with 2 and see if both sides are equal.

$$5(2 + 3) \overset{?}{=} 25$$

Add inside parentheses.

$$5(5) \overset{?}{=} 25$$

Multiply.

$$25 = 25$$

**The solution is 2.**

---

## TIP

**Having Parentheses in a Series of Calculations Expands the Order of Operations.**

To perform a series of calculations:

1. Perform the operations inside the parentheses or eliminate the parentheses by multiplying.
2. Perform multiplication and division as they appear from left to right.
3. Perform addition and subtraction as they appear from left to right.

To solve an equation:

1. Eliminate parentheses by multiplying each addend inside the parentheses by the factor outside the parentheses.
2. Undo addition or subtraction.
3. Undo multiplication or division.

In the preceding example, examine the sequence of steps.

To solve:  Eliminate parentheses.
Undo addition.
Undo multiplication.

To check:  Add inside parentheses.
Multiply.

---

##  STOP AND CHECK

*Solve.*

**1.** $2(N + 4) = 26$

**2.** $3(N - 30) = 45$

**3.** $4(R - 3) = 8$

**4.** $7(2R - 3) = 21$

**5.** $5(3R + 2) = 40$

**6.** $30 = 6(2A + 3)$

---

## 6 Solve equations that are proportions.

**Ratio:** the comparison of two numbers through division. Ratios are most often written as fractions.

**Proportion:** two fractions or ratios that are equal.

**Cross product:** the product of the numerator of one fraction times the denominator of the other fraction of a proportion.

A proportion is based on two pairs of related quantities. The most common way to write proportions is to use fraction notation. A number written in fraction notation is also called a **ratio**. When two fractions or ratios are equal, they form a **proportion**.

An important property of proportions is that the cross products are equal. A **cross product** is the product of the numerator of one fraction times the denominator of another fraction. In the proportion $\frac{1}{2} = \frac{2}{4}$, one cross product is $1 \times 4$ and the other cross product is $2 \times 2$. Notice that the two cross products are both equal to 4. Let's look at other proportions.

$$\frac{3}{6} = \frac{5}{10}$$
$$3(10) = 6(5)$$
$$30 = 30$$

$$\frac{2}{4} = \frac{5}{10}$$
$$2(10) = 4(5)$$
$$20 = 20$$

$$\frac{4}{8} = \frac{6}{12}$$
$$4(12) = 8(6)$$
$$48 = 48$$

## HOW TO — Verify that two fractions form a proportion

1. Find the two cross products.
2. Compare the two cross products.
3. If the cross products are equal, the two fractions form a proportion.

Do $\frac{4}{12}$ and $\frac{6}{18}$ form a proportion?
$4(18) = 72 \quad 12(6) = 72$
Cross products are equal. $\quad 72 = 72$
Fractions form a proportion.

## EXAMPLE 1

Of the fractions $\frac{2}{3}$ and $\frac{3}{4}$, which one is proportional to $\frac{12}{16}$?

Are $\frac{2}{3}$ and $\frac{12}{16}$ proportional?

$$\frac{2}{3} \stackrel{?}{=} \frac{12}{16}$$ — Find the cross products.
$$2(16) \stackrel{?}{=} 3(12)$$ — Multiply.
$$32 \stackrel{?}{=} 36$$ — Not equal, not a proportion.

Are $\frac{3}{4}$ and $\frac{12}{16}$ proportional?

$$\frac{3}{4} \stackrel{?}{=} \frac{12}{16}$$ — Find the cross products.
$$3(16) \stackrel{?}{=} 4(12)$$ — Multiply.
$$48 \stackrel{?}{=} 48$$ — Equal, proportional.

$\frac{3}{4}$ **is proportional to** $\frac{12}{16}$.

## HOW TO — Solve a proportion

1. Find the cross products.
2. Isolate the unknown by undoing the multiplication.

## EXAMPLE 2

Solve: $\frac{3}{8} = \frac{21}{N}$

$$\frac{3}{8} = \frac{21}{N}$$ — Find the cross products.
$$3N = 8(21)$$ — Multiply.
$$3N = 168$$ — Undo multiplication.
$$\frac{3N}{3} = \frac{168}{3}$$ — Divide.
$$N = \mathbf{56}$$

## ✓ STOP AND CHECK

1. Which of the fractions $\frac{5}{7}$ or $\frac{3}{4}$ is proportional to $\frac{20}{28}$?

2. Which of the fractions $\frac{1}{2}$ or $\frac{2}{3}$ is proportional to $\frac{12}{18}$?

3. Solve: $\frac{3}{4} = \frac{N}{8}$

4. Solve: $\frac{5}{N} = \frac{4}{12}$

5. Solve: $\frac{N}{4} = \frac{9}{6}$

6. Solve: $\frac{5}{12} = \frac{15}{N}$

## SKILL BUILDERS

*Solve for the unknown in each equation.*

**1.** $5A = 20$

**2.** $\dfrac{B}{7} = 4$

**3.** $7C = 56$

**4.** $4M = 48$

**5.** $\dfrac{R}{12} = 3$

**6.** $\dfrac{P}{5} = 8$

**7.** $B + 7 = 12$

**8.** $A - 9 = 15$

**9.** $R + 7 = 28$

**10.** $A - 16 = 3$

**11.** $X - 48 = 36$

**12.** $C + 5 = 21$

**13.** $4A + 3 = 27$

**14.** $\dfrac{B}{3} + 2 = 7$

**15.** $3B - 1 = 11$

**16.** $\dfrac{K}{4} - 5 = 3$

**17.** $\dfrac{K}{2} + 3 = 5$

**18.** $7B - 1 = 6$

**19.** $\dfrac{C}{2} - 1 = 9$

**20.** $8A - 1 = 19$

**21.** $2A + 5A = 35$

**22.** $B + 2B = 27$

**23.** $5K - 3K = 40$

**24.** $8K - 2K = 42$

**25.** $3J + J = 28$  **26.** $2J - J = 21$  **27.** $3B + 2B - 6 = 9$  **28.** $8C - C + 6 = 48$

**29.** $2(X - 3) = 6$  **30.** $4(A + 3) = 16$  **31.** $3(B - 1) = 21$  **32.** $6(B + 2) = 30$

*Solve each proportion for* N.

**33.** $\dfrac{N}{5} = \dfrac{9}{15}$  **34.** $\dfrac{3}{N} = \dfrac{4}{12}$  **35.** $\dfrac{2}{5} = \dfrac{N}{20}$  **36.** $\dfrac{2}{4} = \dfrac{9}{N}$

## 5-2 USING EQUATIONS TO SOLVE PROBLEMS

### LEARNING OUTCOME

1 Use the problem-solving approach to analyze and solve word problems.

Equations are powerful business tools because equations use mathematical shorthand for expressing relationships. As we know from our problem-solving strategies, developing a solution plan is a critical step.

### 1 Use the problem-solving approach to analyze and solve word problems.

Certain key words in a problem give you clues as to whether a certain quantity is added to, subtracted from, or multiplied or divided by another quantity. For example, if a word problem tells you that Carol's salary in 2008 *exceeds* her 2007 salary by $2,500, you know that you should *add* $2,500 to her 2007 salary to find her 2008 salary. Many times, when you see the word *of* in a problem, the problem often involves multiplication. Table 5-1 summarizes important key words and what they generally imply when they are used in a word problem. This list should help you analyze the information in word problems and write the information in symbols.

TABLE 5-1
Key Words and What They Generally Imply in Word Problems

| Addition | Subtraction | Multiplication | Division | Equality |
|---|---|---|---|---|
| The sum of | Less than | Times | Divide(s) | Equals |
| Plus/total | Decreased by | Multiplied by | Divided by | Is/was/are |
| Increased by | Subtracted from | Of | Divided into | Is equal to |
| More/more than | Difference between | The product of | Half of (divided by two) | The result is |
| Added to | Diminished by | Twice (two times) | Third of (divided by three) | What is left |
| Exceeds | Take away | Double (two times) | Per | What remains |
| Expands | Reduced by | Triple (three times) | | The same as |
| Greater than | Less/minus | Half ($\frac{1}{2}$ times) | | Gives/giving |
| Gain/profit | Loss | Third of ($\frac{1}{3}$ times) | | Makes |
| Longer | Lower | | | Leaves |
| Older | Shrinks | | | |
| Heavier | Smaller than | | | |
| Wider | Younger | | | |
| Taller | Slower | | | |

We can relate the steps in our five-step problem-solving approach to writing and solving equations.

**What You Know** — Known or given facts

**What You Are Looking For** — Unknown amounts (Assign a letter to represent an unknown amount. Other unknown amounts are written related to the assigned letter.)

**Solution Plan** — Equation or relationship among the known and unknown facts

**Solution** — Solving the equation

**Conclusion** — Solution interpreted within the context of the problem

---

**EXAMPLE 1** Full-time employees at Charlie's Steakhouse work more hours per day than part-time employees. If the difference of working hours is 4 hours per day, and if part-timers work 6 hours per day, how many hours per day do full-timers work?

| What You Know | What You Are Looking For | Solution Plan |
|---|---|---|
| Hours per day that part-timers work: 6 <br><br> Difference between hours worked by full-timers and hours worked by part-timers: 4 | Hours per day that full-timers work: $N$ | The word *difference* implies subtraction. <br><br> Full-time hours − part-time hours = difference of hours <br> $N - 6 = 4$ |

**Solution**

$$N - 6 = 4 \qquad \text{Undo subtraction.}$$
$$\underline{+6 \quad +6}$$
$$N = 10 \qquad \text{The solution is 10.}$$

*Check:*

$$10 - 6 \overset{?}{=} 4 \qquad \text{Replace } N \text{ with 4. Subtract.}$$
$$4 = 4 \qquad \text{The sides are equal.}$$

**Conclusion**

**The hours per day that full-timers work is 10.**

## EXAMPLE 2

Wanda plans to save $\frac{1}{10}$ of her salary each week. If her weekly salary is \$350, how much will she save each week?

| What You Know | What You Are Looking For | Solution Plan |
|---|---|---|
| Salary = \$350<br>Rate of saving: $\frac{1}{10}$ | Amount to be saved: $S$ | The word *of* implies multiplication.<br><br>$\begin{aligned}\text{Amount to be saved} &= \text{rate of saving} \times \text{salary}\end{aligned}$<br><br>$S = \frac{1}{10}(\$350)$ |

### Solution

$S = \dfrac{1}{10}(\$350)$      Reduce and multiply.

$S = \$35$      The solution is 35.

*Check:*

$\$35 \overset{?}{=} \dfrac{1}{10}(\$350)$      Replace $S$ with \$35 and see if the sides are equal.

$\$35 = \$35$

### Conclusion

**Wanda will save \$35 per week.**

---

## TIP

**The Process Is Important!**

Learn the process for solving applied problems with intuitive examples. In Examples 1 and 2 you may have been able to determine the solutions mentally, even intuitively. Learn the process for easier applications so that you can use the process for more complex applications.

---

Many times a problem requires finding more than one unknown value. Our strategy will be to choose a letter to represent one unknown value. Using known facts, we can then express all other unknown values *in terms of* the one letter. For instance, if we know that twice as many men as women attended a conference, then we might represent the number of women as $W$ and the number of men as $2W$, twice as many as $W$.

## EXAMPLE 3

At Alexander's Cafe last Wednesday, there were twice as many requests for seats in the nonsmoking section as there were requests for seats in the smoking section. If 342 customers came to the cafe that day, how many requested the smoking section? How many requested the nonsmoking section?

| What You Know | What You Are Looking For | Solution Plan |
|---|---|---|
| Total customers: 342<br>There are twice as many nonsmokers as smokers. | Both the number of smokers and the number of non-smokers are unknown, but we choose one—smokers— to be represented by a letter, $S$.<br>Number of smokers: $S$<br>Since the number of non-smokers is *twice* the number of smokers, we represent the number of nonsmokers as $2S$, or 2 times $S$.<br>Number of nonsmokers: $2S$ | Smoker + nonsmokers = total customers<br>$S + 2S = 342$ |

**Solution**

$$S + 2S = 342$$ — Combine addends.
$$3S = 342$$

$$\frac{3S}{3} = \frac{342}{3}$$ — Divide both sides by 3.

$$S = 114$$ — The solution is 114, which represents the number of smokers.
$$2S = 2(114)$$
$$= 228$$ — Twice $S$ is twice 114, or 228 nonsmokers.

*Check:*
$$S + 2S = 342$$ — Substitute $S = 114$ and $2S = 228$.
$$114 + 228 \overset{?}{=} 342$$
$$342 = 342$$

**Conclusion**

**There were 114 smokers and 228 nonsmokers.**

Many problems give a *total* number of two types of items. You want to know the number of each of the two types of items. The next example illustrates this type of problem.

**EXAMPLE 4**  Diane's Card Shop spent a total of $950 ordering 600 cards from Wit's End Co., whose humorous cards cost $1.75 each and whose nature cards cost $1.50 each. How many of each style of card did the card shop order?

**What You Know**

| Total cost of cards: $950 | Cost per humorous card: $1.75 |
|---|---|
| Total number of cards: 600 | Cost per nature card: $1.50 |

**What You Are Looking For**

There are two unknown facts, but we choose one—the number of humorous cards—to be represented by a letter, $H$.
Number of humorous cards: $H$
Knowing that the total number of cards is 600, we represent the number of nature cards as 600 minus the humorous cards, or $600 - H$.

**Solution Plan**

Total cost = (cost per humorous card)(number of humorous cards)
    + (cost per nature card)(number of nature cards)
$$950 = (1.75)(H) + (1.50)(600 - H)$$

**Solution**

$$950 = 1.75H + 1.50(600 - H)$$ — Eliminate parentheses showing grouping.
$$950 = 1.75H + (1.50)(600) - 1.50H$$ — Multiply 1.50(600).
$$950 = 1.75H + 900 - 1.50H$$ — Combine letter terms.
$$950 = 0.25H + 900$$
$$\underline{-900 \qquad\qquad -900}$$ — Subtract 900 from both sides.
$$50 = 0.25H$$
$$\frac{50}{0.25} = \frac{0.25H}{0.25}$$ — Divide both sides by 0.25.
$$200 = H$$ — The solution is 200, which represents the number of humorous cards.

$$600 - H = 600 - 200$$ — Subtract 200 from 600 to find $600 - H$,
$$= 400$$ — or 400, the number of nature cards.

*Check:*
$$950 \overset{?}{=} (1.75)(200) + (1.50)(600 - 200)$$ — Substitute 200 in place of $H$. Then perform
$$950 \overset{?}{=} (1.75)(200) + (1.50)(400)$$ — calculations using the order of operations.
$$950 \overset{?}{=} 350 + 600$$ — Subtract inside parentheses first.
$$950 = 950$$

**Conclusion**

**The card shop ordered 200 humorous cards and 400 nature cards.**

Many problems encountered daily involve two pairs of values that are proportional.

## EXAMPLE 5

Your car gets 23 miles to a gallon of gas. How far can you go on 16 gallons of gas?

| What You Know | What You Are Looking For | Solution Plan |
|---|---|---|
| Distance traveled using 1 gallon: 23 miles (Pair 1) | Distance traveled using 16 gallons: $M$ miles (Pair 2) | Miles traveled per 16 gallons is proportional to miles traveled for each 1 gallon. $$\frac{1 \text{ gallon}}{23 \text{ miles}} = \frac{16 \text{ gallons}}{M \text{ miles}}$$ Pair 1  Pair 2 |

**Solution**

$$\frac{1}{23} = \frac{16}{M}$$   Cross multiply.

$1M = (16)(23)$   Multiply.

$M = 368$

*Check:*

$$\frac{1}{23} \overset{?}{=} \frac{16}{368}$$   Substitute 368 for $M$ and cross multiply.

$(1)(368) \overset{?}{=} (23)(16)$   Multiply.

$368 = 368$

**Conclusion**

**You can travel 368 miles using 16 gallons of gas.**

## TIP

**Arranging the Proportion**

Many business-related problems that involve pairs of numbers that are proportional are *direct proportions*. That means an increase in one amount causes an increase in the number that pairs with it. Or, a decrease in one amount causes a decrease in the second amount.

In the preceding example, for 1 gallon of gas, the car can travel 23 miles. It is a direct proportion: More gas *yields* more miles.

The pairs of values in a direct proportion can be arranged in other ways. Another way to arrange the pairs from the preceding example is *across* the equal sign.

$$\frac{1 \text{ gallon}}{16 \text{ gallons}} = \frac{23 \text{ miles}}{M \text{ miles}} \quad \begin{array}{l} \text{Pair 1} \\ \text{Pair 2} \end{array}$$

$$1M = 16(23)$$

$$M = 368$$

## EXAMPLE 6

The label on a container of concentrated weed killer gives directions to mix 3 ounces of weed killer with every 2 gallons of water. For 5 gallons of water, how many ounces of weed killer should you use?

| What You Know | What You Are Looking For | Solution Plan |
|---|---|---|
| Amount of weed killer for 2 gallons of water: 3 ounces (Pair 1) | Amount of weed killer for 5 gallons of water: $W$ ounces (Pair 2) | Amount of weed killer per 5 gallons is proportional to an amount of weed killer for each 2 gallons. $$\frac{2 \text{ gallons}}{3 \text{ ounces}} = \frac{5 \text{ gallons}}{W \text{ ounces}}$$ Pair 1  Pair 2 |

$$\frac{2}{3} = \frac{5}{W}$$     Cross multiply.

$$2W = (3)(5)$$     Multiply.

$$2W = 15$$     Divide both sides by 2.

$$\frac{2W}{2} = \frac{15}{2}$$

$$W = 7\frac{1}{2}$$     The solution is $7\frac{1}{2}$.

Check:   $\frac{2}{3} \overset{?}{=} \frac{5}{7\frac{1}{2}}$     Substitute $7\frac{1}{2}$ for $W$ and simplify each side.

$$\frac{2}{3} \overset{?}{=} 5 \div 7\frac{1}{2}$$

$$\frac{2}{3} \overset{?}{=} 5 \div \frac{15}{2}$$

$$\frac{2}{3} \overset{?}{=} 5\left(\frac{2}{15}\right)$$

$$\frac{2}{3} = \frac{2}{3}$$

**Conclusion**

**You should use $7\frac{1}{2}$ ounces of weed killer for 5 gallons of water.**

 ## STOP AND CHECK

1. Carrie McConnell spends $\frac{1}{6}$ of her weekly earnings on groceries. What are her weekly earnings if she spends $117.50 on groceries each week?

2. Marcus James purchased 2,500 pounds of produce. Records indicate he purchased 800 pounds of potatoes, 150 pounds of broccoli, and 390 pounds of tomatoes. He also purchased apples. How many pounds of apples did he purchase?

3. Hilton Hotel has 8 times as many nonsmoking rooms as it has smoking rooms. If the hotel has 873 rooms in its inventory, how many are smoking rooms?

4. Four hundred eighty notebooks can be purchased for $1,656. How many notebooks can be purchased for $2,242.50?

## 5-2 SECTION EXERCISES

### APPLICATIONS

1. The difference in hours between full-timers and the part-timers who work 5 hours a day is 4 hours. How long do full-timers work?

2. Manny plans to save $\frac{1}{12}$ of his salary each week. If his weekly salary is $372, find the amount he will save each week.

3. Last week at the Sunshine Valley Rock Festival, Joel sold 3 times as many tie-dyed T-shirts as silk-screened shirts. He sold 176 shirts altogether. How many tie-dyed shirts did he sell?

4. Elaine sold 3 times as many magazine subscriptions as Ron did. Ron sold 16 fewer subscriptions than Elaine did. How many subscriptions did each sell?

**5.** Will ordered 2 times as many boxes of ballpoint pens as boxes of felt-tip pens. Ballpoint pens cost $3.50 per box, and felt-tip pens cost $4.50. If Will's order of pens totaled $46, how many boxes of each type of pen did he buy?

**6.** A real estate salesperson bought promotional calendars and date books to give to her customers at the end of the year. The calendars cost $0.75 each, and the date books cost $0.50 each. She ordered a total of 500 promotional items and spent $300. How many of each item did she order?

*Use proportions to solve each problem.*

**7.** Hershey Foods stock earned $151,000,000. If these earnings represent $1.15 per share, how many shares of stock are there?

**8.** A scale drawing of an office building is not labeled, but indicates $\frac{1}{4}$ inches = 5 feet. On the drawing, one wall measures 2 inches. How long is the wall?

**9.** A recipe uses 3 cups of flour to $1\frac{1}{4}$ cups of milk. If you have 2 cups of flour, how much milk should you use?

**10.** For 32 hours of work, you are paid $241.60. How much would you receive for 37 hours?

**11.** The annual real estate tax on a duplex house is $2,321 and the owner sells the house after 9 months of the tax year. How much of the annual tax will the seller pay? How much will the buyer pay?

**12.** A wholesale price list shows that 18 dozen headlights cost $702. If 16 dozen can be bought at the same rate, how much will they cost?

**13.** Two part-time employees share one full-time job. Charris works Mondays, Wednesdays, and Fridays, and Chloe works Tuesdays and Thursdays. The job pays an annual salary of $28,592. What annual salary does each employee earn?

**14.** A car that leases for $5,400 annually is leased for 8 months of the year. How much will it cost to lease the car for the 8 months?

**15.** If 1.0000 U.S. Dollar is equivalent to 0.1273 Chinese Yuan, convert $12,000 to Yuan.

## 5-3 FORMULAS

### LEARNING OUTCOMES

1 Evaluate a formula.
2 Find a variation of a formula by rearranging the formula.

### 1 Evaluate a formula.

**Formulas** are procedures that have been used so frequently to solve certain types of problems that they have become the accepted means of solving these problems. Formulas are composed of numbers, letters, or **variables**, used to represent unknown numbers, and operations that relate these known and unknown values. To **evaluate** a formula is to substitute known values for the appropriate letters of the formula and perform the indicated operations to find the unknown value. Sometimes the equation must be solved to isolate the unknown value in the formula.

> **HOW TO** Evaluate a formula
>
> 1. Write the formula.
> 2. Rewrite the formula substituting known values for the letters of the formula.
> 3. Solve the equation for the unknown letter or perform the indicated operations, applying the order of operations.
> 4. Interpret the solution within the context of the formula.

**EXAMPLE 1**   Wal-Mart purchases a Sony plasma television for $875 and marks it up $400. What is the selling price of the television? Use the formula $S = C + M$ where $S$ is the selling price, $C$ is the cost, and $M$ is the markup.

$S = C + M$        Write the formula. Substitute known values for $C$ and $M$.

$S = \$875 + \$400$        Add.

$S = \$1{,}275$

**The selling price for the television is $1,275.**

In some instances, the missing value is not the value that is isolated in the formula. After the known values are substituted into the formula, use the techniques for solving equations to find the missing value.

**EXAMPLE 2**   A DVD player that costs $85 sells for $129. What is the markup on the player? Use the formula $S = C + M$ where $S$ is the selling price, $C$ is the cost, and $M$ is the markup.

$S = C + M$        Write the formula. Substitute known values for $C$ and $S$.

$\$129 = \$85 + M$        Subtract $85 from each side of the equation.

$\underline{-85 \quad\;\; -85}$

$\$44 = M$

**The markup for the DVD player is $44.**

---

**TIP**

**Interchanging the Sides of an Equation**

In Example 2, the solved equation was $\$44 = M$. Since equations show equality, it is allowable to interchange the sides of the equation. The equation can also be written as $M = \$44$.

---

 **STOP AND CHECK**

1. Office Depot purchased an office chair for $317 and marked it up $250. Find the selling price of the chair. Use the formula $S = C + M$.

2. Office Max purchased a computer workstation for $463 and marked its retail (selling) price at $629. Use the formula $S = C + M$ to find the markup on the workstation.

3. Trios Mixon worked 40 hours at $19.26 per hour. Find his pay. Use the formula $P = RH$, where $P$ is the pay, $R$ is the rate per hour, and $H$ is the number of hours worked.

4. Luis Pardo earned $612 for a 40-hour week. Use the formula $P = RH$ to find his hourly rate.

## 2   Find a variation of a formula by rearranging the formula.

A formula can have as many variations as there are letters or variables in the formula. Using the techniques for solving equations, any missing number can be found no matter where it appears in the formula. Variations of formulas are desirable when the variation is used frequently. Also, in using an electronic spreadsheet, the missing number should be isolated on the left side of the equation. To **isolate** a variable is to **solve for** that variable.

**HOW TO**   Find a variation of a formula by rearranging the formula

1. Determine which variable of the formula is to be isolated (solved for).
2. Highlight or mentally locate all instances of the variable to be isolated.
3. Treat all other variables of the formula as you would treat a number in an equation, and perform normal steps for solving an equation.
4. If the isolated variable is on the right side of the equation, interchange the sides so that it appears on the left side.

**EXAMPLE 1**    Solve the formula $S = C + M$ for $C$.

$$S = C + M$$    Isolate $C$. Subtract $M$ from both sides of the equation.

$$S - M = C + M - M$$    Simplify. $M - M = 0$. $C + 0 = C$.

$$S - M = C$$    Interchange the sides of the equation.

$$C = S - M$$    Formula variation

The unit price of a product is used when comparing prices of a product available in different quantities. The formula for finding the unit price is $U = \frac{P}{N}$, where $U$ is the unit price of a specified amount of a product, $P$ is the total price of the product, and $N$ is the number of specified units contained in the product. The specified unit can be identified in many ways. The unit could be any measuring unit such as pounds (lb) or ounces (oz) or the number of items such as an individual snack cake in a package of cakes.

**EXAMPLE 2**    Find a variation of the formula $U = \dfrac{P}{N}$ that is solved for $P$.

$$U = \frac{P}{N}$$    Isolate $P$. Multiply both sides of the equation by $N$.

$$N(U) = \left(\frac{P}{N}\right)N$$    Simplify. $\dfrac{N}{N} = 1$. $P(1) = P$.

$$NU = P$$    Interchange the sides of the equation.

$$P = NU$$    Formula variation.

##  STOP AND CHECK

1. Solve the formula $S = C + M$ for $M$.

2. Solve the formula $M = S - N$ for $S$.

3. Solve the formula $U = \dfrac{P}{N}$ for $N$.

4. The unit depreciation formula, Unit depreciation $= \dfrac{\text{depreciable Value}}{\text{units Produced during expected life}}$ can be written in symbols as $U = \dfrac{V}{P}$. Solve the formula to find $V$, the depreciable value.

## 5-3 SECTION EXERCISES

### SKILL BUILDERS

1. Sears purchased 10,000 pairs of men's slacks for $18.46 a pair and marked them up $21.53. What was the selling price of each pair of slacks? Use the formula $S = C + M$.

2. K-Mart had 896 swimsuits that were marked to sell at $49.99. Each suit was marked down $18.95. Find the reduced price using the formula $M = S - N$, where $M$ is the markdown, $S$ is the original selling price, and $N$ is the reduced price.

3. Home Depot sold bird feeders for $69.99 and had marked them up $36.12. What was the cost of the feeders? Use the formula $S = C + M$.

4. Dollar General sold garden hoses at a reduced price of $7.64 and took an end-of-season markdown of $12.35. What was the original selling price of each hose? Use the formula $M = S - N$.

**5.** The formula Total cost $=$ Cost $+$ Shipping $+$ Installation is used to find the total cost of a business asset when setting up a depreciation schedule for the asset. The formula can be written in symbols as $T = C + S + I$. Solve the formula for $C$, the cost of the asset.

**6.** The formula, depreciable Value $=$ total Cost $-$ Salvage value is used to set up a depreciation schedule for an asset. The formula can be written in symbols as $V = C - S$. Solve the formula for C.

**7.** The formula, **Yearly depreciation** $= \dfrac{\text{depreciable Value}}{\text{years of expected Life}}$ is used to find yearly depreciation using the straight line depreciation method. The formula can be written in symbols as $Y = \dfrac{V}{L}$. Solve the formula for $V$.

**8.** Solve the formula $Y = \dfrac{V}{L}$ for $L$.

## Learning Outcomes

### Section 5-1

## What to Remember with Examples

**1** Solve equations using multiplication or division. (p. 146)

1. Isolate the unknown value:
   (a) If the equation contains the *product* of the unknown value and a number, then *divide* both sides of the equation by the number.
   (b) If the equation contains the *quotient* of the unknown value and the divisor, then *multiply* both sides of the equation by the divisor.
2. Identify the solution: The solution is the number on the side opposite the isolated unknown-value letter.
3. Check the solution: In the original equation, replace the unknown-value letter with the solution, perform the indicated operations, and verify that both sides of the equation are the same number.

Find the value of $A$.

$$4A = 36 \quad \text{Divide both sides by 4.} \qquad \text{check:} \qquad 4(9) \stackrel{?}{=} 36$$
$$\frac{4A}{4} = \frac{36}{4} \qquad\qquad\qquad\qquad\qquad\qquad 36 = 36$$
$$A = 9$$

Find the value of $B$.

$$\frac{B}{7} = 6 \qquad \text{Multiply both sides by 7.} \qquad \text{check:} \ \frac{42}{7} \stackrel{?}{=} 6$$
$$\left(\frac{B}{7}\right)(7) = 6(7) \qquad\qquad\qquad\qquad\qquad\qquad 6 = 6$$
$$B = 42$$

**2** Solve equations using addition or subtraction. (p. 147)

1. Isolate the unknown value:
   (a) If the equation contains the *sum* of the unknown value and another number, then *subtract* the number from both sides of the equation.
   (b) If the equation contains the *difference* of the unknown value and another number, then *add* the number to both sides of the equation.
2. Identify the solution: The solution is the number on the side opposite the isolated unknown-value letter.
3. Check the solution: In the original equation, replace the unknown-value letter with the solution, perform the indicated operations, and verify that both sides of the equation are the same number.

Find the value of $A$.

$$
\begin{array}{rl}
A - 7 = & 12 \quad \text{Add 7 to both sides.} \\
\underline{+ 7} & \underline{+ 7} \\
A \ \ = & 19
\end{array}
$$

Find the value of $B$.

$$
\begin{array}{rl}
B + 5 = & 32 \quad \text{Subtract 5 from both sides.} \\
\underline{- 5} & \underline{- 5} \\
B \ \ = & 27
\end{array}
$$

**3** Solve equations using more than one operation. (p. 148)

1. Isolate the unknown value:
   (a) Add or subtract as necessary *first*.
   (b) Multiply or divide as necessary *second*.
2. Identify the solution: The solution is the number on the side opposite the isolated unknown-value letter.
3. Check the solution: In the original equation, replace the unknown-value letter with the solution, and perform the indicated operations.

Find the value of $A$.

$$4A + 4 = 20 \quad \text{Undo addition first.}$$
$$\underline{-4 \quad -4}$$
$$4A = 16 \quad \text{Undo multiplication.}$$
$$\frac{4A}{4} = \frac{16}{4}$$
$$A = 4$$

Find the value of $B$.

$$\frac{B}{3} - 5 = 12 \quad \text{Undo subtraction first.}$$
$$\underline{\quad +5 \quad +5}$$
$$\frac{B}{3} = 17 \quad \text{Undo division.}$$
$$\left(\frac{B}{3}\right)(3) = 17(3)$$
$$B = 51$$

**4** Solve equations containing multiple unknown terms. (p. 150)

**Solve an equation when the unknown value occurs in two or more addends.**

1. Combine the unknown-value addends when the addends are on the same side of the equal sign:
   (a) Add the numbers in each addend.
   (b) Multiply their sum by the unknown value.
2. Solve the resulting equation.

Find the value of $A$.

$$A - 5 + 5A = 25 \quad \text{Combine addends that have unknown factors. } A + 5A = 6A$$
$$6A - 5 = 25 \quad \text{Add 5 to both sides.}$$
$$\underline{\quad +5 \quad +5}$$
$$6A = 30 \quad \text{Divide both sides by 6.}$$
$$\frac{6A}{6} = \frac{30}{6}$$
$$A = 5$$

**5** Solve equations containing parentheses. (p. 151)

1. Eliminate the parentheses:
   (a) Multiply the number just outside the parentheses by each addend inside the parentheses.
   (b) Show the resulting products as addition or subtraction as indicated.
2. Solve the resulting equation.

Find the value of $A$.

$$3(A + 4) = 27 \quad \text{Eliminate parentheses first. } 3(A) = 3A; \ 3(4) = 12$$
$$3A + 12 = 27 \quad \text{Subtract 12 from both sides.}$$
$$\underline{\quad -12 \quad -12}$$
$$3A = 15 \quad \text{Divide both sides by 3.}$$
$$\frac{3A}{3} = \frac{15}{3}$$
$$A = 5$$

**6** Solve equations that are proportions. (p. 152)

1. Find the cross products.
2. Isolate the unknown by undoing the multiplication.

Solve the proportion $\dfrac{5}{x} = \dfrac{7}{12}$.

$$\frac{5}{x} = \frac{7}{12} \quad \text{Cross multiply.}$$
$$7x = 5(12) \quad \text{Multiply.}$$
$$7x = 60 \quad \text{Divide.}$$
$$\frac{7x}{7} = \frac{60}{7} \quad \text{Convert } \frac{60}{7} \text{ to a mixed number.}$$
$$x = 8\frac{4}{7}$$

## Section 5-2

**1** Use the problem-solving approach to analyze and solve word problems. (p. 155)

**Keywords and what they generally imply in word problems.**

| Addition | Subtraction | Multiplication | Division | Equality |
|---|---|---|---|---|
| The sum of | Less than | Times | Divide(s) | Equals |
| Plus/total | Decreased by | Multiplied by | Divided by | Is/was/are |
| Increased by | Subtracted from | Of | Divided into | Is equal to |
| More/more than | Difference between | The product of | Half of (divided by two) | The result is |
| Added to | Diminished by | Twice (two times) | Per | What is left |
| Exceeds | Take away | Double (two times) | Third of | What remains |
| Expands | Reduced by | Triple | (divide by 3) | The same as |
| Greater than | Less/minus | (three times) | | Gives/giving |
| Gain/profit | Loss | Half of | | Makes |
| Longer | Lower | ($\frac{1}{2}$ times) | | Leaves |
| Older | Shrinks | Third of | | |
| Heavier | Smaller than | ($\frac{1}{3}$ times) | | |
| Wider | Younger | | | |
| Taller | Slower | | | |

**Use the five-step problem-solving approach.**

| | |
|---|---|
| **What You Know** | Known or given facts |
| **What You Are Looking For** | Unknown or missing amounts |
| **Solution Plan** | Equation or relationship among the known and unknown facts |
| **Solution** | Solve the equation. |
| **Conclusion** | Solution interpreted within the context of the problem |

If 4 printer cartridges cost $56.80, how much would 7 cartridges cost?

| What You Know | What You Are Looking For | Solution Plan |
|---|---|---|
| 4 cartridges cost $56.80 Pair 1 | 7 cartridges cost $N   Pair 2 | $\dfrac{4 \text{ cartridges}}{\$56.80} = \dfrac{7 \text{ cartridges}}{\$N}$ <br> Pair 1        Pair 2 |

**Solution**

$$\frac{4}{\$56.80} = \frac{7}{N}$$  Cross multiply.

$$4N = \$56.80(7)$$  Multiply.

$$4N = \$397.60$$  Divide.

$$\frac{4N}{4} = \frac{\$397.60}{4}$$

$$N = \$99.40$$

**Conclusion**

**7 cartridges cost $99.40.**

## Section 5-3

**1** Evaluate a formula. (p. 162)

1. Write the formula.
2. Rewrite the formula substituting known values for the letters of the formula.
3. Perform the indicated operations, applying the order of operations.
4. Interpret the solution within the context of the formula.

Find the unit price of a snack cake that is available in a package of 6 cakes for $1.98. Use the formula $U = \frac{P}{N}$, where $U$ is the unit price of a specified amount of a product, $P$ is the total price of the product, and $N$ is the number of specified units contained in the product.

$$U = \frac{P}{N}$$  Substitute known values.

$$U = \frac{\$1.98}{6}$$  Divide.

$$U = \$0.33$$  Cost per cake

**2** Find a variation of a formula by rearranging the formula. (p. 163)

1. Determine which variable of the formula is to be isolated (solved for).
2. Highlight or mentally locate all instances of the variable to be isolated.
3. Treat all other variables of the formula as you would treat a number in an equation, and perform the normal steps for solving an equation.
4. If the isolated variable is on the right side of the equation, interchange the sides so that it appears on the left side.

The distance formula is $D = RT$, where $D$ is the distance traveled, $R$ is the rate or speed traveled, and $T$ is the time traveled. Find a variation of the distance formula that is solved for the time traveled.

| | |
|---|---|
| $D = RT$ | Isolate $T$. Divide both sides of the equation by $R$. |
| $\dfrac{D}{R} = \dfrac{RT}{R}$ | Simplify. $\dfrac{R}{R} = 1$. $1(T) = T$. |
| $\dfrac{D}{R} = T$ | Interchange the sides of the equation. |
| $T = \dfrac{D}{R}$ | Formula variation. |

## EXERCISES SET A

*Find the value of the variable:*

**1.** $5N = 35$

**2.** $\dfrac{A}{6} = 2$

**3.** $N - 5 = 12$

**4.** $2N + 4 = 12$

**5.** $\dfrac{A}{3} + 4 = 12$

**6.** $2(x - 3) = 8$

**7.** $3(x - 1) = 30$

**8.** $8A - 3A = 40$

**9.** $4X - X = 21$

**10.** $12N + 5 - 7N = 45$

**11.** Ace Motors sold a total of 15 cars and trucks during one promotion sale. Six of the vehicles sold were trucks. What is the number of cars that were sold?

**12.** Bottletree Bakery and Card Shop ordered an equal number of 12 different cards. If a total of 60 cards were ordered, how many of each type of card were ordered?

**13.** An electrician pays $\frac{2}{5}$ of the amount he charges for a job for supplies. If he was paid $240 for a certain job, how much did he spend on supplies?

**14.** An inventory clerk is expected to have 2,000 fan belts in stock. If the current count is 1,584 fan belts, how many more should be ordered?

**15.** Shaquita Davis earns \$350 for working 40 hours. How much does she make for each hour of work?

**16.** Wallpaper costs \$12.97 per roll and a kitchen requires 9 rolls. What is the cost of the wallpaper needed to paper the kitchen?

**17.** Bright Ideas purchased 1,000 lightbulbs. Headlight bulbs cost \$13.95 each, and taillight bulbs cost \$7.55 each. If Bright Ideas spent \$9,342 on lightbulb stock, how many headlights and how many taillights did it get? What was the dollar value of the headlights ordered? What was the dollar value of the taillights ordered?

**18.** If 5 dozen roses can be purchased for \$62.50, how much will 8 dozen cost?

**19.** For an installment loan, a formula is used to find the total amount of installment payments. The formula is Total installment payments = installment Price − Down payment. The formula can be written in symbols as $T = P - D$. Find the total installment payments if $P = \$6,508.72$ and $D = \$2,250$.

**20.** In the formula $T = P - D$, $T$ represents total installment payments, $P$ represents installment price, and $D$ represents down payment amount. Find the installment price if the total of installment payments is \$15,892.65 and the down payment is \$3,973.16.

**21.** To find the amount of each installment payment for a loan, use the formula $p = \frac{T}{N}$, where $p$ is the installment payment, $T$ is the total of installment payments, and $N$ is the number of payments. Solve the formula to find the total of installment payments.

**22.** Solve the installment payment formula $p = \frac{T}{N}$ for $N$.

## EXERCISES SET B

*Solve.*

**1.** $3N = 27$

**2.** $\dfrac{A}{2} = 3$

**3.** $N + 8 = 20$

**4.** $3N - 5 = 10$

**5.** $\dfrac{A}{2} - 5 = 1$

**6.** $5A - 45 = 10$

**7.** $7B - 14 = 21$

**8.** $3A = 3$

**9.** $5X - 4 = 11$

**10.** $5(2A - 3) = 15$

**11.** Edna's Book Carousel ordered several cookbooks and received 12. The shipping invoice indicated that 6 books would be shipped later. What was the original number of books ordered?

**12.** The Stork Club is a chain of baby clothing stores. The owner of the chain divided a number of bonnets equally among the 7 stores in the chain. If each store got 9 bonnets, what was the number of bonnets distributed by the owner of the chain?

**13.** Liz Bliss spends 18 hours on a project and estimates that she has completed $\frac{2}{3}$ of the project. How many hours does she expect the project to take?

**14.** A personal computer costs $4,000 and a printer costs $1,500. What is the total cost of the equipment?

**15.** A purse that sells for $68.99 is reduced by $25.50. What is the price of the purse after the reduction?

**16.** Wilson's Auto, Inc., has 37 employees and a weekly payroll of $10,878. If each employee makes the same amount, how much does each make?

**17.** An imprint machine makes 22,764 imprints in 12 hours. How many imprints can be made in 1 hour?

**18.** If a delivery van travels 252 miles on 12 gallons of gasoline, how many gallons are needed to travel 378 miles?

**19.** Financial statements use the formula working Capital = current Assets − current Liabilities. This formula can be written in symbols as $C = A - L$. Find the working capital if current assets are $483,596 and current liabilities are $346,087.

**20.** In the formula $C = A - L$, $C$ represents working capital, $A$ represents current assets, and $L$ represents current liabilities. Find the current assets of Premier Travel Company if working capital is $1,803,516 and current liabilities are $483,948.

**21.** Financial ratios are used to evaluate the performance of a business. One ratio is expressed by the formula Current ratio $= \frac{\text{current Assets}}{\text{current Liabilities}}$. The formula can be written in symbols as $C = \frac{A}{L}$. Solve the formula for $A$.

**22.** Solve the current ratio formula $C = \frac{A}{L}$ for $L$.

# PRACTICE TEST

*Solve.*

**1.** $N + 7 = 18$

**2.** $\dfrac{A}{3} = 6$

**3.** $3A - 5 = 10$

**4.** $2(N + 1) = 14$

**5.** $4A = 48$

**6.** $3R + 5 - R = 7$

**7.** $5N = 45$

**8.** $B - 8 = 7$

**9.** $5A + 8 = 33$

**10.** $5A + A = 30$

**11.** An employee who was earning $249 weekly received a raise of $36. How much is the new salary?

**12.** A container of oil holds 585 gallons. How many containers each holding 4.5 gallons will be needed if all the oil is to be transferred to the smaller containers?

**13.** A discount store sold plastic cups for $3.50 each and ceramic cups for $4 each. If 400 cups were sold for a total of $1,458, how many cups of each type were sold? What was the dollar value of each type of cup sold?

**14.** Find the cost of 200 suits if 75 suits cost $10,200.

**15.** Lashonna Harris is a buyer for Plough. She can purchase 100 pounds of chemicals for $97. At this same rate, how much would 2,000 pounds of the chemical cost?

**16.** From the currency exchange rate table shown in Table 5-2, 1.0000 EUR (Euro) is equivalent to 0.7615 USD (U.S. Dollars). Use a proportion to convert $2,500 to EUR.

**17.** From Table 5-2, 1.0000 USD is equivalent to 0.008626 JPY. Use a proportion to convert 250 USD to the equivalent amount of JPY currency.

## TABLE 5-2
### Currency Exchange Rate Table

| Currency names | United Kingdom Pound (GBP) | Canadian Dollar (CAD) | Euro (EUR) | Japanese Yen (JPY) | US Dollar (USD) | Chinese Yuan Renminbi (CNY) |
|---|---|---|---|---|---|---|
| United Kingdom Pound | 1.0000 | 0.4552 | 0.6774 | 0.004450 | 0.5159 | 0.06569 |
| Canadian Dollar | 2.1957 | 1.0000 | 1.4876 | 0.009773 | 1.1330 | 0.1443 |
| Euro | 1.4756 | 0.6718 | 1.0000 | 0.006569 | 0.7615 | 0.09696 |
| Japanese Yen | 224.610 | 102.249 | 152.196 | 1.0000 | 115.899 | 14.7577 |
| US Dollar | 1.9379 | 0.8822 | 1.3130 | 0.008626 | 1.0000 | 0.1273 |
| Chinese Yuan Renminbi | 15.1806 | 6.9109 | 10.2853 | 0.06757 | 7.8335 | 1.0000 |

Source: Currency Exchange Rates provided by OANDA, the currency site.

**18.** The formula for the installment price of an item purchased with financing is Installment price = Total of installment payments + Down payment. The formula can be written in symbols as $I = T + D$. Find the installment price $I$ if $T = \$24,846.38$ and $D = \$2,500$.

**19.** In the formula $I = T + D$, the letter $I$ represents installment price, $T$ represents total of installment payments, and $D$ represents the amount of down payment. Find the down payment for an installment loan if the installment price is $13,846.76 and the total of installment payments is $10,673.26.

**20.** Rearrange the formula $I = T + D$ to solve for $D$.

1. Give some instances when it would be desirable to have more than one version of a formula. For example,

$$P = R \times B, R = \frac{P}{B}, B = \frac{P}{R}.$$

2. Explain why $1.2 + n = 1.7$ and $1.7 - 1.2 = n$ will give the same result for $n$.

3. Explain why $5n = 4.5$ and $n = \frac{4.5}{5}$ give the same result for $n$.

4. Either of these two formulas, $P = 2l + 2w$ or $P = 2(l + w)$, can be used to find the perimeter of a rectangle. Explain why.

5. Test both of the formulas $P = s + s + s + s$ and $P = 4s$ to see if each formula gives the same perimeter for a square of your choosing. If each formula gives the same result, explain why.

6. Find the mistake in the following problem. Explain the mistake and rework the problem correctly.

$$10 + 7(8 + 4) =$$
$$17(8 + 4) =$$
$$17(12) = 204$$

7. If the wholesale cost of 36 printer cartridges is $188, explain how a proportion can be used to find the cost of one cartridge.

## Challenge Problem

Solve $\frac{5}{8}X + \frac{3}{5} = 8$

## 5.1 Shiver Me Timbers

Cape Fear Riverwood is a lumber company that specializes in recovering, cutting, and selling wood from trees discarded long ago, even those that have been underwater or buried in the ground for more than 100 years! Historically, the logging industry used rafts made of wood to transport cut trees to logging pens along the Cape Fear River in North Carolina. Some of the heavier trees sank during transportation. Other trees were intentionally dumped in the river for disposal after being bled for turpentine. The company used side-scan penetrating radar to find large quantities of logs in 30 locations in and around the river. The first two sites the company salvaged contained heart pine and river pine. A more recent site contained a treasure trove of perfectly preserved 38,000-year-old cypress trees buried 30 feet in a sand pit. Scientists have identified these as trees that became extinct more than 20,000 years ago.

1. The cypress trees are 60 to 80 feet long. If there are 14,285 trees at an average length of 70 feet, how many feet of wood will the company have?

2. If the cypress is worth $80 per foot, what are the 14,285 trees worth?

3. If the cost to recover the 60- to 70-foot cypress trees is $375.00 each and the cost to harvest the larger trees is $500.00, how much would it cost to recover all of the trees if $\frac{2}{5}$ of the trees are more than 70 feet long?

4. Because the harvested lumber depletes the total amount of natural resources available to the citizens of North Carolina, the state of North Carolina places an excise tax of $\frac{1}{20}$ of all profits earned by lumber companies within the state. If the wood is worth approximately $80,000,000 and the only expense of obtaining the wood is the recovery cost, how much excise tax is owed to North Carolina?

## 5.2 Artist's Performance Royalties

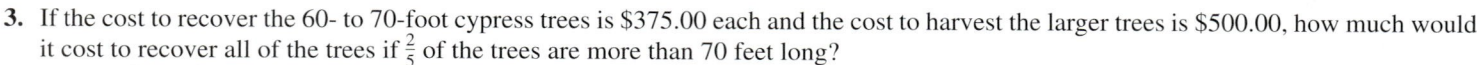

Performance rights organizations track and pay royalties to song writers, publishers, and musicians. Royalties are paid to an artist based on a complicated credit system using a formula with weights assigned for a variety of factors, including the following:

- **Use:** weight based on the type of song or performance (theme, underscore, or promotional).
- **Licensee:** weight based on the station's licensing fee, which is determined by the size of the licensee's markets and number of stations carrying its broadcast signal.
- **Time-of-Day:** weight assigned according to whether the performances are during peak viewing or listening times.
- **Follow-the-Dollar:** factor based on the medium from which the money came (radio play, live performance, TV performance, etc.).
- **General Licensing Allocation:** based on fees collected from bars, hotels, and other non-broadcast licensees.

These amounts are multiplied together, and then a **radio feature premium** is added, if applicable, to arrive at a total number of credits for the particular artist, or his or her **credit total** for a particular reporting period. Royalties are usually split among the writer, the publisher, and possibly a performer if the writer does not perform his or her own work. The proportion that each party receives is called the **share value.** All of the money collected for the reporting period divided by the total number of credits for all performers is called the **credit value.** An artist who wants to figure out what money he or she will receive for a period has to multiply the three factors; credit total, share value, and credit value.

1. Ziam wants to know how much his royalty will be for a song he has written. How will it be calculated? Write the steps or the formulas that will be used to calculate his royalty payment.

Source: Rachel Wimberly, "Shiver Me Timbers," *Wilmington Star-News,* November 2, 2003, p. El.

2. Ziam has written a popular song entitled "Going There," which has been recorded by a well-known performer. He recently received a royalty check for $7,000. If Ziam gets a 0.5 share of the royalties and the credit value is $3.50, what was the credit total that his song earned? Write out the problem in the form of an equation and solve it.

3. Ziam quickly published another song, "Take Me There," that is played even more often than "Going There." If his first song earns 4,000 credits and his second song earns 6,000 credits, what will the royalty payment be from the two songs if the credit value remains at $3.50?

4. Ziam is considering an offer to perform his own songs on a CD to be titled "Waiting There." In the past he has written, but not performed, his music. If Ziam's royalty is 0.12 of the suggested retail price of $15.00, but 0.25 of the retail price is deducted for packaging before Ziam's royalty is calculated, how much will he receive for sale of the CD? Write your answer in the form of an equation and solve it.

# 5.3 Educational Consultant

Jerome Erickson is a retired school district administrator who now works as a consultant specializing in hiring administrators for school districts. Jerome used to charge a flat fee of $5,000 for each administrator hired, but decided to develop a new pricing structure. The new structure is as follows:

| | |
|---|---|
| Due at signing: | $1,500 |
| Contract review: | $125/hr capped at 8 hours |
| Contract formulation: | $125/hr capped at 12 hours |
| Applicant screening: | $25 per applicant |
| Preliminary interviews: | $125 per interview |
| Final interviews: | $175 per interview |

Carol Ferguson is an overworked accounting clerk in a small school district. She sits at her desk, reviewing the pricing structure in the brochure from Erickson Consulting. She knows that Mr. Erickson is one of the most highly regarded educational consultants in the state, but is not sure that the district can afford him. The school board had voted to budget $5,000 for the District Administrator search, based on Carol's recommendation.

1. Write a formula reflecting the pricing structure for Erickson Consulting.

2. Carol presumes that there will be approximately 90 applicants, 10 preliminary interviews, and 3 final interviews. Using her numbers, what is the maximum that the district will have to pay Mr. Erickson?

3. Presuming that Carol is correct about the number of applicants, what are some ways that Carol can reduce her costs? What would you recommend?

4. Why do you think Jerome Erickson changed his pricing structure? What were some of those inherent problems? What are the benefits of the current pricing structure?

Source: http://entertainment.howstuffworks.com/music-royalties.htm

# Percents

# World Series of Poker: Do You Have What It Takes?

In 2006, over 8,000 players participated in World Series of Poker, with an entry fee of $10,000 each and a first prize of $12 million—incredibly high stakes. Texas Hold'em was the name of the game. But does the average player stand a chance? Perhaps, but the probability of winning first place is 0.0001139 or 0.01139%.

Probability is a huge factor in Texas Hold'em. Players use odds or percentages—the focus of this chapter—to determine their actions. The knowledge of poker odds helps them decide on a course of action. Why are poker odds so important? Knowing odds gives players an idea of whether they are in a good or bad situation. Most good players trust the numbers and take the time to learn the odds.

Hand odds are the chances of making a hand in Texas Hold'em poker. Pot odds are calculated as the ratio of the amount of money in the pot to the amount of money it costs to call. Pot odds ratios are useful to see how often you need to win the hand to break even. For instance, if there is $100 in the pot and it takes $10 to call, you must win this hand 1 out of 11 times in order to break even. The rationale is, if you play 11 times, it will cost you $110, but if you win once, you will get $110 ($100 + your $10 call). Sometimes pot odds can be precisely calculated; other times you may have to take your best guess.

Knowing the odds is very helpful, but there are many more aspects of the game you will need to learn if you want to become a winning player.

So whether you play with friends or online, knowledge of percents is essential for knowing your odds. By studying percents in this chapter, who knows—maybe you will discover many ways to use percents.

## LEARNING OUTCOMES

### 6-1  Percent Equivalents
1. Write a whole number, fraction, or decimal as a percent.
2. Write a percent as a whole number, fraction, or decimal.

### 6-2  Solving Percentage Problems
1. Identify the rate, base, and portion in percent problems.
2. Use the percentage formula to find the unknown value when two values are known.

### 6-3  Increases and Decreases
1. Find the amount of increase or decease in percent problems.
2. Find the new amount directly in percent problems.
3. Find the rate or the base in increase or decrease problems.

 A corresponding Business Math Case Video for this chapter, *How Many Hamburgers?* can be found in Appendix A.

## LEARNING OUTCOMES

**1** Write a whole number, fraction, or decimal as a percent.

**2** Write a percent as a whole number, fraction, or decimal.

**Percent:** a standardized way of expressing quantities in relation to a standard unit of 100 (hundredth, per 100, out of 100, over 100).

With fractions and decimals, we compare only like quantities, that is, fractions with common denominators and decimals with the same number of decimal places. We can standardize our representation of quantities so that they can be more easily compared. We standardize by expressing quantities in relation to a standard unit of 100. This relationship, called a **percent**, is used to solve many different types of business problems.

The word *percent* means *hundredths* or *out of 100* or *per 100* or *over 100* (in a fraction). That is, 44 percent means 44 hundredths, or 44 out of 100, or 44 per 100, or 44 over 100. We can write 44 hundredths as 0.44 or $\frac{44}{100}$.

The symbol for *percent* is %. You can write 44 percent using the percent symbol: 44%; using fractional notation: $\frac{44}{100}$; or using decimal notation: 0.44.

$$44\% = 44 \text{ percent} = 44 \text{ hundredths} = \frac{44}{100} = 0.44$$

**Mixed percents:** percents with mixed numbers or mixed decimals.

Percents can contain whole numbers, decimals, fractions, mixed numbers, or mixed decimals. Percents with mixed numbers and mixed decimals are often referred to as **mixed percents**. Examples are $33\frac{1}{3}\%$, $0.05\frac{3}{4}\%$, and $0.23\frac{1}{3}\%$.

## 1 Write a whole number, fraction, or decimal as a percent.

The businessperson must be able to write whole numbers, decimals, or fractions as percents, and to write percents as whole numbers, decimals, or fractions. First we examine writing whole numbers, decimals, and fractions as percents.

Hundredths and percent have the same meaning: per hundred. Just as 100 cents is the same as 1 dollar, 100 percent is the same as 1 whole quantity.

$$100\% = 1$$

This fact is used to write percent equivalents of numbers, and to write numerical equivalents of percents. It is also used to calculate markups, markdowns, discounts, and numerous other business applications.

When we multiply a number by 1, the product has the same value as the original number. $N \times 1 = N$. We have used this concept to change a fraction to an equivalent fraction with a higher denominator. For example,

$$1 = \frac{2}{2} \quad \text{and} \quad \frac{1}{2}\left(\frac{2}{2}\right) = \frac{2}{4}$$

We can also use the fact that $N \times 1 = N$ to change numbers to equivalent percents.

$$1 = 100\% \qquad \frac{1}{2} = \frac{1}{2}(100\%) = \frac{1}{2}\left(\frac{\cancel{100}\%}{1}\right) = 50\%$$

$$0.5 = 0.5(100\%) = 050.\% = 50\%$$

In each case when we multiply by 1 in some form, the value of the product is equivalent to the value of the original number even though the product *looks different*.

---

**HOW TO** **Write a number as its percent equivalent**

Write 0.3 as a percent.

1. Multiply the number by 1 in the form of 100%. ⟶ $0.3 = 0.3(100\%) =$

2. The product has a % symbol. ⟶ $030.\% = 30\%$

---

**EXAMPLE 1**    Write the decimal or whole number as a percent.

(a) 0.27    (b) 0.875    (c) 1.73    (d) 0.004    (e) 2

(a) $0.27 = 0.27(100\%) = 027.\% = 27\%$    Multiply 0.27 by 100% (move the decimal point two places to the right).
**0.27 as a percent is 27%.**

(b) $0.875 = 0.875(100\%) = 087.5\% = 87.5\%$    Multiply 0.875 by 100% (move the decimal point two places to the right).
**0.875 as a percent is 87.5%.**

(c) $1.73 = 1.73(100\%) = 173.\% = 173\%$    Multiply 1.73 by 100% (move the decimal point two places to the right).
**1.73 as a percent is 173%.**

(d) $0.004 = 0.004(100\%) = 000.4\% = 0.4\%$    Multiply 0.004 by 100% (move the decimal point two places to the right).
**0.004 as a percent is 0.4%**

(e) $2 = 2(100\%) = 200.\% = 200\%$    Multiply 2 by 100% (move the decimal point two places to the right).
**2 as a percent is 200%.**

As you can see, the procedure is the same regardless of the number of decimal places in the number and regardless of whether the number is greater than, equal to, or less than 1.

**EXAMPLE 2**    Write the fraction as a percent.

(a) $\frac{67}{100}$    (b) $\frac{1}{4}$    (c) $3\frac{1}{2}$    (d) $\frac{7}{4}$    (e) $\frac{2}{3}$

(a) $\frac{67}{100} = \frac{67}{100}\left(\frac{100\%}{1}\right) = 67\%$    Reduce and multiply.

(b) $\frac{1}{4} = \frac{1}{4}\left(\frac{100\%}{1}\right) = 25\%$    Reduce and multiply.

(c) $3\frac{1}{2} = 3\frac{1}{2}\left(\frac{100\%}{1}\right) = \frac{7}{2}\left(\frac{100\%}{1}\right) = 350\%$    Change to an improper fraction, reduce, and multiply.

(d) $\frac{7}{4} = \frac{7}{4}\left(\frac{100\%}{1}\right) = 175\%$    Reduce and multiply.

(e) $\frac{2}{3} = \frac{2}{3}\left(\frac{100\%}{1}\right) = \frac{200\%}{3} = 66\frac{2}{3}\%$    Multiply.

✔ **STOP AND CHECK**

*Write the decimal or whole number as a percent.*

**1.** 0.82      **2.** 3.45      **3.** 0.0007      **4.** 5

*Write the fraction or mixed number as a percent.*

**5.** $\frac{43}{100}$      **6.** $\frac{3}{10}$      **7.** $8\frac{1}{4}$      **8.** $\frac{1}{6}$

## 2   Write a percent as a whole number, fraction, or decimal.

When a number is divided by 1, the quotient has the same value as the original number. $N \div 1 = N$ or $\frac{N}{1} = N$. We have used this concept to reduce fractions. For example,

$$1 = \frac{2}{2} \qquad \frac{2}{4} \div \frac{2}{2} = \frac{1}{2}$$

We can also use the fact that $N \div 1 = N$ or $\frac{N}{1} = N$ to change percents to numerical equivalents.

$$50\% \div 100\% = \frac{50\%}{100\%} = \frac{50}{100} = \frac{1}{2}$$
$$50\% \div 100\% = 50 \div 100 = 0.50 = 0.5$$

---

**HOW TO**    **Write a percent as a number**

1. Divide the number by 1 in the form of $100\%$ or multiply by $\frac{1}{100\%}$.
2. The quotient does not have a % symbol.

---

**EXAMPLE 1**    Write the percent as a decimal.

(a) 37%    (b) 26.5%    (c) 127%    (d) 7%    (e) 0.9%    (f) $2\frac{19}{20}\%$    (g) $167\frac{1}{3}\%$

(a) $37\% = 37\% \div 100\% = 0.37 = \mathbf{0.37}$    Divide by 100 mentally.
(b) $26.5\% = 26.5\% \div 100\% = 0.265 = \mathbf{0.265}$    Divide by 100 mentally.
(c) $127\% = 127\% \div 100\% = 1.27 = \mathbf{1.27}$    Divide by 100 mentally.
(d) $7\% = 7\% \div 100\% = 0.07 = \mathbf{0.07}$    Divide by 100 mentally.
(e) $0.9\% = 0.9\% \div 100\% = 0.009 = \mathbf{0.009}$    Divide by 100 mentally.

(f) $2\frac{19}{20}\% = 2.95\% \div 100\% = 0.0295 = \mathbf{0.0295}$    Write the mixed number in front of the percent symbol as a mixed decimal before dividing by 100%.

(g) $167\frac{1}{3}\% = 167.3\overline{3}\% \div 100\%$    Write the mixed number in front of the percent symbol as a repeating decimal before dividing by 100.

$\quad = 1.673\overline{3} = \mathbf{1.673\overline{3}}$ **or 1.673 (rounded)**

---

**TIP**

**What Happens to the % (Percent) Sign?**

In multiplying fractions we reduce or cancel common factors from a numerator to a denominator. Percent signs and other types of labels also cancel.

$$\frac{\%}{\%} = 1$$

---

**EXAMPLE 2**    Write the percent as a fraction or mixed number.

(a) 65%    (b) $\frac{1}{4}\%$    (c) 250%    (d) $83\frac{1}{3}\%$    (e) 12.5%

(a) $65\% = 65\% \div 100\% = \frac{65\%}{1}\left(\frac{1}{100\%}\right) = \frac{\mathbf{13}}{\mathbf{20}}$    Convert division to multiplication.

(b) $\frac{1}{4}\% = \frac{1}{4}\% \div 100\% = \frac{1\%}{4}\left(\frac{1}{100\%}\right) = \frac{\mathbf{1}}{\mathbf{400}}$

(c) $250\% = 250\% \div 100\% = \frac{250\%}{1}\left(\frac{1}{100\%}\right) = \frac{5}{2} = \mathbf{2\frac{1}{2}}$

$$\text{(d)} \quad 83\frac{1}{3}\% = 83\frac{1}{3}\% \div 100\% = \frac{250\%}{3}\left(\frac{1}{100\%}\right) = \frac{5}{6}$$

Convert to improper fraction.

$$\text{(e)} \quad 12.5\% = 12\frac{1}{2}\% = 12\frac{1}{2}\% \div 100\% = \frac{25\%}{2}\left(\frac{1}{100\%}\right) = \frac{1}{8}$$

Convert mixed decimal to mixed number.

 ## STOP AND CHECK

*Write the percent as a decimal.*

**1.** 52%          **2.** 38.5%          **3.** 143%          **4.** 0.72%

*Write the percent as a fraction or mixed number.*

**5.** 72%          **6.** $\frac{1}{8}\%$          **7.** 325%          **8.** $16\frac{2}{3}\%$

## 6-1 SECTION EXERCISES

### SKILL BUILDERS

*Write the decimal as a percent.*

**1.** 0.39          **2.** 0.693          **3.** 0.75

**4.** 0.2          **5.** 2.92          **6.** 0.0007

*Write the fraction and mixed number as a percent.*

**7.** $\frac{39}{100}$          **8.** $\frac{3}{4}$          **9.** $3\frac{2}{5}$

**10.** $5\frac{1}{4}$          **11.** $\frac{9}{4}$          **12.** $\frac{7}{5}$

**13.** $\frac{2}{300}$          **14.** $\frac{3}{8}$          **15.** $\frac{4}{5}$

*Write the percent as a decimal. Round to the nearest thousandth if the division does not terminate.*

**16.** $15\frac{1}{2}\%$

**17.** $\frac{1}{8}\%$

**18.** $45\%$

**19.** $150\%$

**20.** $125\frac{1}{3}\%$

**21.** $\frac{3}{7}\%$

*Write the percent as a fraction or mixed number.*

**22.** $45\%$

**23.** $60\%$

**24.** $250\%$

**25.** $180\%$

**26.** $\frac{3}{4}\%$

**27.** $33\frac{1}{3}\%$

## 6-2 SOLVING PERCENTAGE PROBLEMS

### LEARNING OUTCOMES

1 Identify the rate, base, and portion in percent problems.
2 Use the percentage formula to find the unknown value when two values are known.

**Formula:** a relationship among quantities expressed in words or numbers and letters.

**Base:** the original number or one entire quantity.

**Percentage:** a part or portion of the base.

**Portion:** another term for percentage.

**Rate:** the relationship of the base and portion expressed as a percent.

### 1 Identify the rate, base, and portion in percent problems.

A **formula** expresses a relationship among quantities. When you use the five-step problem-solving approach, the third step, the Solution Plan, is often a formula written in words and letters.

The percentage formula, <u>P</u>ercentage = <u>R</u>ate × <u>B</u>ase, can be written as $P = RB$. The letters or words represent numbers.

In the formula $P = RB$, the **base** ($B$) represents the original number or one entire quantity. The **percentage** ($P$) represents a **portion** of the base. The **rate** ($R$) is a percent that tells us how the base and portion are related. In the statement "50 is 20% of 250," 250 is the base (the entire quantity), 50 is the portion (part), and 20% is the rate (percent).

**EXAMPLE 1**    Identify the given and missing elements for each example.

(a) 20% of 75 is what number?
(b) What percent of 50 is 30?
(c) Eight is 10% of what number?

     $R$    $B$      $P$
(a) 20% of 75 is what number?
     Percent Total    Part

       $R$        $B$   $P$
(b) What percent of 50 is 30?
       Percent Total Part

  $P$     $R$          $B$
(c) Eight is 10% of what number?
  Part Percent       Total

Use the identifying key words for rate (*percent* or %), base (*total*, *original*, associated with the word *of*), and portion (*part*, associated with the word *is*).

## 2   Use the percentage formula to find the unknown value when two values are known.

The percentage formula, Percentage = Rate × Base, can be written as $P = RB$. Another word for percentage is portion. When the numbers are put in place of the letters, the formula guides you through the calculations.

The three percentage formulas are

Portion = Rate × Base     $P = RB$     For finding the percentage or portion.

$$\text{Base} = \frac{\text{Portion}}{\text{Rate}} \qquad B = \frac{P}{R} \qquad \text{For finding the base.}$$

$$\text{Rate} = \frac{\text{Portion}}{\text{Base}} \qquad R = \frac{P}{B} \qquad \text{For finding the rate.}$$

Circles can help us visualize these formulas. The shaded part of the circle in Figure 6-1 represents the missing amount. The unshaded parts represent the known amounts. If the unshaded parts

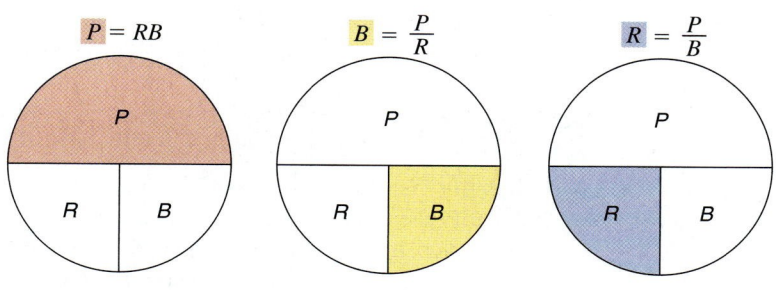

**FIGURE 6-1**
Forms of the Portion (Percentage) Formula

are *side by side, multiply* their corresponding numbers to find the unknown number. If the unshaded parts are *one on top of the other, divide* the corresponding numbers to find the unknown number.

**HOW TO** Use the percentage (portion) formula to solve percentage problems

1. Identify and classify the two known values and the one unknown value.
2. Choose the appropriate portion (percentage) formula for finding the unknown value.
3. Substitute the known values into the formula. For the rate, use the decimal or fractional equivalent of the percent.
4. Perform the calculation indicated by the formula.
5. Interpret the result. If finding the rate, convert decimal or fractional equivalents of the rate to a percent.

**EXAMPLE 1** Solve the problems.

(a) 20% of 400 is what number?
(b) 20% of what number is 80?
(c) 80 is what percent of 400?

(a) 20% = Rate  Identify known values and unknown value.
400 = Base
Portion is unknown
$P = RB$  Choose the appropriate formula.
$P = 0.2(400)$  Substitute values using the decimal equivalent of 20%.
$P = \mathbf{80}$  Perform calculation.
**20% of 400 is 80.**  Interpret result.

(b) 20% = Rate  Identify known values and unknown value.
80 = Portion
Base is unknown
$B = \dfrac{P}{R}$  Choose the appropriate formula.
$B = \dfrac{80}{0.2}$  Substitute values. Perform calculation.
$B = \mathbf{400}$
**20% of 400 is 80.**  Interpret result.

(c) 80 = Portion  Identify known values and unknown value.
400 = Base
Rate is unknown
$R = \dfrac{P}{B}$  Choose the appropriate formula.
$R = \dfrac{80}{400}$  Substitute values. Perform calculation.
$R = 0.2$ or **20%**
**80 is 20% of 400.**  Interpret result. $0.2 = 20\%$.

Very few percentage problems that you encounter in business tell you the values of *P*, *R*, and *B* directly. Percentage problems are usually written in words that must be interpreted before you can tell which form of the percentage formula you should use.

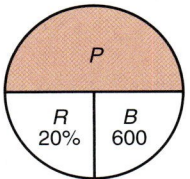

FIGURE 6-2

## EXAMPLE 2

During a special one-day sale, 600 customers bought the on-sale pizza. Of these customers, 20% used coupons. The manager will run the sale again the next day if more than 100 coupons were used. Should she run the sale again?

| What You Know | What You Are Looking For | Solution Plan |
|---|---|---|
| Total customers: 600 <br><br> Coupon-using customers as a percent of total customers: 20% | Quantity of coupon-using customers <br><br> Should the manager run the sale again? | The quantity of coupon-using customers is a *portion* of the *base* of total customers, at a *rate* of 20% (Figure 6-2). <br><br> $P = RB$ <br><br> Quantity of coupon-using customers $= RB$ |

### Solution

| | |
|---|---|
| $P = RB$ | $P$ is unknown; $R = 20\%$; $B = 600$ |
| $P = 20\%(600)$ | Substitute known values. Change % to decimal equivalent. |
| $P = 0.2(600)$ | Multiply. |
| $P = 120$ | |

### Conclusion

**The quantity of coupon-using customers is 120.**
**Since 120 is more than 100, the manager should run the sale again.**

## EXAMPLE 3

If $66\frac{2}{3}\%$ of the 900 employees in a company choose the Preferred Provider insurance plan, how many people from that company are enrolled in the plan?

First, identify the terms. The rate is the percent, and the base is the total number of employees. The portion is the quantity of employees enrolled in the plan.

| | |
|---|---|
| $P = RB$ | The portion is the unknown. |
| $P = 66\frac{2}{3}\%(900)$ | The rate is $66\frac{2}{3}\%$; the base is 900. Write $66\frac{2}{3}\%$ as a fraction. |
| $P = \frac{2}{3}\left(\frac{900}{1}\right) = 600$ | Multiply. |

**The Preferred Provider plan has 600 people enrolled.**

### TIP

**Continuous Sequence Versus Noncontinuous Sequence**

We can write the fractional equivalent of the percent as a rounded decimal and divide using a calculator.

$\boxed{AC}$ 2 $\boxed{÷}$ 3 $\boxed{=}$ $\Rightarrow$ 0.6666666667
$\boxed{AC}$ 900 $\boxed{×}$ .6666666667 $\boxed{=}$ $\Rightarrow$ 599.9999994

As one continuous sequence, enter

$\boxed{AC}$ 2 $\boxed{÷}$ 3 $\boxed{×}$ 900 $\boxed{=}$ $\Rightarrow$ 600

Note slight discrepancies due to rounding. However, the answer obtained by using a continuous sequence of steps is more accurate.

## EXAMPLE 4

Stan sets aside 15% of his weekly income for rent. If he sets aside $75 each week, what is his weekly income?

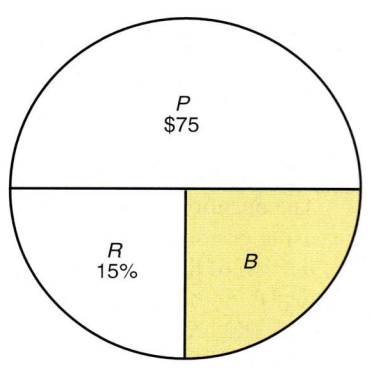

Identify the terms: The rate is the number written as a percent, 15%. The portion is given, $75; it is a portion of his weekly income, the unknown base.

$$B = \frac{P}{R}$$     The rate is 15% and the portion is $75 (Figure 6-3). The base is the weekly income to be found.

$$B = \frac{\$75}{15\%}$$     Convert 15% to a decimal equivalent.

$$B = \frac{75}{0.15}$$     Divide.

$$B = \$500$$

**Stan's weekly income is $500.**

**FIGURE 6-3**

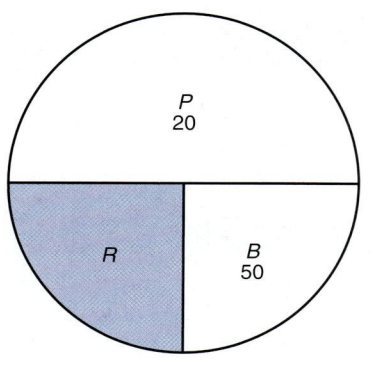

## EXAMPLE 5

If 20 cars were sold from a lot that had 50 cars, what percent of the cars were sold?

$$R = \frac{P}{B}$$     The portion is 20; the base is 50 (Figure 6-4). The rate is the unknown to find.

$$R = \frac{20}{50}$$     Divide.

$$R = 0.4$$     Convert to % equivalent.

$$R = 0.4(100\%)$$

$$R = 40\%$$

**Of the cars on the lot, 40% were sold.**

**FIGURE 6-4**

Many students mistakenly think that the portion can never be larger than the base. The portion (percentage) is smaller than the base only when the rate is less than 100%. The portion is larger than the base when the rate is larger than 100%.

## EXAMPLE 6

48 is what percent of 24?

$$R = \frac{P}{B}$$     The rate is unknown. The percentage is 48. The base is 24.

$$R = \frac{48}{24}$$     Divide.

$$R = 2$$     Rate written as a whole number.

$$\boldsymbol{R = 200\%}$$     Rate written as a percent.

## STOP AND CHECK

1. 15% of 200 is what number?

2. 25% of what number is 120?

3. 150 is what percent of 750?

4. Find $12\frac{1}{2}\%$ of 64.

5. Seventy-five percent of students in a class of 40 passed the first test. How many passed?

6. What percent of 500 is 150?

## 6-2 SECTION EXERCISES

### SKILL BUILDERS

*Identify the rate, base, and portion.*

1. 48% of 12 is what number?

2. 32% of what number is 28?

3. What percent of 158 is 47.4?

**4.** What number is 130% of 149?

**5.** 15% of what number is 80?

**6.** 48% of what number is 120?

*Use the appropriate form of the percentage formula. Round division to the nearest hundredth if necessary.*

**7.** Find $P$ if $R = 25\%$ and $B = 300$.

**8.** Find 40% of 160.

**9.** What number is $33\frac{1}{3}\%$ of 150?

**10.** What number is 154% of 30?

**11.** Find $B$ if $P = 36$ and $R = 66\frac{2}{3}\%$

**12.** Find $R$ if $P = 70$ and $B = 280$.

**13.** 40% of 30 is what number?

**14.** 52% of 17.8 is what number?

**15.** 30% of what number is 21?

**16.** 17.5% of what number is 18? Round to hundredths.

**17.** What percent of 16 is 4?

**18.** What percent of 50 is 30?

**19.** 172% of 50 is what number?

**20.** 0.8% of 50 is what number?

**21.** What percent of 15.2 is 12.7? Round to the nearest hundredth of a percent.

**22.** What percent of 73 is 120? Round to the nearest hundredth of a percent.

**23.** 0.28% of what number is 12? Round to the nearest hundredth.

**24.** 1.5% of what number is 20? Round to the nearest hundredth.

## APPLICATIONS

**25.** At the Evans Formal Wear department store, all suits are reduced 20% from the retail price. If Charles Stewart purchased a suit that originally retailed for $258.30, how much did he save?

**26.** Joe Passarelli earns $8.67 per hour working for Dracken International. If Joe earns a merit raise of 12%, how much was his raise?

**27.** An ice cream truck began its daily route with 95 gallons of ice cream. The truck driver sold 78% of the ice cream. How many gallons of ice cream were sold?

**28.** Stacy Bauer sold 80% of the tie-dyed T-shirts she took to the Green Valley Music Festival. If she sold 42 shirts, how many shirts did she take?

**29.** A stockholder sold her shares and made a profit of $1,466. If this is a profit of 23%, how much were the shares worth when she originally purchased them?

**30.** The Drammelonnie Department Store sold 30% of its shirts in stock. If the department store sold 267 shirts, how many shirts did the store have in stock?

**31.** Ali gave correct answers to 23 of the 25 questions on the driving test. What percent of the questions did he get correct?

**32.** A soccer stadium in Manchester, England, has a capacity of 78,753 seats. If 67,388 seats were filled, what percent of the stadium seats were vacant? Round to the nearest hundredth of a percent.

**33.** Holly Hobbs purchased a magazine at the Atlanta airport for $2.99. The tax on the purchase was $0.18. What is the tax rate at the Atlanta airport? Round to the nearest percent.

**34.** A receipt from Wal-Mart in Memphis showed $4.69 tax on a subtotal of $53.63. What is the tax rate? Round to the nearest tenth percent.

## 6-3 INCREASES AND DECREASES

### LEARNING OUTCOMES

1 Find the amount of increase or decrease in percent problems.
2 Find the new amount directly in percent problems.
3 Find the rate or the base in increase or decrease problems.

**New amount:** the ending amount after an amount has changed (increased or decreased).

In many business applications an original amount is increased or decreased to give a **new amount**. Some examples of increases are the sales tax on a purchase, the raise in a salary, and the markup on a wholesale price. Some examples of decreases are the deductions on your paycheck and the markdown or the discount on an item for sale.

### 1 Find the amount of increase or decrease in percent problems.

The amount of increase or decrease is the amount that an original number changes. Subtraction is used to find the amount of change when the beginning and ending (or new) amounts are known.

| HOW TO | Find the amount of increase or decrease from the beginning and ending amounts |
|---|---|

1. To find the amount of increase:

   Amount of increase = new amount − beginning amount

2. To find the amount of decrease:

   Amount of decrease = beginning amount − new amount

## EXAMPLE 1

David Spear's salary increased from $58,240 to $63,190. What is the amount of increase?

Beginning amount = $58,240
New amount = $63,190
Increase = new amount − beginning amount
= $63,190 − $58,240
= $4,950

**David's salary increase was $4,950.**

## EXAMPLE 2

A coat was marked down from $98 to $79. What is the amount of markdown?

Beginning amount = $98
New amount = $79
Decrease = beginning amount − new amount
= $98 − $79
= $19

**The coat was marked down $19.**

**Percent of change:** the percent by which a beginning amount has changed (increased or decreased).

A change is often expressed as a **percent of change.** The amount of change is a percent of the original or beginning amount.

---

**HOW TO**    **Find the amount of change (increase or decrease) from a percent of change**

1. Identify the original or beginning amount and the percent or rate of change.
2. Multiply the decimal or fractional equivalent of the rate of change times the original or beginning amount.

Amount of change = percent of change × original amount

---

## EXAMPLE 3

Your company has announced that you will receive a 3.2% raise. If your current salary is $42,560, how much will your raise be?

| What You Know | What You Are Looking For |
|---|---|
| Current salary = $42,560<br>Rate of change = 3.2% | Amount of raise |

| Solution Plan |
|---|
| $\text{Amount of raise} = \left(\begin{array}{c}\text{percent of}\\\text{change}\end{array}\right)\left(\begin{array}{c}\text{original}\\\text{amount}\end{array}\right)$ |

**Solution**

Amount of raise = percent of change × original amount
= 3.2%($42,560)
= 0.032($42,560)          Multiply.
= $1,361.92

**Conclusion**

**The raise will be $1,361.92.**

1. The price of a new Lexus is $53,444. The previous year's model cost $51,989. What is the amount of increase?

2. In trading on the New York Stock Exchange, Bank of America fell to $73.57. The stock had sold for $81.99. What is the amount of decrease in the stock price per share?

3. Marilyn Bauer earns $62,870 and gets a 4.3% raise. How much is her raise?

4. International Paper reported third-quarter earnings were down 16% from $145 million. What was the amount of decrease?

5. Zack weighed 230 pounds before experiencing a 12% weight loss. How many pounds did he lose?

6. The number of active registered nurses is currently 2,249,000. A 20.3% increase by 2020 will be needed. How many nurses will need to be added to the existing workforce?

## 2 Find the new amount directly in percent problems.

Often in increase or decrease problems we are more interested in the new amount than the amount of change. We can find the new amount directly by adding or subtracting percents first. The original or beginning amount is always considered to be our *base* and is represented by 100%.

---

**HOW TO** Find the new amount directly in a percent problem

1. Find the rate of the new amount.

For increase: 100% + rate of increase
For decrease: 100% − rate of decrease

2. Find the new amount.

$$P = RB$$

New amount = rate of new amount × original amount

---

**EXAMPLE 1** Medical assistants are to receive a 9% increase in wages per hour. If they were making $15.25 an hour, what is the *new wage per hour* to the nearest cent?

Rate of new amount = 100% + rate of increase
= 100% + 9%
= 109%

New amount = rate of new amount × original amount
= 109%($15.25)　　　Change % to its decimal equivalent.
= 1.09(15.25)　　　　Multiply.
= $16.6225　　　　　New amount
= $16.62　　　　　　Nearest cent

**The new hourly wage is $16.62.**

---

**EXAMPLE 2** A pair of jeans that cost $49.99 is advertised as 70% off. What is the sale price of the jeans?

Rate of new amount = 100% − rate of decrease
= 100% − 70%
= 30%

New amount = rate of new amount × original amount
= 30%($49.99)　　　Change % to its decimal equivalent.
= 0.3(49.99)　　　　Multiply.
= $14.997　　　　　New amount
= $15.00　　　　　Nearest cent

1. Marilyn Bauer earns $62,870 and gets a 4.3% raise. How much is her new salary?

2. International Paper reported third-quarter earnings were down 16% from $145 million. Find the third-quarter earnings.

3. Zack weighed 230 pounds before experiencing a 12% weight loss. How many pounds does he now weigh?

4. Over the next ten years Stacy Bauer plans to increase her investment of $9,500 by 250%. How much will she have invested altogether?

5. Shares of McDonald's, the world's largest hamburger restaurant chain, rose 51% this year. Find the new share price if the stock sold for $24.25 last year.

6. The number of registered nurses is currently 2,249,000. If a 20.3% increase in this number is projected for 2020, how many nurses will be needed in 2020?

## 3 Find the rate or the base in increase or decrease problems.

Many kinds of increase or decrease problems involve finding either the rate or the base.

The rate is the *percent of change* or the *percent of increase or decrease.* The base is still the *original amount.*

---

**HOW TO**    Find the rate or the base in increase or decrease problems

1. Identify or find the amount of increase or decrease.
2. To find the rate of increase or decrease, use the percentage formula $R = \dfrac{P}{B}$.

$$R = \frac{\text{amount of change}}{\text{original amount}}$$

3. To find the base or original amount, use the percentage formula $B = \dfrac{P}{R}$.

$$B = \frac{\text{amount of change}}{\text{rate of change}}$$

---

**EXAMPLE 1**    During the month of May, a graphic artist made a profit of $1,525. In June she made a profit of $1,708. What is the percent of increase in profit?

| What You Know | What You Are Looking For |
|---|---|
| Original amount = $1,525<br>New amount = $1,708 | Percent of increase |

| Solution Plan |
|---|
| Amount of increase = new amount − original amount<br>Percent of increase = $\dfrac{\text{amount of increase}}{\text{original amount}}$ |

| | | |
|---|---|---|
| Amount of increase | $= \$1,708 - \$1,525$ | Subtract. |
| | $= \$183$ | |
| Percent of increase | $= \dfrac{\$183}{\$1,525}$ | Divide. |
| | $= 0.12$ | Convert to % equivalent. |
| | $= 0.12(100\%)$ | |
| | $= 12\%$ | |

**Conclusion**

**The percent of increase in profit is 12%.**

In some cases you may not have enough information to determine the amount of increase or decrease. Then we must match the rate with the information we are given.

## EXAMPLE 2
At Best Buy the price of a DVD player dropped by 20% to $179. What was the original price to the nearest dollar?

| What You Know | What You Are Looking For |
|---|---|
| Reduced price = new amount = $179<br>Rate of decrease = 20% | Original price |

**Solution Plan**

Rate of reduced price $= 100\% - $ rate of decrease

$$B = \dfrac{P}{R}$$

Original price $= \dfrac{\text{reduced price}}{\text{rate of reduced price}}$

**Solution**

| | | |
|---|---|---|
| Rate of reduced price | $= 100\% - 20\%$ | |
| | $= 80\%$ | |
| Original price | $= \dfrac{\$179}{80\%}$ | Convert % to decimal equivalent. |
| | $= \dfrac{179}{0.8}$ | Divide. |
| | $= \$223.75$ | Round to nearest dollar. |
| | $= \$224$ | |

**Conclusion**

**The original price of the DVD player was $224.**

---

## TIP

**Be Sure to Use the Correct Rate**

When using the percentage formula, the description for the rate must match the description of the portion.

| | Example 2 above<br>DVD Problem | Example 2 on p. 194<br>Jeans Problem |
|---|---|---|
| Form of percentage formula | $B = \dfrac{P}{R}$ | $P = RB$ |
| Description of rate | Rate of *reduced price* | Rate of *new amount* |
| Description of portion | *Reduced price* | *New amount* |

# STOP AND CHECK

1. Emily Sien reported sales of $23,583,000 for the third quarter and $38,792,000 for the fourth quarter. What is the percent of increase in profit? Round to the nearest tenth of a percent.

2. Ken Sien reduced his college spending from $9,524 in the fall semester to $8,756 in the spring semester. What percent was the decrease? Round to the nearest percent.

3. Sydney Sien showed a house that was advertised as a 10% decrease on the original price. The sale price is $148,500. What was the original price?

4. You know that a DVD is reduced 25% and the amount of reduction is $6.25. Find the original price and the discounted price of the movie.

5. A used truck is reduced by 48% of its new price. You know the used price is $14,799. Find the new price to the nearest dollar.

6. The average NFL ticket price was $62.38 for 2006 and for 2005 it was $58.95. What was the percent increase in ticket price? Round to the nearest tenth percent.

# 6-3 SECTION EXERCISES

## SKILL BUILDERS

1. A number increased from 5,286 to 7,595. Find the amount of increase.

2. A number decreased from 486 to 104. Find the amount of decrease.

3. Find the amount of increase if 432 is increased by 25%.

4. Find the amount of decrease if 68 is decreased by 15%.

5. If 135 is decreased by 75%, what is the new amount?

6. If 78 is increased by 40%, what is the new amount?

7. A number increased from 224 to 336. Find the percent of increase.

8. A number decreased from 250 to 195. Find the rate of decrease.

9. A number is decreased by 40% to 525. What is the original amount?

10. A number is increased by 15% to 43.7. Find the original amount.

## APPLICATIONS

**11.** The cost of a pound of nails increased from $2.36 to $2.53. What is the percent of increase to the nearest whole-number percent?

**12.** Wrigley announced the first increase in 16 years in the price of a five-stick pack of gum. The price was raised by 5 cents to 30 cents. Find the percent of increase. Round to the nearest percent.

**13.** Bret Davis is getting a 4.5% raise. His current salary is $38,950. How much will his raise be?

**14.** Kewanna Johns plans to lose 12% of her weight in the next 12 weeks. She currently weighs 218 pounds. How much does she expect to lose?

**15.** DeMarco Jones makes $13.95 per hour but is getting a 5.5% increase. What is his new wage per hour to the nearest cent?

**16.** Carol Wynne bought a silver tray that originally cost $195 and was advertised at 65% off. What was the sale price of the tray?

**17.** A laptop computer that was originally priced at $2,400 now sells for $2,700. What is the percent of increase?

**18.** Federated Department Stores dropped the price of a winter coat by 15% to $149. What was the original price to the nearest cent?

## Learning Outcomes

## What to Remember with Examples

### Section 6-1

**1** Write a whole number, fraction, or decimal as a percent. (p. 182)

1. Multiply the number by 1 in the form of 100%.
2. The product has a % symbol.

$$6 = 6(100\%) = 600\%$$

$$\frac{3}{5} = \frac{3}{5}\left(\frac{100}{1}\%\right) = 60\%$$

$$0.075 = 0.075(100\%) = 7.5\%$$

**2** Write a percent as a whole number, fraction, or decimal. (p. 184)

1. Divide by 1 in the form of 100% or multiply by $\frac{1}{100\%}$.
2. The quotient does not have a % symbol.

$$48\% = 48\% \div 100\% = 0.48$$

$$20\% = 20\% \div 100\% = \frac{20}{100} = \frac{1}{5}$$

$$157\% = 157\% \div 100\% = 1.57$$

$$33\frac{1}{3}\% = 33\frac{1}{3}\% \div 100\% = 0.33\frac{1}{3} \text{ or } 0.3\overline{3}$$

### Section 6-2

**1** Identify the rate, base, and portion in percent problems. (p. 186)

1. *Rate* is usually written as a percent, but may be a decimal or fraction.
2. *Base* is the total or original amount.
3. *Portion* is the part, or amount of increase or decrease. It is also called the *percentage*.

Identify the rate, base, and portion.
42% of 18 is what number?
42% is the rate.
18 is the base.
The missing number is the portion.

**2** Use the percentage formula to find the unknown value when two values are known. (p. 187)

1. Identify and classify the two known values and the one missing value.
2. Choose the appropriate percentage formula for finding the missing value.
3. Substitute the known values into the formula. For the rate, use the decimal or fractional equivalent of the percent.
4. Perform the calculation indicated by the formula.
5. Interpret the result. If finding the rate, convert decimal or fractional equivalents of the rate to a percent.

Find *P* if $B = 20$ and $R = 15\%$.

$$P = RB$$

$$P = 15\%(20) = 0.15(20)$$

$$P = 3$$

Find *B* if $P = 36$ and $R = 9\%$.

$$B = \frac{P}{R}$$

$$B = \frac{36}{9\%} = \frac{36}{0.09}$$

$$B = 400$$

**1** Find the amount of increase or decrease in percent problems. (p. 192)

1. To find the amount of increase:

   Amount of increase = new amount − beginning amount

2. To find the amount of decrease:

   Amount of decrease = beginning amount − new amount.

A truck odometer increased from 37,580.3 to 42,719.6. What was the increase?

$42,719.6 - 37,580.3 = 5,139.3$

A truck carrying 62,980 pounds of food delivered 36,520 pounds. What was the amount of food (in pounds) remaining on the truck?

$62,980 - 36,520 = 26,460$ pounds

**2** Find the new amount directly in percent problems. (p. 194)

1. Find the rate of the new amount.

   For increase: 100% + rate of increase

   For decrease: 100% − rate of decrease

2. Find the new amount.

   $P = RB$

   New amount = rate of new amount × original amount

Emily Denly works 30 hours a week but plans to increase her work hours by 20%. How many hours will she be working after the increase?

For increase: 100% + 20% = 120%
$P = RB$
$P = 120\%(30 \text{ hours})$
$\quad = 1.20(30)$
$\quad = 36 \text{ hours}$

**3** Find the rate or the base in increase or decrease problems. (p. 195)

1. Identify or find the amount of increase or decrease.
2. To find the rate of increase or decrease, use the percentage formula $R = \dfrac{P}{B}$.

   $R = \dfrac{\text{amount of change}}{\text{original amount}}$

3. To find the base or original amount, use the percentage formula $B = \dfrac{P}{R}$.

   $B = \dfrac{\text{amount of change}}{\text{rate of change}}$

Tancia Brown made a profit of $5,896 in June and a profit of $6,265 in July. What is the percent of increase? Round to tenths of a percent.

$$\text{Amount of increase} = \$6,265 - \$5,896 = \$369$$
$$R = \frac{\text{amount of change}}{\text{original amount}}$$
$$= \frac{\$369}{\$5,896}$$
$$= 0.06258(100\%)$$
$$= 6.3\% \text{ (rounded)}$$

# EXERCISES SET A

*Write the decimal as a percent.*

**1.** 0.23

**2.** 0.82

**3.** 0.03

**4.** 0.34

**5.** 0.601

**6.** 1

**7.** 3

**8.** 0.37

**9.** 0.2

**10.** 4

*Write the fraction or mixed number as a percent. Round to the nearest hundredth of a percent if necessary.*

**11.** $\dfrac{17}{100}$

**12.** $\dfrac{6}{100}$

**13.** $\dfrac{52}{100}$

**14.** $\dfrac{1}{10}$

**15.** $\dfrac{5}{4}$

**16.** $2\dfrac{3}{5}$

*Write the percent as a decimal.*

**17.** 0.25%

**18.** 98%

**19.** 256%

**20.** 91.7%

**21.** 0.5%

**22.** 6%

*Write the percent as a whole number, mixed number, or fraction, reduced to lowest terms.*

**23.** 10%

**24.** 6%

**25.** 89%

**26.** 45%

**27.** 225%

| Percent | Fraction | Decimal |
|---|---|---|
| **28.** $33\dfrac{1}{3}\%$ | _____ | _____ |
| **29.** _____ | _____ | 0.125 |
| **30.** _____ | _____ | 0.8 |

*Find P, R, or B using the percentage formula or one of its forms. Round decimals to the nearest hundredth and percents to the nearest whole number percent.*

**31.** $B = 300$,   $R = 27\%$

**32.** $P = 25$,   $B = 100$

**33.** $P = \$600$,   $R = 5\%$

**34.** $P = \$835$,   $R = 3.2\%$

**35.** $P = 125$,   $B = 50$

**36.** Find 30% of 80.

**37.** 90% of what number is 27?

**38.** 51.52 is what percent of 2,576?

**39.** Jaime McMahan received a 7% pay increase. If he was earning $2,418 per month, what was the amount of the pay increase?

**40.** Eighty percent of one store's customers paid with credit cards. Forty customers came in that day. How many customers paid for their purchases with credit cards?

**41.** Seventy percent of a town's population voted in an election. If 1,589 people voted, what is the population of the town?

**42.** Thirty-seven of 50 shareholders attended a meeting. What percent of the shareholders attended the meeting?

**43.** The financial officer allows $3,400 for supplies in the annual budget. After three months, $898.32 has been spent on supplies. Is this figure within 25% of the annual budget?

**44.** Chloe Denley's rent of $940 per month was increased by 8%. What is her new monthly rent?

**45.** The price of a wireless phone increased by 14% to $165. What was the original price to the nearest dollar?

EXCEL

**46.** Global wind energy had a record growth in 2006 achieving a level of 11,531 megawatts compared to 8,207 megawatts for 2005. What was the percent increase in additional megawatts to the global market? Round to the nearest tenth percent.

# EXERCISES SET B

*Write the decimal as a percent.*

**1.** 0.675        **2.** 2.63        **3.** 0.007

**4.** 3.741        **5.** 0.0004        **6.** 0.6

**7.** 0.242        **8.** 0.811

*Write the fraction or mixed number as a percent. Round to the nearest hundredth of a percent if necessary.*

**9.** $\dfrac{99}{100}$        **10.** $\dfrac{20}{100}$        **11.** $\dfrac{13}{20}$

**12.** $3\dfrac{2}{5}$        **13.** $\dfrac{2}{5}$        **14.** $2\dfrac{3}{4}$

*Write the percent as a decimal.*

**15.** 328.4%        **16.** 84.6%        **17.** 52%

**18.** 3%        **19.** 0.02%        **20.** 274%

*Write the percent as a whole number, mixed number, or fraction, reduced to lowest terms.*

**21.** 20%        **22.** 170%        **23.** 361%

**24.** 25%        **25.** $12\dfrac{1}{2}\%$

| | Percent | Fraction | Decimal |
|---|---|---|---|
| **26.** | _____ | $\dfrac{2}{5}$ | _____ |
| **27.** | 50% | _____ | _____ |
| **28.** | $87\dfrac{1}{2}\%$ | _____ | _____ |
| **29.** | _____ | _____ | 0.45 |

*Find P, R, or B using the percentage formula or one of its forms.*

**30.** $B = \$1,900, R = 106\%$ **31.** $P = 170, B = 85$ **32.** $P = \$15.50, R = 7.75\%$

*Round decimals to the nearest hundredth and percents to the nearest whole number percent.*

**33.** $P = 68, B = 85$ **34.** $R = 72\%, B = 16$ **35.** $P = 52, R = 17\%$

*Use the percentage formula or one of its forms.*

**36.** Find 150% of 20.

**37.** 82% of what number is 94.3?

**38.** 27 is what percent of 9?

**39.** Ernestine Monahan draws $1,800 monthly retirement. On January 1, she received a 3% cost of living increase. How much was the increase?

**40.** If a picture frame costs $30 and the tax on the frame is 6% of the cost, how much is the tax on the picture frame?

**41.** Five percent of a batch of fuses were found to be faulty during an inspection. If 27 fuses were faulty, how many fuses were inspected?

**42.** The United Way expects to raise $63 million in its current drive. The chairperson projects that 60% of the funds will be raised in the first 12 weeks. How many dollars are expected to be raised in the first 12 weeks?

**43.** An accountant who is currently earning $42,380 annually expects a 6.5% raise. What is the amount of the expected raise?

**44.** Last year Docie Johnson had net sales of $582,496. This year her sales decreased by 12%. What were her net sales this year?

**45.** The price of Internet service decreased by 7% to $52. What was the original price to the nearest dollar?

# PRACTICE TEST

*Write the decimal as a percent.*

**1.** 0.24

**2.** 0.925

**3.** 0.6

*Write the fraction or mixed number as a percent.*

**4.** $\dfrac{21}{100}$

**5.** $\dfrac{3}{8}$

**6.** Write $\dfrac{1}{4}\%$ as a fraction.

*Use the percentage formula or one of its forms.*

**7.** Find 30% of $240.

**8.** 50 is what percent of 20?

**9.** What percent of 8 is 7?

**10.** What is the sales tax on an item that costs $42 if the tax rate is 6%?

**11.** If 100% of 22 rooms are full, how many rooms are full?

**12.** Twelve employees at a meat packing plant were sick on Monday. If the plant employs 360 people, what percent to the nearest whole percent of the employees was sick on Monday?

**13.** A department store had 15% turnover in personnel last year. If the store employs 600 people, how many employees were replaced last year?

**14.** The Dawson family left a 15% tip for a restaurant check. If the check totaled $19.47, find the amount of the tip. What was the total cost of the meal, including the tip?

**15.** A certain make and model of automobile was projected to have a 3% rate of defective autos. If the number of defective automobiles was projected to be 1,698, how many automobiles were to be produced?

**16.** Of the 20 questions on this practice test, 11 are word problems. What percent of the problems are word problems? (Round to the nearest whole number percent.)

**17.** Frances Johnson received a 6.2% increase in earnings. She was earning $86,900 annually. What is her new annual earnings?

**18.** Byron Johnson took a pay cut of 5%. He was earning $148,200 annually. What is his new annual salary?

**19.** Sylvia Williams bought a microwave oven that had been reduced by 30% to $340. What was the original price of the oven? Round to the nearest dollar.

**20.** Sony decided to increase the wholesale price of its DVD players by 18% to $320. What was the original price rounded to the nearest cent?

1. Numbers between $\frac{1}{100}$ and 1 are equivalent to percents that are between 1% and 100%. Numbers greater than 1 are equivalent to percents that are _____.

2. Percents between 0% and 1% are equivalent to fractions or decimals in what interval?

3. Explain why any number can be multiplied by 100% without changing the value of the number.

4. Can any number be divided by 100% without changing the value of the number? Explain.

5. A conjugate of a percent is the difference of 100% and the given percent. What is the conjugate percent of 48%?

6. Finding which one of the three elements of the percentage formula requires multiplication?

7. If the cost of an item increases by 100%, what is the effect of the increase on the original amount? Give an example to illustrate your point.

8. Describe two ways to find the new amount when a given number is increased by a given percent.

## Challenge Problem

Brian Sangean has been offered a job in which he will be paid strictly on a commission basis. He expects to receive a 4% commission on all sales of computer hardware he closes. Brian's goal for a gross yearly salary is $60,000. How much computer hardware must Brian sell in order to meet his target salary?

## 6.1  Wasting Money or Shaping Up?

Sarah belongs to a gym and health spa that is conveniently located between her home and her job. It is one of the nicer gyms in town, and Sarah pays $90 a month for membership. Sarah works out three times a week regularly. While she was getting off the treadmill one day, one of the club's personal trainers came by to talk and offered to plan a routine for Sarah that would help her train for an upcoming marathon. The trainer had noticed that Sarah came in regularly, and she commented that most members don't have the self-control to do that. In fact, she explained that there is a study of 8,000 members in Boston area gyms that showed that members went to the gym only about five times per month. The study also found that people who choose a pay-per-visit membership spend less money than people who choose a monthly or annual membership fee.

1. At Sarah's club the pay-per-visit fee is $5 per day. Would Sarah save money paying per visit? Assume that a month has 4.3 weeks. What percentage of her monthly $90 fee would she spend if she paid on a per-visit basis?

2. If Sarah goes to the gym three times per week, what portion of the year does she use the gym?

3. If Sarah went to the gym every day, how much would she pay per day on the monthly payment plan? Assume 30 days in a month. If she went every day and paid $5 per day, how much would she be spending per month? How much more is this in percentage terms compared to the $90 monthly rate rounded to the nearest percent?

## 6.2  Customer Relationship Management

Minh Phan is going over the numbers one more time. He is about to make the most important sales presentation of his young career, and wants everything to be right. His prospective client, Media Systems, Inc., is one of the country's leading media and communications organizations. Media Systems' primary challenge is how to effectively manage its diverse customer base. The company has 70,000 publication subscribers, 58,000 advertisers, 30,000 telephone services customers, and 18,000 ISP (Internet service provider) customers. The company had little information about who its customers truly were, which products they were using, and how satisfied they were with the service they received. That's where Minh and his company, Customer Solution Technologies, LLC, came in. Through the use of customer relationship management software, Minh believed Media Systems would be able to substantially improve its ability to cross-sell and up-sell multiple media and communications services to customers, while substantially reducing customer complaints.

Source: "Why You Waste So Much Money," *Wall Street Journal,* Wednesday, July 14, 2003, p. D1.

1. What percentage of the total does each of the four customer groups represent?

2. Minh's data shows that on average, only 4.6% of customers were purchasing complementary services available within Media Systems. By using his company's services, Minh was projecting that these percentages would triple across all user groups within one year. How many customers would that equate to in total for each group? What would the difference be compared to current levels?

3. Customer complaint data showed that within the last year, complaints by category were as follows: publication subscribers, 1,174; advertisers, 423; telephone service customers, 4,411; and ISP customers 823. What percentage of customers (round to two decimal places) complained within the last year in each category? If the CRM software were able to reduce complaints by 50% each year over the next two years, how many complaints would there be by category at the end of that time period? What would the number of complaints at the end of two years represent on a percentage basis?

# 6.3 Buying a New Home

Knowing that home ownership is a good step toward a sound financial future, Jeremy and Catherine are excited about buying their first home. They saved and lived frugally the first four years of their marriage and added their savings to the money they received as wedding gifts. They are now ready to pay $20,000 toward their down payment. The house they are buying is in Lakeland, a good family-oriented location, and the results of a home inspection indicate that the house is built soundly. The foundation and roof are in good repair, but they would like to make several improvements on the home in the near future. The mortgage payments on their new home fit well within their budget, but they want to make certain they can afford the improvements as well.

Their first-priority improvement is to replace the carpeting. Jeremy recognized that their house was priced below market because the sellers knew the carpeting would need to be replaced. Catherine also knows that should they want to sell their home in the foreseeable future, nice carpeting would help the resale value and perhaps help it to sell more quickly. Their plan is to recarpet the three bedrooms, the living room, and the hallway. The dimensions of the rooms are as follows:

| Room | Dimensions | Square Feet | Cost to Carpet |
|---|---|---|---|
| Master bedroom | 16 ft by 18 ft | | |
| Bedroom #1 | 12 ft by 13 ft | | |
| Bedroom #2 | 10 ft by 12 ft | | |
| Hallway | 10 ft by 3 ft | | |
| Living room | 15 ft by 20 ft | | |
| **Total Cost** | | | |

1. Find the area of each room and record your results in the chart above. Hint: The area is found by multiplying length by width. The result is "square feet" and is written $ft^2$.

2. Jeremy and Catherine have comparison shopped the carpet retailers in their area. Because Lowe's can guarantee completion of the carpeting job within a week of closing, Jeremy and Catherine have decided to buy their carpet from Lowe's. Although they have not yet decided on a color, the grade of carpet Jeremy and Catherine are interested in costs $36 a square yard. How much does it cost per square foot? Hint: There are 9 square feet in a square yard.

3. How much will it cost to carpet the areas listed above? Report your answers by room in the chart above and then determine the total cost.

4. Lowe's is offering Jeremy and Catherine a 10% discount if they carpet the whole area with the same color carpet. How much will they save if they decide to do this?

5. Jeremy and Catherine feel they can pay $2,000 in cash for carpeting right now. How many square feet of carpet can they afford to buy with the cash they have? How much would they need to borrow if they decide to carpet all the areas listed above with the same color carpet?

6. How much would it cost to carpet only the bedrooms (assume no 10% discount)? How much would it cost to carpet only the living room and hallway (again, assume no discount)?

7. Jeremy would prefer to carpet the whole area at once with the same color carpeting rather than doing it room by room; however, he is hesitant to take out another loan since they will be taking out a mortgage at the same time. He would prefer to save the full amount so that they can pay cash for their entire purchase. How long would it take for them to have enough money if they can save $300 each month? Remember, they already have $2,000 to put toward their purchase.

# Business Statistics

# Big Business in the NFL

The sports business means many different things to different people. This is a truly global industry, and sports stir up deep passion within spectators and players alike in countries around the world. To athletes, sports may lead to high levels of personal achievement; and to professionals, sports can bring fame and fortune. To businesspeople, sports provide a lucrative and continually growing marketplace worthy of immense investment.

When the astonishing variety of sports-related sectors are considered, a significant portion of the workforce in developed nations such as the U.S., the U.K., Australia, and Japan rely on the sports industry for their livelihoods. Official U.S. Bureau of Labor Statistics figures state that 128,070 people work in U.S. spectator sports alone (including about 12,200 professional athletes), while 467,860 work in fitness centers, about 30,000 work in snow skiing facilities, and about 300,000 work at country clubs or golf courses. In total, approximately 1,339,000 Americans work directly in the amusement and recreation sectors.

Nowhere is the impact of sports-related marketing as prevalent as in the NFL. Experts say that the marketing of top stars has played a big role in driving the NFL's business to new heights, which has benefited everyone. Today's $1.4 million average salary is more than double the level in 1994. A look at NFL MVP salaries over the past 25 years shows that, overall, they made 3.3 times the average league salary during the 1980s, a ratio that rose to 5.3 in the 1990s, and to 6.2 times the average in the 2000s. Peyton Manning's $14.1 million salary in 2004 was more than ten times the $1.3 million average. The league's current television package brings in over $2 billion a year, or about $75 million per team.

Coinciding with the birth of the salary cap in the mid-1990s, of course, was the high-tech age. In the new media world, in which fans are interactively involved through games and online fantasy leagues in addition to television, football's "top down" star system is working. Business is booming in the NFL, with both television revenue and player salaries at record levels. Fantasy football and Madden video games, which help drive TV viewership, surely wouldn't be what they are without identifiable names like Peyton Manning, LaDainian Tomlinson, and Brett Favre.

## LEARNING OUTCOMES

### 7-1 Measures of Central Tendency

1. Find the mean.
2. Find the median.
3. Find the mode.
4. Make and interpret a frequency distribution.
5. Find the mean of grouped data.

### 7-2 Graphs and Charts

1. Interpret and draw a bar graph.
2. Interpret and draw a line graph.
3. Interpret and draw a circle graph.

### 7-3 Measures of Dispersion

1. Find the range.
2. Find the standard deviation.

 A corresponding Business Math Case Video for this chapter, *How Many Baseball Cards?* can be found in Appendix A.

Galileo once said that mathematics is the language of science. In the 21st century, he might have said that mathematics is also the language of business. Through numbers, businesspeople communicate their business history, status, and goals. Statistics, tables, and graphs are three important tools with which to do so.

## 7-1 MEASURES OF CENTRAL TENDENCY

### LEARNING OUTCOMES

1 Find the mean.
2 Find the median.
3 Find the mode.
4 Make and interpret a frequency distribution.
5 Find the mean of grouped data.

**Data set:** a collection of values or measurements that have a common characteristic.

**Statistic:** a standardized, meaningful measure of a set of data that reveals a certain feature or characteristic of the data.

All through the year, a business records its daily sales. At the end of the year, 365 values—one for each day—are on record. These values are a **data set**. With this data set, and using the right *statistical* methods, we may calculate manageable and meaningful information; this information is called **statistics**. Recording the statistics, we should be able to reconstruct—well enough—the original data set or make predictions about a future data set.

### 1  Find the mean.

**Mean:** the arithmetic average of a set of data or the sum of the values divided by the number of values.

One common statistic we may calculate for a data set is its mean. The **mean** is the statistical term for the ordinary arithmetic average. To find the mean, or arithmetic average, we divide the sum of the values by the total number of values.

---

**HOW TO**  Find the mean of a data set

Find the mean for these scores: 96, 86, 95, 89, 92.

1. Find the sum of the values.

$96 + 86 + 95 + 89 + 92 = 458$

2. Divide the sum by the total number of values.

$$\text{Mean} = \frac{\text{sum of values}}{\text{number of values}}$$

$$\text{Mean} = \frac{458}{5} = 91.6$$

---

**TABLE 7-1**
Prices of Used Automobiles Sold in Tyreville over the Weekend of May 1–2

| | |
|---|---|
| $7,850 | $ 9,600 |
| 6,300 | 6,100 |
| 9,600 | 7,800 |
| 6,750 | 9,400 |
| 8,800 | 11,500 |
| 8,200 | 15,450 |

**EXAMPLE 1**  Find the mean used car price for the prices in Table 7-1. Round to the nearest ten dollars.

First find the sum of the values.

$$
\begin{array}{rl}
\$ \quad 7,850 & \text{Add all the prices.} \\
6,300 & \\
9,600 & \\
6,750 & \\
8,800 & \\
8,200 & \\
9,600 & \\
6,100 & \\
7,800 & \\
9,400 & \\
11,500 & \\
+ \quad 15,450 & \\
\hline
\$107,350 &
\end{array}
$$

$\$107,350 \div 12 = \$8,945.8\overline{3}$    There are 12 prices listed, so find the mean by dividing the sum of the values by 12.

**The mean price is $8,950, rounded to the nearest 10 dollars.**

## STOP AND CHECK

1. Find the mean salary to the nearest dollar: $37,500; $32,000; $28,800; $35,750; $29,500; $47,300.

2. Find the mean number of hours for the life of a lightbulb to the nearest whole hour: 2,400; 2,100; 1,800; 2,800; 3,450.

3. Find the mean number of days a patient stays in the hospital rounded to the nearest whole day: 2 days; 15 days; 7 days; 3 days; 1 day; 3 days; 5 days; 2 days; 4 days; 1 day; 2 days; 6 days; 4 days; 2 days.

4. Find the mean number of CDs purchased per month by college students: 12, 7, 5, 2, 1, 8, 0, 3, 1, 2, 7, 5, 30, 5, 2.

5. Find the mean for the Internal Revenue gross collection of estate taxes for a recent 10-year period: $9,633,736,000; $10,237,247,000; $10,411,450,000; $11,433,495,000; $13,500,126,000; $13,326,051,000; $15,350,591,000; $17,595,484,000; $21,314,933,000; $23,627,320,000. (*Source: IRS Data Book FY 2002*, Publication 55b)

## 2  Find the median.

**Median:** the middle value of a data set when the values are arranged in order of size.

A second kind of average is a statistic called the **median**. To find the median of a data set, we arrange the values in order from the smallest to the largest or from the largest to the smallest and select the value in the middle.

---

**HOW TO**  Find the median of a data set

Find the median for 22, 25, 28, 21, and 30.

1. Arrange the values in order from smallest to largest or largest to smallest.

    21, 22, 25, 28, 30

2. Count the number of values.

    five values

    (a) If the number of values is odd, identify the value in the middle.

    25

    (b) If the number of values is even, find the mean of the middle two values.

Median = middle value or mean of middle two values

median = 25

---

**EXAMPLE 1**  Find the median price of used cars in Table 7-1.

$15,450
11,500
9,600
9,600
9,400
8,800 ←
8,200 ←
7,850
7,800
6,750
6,300
6,100

Arrange the values from largest to smallest. There are 12 prices, an even number, so there are two "middle" prices.

These two are the "middle" values. Five values are above and 5 values are below these two values.

$$\frac{8,800 + 8,200}{2} = \frac{17,000}{2} = 8,500$$  Find the mean of the two middle values.

**The median price is $8,500.**

## 3  Find the mode.

**Mode:** the value or values that occur most frequently in a data set.

A third kind of average is the **mode**. The mode is the value or values that occur most frequently in a data set. If no value occurs most frequently, then there is no mode for that data set. In Table 7-1 there are two cars priced at $9,600. The mode for that set of prices is $9,600.

| HOW TO | Find the mode(s) of a data set |
|---|---|
| | Find the mode(s) for 95, 96, 98, 72, 96, 95, 96. |
| 1. For each value, count the number of times the value occurs. | 95 occurs twice. 96 occurs three times. All others occur only once. |
| 2. Identify the value or values that occur most frequently.   Mode = most frequent value(s) | 96 occurs most frequently.  96 is the mode. |

**EXAMPLE 1**  Find the mode(s) for this set of test grades in a business class: 76, 83, 94, 76, 53, 83, 74, 76, 97, 83, 65, 77, 76, 83

The grade of 76 occurs four times. The grade of 83 also occurs four times. All other grades occur only once. Therefore, both 76 and 83 occur the same number of times and are modes.

**Both 76 and 83 are modes for this set of test grades.**

The mean, median, and mode may each be called an *average*. Taken together, the mean, median, and mode describe the tendencies of a data set to cluster between the smallest and largest values. Sometimes it is useful to know all three of these statistical averages, since each represents a different way of describing the data set. It is like looking at the same thing from three different points of view.

Looking at just one statistic for a set of numbers often distorts the total picture. It is advisable to find the mean, median, and mode of a data set and then analyze the results.

**EXAMPLE 2**  A real estate agent told a prospective buyer that the average cost of a home in Tyreville was $171,000 during the past three months. The agent based this statement on this list of selling prices: $270,000, $250,000, $150,000, $150,000, $150,000, $150,000, $149,000, $145,000, $125,000.

Which statistic—the mean, the median, or the mode—gives the most realistic picture of how much a home in Tyreville is likely to cost?

| What You Know | What You Are Looking For | Solution Plan |
|---|---|---|
| Houses sold during the period: 9<br>Prices of these houses: $270,000, $250,000, $150,000, $150,000, $150,000, $150,000, $149,000, $145,000, and $125,000 | Which statistic gives the most realistic picture of how much a home in Tyreville is likely to cost?<br>Find the mean, median, and mode. | Mean = sum of values ÷ number of values<br>Median = middle value when values are arranged in order<br>Mode = most frequent value |

**Solution**

Mean = sum of values ÷ number of values
$$= \$1,539,000 \div 9$$
$$= \$171,000$$

The values are listed in order from largest to smallest, and the middle value is $150,000.
Median = middle value = $150,000
Mode = most frequent amount = $150,000
The mean is $171,000. The median is $150,000. The mode is $150,000.

**Conclusion**

Since two values are significantly different from the other values, the mean is probably not the most useful statistic.

**The median and mode give a more realistic picture of how much a home is likely to cost—about $150,000.**

 **STOP AND CHECK**

1. From Table 7-2 find the mode score for vacation days.

2. State sales tax rates are given in Table 7-3. What is the mode?

**TABLE 7-2**
Number of Vacation Days Accumulated by Staff at Tulsa Community College

| | | | | | | | | |
|---|---|---|---|---|---|---|---|---|
| 2 | 62 | 7 | 23 | 32 | 48 | 32 | 92 | 48 |
| 56 | 17 | 0 | 12 | 19 | 21 | 9 | 17 | 32 |
| 32 | 86 | 73 | 74 | 18 | 32 | 18 | 66 | 6 |
| 38 | 62 | 32 | 48 | 32 | 48 | 83 | 32 | 23 |

**TABLE 7-3**
State Sales Tax Rates

| State | Tax Rate | State | Tax Rate | State | Tax Rate |
|---|---|---|---|---|---|
| Alabama | 4 | Louisiana | 4 | Ohio | 5 |
| Alaska | 0 | Maine | 5 | Oklahoma | 4.5 |
| Arizona | 5.6 | Maryland | 5 | Oregon | 0 |
| Arkansas | 5.125 | Massachusetts | 5 | Pennsylvania | 6 |
| California | 7.25 | Michigan | 6 | Rhode Island | 7 |
| Colorado | 2.9 | Minnesota | 6.5 | South Carolina | 5 |
| Connecticut | 6 | Mississippi | 7 | South Dakota | 4 |
| Delaware | 0 | Missouri | 4.225 | Tennessee | 7 |
| Florida | 6 | Montana | 0 | Texas | 6.25 |
| Georgia | 4 | Nebraska | 5.5 | Utah | 4.75 |
| Hawaii | 4 | Nevada | 6.5 | Vermont | 5 |
| Idaho | 5 | New Hampshire | 0 | Virginia | 4.5 |
| Illinois | 6.25 | New Jersey | 6 | Washington | 6.5 |
| Indiana | 6 | New Mexico | 5 | West Virginia | 6 |
| Iowa | 5 | New York | 4 | Wisconsin | 5 |
| Kansas | 5.3 | North Carolina | 4.5 | Wyoming | 4 |
| Kentucky | 6 | North Dakota | 5 | | |

Compiled by Federation of Tax Administrators from various sources.

(continued)

3. Michelle Baragona recorded the test scores on a biology exam. Find the mode score: 98, 92, 76, 48, 97, 83, 42, 86, 79, 100.

4. What is the mode score for number of points scored by players in the season-opening basketball game?

| | |
|---|---|
| Baragona 11 | Kennedy 7 |
| Byrd 8 | Nock 22 |
| Freese 2 | Pounds 0 |
| Guest 12 | Ramsey 11 |

5. What is the mode weight of soccer players?
148, 172, 158, 160, 170, 158, 170, 165, 162, 173, 155, 161

## 4  Make and interpret a frequency distribution.

Suppose for a class of 25 students the instructor records the following grades:

| 76 | 91 | 71 | 83 | 97 | 87 | 77 | 88 | 93 | 77 | 93 | 81 | 63 |
|----|----|----|----|----|----|----|----|----|----|----|----|----|
| 79 | 74 | 77 | 76 | 97 | 87 | 89 | 68 | 90 | 84 | 88 | 91 | |

**Class intervals:** special categories for grouping the values in a data set.

**Tally:** a mark that is used to count data in class intervals.

**Class frequency:** the number of tallies or values in a class interval.

**Grouped frequency distribution:** a compilation of class intervals, tallies, and class frequencies of a data set.

It is difficult to make sense of all these numbers as they appear here. But the instructor can arrange the scores into several smaller groups, called **class intervals**. The word *class* means a special category.

These scores can be grouped into class intervals of 5, such as 60–64, 65–69, 70–74, 75–79, 80–84, 85–89, 90–94, and 95–99. Each class interval has an odd number of scores.

The instructor can now **tally** the number of scores that fall into each class interval to get a **class frequency**, the number of scores in each class interval.

A compilation of class intervals, tallies, and class frequencies is called a **grouped frequency distribution**.

> **HOW TO**  Make a frequency distribution
>
> 1. Identify appropriate intervals for the data.
> 2. Tally the data for the intervals.
> 3. Count the number in each interval.

**EXAMPLE 1**  Examine the grouped frequency distribution in Table 7-4, and answer the questions.

(a) How many students scored 70 or above?

$$2 + 6 + 3 + 5 + 5 + 2 = 23$$    Add the frequencies for class intervals with scores 70 or higher.

**23 students scored 70 or above.**

**TABLE 7-4**
**Frequency Distribution of 25 Scores**

| Class Interval | Tally | Class Frequency |
|---|---|---|
| 60–64 | / | 1 |
| 65–69 | / | 1 |
| 70–74 | // | 2 |
| 75–79 | ⊬⊬ / | 6 |
| 80–84 | /// | 3 |
| 85–89 | ⊬⊬ | 5 |
| 90–94 | ⊬⊬ | 5 |
| 95–99 | // | 2 |
| | | 25 |

(b) How many students made As (90 or higher)?

$$5 + 2 = 7$$

Add the frequencies for class intervals 90–94 and 95–99.

**7 students made As (90 or higher).**

(c) What percent of the total grades were As (90s)?

$$\frac{7 \text{ As}}{25 \text{ total}} = \frac{7}{25} = 0.28 = 28\% \text{ As}$$

The portion or part is 7 and the base or total is 25.

(d) Were the students prepared for the test or was the test too difficult?
The relatively high number of 90s (7) compared to the relatively low number of 60s (2) suggests that **in general, most students were prepared for the test**.

(e) What is the ratio of As (90s) to Fs (60s)?

$$\frac{7 \text{ As}}{2 \text{ Fs}} = \frac{7}{2}$$

**The ratio is** $\dfrac{7}{2}$.

---

Sometimes you want more information about how data are distributed. For instance, you may want to know how each class interval of a frequency distribution relates to the whole set of data. This information is called a relative frequency distribution. A **relative frequency distribution** is the percent that each class interval of a frequency distribution relates to the whole.

**Relative frequency distribution:** the percent that each class interval of a frequency distribution relates to the whole.

### HOW TO    Make a relative frequency distribution

1. Make the frequency distribution.
2. Calculate the percent that the frequency of each class interval is of the total number of data items in the set.

$$\text{Relative frequency} = \frac{\text{class interval frequency}}{\text{total number in the data set}} \times 100\%$$

### EXAMPLE 2    Make a relative frequency distribution of the data in Table 7-4.

| Class interval | Class frequency | Calculations | Relative frequency |
|---|---|---|---|
| 60–64 | 1 | $\frac{1}{25}(100\%) = \frac{100\%}{25} = 4\%$ | 4% |
| 65–69 | 1 | $\frac{1}{25}(100\%) = \frac{100\%}{25} = 4\%$ | 4% |
| 70–74 | 2 | $\frac{2}{25}(100\%) = \frac{200\%}{25} = 8\%$ | 8% |
| 75–79 | 6 | $\frac{6}{25}(100\%) = \frac{600\%}{25} = 24\%$ | 24% |
| 80–84 | 3 | $\frac{3}{25}(100\%) = \frac{300\%}{25} = 12\%$ | 12% |
| 85–89 | 5 | $\frac{5}{25}(100\%) = \frac{500\%}{25} = 20\%$ | 20% |
| 90–94 | 5 | $\frac{5}{25}(100\%) = \frac{500\%}{25} = 20\%$ | 20% |
| 95–99 | 2 | $\frac{2}{25}(100\%) = \frac{200\%}{25} = 8\%$ | 8% |
| Total | 25 | | 100% |

1. Make a frequency distribution for the number of vacation days accumulated by staff at Tulsa Community College (Table 7-2). Use intervals 0–19, 20–39, 40–59, 60–79, and 80–99.

Use the frequency distribution to answer the questions.

2. How many staff have more than 39 vacation days?

3. How many staff have fewer than 40 vacation days?

4. What percent of the staff have 80 or more vacation days? Round to the nearest tenth of a percent.

5. What percent of the staff have 20 to 59 vacation days? Round to the nearest tenth of a percent.

6. Make a relative frequency distribution of the data in Table 7-2 on page 217. Round percents to the nearest tenth percent.

## 5 Find the mean of grouped data.

When data are grouped, it may be desirable to find the mean of the grouped data. To do this we extend our frequency distribution.

### HOW TO Find the mean of grouped data

1. Make a frequency distribution.
2. Find the products of the midpoint of the interval and the frequency for each interval for all intervals.
3. Find the sum of the frequencies.
4. Find the sum of the products from Step 2.
5. Divide the sum of the products by the sum of the frequencies.

$$\text{Mean of grouped data} = \frac{\text{sum of the products of the midpoints and the frequencies}}{\text{sum of the frequencies}}$$

## EXAMPLE 1

Find the grouped mean of the scores in Table 7-4.

Find the midpoint of each class interval:

$$\frac{60 + 64}{2} = \frac{124}{2} = 62 \qquad \frac{65 + 69}{2} = \frac{134}{2} = 67 \qquad \frac{70 + 74}{2} = \frac{144}{2} = 72$$

$$\frac{75 + 79}{2} = \frac{154}{2} = 77 \qquad \frac{80 + 84}{2} = \frac{164}{2} = 82 \qquad \frac{85 + 89}{2} = \frac{174}{2} = 87$$

$$\frac{90 + 94}{2} = \frac{184}{2} = 92 \qquad \frac{95 + 99}{2} = \frac{194}{2} = 97$$

| Class interval | Class frequency | Midpoint | Product of midpoint and frequency |
|---|---|---|---|
| 60–64 | 1 | 62 | 62 |
| 65–69 | 1 | 67 | 67 |
| 70–74 | 2 | 72 | 144 |
| 75–79 | 6 | 77 | 462 |
| 80–84 | 3 | 82 | 246 |
| 85–89 | 5 | 87 | 435 |
| 90–94 | 5 | 92 | 460 |
| 95–99 | 2 | 97 | 194 |
| Total | 25 | | 2,070 |

$$\text{Mean of grouped data} = \frac{\text{sum of the products of the midpoints and the frequencies}}{\text{sum of the frequencies}}$$

$$= \frac{2,070}{25}$$

$$= 82.8$$

**The grouped mean of the scores is 82.8.**

---

## TIP

**Is the Mean of Grouped Data Exact?**

No. The mean of grouped data is based on the assumption that all the data in an interval have a mean that is exactly equal to the midpoint of the interval. Because this is usually not the case, the mean of grouped data is a reasonable approximation.

---

 STOP AND CHECK

1. Find the grouped mean of the scores in Table 7-2 on page 217. Round to tenths.

2. Use the grouped frequency distribution in Table 7-5 to find the grouped mean. Round to hundredths.

3. Find the grouped mean to the nearest whole number of the data in the frequency distribution in Table 7-6. Round to hundredths.

**TABLE 7-5**
Frequency Distribution of 25 Scores

| Class interval | Midpoint | Class frequency |
|---|---|---|
| 60–64 | 62 | 6 |
| 65–69 | 67 | 8 |
| 70–74 | 72 | 12 |
| 75–79 | 77 | 22 |
| 80–84 | 82 | 18 |
| 85–89 | 87 | 9 |

**TABLE 7-6**
Frequency Distribution of Credit-Hour Loads

| Class interval | Midpoint | Class frequency |
|---|---|---|
| 0–4 | 2 | 3 |
| 5–9 | 7 | 7 |
| 10–14 | 12 | 4 |
| 15–19 | 17 | 2 |
| Total | | 16 |

Mean of grouped data = 8.56

## SKILL BUILDERS

1. Find the mean for the scores: 3,850; 5,300; 8,550; 4,300; 5,350.

2. Find the mean for the amounts: 92, 68, 72, 83, 72, 95, 88, 76, 72, 89, 89, 96, 74, 72. Round to the nearest whole number.

3. Find the mean for the amounts: $17,485; $14,978; $13,592; $14,500; $18,540; $14,978. Round to the nearest whole number.

4. Find the median for the scores: 3,850; 5,300; 8,550; 4,300; 5,350.

5. Find the median for the scores: 92, 68, 72, 83, 72, 95, 88, 76, 72, 89, 89, 96, 74, 72.

6. Find the median for the amounts: $17,485; $14,978; $13,592; $14,500; $18,540; $14,978.

7. Find the mode for the scores: 3,850; 5,300; 8,550; 4,300; 5,350.

8. Find the mode for the scores: 92, 68, 72, 83, 72, 95, 88, 76, 72, 89, 89, 96, 74, 72.

9. Find the mode for the amounts: $17,485; $14,978; $13,592; $14,500; $18,540; $14,978.

## APPLICATIONS

10. Weekly expenses of students taking a business mathematics class are shown in Table 7-7.
    a. Find the mean rounded to the nearest whole number.
    b. Find the median.
    c. Find the mode.

| TABLE 7-7 Weekly Expenses of Students | | | | | | | | | | | | | |
|----|----|----|-----|----|----|----|----|----|----|----|----|-----|----|
| 89 | 42 | 78 | 156 | 67 | 85 | 92 | 80 | 55 | 75 | 85 | 99 | 88 |    |
| 90 | 85 | 95 | 100 | 95 | 79 | 93 | 56 | 78 | 81 | 84 | 105 | 77 |   |

11. Salaries for the research and development department of Richman Chemical are given as $48,397; $27,982; $42,591; $19,522; $32,400; and $37,582.
    a. Find the mean rounded to the nearest dollar.
    b. Find the median.
    c. Find the mode.

12. Sales in thousands of dollars for men's suits at a Macy's department store for a 12-month period were $127; $215; $135; $842; $687; $512; $687; $742; $984; $752; $984; $1,992.
   a. Find the mean rounded to the nearest whole thousand.
   b. Find the median.
   c. Find the mode.

13. Accountants often use the median when studying salaries for various businesses. What is the median of the following salary list: $32,084, $21,983, $27,596, $43,702, $38,840, $25,997?

14. Weather forecasters sometimes give the average (mean) temperature for a particular city. The following temperatures were recorded as highs on June 30 of the last 10 years in a certain city: 89°, 88°, 90°, 92°, 95°, 89°, 93°, 98°, 93°, 97°. What is the mean high temperature for June 30 for the last 10 years?

15. The following grades were earned by students on a mid-term business math exam:

| 75 | 82 | 63 | 88 | 94 |
|----|----|----|----|----|
| 81 | 90 | 72 | 84 | 87 |
| 98 | 93 | 85 | 68 | 91 |
| 78 | 86 | 91 | 83 | 92 |

Make a frequency distribution of the data using the intervals 60–69, 70–79, 80–89, and 90–99.

16. What percent of the students in Exercise 15 earned a grade that was below 80?

17. The 7th Inning wants to group a collection of autographed photos by price ranges. Make a frequency distribution of the prices using the intervals $0–$9.99, $10–$19.99, $20–$29.99, $30–$39.99, and $40–$49.99.

| $2.50 | $3.75 | $1.25 | $21.50 | $43.00 | $15.00 |
|-------|-------|-------|--------|--------|--------|
| $26.00 | $14.50 | $12.75 | $35.00 | $37.50 | $48.00 |
| $7.50 | $6.50 | $7.50 | $8.00 | $12.50 | $15.00 |
| $9.50 | $8.25 | $14.00 | $25.00 | $18.50 | $45.00 |
| $32.50 | $20.00 | $10.00 | $17.50 | $6.75 | $28.50 |

18. In Exercise 17, what percent to the nearest whole percent of the collection is priced below $20?

19. In Exercise 17, what percent of the collection is priced $40 or over?

**20.** Use the given hourly rates (rounded to the nearest whole dollar) for 35 support employees in a private college to complete the frequency distribution and find the grouped mean rounded to the nearest cent.

| $14 | $16 | $9  | $10 | $12 | $13 | $15 |
|-----|-----|-----|-----|-----|-----|-----|
| $11 | $12 | $16 | $17 | $22 | $19 | $28 |
| $18 | $16 | $12 | $9  | $11 | $12 | $17 |
| $26 | $16 | $18 | $21 | $18 | $16 | $14 |
| $10 | $13 | $12 | $15 | $12 | $12 | $9  |

| Class interval | Tally | Class frequency | Midpoint | Product of midpoint and frequency |
|----------------|-------|-----------------|----------|-----------------------------------|
| 6–10 | | | | |
| 11–15 | | | | |
| 16–20 | | | | |
| 21–25 | | | | |
| 26–30 | | | | |
| Total | | | | |

## 7-2 GRAPHS AND CHARTS

### LEARNING OUTCOMES

1 Interpret and draw a bar graph.
2 Interpret and draw a line graph.
3 Interpret and draw a circle graph.

Scan a newspaper, a magazine, or a business report, and you are likely to see graphs. Graphs do more than present sets of data. They make visual the relationship between the sets. The relationship between data sets might be visualized by a bar graph, a line graph, or a circle graph. Depending on "what you want to see," one of these forms helps you to see the relationship more meaningfully.

## 1 Interpret and draw a bar graph.

**Bar graph:** a graph that uses horizontal or vertical bars to show how values compare to each other.

**Bar graphs** are used to make visual the relationship between data. As its name implies, a bar graph uses horizontal or vertical bars to show relative quantities. Figure 7-1 is a bar graph representing the data in the frequency distribution of the 25 scores in Table 7-4.

Along the bottom of the bar graph are the class intervals that correspond to the first column of Table 7-4. Along the left side of the bar graph is a scale from 0 to 6. In relation to the scale, each bar corresponds to the class frequency.

Figure 7-1 demonstrates why bar graphs are so useful: We can easily compare the scores for grade intervals at a glance.

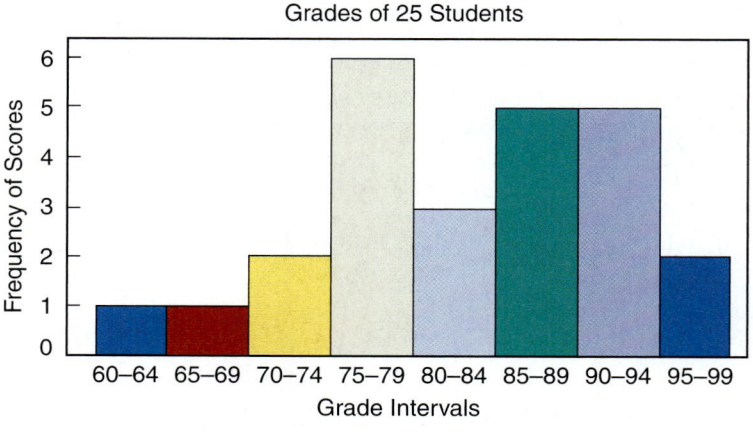

**FIGURE 7-1**
**Distribution of 25 Scores Grouped**

Answer the questions using the data represented in Figure 7-1.

(a) Which grade interval(s) had the highest number of scores?
(b) Which grade interval(s) had the lowest number of scores?
(c) If 90–99 is a grade of A, how many As were there?

(a) Which grade interval(s) had the highest number of scores?

**The interval 75–79 had the highest number of scores, 6.**

(b) Which grade interval(s) had the lowest number of scores?

**The intervals 60–64 and 65–69 had the lowest number of scores, 1.**

(c) If 90–99 is a grade of A, how many As were there?

There are 5 scores in the 90–94 interval and 2 scores in the 95–99 interval. There are 5 + 2 or **7 scores that are As.**

**Histogram:** a special type of bar graph that represents the data from a frequency distribution.

A **histogram** is a special type of bar graph that represents the data from a frequency distribution. Figure 7-1 is a histogram. Since there are no gaps in the intervals, the bars in a histogram are drawn with no space between them.

**HOW TO** Draw a bar graph

1. Write an appropriate title.
2. Make appropriate labels for the bars and scale. The intervals on the scale should be equally spaced and include the smallest and largest values.
3. Draw bars to represent the data. Bars should be of uniform width.
4. Make additional notes as appropriate. For example, "Amounts in Thousands of Dollars" allows values such as $30,000 to be represented as 30.

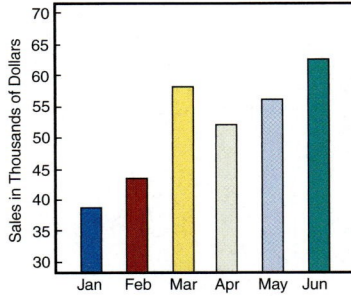

**FIGURE 7-2**
**Horizontal Bar Graph Showing Corky's Barbecue Restaurant Sales, January–June**

**EXAMPLE 2** The data show Corky's Barbecue Restaurant sales during January through June. Draw a bar graph that represents the data.

| January | $37,734 | April | $52,175 |
| February | $43,284 | May | $56,394 |
| March | $58,107 | June | $63,784 |

The title of the graph is "Corky's Barbecue Restaurant Sales, January–June."

The smallest value is $37,734 and the largest value is $63,784. Therefore, the graph should show values from $30,000 to $70,000. To avoid using very large numbers, indicate on the graph that the numbers represent dollars in thousands. Therefore, 65 on the graph would represent $65,000. The bars can be either horizontal or vertical. In Figure 7-2 we make the bars horizontal. Months are labeled along the vertical line, and the dollar scale is labeled along the horizontal line. For each month, the length of the bar corresponds to the sales for the month.

Figure 7-3 interchanges the labeling of the scales, and the bars are drawn vertically.

Bar graphs may illustrate relationships among more than one variable. A **standard bar graph** illustrates the change in magnitude of just one variable. Figure 7-2 is a standard bar graph. A **comparative bar graph** is used to illustrate two or more related variables. The bars representing each variable are shaded or colored differently so that visual comparisons can be made more easily. Figure 7-4 is a comparative bar graph.

A **component bar graph** is used to show that each bar is the total of various components. The components are stacked immediately next to each other and shaded or colored differently. Figure 7-5 is a component bar graph.

**FIGURE 7-3**
**Vertical Bar Graph Showing Corky's Barbecue Restaurant Sales, January–June**

**TIP**

**Constructing Graphs Electronically**
Electronic spreadsheets have a function that translates the data from a spreadsheet to various types of graphs, also called *charts*. The type of graph (bar, line, circle), titles of scales, and labels are still determined by the user. The software then produces the graph electronically.

**Standard bar graph:** bar graph with just one variable.

**Comparative bar graph:** bar graph with two or more variables.

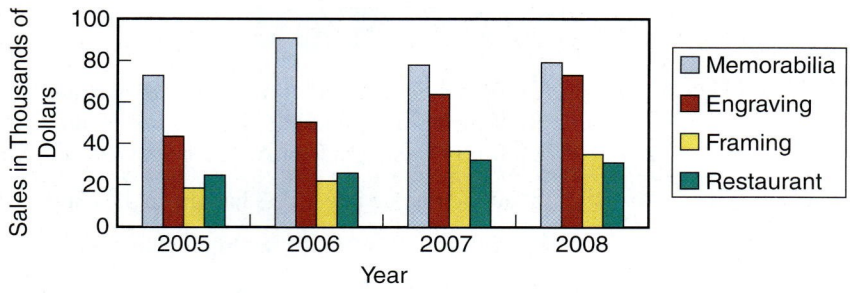

**FIGURE 7-4**
**The 7th Inning Sales by Department**

**Component bar graph:** bar graph with each bar having more than one component.

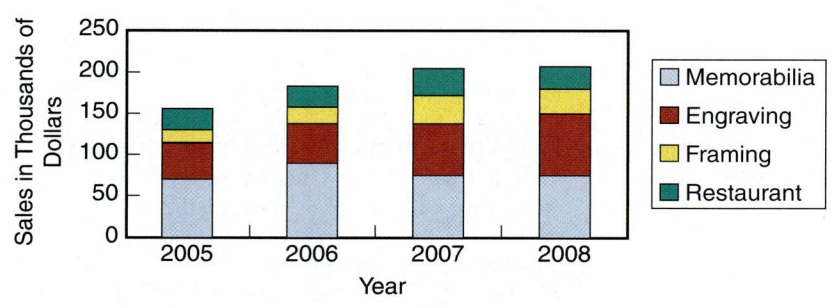

**FIGURE 7-5**
**The 7th Inning Annual Sales**

## ✓ STOP AND CHECK

1. Use the frequency distribution for Table 7-2 (Stop and Check, Exercise 1 on page 217) to construct a bar graph.

2. From the graph identify the number of vacation days (interval) that 12 staff members have.

*Fifty business students were given a project to complete. The bar graph in Figure 7-6 shows the number of days it took the students to complete the assignment.*

3. How many students took 4 days to complete the assignment?

4. How many students completed the project in 3 days or less?

5. What percent of students completed the project in 3 days or less?

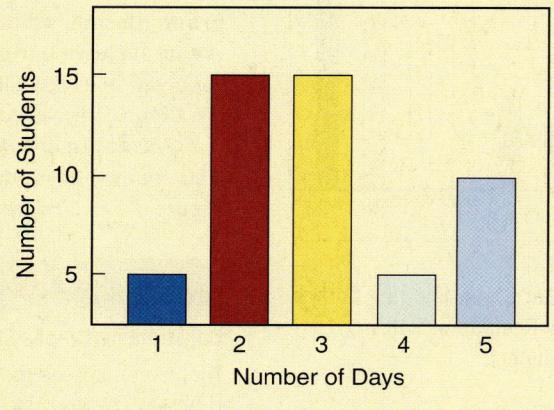

**FIGURE 7-6**

## 2 Interpret and draw a line graph.

**Line graphs** are very similar to vertical bar graphs. The difference is that a line graph uses a single dot to represent height, rather than a whole bar. When the dots are in place, they are connected by a line. Line graphs make even more apparent the rising and falling trends of the data. Figure 7-7 is a line graph representing the data in the vertical bar graph in Figure 7-3.

Line graphs may have enough points that connecting them yields a curve rather than angles. Figure 7-8 shows such a line graph, relating the time film is developed to the degree of contrast achieved in the developed film. To read the graph, we locate a specific degree of contrast on the vertical scale, and then move horizontally until we intersect the curve. From that point, we move down to locate the corresponding number of minutes on the horizontal scale.

**EXAMPLE 1**  Use Figure 7-8 to answer the following questions:

(a) If the film is to be developed to a contrast of 0.5, how long must it be developed?
(b) If the film is developed for 13 minutes, what is its degree of contrast?

(a) Find 0.5 on the vertical scale, and then move horizontally until you intersect the curve. From the point of intersection, move down to locate the corresponding number of minutes on the horizontal scale. **Figure 7-9 shows the minutes are 9.**
(b) Find 13 minutes on the horizontal scale, and move up until you intersect the curve. From the point of intersection, move across to locate the corresponding degree of contrast. **Figure 7-9 shows the degree of contrast is 0.7.**

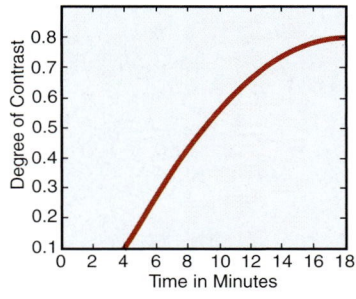

**FIGURE 7-7**
Line Graph Showing Corky's Barbecue Restaurant Sales, January–June

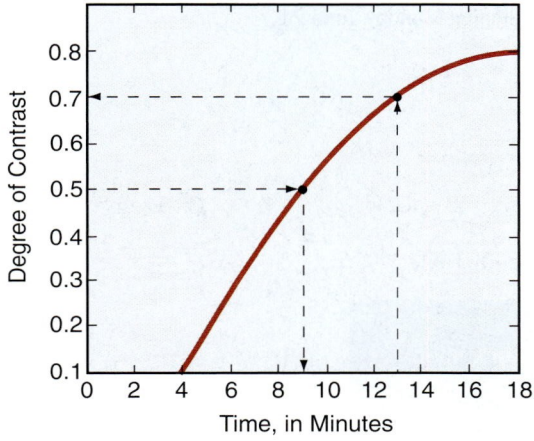

**FIGURE 7-9**
Reading a Line Graph

**FIGURE 7-8**
Developing Time Required for Degrees of Contrast

As in drawing bar graphs, drawing line graphs often means using approximations of the given data.

**HOW TO** Draw a line graph

1. Write an appropriate title.
2. Make and label appropriate horizontal and vertical scales, each with equally spaced intervals. Often, the horizontal scale represents time.
3. Use points to locate data on the graph.
4. Connect data points with line segments or a smooth curve.

**TABLE 7-8**
Neighborhood Grocery Daily Sales for Week Beginning Monday, June 21

| | |
|---|---|
| Monday | $1,567 |
| Tuesday | 1,323 |
| Wednesday | 1,237 |
| Thursday | 1,435 |
| Friday | 1,848 |
| Saturday | 1,984 |

**EXAMPLE 2**  Draw a line graph to represent the data in Table 7-8.

The smallest and greatest values in the table are $1,237 and $1,984, respectively, so the graph may go from $1,000 to $2,000 in $100 increments. Do not label every increment. This would crowd the side of the graph and make it hard to read. The purpose of any graph is to give information that is quick and easy to understand and interpret.

The horizontal side of the graph will show the days of the week, and the vertical side will show the daily sales. Plot each day's sales by placing a dot directly above the appropriate day of the week across from the approximate value. For example, the sales for Monday totaled $1,567. Place the dot above Monday between $1,500 and $1,600. After each amount has been plotted, connect the dots with straight lines.

**Figure 7-10 shows the resulting graph.**

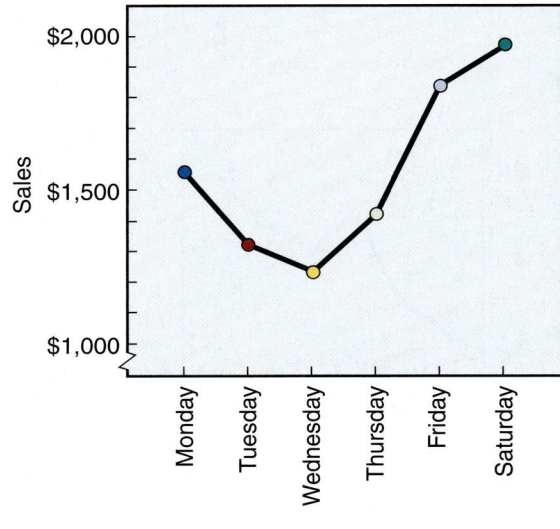

**FIGURE 7-10**
**Neighborhood Grocery Daily Sales for Week Beginning Monday, June 21**

Days of the Week

## ✔ STOP AND CHECK

**1.** Draw a line graph to represent the data in Table 7-9.

| TABLE 7-9 | |
|---|---|
| Personal Income for March 2003–September 2003 (Billions of dollars) | |
| March 2003 | 9,102.0 |
| April 2003 | 9,119.8 |
| May 2003 | 9,155.4 |
| June 2003 | 9,192.9 |
| July 2003 | 9,219.4 |
| August 2003 | 9,248.9 |
| September 2003 | 9,277.5 |

*Source:* Bureau of Economic Analysis, an agency of the U.S. Department of Commerce.

**2.** Is the graph in Exercise 1 increasing, decreasing, or fluctuating?

**3.** Which month showed the highest personal income?

**4.** Is the graph in Figure 7-11 increasing, decreasing, or fluctuating?

**5.** Find the monthly average number of CDs sold by House of Music for the 6-month period January–June.

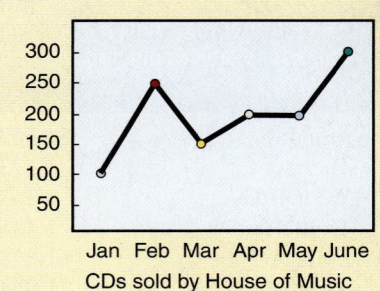

**FIGURE 7-11**

Jan Feb Mar Apr May June
CDs sold by House of Music

## 3 Interpret and draw a circle graph.

**Circle graph:** a circle that is divided into parts to show how a whole quantity is being divided.

A **circle graph** is a circle divided into sections to give a visual picture of *how some whole quantity* (represented by the whole circle) *is being divided*. Each section represents a portion of the total amount. Figure 7-12 shows a circle graph illustrating how different portions of a family's total take-home income are spent on nine categories of expenses: food, housing, contributions, savings, clothing, insurance, education, personal items, and miscellaneous items.

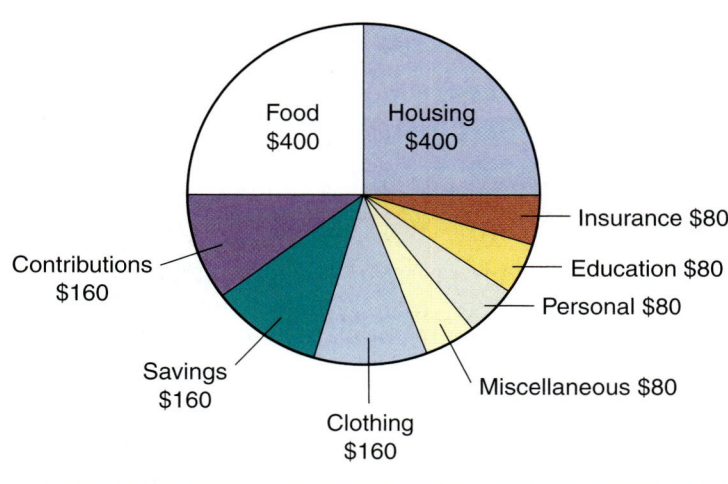

**FIGURE 7-12**
**Distribution of Family Monthly Take-Home Pay**

Circle graphs are relatively easy to read, and they make it easy to visually compare categories. Constructing a circle graph requires that you make several calculations and use a measuring device called a **protractor** that measures angles. Each value in the data set should be represented as a fraction of the sum of all the values. We calculate these fractions and then draw the graph.

**Protractor:** a measuring device that measures angles.

---

### HOW TO    Draw a circle graph

1. Write an appropriate title.
2. Find the sum of the values in the data set.
3. Represent each value as a fractional or decimal part of the sum of values.
4. For each fraction or decimal, find the number of degrees in the **sector** of the circle to be represented by the fraction or decimal: Multiply the fraction or decimal by 360 degrees. The sum of the degrees for all sectors should be 360 degrees.
5. Use a **compass** (a tool for drawing circles) to draw a circle. Indicate the center of the circle and a starting point on the circle.
6. For each degree value, draw a sector: Use a protractor (a measuring instrument for angles) to measure the number of degrees for the sector of the circle to be represented by the value. Where the first sector ends, the next sector begins. The last sector should end at the starting point.
7. Label each sector of the circle and make additional explanatory notes as necessary.

**Sector:** portion or wedge of a circle identified by two lines from the center to the outer edge of the circle.

**Compass:** a tool for drawing circles.

---

### EXAMPLE 1

Construct a circle graph showing the budgeted operating expenses for one month for Silver's Spa: salary, $25,000; rent, $8,500; depreciation, $2,500; miscellaneous, $2,000; taxes and insurance, $10,000; utilities, $2,000; advertising, $3,000. The title of the graph is "Silver's Spa Monthly Budgeted Operating Expenses."

Since several calculations are required, it is helpful to organize the calculation results in a chart (Table 7-10).

**TABLE 7-10**
Silver's Spa Monthly Budgeted Operating Expenses

| Type of Expense | Amount of Expense | Expense as Fraction of Total Expenses | Degrees in Sector: Fraction × 360 |
|---|---|---|---|
| Salary | $25,000 | $\dfrac{25,000}{53,000}$ or $\dfrac{25}{53}$ | $\dfrac{25}{53}(360)$, or 170 |
| Rent | 8,500 | $\dfrac{8,500}{53,000}$ or $\dfrac{17}{106}$ | $\dfrac{17}{106}(360)$, or 58 |
| Depreciation | 2,500 | $\dfrac{2,500}{53,000}$ or $\dfrac{5}{106}$ | $\dfrac{5}{106}(360)$, or 17 |
| Miscellaneous | 2,000 | $\dfrac{2,000}{53,000}$ or $\dfrac{2}{53}$ | $\dfrac{2}{53}(360)$, or 14 |
| Taxes and insurance | 10,000 | $\dfrac{10,000}{53,000}$ or $\dfrac{10}{53}$ | $\dfrac{10}{53}(360)$, or 68 |
| Utilities | 2,000 | $\dfrac{2,000}{53,000}$ or $\dfrac{2}{53}$ | $\dfrac{2}{53}(360)$, or 14 |
| Advertising | 3,000 | $\dfrac{3,000}{53,000}$ or $\dfrac{3}{53}$ | $\dfrac{3}{53}(360)$, or 20 |
| Total | $53,000 | 1 | 361* |

*Extra degree due to rounding.

Decimal equivalents can be used instead of fractions of total expenses. The sum of the fractions or decimal equivalents is 1. To the nearest thousandth, the decimal equivalents are 0.472, 0.160, 0.047, 0.038, 0.189, 0.038, and 0.057. The sum is 1.001. Rounding causes the sum to be slightly more than 1, just as the sum of the degrees is slightly more than 360°.

Use a compass to draw a circle. Measure the sectors of the circle with a protractor, using the calculations you just made. **The finished circle graph is shown in Figure 7-13.**

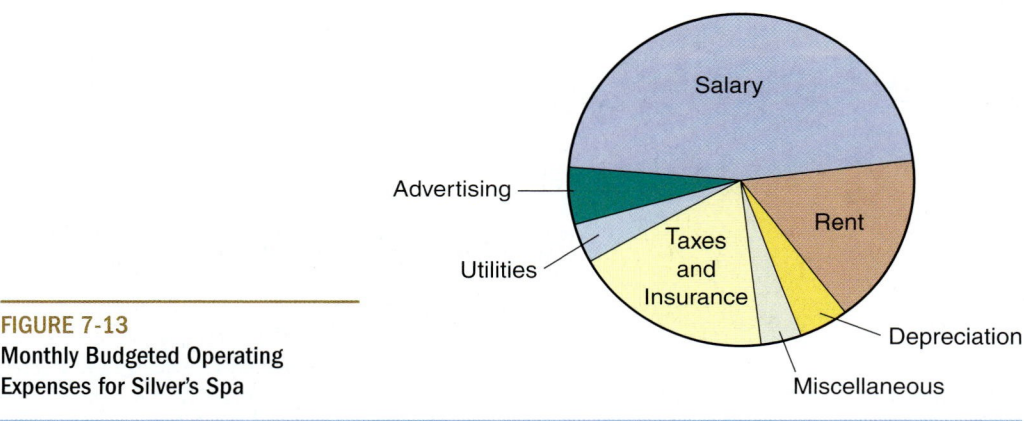

**FIGURE 7-13**
**Monthly Budgeted Operating Expenses for Silver's Spa**

 **STOP AND CHECK**

1. Construct a circle graph showing the distribution of market share using data in Table 7-11.

**TABLE 7-11**
Percent Dollar Market Share of Comics and Magazine Sales for September (Rounded to the Nearest Whole Percent)

| Publisher | Market Share |
|---|---|
| Marvel Comics | 35% |
| DC Comics | 32% |
| Image Comics | 5% |
| Dark Horse Comics | 4% |
| Dreamweave Productions | 4% |
| All others | 20% |

**2.** What percent of market share is held by the largest three companies?

**4.** What was Image Comics' sales for September if the total market was $80,000,000?

**3.** If the total market had $80,000,000 in comics and magazine sales for September, what were the sales for Marvel Comics?

# 7-2 SECTION EXERCISES

## APPLICATIONS

*Use Table 7-12 for Exercises 1–4.*

**TABLE 7-12**
Sales by Each Salesperson at Happy's Gift Shoppe

| Salesperson | Mon. | Tues. | Wed. | Thurs. | Fri. | Sat. | Total |
|---|---|---|---|---|---|---|---|
| | | | Sales | | | | |
| Brown | Off | $110.25 | $114.52 | $186.42 | $126.81 | $315.60 | $ 853.60 |
| Jackson | $121.68 | Off | $118.29 | Off | $125.42 | Off | $ 365.39 |
| Ulster | $112.26 | $119.40 | $122.35 | $174.51 | $116.78 | Off | $ 645.30 |
| Young | Off | $122.90 | Off | $181.25 | Off | $296.17 | $ 600.32 |
| **Totals** | **$233.94** | **$352.55** | **$355.16** | **$542.18** | **$369.01** | **$611.77** | **$2,464.61** |

**1.** What day of the week had the highest amount in sales? What day had the lowest amount in sales?

**2.** Which salesperson made the most sales for the week? Which salesperson made the second highest amount in sales?

**3.** Construct a bar graph showing total sales by salesperson for Happy's Gift Shoppe in Table 7-12.

**4.** Construct a bar graph showing total sales by the days of the week for Happy's Gift Shoppe in Table 7-12.

*Use Figure 7-14 for Exercises 5–7.*

**5.** Which quarter had the highest dollar volume?

**6.** What percent of the yearly sales were the sales for October–December?

**7.** What was the percent of increase in sales from the first to the second quarter?

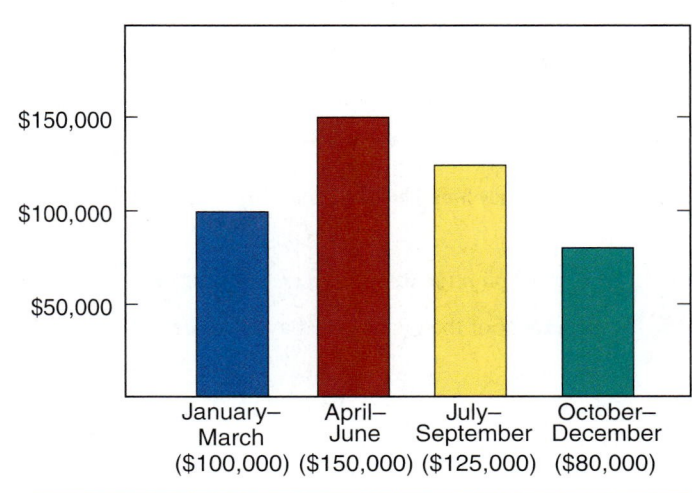

**FIGURE 7-14**
Quarterly Dollar Volume of Batesville Tire Company

**8.** Draw a bar graph comparing the quarterly sales of the Oxford Company: January–March, $280,000; April–June, $310,000; July–September, $250,000; October–December, $400,000.

*Use Figure 7-15 for Exercises 9–12.*

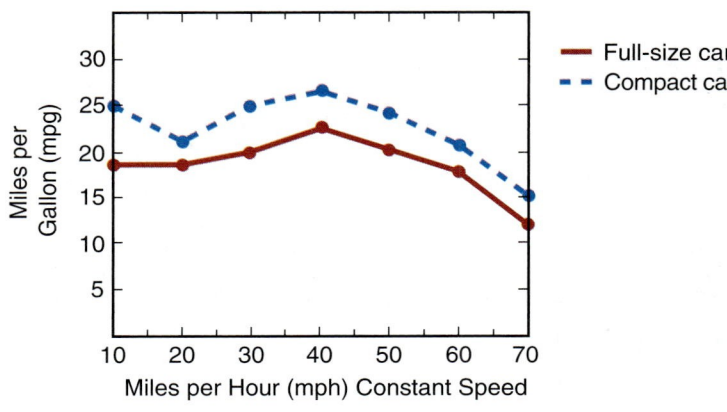

**FIGURE 7-15**
**Automobile Gasoline Mileage Comparisons**

**9.** What speed gave the highest gasoline mileage for both types of automobiles?

**10.** What speed gave the lowest gasoline mileage for both types of automobiles?

**11.** At what speed did the first noticeable decrease in gasoline mileage occur? Which car showed this decrease?

**12.** Identify factors other than gasoline mileage that should be considered when deciding which type of car to purchase, full size or compact.

**13.** The family budget is illustrated in Figure 7-16. What is the total take-home pay and what percent is allocated for transportation?

**14.** Match the dollar values with the names in the circle graph of Figure 7-17: $192, $144, $96, $72, $72.

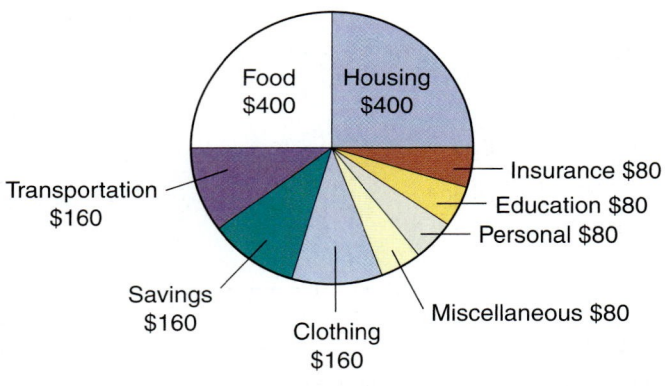

**FIGURE 7-16**
**Distribution of Family Monthly Take-Home Pay**

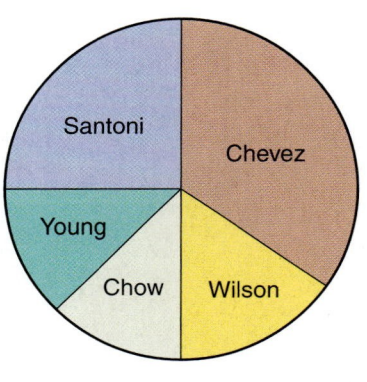

**FIGURE 7-17**
**Daily Sales by Salesperson**

*Use Figure 7-12 on page 229 for Exercises 15 through 17.*

**15.** What percent of the take-home pay is allocated for food?

**16.** What percent of take-home pay is spent for education?

**17.** What percent of take-home pay is spent for education if education, savings, and miscellaneous funds are used for education?

*Use Figure 7-18 for Exercises 18–21. Round to the nearest tenth of a percent.*

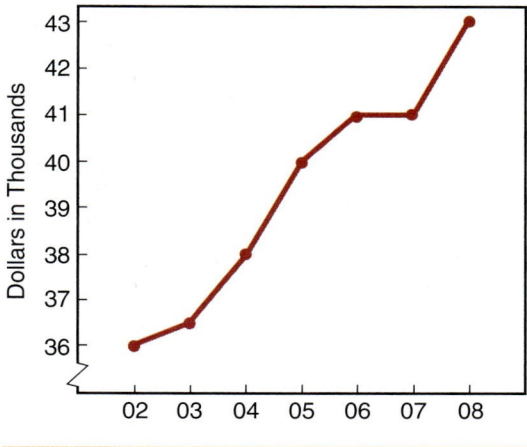

**FIGURE 7-18**
**Dale Crosby's Salary History**

**18.** What is the percent of increase in Dale's salary from 2003 to 2004?

**19.** Calculate the amount and percent of increase in Dale's salary from 2005 to 2006.

**20.** Calculate the amount and percent of increase in Dale's salary from 2007 to 2008.

**21.** If the cost-of-living increase was 10% from 2002 to 2008, determine if Dale's salary for this period of time kept pace with inflation.

## 7-3 MEASURES OF DISPERSION

### LEARNING OUTCOMES

1 Find the range.
2 Find the standard deviation.

**Measures of central tendency:** statistical measurements such as the mean, median, or mode that indicate how data group toward the center.

**Measures of variation or dispersion:** statistical measurements such as the range and standard deviation that indicate how data are dispersed or spread.

**Spread:** the variation or dispersion of a set of data.

**Range:** the difference between the highest and lowest values in a data set.

The mean, the median, and the mode are **measures of central tendency**. Another group of statistical measures is **measures of variation or dispersion**. The variation or dispersion of a set of data may also be referred to as the **spread**.

### 1 Find the range.

One measure of dispersion of a set of data is the **range**. The range is the difference between the highest value and the lowest value in a set of data.

> **HOW TO** Find the range
>
> 1. Find the highest and lowest values.
> 2. Find the difference between the highest and lowest values.

**EXAMPLE 1** Find the range for the data in Table 7-1 in the example on page 214 for prices of used automobiles sold.

The high value is $15,450. The low value is $6,100.
Range = $15,450 − $6,100 = **$9,350.**

**TIP**

**Use More Than One Statistical Measure**

A common mistake when making conclusions or inferences from statistical measures is to examine only one statistic, such as the range. To obtain a complete picture of the data requires looking at more than one statistic.

 **STOP AND CHECK**

1. Find the range for salary: $37,500; $32,000; $28,800; $35,750; $29,500; $47,300.

2. Find the range for the number of hours for the life of a lightbulb: 2,400; 2,100; 1,800; 2,800; 3,450.

3. Find the range for the number of days a patient stays in the hospital: 2 days; 15 days; 7 days; 3 days; 1 day; 3 days; 5 days; 2 days; 4 days; 1 day; 2 days; 6 days; 4 days; 2 days.

4. Find the range for the number of CDs purchased per month by college students: 12, 7, 5, 2, 1, 8, 0, 3, 1, 2, 7, 5, 30, 5, 2.

5. Find the range for the Internal Revenue gross collection of estate taxes for a recent 10-year period: $9,633,736,000; $10,237,247,000; $10,411,450,000; $11,433,495,000; $13,500,126,000; $13,326,051,000; $15,350,591,000; $17,595,484,000; $21,314,933,000; $23,627,320,000. (*Source: IRS Data Book FY 2002*, Publication 55b)

## 2  Find the standard deviation.

Although the range gives us some information about dispersion, it does not tell us whether the highest or lowest values are typical values or extreme *outliers*. We can get a clearer picture of the data set by examining how much each data point *differs* or *deviates* from the mean.

**Deviation from the mean:** the difference between a value of a data set and the mean.

The **deviation from the mean** of a data value is the difference between the value and the mean.

**HOW TO** Find the deviations from the mean

Data set: 38, 43, 45, 44.

1. Find the mean of the set of data.

$$\text{Mean} = \frac{\text{sum of data values}}{\text{number of values}}$$

$$\frac{38 + 43 + 45 + 44}{4} = \frac{170}{4} = 42.5$$

2. Find the amount that each data value deviates or is different from the mean.

Deviation from the mean = data value − mean

$38 - 42.5 = -4.5$ (below the mean)
$43 - 42.5 = 0.5$ (above the mean)
$45 - 42.5 = 2.5$ (above the mean)
$44 - 42.5 = 1.5$ (above the mean)

When the value is smaller than the mean, the difference is represented by a *negative* number, indicating the value is *below* or less than the mean. When the value is larger than the mean, the difference is represented by a positive number, indicating the value is *above* or greater than the mean. In the example in the How To feature, only one value is below the mean, and its deviation is $-4.5$. Three values are above the mean, and the sum of these deviations is $0.5 + 2.5 + 1.5 = 4.5$. We say that *the sum of all deviations from the mean is zero*. This is true for all sets of data.

---

**EXAMPLE 1**  Find the deviations from the mean for the set of data 45, 63, 87, and 91.

$$\frac{\text{Sum of values}}{\text{Number of values}} = \frac{45 + 63 + 87 + 91}{4} = \frac{286}{4} = 71.5 \quad \text{Mean}$$

To find the deviation from the mean, subtract the mean from each value. We arrange these values in a table.

| Data Values | Deviations (Data Value − Mean) |
|-------------|-------------------------------|
| 45 | $45 - 71.5 = \mathbf{-26.5}$ |
| 63 | $63 - 71.5 = \mathbf{-8.5}$ |
| 87 | $87 - 71.5 = \mathbf{15.5}$ |
| 91 | $91 - 71.5 = \mathbf{19.5}$ |

---

The sum of deviations are found as follows:

$-26.5 + -8.5 = -35$  The sum of two negative numbers is negative.

$15.5 + 19.5 = 35$  The sum of two positive numbers is positive.

$-35 + 35 = 0$  $-35$ and 35 are **opposites**.  The sum of opposites is 0.

**Opposites:** a positive and negative number that represent the same distance from 0 but in opposite directions.

---

**TIP**

**Adding and Subtracting Negative Numbers**

Some business applications involve negative numbers. A combination of positive and negative numbers is referred to as **signed numbers**. We will introduce the appropriate rules for signed numbers as they are needed.

When subtracting a larger number from a smaller number, the result is a negative number.

$$45 - 71.5 = -26.5$$

To perform the subtraction, subtract 45 from 71.5 and assign the difference the negative sign. When adding two negative numbers, the sum is also negative. $-26.5 + -8.5 = -35$.

**Signed numbers:** a combination of positive and negative numbers.

---

We have not gained any statistical insight or new information by analyzing the sum of the deviations from the mean or even by analyzing the average of the deviations.

$$\text{Average deviation} = \frac{\text{sum of deviations}}{\text{number of values}} = \frac{0}{n} = 0$$

To compensate for this situation, we use a statistical measure called the **standard deviation**, which uses the square of each deviation from the mean. The square of a negative value is always positive. The squared deviations are averaged (mean), and the result is called the **variance**.

The square root of the variance is taken so that the result can be interpreted within the context of the problem. Various formulas exist for finding the standard deviation of a set of values, but we examine only one formula, the formula for a sample of data or a small data set. This formula averages the values by dividing by 1 less than the number of values $(n - 1)$. Several calculations are necessary and are best organized in a table.

**Standard deviation:** a statistical measurement that shows how data are spread above and below the mean. The square root of the variance is the standard deviation.

**Variance:** a statistical measurement that is the average of the squared deviations of data from the mean.

**Find the standard deviation of a sample of a set of data**

1. Find the mean of the sample.

$$\dfrac{\text{Sum of values}}{\text{Number of values}}$$

2. Find the deviation of each value from the mean.

Data value − mean

3. Square each deviation.

Deviation × deviation

4. Find the sum of the squared deviations.

5. Divide the sum of the squared deviations by 1 *less than* the number of values in the data set. This amount is called the *variance*.

$$\dfrac{\text{Sum of squared deviations}}{n - 1}$$

6. Find the standard deviation by taking the square root of the variance found in Step 5.

**EXAMPLE 1** Find the standard deviation for the values 45, 63, 87, and 91.

From the previous example the mean is 71.5 and the number of values is 4.

| Data Values | Deviations from the Mean: Data Value − Mean | Squares of the Deviations from the Mean |
|---|---|---|
| 45 | $45 - 71.5 = -26.5$ | $(-26.5)(-26.5) = 702.25$ |
| 63 | $63 - 71.5 = -8.5$ | $(-8.5)(-8.5) = 72.25$ |
| 87 | $87 - 71.5 = 15.5$ | $(15.5)(15.5) = 240.25$ |
| 91 | $91 - 71.5 = 19.5$ | $(19.5)(19.5) = 380.25$ |
| Sum of Values = 286 | Sum of Deviations = 0 | Sum of Squared Deviations = 1,395 |

$$\text{Variance} = \dfrac{\text{sum of squared deviations}}{n - 1} = \dfrac{1{,}395}{4 - 1} = \dfrac{1{,}395}{3} = 465$$

$$\text{Standard deviation} = \text{square root of variance} = \sqrt{465}$$
$$= 21.56385865 \ or \ \mathbf{21.6}$$

A small standard deviation indicates that the mean is a typical value in the data set. A large standard deviation indicates that the mean is not typical, and other statistical measures should be examined to better understand the characteristics of the data set.

Examine the various statistics for the data set on a number line (Figure 7-19). We can confirm visually that the dispersion of the data is broad and the mean is not a typical value in the data set.

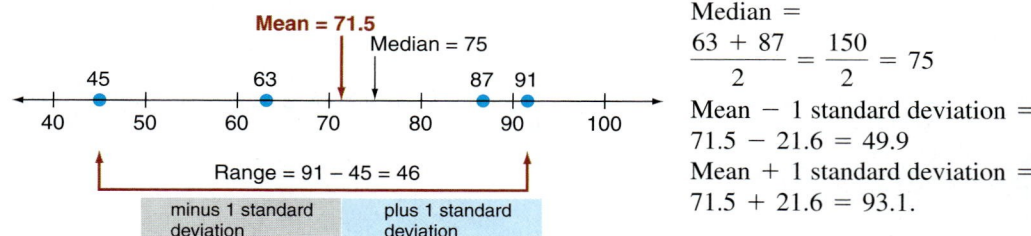

$$\text{Median} = \dfrac{63 + 87}{2} = \dfrac{150}{2} = 75$$

Mean − 1 standard deviation = $71.5 - 21.6 = 49.9$

Mean + 1 standard deviation = $71.5 + 21.6 = 93.1$.

**FIGURE 7-19**
**Dispersion of Data Using a Number Line**

**Normal distribution:** a characteristic of many data sets that shows that data graphs into a bell-shaped curve around the mean.

**Symmetrical:** a figure that if folded at a middle point, the two halves will match.

Another interpretation of the standard deviation is in its relationship to the **normal distribution**. Many data sets are normally distributed, and the graph of a normal distribution is a bell-shaped curve, as in Figure 7-20. The curve is **symmetrical**; that is, if folded at the highest point of the curve, the two halves would match. The mean of the data set is at the highest point or fold line. Then, half the data (50%) is to the left or *below* the mean and half the data (50%) is to the right or *above* the mean. Other characteristics of the normal distribution are:

68.3% of the data are within **1** standard deviation of the mean.
95.4% of the data are within **2** standard deviations of the mean.
99.7% of the data are within **3** standard deviations of the mean.

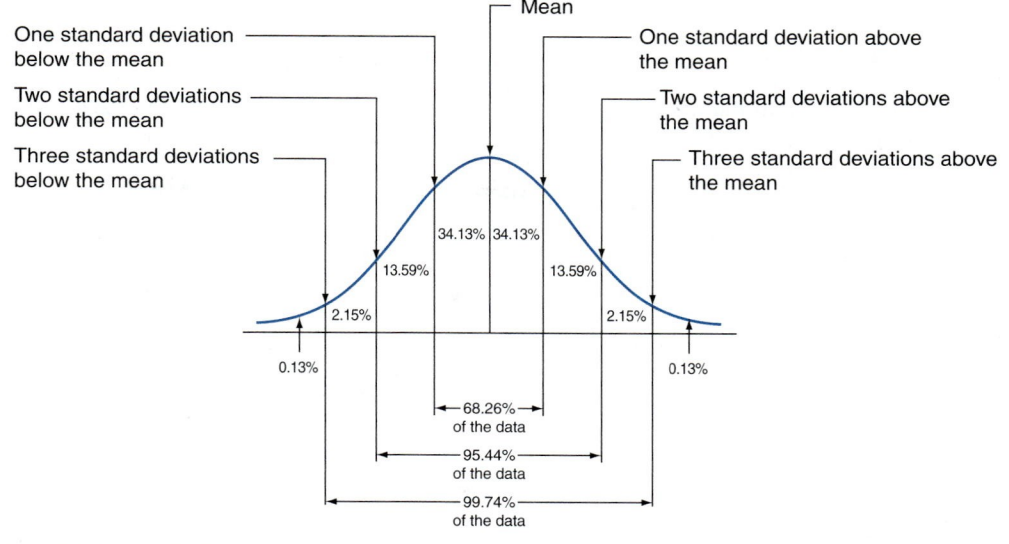

**FIGURE 7-20**
**The Normal Distribution**

**EXAMPLE 3**   An Auto Zone Duralast Gold automobile battery has an expected mean life of 46 months with a standard deviation of 4 months. In an order of 100 batteries, how many do you expect to last 54 months? Round to the nearest battery.

54 months is 8 months above the mean.
4 months is 1 standard deviation.
8 months is 2 standard deviations.
Visualize the facts (Figure 7-21).
   $50\% + 34.13\% + 13.59\% = 97.72\%$

$54 - 46 = 8$
$\dfrac{8}{4} = 2$

Sum of percents

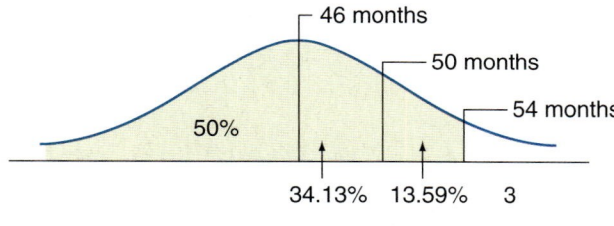

**FIGURE 7-21**
**Mean Life for Automotive Batteries**

97.72% of the batteries should last *less* than 54 months.

   $100\% - 97.72\% = 2.28\%$                              Complement of 97.72%

2.28% of the batteries should last 54 months or longer.

   $2.28\% \times 100 \text{ batteries} = 0.0228(100) = 2.28 \text{ batteries}$

**2 batteries (rounded) should last 54 months or longer.**

 **STOP AND CHECK**

1. Find the deviations from the mean for the set of data: 72, 75, 68, 73, 69.

2. Show that the sum of the deviations from the mean in Exercise 1 is 0.

*(continued)*

3. Find the sum of the squares of the deviations from the mean in Exercise 1.

4. Find the variance for the data in Exercise 1.

5. Find the standard deviation for the data in Exercise 1.

6. Refer to Example 3 on Auto Zone Duralast Gold batteries. In an order of 100 batteries, how many do you expect to last less than 50 months?

## 7-3 SECTION EXERCISES

### SKILL BUILDERS

*Use the sample ACT test scores 24, 30, 17, 22, 22 for Exercises 1–7.*

1. Find the range.

2. Find the mean.

3. Find the deviations from the mean.

4. Find the sum of squares of the deviations from the mean.

5. Find the variance.

6. Find the standard deviation.

7. In a set of 100 ACT scores that are normally distributed and based on the information in Exercises 1–6, (a) how many scores are expected to be lower than 18.31 (one standard deviation below the mean)? (b) How many of the 100 scores are expected to be below 32.38 (two standard deviations above the mean)?

### APPLICATIONS

*The data shows the total number of employee medical leave days taken for on-the-job accidents in the first six months of the year: 12, 6, 15, 9, 18, 12. Use the data for Exercises 8–14.*

8. Find the range of days taken for medical leave for each month.

9. Find the mean number of days taken for medical leave each month.

**10.** Find the deviations from the mean.

**11.** Find the sum of squares of the deviations from *the mean*.

**12.** Find the variance.

**13.** Find the standard deviation.

**14.** In a set of 36 months and based on the information in Exercises 8–13, how many months are expected to have fewer than 16.24 days per month reported medical leave (one standard deviation above the mean)?

## Learning Outcomes

**Section 7-1**

## What to Remember with Examples

**1** Find the mean. (p. 214)

1. Find the sum of the values.
2. Divide the sum by the total number of values.

$$\text{Mean} = \frac{\text{sum of values}}{\text{number of values}}$$

Find the mean price of the printers: $435, $398, $429, $435, $479, $495, $435

$$\text{Mean} = \frac{\text{sum of values}}{\text{number of values}}$$

$$= \$435 + \$398 + \$429 + \$479 + \$435 + \$495 + \$435 = \frac{\$3,106}{7}$$

$$= \$443.71 \text{ (rounded)}$$

**2** Find the median. (p. 215)

1. Arrange the values in order from smallest to largest or largest to smallest.
2. Count the number of values:
   (a) If the number of values is odd, identify the value in the middle.
   (b) If the number of values is even, find the mean of the middle two values.

$$\text{Median} = \text{middle value or mean of middle two values}$$

Find the median price of the printers.

Median = middle value of $495, $479, $435, $435, $435, $429, $398
       = $435

**3** Find the mode. (p. 216)

1. For each value, count the number of times the value occurs.
2. Identify the value or values that occur most frequently.

$$\text{Mode} = \text{most frequent value(s)}$$

Find the mode price of the printers for the prices given above.

Mode = most frequent value
     = $435

**4** Make and interpret a frequency distribution. (p. 218).

1. Identify the appropriate interval for classifying the data.
2. Tally the data.
3. Count the number in each interval.

Make a frequency distribution with the following data, indicating leave days for State College employees (see Table 7-13).

| 2 | 2 | 4 | 4 | 4 | 5 | 5 | 6 | 6 | 8 |
|---|---|---|---|---|---|---|---|---|---|
| 8 | 8 | 9 | 12 | 12 | 12 | 14 | 15 | 20 | 20 |

**TABLE 7-13**
Annual Leave Days of 20 State College Employees

| Class Interval | Tally | Class Frequency |
|---|---|---|
| 16–20 | // | 2 |
| 11–15 | ₩ | 5 |
| 6–10 | ₩ / | 6 |
| 1–5 | ₩ // | 7 |

To make a relative frequency distribution:

1. Make the frequency distribution.
2. Calculate the percent that the frequency of each class interval is of the total number of data items in the set.

$$\text{Relative frequency} = \frac{\text{class interval frequency}}{\text{total number in the data set}} \times 100\%$$

Make a relative frequency distribution for the leave days for State College employees.

| Class interval | Class frequency | Relative frequency |
|---|---|---|
| 16–20 | 2 | $\frac{2}{20}(100\%) = \frac{200\%}{20} = 10\%$ |
| 11–15 | 5 | $\frac{5}{20}(100\%) = \frac{500\%}{20} = 25\%$ |
| 6–10 | 6 | $\frac{6}{20}(100\%) = \frac{600\%}{20} = 30\%$ |
| 1–5 | 7 | $\frac{7}{20}(100\%) = \frac{700\%}{20} = 35\%$ |
| Total | 20 | 100% |

**5** Find the mean of grouped data. (p. 220)

1. Make a frequency distribution.
2. Find the products of the midpoint of the interval and the frequency for each interval for all intervals.
3. Find the sum of the frequencies.
4. Find the sum of the products from Step 2.
5. Divide the sum of the products by the sum of the frequencies.

$$\text{Mean of grouped data} = \frac{\text{Sum of the products of the midpoints and the frequencies}}{\text{sum of the frequencies}}$$

Find the grouped mean of the number of leave days taken by the State College employees (see Table 7-12).

Find the midpoint of each class interval:

$$\frac{16 + 20}{2} = \frac{36}{2} = 18 \qquad \frac{11 + 15}{2} = \frac{26}{2} = 13$$

$$\frac{6 + 10}{2} = \frac{16}{2} = 8 \qquad \frac{1 + 5}{2} = \frac{6}{2} = 3$$

| | Class frequency | Midpoint | Product of midpoint and frequency |
|---|---|---|---|
| 16–20 | 2 | 18 | 36 |
| 11–15 | 5 | 13 | 65 |
| 6–10 | 6 | 8 | 48 |
| 1–5 | 7 | 3 | 21 |
| Total | 20 | | 170 |

$$\text{mean of grouped data} = \frac{170}{20}$$
$$= 8.5$$

## Section 7-2

**1** Interpret and draw a bar graph. (p. 224)

**Draw a bar graph.**

1. Write an appropriate title.
2. Make appropriate labels for the bars and scale. The intervals on the scale should be equally spaced and include the smallest and largest values.
3. Draw bars to represent the data. Bars should be of uniform width.
4. Make additional notes as appropriate. For example, "Amounts in Thousands of Dollars" allows values such as $30,000 to be represented by 30.

Draw a bar graph to represent daily sales for the week.

| | |
|---|---|
| Monday: | $18,000 |
| Tuesday: | $30,000 |
| Wednesday: | $50,000 |
| Thursday: | $29,000 |
| Friday: | $40,000 |
| Saturday: | $32,000 |
| Sunday: | $8,000 |

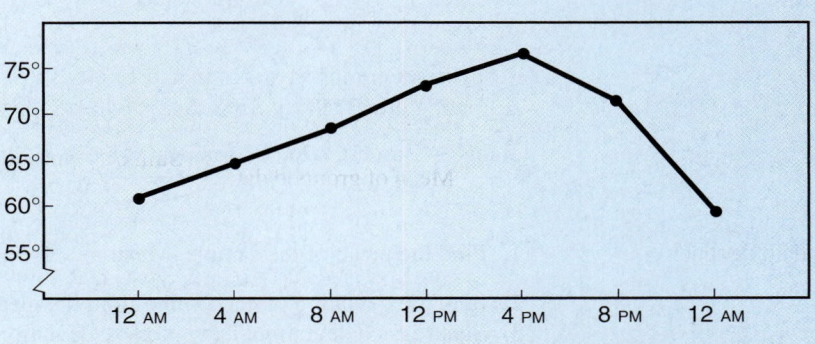

**FIGURE 7-22**
**Daily Sales in Thousands of Dollars**

## 2 Interpret and draw a line graph. (p. 227)

**Draw a line graph.**

1. Write an appropriate title.
2. Make and label appropriate horizontal and vertical scales, each with equally spaced intervals. Often, the horizontal scale represents time.
3. Use points to locate data on the graph.
4. Connect data points with line segments or a smooth curve.

Draw a line graph to show temperature changes: 12 A.M., 62°; 4 A.M., 65°; 8 A.M., 68°; 12 P.M., 73°; 4 P.M., 76°; 8 P.M., 72°; 12 A.M., 59°.

**FIGURE 7-23**
**Temperature for a 24-Hour Period**

## 3 Interpret and draw a circle graph. (p. 229)

**Draw a circle graph.**

1. Write an appropriate title.
2. Find the sum of the values in the data set.
3. Represent each value as a fractional or decimal part of the sum of values.
4. For each fraction or decimal, find the number of degrees in the sector of the circle to be represented by the fraction or decimal: Multiply the fraction or decimal by 360 degrees. The sum of the degrees for all sectors should be 360 degrees.
5. Use a compass (a tool for drawing circles) to draw a circle. Indicate the center of the circle and a starting point on the circle.
6. For each degree value, draw a sector: Use a protractor (a measuring instrument for angles) to measure the number of degrees for the sector of the circle to be represented by the value. Where the first sector ends, the next sector begins. The last sector should end at the starting point.
7. Label each sector of the circle and make additional explanatory notes as necessary.

Draw a circle graph to represent the data.

Total salary: $28,000
Housing: $8,000
Food: $6,000
Clothing: $1,000
Transportation: $2,000

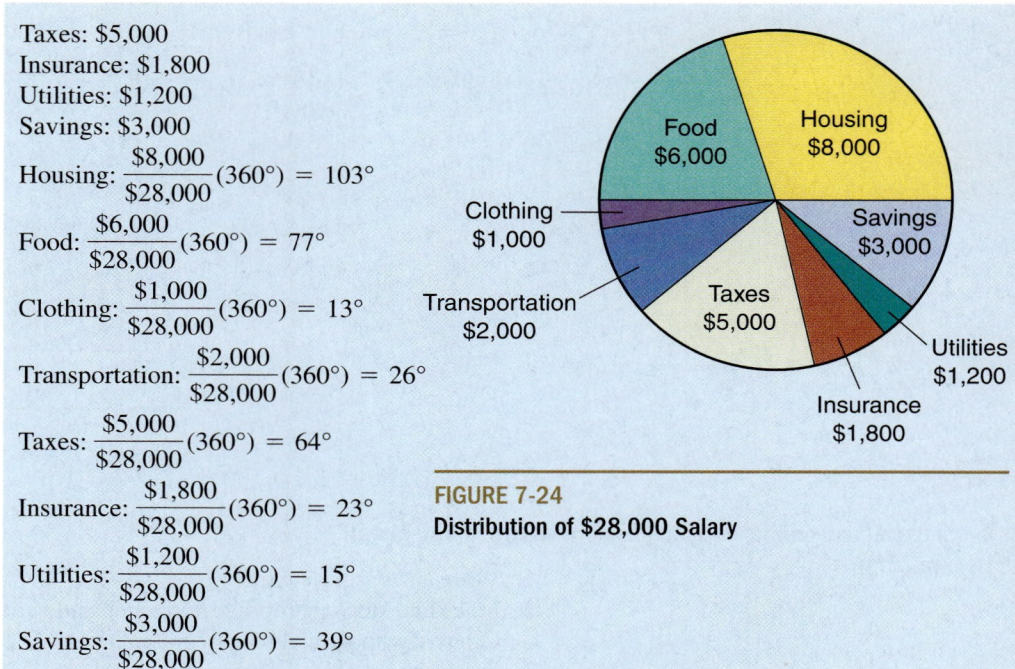

Taxes: $5,000
Insurance: $1,800
Utilities: $1,200
Savings: $3,000
Housing: $\dfrac{\$8,000}{\$28,000}(360°) = 103°$

Food: $\dfrac{\$6,000}{\$28,000}(360°) = 77°$

Clothing: $\dfrac{\$1,000}{\$28,000}(360°) = 13°$

Transportation: $\dfrac{\$2,000}{\$28,000}(360°) = 26°$

Taxes: $\dfrac{\$5,000}{\$28,000}(360°) = 64°$

Insurance: $\dfrac{\$1,800}{\$28,000}(360°) = 23°$

Utilities: $\dfrac{\$1,200}{\$28,000}(360°) = 15°$

Savings: $\dfrac{\$3,000}{\$28,000}(360°) = 39°$

**FIGURE 7-24**
**Distribution of $28,000 Salary**

## Section 7-3

**1** Find the range. (p. 233)

1. Find the highest and lowest value.
2. Find the difference between the highest and lowest values.

$$\text{Range} = \text{highest value} - \text{lowest value}$$

A survey of computer stores in a large city shows that a certain printer was sold for the following prices: $435, $398, $429, $479, $435, $495, and $435. Find the range.

$\text{Range} = \text{largest value} - \text{smallest value} = \$495 - \$398 = \$97$

**2** Find the standard deviation (p. 234)

1. Find the mean of the sample. $\text{Mean} = \dfrac{\text{sum of data values}}{\text{number of values}}$
2. Find the deviation of each value from the mean. $\text{Deviation} = \text{data value} - \text{mean}$
3. Square each deviation. Deviation $\times$ deviation
4. Find the sum of the squared deviations.
5. Divide the sum of the squared deviations by 1 *less* than the number of values in the data set. This is called the *variance*.

$$\dfrac{\text{sum of squared deviations}}{n - 1}$$

6. Find the standard deviation by taking the square root of the *variance*.

Find the standard deviation of these test scores: 68, 76, 76, 86, 87, 88, 93.

$$\text{Mean} = \dfrac{68 + 76 + 76 + 86 + 87 + 88 + 93}{7} = \dfrac{574}{7} = 82$$

| Deviations | Squared Deviations |
|---|---|
| $68 - 82 = -14$ | 196 |
| $76 - 82 = -6$ | 36 |
| $76 - 82 = -6$ | 36 |
| $86 - 82 = 4$ | 16 |
| $87 - 82 = 5$ | 25 |
| $88 - 82 = 6$ | 36 |
| $93 - 82 = 11$ | 121 |
| | 466   Sum of squared deviations |

$$\text{Variance} = \dfrac{\text{sum of squared deviations}}{n - 1} = \dfrac{466}{6} = 77.66666667$$

$$\text{Standard deviation} = \sqrt{\text{variance}} = \sqrt{77.66666667} = 8.812869378 = 8.8 \quad \text{Rounded}$$

# EXERCISES SET A

*Find the range, mean, median, and mode for the following. Round to the nearest hundredth if necessary.*

**1.** New car mileages

| | |
|---|---|
| 17 mi/gal | 16 mi/gal |
| 25 mi/gal | 22 mi/gal |
| 30 mi/gal | |

**2.** Sandwiches

| | |
|---|---|
| $0.95 | $1.65 |
| $1.27 | $1.97 |
| $1.65 | $1.15 |

**3.** Find the range, mean, median, and mode of the hourly pay rates for the employees.

| | | | |
|---|---|---|---|
| Thompson | $13.95 | Cleveland | $ 5.25 |
| Chang | $ 5.80 | Gandolfo | $ 4.90 |
| Jackson | $ 4.68 | DuBois | $13.95 |
| Smith | $ 4.90 | Serpas | $13.95 |

**4.** During the past year, Piazza's Clothiers sold a certain sweater at different prices: $42.95, $36.50, $40.75, $38.25, and $43.25. Find the range, mean, median, and mode of the selling prices.

*Use Table 7-14 for Exercises 5–9.*

**TABLE 7-14**
**Class Enrollment by Period and Days of the First Week for the Second Semester**

| Period | | Mon. | Tues. | Wed. | Thur. | Fri. |
|---|---|---|---|---|---|---|
| 1. | 7:00–7:50 A.M. | 277 | 374 | 259 | 340 | 207 |
| 2. | 7:55–8:45 A.M. | 653 | 728 | 593 | 691 | 453 |
| 3. | 8:50–9:40 A.M. | 908 | 863 | 824 | 798 | 604 |
| 4. | 9:45–10:35 A.M. | 962 | 782 | 849 | 795 | 561 |
| 5. | 10:40–11:30 A.M. | 914 | 858 | 795 | 927 | 510 |
| 6. | 11:35–12:25 P.M. | 711 | 773 | 375 | 816 | 527 |
| 7. | 12:30–1:20 P.M. | 686 | 734 | 696 | 733 | 348 |
| 8. | 1:25–2:15 P.M. | 638 | 647 | 659 | 627 | 349 |
| 9. | 2:20–3:10 P.M. | 341 | 313 | 325 | 351 | 136 |
| 10. | 3:15–4:05 P.M. | 110 | 149 | 151 | 160 | 45 |

5. Find the mean number of students for each period in Table 7-14. Round to the nearest whole number.

6. Which period had the highest average enrollment?

7. Which period had the lowest average enrollment?

8. Draw a bar graph representing the mean enrollment for each period.

9. Identify enrollment trends for the 10 periods from the bar graph in Exercise 8.

*Use Table 7-15 for Exercises 10–13.*

10. What is the least value for 2006 sales? For 2007 sales?

11. What is the greatest value for 2006 sales? For 2007 sales?

**TABLE 7-15**
**Sales for The Family Store, 2006–2007**

| | 2006 | 2007 |
|---|---|---|
| Girls' clothing | $ 74,675 | $ 81,534 |
| Boys' clothing | 65,153 | 68,324 |
| Women's clothing | 125,115 | 137,340 |
| Men's clothing | 83,895 | 96,315 |

12. Using the values in Table 7-15, which of the following interval sizes would be more appropriate in making a bar graph? Why?
    (a) $1,000 intervals ($60,000, $61,000, $62,000, . . .)
    (b) $10,000 intervals ($60,000, $70,000, $80,000, . . .)

13. Draw a comparative bar graph to show both the 2006 and 2007 values for The Family Store (see Table 7-15). Be sure to include a title, explanation of the scales, and any additional information needed.

*Use Figure 7-25 for Exercises 14–15.*

**14.** What three-month period maintained a fairly constant sales record?

**15.** What month showed a dramatic drop in sales?

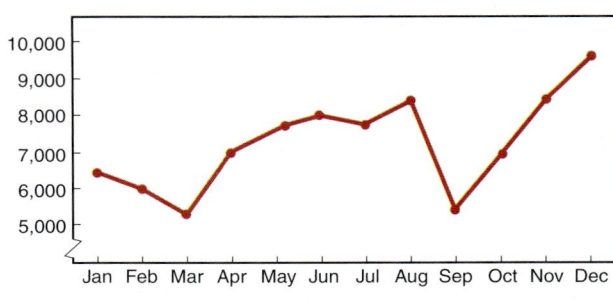

**FIGURE 7-25**
Monthly Sales for 7th Inning Sports Memorabilia

*Use Figure 7-26 for Exercises 16–19.*

**16.** What percent of the gross pay goes into savings? (Round to tenths.)

**17.** What percent of the gross pay is federal income tax? (Round to tenths.)

**18.** What percent of the gross pay is the take-home pay? (Round to tenths.)

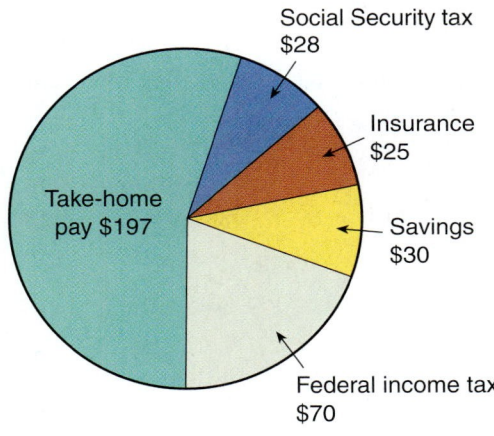

**FIGURE 7-26**
Distribution of Gross Pay ($350)

**19.** What are the total deductions for this payroll check?

**20.** Find the range for the data set: 90, 89, 82, 87, 93, 92, 98, 79, 81, 80.

**21.** Find the mean, median, and mode for the data set: 90, 89, 82, 87, 93, 92, 98, 79, 81, 80.

**22.** Find the variance for the scores in the following data set: 90, 89, 82, 87, 93, 92, 98, 79, 81, 80.

**23.** Find the standard deviation from the variance in Exercise 22.

**24.** Use the test scores of 24 students taking Marketing 235 to complete the frequency distribution and find the grouped mean rounded to the nearest whole number.

| | | | | | | | |
|---|---|---|---|---|---|---|---|
| 57 | 91 | 76 | 89 | 82 | 59 | 72 | 88 |
| 76 | 84 | 67 | 59 | 77 | 66 | 56 | 76 |
| 77 | 84 | 85 | 79 | 69 | 88 | 75 | 58 |

# EXERCISES SET B

*Find the range, mean, median, and mode for the following. Round to the nearest hundredth if necessary.*

**1.** Test scores

| | |
|---|---|
| 61 | 72 |
| 63 | 70 |
| 93 | 87 |

**2.** Credit hours

| | |
|---|---|
| 16 | 12 |
| 18 | 15 |
| 16 | 12 |
| 12 | |

**3.** Find the range, mean, median, and mode of the weights of the metal castings after being milled.

| | | | |
|---|---|---|---|
| Casting A | 1.08 kg | Casting D | 1.1 kg |
| Casting B | 1.15 kg | Casting E | 1.25 kg |
| Casting C | 1.19 kg | Casting F | 1.1 kg |

*Use Figure 7-27 for Exercises 4–7.*

**4.** What expenditure is expected to be the same next year as this year?

**5.** What two expenditures are expected to increase next year?

**6.** What two expenditures are expected to decrease next year?

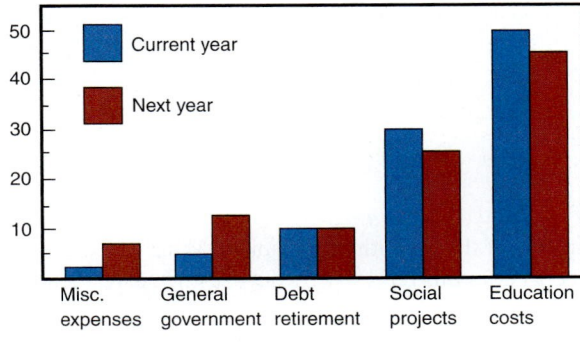

**FIGURE 7-27**
**Distribution of Tax Dollars**

**7.** What expenditure was greatest both years?

*Use the following information for Exercises 8–11. The temperatures were recorded at two-hour intervals on June 24.*

| | | | | | | | |
|---|---|---|---|---|---|---|---|
| 12 A.M. | 76° | 8 A.M. | 70° | 2 P.M. | 84° | 8 P.M. | 82° |
| 2 A.M. | 75° | 10 A.M. | 76° | 4 P.M. | 90° | 10 P.M. | 79° |
| 4 A.M. | 72° | 12 P.M. | 81° | 6 P.M. | 90° | 12 A.M. | 77° |
| 6 A.M. | 70° | | | | | | |

**8.** What is the smallest value?

**9.** What is the greatest value?

**10.** Which interval size is most appropriate when making a line graph for the data? Why?
  a. 1°
  b. 5°
  c. 50°
  d. 100°

**11.** Draw a line graph representing the data. Be sure to include the title, explanation of the scales, and any additional information needed.

**12.** Which of the following terms would describe the line graph in Exercise 11.
  a. Continually increasing
  b. Continually decreasing
  c. Fluctuating

*Use Figure 7-28 for Exercises 13–15.*

**13.** What percent of the overall cost does the lot represent? (Round to the nearest tenth.)

**14.** What is the cost of the lot with landscaping? What percent of the total cost does this represent? Round to the nearest tenth.

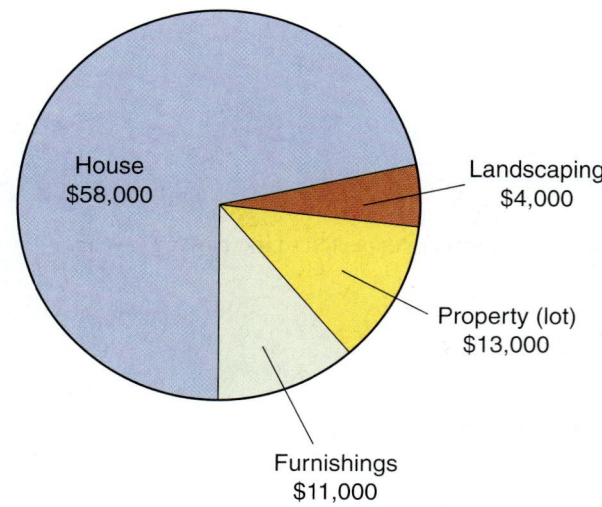

**FIGURE 7-28**
**Distribution of Costs for an $86,000 Home**

**15.** What is the cost of the house with furnishings? What percent of the total cost does this represent? Round to the nearest tenth.

*Use Table 7-16 for Exercises 16–19.*

**TABLE 7-16**
Automobile Dealership's New and Repeat Business

| Customer | Cars Sold |
|---|---|
| New | 920 |
| Repeat | 278 |

**16.** What was the total number of cars sold?

**17.** How many degrees should be used to represent the new car business on a circle (to the nearest whole degree)?

**18.** How many degrees should be used to represent the repeat business on the circle graph (to the nearest whole degree)?

**19.** Construct a circle graph for the data in Table 7-16. Label the parts of the graph as "New" and "Repeat." Be sure to include a title and any additional information needed.

*Use Table 7-17 for Exercises 20 and 21.*

**TABLE 7-17**

| First Semester Fall | | | Second Semester Spring | | | Third Semester Fall | | | Fourth Semester Spring | | |
|---|---|---|---|---|---|---|---|---|---|---|---|
| Course | Cr. Hr. | Gr. | Course | Cr. Hr. | Gr. | Course | Cr. Hr. | Gr. | Course | Cr. Hr. | Gr. |
| BUS MATH | 4 | 90 | SOC | 3 | 92 | FUNS | 4 | 88 | CAL I | 4 | 89 |
| ACC I | 4 | 89 | PSYC | 3 | 91 | ACC II | 4 | 89 | ACC IV | 4 | 90 |
| ENG I | 3 | 91 | ENG II | 3 | 90 | ENG III | 3 | 95 | ENG IV | 3 | 96 |
| HISTORY | 3 | 92 | ACC II | 4 | 88 | PURCH | 3 | 96 | ADV | 3 | 93 |
| ECON | 5 | 85 | ECON II | 4 | 86 | MGMT I | 5 | 84 | MGMT II | 5 | 83 |

**20.** Give the range and mode of grades for each semester.

**21.** Give the range and mode of grades for the entire two-year program.

**22.** Find the mean, variance, and standard deviation for the scores: 82, 60, 78, 81, 65, 72, 72, 78.

**EXCEL**

**23.** Use the test scores of 32 students taking Business 205 to complete the frequency distribution and find the grouped mean rounded to the nearest whole number.

| | | | | | | | |
|---|---|---|---|---|---|---|---|
| 88 | 91 | 68 | 83 | 72 | 69 | 82 | 94 |
| 86 | 94 | 69 | 59 | 75 | 66 | 62 | 66 |
| 87 | 88 | 95 | 92 | 95 | 90 | 89 | 60 |
| 92 | 83 | 79 | 78 | 74 | 70 | 79 | 68 |

# PRACTICE TEST

CHAPTER 7

**1.** Use the data to find the statistical measures.

42  86  92  15  32  67  48  19  87  63
15  19  21  17  53  27  21  15  82  15

a. What is the range?    b. What is the mean?    c. What is the median?    d. What is the mode?

*The costs of producing a piece of luggage at ACME Luggage Company are labor, $45; materials, $40; overhead, $35. Use this information for Exercises 2–7.*

**2.** What is the total cost of producing a piece of luggage?

**3.** What percent of the total cost is attributed to labor?

**4.** What percent of the total cost is attributed to materials?

**5.** What percent of the total cost is attributed to overhead?

**6.** Compute the number of degrees for labor, materials, and overhead needed for a circle graph.

**7.** Construct a circle graph for the cost of producing a piece of luggage.

*Katz Florist recorded the sales for a six-month period for fresh and silk flowers in Table 7-18. Use the table for Exercises 8–11.*

**8.** What is the greatest value of fresh flowers? Of silk flowers?

**TABLE 7-18**
Sales for Katz Florist, January–June

|        | January | February | March   | April   | May     | June    |
|--------|---------|----------|---------|---------|---------|---------|
| Fresh  | $11,520 | $22,873  | $10,380 | $12,562 | $23,712 | $15,816 |
| Silk   | $ 8,460 | $14,952  | $ 5,829 | $10,621 | $17,892 | $ 7,583 |

**9.** What is the smallest value of fresh flowers? Of silk flowers?

**10.** What interval size would be most appropriate when making a bar graph? Why?

a. $100

b. $1,000

c. $5,000

d. $10,000

**11.** Construct a bar graph for the sales at Katz Florist.

*Use the following data for Exercises 12–13. The totals of the number of laser printers sold in the years 2006 through 2011 by Smart Brothers Computer Store are as follows:*

| 2006 | 2007 | 2008 | 2009 | 2010 | 2011 |
|------|------|------|------|------|------|
| 983 | 1,052 | 1,117 | 615 | 250 | 400 |

**12.** What is the smallest value? The greatest value?

**13.** Draw a line graph representing the data. Use an interval of 250. Be sure to include a title and explanation of the scales.

**14.** A dusk-to-dawn outdoor lightbulb has an expected (mean) life of 8,000 hours with a standard deviation of 250 hours. How many bulbs in a batch of 500 can be expected to last no longer than 7,500 hours?

1. What type of information does a circle graph show?

2. Give a situation in which it would be appropriate to organize the data in a circle graph.

3. What type of information does a bar graph show?

4. Give a situation in which it would be appropriate to organize the data in a bar graph.

5. What type of information does a line graph show?

6. Give a situation in which it would be appropriate to organize the data in a line graph.

7. Explain the differences among the three types of averages: the mean, the median, and the mode.

8. What can we say about the mean for a data set with a large range?

9. What can we say about the mean for a data set with a small range?

10. What components of a graph enable us to analyze and interpret the data given in the graph?

# Challenge Problem

Have the computers made a mistake? You have been attending Northeastern State College (which follows a percentage grading system) for two years. You have received good grades, but after four semesters you have not made the Dean's List, which requires an overall average of 90% for all accumulated credits or 90% for any given semester. Your grade reports are shown in Table 7-19.

### TABLE 7-19

| First Semester Fall | | | Second Semester Spring | | | Third Semester Fall | | | Fourth Semester Spring | | |
|---|---|---|---|---|---|---|---|---|---|---|---|
| Course | Cr. Hr. | Gr. | Course | Cr. Hr. | Gr. | Course | Cr. Hr. | Gr. | Course | Cr. Hr. | Gr. |
| BUS MATH | 4 | 90 | SOC | 3 | 92 | FUNS | 4 | 88 | CAL I | 4 | 89 |
| ACC I | 4 | 89 | PSYC | 3 | 91 | ACC II | 4 | 89 | ACC IV | 4 | 90 |
| ENG I | 3 | 91 | ENG II | 3 | 90 | ENG III | 3 | 95 | ENG IV | 3 | 96 |
| HISTORY | 3 | 92 | ACC II | 4 | 88 | PURCH | 3 | 96 | ADV | 3 | 93 |
| ECON | 5 | 85 | ECON II | 4 | 86 | MGMT I | 5 | 84 | MGMT II | 5 | 83 |

To find the grade point average for a semester, multiply each grade by the credit hours. Add the products and then divide by the total number of credit hours for the semester. To calculate the overall grade point average, proceed similarly, but divide the sum of the products for all semesters by the total accumulated credit hours. Find the grade point average for each semester and the overall grade point average.

## 7.1 Cell Phone Company Uses Robotic Assembly Line

A small cell phone manufacturing company using a robotic assembly line employs 13 people with the following annual salaries:

| | |
|---|---|
| $120,000 President | $100,000 Vice president |
| $ 75,000 Financial manager | $ 65,000 Sales manager |
| $ 40,000 Production manager | $ 30,000 Production supervisor |
| $ 30,000 Warehouse supervisor | $ 16,000 Six unskilled laborers |

1. Calculate the mean, median, and mode for the salaries rounded up to the nearest thousand.

2. The statistic most often used to describe company salaries is the median or the mean. For this company, does the mean give an accurate description of the salaries? Why or why not?

3. Which statistic would this company's labor union representative be most likely to cite during contract negotiations and why? Which statistic would the company president most likely report at the annual shareholders' meeting and why?

4. Name another situation in which it would be beneficial to report the highest average salary, and name another situation where it would be beneficial to use the lowest average salary.

## 7.2 Ink Hombre: Tattoos and Piercing

At 42 years of age, Enrique Chavez was starting to think more and more about retirement. After 17 years of running one of the bay area's most popular tattoo parlors, Ink Hombre, he decided to take on a partner—his 21-year-old bilingual niece Diana. Her words still echoed in his head—the same words she repeated every time someone left his shop to go elsewhere: "Tío, debe ofrecer la perforación del cuerpo: You should offer body piercing." She would go on to say, "Piercing gives people the opportunity to express their identity, just like a tattoo." She was right, of course. After she got her piercing certification, Diana came to work with Enrique full-time. But she didn't come cheaply. Between her salary and benefits, she was costing the business $1,000 per month! Enrique kept very detailed records, and her first month's sales were a bit disappointing. Piercings were offered as Category I, II, or III, and cost $35, $55, and $75 for stainless steel jewelry, respectively, and $55, $85, and $120 for gold. Diana sold five Category I, two Category II, and three Category III in stainless, and one each of categories I, II, and III in gold.

1. Find the mean, median, and mode for Diana's first month of sales.

2. Given the total sales value for Diana's first month, how long will it take for her to break even with her salary and benefits, assuming a 10 percent increase in sales value each month? Is the increase more likely to come from increased number of sales or a higher average sales value?

3. Diana's second month results show that she made six sales at $35, two at $55, three at $75, three at $85, and two at $120. Calculate the standard deviation for this data set. Does your answer for the standard deviation indicate that this is a normal distribution? If not, what are the implications?

# Trade and Cash Discounts

## Wisconsin Dells: Mount Olympus

Wisconsin Dells is known as "The Waterpark Capital of the World." One of the newer attractions, Mount Olympus Water and Theme Park, is the Dells' first "mega park," and it has a theme of Greek mythology. The park has 37 water slides, 15 kiddie rides, 9 go-cart tracks, 7 rollercoasters, a wave pool, water play areas, and much more.

The main attraction is a wooden roller coaster named Hades. With a 65-degree drop, the world's longest underground tunnel, and speeds up to 70 mph, it was voted "Best New Ride" in 2005 by *Amusement Today*. Slowly you scale the 160-foot height of Hades, then with heart-pounding speed, reach the bottom of the first 140-foot drop, make a 90-degree turn underground in complete darkness, then blast into daylight to dip, spin around, and do it again. You won't forget the experience of riding Hades, the master of the Underworld!

How do you get tickets to Mount Olympus, or one of over 70 other Wisconsin Dells attractions? More importantly, how can you get the best discounts available? One of the best places to start is www.wisdells.com, where you can find a number of vacation packages offering substantial discounts. There are waterpark packages, a Murder Mystery Dinner Party package, and even a Will You Marry Me? package. Some packages offer discounts of $100 or more per day.

Angela was organizing a youth trip for her church, and decided to check out ticket prices at the Mount Olympus website at: www.mtolympusthemepark.com. There she learned she could receive a $3 discount off the regular price of $21, on an all day unlimited pass for tickets purchased online. She also discovered the discount could be as much as $6 per person for a group of 15 or more. Although Angela wasn't sure yet which would be the best deal, she knew that she wanted to save her church group as much as possible—in this case it could be $60 or more. Either way, Angela, enjoy the rides and hang on to your hat.

## LEARNING OUTCOMES

### 8-1 Single Trade Discounts

1. Find the trade discount using a single trade discount rate; find the net price using the trade discount.
2. Find the net price using the complement of the single trade discount rate.

### 8-2 Trade Discount Series

1. Find the net price applying a trade discount series and using the net decimal equivalent.
2. Find the trade discount, applying a trade discount series and using the single discount equivalent.

### 8-3 Cash Discounts and Sales Terms

1. Find the cash discount and the net amount using ordinary dating terms.
2. Interpret and apply end-of-month (EOM) terms.
3. Interpret and apply receipt-of-goods (ROG) terms.
4. Find the amount credited and the outstanding balance from partial payments.
5. Interpret freight terms.

A discount is money deducted from the list price. Manufacturers and distributors give *trade discounts* as incentives for a sale and *cash discounts* as incentives for paying promptly. Discounts are usually established by *discount rates,* given in percent or decimal form, based on the money owed. The discount, then, is a percentage of the list price.

## 8-1 SINGLE TRADE DISCOUNTS

### LEARNING OUTCOMES

1 Find the trade discount using a single trade discount rate; find the net price using the trade discount.
2 Find the net price using the complement of the single trade discount rate.

Most products go from the manufacturer to the consumer by way of the wholesale merchant (wholesaler or distributor) and the retail merchant (retailer).

*Product flow*

Manufacturer → Wholesaler → Retailer → Consumer

*Price flow*

| Consumer → | Retailer → | Wholesaler → | Manufacturer |
|---|---|---|---|
| List price | Net price | Net price | Cost |
| | Discount off list | Discount off list | |
| $80 | $56 | $40 | $20 |
| | 30% off list | 50% off list | |

Manufacturers often describe each of their products in a book or catalog that is made available to wholesalers or retailers. In such catalogs, manufacturers suggest a price at which each product should be sold to the consumer. This price is called the **suggested retail price**, the **catalog price**, or, most commonly, the **list price**.

When a manufacturer sells an item to the wholesaler, the manufacturer deducts a certain amount from the list price of the item. The amount deducted is called the **trade discount**. The wholesaler pays the **net price**, which is the difference between the list price and the trade discount. Likewise, the wholesaler discounts the list price when selling to the retailer. The discount rate that the wholesaler gives the retailer is smaller than the discount rate that the manufacturer gives the wholesaler. The consumer pays the list price.

The trade discount is not usually stated in the published catalog. Instead, the wholesaler or retailer calculates it using the list price and the **discount rate**. The discount rate is a *percent* of the list price.

The manufacturer makes available lists of discount rates for all items in the catalog. The discount rates vary considerably depending on such factors as the wholesaler's and retailer's purchasing history, the season, the condition of the economy, whether a product is being discontinued, and the manufacturer's efforts to encourage volume purchases. Each time the discount rate changes, the manufacturer updates the listing. Each new discount rate applies to the original list price in the catalog.

**Suggested retail price, catalog price, list price:** three common terms for the price at which the manufacturer suggests an item should be sold to the consumer.

**Trade discount:** the amount of discount that the wholesaler or retailer receives off the list price, or the difference between the list price and the net price.

**Net price:** the price the wholesaler or retailer pays or the list price minus the trade discount.

**Discount rate:** a percent of the list price.

## 1 Find the trade discount using a single trade discount rate; find the net price using the trade discount.

List prices and discounts apply the percentage formula.

$$\text{Portion (part)} = \text{rate (percent)} \times \text{base (whole)}$$

The portion is the trade discount $T$, the rate is the single trade discount rate $R$, and the base is the list price $L$.

$$P = RB$$
$$T = RL$$

**HOW TO**    Find the trade discount using a single trade discount rate

1. Identify the single discount rate and the list price.
2. Multiply the list price by the decimal equivalent of the single trade discount rate.

$$\text{Trade discount} = \text{single trade discount rate} \times \text{list price}$$
$$T = RL$$

Since the trade discount is deducted from the list price to get the net price, once you know the trade discount, you can calculate the net price.

1. Identify the list price and the trade discount.
2. Subtract the trade discount from the list price.

$$\text{Net price} = \text{list price} - \text{trade discount}$$
$$N = L - T$$

**EXAMPLE 1** The list price of a refrigerator is $1,200. Young's Appliance Store can buy the refrigerator at the list price less 20%. (a) Find the trade discount. (b) Find the net price of the refrigerator.

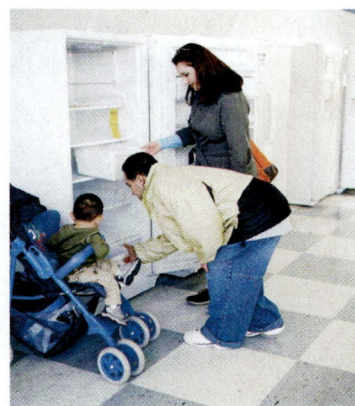

(a) Trade discount = single trade discount rate × list price

$$20\%(\$1,200) = 0.2(\$1,200)$$
$$= \$240$$

Discount rate is 20%; list price is $1,200. Change the percent to a decimal equivalent. Multiply.

**The trade discount is $240.**

(b) Net price = list price − trade discount
$$= \$1,200 - \$240$$
$$= \$960$$

List price is $1,200; trade discount is $240. Subtract.

**The net price is $960.**

 **STOP AND CHECK**

1. The list price of an NSX-T Acura is $89,765. Shavells Automobiles can buy the car at the list price less 12%.
   a. Find the trade discount.

   b. Find the net price of the car.

2. Find the trade discount and net price of an electric VeloBinder that has a retail price of $124 and a trade discount of 32%.

3. Direct Safes offers a Depository Safe for $425 with an 8% trade discount. Find the amount of the trade discount and the net price.

4. PlumbingStore.com buys one model of tankless water heater that has a list price of $395. The trade discount is 18%. What is the trade discount and net price of the heater?

5. The *Generation Money Book* has a suggested list price of $21.00 and ECampus.com can get a 24% trade discount on each copy of the book. Find the trade discount and net price.

6. Duty Free Stores purchased handbags, wallets, and key fobs for a total of $20,588.24 from Gucci, the manufacturer. The order has a trade discount of 15%. Find the amount of trade discount and find the net price of the goods.

## 2 Find the net price using the complement of the single trade discount rate.

**Complement of a percent:** the difference between 100% and the given percent.

Another method for calculating the net price uses the *complement* of a percent. The **complement of a percent** is the difference between 100% and the given percent. For example, the complement of 35% is 65%, since $100\% - 35\% = 65\%$. The complement of 20% is 80% because $100\% - 20\% = 80\%$.

The complement of the single trade discount rate can be used to find the net price. Observe the relationships among the rates for the list price, discount, and net price.

| List price | Discount (amount off list) | Net price (amount paid) |
|---|---|---|
| 100% | 25% of list price | 75% of list price |
| 100% | 20% of list price | 80% of list price |
| 100% | 40% of list price | 60% of list price |
| 100% | 50% of list price | 50% of list price |

Since the complement is a percent, it is a rate. The complement of the trade discount rate is the **net price rate**. The single trade discount rate is used to calculate the amount the retailer *does not* pay: the trade discount. The net price rate is used to calculate the amount the retailer *does* pay: the net price.

---

## HOW TO · Find the net price using the complement of the single trade discount rate

Find the net price of a computer that lists for \$3,200 with a trade discount of 35%.

1. Find the net price rate: Subtract the single trade discount rate from 100%.

$$100\% - 35\% = 65\%$$

2. Multiply the decimal equivalent of the net price rate by the list price.

$$\text{Net price} = 0.65(\$3{,}200)$$
$$= \$2{,}080$$

$$\text{Net price} = \text{Net price rate} \times \text{list price}$$

or

$$\text{Net Price} = (100\% - \text{single trade discount rate}) \times \text{list price}$$

---

## TIP

**To Summarize the Concept of Trade Discounts**

$$\text{Trade discount} = \text{amount list price is reduced}$$
$$= \text{part of list price you } do\ not \text{ pay}$$
$$\text{Net price} = \text{part of list price you } do \text{ pay}$$

---

### EXAMPLE 1

Mays' Stationery Store buys 300 pens at \$0.30 each, 200 legal pads at \$0.60 each, and 100 boxes of paper clips at \$0.90 each. The single trade discount rate for the order is 12%. Find the net price of the order.

| | |
|---|---|
| $300(\$0.30) = \$\ 90$ | Find the list price of the pens. |
| $200(\$0.60) = \$120$ | Find the list price of the legal pads. |
| $100(\$0.90) = \$\ 90$ | Find the list price of the paper clips. |
| $\$300$ | Add to find the total list price. |

$$\text{Net price} = (100\% - \text{single trade discount rate}) \times \text{list price}$$

The single trade discount rate is 12%; the list price is \$300.

$$= (100\% - 12\%)(\$300)$$

The complement of 12% is 88%.

$$= 88\%(\$300)$$

Write 88% as a decimal.

$$= 0.88(\$300)$$

Multiply.

$$= \$264$$

**The net price is \$264.**

---

 **STOP AND CHECK**

1. Find the net price of the PC software SystemWorks that lists for \$70 and has a discount rate of 12%.

2. The InFocus LP 120 projector lists for \$3,200 and has a trade discount rate of 15%. Find the net price.

3. Canon has a fancy new digital camera that lists for \$1,299 and has a trade discount of 18%. What is the net price?

4. Find the net price of 100 sheets of display board that list for \$3.99 each, 40 pairs of scissors that list for \$1.89 each, and 20 boxes of push pins that list for \$3.99 if a 22% trade discount is allowed.

## SKILL BUILDERS

1. Find the trade discount on a computer that lists for $400 if a discount rate of 30% is offered.

2. Find the net price of the computer in Exercise 1.

3. Calculate the trade discount for 20 boxes of computer paper if the unit price is $14.67 and a single trade discount rate of 20% is allowed.

4. Calculate the trade discount for 30 cases of antifreeze coolant if each case contains 6 one-gallon units that cost $2.18 per gallon and a single trade discount rate of 18% is allowed.

5. Calculate the net price for the 20 boxes of computer paper in Exercise 3.

6. Calculate the net price for the 30 cases of antifreeze coolant in Exercise 4.

7. Use the net price rate to calculate the net price for the 20 boxes of computer paper in Exercise 3. Compare this net price with the net price found in Exercise 5.

8. Use the net price rate to calculate the net price for the 30 cases of antifreeze coolant in Exercise 4. Compare this net price with the net price found in Exercise 6.

9. Which method of calculating net price do you prefer? Why?

**EXCEL** 10. If you were writing a spreadsheet program to calculate the net price for several items and you were not interested in showing the trade discount, which method would you be likely to use? Why?

11. Complete the following invoice 2501, finding the net price using the single trade discount rate.

12. Verify that the net price calculated in Exercise 11 is correct by recalculating the net price using the net price rate.

Invoice No. 2501
October 15, 20XX

| Qty. | Item | Unit price | List price |
|------|------|-----------|-----------|
| 15 | Notebooks | $1.50 | |
| 10 | Loose leaf paper | 0.89 | |
| 30 | Ballpoint pens | 0.79 | |
| | | Total list price | |
| | | 40% trade discount | |
| | | Net price | |

13. Best Buy Company, Inc. purchased video and digital cameras from Sony for its new store in Shanghai, China, with a total of $148,287. The order has a trade discount of 28%. Use the net price rate to find the net price of the merchandise.

# 8-2 TRADE DISCOUNT SERIES

## LEARNING OUTCOMES

1 Find the net price applying a trade discount series and using the net decimal equivalent.
2 Find the trade discount, applying a trade discount series and using the single discount equivalent.

Sometimes a manufacturer wants to promote a particular item or encourage additional business from a buyer. Also, buyers may be entitled to additional discounts as a result of buying large quantities. In such cases, the manufacturer may offer additional discounts that are deducted one after another from the list price. Such discounts are called a **trade discount series** or **chain discounts**. An example of a discount series is $400 (list price) with a discount series of 20/10/5 (discount rates). That is, a discount of 20% is allowed off the list price, a discount of 10% is allowed off the amount that was left after the first discount, and a discount of 5% is allowed off the amount that was left after the second discount. It *does not* mean a total discount of 35% is allowed on the original list price.

One way to calculate the net price is to make a series of calculations:

| | | |
|---|---|---|
| $400(0.2) = $80 | $400 - $80 = $320 | The first discount is taken on the list price of $400, which leaves $320. |
| $320(0.1) = $32 | $320 - $32 = $288 | The second discount is taken on $320, which leaves $288. |
| $288(0.05) = $14.40 | $288 - $14.40 = $273.60 | The third discount is taken on $288, which leaves the net price of $273.60. |

Thus, the net price of a $400 order with a discount series of 20/10/5 is $273.60.

It is time-consuming to calculate a trade discount series this way. The business world uses a faster way of calculating the net price of a purchase when a series of discounts are taken.

## 1 Find the net price applying a trade discount series and using the net decimal equivalent.

Complements are used to find net prices directly. For the $400 purchase with discounts of 20/10/5, the net price after the first discount is 80% of $400 since $100\% - 20\% = 80\%$.

$$0.8(400) = \$320$$

The net price after the second discount is 90% of $320.

$$0.9(\$320) = \$288$$

The net price after the third discount is 95% of $288.

$$0.95(\$288) = \$273.60$$

To condense this process, the decimal equivalents of the complements of the discount rates can be multiplied in a continuous sequence.

$$(0.8)(0.9)(0.95)(\$400) = 0.684(\$400) = \$273.60$$

The product of the decimal equivalents of the complements of the discount rates in a series is the **net decimal equivalent** of the net price rate.

---

**HOW TO** Find net price using the net decimal equivalent of a trade discount series

Find the net price of a copy machine if the list price is $1,830 with a series discount of 10/10.

1. Find the net decimal equivalent: Multiply the decimal form of the complement of each trade discount rate in the series.

$$0.9(0.9) = 0.81$$

2. Multiply the net decimal equivalent by the list price.

Net price = 0.81($1,830)
Net price = $1,482.30

Net price = net decimal equivalent × list price

---

**EXAMPLE 1** Find the net price of an order with a list price of $600 and a trade discount series of 15/10/5.

$100\% - 15\% = 85\% = 0.85$    Find the complement of each discount rate and write it as an
$100\% - 10\% = 90\% = 0.9$    equivalent decimal.
$100\% - 5\% = 95\% = 0.95$
$0.85(0.9)(0.95) = 0.72675$    Multiply the complements to find the net decimal equivalent.

Net price = net decimal equivalent × list price
= 0.72675($600)
= $436.05

The net decimal equivalent is 0.72675; the list price is $600.

**The net price for a $600 order with a trade discount series of 15/10/5 is $436.05.**

---

## TIP

**A Trade Discount Series Does Not Add Up!**

The trade discount series of 15/10/5 is *not* equivalent to the single discount rate of 30% (which is the *sum* of 15%, 10%, and 5%). Look at Example 1 worked incorrectly.

Net price = net decimal equivalent × list price
= (100% − 30%) × list price
= 0.70($600)
= $420

### INCORRECT

To add the discount rates implies that all the discounts are taken from the list price. In a series of discounts, each successive discount is taken from the remaining price.

---

### EXAMPLE 2

One manufacturer lists a desk at $700 with a discount series of 20/10/10. A second manufacturer lists the same desk at $650 with a discount series of 10/10/10. Which is the better deal?

| What You Know | What You Are Looking For | Solution Plan |
|---|---|---|
| List price for first deal: $700<br><br>Discount series for first deal: 20/10/10<br><br>List price for second deal: $650<br><br>Discount series for second deal: 10/10/10 | Net price for the first deal<br><br>Net price for the second deal<br><br>Which deal on the desk is better? | Net price = net decimal equivalent × list price |

**Solution**

Decimal equivalents of complements of 20%, 10%, and 10% are 0.8, 0.9, and 0.9, respectively.

Net decimal equivalent = 0.8(0.9)(0.9)      Deal 1
= 0.648
Net price for first deal = (0.648)$700
= $453.60

Decimal equivalents of complements of 10%, 10%, and 10% are 0.9, 0.9, and 0.9, respectively.

Net decimal equivalent = 0.9(0.9)(0.9)      Deal 2
= 0.729
Net price for second deal = (0.729)$650
= $473.85

**Conclusion**

The net price for the first deal is $20.25 less than the net price for the second deal ($473.85 − $453.60 = $20.25).

**The first deal—the $700 desk with the 20/10/10 discount series—is the better deal.**

---

## ✔ STOP AND CHECK

1. Find the net price of a piano that has a list price of $4,800 and a trade discount series of 10/5.

2. The website www.Mobile-Tronics.com offers a three-deck Instrument Cart at a retail (list) price of $535 and a trade discount series of 12/6. What is the net price?

*(continued)*

**3.** A five-shelf Instrument Cart that lists for $600 has a trade discount series of 15/10. What is the net price?

**4.** A Tuffy Utility Cart listing for $219 has a chain discount of 10/6/5. What is the net price?

**5.** One manufacturer lists a Stand-up Workstation for $448 with a chain discount of 10/6/4. Another manufacturer lists a station of similar quality for $550 with a discount series of 15/10/10. Which is the better deal?

**6.** Home Depot can purchase gas grills from one manufacturer for $695 with a 5/10/10 discount. Another manufacturer offers a similar grill for $705 with a 6/10/12 discount. Which is the better deal?

## 2 Find the trade discount, applying a trade discount series and using the single discount equivalent.

If you want to know how much you have *saved* by using a discount series, you can calculate the savings—the trade discount—the long way, by finding the net price and then subtracting the net price from the list price. Or you can apply another, quicker complement method. In percent form, the complement of the net decimal equivalent is the **single discount equivalent**.

> **Single discount equivalent:** the complement of net decimal equivalent. It is the decimal equivalent of a single discount rate that is equal to the series of discount rates.

Total amount of a series of discounts = single discount equivalent × list price
Net amount you pay after a series of discounts = net decimal equivalent × list price

---

**HOW TO** Find the trade discount using the single discount equivalent

1. Find the single discount equivalent: Subtract the net decimal equivalent from 1.

   Single discount equivalent = 1 − net decimal equivalent

2. Multiply the single discount equivalent by the list price.

   Trade discount = single discount equivalent × list price

---

**EXAMPLE 1** Use the single discount equivalent to calculate the trade discount on a $1,500 fax machine with a discount series of 30/20/10.

The single discount equivalent is the complement of the net decimal equivalent. So first find the net decimal equivalent.

| | |
|---|---|
| 100% − 30% = 70% = 0.7 | Find the complement of each discount rate and write it as |
| 100% − 20% = 80% = 0.8 | an equivalent decimal. |
| 100% − 10% = 90% = 0.9 | |
| 0.7(0.8)(0.9) = 0.504 | Net decimal equivalent |
| 1.000 − 0.504 = 0.496 | Subtract the net decimal equivalent from 1 to find the single discount equivalent. |

Thus, the single discount equivalent for the trade discount series 30/20/10 is 0.496, or 49.6%.

Trade discount = single discount equivalent × list price   The single discount equivalent
$\qquad$ = 0.496($1,500$)   is 0.496; the list price is $1,500.
$\qquad$ = $744

**The trade discount on the $1,500 fax machine with a trade discount series of 30/20/10 is $744.**

Some calculators have a key labeled $\boxed{ANS}$ which allows you to enter the answer from the last calculation. To find the single discount equivalent and the trade discount using the $\boxed{ANS}$ key and parentheses:

$\boxed{AC}\ 1 - \boxed{(}\ \boxed{.}7\ \boxed{\times}\ .8\ \boxed{\times}\ .9\ \boxed{)}\ \boxed{=}\ \Rightarrow 0.496$

$\boxed{ANS}\ \boxed{\times}\ 1500\ \boxed{=}\ \Rightarrow 744$

##  STOP AND CHECK

1. Use the single discount equivalent to find the trade discount on a wood desk that lists for $504 and has a trade discount series of 12/10/5.

2. A child's adjustable computer workstation lists for $317 and has a chain discount of 10/5. What is the discount amount?

3. A children's chair lists for $24.00 with a chain discount of 10/5/3. Find the amount of discount.

4. What is the discount amount of a toddler's work desk that lists for $74 with discounts of 12/8/6?

5. Tots Room offers a play-a-round table and chairs at a list price of $289.95 with a chain discount of 8/6/5. What is the trade discount?

6. If you want to know how much you have *saved* by using a discount series, would you use the net decimal equivalent or the single discount equivalent? Explain the reason for your choice.

## 8-2 SECTION EXERCISES

### SKILL BUILDERS

1. Guadalupe Mesa manages an electronic equipment store and has ordered 100 color TVs with remote control for a special sale. The list price for each TV is $215 with a trade discount series of 7/10/5. Find the net price of the order by using the net decimal equivalent.

2. Tim Warren purchased computers for his computer store. Find the net price of the order of 36 computers if each one has a list price of $1,599 and a trade discount series of 5/5/10 is offered by the distributor.

3. Donna McAnally needs to calculate the net price of an order with a list price of $800 and a trade discount series of 12/10/6. Use the net decimal equivalent to find the net price.

4. Shinder Blunt is responsible for Cummins Appliance Store's accounts payable department and has an invoice that shows a list price of $2,200 with a trade discount series of 25/15/10. Use the single discount equivalent to calculate the trade discount on the purchase.

5. Mary Harrington is calculating the trade discount on a dog kennel with a list price of $269 and a trade discount series of 10/10/10. What is the trade discount? What is the net price for the kennel?

6. Christy Hunsucker manages a computer software distributorship and offers a desktop publishing software package for $395 with a trade discount series of 5/5/8. What is the trade discount on this package?

## APPLICATIONS

7. One distributor lists ink jet printers with 360 dpi and six scalable fonts that can print envelopes, labels, and transparencies for $189.97 with a trade discount series of 5/5/10. Another distributor lists the same brand and model printer at $210 with a trade discount series of 5/10/10. Which is the better deal if all other aspects of the deal, such as shipping, time of availability, and warranty are the same or equivalent?

8. Two distributors offer the same brand and model PC computer. One distributor lists the computer at $1,899 with a trade discount series of 8/8/5 and free shipping. The other distributor offers the computer at $2,000 with a trade discount series of 10/5/5 and $50 shipping cost added to the net price. Which computer is the better deal?

9. Stephen Black currently receives a trade discount series of 5/10/10 on merchandise purchased from a furniture company. He is negotiating with another furniture manufacturer to purchase similar furniture of the same quality. The first company lists a dining room table and six chairs for $1,899. The other company lists a similar set for $1,800 and a trade discount series of 5/5/10. Which deal is better?

10. We have seen that the trade discount series 20/10/5 is *not* equal to a single trade discount rate of 35%. Does the trade discount series 20/10/5 equal the trade discount series 5/10/20? Use an item with a list price of $1,000 and calculate the trade discount for both series to justify your answer.

**11.** One distributor lists a printer at $460 with a trade discount series of 15/12/5. Another distributor lists the same printer at $410 with a trade discount series of 10/10/5. Which is the better deal?

**12.** A Sony Playstation has a list price of $289 and a trade discount series of 8/8. Find the net price and trade discount.

### LEARNING OUTCOMES

1 Find the cash discount and the net amount using ordinary dating terms.
2 Interpret and apply end-of-month (EOM) terms.
3 Interpret and apply receipt-of-goods (ROG) terms.
4 Find the amount credited and the outstanding balance from partial payments.
5 Interpret freight terms.

## 1 Find the cash discount and the net amount using ordinary dating terms.

**Cash discount:** a discount on the amount due on an invoice that is given for prompt payment.

To encourage prompt payment, many manufacturers and wholesalers allow buyers to take a **cash discount**, a reduction of the amount due on an invoice. The cash discount is a specified percentage of the price of the goods. Customers who pay their bills within a certain time receive a cash discount. Many companies use computerized billing systems to compute the exact amount of a cash discount and show it on the invoice, so the customer does not need to calculate the discount and resulting net price. But the customer still determines when the bill must be paid to receive the discount.

Bills are often due within 30 days from the date of the invoice. To determine the exact day of the month the payment is due, you have to know how many days are in the month, 30, 31, 28, or 29 in the case of February. There are two ways to help remember which months have 31 days and which have 30 or fewer days. The first method, shown in Figure 8-1, is called the *knuckle method*. Each knuckle represents a month with 31 days and each space between knuckles represents a month with 30 days (except February, which has 28 days except in a leap year, when it has 29).

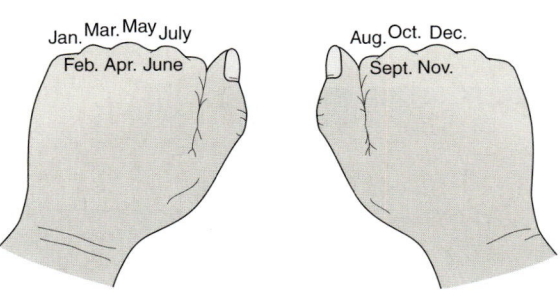

**FIGURE 8-1**
The knuckle months (Jan., Mar., May, July, Aug., Oct., and Dec.) have 31 days. The other months have 30 or fewer days.

Another way to remember which months have 30 days and which months have 31 is the following rhyme:

Thirty days has September,

April, June, and November.

All the rest have 31,

'cept February has 28 alone.

And leap year, that's the time

when February has 29.

## HOW TO  Find the ending date of an interval of time

1. Add the beginning date and the number of days in the interval.
2. If the sum exceeds the number of days in the month, subtract the number of days in the month from the sum.
3. The result of Step 2 will be the ending date in the next month of the interval.

## EXAMPLE 1

If an invoice is dated March 19, what is the date (a) 10 days later and (b) 15 days later?

(a) $19 + 10 = 29$

**Ten days later is March 29.**

(b) $19 + 15 = 34$      March has 31 days.
$34 - 31 = 3$

**Fifteen days later is April 3.**

With this in mind, let's look at one of the most common credit terms and dating methods.

Many firms offer credit terms 2/10, n/30 (read *two ten, net thirty*). The 2/10 means a 2% cash discount rate may be applied if the bill is paid within 10 days of the invoice date. The n/30 means that the full amount or net amount of the bill is due within 30 days. After the 30th day, the bill is overdue, and the buyer may have to pay interest charges or late fees.

For example, say an invoice is dated January 4 with credit terms of 2/10, n/30. If the buyer pays on or before January 14, then a 2% cash discount rate is applied. If the buyer pays on or after January 15, no cash discount is allowed. Finally, since 30 days from January 4 is February 3, if the buyer pays on or after February 4, interest charges or a late fee may be added to the bill.

## HOW TO  Find the cash discount

1. Identify the cash discount rate and the net price.
2. Multiply the cash discount rate by the net price.

$$\text{Cash discount} = \text{cash discount rate} \times \text{net price}$$

## EXAMPLE 2

An invoice dated July 27 shows a net price of $450 with the terms 2/10, n/30. (a) Find the latest date the cash discount is allowed. (b) Find the cash discount.

(a) The cash discount is allowed up to and including 10 days from the invoice date, July 27.

| | |
|---|---|
| 27th of July | Invoice date |
| + 10 days | Days allowed according to terms 2/10 |
| "37th of July" | If July had 37 days . . . |
| − 31 days in July | July has 31 days. |
| 6th of August | Latest date allowed |

**August 6 is the latest date the cash discount is allowed.**

(b) Cash discount = Cash discount rate × net price

$$\text{Cash discount} = 2\%(\$450)$$
$$= 0.02(\$450)$$
$$= \$9.00$$

**The cash discount is $9.00.**

Once a cash discount is deducted from a net price, the amount remaining is called the **net amount**. The net amount is the amount the buyer actually pays. Like the net price, there are two ways to calculate the net amount.

Because we attempt to use terms that are commonly used in the business world, the terms *net price* and *net amount* can be confusing. The list price is the suggested retail price, the net price is the price a retailer pays to the distributor or manufacturer for the merchandise, and the net amount is the net price minus any additional discount for paying the bill promptly.

> **Net amount:** the amount you owe if a cash discount is applied.

## HOW TO     Find the net amount

**Using the cash discount:**
1. Identify the net price and the cash discount.
2. Subtract the cash discount from the net price.

$$\text{Net amount} = \text{net price} - \text{cash discount}$$

**Using the complement of the cash discount rate:**
1. Identify the net price and the complement of the cash discount rate.
2. Multiply the complement of the cash discount rate by the net price.

$$\text{Net amount} = \text{complement of cash discount rate} \times \text{net price}$$

**TIP**

**The Check Is in the Mail**

The requirement for a bill to be paid on or before a specific date means that the payment must be *received* by the supplier on or before that date. For the payment to be postmarked by the due date does not generally count.

**EXAMPLE 3**   Find the net amount for the invoice in Example 2.

**Using the cash discount:**

$$\text{Net amount} = \text{net price} - \text{cash discount}$$
$$= \$450 - \$9$$
$$= \$441$$

**Using the complement of cash discount rate:**

$$\text{Net amount} = \text{complement of cash discount rate} \times \text{net price}$$
$$= (100\% - 2\%)(\$450)$$
$$= 0.98(\$450)$$
$$= \$441$$

**The net amount is $441.**

Another common set of discount terms is 2/10, 1/15, n/30. These terms are read *two ten, one fifteen, net thirty*. A 2% cash discount is allowed if the bill is paid within 10 days after the invoice date, a 1% cash discount is allowed if the bill is paid during the 11th through 15th days, and no discount is allowed during the 16th through 30th days. Interest charges or late fees may accrue if the bill is paid after the 30th day from the date of the invoice.

**EXAMPLE 4**   Charming Shoppes received a $1,248 invoice for computer supplies, dated September 2, with sales terms 2/10, 1/15, n/30. A 5% late fee is charged for payment after 30 days. Find the amount due if the bill is paid (a) on or before September 12; (b) on or between September 13 and September 17; (c) on or between September 18 and October 2; and (d) on or after October 3.

(a) If the bill is paid on or before September 12 (within 10 days), the 2% discount applies:

$$\text{Cash discount} = 2\%(\$1,248) = 0.02(\$1,248) = \$24.96$$
$$\text{Net amount} = \$1,248 - \$24.96 = \$1,223.04$$

**The net amount due on or before September 12 is $1,223.04.**

(b) If the bill is paid on or between September 13 and September 17 (within 15 days), the 1% discount applies:

$$\text{Cash discount} = 1\%(\$1{,}248) = 0.01(\$1{,}248) = \$12.48$$
$$\text{Net amount} = \$1{,}248 - \$12.48 = 1{,}235.52$$

**The net amount due on or between September 13 and September 17 is $1,235.52.**

(c) If the bill is paid on or between September 18 and October 2, no cash discount applies.

**The net price of $1,248 is due.**

(d) If the bill is paid on or after October 3, a 5% late fee is added:

$$\text{Late fee} = 5\%(\$1{,}248) = 0.05(\$1{,}248) = \$62.40$$
$$\text{Net amount} = \$1{,}248 + \$62.40 = \$1{,}310.40$$

**The net amount due on or after October 3 is $1,310.40.**

## ✔ STOP AND CHECK

1. An invoice received by Circuit City and dated March 15 has a net price of $985 with terms 2/15, n/30. Find the latest date a cash discount is allowed and find the cash discount. Find the net amount.

2. Dillard's Department Stores received an invoice dated April 18 that shows a billing for $3,848.96 with terms 2/10, 1/15, n/30. Find the cash discount and net amount if the invoice is paid within 15 days but after 10 days.

3. The Gap has an invoice dated August 20 with terms 3/15, n/30. It must be paid by what date to get the discount?

4. Office Depot has an invoice for $3,814 dated May 8, with terms of 3/10, 2/15, n/30. The invoice also has a 1% penalty per month for payment after 30 days.
   a. What amount is due if paid on May 12?

   b. What amount is due if paid on May 25?

   c. What amount is due if paid on June 7?

   d. What amount is due if paid on June 13?

## 2  Interpret and apply end-of-month (EOM) terms.

Another type of sales terms is **end-of-month (EOM) terms**. For example, the term might be 2/10 EOM, meaning that a 2% discount is allowed if the bill is paid during the first 10 days of the month *after* the month in the date of the invoice. Thus, if a bill is dated November 19, a 2% discount is allowed as long as the bill is paid on or before December 10.

An exception to the EOM rule occurs when the invoice is dated *on or after the 26th of the month*. When this happens, the discount is allowed if the bill is paid during the first 10 days of the month after the next month. If an invoice is dated May 28 with terms 2/10 EOM, a 2% discount is allowed as long as the bill is paid on or before *July* 10. This exception allows retailers adequate time to receive and pay the invoice.

### HOW TO    Apply EOM terms

To an invoice dated **before the 26th** day of the month:

1. A cash discount is allowed when the bill is paid by the specified day of the *next month*.
2. To find the net amount, multiply the invoice amount times the complement of the discount rate.

To an invoice dated **on or after the 26th day** of the month:

1. A cash discount is allowed when the bill is paid by the specified day of the *month after the next month*.
2. To find the net amount, multiply the invoice amount times the complement of the discount rate.

**EXAMPLE 1**    Newman, Inc., received a bill for cleaning services dated September 17 for $5,000 with terms 2/10 EOM. The invoice was paid on October 9. How much did Newman, Inc., pay?

Since the bill was paid within the first 10 days of the next month, a 2% discount was allowed. The complement of 2% is 98%. Thus, 98% is the rate that is paid.

$$\text{Net amount} = 98\%(\$5,000) = 0.98(\$5,000) = \$4,900$$

**The net amount paid on October 9 is $4,900.**

**EXAMPLE 2**    H-E-B of San Antonio received a $200 bill for copying services dated April 27. The terms on the invoice were 3/10 EOM. The firm paid the bill on June 2. How much did it pay?

Since the bill was paid within the first 10 days of the second month after the month on the invoice, a 3% discount was allowed. The complement of 3% is 97%.

$$\text{Net amount} = 97\%(\$200) = 0.97(\$200) = \$194$$

**The net amount paid was $194.**

 **STOP AND CHECK**

1. An invoice dated November 2 for $2,697 with terms 3/15 EOM was paid on November 14. How much was paid?

2. An invoice dated December 1 for $598.46 with terms 2/10 EOM must be paid by what date to get a cash discount? How much is the cash discount?

3. Domino's Pizza received an invoice dated April 29 with terms 2/10 EOM. What is the latest date the invoice can be paid at a discount? What percent of the invoice must be paid if the discount applies?

4. Find the net amount to be paid on an invoice for $1,096.82 dated May 26 with terms of 1/10 EOM if the invoice is paid on July 7.

5. Find the net amount required on an invoice for $187.17 with terms of 2/10 EOM if it is dated February 15 and paid March 12.

6. Target Stores received an invoice for $84,896 dated July 28 with terms 3/15 EOM. If the invoice is paid on September 10, what is the net amount due?

## 3    Interpret and apply receipt-of-goods (ROG) terms.

**Receipt-of-goods (ROG) terms:** a discount applied if the bill is paid within the specified number of days of the receipt of the goods.

Sometimes sales terms apply to the day the *goods are received* instead of the invoice date. For example, the terms may be written 1/10 ROG, where **ROG** stands for **receipt of goods**. The terms 1/10 ROG mean that a 1% discount is allowed on the bill if it is paid within 10 days of the receipt of goods.

An invoice is dated September 6 but the goods do not arrive until the 14th. If the sales terms are 2/15 ROG, then a 2% discount is allowed if the bill is paid on any date up to and including September 29.

**HOW TO**    Apply ROG terms

1. A cash discount is allowed when the bill is paid within the specified number of days from the **receipt of goods**, not from the date of the invoice.
2. To find the net amount, multiply the invoice amount times the complement of the discount rate.

(a) If the bill is paid on November 21, what is the net amount due?

(b) If the bill is paid on December 2, what is the net amount due?

(a) Since the bill is being paid within 10 days of the receipt of goods, a 2% discount is allowed. The complement of 2% is 98%.

$$\text{Net amount} = 98\%(\$400) = 0.98(\$400) = \$392$$

**The net amount due is $392.**

(b) No discount is allowed since the bill is not being paid within 10 days of the receipt of goods.

**Thus, $400 is due**.

---

##  STOP AND CHECK

1. An invoice for $3,097.15 is dated September 8 with terms of 3/15 ROG. The goods being invoiced arrived on September 12. By what date must the invoice be paid to get the cash discount? How much should be paid?

2. Johnson's Furniture purchased furniture that totaled $8,917.48 and received the furniture on March 12. The invoice dated March 5 arrived on March 15 and had discount terms of 2/10, n/30, ROG. Explain the discount terms. How much is paid if the invoice is paid on March 20?

3. Columbus Fitness Center received three new weight machines on May 15 and the invoice in the amount of $1,215 for these goods arrived on May 1 with discount terms of 2/15, n/30, ROG. How much must be paid if the invoice is paid on May 28? June 14?

4. Tracy Burford purchased two new dryers for Fashion Flair Beauty Salon at a cost of $797. The dryers were delivered on June 17 and the invoice arrived on June 13 with cash terms of 3/15, n/30, ROG. Tracy decided to pay the invoice on July 12. How much did she pay?

---

**Partial payment:** a payment that does not equal the full amount of the invoice less any cash discount.

**Partial cash discount:** a cash discount applied only to the amount of the partial payment.

**Amount credited:** the sum of the partial payment and the partial discount.

**Outstanding balance:** the invoice amount minus the amount credited.

## 4 Find the amount credited and the outstanding balance from partial payments.

A company sometimes cannot pay the full amount due in time to take advantage of cash discount terms. Most sellers allow buyers to make a **partial payment** and still get a **partial cash discount** off the net price if the partial payment is made within the time specified in the credit terms. The **amount credited** to the account, then, is the partial payment plus this partial cash discount. The **outstanding balance** is the amount still owed and is expected to be paid within the time specified by the sales terms.

**HOW TO** Find the amount credited and the outstanding balance from partial payments

1. Find the amount credited to the account: Divide the partial payment by the complement of the cash discount rate.

$$\text{Amount credited} = \frac{\text{partial payment}}{\text{complement of cash discount rate}}$$

2. Find the outstanding balance: Subtract the amount credited from the net price.

$$\text{Outstanding balance} = \text{net price} - \text{amount credited}$$

**EXAMPLE 1** The Semmes Corporation received an $875 invoice for cardboard cartons with terms of 3/10, n/30. The firm could not pay the entire bill within 10 days but sent a check for $500. What amount was credited to Semmes' account?

$$\text{Amount credited} = \frac{\text{partial payment}}{\text{complement of rate}} = \frac{\$500}{0.97}$$
$$= \$515.46$$

Divide the amount of the partial payment by the complement of the discount rate to find the amount credited.

$$\text{Outstanding balance} = \$875 - \$515.46 = \$359.54$$

Subtract the amount credited from the net price to find the outstanding balance.

**A $515.46 payment was credited to the account, and the outstanding balance was $359.54.**

---

## TIP

**Get Proper Credit for Partial Payments**

Remember to find the *complement* of the discount rate and then divide the partial payment by this complement. Students sometimes just multiply the discount rate times the partial payment, which does not allow the proper credit.

From Example 1,

$$\frac{\$500}{0.97} = \$515.46$$

$$\$875 - \$515.46 = \$359.54$$

**CORRECT**

From Example 1,

$$\$500(0.03) = \$15$$
$$\$500 + \$15 = \$515$$
$$\$875 - \$515 = \$360$$

**INCORRECT**

---

## ✔ STOP AND CHECK

1. Coach of New York sold DFS in San Francisco $340,800 in leather goods with terms of 3/10, n/30. DFS decided to make a partial payment of $200,000 within 10 days. What amount was credited to DFS's invoice?

2. DFS purchased handbags from Burberry in the amount of $2,840,000 with terms of 2/10, n/30, ROG. If the goods arrived on November 12 and DFS made a partial payment of $1,900,000 on November 15, how much should be credited to the DFS account?

3. Office Max purchased office furniture in the amount of $89,517 and was invoiced with terms of 2/10, n/30. Cash-strapped at the time, Office Max decided to make a partial payment of $50,000 within 10 days. How much should be credited to its account?

4. Cellular North sold 6,000 new phones to BellSouth Wireless for $79 each. The invoice arrived with terms of 3/10, n/30, and BellSouth paid $400,000 immediately. How much should be credited to BellSouth Wireless's account? How much was still to be paid on the invoice?

---

## 5 Interpret freight terms.

**Bill of lading:** shipping document that includes a description of the merchandise, number of pieces, weight, name of consignee (sender), destination, and method of payment of freight charges.

**FOB shipping point:** free on board at the shipping point. The buyer pays the shipping when the shipment is received.

**Freight collect:** The buyer pays the shipping when the shipment is received.

Manufacturers rely on a wide variety of carriers (truck, rail, ship, plane, and the like) to distribute their goods. The terms of freight shipment are indicated on a document called a **bill of lading** that is attached to each shipment. This document includes a description of the merchandise, number of pieces, weight, name of consignee, destination, and method of payment of freight charges. Freight payment terms are usually specified on the *manufacturer's price list* so that purchasers clearly understand who is responsible for freight charges and under what circumstances before purchases are made. The cost of shipping may be paid by the buyer or seller. If the freight is paid by the buyer, the bill of lading is marked **FOB shipping point**—meaning "free on board" at the shipping point—or **freight collect**. For example, CCC Industries located in Tulsa purchased

**FOB destination:** free on board at the destination point. The seller pays the shipping when the merchandise is shipped.

**Freight paid:** the seller pays the shipping when the merchandise is shipped.

**Prepay and add:** the seller pays the shipping when the merchandise is shipped, but the shipping costs are added to the invoice for the buyer to pay.

parts from Rawhide in Chicago. Rawhide ships FOB Chicago, so CCC Industries must pay the freight from Chicago to Tulsa. The freight company then collects freight charges from CCC upon delivery of the goods.

If the freight is paid by the seller, the bill of lading may be marked **FOB destination**—meaning "free on board" at the destination point—or **freight paid**. If Rawhide paid the freight in the preceding example, the term *FOB Tulsa* could also have been used. Many manufacturers pay shipping charges for shipments above some minimum dollar value. Some shipments of very small items may be marked **prepay and add**. That is, the seller pays the shipping charge and adds it to the invoice, so the buyer pays the shipping charge to the seller rather than to the freight company. **Cash discounts do *not* apply to freight or shipping charges.**

---

**EXAMPLE 1** Calculate the cash discount and the net amount paid for an $800 order of business forms with sales terms of 3/10, 1/15, n/30 if the cost of shipping was $40 (which is included in the $800). The invoice was dated June 13, marked *freight prepay and add*, and paid June 24.

Net price of merchandise

= total invoice − shipping fee
= $800 − $40 = $760

Cash discount
= $760(0.01) = $7.60

Net amount
= $800 − $7.60 = $792.40

Apply the cash discount rate *only* to the net amount of the merchandise.

The net price is $760.

The bill was paid after 10 days but within 15 days, so the 1% discount applies.

Discount is taken from total bill.

**The cash discount was $7.60 and the net amount paid was $792.40, which included the shipping fee.**

---

### TIP

**Who Pays and When**

The chart summarizes the most common shipping terms.

| Term | Who Pays | When | Who Doesn't Pay |
|---|---|---|---|
| FOB-shipping | Buyer | On receipt | Seller |
| Freight collect | Buyer | On receipt | Seller |
| FOB-destination | Seller | When shipped | Buyer |
| Freight paid | Seller | When shipped | Buyer |
| Prepay and add | Both | Shipper pays when shipped; buyer pays with invoice payment | Shipper gets reimbursed for shipping |

---

 ## STOP AND CHECK

1. Windshield Rescue received a shipment of glass on May 3 marked *freight prepay and add*. The invoice dated April 25 showed the cost of the glass to be $2,896 and the freight to be $72. The invoice also showed sales terms of 2/10, n/30. Find the cash discount and the net amount if the invoice is paid within the discount period. Find the total amount to be paid within the discount period.

2. Stout's Carpet, Inc., in Oxford, MS, received a shipment of carpet from Nortex Mills in Dalton, GA, delivered by M.S. Carriers truck line. The shipment was marked *FOB destination*. Who is responsible for paying shipping costs?

3. Dee's Discount Tires received a shipment from Cooper Tires in Novi, MI, that was marked *Freight collect* $215. The invoice Dee received was dated March 21 with terms 2/10, 1/15, n/30. Find the total amount paid for the tires if the invoice showed a balance of $7,925 before discounts and the invoice was paid 7 days after it was dated.

4. Memphis Hardwood Lumber in Memphis, NY, shipped 10 teak boards $6'' \times 24'' \times \frac{1}{2}''$ that cost $26.50 per board and 25 mahogany boards $6'' \times 24'' \times \frac{1}{2}''$ that cost $7.95 per board. High Point Furniture received the shipment marked *Prepay and add*. The invoice showed $65 for freight and was dated July 15 with terms 3/10, n/30. The invoice was paid on July 23. How much was paid?

## 8-3 SECTION EXERCISES

### SKILL BUILDERS

*Ken Bonnett received an invoice dated March 9, with terms 2/10, n/30, amounting to $540. He paid the bill on March 12.*

1. How much was the cash discount?

2. What is the net amount Ken will pay?

*Jim Bettendorf gets an invoice for $450 with terms 4/10, 1/15, n/30.*

3. How much would Jim pay 7 days after the invoice date?

4. How much would Jim pay 15 days after the invoice date?

5. How much would Jim pay 25 days after the invoice date?

*Alexa May, director of accounts, received a bill for $648, dated April 6, with sales terms 2/10, 1/15, n/30. A 3% penalty is charged for payment after 30 days.*

6. Find the amount due if the bill is paid on or before April 16.

7. What amount is due if the bill is paid on or between April 17 and April 21?

8. What amount is due if Alexa pays on or between April 22 and May 6?

9. If Alexa pays on or after May 7, how much must she pay?

*Chloe Duke is an accounts payable officer for her company and must calculate cash discounts before paying invoices. She is paying bills on June 18 and has an invoice dated June 12 with terms 3/10, n/30.*

10. If the net price of the invoice is $1,296.45, how much cash discount can she take?

11. What is the net amount Chloe will need to pay?

12. Charlene Watson received a bill for $800 dated July 5, with sales terms of 2/10 EOM. She paid the bill on August 8. How much did Charlene pay?

13. An invoice for a camcorder that cost $1,250 is dated August 1, with sales terms of 2/10 EOM. If the bill is paid on September 8, how much is due?

14. Ruby Wossum received an invoice for $798.53 dated February 27 with sales terms of 3/10 EOM. How much should she pay if she pays the bill on April 15?

15. Sylvester Young received an invoice for a leaf blower for $493 dated April 15 with sales terms of 3/10 EOM. How much should he pay if he pays the bill on April 30?

*An invoice for $900 is dated October 15 and has sales terms of 2/10 ROG. The merchandise arrives October 21.*

16. How much is due if the bill is paid October 27?

17. How much is due if the bill is paid on November 3?

18. Sharron Smith is paying an invoice showing a total of $5,835 and dated June 2. The invoice shows sales terms of 2/10 ROG. The merchandise delivery slip shows a receiving date of 6/5. How much is due if the bill for the merchandise is paid on June 12?

19. Kariem Salaam is directing the accounts payable office and is training a new accounts payable associate. They are processing an invoice for a credenza that is dated August 19 in the amount of $392.34. The delivery ticket for the credenza is dated August 23. If the sales terms indicated on the invoice are 3/10 ROG, how much needs to be paid if the bill is paid on September 5?

20. Clordia Patterson-Nathanial handles all accounts payable for her company. She has a bill for $730 and plans to make a partial payment of $400 within the discount period. If the terms of the transaction were 3/10, n/30, find the amount credited to the account and find the outstanding balance.

21. Robert Palinchak has an invoice for a complete computer system for $3,982.48. The invoice shows terms of 3/10, 2/15, n/30. He can afford to pay $2,000 within 10 days of the date on the invoice and the remainder within the 30-day period. How much should be credited to the account for the $2,000 payment, and how much is still due?

22. Ada Shotwell has been directed to pay all invoices in time to receive any discounts offered by vendors. However, she has an invoice with terms of 2/10, n/30 for $2,983 and the fund for accounts payable has a balance of $2,196.83. So she elects to pay $2,000 on the invoice within the 10-day discount period and the remainder within the 30-day period. How much should be credited to the account for the $2,000 payment and how much remains to be paid?

23. Dorothy Rogers' Bicycle Shop received a shipment of bicycles via truck from Better Bilt Bicycles. The bill of lading was marked FOB destination. Who paid the freight? To whom was the freight paid?

24. Joseph Denatti is negotiating the freight payment for a large shipment of office furniture and will take a discount on the invoice offered by the vendor since the freight terms are FOB destination. Who is to pay the freight?

25. Phyllis Porter receives a shipment with the bill of lading marked "prepay and add." Who is responsible for freight charges? Who pays the freight company?

26. Explain the difference in the freight terms *FOB shipping point* and *prepay and add*.

## Learning Outcomes

### Section 8-1

**1** Find the trade discount using a single trade discount rate; find the net price using the trade discount. (p. 260)

## What to Remember with Examples

Find the trade discount using a single trade discount rate.

1. Identify the single discount rate and the list price.
2. Multiply the list price by the single trade discount rate.

$$\text{Trade discount} = \text{single trade discount rate} \times \text{list price}$$

> The list price of a laminating machine is \$76 and the single trade discount rate is 25%. Find the trade discount.
>
> $$\begin{aligned} \text{Trade discount} &= 25\%(\$76) \\ &= 0.25(76) \\ &= \$19 \end{aligned}$$

Find the net price using the trade discount.

1. Identify the list price and the trade discount.
2. Subtract the trade discount from the list price.

$$\text{Net price} = \text{list price} - \text{trade discount}$$

> Find the net price when the list price is \$76 and the trade discount is \$19.
>
> $$\begin{aligned} \text{Net price} &= \$76 - \$19 \\ &= \$57 \end{aligned}$$

**2** Find the net price using the complement of the single trade discount rate. (p. 261)

1. Find the net price rate: Subtract the single trade discount rate from 100%.
2. Multiply the decimal equivalent of the net price rate by the list price.

$$\text{Net price} = (100\% - \text{single trade discount rate}) \times \text{list price}$$

> The list price is \$480 and the single trade discount rate is 15%. Find the net price.
>
> $$\begin{aligned} \text{Net price} &= (100\% - 15\%)(\$480) \\ &= 0.85(\$480) \\ &= \$408 \end{aligned}$$

### Section 8-2

**1** Find the net price, applying a trade discount series and using the net decimal equivalent. (p. 264)

1. Find the net decimal equivalent: Multiply the complement of each trade discount rate, in decimal form, in the series.
2. Multiply the net decimal equivalent by the list price.

$$\text{Net price} = \text{net decimal equivalent} \times \text{list price}$$

> The list price is \$960 and the discount series is 10/5/2. Find the net price.
>
> $$\text{Net decimal equivalent} = (0.9)(0.95)(0.98) = 0.8379$$
> $$\begin{aligned} \text{Net price} &= (0.8379)(\$960) \\ &= \$804.38 \end{aligned}$$

**2** Find the trade discount, applying a trade discount series and using the single discount equivalent. (p. 266)

1. Find the single discount equivalent: Subtract the net decimal equivalent from 1.

$$\text{Single discount equivalent} = 1 - \text{net decimal equivalent}$$

2. Multiply the single discount equivalent by the list price.

$$\text{Trade discount} = \text{single discount equivalent} \times \text{list price}$$

> The list price is $2,800 and the discount series is 25/15/10. Find the trade discount.
>
> Net decimal equivalent $= (0.75)(0.85)(0.9) = 0.57375$
> Single decimal equivalent $= 1 - 0.57375 = 0.42625$
> Trade discount $= (0.42625)(\$2,800)$
> $\qquad\qquad = \$1,193.50$

## Section 8-3

**1** Find the cash discount and the net amount using ordinary dating terms. (p. 269)

Find the ending date of an interval of time:

1. Add the beginning date and the number of days in the interval.
2. If the sum exceeds the number of days in the month, subtract the number of days in the month from the sum.
3. The result of Step 2 will be the ending date in the next month of the interval.

Interpret ordinary dating terms:

To find the last day to receive a discount, add to the invoice date the number of days specified in the terms. If this sum is greater than the number of days in the month the invoice is dated, subtract from the sum the number of days in the month the invoice is dated. The result is the last date the cash discount is allowed in the next month. Use the knuckle method to remember how many days are in each month or use the days-in-a-month rhyme.

> By what date must an invoice dated July 10 be paid if it is due in 10 days?
>
> July 10 + 10 days = July 20
>
> By what date must an invoice dated May 15 be paid if it is due in 30 days?
>
> May 15 + 30 = "May 45"
>
> May is a "knuckle" month, so it has 31 days.
>
> "May 45" − 31 days in May = June 14
>
> The invoice must be paid on or before June 14.

1. Find the cash discount: Multiply the cash discount rate by the net price.

$$\text{Cash discount} = \text{cash discount rate} \times \text{net price}$$

2. Find the net amount using the cash discount: Subtract the cash discount from the net price.

$$\text{Net amount} = \text{net price} - \text{cash discount}$$

3. Find the net amount using the complement of the cash discount rate: Multiply the complement of the cash discount rate by the net price.

$$\text{Net amount} = \text{complement of cash discount rate} \times \text{net price}$$

> An invoice is dated July 17 with terms 2/10, n/30 on a $2,500 net price. What is the latest date a cash discount is allowed? What is the net amount due on that date? On what date may interest begin accruing? What is the net amount due one day earlier?
>
> Sale terms 2/10, n/30 mean the buyer takes a 2% cash discount if he or she pays within 10 days of the invoice date; interest may accrue after the 30th day.
>
> Latest discount date $=$ July 17 + 10 days $=$ July 27
>
> Net amount $= (100\% - 2\%)(\$2,500)$
> $\qquad\qquad = (0.98)(\$2,500)$
> $\qquad\qquad = \$2,450$
>
> Latest no-interest date $=$ July 17 + 30 $=$ "July 47"
>
> "July 47" − 31 days in July $=$ August 16
>
> Interest begins accruing August 17. On August 16 the amount due is the net price of $2,500.

**2** Interpret and apply end-of-month (EOM) terms. (p. 272)

For an invoice dated *before the 26th* day of the month, a cash discount is allowed when the bill is paid by the specified day of the *next month*. For an invoice dated *on or after the 26th* day of the month, a cash discount is allowed when the bill is paid by the specified day of the *month after the next month*.

An invoice dated November 5 shows terms of 2/10 EOM on an $880 net price. By what date does the invoice have to be paid in order to get the cash discount? What is the net amount due on that date?

Sale terms 2/10 EOM for an invoice dated before the 26th day of a month mean that a 2% cash discount is allowed if the invoice is paid on or before the 10th day of the next month.

Latest discount day $=$ December 10
Net amount $= (100\% - 2\%)(\$880)$
$\qquad = (0.98)(\$880)$
$\qquad = \$862.40$

**3** Interpret and apply receipt-of-goods (ROG) terms. (p. 273)

A cash discount is allowed when the bill is paid within the specified number of days from the *receipt of goods,* not from the date of the invoice.

What is the net amount due on April 8 for an invoice dated March 28 with terms of 1/10 ROG on a net price of $500? The shipment arrived April 1.

Sales terms 1/10 ROG mean that a 1% cash discount is allowed if the invoice is paid within 10 days of the receipt of goods.

April 8 is within 10 days of April 1, the date the shipment is received, so the cash discount is allowed.

Net amount $= (100\% - 1\%)(\$500)$
$\qquad = (0.99)(\$500)$
$\qquad = \$495$

**4** Find the amount credited and the outstanding balance from partial payments. (p. 274)

1. Find the amount credited to the account: Divide the partial payment by the complement of the cash discount rate.

$$\text{Amount credited} = \frac{\text{partial payment}}{\text{complement of cash discount rate}}$$

2. Find the outstanding balance: Subtract the amount credited from the net price.

$$\text{Outstanding balance} = \text{net price} - \text{amount credited}$$

Estrada's Restaurant purchased carpet for $1,568 with sales terms of 3/10, n/30 and paid $1,000 on the bill within the 10 days specified. How much was credited to Estrada's account and what balance remained?

Amount credited to account $= \$1,000 \div 0.97 = \$1,030.93$
Outstanding balance $= \$1,568 - \$1,030.93 = \$537.07$

**5** Interpret freight terms. (p. 275)

If the bill of lading is marked FOB (free on board) *shipping point,* or *freight collect,* the buyer is responsible for paying freight expenses directly to the freight company. If the bill of lading is marked *FOB destination* or *freight paid,* the shipper is responsible for paying freight expenses directly to the freight company. If the bill of lading is marked *prepay and add,* the buyer is responsible for paying the freight expenses to the seller, who pays the freight company. Cash discounts do not apply to freight charges.

A shipment is sent from a manufacturer in Boston to a wholesaler in Dallas and is marked FOB destination. Who is responsible for the freight cost?

The manufacturer is responsible and pays the shipper.

## EXERCISES SET A

## Skill Builders

*Find the trade discount. Round to the nearest cent.*

| | Item | List price | Single discount rate | Trade discount |
|---|---|---|---|---|
| **1.** | Water heater | $300 | 15% | _____ |
| **2.** | Mountain bike | $149.50 | 20% | _____ |
| **3.** | Sun Unicycle | $49.97 | 12% | _____ |

*Find the net price. Round to the nearest cent.*

| | Item | List price | Trade discount | Net price |
|---|---|---|---|---|
| **4.** | Home Gym | $279 | $49 | _____ |
| **5.** | Dagger Kayak | $399 | $91.77 | _____ |

*Find the trade discount and net price. Round to the nearest cent.*

| | Item | List price | Single discount rate | Trade discount | Net price |
|---|---|---|---|---|---|
| **6.** | Spaulding golf club | $25 | 5% | _____ | _____ |
| **7.** | Minolta camera | $199.95 | 2% | _____ | _____ |
| **8.** | Jeep radio | $100 | 17% | _____ | _____ |

*Find the complement and net price. Round the net price to the nearest cent.*

| | Item | List price | Single discount rate | Net price rate | Net price |
|---|---|---|---|---|---|
| **9.** | Casio camera watch | $329 | 4% | _____ | _____ |
| **10.** | MP3 Player | $399.98 | 6% | _____ | _____ |
| **11.** | Teslar watch | $1,595 | 11% | _____ | _____ |

*Find the decimal equivalents of complements, net decimal equivalent, and net price. Round the net price to the nearest cent.*

| | Item | List price | Trade discount series | Decimal equivalents of complements | Net decimal equivalent | Net price |
|---|---|---|---|---|---|---|
| **12.** | Ralph sunglasses | $200 | 20/10 | _____ | _____ | _____ |
| **13.** | HDTV monitor | $1,399.99 | 10/15/10 | _____ | _____ | _____ |
| **14.** | Nintendo Gameboy | $99.99 | 15/5 | _____ | _____ | _____ |

*Round to the nearest hundredth of a percent when necessary.*

| Net decimal equivalent | Net decimal equivalent in percent form | Single discount equivalent in percent form |
|---|---|---|
| **15.** 0.765 | _____ | _____ |
| **16.** 0.6835 | _____ | _____ |
| **17.** 0.7434 | _____ | _____ |

*Find the single discount equivalent in percent form for the discount series.*

**18.** 20/10          **19.** 10%, 5%, 2%          **20.** 10/5

## Applications

**21.** Find the trade discount on a conference table listed at $1,025 less 10% (single discount rate).

**22.** Find the trade discount on a suite listed for $165 less 12%.

**23.** Find the trade discount on an order of 30 lamps listed at $35 each less 9%.

**24.** The list price on slacks is $22, and the list price on jumpers is $37. If Petit's Clothing Store orders 30 pairs of slacks and 40 jumpers at a discount rate of 11%, what is the trade discount on the purchase?

**25.** A trade discount series of 10/5 was given on ladies' scarves listed at $4. Find the net price of each scarf.

**26.** A trade discount series of 10/5/5 is offered on a printer, which is listed at $800. Also, a trade discount series of 5/10/5 is offered on a desk chair listed at $250. Find the total net price for the printer and the chair. Round to the nearest cent.

**27.** One manufacturer lists an aquarium for $58.95 with a trade discount of $5.90. Another manufacturer lists the same aquarium for $60 with a trade discount of $9.45. Which is the better deal?

**28.** Beverly Vance received a bill dated March 1 with sales terms of 3/10, n/30. What percent discount will she receive if she pays the bill on March 5?

**29.** Find the cash discount on an invoice for $270 dated April 17 with terms of 2/10, n/30 if the bill was paid April 22.

**30.** Christy Hunsucker received an invoice for $650 dated January 26. The sales terms in the invoice were 2/10 EOM. She paid the bill on March 4. How much did Christy pay?

**31.** An invoice for $5,298 has terms of 3/10 ROG and is dated March 15. The merchandise is received on March 20. How much should be paid if the invoice is paid on March 25?

**32.** An invoice for $1,200 is dated on June 3, and terms of 3/10, n/30 are offered. A payment of $800 is made on June 12, and the remainder is paid on July 12. Find the amount remitted on July 12 and the total amount paid.

## EXERCISES SET B

## Skill Builders

*Find the trade discount or net price as indicated. Round to the nearest cent.*

| | List price | Single discount rate | Trade discount | | List price | Trade discount | Net price |
|---|---|---|---|---|---|---|---|
| 1. | $48 | 10% | _____ | 4. | $24.62 | $5.93 | _____ |
| 2. | $100 | 12% | _____ | 5. | $0.89 | $0.12 | _____ |
| 3. | $425 | 15% | _____ | | | | |

*Find the net price. Round to the nearest cent.*

| | List price | Single discount rate | Trade discount | Net price | | List price | Single discount rate | Complement | Net price |
|---|---|---|---|---|---|---|---|---|---|
| 6. | $1,263 | 12% | _____ | _____ | 9. | $421 | 5% | _____ | _____ |
| 7. | $27.50 | 3% | _____ | _____ | 10. | $721.18 | 3% | _____ | _____ |
| 8. | $8,952 | 18% | _____ | _____ | 11. | $3,983.00 | 8% | _____ | _____ |

*Find the decimal equivalents of complements, net decimal equivalent, and net price. Round to the nearest cent.*

| | List price | Trade discount series | Decimal equivalents of complements | Net decimal equivalent | Net price |
|---|---|---|---|---|---|
| 12. | $50 | 10/7/5 | _____ | _____ | _____ |
| 13. | $35 | 20/15/5 | _____ | _____ | _____ |
| 14. | $2,834 | 5/10/10 | _____ | _____ | _____ |

*Round to the nearest hundredth of a percent when necessary.*

| | Net decimal equivalent | Net decimal equivalent in percent form | Single discount equivalent in percent form |
|---|---|---|---|
| 15. | 0.82 | _____ | _____ |

|  | Net decimal equivalent | Net decimal equivalent in percent form | Single discount equivalent in percent form |
|---|---|---|---|
| **16.** 0.6502 | | _____ | _____ |
| **17.** 0.758 | | _____ | _____ |

*Find the single discount equivalent.*

**18.** 30/20/5

**19.** 10%, 10%, 5%

**20.** 20/15

# Applications

**21.** The list price for velvet at Harris Fabrics is $6.25 per yard less 6%. What is the trade discount?

**22.** Rocha Bros. offered a $12\frac{1}{2}\%$ trade discount on a tractor listed at $10,851. What was the trade discount?

**23.** The list price for a big-screen TV is $1,480 and the trade discount is $301. What is the net price?

**24.** A stationery shop bought 10 boxes of writing paper listed at $5 each and 200 greeting cards listed at $3.00 each. If the single discount rate for the purchase is 15%, find the trade discount.

**25.** Find the net price of an item listed at $800 with a trade discount series of 25/10/5.

**26.** Five desks are listed at $400 each, with a trade discount series of 20/10/10. Also, 10 bookcases are listed at $200 each, discounted 10/20/10. Find the total net price for the desks and bookcases.

**27.** One manufacturer lists a table at $200 less 12%. Another manufacturer lists the same table at $190 less 10%. Which is the better deal?

**28.** Chris Merillat received a bill dated September 3 with sales terms of 2/10, n/30. Did she receive a discount if she paid the bill on September 15?

**29.** Find the cash discount on an invoice for $50 dated May 3 with terms 1/15, n/30 if the bill was paid May 14.

**30.** How much would have to be paid on an invoice for $328 with terms of 2/10 ROG if the merchandise invoice is dated January 3, the merchandise arrives January 8, and the invoice is paid (a) January 11; (b) January 25?

**31.** Find the amount credited and the outstanding balance on an invoice dated August 19 if a partial payment of $500 is paid on August 25 and has terms of 3/10, 1/15, n/30. The amount of the invoice is $826.

**EXCEL 32.** Campbell Sales purchased merchandise worth $745 and made a partial payment of $300 on day 13. If the sales terms were 2/15, n/30, how much was credited to the account? What was the outstanding balance?

# PRACTICE TEST

## CHAPTER 8

1. The list price of a refrigerator is $550. The retailer can buy the refrigerator at the list price minus 20%. Find the trade discount.

2. The list price of a television is $560. The trade discount is $27.50. What is the net price?

3. A retailer can buy a lamp that is listed at $36.55 for 20% less than the list price. How much does the retailer have to pay for the lamp?

4. One manufacturer lists a chair for $250 less 20%. Another manufacturer lists the same chair at $240 less 10%. Which manufacturer offers the better deal?

5. Find the net price if a discount series of 20/10/5 is deducted from $70.

6. Find the single discount equivalent for the discount series 20/20/10.

7. Find the net decimal equivalent of the series 20/10/5.

8. What is the complement of 15%?

9. A retailer buys 20 boxes of stationery at $4 each and 400 greeting cards at $0.50 each. The discount rate for the order is 15%. Find the trade discount.

10. A retailer buys 30 electric frying pans listed at $40 each for 10% less than the list price. How much does the retailer have to pay for the frying pans?

11. Domingo Castro received an invoice for $200 dated March 6 with sales terms 1/10, n/30. He paid the bill on March 9. What was his cash discount?

12. Shareesh Raz received a bill dated September 1 with sales terms of 3/10, 1/15, n/30. What percent discount will she receive if she pays the bill on September 6?

13. An invoice for $400 dated December 7 has sales terms of 2/10 ROG. The merchandise arrived December 11. If the bill is paid on December 18, what is the amount due?

14. Gladys Quaweay received a bill for $300 dated April 7. The sales terms on the invoice were 2/10 EOM. If she paid the bill on May 2, how much did she pay?

15. If the bill in Exercise 13 is paid on January 2, what is the amount due?

16. Zing Manufacturing lists artificial flower arrangements at $30 less 10% and 10%. Another manufacturer lists the same flower arrangements at $31 less 10%, 10%, and 5%. Which is the better deal?

17. A trade discount series of 10% and 20% is offered on 20 dartboards that are listed at $14 each. Also, a trade discount series of 20% and 10% is offered on 10 bowling balls that are listed at $40 each. Find the total net price for the dartboards and bowling balls.

18. The monogrammed items purchased by Dean Specialty Company are shipped by rail from the manufacturer. The bill of lading is marked "FOB destination." Who is responsible for paying freight expenses?

1. Who generally pays the list price? Who generally pays the net price?

2. Use an example to illustrate that a trade discount series of 20/10 is not the same as a discount of 30%. Why are the discounts not the same?

3. The net price can be found by first finding the trade discount as discussed in Outcome 1 in Section 8.1, then subtracting to get the net price. When is it advantageous to use the complement of the discount rate for finding the net price directly?

4. To find the amount credited for a partial payment, we must find the complement of the discount rate and then divide the partial payment by this complement. Explain why we cannot multiply the payment by the discount rate and then add the product to the payment to find the amount to be credited to the account balance.

5. If the single discount rate is 20%, the complement is 80%. What does the complement represent?

6. Describe a procedure for mentally finding a 1% discount on an invoice. Illustrate with an example.

7. Describe the calculations used to project a due date of 60 days from a date of purchase, assuming the 60 days are within the same year.

8. Expand the mental process for using a 1% discount on an invoice to find a 2% discount. Illustrate with an example.

9. Develop a process for estimating a cash discount on an invoice. Illustrate with an example.

10. Why is it important to estimate the discount amount on an invoice?

# Challenge Problems

1. Swift's Dairy Mart receives a shipment of refrigeration units totaling $2,386.50 including a shipping charge of $32. Swift's returns $350 worth of the units. Terms of the purchase are 2/10, n/30. If Swift's takes advantage of the discount, what is the net amount payable?

2. An important part of owning a business is the purchasing of equipment and supplies to run the office. Before paying an invoice, all items must be checked and amounts refigured before writing the check for payment. At this time the terms of the invoice can be applied.

   Using the information on the invoice in Figure 8-2, fill in the extended amount for each line, the merchandise total, the tax amount, and the total invoice amount. Locate the terms of the invoice and find what you would write on a check to pay Harper on each of the following dates:
   Discounts are applied before sales tax is calculated.
   March 5, 20XX
   March 12, 20XX
   March 25, 20XX

| INVOICE DATE | TERMS | DATE OF ORDER | ORDERED BY | PHONE NO. | REMIT TO ▶ | HARPER General Accounting Office |
|---|---|---|---|---|---|---|
| 02/27/XX | 2/10, 1/15, n/30 | 02/27/XX | | 803-000-4488 | | |

| LINE NO. | MANUFACTURER PRODUCT NUMBER | QTY. ORD. | QTY. B.O. | QTY. SHP. | U/M | DESCRIPTION | UNIT PRICE | | EXTENDED AMOUNT |
|---|---|---|---|---|---|---|---|---|---|
| 001 | REMYY370/02253 | 3 | 0 | 3 | EA | TONER, F/ROYAL TA210 COP 1 | 11.90 | | |
| 002 | Sk 1230M402 | 5 | 2 | 3 | PK | CORRECTABLE FILM RIBBON | 10.95 | | |
| 003 | JRLM01023 | 10 | 0 | 10 | PK | COVER-UP CORRECTION TAPE | 9.90 | | |
| 004 | rTu123456 | 9 | 0 | 9 | CS | PAPER, BOND, WHITE 8 1/2 x 11 | 58.23 | | |

| DATE REC'D. | 01460900001 | | 5% | | $0.00 | TOTAL INVOICE AMOUNT ▶ | |
|---|---|---|---|---|---|---|---|
| | OUR ORDER NO. | MDSE. TOTAL | TAX RATE | TAX AMOUNT | FREIGHT AMOUNT | | |

**FIGURE 8-2**
**Harper Invoice**

## 8.1 Image Manufacturing's Rebate Offer

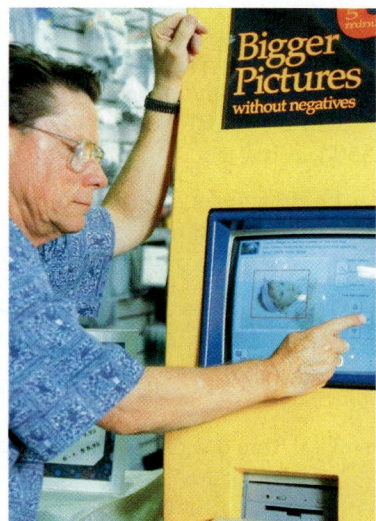

Misuse and abuse of trade discounts infringe on fair trade laws and can cost companies stiff fines and legal fees. One way to avoid misuse is to establish the same discount for everyone and give rebates based solely on volume. Image Manufacturing, Inc., uses this policy for equipment sales to companies that develop photographs. For example, one developing machine component, a special hinge, sells for about $3 to a company buying 15,000 pieces per month. In an effort to run more cost-efficient large jobs and capture market share, Image Manufacturing will give an incentive for higher volume. It offers a 5% rebate on orders of 20,000 pieces per month, or a 17–18 cents apiece rebate for orders of at least 22,000 pieces per month. The increased volume needed for a rebate is determined by market research that tells Image Manufacturing factors such as the volume a customer is capable of ordering per month, the volume and cost of the same part a customer currently buys from other suppliers. The rebate amount is determined by Image Manufacturing's profit margin and the company's ability to acquire sufficient raw materials to produce larger volumes without raising production costs. In some industries this is called a bill-back because the buyer receives credit toward the next order rather than a rebate check.

1. Suppose Photo Magic currently orders 15,000 hinges per month from Image Manufacturing at $3 each, which is about half of what they buy each month from other suppliers. If they move 5,000 pieces per month from another company to Image Manufacturing, what will be their rebate on the total order? What will be the discounted cost per piece?

2. If Photo Magic increases its order to 22,000 pieces per month and negotiates an 18 cents-per-piece trade discount, what will be the rebate? What is the percent of the discount?

3. If Photo Magic also receives a $\frac{1}{2}$% cash discount (10 days, net 30), calculate the cash discount and total rebate on a 30,000-piece-per-month order, and then find the net price. Note: Cash discount of $\frac{1}{2}$% is allowed to be taken on total purchase before the rebate is applied.

4. Another company currently orders about 6,000 hinges per month from Image Manufacturing at $3 each. Image Manufacturing's marketing manager believes this company is capable of expanding its business to 8,000 pieces per month and recommends a rebate of 17 cents per piece if they do so. Rounded to the nearest tenth, what is the rebate percentage? Do you think this trade discount violates fair trade laws? Why and why not?

## 8.2 Shopping for a New Car

Tom Zahlia is shopping for a new car. Tom looked at the Toyota Camry, the Nissan Altima, and the Honda Accord. Tom decided that the Nissan Altima meets his needs at a lower price than its competitors. The manufacturer's suggested retail price (MSRP) for the car he likes best is $23,200. The car has several upgrades. The base invoice price is $21,456 and the destination charge is $560 and will be added to any negotiated price of a car. The dealership has offered to give Tom $500 cash toward his down payment since he has just graduated from college. They explained that the current discount being offered is 5% off the MSRP of any car until the end of the week, and Tom can have either the 5% discount or the $500 cash discount, but not both. Tom decided he would think about this and return the next day.

1. How much bargaining room is there between the base invoice price and the suggested retail price for the Altima?

2. If the dealer gives Tom $500 toward a down payment, how much will the car cost without regard to the destination charge? How much above invoice is the car now?

3. If Tom decides to take the 5% discount, how much will he pay for the car without regard to the destination charge? How much over invoice is this?

4. Tom has decided to take the 5% discount. If a 5% sales tax is added to the price of the car and then the destination charge and a $200 title and licensing fee is added, what is the total amount to be paid or financed?

## 8.3 The Artist's Palette

The Artist's Palette sells high-end art supplies to the art students at three regional art and design schools in Philadelphia, Washington, D.C., and Baltimore. They carry paints, brushes, drawing pads, frames, charcoal, pastels, and other supplies used in a variety of artistic media. Because their clientele is very discriminating, The Artist's Palette tends to carry only the top lines in their inventory and they are known for having the best selection on hand. It is rare that an item is out of stock. Artists can visit the store, purchase from The Artist's Palette catalog, or from the secure web site.

1. The Artist's Palette purchases their inventory from a number of suppliers and each supplier offers different purchasing discounts. The manager of The Artist's Palette, Parma, is currently comparing two offers for purchasing modeling clay and supplies. The first company offers a chain discount of 20/10/5, and the second company offers a chain discount of 18/12/7 as long as the total purchases are $300 or more. Assuming Parma purchases $300 worth of supplies, what is the net price from supplier 1? From supplier 2? From which supplier would you recommend Parma purchase her modeling clay and supplies?

2. What is the net decimal equivalent for supplier 1? For supplier 2?

3. What is the trade discount from supplier 1? From supplier 2?

**4.** The Artist's Palette recognizes that students may purchase supplies at the beginning of the term to cover all of their art class needs. Because this could represent a fairly substantial outlay, The Artist's Palette offers discounts to those students who pay sooner than required. Assume that if students buy more than $250 of art supplies in one visit, they may put it on a student account with terms of 2/10, n/30. If a student purchases $250 of supplies on September 16, what amount is due by September 26? How much would the student save by paying early?

**5.** Assume that if students buy more than $250 of art supplies in one visit, they may put it on a student account with terms of 2/10 EOM. If a student makes the purchase on September 16, on what day does the 2% discount expire? If the purchase is made on September 26, on what day does the 2% discount expire? If you were an art student, which method would you prefer: 2/10, n/30, or 2/10 EOM?

# Markup and Markdown

## Hip Hop Clothing

Kendra and Mikala were excited about opening their own hip hop clothing store, 'Nue Rhythm. 'Nue was short for Avenue, and they wanted their clothing to capture the "rhythm of the street." They know that the urban clothing market is one of the most exciting and fastest growing markets for today's consumers. Urban wear has increased in popularity as the number of new, musical hip hop artists has increased. This style of baggy pants, baseball caps worn backwards (NBA, NFL, or successful university teams), oversized rugby or polo shirts, and expensive tennis shoes, although still very popular, is being replaced in some areas with a trend toward tighter hipster-inspired items such as polo shirts, sports coats, large ornamental belt buckles, and tighter jeans. But what really concerned Kendra and Mikala was pricing their new hip hop clothing lines. While typical markups on clothing and accessories can be 30–85%, they knew from research that the markup for hip hop clothing is often 100–200% or more.

What if you're a new business owner (like Kendra and Mikala) and don't have any experience on which to base an estimate? Then you need to research material costs by getting quotes from suppliers as well as study the labor rates in the area. You should also research industry manufacturing prices, as well as competitor's prices. Armed with this information, you will have a well-educated "guess" on which to base your pricing.

For now, 'Nue Rhythm is strictly a retail operation; however, the owners have hopes of introducing their own retail line, "Hip Hop Tops," in the future. Kendra and Mikala felt they were on the right track, and decided to take a seasonal approach to pricing. For the peak shopping months during the summer and leading up to Christmas, they would institute markups of 150% across the board on all lines. To draw customers into the store, a specific designer or line would be marked down as much as 50% off the normal price, and would still be profitable for them. During the rest of the year, 10–50% markdowns would be taken to generate interest among shoppers or to move obsolete inventory. Their focus would be creating competitive prices on truly unique hip hop clothing pieces that their customers would not hesitate to buy.

## LEARNING OUTCOMES

### 9-1 Markup Based on Cost

1. Find the cost, markup, or selling price when any two of the three are known.
2. Find the percent of markup based on the cost when the cost and selling price are known.
3. Find the selling price when the cost and the percent of markup based on the cost are known.
4. Find the cost when the amount of markup and the percent of markup based on the cost are known.
5. Find the cost when the selling price and the percent of markup based on the cost are known.

### 9-2 Markup Based on Selling Price and Markup Comparisons

1. Find the amount of markup and the percent of markup based on the selling price when the cost and selling price are known.
2. Find the selling price when the amount of markup and the percent of markup based on the selling price are known.
3. Find the selling price when the cost and the percent of markup based on the selling price are known.
4. Find the cost when the selling price and the percent of markup based on the selling price are known.
5. Compare the markup based on the cost with the markup based on the selling price.

### 9-3 Markdown, Series of Markdowns, and Perishables

1. Find the amount of markdown, the reduced (new) price, and the percent of markdown.
2. Find the final selling price for a series of markups and markdowns.
3. Find the selling price for a desired profit on perishable and seasonal goods.

 A corresponding Business Math Case Video for this chapter, *An All-Star Signing!* can be found in Appendix A.

**Cost:** price at which a business purchases merchandise.

**Selling price (retail price):** price at which a business sells merchandise.

**Markup (gross profit or gross margin):** difference between the selling price and the cost.

**Net profit:** difference between markup (gross profit or gross margin) and operating expenses and overhead.

**Markdown:** amount the original selling price is reduced.

Chapter 8 introduced the mathematics associated with buying for a small business. This chapter will focus on the mathematics of selling. Any successful business must keep prices low enough to attract customers, yet high enough to pay expenses and make a profit.

The price at which a retail business purchases merchandise is called the **cost**. The merchandise is then sold at a higher price called the **selling price** or the **retail price**. The difference between the selling price and the cost is the **markup**. The markup is also called the **gross profit** or **gross margin**. The gross profit or margin includes operating expenses and the overhead. The difference between the gross profit and the expenses and overhead is the **net profit**. In Chapter 20 we will look at these concepts. For now, we will only consider the gross profit or markup.

Merchandise may also be reduced from the original selling price. The amount the original selling price is reduced is the **markdown**.

## 9-1 MARKUP BASED ON COST

### LEARNING OUTCOMES

1 Find the cost, markup, or selling price when any two of the three are known.
2 Find the percent of markup based on the cost when the cost and selling price are known.
3 Find the selling price when the cost and the percent of markup based on the cost are known.
4 Find the cost when the amount of markup and the percent of markup based on the cost are known.
5 Find the cost when the selling price and the percent of markup based on the cost are known.

In business situations it is common to need to find missing information. The cost, markup, and selling price are related so that when any two amounts are known, the third amount can be found.

### 1 Find the cost, markup, or selling price when any two of the three are known.

Visualize the relationships among the cost, markup, and the selling price. The basic relationship can be written as the formula

$$\text{Selling price} = \text{cost} + \text{markup}$$
$$S = C + M$$

Relate this to the concept that two parts add together to get a sum or total. Then we can develop variations of the formula using the concept that the sum or total minus one part gives the other part.

$$\text{Cost} = \text{selling price} - \text{markup}$$
$$C = S - M$$
$$\text{Markup} = \text{selling price} - \text{cost}$$
$$M = S - C$$

| HOW TO | Find the cost, markup, or selling price when any two of the three are known |
| --- | --- |

1. Identify the two known amounts.
2. Identify the missing amount.
3. Select the appropriate formula.
4. Substitute the known amounts into the formula.
5. Evaluate the formula.

**EXAMPLE 1** What is the selling price of an item if the cost is $28.35 and the markup is $5.64?

| What You Know | What You Are Looking For | Solution Plan |
| --- | --- | --- |
| Cost = $28.35 | Selling price | Selling price = cost + markup |
| Markup = $5.64 | | |

**Solution**

| | |
|---|---|
| $S = C + M$ | Substitute known values. |
| $S = \$28.35 + \$5.64$ | Add. |
| $S = \$33.99$ | |

**Conclusion**

**The selling price is \$33.99.**

---

### EXAMPLE 2

Mapco buys travel mugs for \$2.45 and sells them for \$5.88. What is the markup?

| What You Know | What You Are Looking For | Solution Plan |
|---|---|---|
| Cost = \$2.45 <br> Selling price = \$5.88 | Markup | Cost = selling price − markup |

**Solution**

| | |
|---|---|
| $M = S - C$ | Substitute known values. |
| $M = \$5.88 - \$2.45$ | Subtract. |
| $M = \$3.43$ | |

**Conclusion**

**The markup is \$3.43.**

---

### EXAMPLE 3

Kroger is selling 2-liter Coke at \$1.29. If the markup is \$0.35, what is the cost?

| What You Know | What You Are Looking For | Solution Plan |
|---|---|---|
| Selling price = \$1.29 <br> Markup = \$0.35 | Cost | Cost = selling price − markup |

**Solution**

| | |
|---|---|
| $C = S - M$ | Substitute known values. |
| $C = \$1.29 - \$0.35$ | Subtract. |
| $M = \$0.94$ | |

**Conclusion**

**The cost of the 2-liter Coke is \$0.94.**

---

 ## STOP AND CHECK

1. Charlie Cook bought a light fixture that cost \$32 and marked it up \$40. Find the selling price.

2. Margaret Davis sells a key fob for \$12.95 and it costs \$7. Find the markup.

3. Sylvia Knight bought a printer cartridge and marked it up \$18 and set the selling price at \$34.95. Find the cost.

4. Berlin Jones introduced a new veggie sandwich at Subway, the sandwich shop. He determines that each sandwich costs \$3 and plans to sell each sandwich for \$5.25, which is 175% of the cost. Find the markup.

## 2 Find the percent of markup based on the cost when the cost and selling price are known.

Whether markup is based on cost or selling price, the *rate* of markup, the *rate* of the selling price, and the *rate* of cost are related in the same way.

Rate of $S$ = rate of $C$ + rate of $M$      $S\% = C\% + M\%$
Rate of $C$ = rate of $S$ − rate of $M$      $C\% = S\% - M\%$
Rate of $M$ = rate of $S$ − rate of $C$      $M\% = S\% - C\%$

When the markup is based on cost, the rate of the cost is known and is 100%. The cost is the base in the basic percentage formulas

$$P = R \times B \quad R = \frac{P}{B} \text{ and } B = \frac{P}{R}.$$

Variations of the percentage formula for markup based on cost are

$$\text{Markup} = \text{Rate of markup based on cost} \times \text{cost}$$

$$\text{Rate of markup based on cost} = \frac{\text{Markup}}{\text{Cost}}$$

$$\text{Cost} = \frac{\text{Markup}}{\text{Rate of markup based on cost}}$$

---

**HOW TO**    **Find the percent or rate of markup based on the cost when the cost and selling price are known**

1. Find the amount of markup using the formula

$$\text{Markup} = \text{Selling price} - \text{Cost}$$
$$M \quad = \quad S \quad\quad - \quad C$$

2. Find the percent of markup based on cost using the formula

$$\text{Rate of markup based on cost} = \frac{\text{markup}}{\text{cost}} \times 100\%$$

$$M\% = \frac{\text{markup}}{\text{cost}} \times 100\%$$

---

**EXAMPLE 1**    Duke's Photography pays $9 for a 5 in.-by-7 in. photograph. If the photograph is sold for $15, what is the percent of markup based on cost? Round to the nearest tenth of a percent.

| What You Know | What You Are Looking For | Solution Plan |
|---|---|---|
| Cost = $9<br>Cost% = 100%<br>Selling price = $15 | Rate of markup | Markup = selling price − cost<br><br>$M\% = \frac{\text{markup}}{\text{cost}} \times 100\%$ |

**Solution**

Find the amount of markup:

| | |
|---|---|
| $M = S - C$ | Substitute known values into the formula. |
| $M = \$15 - \$9$ | Subtract. |
| $M = \$6$ | Amount of markup |

Find the rate of markup:

| | |
|---|---|
| $M\% = \frac{\text{markup}}{\text{cost}} \times 100\%$ | Substitute known values into the formula. |
| $M\% = \frac{\$6}{\$9}(100\%)$ | Divide. |
| $M\% = 0.667(100\%)$ | Rounded to thousandths. Change to percent equivalent. |
| $M\% = 66.7\%$ | Rate or percent of markup |

**Conclusion**

**The percent of markup based on cost is 66.7%.**

1. Find the percent of markup based on cost for a table that costs $220 and sells for $599. Round to the nearest tenth of a percent.

2. A file cabinet costs $145 and sells for $197.20. Find the percent of markup based on cost.

3. A bicycle costs $245 and sells for $395. Find the percent of markup based on cost. Round to the nearest tenth percent.

4. A motorcycle costs $690 and sells for $1,420. Find the percent of markup based on cost. Round to the nearest tenth percent.

5. A patio lounger costs $89 and is sold for $249. What is the percent of markup based on cost? Round to the nearest tenth percent.

6. Lowe's can purchase a KitchenAid Energy Star dishwasher for $738. Find the percent markup based on cost if the dishwasher sells for $1,048.00. Round to the nearest tenth percent.

## 3 Find the selling price when the cost and the percent of markup based on the cost are known.

When the markup is based on the cost, the cost is 100% and represents the base in the percentage formula. The selling price percent or rate is found by adding the cost percent and the markup percent. The selling price rate will be more than 100%.

---

**HOW TO** Find the selling price when the cost and the percent of markup based on the cost are known

1. Find the rate of the selling price based on cost using the formula

$$\text{Rate of } S = \text{rate of } C + \text{rate of } M$$
$$S\% = C\% + M\%$$

2. Find the selling price using the formula

$$\text{Selling price} = \text{rate of selling price based on cost} \times \text{cost}$$
$$S = S\% \times C$$

---

**TIP**

**Alternative Procedure for Finding the Selling Price when the Cost and the Percent of Markup Based on the Cost Are Known**

1. Find the amount of markup using the formula

$$M = M\% \times C$$

2. Find the selling price using the formula

$$S = C + M$$

---

**EXAMPLE 1** A boutique pays $5 a pair for handmade earrings and sells them at a 50% markup rate based on cost. Find the selling price of the earrings.

| What You Know | What You Are Looking For | Solution Plan |
|---|---|---|
| Cost = $5<br>C% = 100%<br>Markup % = 50% | Selling price | S% = C% + M%<br>S = S% × C |

**Solution**

Find the rate of selling price:

| | |
|---|---|
| S% = C% + M% | Substitute known amounts. |
| S% = 100% + 50% | Add. |
| S% = 150% | |

Find the selling price:

| | |
|---|---|
| $S = S\% \times C$ | Substitute known amounts. |
| $S = 150\%(\$5)$ | Change percent to equivalent decimal. |
| $S = 1.5(\$5)$ | Multiply. |
| $S = \$7.50$ | Selling price |

**Conclusion**

The selling price is **$7.50**.

 STOP AND CHECK

1. Ed's Camera Shop pays $218 for a camera and sells it at a 78% markup based on cost. What is the selling price of the camera?

2. Holly's Leather Shop pays $87.50 for a Coach bag and sells it at a 95% markup based on cost. What is the selling price of the bag rounded to the nearest cent?

3. Wimberly Computers buys computers for $465 and sells them at an 80% markup based on cost. What will the computers sell for?

4. The National Parks Conservation Association purchases calendars for $0.86 and sells them at a 365% markup based on cost. What will the calendars sell for rounded to the nearest cent?

5. A 4-oz bottle of Vanilla Bean Panache lotion is purchased for $0.45 and sells at a 110% markup based on cost. What is the selling price of the lotion?

6. J. C. Penney buys Casio watches for $58.82 and sells them at a 70% markup based on cost. Find the selling price of the watches.

## 4  Find the cost when the amount of markup and the percent of markup based on the cost are known.

When markup is based on cost, the rate of cost is 100%. The cost is found by dividing the markup by the percent of markup.

$$B = \frac{P}{R} \qquad \text{Cost} = \frac{\text{markup}}{\text{rate of markup based on cost}}$$

**HOW TO**  Find the cost when the amount of markup and the percent of markup based on the cost are known

1. Find the cost using the formula

$$\text{Cost} = \frac{\text{markup}}{\text{rate of markup based on cost}} \qquad C = \frac{M}{M\%}$$

2. Change the rate of markup to a numerical equivalent and divide.

**EXAMPLE 1**  A DVD movie was marked up $6.50, which was a 40% markup based on cost. What was the cost of the DVD?

| What You Know | What You Are Looking For | Solution Plan |
|---|---|---|
| Markup = $6.50<br>$M\% = 40\%$ | Cost | $C = \dfrac{M}{M\%}$ |

**Solution**

$$C = \frac{M}{M\%}$$  Substitute known amounts.

$$C = \frac{\$6.50}{40\%}$$  Change percent to its decimal equivalent.

$$C = \frac{\$6.50}{0.4}$$  Divide.

$$C = \$16.25$$

**Conclusion**

**The cost of the DVD movie was $16.25.**

## STOP AND CHECK

1. A pair of New Balance running shoes is marked up $38, which is a 62% markup based on cost. Find the cost of the shoes.

2. Bradley's Sound Shop marks up a music system $650 and sells it at a 92% markup based on cost. What is the cost of the system? Round to the nearest cent.

3. Wiggins Clock Shop marked up an order of marble clocks $358 each and sells them at a 65% markup based on cost. What is the cost of each clock? Round to the nearest cent.

4. EnviroTote can purchase laundry bags in large quantities and mark them up $4.14 each. What is the cost of each bag if it is marked up 125% of cost? Round to the nearest cent.

5. EnviroTote can purchase a 10-oz Organic Barrel Bag with 25″ handles and mark it up $7.82. What is the cost of each bag if it is marked up 80% of cost? Round to the nearest cent.

6. Kroger marks up Armour chili $0.24 and sells it at a 32% markup. What is the cost of each can of chili?

## 5 Find the cost when the selling price and the percent of markup based on the cost are known.

If the markup is based on cost, the cost percent is 100% and the selling price percent is 100% + the markup percent.

**HOW TO** Find the cost when the selling price and the percent of markup based on the cost are known

1. Find the rate of selling price.

$$\text{Rate of selling price} = \text{rate of cost} + \text{rate of markup}$$
$$S\% = 100\% + M\%$$

2. Find the cost using the formula

$$\text{Cost} = \frac{\text{selling price}}{\text{rate of selling price based on cost}} \qquad C = \frac{S}{S\%}$$

3. Change the rate of selling price to a numerical equivalent and divide.

**EXAMPLE 1** A camera sells for $20. The markup rate is 50% of the cost. Find the cost of the camera and the markup.

| What You Know | What You Are Looking For | Solution Plan |
|---|---|---|
| Selling price = $20<br>$M\% = 50\%$<br>$C\% = 100\%$ | Cost<br><br>Markup | $S\% = 100\% + M\%$<br><br>$C = \dfrac{S}{S\%}$<br><br>$M = S - C$ |

Find the selling price rate:

| | |
|---|---|
| $S\% = 100\% + M\%$ | Substitute known amounts. |
| $S\% = 100\% + 50\%$ | Add. |
| $S\% = 150\%$ | |

Find the cost:

| | |
|---|---|
| $C = \dfrac{S}{S\%}$ | Substitute known amounts. |
| $C = \dfrac{\$20}{150\%}$ | Change percent to its decimal equivalent. |
| $C = \dfrac{\$20}{1.5}$ | Divide. |
| $C = \$13.33$ | Rounded to the nearest cent |

Find the markup:

| | |
|---|---|
| $M = S - C$ | Substitute known amounts. |
| $M = \$20 - \$13.33$ | Subtract. |
| $M = \$6.67$ | |

**The cost of the camera is $13.33 and the markup is $6.67.**

 ## STOP AND CHECK

*Round to the nearest cent.*

1. A paper cutter sells for $39. The markup rate is 60% of the cost. Find the cost of the camera and find the markup.

2. A leather jacket sells for $149. The markup rate is 110% of the cost. Find the cost of the jacket and find the markup.

3. Find the cost and markup of a box of cereal that sells for $4.65 and has a markup rate of 85% based on the cost.

4. A model train engine sells for $595 and has a markup rate of 165% based on the cost. What is the cost and markup of the engine?

5. Charlie at The 7th Inning sells Topps baseball cards for $65 a box and has a markup rate of 45% based on cost. Find the cost and markup of each box of cards.

6. AutoZone sells Anco windshield wiper blades for $9.99 and has a markup rate of 62% based on cost. What is the cost and markup for the wiper blades?

## 9-1 SECTION EXERCISES

### SKILL BUILDERS

*Round amounts to the nearest cent and percents to the nearest whole percent.*

1. Cost = $30; Markup = $20. Find the selling price.

2. Selling price = $75; Cost = $50. Find the markup.

3. Selling price = $36.99; Markup = $12.99. Find the cost.

4. Cost = $40; Rate of markup based on cost = 35%.
   a. Find the markup.

   b. Find the selling price.

**5.** Markup = $70; Rate of markup based on cost = 83%.
   a. Find the cost.

   b. Find the selling price.

**6.** Selling price = $148.27; Rate of markup based on cost = 40%.
   a. Find the cost.

   b. Find the markup.

**7.** Cost = $60; Selling price = $150.
   a. Find the markup.

   b. Find the rate of markup based on cost.

**8.** Cost = $82; Markup = $46.
   a. Find the rate of markup based on cost.

   b. Find the selling price.

## APPLICATIONS

**9.** Mugs cost $2 each and sell for $6 each. Find the markup.

**10.** Belts cost $4 and sell with a markup of $2.40. Find the selling price of the belts.

**11.** A compact disc player sells for $300. The cost is $86. Find the markup of the CD player.

**12.** Twenty decorative enamel balls cost $12.75 each and are marked up $9.56.
   a. Find the selling price for each one.

   b. Find the total amount of margin or markup for the 20 balls.

**13.** A DVD costs $4 and sells for $12. Find the amount of markup.

**14.** Find the cost if a hard hat is marked up $5 and has a selling price of $12.50.

**15.** Find the cost of a magazine that sells for $3.50 and is marked up $1.75.

**16.** Find the selling price if a case of photocopier paper costs $8 and is marked up $14.

**17.** A sofa costs $398 and sells for $716.40, which is 180% of the cost.
   a. Find the rate of markup.

   b. Find the markup.

**18.** An audio system sells for $2,980, which is 160% of the cost. The cost is $1,862.50.
   a. What is the rate of markup?

   b. What is the markup?

**19.** A lamp costs $32 and is marked up based on cost. If the lamp sold for $72, what was the percent of markup?

**20.** A TV that costs $1,899 sells for a 63% markup based on the cost. What is the selling price of the TV?

**21.** A computer desk costs $196 and sells for $395. What is the percent of markup based on cost? Round to the nearest tenth percent.

**22.** Battery-powered massagers cost $8.50 if they are purchased in lots of 36 or more. The Gift Horse Shoppe purchased 48 and sells them at a 45% markup based on cost. Find the selling price of each massager.

**23.** What is the cost of a sink that is marked up $188 if the markup rate is 70% based on cost?

**24.** A wristwatch sells for $289. The markup rate is 250% of cost.
a. Find the cost of the watch.

b. Find the markup.

**25.** A wallet is marked up $12, which is an 80% markup based on cost. What is the cost of the wallet?

**26.** Tombo Mono Correction Tape sells for $3.29. The markup rate is 65% of the cost.
a. What is the cost?

b. What is the markup of the tape?

## 9-2 MARKUP BASED ON SELLING PRICE AND MARKUP COMPARISONS

### LEARNING OUTCOMES

1 Find the amount of markup and the percent of markup based on the selling price when the cost and selling price are known.
2 Find the selling price when the amount of markup and the percent of markup based on the selling price are known.
3 Find the selling price when the cost and the percent of markup based on the selling price are known.
4 Find the cost when the selling price and the percent of markup based on the selling price are known.
5 Compare the markup based on the cost with the markup based on the selling price.

The markup rate can be calculated as a portion of either the cost or the selling price of an item. Most manufacturers and distributors calculate markup as a portion of *cost,* since they typically keep their records in terms of cost. Some wholesalers and a few retailers also use this method. Many retailers, however, use the *selling price* or *retail price* as a base in computing markup since they keep most of their records in terms of selling price.

## 1 Find the amount of markup and the percent of markup based on the selling price when the cost and selling price are known.

When the markup is based on selling price, the rate of the selling price is known and is 100%. The amount of the selling price is the base in the basic percentage formulas $P = RB$, $R = \dfrac{P}{B}$, and $B = \dfrac{P}{R}$.

Variations of the percentage formula for markup based on selling price are

$$\text{Markup} = \text{rate of markup based on selling price} \times \text{selling price}$$

$$\text{Rate of markup based on selling price} = \frac{\text{markup}}{\text{selling price}} \times 100\%$$

$$\text{Selling price} = \frac{\text{markup}}{\text{rate of markup based on selling price}}$$

| **HOW TO** | Find the amount of markup and the percent of markup based on the selling price when the cost and selling price are known: |

1. Find the amount of markup using the formula

$$\text{Markup} = \text{Selling price} - \text{Cost}$$
$$M \quad = \quad S \quad - \quad C$$

2. Find the percent of markup based on selling price using the formula

$$\text{Rate of markup based on selling price} = \frac{\text{markup}}{\text{selling price}} \times 100\%$$

$$M\% = \frac{\text{markup}}{\text{selling price}} \times 100\%$$

### EXAMPLE 1
A calculator costs $4 and sells for $10. Find the rate of markup based on the selling price.

| What You Know | What You Are Looking For | Solution Plan |
|---|---|---|
| Cost = $4 <br> Selling price = $10 <br> $S\% = 100\%$ | Rate of markup | Markup = selling price − cost <br><br> $M\% = \dfrac{\text{markup}}{\text{selling price}} \times 100\%$ |

**Solution**

Find the markup:

| | |
|---|---|
| $M = S - C$ | Substitute known values into the formula. |
| $M = \$10 - \$4$ | Subtract. |
| $M = \$6$ | Amount of markup |

Find the rate of markup:

$$M\% = \frac{\text{markup}}{\text{selling price}} \times 100\%$$      Substitute known values into the formula.

$$M\% = \frac{\$6}{\$10}(100\%)$$      Divide.

$$M\% = 0.6(100\%)$$      Change to percent equivalent.

$$M\% = 60\%$$      Rate or percent of markup

**Conclusion**

**The rate of markup for the calculator is 60%.**

---

 ## STOP AND CHECK

1. A textbook costs $58 and sells for $70. Find the rate of markup based on the selling price. Round to the nearest tenth percent.

2. The manufacturer's suggested retail price for a refrigerator is $1,499 and it costs $385. What is the rate of markup based on the suggested retail price?

3. Hale's Trailers purchases 16-ft trailers for $395 and sells them for $795. What is the rate of markup based on the selling price? Round to the nearest tenth percent.

4. Martha's Birding Society purchases humming bird feeders for $2.40 and sells them for $6.00. Find the rate of markup based on the selling price.

5. AutoZone purchases tire cleaner for $0.84 and sells it for $2.39. What is the rate of markup based on the selling price? Round to the nearest tenth percent.

6. Federated Department Stores purchased men's shoes for $132 and sells them for $229. What is the rate of markup based on selling price? Round to the nearest cent.

---

## 2   Find the selling price when the amount of markup and the percent of markup based on the selling price are known.

When the percent of markup is based on the selling price, the selling price is found by dividing the markup by the percent of markup.

> **HOW TO**   Find the selling price when the amount of markup and the percent of markup based on the selling price are known
>
> 1. Find the selling price using the formula
>
> $$\text{Selling price} = \frac{\text{markup}}{\text{rate of markup based on selling price}} \qquad S = \frac{M}{M\%}$$
>
> 2. Change the rate of markup to the numerical equivalent and divide.

**EXAMPLE 1**   Find the cost and selling price if a handbook is marked up $5 with a 20% markup rate based on selling price.

| What You Know | What You Are Looking For | Solution Plan |
|---|---|---|
| Markup = $5<br>$M\% = 20\%$ | Selling price<br>Cost | $S = \dfrac{M}{M\%}$<br>$C = S - M$ |

Find the selling price:

$$S = \frac{M}{M\%}$$       Substitute known amounts.

$$S = \frac{\$5}{20\%}$$       Change percent to its decimal equivalent.

$$S = \frac{\$5}{0.2}$$       Divide.

$$S = \$25$$       Selling price

Find the cost:

$$C = S - M$$       Substitute known amounts.

$$C = \$25 - \$5$$       Subtract.

$$C = \$20$$       Cost

**Conclusion**

**The selling price of the handbook is $25 and the cost is $20.**

 ## STOP AND CHECK

1. Find the cost and selling price if a handbook is marked up $195 with a 60% markup rate based on selling price.

2. Find the cost and selling price of a baseball that is marked up $21 with an 80% markup based on the selling price.

3. The 7th Inning marks a soccer trophy up $14, a 75% markup based on the selling price. What is the cost and selling price of the trophy?

4. Wolf Camera marks a camera up 25% of the selling price. If the markup is $145, what is the cost and selling price of the camera?

5. Shekenna's Dress Shop marks up a Sag Harbor suit $38. This represents a 70% markup based on the selling price. What is the cost and selling price of the suit?

6. May Department Store marks one stock keeping unit (SKU) of its Coach handbags up $70.08 or 32% of the selling price. Find the cost and selling price of the handbags.

### 3 Find the selling price when the cost and the percent of markup based on the selling price are known.

When the percent of markup is based on the selling price, the selling price is found by dividing the cost by the rate of cost based on the selling price. The rate of cost based on the selling price is 100% − rate of markup. The rate of cost based on selling price will be less than 100%.

**HOW TO**    **Find the selling price when the cost and the percent of markup based on the selling price are known**

1. Find the rate of the cost using the formula

$$\text{Rate of } C = \text{rate of } S - \text{rate of } M$$
$$C\% = 100\% - M\%$$

2. Find the selling price using the formula

$$\text{Selling price} = \frac{\text{cost}}{\text{rate of cost based on selling price}}$$
$$S = \frac{C}{C\%}$$

**EXAMPLE 1** Find the selling price and markup for a pair of jeans that costs the retailer $28 and is marked up 30% of the selling price.

| What You Know | What You Are Looking For | Solution Plan |
|---|---|---|
| Cost = $28 | Rate of cost | $C\% = 100\% - M\%$ |
| Markup % = 30% | Selling price | $S = \dfrac{C}{C\%}$ |
| Selling price % = 100% | Markup | $M = S - C$ |

**Solution**

Find the rate of cost:

| | |
|---|---|
| $C\% = 100\% - M\%$ | Substitute known amounts. |
| $C\% = 100\% - 30\%$ | Subtract. |
| $C\% = 70\%$ | Rate of cost |

Find the selling price:

| | |
|---|---|
| $S = \dfrac{C}{C\%}$ | Substitute known amounts. |
| $S = \dfrac{\$28}{70\%}$ | Change percent to its decimal equivalent. |
| $S = \dfrac{\$28}{0.7}$ | Divide. |
| $S = \$40$ | Selling price |

Find the markup:

| | |
|---|---|
| $M = S - C$ | Substitute known amounts. |
| $M = \$40 - \$28$ | Subtract. |
| $M = \$12$ | Markup |

**Conclusion**

**The selling price is $40 and the markup is $12.**

 **STOP AND CHECK**

1. Dollar General Stores buys detergent from the manufacturer for $2.99 and marks it up 25% of the selling price. Find the selling price and markup for the detergent.

2. Best Buy buys a digital camera for $187 and marks it up 38% of the selling price. Find the selling price and markup for the camera.

3. Lucinda Gallegos buys scissors for $3.84 and sells them with a 27% markup based on selling price. What is the selling price and markup for the scissors?

4. A Singer sewing machine costs $127.59 and the Fabric Center marks it up 23% of the selling price. What is the selling price and markup for the machine?

5. The Fabric Center pays $1.92 per yard for bridal satin then marks it up 65% of the selling price. What is the selling price and markup for the fabric?

6. IZZE sparkling grapefruit soda costs $32.49 per case and Trader Joe's marks it up 35% of the selling price. Find the selling price and markup per case.

## 4   Find the cost when the selling price and the percent of markup based on the selling price are known.

When the percent of markup is based on the selling price, the cost percent equals 100% minus the markup percent.

**Find the cost when the selling price and the percent of markup based on the selling price are known**

1. Find the rate of cost.

$$\text{Rate of cost} = \text{rate of selling price} - \text{rate of markup}$$
$$C\% = 100\% - M\%$$

2. Find the cost.

$$\text{Cost based on selling price} = \text{rate of cost} \times \text{selling price}$$
$$C = C\% \times S$$

3. Change $C\%$ to a numerical equivalent and multiply.

**EXAMPLE 1** Find the markup and cost of a box of pencils that sells for $2.99 and is marked up 25% of the selling price.

| What You Know | What You Are Looking For | Solution Plan |
|---|---|---|
| Selling price = $2.99<br>$S\% = 100\%$<br>$M\% = 25\%$ | Cost<br>Markup | $C\% = 100\% - M\%$<br>$C = C\% \times S$<br>$M = S - C$ |

**Solution**

Find the cost rate:

| | |
|---|---|
| $C\% = 100\% - M\%$ | Substitute known amounts. |
| $C\% = 100\% - 25\%$ | Subtract. |
| $C\% = 75\%$ | Cost rate |

Find the cost:

| | |
|---|---|
| $C = C\% \times S$ | Substitute known amounts. |
| $C = 75\%(\$2.99)$ | Change percent to its decimal equivalent. |
| $C = 0.75(\$2.99)$ | Multiply. |
| $C = \$2.24$ | Rounded to the nearest cent |

Find the markup:

| | |
|---|---|
| $M = S - C$ | Substitute known amounts. |
| $M = \$2.99 - \$2.24$ | Subtract. |
| $M = \$0.75$ | |

**Conclusion**

**The cost of the box of pencils is $2.24 and the markup is $0.75.**

To summarize the concepts we have covered in this chapter to this point, all markup problems are solved in basically the same way. One key point is that one rate is known when you know if the markup is based on the cost or the selling price. When the markup is based on cost, the rate of the cost is 100%. When the markup is based on selling price, the rate of the selling price is 100%.

In markup problems there are three amounts and three percents (rates). If three of the six parts are known and at least one known part is an amount and another is whether the markup is based on the cost or the selling price, the other three parts can be determined.

To organize the known and unknown parts, we can use a chart. This chart can guide you in selecting the appropriate formula.

**Find all the missing parts if three parts are known and at least one part is an amount and it is known whether the markup is based on the cost or the selling price**

1. Place the three known parts into the chart.

| | $ | % |
|---|---|---|
| $C$ | | |
| $M$ | | |
| $S$ | | |

## EXAMPLE 2

Wal-Mart plans to mark up a package of 8 AA batteries $3.50 over cost. This will be a 50% markup based on cost. Find the missing information.

| What You Know | What You Are Looking For | Solution Plan |
|---|---|---|
| $C\% = 100\%$ <br> $M\% = 50\%$ <br> $M = \$3.50$ | $S\%$, $C$, and $S$ | $S\% = C\% + M\%$ <br> $B = \dfrac{P}{R}$ or $C = \dfrac{M}{M\%}$ <br> $S = C + M$ |

| | $ | % |
|---|---|---|
| $C$ | | 100 |
| $M$ | 3.50 | 50 |
| $S$ | | |

### Solution

Find the rate of the selling price:

$S\% = C\% + M\%$     Two percents are known.

$S\% = 100\% + 50\%$     Substitute known percents.

$S\% = 150\%$     Add.

Rate of selling price

Find the cost:

$C = \dfrac{M}{M\%}$     Substitute known amounts.

$C = \dfrac{\$3.50}{50\%}$     Change percent to its decimal equivalent.

$C = \dfrac{\$3.50}{0.5}$     Divide.

$C = \$7.00$     Cost

Find the selling price:

$S = C + M$     Substitute known amounts.

$S = \$7.00 + \$3.50$     Add.

$S = \$10.50$     Selling price

| | $ | % |
|---|---|---|
| $C$ | 7.00 | 100 |
| $M$ | 3.50 | 50 |
| $S$ | 10.50 | 150 |

### Conclusion

**The rate of the selling price is 150%, the cost is $7.00, and the selling price is $10.50.**

**STOP AND CHECK**

1. Find the markup and cost of a fishing lure that sells for $18.99 and is marked up 38% of the selling price.

2. Al's Golf Supply plans to mark up its persimmon wood drivers by 60% based on cost, or $135. Find the cost and selling price for the drivers.

3. What is the markup and cost of a chair that sells for $349 and is marked up 58% of the selling price?

4. Ronin Copies marks up signs that sell for $49. The markup is 80% based on the selling price. What is the amount of the markup and cost of a sign?

5. A scanner that is marked up 46% of the selling price sells for $675. Find the amount of markup and the cost of the scanner.

6. A Canon copier is marked up 38% of the selling price. It costs $3,034.90. Find the markup and selling price of the copier.

## 5 Compare the markup based on the cost with the markup based on the selling price.

If a store manager tells you that the standard markup rate is 25%, you don't know if that means markup based on cost or on selling price. What's the difference?

**EXAMPLE 1** Find the rate of markup based on cost and based on selling price of a computer that costs $1,500 and sells for $2,000.

| What You Know | What You Are Looking For | Solution Plan |
|---|---|---|
| $C = \$1,500$ <br> $S = \$2,000$ | $M\%$ based on cost <br> $M\%$ based on selling price | $M = S - C$ <br><br> $M\%_{cost} = \dfrac{M}{C} \times 100\%$ <br><br> $M\%_{selling\ price} = \dfrac{M}{S} \times 100\%$ |

**Solution**

Find the markup:

$M = S - C$       Substitute known amounts.

$M = \$2,000 - \$1,500$       Subtract.

$M = \$500$       Amount of markup

Find the rate of markup based on cost:

$M\%_{cost} = \dfrac{M}{C} \times 100\%$       Substitute known amounts.

$M\%_{cost} = \dfrac{\$500}{\$1,500}(100\%)$       Divide and write percent equivalent.

$M\%_{cost} = 33\dfrac{1}{3}\%$       Markup rate based on cost

Find the rate of markup based on selling price:

$M\%_{selling\ price} = \dfrac{M}{S} \times 100\%$       Substitute known amounts.

$M\%_{selling\ price} = \dfrac{\$500}{\$2,000}(100\%)$       Divide and write percent equivalent.

$M\%_{selling\ price} = 25\%$       Markup rate based on selling price

**Conclusion**

**The markup rate based on cost is $33\dfrac{1}{3}\%$ and the markup rate based on selling price is 25%.**

Sometimes it is necessary to switch from a markup based on selling price to a markup based on cost, or vice versa.

## HOW TO   Convert a markup rate based on selling price to a markup rate based on cost

1. Find the complement of the markup rate based on the selling price. That is, subtract the markup rate from 100%.
2. Divide the decimal equivalent of the markup rate based on the selling price by the decimal equivalent of the complement of the rate.

$$M\%_{cost} = \frac{M\%_{selling\ price}}{100\% - M\%_{selling\ price}}(100\%)$$

## EXAMPLE 2   A desk is marked up 30% based on selling price. What is the equivalent markup based on the cost?

| What You Know | What You Are Looking For | Solution Plan |
|---|---|---|
| $M\%_{selling\ price} = 30\%$ | $M\%_{cost}$ | $M\%_{cost} = \dfrac{M\%_{selling\ price}}{100\% - M\%_{selling\ price}}(100\%)$ |

### Solution

$$M\%_{cost} = \frac{M\%_{selling\ price}}{100\% - M\%_{selling\ price}} \times 100\%$$   Substitute known amounts.

$$M\%_{cost} = \frac{30\%}{100\% - 30\%} \times 100\%$$   Subtract in denominator.

$$M\%_{cost} = \frac{30\%}{70\%}(100\%)$$   Change percents to decimal equivalents.

$$M\%_{cost} = \frac{0.3}{0.7}(100\%)$$   Divide and round to hundredths.

$$M\%_{cost} = 0.43(100\%)$$   Change to percent equivalent rounded to the
$$M\%_{cost} = 43\%$$   nearest whole-number percent.

### Conclusion

**A 30% markup based on selling price is equivalent to a 43% markup based on cost.**

## HOW TO   Convert a markup rate based on cost to a markup rate based on selling price

1. Add 100% to the markup rate based on the cost.
2. Divide the decimal equivalent of the markup rate based on the cost by the decimal equivalent of the sum found in step 1.

$$M\%_{selling\ price} = \frac{M\%_{cost}}{100\% + M\%_{cost}} \times 100\%$$

**EXAMPLE 3** A DVD player is marked up 40% based on cost. What is the markup rate based on selling price?

| What You Know | What You Are Looking For | Solution Plan |
|---|---|---|
| $M\%_{cost} = 40\%$ | $M\%_{selling\ price}$ | $M\%_{selling\ price} = \dfrac{M\%_{cost}}{100\% + M\%_{cost}}(100\%)$ |

**Solution**

$$M\%_{selling\ price} = \frac{M\%_{cost}}{100\% + M\%_{cost}} \times 100\%$$ 
Substitute known amounts.

$$M\%_{selling\ price} = \frac{40\%_{cost}}{100\% + 40\%_{cost}}(100\%)$$ 
Add in denominator.

$$M\%_{selling\ price} = \frac{40\%}{140\%}(100\%)$$ 
Change percents to decimal equivalents.

$$M\%_{selling\ price} = \frac{0.4}{1.4}(100\%)$$ 
Divide and round to hundredths.

$$M\%_{selling\ price} = 0.29(100\%)$$ 
Change to percent equivalent rounded to the nearest whole-number percent.

$$M\%_{selling\ price} = 29\%$$

**Conclusion**

**A 40% markup based on cost is equivalent to a 29% markup based on selling price.**

---

## TIP

**Estimating Markup Equivalencies**

| Known | Unknown | Estimate |
|---|---|---|
| $M\%_{cost}$ | $M\%_{selling\ price}$ | $M\%_{selling\ price}$ will be smaller |
| $M\%_{selling\ price}$ | $M\%_{cost}$ | $M\%_{cost}$ will be larger |

---

 **STOP AND CHECK**

1. Find the rate of markup based on cost and based on selling price of a blanket that costs $12.50 and sells for $38. Round to the nearest tenth percent.

2. Find the rate of markup based on cost and based on selling price of a copy machine that costs $12,500 and sells for $18,900. Round to the nearest tenth of a percent.

3. Find the rate of markup based on cost and based on selling price of a postage meter that costs $375 and sells for $535. Round to the nearest tenth percent.

4. A stroller is marked up 40% based on selling price. What is the equivalent markup based on cost? Round to the nearest tenth percent.

5. A DVD is marked up 120% of cost. What is the equivalent rate of markup based on selling price? Round to the nearest tenth percent.

6. A diamond ring is marked up 75% based on selling price. Find the equivalent markup based on cost. Round to the nearest tenth percent.

## SKILL BUILDERS

*Round to the nearest cent or tenth of a percent.*

1. Cost = $32; selling price = $40. Find the rate of markup based on the selling price.

2. Markup = $75; markup rate of 60% based on the selling price.
   a. Find the selling price.

   b. Find the cost.

3. Selling price = $1,980; cost = $795. Find the rate of markup based on the selling price.

4. Markup = $2,050; markup rate is 42% of the selling price.
   a. Find the selling price.

   b. Find the cost.

5. Markup rate based on selling price = 15%; markup = $250. Find the selling price.

6. Find the selling price for an item that costs $792 and is marked up 42% of the selling price.
   a. Find the cost.

   b. Find the selling price.

7. An item is marked up $12. The markup rate based on selling price is 65%.
   a. Find the selling price.

   b. Find the cost.

8. Selling price = $1.98; markup is 48% of the selling price.
   a. What is the cost?

   b. What is the markup?

9. An item sells for $5,980 and costs $3,420. What is the rate of markup based on selling price?

10. The selling price of an item is $18.50 and the markup rate is 86% of the selling price.
   a. Find the markup.

   b. Find the cost.

11. An item has a 30% markup based on selling price. The markup is $100.
   a. Find the selling price.

   b. Find the cost.

12. An item costs $20 and sells for $50.
   a. Find the rate of markup based on cost.

   b. Find the rate of markup based on selling price.

13. An item has a 60% markup based on selling price. What is the equivalent markup percent based on the cost?

14. A 40% markup based on cost is equivalent to what percent based on selling price (retail)?

## APPLICATIONS

15. An air compressor costs $350 and sells for $695. Find the rate of markup based on the selling price.

16. A lateral file is marked up $140, which represents a 28% markup based on the selling price.
   a. Find the selling price.

   b. Find the cost.

17. A lawn tractor that costs the retailer $599 is marked up 36% of the selling price.
   a. Find the selling price.

   b. Find the markup.

18. A recliner chair that sells for $1,499 is marked up 60% of the selling price.
   a. What is the cost?

   b. What is the markup?

19. Lowe's plans to sell its best-quality floor tiles for $15 each. This is a 48% markup based on selling price.
   a. Find the cost.

   b. Find the markup.

20. A serving tray costs $1,400 and sells for $2,015.
   a. Find the rate of markup based on cost.

   b. Find the rate of markup based on selling price.

21. What is the equivalent markup based on cost of a water fountain that is marked up 63% based on the selling price?

22. A box of Acco paper clips is marked up 46% based on cost. What is the markup based on selling price?

# 9-3 MARKDOWN, SERIES OF MARKDOWNS, AND PERISHABLES

## LEARNING OUTCOMES

1 Find the amount of markdown, the reduced (new) price, and the percent of markdown.
2 Find the final selling price for a series of markups and markdowns.
3 Find the selling price for a desired profit on perishable and seasonal goods.

**Markdown:** amount by which an original selling price is reduced.

**Perishable:** an item for sale that has a relatively short time during which the quality of the item is acceptable for sale.

Merchants often have to reduce the price of merchandise from the price at which it was originally sold. The amount that the original selling price is reduced is called the **markdown**.

There are many reasons for making markdowns. Sometimes merchandise is marked too high to begin with. Sometimes it gets worn or dirty or goes out of style. Flowers, fruits, vegetables, and baked goods are called **perishables** and are sold for less when the quality of the item is not as good as the original quality. Competition from other stores may also require that a retailer mark prices down.

## 1 Find the amount of markdown, the reduced (new) price, and the percent of markdown.

Markdowns are generally based on the original selling price. That is, the original selling price is the base in the percentage formulas and the rate of the selling price is 100%.

---

**HOW TO** Find the amount of markdown, the reduced (new) price, and the percent of markdown

1. Place the known values into the chart:

|  | $ | % |
|---|---|---|
| Original Selling Price ($S$) |  | 100% |
| Markdown ($M$) |  |  |
| Reduced (New) Price ($N$) |  |  |

2. Select the appropriate formula based on the known values:

Markdown = original selling price − reduced price   $M = S - N$
Reduced price = original selling price − markdown   $N = S - M$

$$M\% = \frac{M}{S}(100\%)$$

---

**EXAMPLE 1**   A lamp originally sold for $36 and was marked down to sell for $30. Find the markdown and the rate of markdown (to the nearest hundredth).

| What You Know | What You Are Looking For | Solution Plan |
|---|---|---|
| $S = \$36$<br>$N = \$30$ | Markdown<br>Rate of markdown | <table><tr><td></td><td>$</td><td>%</td></tr><tr><td>$S$</td><td>36</td><td>100%</td></tr><tr><td>$M$</td><td></td><td></td></tr><tr><td>$N$</td><td>30</td><td></td></tr></table>$M = S - N$<br>$M\% = \dfrac{M}{S} \times 100\%$ |

### Solution

Find the markdown:

$M = S - N$      Substitute known values.
$M = \$36 - \$30$      Subtract.
$M = \$6$      Markdown

Find the rate of markdown:

$M\% = \dfrac{M}{S} \times 100\%$      Substitute known values.

$M\% = \dfrac{\$6}{\$36}(100\%)$      Perform calculations.

$M\% = 0.166666667(100\%)$      Rate of markdown
$M\% = 16.7\%$      Rounded

### Conclusion

**The markdown is \$6 and the rate of markdown is 16.7%.**

---

## TIP

**Making Connections between Markup and Markdown**

Some business processes use the same or similar terminology in different contexts. Examine the terms *original price* and *new price* when associated with markup and markdown.

**Markup**
Original price = cost ($C$)
Upward change = markup ($M$)
New price = selling price ($S$)
$S = C + M$

**Markdown**
Original price = selling price ($S$)
Downward change = markdown ($M$)
New price = reduced or sale price ($N$)
$N = S - M$

---

## EXAMPLE 2

A wallet was originally priced at \$12 and was reduced by 25%. Find the markdown and the sale (new) price.

| What You Know | What You Are Looking For | Solution Plan | | |
|---|---|---|---|---|
| $S = \$12$ <br> $M\% = 25\%$ | Markdown <br> Sale price | | $ | % |
| | | $S$ | 12 | 100% |
| | | $M$ | | 25% |
| | | $N$ | | |

$M = M\% \times S$
$N = S - M$

### Solution

Find the markdown:

$M = M\% \times S$      Substitute known values.
$M = 25\%(\$12)$      Change percent to its decimal equivalent.
$M = 0.25(\$12)$      Multiply.
$M = \$3$      Markdown

Find the sale (new) price:

$N = S - M$      Substitute known values.
$N = \$12 - \$3$      Subtract.
$N = \$9$

### Conclusion

**The markdown is \$3 and the sale price is \$9.**

1. A purse originally sold for $135 and was marked down to sell for $75. Find the markdown and the rate of markdown (to the nearest tenth).

2. An umbrella originally sold for $15 and was marked down to sell for $8. Find the markdown and rate of markdown rounded to the nearest tenth of a percent.

3. A ladder was originally priced to sell for $249 and was reduced by 35%. Find the amount of markdown and the reduced price.

4. A book bag is priced to sell for $38.99. If the bag was reduced 25%, find the amount of markdown and the reduced price.

5. A corkboard was originally priced to sell at $85 and was reduced by 40%. Find the amount of markdown and the reduced price.

6. Lowe's reduced a Maytag dishwasher 12.563%. If the dishwasher was priced at $398, find the amount of markdown and the reduced price.

## 2  Find the final selling price for a series of markups and markdowns.

Prices are in a continuous state of flux in the business world. Markups are made to cover increased costs. Markdowns are made to move merchandise more rapidly, to move dated or perishable merchandise, or to draw customers into a store.

Sometimes prices are marked down several times or marked up between markdowns before the merchandise is sold. In calculating each stage of prices, markups, markdowns, and rates, we use exactly the same markup/markdown formulas and procedures as before. To apply these formulas and procedures, we agree that both the markup and the markdown are based on the *previous selling price* in the series.

> **HOW TO**  Find the final selling price for a series of markups and markdowns
>
> 1. Find the first selling price using the given facts and markup procedures in Sections 9-1 and 9-2.
> 2. For each remaining stage in the series:
>    (a) If the stage requires a *markdown*, identify the previous selling price as the *original selling price S* for this stage. Find the *reduced price N*. This reduced price is the new selling price for this stage.
>    (b) If the stage requires a *markup*, identify the previous selling price as the *cost C* for this stage. Find the *selling price S*. This price is the new selling price for this stage.
> 3. Identify the selling price for the last stage as the *final selling price*.

> **EXAMPLE 1**  Belinda's China Shop paid a wholesale price of $800 for a set of imported china. On August 8, Belinda marked up the china 50% based on the cost. On October 1, she marked the china down 25% for a special 10-day promotion. On October 11, she marked the china up 15%. The china was again marked down 30% for a preholiday sale. What was the final selling price of the china?

| What You Know | What You Are Looking For | Solution Plan |
|---|---|---|
| Cost = $800 | Selling price for stage 1 ($S_1$) | Find the selling price for each stage using the formulas: |
| Stage 1: markup of 50% based on cost | Selling price for stage 2 ($N_2$) | |
| | Selling price for stage 3 ($S_3$) | $S\% = C\% + M\%$ |
| Stage 2: markdown of 25% based on selling price | Selling price for stage 4 ($N_4$) | $N\% = S\% - M\%$ |
| | | $S = S\% \times C$ |
| Stage 3: markup of 15% based on new selling price | | $N = N\% \times S$ |
| Stage 4: markdown of 30% based on new selling price | | |

Stage 1: August 8

Find the first selling price ($S_1$), which is a markup, based on cost:

|   | $ | % |
|---|---|---|
| $C$ | 800 | 100 |
| $M$ |  | 50 |
| $S$ | 1,200 | 150 |

$S_1\% = C\% + M\%$
$S_1\% = 100\% + 50\%$
$S_1\% = 150\%$

$S_1 = S_1\% \times C$
$S_1 = 150\%(\$800)$
$S_1 = 1.5(\$800)$
$S_1 = \$1,200$

Stage 2: October 1

Find the second selling price ($N_2$), which is a markdown, using $S_1$ as the original selling price:

|   | $ | % |
|---|---|---|
| $S_1$ | 1,200 | 100 |
| $M$ |  | 25 |
| $N_2$ | 900 | 75 |

$N_2\% = S\% - M\%$
$N_2\% = 100\% - 25\%$
$N_2\% = 75\%$

$N_2 = N\% \times S_1$
$N_2 = 75\%(\$1,200)$
$N_2 = 0.75(\$1,200)$
$N_2 = \$900$

Stage 3: October 11

Find the third selling price ($S_3$), which is a markup, using $N_2$ as the cost:

|   | $ | % |
|---|---|---|
| $N_2$ | 900 | 100 |
| $M$ |  | 15 |
| $S_3$ | 1,035 | 115 |

$S_3\% = N_2\% + M\%$
$S_3\% = 100\% + 15\%$
$S_3\% = 115\%$

$S_3 = S_3\% \times N_2$
$S_3 = 115\%(\$900)$
$S_3 = 1.15(\$900)$
$S_3 = \$1,035$

Stage 4: Final markdown

Find the final selling price ($N_4$), which is a markup, using $S_3$ as the selling price:

|   | $ | % |
|---|---|---|
| $S_3$ | 1,035 | 100 |
| $M$ |  | 30 |
| $N_4$ | 724.50 | 70 |

$N_4\% = S\% - M\%$
$N_4\% = 100\% - 30\%$
$N_4\% = 70\%$

$N_4 = N_4\% \times S_3$
$N_4 = 70\%(\$1,035)$
$N_4 = 0.7(\$1,035)$
$N_4 = \$724.50$

**Conclusion**

**The final price in the series is \$724.50.**

Sometimes in retail marketing the series of changes are all markdowns. We can adapt our procedure for finding the net price after applying a trade discount series, which was discussed in Chapter 8. Repricing individual items can be very time-consuming, and many department stores have chosen to use a single sign on an entire table or rack to indicate the same percent markdown on a variety of items. Also, as a further incentive to buy, they may publish a coupon that entitles you to "take an extra 10% off already reduced prices." This is a situation that can model the procedure for finding the net price after applying a trade discount series.

Net decimal equivalent = product of decimal equivalents of the complements of each discount rate

Net price = net decimal equivalent × original price

Total rate of reduction = (1 − net decimal equivalent)(100%)

**EXAMPLE 2** Burdines' has various sales racks throughout the store. Chloe Duke finds a coat that she would like to purchase from a rack labeled 40% off. She also has a newspaper coupon that reads "Take an additional 10% off any already reduced price." How much will a coat cost (net price) that was originally priced at $145? What is the total percent of reduction?

| What You Know | What You Are Looking For | Solution Plan |
|---|---|---|
| Original price = $145<br><br>Discount rates are 40% and 10%. | Final reduced price<br><br>Total percent of reduction | Find the net decimal equivalent of the rate you pay:<br><br>Net price = net decimal equivalent × original price<br><br>Total rate of reduction = (1 − net decimal equivalent) × 100% |

**STOP AND CHECK**

1. Holly's Interior Design Shoppe paid $189 for a fern stand and marked it up 60% based on the cost. Holly included it in a special promotional markdown of 30%. The stand was damaged during the sale and was marked down an additional 40%. What was the final selling price of the stand?

2. Rich's placed a "10% off" coupon in a newspaper for a holiday sale. Becca selected shoes from the sale rack that were marked 30% off and also used the coupon. How much will Becca pay for the shoes if they were originally priced at $128? What is the total percent reduction?

3. Johnson's Furniture bought a table for $262 and marked it up 85% based on the cost. For a special promotion, it was marked down 25%. Store management decided to mark it down an additional 30%. What was the final reduced price?

4. Neilson's Department Store placed a "15% off" coupon in the newspaper for an after-Thanksgiving sale. Lakisha purchased a formal dress that was marked 40% off and used the coupon. The dress was originally priced at $249. How much did Lakisha pay for the dress?

## 3  Find the selling price for a desired profit on perishable and seasonal goods.

Most businesses anticipate that some seasonal merchandise will not sell at the original selling price. Stores that sell perishable or strictly seasonal items (fresh fruits, vegetables, swimsuits, or coats, for example) usually anticipate from past experience how much merchandise will be marked down or discarded due to spoilage or merchandise out of date. For example, most retail stores mark down holiday items to 50% of the original price the day after the holiday. Thus, merchants set the original markup of such items to obtain the desired profit level based on the projected number of items sold at "full price" (the original selling price).

**HOW TO**  Find the selling price to achieve a desired profit

1. Establish the rate of profit (markup)—based on cost—desired on the sale of the merchandise.
2. Find the total cost of the merchandise by multiplying the unit cost by the quantity of merchandise. Add in additional charges such as shipping.
3. Find the total desired profit (markup) based on cost by multiplying the rate of profit (markup) by the total cost.
4. Find the total selling price by adding the total cost and the total desired profit.
5. Establish the quantity expected to sell.
6. Divide the total selling price (step 4) by the expect-to-sell quantity (step 5).

$$\text{Selling price per item to achieve desired profit (markup)} = \frac{\text{total selling price}}{\text{expect-to-sell quantity}}$$

## EXAMPLE 1

Green's Grocery specializes in fresh fruits and vegetables. Merchandise is priced for quick sale and some must be discarded because of spoilage. Hardy Green, the owner, receives 400 pounds of bananas, for which he pays $0.15 per pound. On the average, 8% of the bananas will spoil. Find the selling price per pound to obtain a 175% markup on cost.

| What You Know | What You Are Looking For | Solution Plan |
|---|---|---|
| 400 lb of bananas at $0.15 per pound<br><br>175% markup on cost (desired profit)<br><br>8% expected spoilage | Selling price per pound | Total cost = cost per pound $\times$ number of pounds<br>Markup = $M\% \times C$<br>Total selling price = $C + M$<br>Pounds expected to sell = 92%(400)<br>Selling price per pound = $\dfrac{\text{total selling price}}{\text{pounds expected to sell}}$ |

### Solution

$C = \$0.15(400) = \$60$      Find the total cost of the bananas.

$M = 1.75(\$60) = \$105$      175% = 1.75. Find the desired profit (markup).

$S = C + M = \$60 + \$105 = \$165$      Find the total selling price.

Hardy must receive $165 for the bananas he expects to sell. He expects 8% not to sell, or 92% to sell.

$0.92(400) = 368$      Establish how many pounds he can expect to sell.

He can expect to sell 368 pounds of bananas.

$$\text{Selling price per pound} = \frac{\text{total selling price}}{\text{pounds expected to sell}}$$

$$= \frac{\$165}{368} = \$0.4483695652 \text{ or } \$0.45$$

### Conclusion

**Hardy must sell the bananas for $0.45 per pound to receive the profit he desires. If he sells more than 92% of the bananas, he will receive additional profit.**

 **STOP AND CHECK**

1. Drewrey's Market pays $0.30 per pound for 300 pounds of peaches. On average 5% of the peaches will spoil before they sell. Find the selling price per pound needed to obtain a 180% markup on cost.

2. Cozort's Produce pays $0.35 per pound for 500 pounds of apples. On average, 8% of the apples will spoil before they sell. Find the selling price per pound needed to obtain a 175% markup on cost.

3. Wesson grocery buys tomatoes for $0.27 per pound. On average, 4% of the tomatoes must be discarded. Find the selling price per pound needed to obtain a 160% markup on cost for 2,000 pounds.

4. EZ Way Produce pays $0.92 per pound for 1,000 lb of mushrooms. On average 10% of the mushrooms will spoil before they sell. Find the selling price per pound needed to obtain a 180% markup based on cost.

## SKILL BUILDERS

*Round dollar amounts to the nearest cent, and percents to the nearest tenth percent.*

1. An item sells for $48 and is reduced to sell for $30. Find the markdown amount and the rate of markdown.

2. An item is reduced from $585 to sell for $499. What is the markdown amount and the rate of markdown?

3. Selling price = $850; reduced (New) price = $500. Find the markdown amount and the rate of markdown.

4. Selling price = $795; reduced price = $650. Find the markdown amount and the rate of markdown.

5. An item is originally priced to sell for $75 and is marked down 40%. A customer has a coupon for an additional 15%. What is the total percent reduction?

6. An item costs $400 and is marked up 60% based on the cost. The first markdown rate is 20% and the second markdown rate is 30%. What is the final selling price?

## APPLICATIONS

7. Jung's Grocery received 1,000 pounds of onions at $0.12 per pound. On the average, 4% of the onions will spoil before selling. Find the selling price per pound to obtain a markup rate of 200% based on cost.

8. Deron marks down pillows at the end of the season. They sell for $35 and are reduced to $20. What is the markdown and the rate of markdown?

9. Desmond found a bicycle with an original price tag of $349 but it had been reduced by 45%. What is the amount of markdown and the sale price?

10. Julia purchased a sweatshirt that was reduced from $42 to sell for $26. How much was her markdown? What was the markdown and the rate of markdown?

11. A ladies' suit selling for $135 is marked down 25% for a special promotion. It is later marked down 15% of the sale price. Since the suit still hasn't sold, it is marked down to a price that is 75% off the original selling price. What are the two sale prices of the suit? What is the final selling price of the suit?

12. The Swim Shop paid a wholesale price of $24 each for Le Paris swimsuits. On May 5 it marked up the suits 50% of the cost. On June 15 the swimsuits were marked down 15% for a two-day sale, and on June 17 they were marked up again to the original selling price. On August 30, the shop sold all remaining swimsuits for 40% off. What was the May 5 price, the June 15 price, and the final selling price of a Le Paris swimsuit?

13. Tancia Boone ordered 600 pounds of Red Delicious apples for the produce section of the supermarket. She paid $0.32 per pound for the apples and expected 15% of them to spoil. If the store wants to make a profit of 90% on the cost, what should be the per-pound selling price?

14. Drewrey's fruit stand sells fresh fruits and vegetables. Becky Drewrey, the manager, must mark the selling price of incoming produce high enough to make the desired profit while taking expected markdowns and spoilage into account. Becky paid $0.35 per pound for 300 pounds of grapes. On average, 12% of the grapes will spoil. Find the selling price per pound needed to achieve a 175% markup on cost.

15. The 7th Inning is buying Ohio State T-shirts. The cost of the shirts, which includes permission fees paid to Ohio State, will be $10.90 each if 1,000 shirts are purchased. Charlie sells 800 shirts before the football season begins at a 50% markup based on cost. What is the gross margin (markup) if Charlie sells the remaining 200 shirts at a 25% reduction from the selling price?

## Learning Outcomes

## What to Remember with Examples

### Section 9-1

**1** Find the cost, markup, or selling price when any two of the three are known. (p. 296)

1. Identify the two known amounts.
2. Identify the missing amount.
3. Select the appropriate formula.
4. Substitute the known amounts into the formula.
5. Evaluate the formula.

> Find the markup based on a cost of $38 if the selling price is $95.
>
> $M = S - C$
> $M = \$95 - \$38$
> $M = \$57$

**2** Find the percent of markup based on the cost when the cost and selling price are known. (p. 298)

1. Find the amount of markup using the formula

$$\text{Markup} = \text{selling price} - \text{cost}$$
$$M = S - C$$

2. Find the percent of markup based on cost using the formula

$$\text{Rate of markup based on cost} = \frac{\text{markup}}{\text{cost}} \times 100\%$$

$$M\% = \frac{\text{markup}}{\text{cost}}(100\%)$$

> Find the percent of markup based on a cost of $86 if the selling price is $124.70.
>
> $M = S - C$
> $M = \$124.70 - \$86$
> $M = \$38.70$
> $M\% = \dfrac{\$38.70}{\$86}(100\%)$
> $M\% = 45\%$

**3** Find the selling price when the cost and the percent of markup based on the cost are known. (p. 299)

1. Find the rate of the selling price based on cost using the formula

$$\text{Rate of } S = \text{rate of } C + \text{rate of } M \qquad S\% = C\% + M\%$$

2. Find the selling price using the formula

$$\text{Selling price} = \text{rate of selling price based on cost} \times \text{cost}$$
$$S = S\% \times C$$

> An item that costs $70 has a 40% markup based on cost. Find the selling price.
>
> $S\% = C\% + M\%$
> $S\% = 100\% + 40\%$
> $S\% = 140\%$
> $S = S\% \times C$
> $S = 140\%(\$70)$
> $S = 1.4(\$70)$
> $S = \$98$

**4** Find the cost when the amount of markup and the percent of markup based on the cost are known. (p. 300)

1. Find the cost using the formula

$$\text{Cost} = \frac{\text{markup}}{\text{rate of markup based on cost}} \qquad C = \frac{M}{M\%}$$

2. Change rate of markup to numerical equivalent and divide.

Find the cost of an item that is marked up $140 and has a markup of 35% of the cost.

$$C = \frac{M}{M\%}$$

$$C = \frac{\$140}{35\%}$$

$$C = \frac{\$140}{0.35}$$

$$C = \$400$$

**5** Find the cost when the selling price and the percent of markup based on the cost are known. (p. 301)

1. Find the rate of selling price.

$$S\% = 100\% + M\%$$

2. Find the cost using the formula

$$C = \frac{S}{S\%}$$

3. Change $S\%$ to a numerical equivalent and divide.

An item that sells for $5,950 has a 42% markup based on cost. Find the cost.

$$S\% = C\% + M\%$$
$$S\% = 100\% + 42\%$$
$$S\% = 142\%$$

$$C = \frac{S}{S\%}$$
$$C = \frac{\$5,950}{142\%}$$
$$C = \frac{\$5,950}{1.42}$$
$$C = \$4,190.14 \text{ rounded}$$

## Section 9-2

**1** Find the amount of markup and the percent of markup based on the selling price when the cost and selling price are known. (p. 305)

1. Find the amount of markup using the formula

$$\text{Markup} = \text{selling price} - \text{cost}$$
$$M = S - C$$

2. Find the percent of markup based on selling price using the formula

$$\text{Rate of markup based on selling price} = \frac{\text{markup}}{\text{selling price}} \times 100\%$$

$$M\% = \frac{\text{markup}}{\text{selling price}} \times 100\%$$

Find the amount of markup and the percent of markup based on the selling price if an item costs $40 and sells for $100.

$$M = S - C$$
$$M = \$100 - \$40$$
$$M = \$60$$

$$M\% = \frac{M}{S} \times 100\%$$
$$M\% = \frac{\$60}{\$100}(100\%)$$
$$M\% = 60\%$$

**2** Find the selling price when the amount of markup and the percent of markup based on the selling price are known. (p. 306)

1. Find the selling price using the formula

$$\text{Selling price} = \frac{\text{markup}}{\text{rate of markup based on selling price}} \qquad S = \frac{M}{M\%}$$

2. Change rate of markup to a numerical equivalent and divide.

Find the selling price of an item that is marked up \$68 when the percent of markup based on the selling price is 54%.

$$S = \frac{M}{M\%}$$

$$S = \frac{\$68}{54\%}$$

$$S = \frac{\$68}{0.54}$$

$$S = \$125.93 \text{ rounded}$$

**3** Find the selling price when the cost and the percent of markup based on the selling price are known. (p. 307)

1. Find the rate of the cost using the formula

$$\text{Rate of } C = \text{rate of } S - \text{rate of } M \quad C\% = 100\% - M\%$$

2. Find the selling price using the formula

$$\text{Selling price} = \frac{\text{cost}}{\text{rate of cost based on selling price}} \quad S = \frac{C}{C\%}$$

Find the selling price of an item that costs \$40 and is marked up 35% based on selling price.

$$C\% = 100\% - M\%$$
$$C\% = 100\% - 35\%$$
$$C\% = 65\%$$

$$S = \frac{C}{C\%}$$

$$S = \frac{\$40}{65\%}$$

$$S = \frac{\$40}{0.65}$$

$$S = \$61.54 \text{ rounded}$$

**4** Find the cost when the selling price and the percent of markup based on the selling price are known. (p. 308)

1. Find the rate of cost.

$$C\% = 100\% - M\%$$

2. Find the cost using the formula

$$C = C\% \times S$$

3. Change $C\%$ to its numerical equivalent and multiply.

An item sells for \$85 and is marked up 60% based on the selling price. Find the cost.

$$C\% = 100\% - 60\%$$
$$C\% = 40\%$$

$$C = C\% \times S$$
$$C = 40\%(\$85)$$
$$C = 0.4(\$85)$$
$$C = \$34$$

To find all the missing parts if three parts are known and at least one part is an amount and it is known whether the markup is based on the cost or the selling price:

1. Place the three known parts into the chart.

|   | \$ | % |
|---|---|---|
| $C$ |  |  |
| $M$ |  |  |
| $S$ |  |  |

*If the \$ column has two entries:*

2. Add or subtract as appropriate to find the third amount.
3. Find a second percent by using the formula $R = \dfrac{P}{B}$.
4. Find the third percent by adding or subtracting as appropriate.

*If the % column has two entries:*

Add or subtract as appropriate to find the third percent.

Find an additional amount using the formula $P = RB$ or $B = \dfrac{P}{R}$.

Find the third amount by adding or subtracting as appropriate.

Find the markup of an item if it is based on the cost of \$38 and the selling price is \$76.

$$M = S - C$$
$$M = \$76 - \$38$$
$$M = \$38$$

$$M\% = \frac{M}{C} \times 100\%$$
$$M\% = \frac{\$38}{\$38}(100\%)$$
$$M\% = 100\%$$

**5** Compare the markup based on the cost with the markup based on the selling price. (p. 311)

To convert a markup rate based on selling price to a markup rate based on cost:

1. Find the complement of the markup rate based on the selling price. That is, subtract the markup rate from 100%.
2. Divide the decimal equivalent of the markup rate based on the selling price by the decimal equivalent of the complement of the rate.

$$M\%_{cost} = \frac{M\%_{selling\ price}}{100\% - M\%_{selling\ price}} \times 100\%$$

A fax machine is marked up 30% based on selling price. What is the rate of markup based on cost?

$$M\%_{cost} = \frac{M\%_{selling\ price}}{100\% - M\%_{selling\ price}} \times 100\%$$ — Substitute known values.

$$M\%_{cost} = \frac{30\%}{100\% - 30\%}(100\%)$$ — Change percent to its decimal equivalent.

$$M\%_{cost} = \frac{0.3}{1 - 0.3}(100\%)$$ — Subtract in the denominator.

$$M\%_{cost} = \frac{0.3}{0.7}(100\%)$$ — Divide. Round to thousandths.

$$M\%_{cost} = 0.429$$ — Change to the percent equivalent.
$$M\%_{cost} = 42.9\%$$

To convert a markup rate based on cost to a markup rate based on selling price:

1. Add 100% to the markup rate based on the cost.
2. Divide the decimal equivalent of the markup rate based on the cost by the decimal equivalent of the sum found in step 1.

$$M\%_{selling\ price} = \frac{M\%_{cost}}{100\% + M\%_{cost}}(100\%)$$

A DVD player is marked up 80% based on cost. What is the rate of markup based on selling price?

$$M\%_{selling\ price} = \frac{M\%_{cost}}{100\% + M\%_{cost}} \times 100\%$$ — Substitute known values.

$$M\%_{selling\ price} = \frac{80\%}{100\% + 80\%}(100\%)$$ — Change percent to its decimal equivalent.

$$M\%_{selling\ price} = \frac{0.8}{1 + 0.8}(100\%)$$ — Add in denominator.

$$M\%_{selling\ price} = \frac{0.8}{1.8}(100\%)$$ — Divide. Round to thousandths.

$$M\%_{selling\ price} = 0.444(100\%)$$ — Change to the percent equivalent.
$$M\%_{selling\ price} = 44.4\%$$

## Section 9-3

**1** Find the amount of markdown, the reduced (new) price, and the percent of markdown. (p. 316)

1. Place the known values into the chart.

|  | \$ | % |
|---|---|---|
| Original Selling Price (S) |  | 100 |
| Markdown (M) |  |  |
| Reduced (New) Price (N) |  |  |

**2.** Select the appropriate formula based on the known values.

$$\text{Markdown} = \text{original selling price} - \text{reduced price} \qquad M = S - N$$
$$\text{Reduced price} = \text{original selling price} - \text{markdown} \qquad N = S - M$$

$$M\% = \frac{M}{S} \times 100\%$$

---

Find the markdown and rate of markdown if the original selling price is $4.50 and the sale (new) price is $3.

$M = S - N$

$M = \$4.50 - \$3$

$M = \$1.50$

$M\% = \dfrac{M}{S} \times 100\%$

$M\% = \dfrac{\$1.50}{\$4.50}(100\%)$

$M\% = 0.333(100\%)$

$M\% = 33.3\%$

|   | $ | % |
|---|---|---|
| S | 4.50 | 100 |
| M |  |  |
| N | 3.00 |  |

---

**2**   Find the final selling price for a series of markups and markdowns. (p. 318)

**1.** Find the first selling price using the given facts and markup procedures in Sections 9-1 and 9-2.

**2.** For each remaining stage in the series:

   **(a)** If the stage requires a *markdown,* identify the previous selling price as the *original selling price S* for this stage. Find the *reduced price N.* This reduced price is the new selling price for this stage.

   **(b)** If the stage requires a *markup,* identify the previous selling price as the *cost C* for this stage. Find the *selling price S.* This price is the new selling price for this stage.

**3.** Identify the selling price for the last stage as the *final selling price.*

---

An item costing $7 was marked up 70% on cost, then marked down 20%, marked up 10%, and finally marked down 20%. What was the final selling price?

| First stage: | $S\% = C\% + M\%$ | $S_1 = S\% \times C$ |
|---|---|---|
| Markup | $S\% = 100\% + 70\%$ | $S_1 = 170\%(\$7)$ |
|  | $S\% = 170\%$ | $S_1 = 1.7(\$7)$ |
|  |  | $S_1 = \$11.90$ |

| Second stage: | $N\% = 100\% - M\%$ | $N_2 = N\% \times S_1$ |
|---|---|---|
| Markdown | $N\% = 100\% - 20\%$ | $N_2 = 80\%(\$11.90)$ |
| $S_1 = S$ | $N\% = 80\%$ | $N_2 = 0.8(\$11.90)$ |
|  |  | $N_2 = \$9.52$ |

| Third stage: | $S\% = C\% + M\%$ | $S_3 = S\% \times N_2$ |
|---|---|---|
| Markup | $S\% = 100\% + 10\%$ | $S_3 = 110\%(\$9.52)$ |
| $N_2 = C$ | $S\% = 110\%$ | $S_3 = 1.1(\$9.52)$ |
|  |  | $S_3 = \$10.47$ |

| Final stage: | $N\% = 100\% - M\%$ | $N_4 = N\% \times S_3$ |
|---|---|---|
| Markdown | $N\% = 100\% - 20\%$ | $N_4 = 80\%(\$10.47)$ |
| $S_3 = S$ | $N\% = 80\%$ | $N_4 = 0.8(\$10.47)$ |
|  |  | $N_4 = \$8.38$ |

The final selling price was $8.38.

---

**3**   Find the selling price for a desired profit on perishable and seasonal goods. (p. 320)

**1.** Establish the rate of profit (markup)—based on cost—desired on the sale of the merchandise.

**2.** Find the total cost of the merchandise by multiplying the unit cost by the quantity of merchandise. Add in additional charges such as shipping.

**3.** Find the total desired profit (markup) based on cost by multiplying the rate of profit (markup) by the total cost.

**4.** Find the total selling price by adding the total cost and the total desired profit.

**5.** Establish the quantity expected to sell.

**6.** Divide the total selling price (step 4) by the expect-to-sell quantity (step 5).

$$\text{Selling price per item to achieve desired profit} = \frac{\text{total selling price}}{\text{expect-to-sell quantity}}$$

At a total cost of $25, 25% of 400 lemons are expected to spoil before being sold. A 75% rate of profit (markup) on cost is needed. At what selling price must each lemon be sold to achieve the needed profit?

$C$ = total cost of lemons = $25
$M\%$ = total rate of profit (markup) = 75%

$M = M\% \times C$ $\qquad\qquad\qquad$ $S = C + M$
$M = 75\%(\$25)$ $\qquad\qquad\qquad$ $S = \$25 + \$18.75$
$M = 0.75(\$25)$ $\qquad\qquad\qquad$ $S = \$43.75$
$M = \$18.75$

Quantity expected to sell $= (100\% - 25\%)(400)$
$\qquad\qquad\qquad\qquad = (75\%)(400)$
$\qquad\qquad\qquad\qquad = 0.75(400)$
$\qquad\qquad\qquad\qquad = 300$ lemons

Selling price per item $= \dfrac{\$43.75}{300 \text{ lemons}}$
$\qquad\qquad\qquad\quad = \$0.15$ per lemon (rounded)

# EXERCISES SET A

*Find the missing numbers in the table if the markup is based on cost.*

**1.**

|  | $ | % |
|---|---|---|
| C | $50 |  |
| +M | $25 | 50% |
| S |  |  |

**2.**

|  | $ | % |
|---|---|---|
| C | $41 |  |
| +M |  | 100% |
| S |  |  |

*Find the missing numbers in the table if the markup is based on the selling price.*

**3.**

|  | $ | % |
|---|---|---|
| C | $38 | 42% |
| +M |  |  |
| S |  |  |

**4.**

|  | $ | % |
|---|---|---|
| C |  |  |
| +M | $8 | 15% |
| S |  |  |

*Fill in the blanks in Exercises 5 through 9. Round amounts to the nearest cent and rates to the nearest hundredth percent.*

|  | Cost | Markup | Selling price | Rate of markup based on cost | Rate of markup based on selling price |
|---|---|---|---|---|---|
| **5.** |  | $32 | $89 |  |  |
| **6.** | $1.56 |  | $2 |  |  |
| **7.** |  | $27.38 |  | 40% |  |
| **8.** |  |  | $124 | 150% |  |
| **9.** |  |  | $18.95 |  | 15% |

10. A hairdryer costs $15 and is marked up 40% of the cost.
    a. Find the markup.

    b. Find the selling price.

11. A blender is marked up $9 and sells for $45.
    a. Find the cost.

    b. Find the rate of markup if the markup is based on cost.

12. A computer table sells for $198.50 and costs $158.70.
    a. Find the markup.

    b. Find the rate of markup based on the cost.

13. A flower arrangement is marked up $12, which is 50% of the cost.
    a. Find the cost.

    b. Find the selling price.

14. A briefcase is marked up $15.30, which is 30% of the selling price.
    a. Find the selling price of the briefcase.

    b. Find the cost.

15. A hole punch costs $40 and sells for $58.50.
    a. Find the markup.

    b. Find the rate of markup based on selling price.

16. A desk organizer sells for $35, which includes a markup rate of 60% of the selling price.
    a. Find the cost.

    b. Find the markup.

17. Find the rate of markup based on cost of a textbook that is marked up 20% based on the selling price.

18. A chest is marked up 63% based on cost. What is the rate of markup based on selling price?

19. A fiberglass shower originally sold for $379.98 and was marked down to sell for $341.98.
    a. Find the markdown.

    b. Find the rate of markdown.

20. An area rug originally sold for $699.99 and was reduced to sell for $500.
    a. Find the markdown.

    b. Find the rate of markdown.

21. A portable DVD player was originally priced at $249.99 and was reduced by 20%.
    a. Find the markdown.

    b. Find the sale (reduced) price.

22. A set of stainless steel cookware was originally priced at $79 and was reduced by 25%.
    a. Find the markdown.

    b. Find the sale price.

23. Crystal stemware originally marked to sell for $49.50 was reduced 20% for a special promotion. The stemware was then reduced an additional 30% to turn inventory. What were the markdown and the sale price for each reduction?

24. James McDonnell operates a vegetable store. He purchases 800 pounds of potatoes at a cost of $0.18 per pound. If he anticipates a spoilage rate of 20% of the potatoes and wishes to make a profit of 140% of the cost, for how much must he sell the potatoes per pound?

# EXERCISES SET B

*Find the missing numbers in the table if the markup is based on cost.*

**1.**

|     | $  | %   |
|-----|-----|-----|
| C   | $4  |     |
| +M  | $1  | 25% |
| S   |     |     |

**2.**

|     | $   | %   |
|-----|-----|-----|
| C   |     |     |
| +M  | $ 5 | 20% |
| S   |     |     |

*Find the missing numbers in the table if the markup is based on the selling price.*

**3.**

|     | $   | %   |
|-----|-----|-----|
| C   | $86 |     |
| +M  |     | 50% |
| S   |     |     |

**4.**

|     | $      | %   |
|-----|--------|-----|
| C   |        | 42% |
| +M  | $22.10 |     |
| S   |        |     |

*Fill in the blanks in Exercises 5 through 9. Round amounts to the nearest cent and rates to the nearest hundredth percent.*

|       | Cost    | Markup   | Selling price | Rate of markup based on cost | Rate of markup based on selling price |
|-------|---------|----------|---------------|------------------------------|---------------------------------------|
| **5.** |         | $208.29  | $694.29       |                              |                                       |
| **6.** | $39.27  |          | $45.16        |                              |                                       |
| **7.** | $25     | $23.08   |               |                              |                                       |
| **8.** |         | $28      |               |                              | 27%                                   |
| **9.** |         |          | $32.20        |                              | 49.44%                                |

10. A hairbrush costs $3 and is marked up 40% of the cost.
    a. Find the markup.

    b. Find the selling price.

11. A package of cassette tapes costs $12 and is marked up $7.20.
    a. Find the selling price.

    b. Find the rate of markup based on the cost.

12. The selling price of an office chair is $75 and this item is marked up 100% of the cost.
    a. Find the cost.

    b. Find the rate of markup based on selling price.

13. A toaster sells for $28.70 and has a markup rate of 50% based on selling price.
    a. Find the cost.

    b. Find the markup.

14. A three-ringed binder costs $4.60 and is marked up $3.07. Find the selling price and the rate of markup based on selling price. Round to the nearest tenth percent.

15. A pair of bookends sells for $15 and costs $10. Find the rate of markup based on the selling price. Round to the nearest tenth percent.

16. A pair of athletic shoes costs $38 and is marked up $20. Find the selling price and rate of markup based on selling price. Round to the nearest tenth percent.

17. A desk has an 84% markup based on selling price. What is the rate of markup based on cost?

18. A dining room suite is marked up 45% based on cost. What is the rate of markup based on selling price? Round to the nearest tenth percent.

19. A three-speed fan originally sold for $29.98 and was reduced to sell for $25.40. Find the markdown and the rate of markdown. Round to the nearest tenth percent.

20. A room air conditioner that originally sold for $599.99 was reduced to sell for $400. Find the markdown and the rate of markdown. Round to the nearest tenth percent.

21. A set of rollers was originally priced at $39.99 and was reduced by 30%. Find the markdown and the sale price.

22. A down comforter was originally priced to sell at $280 and was reduced by 65%. Find the markdown and the sale price.

23. A camcorder that originally sold for $1,199 was reduced to sell for $999. What is the amount of reduction? What is the percent of reduction? Round to the nearest tenth percent.

# PRACTICE TEST

## CHAPTER 9

1. A calculator sells for $23.99 and costs $16.83. What is the markup?

2. A mixer sells for $109.98 and has a markup of $36.18. Find the cost.

3. A cookbook has a 34% markup rate based on cost. If the markup is $5.27, find the cost of the cookbook.

4. A computer stand sells for $385. What is the markup if it is 45% of the selling price?

5. A box of printer paper costs $16.80. Find the selling price if there is a 35% markup rate based on cost.

6. The reduced price of a dress is $54.99. Find the original selling price if a reduction of 40% has been taken.

7. A daily organizer that originally sold for $86.90 was marked down by 30%. What is the markdown?

8. What is the sale price of the organizer in Exercise 7?

9. If a television costs $498.15 and was marked up $300, what is the selling price?

10. A refrigerator that sells for $589.99 was marked down $100. What is the sale price?

11. What is the rate of markdown of a scanner that sells for $498 and is marked down $142? Round to the nearest tenth percent.

12. A wallet costs $16.05 to produce. The wallet sells for $25.68. What is the rate of markup based on the cost?

13. A lamp costs $88. What is the selling price if the markup is 45% of the selling price?

14. A file cabinet originally sold for $215 but was damaged and had to be reduced. If the reduced cabinet sold for $129, what was the rate of markdown based on the original selling price?

15. A desk that originally sold for $589 was marked down 25%. During the sale it was scratched and had to be reduced an additional 25% of the original price. What was the final selling price of the desk?

16. Brenda Wimberly calculates the selling price for all produce at Quick Stop Produce. If 400 pounds of potatoes were purchased for $0.13 per pound and 18% of the potatoes were expected to spoil before being sold, determine the price per pound that the potatoes must sell for if a profit of 120% of the purchase price is desired.

17. The college bookstore marks up loose-leaf paper 40% of its cost. Find the cost if the selling price is $2.34 per package.

18. A CD costs $0.90 and sells for $1.50. Find the rate of markup based on selling price. Find the rate of markup based on cost. Round to the nearest whole percent.

19. A radio sells for $45, which includes a markup of 65% of the selling price. Find the cost and the markup.

20. Becky Drewery purchased a small refrigerator for her dorm room for $159, which included a markup of $32 based on the cost. Find the cost and the rate of markup based on cost. Round the rate to the nearest tenth percent.

1. Will the series markdown of 25% and 30% be more than or less than 55%? Explain why.

2. Explain why taking a series of markdowns of 25% and 30% is not the same as taking a single markdown of 55%. Illustrate your answer with a specific example.

3. Under what circumstances would you be likely to base the markup of an item on the selling price?

4. Under what circumstances would you be likely to base the markup for an item on cost?

5. What clues do you look for to determine whether the cost or selling price represents 100% in a markup problem?

6. If you were a retailer, would you prefer to base your markup on selling price or cost? Why? Give an example to illustrate your preference.

7. When given the rate of markup, describe at least one situation that leads to adding the rate to 100%. Describe at least one situation that leads to subtracting the rate from 100%.

8. Show by giving an example that the final reduced price in a series markdown can be found by doing a series of computations or by using the net decimal equivalent.

9. An item is marked up 60% based on a selling price of $400. What is the cost of the item? Find and correct the error in the solution.

$$C\% = S\% - M\%$$
$$C\% = 100\% - 60\%$$
$$C\% = 40\%$$

$$C = \frac{S}{S\%}$$

$$C = \frac{\$400}{100\%}$$

$$C = \frac{\$400}{1}$$

$$C = \$400$$

10. Explain why the percent of markup based on selling price cannot be greater than 100%.

## Challenge Problem

Pro Peds, a local athletic shoe manufacturer, makes a training shoe at a cost of $22 per pair. This cost includes raw materials and labor only. A check of previous factory runs indicates that 10% of the training shoes will be defective and must be sold to Odd Tops, Inc., as irregulars for $32 per pair. If Pro Peds produces 1,000 pairs of the training shoes and desires a markup of 100% on cost, find the selling price per pair of the regular shoes to the nearest cent.

## 9.1 Acupuncture, Tea, and Rice-Filled Heating Pads

Karen is an acupuncturist with a busy practice. In addition to acupuncture services Karen sells teas, herbal supplements, and rice-filled heating pads. Because Karen's primary income is from acupuncture, she feels that she is providing the other items simply to fill a need and not as an important source of profits. As a matter of fact, the rice filled heating pads are made by a patient who receives acupuncture instead of cash. The rice filled pads cost her $5.00, $8.00, and $12.00 respectively for small, medium, and large sizes. The ginger tea, relaxing tea, cold & flu tea, and detox tea cost her $2.59 per box plus $5.00 shipping and handling for 24 boxes. Karen uses a cost plus markup method, whereby she adds the same set amount to each box of tea. She figures that each box costs $2.59 plus $0.21 shipping and handling, which totals $2.80, then she adds $0.70 profit to each box and sells it for $3.50. Do you think this is a good pricing strategy? How would it compare to marking up by a percentage of the cost?

1. What is the markup percentage for a box of ginger tea?

2. If the rice-filled heating pads sell for $7.00, $10.00, and $15.00 for small, medium, and large, respectively, what is the markup percentage on each one?

3. Karen wants to compare using the cost plus method to the percentage markup method. If she sells 2 small rice pads, 4 medium rice pads, 2 large rice pads, and 20 boxes of $3.50 tea in a month, how much profit does she accumulate? What markup percentage would she have to use to make the same amount of profit on this month's sales?

4. What prices should Karen charge (using the markup percentage) to obtain the same amount of profit as she did with the cost plus method? Do not include shipping.

## 9.2 Carolina Crystals

Carolina Crystals, a mid-range jewelry store located at Harbor Village in San Diego, serves two clienteles: regular customers who purchase gifts and special-occasion jewelry year-round, and tourists visiting the city. Although tourism is high in San Diego most months of the year, the proprietor of Carolina Crystals, Amanda, knows that her regular customers tend to purchase more jewelry during November and December for Christmas presents; in late January and early February for Valentine's Day; and in late April and May for summer weddings. Typically, jewelry is marked up 100% based on cost, but Amanda adjusts her pricing throughout the year to reflect seasonal needs. Amanda always carries a selection of diamond engagement and eternity rings, a wide array of gold charms that appeal to tourists, both regular and baroque pearl strands, and other types of jewelry.

1. If Amanda purchases diamond rings at $1,200 each, what would be the regular selling price to her customers, assuming a 100% markup on cost?

2. If Amanda feels that an 85% markup on cost is more appropriate for gold charms, what would be the selling price on a gold sailboat charm Amanda purchases for $135?

Source: Cape Fear Community College Website, North Carolina

3. Amanda also sells gold bracelets on which the charms can be mounted. She runs a special all year that allows a customer to purchase a gold charm bracelet at 50% off if the customer also buys three gold charms at the same time. If a 7" gold bracelet costs Amanda $125, what would the price be if the customer bought only the bracelet (without the charms) at a regular 100% markup on cost?

4. What would be the total price of the purchase if a customer purchased 3 charms and the bracelet, assuming the first charm cost Amanda $150, the second $185, and the third $125, and were marked up 85% based on cost?

5. Amanda often suggests to her male customers who buy diamond engagement rings, that they also purchase a pearl necklace as a wedding gift for their bride. As a courtesy to men purchasing diamond engagement rings, Amanda discounts pearl strands 18" and shorter by 35% and pearl strands longer than 18" by 45%. If the diamond rings have a 100% markup on cost and the pearl necklaces have a 60% markup on cost, what would be Amanda's cost for a ring selling at $4,500 and a 22" pearl necklace selling for $1,500?

6. If a customer purchases both the diamond ring for $4,500 and the 22" pearl strand for $1,500 and receives the 45% discount applied, what would be the total purchase price? How much did the customer save by purchasing the ring and necklace together?

# 9.3 Deer Valley Organics, LLC

With an original goal of selling fresh apples from the family orchard at a roadside stand, Deer Valley Organics has become a unique operation featuring a wide variety of locally grown organic produce and farm products that include their own fruit as well as products from the area's finest growers. A number of different products are available, including: apples, strawberries, and raspberries as either prepackaged or pick your own; assorted fresh vegetables; ciders, jams, and jellies; and organic fresh eggs and free-range chicken whole fryers. Prepackaged apples are still the mainstay of the business, and after adding all production and labor costs, Deer Valley determined that the cost of these apples was 64 cents per pound.

1. What would be the selling price per pound for the prepackaged apples using a 30% markup based on cost? A 40% markup? A 50% markup?

2. Based on the national average for apples sold on a retail basis, Deer Creek sets a target price of $1.10 per pound for the prepackaged apples. Using this selling price, compute the percent of markup **based on cost** for the prepackaged apples. Then, compute the percent of markup **based on selling price**.

3. Deer Valley allows customers to pick their own apples for $8 a bag, which works out to approximately 47 cents per pound. How is that possible given the cost data in the introductory paragraph? Would the orchard be losing money? Explain.

4. Deer Valley receives a delivery of 1,250 lb of tomatoes from a local supplier, for which they pay 18 cents per pound. Normally, 6% of the tomatoes will be discarded due to appearance or spoilage. Find the selling price needed per pound to obtain a 120% markup based on cost.

# Your First Job: Understanding Your Paycheck

"My paycheck isn't right!" Tom can't believe it: $461.69? He's supposed to be paid $600 each week! That's the salary he was quoted when he was hired.

Many people, when they receive their first paycheck, are surprised at the amount of money that is deducted from it before they get paid. These are payroll taxes. There's a big difference between gross income, salary or hourly rate times the number of hours; and net income, or take-home pay.

In Tom's case, his tax filing status is single with zero exemptions. His withholding is calculated using state tax tables and IRS information. The deductions from his pay are:

- Federal taxes, money sent to the IRS to pay federal income taxes. Federal taxes pay for a number of programs such as national defense, foreign affairs, law enforcement, education, and transportation.

- Social Security, money set aside for a federal program that provides monthly benefits to retired and disabled workers, their dependents, and their survivors.
- Medicare provides health care coverage for older Americans and people with disabilities.
- State tax, money withheld and sent to your state of residence to pay state income taxes. State taxes pay for state programs such as education, health, and welfare, public safety, and the court justice system. Some states may require additional deductions for state disability insurance and local taxes.

Always check your pay stub. It should include your identification information and the pay period (dates you worked for this check). It also lists your gross income, all your deductions, and your net income (the amount you get to keep).

## LEARNING OUTCOMES

### 10-1 Gross Pay

1. Find the gross pay per paycheck based on salary.
2. Find the gross pay per weekly paycheck based on hourly wage.
3. Find the gross pay per paycheck based on piecework wage.
4. Find the gross pay per paycheck based on commission.

### 10-2 Payroll Deductions

1. Find federal tax withholding per paycheck using IRS tax tables.
2. Find federal tax withholding per paycheck using the IRS percentage method.
3. Find Social Security tax and Medicare tax per paycheck.
4. Find net earnings per paycheck.

### 10-3 The Employer's Payroll Taxes

1. Find an employer's total deposit for withholding tax, Social Security tax, and Medicare tax per pay period.
2. Find an employer's SUTA tax and FUTA tax due for a quarter.

Pay is an important concern of employees and employers alike. If you have worked and received a paycheck, you know that part of your earnings is taken out of your paycheck before you ever see it. Your employer *withholds* (deducts) taxes, union dues, medical insurance payments, and so on. Thus, there is a difference between **gross earnings (gross pay)**, the amount earned before deductions, and **net earnings (net pay)—take-home pay**—the amount of your paycheck.

Employers have the option of paying their employees in salary or in wages and of distributing these earnings at various time intervals. **Wages** are based on an hourly rate of pay and the number of hours worked. **Salary** is most often stated as a certain amount of money paid each year. Salaried employees are paid the agreed-upon salary, whether they work fewer or more than the usual number of hours.

**Gross earnings (gross pay):** the amount earned before deductions.

**Net earnings (net pay)** or **(take-home pay):** the amount of your paycheck.

**Wages:** earnings based on an hourly rate of pay and the number of hours worked.

**Salary:** an agreed-upon amount of pay that is not based on the number of hours worked.

## 10-1 GROSS PAY

### LEARNING OUTCOMES

1. Find the gross pay per paycheck based on salary.
2. Find the gross pay per weekly paycheck based on hourly wage.
3. Find the gross pay per paycheck based on piecework wage.
4. Find the gross pay per paycheck based on commission.

Employees may be paid according to a salary, an hourly wage, a piecework rate, or a commission rate. Employers are required to withhold taxes from employee paychecks and forward these taxes to federal, state, and local governments.

### 1 Find the gross pay per paycheck based on salary.

Companies differ in how often they pay salaried employees, which determines how many paychecks an employee receives in a year. If employees are paid **weekly**, they receive 52 paychecks a year; if they are paid **biweekly** (every two weeks), they receive 26 paychecks a year. **Semimonthly** (twice a month) paychecks are issued 24 times a year, and **monthly** paychecks come 12 times a year.

**Weekly:** once a week or 52 times a year.

**Biweekly:** every two weeks or 26 times a year.

**Semimonthly:** twice a month or 24 times a year.

**Monthly:** once a month or 12 times a year.

| HOW TO | Find the gross pay per paycheck based on annual salary |
| --- | --- |

1. Identify the number of pay periods per year:
   Monthly—12 pay periods per year
   Semimonthly—24 pay periods per year
   Biweekly—26 pay periods per year
   Weekly—52 pay periods per year
2. Divide the annual salary by the number of pay periods per year.

**EXAMPLE 1** Charles Demetriou earns a salary of $30,000 a year.

(a) If Charles is paid biweekly, how much is his gross pay per pay period before taxes are taken out?
(b) If Charles is paid semimonthly, how much is his gross pay per pay period?

(a) $30,000 ÷ 26 = $1,153.85
   **Charles earns $1,153.85 biweekly before deductions.**

Biweekly paychecks are issued 26 times a year, so divide Charles's salary by 26.

(b) $30,000 ÷ 24 = $1,250
   **Charles earns $1,250 semimonthly before deductions.**

Semimonthly paychecks are issued 24 times a year, so divide Charles's salary by 24.

## ✔ STOP AND CHECK

1. Ryan Thomas earns $42,822 a year. What is his biweekly gross pay?

2. Jaswant Jain earns $32,928 annually and is paid semimonthly. Find his earnings per pay period.

3. Alison Bishay earns $1,872 each pay period and is paid weekly. Find her annual gross pay.

4. Annette Ford earns $3,315 monthly. What is her gross annual pay?

## 2 Find the gross pay per weekly paycheck based on hourly wage.

**Hourly rate** or **hourly wage:** the amount of pay per hour worked based on a standard 40-hour work week.

**Overtime rate:** rate of pay for hours worked that are more than 40 hours in a week.

**Time and a half:** standard overtime rate that is $1\frac{1}{2}$ (or 1.5) times the hourly rate.

**Regular pay:** earnings based on hourly rate of pay.

**Overtime pay:** earnings based on overtime rate of pay.

Many jobs pay according to an *hourly wage*. The **hourly rate**, or **hourly wage**, is the amount of money paid for each hour the employee works in a standard 40-hour work week. The Fair Labor Standards Act of 1938 set the standard work week at 40 hours. When hourly employees work more than 40 hours in a week, they earn the hourly wage for the first 40 hours, and they earn an **overtime rate** for the remaining hours. The standard overtime rate is often called **time and a half**. By law, it must be at least 1.5 (one and one-half) times the hourly wage. Earnings based on the hourly wage are called **regular pay**. Earnings based on the overtime rate are called **overtime pay**. An hourly employee's gross pay for a pay period is the sum of his or her regular pay and his or her overtime pay.

> ### HOW TO　Find the gross pay per week based on hourly wages
>
> 1. Find the regular pay:
>    (a) If the hours worked in the week are 40 or fewer, multiply the hours worked by the hourly wage.
>    (b) If the hours worked are more than 40, multiply 40 hours by the hourly wage.
> 2. Find the overtime pay:
>    (a) If the hours worked are 40 or fewer, the overtime pay is $0.
>    (b) If the hours worked are more than 40, subtract 40 from the hours worked and multiply the difference by the overtime rate.
> 3. Add the regular pay and the overtime pay.

*When Does the Week Start?* Even if an employee is paid biweekly, overtime pay is still based on the 40-hour standard work week. So overtime pay for each week in the pay period must be calculated separately. Also, each employer establishes the formal work week. For example, an employer's work week may begin at 12:01 A.M. Thursday and end at 12:00 midnight on Wednesday of the following week, allowing the payroll department to process payroll checks for distribution on Friday. Another employer may begin the work week at 11:01 P.M. on Sunday evening and end at 11:00 P.M. on Sunday the following week so that the new week coincides with the beginning of the 11 P.M.–7 A.M. shift on Sunday.

**EXAMPLE 1**　Marcia Scott, whose hourly wage is $10.25, worked 46 hours last week. Find her gross pay for last week if she earns time and a half for overtime.

| | |
|---|---|
| $40(\$10.25) = \boxed{\$410}$ | Find the regular pay for 40 hours of work at the hourly wage. |
| $46 - 40 = 6$ | Find the overtime hours. |
| $\underbrace{6(\$10.25)(1.5)}_{\text{overtime rate}} = \boxed{\$92.25}$ | Find the overtime pay by multiplying the overtime hours by the overtime rate, which is the hourly wage times 1.5. Round to the nearest cent. |
| $\boxed{\$410} + \boxed{\$92.25} = \$502.25$ | Add the regular pay and the overtime pay to find Marcia's total gross earnings. |

**Marcia's gross pay is $502.25.**

1. Shekenna Chapman earns $15.83 per hour and worked 48 hours in a week. Overtime is paid at 1.5 times hourly pay. What is her gross pay?

2. McDonald's pays Kelyn Blackburn 1.5 times her hourly pay for overtime. She worked 52 hours one week and her hourly pay is $13.56. Find her gross pay for the week.

3. Mark Kozlowski earns $14.27 per hour and worked 55 hours in one weekly pay period. What is his gross pay?

4. Marc Showalter earns $22.75 per hour with time and a half for regular overtime and double time on holidays. He worked 62 hours the week of July 4th and 8 of those hours were on July 4th. Find his gross pay.

## 3 Find the gross pay per paycheck based on piecework wage.

**Piecework rate:** amount of pay for each acceptable item produced.

**Straight piecework rate:** piecework rate where the pay is the same per item no matter how many items are produced.

**Differential piece rate (escalating piece rate):** piecework rate that increases as more items are produced.

Many employers motivate employees to produce more by paying according to the quantity of acceptable work done. Such **piecework rates** are typically offered in production or manufacturing jobs. Garment makers and some other types of factory workers, agricultural workers, and employees who perform repetitive tasks such as stuffing envelopes or packaging parts may be paid by this method. In the simplest cases, the gross earnings of such workers are calculated by multiplying the number of items produced by the **straight piecework rate**.

Sometimes employees earn wages at a **differential piece rate**, also called an **escalating piece rate**. As the number of items produced by the worker increases, so does the pay per item. This method of paying wages offers employees an even greater incentive to complete more pieces of work in a given period of time.

---

**HOW TO** Find the gross pay per paycheck based on piecework wage

1. If a *straight piecework rate* is used, multiply the number of items completed by the straight piecework rate.
2. If a *differential piecework rate* is used:
   (a) For each rate category, multiply the number of items produced for the category by the rate for the category.
   (b) Add the pay for all rate categories.

---

**EXAMPLE 1** A shirt manufacturer pays a worker $0.47 for each acceptable shirt inspected under the prescribed job description. If the worker had the following work record, find the gross earnings for the week: Monday, 250 shirts; Tuesday, 300 shirts; Wednesday, 178 shirts; Thursday, 326 shirts; Friday, 296 shirts.

| | |
|---|---|
| $250 + 300 + 178 + 326 + 296$ | Find the total number of shirts inspected. |
| $= 1,350$ shirts | |
| $1,350($0.47) = $634.50$ | Multiply the number of shirts by the piecework rate. |

**The weekly gross earnings are $634.50.**

---

**EXAMPLE 2** Last week, Jorge Sanchez assembled 317 game boards. Find Jorge's gross earnings for the week if the manufacturer pays at the following differential piece rates:

| Boards assembled per week | Pay per board |
|---|---|
| First 100 | $1.82 |
| Next 200 | $1.92 |
| Over 300 | $2.08 |

Find how many boards were completed at each pay rate, multiply the number of boards by the rate, and add the amounts.

First 100 items: 100($1.82) = $182.00
Next 200 items: 200($1.92) = $384.00
Last 17 items: 17($2.08)  = $ 35.36
                            $601.36

**Jorge's gross earnings were $601.36.**

# STOP AND CHECK

1. JR Tinkler and Co. employs pear and peach pickers on a piecework basis. Paul Larson picks enough pears to fill 12 bins in the 40-hour work week. He is paid at the rate of $70 per bin. What is his pay for the week?

2. A rubber worker is paid $5.50 for each finished tire. In a given week, Dennis Swartz completed 21 tires on Monday, 27 tires on Tuesday, 18 tires on Wednesday, 29 tires on Thursday, and 24 tires on Friday. How much were his gross weekly earnings?

3. A tool assembly company pays differential piecework wages:

| Units Assembled | Pay per Unit |
|---|---|
| 1–200 | $1.18 |
| 201–400 | $1.35 |
| 401 and over | $1.55 |

Find Virginia March's gross pay if she assembled 535 units in one week.

4. Thai Notebaert assembles computer keyboards according to this differential piecework scale on a weekly basis.

| Units Assembled | Pay per Unit |
|---|---|
| 1–50 | $2.95 |
| 51–150 | $3.10 |
| Over 150 | $3.35 |

He assembled 37 keyboards on Monday, 42 on Tuesday, 40 on Wednesday, 46 on Thursday, and 52 keyboards on Friday. What is his gross pay for the week?

## 4 Find the gross pay per paycheck based on commission.

**Commission:** earnings based on sales.

**Straight commission:** entire pay based on sales.

**Salary-plus-commission:** a set amount of pay plus an additional amount based on sales.

**Commission rate:** the percent used to calculate the commission based on sales.

**Quota:** a minimum amount of sales that is required before a commission is applicable.

Many salespeople earn a **commission**, a percentage based on sales. Those whose entire pay is commission are said to work on **straight commission**. Those who receive a salary in addition to a commission are said to work on a **salary-plus-commission** basis. A **commission rate** can be a percent of total sales or a percent of sales greater than a specified **quota** of sales.

> **HOW TO** Find the gross pay per paycheck based on commission
>
> 1. Find the commission:
>    (a) If the commission is *commission based on total sales,* multiply the commission rate by the total sales for the pay period.
>    (b) If the commission is *commission based on quota,* subtract the quota from the total sales and multiply the difference by the commission rate.
> 2. Find the salary:
>    (a) If the wage is *straight commission,* the salary is $0.
>    (b) If the wage is *commission-plus-salary,* determine the gross pay based on salary.
> 3. Add the commission and the salary.

**EXAMPLE 1** Shirley Garcia is a restaurant supplies salesperson and receives 8% of her total sales as commission. Her sales totaled $15,000 during a given week. Find her gross earnings.

Use the percentage formula $P = RB$.

$P = 0.08(\$15,000) = \$1,200$    Change the rate of 8% to an equivalent decimal and multiply it times the base of $15,000.

**Shirley's gross earnings were $1,200.**

**EXAMPLE 2** Eloise Brown is paid on a salary-plus-commission basis. She receives $450 weekly in salary and 3% of all sales over $8,000. If she sold $15,000 worth of goods, find her gross pay.

| | |
|---|---|
| $15,000 - \$8,000 = \$7,000$ | Subtract the quota from total sales to find the sales on which commission is paid. |
| $P = RB$ | Change the rate of 3% to an equivalent decimal. |
| $P = 0.03(\$7,000)$ | Multiply the rate by the base of $7,000. |
| $P = \$210$ (commission) | |
| $\$210 + \$450 = \$660$ | Add the commission and salary to find gross pay. |

**Eloise Brown's gross earnings were $660.**

---

 ## STOP AND CHECK

1. Reyna Mata sells furniture and is paid 6% of her total sales as commission. One week her sales totaled $17,945. What are her gross earnings?

2. Acacio Sweazea receives 1% of eBay sales plus $4.00 for each item he lists through his eBay listing service. One month he listed 547 items that sold for a total of $30,248. Find his gross earnings.

3. Kate Citrino is paid $200 weekly plus 2% of her sales above $3,000. One week she sold $26,572 in merchandise. Find her gross pay. Find her estimated annual gross pay.

4. Arita Hannus earns $275 biweekly and 4% of her sales. In one pay period her sales were $32,017. Find her gross pay. At this same rate find her estimated annual gross pay.

---

## 10-1 SECTION EXERCISES

### SKILL BUILDERS

1. If Timothy Oaks earns a salary of $35,204 a year and is paid weekly, how much is his weekly paycheck before taxes?

2. If Nita McMillan earns a salary of $31,107.96 a year and is paid biweekly, how much is her biweekly paycheck before taxes are taken out?

3. Gregory Maksi earns a salary of $52,980 annually and is paid monthly. How much is his gross monthly income?

4. Amelia Mattix is an accountant and is paid semimonthly. Her annual salary is $38,184. How much is her gross pay per period?

5. William Melton worked 47 hours in one week. His regular pay was $7.60 per hour with time and a half for overtime. Find his gross earnings for the week.

6. Bethany Colangelo, whose regular rate of pay is $8.25 per hour, with time and a half for overtime, worked 44 hours last week. Find her gross pay for the week.

7. Carlos Espinosa earns $15.90 per hour with time and a half for overtime and worked 47 hours during a recent week. Find his gross pay for the week.

8. A belt manufacturer pays a worker $0.84 for each buckle she correctly attaches to a belt. If Yolanda Jackson had the following work record, find the gross earnings for the week: Monday, 132 buckles; Tuesday, 134 buckles; Wednesday, 138 buckles; Thursday, 134 buckles; Friday, 130 buckles.

9. Last week, Laurie Golson packaged 289 boxes of Holiday Cheese Assortment. Find her gross weekly earnings if she is paid at the following differential piece rate.

| Cheese boxes packaged per week | Pay per package |
|---|---|
| 1–100 | $1.88 |
| 101–300 | $2.08 |
| 301 and over | $2.18 |

10. Joe Thweatt makes icons for a major distributor. He is paid $9.13 for each icon and records the following number of completed icons: Monday, 14; Tuesday, 11; Wednesday, 10; Thursday, 12; Friday, 12. How much will he be paid for his work for the week?

11. Mark Moses is a paper mill sales representative who receives 6% of his total sales as commission. His sales last week totaled $8,972. Find his gross earnings for the week.

12. Mary Lee Strode is paid a straight commission on sales as a real estate salesperson. In one pay period she had a total of $452,493 in sales. What is her gross pay if the commission rate is $3\frac{1}{2}\%$?

13. Dwayne Moody is paid on a salary-plus-commission basis. He receives $275 weekly in salary and a commission based on 5% of all weekly sales over $2,000. If he sold $7,821 in merchandise in one week, find his gross earnings for the week.

14. Vincent Ores sells equipment to receive satellite signals. He earns a 3% commission on monthly sales above $2,000. One month his sales totaled $145,938. What is his commission for the month?

## 10-2 PAYROLL DEDUCTIONS

### LEARNING OUTCOMES

1 Find federal tax withholding per paycheck using IRS tax tables.
2 Find federal tax withholding per paycheck using the IRS percentage method.
3 Find Social Security tax and Medicare tax per paycheck.
4 Find net earnings per paycheck.

As anyone who has ever drawn a paycheck knows, many deductions may be subtracted from gross pay. Deductions may include federal, state, and local income or payroll taxes, Social Security and Medicare taxes, union dues, medical insurance payments, credit union payments, and a host of others. By law, employers are responsible for withholding and paying their employee's payroll taxes.

One of the largest deductions from an employee's paycheck usually comes in the form of **income tax**. The tax paid to the federal government is called **federal tax withholding**. The tax withheld is based on three things: the employee's gross earnings, the employee's **tax-filing status**, and the number of *withholding allowances* the person claims.

The employee's filing status is determined by marital status and eligibility to be classified as a head of household. A **withholding allowance**, called an **exemption**, is a portion of gross earnings that is not subject to tax. Each employee is permitted one withholding allowance for himself or herself, one for a spouse, and one for each eligible dependent (such as a child or elderly parent). A detailed discussion on eligibility for various allowances can be found in several IRS publications, such as Publication 15 [Circular E, Employer's Tax Guide], Publication 505 [Tax Withholding and Estimated Tax], and Publication 17 [Your Federal Income Tax for Individuals].

There are several ways to figure the withholding tax for an employee. The most common methods use tax tables and tax rates. These and other methods are referenced in IRS Publication 15 (Circular E, Employer's Tax Guide).

**Income tax:** local, state, or federal tax paid on one's income.

**Federal tax withholding:** the amount required to be withheld from a person's pay to be paid to the federal government.

**Tax-filing status:** status based on whether the employee is married, single, or a head of household that determines the tax rate.

**Withholding allowance (exemption):** a portion of gross earnings that is not subject to tax.

# 1 Find federal tax withholding per paycheck using IRS tax tables.

To calculate federal withholding tax using IRS tax tables, an employer must know the employee's filing status (single, married, or head of household), the number of withholding allowances the employee claims, the type of pay period (weekly, biweekly, and so on), and the employee's *adjusted gross income*. When an employee is hired for a job, he or she is asked for payroll purposes to complete a federal W-4 form. Figure 10-1 shows a 2007 W-4 form. On this form an

**W-4 form:** form required to be held by the employer for determining the amount of federal tax to be withheld.

## Form W-4 (2007)

**Purpose.** Complete Form W-4 so that your employer can withhold the correct federal income tax from your pay. Because your tax situation may change, you may want to refigure your withholding each year.

**Exemption from withholding.** If you are exempt, complete **only** lines 1, 2, 3, 4, and 7 and sign the form to validate it. Your exemption for 2007 expires February 16, 2008. See Pub. 505, Tax Withholding and Estimated Tax.

**Note.** You cannot claim exemption from withholding if (a) your income exceeds $850 and includes more than $300 of unearned income (for example, interest and dividends) and (b) another person can claim you as a dependent on their tax return.

**Basic instructions.** If you are not exempt, complete the **Personal Allowances Worksheet** below. The worksheets on page 2 adjust your withholding allowances based on

itemized deductions, certain credits, adjustments to income, or two-earner/multiple job situations. Complete all worksheets that apply. However, you may claim fewer (or zero) allowances.

**Head of household.** Generally, you may claim head of household filing status on your tax return only if you are unmarried and pay more than 50% of the costs of keeping up a home for yourself and your dependent(s) or other qualifying individuals.

**Tax credits.** You can take projected tax credits into account in figuring your allowable number of withholding allowances. Credits for child or dependent care expenses and the child tax credit may be claimed using the **Personal Allowances Worksheet** below. See Pub. 919, How Do I Adjust My Tax Withholding, for information on converting your other credits into withholding allowances.

**Nonwage income.** If you have a large amount of nonwage income, such as interest or dividends, consider making estimated tax payments using Form 1040-ES, Estimated Tax

for Individuals. Otherwise, you may owe additional tax. If you have pension or annuity income, see Pub. 919 to find out if you should adjust your withholding on Form W-4 or W-4P.

**Two earners/Multiple jobs.** If you have a working spouse or more than one job, figure the total number of allowances you are entitled to claim on all jobs using worksheets from only one Form W-4. Your withholding usually will be most accurate when all allowances are claimed on the Form W-4 for the highest paying job and zero allowances are claimed on the others.

**Nonresident alien.** If you are a nonresident alien, see the Instructions for Form 8233 before completing this Form W-4.

**Check your withholding.** After your Form W-4 takes effect, use Pub. 919 to see how the dollar amount you are having withheld compares to your projected total tax for 2007. See Pub. 919, especially if your earnings exceed $130,000 (Single) or $180,000 (Married).

---

**Personal Allowances Worksheet** (Keep for your records.)

**A** Enter "1" for **yourself** if no one else can claim you as a dependent . . . . . . . . . . . . . **A** \_\_\_\_\_

**B** Enter "1" if:
- You are single and have only one job; or
- You are married, have only one job, and your spouse does not work; or
- Your wages from a second job or your spouse's wages (or the total of both) are $1,000 or less.

**B** \_\_\_\_\_

**C** Enter "1" for your **spouse.** But, you may choose to enter "-0-" if you are married and have either a working spouse or more than one job. (Entering "-0-" may help you avoid having too little tax withheld.) . . . . . . . . . **C** \_\_\_\_\_

**D** Enter number of **dependents** (other than your spouse or yourself) you will claim on your tax return . . . . . . **D** \_\_\_\_\_

**E** Enter "1" if you will file as **head of household** on your tax return (see conditions under **Head of household** above) . **E** \_\_\_\_\_

**F** Enter "1" if you have at least $1,500 of **child or dependent care expenses** for which you plan to claim a credit . . **F** \_\_\_\_\_
(**Note.** Do **not** include child support payments. See Pub. 503, Child and Dependent Care Expenses, for details.)

**G** **Child Tax Credit** (including additional child tax credit). See Pub 972, Child Tax Credit, for more information.
- If your total income will be less than $57,000 ($85,000 if married), enter "2" for each eligible child.
- If your total income will be between $57,000 and $84,000 ($85,000 and $119,000 if married), enter "1" for each eligible child plus "1" **additional** if you have 4 or more eligible children.

**G** \_\_\_\_\_

**H** Add lines A through G and enter total here. (**Note.** This may be different from the number of exemptions you claim on your tax return.) ▶ **H** \_\_\_\_\_

For accuracy, complete all worksheets that apply.
- If you plan to **itemize or claim adjustments to income** and want to reduce your withholding, see the **Deductions and Adjustments Worksheet** on page 2.
- If you have **more than one job** or are **married and you and your spouse both work** and the combined earnings from all jobs exceed $40,000 ($25,000 if married) see the **Two-Earners/Multiple Jobs Worksheet** on page 2 to avoid having too little tax withheld.
- If **neither** of the above situations applies, **stop here** and enter the number from line H on line 5 of Form W-4 below.

---

- - - - - - - - - - Cut here and give Form W-4 to your employer. Keep the top part for your records. - - - - - - - - - -

**Form W-4**

Department of the Treasury
Internal Revenue Service

**Employee's Withholding Allowance Certificate**

▶ Whether you are entitled to claim a certain number of allowances or exemption from withholding is subject to review by the IRS. Your employer may be required to send a copy of this form to the IRS.

OMB No. 1545-0074

**2007**

| 1 Type or print your first name and middle initial. | Last name | 2 Your social security number |
|---|---|---|

| Home address (number and street or rural route) | 3 ☐ Single ☐ Married ☐ Married, but withhold at higher Single rate.<br>**Note.** If married, but legally separated, or spouse is a nonresident alien, check the "Single" box. |
|---|---|
| City or town, state, and ZIP code | 4 If your last name differs from that shown on your social security card, check here. You must call 1-800-772-1213 for a replacement card. ▶ ☐ |

**5** Total number of allowances you are claiming (from line **H** above **or** from the applicable worksheet on page 2) | **5** \_\_\_\_

**6** Additional amount, if any, you want withheld from each paycheck . . . . . . . . . . . | **6** $ \_\_\_\_

**7** I claim exemption from withholding for 2007, and I certify that I meet **both** of the following conditions for exemption.
- Last year I had a right to a refund of **all** federal income tax withheld because I had **no** tax liability **and**
- This year I expect a refund of **all** federal income tax withheld because I expect to have **no** tax liability.

If you meet both conditions, write "Exempt" here . . . . . . . . . . . ▶ | **7** \_\_\_\_

Under penalties of perjury, I declare that I have examined this certificate and to the best of my knowledge and belief, it is true, correct, and complete.

**Employee's signature**
(Form is not valid unless you sign it.) ▶

**Date** ▶

| 8 Employer's name and address (Employer: Complete lines 8 and 10 only if sending to the IRS.) | 9 Office code (optional) | 10 Employer identification number (EIN) |
|---|---|---|

**For Privacy Act and Paperwork Reduction Act Notice, see page 2.** | Cat. No. 10220Q | Form **W-4** (2007)

---

**FIGURE 10-1**

Employee's Withholding Allowance Certificate

**Adjustment:** amount that can be subtracted from the gross income, such as qualifying IRAs, tax-sheltered annuities, 401Ks, or employer-sponsored child care of medical plans.

**Adjusted gross income:** the income that remains after allowable adjustments have been made.

employee must indicate tax-filing status and number of exemptions claimed. This information is necessary in order to compute the amount of federal income tax to be withheld from the employee's earnings.

In many cases, adjusted gross income is the same as gross pay. However, earnings contributed to funds such as qualifying IRAs, tax-sheltered annuities, 401ks, or some employer-sponsored child care and medical plans are called **adjustments** to income and are subtracted from gross pay to determine the **adjusted gross income**.

Figures 10-2 and 10-3 show a portion of two IRS tax tables.

## SINGLE Persons—SEMIMONTHLY Payroll Period
### (For Wages Paid in 2007)

| If the wages are— | | And the number of withholding allowances claimed is— | | | | | | | | | | |
|---|---|---|---|---|---|---|---|---|---|---|---|---|
| At least | But less than | 0 | 1 | 2 | 3 | 4 | 5 | 6 | 7 | 8 | 9 | 10 |
| | | The amount of income tax to be withheld is— | | | | | | | | | | |
| $840 | $860 | $95 | $74 | $53 | $32 | $17 | $3 | $0 | $0 | $0 | $0 | $0 |
| 860 | 880 | 98 | 77 | 56 | 35 | 19 | 5 | 0 | 0 | 0 | 0 | 0 |
| 880 | 900 | 101 | 80 | 59 | 38 | 21 | 7 | 0 | 0 | 0 | 0 | 0 |
| 900 | 920 | 104 | 83 | 62 | 41 | 23 | 9 | 0 | 0 | 0 | 0 | 0 |
| 920 | 940 | 107 | 86 | 65 | 44 | 25 | 11 | 0 | 0 | 0 | 0 | 0 |
| 940 | 960 | 110 | 89 | 68 | 47 | 27 | 13 | 0 | 0 | 0 | 0 | 0 |
| 960 | 980 | 113 | 92 | 71 | 50 | 29 | 15 | 1 | 0 | 0 | 0 | 0 |
| 980 | 1,000 | 116 | 95 | 74 | 53 | 31 | 17 | 3 | 0 | 0 | 0 | 0 |
| 1,000 | 1,020 | 119 | 98 | 77 | 56 | 34 | 19 | 5 | 0 | 0 | 0 | 0 |
| 1,020 | 1,040 | 122 | 101 | 80 | 59 | 37 | 21 | 7 | 0 | 0 | 0 | 0 |
| 1,040 | 1,060 | 125 | 104 | 83 | 62 | 40 | 23 | 9 | 0 | 0 | 0 | 0 |
| 1,060 | 1,080 | 128 | 107 | 86 | 65 | 43 | 25 | 11 | 0 | 0 | 0 | 0 |
| 1,080 | 1,100 | 131 | 110 | 89 | 68 | 46 | 27 | 13 | 0 | 0 | 0 | 0 |
| 1,100 | 1,120 | 134 | 113 | 92 | 71 | 49 | 29 | 15 | 1 | 0 | 0 | 0 |
| 1,120 | 1,140 | 137 | 116 | 95 | 74 | 52 | 31 | 17 | 3 | 0 | 0 | 0 |
| 1,140 | 1,160 | 140 | 119 | 98 | 77 | 55 | 34 | 19 | 5 | 0 | 0 | 0 |
| 1,160 | 1,180 | 143 | 122 | 101 | 80 | 58 | 37 | 21 | 7 | 0 | 0 | 0 |
| 1,180 | 1,200 | 146 | 125 | 104 | 83 | 61 | 40 | 23 | 9 | 0 | 0 | 0 |
| 1,200 | 1,220 | 149 | 128 | 107 | 86 | 64 | 43 | 25 | 11 | 0 | 0 | 0 |
| 1,220 | 1,240 | 152 | 131 | 110 | 89 | 67 | 46 | 27 | 13 | 0 | 0 | 0 |
| 1,240 | 1,260 | 155 | 134 | 113 | 92 | 70 | 49 | 29 | 15 | 1 | 0 | 0 |
| 1,260 | 1,280 | 158 | 137 | 116 | 95 | 73 | 52 | 31 | 17 | 3 | 0 | 0 |
| 1,280 | 1,300 | 161 | 140 | 119 | 98 | 76 | 55 | 34 | 19 | 5 | 0 | 0 |
| 1,300 | 1,320 | 164 | 143 | 122 | 101 | 79 | 58 | 37 | 21 | 7 | 0 | 0 |
| 1,320 | 1,340 | 167 | 146 | 125 | 104 | 82 | 61 | 40 | 23 | 9 | 0 | 0 |
| 1,340 | 1,360 | 170 | 149 | 128 | 107 | 85 | 64 | 43 | 25 | 11 | 0 | 0 |
| 1,360 | 1,380 | 173 | 152 | 131 | 110 | 88 | 67 | 46 | 27 | 13 | 0 | 0 |
| 1,380 | 1,400 | 176 | 155 | 134 | 113 | 91 | 70 | 49 | 29 | 15 | 0 | 0 |
| 1,400 | 1,420 | 181 | 158 | 137 | 116 | 94 | 73 | 52 | 31 | 17 | 2 | 0 |
| 1,420 | 1,440 | 186 | 161 | 140 | 119 | 97 | 76 | 55 | 34 | 19 | 4 | 0 |
| 1,440 | 1,460 | 191 | 164 | 143 | 122 | 100 | 79 | 58 | 37 | 21 | 6 | 0 |
| 1,460 | 1,480 | 196 | 167 | 146 | 125 | 103 | 82 | 61 | 40 | 23 | 8 | 0 |
| 1,480 | 1,500 | 201 | 170 | 149 | 128 | 106 | 85 | 64 | 43 | 25 | 10 | 0 |
| 1,500 | 1,520 | 206 | 173 | 152 | 131 | 109 | 88 | 67 | 46 | 27 | 12 | 0 |
| 1,520 | 1,540 | 211 | 176 | 155 | 134 | 112 | 91 | 70 | 49 | 29 | 14 | 0 |
| 1,540 | 1,560 | 216 | 180 | 158 | 137 | 115 | 94 | 73 | 52 | 31 | 16 | 2 |
| 1,560 | 1,580 | 221 | 185 | 161 | 140 | 118 | 97 | 76 | 55 | 33 | 18 | 4 |
| 1,580 | 1,600 | 226 | 190 | 164 | 143 | 121 | 100 | 79 | 58 | 36 | 20 | 6 |
| 1,600 | 1,620 | 231 | 195 | 167 | 146 | 124 | 103 | 82 | 61 | 39 | 22 | 8 |
| 1,620 | 1,640 | 236 | 200 | 170 | 149 | 127 | 106 | 85 | 64 | 42 | 24 | 10 |
| 1,640 | 1,660 | 241 | 205 | 173 | 152 | 130 | 109 | 88 | 67 | 45 | 26 | 12 |
| 1,660 | 1,680 | 246 | 210 | 176 | 155 | 133 | 112 | 91 | 70 | 48 | 28 | 14 |
| 1,680 | 1,700 | 251 | 215 | 180 | 158 | 136 | 115 | 94 | 73 | 51 | 30 | 16 |
| 1,700 | 1,720 | 256 | 220 | 185 | 161 | 139 | 118 | 97 | 76 | 54 | 33 | 18 |
| 1,720 | 1,740 | 261 | 225 | 190 | 164 | 142 | 121 | 100 | 79 | 57 | 36 | 20 |
| 1,740 | 1,760 | 266 | 230 | 195 | 167 | 145 | 124 | 103 | 82 | 60 | 39 | 22 |
| 1,760 | 1,780 | 271 | 235 | 200 | 170 | 148 | 127 | 106 | 85 | 63 | 42 | 24 |
| 1,780 | 1,800 | 276 | 240 | 205 | 173 | 151 | 130 | 109 | 88 | 66 | 45 | 26 |
| 1,800 | 1,820 | 281 | 245 | 210 | 176 | 154 | 133 | 112 | 91 | 69 | 48 | 28 |
| 1,820 | 1,840 | 286 | 250 | 215 | 179 | 157 | 136 | 115 | 94 | 72 | 51 | 30 |
| 1,840 | 1,860 | 291 | 255 | 220 | 184 | 160 | 139 | 118 | 97 | 75 | 54 | 33 |
| 1,860 | 1,880 | 296 | 260 | 225 | 189 | 163 | 142 | 121 | 100 | 78 | 57 | 36 |
| 1,880 | 1,900 | 301 | 265 | 230 | 194 | 166 | 145 | 124 | 103 | 81 | 60 | 39 |
| 1,900 | 1,920 | 306 | 270 | 235 | 199 | 169 | 148 | 127 | 106 | 84 | 63 | 42 |
| 1,920 | 1,940 | 311 | 275 | 240 | 204 | 172 | 151 | 130 | 109 | 87 | 66 | 45 |
| 1,940 | 1,960 | 316 | 280 | 245 | 209 | 175 | 154 | 133 | 112 | 90 | 69 | 48 |
| 1,960 | 1,980 | 321 | 285 | 250 | 214 | 179 | 157 | 136 | 115 | 93 | 72 | 51 |
| 1,980 | 2,000 | 326 | 290 | 255 | 219 | 184 | 160 | 139 | 118 | 96 | 75 | 54 |
| 2,000 | 2,020 | 331 | 295 | 260 | 224 | 189 | 163 | 142 | 121 | 99 | 78 | 57 |
| 2,020 | 2,040 | 336 | 300 | 265 | 229 | 194 | 166 | 145 | 124 | 102 | 81 | 60 |
| 2,040 | 2,060 | 341 | 305 | 270 | 234 | 199 | 169 | 148 | 127 | 105 | 84 | 63 |
| 2,060 | 2,080 | 346 | 310 | 275 | 239 | 204 | 172 | 151 | 130 | 108 | 87 | 66 |
| 2,080 | 2,100 | 351 | 315 | 280 | 244 | 209 | 175 | 154 | 133 | 111 | 90 | 69 |
| 2,100 | 2,120 | 356 | 320 | 285 | 249 | 214 | 179 | 157 | 136 | 114 | 93 | 72 |
| 2,120 | 2,140 | 361 | 325 | 290 | 254 | 219 | 184 | 160 | 139 | 117 | 96 | 75 |

**$2,140 and over**          Use Table 3(a) for a **SINGLE person** on page 37. Also see the instructions on page 35.

## FIGURE 10-2

Portion of IRS Withholding Table for Single Persons Paid Semimonthly

# MARRIED Persons—WEEKLY Payroll Period

**(For Wages Paid in 2007)**

| If the wages are— | | And the number of withholding allowances claimed is— | | | | | | | | | | |
|---|---|---|---|---|---|---|---|---|---|---|---|---|
| At least | But less than | 0 | 1 | 2 | 3 | 4 | 5 | 6 | 7 | 8 | 9 | 10 |
| | | The amount of income tax to be withheld is— | | | | | | | | | | |
| $0 | $125 | $0 | $0 | $0 | $0 | $0 | $0 | $0 | $0 | $0 | $0 | $0 |
| 125 | 130 | 0 | 0 | 0 | 0 | 0 | 0 | 0 | 0 | 0 | 0 | 0 |
| 130 | 135 | 0 | 0 | 0 | 0 | 0 | 0 | 0 | 0 | 0 | 0 | 0 |
| 135 | 140 | 0 | 0 | 0 | 0 | 0 | 0 | 0 | 0 | 0 | 0 | 0 |
| 140 | 145 | 0 | 0 | 0 | 0 | 0 | 0 | 0 | 0 | 0 | 0 | 0 |
| 145 | 150 | 0 | 0 | 0 | 0 | 0 | 0 | 0 | 0 | 0 | 0 | 0 |
| 150 | 155 | 0 | 0 | 0 | 0 | 0 | 0 | 0 | 0 | 0 | 0 | 0 |
| 155 | 160 | 0 | 0 | 0 | 0 | 0 | 0 | 0 | 0 | 0 | 0 | 0 |
| 160 | 165 | 1 | 0 | 0 | 0 | 0 | 0 | 0 | 0 | 0 | 0 | 0 |
| 165 | 170 | 1 | 0 | 0 | 0 | 0 | 0 | 0 | 0 | 0 | 0 | 0 |
| 170 | 175 | 2 | 0 | 0 | 0 | 0 | 0 | 0 | 0 | 0 | 0 | 0 |
| 175 | 180 | 2 | 0 | 0 | 0 | 0 | 0 | 0 | 0 | 0 | 0 | 0 |
| 180 | 185 | 3 | 0 | 0 | 0 | 0 | 0 | 0 | 0 | 0 | 0 | 0 |
| 185 | 190 | 3 | 0 | 0 | 0 | 0 | 0 | 0 | 0 | 0 | 0 | 0 |
| 190 | 195 | 4 | 0 | 0 | 0 | 0 | 0 | 0 | 0 | 0 | 0 | 0 |
| 195 | 200 | 4 | 0 | 0 | 0 | 0 | 0 | 0 | 0 | 0 | 0 | 0 |
| 200 | 210 | 5 | 0 | 0 | 0 | 0 | 0 | 0 | 0 | 0 | 0 | 0 |
| 210 | 220 | 6 | 0 | 0 | 0 | 0 | 0 | 0 | 0 | 0 | 0 | 0 |
| 220 | 230 | 7 | 1 | 0 | 0 | 0 | 0 | 0 | 0 | 0 | 0 | 0 |
| 230 | 240 | 8 | 2 | 0 | 0 | 0 | 0 | 0 | 0 | 0 | 0 | 0 |
| 240 | 250 | 9 | 3 | 0 | 0 | 0 | 0 | 0 | 0 | 0 | 0 | 0 |
| 250 | 260 | 10 | 4 | 0 | 0 | 0 | 0 | 0 | 0 | 0 | 0 | 0 |
| 260 | 270 | 11 | 5 | 0 | 0 | 0 | 0 | 0 | 0 | 0 | 0 | 0 |
| 270 | 280 | 12 | 6 | 0 | 0 | 0 | 0 | 0 | 0 | 0 | 0 | 0 |
| 280 | 290 | 13 | 7 | 0 | 0 | 0 | 0 | 0 | 0 | 0 | 0 | 0 |
| 290 | 300 | 14 | 8 | 1 | 0 | 0 | 0 | 0 | 0 | 0 | 0 | 0 |
| 300 | 310 | 15 | 9 | 2 | 0 | 0 | 0 | 0 | 0 | 0 | 0 | 0 |
| 310 | 320 | 16 | 10 | 3 | 0 | 0 | 0 | 0 | 0 | 0 | 0 | 0 |
| 320 | 330 | 17 | 11 | 4 | 0 | 0 | 0 | 0 | 0 | 0 | 0 | 0 |
| 330 | 340 | 18 | 12 | 5 | 0 | 0 | 0 | 0 | 0 | 0 | 0 | 0 |
| 340 | 350 | 19 | 13 | 6 | 0 | 0 | 0 | 0 | 0 | 0 | 0 | 0 |
| 350 | 360 | 20 | 14 | 7 | 1 | 0 | 0 | 0 | 0 | 0 | 0 | 0 |
| 360 | 370 | 21 | 15 | 8 | 2 | 0 | 0 | 0 | 0 | 0 | 0 | 0 |
| 370 | 380 | 22 | 16 | 9 | 3 | 0 | 0 | 0 | 0 | 0 | 0 | 0 |
| 380 | 390 | 23 | 17 | 10 | 4 | 0 | 0 | 0 | 0 | 0 | 0 | 0 |
| 390 | 400 | 24 | 18 | 11 | 5 | 0 | 0 | 0 | 0 | 0 | 0 | 0 |
| 400 | 410 | 25 | 19 | 12 | 6 | 0 | 0 | 0 | 0 | 0 | 0 | 0 |
| 410 | 420 | 26 | 20 | 13 | 7 | 0 | 0 | 0 | 0 | 0 | 0 | 0 |
| 420 | 430 | 27 | 21 | 14 | 8 | 1 | 0 | 0 | 0 | 0 | 0 | 0 |
| 430 | 440 | 28 | 22 | 15 | 9 | 2 | 0 | 0 | 0 | 0 | 0 | 0 |
| 440 | 450 | 29 | 23 | 16 | 10 | 3 | 0 | 0 | 0 | 0 | 0 | 0 |
| 450 | 460 | 30 | 24 | 17 | 11 | 4 | 0 | 0 | 0 | 0 | 0 | 0 |
| 460 | 470 | 32 | 25 | 18 | 12 | 5 | 0 | 0 | 0 | 0 | 0 | 0 |
| 470 | 480 | 33 | 26 | 19 | 13 | 6 | 0 | 0 | 0 | 0 | 0 | 0 |
| 480 | 490 | 35 | 27 | 20 | 14 | 7 | 0 | 0 | 0 | 0 | 0 | 0 |
| 490 | 500 | 36 | 28 | 21 | 15 | 8 | 1 | 0 | 0 | 0 | 0 | 0 |
| 500 | 510 | 38 | 29 | 22 | 16 | 9 | 2 | 0 | 0 | 0 | 0 | 0 |
| 510 | 520 | 39 | 30 | 23 | 17 | 10 | 3 | 0 | 0 | 0 | 0 | 0 |
| 520 | 530 | 41 | 31 | 24 | 18 | 11 | 4 | 0 | 0 | 0 | 0 | 0 |
| 530 | 540 | 42 | 33 | 25 | 19 | 12 | 5 | 0 | 0 | 0 | 0 | 0 |
| 540 | 550 | 44 | 34 | 26 | 20 | 13 | 6 | 0 | 0 | 0 | 0 | 0 |
| 550 | 560 | 45 | 36 | 27 | 21 | 14 | 7 | 1 | 0 | 0 | 0 | 0 |
| 560 | 570 | 47 | 37 | 28 | 22 | 15 | 8 | 2 | 0 | 0 | 0 | 0 |
| 570 | 580 | 48 | 39 | 29 | 23 | 16 | 9 | 3 | 0 | 0 | 0 | 0 |
| 580 | 590 | 50 | 40 | 30 | 24 | 17 | 10 | 4 | 0 | 0 | 0 | 0 |
| 590 | 600 | 51 | 42 | 32 | 25 | 18 | 11 | 5 | 0 | 0 | 0 | 0 |
| 600 | 610 | 53 | 43 | 33 | 26 | 19 | 12 | 6 | 0 | 0 | 0 | 0 |
| 610 | 620 | 54 | 45 | 35 | 27 | 20 | 13 | 7 | 0 | 0 | 0 | 0 |
| 620 | 630 | 56 | 46 | 36 | 28 | 21 | 14 | 8 | 1 | 0 | 0 | 0 |
| 630 | 640 | 57 | 48 | 38 | 29 | 22 | 15 | 9 | 2 | 0 | 0 | 0 |
| 640 | 650 | 59 | 49 | 39 | 30 | 23 | 16 | 10 | 3 | 0 | 0 | 0 |
| 650 | 660 | 60 | 51 | 41 | 31 | 24 | 17 | 11 | 4 | 0 | 0 | 0 |
| 660 | 670 | 62 | 52 | 42 | 32 | 25 | 18 | 12 | 5 | 0 | 0 | 0 |
| 670 | 680 | 63 | 54 | 44 | 34 | 26 | 19 | 13 | 6 | 0 | 0 | 0 |
| 680 | 690 | 65 | 55 | 45 | 35 | 27 | 20 | 14 | 7 | 1 | 0 | 0 |
| 690 | 700 | 66 | 57 | 47 | 37 | 28 | 21 | 15 | 8 | 2 | 0 | 0 |
| 700 | 710 | 68 | 58 | 48 | 38 | 29 | 22 | 16 | 9 | 3 | 0 | 0 |
| 710 | 720 | 69 | 60 | 50 | 40 | 30 | 23 | 17 | 10 | 4 | 0 | 0 |
| 720 | 730 | 71 | 61 | 51 | 41 | 32 | 24 | 18 | 11 | 5 | 0 | 0 |
| 730 | 740 | 72 | 63 | 53 | 43 | 33 | 25 | 19 | 12 | 6 | 0 | 0 |

**FIGURE 10-3**

Portion of IRS Withholding Table for Married Persons Paid Weekly

## HOW TO  Find federal tax withholding per paycheck using the IRS tax tables

1. Find the adjusted gross income by subtracting the total *allowable* adjustments from the gross pay per pay period. Select the appropriate table according to the employee's filing status (single, married, or head of household) and according to the type of pay period (weekly, biweekly, and so on).
2. Find the income row: In the columns labeled "If the wages are—," select the "At least" and "But less than" interval that includes the employee's adjusted gross income for the pay period.
3. Find the allowances column: In the columns labeled "And the number of withholding allowances claimed is—," select the number of allowances the employee claims.
4. Find the cell where the income row and allowance column intersect. The correct tax is given in this cell.

### EXAMPLE 1

Jeremy Dawson has a gross semimonthly income of $1,240, is single, claims three withholding allowances, and has no qualified adjustments. Find the amount of federal tax withholding to be deducted from his gross earnings.

Use Figure 10-2.                         Select appropriate tax table for a single person who is paid semimonthly.

Use row for interval "At least        $1,240 is in the selected interval.
$1,240 but less than $1,260."
Use the column for three
withholding allowances.                Find the intersection of the row and column.

**The withholding tax is $92.**

### EXAMPLE 2

Haruna Jing is married, has a gross weekly salary of $585, claims two withholding allowances, and has no qualified adjustments. Find the amount of withholding tax to be deducted from her gross salary.

Use Figure 10-3.                         Select appropriate tax table for a married person who is paid weekly.

Use row for interval "At            $585 is in the selected interval.
least $580 but less than $590."
Use the column for two
withholding allowances.                Find the intersection of the row and column.

**The withholding tax is $30.**

##  STOP AND CHECK

1. W. F. Kenoyer is single, claims two withholding allowances, has no allowable adjustments, and has a gross semimonthly income of $1,685. Find the amount of withholding tax to be deducted.

2. Kiyoshi Maruyama is married, has a weekly gross salary of $705, and has no allowable adjustments. He claims four withholding allowances. How much withholding tax will be deducted?

3. Karita Merrill is single and has no allowable adjustments but claims one exemption for herself. Her semimonthly earnings are $2,020. How much withholding tax will be deducted?

4. D. M. Park earns $640 weekly and has allowable adjustments of $30. Find his withholding tax if he is married and claims seven withholding allowances.

## 2 Find federal tax withholding per paycheck using the IRS percentage method.

**Percentage method income:** the result of subtracting the appropriate withholding allowances when using the percentage method of withholding.

**Percentage method of withholding:** an alternative method to the tax tables for calculating employees' withholding taxes.

Instead of using the tax tables, many companies calculate federal tax withholding using software such as QuickBooks or Peachtree Accounting that uses the tax rates. In order to use tax rates, the employer must deduct from the employee's adjusted gross income a tax-exempt amount based on the number of withholding allowances the employee claims. The resulting amount is sometimes called the **percentage method income**.

Figure 10-4 shows how much of an employee's adjusted gross income is exempt for each withholding allowance claimed, according to the type of pay period—weekly, biweekly, and so on. The table in Figure 10-4 is available from the IRS and is one of the tables used for calculating employees' withholding taxes. This method is called the **percentage method of withholding**.

**FIGURE 10-4**

IRS Table for Figuring Withholding Allowance According to the Percentage Method

| Payroll Period | One Withholding Allowance |
|---|---|
| Weekly. . . . . . . . . . . . . . . . . . . . . . | $ 65.38 |
| Biweekly . . . . . . . . . . . . . . . . . . . . | 130.77 |
| Semimonthly . . . . . . . . . . . . . . . . . | 141.67 |
| Monthly . . . . . . . . . . . . . . . . . . . . . | 283.33 |
| Quarterly . . . . . . . . . . . . . . . . . . . . | 850.00 |
| Semiannually. . . . . . . . . . . . . . . . . | 1,700.00 |
| Annually . . . . . . . . . . . . . . . . . . . . | 3,400.00 |
| Daily or miscellaneous (each day of the payroll period) . . . . . . . . . . . . . | 13.08 |

### HOW TO    Find the percentage method income per paycheck

1. Find the exempt-per-allowance amount: From the withholding allowance table (in Figure 10-4), identify the amount exempt for one withholding allowance according to the type of pay period.
2. Find the total exempt amount: Multiply the number of withholding allowances the employee claims by the exempt-per-allowance amount.
3. Subtract the total exempt amount from the employee's adjusted gross income for the pay period.

### EXAMPLE 1    Find the percentage method income on Dollie Calloway's biweekly gross earnings of $3,150. She has no adjustments to income, is single, and claims two withholding allowances on her W-4 form.

Since Dollie has no adjustments to income, her gross earnings of $3,150 is her adjusted gross income. From the table in Figure 10-4, the amount exempt for one withholding allowance in a biweekly pay period is $130.77.

$2(\$130.77) = \$261.54$      Multiply the number of withholding allowances by the exempt-per-allowance amount.

$\$3,150 - \$261.54 = \$2,888.46$      Subtract the total exempt amount from the adjusted gross income.

**The percentage method income is $2,888.46.**

Once an employee's percentage method income is found, the employer consults the percentage method tables, also available from the IRS, to know how much of this income should be taxed at the appropriate tax rate, according to the employee's marital status and the type of pay period. Figure 10-5 shows the IRS percentage method tables.

# Tables for Percentage Method of Withholding
## (For Wages Paid in 2007)

## TABLE 1—WEEKLY Payroll Period

**(a) SINGLE person** (including head of household)—

| If the amount of wages (after subtracting withholding allowances) is: | | The amount of income tax to withhold is: | |
|---|---|---|---|
| Not over $51 . . . . . | | $0 | |
| Over— | But not over— | | of excess over— |
| $51 | —$195 . . | 10% | —$51 |
| $195 | —$645 . . | $14.40 plus 15% | —$195 |
| $645 | —$1,482 . . | $81.90 plus 25% | —$645 |
| $1,482 | —$3,131 . . | $291.15 plus 28% | —$1,482 |
| $3,131 | —$6,763 . . | $752.87 plus 33% | —$3,131 |
| $6,763 | . . . . . . | $1,951.43 plus 35% | —$6,763 |

**(b) MARRIED person**—

| If the amount of wages (after subtracting withholding allowances) is: | | The amount of income tax to withhold is: | |
|---|---|---|---|
| Not over $154 . . . . | | $0 | |
| Over— | But not over— | | of excess over— |
| $154 | —$449 . . | 10% | —$154 |
| $449 | —$1,360 . . | $29.50 plus 15% | —$449 |
| $1,360 | —$2,573 . . | $166.15 plus 25% | —$1,360 |
| $2,573 | —$3,907 . . | $469.40 plus 28% | —$2,573 |
| $3,907 | —$6,865 . . | $842.92 plus 33% | —$3,907 |
| $6,865 | . . . . . . | $1,819.06 plus 35% | —$6,865 |

## TABLE 2—BIWEEKLY Payroll Period

**(a) SINGLE person** (including head of household)—

| If the amount of wages (after subtracting withholding allowances) is: | | The amount of income tax to withhold is: | |
|---|---|---|---|
| Not over $102 . . . . | | $0 | |
| Over— | But not over— | | of excess over— |
| $102 | —$389 . . | 10% | —$102 |
| $389 | —$1,289 . . | $28.70 plus 15% | —$389 |
| $1,289 | —$2,964 . . | $163.70 plus 25% | —$1,289 |
| $2,964 | —$6,262 . . | $582.45 plus 28% | —$2,964 |
| $6,262 | —$13,525 . . | $1,505.89 plus 33% | —$6,262 |
| $13,525 | . . . . . . | $3,902.68 plus 35% | —$13,525 |

**(b) MARRIED person**—

| If the amount of wages (after subtracting withholding allowances) is: | | The amount of income tax to withhold is: | |
|---|---|---|---|
| Not over $308 . . . . | | $0 | |
| Over— | But not over— | | of excess over— |
| $308 | —$898 . . | 10% | —$308 |
| $898 | —$2,719 . . | $59.00 plus 15% | —$898 |
| $2,719 | —$5,146 . . | $332.15 plus 25% | —$2,719 |
| $5,146 | —$7,813 . . | $938.90 plus 28% | —$5,146 |
| $7,813 | —$13,731 . . | $1,685.66 plus 33% | —$7,813 |
| $13,731 | . . . . . . | $3,638.60 plus 35% | —$13,731 |

## TABLE 3—SEMIMONTHLY Payroll Period

**(a) SINGLE person** (including head of household)—

| If the amount of wages (after subtracting withholding allowances) is: | | The amount of income tax to withhold is: | |
|---|---|---|---|
| Not over $110 . . . . | | $0 | |
| Over— | But not over— | | of excess over— |
| $110 | —$422 . . | 10% | —$110 |
| $422 | —$1,397 . . | $31.20 plus 15% | —$422 |
| $1,397 | —$3,211 . . | $177.45 plus 25% | —$1,397 |
| $3,211 | —$6,783 . . | $630.95 plus 28% | —$3,211 |
| $6,783 | —$14,652 . . | $1,631.11 plus 33% | —$6,783 |
| $14,652 | . . . . . . | $4,227.88 plus 35% | —$14,652 |

**(b) MARRIED person**—

| If the amount of wages (after subtracting withholding allowances) is: | | The amount of income tax to withhold is: | |
|---|---|---|---|
| Not over $333 . . . . | | $0 | |
| Over— | But not over— | | of excess over— |
| $333 | —$973 . . | 10% | —$333 |
| $973 | —$2,946 . . | $64.00 plus 15% | —$973 |
| $2,946 | —$5,575 . . | $359.95 plus 25% | —$2,946 |
| $5,575 | —$8,465 . . | $1,017.20 plus 28% | —$5,575 |
| $8,465 | —$14,875 . . | $1,826.40 plus 33% | —$8,465 |
| $14,875 | . . . . . . | $3,941.70 plus 35% | —$14,875 |

## TABLE 4—MONTHLY Payroll Period

**(a) SINGLE person** (including head of household)—

| If the amount of wages (after subtracting withholding allowances) is: | | The amount of income tax to withhold is: | |
|---|---|---|---|
| Not over $221 . . . . | | $0 | |
| Over— | But not over— | | of excess over— |
| $221 | —$843 . . | 10% | —$221 |
| $843 | —$2,793 . . | $62.20 plus 15% | —$843 |
| $2,793 | —$6,423 . . | $354.70 plus 25% | —$2,793 |
| $6,423 | —$13,567 . . | $1,262.20 plus 28% | —$6,423 |
| $13,567 | —$29,304 . . | $3,262.52 plus 33% | —$13,567 |
| $29,304 | . . . . . . | $8,455.73 plus 35% | —$29,304 |

**(b) MARRIED person**—

| If the amount of wages (after subtracting withholding allowances) is: | | The amount of income tax to withhold is: | |
|---|---|---|---|
| Not over $667 . . . . | | $0 | |
| Over— | But not over— | | of excess over— |
| $667 | —$1,946 . . | 10% | —$667 |
| $1,946 | —$5,892 . . | $127.90 plus 15% | —$1,946 |
| $5,892 | —$11,150 . . | $719.80 plus 25% | —$5,892 |
| $11,150 | —$16,929 . . | $2,034.30 plus 28% | —$11,150 |
| $16,929 | —$29,750 . . | $3,652.42 plus 33% | —$16,929 |
| $29,750 | . . . . . . | $7,883.35 plus 35% | —$29,750 |

**FIGURE 10-5**

IRS Tables for Percentage Method of Withholding

> **HOW TO** Find federal tax withholding per paycheck using the IRS percentage method tables
>
> 1. Select the appropriate table according to the employee's filing status and the type of pay period.
> 2. Find the income row: In the columns labeled "If the amount of wages (after subtracting withholding allowances) is:" select the "Over—" and "But not over—" interval that includes the employee's percentage method income for the pay period.
> 3. Find the cell where the income row and the column labeled "of excess over—" intersect, and subtract the amount given in this cell from the employee's percentage method income for the pay period.
> 4. Multiply the difference from step 3 by the percent given in the income row.
> 5. Add the product from step 4 to the amount given with the *percent* in the income row and "The amount of income tax to withhold is:" column.

**EXAMPLE 2** Find the federal tax withholding to be deducted from Dollie's income in Example 1.

From Figure 10-5 select Table 2(a) for single employees paid biweekly. We found Dollie's percentage method income to be $2,888.46 for the pay period. Table 2(a) tells us that the tax for that income is $163.70 plus 25% of the income in excess of $1,289.

| | |
|---|---|
| $2,888.46 − $1,289 = $1,599.46 | Subtract $1,289 from the percentage method income to find the amount in excess of $1,289. |
| $1,599.46(0.25) = $399.87 | Find 25% of the income in excess of $1,289. |
| $163.70 + $399.87 = $563.57 | Add $399.87 to $163.70 to find the withholding tax. |

**The federal tax withholding is $563.57 for the pay period.**

The withholding tax calculated by the percentage method may differ slightly from the withholding tax given in the tax table. The tax table uses $20 income intervals and tax amounts are rounded to the nearest dollar.

## STOP AND CHECK

1. Use the percentage method to find the total withholding allowance for weekly gross earnings of $850 with no adjustments if the wage earner is single and claims three withholding allowances.

2. Find the adjusted gross income for the wage earner in Exercise 1.

3. Find the amount of income tax to withhold for the wage earner in Exercise 1.

4. Emily Harrington earns $1,700 semimonthly and claims four withholding allowances and no other income adjustments. Emily is married. Find the amount of income tax to be withheld each pay period.

## 3  Find Social Security tax and Medicare tax per paycheck.

Two other amounts withheld from an employee's paycheck are the deductions for Social Security and Medicare taxes. The Federal Insurance Contribution Act (FICA) was established by Congress during the depression of the 1930s. Prior to 1991, funds collected under the Social Security tax act were used for both Social Security and Medicare benefits. Beginning in 1991, funds were collected separately for these two programs.

The Social Security tax rate and the income subject to Social Security tax change periodically as Congress passes new legislation. In a recent year, the Social Security tax rate was 6.2% (0.062) of the first $97,500 of gross earnings. This means that after a person has earned $97,500 in a year, no Social Security tax will be withheld on any additional money he or she earns during that year. A person who earns $100,000 in a year pays exactly the same Social Security tax as a person who earns $97,500. In this same year, the rate for Medicare was 1.45% (0.0145). All wages earned are subject to Medicare tax, unless the employee participates in a flexible benefits plan that is exempt from Medicare tax and under certain other conditions specified in the Internal Revenue Code. These plans are written to provide employees with a choice or "menu" of benefits such as health insurance, child care, and so on. In some instances, the wages used to pay for these benefits are subtracted from gross earnings to give an adjusted gross income that is used as the basis for withholding tax, Social Security tax, and Medicare tax.

Employers also pay a share of Social Security and Medicare taxes: The employer contributes the same amount as the employee contributes to that employee's Social Security account and Medicare account.

**Find the amount of Social Security and Medicare tax to be paid by an employee**

**Social Security tax:**
1. Determine the amount of the earnings subject to tax.
   (a) If the year-to-date earnings for the previous pay period exceeded $97,500, no additional Social Security tax is to be paid.
   (b) If the year-to-date earnings exceed $97,500 for the first time this pay period, from this period's year-to-date earnings subtract $97,500.
   (c) If the year-to-date earnings for this period are less than $97,500, the entire earnings for this period are subject to tax.
2. Multiply the earnings to be taxed by 6.2% (0.062). Round to the nearest cent.

**Medicare tax:**
Multiply the earnings to be taxed by 1.45% (0.0145). Round to the nearest cent.

**EXAMPLE 1**   Mickey Beloate has a gross weekly income of $967. How much Social Security tax and Medicare tax should be withheld?

$967(52) = $50,284     The salary for the entire year will not exceed $97,500. The entire salary is to be taxed.

$967(0.062) = $59.95     Social Security tax on $967

$967(0.0145) = $14.02     Medicare tax on $967

**The Social Security tax withheld per week should be $59.95, and the Medicare tax withheld should be $14.02.**

**EXAMPLE 2**   John Friedlander, vice president of marketing for Golden Sun Enterprises, earns $99,580 annually, or $1,915 per week. Find the amount of Social Security and Medicare taxes that should be withheld for the 51st week.

At the end of the 50th week, John will have earned a total gross salary for the year of $95,750. Since Social Security tax is withheld on the first $97,500 annually, he needs to pay Social Security tax on $1,750 for the remainder of the year ($97,500 − $95,750 = $1,750).

$1,750(0.062) = $108.50     Multiply $1,750 by the 6.2% tax rate to find the Social Security tax for the 51st week.

Since Medicare tax is paid on the entire salary, John must pay the Medicare tax on the full week's salary of $1,915.

$$\$1,915(0.0145) = \$27.77$$

**The Social Security tax for the 51st week is $108.50 and the Medicare tax is $27.77.**

**Self-employment (SE) tax:** the equivalent of both the employee's and the employer's tax for both Social Security and Medicare. It is two times the employee's rate.

A person who is self-employed must also pay Social Security tax and Medicare tax. Since there is no employer involved to make matching contributions, the self-employed person must pay the equivalent of both amounts. The self-employment rates are 12.4% Social Security and 2.9% Medicare tax for a total of 15.3%. The tax is called the **self-employment (SE) tax**. However, one-half of the self-employment tax can be deducted as an adjustment to income when finding the adjusted income for paying income tax. Self-employed persons report and pay taxes differently.

1. Lars Pacheco has a gross biweekly income of $1,730. How much Social Security tax and Medicare tax should be withheld?

2. George Pacheco earns $6,230 monthly. How much Social Security tax and Medicare tax should be withheld from his monthly pay?

3. Sarah Grafe earns $99,240 annually or $4,135 semimonthly. How much Social Security tax and Medicare tax should be withheld from her 24th paycheck of the year?

4. Sollaug Pacheco earns $98,384 annually or $1,892 per week. How much Social Security tax and Medicare tax should be withheld for the 47th week?

## 4 Find net earnings per paycheck.

In addition to federal taxes, a number of other deductions may be made from an employee's paycheck. Often, state and local income taxes must also be withheld by the employer. Other deductions are made at the employee's request, such as insurance payments or union dues. Some retirement plans and insurance plans are tax exempt; others are not. When all these deductions have been made, the amount left is called net earnings, net pay, or take-home pay.

### HOW TO     Find net earnings per paycheck

1. Find the gross pay for the pay period.
2. Find the adjustments-to-income deductions, such as tax-exempt retirement, tax-exempt medical insurance, and so on.
3. Find the Social Security tax and Medicare tax based on the adjusted gross income.
4. Find the federal tax withholding based on (a) or (b):
   (a) Adjusted gross income (gross pay minus adjustments to income) using IRS tax tables
   (b) Percentage method income (adjusted gross income minus amount exempt for withholding allowances) using IRS percentage method tables
5. Find other withholding taxes, such as local or state taxes.
6. Find other deductions, such as insurance payments or union dues.
7. Find the sum of all deductions from steps 2–6, and subtract the sum from the gross pay.

### EXAMPLE 1

Jeanetta Grandberry's gross weekly earnings are $676. She is married and claims two withholding allowances. Five percent of her gross earnings is deducted for her nonexempt retirement fund and $25.83 is deducted for nonexempt insurance. Find her net earnings.

| | |
|---|---|
| Income tax withholding: $44 | In Figure 10-3, find the amount of income tax to be withheld. |
| Social Security tax withholding: $676(0.062) = $41.91 | Find the Social Security tax by the percentage method. |
| Medicare tax withholding: $676(0.0145) = $9.80 | Find the Medicare tax by the percentage method. |
| Retirement fund withholding: 0.05($676) = $33.80 | Use the formula $P = R \times B$. Multiply rate (5% = 0.05) by base (gross pay of $676). |
| Total deductions | Add all deductions including the nonexempt insurance. |

= withholding tax + Social Security tax + Medicare tax + retirement fund + insurance
= $44.00         + $41.91         + $9.80         + $33.80         + $25.83 = $155.34

Net earnings:
Gross earnings − total deductions
    $676      −      $155.34      = $520.66     Subtract total deductions from the gross earnings.

**The net earnings are $520.66.**

## STOP AND CHECK

1. Olena Koduri earns $732 weekly. She is married and claims three withholding allowances. $110.15 is deducted for nonexempt insurance and 6% of her gross earnings is deducted for nonexempt retirement. Find the amount deducted for retirement and Social Security and Medicare taxes.

2. Find the amount of withholding tax deducted.

3. Find the total deductions.

4. Find the net pay for Olena.

## 10-2 SECTION EXERCISES

1. Khalid Khouri is married, has a gross weekly salary of $486 (all of which is taxable), and claims three withholding allowances. Use the tax tables to find the federal tax withholding to be deducted from his weekly salary.

2. Mae Swift is married and has a gross weekly salary of $583. She has $32 in adjustments to income for tax-exempt health insurance and claims two withholding allowances. Use the tax tables to find the federal tax withholding to be deducted from her weekly salary.

3. Jacob Drewrey is paid semimonthly an adjusted gross income of $1,431. He is single and claims two withholding allowances. Use the tax tables to find the federal tax withholding to be deducted from his salary.

4. Dieter Tillman earns a semimonthly salary of $1,698. He has a $100 adjustment-to-income flexible benefits package, is single, and claims three withholding allowances. Find the federal tax withholding to be deducted from his salary using the percentage method tables.

5. Mohammad Hajibeigy has a weekly adjusted gross income of $580, is single, and claims one withholding allowance. Find the federal tax withholding to be deducted from his weekly paycheck using the percentage method tables.

6. Margie Young is an associate professor at a major research university and earns $4,598 monthly with no adjustments to income. She is married and claims one withholding allowance. Find the federal tax withholding that is deducted from her monthly paycheck using the percentage method tables.

7. Dr. Josef Young earns an adjusted gross weekly income of $2,583. How much Social Security tax should be withheld the first week of the year? How much Medicare tax should be withheld?

8. Dierdri Williams earns a gross biweekly income of $1,020 and has no adjustments to income. How much Social Security tax should be withheld? How much Medicare tax should be withheld?

9. Rodney Whitaker earns $98,604 annually and is paid monthly. How much Social Security tax will be deducted from his December earnings? How much Medicare tax will be deducted from his December earnings?

10. Pam Trim earns $5,291 monthly, is married, and claims four withholding allowances. Her company pays her retirement, but she pays $52.83 each month for nonexempt insurance premiums. Find her net pay.

11. Shirley Riddle earns $1,319 biweekly. She is single and claims no withholding allowances. She pays 2% of her salary for retirement and $22.80 in nonexempt insurance premiums each pay period. What are her net earnings for each pay period?

12. Donna Wood's gross weekly earnings are $615. Three percent of her gross earnings is deducted for her nonexempt retirement fund and $25.97 is deducted for nonexempt insurance. Find the net earnings if Donna is married and claims two withholding allowances.

## 10-3 THE EMPLOYER'S PAYROLL TAXES

### LEARNING OUTCOMES

1 Find an employer's total deposit for withholding tax, Social Security tax, and Medicare tax per pay period.
2 Find an employer's SUTA tax and FUTA tax due for a quarter.

### 1 Find an employer's total deposit for withholding tax, Social Security tax, and Medicare tax per pay period.

The employer must pay to the Internal Revenue Service the income tax withheld and both the employees' and employer's Social Security and Medicare taxes. This payment is made by making a deposit at an authorized financial institution or Federal Reserve bank. If the employer's accumulated tax is less than $500, this payment may be made with the tax return (generally Form 941, Employer's Quarterly Federal Tax Return). Other circumstances create a different employer's deposit schedule. This schedule varies depending on the amount of tax liability and other criteria. IRS Publication 15 (Circular E, Employer's Tax Guide) and Publication 334 (Tax Guide for Small Business) give the criteria for depositing and reporting these taxes.

## HOW TO Find an employer's total deposit for withholding tax, Social Security tax, and Medicare tax per pay period

1. Find the withholding tax deposit: From employee payroll records, find the total withholding tax for all employees for the period.
2. Find the Social Security tax deposit: Find the total Social Security tax paid by all employees and multiply this total by 2 to include the employer's matching tax.
3. Find the Medicare tax deposit: Find the total Medicare tax paid by all employees for the pay period and multiply the total by 2 to include the employer's matching tax.
4. Add the withholding tax deposit, Social Security tax deposit, and Medicare tax deposit.

## EXAMPLE 1

Determine the employer's total deposit of withholding tax, Social Security tax, and Medicare tax for the payroll register.

Payroll for June 1 through June 15, 2007

| Employee | Gross earnings | Withholding | Social Security | Medicare | Net earnings |
|---|---|---|---|---|---|
| Plumlee, C. | $1,050.00 | $ 57.73 | $ 65.10 | $15.23 | $ 911.94 |
| Powell, M. | 2,085.00 | 168.05 | 129.27 | 30.23 | 1,757.45 |
| Randle, M. | 1,995.00 | 174.80 | 123.69 | 28.93 | 1,667.58 |
| Robinson, J. | 2,089.00 | 350.45 | 129.52 | 30.29 | 1,578.74 |

Total withholding = $57.73 + $168.05 + $174.80 + $350.45 = $751.03
Total Social Security = $65.10 + $129.27 + $123.69 + $129.52 = $447.58
Total Medicare = $15.23 + $30.23 + $28.93 + $30.29 = $104.68
Total Social Security and Medicare(2) = ($447.58 + $104.68)(2) = $552.26(2) = $1,104.52
Total employer's deposit = $751.03 + $1,104.52 = $1,855.55

**The total amount of the employer's deposit for this payroll is $1,855.55.**

Bookkeeping software will compile payroll records and generate a report of tax liability for a month, quarter, or any selected time interval.

 ## STOP AND CHECK

*Use the following weekly payroll register to answer questions 1–4.*

**Weekly Payroll Register**

| Employee | Gross earnings | Withholding | Social Security | Medicare | Net earnings |
|---|---|---|---|---|---|
| Cohen, P. | $740 | $63 | $45.88 | $10.73 | $620.39 |
| Faneca, T. | 867 | 88.37 | 53.75 | 12.57 | 712.32 |
| Gex, M. | 630 | 29 | 39.06 | 9.14 | 552.80 |
| Hasan, F. | 695 | 57 | 43.09 | 10.08 | 584.83 |

1. Find the total withholding tax for the employer payroll register.

2. Find the total Social Security tax withheld from employees' pay.

3. Find the total Medicare tax withheld from employees' pay.

4. Find the employer's total deposit for the payroll register.

## 2  Find an employer's SUTA tax and FUTA tax due for a quarter.

The major employee-related taxes paid by employers are the employer's share of the Social Security and Medicare taxes, which we have already discussed, and federal and state unemployment taxes. Federal and state unemployment taxes do not affect the paycheck of the employee. They are paid entirely by the employer. Under the Federal Unemployment Tax Act (FUTA) most employers pay a federal unemployment tax. This tax, along with state unemployment tax, provides for payment of unemployment compensation to workers who have lost their job. **Federal unemployment (FUTA) tax** is currently 6.2% of the first $7,000 earned by an employee in a year *minus* any amount that the employer has paid in **state unemployment (SUTA) tax**, up to a limit of 5.4% on the first $7,000. In most states SUTA rates vary depending on a company's unemployment history. FUTA tax is accumulated for all employees and is deposited quarterly if the amount exceeds $100. Amounts less than $100 are paid with the annual tax return that is due January 31 of the following year.

### HOW TO  Find the SUTA tax due for a quarter

1. For each employee, multiply 5.4% or the employer's appropriate rate by the employee's cumulative earnings for the quarter (up to $7,000 annually).
2. Add the SUTA tax owed on all employees.

### HOW TO  Find the FUTA tax due for a quarter

1. For each employee:
   (a) If no SUTA tax is paid, multiply 6.2% by the employee's cumulative earnings for the quarter (up to $7,000 annually).
   (b) If 5.4% of the employee's cumulative earnings for the quarter (up to $7,000 annually) is paid as SUTA tax, multiply 0.8% by the employee's cumulative earnings for the quarter (up to $7,000 annually).
2. Add the FUTA tax owed on all employees' wages for the quarter.
3. If the total from step 2 is less than $100, no FUTA tax is due for the quarter, but the total from step 2 must be added to the amount due for the next quarter.

### EXAMPLE 1

Melanie McFarren earned $32,500 last year and over $7,000 in the first quarter of this year. If the state unemployment (SUTA) tax rate for her employer is 5.4% of the first $7,000 earned in a year, how much SUTA tax must Melanie's employer pay on her behalf? Also, how much FUTA must be paid?

SUTA = tax rate × taxable wages          $7,000 is subject to SUTA tax in the first quarter.
SUTA = 5.4%($7,000)
SUTA = 0.054($7,000) = $378
FUTA = 0.8% × taxable wages              $7,000 is subject to FUTA tax in the first quarter.
       0.008($7,000) = $56

**SUTA tax is $378 and FUTA tax is $56.**

### EXAMPLE 2

Leak Busters has two employees who are paid semimonthly. One employee earns $1,040 per pay period and the other earns $985 per pay period. Based on the SUTA tax rate of 5.4%, the FUTA tax rate is 0.8% of the first $7,000 of each employee's annual gross pay. At the end of which quarter should the FUTA tax first be deposited?

| What You Know | What You Are Looking For | Solution Plan |
|---|---|---|
| Employee 1 pay = $1,040<br>Employee 2 pay = $985<br>Semimonthly pay period<br>FUTA rate = 0.8% of 1st $7,000<br><br>FUTA deposit not required until accumulated amount is more than $100. | First FUTA deposit should be made at the end of which quarter? | Find the FUTA tax for each employee for each pay period and total the tax by quarters. |

### Solution

| Pay period | Employee 1 salary | Accumulated salary subject to FUTA tax | FUTA tax | Employee 2 salary | Accumulated salary subject to FUTA tax | FUTA tax |
|---|---|---|---|---|---|---|
| Jan. 15 | $1,040 | $1,040 | $8.32 | $985 | $ 985 | $7.88 |
| Jan. 31 | 1,040 | 2,080 | 8.32 | 985 | 1,970 | 7.88 |
| Feb. 15 | 1,040 | 3,120 | 8.32 | 985 | 2,955 | 7.88 |
| Feb. 28 | 1,040 | 4,160 | 8.32 | 985 | 3,940 | 7.88 |
| Mar. 15 | 1,040 | 5,200 | 8.32 | 985 | 4,925 | 7.88 |
| Mar. 31 | 1,040 | 6,240 | 8.32 | 985 | 5,910 | 7.88 |

First quarter FUTA tax totals: $8.32(6) + $7.88(6) = 49.92 + 47.28 = $97.20
$97.20 is less than $100.00, so no deposit should be made at the end of the first quarter.

| Pay period | Employee 1 salary | Accumulated salary subject to FUTA tax | FUTA tax | Employee 2 salary | Accumulated salary subject to FUTA tax | FUTA tax |
|---|---|---|---|---|---|---|
| Apr. 15 | $1,040 | $7,000 | $6.08* | $985 | $6,895 | $7.88 |
| Apr. 30 | 1,040 | | | 985 | 7,000 | 0.84** |
| May 15 | 1,040 | | | 985 | | |
| May 31 | 1,040 | | | 985 | | |
| Jun. 15 | 1,040 | | | 985 | | |
| Jun. 30 | 1,040 | | | 985 | | |

*$7,000 − $6,240 = $760; $760(0.008) = $6.08
**$7,000 − $6,895 = $105; $105(0.008) = $0.84

Second quarter FUTA tax totals: $6.08 + $8.72 = $14.80
Total FUTA tax for first two quarters = $97.20 + $14.80 = $112.00

### Conclusion

**FUTA tax in the amount of $112 should be deposited by the end of the month following the second quarter. It should be deposited by July 31.**

 ## STOP AND CHECK

1. Kumar Konde earned $35,200 last year and over $7,000 in the first quarter of this year. State unemployment tax for Kumar's employer is 5.4% of the first $7,000 earned in a year. How much SUTA tax must Kumar's employer pay on his behalf?

2. How much FUTA tax must Kumar's employer pay on his behalf?

3. Powell's Lumber Company has two employees who are paid semimonthly. One employee earns $1,320 and the other earns $1,275 per pay period. At the end of which quarter must the first FUTA tax be deposited for the year if the company's rate is 5.4% of the first $7,000 earnings for each employee?

4. How much FUTA tax should be deposited by Powell's Lumber Company with the first payment of the year?

### SKILL BUILDERS

1. Carolyn Luttrell owns Just the Right Thing, a small antiques shop with four employees. For one payroll period the total withholding tax for all employees was $1,633. The total Social Security tax was $482, and the total Medicare tax was $113. How much tax must Carolyn deposit as the employer's share of Social Security and Medicare? What is the total tax that must be deposited?

2. Hughes' Trailer Manufacturer makes utility trailers and has seven employees who are paid weekly. For one payroll period the withholding tax for all employees was $1,661. The total Social Security tax withheld from employees' paychecks was $608, and the total Medicare tax withheld was $142. What is the total tax that must be deposited by Hughes?

3. Determine the employer's deposit of withholding, Social Security, and Medicare for the payroll register.

| Employee | Gross earnings | Withholding | Social Security | Medicare | Net earnings |
|---|---|---|---|---|---|
| Paszel, J. | $1,905 | $169 | $118.11 | $27.62 | $1,590.27 |
| Thomas, P. | 1,598 | 143 | 99.08 | 23.17 | 1,332.75 |
| Tillman, D. | 1,431 | 97 | 88.72 | 20.75 | 1,224.53 |

4. Heaven Sent Gifts, a small business that provides custom meals, flowers, and other specialty gifts, has three employees who are paid weekly. One employee earns $475 per week, is single, and claims one withholding allowance. Another employee earns $450 per week, is single, and claims two withholding allowances. The manager earns $740 per week, is married, and claims one withholding allowance. Calculate the amount of withholding tax, Social Security tax, and Medicare tax that will need to be deposited by Heaven Sent Gifts.

## APPLICATIONS

*Bruce Young earned $20,418 last year. His employer's SUTA tax rate is 5.4% of the first $7,000.*

**5.** How much SUTA tax must Bruce's employer pay for him?

**6.** How much FUTA tax must Bruce's company pay for him?

**7.** Bailey Plyler has three employees in his carpet cleaning business. The payroll is semimonthly and the employees earn $745, $780, and $1,030 per pay period. Calculate when and in what amounts FUTA tax payments are to be made for the year.

## Learning Outcomes

### Section 10-1

## What to Remember with Examples

**1** Find the gross pay per paycheck based on salary. (p. 342)

1. Identify the number of pay periods per year: monthly, 12; semimonthly, 24; biweekly, 26; weekly, 52
2. Divide the annual salary by the number of pay periods per year.

If Barbara earns $23,500 per year, how much is her weekly gross pay?

$$\frac{\$23,500}{52} = \$451.92$$

Clemetee earns $32,808 annually and is paid twice a month. What is her gross pay per pay period?

$$\frac{\$32,808}{24} = \$1,367$$

**2** Find the gross pay per weekly paycheck based on hourly wage. (p. 343)

1. Find the regular pay:
   (a) If the hours worked in the week are 40 or fewer, multiply the hours worked by the hourly wage.
   (b) If the hours worked are more than 40, multiply 40 hours by the hourly wage.
2. Find the overtime pay:
   (a) If the hours worked are 40 or fewer, the overtime pay is $0.
   (b) If the hours worked are more than 40, subtract 40 from the hours worked and multiply the difference by the overtime rate.
3. Add the regular pay and the overtime pay.

Aldo earns $10.25 per hour. He worked 38 hours this week. What is his gross pay?

38($10.25) = $389.50

Belinda worked 44 hours one week. Her regular pay was $7.75 per hour and time and a half for overtime. Find her gross earnings.

$$40(\$7.75) = \$310$$
$$4(\$7.75)(1.5) = \$46.50$$
$$\$310 + \$46.50 = \$356.50$$

**3** Find the gross pay per paycheck based on piecework wage. (p. 344)

1. If a *straight piecework* rate is used, multiply the number of items completed by the straight piecework rate.
2. If a *differential piecework* rate is used:
   (a) For each rate category, multiply the number of items produced for the category by the rate for the category.
   (b) Add the pay for all rate categories.

Willy earns $0.53 for each widget he twists. He twisted 1,224 widgets last week. Find his gross earnings.

1,224($0.53) = $648.72

Nadine does piecework for a jeweler and earns $0.65 per piece for finishing 1 to 25 pins, $0.70 per piece for 26 to 50 pins, and $0.75 per piece for pins over 50. Yesterday she finished 130 pins. How much did she earn?

$$25(\$0.65) + 25(\$0.70) + 80(\$0.75) =$$
$$\$16.25 + \$17.50 + \$60 = \$93.75$$

**4** Find the gross pay per paycheck based on commission. (p. 345)

1. Find the commission:
   (a) If the commission is *commission based on total sales,* multiply the commission rate by the total sales for the pay period.
   (b) If the commission is *commission based on quota,* subtract the quota from the total sales and multiply the difference by the commission rate.

2. Find the salary:
   (a) If the wage is *straight commission,* the salary is $0.
   (b) If the wage is *commission-plus-salary,* use the How To steps for finding gross pay based on salary.
3. Add the commission and the salary.

Bart earns a 4% commission on the appliances he sells. His sales last week totaled $18,000. Find his gross earnings.

0.04($18,000) = $720

Elaine earns $250 weekly plus 6% of all sales over $1,500. Last week she had $9,500 worth of sales. Find her gross earnings.

$$\$9,500 - \$1,500 = \$8,000$$
$$\text{Commission} = 0.06(\$8,000) = \$480$$
$$\$250 + \$480 = \$730$$

## Section 10-2

**1** Find federal tax withholding per paycheck using IRS tax tables. (p. 348)

1. Find the adjusted gross income by subtracting the total allowable adjustments from the gross pay per pay period. Select the appropriate table according to the employee's filing status (single, married, or head of household) and according to the type of pay period (weekly, biweekly, and so on).
2. Find the income row: In the columns labeled "If the wages are—," select the "At least" and "But less than" interval that includes the employee's adjusted gross income for the pay period.
3. Find the allowances column: In the columns labeled "And the number of withholding allowances claimed is—," select the number of allowances the employee claims.
4. Find the cell where the income row and allowance column intersect. The correct tax is given in this cell.

Archy is married, has a gross weekly salary of $680, and claims two withholding allowances. Find his withholding tax.

Look in the first two columns of Figure 10-3 to find the range for $680. Move across to the column for two withholding allowances. The amount of federal tax to be withheld is $45.

Lexie Lagen is married and has a gross weekly salary of $655. He claims three withholding allowances and has $20 deducted weekly from his paycheck for a flexible benefits plan, which is exempted from federal income taxes. Find the amount of his withholding tax.

Adjusted gross income = $655 − $20 = $635

Find the range for $635 and three withholding allowances in Figure 10-3. The tax is $29.

**2** Find federal tax withholding per paycheck using the IRS percentage method. (p. 352)

**Find the percentage method income per paycheck.**

1. Find the exempt-per-allowance amount: From the withholding allowance table (Figure 10-4), identify the amount exempt for one withholding allowance according to the type of pay period.
2. Find the total exempt amount: Multiply the number of withholding allowances the employee claims by the exempt-per-allowance amount.
3. Subtract the total exempt amount from the employee's adjusted gross income for the pay period.

Edith Sailor has weekly gross earnings of $890. Find her percentage method income if she has no adjustments to income, is married, and claims three withholding allowances.

Use Figure 10-4 to find one withholding allowance for a weekly payroll period. Multiply by 3.

$65.38(3) = $196.14

Percentage method income = $890.00 − $196.14 = $693.86.

**Find the federal tax withholding per paycheck using the IRS percentage method tables.**

1. Select the appropriate table in Figure 10-5 according to the employee's filing status and the type of pay period.
2. Find the income row: In the columns labeled "If the amount of wages (after subtracting withholding allowances) is:" select the "Over—" and "But not over—" interval that includes the employee's percentage method income for the pay period.

3. Find the cell where the income row and the column labeled "of excess over—" intersect, and subtract the amount given in this cell from the employee's percentage method income for the pay period.
4. Multiply the difference from step 3 by the percent given in the income row.
5. Add the product from step 4 to the amount given with the *percent* in the income row and "The amount of tax to withhold is:" column.

---

Find the federal tax on Ruth's monthly income of $1,938. She is single and claims one exemption.

1 exemption = $283.33          (Figure 10-4)
$1,938 − $283.33 = $1,654.67
$1,654.67 is in the $843 to $2,793 range (Figure 10-5, Table 4a), so the amount of withholding tax is $62.20 plus 15% of the amount over $843.

$1,654.67 − $843 = $811.67
$811.67(0.15) = $121.75
$62.20 + $121.75 = $183.95

---

**3** Find Social Security tax and Medicare tax per paycheck. (p. 354)

Social Security tax:

1. Determine the amount of the earnings subject to tax.
   (a) If the year-to-date earnings for the previous pay period exceeded $97,500, no additional Social Security tax is to be paid.
   (b) If the year-to-date earnings exceed $97,500 for the first time this pay period, from this period's year-to-date earnings subtract $97,500.
   (c) If the year-to-date earnings for this period are less than $97,500, the entire earnings for this period are subject to tax.
2. Multiply the earnings to be taxed by 6.2% (0.062). Round to the nearest cent.

Medicare tax:
   Multiply the earnings to be taxed by 1.45% (0.0145). Round to the nearest cent.

---

Find the Social Security and Medicare taxes for Abbas Laknahour, who earns $938 every two weeks.

Social Security = $938(0.062) = $58.16
Medicare = $938(0.0145) = $13.60

Donna Shroyer earns $9,170 monthly. Find the Social Security and Medicare taxes that will be deducted from her November paycheck.

Pay for first 10 months = $9,170(10) = $91,700
November pay subject to Social Security = $97,500 − $91,700 = $5,800
Social Security tax = $5,800(0.062) = $359.60
Medicare tax = $9,170(0.0145) = $132.97

---

**4** Find net earnings per paycheck. (p. 356)

1. Find the gross pay for the pay period.
2. Find the adjustments-to-income deductions, such as retirement, insurance, and so on.
3. Find the Social Security tax and Medicare tax based on the adjusted gross income.
4. Find the federal tax withholding based on (a) or (b):
   (a) adjusted gross income (gross pay minus adjustments to income) using IRS tax tables;
   (b) percentage method income (adjusted gross income minus amount exempt for withholding allowances) using IRS percentage method tables.
5. Find other withholding taxes, such as local or state taxes.
6. Find other deductions, such as insurance payments or union dues.
7. Find the sum of all deductions from steps 2–6, and subtract the sum from the gross pay.

---

Beth Cooley's gross weekly earnings are $588. Four percent of her gross earnings is deducted for her nonexempt retirement fund and $27.48 is deducted for insurance. Find her net earnings if Beth is married and claims three withholding allowances.

Retirement fund = $588(0.04) = $23.52
Withholding tax = $24.00 (from Figure 10-3)
Social Security = $588(0.062) = $36.46
Medicare = $588(0.0145) = $8.53
Total deductions = $23.52 + $27.48 + $24.00 + $36.46 + $8.53 = $119.99
Net earnings = $588 − $119.99 = $468.01

**1** Find an employer's total deposit for withholding tax, Social Security tax, and Medicare tax per pay period. (p. 358)

1. Find the withholding tax deposit: From employee payroll records, find the total withholding tax for all employees for the pay period.
2. Find the Social Security tax deposit: Find the total Social Security tax for all employees for the pay period and multiply this total by 2 to include the employer's matching tax.
3. Find the Medicare tax deposit: Find the total Medicare tax for all employees for the pay period and multiply this total by 2 to include the employer's matching tax.
4. Add the withholding tax deposit, Social Security tax deposit, and Medicare tax deposit.

Determine the employer's total deposit.

| Employee | Gross earnings | Withholding | Social Security | Medicare | Net earnings |
|---|---|---|---|---|---|
| Davis, T. | $ 485.00 | $ 27.00 | $ 30.07 | $ 7.03 | $ 420.90 |
| Dobbins, L. | 632.00 | 57.00 | 39.18 | 9.16 | 526.66 |
| Harris, M. | 590.00 | 51.00 | 36.58 | 8.56 | 493.86 |
| Totals | $1,707.00 | $135.00 | $105.83 | $24.75 | $1,441.42 |

Employer's tax deposit = $135 + 2($105.83 + $24.75) = $396.16

**2** Find an employer's SUTA tax and FUTA tax due for a quarter. (p. 360)

**Find the SUTA tax due for a quarter.**

1. For each employee, multiply 5.4% or the appropriate rate by the employee's cumulative earnings for the quarter (up to $7,000 annually).
2. Add the SUTA tax owed on all employees.

Kim Brown has three employees who each earn $8,250 in the first three months of the year. How much SUTA tax should Kim pay for the first quarter if the SUTA rate is 5.4% of the first $7,000 earnings?

$7,000(0.054)(3) = $1,134

Kim should pay $1,134 in SUTA tax for the first quarter.

**Find the FUTA tax due for a quarter.**

1. For each employee:
   (a) If no SUTA tax is paid, multiply 6.2% by the employee's cumulative earnings for the quarter (up to $7,000 annually).
   (b) If 5.4% of the employee's cumulative earnings for the quarter (up to $7,000 annually) is paid as SUTA tax, multiply 0.8% by the employee's cumulative earnings for the quarter (up to $7,000 annually).
2. Add the FUTA tax owed on all employees' wages for the quarter.
3. If the total from step 2 is less than $100, no FUTA tax is due for the quarter, but the total from step 2 must be added to the amount due for the next quarter.

How much FUTA tax should Kim pay for the three employees?

$7,000(0.008)(3) = $168

## EXERCISES SET A

### SKILL BUILDERS

*Find the gross earnings for each employee in Table 10-1. A regular week is 40 hours and the overtime rate is 1.5 times the regular rate.*

**TABLE 10-1**

| Employee | M | T | W | T | F | S | S | Hourly wage | Regular hours | Regular pay | Overtime hours | Overtime pay | Gross pay |
|----------|---|---|---|---|---|---|---|-------------|---------------|-------------|----------------|--------------|-----------|
| **1.** Allen, H. | 8 | 9 | 8 | 7 | 10 | 4 | 0 | $ 9.86 | | | | | |
| **2.** Pick, J. | 8 | 8 | 8 | 8 | 8 | 4 | 0 | $11.35 | | | | | |
| **3.** Lovett, L. | 8 | 8 | 8 | 8 | 0 | 0 | 0 | $14.15 | | | | | |
| **4.** Mitze, A. | 8 | 8 | 8 | 8 | 8 | 2 | 4 | $12.00 | | | | | |

**5.** Brian Williams is a salaried employee who earns $95,256 and is paid monthly. What is his pay each payroll period?

**6.** Varonia Reed is paid a weekly salary of $1,036. What is her annual salary?

**7.** Melanie Michael has a salaried job. She earns $425 a week. One week she worked 46 hours. Find her gross weekly earnings.

**8.** Glenda Chaille worked 27 hours in one week at $9.45 per hour. Find her gross earnings.

**9.** Susan Wood worked 52 hours in a week. She was paid at the hourly rate of $12.45 with time and a half for overtime. Find her gross earnings.

**10.** Ronald James is paid 1.5 times his hourly wage for all hours worked in a week exceeding 40. His hourly pay is $11.55 and he worked 52 hours in a week. Calculate his gross pay.

**11.** For sewing buttons on shirts, employees are paid $0.28 a shirt. Marty Hughes completes an average of 500 shirts a day. Find her average gross weekly earnings for a five-day week.

**12.** Patsy Hilliard is paid 5% commission on sales of $18,200. Find her gross pay.

**13.** Vincent Ores is paid a salary of $400 plus 8% of sales. Calculate his gross income if his sales total $9,890 in the current pay period.

**14.** Find the gross earnings if Juanita Wilson earns $275 plus 4% of all sales over $3,000 and the sales for a week are $8,756.

*Use Figure 10-3 to find the amount of federal tax withholding for the gross earnings of the following married persons who are paid weekly and have the indicated number of withholding allowances.*

**15.** $525, four allowances

**16.** $682, zero allowances

**17.** $495, three allowances

**18.** $709, five allowances

*Use Figures 10-4 and 10-5, the percentage method tables, to find the amount of federal income tax to be withheld from the gross earnings of married persons who are paid weekly and have the indicated number of withholding allowances in Exercises 19 and 20.*

**19.** $755, five allowances

**20.** $2,215, two allowances

*Find the Social Security and Medicare taxes deducted for each pay period in Exercises 21–24.*

**21.** Weekly gross income of $842

**22.** Yearly gross income of $24,000

**23.** Semimonthly gross income of $1,856

**24.** Biweekly gross income of $1,426

## APPLICATIONS

**25.** Irene Gamble earns $675 weekly and is married with 1 withholding allowance. She has a deduction for nonexempt insurance of $12.45. A 5% deduction is made for retirement. Find her total deductions including Social Security and Medicare taxes and find her net earnings.

**26.** Vince Bremaldi earned $32,876 last year. The state unemployment tax paid by his employer is 5.4% of the first $7,000 earned in a year. How much SUTA tax must Vince's employer pay for him? How much FUTA tax must Vince's employer pay?

**27.** Media Services, Inc. has a payroll in which the total employee withholding is $765.26; the total employee Social Security is $273.92; the total employee Medicare is $64.06. How much must the employer pay for this payroll? What is the total amount of taxes that must be paid for the payroll?

# EXERCISES SET B

## SKILL BUILDERS

*Find the gross earnings for each employee in Table 10-2. A regular week is 40 hours and the overtime rate is 1.5 times the regular rate.*

### TABLE 10-2

| Employee | M | T | W | T | F | S | S | Hourly wage | Regular hours | Regular pay | Overtime hours | Overtime pay | Gross pay |
|----------|---|---|---|---|---|---|---|-------------|---------------|-------------|----------------|--------------|-----------|
| **1.** Brown, J. | 4 | 6 | 8 | 9 | 9 | 5 | 0 | $10.43 | | | | | |
| **2.** Sayer, C. | 9 | 10 | 8 | 9 | 11 | 9 | 0 | $ 8.45 | | | | | |
| **3.** Lovett, L. | 8 | 8 | 8 | 8 | 0 | 0 | 0 | $ 9.95 | | | | | |
| **4.** James, M. | 8 | 8 | 4 | 8 | 8 | 8 | 0 | $11.10 | | | | | |

**5.** Arsella Gallagher earns a salary of $63,552 and is paid semimonthly. What is her gross salary for each payroll period?

**6.** John Edmonds is paid a biweekly salary of $1,398. What is his annual salary?

**7.** Fran Coley earns $1,896 biweekly on a salaried job. If she works 89 hours in one pay period, how much does she earn?

**8.** Robert Stout worked 40 hours at $12 per hour. Find his gross earnings for the week.

**9.** Leslie Jinkins worked a total of 58 hours in one week. Eight hours were paid at 1.5 times his hourly wage and 10 hours were paid at the holiday rate of 2 times his hourly wage. Find his gross earnings for the week if his hourly wage is $14.95.

**10.** Mike Kelly earns $21.30 per hour as a chemical technician. One week he works 38 hours. What is his gross pay for the week?

**11.** Employees are paid $3.50 per piece for a certain job. In a week's time, Maria Sanchez produced a total of 218 pieces. Find her gross earnings for the week.

**12.** Ada Shotwell is paid 4% commission on all computer sales. If she needs a monthly income of $2,500, find the monthly sales volume she must meet.

**13.** Cassie Lyons earns $350 plus 7% commission on all sales over $2,000. What are the gross earnings if sales for a week are $5,276?

**14.** Dieter Tillman is paid $2,000 plus 5% of the total sales volume. If he sold $3,000 in merchandise, find the gross earnings.

*Use Figure 10-3 to find the amount of federal tax withholding for the gross earnings of the following married persons with the indicated number of withholding allowances.*

**15.** $724, two allowances

**16.** $695, three allowances

**17.** $728, three allowances

**18.** $694, zero allowances

*Use Figures 10-4 and 10-5, the percentage method tables, to find the amount of federal income tax to be withheld from the gross earnings of married persons who are paid weekly and have the indicated number of withholding allowances.*

**19.** $620, eight allowances

**20.** $7,290, four allowances

*Find the Social Security and Medicare taxes deducted for each pay period for Exercises 21–24.*

**21.** Monthly gross income of $3,500

**22.** Yearly gross income of $78,500

**23.** Semimonthly gross income of $1,226

**24.** Biweekly gross income of $1,684

## APPLICATIONS

**25.** Anita Loyd earns $1,775 semimonthly. She is single and claims two withholding allowances. She also pays $12.83 each pay period for nonexempt health insurance. What is her net pay?

**26.** Elisa Marus has three employees who earn $2,500, $2,980, and $3,200 monthly. How much SUTA tax will she need to pay at the end of the first quarter if the SUTA tax rate is 5.4% of the first $7,000 for each employee?

**27.** Computer Solutions, Inc. has a payroll in which the total employee withholding is $1,250.37; the total employee Social Security is $395.56; the total employee Medicare is $92.51. How much must the employer pay for this payroll? What is the total amount of taxes that must be paid for the payroll?

# PRACTICE TEST

## CHAPTER 10

1. Cheryl Douglas works 43 hours in a week for a salary of $1,827 per week. What are Cheryl's gross weekly earnings?

2. June Jackson earns $7.59 an hour. Find her gross earnings if she worked 46 hours (time and a half for overtime over 40 hours).

3. Willy Bell checks wrappers on cans in a cannery. He receives $0.15 for each case of cans. If he checks 1,400 cases on an average day, find his gross weekly salary. (A work week is five days.)

4. Stacey Ellis is paid at the following differential piece rate: 1–100, $2.58; 101–250, $2.72; 251 and up, $3.15. Find her gross earnings for completing 475 pieces.

5. Dorothy Ford, who sells restaurant supplies, works on 6% commission. If her sales for a week are $18,200, find her gross earnings.

6. Carlo Mason works on 5% commission. If he sells $17,500 in merchandise, find his gross earnings.

7. Find the gross earnings of Sallie Johnson who receives a 9% commission and whose sales totaled $7,852.

8. Find the Social Security tax (at 6.2%) and the Medicare tax (at 1.45%) for Anna Jones, whose gross earnings are $513.86. Round to the nearest cent.

9. Find the Social Security and Medicare taxes for Michele Cottrell, whose gross earnings are $861.25.

10. How much income tax should be withheld for Terry McLean, a married employee who earns $486 weekly and claims two allowances? (Use Figure 10-3.)

11. Use Figure 10-3 to find the federal income tax paid by Charlotte Jordan, who is married with four exemptions, if her weekly gross earnings are $576.

12. If LaQuita White had net earnings of $877.58 and total deductions of $261.32, find her gross earnings.

*Complete the weekly register for married employees in Table 10-3. The number of each person's allowances is listed after each name. Round to the nearest cent. Use Figure 10-3.*

**TABLE 10-3**

| Employee (exemptions) | Gross earnings | Social Security | Medicare | Withholding tax | Other nonexempt deductions | Net earnings |
|---|---|---|---|---|---|---|
| **13.** Jackson (0) | $735.00 | | | | $25.12 | |
| **14.** Love (1) | $673.80 | | | | $12.87 | |
| **15.** Chow (2) | $492.17 | | | | 0 | |
| **16.** Ferrante (3) | $577.15 | | | | $ 4.88 | |
| **17.** Towns (4) | $610.13 | | | | 0 | |

**18.** How much SUTA tax must Anaston, Inc., pay to the state for a part-time employee who earns $5,290 in the first quarter? The SUTA tax rate is 5.4% of the wages.

**19.** How much SUTA tax must University Dry Cleaners pay to the state for an employee who earns $38,200?

**20.** How much FUTA tax must University Dry Cleaners pay for the employee in Exercise 19? The FUTA tax rate is 6.2% of the first $7,000 minus the SUTA tax.

**21.** Use Figures 10-4 and 10-5 to find the amount of federal income tax to be withheld from Joey Surrette's gross biweekly earnings of $2,555 if Joey is married and claims 3 withholding allowances.

1. Anita Loyd works 45 hours in one week, is paid $8.98 per hour, and earns 1.5 times her hourly wage for all hours worked over 40 in a given week. Calculate Anita's gross pay using the method described in the chapter.

2. Calculate Anita Loyd's gross pay by multiplying the total number of hours worked by the hourly rate and multiplying the hours over 40 by 0.5 the hourly rate. Compare this gross pay to the gross pay found in Exercise 1.

3. Explain why the methods for calculating gross pay in Exercises 1 and 2 are mathematically equivalent.

4. Most businesses prefer to use the method used in Exercise 1 to calculate gross pay. Discuss reasons for this preference.

*Assume that the taxpayers in questions 5–7 claim zero withholding allowances.*

5. If a person is paid weekly and is married, use Figure 10-5 to find the annual salary range that causes a portion of the person's salary to fall in the "28% bracket" for withholding purposes.

6. Compare the annual salary range found in Exercise 5 with the annual salary range for a person who is paid biweekly, is married, and whose salary is in the "28% bracket."

7. Predict the annual salary range a married person who is paid semimonthly would need to earn to fall in the "28% bracket." Use Table 3 of Figure 10-5 to verify or refute your prediction.

8. Use Exercises 5, 6, and 7 to make a general statement about the amount of withholding tax on an annual salary for the various types of pay periods. To what can you attribute any differences you noted?

9. Many people think that if an increase in earnings moves their salary to a higher tax bracket, their entire salary will be taxed at the higher rate. Is this true? Give an example to justify your answer.

10. Shameka Jones earns $98,520 and is paid semimonthly. Her last pay stub for the year shows $254.51 is deducted for Social Security and $59.52 is deducted for Medicare. Should she call her payroll office for a correction? If so, what would that correction be?

# Challenge Problem

Complete the following time card for Janice Anderson in Figure 10-6. She earns time and a half overtime when she works more than eight hours on a weekday or on Saturday. She earns double time on Sundays and holidays. Calculate Janice's net pay if she earns $9.75 per hour, is married, and claims one withholding allowance.

**WEEKLY TIME CARD**
**CHD Company**

Name: *Janice Anderson*  SS# *000-00-0000*

Pay for period ending

| DATE | IN | OUT | IN | OUT | Total Regular Hours | Total Overtime Hours |
|------|-----|-------|-------|------|---------------------|----------------------|
| M 8/4 | 7:00 | 11:00 | 11:30 | 7:30 | | |
| Tu 8/5 | 8:00 | 12:00 | 12:30 | 4:30 | | |
| W 8/6 | 8:00 | 12:00 | 12:30 | 4:30 | | |
| Th 8/7 | 7:00 | 11:00 | 12:30 | 5:30 | | |
| F 8/8 | 8:00 | 12:00 | 12:30 | 4:30 | | |
| Sa 8/9 | 7:00 | 12:00 | | | | |
| Su 8/10 | | | | | | |

|  | HOURS | RATE | GROSS PAY |
|------|-------|------|-----------|
| Regular | | | |
| Overtime (1.5X) | | | |
| Overtime (2X) | | | |
| Total | | | |

## 10.1  Score Skateboard Company

Score Skateboard Company is a small firm that designs and manufactures skateboards for high school and college students who want effective, fast transportation around campus. Score has two employees who receive $1,100 gross pay per semimonthly pay period and four employees who receive $850 gross pay per semimonthly pay period. The company owner and manager, Christie, needs to determine how much to include in her budget for each employee. Starting in January, Score will be contributing $75 per pay period to each employee's retirement fund. Score is in a state that has a maximum of $7,000 gross pay for SUTA and Score is required to pay 5.4% of the first $7,000 for each employee.

1.  Calculate the cost to Score for an employee with $1,100 gross pay in the first period in January.

2.  Calculate the cost to Score for an employee with $850 gross pay in the first period in January.

3.  Find the total gross semimonthly pay for all six employees and compare this to the total amount Score must include in its budget. How much extra is needed in the budget?

4.  Calculate the total amount Score will need for its first quarter FUTA and SUTA deposit. There are six semimonthly pay periods in the first quarter of the year.

## 10.2  Welcome Care

Welcome Care, a senior citizen day care center, pays the major portion of its employees' medical insurance—$150 of the $204 monthly premium for an individual employee. If an employee wishes coverage for a spouse or family, the employee must pay $126 or $212 per month respectively to cover herself or himself and the additional person(s). The center hires three new employees. Calculate their semimonthly take-home pay using the percentage method tables. The company pays time and a half for overtime hours in excess of 40 hours in a given week. Medical insurance premiums can be paid with pretax dollars. Withholding taxes, Social Security, and Medicare deductions are calculated on the lower adjusted gross salary.

1.  An activities director is hired at an annual salary of $32,000. He is single with two dependent children (three withholding allowances) and wants family medical insurance coverage. Find his total deductions and his net income.

**2.** A dietitian is hired at a monthly salary of $3,500 a month paid semimonthly. She is married with one withholding allowance and wants medical insurance for herself and her spouse. Find her take-home pay if she is subject to an IRS garnishment of $100 per month for back taxes. Use the percentage method of withholding.

**3.** A vehicle driver is hired at $12 per hour to transport seniors to appointments and leisure activities. The driver is single and claims no withholding allowances. He needs medical coverage for himself only. Find his net pay if he worked 77 hours regular time, 8 hours overtime, and has $200 per month taken out for court-ordered child support payments.

**4.** A part-time caregiver comes daily to sit with and talk with senior citizens at Welcome Care. He is paid $8 per hour and works 4 hours each day for 10 days in the pay period. He is single and claims one withholding allowance. He has medical insurance coverage through another job. Find his net pay for a semimonthly paycheck using the percentage method of withholding.

# 10.3 First Foreign Auto Parts

Ryan Larson, owner of First Foreign Auto Parts, is considering expanding his operation for the new year by manufacturing rebuilt shock absorbers. This will require two additional full-time employees. Due to a tight labor market, Ryan presumes he will have to pay $10 per hour, along with health insurance, to attract quality employees. He decides he will contribute 50% towards the $260 monthly health insurance premium, in addition to the federal and state unemployment taxes and Medicare and Social Security taxes that he must pay on the employees' behalf. Ryan needs to decide how much to include in his budget for each employee.

**1.** Based on a 40-hour work week, calculate the cost to First Foreign Auto Parts for each employee in the first month in January.

**2.** Ryan hires a new employee at $10 per hour to rebuild shock absorbers. The employee is single and claims no withholding allowances, and needs the health coverage. Calculate his weekly take-home pay using the percentage method tables, assuming he works 40 regular hours and 10 overtime hours, and pays 29% of his earnings for court-ordered child support. His health insurance premiums can be paid with pre-tax dollars. Use Table 10-4 to determine the federal tax to be withheld.

**3.** Ryan is considering a differential piecework rate to give his new employees incentive to produce more and increase their wages. Ryan came up with the following schedule:

| Shocks assembled per week | Pay per shock |
|---|---|
| First 40 shocks | $4.50 |
| Next 40 shocks | $5.50 |
| Over 80 shocks | $6.50 |

**4.** How much would each employee make for completing 75 shocks per week? How much more would each employee make by completing just 15 additional shocks per week beyond the first 75 shocks?

# CHAPTER
# 11
# Simple Interest and Simple Discount

## 18 Months Same as Cash Financing on New TVs*

Radhika had just received mail for the first time in her new apartment, and there it was in big bold letters: 18 MONTHS SAME AS CASH FINANCING*. The ad read: The minimum monthly payment for this purchase does not include interest charges during the promotional period. You'll pay no interest for 18 months. Simply pay at least the total minimum monthly payment due as indicated on your billing statement. There's no prepayment penalty, and this offer provides you with the flexibility you need to meet your specific budget and purchasing requirements.

It sounded like a great deal. She really wanted to buy a flat panel TV and was short on cash. But Radhika had some concerns. First, she didn't know much about financing or how interest was computed; and second, she knew that the asterisk would probably mean trouble. After reading further, she found the following:

*The 18-month promotion is for televisions with a minimum value of $499.99. The 12-month promotion requires a minimum purchase of $299.99. These are "same as cash" promotions. If the balance on these purchases is paid in full before the expiration of the promotional period indicated on your billing statement and your account is kept current, then accrued finance

charges will not be imposed on these purchases. If the balance on these purchases is not paid in full, finance charges will be assessed from the purchase date at the annual simple interest rate of 24.99%. For accounts not kept current, the default simple interest rate of 27.99% will be applied to all balances on your account. Minimum monthly payments are required. The minimum finance charge is $2.00. Certain rules apply to the allocation of payments and finance charges on your promotional purchase if you make more than one purchase on your account.

Wow! That was a lot to digest. Radhika had her heart set on a TV that cost about $800, and she was hoping to keep her payments under $20 per month. Would that be enough to pay the account in full in 18 months? And if she came up short by a few hundred dollars, would she still be charged all of that interest? If so, how much would 24.99% cost her during that time? What was simple interest, anyway? None of this sounded simple to her. And the late penalties—she didn't even want to think about those.

Radhika took a deep breath. Maybe this wasn't such a good idea, she thought as she reached for her keys. But she really wanted that TV.

## LEARNING OUTCOMES

### 11-1 The Simple Interest Formula

1. Find simple interest using the simple interest formula.
2. Find the maturity value of a loan.
3. Convert months to a fractional or decimal part of a year.
4. Find the principal, rate, or time using the simple interest formula.

### 11-2 Ordinary and Exact Interest

1. Find the exact time.
2. Find the due date.
3. Find the ordinary interest and the exact interest.
4. Make a partial payment before the maturity date.

### 11-3 Promissory Notes

1. Find the bank discount and proceeds for a simple discount note.
2. Find the true or effective interest rate of a simple discount note.
3. Find the third-party discount and proceeds for a third-party discount note.

*A corresponding Business Math Case Video for this chapter, *The Real World: Video Case: Should I Buy New Equipment Now?* can be found in Appendix A.

Every business and every person at some time borrows or invests money. A person (or business) who borrows money must pay for the use of the money. A person who invests money must be paid by the person or firm who uses the money. The price paid for using money is called **interest**.

In the business world, we encounter two basic kinds of interest, *simple* and *compound*. **Simple interest** applies when a loan or investment is repaid in a lump sum. The person using the money has use of the full amount of money for the entire time of the loan or investment. Compound interest, which is explained in Chapter 13, most often applies to savings accounts, installment loans, and credit cards.

Both types of interest take into account three factors: the principal, the interest rate, and the time period involved. **Principal** is the amount of money borrowed or invested. **Rate** is the percent of the principal paid as interest per time period. **Time** is the number of days, months, or years that the money is borrowed or invested.

## 11-1 THE SIMPLE INTEREST FORMULA

### LEARNING OUTCOMES

1 Find simple interest using the simple interest formula.
2 Find the maturity value of a loan.
3 Convert months to a fractional or decimal part of a year.
4 Find the principal, rate, or time using the simple interest formula.

### 1 Find simple interest using the simple interest formula.

The interest formula $I = PRT$ shows how interest, principal, rate, and time are related and gives us a way of finding one of these values if the other three values are known.

> **HOW TO** Find simple interest using the simple interest formula
>
> 1. Identify the principal, rate, and time.
> 2. Multiply the principal by the rate and time.
>
> $$\text{Interest} = \text{principal} \times \text{rate} \times \text{time}$$
> $$I = PRT$$

The rate of interest is a percent for a given time period, usually one year. The time in the interest formula must be expressed in the same unit of time as the rate. If the rate is a percent per year, the time must be expressed in years or a decimal or fractional part of a year. Similarly, if the rate is a percent per month, the time must be expressed in months.

> **EXAMPLE 1** Find the interest paid on a loan of $1,500 for one year at a simple interest rate of 9% per year.
>
> $I = PRT$          Use the simple interest formula. Principal $P$ is $1,500, rate $R$ is 9% per year, and time $T$ is one year.
> $I = (\$1,500)(9\%)(1)$    Write 9% as a decimal. Multiply.
> $I = (\$1,500)(0.09)(1)$
> $I = \$135$
>
> **The interest on the loan is $135.**

> **EXAMPLE 2** Kanette's Salon borrowed $5,000 at $8\frac{1}{2}\%$ per year simple interest for two years to buy new hair dryers. How much interest must be paid?
>
> $I = PRT$          Use the simple interest formula. Principal $P$ is $5,000, rate $R$ is $8\frac{1}{2}\%$ per year, and time $T$ is two years.
> $I = (\$5,000)(8\frac{1}{2}\%)(2)$
> $I = (\$5,000)(0.085)(2)$    Write $8\frac{1}{2}\%$ as a decimal. Multiply.
> $I = \$850$
>
> **Kanette's Salon will pay $850 interest.**

**Prime interest rate (prime):** the lowest rate of interest charged by banks for short-term loans to their most creditworthy customers.

A loan that is made using simple interest is to be repaid in a lump sum at the end of the time of the loan. Banks and lending institutions make loans at a variety of different rates based on factors such as prime interest rate and the amount of risk that the loan will be repaid. The **prime interest rate** is the lowest rate of interest charged by banks for short-term loans to their most creditworthy customers. Banks establish the rate of a loan based on the current prime rate and the likelihood that it will not change significantly over the time of the loan.

Loans are made at the prime rate or higher, often significantly higher. Investments such as savings accounts and certificates of deposit earn interest at a rate less than prime. Lending institutions make a profit based on the difference between the rate of interest charged for loans and the rate of interest given for investments.

## ✔ STOP AND CHECK

1. Find the interest paid on a loan of $38,000 for one year at a simple interest rate of 10.5%.

2. A loan of $17,500 for six years has a simple interest rate of 7.75%. Find the interest.

3. The 7th Inning borrowed $6,700 at 9.5% simple interest for three years. How much interest is paid?

4. Find the interest on a $38,500 loan at a simple interest rate of 12.3% for five years.

## 2    Find the maturity value of a loan.

**Maturity value:** the total amount of money due at the end of a loan period–the amount of the loan and the interest.

The *total* amount of money due at the end of a loan period—the amount of the loan *and* the interest—is called the **maturity value** of the loan. When the principal and interest of a loan are known, the maturity value is found by adding the principal and the interest. The maturity value can also be found directly from the principal, rate, and time.

---

### HOW TO    Find the maturity value of a loan

1. If the principal and interest are known, add them.

$$\text{Maturity value} = \text{principal} + \text{interest}$$
$$MV = P + I$$

2. If the principal, rate, and time are known, use either of the formulas:
   (a) Maturity value = principal + (principal × rate × time)
$$MV = P + PRT$$
   (b) Maturity value = principal (1 + rate × time)
$$MV = P(1 + RT)$$

---

Both variations of the formula for finding the maturity value when the principal, rate, and time are known require that the operations be performed according to the standard order of operations. To review briefly, when more than one operation is to be performed, perform operations within parentheses first. Perform multiplications and divisions before additions and subtractions. Perform additions and subtractions last. For a more detailed discussion of the order of operations, review Chapter 5, Section 1, Learning Outcome 3.

**EXAMPLE 1**    In Example 2 on page 382, we found that Kanette's Salon would pay $850 interest on a $5,000 loan. How much money will Kanette's Salon pay at the end of two years?

Maturity value = principal + interest          *P* and *I* are known.
$$MV = P + I$$                                      Substitute known values.
$$= \$5,000 + \$850 = \$5,850$$

**Kanette's Salon will pay $5,850 at the end of the loan period.**

## EXAMPLE 2

Marcus Logan can purchase furniture with a two-year simple interest loan at 9% interest per year. What is the maturity value for a $2,500 loan?

Maturity value = principal (1 + rate × time)

$$MV = P(1 + RT)$$

*P, R,* and *T* are known.
Substitute $P = \$2,500$,
$R = 9\%$ or 0.09,
$T = 2$ years.

$$MV = \$2,500(1 + 0.09 \times 2)$$
$$MV = \$2,500(1 + 0.18)$$
$$MV = \$2,500(1.18)$$
$$MV = \$2,950$$

Multiply in parentheses.
Add in parentheses.
Multiply.

**Marcus will pay $2,950 at the end of two years.**

---

## TIP

**Does a Calculator Know the Proper Order of Operations? Some Do, Some Don't.**

Using a basic calculator, you enter calculations as they should be performed according to the standard order of operations.

$$\boxed{AC}\ .09\ \boxed{\times}\ 2\ \boxed{=}\boxed{+}\ 1\ \boxed{=}\ \boxed{\times}\ 2500\ \boxed{=}\ \Rightarrow 2950$$

Using a business or scientific calculator with parentheses keys allows you to enter values for the maturity value formula as they appear. The calculator is programmed to perform the operations in the standard order. The calculator has special keys for entering parentheses, $\boxed{(}$ and $\boxed{)}$.

$$\boxed{AC}\ 2500\ \boxed{\times}\boxed{(}\ 1\ \boxed{+}\ .09\ \boxed{\times}\ 2\ \boxed{)}\boxed{=}\ \Rightarrow 2950$$

---

 **STOP AND CHECK**

1. How much is paid at the end of two years for a loan of $8,000 if the total interest is $660?

2. A loan of $7,250 is to be repaid in three years and has a simple interest rate of 12%. How much is paid after the three years?

3. Find the maturity value of a $1,800 loan made for two years at $9\frac{3}{4}\%$ simple interest per year.

4. Find the maturity value of a three-year, simple interest loan at 11% per year in the amount of $7,275.

---

## 3   Convert months to a fractional or decimal part of a year.

Not all loans or investments are made for a whole number of years; but, since the interest rate is most often given per year, the time must also be expressed in the same unit of time as the rate.

---

### HOW TO   Convert months to a fractional or decimal part of a year

1. Write the number of months as the numerator of a fraction.
2. Write 12 as the denominator of the fraction.
3. Reduce the fraction to lowest terms if using the fractional equivalent.
4. Divide the numerator by the denominator to get the decimal equivalent of the fraction.

## EXAMPLE 1

Convert (a) 5 months and (b) 15 months to years, expressed in both fraction or mixed-number and decimal form.

(a) 5 months $= \dfrac{5}{12}$ year

5 months equal $\frac{5}{12}$ year.

$$12)\overline{5.0000000} \quad 0.4166666 \text{ year} = 0.42 \text{ year}$$

To write the fraction as a decimal, divide the number of months (the numerator) by the number of months in a year (the denominator).

**5 months $= \frac{5}{12}$ year or 0.42 year (rounded)**

(b) 15 months $= \dfrac{15}{12}$ years $= \dfrac{5}{4}$ or $1\dfrac{1}{4}$ years

15 months equal $\frac{15}{12}$ years.

$$
\begin{array}{r}
1.25 \text{ years} \\
12)\overline{15.00} \\
\underline{12}\phantom{.00} \\
3\,0 \\
\underline{2\,4} \\
60 \\
\underline{60} \\
0
\end{array}
$$

To write the fraction as a decimal, divide the number of months (the numerator) by the number of months in a year (the denominator).

**15 months $= 1\frac{1}{4}$ years or 1.25 years**

## EXAMPLE 2

To save money for a shoe repair shop, Stan Wright invested $2,500 for 45 months at $3\frac{1}{2}\%$ simple interest per year. How much interest did he earn?

$T = 45$ months $= \dfrac{45}{12}$ years $= 3\dfrac{3}{4}$ or 3.75 years

Write the time in terms of years.

$I = PRT$

Use the simple interest formula.

$I = \$2,500\,(0.035)(3.75)$

Principal $P$ is $2,500, rate $R$ is 0.035, and time $T$ is $\frac{45}{12}$ or 3.75. Multiply.

$I = \$328.13$

Round to the nearest cent.

**Stan Wright earned $328.13 in interest.**

---

**TIP**

**Check Calculations by Estimating**

As careful as we are, there will always be times that we hit an incorrect key or use an improper sequence of steps and produce an incorrect solution. You can catch most of these mistakes by first anticipating what a reasonable answer should be.

In the preceding example, 1% interest for one year would be $25. At that rate the interest for four years would be $100. The actual rate is $3\frac{1}{2}$ times one percent and the time is less than four years, so a reasonable estimate would be $350.

**TIP**

**So Many Choices!**

When time is expressed in months, the calculator sequence is the same as when time is expressed in years, except that you do not enter a whole number for the time. Months can be changed to years in the sequence rather than as a separate calculation. All other steps are the same. To solve the equation using a calculator without the percent key, use the decimal equivalent of $3\frac{1}{2}\%$ and the fraction for the time.

$$\boxed{AC}\ 2500\ \boxed{\times}\ .035\ \boxed{\times}\ 45\ \boxed{\div}\ 12\ \boxed{=}\ \Rightarrow 328.125$$

It is not necessary to find the decimal equivalent of $\frac{45}{12}$ or to reduce $\frac{45}{12}$. However, you will get the same result if you use 3.75 or $\frac{15}{4}$.

$$\boxed{AC}\ 2500\ \boxed{\times}\ .035\ \boxed{\times}\ 3.75\ \boxed{=}\ \Rightarrow 328.125$$
$$\boxed{AC}\ 2500\ \boxed{\times}\ .035\ \boxed{\times}\ 15\ \boxed{\div}\ 4\ \boxed{=}\ \Rightarrow 328.125$$

---

 ## STOP AND CHECK

1. Change eight months to years, expressed in fraction and decimal form. Round to the nearest millionth.

2. Change 15 months to years, expressed in both fraction and decimal form.

3. Carrie made a $1,200 loan for 18 months at 9.5% simple interest. How much interest was paid?

4. Find the maturity value of a loan of $1,750 for 28 months at 9.8% simple interest.

## 4 Find the principal, rate, or time using the simple interest formula.

So far in this chapter, we have used the formula $I = PRT$ to find the simple interest on a loan. However, sometimes you need to find the principal or the rate or the time instead of the interest. You can remember the different forms of this formula with a circle diagram (see Figure 11-1) like the one used for the percentage formula. Cover the unknown term to see the form of the simple interest formula needed to find the missing value.

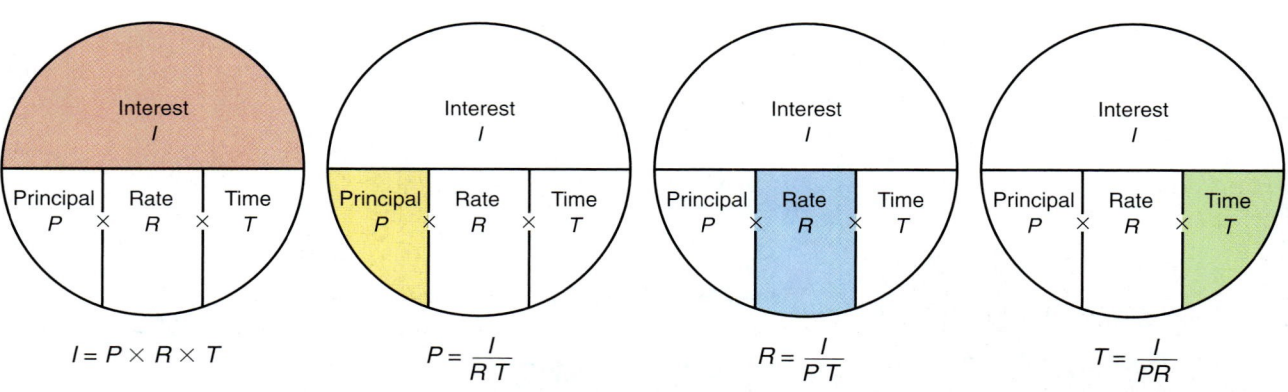

$$I = P \times R \times T \qquad P = \frac{I}{RT} \qquad R = \frac{I}{PT} \qquad T = \frac{I}{PR}$$

**FIGURE 11-1**
**Various Forms of the Simple Interest Formula**

**HOW TO** Find the principal, rate, or time using the simple interest formula

1. Select the appropriate form of the formula.
   (a) If the principal is unknown, use

$$P = \frac{I}{RT}$$

   (b) If the rate is unknown, use

$$R = \frac{I}{PT}$$

   (c) If the time is unknown, use

$$T = \frac{I}{PR}$$

2. Replace letters with known values and perform the indicated operations.

**EXAMPLE 1** To buy a food preparation table for his restaurant, the owner of The 7th Inning borrowed $1,800 for $1\frac{1}{2}$ years and paid $202.50 simple interest on the loan. What rate of interest did he pay?

$R = \dfrac{I}{PT}$    *R is unknown. Select the correct form of the simple interest formula. Replace letters with known values: I is $202.50, P is $1,800, T is 1.5 years. Perform the operations.*

$R = \dfrac{\$202.50}{(\$1,800)(1.5)}$

$R = 0.075$    *Write the rate in percent form by moving the decimal point two places to the right and attaching a % symbol.*

$R = 7.5\%$

**The owner paid 7.5% interest.**

## EXAMPLE 2

Phyllis Cox wanted to borrow some money to expand her photography business. She was told she could borrow a sum of money for 18 months at 6% simple interest per year. She thinks she can afford to pay as much as $540 in interest charges. How much money could she borrow?

$$P = \frac{I}{RT}$$

$I = \$540$

$R = 6\% = 0.06$

$T = 18 \text{ months} = \dfrac{18}{12}$

$= 1.5 \text{ years}$

$P = \dfrac{\$540}{0.06(1.5)}$

$P = \$6,000$

*P* is unknown. Select the correct form of the simple interest formula.

Write the percent as a decimal equivalent.

The interest rate is per year, so write 18 months as 1.5 years.

Replace letters with known values: *I* is $540, *R* is 0.06, *T* is 1.5.

Perform the operations.

**The principal is $6,000.**

---

## TIP

**Numerator Divided by Denominator**

When a series of calculations has fractions and a calculation in the denominator, the numerator must be divided by the entire denominator.

With a basic calculator and using memory, multiply 0.06 × 1.5, store the result in memory and clear the display, and divide 540 by the stored product:

$$\boxed{\text{AC}} \ \ .06 \ \boxed{\times} \ 1.5 \ \boxed{=} \ \boxed{\text{M}^+} \ \text{CE/C} \ 540 \ \boxed{\div} \ \text{MRC} \ \boxed{=} \ \Rightarrow 6000$$

Using repeated division, divide 540 by both .06 and 1.5:

$$\boxed{\text{AC}} \ 540 \ \boxed{\div} \ .06 \ \boxed{\div} \ 1.5 \ \boxed{=} \ \Rightarrow 6000$$

With a business or scientific calculator and parentheses, group the calculation in the denominator using parentheses:

$$\boxed{\text{AC}} \ 540 \ \boxed{\div} \ \boxed{(} \ .06 \ \boxed{\times} \ 1.5 \ \boxed{)} \ \boxed{=} \ \Rightarrow 6000$$

---

## EXAMPLE 3

The 7th Inning borrowed $2,400 at 7% simple interest per year to buy new tables for Brubaker's Restaurant. If it paid $420 interest, what was the duration of the loan?

$$T = \frac{I}{PR}$$

$$T = \frac{\$420}{\$2,400(0.07)} = 2.5 \text{ years}$$

*T* is unknown. Select the correct form of the simple interest formula. Replace letters with known values: $I = \$420$, $P = \$2,400$, $R = 0.07$.

Perform the operations.

**The duration of the loan is 2.5 years.**

---

## TIP

**Is the Answer Reasonable?**

Suppose in the previous example we had mistakenly made the following calculations:

$$420 \div 2400 \times 0.07 = \Rightarrow 0.01225$$

Is it reasonable to think that $420 in interest would be paid on a $2,400 loan that is made for such a small portion of a year? The interest on a 10% loan for one year would be $240. The interest on a 10% loan for two years would be $480. This type of reasoning draws attention to an unreasonable answer.

You can reexamine your steps to discover that you should have used your memory function, repeated division, or your parentheses keys.

1. What is the simple interest rate of a loan of $2,680 for $2\frac{1}{2}$ years if $636.50 interest is paid?

2. Find the simple interest rate of a loan of $5,000 that is made for three years and requires $1,762.50 in interest.

3. How much money is borrowed if the interest rate is $9\frac{1}{4}\%$ simple interest and the loan is made for 3.5 years and has $904.88 interest?

4. A loan of $16,840 is borrowed at 9% simple interest and is repaid with $4,167.90 interest. What is the duration of the loan?

## 11-1 SECTION EXERCISES

### SKILL BUILDERS

1. Find the interest paid on a loan of $2,400 for one year at a simple interest rate of 11% per year.

2. Find the interest paid on a loan of $800 at $8\frac{1}{2}\%$ annual simple interest for two years.

3. How much interest will have to be paid on a loan of $7,980 for two years at a simple interest rate of 6.2% per year?

4. Find the total amount of money (maturity value) that the borrower will pay back on a loan of $1,400 at $12\frac{1}{2}\%$ annual simple interest for three years.

5. Find the maturity value of a loan of $2,800 after three years. The loan carries a simple interest rate of 7.5% per year.

6. Susan Duke borrowed $20,000 for four years to purchase a car. The simple interest loan has a rate of 8.2% per year. What is the maturity value of the loan?

*Convert to years, expressed in decimal form to the nearest hundredth.*

7. 9 months

8. 40 months

9. A loan is made for 18 months. Convert the time to years.

10. Express 28 months as years in decimal form.

### APPLICATIONS

11. Alexa May took out a $42,000 construction loan to remodel a house. The loan rate is 8.3% simple interest per year and will be repaid in six months. How much is paid back?

12. Madison Duke needed start-up money for her bakery. She borrowed $1,200 for 30 months and paid $360 simple interest on the loan. What interest rate did she pay?

**13.** Raul Fletes needed money to buy lawn equipment. He borrowed $500 for seven months and paid $53.96 in interest. What was the rate of interest?

**14.** Linda Davis agreed to lend money to Alex Luciano at a special interest rate of 9% per year, on the condition that he borrow enough that he would pay her $500 in interest over a two-year period. What was the minimum amount Alex could borrow?

**15.** Jake McAnally needed money for college. He borrowed $6,000 at 12% simple interest per year. If he paid $360 interest, what was the duration of the loan?

**16.** Keaton Smith borrowed $25,000 to purchase stock for his baseball card shop. He repaid the simple interest loan after three years. He paid interest of $6,750. What was the interest rate?

## 11-2 ORDINARY AND EXACT INTEREST

### LEARNING OUTCOMES

1 Find the exact time.
2 Find the due date.
3 Find the ordinary interest and the exact interest.
4 Make a partial payment before the maturity date.

Sometimes the time period of a loan is indicated by the beginning date and the due date of the loan rather than by a specific number of months or days. In such cases, you must first determine the time of the loan.

### 1 Find the exact time.

**Exact time:** time that is based on counting the exact number of days in a time period.

In Chapter 8, Section 3, Learning Outcome 1 we found the exact days in each month of a year. The exact number of days in a time period is called **exact time**.

**EXAMPLE 1** Find the exact time of a loan made on July 12 and due on September 12.

| | | |
|---|---|---|
| Days in July | $31 - 12 = 19$ | July has 31 days. |
| Days in August | $= 31$ | August has 31 days. |
| Days in September | $= 12$ | |
| Total days | $62$ | |

**The exact time from July 12 to September 12 is 62 days.**

Another way to calculate exact time is by using a table or calendar that assigns each day of the year a numerical value. See Table 11-1.

| HOW TO | Find the exact time of a loan using the sequential numbers table (Table 11-1) |

1. If the beginning and due dates of the loan fall within the same year, subtract the beginning date's sequential number from the due date's sequential number.

From May 15 to Oct. 15
$288 - 135 = 153$ days

2. If the beginning and due dates of the loan do not fall within the same year:

From May 15 to March 15

(a) Subtract the beginning date's sequential number from 365.

$365 - 135 = 230$

(b) Add the due date's sequential number to the difference from step 2a.

$230 + 74 = 304$ days
(non-leap year)

3. If February 29 is between the beginning and due dates, add 1 to the difference from step 1 or the sum from step 2b.

$304 + 1 = 305$ days
(leap year)

**EXAMPLE 2** Find the exact time of a loan from July 12 to September 12.

255     Sequence number for September 12
−193     Sequence number for July 12
62 days

## TABLE 11-1
Sequential Numbers for Dates of the Year

| Day of Month | Jan. | Feb. | Mar. | Apr. | May | June | July | Aug. | Sept. | Oct. | Nov. | Dec. |
|---|---|---|---|---|---|---|---|---|---|---|---|---|
| 1 | 1 | 32 | 60 | 91 | 121 | 152 | 182 | 213 | 244 | 274 | 305 | 335 |
| 2 | 2 | 33 | 61 | 92 | 122 | 153 | 183 | 214 | 245 | 275 | 306 | 336 |
| 3 | 3 | 34 | 62 | 93 | 123 | 154 | 184 | 215 | 246 | 276 | 307 | 337 |
| 4 | 4 | 35 | 63 | 94 | 124 | 155 | 185 | 216 | 247 | 277 | 308 | 338 |
| 5 | 5 | 36 | 64 | 95 | 125 | 156 | 186 | 217 | 248 | 278 | 309 | 339 |
| 6 | 6 | 37 | 65 | 96 | 126 | 157 | 187 | 218 | 249 | 279 | 310 | 340 |
| 7 | 7 | 38 | 66 | 97 | 127 | 158 | 188 | 219 | 250 | 280 | 311 | 341 |
| 8 | 8 | 39 | 67 | 98 | 128 | 159 | 189 | 220 | 251 | 281 | 312 | 342 |
| 9 | 9 | 40 | 68 | 99 | 129 | 160 | 190 | 221 | 252 | 282 | 313 | 343 |
| 10 | 10 | 41 | 69 | 100 | 130 | 161 | 191 | 222 | 253 | 283 | 314 | 344 |
| 11 | 11 | 42 | 70 | 101 | 131 | 162 | 192 | 223 | 254 | 284 | 315 | 345 |
| 12 | 12 | 43 | 71 | 102 | 132 | 163 | 193 | 224 | 255 | 285 | 316 | 346 |
| 13 | 13 | 44 | 72 | 103 | 133 | 164 | 194 | 225 | 256 | 286 | 317 | 347 |
| 14 | 14 | 45 | 73 | 104 | 134 | 165 | 195 | 226 | 257 | 287 | 318 | 348 |
| 15 | 15 | 46 | 74 | 105 | 135 | 166 | 196 | 227 | 258 | 288 | 319 | 349 |
| 16 | 16 | 47 | 75 | 106 | 136 | 167 | 197 | 228 | 259 | 289 | 320 | 350 |
| 17 | 17 | 48 | 76 | 107 | 137 | 168 | 198 | 229 | 260 | 290 | 321 | 351 |
| 18 | 18 | 49 | 77 | 108 | 138 | 169 | 199 | 230 | 261 | 291 | 322 | 352 |
| 19 | 19 | 50 | 78 | 109 | 139 | 170 | 200 | 231 | 262 | 292 | 323 | 353 |
| 20 | 20 | 51 | 79 | 110 | 140 | 171 | 201 | 232 | 263 | 293 | 324 | 354 |
| 21 | 21 | 52 | 80 | 111 | 141 | 172 | 202 | 233 | 264 | 294 | 325 | 355 |
| 22 | 22 | 53 | 81 | 112 | 142 | 173 | 203 | 234 | 265 | 295 | 326 | 356 |
| 23 | 23 | 54 | 82 | 113 | 143 | 174 | 204 | 235 | 266 | 296 | 327 | 357 |
| 24 | 24 | 55 | 83 | 114 | 144 | 175 | 205 | 236 | 267 | 297 | 328 | 358 |
| 25 | 25 | 56 | 84 | 115 | 145 | 176 | 206 | 237 | 268 | 298 | 329 | 359 |
| 26 | 26 | 57 | 85 | 116 | 146 | 177 | 207 | 238 | 269 | 299 | 330 | 360 |
| 27 | 27 | 58 | 86 | 117 | 147 | 178 | 208 | 239 | 270 | 300 | 331 | 361 |
| 28 | 28 | 59 | 87 | 118 | 148 | 179 | 209 | 240 | 271 | 301 | 332 | 362 |
| 29 | 29 | * | 88 | 119 | 149 | 180 | 210 | 241 | 272 | 302 | 333 | 363 |
| 30 | 30 | | 89 | 120 | 150 | 181 | 211 | 242 | 273 | 303 | 334 | 364 |
| 31 | 31 | | 90 | | 151 | | 212 | 243 | | 304 | | 365 |

*For centennial years (those at the turn of the century), leap years occur only when the number of the year is divisible by 400. Thus, 2000 was a leap year (2000/400 divides exactly), but 1700, 1800, and 1900 were not leap years.

**EXAMPLE 3**   A loan made on September 5 is due July 5 of the *following year*. Find (a) the exact time for the loan in a non-leap year and (b) the exact time in a leap year.

(a) *Exact time in a non-leap year*
From Table 11-1, September 5 is the 248th day.

$$\begin{array}{r} 365 \\ -248 \\ \hline 117 \text{ days} \end{array}$$   Subtract 248 from 365.
Days from September 5 through December 31

July 5 is the 186th day.
117 + 186 = 303 days   Add 117 and 186 to find the exact time of the loan.

(b) *Exact time in a leap year*
303 + 1 = 304 days   Since Feb. 29 is between the beginning and due dates, add 1 to the non-leap year total.

**Exact time is 303 days in a non-leap year and 304 days in a leap year.**

---

## STOP AND CHECK

1. Find the exact time of a loan made on April 15 and due on October 15.

2. Find the exact time of a loan made on March 20 and due on September 20.

3. Find the exact number of days of a loan made on October 14 and due on December 21.

4. A loan made on November 1 is due on March 1 of the following year. How many days are in the loan using exact time?

---

## 2   Find the due date.

Sometimes the beginning date of a loan and the time period of the loan are known and the due date must be determined.

**HOW TO**   Find the due date of a loan given the beginning date and the time period in days

1. Add the sequential number of the beginning date to the number of days in the time period.
2. If the sum is less than or equal to 365, find the date (Table 11-1) corresponding to the sum.
3. If the sum is more than 365, subtract 365 from the sum. Then find the date (Table 11-1) in the following year corresponding to the difference.
4. Adjust for February 29 in a leap year if appropriate by *subtracting* 1 from the result in step 2 or 3.

60-day loan beginning on July 1:
July 1 = Day 182
182 + 60 = 242
242nd day = August 30

**EXAMPLE 1**   Find the due date for a 90-day loan made on November 15.

From Table 11-1, November 15 is the 319th day.

$$\begin{array}{r} 319 \\ +\ 90 \\ \hline 409 \end{array}$$   Add 319 to 90 days in the time period.

409 is greater than 365, so the loan is due in the following year.

$$\begin{array}{r} 409 \\ -365 \\ \hline 44 \end{array}$$   Subtract 365 from 409.

In Table 11-1, day 44 corresponds to February 13.

**The loan is due February 13 of the following year.**

## STOP AND CHECK

1. Find the due date for a 120-day loan made on June 12.

2. What is the due date for a loan made on July 17 for 150 days?

3. Use exact time and find the due date of a $3,200 loan made on January 29 for 90 days.

4. Use exact time and find the due date of a $2,582 loan made on November 22 for 120 days.

### 3  Find the ordinary interest and the exact interest.

**Ordinary interest:** assumes 360 days per year.

**Exact interest:** assumes 365 days per year.

An interest rate is normally given as a rate *per year*. But if the time period of the loan is in days, then using the simple interest formula requires that the rate *also* be expressed as a rate *per day*. We convert a rate per year to a rate per day in two different ways, depending on whether the rate per day is to be an **ordinary interest** or an **exact interest**. Ordinary interest assumes 360 days per year; exact interest assumes 365 days per year.

> ### HOW TO  Find the ordinary interest and the exact interest
>
> 1. To find the ordinary interest, use 360 as the number of days in a year.
> 2. To find the exact interest, use 365 as the number of days in a year.

#### EXAMPLE 1
Find the ordinary interest for a loan of $500 at a 7% annual interest rate. The loan was made on March 15 and is due May 15.

| | |
|---|---|
| Exact time $= 135 - 74 = 61$ days | Find each date's sequential number in Table 11-1 and subtract. |
| $I = PRT$ | Replace with known values. |
| $I = \$500(0.07)\left(\dfrac{61}{360}\right)$ | Perform the operations. |
| $I = \$5.93$ | Round to the nearest cent. |

**The interest is $5.93.**

#### EXAMPLE 2
Find the exact interest on the loan in Example 1.

| | |
|---|---|
| Exact time $= 61$ days | |
| $I = PRT$ | Replace with known values. |
| $I = \$500(0.07)\left(\dfrac{61}{365}\right)$ | Perform the operations. |
| $I = \$5.85$ | Round to the nearest cent. |

**The interest is $5.85.**

> ### TIP
>
> **Make Comparisons Quickly by Storing Common Portions of Problems**
>
> The two preceding examples can be calculated and compared using the memory function of a calculator.
>
> Be sure memory is clear or equal to 0 before you begin. Store the first calculation $(500 \times 0.07)$ in memory.
>
> $\boxed{AC}$ $500$ $\boxed{\times}$ $.07$ $\boxed{=}$ $\boxed{M^+}$
>
> $\boxed{AC}$ $\boxed{MR}$ $\boxed{\times}$ $61$ $\boxed{\div}$ $360$ $\boxed{=}$ $\Rightarrow 5.930555556$
>
> $\boxed{AC}$ $\boxed{MR}$ $\boxed{\times}$ $61$ $\boxed{\div}$ $365$ $\boxed{=}$ $\Rightarrow 5.849315068$

Note that the interest varies in the two cases. The first method illustrated, *ordinary interest,* is most often used by bankers when they are *lending* money because it yields a slightly higher amount of interest. It is sometimes called the **banker's rule**. On the other hand, when bankers *pay* interest on savings accounts, they normally use a 365-day year—exact interest—which yields the most accurate amount of interest but is less than the amount yielded by the banker's rule.

## EXAMPLE 3

Borrowing money to pay cash for large purchases is sometimes profitable when a cash discount is allowed on the purchases. Joann Jimanez purchased a computer, printer, copier, and fax machine for her consulting firm that regularly sold for $5,999. A special promotion offered the equipment for $5,890, with cash terms of 3/10, n/30. She does not have the cash to pay the bill now, but she will within the next three months. She finds a bank that will loan her the money for the equipment at 10% (using ordinary interest) for 90 days. Should she take out the loan to take advantage of the special promotion and cash discount?

| What You Know | What You Are Looking For | Solution Plan |
|---|---|---|
| Regular price: $5,999 <br> Special price: $5,890 <br> Cash discount rate: 0.03 <br> Exact term of loan: 90 days <br> Ordinary interest uses 360 days. | Should Joann Jimanez take out the loan? <br><br> Cash discount on special price, compared with interest on loan | Cash discount = special price × discount rate <br><br> Ordinary interest on loan = principal × rate × time <br><br> The principal of the loan is the net amount Joann would pay, once the cash discount is allowed on the special price, or 97% of the cash price. |

**Solution**

$$\text{Cash discount} = \$5,890(0.03)$$
$$= \$176.70$$
$$\text{Principal} = \$5,890(0.97)$$
$$= \$5,713.30$$
$$\text{Interest on loan} = \$5,713.30(0.1)\left(\frac{90}{360}\right)$$
$$= \$142.83$$
$$\text{Difference} = \$176.70 - \$142.83$$
$$= \$33.87$$

**Conclusion**

The interest on the loan is $142.83, which is $33.87 less than the cash discount of $176.70. Since the cash discount is more than the interest on the loan, Joann will not lose money by borrowing to take advantage of the discount terms of the sale. But other factors—the time she spends to take out the loan, for example—should be considered.

 **STOP AND CHECK**

1. Find the ordinary interest on a loan of $1,350 at 6.5% annual interest rate if the loan is made on March 3 and due on September 3.

2. Find the exact interest for the loan in Exercise 1.

3. Compare the interest amounts from the two methods. Which method would you guess bankers offer to borrowers?

4. Use the banker's rule to find the maturity value of a loan of $4,250 made on April 12 and repaid on October 12. The interest rate is 7.2% simple interest.

## 4 Make a partial payment before the maturity date.

Simple interest loans are intended to be paid with a lump sum payment at the maturity date. To save some interest, a borrower may decide to make one or more partial payments before the maturity date. The most common method for properly crediting a partial payment is to first apply the loan payment to the accumulated interest. The remainder of the partial payment is applied to the principal. This process is called the **U. S. Rule**.

Some states have passed legislation that forbids a lender from charging interest on interest. That means if the partial payment does not cover the accumulated interest, the principal for calculating the interest cannot be increased by the unpaid interest.

**U. S. rule:** any partial loan payment first covers any interest that has accumulated. The remainder of the partial payment reduces the loan principal.

**Adjusted principal:** the remaining principal after a partial payment has been properly credited.

**Adjusted balance due at maturity:** the remaining balance due at maturity after one or more partial payments have been made.

> ### HOW TO   Find the adjusted principal and adjusted balance due at maturity for a partial payment made before the maturity date.
>
> 1. Determine the exact time from the date of the loan to the first partial payment.
> 2. Calculate the interest using the time found in Step 1.
> 3. Subtract the amount of interest found in Step 2 from the partial payment.
> 4. Subtract the remainder of the partial payment (Step 3) from the original principal. This is the **adjusted principal**.
> 5. Repeat the process with the adjusted principal if additional partial payments are made.
> 6. At maturity, calculate the interest from the last partial payment. Add this interest to the adjusted principal from the last partial payment. This is the **adjusted balance due at maturity**.

### EXAMPLE 1
Tony Powers borrows $5,000 on a 10%, 90 day note. On the 30th day, Tony pays $1,500 on the note. If ordinary interest is applied, what is Tony's adjusted principal after the partial payment? What is the adjusted balance due at maturity?

$$\$5,000(0.1)\left(\frac{30}{360}\right) = \$41.67$$  Calculate the ordinary interest on 30 days.

$$\$1,500 - \$41.67 = \$1,458.33$$  Amount of partial payment applied to principal

$$\$5,000 - \$1,458.33 = \$3,541.67$$  Adjusted principal

$$\$3,541.67(0.1)\left(\frac{60}{360}\right) = \$59.03$$  Interest on adjusted principal

$$\$3,541.67 + \$59.03 = \$3,600.70$$  Adjusted balance due at maturity

**The adjusted principal after 30 days is $3,541.67 and the adjusted balance due at maturity is $3,600.70.**

### EXAMPLE 2
How much interest was saved by making the partial payment in Example 1?

$$\$41.67 + \$59.03 = \$100.70$$  Total interest paid

$$\$5,000(0.1)\left(\frac{90}{360}\right) = \$125$$  Interest if no partial payment is made

$$\$125 - \$100.70 = \$24.30$$  Interest saved

**The interest saved by making a partial payment is $24.30.**

##  STOP AND CHECK

1. James Ligon borrowed $10,000 at 9% for 270 days with ordinary interest applied. On the 60th day he paid $3,000 on the note. What is the adjusted balance due at maturity?

2. Jennifer Raymond borrowed $5,800 on a 120 day note that required ordinary interest at 7.5%. Jennifer paid $2,500 on the note on the 30th day. How much interest did she save by making the partial payment?

# 11-2 SECTION EXERCISES

## SKILL BUILDERS

1. Find the exact interest on a loan of $32,400 at 8% annually for 30 days.

2. Find the exact interest on a loan of $12,500 at 7.75% annually for 45 days.

3. Find the exact interest on a loan of $6,000 at 8.25% annually for 50 days.

4. Find the exact interest on a loan of $9,580 at 8.5% annually for 40 days.

5. A loan made on March 10 is due September 10 of the *following year*. Find the exact time for the loan in a non-leap year and a leap year.

6. Find the exact time of a loan made on March 25 and due on November 15 of the same year.

7. A loan is made on January 15 and has a due date of October 20 during a leap year. Find the exact time of the loan.

8. Find the due date for a loan made on October 15 for 120 days.

9. A loan is made on March 20 for 180 days. Find the due date.

10. Find the due date of a loan that is made on February 10 of a leap year and is due in 60 days.

## APPLICATIONS

*Exercises 11–12: A loan for $3,000 with a simple annual interest rate of 15% was made on June 15 and was due on August 15.*

11. Find the exact interest.

12. Find the ordinary interest.

**13.** Find the adjusted balance due at maturity for a 90-day note of $15,000 at 13.8% ordinary interest if a partial payment of $5,000 is made on the 60th day of the loan.

**14.** Raul Fletes borrowed $8,500 on a 300-day note that required ordinary interest at 11.76%. Raul paid $4,250 on the note on the 60th day. How much interest did he save by making the partial payment?

## 11-3 PROMISSORY NOTES

### LEARNING OUTCOMES

1  Find the bank discount and proceeds for a simple discount note.
2  Find the true or effective interest rate of a simple discount note.
3  Find the third-party discount and proceeds for a third-party discount note.

**Promissory note:** a legal document promising to repay a loan.

**Maker:** the person or business that borrows the money.

**Payee:** the person or business loaning the money.

**Term:** the length of time for which the money is borrowed.

**Maturity date:** the date on which the loan is due to be repaid.

**Face value:** the amount borrowed.

When a business or individual borrows money, it is customary for the borrower to sign a legal document promising to repay the loan. The document is called a **promissory note**. The note includes all necessary information about the loan. The **maker** is the person borrowing the money. The **payee** is the person loaning the money. The **term** of the note is the length of time for which the money is borrowed; the **maturity date** is the date on which the loan is due to be repaid. The **face value** of the note is the amount borrowed.

### 1  Find the bank discount and proceeds for a simple discount note.

If money is borrowed from a bank at a simple interest rate, the bank sometimes collects the interest, which is also called the **bank discount**, at the time the loan is made. Thus, the maker receives the face value of the loan minus the bank discount. This difference is called the **proceeds**. Such a loan is called a **simple discount note**. Loans of this type allow the bank or payee of the loan to receive all fees and interest at the time the loan is made. This increases the yield on the loan since the interest and fees can be reinvested immediately. Besides increased yields, a bank may require this type of loan when the maker of the loan has an inadequate or poor credit history. This decreases the amount of risk to the bank or lender.

> **HOW TO**  Find the bank discount and proceeds for a simple discount note
>
> 1. For the bank discount, use:
>
> $$\text{Bank discount} = \text{face value} \times \text{discount rate} \times \text{time}$$
> $$I = PRT$$
>
> 2. For the proceeds, use:
>
> $$\text{Proceeds} = \text{face value} - \text{bank discount}$$
> $$A = P - I$$

> **EXAMPLE 1**  Find the (a) bank discount and (b) proceeds using ordinary interest on a promissory note to Mary Fisher for $4,000 at 8% annual simple interest from June 5 to September 5.
>
> (a) Exact days = 248 − 156 = 92          Subtract sequential numbers (Table 11-1).
> Bank discount = $PRT$
>
> Bank discount = $\$4,000(0.08)\left(\dfrac{92}{360}\right)$          Multiply.
>
> Bank discount = $81.78          Rounded to the nearest cent.
>
> **The bank discount is $81.78.**

(b) Proceeds $= A = P - I$
Proceeds $= \$4{,}000 - \$81.78$     Subtract the bank discount from the face value of the
Proceeds $= \$3{,}918.22$     note.

**The proceeds are \$3,918.22.**

**Undiscounted note:** another term for a simple interest note.

The difference between the simple interest note—which is also called an **undiscounted note**—and the simple discount note is the amount of money the borrower has use of for the length of the loan, and also the maturity value of the loan—the amount owed at the end of the loan term. Interest is paid on the same amount for the same period of time in both cases. In the simple interest note, the borrower has use of the full principal of the loan, but the maturity value is principal plus interest. In the simple discount note, the borrower has use of only the proceeds (face value − discount), but the maturity value is just the face value, since the interest (the discount) was paid "in advance."

Suppose Bill borrows \$5,000 with a discount (interest) rate of 10%. The discount is 10% × \$5,000, or \$500, so he gets the use of only \$4,500, though the bank charges interest on the full \$5,000. The maturity value is \$5,000.

Here is a comparison of simple interest notes versus simple discount notes:

| | Simple interest note | Simple discount note |
|---|---|---|
| Principal or face value | \$5,000 | \$5,000 |
| Interest or discount | 500 | 500 |
| Amount available to borrower or proceeds | 5,000 | 4,500 |
| Amount to be repaid or maturity value | 5,500 | 5,000 |

 **STOP AND CHECK**

1. Find the bank discount and proceeds using ordinary interest for a loan to Michelle Anders for \$7,200 at 8.25% annual simple interest from August 8 to November 8.

2. Find the bank discount and proceeds using ordinary interest for a loan to Andre Peters for \$9,250 at 7.75% annual simple interest from January 17 to July 17.

3. Find the bank discount and proceeds using ordinary interest for a loan to Megan Anders for \$3,250 at 8.75% annual simple interest from February 23 to November 23.

4. Frances Johnson is making a bank loan for \$32,800 at 7.5% annual simple interest from May 10 to July 10. Find the bank discount and proceeds using ordinary interest.

## 2   Find the true or effective interest rate of a simple discount note.

For a simple interest note, the borrower uses the full face value of the loan for the entire period of the loan. In a simple discount note, the borrower only uses the proceeds of the loan for the period of the loan. Since the proceeds are less than the face value of the loan, the stated discount rate is not the true or effective rate of interest of the note. To find the **effective interest rate of a simple discount note**, the proceeds of the loan is used as the principal in the interest formula.

**Effective interest rate for a simple discount note:** the actual interest rate based on the proceeds of the loan.

**HOW TO**   Find the true or effective interest rate of a simple discount note

1. Find the bank discount (interest).

$$I = PRT$$

2. Find the proceeds.

$$\text{Proceeds} = \text{principal} - \text{bank discount}$$

3. Find the effective interest rate.

$$R = \frac{I}{PT} \text{ using the proceeds as the principal.}$$

**EXAMPLE 1** What is the effective interest rate of a simple discount note for $5,000, at an ordinary bank discount rate of 12%, for 90 days? Round to the nearest tenth of a percent.

Find the bank discount:

$$I = PRT$$

$$I = \$5,000(0.12)\left(\frac{90}{360}\right)$$

$$I = \$150 \qquad\qquad \text{Bank discount}$$

Find the proceeds:

Proceeds = principal − bank discount
Proceeds = $5,000 − $150
Proceeds = $4,850

Find the effective interest rate:

$$R = \frac{I}{PT} \qquad\qquad \text{Substitute proceeds for principal.}$$

$$R = \frac{\$150}{\$4,850\left(\dfrac{90}{360}\right)}$$

$$R = \frac{\$150}{\$1,212.50}$$

$$R = 0.1237113402$$

$$R = 12.4\% \qquad\qquad \text{Effective interest rate}$$

**The effective interest rate for a simple discount note of $5,000 for 90 days is 12.4%.**

## STOP AND CHECK

1. What is the effective interest rate of a simple discount note for $8,000, at an ordinary bank discount rate of 11%, for 120 days? Round to the nearest tenth of a percent.

2. What is the effective interest rate of a simple discount note for $22,000, at an ordinary bank discount rate of 8.36%, for 90 days? Round to the nearest tenth of a percent.

## 3 Find the third-party discount and proceeds for a third-party discount note.

**Third party:** an investment group or individual that assumes a note that was made between two other parties.

**Third-party discount note:** a note that is sold to a third party (usually a bank) so that the original payee gets the proceeds immediately and the maker pays the third party the original amount at maturity.

**Discount period:** the amount of time that the third party owns the third-party discounted note.

Many businesses agree to be the payee for a promissory note as payment for the sale of goods. If these businesses in turn need cash, they may sell such a note to an investment group or person who is the **third party** of the note. Selling a note to a third party in return for cash is called *discounting* a note. The note is called a **third-party discount note**.

When the third party discounts a note, it gives the business owning the note the maturity value of the note minus a third-party discount. The discount is based on how long the third party holds the note, called the **discount period**. The third party receives the full maturity value of the note from the maker when it comes due. From the standpoint of the note maker (the borrower), the term of the note is the same because the maturity (due) date is the same, and the maturity value is the same.

The following diagram shows how the discount period is determined.

| Original date of loan | Date loan is discounted | Maturity date |
|---|---|---|
| July 14 | Aug. 3 | Sept. 12 |

Discount period

1. For the third-party discount, use:

Third-party discount = maturity value of original note × discount rate
× discount period

$$I = PRT$$

2. For the proceeds to the original payee, use:

Proceeds = maturity value of original note − third-party discount
$$A = P - I$$

**EXAMPLE 1** Alpine Pleasures, Inc., delivers ski equipment to retailers in July but does not expect payment until mid-September, so the retailers agree to sign promissory notes for the equipment. These notes are based on exact interest, with a 10% annual simple interest rate. One promissory note held by Alpine is for $8,000, was made on July 14, and is due September 12. Alpine needs cash, so it takes the note to an investment group. On August 3, the group agrees to buy the note at a 12% discount rate using the banker's rule (ordinary interest). Find the proceeds for the note.

A table can help you organize the facts:

| Date of original note | Principal of note | Simple interest rate | Date of discount note | Third-party discount rate | Maturity date |
|---|---|---|---|---|---|
| July 14 | $8,000 | 10% | Aug. 3 | 12% | Sept. 12 |

Calculate the time and maturity value of the original note.

| | |
|---|---|
| 255 | September 12 (Table 11-1) |
| −195 | July 14 (Table 11-1) |
| 60 days | Exact days of the original loan |
| $I = PRT$ | Use the simple interest formula to find exact interest. |
| $I = \$8,000(0.1)\left(\dfrac{60}{365}\right)$ | Use 365 days in a year. |
| $I = \$131.51$ (rounded) | |

**The simple interest for the original loan is $131.51.**

To find the maturity value, add the principal and interest.

Maturity value = principal + interest
Maturity value = $8,000 + $131.51
Maturity value = $8,131.51

**The maturity value of the original loan is $8,131.51.**

Now calculate the discount period.

Discount period = number of days from August 3 to September 12

August 3 is the 215th day.

| | |
|---|---|
| 255 | September 12 |
| −215 | August 3 |
| 40 days | Exact days of discount period |

**The discount period for the discount note is 40 days.**

Now calculate the third-party discount based on the banker's rule (ordinary interest).

Third-party discount = maturity value × third-party discount rate × discount period

Third-party discount = $8,131.51(0.12)$\left(\dfrac{40}{360}\right)$    Use 360 days in a year.

Third-party discount = $108.42

**The third-party discount is $108.42.**

Now calculate the proceeds that will be received by Alpine.

$$\text{Proceeds} = \text{maturity value} - \text{third-party discount}$$
$$\text{Proceeds} = \$8,131.51 - \$108.42$$
$$\text{Proceeds} = \$8,023.09$$

**The proceeds to Alpine are $8,023.09.**

##  STOP AND CHECK

1. Hugh's Trailers delivers trailers to retailers in February and expects payment in July. The retailers sign promissory notes based on exact interest with 8.25% annual simple interest. One promissory note held by Hugh's for $19,500 was made on February 15 and is due July 20. On May 5 a third party buys the note at a 10% discount using the banker's rule. Find the maturity exact time of the original note.

2. Find the maturity value of the original note in Exercise 1.

3. Find the third-party discount for the note in Exercise 1.

4. Find the proceeds to Hugh's Trailers for the discounted note in Exercise 1.

## 11-3 SECTION EXERCISES

### SKILL BUILDERS

*Use the banker's rule unless otherwise specified.*

1. José makes a simple discount note with a face value of $2,500, a term of 120 days, and a 9% discount rate. Find the discount.

2. Find the proceeds for Exercise 1.

3. Find the discount and proceeds on a $3,250 face-value note for six months if the discount rate is 9.2%.

4. Find the maturity value of the undiscounted promissory note shown in Figure 11-2.

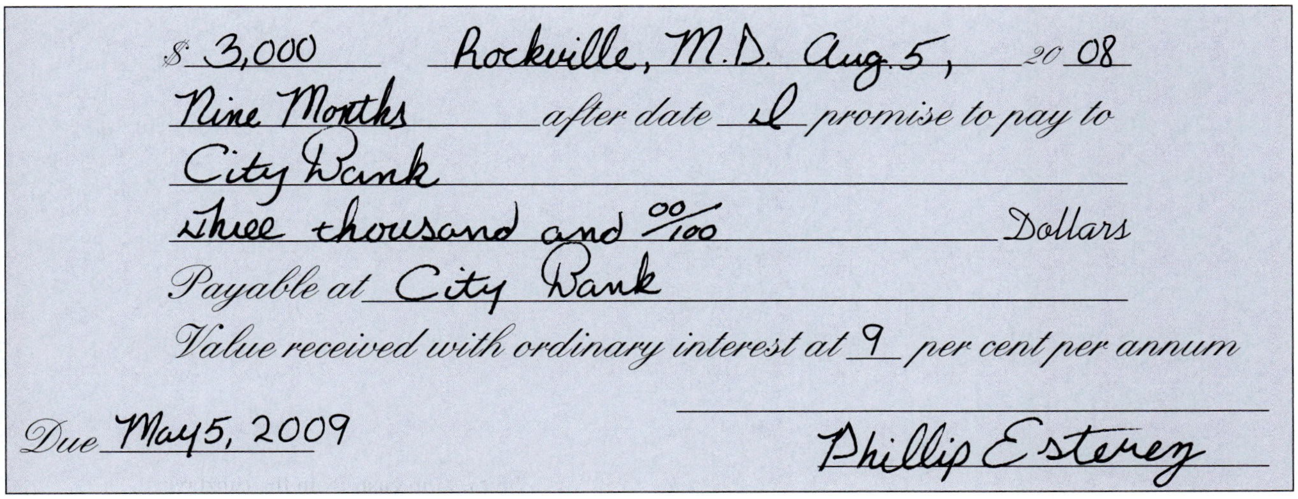
$ 3,000 Rockville, M.D. Aug. 5, 20 08

Nine Months after date I promise to pay to

City Bank

three thousand and 00/100 Dollars

Payable at City Bank

Value received with ordinary interest at 9 per cent per annum

Due May 5, 2009 Phillip Estevez

FIGURE 11-2
**Promissory Note**

5. Roland Clark has a simple discount note for $6,500, at an ordinary bank discount rate of 8.74%, for 60 days. What is the effective interest rate? Round to the nearest tenth of a percent.

6. What is the effective interest rate of a simple discount note for $30,800, at an ordinary bank discount rate of 14%, for 20 days? Round to the nearest tenth of a percent.

7. Carter Manufacturing holds a note of $5,000 that has an interest rate of 11% annually. The note was made on March 18 and is due November 13. Carter sells the note to a bank on June 13 at a discount rate of 10% annually. Find the proceeds on the third-party discount note.

8. Discuss reasons a payee might agree to a non-interest-bearing note.

9. Discuss reasons a payee would sell a note to a third party and lose money in the process.

## Learning Outcomes

## What to Remember with Examples

### Section 11-1

**1** Find simple interest using the simple interest formula. (p. 382)

1. Identify the principal, rate, and time.
2. Multiply the principal by the rate and time.

$$\text{Interest} = \text{principal} \times \text{rate} \times \text{time}$$
$$I = PRT$$

| | |
|---|---|
| Find the interest paid on a loan of \$8,400 for one year at $9\frac{1}{2}\%$ annual simple interest rate. | Find the interest paid on a loan of \$4,500 for two years at a simple interest rate of 12% per year. |
| $\text{Interest} = \text{principal} \times \text{rate} \times \text{time}$ <br> $= \$8,400(0.095)(1)$ <br> $= \$798$ | $\text{Interest} = \text{principal} \times \text{rate} \times \text{time}$ <br> $= \$4,500(0.12)(2)$ <br> $= \$1,080$ |

**2** Find the maturity value of a loan. (p. 383)

1. If the principal and interest are known, add them.

$$\text{Maturity value} = \text{principal} + \text{interest}$$
$$MV = P + I$$

2. If the principal, rate, and time are known, use either of the formulas:
   **(a)** $\text{Maturity value} = \text{principal} + \text{principal} \times \text{rate} \times \text{time}$
   $$MV = P + PRT$$

   **(b)** $\text{Maturity value} = \text{principal}\,(1 + \text{rate} \times \text{time})$
   $$MV = P(1 + RT)$$

| | |
|---|---|
| Find the maturity value of a loan of \$8,400 with \$798 interest. | Find the maturity value of a loan of \$4,500 for two years at a simple interest rate of 12% per year. |
| $MV = P + I$ <br> $MV = \$8,400 + \$798$ <br> $MV = \$9,198$ | $MV = P(1 + RT)$ <br> $MV = \$4,500[1 + 0.12(2)]$ <br> $MV = \$4,500(1.24)$ <br> $MV = \$5,580$ |

**3** Convert months to a fractional or decimal part of a year. (p. 384)

1. Write the number of months as the numerator of a fraction.
2. Write 12 as the denominator of the fraction.
3. Reduce the fraction to lowest terms if using the fractional equivalent.
4. Divide the numerator by the denominator to get the decimal equivalent of the fraction.

| | |
|---|---|
| Convert 42 months to years. | Convert 3 months to years. |
| $\dfrac{42}{12} = \dfrac{7}{2} = 3.5$ years | $\dfrac{3}{12} = \dfrac{1}{4} = 0.25$ years |

**4** Find the principal, rate, or time using the simple interest formula. (p. 386)

1. Select the appropriate form of the formula.
   **(a)** If the principal is unknown, use $P = \dfrac{I}{RT}$

   **(b)** If the rate is unknown, use $R = \dfrac{I}{PT}$

   **(c)** If the time is unknown, use $T = \dfrac{I}{PR}$

2. Replace letters with known values and perform the indicated operations.

| | |
|---|---|
| Nancy Jeggle borrowed \$6,000 for $3\frac{1}{2}$ years and paid \$2,800 simple interest. What was the annual interest rate? | $R$ is unknown.<br><br>$R = \dfrac{I}{PT}$<br><br>$R = \dfrac{\$2,800}{(\$6,000)(3.5)}$<br><br>$R = 0.133$<br><br>$R = 13.3\%$ annually |
| Donna Ruscitti paid \$675 interest on an 18-month loan at 10% annual simple interest. What was the principal? | $P$ is unknown.<br><br>$P = \dfrac{I}{RT}$      $\dfrac{18}{12} = \dfrac{3}{2} = 1.5$<br><br>$P = \dfrac{\$675}{0.10(1.5)}$<br><br>$P = \$4,500$ |
| Ashish Paranjape borrowed \$1,500 at 8% annual simple interest. If he paid \$866.25 interest, what was the time period of the loan? | $T$ is unknown.<br><br>$T = \dfrac{I}{PR}$<br><br>$T = \dfrac{\$866.25}{\$1,500(0.08)}$<br><br>$T = 7.2$ years (rounded) |

## Section 11-2

**1** Find the exact time. (p. 389)

### Change months and years to exact time in days.

$$1 \text{ month} = \text{exact number of days in the month}$$
$$1 \text{ year} = 365 \text{ days (or 366 days in a leap year)}$$

| |
|---|
| Find the exact time of a loan made October 1 and due May 1 (non-leap year).<br><br>October, December, January, and March have 31 days. November and April have 30 days. February has 28 days.<br><br>$4(31) + 2(30) + 28 = 212 \text{ days}$ |

### Find the exact time of a loan using the sequential numbers table (Table 11-1).

1. If the beginning and due dates of the loan fall within the same year, subtract the beginning date's sequential number from the due date's sequential number.
2. If the beginning and due dates of the loan do not fall within the same year:
   (a) Subtract the beginning date's sequential number from 365.
   (b) Add the due date's sequential number to the difference from step 2a.
3. If February 29 is between the beginning and due dates, add 1 to the difference from step 1 or to the sum from step 2b.

| | |
|---|---|
| Find the exact time of a loan made on March 25 and due on October 10.<br><br>October 10 = day 283<br>March 25 = day  84<br>          199 days<br><br>The loan is made for 199 days. | Find the exact time of a loan made on June 7 and due the following March 7 in a non-leap year.<br><br>December 31 = day 365<br>June 7 = day 158<br>        207 days<br><br>March 7 =  + 66 days<br>        273 days<br><br>The loan is made for 273 days in all. |

| **2** | Find the due date. (p. 391) | **Find the due date of a loan given the beginning date and the time period in days.** |
|---|---|---|

1. Add the sequential number of the beginning date to the number of days in the time period.
2. If the sum is less than or equal to 365, find the date (Table 11-1) corresponding to the sum.
3. If the sum is more than 365, subtract 365 from the sum. Then find the date (Table 11-1) in the following year corresponding to the difference.
4. Adjust for February 29 in a leap year if appropriate by subtracting 1 from the difference.

Figure the due date for a 60-day loan made on August 12.

August 12 = day 224
$$\begin{array}{r} 224 \\ +\ 60 \\ \hline 284 \end{array}$$

Day 284 is October 11.

| **3** | Find the ordinary interest and the exact interest. (p. 392) | 1. To find the ordinary interest, use 360 as the number of days in a year. |
|---|---|---|
| | | 2. To find the exact interest, use 365 as the number of days in a year. |

On May 15, Roberta Krech borrowed $6,000 at 12.5% annual simple interest. The loan was due on November 15. Find the ordinary interest due on the loan.

Use Table 11-1 to find exact time. November 15 is day 319. May 15 is day 135. So time is 319 − 135 = 184 days.

$$I = PRT$$
$$I = (\$6,000)(0.125)\left(\frac{184}{360}\right)$$
$$I = \$383.33$$

Find the exact interest due on Roberta's loan (see above).

$$I = PRT$$
$$I = (\$6,000)(0.125)\left(\frac{184}{365}\right)$$
$$I = \$378.08$$

| **4** | Make a partial payment before the maturity date. (p. 394) | 1. Determine the exact time from the date of the loan to the first partial payment. |
|---|---|---|

2. Calculate the interest using the time found in Step 1.
3. Subtract the amount of interest found in Step 2 from the partial payment.
4. Subtract the remainder of the partial payment (Step 3) from the original principal. This is the **adjusted principal**.
5. Repeat the process with the adjusted principal if additional partial payments are made.
6. At maturity, calculate the interest from the last partial payment. Add this interest to the adjusted principal from the last partial payment. This is the **adjusted balance due at maturity**.

Tony Powers borrows $7,000 on a 12%, 90 day note. On the 60th day, Tony pays $1,500 on the note. If ordinary interest is applied, what is Tony's adjusted principal after the partial payment? What is the adjusted balance due at maturity?

$$\$7,000(0.12)\left(\frac{60}{360}\right) = \$140 \qquad \text{Calculate the ordinary interest on 60 days.}$$

$$\$1,500 - \$140 = \$1,360 \qquad \text{Amount of partial payment applied to principal}$$
$$\$7,000 - \$1,360 = \$5,640 \qquad \text{Adjusted principal}$$

$$\$5,640(0.12)\left(\frac{30}{360}\right) = \$56.40 \qquad \text{Interest on adjusted principal}$$

$$\$5,640 + \$56.40 = \$5,696.40 \qquad \text{Adjusted balance due at maturity}$$

The adjusted principal after 90 days is $5,640 and the adjusted balance due at maturity is $5,696.40.

**1** Find the bank discount and proceeds for a simple discount note. (p. 396)

1. For the bank discount, use:

$$\text{Bank discount} = \text{face value} \times \text{discount rate} \times \text{time}$$
$$I = PRT$$

2. For the proceeds, use:

$$\text{Proceeds} = \text{face value} - \text{bank discount}$$
$$A = P - I$$

The bank charged Robert Milewsky a 11.5% annual discount rate on a bank note of $1,500 for 120 days. Find the proceeds of the note using the banker's rule.

First find the discount, and then subtract the discount from the face value of $1,500.

$$\text{Discount} = I = PRT$$

$$\text{Discount} = \$1,500(0.115)\left(\frac{120}{360}\right) \qquad \text{Ordinary interest}$$

$$\text{Discount} = \$57.50$$
$$\text{Proceeds} = A = P - I$$
$$\text{Proceeds} = \$1,500 - \$57.50$$
$$\text{Proceeds} = \$1,442.50$$

**2** Find the true or effective interest rate of a simple discount note. (p. 397)

1. Find the bank discount (interest).

$$I = PRT$$

2. Find the proceeds.

$$\text{Proceeds} = \text{principal} - \text{bank discount}$$

3. Find the effective interest rate.

$$R = \frac{I}{PT} \qquad \text{Use the proceeds as the principal.}$$

Larinda Temple has a simple discount note for $5,000, at an ordinary bank discount rate of 8%, for 90 days. What is the effective interest rate? Round to the nearest tenth of a percent.

Find the bank discount:

$$I = PRT$$
$$I = \$5,000(0.08)\left(\frac{90}{360}\right)$$
$$I = \$100$$
$$\text{Proceeds} = \text{principal} - \text{bank discount}$$
$$\text{Proceeds} = \$5,000 - \$100$$
$$\text{Proceeds} = \$4,900$$
$$R = \frac{I}{PT}$$
$$R = \frac{\$100}{\$4,900\left(\dfrac{90}{360}\right)}$$
$$R = \frac{\$100}{\$1,225}$$
$$R = 0.0816326531$$
$$R = 8.1\%$$

The effective interest rate for a simple discount note of $5,000 for 90 days is 8.1%.

**3** Find the third-party discount and proceeds for a third-party discount note. (p. 398)

1. For the third-party discount, use:

$$\text{Third-party discount} = \text{maturity value of original note} \times \text{discount rate} \times \text{discount period}$$
$$I = PRT$$

2. For the proceeds, use:

$$\text{Proceeds} = \text{maturity value of original note} - \text{third-party discount}$$
$$A = P - I$$

Mihoc Trailer Sales made a note of $10,000 with Darcy Mihoc, company owner, at 9% simple interest based on exact interest. The note is made on August 12 and due on November 10. However, Mihoc Trailer Sales needs cash, so the note is taken to a third party on September 5. The third party agrees to accept the note with a 13% annual discount rate using the banker's rule. Find the proceeds of the note to the original payee.

To find the proceeds, we find the maturity value of the original note and then find the third-party discount. Exact time is 90 days (314 − 224).

$$\text{Maturity value} = P(1 + RT)$$
$$\text{Maturity value} = \$10,000\left(1 + 0.09 \cdot \frac{90}{365}\right) \quad \text{Exact interest}$$
$$\text{Maturity value} = \$10,221.92$$

Exact time of the discount period is 66 days (314 − 248). Use the banker's rule.

$$\text{Third-party discount} = I = PRT$$
$$\text{Third-party discount} = \$10,221.92(0.13)\left(\frac{66}{360}\right) \quad \text{Ordinary interest}$$
$$\text{Third-party discount} = \$243.62$$
$$\text{Proceeds} = A = P - I$$
$$\text{Proceeds} = \$10,221.92 - \$243.62$$
$$\text{Proceeds} = \$9,978.30$$

## EXERCISES SET A

## SKILL BUILDERS

*Find the simple interest. Round to the nearest cent when necessary.*

| | Principal | Annual rate | Time | Interest |
|---|---|---|---|---|
| CEL **1.** | $500 | 12% | 2 years | ____ |
| CEL **2.** | $3,575 | 11% | 3 years | ____ |

**3.** Capco, Inc., borrowed $4,275 for three years at 12% interest. (a) How much simple interest did the company pay? (b) What is the maturity value?

*Find the rate of annual simple interest in each of the following problems.*

| | Principal | Interest | Time | Rate |
|---|---|---|---|---|
| **4.** | $800 | $124 | 1 year | ____ |
| **5.** | $175 | $ 31.50 | 2 years | ____ |

*Find the time period of the loan using the formula for simple interest.*

| | Principal | Annual rate | Interest | Time |
|---|---|---|---|---|
| **6.** | $450 | 10% | $135 | ____ |
| **7.** | $1,500 | $8\frac{1}{2}$% | $478.13 | ____ |

*In each of the following problems, find the principal, based on simple interest.*

| | Interest | Annual rate | Time | Principal |
|---|---|---|---|---|
| **8.** | $300 | 3% | 2 years | ____ |
| **9.** | $90 | 3.2% | 1 year | ____ |

**10.** A loan for three years with an annual simple interest rate of 9% costs $486 interest. Find the principal.

*Write a fraction expressing each amount of time as a part of a year (12 months = 1 year).*

**11.** 7 months

**12.** 16 months

## APPLICATIONS

**13.** Carol Stoy invested $500 at 2% annually for six months. How much interest did she receive?

**14.** Find the interest paid on a loan of $1,200 for 60 days at a simple interest rate of 6% annually.

**15.** Find the interest paid on a loan of $800 for 120 days at a simple interest rate of 6% annually.

**16.** Interest figured using 360 days per year is called what kind of interest?

*Use Table 11-1 to find the exact time from the first date to the second date for non-leap years unless a leap year is identified.*

**17.** March 15 to July 10

**18.** January 27, 2008, to September 30, 2008

*If a loan is made on the given date, find the date it is due.*

**19.** January 10 for 210 days

**20.** August 12 for 60 days

*For exercise 27, find (a) the exact interest and (b) the ordinary interest. Round answers to the nearest cent.*

**21.** A loan of $1,200 at 10% annually made on October 15 and due on March 20 of the following year

**22.** Find the discount (ordinary interest) and proceeds on a promissory note for $2,000 made by Barbara Jones on February 10, 2007, and payable to First State Bank on August 10, 2007, with a discount rate of 9%.

**23.** MAK, Inc., accepted an interest-bearing note for $10,000 with 9% annual ordinary interest. The note was made on April 10 and was due December 6. MAK needed cash and took the note to First United Bank, which offered to buy the note at a discount rate of $12\frac{1}{2}$%. The transaction was made on July 7. How much cash did MAK receive for the note?

**24.** Malinda Levi borrows $12,000 on a 9.5%, 90-day note. On the 30th day, Malinda pays $4,000 on the note. If ordinary interest is applied, what is Malinda's adjusted principal after the partial payment? What is the adjusted balance due at maturity?

**25.** Shameka Bonner has a simple discount note for $11,000, at an ordinary bank discount rate of 11%, for 120 days. What is the effective interest rate? Round to the nearest tenth of a percent.

## SKILL BUILDERS

*Find the simple interest. Round to the nearest cent when necessary.*

| | Principal | Annual rate | Time | Interest |
|---|---|---|---|---|
| **CEL 1.** | $1,000 | $9\frac{1}{2}\%$ | 3 years | _____ |
| **CEL 2.** | $2,975 | $12\frac{1}{2}\%$ | 2 years | _____ |

**3.** Legan Company borrowed $15,280 at $10\frac{1}{2}\%$ for 12 years. How much simple interest did the company pay? What was the total amount paid back?

*Find the rate of annual simple interest in each of the following problems.*

| | Principal | Interest | Time | Rate |
|---|---|---|---|---|
| **4.** | $1,280 | $256 | 2 years | _____ |
| **5.** | $40,000 | $32,000 | 10 years | _____ |

*Find the time period of the loan using the formula for simple interest.*

| | Principal | Annual rate | Interest | Time |
|---|---|---|---|---|
| **6.** | $700 | 6% | $84 | _____ |
| **7.** | $3,549 | 9.2% | $979.52 | _____ |

*In each of the following problems, find the principal, based on simple interest.*

| | Interest | Annual rate | Time | Principal |
|---|---|---|---|---|
| **8.** | $56.25 | $2\frac{1}{2}\%$ | 3 years | _____ |
| **9.** | $20 | 1.25% | 2 years | _____ |

**10.** An investor earned $1,170 interest on funds invested at $9\frac{3}{4}\%$ annual simple interest for four years. How much was invested?

*Write a fraction expressing each amount of time as a part of a year (12 months = 1 year).*

**11.** 18 months

**12.** 9 months

## APPLICATIONS

**13.** Alpha Hodge borrowed $500 for three months and paid $12.50 interest. What was the annual rate of interest?

**14.** Find the ordinary interest paid on a loan of $2,100 for 90 days at a simple interest rate of 4% annually.

**15.** Find the ordinary interest paid on a loan of $15,835 for 45 days at a simple interest rate of 8.1% annually.

**16.** When the exact number of days in a year is used to figure time, it is called what kind of interest?

*Use Table 11-1 to find the exact time from the first date to the second date for non-leap years unless a leap year is identified.*

**17.** April 12 to November 15

**18.** November 12 to April 15 of the next year

**19.** February 3, 2008, to August 12, 2008

*If a loan is made on the given date, find the date it is due.*

**20.** May 30 for 240 days

**21.** June 13 for 90 days

*For problem 27, find (a) the exact interest and (b) the ordinary interest. Round answers to the nearest cent.*

**22.** A loan of $8,900 at 7.75% annually made on September 10 and due on December 10

**23.** Find the discount and proceeds using the banker's rule on a promissory note for $1,980 at 8% made by Alexa Green on January 30, 2007, and payable to Enterprise Bank on July 30, 2007.

**24.** Find the exact interest on a loan of $2,100 at 7.75% annual interest for 40 days.

**25.** Allan Stojanovich can purchase an office desk for $1,500 with cash terms of 2/10, n/30. If he can borrow the money at 12% annual simple ordinary interest for 20 days, will he save money by taking advantage of the cash discount offered?

**26.** Shaunda Sanders borrows $16,000 on a 10.8%, 120-day note. On the 60th day, Shaunda pays $10,000 on the note. If ordinary interest is applied, what is Shaunda's adjusted principal after the partial payment? What is the adjusted balance due at maturity?

**27.** Bam Doyen has a simple discount note for $6,250, at an ordinary bank discount rate of 9%, for 90 days. What is the effective interest rate? Round to the nearest tenth of a percent.

# PRACTICE TEST

1. Find the simple interest on $500 invested at 4% annually for three years.

2. How much money was borrowed at 12% annually for 6 months if the interest was $90?

3. A loan of $3,000 was made for 210 days. If ordinary interest is $218.75, find the rate.

4. A loan of $5,000 at 12% annually requires $1,200 interest. For how long is the money borrowed?

5. Find the exact time from February 13 to November 27 in a non-leap year.

6. Find the exact time from October 12 to March 28 of the following year (a leap year).

7. Find the exact time from January 28, 2008, to July 5, 2008.

8. Sondra Davis borrows $6,000 on a 10%, 120 day note. On the 60th day, Sondra pays $2,000 on the note. If ordinary interest is applied, what is Sondra's adjusted principal after the partial payment? What is the adjusted balance due at maturity?

9. Find the ordinary interest on a loan of $2,800 at 10% annually made on March 15 for 270 days.

10. A bread machine with a cash price of $188 can be purchased with a one-year loan at 10% annual simple interest. Find the total amount to be repaid.

11. A copier that originally cost $3,000 was purchased with a loan for 12 months at 15% annual simple interest. What was the *total* cost of the copier?

12. Find the exact interest on a loan of $850 at 11% annually. The loan was made January 15 and was due March 15.

**13.** Michael Denton has a simple discount note for $2,000, at an ordinary bank discount rate of 12%, for 240 days. What is the effective interest rate? Round to the nearest tenth of a percent.

**14.** Find the duration of a loan of $3,000 if the loan required interest of $213.75 and was at a rate of $9\frac{1}{2}\%$ annual simple interest.

**15.** Find the rate of simple interest on a $1,200 loan that requires the borrower to repay a total of $1,302 after one year.

**16.** A promissory note using the banker's rule has a face value of $5,000 and is discounted by the bank at the rate of 14%. If the note is made for 180 days, find the discount of the note.

**17.** Find the ordinary interest paid on a loan of $1,600 for 90 days at a simple interest rate of 13% annually.

**18.** Jerry Brooks purchases office supplies totaling $1,890. He can take advantage of cash terms of 2/10, n/30 if he obtains a short-term loan. If he can borrow the money at $10\frac{1}{2}\%$ annual simple ordinary interest for 20 days, will he save money if he borrows to take advantage of the cash discount? How much will he save?

**19.** Find the exact interest on a loan of $25,000 at $8\frac{1}{2}\%$ annually for 21 days.

**20.** Find the exact interest on a loan of $1,510 at $7\frac{3}{4}\%$ annual interest for 27 days.

1. In applying most formulas involving a rate, a fractional or decimal equivalent of the rate is used. Explain how a rate can be mentally changed to a decimal equivalent.

2. When solving problems, one should devise a method to estimate the solution. Describe a strategy for estimating the interest in the first example of Section 11-1 on page 382.

3. Explain how the rate can be estimated in Example 1 on page 386.

4. Use the formula $I = P\left(R \times \dfrac{D}{365}\right)$ to find the exact interest on $100 for 30 days and 7.50%.

5. Find the exact interest on $1,000 for 60 days at 5.3% annual interest rate.

6. The ordinary interest using exact time (banker's rule) will always be higher than exact interest using exact time. Explain why this is true.

7. Show how the formulas $I = PRT$ and $MV = P + I$ lead to the formula $MV = P(I + RT)$.

8. The maturity value for a loan of $2,000 at 9% interest for two years was found to be $4,360. Examine the solution to identify the incorrect mathematical process. Explain the correct process and rework the problem correctly.

$$MV = P(1 + RT)$$
$$MV = \$2{,}000(1 + 0.09 \times 2)$$
$$MV = \$2{,}000(1.09 \times 2)$$
$$MV = \$2{,}000(2.18)$$
$$MV = \$4{,}360$$

## Challenge Problem

A simple interest loan with a final "balloon payment" can be a good deal for both the consumer and the banker. For the banker, this loan reduces the rate risk, since the loan rate is locked in for a short period of time. For the consumer, this loan allows lower monthly payments.

You borrow $5,000 at 13% simple interest rate for a year.

For 12 monthly payments:

$$\$5{,}000(13\%)(1) = \$650 \text{ interest}$$

$$\frac{\$5{,}650}{12} = \$470.83 \text{ monthly payment}$$

Your banker offers to make the loan as if it is to be extended over five years but with interest for only one year, or 60 monthly payments, but with a final balloon payment on the 12th payment. This means a much lower monthly payment.

For 60 monthly payments:

$$\frac{\$5{,}650}{60} = \$94.17 \text{ monthly payment}$$

The lower monthly payment is tempting! The banker will expect you to make these lower payments for *one* year. You will actually make 11 payments of $94.17: $94.17(11) = \$1{,}035.87$, which is the amount paid during the first 11 months.

The 12th and final payment, the *balloon payment,* is the *remainder* of the loan.

$$\$5{,}650 - \$1{,}035.87 = \$4{,}614.13$$

At this time you are expected to pay the balance of the loan in the balloon payment shown above. Don't panic! Usually the loan is refinanced for another year. But beware—you may have to pay a higher interest rate for the next year.

a. Find the monthly payment for a $2,500 loan at 12% interest for one year, extended over a three-year period with a balloon payment at the end of the first year.

b. What is the amount of the final balloon payment for a $1,000 loan at 10% interest for one year, extended over five years?

c. You need a loan of $5,000 at 10% interest for one year. What is the amount of the monthly payment?

# CASE STUDIES

## 11.1 90 Days Same as Cash!

Sara has just rented her first apartment starting December 1 before beginning college in January. The apartment has washer and dryer hook-ups, so Sara wanted to buy the appliances to avoid trips to the laundromat. The Saturday newspaper had an advertisement for a local appliance store offering "90 days, same as cash!" financing. Sara asked how the financing worked and learned that she could pay for the washer and dryer anytime during the first 90 days for the purchase price plus sales tax. If she waited longer, she would have to pay the purchase price, plus sales tax, plus 26.8% annual simple interest for the first 90 days, plus 2% simple interest per month on the unpaid balance after 90 days, with minimum payments of $50 per month after the 90-day period. Together, the washer and dryer cost $699 plus the 8.25% sales tax. Sara knew that her tax refund from the IRS would be $1,000 so she bought the washer and dryer confident that she could pay off the balance within the 90 days.

1. If Sara pays off the balance within 90 days how much will she pay?

2. If Sara bought the washer and dryer on December 15, using the exact interest, what is her deadline for paying no interest in a non-leap year? In a leap year? Is the finance company likely to use exact or ordinary interest and why?

3. If Sara's IRS refund does not come until April 1, what is her payoff amount? (Assume ordinary interest and a non-leap year.)

4. How much did it cost her to pay off this loan 17 days late? What annual simple interest rate does this amount to?

## 11.2 The Price of Money

James wants to buy a flat screen television for his new apartment. He has saved $700, but still needs $500 more. The bank where he has a checking and savings account will loan him $500 at 12% annual interest using a 90-day promissory note. James also visited the PayDay Loan store to compare the cost of borrowing. The manager told James that he could borrow $500 at 12% for two weeks. If James needed more time to repay the loan, he would be charged 16% on the balance due for each additional week. He wondered how much it would cost to pay the loan back in 12 weeks so he could compare the cost to the bank's lending rate. He recognized that 12 weeks is a few days less than 90 days.

1. Calculate the total cost (principal plus interest) for the 90-day promissory note from the bank.

2. How much will James pay if he gets the loan from the PayDay Loan store and pays the balance back in two weeks?

**3.** How much will it cost if James gets his loan from the PayDay Loan store and pays it back in 12 weeks (nearly 90 days)?

**4.** James wondered how PayDay Loan can stay in business unless its customers neglect to determine how much they owe before agreeing to borrow. What do you think? When would a PayDay loan be an appropriate choice?

# 11.3  Quality Photo Printing

As a professional photographer, Jillian had seen a significant shift in customer demand for digital technologies in photography. Many customers, attempting to save a few dollars, had invested in low-end digital cameras (and even lower-end printers) to avoid processing fees typically associated with printing photographs. The end result, for most customers, was a bounty of digital photographic images but with limited options for creating quality printed digital photographs. Jillian was hoping to tap into this underserved market by offering customers superior quality digital printing using advanced pigment inks to produce exquisite color prints. In order to provide this service, Jillian needs to purchase a state-of-the-art photo printer she found listed through a photography supply company for $8,725, plus sales tax of 5.5%. The supply company is offering cash terms of 3/15, n/30, with a 1.5% service charge on late payments, or 90 days same as cash financing if Jillian will apply and is approved for a company credit card. If she is unable to pay within 90 days under the second option, she would have to pay 24.9% annual simple interest for the first 90 days, plus 2% simple interest per month on the unpaid balance after 90 days. Jillian has an excellent credit rating, but is not sure what to do.

1. If Jillian took the cash option and was able to pay off the printer within the 15-day discount period, how much would she save? How much would she owe?

2. If Jillian takes the 90 days same as cash option and purchases the printer on December 30 to get a current-year tax deduction, using exact time, what is her deadline for paying no interest in a non-leap year? In a leap year? Find the dates in ordinary time. Is the finance company likely to use exact or ordinary interest and why?

3. If Jillian takes the 90 days same as cash and pays within 90 days, what is her payoff amount? If she can't pay until April 30, how much additional money would she owe? (Assume ordinary interest and exact time and a non-leap year.)

4. Jillian finds financing available through a local bank. Find the bank discount and proceeds using ordinary interest and ordinary time for a 90-day promissory note for $9,200 at 8% annual simple interest. Is this enough money for Jillian to cover the purchase price of the printer? Is this a better option for Jillian to pursue, and why or why not?

# Consumer Credit

## Get Out of Debt Diet

Having trouble paying your bills? Constantly making minimum payments each month? Don't know how much you owe? Worried about getting a bad credit report? According to CardWeb.com, the average U.S. household has credit card debt of over $9,000, with interest rates ranging from the mid to high teens. Credit card companies have made running up that balance deceptively easy.

However, there are a number of steps you can take to pay off the debt and get back on track. Of course, this will require you to adjust your spending habits and become more careful about your spending.

1. **Determine what you owe.** Make a list of all the debts you have including the name of the creditor, your total balance, your minimum monthly payment, and your interest rate. This will help you determine in which order you should pay down your debts.
2. **Pay it down.** Work overtime or take on a second job and devote that income to paying down debt. Cash in CDs, pay down home equity loans, and pay down loans against retirement. Have a garage sale. Do whatever you can to earn extra money and devote that money to paying down your debt.
3. **Reduce expenses.** Eliminate any unnecessary expenses such as eating out and expensive entertainment. Clip coupons, shop at sales, and avoid impulse purchases. Brown bag it at work and be creative about gifts. Above all, stop using credit cards. Just giving up that expensive cup of coffee each morning can save you more than $750 dollars a year.
4. **Record your spending.** This is actually your key to getting out of debt. You're in debt because you spent money you didn't have. Avoiding more debt starts with knowing what you are spending your money on. Each day for at least one month, write down every amount you spend, no matter how small. Reviewing how you spend your money allows you to set priorities.
5. **Make a budget based on your spending record.** Write down the amount you spent in each category of spending last month as you budget for spending for the next month. Categorize your monthly expenses into logical groups such as *necessities* (food, rent, medicine, pet food, etc.), *should have* (things you need but not immediately, such as new workout gear), and *like to have* (things you don't need but enjoy (magazines, cable television). One expense should be paying off your debt. Did you know that making a minimum payment of $26 on a single credit card with a $1,000 balance and 19% interest will take more than five years to pay off?
6. **Pay cash.** This results in a significant savings in terms of what you purchase and not having to pay interest on those purchases. When you don't have the cash, you don't buy.
7. **Resolve to spend less than you make.** Realize once and for all that if you can't pay for it today then you can't afford it.

Managing your credit and knowing exactly how much you are paying for using credit are important concepts that you will learn in this chapter.

## LEARNING OUTCOMES

### 12-1 Installment Loans and Closed-End Credit

1. Find the amount financed, the installment price, and the finance charge of an installment loan.
2. Find the installment payment of an installment loan.
3. Find the estimated annual percentage rate (APR) using a table.

### 12-2 Paying a Loan Before It Is Due: The Rule of 78

1. Find the interest refund using the rule of 78.

### 12-3 Open-End Credit

1. Find the finance charge and new balance using the average daily balance method.
2. Find the finance charge and new balance using the unpaid or previous month's balance.

 Two corresponding Business Math Case Videos for this chapter, *Which Credit Card Deal is Best?* and *Should I Buy or Lease a Car?* can be found in Appendix A.

Many individuals and businesses make purchases for which they do not pay the full amount at the time of purchase. These purchases are paid for by paying a portion of the amount owed in regular payments until the loan is completely paid. This type of loan or credit is often referred to as **consumer credit**.

In the preceding chapters we discussed the interest to be paid on loans that are paid in full on the date of maturity of the loan. Many times, loans are made so that the maker (the borrower) pays a given amount in regular payments. Loans with regular payments are called **installment loans**.

There are two kinds of installment loans. **Closed-end credit** is a type of loan in which the amount borrowed plus interest is repaid in a specified number of equal payments. Examples include bank loans and loans for large purchases such as cars and appliances. **Open-end credit** is a type of loan in which there is no fixed number of payments—the person keeps making payments until the amount is paid off, and the interest is computed on the unpaid balance at the end of each payment period. Credit card accounts, retail store accounts, and line-of-credit accounts are types of open-end credit.

## 12-1 INSTALLMENT LOANS AND CLOSED-END CREDIT

### LEARNING OUTCOMES

1 Find the amount financed, the installment price, and the finance charge of an installment loan.
2 Find the installment payment of an installment loan.
3 Find the estimated annual percentage rate (APR) using a table.

Should you or your business take out an installment loan? That depends on the interest you will pay and how it is computed. The interest associated with an installment loan is part of the charges referred to as **finance charges** or **carrying charges**. In addition to accrued interest charges, installment loans often include charges for insurance, credit-report fees, or loan fees. Under the truth-in-lending law, all of these charges must be disclosed in writing to the consumer.

### 1 Find the amount financed, the installment price, and the finance charge of an installment loan.

The **cash price** is the price you pay if you pay all at once at the time of the purchase. If you pay on an installment basis instead, the **down payment** is a partial payment of the cash price at the time of the purchase. The **amount financed** is the cash price minus the down payment. The **installment payment** is the amount you pay each period, including interest, to pay off the loan. The **installment price** is the total paid, including all of the installment payments, the finance charges, and the down payment.

> **HOW TO** Find the amount financed and the installment price
>
> 1. Find the amount financed: Subtract the down payment from the cash price.
>
> $$\text{Amount financed} = \text{cash price} - \text{down payment}$$
>
> 2. Find the installment price: Add the down payment to the total of the installment payments.
>
> $$\text{Installment price} = \text{total of installment payments} + \text{down payment}$$

**EXAMPLE 1** The 7th Inning purchased a mat cutter for the framing department on the installment plan with a $600 down payment and 12 payments of $145.58. Find the installment price of the mat cutter.

$$\begin{array}{c}\text{Total of}\\ \text{installment}\\ \text{payments}\end{array} = \begin{pmatrix}\text{number of}\\ \text{installments}\end{pmatrix} \times \begin{pmatrix}\text{installment}\\ \text{payment}\end{pmatrix}$$

$$= \quad 12 \quad \times \quad \$145.58$$

$$= \$1,746.96$$

$$\text{Installment price} = \text{total of installment payments} + \text{down payment}$$
$$= \$1,746.96 + \$600$$
$$= \$2,346.96$$

**The installment price is $2,346.96.**

## HOW TO    Find the finance charge of an installment loan

1. Determine the cash price of the item.
2. Find the installment price of the item.
3. Subtract the result found in step 2 from the result of step 1.

$$\text{Finance charge} = \text{installment price} - \text{cash price}$$

### EXAMPLE 2
If the cash price of the mat cutter in Example 1 was $2,200, find the finance charge and the amount financed.

| | |
|---|---|
| Finance charge $=$ installment price $-$ cash price | Installment price $= \$2,346.96$ |
| $= \$2,346.96 - \$2,200.00$ | Cash price $= \$2,200.00$ |
| $= \$146.96$ | Down payment $= \$600$ |

$$\text{Amount financed} = \text{cash price} - \text{down payment.}$$
$$= \$2,200 - \$600$$
$$= \$1,600$$

**The finance charge is $146.96 and the amount financed is $1,600.**

## STOP AND CHECK

1. An ice machine with a cash price of $1,095 is purchased on the installment plan with a $100 down payment and 18 monthly payments of $62.50. Find the amount financed, installment price, and finance charge for the machine.

2. A copy machine is purchased on the installment plan with a $200 down payment and 24 monthly payments of $118.50. The cash price is $2,695. Find the amount financed, installment price, and finance charge for the machine.

3. An industrial freezer with a cash price of $2,295 is purchased on the installment plan with a $275 down payment and 30 monthly installment payments of $78.98. Find the amount financed, installment price, and finance charge for the freezer.

4. The cash price of a music system is $2,859 and the installment price is $3,115.35. How much is the finance charge?

## 2   Find the installment payment of an installment loan.

Since the installment price is the total of the installment payments plus the down payment, we can find the installment payment if we know the installment price, the down payment, and the number of payments.

### HOW TO    Find the installment payment, given the installment price, the down payment, and the number of payments

1. Find the total of the installment payments: Subtract the down payment from the installment price.

$$\text{Total of installment payments} = \text{installment price} - \text{down payment}$$

2. Divide the total of the installment payments by the number of installment payments.

$$\text{Installment payment} = \frac{\text{total of installment payments}}{\text{number of payments}}$$

## EXAMPLE 1

The installment price of a drafting table was $1,627 for a 12-month loan. If a $175 down payment had been made, find the installment payment.

Total of installment payments = installment price − down payment

$$= \$1,627 - \$175 = \$1,452 \qquad \text{Subtract.}$$

$$\text{Installment payment} = \frac{\text{total of installment payments}}{\text{number of payments}}$$

$$= \frac{\$1,452}{12} = \$121 \qquad \text{Divide.}$$

**The installment payment is $121.**

 ## STOP AND CHECK

1. The installment price of a refrigerator is $2,087 for a 24-month loan. If a down payment of $150 had been made, what is the installment payment?

2. The installment price of a piano is $8,997.40 and a down payment of $1,000 is made. What is the monthly installment payment if the piano is financed for 36 months?

3. The installment price of a tire machine is $2,795.28. A down payment of $600 is made. What is the installment payment if the machine is financed for 36 months?

4. Find the installment payment for a trailer if its installment price is $3,296.96 over 30 months and an $800 down payment is made.

## 3  Find the estimated annual percentage rate (APR) using a table.

In 1969 the federal government passed the Consumer Credit Protection Act, Regulation Z, also known as the Truth-in-Lending Act. It requires that a lending institution tell the borrower, in writing, what the actual annual rate of interest is as it applies to the balance due on the loan each period. This interest rate tells the borrower the true cost of the loan.

For example, if you borrowed $1,500 for a year and paid an interest charge of $165, you would be paying an interest rate of 11% annually on the entire $1,500 (165 ÷ $1,500 = 0.11 = 11%). But if you paid the money back in 12 monthly installments of $138.75 ([$1,500 + $165] ÷ 12 = $138.75), you would not have the use of the $1,500 for a full year. Instead, you would be paying it back in 12 payments of $138.75 each. Thus, you are losing the use of some of the money every month but are still paying interest at the rate of 11% of *the entire amount*. This means that you are actually paying *more than* 11% interest. The true rate is the **annual percentage rate (APR)**. Applied to installment loans, the APR is the *annual simple interest rate equivalent* that is actually being paid on the unpaid balances. The APR can be determined using a government-issued table.

The federal government issues annual percentage rate tables, which are used to find APR rates (within $\frac{1}{4}\%$, which is the federal standard). A portion of one of these tables, based on the number of monthly payments, is shown in Table 12-1.

**Annual percentage rate (APR):** the true rate of an installment loan that is equivalent to an annual simple interest rate.

## HOW TO  Find the estimated annual percentage rate using a per $100 of amount financed table

1. Find the interest per $100 of amount financed: Divide the finance charge including interest by the amount financed and multiply by $100.

$$\text{Interest per } \$100 = \frac{\text{finance charge}}{\text{amount financed}} \times \$100$$

2. Find the row corresponding to the number of monthly payments. Move across the row to find the number closest to the value from step 1. Read up the column to find the annual percentage rate for that column. If the result in step 1 is exactly halfway between two table values, a rate halfway between the two rates can be used.

## TABLE 12-1
### Interest per $100 of Amount Financed

| Number of monthly payments | \multicolumn{16}{c}{APR (Annual Percentage Rate)} | | | | | | | | | | | | | | | |
|---|---|---|---|---|---|---|---|---|---|---|---|---|---|---|---|---|
| | 10.00% | 10.25% | 10.50% | 10.75% | 11.00% | 11.25% | 11.50% | 11.75% | 12.00% | 12.25% | 12.50% | 12.75% | 13.00% | 13.25% | 13.50% | 13.75% |
| 1 | 0.83 | 0.85 | 0.87 | 0.90 | 0.92 | 0.94 | 0.96 | 0.98 | 1.00 | 1.02 | 1.04 | 1.06 | 1.08 | 1.10 | 1.12 | 1.15 |
| 2 | 1.25 | 1.28 | 1.31 | 1.35 | 1.38 | 1.41 | 1.44 | 1.47 | 1.50 | 1.53 | 1.57 | 1.60 | 1.63 | 1.66 | 1.69 | 1.72 |
| 3 | 1.67 | 1.71 | 1.76 | 1.80 | 1.84 | 1.88 | 1.92 | 1.96 | 2.01 | 2.05 | 2.09 | 2.13 | 2.17 | 2.22 | 2.26 | 2.30 |
| 4 | 2.09 | 2.14 | 2.20 | 2.25 | 2.30 | 2.35 | 2.41 | 2.46 | 2.51 | 2.57 | 2.62 | 2.67 | 2.72 | 2.78 | 2.83 | 2.88 |
| 5 | 2.51 | 2.58 | 2.64 | 2.70 | 2.77 | 2.83 | 2.89 | 2.96 | 3.02 | 3.08 | 3.15 | 3.21 | 3.27 | 3.34 | 3.40 | 3.46 |
| 6 | 2.94 | 3.01 | 3.08 | 3.16 | 3.23 | 3.31 | 3.38 | 3.45 | 3.53 | 3.60 | 3.68 | 3.75 | 3.83 | 3.90 | 3.97 | 4.05 |
| 7 | 3.36 | 3.45 | 3.53 | 3.62 | 3.70 | 3.78 | 3.87 | 3.95 | 4.04 | 4.12 | 4.21 | 4.29 | 4.38 | 4.47 | 4.55 | 4.64 |
| 8 | 3.79 | 3.88 | 3.98 | 4.07 | 4.17 | 4.26 | 4.36 | 4.46 | 4.55 | 4.65 | 4.74 | 4.84 | 4.94 | 5.03 | 5.13 | 5.22 |
| 9 | 4.21 | 4.32 | 4.43 | 4.53 | 4.64 | 4.75 | 4.85 | 4.96 | 5.07 | 5.17 | 5.28 | 5.39 | 5.49 | 5.60 | 5.71 | 5.82 |
| 10 | 4.64 | 4.76 | 4.88 | 4.99 | 5.11 | 5.23 | 5.35 | 5.46 | 5.58 | 5.70 | 5.82 | 5.94 | 6.05 | 6.17 | 6.29 | 6.41 |
| 11 | 5.07 | 5.20 | 5.33 | 5.45 | 5.58 | 5.71 | 5.84 | 5.97 | 6.10 | 6.23 | 6.36 | 6.49 | 6.62 | 6.75 | 6.88 | 7.01 |
| 12 | 5.50 | 5.64 | 5.78 | 5.92 | 6.06 | 6.20 | 6.34 | 6.48 | 6.62 | 6.76 | 6.90 | 7.04 | 7.18 | 7.32 | 7.46 | 7.60 |
| 13 | 5.93 | 6.08 | 6.23 | 6.38 | 6.53 | 6.68 | 6.84 | 6.99 | 7.14 | 7.29 | 7.44 | 7.59 | 7.75 | 7.90 | 8.05 | 8.20 |
| 14 | 6.36 | 6.52 | 6.69 | 6.85 | 7.01 | 7.17 | 7.34 | 7.50 | 7.66 | 7.82 | 7.99 | 8.15 | 8.31 | 8.48 | 8.64 | 8.81 |
| 15 | 6.80 | 6.97 | 7.14 | 7.32 | 7.49 | 7.66 | 7.84 | 8.01 | 8.19 | 8.36 | 8.53 | 8.71 | 8.88 | 9.06 | 9.23 | 9.41 |
| 16 | 7.23 | 7.41 | 7.60 | 7.78 | 7.97 | 8.15 | 8.34 | 8.53 | 8.71 | 8.90 | 9.08 | 9.27 | 9.46 | 9.64 | 9.83 | 10.02 |
| 17 | 7.67 | 7.86 | 8.06 | 8.25 | 8.45 | 8.65 | 8.84 | 9.04 | 9.24 | 9.44 | 9.63 | 9.83 | 10.03 | 10.23 | 10.43 | 10.63 |
| 18 | 8.10 | 8.31 | 8.52 | 8.73 | 8.93 | 9.14 | 9.35 | 9.56 | 9.77 | 9.98 | 10.19 | 10.40 | 10.61 | 10.82 | 11.03 | 11.24 |
| 19 | 8.54 | 8.76 | 8.98 | 9.20 | 9.42 | 9.64 | 9.86 | 10.08 | 10.30 | 10.52 | 10.74 | 10.96 | 11.18 | 11.41 | 11.63 | 11.85 |
| 20 | 8.98 | 9.21 | 9.44 | 9.67 | 9.90 | 10.13 | 10.37 | 10.60 | 10.83 | 11.06 | 11.30 | 11.53 | 11.76 | 12.00 | 12.23 | 12.46 |
| 21 | 9.42 | 9.66 | 9.90 | 10.15 | 10.39 | 10.63 | 10.88 | 11.12 | 11.36 | 11.61 | 11.85 | 12.10 | 12.34 | 12.59 | 12.84 | 13.08 |
| 22 | 9.86 | 10.12 | 10.37 | 10.62 | 10.88 | 11.13 | 11.39 | 11.64 | 11.90 | 12.16 | 12.41 | 12.67 | 12.93 | 13.19 | 13.44 | 13.70 |
| 23 | 10.30 | 10.57 | 10.84 | 11.10 | 11.37 | 11.63 | 11.90 | 12.17 | 12.44 | 12.71 | 12.97 | 13.24 | 13.51 | 13.78 | 14.05 | 14.32 |
| 24 | 10.75 | 11.02 | 11.30 | 11.58 | 11.86 | 12.14 | 12.42 | 12.70 | 12.98 | 13.26 | 13.54 | 13.82 | 14.10 | 14.38 | 14.66 | 14.95 |
| 25 | 11.19 | 11.48 | 11.77 | 12.06 | 12.35 | 12.64 | 12.93 | 13.22 | 13.52 | 13.81 | 14.10 | 14.40 | 14.69 | 14.98 | 15.28 | 15.57 |
| 26 | 11.64 | 11.94 | 12.24 | 12.54 | 12.85 | 13.15 | 13.45 | 13.75 | 14.06 | 14.36 | 14.67 | 14.97 | 15.28 | 15.59 | 15.89 | 16.20 |
| 27 | 12.09 | 12.40 | 12.71 | 13.03 | 13.34 | 13.66 | 13.97 | 14.29 | 14.60 | 14.92 | 15.24 | 15.56 | 15.87 | 16.19 | 16.51 | 16.83 |
| 28 | 12.53 | 12.86 | 13.18 | 13.51 | 13.84 | 14.16 | 14.49 | 14.82 | 15.15 | 15.48 | 15.81 | 16.14 | 16.47 | 16.80 | 17.13 | 17.46 |
| 29 | 12.98 | 13.32 | 13.66 | 14.00 | 14.33 | 14.67 | 15.01 | 15.35 | 15.70 | 16.04 | 16.38 | 16.72 | 17.07 | 17.41 | 17.75 | 18.10 |
| 30 | 13.43 | 13.78 | 14.13 | 14.48 | 14.83 | 15.19 | 15.54 | 15.89 | 16.24 | 16.60 | 16.95 | 17.31 | 17.66 | 18.02 | 18.38 | 18.74 |
| 31 | 13.89 | 14.25 | 14.61 | 14.97 | 15.33 | 15.70 | 16.06 | 16.43 | 16.79 | 17.16 | 17.53 | 17.90 | 18.27 | 18.63 | 19.00 | 19.38 |
| 32 | 14.34 | 14.71 | 15.09 | 15.46 | 15.84 | 16.21 | 16.59 | 16.97 | 17.35 | 17.73 | 18.11 | 18.49 | 18.87 | 19.25 | 19.63 | 20.02 |
| 33 | 14.79 | 15.18 | 15.57 | 15.95 | 16.34 | 16.73 | 17.12 | 17.51 | 17.90 | 18.29 | 18.69 | 19.08 | 19.47 | 19.87 | 20.26 | 20.66 |
| 34 | 15.25 | 15.65 | 16.05 | 16.44 | 16.85 | 17.25 | 17.65 | 18.05 | 18.46 | 18.86 | 19.27 | 19.67 | 20.08 | 20.49 | 20.90 | 21.31 |
| 35 | 15.70 | 16.11 | 16.53 | 16.94 | 17.35 | 17.77 | 18.18 | 18.60 | 19.01 | 19.43 | 19.85 | 20.27 | 20.69 | 21.11 | 21.53 | 21.95 |
| 36 | 16.16 | 16.58 | 17.01 | 17.43 | 17.86 | 18.29 | 18.71 | 19.14 | 19.57 | 20.00 | 20.43 | 20.87 | 21.30 | 21.73 | 22.17 | 22.60 |
| 37 | 16.62 | 17.06 | 17.49 | 17.93 | 18.37 | 18.81 | 19.25 | 19.69 | 20.13 | 20.58 | 21.02 | 21.46 | 21.91 | 22.36 | 22.81 | 23.25 |
| 38 | 17.08 | 17.53 | 17.98 | 18.43 | 18.88 | 19.33 | 19.78 | 20.24 | 20.69 | 21.15 | 21.61 | 22.07 | 22.52 | 22.99 | 23.45 | 23.91 |
| 39 | 17.54 | 18.00 | 18.46 | 18.93 | 19.39 | 19.86 | 20.32 | 20.79 | 21.26 | 21.73 | 22.20 | 22.67 | 23.14 | 23.61 | 24.09 | 24.56 |
| 40 | 18.00 | 18.48 | 18.95 | 19.43 | 19.90 | 20.38 | 20.86 | 21.34 | 21.82 | 22.30 | 22.79 | 23.27 | 23.76 | 24.25 | 24.73 | 25.22 |
| 41 | 18.47 | 18.95 | 19.44 | 19.93 | 20.42 | 20.91 | 21.40 | 21.89 | 22.39 | 22.88 | 23.38 | 23.88 | 24.38 | 24.88 | 25.38 | 25.88 |
| 42 | 18.93 | 19.43 | 19.93 | 20.43 | 20.93 | 21.44 | 21.94 | 22.45 | 22.96 | 23.47 | 23.98 | 24.49 | 25.00 | 25.51 | 26.03 | 26.55 |
| 43 | 19.40 | 19.91 | 20.42 | 20.94 | 21.45 | 21.97 | 22.49 | 23.01 | 23.53 | 24.05 | 24.57 | 25.10 | 25.62 | 26.15 | 26.68 | 27.21 |
| 44 | 19.86 | 20.39 | 20.91 | 21.44 | 21.97 | 22.50 | 23.03 | 23.57 | 24.10 | 24.64 | 25.17 | 25.71 | 26.25 | 26.79 | 27.33 | 27.88 |
| 45 | 20.33 | 20.87 | 21.41 | 21.95 | 22.49 | 23.03 | 23.58 | 24.12 | 24.67 | 25.22 | 25.77 | 26.32 | 26.88 | 27.43 | 27.99 | 28.55 |
| 46 | 20.80 | 21.35 | 21.90 | 22.46 | 23.01 | 23.57 | 24.13 | 24.69 | 25.25 | 25.81 | 26.37 | 26.94 | 27.51 | 28.08 | 28.65 | 29.22 |
| 47 | 21.27 | 21.83 | 22.40 | 22.97 | 23.53 | 24.10 | 24.68 | 25.25 | 25.82 | 26.40 | 26.98 | 27.56 | 28.14 | 28.72 | 29.31 | 29.89 |
| 48 | 21.74 | 22.32 | 22.90 | 23.48 | 24.06 | 24.64 | 25.23 | 25.81 | 26.40 | 26.99 | 27.58 | 28.18 | 28.77 | 29.37 | 29.97 | 30.57 |
| 49 | 22.21 | 22.80 | 23.39 | 23.99 | 24.58 | 25.18 | 25.78 | 26.38 | 26.98 | 27.59 | 28.19 | 28.80 | 29.41 | 30.02 | 30.63 | 31.24 |
| 50 | 22.69 | 23.29 | 23.89 | 24.50 | 25.11 | 25.72 | 26.33 | 26.95 | 27.56 | 28.18 | 28.80 | 29.42 | 30.04 | 30.67 | 31.29 | 31.92 |
| 51 | 23.16 | 23.78 | 24.40 | 25.02 | 25.64 | 26.26 | 26.89 | 27.52 | 28.15 | 28.78 | 29.41 | 30.05 | 30.68 | 31.32 | 31.96 | 32.60 |
| 52 | 23.64 | 24.27 | 24.90 | 25.53 | 26.17 | 26.81 | 27.45 | 28.09 | 28.73 | 29.38 | 30.02 | 30.67 | 31.32 | 31.98 | 32.63 | 33.29 |
| 53 | 24.11 | 24.76 | 25.40 | 26.05 | 26.70 | 27.35 | 28.00 | 28.66 | 29.32 | 29.98 | 30.64 | 31.30 | 31.97 | 32.63 | 33.30 | 33.97 |
| 54 | 24.59 | 25.25 | 25.91 | 26.57 | 27.23 | 27.90 | 28.56 | 29.23 | 29.91 | 30.58 | 31.25 | 31.93 | 32.61 | 33.29 | 33.98 | 34.66 |
| 55 | 25.07 | 25.74 | 26.41 | 27.09 | 27.77 | 28.44 | 29.13 | 29.81 | 30.50 | 31.18 | 31.87 | 32.56 | 33.26 | 33.95 | 34.65 | 35.35 |
| 56 | 25.55 | 26.23 | 26.92 | 27.61 | 28.30 | 28.99 | 29.69 | 30.39 | 31.09 | 31.79 | 32.49 | 33.20 | 33.91 | 34.62 | 35.33 | 36.04 |
| 57 | 26.03 | 26.73 | 27.43 | 28.13 | 28.84 | 29.54 | 30.25 | 30.97 | 31.68 | 32.39 | 33.11 | 33.83 | 34.56 | 35.28 | 36.01 | 36.74 |
| 58 | 26.51 | 27.23 | 27.94 | 28.66 | 29.37 | 30.10 | 30.82 | 31.55 | 32.27 | 33.00 | 33.74 | 34.47 | 35.21 | 35.95 | 36.69 | 37.43 |
| 59 | 27.00 | 27.72 | 28.45 | 29.18 | 29.91 | 30.65 | 31.39 | 32.13 | 32.87 | 33.61 | 34.36 | 35.11 | 35.86 | 36.62 | 37.37 | 38.13 |
| 60 | 27.48 | 28.22 | 28.96 | 29.71 | 30.45 | 31.20 | 31.96 | 32.71 | 33.47 | 34.23 | 34.99 | 35.75 | 36.52 | 37.29 | 38.06 | 38.83 |

**TABLE 12-1**
Interest per $100 of Amount Financed—*Continued*

| Number of monthly payments | APR (Annual Percentage Rate) | | | | | | | | | | | | | | | |
|---|---|---|---|---|---|---|---|---|---|---|---|---|---|---|---|---|
| | 14.00% | 14.25% | 14.50% | 14.75% | 15.00% | 15.25% | 15.50% | 15.75% | 16.00% | 16.25% | 16.50% | 16.75% | 17.00% | 17.25% | 17.50% | 17.75% |
| 1 | 1.17 | 1.19 | 1.21 | 1.23 | 1.25 | 1.27 | 1.29 | 1.31 | 1.33 | 1.35 | 1.37 | 1.40 | 1.42 | 1.44 | 1.46 | 1.48 |
| 2 | 1.75 | 1.78 | 1.82 | 1.85 | 1.88 | 1.91 | 1.94 | 1.97 | 2.00 | 2.04 | 2.07 | 2.10 | 2.13 | 2.16 | 2.19 | 2.22 |
| 3 | 2.34 | 2.38 | 2.43 | 2.47 | 2.51 | 2.55 | 2.59 | 2.64 | 2.68 | 2.72 | 2.76 | 2.80 | 2.85 | 2.89 | 2.93 | 2.97 |
| 4 | 2.93 | 2.99 | 3.04 | 3.09 | 3.14 | 3.20 | 3.25 | 3.30 | 3.36 | 3.41 | 3.46 | 3.51 | 3.57 | 3.62 | 3.67 | 3.73 |
| 5 | 3.53 | 3.59 | 3.65 | 3.72 | 3.78 | 3.84 | 3.91 | 3.97 | 4.04 | 4.10 | 4.16 | 4.23 | 4.29 | 4.35 | 4.42 | 4.48 |
| 6 | 4.12 | 4.20 | 4.27 | 4.35 | 4.42 | 4.49 | 4.57 | 4.64 | 4.72 | 4.79 | 4.87 | 4.94 | 5.02 | 5.09 | 5.17 | 5.24 |
| 7 | 4.72 | 4.81 | 4.89 | 4.98 | 5.06 | 5.15 | 5.23 | 5.32 | 5.40 | 5.49 | 5.58 | 5.66 | 5.75 | 5.83 | 5.92 | 6.00 |
| 8 | 5.32 | 5.42 | 5.51 | 5.61 | 5.71 | 5.80 | 5.90 | 6.00 | 6.09 | 6.19 | 6.29 | 6.38 | 6.48 | 6.58 | 6.67 | 6.77 |
| 9 | 5.92 | 6.03 | 6.14 | 6.25 | 6.35 | 6.46 | 6.57 | 6.68 | 6.78 | 6.89 | 7.00 | 7.11 | 7.22 | 7.32 | 7.43 | 7.54 |
| 10 | 6.53 | 6.65 | 6.77 | 6.88 | 7.00 | 7.12 | 7.24 | 7.36 | 7.48 | 7.60 | 7.72 | 7.84 | 7.96 | 8.08 | 8.19 | 8.31 |
| 11 | 7.14 | 7.27 | 7.40 | 7.53 | 7.66 | 7.79 | 7.92 | 8.05 | 8.18 | 8.31 | 8.44 | 8.57 | 8.70 | 8.83 | 8.96 | 9.09 |
| 12 | 7.74 | 7.89 | 8.03 | 8.17 | 8.31 | 8.45 | 8.59 | 8.74 | 8.88 | 9.02 | 9.16 | 9.30 | 9.45 | 9.59 | 9.73 | 9.87 |
| 13 | 8.36 | 8.51 | 8.66 | 8.81 | 8.97 | 9.12 | 9.27 | 9.43 | 9.58 | 9.73 | 9.89 | 10.04 | 10.20 | 10.35 | 10.50 | 10.66 |
| 14 | 8.97 | 9.13 | 9.30 | 9.46 | 9.63 | 9.79 | 9.96 | 10.12 | 10.29 | 10.45 | 10.67 | 10.78 | 10.95 | 11.11 | 11.28 | 11.45 |
| 15 | 9.59 | 9.76 | 9.94 | 10.11 | 10.29 | 10.47 | 10.64 | 10.82 | 11.00 | 11.17 | 11.35 | 11.53 | 11.71 | 11.88 | 12.06 | 12.24 |
| 16 | 10.20 | 10.39 | 10.58 | 10.77 | 10.95 | 11.14 | 11.33 | 11.52 | 11.71 | 11.90 | 12.09 | 12.28 | 12.46 | 12.65 | 12.84 | 13.03 |
| 17 | 10.82 | 11.02 | 11.22 | 11.42 | 11.62 | 11.82 | 12.02 | 12.22 | 12.42 | 12.62 | 12.83 | 13.03 | 13.23 | 13.43 | 13.63 | 13.83 |
| 18 | 11.45 | 11.66 | 11.87 | 12.08 | 12.29 | 12.50 | 12.72 | 12.93 | 13.14 | 13.35 | 13.57 | 13.78 | 13.99 | 14.21 | 14.42 | 14.64 |
| 19 | 12.07 | 12.30 | 12.52 | 12.74 | 12.97 | 13.19 | 13.41 | 13.64 | 13.86 | 14.09 | 14.31 | 14.54 | 14.76 | 14.99 | 15.22 | 15.44 |
| 20 | 12.70 | 12.93 | 13.17 | 13.41 | 13.64 | 13.88 | 14.11 | 14.35 | 14.59 | 14.82 | 15.06 | 15.30 | 15.54 | 15.77 | 16.01 | 16.25 |
| 21 | 13.33 | 13.58 | 13.82 | 14.07 | 14.32 | 14.57 | 14.82 | 15.06 | 15.31 | 15.56 | 15.81 | 16.06 | 16.31 | 16.56 | 16.81 | 17.07 |
| 22 | 13.96 | 14.22 | 14.48 | 14.74 | 15.00 | 15.26 | 15.52 | 15.78 | 16.04 | 16.30 | 16.57 | 16.83 | 17.09 | 17.36 | 17.62 | 17.88 |
| 23 | 14.59 | 14.87 | 15.14 | 15.41 | 15.68 | 15.96 | 16.23 | 16.50 | 16.78 | 17.05 | 17.32 | 17.60 | 17.88 | 18.15 | 18.43 | 18.70 |
| 24 | 15.23 | 15.51 | 15.80 | 16.08 | 16.37 | 16.65 | 16.94 | 17.22 | 17.51 | 17.80 | 18.09 | 18.37 | 18.66 | 18.95 | 19.24 | 19.53 |
| 25 | 15.87 | 16.17 | 16.46 | 16.76 | 17.06 | 17.35 | 17.65 | 17.95 | 18.25 | 18.55 | 18.85 | 19.15 | 19.45 | 19.75 | 20.05 | 20.36 |
| 26 | 16.51 | 16.82 | 17.13 | 17.44 | 17.75 | 18.06 | 18.37 | 18.68 | 18.99 | 19.30 | 19.62 | 19.93 | 20.24 | 20.56 | 20.87 | 21.19 |
| 27 | 17.15 | 17.47 | 17.80 | 18.12 | 18.44 | 18.76 | 19.09 | 19.41 | 19.74 | 20.06 | 20.39 | 20.71 | 21.04 | 21.37 | 21.69 | 22.02 |
| 28 | 17.80 | 18.13 | 18.47 | 18.80 | 19.14 | 19.47 | 19.81 | 20.15 | 20.48 | 20.82 | 21.16 | 21.50 | 21.84 | 22.18 | 22.52 | 22.86 |
| 29 | 18.45 | 18.79 | 19.14 | 19.49 | 19.83 | 20.18 | 20.53 | 20.88 | 21.23 | 21.58 | 21.94 | 22.29 | 22.64 | 22.99 | 23.35 | 23.70 |
| 30 | 19.10 | 19.45 | 19.81 | 20.17 | 20.54 | 20.90 | 21.26 | 21.62 | 21.99 | 22.35 | 22.72 | 23.08 | 23.45 | 23.81 | 24.18 | 24.55 |
| 31 | 19.75 | 20.12 | 20.49 | 20.87 | 21.24 | 21.61 | 21.99 | 22.37 | 22.74 | 23.12 | 23.50 | 23.88 | 24.26 | 24.64 | 25.02 | 25.40 |
| 32 | 20.40 | 20.79 | 21.17 | 21.56 | 21.95 | 22.33 | 22.72 | 23.11 | 23.50 | 23.89 | 24.28 | 24.68 | 25.07 | 25.46 | 25.86 | 26.25 |
| 33 | 21.06 | 21.46 | 21.85 | 22.25 | 22.65 | 23.06 | 23.46 | 23.86 | 24.26 | 24.67 | 25.07 | 25.48 | 25.88 | 26.29 | 26.70 | 27.11 |
| 34 | 21.72 | 22.13 | 22.54 | 22.95 | 23.37 | 23.78 | 24.19 | 24.61 | 25.03 | 25.44 | 25.86 | 26.28 | 26.70 | 27.12 | 27.54 | 27.97 |
| 35 | 22.38 | 22.80 | 23.23 | 23.65 | 24.08 | 24.51 | 24.94 | 25.36 | 25.79 | 26.23 | 26.66 | 27.09 | 27.52 | 27.96 | 28.39 | 28.83 |
| 36 | 23.04 | 23.48 | 23.92 | 24.35 | 24.80 | 25.24 | 25.68 | 26.12 | 26.57 | 27.01 | 27.46 | 27.90 | 28.35 | 28.80 | 29.25 | 29.70 |
| 37 | 23.70 | 24.16 | 24.61 | 25.06 | 25.51 | 25.97 | 26.42 | 26.88 | 27.34 | 27.80 | 28.26 | 28.72 | 29.18 | 29.64 | 30.10 | 30.57 |
| 38 | 24.37 | 24.84 | 25.30 | 25.77 | 26.24 | 26.70 | 27.17 | 27.64 | 28.11 | 28.59 | 29.06 | 29.53 | 30.01 | 30.49 | 30.96 | 31.44 |
| 39 | 25.04 | 25.52 | 26.00 | 26.48 | 26.96 | 27.44 | 27.92 | 28.41 | 28.89 | 29.38 | 29.87 | 30.36 | 30.85 | 31.34 | 31.83 | 32.32 |
| 40 | 25.71 | 26.20 | 26.70 | 27.19 | 27.69 | 28.18 | 28.68 | 29.18 | 29.68 | 30.18 | 30.68 | 31.18 | 31.68 | 32.19 | 32.69 | 33.20 |
| 41 | 26.39 | 26.89 | 27.40 | 27.91 | 28.41 | 28.92 | 29.44 | 29.95 | 30.46 | 30.97 | 31.49 | 32.01 | 32.52 | 33.04 | 33.56 | 34.08 |
| 42 | 27.06 | 27.58 | 28.10 | 28.62 | 29.15 | 29.67 | 30.19 | 30.72 | 31.25 | 31.78 | 32.31 | 32.84 | 33.37 | 33.90 | 34.44 | 34.97 |
| 43 | 27.74 | 28.27 | 28.81 | 29.34 | 29.88 | 30.42 | 30.96 | 31.50 | 32.04 | 32.58 | 33.13 | 33.67 | 34.22 | 34.76 | 35.31 | 35.86 |
| 44 | 28.42 | 28.97 | 29.52 | 30.07 | 30.62 | 31.17 | 31.72 | 32.28 | 32.83 | 33.39 | 33.95 | 34.51 | 35.07 | 35.63 | 36.19 | 36.76 |
| 45 | 29.11 | 29.67 | 30.23 | 30.79 | 31.36 | 31.92 | 32.49 | 33.06 | 33.63 | 34.20 | 34.77 | 35.35 | 35.92 | 36.50 | 37.08 | 37.66 |
| 46 | 29.79 | 30.36 | 30.94 | 31.52 | 32.10 | 32.68 | 33.26 | 33.84 | 34.43 | 35.01 | 35.60 | 36.19 | 36.78 | 37.37 | 37.96 | 38.56 |
| 47 | 30.48 | 31.07 | 31.66 | 32.25 | 32.84 | 33.44 | 34.03 | 34.63 | 35.23 | 35.83 | 36.43 | 37.04 | 37.64 | 38.25 | 38.86 | 39.46 |
| 48 | 31.17 | 31.77 | 32.37 | 32.98 | 33.59 | 34.20 | 34.81 | 35.42 | 36.03 | 36.65 | 37.27 | 37.88 | 38.50 | 39.13 | 39.75 | 40.37 |
| 49 | 31.86 | 32.48 | 33.09 | 33.71 | 34.34 | 34.96 | 35.59 | 36.21 | 36.84 | 37.47 | 38.10 | 38.74 | 39.37 | 40.01 | 40.65 | 41.29 |
| 50 | 32.55 | 33.18 | 33.82 | 34.45 | 35.09 | 35.73 | 36.37 | 37.01 | 37.65 | 38.30 | 38.94 | 39.59 | 40.24 | 40.89 | 41.55 | 42.20 |
| 51 | 33.25 | 33.89 | 34.54 | 35.19 | 35.84 | 36.49 | 37.15 | 37.81 | 38.46 | 39.12 | 39.79 | 40.45 | 41.11 | 41.78 | 42.45 | 43.12 |
| 52 | 33.95 | 34.61 | 35.27 | 35.93 | 36.60 | 37.27 | 37.94 | 38.61 | 39.28 | 39.96 | 40.63 | 41.31 | 41.99 | 42.67 | 43.36 | 44.04 |
| 53 | 34.65 | 35.32 | 36.00 | 36.68 | 37.36 | 38.04 | 38.72 | 39.41 | 40.10 | 40.79 | 41.48 | 42.17 | 42.87 | 43.57 | 44.27 | 44.97 |
| 54 | 35.35 | 36.04 | 36.73 | 37.42 | 38.12 | 38.82 | 39.52 | 40.22 | 40.92 | 41.63 | 42.33 | 43.04 | 43.75 | 44.47 | 45.18 | 45.90 |
| 55 | 36.05 | 36.76 | 37.46 | 38.17 | 38.88 | 39.60 | 40.31 | 41.03 | 41.74 | 42.47 | 43.19 | 43.91 | 44.64 | 45.37 | 46.10 | 46.83 |
| 56 | 36.76 | 37.48 | 38.20 | 38.92 | 39.65 | 40.38 | 41.11 | 41.84 | 42.57 | 43.31 | 44.05 | 44.79 | 45.53 | 46.27 | 47.02 | 47.77 |
| 57 | 37.47 | 38.20 | 38.94 | 39.68 | 40.42 | 41.16 | 41.91 | 42.65 | 43.40 | 44.15 | 44.91 | 45.66 | 46.42 | 47.18 | 47.94 | 48.71 |
| 58 | 38.18 | 38.93 | 39.68 | 40.43 | 41.19 | 41.95 | 42.71 | 43.47 | 44.23 | 45.00 | 45.77 | 46.54 | 47.32 | 48.09 | 48.87 | 49.65 |
| 59 | 38.89 | 39.66 | 40.42 | 41.19 | 41.96 | 42.74 | 43.51 | 44.29 | 45.07 | 45.85 | 46.64 | 47.42 | 48.21 | 49.01 | 49.80 | 50.60 |
| 60 | 39.61 | 40.39 | 41.17 | 41.95 | 42.74 | 43.53 | 44.32 | 45.11 | 45.91 | 46.71 | 47.51 | 48.31 | 49.12 | 49.92 | 50.73 | 51.55 |

**TABLE 12-1**

Interest per $100 of Amount Financed—*Continued*

| Number of monthly payments | APR (Annual Percentage Rate) | | | | | | | | | | | | | | | |
|---|---|---|---|---|---|---|---|---|---|---|---|---|---|---|---|---|
| | 18.00% | 18.25% | 18.50% | 18.75% | 19.00% | 19.25% | 19.50% | 19.75% | 20.00% | 20.25% | 20.50% | 20.75% | 21.00% | 21.25% | 21.50% | 21.75% |
| 1 | 1.50 | 1.52 | 1.54 | 1.56 | 1.58 | 1.60 | 1.62 | 1.65 | 1.67 | 1.69 | 1.71 | 1.73 | 1.75 | 1.77 | 1.79 | 1.81 |
| 2 | 2.26 | 2.29 | 2.32 | 2.35 | 2.38 | 2.41 | 2.44 | 2.48 | 2.51 | 2.54 | 2.57 | 2.60 | 2.63 | 2.66 | 2.70 | 2.73 |
| 3 | 3.01 | 3.06 | 3.10 | 3.14 | 3.18 | 3.23 | 3.27 | 3.31 | 3.35 | 3.39 | 3.44 | 3.48 | 3.52 | 3.56 | 3.60 | 3.65 |
| 4 | 3.78 | 3.83 | 3.88 | 3.94 | 3.99 | 4.04 | 4.10 | 4.15 | 4.20 | 4.25 | 4.31 | 4.36 | 4.41 | 4.47 | 4.52 | 4.57 |
| 5 | 4.54 | 4.61 | 4.67 | 4.74 | 4.80 | 4.86 | 4.93 | 4.99 | 5.06 | 5.12 | 5.18 | 5.25 | 5.31 | 5.37 | 5.44 | 5.50 |
| 6 | 5.32 | 5.39 | 5.46 | 5.54 | 5.61 | 5.69 | 5.76 | 5.84 | 5.91 | 5.99 | 6.06 | 6.14 | 6.21 | 6.29 | 6.36 | 6.44 |
| 7 | 6.09 | 6.18 | 6.26 | 6.35 | 6.43 | 6.52 | 6.60 | 6.69 | 6.78 | 6.86 | 6.95 | 7.04 | 7.12 | 7.21 | 7.29 | 7.38 |
| 8 | 6.87 | 6.96 | 7.06 | 7.16 | 7.26 | 7.35 | 7.45 | 7.55 | 7.64 | 7.74 | 7.84 | 7.94 | 8.03 | 8.13 | 8.23 | 8.33 |
| 9 | 7.65 | 7.76 | 7.87 | 7.97 | 8.08 | 8.19 | 8.30 | 8.41 | 8.52 | 8.63 | 8.73 | 8.84 | 8.95 | 9.06 | 9.17 | 9.28 |
| 10 | 8.43 | 8.55 | 8.67 | 8.79 | 8.91 | 9.03 | 9.15 | 9.27 | 9.39 | 9.51 | 9.63 | 9.75 | 9.88 | 10.00 | 10.12 | 10.24 |
| 11 | 9.22 | 9.35 | 9.49 | 9.62 | 9.75 | 9.88 | 10.01 | 10.14 | 10.28 | 10.41 | 10.54 | 10.67 | 10.80 | 10.94 | 11.07 | 11.20 |
| 12 | 10.02 | 10.16 | 10.30 | 10.44 | 10.59 | 10.73 | 10.87 | 11.02 | 11.16 | 11.31 | 11.45 | 11.59 | 11.74 | 11.88 | 12.02 | 12.17 |
| 13 | 10.81 | 10.97 | 11.12 | 11.28 | 11.43 | 11.59 | 11.74 | 11.90 | 12.05 | 12.21 | 12.36 | 12.52 | 12.67 | 12.83 | 12.99 | 13.14 |
| 14 | 11.61 | 11.78 | 11.95 | 12.11 | 12.28 | 12.45 | 12.61 | 12.78 | 12.95 | 13.11 | 13.28 | 13.45 | 13.62 | 13.79 | 13.95 | 14.12 |
| 15 | 12.42 | 12.59 | 12.77 | 12.95 | 13.13 | 13.31 | 13.49 | 13.67 | 13.85 | 14.03 | 14.21 | 14.39 | 14.57 | 14.75 | 14.93 | 15.11 |
| 16 | 13.22 | 13.41 | 13.60 | 13.80 | 13.99 | 14.18 | 14.37 | 14.56 | 14.75 | 14.94 | 15.13 | 15.33 | 15.52 | 15.71 | 15.90 | 16.10 |
| 17 | 14.04 | 14.24 | 14.44 | 14.64 | 14.85 | 15.05 | 15.25 | 15.46 | 15.66 | 15.86 | 16.07 | 16.27 | 16.48 | 16.68 | 16.89 | 17.09 |
| 18 | 14.85 | 15.07 | 15.28 | 15.49 | 15.71 | 15.93 | 16.14 | 16.36 | 16.57 | 16.79 | 17.01 | 17.22 | 17.44 | 17.66 | 17.88 | 18.09 |
| 19 | 15.67 | 15.90 | 16.12 | 16.35 | 16.58 | 16.81 | 17.03 | 17.26 | 17.49 | 17.72 | 17.95 | 18.18 | 18.41 | 18.64 | 18.87 | 19.10 |
| 20 | 16.49 | 16.73 | 16.97 | 17.21 | 17.45 | 17.69 | 17.93 | 18.17 | 18.41 | 18.66 | 18.90 | 19.14 | 19.38 | 19.63 | 19.87 | 20.11 |
| 21 | 17.32 | 17.57 | 17.82 | 18.07 | 18.33 | 18.58 | 18.83 | 19.09 | 19.34 | 19.60 | 19.85 | 20.11 | 20.36 | 20.62 | 20.87 | 21.13 |
| 22 | 18.15 | 18.41 | 18.68 | 18.94 | 19.21 | 19.47 | 19.74 | 20.01 | 20.27 | 20.54 | 20.81 | 21.08 | 21.34 | 21.61 | 21.88 | 22.15 |
| 23 | 18.98 | 19.26 | 19.54 | 19.81 | 20.09 | 20.37 | 20.65 | 20.93 | 21.21 | 21.49 | 21.77 | 22.05 | 22.33 | 22.61 | 22.90 | 23.18 |
| 24 | 19.82 | 20.11 | 20.40 | 20.69 | 20.98 | 21.27 | 21.56 | 21.86 | 22.15 | 22.44 | 22.74 | 23.03 | 23.33 | 23.62 | 23.92 | 24.21 |
| 25 | 20.66 | 20.96 | 21.27 | 21.57 | 21.87 | 22.18 | 22.48 | 22.79 | 23.10 | 23.40 | 23.71 | 24.02 | 24.32 | 24.63 | 24.94 | 25.25 |
| 26 | 21.50 | 21.82 | 22.14 | 22.45 | 22.77 | 23.09 | 23.41 | 23.73 | 24.04 | 24.36 | 24.68 | 25.01 | 25.33 | 25.65 | 25.97 | 26.29 |
| 27 | 22.35 | 22.68 | 23.01 | 23.44 | 23.67 | 24.00 | 24.33 | 24.67 | 25.00 | 25.33 | 25.67 | 26.00 | 26.34 | 26.67 | 27.01 | 27.34 |
| 28 | 23.20 | 23.55 | 23.89 | 24.23 | 24.58 | 24.92 | 25.27 | 25.61 | 25.96 | 26.30 | 26.65 | 27.00 | 27.35 | 27.70 | 28.05 | 28.40 |
| 29 | 24.06 | 24.41 | 24.27 | 25.13 | 25.49 | 25.84 | 26.20 | 26.56 | 26.92 | 27.28 | 27.64 | 28.00 | 28.37 | 28.73 | 29.09 | 29.46 |
| 30 | 24.92 | 25.29 | 25.66 | 26.03 | 26.40 | 26.77 | 27.14 | 27.52 | 27.89 | 28.26 | 28.64 | 29.01 | 29.39 | 29.77 | 30.14 | 30.52 |
| 31 | 25.78 | 26.16 | 26.55 | 26.93 | 27.32 | 27.70 | 28.09 | 28.47 | 28.86 | 29.25 | 29.64 | 30.03 | 30.42 | 30.81 | 31.20 | 31.59 |
| 32 | 26.65 | 27.04 | 27.44 | 27.84 | 28.24 | 28.64 | 29.04 | 29.44 | 29.84 | 30.24 | 30.64 | 31.05 | 31.45 | 31.85 | 32.26 | 32.67 |
| 33 | 27.52 | 27.93 | 28.34 | 28.75 | 29.16 | 29.57 | 29.99 | 30.40 | 30.82 | 31.23 | 31.65 | 32.07 | 32.49 | 32.91 | 33.33 | 33.75 |
| 34 | 28.39 | 28.81 | 29.24 | 29.66 | 30.09 | 30.52 | 30.95 | 31.37 | 31.80 | 32.23 | 32.67 | 33.10 | 33.53 | 33.96 | 34.40 | 34.83 |
| 35 | 29.27 | 29.71 | 30.14 | 30.58 | 31.02 | 31.47 | 31.91 | 32.35 | 32.79 | 33.24 | 33.68 | 34.13 | 34.58 | 35.03 | 35.47 | 35.92 |
| 36 | 30.15 | 30.60 | 31.05 | 31.51 | 31.96 | 32.42 | 32.87 | 33.33 | 33.79 | 34.25 | 34.71 | 35.17 | 35.63 | 36.09 | 36.56 | 37.02 |
| 37 | 31.03 | 31.50 | 31.97 | 32.43 | 32.90 | 33.37 | 33.84 | 34.32 | 34.79 | 35.26 | 35.74 | 36.21 | 36.69 | 37.16 | 37.64 | 38.12 |
| 38 | 31.92 | 32.40 | 32.88 | 33.37 | 33.85 | 34.33 | 34.82 | 35.30 | 35.79 | 36.28 | 36.77 | 37.26 | 37.75 | 38.24 | 38.73 | 39.23 |
| 39 | 32.81 | 33.31 | 33.80 | 34.30 | 34.80 | 35.30 | 35.80 | 36.30 | 36.80 | 37.30 | 37.81 | 38.31 | 38.82 | 39.32 | 39.83 | 40.34 |
| 40 | 33.71 | 34.22 | 34.73 | 35.24 | 35.75 | 36.26 | 36.78 | 37.29 | 37.81 | 38.33 | 38.85 | 39.37 | 39.89 | 40.41 | 40.93 | 41.46 |
| 41 | 34.61 | 35.13 | 35.66 | 36.18 | 36.71 | 37.24 | 37.77 | 38.30 | 38.83 | 39.36 | 39.89 | 40.43 | 40.96 | 41.50 | 42.04 | 42.58 |
| 42 | 35.51 | 36.05 | 36.59 | 37.13 | 37.67 | 38.21 | 38.76 | 39.30 | 39.85 | 40.40 | 40.95 | 41.50 | 42.05 | 42.60 | 43.15 | 43.71 |
| 43 | 36.42 | 36.97 | 37.52 | 38.08 | 38.63 | 39.19 | 39.75 | 40.31 | 40.87 | 41.44 | 42.00 | 42.57 | 43.13 | 43.70 | 44.27 | 44.84 |
| 44 | 37.33 | 37.89 | 38.46 | 39.03 | 39.60 | 40.18 | 40.75 | 41.33 | 41.90 | 42.48 | 43.06 | 43.64 | 44.22 | 44.81 | 45.39 | 45.98 |
| 45 | 38.24 | 38.82 | 39.41 | 39.99 | 40.58 | 41.17 | 41.75 | 42.35 | 42.94 | 43.53 | 44.13 | 44.72 | 45.32 | 45.92 | 46.52 | 47.12 |
| 46 | 39.16 | 39.75 | 40.35 | 40.95 | 41.55 | 42.16 | 42.76 | 43.37 | 43.98 | 44.58 | 45.20 | 45.81 | 46.42 | 47.03 | 47.65 | 48.27 |
| 47 | 40.08 | 40.69 | 41.30 | 41.92 | 42.54 | 43.15 | 43.77 | 44.40 | 45.02 | 45.64 | 46.27 | 46.90 | 47.53 | 48.16 | 48.79 | 49.42 |
| 48 | 41.00 | 41.63 | 42.26 | 42.89 | 43.52 | 44.15 | 44.79 | 45.43 | 46.07 | 46.71 | 47.35 | 47.99 | 48.64 | 49.28 | 49.93 | 50.58 |
| 49 | 41.93 | 42.57 | 43.22 | 43.86 | 44.51 | 45.16 | 45.81 | 46.46 | 47.12 | 47.77 | 48.43 | 49.09 | 49.75 | 50.41 | 51.08 | 51.74 |
| 50 | 42.86 | 43.52 | 44.18 | 44.84 | 45.50 | 46.17 | 46.83 | 47.50 | 48.17 | 48.84 | 49.52 | 50.19 | 50.87 | 51.55 | 52.23 | 52.91 |
| 51 | 43.79 | 44.47 | 45.14 | 45.82 | 46.50 | 47.18 | 47.86 | 48.55 | 49.23 | 49.92 | 50.61 | 51.30 | 51.99 | 52.69 | 53.38 | 54.08 |
| 52 | 44.73 | 45.42 | 46.11 | 46.80 | 47.50 | 48.20 | 48.89 | 49.59 | 50.30 | 51.00 | 51.71 | 52.41 | 53.12 | 53.83 | 54.55 | 55.26 |
| 53 | 45.67 | 46.38 | 47.08 | 47.79 | 48.50 | 49.22 | 49.93 | 50.65 | 51.37 | 52.09 | 52.81 | 53.53 | 54.26 | 54.98 | 55.71 | 56.44 |
| 54 | 46.62 | 47.34 | 48.06 | 48.79 | 49.51 | 50.24 | 50.97 | 51.70 | 52.44 | 53.17 | 53.91 | 54.65 | 55.39 | 56.14 | 56.88 | 57.63 |
| 55 | 47.57 | 48.30 | 49.04 | 49.78 | 50.52 | 51.27 | 52.02 | 52.76 | 53.52 | 54.27 | 55.02 | 55.78 | 56.54 | 57.30 | 58.06 | 58.82 |
| 56 | 48.52 | 49.27 | 50.03 | 50.78 | 51.54 | 52.30 | 53.06 | 53.83 | 54.60 | 55.37 | 56.14 | 56.91 | 57.68 | 58.46 | 59.24 | 60.02 |
| 57 | 49.47 | 50.24 | 51.01 | 51.79 | 52.56 | 53.34 | 54.12 | 54.90 | 55.68 | 56.47 | 57.25 | 58.04 | 58.84 | 59.63 | 60.43 | 61.22 |
| 58 | 50.43 | 51.22 | 52.00 | 52.79 | 53.58 | 54.38 | 55.17 | 55.97 | 56.77 | 57.57 | 58.38 | 59.18 | 59.99 | 60.80 | 61.62 | 62.43 |
| 59 | 51.39 | 52.20 | 53.00 | 53.80 | 54.61 | 55.42 | 56.23 | 57.05 | 57.87 | 58.68 | 59.51 | 60.33 | 61.15 | 61.98 | 62.81 | 63.64 |
| 60 | 52.36 | 53.18 | 54.00 | 54.82 | 55.64 | 56.47 | 57.30 | 58.13 | 58.96 | 59.80 | 60.64 | 61.48 | 62.32 | 63.17 | 64.01 | 64.86 |

**EXAMPLE 1** Lewis Strang bought a motorcycle for $3,500, which was financed at $142 per month for 24 months. The down payment was $500. Find the APR.

Installment price $= 24(\$142) + \$500 = \$3,408 + \$500 = \$3,908$
Finance charge $= \$3,908 - \$3,500 = \$408$
Amount financed $= \$3,500 - \$500 = \$3,000$
Interest per $100 $= \dfrac{\text{finance charge}}{\text{amount financed}} \times \$100 = \dfrac{\$408}{\$3,000}(\$100) = \$13.60$

Find the row for 24 monthly payments. Move across to find the number nearest to $13.60.

| $13.60 | $13.82 | Find the table value closest to $13.60. |
| $-\$13.54$ | $-13.60$ | |
| $0.06 | $0.22 | |
| Closest | | |
| value | | |

Move up to the top of that column to find the **annual percentage rate, which is 12.5%.**

---

## TIP

**Finding the Closest Table Value**

Another way to find the closest table value to the interest per $100 is to compare the interest to the amount halfway between two table values. The halfway amount is the average of the two table values.

$$\text{Halfway} = \frac{\text{larger value} + \text{smaller value}}{2}$$

In the previous example, $13.60 is between $13.54 and $13.82.

$$\text{Halfway} = \frac{\$13.54 + \$13.82}{2} = \frac{\$27.36}{2}$$
$$= \$13.68$$

Since $13.60 is less than the halfway amount ($13.68), it is closer to the lower table value ($13.54).

---

 **STOP AND CHECK**

1. Jaime Lopez purchased a preowned car that listed for $11,935. After making a down payment of $1,500, he financed the balance over 36 months with payments of $347.49 per month. Use Table 12-1 to find the annual percentage rate (APR) of the loan.

2. Peggy Portzen purchased new kitchen appliances with a cash price of $6,800. After making a down payment of $900, she financed the balance over 24 months with payments of $279.65. Find the annual percentage rate (APR) of the loan.

3. Alan Dan could purchase a jet ski for $9,995 cash. He paid $2,000 down and financed the balance with 36 monthly payments of $295.34. Find the APR of the loan.

4. Nellie Chapman bought a Harley-Davidson motorcycle that had a cash price of $12,799 with a $2,500 down payment. She paid for the motorcycle in 48 monthly payments of $296.37. Find the APR for the loan.

---

## 12-1 SECTION EXERCISES

### SKILL BUILDERS

1. Find the installment price of a recliner bought on the installment plan with a down payment of $100 and six payments of $108.20.

2. Find the amount financed if a $125 down payment is made on a TV with a cash price of $579.

**3.** Stephen Helba purchased a TV with surround sound and remote control on an installment plan with $100 down and 12 payments of $106.32. Find the installment price of the TV.

**4.** A queen-size bedroom suite can be purchased on an installment plan with 18 payments of $97.42 if an $80 down payment is made. What is the installment price of the suite?

**5.** Zack's Trailer Sales will finance a 16-foot utility trailer with ramps and electric brakes. If a down payment of $100 and eight monthly payments of $82.56 are required, what is the installment price of the trailer?

**6.** A forklift is purchased for $10,000. The forklift is used as collateral and no down payment is required. Twenty-four monthly payments of $503 are required to repay the loan. What is the installment price of the forklift?

**7.** A computer with software costs $2,987, and Docie Johnson has agreed to pay a 19% per year finance charge on the cash price. If she contracts to pay the loan in 18 months, how much will she pay each month?

**8.** The cash price of a bedroom suite is $2,590. There is a 24% finance charge on the cash price and 12 monthly payments. Find the monthly payment.

**9.** Find the monthly payment on a VCR with an installment price of $929, 12 monthly payments, and a down payment of $100.

**10.** The installment price of a teakwood extension table and four chairs is $625 with 18 monthly payments and a down payment of $75. What is the monthly payment?

## APPLICATIONS

**11.** An entertainment center is financed at a total cost of $2,357 including a down payment of $250. If the center is financed over 24 months, find the monthly payment.

**12.** A Hepplewhite sofa costs $3,780 in cash. Jaquanna Wilson will purchase the sofa in 36 monthly installment payments. A 13% per year finance charge will be assessed on the amount financed. Find the finance charge, the installment price, and the monthly payment.

**13.** A fishing boat is purchased for $5,600 and financed for 36 months. If the total finance charge is $1,025, find the annual percentage rate using Table 12-1.

**14.** An air compressor costs $780 and is financed with monthly payments for 12 months. The total finance charge is $90. Find the annual percentage rate using Table 12-1.

**15.** Jim Meriweather purchased an engraving machine for $28,000 and financed it for 36 months. The total finance charge was $5,036. Use Table 12-1 to find the annual percentage rate.

## 12-2 PAYING A LOAN BEFORE IT IS DUE: THE RULE OF 78

### LEARNING OUTCOME

1 Find the interest refund using the rule of 78.

If a closed-end installment loan is paid entirely before the last payment is actually due, is part of the interest refundable? In most cases it is, but not always at the rate you might hope. If you paid a 12-month loan in 6 months, you might expect a refund of half the total interest. However, this is often not the case because the portion of the monthly payment that is interest is not the same from month to month. In some cases, interest or finance charge refunds are made according to the **rule of 78**. Some states allow this method to be used for short-term loans, generally 60 months or less. Laws and court rulings protect and inform the consumer in matters involving interest.

## 1  Find the interest refund using the rule of 78.

The rule of 78 is not based on the actual unpaid balance after a payment is made. Instead, it is an approximation that assumes the amount financed (which includes the interest) of a one-year loan is paid in 12 equal parts. For the first payment, the interest is based on the total amount financed, or $\frac{12}{12}$ of the loan. The interest for the second payment is based on $\frac{11}{12}$ of the amount financed since $\frac{1}{12}$ of this amount has already been paid. The interest for the third payment is $\frac{10}{12}$ of the amount financed, and so on. The interest on the last payment is based on $\frac{1}{12}$ of the amount financed.

The sum of all the parts accruing interest for a 12-month loan is $12 + 11 + 10 + 9 + 8 + 7 + 6 + 5 + 4 + 3 + 2 + 1$, or 78.

Thus, 78 equal parts accrue interest. The interest each part accrues is the same because the rate is the same and the parts are the same (each is $\frac{1}{12}$ of the principal). Since 78 equal parts each accrue equal interest, the interest each part accrues must be $\frac{1}{78}$ of the total interest for the one-year loan. So if the loan is paid in full with three months remaining, then the interest that would have accrued in the 10th, 11th, and 12th months is refunded. In the 10th month, three parts each accrue $\frac{1}{78}$ of the total interest; in the 11th month, two parts each accrue $\frac{1}{78}$ of the total interest; and in the 12th month, one part accrues $\frac{1}{78}$ of the total interest. So each of the $3 + 2 + 1$ parts, or 6 parts, accrues $\frac{1}{78}$ of the total interest. Thus $\frac{6}{78}$ of the total interest is refunded. The fraction $\frac{6}{78}$ is called the **refund fraction**.

All installment loans are not for 12 months, but the rule of 78 gives us a pattern that we can apply to loans of any allowable length.

---

**HOW TO**  Find the refund fraction for the interest refund

1. The numerator is the sum of the digits from 1 through the number of months remaining of a loan paid off before it was due.
2. The denominator is the sum of the digits from 1 through the original number of months of the loan.
3. The original fraction, the reduced fraction, or the decimal equivalent of the fraction can be used.

---

The sum-of-digits table in Table 12-2 can be used to find the numerator and denominator of the refund fraction.

**TABLE 12-2**
Sum-of-Digits

| Months | Sum of digits | Months | Sum of digits | Months | Sum of digits |
|--------|---------------|--------|---------------|--------|---------------|
| 1  | 1   | 21 | 231 | 41 | 861   |
| 2  | 3   | 22 | 253 | 42 | 903   |
| 3  | 6   | 23 | 276 | 43 | 946   |
| 4  | 10  | 24 | 300 | 44 | 990   |
| 5  | 15  | 25 | 325 | 45 | 1,035 |
| 6  | 21  | 26 | 351 | 46 | 1,081 |
| 7  | 28  | 27 | 378 | 47 | 1,128 |
| 8  | 36  | 28 | 406 | 48 | 1,176 |
| 9  | 45  | 29 | 435 | 49 | 1,225 |
| 10 | 55  | 30 | 465 | 50 | 1,275 |
| 11 | 66  | 31 | 496 | 51 | 1,326 |
| 12 | 78  | 32 | 528 | 52 | 1,378 |
| 13 | 91  | 33 | 561 | 53 | 1,431 |
| 14 | 105 | 34 | 595 | 54 | 1,485 |
| 15 | 120 | 35 | 630 | 55 | 1,540 |
| 16 | 136 | 36 | 666 | 56 | 1,596 |
| 17 | 153 | 37 | 703 | 57 | 1,653 |
| 18 | 171 | 38 | 741 | 58 | 1,711 |
| 19 | 190 | 39 | 780 | 59 | 1,770 |
| 20 | 210 | 40 | 820 | 60 | 1,830 |

There is a shortcut for finding the sum of consecutive numbers beginning with 1. You may be interested to know that a young boy in elementary school discovered this shortcut in the late 18th century. He later went on to be one of the greatest mathematicians of all time. His name was Carl Friedrich Gauss (1777–1855).

## TIP

**The Sum of Consecutive Numbers Beginning with 1**

Multiply the largest number by 1 more than the largest number and divide the product by 2.

$$\text{Sum of consecutive numbers beginning with 1} = \frac{\text{largest number} \times (\text{largest number} + 1)}{2}$$

$$\text{Sum of consecutive numbers from 1 through 4} = \frac{4(5)}{2} = \frac{20}{2} = 10$$

$$\text{Sum of consecutive numbers from 1 through 12} = \frac{12(13)}{2} = \frac{156}{2} = 78$$

## HOW TO    Find the interest refund using the rule of 78

1. Find the refund fraction.
2. Multiply the total interest by the refund fraction.

$$\text{Interest refund} = \text{total interest} \times \text{refund fraction}$$

## EXAMPLE 1
A loan for 12 months with interest of $117 is paid in full with four payments remaining. Find the refund fraction for the interest refund.

$$\text{Refund fraction} = \frac{\text{sum of the digits for number of payments remaining}}{\text{sum of the digits for total number of payments}}$$

$$= \frac{1 + 2 + 3 + 4}{1 + 2 + 3 + 4 + 5 + 6 + 7 + 8 + 9 + 10 + 11 + 12}$$

$$= \frac{10}{78} = \frac{5}{39} \text{ or } 0.1282051282 \qquad\qquad 10 \div 78 = 0.1282051282$$

**The refund fraction is $\frac{10}{78}$ or $\frac{5}{39}$ or 0.1282051282.**

## EXAMPLE 2
Find the interest refund for the installment loan in Example 1.

$\text{Interest refund} = \text{total interest} \times \text{refund fraction}$   Total interest = $117

Refund fraction $= \dfrac{10}{78}$ or $\dfrac{5}{39}$ or 0.1282051282

$= \$117(0.1282051282)$    Multiply.

$= \$15$

**The interest refund is $15.**

## TIP

**Continuous Sequence of Steps Using a Calculator**

It is advisable in making calculations as in Example 2 that you use a continuous sequence of steps in a calculator. It is time consuming and more mistakes are made if you reenter the result of a previous calculation to make another calculation.

For Example 2, the continuous sequence of steps is:

$\boxed{\text{CLEAR}}\ 117\ \boxed{\times}\ 10\ \boxed{\div}\ 78\ \boxed{=}\ \Rightarrow 15$

When using a calculator, there is no need to reduce fractions first.

## EXAMPLE 3

A loan for 36 months, with a finance charge of $1,276.50, is paid in full with 15 payments remaining. Find the finance charge to be refunded.

$$\text{Refund fraction} = \frac{\text{sum of the digits for number of payments remaining}}{\text{sum of the digits for total number of payments}}$$

$$= \frac{\text{sum of digits from 1 through 15}}{\text{sum of digits from 1 through 36}} \qquad 15 \times 16 \div 2 = \Rightarrow 120$$
$$\qquad\qquad\qquad\qquad\qquad\qquad\qquad\qquad\qquad 36 \times 37 \div 2 = \Rightarrow 666$$

$$\text{Refund fraction} = \frac{120}{666}$$

$$\text{Finance charge refund} = \text{finance charge} \times \text{refund fraction}$$

$$= \$1{,}276.50\left(\frac{120}{666}\right)$$

$$= \$230$$

Calculator sequence: $1276.50 \times 120 \div 666 =$

**The finance charge refund is $230.**

---

## STOP AND CHECK

1. A loan for 12 months with interest of $397.85 is paid in full with five payments remaining. What is the refund fraction for the interest refund?

2. A loan for 48 months has interest of $2,896 and is paid in full with 18 months remaining. What is the refund fraction for the interest refund?

3. A loan for 36 months requires $1,798 interest. The loan is paid in full with 6 months remaining. How much interest is refunded?

4. Ruth Brechner borrowed money to purchase a retail business. The 60-month loan had $4,917 interest. Ruth's business flourished and she repaid the loan after 50 months. How much interest refund did she receive?

---

## 12-2 SECTION EXERCISES

### SKILL BUILDERS

1. Calculate the refund fraction for a 60-month loan that is paid off with 18 months remaining.

2. Find the refund fraction on an 18-month loan if it is paid off with 8 months remaining.

3. Find the interest refund on a 36-month loan with interest of $2,817 if the loan is paid in full with 9 months remaining.

4. Stephen Helba took out a loan to purchase a computer. He originally agreed to pay off the loan in 18 months with a finance charge of $205. He paid the loan in full after 12 payments. How much finance charge refund should he get?

**5.** John Paszel took out a loan for 48 months but paid it in full after 28 months. Find the refund fraction he should use to calculate the amount of his refund.

**6.** If the finance charge on a loan made by Marjorie Young is $1,645 and the loan is to be paid in 48 monthly payments, find the finance charge refund if the loan is paid in full with 28 months remaining.

**7.** Phillamone Berry has a car loan with a company that refunds interest using the rule of 78 when loans are paid in full ahead of schedule. He is using an employee bonus to pay off his Taurus, which is on a 42-month loan. The total interest for the loan is $2,397, and he has 15 more payments to make. How much finance charge will he get credit for if he pays the loan in full immediately?

**8.** Dwayne Moody purchased a four-wheel drive vehicle and is using severance pay from his current job to pay off the vehicle loan before moving to his new job. The total interest on the 36-month loan is $3,227. How much finance charge refund will he receive if he pays the loan in full with 10 more payments left?

## 12-3 OPEN-END CREDIT

### LEARNING OUTCOMES

1 Find the finance charge and new balance using the average daily balance method.
2 Find the finance charge and new balance using the unpaid or previous month's balance.

**Line-of-credit accounts:** a type of open-end loan.

Open-end loans are often called **line-of-credit accounts**. While a person or company is paying off loans, that person or company may also be adding to the total loan account by making a new purchase or otherwise borrowing money on the account.

For example, you may want to use your Visa card to buy new textbooks even though you still owe for clothes bought last winter. Likewise, a business may use an open-end credit account to buy a new machine this month even though it still owes the bank for funds used to pay a major supplier six months ago.

Nearly all open-end accounts are billed monthly. Interest rates are most often stated as annual rates. The Fair Credit and Charge Card Disclosure Act of 1988 and updates passed since that time specify the required details that must be disclosed for charge cards and line-of-credit accounts. These details include all fees, grace period, how finance charges are calculated, how late fees are assessed, and so on. Interest on many open-end credit accounts is figured according to the *average daily balance method.*

### 1 Find the finance charge and new balance using the average daily balance method.

**Average daily balance:** the average of the daily balances for each day of the billing cycle.

Many lenders determine the finance charge using the **average daily balance** method. In this method, the daily balances of the account are determined, and then the sum of these balances is divided by the number of days in the billing cycle. This average daily balance is then multiplied by the monthly interest rate to find the finance charge for the month.

**Billing cycle:** the days that are included on a statement or bill.

Even though open-end credit accounts are billed monthly, the monthly period may not coincide with the first and last days of a calendar month. To spread out the workload for the billing department, each account is given a monthly billing cycle. The **billing cycle** is the days that are included on a statement or bill. This cycle can start on any day of a month. For example, a billing cycle may start on the 22nd of one month and end on the 21st of the next month. This means that the number of days of a billing cycle will vary from month to month based on the number of days in the months involved.

1. Find the daily unpaid balance for each day in the billing cycle.
   (a) Find the total purchases and cash advances charged to the account during the day.
   (b) Find the total credits (payments and adjustments) credited to the account during the day.
   (c) To the previous daily unpaid balance, add the total purchases and cash advances for the day (from step 1a). Then subtract the total credits for the day (from step 1b).

   > Daily unpaid balance = previous daily unpaid balance + total purchases and cash advances for the day − total credits for the day

2. Add the unpaid balances from step 1 for each day of the billing cycle, and divide the sum by the number of days in the cycle.

$$\text{Average daily balance} = \frac{\text{sum of daily unpaid balances}}{\text{number of days in billing cycle}}$$

---

**HOW TO**    Find the finance charge using the average daily balance

1. Determine the decimal equivalent of the rate per period.
2. Multiply the average daily balance by the decimal equivalent of the rate per period.

---

**TIP**

**When Does the Balance Change?**
In most cases, if a transaction reaches a financial institution at any time during the day, the transaction is posted and the balance is updated at the end of the business day. Thus, the new balance takes effect at the beginning of the next day. **Calculations on the day's unpaid balance are made on the end-of-day amount** (same as beginning of next day).

**EXAMPLE 1**    Use the chart showing May activity in the Hodge's Tax Service charge account to determine the average daily balance and finance charge for the month. The bank's finance charge is 1.5% per month on the average daily balance.

| Date transaction posted | Transaction | Transaction amount |
|---|---|---|
| May 1 | Billing date | Balance $122.70 |
| May 7 | Payment | 25.00 |
| May 10 | Purchase (pencils) | 12.00 |
| May 13 | Purchase (envelopes) | 20.00 |
| May 20 | Cash advance | 50.00 |
| May 23 | Purchase (business forms) | 100.00 |

To find the average daily balance, we must find the unpaid balance for each day, add these balances, and divide by the number of days.

| Day | Balance | Day | Balance | Day | Balance |
|---|---|---|---|---|---|
| 1 | 122.70 | 11 | 109.70 | 21 | 179.70 |
| 2 | 122.70 | 12 | 109.70 | 22 | 179.70 |
| 3 | 122.70 | 13 | 129.70 (109.70 + 20) | 23 | 279.70 (179.70 + 100) |
| 4 | 122.70 | 14 | 129.70 | 24 | 279.70 |
| 5 | 122.70 | 15 | 129.70 | 25 | 279.70 |
| 6 | 122.70 | 16 | 129.70 | 26 | 279.70 |
| 7 | 97.70 (122.70 − 25) | 17 | 129.70 | 27 | 279.70 |
| 8 | 97.70 | 18 | 129.70 | 28 | 279.70 |
| 9 | 97.70 | 19 | 129.70 | 29 | 279.70 |
| 10 | 109.70 (97.70 + 12) | 20 | 179.70 (129.70 + 50) | 30 | 279.70 |
| | | | | 31 | 279.70 |

Total:    $5,322.70          Average Daily Balance:    $171.70

The average daily balance can also be determined by grouping days that have the same balance.

For the first six days, May 1–May 6, there is no activity, so the daily unpaid balance is the previous unpaid balance of $122.70. The sum of daily unpaid balances for these six days, then, is 122.70(6).

$$\$122.70(6) = \$736.20$$

On May 7 there is a payment of $25, which reduces the daily unpaid balance.

$$\$122.70 - \$25 = \$97.70$$

The new balance of $97.70 holds for the three days (May 7, 8, and 9) until May 10.

$$\$97.70(3) = \$293.10$$

Continue doing this until you get to the end of the cycle. The calculations can be organized in a chart.

| Date | Change | Daily unpaid balance | Number of days | Partial sum |
|------|--------|---------------------|----------------|-------------|
| May 1–May 6 | | $122.70 | 6 | $ 736.20 |
| May 7–May 9 | −$25.00 | 97.70 | 3 | 293.10 |
| May 10–May 12 | +10.00 | 109.70 | 3 | 329.10 |
| May 13–May 19 | +20.00 | 129.70 | 7 | 907.90 |
| May 20–May 22 | +50.00 | 179.70 | 3 | 539.10 |
| May 23–May 31 | +100.00 | 279.70 | 9 | 2,517.30 |
| | | | Total 31 | $5,322.70 |

Divide the sum of $5,322.70 by the 31 days.

$$\text{Average daily balance} = \frac{\text{sum of daily unpaid balances}}{\text{number of days}}$$

$$= \frac{\$5,322.70}{31} = \$171.70$$

To find the interest, multiply the average daily balance by the monthly interest rate of 1.5%.

$$\text{Finance charge} = \$171.70(0.015)$$
$$= \$2.58$$

**The average daily balance is $171.70 and the finance charge is $2.58.**

## ✔ STOP AND CHECK

| Account Number | Credit Limit | Available Credit | Billing Period |
|----------------|--------------|------------------|----------------|
| xxxx-xxxx-xxxx-xxxx | $5,000 | $ | 9/24/05 to 10/24/05 |

| Posting Date | Transaction Date | Description | Amount CR–Credit  PY–Payment | |
|--------------|------------------|-------------|--------|--|
| 9/26 | 9/24 | The Store Oxford MS | $11.93 | CR |
| 10/6 | 10/02 | Chili's Oxford MS | $15.24 | CR |
| 10/8 | 10/06 | Durall St Cloud FL | $86.98 | CR |
| 10/10 | 10/10 | Payment Received–Thank You | $927.86 | PY |
| 10/14 | 10/12 | Foley's Knitwear San Antonio TX | $113.19 | CR |
| 10/20 | 10/16 | Red Lobster Tupelo MS | $22.88 | CR |
| 10/20 | 10/19 | JC Penny Co Oxford MS | $47.36 | CR |

| Finance Charge | | | | | Balance | | |
|----------------|--|--|--|--|---------|--|--|
| Average Daily Balance | Monthly Periodic Rate | Corresponding Annual Percentage Rate | Finance Charge | | Previous Balance | $ | 1,406.54 |
| | | | | | Purchases | + | 297.58 |
| | | | | | Other Charges | + | .00 |
| Purchases | | Variable | | | Cash Advances | + | 0.00 |
| | 1.0750% | 12.90% | | | Credits | − | .00 |
| | | | | | Payments | − | 927.86 |
| Cash Advances | | Variable | | | Late Charges | + | .00 |
| $0.00 | 1.0750% | 12.90% | | | Finance Charges | + | |
| | | | | | New Balance | $ | |

FIGURE 12-1

*Use the statement in Figure 12-1 for Exercises 1–4.*

1. Make a table showing the unpaid balance for each day in the billing period.

2. Find the average daily balance for the month.

3. Find the finance charge for the month.

4. Find the new balance for the month.

## 2  Find the finance charge and new balance using the unpaid or previous month's balance.

Not all open-end credit accounts use the average daily balance method for determining the monthly finance charge. Another method uses the unpaid or previous month's balance as the basis for determining the finance charge. In this method, the new purchases or payments made during a month do not affect the finance charge for that month.

---

**HOW TO**  Find the finance charge and new balance using the unpaid or previous month's balance.

Finance charge:

1. Find the monthly rate.

$$\text{Monthly rate} = \frac{\text{Annual percentage rate}}{12}$$

2. Multiply the unpaid or previous month's balance by the monthly rate.

$$\text{Finance charge} = \text{Unpaid balance} \times \text{Monthly rate}$$

New balance:

1. Total the purchases and cash advances for the billing cycle.
2. Total the payments and credits for the billing cycle.
3. Adjust the unpaid balance of the previous month using the totals in steps 1 and 2.

   New balance = Previous balance + Finance charge + Purchases and cash advances − Payments and credits

---

**EXAMPLE 1**  Hanna Stein has a department store revolving credit account with an annual percentage rate of 21%. Her unpaid balance for her March billing cycle is $285.45. During the billing cycle she purchased shoes for $62.58 and a handbag for $35.18. She returned a blouse that she had purchased in the previous billing cycle and received a credit of $22.79 and she made a payment of $75. If the store uses the unpaid balance method, what are the finance charge and the new balance?

Monthly rate:

$$\text{Monthly rate} = \frac{\text{Annual percentage rate}}{12}$$

$$\text{Monthly rate} = \frac{21\%}{12} = \frac{0.21}{12} = 0.0175$$

Finance charge:

Finance charge = Unpaid balance × Monthly rate

Finance charge = $285.45(0.0175) = $5.00     Rounded from $4.995375

New balance:

Total purchases and cash advances = $62.58 + $35.18 = $97.76

Total payments and credits = $75 + $22.79 = $97.79

New balance = Previous balance + Finance charge + Purchases and cash advances − Payments and credits

New balance = $285.45 + $5 + $97.76 − $97.79 = $290.42

 ## STOP AND CHECK

1. Shakina Brewster has a Target revolving credit account that has an annual percentage rate of 18% on the unpaid balance. Her unpaid balance for the July billing cycle is $1,285.96. During the billing cycle, Shakina purchased groceries for $98.76 and received $50 in cash. She purchased linens for $46.98. Shakina made a payment of $135. Find the finance charge and new balance if Target uses the unpaid balance method.

2. Shameka Brown has a Best Buy Stores revolving credit account that has an annual percentage rate of 15% on the unpaid balance. Her unpaid balance for the October billing cycle is $2,531.77. During the billing cycle, Shameka purchased movies for $58.63 and received $70 in cash. She purchased a camera for $562.78 and returned a printer purchased in September for credit of $85.46. Shameka made a payment of $455. Find the finance charge and new balance if Best Buy uses the unpaid balance method.

3. Dallas Hunsucker has a Master Card account with an annual percentage rate of 24%. The unpaid balance for his January billing cycle is $2,094.54. During the billing cycle he made grocery purchases of $65.82, $83.92, $12.73, and gasoline purchases of $29.12 and $28.87. He made a payment of $400. If the account applies the unpaid balance method, what were the finance charge and the new balance?

4. Ryan Bradley has a Visa Card with an introductory annual percentage rate of 9%. The unpaid balance for his February billing cycle is $245.18. During the billing cycle he purchased fresh flowers for $45.00, candy for $22.38, and gasoline for $36.53. He made a payment of $100 and had a return for credit of $74.93. If the account applies the unpaid balance method, what are the finance charge and the new balance?

## 12-3 SECTION EXERCISES

### SKILL BUILDERS

1. What is the monthly interest rate if an annual rate is 13.8%?

2. Find the monthly interest rate if the annual rate is 15.6%.

3. A credit card has an average daily balance of $2,817.48 and the monthly periodic rate is 1.325%. What is the finance charge for the month?

4. What is the finance charge on a credit card account that has an average daily balance of $5,826.42 and the monthly interest rate is 1.55%?

## APPLICATIONS

**5.** Jim Riddle has a credit card that charges 10% annual interest on the monthly average daily balance for the billing cycle. The current billing cycle has 29 days. For 15 days his balance was $2,534.95. For 7 days the balance was $1,534.95. And for 7 days the balance was $1,892.57. Find the average daily balance. Find the amount of interest.

**6.** Suppose the charge account of Strong's Mailing Service at the local supply store had a 1.8% interest rate per month on the average daily balance. Find the average daily balance if Strong's had an unpaid balance on March 1 of $128.50, a payment of $20 posted on March 6, and a purchase of $25.60 posted on March 20. The billing cycle ends March 31.

**7.** Using Exercise 6, find Strong's finance charge on April 1.

**8.** Make a chart to show the transactions for Rick Schiendler's credit card account in which interest is charged on the average daily balance. The cycle begins on May 4, and the cycle ends on June 3. The beginning balance is $283.57. A payment of $200 is posted on May 18. A charge of $19.73 is posted on May 7. A charge of $53.82 is posted on May 12. A charge of $115.18 is posted on May 29. How many days are in the cycle? What is the average daily balance?

**9.** Rick is charged 1.42% per period. What is the finance charge for the cycle?

**10.** What is the beginning balance for the next cycle of Rick's credit card account?

**11.** Jamel Cisco has a Visa Card with an annual percentage rate of 16.8%. The unpaid balance for his June billing cycle is $1,300.84. During the billing cycle he purchased a printer cartridge for $42.39, books for $286.50 and gasoline for $16.71. He made a payment of $1,200. If the account applies the unpaid balance method, what are the finance charge and the new balance?

**12.** Chaundra Mixon has a Master Card with an annual percentage rate of 19.8%. The unpaid balance for her August billing cycle is $675.21. During the billing cycle she purchased shoes for $87.52, a suit for $132.48, and a wallet for $28.94. She made a payment of $225. If the account applies the unpaid balance method, what are the finance charge and the new balance?

## Learning Outcomes

## What to Remember with Examples

### Section 12-1

**1** Find the amount financed, the installment price, and the finance charge of an installment loan. (p. 422)

**1.** Find the amount financed: Subtract the down payment from the cash price.

$$\text{Amount financed} = \text{cash price} - \text{down payment}$$

**2.** Find the installment price: Add the down payment to the total of the installment payments.

$$\text{Installment price} = \text{total of installment payments} + \text{down payment}$$

> Find the installment price of a computer that is paid for in 24 monthly payments of $113 if a down payment of $50 is made.
>
> $$(24)(\$113) + \$50 = \$2,712 + \$50 = \$2,762$$

Find the finance charge of an installment loan: Subtract the cash price from the installment price.

$$\text{Finance charge} = \text{installment price} - \text{cash price}$$

> If the cash price of the computer in the previous example was $2,499, how much is the finance charge?
>
> $$\$2,762 - \$2,499 = \$263$$

**2** Find the installment payment of an installment loan. (p. 423)

**1.** Find the total of the installment payments: Subtract the down payment from the installment price.

$$\text{Total of installment payments} = \text{installment price} - \text{down payment}$$

**2.** Divide the total of installment payments by the number of installment payments.

$$\text{Installment payment} = \frac{\text{total of installment payments}}{\text{number of payments}}$$

> Find the monthly payment on a computer if the cash price is $3,285. A 14% interest rate is charged on the cash price, and there are 12 monthly payments.
>
> $$\$3,285(0.14)(1) = \$459.90$$
> $$\text{Installment price} = \$3,285 + \$459.90 = \$3,744.90$$
> $$\text{Monthly payment} = \frac{\$3,744.90}{12} = \$312.08$$
>
> A computer has an installment price of $2,187.25 when financed over 18 months. If a $100 down payment is made, find the monthly payment.
>
> $$\$2,187.25 - \$100 = \$2,087.25$$
> $$\text{Monthly payment} = \frac{\$2,087.25}{18} = \$115.96$$

**3** Find the estimated annual percentage rate (APR) using a table. (p. 424)

**1.** Find the interest per $100 of amount financed: Divide the finance charge by the amount financed and multiply by $100.

$$\text{Interest per } \$100 = \frac{\text{total finance charge}}{\text{amount financed}} \times \$100$$

**2.** Find the row corresponding to the number of monthly payments. Move across the row to find the number closest to the value from step 1. Read up the column to find the annual percentage rate for that column.

Find the annual percentage rate on a loan of $500 that is repaid in 36 monthly installments. The interest for the loan is $95.

$$\text{Interest per }\$100 = \frac{\$95}{\$500}(\$100) = \$19$$

In the row for 36 months, move across to 19.14 (nearest to 19). APR is at the top of the column, 11.75%.

**Section 12-2**

**1** Find the interest refund using the rule of 78. (p. 430)

**Find the refund fraction.**

1. The numerator is the sum of the digits from 1 through the number of months remaining of a loan paid off before it was due.
2. The denominator is the sum of the digits from 1 through the original number of months of the loan.
3. The original fraction, the reduced fraction or the decimal equivalent of the fraction can be used.

Find the refund fraction on a loan that has a total finance charge of $892 and was made for 24 months. The loan is paid in full with 10 months (payments) remaining.

$$\begin{aligned}\text{Refund fraction} &= \frac{\text{sum of digits from 1 to the number of periods remaining}}{\text{sum of digits from 1 through original number of periods}}\\ &= \frac{\text{sum of 1 to 10}}{\text{sum of 1 to 24}}\\ &= \frac{55}{300} \text{ or } \frac{11}{60} \text{ or } 0.1833333333\end{aligned}$$

**Find the interest refund using the rule of 78.**

1. Find the refund fraction.
2. Multiply the total interest by the refund fraction.

$$\text{Interest refund} = \text{total interest} \times \text{refund fraction}$$

Find the interest refund for the previous example.

$$\text{Interest refund} = \$892\left(\frac{11}{60}\right) = \$163.53 \quad 892\ \boxed{\times}\ 11\ \boxed{\div}\ 60\ \boxed{=}\ \Rightarrow 163.5333333$$

**Section 12-3**

**1** Find the finance charge and new balance using the average daily balance method. (p. 433)

1. Find the daily unpaid balance for each day in the billing cycle.
   (a) Find the total purchases and cash advances charged to the account during the day.
   (b) Find the total credits (payments and adjustments) credited to the account during the day.
   (c) To the previous daily unpaid balance, add the total purchases and cash advances for the day (from step 1a). Then subtract the total payments for the day (from step 1b).

$$\text{Daily unpaid balance} = \text{previous daily unpaid balance} + \text{total purchases}$$
$$\text{and cash advances for the day} - \text{total credits for the day}$$

2. Add the unpaid balances from step 1 for each day of the billing cycle, and divide the sum by the number of days in the cycle.

$$\text{Average daily balance} = \frac{\text{sum of daily unpaid balances}}{\text{number of days in billing cycle}}$$

A credit card has a balance of $398.42 on September 14, the first day of the billing cycle. A charge of $182.37 is posted to the account on September 16. Another charge of $82.21 is posted to the account on September 25. The amount of a returned item ($19.98) is posted to the account on October 10 and a payment of $500 is made on October 12. The billing period ends on October 13. Find the average daily balance.

| Date | Change | Daily Unpaid Balance | Number of Days | Partial Sum |
|---|---|---|---|---|
| September 14–15 | | $398.42 | 2 days | $ 796.84 |
| September 16–24 | +$182.37 | 580.79 | 9 days | 5,227.11 |
| September 25–October 9 | +82.21 | 663.00 | 15 days | 9,945.00 |
| October 10–11 | −19.98 | 643.02 | 2 days | 1,286.04 |
| October 12–13 | −500.00 | 143.02 | 2 days | 286.04 |
| | | | Total  30 days | $17,541.03 |

Average daily balance = $17,541.03 ÷ 30 = $584.70

Find the finance charge using the average daily balance.

1. Determine the decimal equivalent of the rate per period.
2. Multiply the average daily balance by the decimal equivalent of the rate per period.

Find the finance charge for the average daily balance in the preceding example if the monthly rate is 1.3%.

$$\text{Finance charge} = \$584.70(0.013) = \$7.60$$

**2** Find the finance charge and new balance using the unpaid or previous month's balance. (p. 436)

Finance charge:

1. Find the monthly rate.

$$\text{Monthly rate} = \frac{\text{Annual percentage rate}}{12}$$

2. Multiply the unpaid or previous month's balance by the monthly rate.

$$\text{Finance charge} = \text{Unpaid balance} \times \text{Monthly rate}$$

New balance:

1. Total the purchases and cash advances for the billing cycle.
2. Total the payments and credits for the billing cycle.
3. Adjust the unpaid balance of the previous month using the totals in steps 1 and 2.

Dakota Beasley has a Visa account with an annual percentage rate of 24%. Her unpaid balance for her September billing cycle is $381.15. During the billing cycle she made gasoline purchases of $25.18, $18.29, $22.75, and $19.12. She made a payment of $100. If the account applies the unpaid balance method, what is the finance charge and the new balance?

$$\text{Monthly rate} = \frac{\text{Annual percentage rate}}{12}$$

$$\text{Monthly rate} = \frac{24\%}{12} = \frac{0.24}{12} = 0.02$$

Finance charge = Unpaid balance × Monthly rate
Finance charge = $381.15(0.02) = $7.62   Rounded from $7.623
Total purchases = $25.18 + $18.29 + $22.75 + $19.12
= $85.34
Payments = $100
New balance = $381.15 + $7.62 + $85.34 − $100
= $374.11

# EXERCISES SET A

1. Find the installment price of a notebook computer system bought on the installment plan with $250 down and 12 payments of $111.33.

2. Find the monthly payment on a water bed if the installment price is $1,050, the down payment is $200, and there are 10 monthly payments.

3. If the cash price of a refrigerator is $879 and a down payment of $150 is made, how much is to be financed?

4. Find the refund fraction for a 60-month loan if it is paid in full with 22 months remaining.

*Use the rule of 78 to find the finance charge (interest) refund in each of the following.*

| | Finance charge | Number of monthly payments | Remaining payments | Interest refund |
|---|---|---|---|---|
| **XCEL 5.** | $238 | 12 | 4 | |
| **XCEL 6.** | $2,175 | 24 | 10 | |
| **XCEL 7.** | $896 | 18 | 4 | |

8. The finance charge on a copier was $1,778. The loan for the copier was to be paid in 18 monthly payments. Find the finance charge refund if it is paid off in eight months.

9. Becky Whitehead has a loan with $1,115 in finance charges, which she paid in full after 10 of the 24 monthly payments. What is her finance charge refund?

10. Alice Dubois was charged $455 in finance charges on a loan for 15 months. Find the finance charge refund if she pays off the loan in full after 10 payments.

11. Find the finance charge refund on a 24-month loan with monthly payments of $103.50 if you decide to pay off the loan with 10 months remaining. The finance charge is $215.55.

12. If you purchase a fishing boat for 18 monthly payments of $106 and an interest charge of $238, how much is the refund after 10 payments?

13. Find the interest on an average daily balance of $265 with an interest rate of $1\frac{1}{2}\%$.

**14.** Find the finance charge on a credit card with an average daily balance of $465 if the rate charged is 1.25%.

**15.** Use the following activity chart to find the unpaid balance on November 1. The billing cycle ended on October 31, and the finance charge is 1.5% of the average daily balance.

| Date posted | Activity | Amount |
|---|---|---|
| October 1 | Billing date | Previous balance $426.40 |
| October 8 | Purchase | 41.60 |
| October 11 | Payment | 70.00 |
| October 16 | Purchase | 31.25 |
| October 21 | Purchase | 26.80 |

*Use Table 12-1 to find the annual percentage rate (APR) for the following exercises.*

**16.** Find the annual percentage rate on a loan of $1,500 for 18 months if the loan requires $190 interest and is repaid monthly.

**17.** Find the annual percentage rate on a loan of $3,820 if the monthly payment is $130 for 36 months.

**18.** A vacuum cleaner was purchased on the installment plan with 12 monthly payments of $36.98 each. If the cash price was $415 and there was no down payment, find the annual percentage rate.

**19.** A merchant charged $420 in cash for a dining room set that could be bought for $50 down and $40.75 per month for 10 months. What is the annual percentage rate?

**20.** An electric mixer was purchased on the installment plan for a down payment of $60 and 11 monthly payments of $11.05 each. The cash price was $170. Find the annual percentage rate.

**21.** A computer was purchased by paying $50 down and 24 monthly payments of $65 each. The cash price was $1,400. Find the annual percentage rate to the nearest tenth of a percent.

# EXERCISES SET B

CHAPTER 12

1. A television set has been purchased on the installment plan with a down payment of $120 and six monthly payments of $98.50. Find the installment price of the television set.

2. A dishwasher sold for a $983 installment price with a down payment of $150 and 12 monthly payments. How much is each payment?

3. What is the cash price of a chair if the installment price is $679, the finance charge is $102, and there was no down payment?

4. Find the refund fraction for a 42-month loan if it is paid in full with 16 months remaining.

*Use the rule of 78 to find the finance charge refund in each of the following.*

| | Finance charge | Number of monthly payments | Remaining payments | Interest refund |
|---|---|---|---|---|
| **XCEL 5.** | $1,076 | 18 | 6 | |
| **XCEL 6.** | $476 | 12 | 5 | |
| **XCEL 7.** | $683 | 15 | 11 | |

8. Find the refund fraction on a 48-month loan if it is paid off after 20 months.

9. Lanny Jacobs made a loan to purchase a computer. Find the refund due on this loan with interest charges of $657 if it is paid off after paying 7 of the 12 monthly payments.

10. Suppose you have borrowed money that is being repaid at $45 a month for 12 months. What is the finance charge refund after making eight payments if the finance charge is $105?

11. You have purchased a new stereo on the installment plan. The plan calls for 12 monthly payments of $45 and a $115 finance charge. After nine months you decide to pay off the loan. How much is the refund?

12. The interest for an automobile loan is $2,843. The automobile is financed for 36 monthly payments, and interest refunds are made using the rule of 78. How much interest should be refunded if the loan is paid in full with 22 months still remaining?

13. Find the finance charge on $371 if the interest charge is 1.4% of the average daily balance.

**14.** A new desk for an office has a cash price of $1,500 and can be purchased on the installment plan with a 12.5% finance charge. The desk will be paid for in 12 monthly payments. Find the amount of the finance charge, the total price, and the amount of each monthly payment, if there was no down payment.

**15.** On January 1 the previous balance for Lynn's charge account was $569.80. On the following days, purchases were posted:

January 13    $38.50    jewelry
January 21    $44.56    clothing

On January 16 a $50 payment was posted. Using the average daily balance method, find the finance charge and unpaid balance on February 1 if the bank charges interest of 1.5% per month.

*Use Table 12-1 to find the annual percentage rate for the following exercises.*

**16.** Find the annual percentage rate on a loan for 25 months if the amount of the loan without interest is $300. The loan requires $40 interest.

**17.** Find the annual percentage rate on a loan of $700 without interest with 12 monthly payments. The loan requires $50 interest.

**18.** A queen-size brass bed costs $1,155 and is financed with monthly payments for three years. The total finance charge is $415.80. Find the annual percentage rate.

**19.** John Edmonds borrowed $500. He repaid the loan in 22 monthly payments of $26.30 each. Find the annual percentage rate.

**20.** A loan of $3,380 was paid back in 30 monthly payments with an interest charge of $620. Find the annual percentage rate.

**21.** A 6 × 6 color enlarger costs $1,295 and is financed with monthly payments for two years. The total finance charge is $310.80. Find the annual percentage rate.

# PRACTICE TEST

1. Find the finance charge on an item with a cash price of $469 if the installment price is $503 and no down payment was made.

2. An item with a cash price of $578 can be purchased on the installment plan in 15 monthly payments of $46. Find the installment price if no down payment was made. Find the finance charge.

3. A copier that originally cost $300 was sold on the installment plan at $28 per month for 12 months. Find the installment price if no down payment was made. Find the finance charge.

4. Use Table 12-1 to find the annual percentage rate for the loan in Exercise 3.

5. Use Table 12-1 to find the APR on a loan of $3,000 for three years if the loan had $810 interest and was repaid monthly.

6. Find the interest on an average daily balance of $165 if the monthly interest rate is $1\frac{3}{4}\%$.

7. Find the yearly rate of interest on a loan if the monthly rate is 2%.

8. Find the interest refunded on a 15-month loan with total interest of $72 if the loan is paid in full with six months remaining.

9. Find the annual percentage rate on a loan of $1,600 for 24 months if $200 interest is charged and the loan is repaid in monthly payments. Use Table 12-1.

10. Find the annual interest rate on a loan that is repaid monthly for 26 months if the amount of the loan is $1,075. The interest charged is $134.85.

11. Office equipment was purchased on the installment plan with 12 monthly payments of $11.20 each. If the cash price was $120 and there was no down payment, find the annual percentage rate.

12. A canoe has been purchased on the installment plan with a down payment of $75 and 10 monthly payments of $80 each. Find the installment price of the canoe.

**13.** Find the monthly payment when the installment price is $2,300, a down payment of $400 is made, and there are 12 monthly payments.

**14.** How much is to be financed on a cash price of $729 if a down payment of $75 is made?

**15.** A 30-month loan that has interest of $3,987 is paid in full with 7 months remaining. Find the amount of interest to be refunded.

**16.** Use the following activity chart to find the average daily balance, finance charge, and unpaid balance for July. The monthly interest rate is 1.75%. The billing cycle has 31 days.

| Date Posted | Activity | Amount |
|---|---|---|
| July 1 | Billing date | Previous balance $441.05 |
| July 5 | Payment | $75.00 |
| July 16 | Purchase | 23.50 |
| July 26 | Purchase | 31.40 |

**17.** Mary Lawson has a credit card account with an annual percentage rate of 18.24%. The unpaid balance for her November billing cycle is $783.56. During the billing cycle she purchased a desk chair for $134.77 and a floor mat for $82.36. Mary returned a grill purchased in the previous month for a credit of $186.21 and she made a payment of $80. If the account applies the unpaid balance method, what are the finance charge and the new balance?

1. Explain the mistake in the solution of the problem and correct the solution.

   Dawn Mayhall financed a car and the loan of 42 months required $3,827 interest. She paid the loan off after making 20 payments. How much interest should be refunded if the rule of 78 is used?

   Solution:

   Refund fraction $= \dfrac{210}{903}$

   $\dfrac{210}{903}(\$3,827) = \$890$

   Thus, $890 should be refunded.

2. Explain the mistake in the solution and correct the solution.

   Ava Landry agreed to pay $2,847 interest for a 36-month loan to redecorate her greeting card shop. However, business was better than expected and she repaid the loan with 16 months remaining. If the rule of 78 was used, how much interest should she get back?

   Solution:

   $\dfrac{16}{36}(\$2,847) = \$1,265.33$

   Thus, $1,265.33 should be refunded.

3. Arrange the consecutive numbers from 1 to 10 in ascending order, then in descending order, so that 1 and 10, 2 and 9, 3 and 8, etc., align vertically. Add vertically. Find the grand total. Finally divide the grand total by 2.

4. Explain why finding the sum of consecutive numbers by using the process in Exercise 3 requires that the product be divided by 2.

5. Explain why the formula for finding the sum of consecutive numbers requires the product of the largest number and one *more* than the largest number rather than one *less* than the largest number.

6. Give three examples of finding the sum of consecutive odd numbers beginning with 1.

# Challenge Problem

It pays to read the details! Bank One Delaware offers a Platinum Visa Credit Card to qualifying persons with an introductory 0% fixed APR on all purchases and balance transfers and, after the 12-month introductory period, a low variable APR on purchases and balance transfers at a current rate of 8.99%. However, the default rate is 24.99% APR. A default occurs if the minimum payment is not received by the due date on the billing statement or if your balance ever exceeds your credit limit. Find the difference in just one month's interest on an average daily balance of $1,000 if the payment is not received by the date.

## 12.1  Know What You Owe

Nancy Tai has recently opened a revolving charge account with MasterCard. Her credit limit is $1,000, but she has not charged that much since opening the account. Nancy hasn't had the time to review her monthly statements promptly as she should, but over the upcoming weekend she plans to catch up on her work. She has been putting it off because she can't tell how much interest she paid or the unpaid balance in November. She spilled watercolor paint on that portion of the statement.

In reviewing November's statement she notices that her beginning balance was $600 and that she made a $200 payment on November 10. She also charged purchases of $80 on November 5, $100 on November 15, and $50 on November 30. She paid $5.27 in interest the month before. She does remember, though, seeing the letters APR and the number 16 percent. Also, the back of her statement indicates that interest was charged using the average daily balance method, including current purchases, which considers the day of a charge or credit.

1. Find the unpaid balance on November 30 before the interest is charged.

2. Assuming a 30-day period in November find the average daily balance.

3. Calculate the interest for November.

4. What was the unpaid balance for November after interest is charged?

## 12.2  Massage Therapy

It was time to expand her massage therapy business, and Arminte had finally found a commercial space that met her needs. With room for herself and the two new massage therapists she planned to hire, and adjacent to a chiropractor's office, the space was everything that she had hoped for. Now all she needed was to finalize purchases for three massage rooms, furniture for the reception area, various artwork, and miscellaneous supplies. Arminte started to make a list of massage equipment: 3 tables at $1,695 each; 3 stools at $189 each; a portable massage chair for $399; and the list went on—bolsters, pillows, sheets, table warmers, and music. By the time Arminte was finished, her massage equipment alone totaled $7,644.25, including sales tax. The supplier offered in-house financing of 24 monthly payments at $365.33 per month, with a 10% down payment.

1. Find the amount financed, installment price, and the finance charge presuming Arminte goes with the financing available through her supplier.

2. Use Table 12-1 to find the annual percentage rate (APR) of the financing.

Source: Adapted from Winger and Frasca, *Personal Finance: An Integrated Approach,* 6th edition, Upper Saddle River, NJ: Prentice Hall, p. 162.

**3.** If Arminte takes the financing but pays it in full with 9 months remaining, what is the amount of the finance charge to be refunded using the rule of 78?

**4.** Arminte had recently opened a revolving charge account with MasterCard, to pick up some miscellaneous supplies for her business. Her credit limit is $1,500, with 18% APR. Her beginning balance for the month of April was $440, and she made a payment of $60, which was received on April 10. She purchased massage oil for $240 on April 6, office supplies for $68.45 on April 14, a CD player for $129.44 on April 20, and $25 in gas on April 27. Arminte's statement indicates that interest is charged using the average daily balance method, including current purchases, which considers the day of a charge or credit. Assuming a 30-day period in April, find the average daily balance and the interest for April.

# Compound Interest, Future Value, and Present Value

# Auto Loans: When Is 4% APR Better Than 0% APR?

What could possibly be wrong with a zero percent auto loan? Nothing could be more enticing than free money, and that's exactly what zero-percent finance deals seem to offer. With an auto loan, zero-percent financing may cost more than you think. Before taking on any loan, there are many things to consider. Compound interest—one of the topics you'll learn about in Chapter 13, is of special concern. With compound interest, you will actually pay more interest than you expect. Look for the annual percentage rate (APR) on your loan information. The APR tells you the effective interest rate that you will actually pay for the term of your loan. Does that mean a lower interest rate is the best deal? Not always. Here are a few things you should know about this special financing arrangement.

Anyone who purchases a vehicle with a cash rebate gets the rebate. But only about 5 percent of all consumers qualify for zero percent financing. You must have an excellent credit rating and a certain amount of income to qualify. Most zero percent loans have short payback terms, which mean higher monthly payments. You may have to make a large down payment and be subject to prepayment penalties. Also, most zero percent financing applies only to certain makes and models of vehicles or those already on the lot.

Want to make the best deal? Consider rebates instead of special financing. Rebates are simply a form of discount, or savings, which may be greater than the amount you would save with zero percent financing. The table below shows a comparison of zero percent financing versus a rebate. In the table, the rebate deals saved money compared to the zero percent financing—more than $800 savings over the life of the loan. Do the math ahead of time to find out whether the rebate or the special financing would save you more money.

| Financing a $20,000 New Car | | | | |
|---|---|---|---|---|
| **Loan terms** | **36 Months** | | **60 Months** | |
| APR | 0% | 4.0% | 2.9% | 5.6% |
| Price of new car | $20,000.00 | $20,000.00 | $20,000.00 | $20,000.00 |
| Less dealer rebate | $0 | $2,000.00 | $0 | $2,000.00 |
| Amount to finance | $20,000.00 | $18,000.00 | $20,000.00 | $18,000.00 |
| Monthly payment | $555.56 | $531.43 | $358.49 | $344.65 |
| Total financing cost | $20,000.00 | $19,131.48 | $21,509.40 | $20,679.00 |
| **Savings** | | **$868.52** | | **$830.40** |

## LEARNING OUTCOMES

### 13-1 Compound Interest and Future Value

1. Find the future value and compound interest by compounding manually.
2. Find the future value and compound interest using a $1.00 future value table.
3. Find the future value and compound interest using a formula (optional).
4. Find the effective interest rate.
5. Find the interest compounded daily using a table.

### 13-2 Present Value

1. Find the present value based on annual compounding for one year.
2. Find the present value using a $1.00 present value table.
3. Find the present value using a formula (optional).

 A corresponding Business Math Case Video for this chapter, *The Real World: Video Case: Should I Invest in Elvis?* can be found in Appendix A.

For some loans made on a short-term basis, interest is computed once, using the simple interest formula. For other loans, interest may be *compounded:* Interest is calculated more than once during the term of the loan or investment and this interest is added to the principal. This sum (principal + interest) then becomes the principal for the next calculation of interest, and interest is charged or paid on this new amount. This process of adding interest to the principal before interest is calculated for the next period is called *compounding interest.*

## 13-1 COMPOUND INTEREST AND FUTURE VALUE

### LEARNING OUTCOMES

1 Find the future value and compound interest by compounding manually.
2 Find the future value and compound interest using a $1.00 future value table.
3 Find the future value and compound interest using a formula (optional).
4 Find the effective interest rate.
5 Find the interest compounded daily using a table.

**Interest period:** the amount of time after which interest is calculated and added to the principal.

Whether the interest rate is simple or compound, interest is calculated for each **interest period**. The entire period of the loan or investment is the single, simple interest period. When the interest is compounded, there are two or more interest periods, each of the same duration. The interest period may be one day, one week, one month, one quarter, one year, or some other designated period of time. The greater the number of interest periods in the time period of the loan or investment, the greater the total interest that accumulates during the time period. The total interest that accumulates is the **compound interest**. The sum of the compound interest and the original principal is the **future value** or **maturity value** or **compound amount** in the case of an investment, or the compound amount in the case of a loan. In this chapter we use the term *future value* to mean future value *or* compound amount, depending on whether the principal is an investment or a loan.

**Compound interest:** the total interest that accumulated after more than one interest period.

**Future value, maturity value, compound amount:** the accumulated principal and interest after one or more interest periods.

### 1 Find the future value and compound interest by compounding manually.

We can calculate the future value of the principal using the simple interest formula method. The terms of a loan or investment indicate the annual number of interest periods and the annual interest rate. Dividing the annual interest rate by the annual number of interest periods gives us the **period interest rate** or interest rate per period. We can use the period interest rate to calculate the interest that accumulates for each period using the familiar simple interest formula: $I = PRT$. $I$ is the interest for the period, $P$ is the principal at the beginning of the period, $R$ is the period interest rate, and $T$ is one period. Since we are calculating the interest for only one period, the length of time is one period. So the value of $T$ in the formula is one period, and the formula is simplified to $I = PR(1)$, or $I = PR$. The value of $P$ is different for each period in turn because the principal at the beginning of each period includes the original principal and all the interest so far accumulated.

**Period interest rate:** the rate for calculating interest for one interest period—the annual interest rate divided by the number of interest periods per year.

### HOW TO  Find the period interest rate

Divide the annual interest rate by the number of interest periods per year.

$$\text{Period interest rate} = \frac{\text{annual interest rate}}{\text{number of interest periods per year}}$$

### HOW TO  Find the future value using the simple interest formula method

1. Find the first end-of-period principal: Multiply the original principal by the sum of 1 and the period interest rate.

$$\text{First end-of-period principal} = \text{original principal} \times (1 + \text{period interest rate})$$
$$A = P(1 + R)$$

2. For each remaining period in turn, find the next end-of-period principal: Multiply the previous end-of-period principal by the sum of 1 and the period interest rate.

$$\text{End-of-period principal} = \text{previous end-of-period principal} \times (1 + \text{period interest rate})$$

3. Identify the last end-of-period principal as the future value.

$$\text{Future value} = \text{last end-of-period principal}$$

The future value is calculated before the compound interest can be calculated.

**HOW TO**  Find the compound interest

Subtract the original principal from the future value.

$$\text{Compound interest} = \text{future value} - \text{original principal}$$
$$I = A - P$$

**EXAMPLE 1**  Duke's Photography secured a small business loan of $8,000 for three years, compounded annually. If the interest rate was 9%, find (a) the future value (compound amount) and (b) the compound interest paid on the loan. (c) Compare the compound interest with simple interest for the same loan period, original principal, and annual interest rate.

$$\text{Period interest rate} = \frac{\text{rate per year}}{\text{number of interest periods per year}}$$

(a) Since the loan is compounded annually, there is one interest period per year. So the period interest rate is 0.09. There are three interest periods, one for each of the three years.

First end-of-period principal $= \$8,000(1 + 0.09)$ $\qquad 8,000(1.09) = 8,720$
$\qquad\qquad\qquad\qquad\qquad = \$8,720$

Next end-of-period principal $= \$8,720(1 + 0.09)$ $\qquad 8,720(1.09) = 9,504.8$
$\qquad\qquad\qquad\qquad\qquad = \$9,504.80$

Third end-of-period principal $= \$9,504.80(1 + 0.09)$ $\qquad 9,504.80(1.09) = 10,360.232$
$\qquad\qquad\qquad\qquad\qquad = \$10,360.23$

**The future value is $10,360.23.**

(b) Compound interest is the future value (compound amount) minus the original principal.

| | |
|---|---|
| $10,360.23 | Future value |
| $- 8,000.00$ | Original principal |
| $\$ 2,360.23$ | Compound interest |

**The compound interest is $2,360.23.**

(c) Use the simple interest formula to find the simple interest on $8,000 at 9% annually for three years.

$$I = PRT$$
$$I = \$8,000(0.09)(3)$$
$$I = \$2,160.00 \qquad\qquad \text{Simple interest}$$
Difference: $\qquad \$2,360.23 - \$2,160.00 = \$200.23$

**The simple interest is $2,160.00, which is $200.23 less than the compound interest.**

**EXAMPLE 2**  Find the future value of a $10,000 investment at 8% annual interest compounded semiannually for three years.

$$\text{Period interest rate} = \frac{8\% \text{ annually}}{2 \text{ periods annually}} = \frac{0.08}{2} = 0.04$$

Number of periods $= \text{years}(2) = 3(2) = 6$

First end-of-period principal $= \$10,000(1 + 0.04)$      $10,000(1.04) = 10,400$
$= \$10,400$

Second end-of-period principal $= \$10,400(1 + 0.04)$      $10,400(1.04) = 10,816$
$= \$10,816$

Third end-of-period principal $= \$11,248.64$      $10,816(1.04) = 11,248.64$

Fourth end-of-period principal $= \$11,698.59$      $11,248.64(1.04) = 11,698.59$

Fifth end-of-period principal $= \$12,166.53$      $11,698.59(1.04) = 12,166.53$

Sixth end-of-period principal $= \$12,653.19$      $12,166.53(1.04) = 12,653.19$

**The future value is $12,653.19.**

---

## TIP

**Calculator Shortcut for Compounding**

Many calculators keep the result of a calculation in the calculator and allow the next calculation to begin with this amount.

Examine the calculator steps that can be used for Example 2.

$10000 \boxed{\times} 1.04 \boxed{=} \Rightarrow 10400$      Record display as first end-of-period principal.

Do not clear the calculator.

$\boxed{\times} 1.04 \boxed{=} \Rightarrow 10816$      Record display as second end-of-period principal.

Continue without clearing the calculator.

$\boxed{\times} 1.04 \boxed{=} \Rightarrow 11248.64$      Record display as third end-of-period principal.
$\boxed{\times} 1.04 \boxed{=} \Rightarrow 11698.5856$      Record display as fourth end-of-period principal.
$\boxed{\times} 1.04 \boxed{=} \Rightarrow 12166.52902$      Record display as fifth end-of-period principal.
$\boxed{\times} 1.04 \boxed{=} \Rightarrow 12653.19018$      Record display as sixth end-of-period principal.

---

## STOP AND CHECK

1. Find the monthly interest rate on a loan that has an annual interest rate of 9.2%.

2. A loan of $2,950 at 8% annually is made for two years compounded annually. Find the future value (compound amount) of the loan. Find the amount of interest paid on the loan.

3. Find the future value of a $20,000 investment at 3.5% annual interest compounded semiannually for two years.

4. Find the future value of a $15,000 money market investment at 2.8% annual interest compounded semiannually for three years.

## 2 Find the future value and compound interest using a $1.00 future value table.

As you may have guessed from the previous examples, compounding interest for a large number of periods is very time-consuming. This task is done more quickly if you use a compound interest table, as shown in Table 13-1.

Table 13-1 gives the future value of $1.00, depending on the number of interest periods per year and the interest rate per period.

TABLE 13-1
Future Value or Compound Amount of $1.00

### Rate per period

| Periods | 1% | 1.5% | 2% | 2.5% | 3% | 4% | 5% | 6% | 8% | 10% | 12% |
|---|---|---|---|---|---|---|---|---|---|---|---|
| 1 | 1.01000 | 1.01500 | 1.02000 | 1.02500 | 1.03000 | 1.04000 | 1.05000 | 1.06000 | 1.08000 | 1.10000 | 1.12000 |
| 2 | 1.02010 | 1.03023 | 1.04040 | 1.05063 | 1.06090 | 1.08160 | 1.10250 | 1.12360 | 1.16640 | 1.21000 | 1.25440 |
| 3 | 1.03030 | 1.04568 | 1.06121 | 1.07689 | 1.09273 | 1.12486 | 1.15763 | 1.19102 | 1.25971 | 1.33100 | 1.40493 |
| 4 | 1.04060 | 1.06136 | 1.08243 | 1.10381 | 1.12551 | 1.16986 | 1.21551 | 1.26248 | 1.36049 | 1.46410 | 1.57352 |
| 5 | 1.05101 | 1.07728 | 1.10408 | 1.13141 | 1.15927 | 1.21665 | 1.27628 | 1.33823 | 1.46933 | 1.61051 | 1.76234 |
| 6 | 1.06152 | 1.09344 | 1.12616 | 1.15969 | 1.19405 | 1.26532 | 1.34010 | 1.41852 | 1.58687 | 1.77156 | 1.97382 |
| 7 | 1.07214 | 1.10984 | 1.14869 | 1.18869 | 1.22987 | 1.31593 | 1.40710 | 1.50363 | 1.71382 | 1.94872 | 2.21068 |
| 8 | 1.08286 | 1.12649 | 1.17166 | 1.21840 | 1.26677 | 1.36857 | 1.47746 | 1.59385 | 1.85093 | 2.14359 | 2.47596 |
| 9 | 1.09369 | 1.14339 | 1.19509 | 1.24886 | 1.30477 | 1.42331 | 1.55133 | 1.68948 | 1.99900 | 2.35795 | 2.77308 |
| 10 | 1.10462 | 1.16054 | 1.21899 | 1.28008 | 1.34392 | 1.48024 | 1.62889 | 1.79085 | 2.15892 | 2.59374 | 3.10585 |
| 11 | 1.11567 | 1.17795 | 1.24337 | 1.31209 | 1.38423 | 1.53945 | 1.71034 | 1.89830 | 2.33164 | 2.85312 | 3.47855 |
| 12 | 1.12683 | 1.19562 | 1.26824 | 1.34489 | 1.42576 | 1.60103 | 1.79586 | 2.01220 | 2.51817 | 3.13843 | 3.89598 |
| 13 | 1.13809 | 1.21355 | 1.29361 | 1.37851 | 1.46853 | 1.66507 | 1.88565 | 2.13293 | 2.71962 | 3.45227 | 4.36349 |
| 14 | 1.14947 | 1.23176 | 1.31948 | 1.41297 | 1.51259 | 1.73168 | 1.97993 | 2.26090 | 2.93719 | 3.79750 | 4.88711 |
| 15 | 1.16097 | 1.25023 | 1.34587 | 1.44830 | 1.55797 | 1.80094 | 2.07893 | 2.39656 | 3.17217 | 4.17725 | 5.47357 |
| 16 | 1.17258 | 1.26899 | 1.37279 | 1.48451 | 1.60471 | 1.87298 | 2.18287 | 2.54035 | 3.42594 | 4.59497 | 6.13039 |
| 17 | 1.18430 | 1.28802 | 1.40024 | 1.52162 | 1.65285 | 1.94790 | 2.29202 | 2.69277 | 3.70002 | 5.05447 | 6.86604 |
| 18 | 1.19615 | 1.30734 | 1.42825 | 1.55966 | 1.70243 | 2.02582 | 2.40662 | 2.85434 | 3.99602 | 5.55992 | 7.68997 |
| 19 | 1.20811 | 1.32695 | 1.45681 | 1.59865 | 1.75351 | 2.10685 | 2.52695 | 3.02560 | 4.31570 | 6.11591 | 8.61276 |
| 20 | 1.22019 | 1.34686 | 1.48595 | 1.63862 | 1.80611 | 2.19112 | 2.65330 | 3.20714 | 4.66096 | 6.72750 | 9.64629 |
| 21 | 1.23239 | 1.36706 | 1.51567 | 1.67958 | 1.86029 | 2.27877 | 2.78596 | 3.39956 | 5.03383 | 7.40025 | 10.80385 |
| 22 | 1.24472 | 1.38756 | 1.54598 | 1.72157 | 1.91610 | 2.36992 | 2.92526 | 3.60354 | 5.43654 | 8.14027 | 12.10031 |
| 23 | 1.25716 | 1.40838 | 1.57690 | 1.76461 | 1.97359 | 2.46472 | 3.07152 | 3.81975 | 5.87146 | 8.95430 | 13.55235 |
| 24 | 1.26973 | 1.42950 | 1.60844 | 1.80873 | 2.03279 | 2.56330 | 3.22510 | 4.04893 | 6.34118 | 9.84973 | 15.17863 |
| 25 | 1.28243 | 1.45095 | 1.64061 | 1.85394 | 2.09378 | 2.66584 | 3.38635 | 4.29187 | 6.84848 | 10.83471 | 17.00006 |
| 26 | 1.29526 | 1.47271 | 1.67342 | 1.90029 | 2.15659 | 2.77247 | 3.55567 | 4.54938 | 7.39635 | 11.91818 | 19.04007 |
| 27 | 1.30821 | 1.49480 | 1.70689 | 1.94780 | 2.22129 | 2.88337 | 3.73346 | 4.82235 | 7.98806 | 13.10999 | 21.32488 |
| 28 | 1.32129 | 1.51722 | 1.74102 | 1.99650 | 2.28793 | 2.99870 | 3.92013 | 5.11169 | 8.62711 | 14.42099 | 23.88387 |
| 29 | 1.33450 | 1.53998 | 1.77584 | 2.04641 | 2.35657 | 3.11865 | 4.11614 | 5.41839 | 9.31727 | 15.86309 | 26.74993 |
| 30 | 1.34785 | 1.56308 | 1.81136 | 2.09757 | 2.42726 | 3.24340 | 4.32194 | 5.74349 | 10.06266 | 17.44940 | 29.95992 |

Table shows future value (*FV*) of $1.00 compounded for *N* periods at *R* rate per period.
Table values can be generated using the formula $FV = \$1(1 + R)^N$.

---

## HOW TO — Find the future value and compound interest using a $1.00 future value table

1. Find the number of interest periods: Multiply the number of years by the number of interest periods per year.

$$\text{Interest periods} = \text{number of years} \times \text{number of interest periods per year}$$

2. Find the period interest rate: Divide the annual interest rate by the number of interest periods per year.

$$\text{Period interest rate} = \frac{\text{annual interest rate}}{\text{number of interest periods per year}}$$

3. Using Table 13-1, select the periods row corresponding to the number of interest periods.
4. Select the rate-per-period column corresponding to the period interest rate.
5. Locate the value in the cell where the periods row intersects the rate-per-period column. This value is sometimes called the *i-factor*.
6. Multiply the original principal by the value from step 5 to find the future value or compound amount.

$$\text{Future value} = \text{principal} \times \text{table value}$$

7. To find the compound interest,

$$\text{Compound interest} = \text{future value} - \text{original principal}$$

**EXAMPLE 1**  Use Table 13-1 to compute the compound interest on a $5,000 loan for six years compounded annually at 8%.

Interest periods = number of years × interest periods per year

$$= 6(1) = 6 \text{ periods}$$

$$\text{Period interest rate} = \frac{\text{annual interest rate}}{\text{interest periods per year}}$$

$$= \frac{8\%}{1} = 8\%$$

Find period row 6 of the table and the 8% rate column. The value in the intersecting cell is 1.58687. This means that $1 would be worth $1.58687, or $1.59 rounded, compounded annually at the end of six years.

$5,000(1.58687) = **$7,934.35**    The loan is for $5,000, so multiply $5,000 by 1.58687 to find the future value of the loan.

The future value is $7,934.35.

**$7,934.35** − $5,000 = $2,934.35    The future value minus the principal is the compound interest.

**The compound interest on $5,000 for six years compounded annually at 8% is $2,934.35.**

**EXAMPLE 2**  An investment of $3,000 at 8% annually is compounded *quarterly* (four times a year) for three years. Find the future value and the compound interest.

Interest periods = number of years × number of interest periods per year

$$= 3(4) = 12 \qquad \text{The investment is compounded four times a year for three years.}$$

$$\text{Period interest rate} = \frac{\text{annual interest rate}}{\text{number of interest periods per year}} \qquad \begin{array}{l}\text{Divide the annual rate of 8\%} \\ \text{by the number of periods} \\ \text{per year to find the period} \\ \text{interest rate.}\end{array}$$

$$= \frac{8\%}{4} = 2\%$$

Future value of $1 = **1.26824**    Find the 12 periods row in Table 13-1. Move across to the 2% column.

$3,000(**1.26824**) = $3,804.72    The principal times the future value per dollar equals the total future value.

**$3,804.72 is the future value.**

Compound interest = future value − original principal

$$= \$3,804.72 - \$3,000$$

$$= \$804.72$$

**The compound interest is $804.72.**

## ✔ STOP AND CHECK

1. Use Table 13-2 to compute the compound interest on $2,890 for five years compounded annually at 4%.

2. A loan of $2,982 is repaid in three years. Find the amount of interest paid on the loan if it is compounded quarterly at 10%.

3. Andre Castello owns a savings account that is paying 2.5% interest compounded annually. His current balance is $7,598.42. How much interest will he earn over five years if the rate remains constant?

4. Natalie Bradley invested $25,000 at 5% for three years compounded semiannually. Find the future value at the end of three years using Table 13-1.

## 3 Find the future value and compound interest using a formula (optional).

Table values are most often generated with a formula. When the table does not include the rate you need or does not have as many periods as you need, the equivalent table value can be found by using the formula. The formula for finding the future value or the compound interest will require a calculator or electronic spreadsheet that has a power function. A business or scientific calculator or an electronic spreadsheet, such as Excel, is normally used.

> **HOW TO** Find the future value using a formula.
>
> The future value formula is
>
> $$FV = P(1 + R)^N$$
>
> where $FV$ is the future value, $P$ is the principal, $R$ is the period interest rate, and $N$ is the number of periods.

Business calculators, scientific calculators, and electronic spreadsheets impose a standard order of operations when making calculations. However, it is helpful to make some of the calculations in a formula mentally or before you begin the evaluation of the formula. For instance, in the future value formula you can find the period interest rate and the number of periods first. Also, you can change the period interest rate to a decimal equivalent and add one mentally.

**EXAMPLE 1** Find the future value of a three-year investment of $5,000 that earns 6% compounded monthly.

Find the period interest rate:

$$R = \frac{6\%}{12} = \frac{0.06}{12} = 0.005$$
Change the annual rate to a decimal equivalent and divide by 12.

Find the number of periods:

$$N = 3(12) = 36$$
Multiply the number of years by 12.

Evaluate the future value formula:

$$FV = P(1 + R)^N$$
Substitute known values.

$$FV = 5,000(1 + 0.005)^{36}$$
Mentally add inside of parentheses.

$$FV = 5,000(1.005)^{36}$$
Evaluate using a calculator or spreadsheet.

$5000\ \boxed{(}\ 1.005\ \boxed{)}\ \boxed{^\wedge}\ 36\ \boxed{=}\ \Rightarrow\ 5983.402624$

$$FV = \$5,983.40$$
Rounded

The compound interest is found by subtracting the original principal from the future value. The compound interest formula is

$$I = P(1 + R)^N - P$$

where $I$ is the compound interest, $P$ is the principal, $R$ is the period rate, and $N$ is the number of periods.

**EXAMPLE 2** Find the compound interest earned on a four-year investment of $3,500 at 4.5% compounded monthly.

Find the period interest rate:

$$R = \frac{4.5\%}{12} = \frac{0.045}{12} = 0.00375$$
Change the annual rate to a decimal equivalent and divide by 12.

Find the number of periods:

$$N = 4(12) = 48$$
Multiply the number of years by 12.

Evaluate the compound interest formula:

$$I = P(1 + R)^N - P$$
Substitute known values.

$$I = 3,500(1 + 0.00375)^{48} - 3,500$$
Mentally add inside of parentheses.

$$I = 3,500(1.00375)^{48} - 3,500$$
Evaluate using a calculator or spreadsheet.

$3500\ \boxed{(}\ 1.00375\ \boxed{)}\ \boxed{^\wedge}\ 48\ \boxed{=}\ \boxed{-}\ 3500\ \boxed{=}\ \Rightarrow\ 688.850321$

$$I = \$688.85$$
Rounded

**EXAMPLE 3** Joe Gallegos can invest $10,000 at 8% compounded quarterly for two years. Or he can invest the same $10,000 at 8.2% compounded annually for the same two years. If all other conditions (such as early withdrawal penalty, etc.) are the same, which deal should he take?

| What You Know | What You Are Looking For |
|---|---|
| Principal: $10,000 | Which deal should Joe take? |
| Time period: 2 years | Future value for each investment |
| Deal 1 annual rate: 8% | |
| Deal 1 interest periods per year: 4 | |
| Deal 2 annual rate: 8.2% | |
| Deal 2 interest periods per year: 1 | |

**Solution Plan**

Number of interest periods = number of years $\times$ number of interest periods per year

Deal 1 interest periods = 2(4) = 8     Deal 2 interest periods = 2(1) = 2

$$\text{Period interest rate} = \frac{\text{annual interest rate}}{\text{number of interest periods per year}}$$

Deal 1 period interest rate = $\dfrac{8\%}{4}$ = 2%     Deal 2 period interest rate = $\dfrac{8.2\%}{1}$ = 8.2%

**Solution**

Deal 1: Using the future value formula for $10,000 at 2% per period for 8 periods

| | |
|---|---|
| $FV = P(1 + R)^N$ | Substitute known values. |
| $FV = \$10,000(1 + 0.02)^8$ | Mentally add inside of parentheses. |
| $FV = 10,000(1.02)^8$ | Evaluate using a calculator or spreadsheet. |
| $10000\ (\ 1.02\ )\ ^\wedge\ 8\ =\ \Rightarrow$ | 11716.59381 |
| $FV = \$11,716.59$ | Future value for Deal 1 |

Deal 2: Using the future value formula for $10,000 at 8.2% per period for 2 periods

| | |
|---|---|
| $FV = P(1 + R)^N$ | Substitute known values. |
| $FV = \$10,000(1 + 0.082)^2$ | Mentally add inside of parentheses. |
| $FV = 10,000(1.082)^2$ | Evaluate using a calculator or spreadsheet. |
| $10000\ (\ 1.082\ )\ ^\wedge\ 2\ =\ \Rightarrow$ | 11707.24 |
| $FV = \$11,707.24$ | Future value for Deal 2 |

**Conclusion**

**Deal 1, the lower interest rate of 8% compounded more frequently (quarterly), is a slightly better deal because it yields the greater future value.**

## ✔ STOP AND CHECK

1. Kellen Davis invested $20,000 that earns 4.68% compounded monthly for four years. Find the future value of Kellen's investment.

2. Jonathan Vergues invested $17,500 that earns 5.2% compounded semiannually for 10 years. What is the future value of the investment after 10 years?

3. Hanna Stein has a $18,200 certificate of deposit (CD) that earns 4.8% interest compounded quarterly for 5 years. Find the compound interest after 5 years.

4. Susan Bertrees can invest $12,000 at 4% interest compounded twice a year or compounded quarterly. If either investment is for five years, which investment results in more interest? How much more interest is yielded by the better investment?

## 4 Find the effective interest rate.

If the investment in Example 2 on page 458 is compounded annually instead of quarterly for three years—three periods at 8% per period—the future value is $3,779.22 (using table value 1.25971), and the compound interest is $779.22. The simple interest at the end of three years is $3,000 × 8% × 3, or $720. $3,000 at 8% for 3 years:

| $720 | $799.22 | $804.72 |
| Simple interest | Compounded annually using table value | Compounded quarterly using table value |

You can see from these comparisons that a loan or investment with an interest rate of 8% compounded quarterly carries higher interest than a loan with an interest rate of 8% compounded annually or a loan with an annual simple interest rate of 8%. When you compare interest rates, you need to know the actual or **effective rate** of interest. The effective rate of interest equates compound interest rates to equivalent simple interest rates so that comparisons can be made.

  The effective rate of interest is also referred to as the **annual percentage yield (APY)** when identifying the rate of earnings on an investment. It is referred to as the **annual percentage rate (APR)** when identifying the rate of interest on a loan.

**Effective rate:** the simple interest rate that is equivalent to a compound rate.

**Annual percentage yield (APY):** effective rate of interest for an investment.

**Annual percentage rate (APR):** effective rate of interest for a loan.

---

**HOW TO**   Find the effective interest rate of a compound interest rate

**Using the manual compound interest method:** Divide the compound interest for the first year by the principal.

$$\text{Effective annual interest rate} = \frac{\text{compound interest for first year}}{\text{principal}} \times 100\%$$

**Using the table method:** Find the future value of $1.00 by using the future value table, Table 13-1. Subtract $1.00 from the future value of $1.00 after one year and divide by $1.00 to remove the dollar sign.

$$\text{Effective annual interest rate} = \frac{\text{future value of \$1.00 after 1 year} - \$1.00}{\$1.00} \times 100\%$$

---

**EXAMPLE 1**   Marcia borrowed $6,000 at 10% compounded semiannually. What is the effective interest rate?

*Using the manual compound interest method:*

$$\text{Period interest rate} = \frac{10\%}{2} = 5\% = 0.05$$

First end-of-period principal $= \$6,000(1 + 0.05)$
$$= \$6,300$$

Second end-of-period principal $= \$6,300(1 + 0.05)$
$$= \$6,615$$

Compound interest after first year $= \$6,615 - \$6,000 = \$615$

$$\text{Effective annual interest rate} = \frac{\$615}{\$6,000}(100\%)$$
$$= 0.1025(100\%)$$
$$= 10.25\%$$

*Using the table method:*
10% compounded semiannually means two periods in the first (and every) year and a period interest rate of 5%. The Table 13-1 value is 1.10250. Subtract 1.00.

$$\text{Effective annual interest rate} = (1.10250 - 1.00)(100\%)$$
$$= 0.10250(100\%)$$
$$= 10.25\%$$

**The effective interest rate is 10.25%.**

## STOP AND CHECK

1. Willy Spears borrowed $2,800 at 8% compounded semiannually. Use the manual compound interest method to find the effective interest rate.

2. Use Table 13-1 to find the effective interest rate on Willy Spears' loan in Exercise 1. Compare the rate using the table with the rate found manually.

3. Mindi Lancaster invested $82,500 at 4% compounded quarterly. Use Table 13-1 to find the annual percentage yield (APY) for her investment.

4. Una Sircy invested $5,000 at 3% compounded semiannually. Use Table 13-1 to find the APY for her investment.

## 5 Find the interest compounded daily using a table.

Some banks compound interest daily and others use continuous compounding to compute interest on savings accounts. There is no significant difference in the interest earned on money using interest compounded daily and interest compounded continuously. A computer is generally used in calculating interest if either daily or continuous compounding is used.

Table 13-2 gives compound interest for $100 compounded daily (using 365 days as a year). Notice that this table gives the *compound interest* rather than the future value of the principal, as is given in Table 13-1.

Using Table 13-2 is exactly like using Table 11-2, which gives the *simple* interest on $100.

### HOW TO     Find the compounded daily interest using a table

1. Determine the amount of money the table uses as the principal ($1, $100, or $1,000).
2. Divide the loan principal by the table principal.
3. Using Table 13-2, select the days row corresponding to the time period (in days) of the loan.
4. Select the interest rate column corresponding to the interest rate of the loan.
5. Locate the value in the cell where the interest column intersects the days row.
6. Multiply the quotient from step 2 by the value from step 5.

### TIP

**Examine Table Title and Footnote Carefully!**

All tables are not alike! Different reference sources may approach finding the same information using different methods.

In working with compound interest, you may more frequently want to know the accumulated amount than the accumulated interest, or vice versa. A table can be designed to give a factor for finding either amount directly.

- Determine whether the table will help you find the compound amount or the compound interest. Table 13-1 finds the compound amount and Table 13-2 finds the compound interest. Also, the principal that is used to determine the table value may be $1, $10, $100, or some other amount.

- Determine the principal amount used in calculating table values. Table 13-1 uses $1 as the principal and Table 13-2 uses $100 as the principal.

### EXAMPLE 1     Find the interest on $800 at 7.5% annually, compounded daily, for 28 days.

$800 ÷ $100 = 8                     Find the number of $100 units in the principal.
                                    Find the 28 days row in Table 13-2. Move across to the 7.5% column and find the interest for $100.

$8(0.576941) = $4.615528            Multiply the table value by 8, the number of $100 units.

**The interest is $4.62.**

| Days | 5.00% | 5.25% | 5.50% | 5.75% | 6.00% | 6.25% | 6.50% | 6.75% | 7.00% |
|---|---|---|---|---|---|---|---|---|---|
| | | | | | **Annual rate** | | | | |
| 1 | 0.013699 | 0.014384 | 0.015068 | 0.015753 | 0.016438 | 0.017123 | 0.017808 | 0.018493 | 0.019178 |
| 2 | 0.027399 | 0.028769 | 0.030139 | 0.031509 | 0.032879 | 0.034250 | 0.035620 | 0.036990 | 0.038360 |
| 3 | 0.041102 | 0.043157 | 0.045212 | 0.047268 | 0.049323 | 0.051379 | 0.053434 | 0.055490 | 0.057545 |
| 4 | 0.054806 | 0.057547 | 0.060288 | 0.063029 | 0.065770 | 0.068511 | 0.071252 | 0.073993 | 0.076734 |
| 5 | 0.068512 | 0.071938 | 0.075365 | 0.078792 | 0.082219 | 0.085646 | 0.089073 | 0.092500 | 0.095927 |
| 6 | 0.082220 | 0.086332 | 0.090445 | 0.094558 | 0.098671 | 0.102784 | 0.106897 | 0.111010 | 0.115124 |
| 7 | 0.095930 | 0.100728 | 0.105527 | 0.110326 | 0.115125 | 0.119925 | 0.124724 | 0.129524 | 0.134324 |
| 8 | 0.109642 | 0.115126 | 0.120612 | 0.126097 | 0.131583 | 0.137068 | 0.142555 | 0.148041 | 0.153528 |
| 9 | 0.123355 | 0.129527 | 0.135698 | 0.141870 | 0.148043 | 0.154215 | 0.160388 | 0.166562 | 0.172735 |
| 10 | 0.137071 | 0.143929 | 0.150787 | 0.157646 | 0.164505 | 0.171365 | 0.178225 | 0.185085 | 0.191946 |
| 11 | 0.150788 | 0.158333 | 0.165878 | 0.173424 | 0.180971 | 0.188518 | 0.196065 | 0.203613 | 0.211161 |
| 12 | 0.164507 | 0.172739 | 0.180972 | 0.189205 | 0.197439 | 0.205673 | 0.213908 | 0.222144 | 0.230380 |
| 13 | 0.178229 | 0.187148 | 0.196068 | 0.204988 | 0.213910 | 0.222832 | 0.231754 | 0.240678 | 0.249602 |
| 14 | 0.191952 | 0.201558 | 0.211166 | 0.220774 | 0.230383 | 0.239993 | 0.249604 | 0.259216 | 0.268828 |
| 15 | 0.205677 | 0.215971 | 0.226266 | 0.236562 | 0.246859 | 0.257157 | 0.267457 | 0.277757 | 0.288058 |
| 16 | 0.219403 | 0.230385 | 0.241369 | 0.252353 | 0.263338 | 0.274325 | 0.285312 | 0.296301 | 0.307291 |
| 17 | 0.233132 | 0.244802 | 0.256473 | 0.268146 | 0.279820 | 0.291495 | 0.303171 | 0.314849 | 0.326528 |
| 18 | 0.246863 | 0.259221 | 0.271581 | 0.283942 | 0.296304 | 0.308668 | 0.321034 | 0.333400 | 0.345769 |
| 19 | 0.260595 | 0.273642 | 0.286690 | 0.299740 | 0.312791 | 0.325844 | 0.338899 | 0.351955 | 0.365013 |
| 20 | 0.274329 | 0.288065 | 0.301802 | 0.315540 | 0.329281 | 0.343023 | 0.356768 | 0.370514 | 0.384261 |
| 21 | 0.288066 | 0.302490 | 0.316916 | 0.331344 | 0.345774 | 0.360205 | 0.374639 | 0.389075 | 0.403513 |
| 22 | 0.301804 | 0.316917 | 0.332032 | 0.347149 | 0.362269 | 0.377390 | 0.392514 | 0.407640 | 0.422769 |
| 23 | 0.315544 | 0.331346 | 0.347150 | 0.362957 | 0.378767 | 0.394578 | 0.410392 | 0.426209 | 0.442028 |
| 24 | 0.329286 | 0.345777 | 0.362271 | 0.378768 | 0.395267 | 0.411769 | 0.428274 | 0.444781 | 0.461291 |
| 25 | 0.343029 | 0.360210 | 0.377394 | 0.394581 | 0.411771 | 0.428963 | 0.446158 | 0.463356 | 0.480557 |
| 26 | 0.356775 | 0.374646 | 0.392520 | 0.410397 | 0.428277 | 0.446160 | 0.464046 | 0.481935 | 0.499827 |
| 27 | 0.370522 | 0.389083 | 0.407647 | 0.426215 | 0.444785 | 0.463359 | 0.481937 | 0.500517 | 0.519101 |
| 28 | 0.384272 | 0.403523 | 0.422777 | 0.442035 | 0.461297 | 0.480562 | 0.499831 | 0.519103 | 0.538379 |
| 29 | 0.398023 | 0.417964 | 0.437909 | 0.457858 | 0.477811 | 0.497768 | 0.517728 | 0.537692 | 0.557660 |
| 30 | 0.411776 | 0.432408 | 0.453044 | 0.473684 | 0.494328 | 0.514976 | 0.535628 | 0.556285 | 0.576945 |
| 35 | 0.480570 | 0.504658 | 0.528751 | 0.552849 | 0.576953 | 0.601063 | 0.625178 | 0.649299 | 0.673426 |
| 40 | 0.549411 | 0.576959 | 0.604514 | 0.632077 | 0.659646 | 0.687223 | 0.714808 | 0.742400 | 0.769999 |
| 45 | 0.618300 | 0.649313 | 0.680335 | 0.711367 | 0.742408 | 0.773458 | 0.804518 | 0.835587 | 0.866665 |
| 50 | 0.687235 | 0.721718 | 0.756213 | 0.790719 | 0.825237 | 0.859766 | 0.894307 | 0.928859 | 0.963424 |
| 55 | 0.756218 | 0.794176 | 0.832148 | 0.870134 | 0.908134 | 0.946148 | 0.984176 | 1.022219 | 1.060275 |
| 60 | 0.825248 | 0.866686 | 0.908140 | 0.949612 | 0.991099 | 1.032604 | 1.074126 | 1.115664 | 1.157219 |
| 90 | 1.240422 | 1.302841 | 1.365298 | 1.427794 | 1.490327 | 1.552898 | 1.615507 | 1.678155 | 1.740841 |
| 120 | 1.657306 | 1.740883 | 1.824528 | 1.908241 | 1.992022 | 2.075871 | 2.159789 | 2.243775 | 2.327830 |
| 150 | 2.075907 | 2.180819 | 2.285838 | 2.390964 | 2.496197 | 2.601538 | 2.706986 | 2.812542 | 2.918205 |
| 180 | 2.496231 | 2.622657 | 2.749237 | 2.875973 | 3.002864 | 3.129911 | 3.257114 | 3.384472 | 3.511987 |
| 240 | 3.342080 | 3.512073 | 3.682344 | 3.852895 | 4.023725 | 4.194835 | 4.366225 | 4.537896 | 4.709848 |
| 360 | 5.054775 | 5.314097 | 5.574058 | 5.834658 | 6.095900 | 6.357785 | 6.620315 | 6.883491 | 7.147315 |
| 365 | 5.126750 | 5.389858 | 5.653624 | 5.918047 | 6.183131 | 6.448876 | 6.715285 | 6.982358 | 7.250098 |
| 730 | 10.516335 | 11.070222 | 11.626882 | 12.186328 | 12.748573 | 13.313633 | 13.881520 | 14.452250 | 15.025836 |
| 1095 | 16.182231 | 17.056750 | 17.937846 | 18.825568 | 19.719965 | 20.621089 | 21.528989 | 22.443716 | 23.365322 |
| 1825 | 28.400343 | 30.015193 | 31.650340 | 33.306041 | 34.982553 | 36.680138 | 38.399060 | 40.139588 | 41.901993 |
| 3650 | 64.866481 | 69.039503 | 73.318120 | 77.705005 | 82.202895 | 86.814600 | 91.542998 | 96.391041 | 101.361756 |

Table shows interest ($I$) on $100 compounded daily for $N$ days at an annual rate of $R$. Table values can be generated using the formula $I = 100(1 + R/365)^N - 100$.

| Days | 7.25% | 7.50% | 7.75% | 8.00% | 8.25% | 8.50% | 8.75% | 9.00% |
|------|-------|-------|-------|-------|-------|-------|-------|-------|
| | | | | Annual rate | | | | |
| 1 | 0.019863 | 0.020548 | 0.021233 | 0.021918 | 0.022603 | 0.023288 | 0.023973 | 0.024658 |
| 2 | 0.039730 | 0.041100 | 0.042470 | 0.043840 | 0.045211 | 0.046581 | 0.047951 | 0.049321 |
| 3 | 0.059601 | 0.061657 | 0.063712 | 0.065768 | 0.067824 | 0.069879 | 0.071935 | 0.073991 |
| 4 | 0.079476 | 0.082217 | 0.084959 | 0.087700 | 0.090442 | 0.093183 | 0.095925 | 0.098667 |
| 5 | 0.099355 | 0.102782 | 0.106209 | 0.109637 | 0.113065 | 0.116493 | 0.119920 | 0.123348 |
| 6 | 0.119237 | 0.123351 | 0.127465 | 0.131579 | 0.135693 | 0.139807 | 0.143922 | 0.148036 |
| 7 | 0.139124 | 0.143924 | 0.148725 | 0.153526 | 0.158327 | 0.163128 | 0.167929 | 0.172730 |
| 8 | 0.159015 | 0.164502 | 0.169989 | 0.175477 | 0.180965 | 0.186453 | 0.191942 | 0.197431 |
| 9 | 0.178909 | 0.185084 | 0.191258 | 0.197433 | 0.203609 | 0.209784 | 0.215960 | 0.222137 |
| 10 | 0.198808 | 0.205670 | 0.212532 | 0.219394 | 0.226257 | 0.233121 | 0.239985 | 0.246849 |
| 11 | 0.218710 | 0.226260 | 0.233810 | 0.241360 | 0.248911 | 0.256463 | 0.264015 | 0.271568 |
| 12 | 0.238617 | 0.246854 | 0.255092 | 0.263331 | 0.271570 | 0.279810 | 0.288051 | 0.296292 |
| 13 | 0.258527 | 0.267453 | 0.276379 | 0.285307 | 0.294234 | 0.303163 | 0.312092 | 0.321023 |
| 14 | 0.278442 | 0.288056 | 0.297671 | 0.307287 | 0.316904 | 0.326521 | 0.336140 | 0.345759 |
| 15 | 0.298360 | 0.308663 | 0.318967 | 0.329272 | 0.339578 | 0.349885 | 0.360193 | 0.370502 |
| 16 | 0.318282 | 0.329274 | 0.340268 | 0.351262 | 0.362258 | 0.373254 | 0.384252 | 0.395251 |
| 17 | 0.338208 | 0.349890 | 0.361573 | 0.373257 | 0.384942 | 0.396629 | 0.408317 | 0.420006 |
| 18 | 0.358139 | 0.370510 | 0.382882 | 0.395256 | 0.407632 | 0.420009 | 0.432387 | 0.444767 |
| 19 | 0.378073 | 0.391134 | 0.404197 | 0.417261 | 0.430327 | 0.443394 | 0.456464 | 0.469534 |
| 20 | 0.398011 | 0.411762 | 0.425515 | 0.439270 | 0.453027 | 0.466785 | 0.480546 | 0.494308 |
| 21 | 0.417953 | 0.432395 | 0.446838 | 0.461284 | 0.475732 | 0.490182 | 0.504633 | 0.519087 |
| 22 | 0.437899 | 0.453031 | 0.468166 | 0.483303 | 0.498442 | 0.513583 | 0.528727 | 0.543873 |
| 23 | 0.457849 | 0.473672 | 0.489498 | 0.505327 | 0.521158 | 0.536991 | 0.552826 | 0.568664 |
| 24 | 0.477803 | 0.494318 | 0.510835 | 0.527355 | 0.543878 | 0.560403 | 0.576931 | 0.593462 |
| 25 | 0.497761 | 0.514967 | 0.532177 | 0.549389 | 0.566604 | 0.583822 | 0.601042 | 0.618266 |
| 26 | 0.517723 | 0.535621 | 0.553523 | 0.571427 | 0.589335 | 0.607245 | 0.625159 | 0.643076 |
| 27 | 0.537688 | 0.556279 | 0.574873 | 0.593470 | 0.612071 | 0.630674 | 0.649281 | 0.667892 |
| 28 | 0.557658 | 0.576941 | 0.596228 | 0.615518 | 0.634812 | 0.654109 | 0.673410 | 0.692714 |
| 29 | 0.577632 | 0.597608 | 0.617587 | 0.637571 | 0.657558 | 0.677549 | 0.697544 | 0.717542 |
| 30 | 0.597610 | 0.618279 | 0.638951 | 0.659628 | 0.680309 | 0.700994 | 0.721684 | 0.742377 |
| 35 | 0.697558 | 0.721696 | 0.745839 | 0.769989 | 0.794143 | 0.818304 | 0.842470 | 0.866641 |
| 40 | 0.797606 | 0.825220 | 0.852841 | 0.880470 | 0.908106 | 0.935749 | 0.963400 | 0.991059 |
| 45 | 0.897753 | 0.928850 | 0.959956 | 0.991072 | 1.022197 | 1.053332 | 1.084476 | 1.115630 |
| 50 | 0.997999 | 1.032586 | 1.067185 | 1.101796 | 1.136418 | 1.171052 | 1.205697 | 1.240354 |
| 55 | 1.098345 | 1.136430 | 1.174528 | 1.212641 | 1.250768 | 1.288909 | 1.327063 | 1.365233 |
| 60 | 1.198791 | 1.240380 | 1.281985 | 1.323608 | 1.365247 | 1.406903 | 1.448575 | 1.490265 |
| 90 | 1.803565 | 1.866327 | 1.929128 | 1.991967 | 2.054844 | 2.117759 | 2.180713 | 2.243705 |
| 120 | 2.411953 | 2.496145 | 2.580405 | 2.664734 | 2.749132 | 2.833599 | 2.918135 | 3.002739 |
| 150 | 3.023977 | 3.129857 | 3.235844 | 3.341940 | 3.448144 | 3.554457 | 3.660878 | 3.767407 |
| 180 | 3.639658 | 3.767486 | 3.895471 | 4.023613 | 4.151911 | 4.280368 | 4.408981 | 4.537753 |
| 240 | 4.882081 | 5.054597 | 5.227396 | 5.400477 | 5.573842 | 5.747491 | 5.921424 | 6.095642 |
| 360 | 7.411788 | 7.676912 | 7.942689 | 8.209120 | 8.476207 | 8.743951 | 9.012354 | 9.281418 |
| 365 | 7.518507 | 7.787585 | 8.057334 | 8.327757 | 8.598855 | 8.870629 | 9.143082 | 9.416214 |
| 730 | 15.602292 | 16.181634 | 16.763875 | 17.349030 | 17.937113 | 18.528139 | 19.122123 | 19.719080 |
| 1095 | 24.293858 | 25.229377 | 26.171931 | 27.121572 | 28.078354 | 29.042331 | 30.013557 | 30.992085 |
| 1825 | 43.686550 | 45.493537 | 47.323235 | 49.175931 | 51.051913 | 52.951474 | 54.874909 | 56.822519 |
| 3650 | 106.458246 | 111.683692 | 117.041357 | 122.534585 | 128.166805 | 133.941534 | 139.862375 | 145.933026 |

Table shows interest ($I$) on $100 compounded daily for $N$ days at an annual rate of $R$. Table values can be generated using the formula $I = 100(1 + R/365)^N - 100$.

## STOP AND CHECK

1. Find the interest on $1,850 at 7.25% annually, compounded daily for 60 days.

2. Find the interest on $3,050 at 6% annually, compounded daily for 365 days.

3. Find the interest on $10,000 at 6.75% annually, compounded daily for 730 days.

4. Bob Weaver has $20,000 invested for three years at a 5.25% annual rate compounded daily. How much interest will he earn?

## 13-1 SECTION EXERCISES

### SKILL BUILDERS

*Find the future value and compound interest. Use Table 13-1 or the future value and compound interest formula.*

1. $5,000 at 6% compounded semiannually for two years

2. $18,500 at 6% compounded quarterly for four years

3. $7,000 at 2% compounded semiannually for six years

4. $500 at 5% compounded semiannually for five years

5. $1,000 at 12% compounded monthly for two years

6. $2,000 at 1.5% compounded annually for ten years

### APPLICATIONS

*Use the simple interest formula method for Exercises 7–10.*

7. Thayer Farm Trust made a farmer a loan of $1,200 at 16% for three years compounded annually. Find the future value and the compound interest paid on the loan. Compare the compound interest with simple interest for the same period.

8. Maeola Killebrew invests $3,800 at 3% compounded semiannually for two years. What is the future value of the investment, and how much interest will she earn over the two-year period?

9. Carolyn Smith borrowed $6,300 at $8\frac{1}{2}\%$ for three years compounded annually. What is the compound amount of the loan and how much interest will she pay on the loan?

10. Margaret Hillman invested $5,000 at 6% compounded quarterly for one year. Find the future value and the interest earned for the year.

*Use Table 13-1 or the appropriate formula for Exercises 11–16.*

11. First State Bank loaned Doug Morgan $2,000 for four years compounded annually at 8%. How much interest was Doug required to pay on the loan?

12. A loan of $8,000 for two acres of woodland is compounded quarterly at an annual rate of 12% for five years. Find the compound amount and the compound interest.

13. Compute the compound amount and the interest on a loan of $10,500 compounded annually for four years at 10%.

14. Find the future value of an investment of $10,500 if it is invested for four years and compounded quarterly at an annual rate of 4%.

15. You have $8,000 that you plan to invest in a compound-interest-bearing instrument. Your investment agent advises you that you can invest the $8,000 at 8% compounded quarterly for three years or you can invest the $8,000 at $8\frac{1}{4}\%$ compounded annually for three years. Which investment should you choose to receive the most interest?

16. Find the future value of $50,000 at 6% compounded semiannually for ten years.

17. Find the effective interest rate for a loan for four years compounded quarterly at an annual rate of 4%. Use the table method.

18. What is the effective interest rate for a loan of $5,000 at 10% compounded semiannually for three years? Use the simple interest formula method.

**19.** Ross Land has a loan of $8,500 compounded quarterly for four years at 6%. What is the effective interest rate for the loan? Use the table method.

**20.** What is the effective interest rate for a loan of $20,000 for three years if the interest is compounded quarterly at a rate of 12%?

*Use Table 13-2 for Exercises 21–24.*

**21.** Find the compound interest on $2,500 at $6\frac{3}{4}$% compounded daily by Leader Financial Bank for 20 days.

**22.** How much compound interest is earned on a deposit of $1,500 at 6.25% compounded daily for 30 days?

**23.** John McCormick has found a short-term investment opportunity. He can invest $8,000 at 8.5% interest for 15 days. How much interest will he earn on this investment if the interest is compounded daily?

**24.** What is the compound interest on $8,000 invested at 8% for 180 days if it is compounded daily?

## 13-2 PRESENT VALUE

### LEARNING OUTCOMES

1 Find the present value based on annual compounding for one year.
2 Find the present value using a $1.00 present value table.
3 Find the present value using a formula (optional).

In Section 1 of this chapter we learned how to find the future value of money invested at the present time. Sometimes businesses and individuals need to know how much to invest at the present time to yield a certain amount at some specified future date. For example, a business may want to set aside a lump sum of money to provide pensions for employees in years to come. Individuals may want to set aside a lump sum of money now to pay for a child's college education or for a vacation. You can use the concepts of compound interest to determine the amount of money that must be set aside at present and compounded periodically to yield a certain amount of money at some specific time in the future. The amount of money set aside now is called *present value*. See Figure 13-1.

### 1 Find the present value based on annual compounding for one year.

**Present value:** the amount that must be invested now and compounded at a specified rate and time to reach a specified future value.

Finding the present value of $100 means finding the *principal* that we must invest today so that $100 is its future value. We know that the future value of principal depends on the period interest rate and the number of interest periods. Just as calculating future value by hand is time-consuming when there are many interest periods, so is calculating **present value** by hand. A present value table is more efficient. For now, we find present value based on the simplest case—annual compounding for one year. In this case, the number of interest periods is 1, and the period interest rate is the annual interest rate. In this case,

$$\text{Future value} = \text{principal}(1 + \text{annual interest rate})$$

If we know the future value and want to know the present value,

$$\text{Principal(present value)} = \frac{\text{future value}}{1 + \text{annual interest rate}}$$

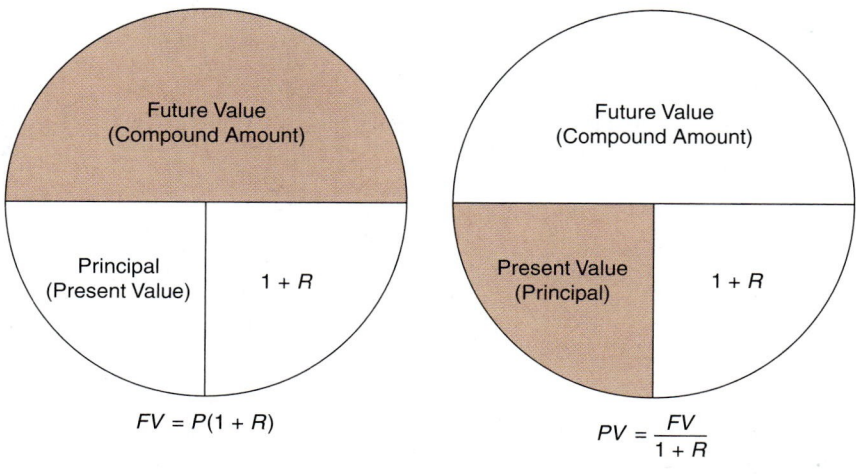

$$FV = P(1 + R)$$

$$PV = \frac{FV}{1 + R}$$

**FIGURE 13-1**
Relationship between future value and present value.

**HOW TO**    **Find the present value based on annual compounding for one year**

Divide the future value by the sum of 1 and the decimal equivalent of the annual interest rate.

$$\text{Present value(principal)} = \frac{\text{future value}}{1 + \text{annual interest rate}}$$

**EXAMPLE 1**    Find the amount of money that The 7th Inning needs to set aside today to ensure that $10,000 will be available to buy a new large-screen plasma television in one year if the annual interest rate is 4% compounded annually.

$1 + 0.04 = 1.04$      Convert the annual interest rate to a decimal and add to 1.

$\dfrac{\$10,000}{1.04} = \$9,615.38$      Divide the future value by 1.04 to get the present value.

**An investment of $9,615.38 at 4% would have a value of $10,000 in one year.**

---

## ✔ STOP AND CHECK

1. How much money needs to be set aside today to have $15,000 in one year if the annual interest rate is 2% compounded annually?

2. How much should be set aside today to have $15,000 in one year if the annual interest rate is 4% compounded annually?

3. Greg Karrass should set aside how much money today to have $30,000 in one year if the annual interest rate is 2.8% compounded annually?

4. Jamie Puckett plans to purchase real estate in one year that costs $148,000. How much should be set aside today at an annual interest rate of 3.46% compounded annually?

## 2 Find the present value using a $1.00 present value table.

If the interest in the preceding example had been compounded more than once a year, you would have to make calculations for each time the money was compounded. One method for finding the present value when the principal is compounded for more than one period is to use Table 13-3, which shows the present value of $1.00 at different interest rates for different periods. Table 13-3 is used like Table 13-1, which gives the future value of $1.00.

### HOW TO  Find the present value using a $1.00 present value table

1. Find the number of interest periods: Multiply the time period, in years, by the number of interest periods per year.

$$\text{Interest periods} = \text{number of years} \times \text{number of interest periods per year}$$

2. Find the period interest rate: Divide the annual interest rate by the number of interest periods per year.

$$\text{Period interest rate} = \frac{\text{annual interest rate}}{\text{number of interest periods per year}}$$

3. Using Table 13-3, select the periods row corresponding to the number of interest periods.
4. Select the rate-per-period column corresponding to the period interest rate.
5. Locate the value in the cell where the periods row intersects the rate-per-period column.
6. Multiply the future value by the value from step 5.

### EXAMPLE 1  The Absorbent Diaper Company needs $20,000 in five years to buy a new diaper edging machine. How much must the firm invest at the present if it receives 5% interest compounded annually?

$R = 5\%$ and $N = 5$ years

Table value = 0.78353   The money is to be compounded for 5 periods, so we find periods row 5 in Table 13-3 and the 5% rate column to find the present value of $1.00.

$20,000(0.78353) = $15,670.60   Multiply the present value factor times the desired future value to find the amount that must be invested at the present.

**The Absorbent Diaper Company should invest $15,670.60 today to have $20,000 in five years.**

### TIP

**Which Table Do I Use?**

Tables 13-1 and 13-3 have entries that are reciprocal. Except for minor rounding discrepancies, the product of corresponding entries is 1. And 1 divided by a table value equals its comparable table value in the other table.

Look at period row 1 at 1% on each table.

Table 13-1: 1.01000      1 ÷ 1.01000 = 0.99010 (rounded)      Table 13-3: 0.99010

Look at period row 16 at 4% on each table.

Table 13-1: 1.87298      1 ÷ 1.87298 = 0.53391 (rounded)      Table 13-3: 0.53391

One way to select the appropriate table is to anticipate whether you expect a larger or smaller amount. You expect a future value to be larger than what you start with. All entries in Table 13-1 are greater than 1 and produce a larger product.

You expect a present value to require a smaller investment to reach a desired amount. All entries in Table 13-3 are less than 1 and produce a smaller product.

FV table factors > 1
PV table factors < 1

## TABLE 13-3
### Present Value of $1.00

| Periods | 1% | 1.5% | 2% | 2.5% | 3% | 4% | 5% | 6% | 8% | 10% | 12% |
|---|---|---|---|---|---|---|---|---|---|---|---|
| 1 | 0.99010 | 0.98522 | 0.98039 | 0.97561 | 0.97087 | 0.96154 | 0.95238 | 0.94340 | 0.92593 | 0.90909 | 0.89286 |
| 2 | 0.98030 | 0.97066 | 0.96117 | 0.95181 | 0.94260 | 0.92456 | 0.90703 | 0.89000 | 0.85734 | 0.82645 | 0.79719 |
| 3 | 0.97059 | 0.95632 | 0.94232 | 0.92860 | 0.91514 | 0.88900 | 0.86384 | 0.83962 | 0.79383 | 0.75131 | 0.71178 |
| 4 | 0.96098 | 0.94218 | 0.92385 | 0.90595 | 0.88849 | 0.85480 | 0.82270 | 0.79209 | 0.73503 | 0.68301 | 0.63552 |
| 5 | 0.95147 | 0.92826 | 0.90573 | 0.88385 | 0.86261 | 0.82193 | 0.78353 | 0.74726 | 0.68058 | 0.62092 | 0.56743 |
| 6 | 0.94205 | 0.91454 | 0.88797 | 0.86230 | 0.83748 | 0.79031 | 0.74622 | 0.70496 | 0.63017 | 0.56447 | 0.50663 |
| 7 | 0.93272 | 0.90103 | 0.87056 | 0.84127 | 0.81309 | 0.75992 | 0.71068 | 0.66506 | 0.58349 | 0.51316 | 0.45235 |
| 8 | 0.92348 | 0.88771 | 0.85349 | 0.82075 | 0.78941 | 0.73069 | 0.67684 | 0.62741 | 0.54027 | 0.46651 | 0.40388 |
| 9 | 0.91434 | 0.87459 | 0.83676 | 0.80073 | 0.76642 | 0.70259 | 0.64461 | 0.59190 | 0.50025 | 0.42410 | 0.36061 |
| 10 | 0.90529 | 0.86167 | 0.82035 | 0.78120 | 0.74409 | 0.67556 | 0.61391 | 0.55839 | 0.46319 | 0.38554 | 0.32197 |
| 11 | 0.89632 | 0.84893 | 0.80426 | 0.76214 | 0.72242 | 0.64958 | 0.58468 | 0.52679 | 0.42888 | 0.35049 | 0.28748 |
| 12 | 0.88745 | 0.83639 | 0.78849 | 0.74356 | 0.70138 | 0.62460 | 0.55684 | 0.49697 | 0.39711 | 0.31863 | 0.25668 |
| 13 | 0.87866 | 0.82403 | 0.77303 | 0.72542 | 0.68095 | 0.60057 | 0.53032 | 0.46884 | 0.36770 | 0.28966 | 0.22917 |
| 14 | 0.86996 | 0.81185 | 0.75788 | 0.70773 | 0.66112 | 0.57748 | 0.50507 | 0.44230 | 0.34046 | 0.26333 | 0.20462 |
| 15 | 0.86135 | 0.79985 | 0.74301 | 0.69047 | 0.64186 | 0.55526 | 0.48102 | 0.41727 | 0.31524 | 0.23939 | 0.18270 |
| 16 | 0.85282 | 0.78803 | 0.72845 | 0.67362 | 0.62317 | 0.53391 | 0.45811 | 0.39365 | 0.29189 | 0.21763 | 0.16312 |
| 17 | 0.84438 | 0.77639 | 0.71416 | 0.65720 | 0.60502 | 0.51337 | 0.43630 | 0.37136 | 0.27027 | 0.19784 | 0.14564 |
| 18 | 0.83602 | 0.76491 | 0.70016 | 0.64117 | 0.58739 | 0.49363 | 0.41552 | 0.35034 | 0.25025 | 0.17986 | 0.13004 |
| 19 | 0.82774 | 0.75361 | 0.68643 | 0.62553 | 0.57029 | 0.47464 | 0.39573 | 0.33051 | 0.23171 | 0.16351 | 0.11611 |
| 20 | 0.81954 | 0.74247 | 0.67297 | 0.61027 | 0.55368 | 0.45639 | 0.37689 | 0.31180 | 0.21455 | 0.14864 | 0.10367 |
| 21 | 0.81143 | 0.73150 | 0.65978 | 0.59539 | 0.53755 | 0.43883 | 0.35894 | 0.29416 | 0.19866 | 0.13513 | 0.09256 |
| 22 | 0.80340 | 0.72069 | 0.64684 | 0.58086 | 0.52189 | 0.42196 | 0.34185 | 0.27751 | 0.18394 | 0.12285 | 0.08264 |
| 23 | 0.79544 | 0.71004 | 0.63416 | 0.56670 | 0.50669 | 0.40573 | 0.32557 | 0.26180 | 0.17032 | 0.11168 | 0.07379 |
| 24 | 0.78757 | 0.69954 | 0.62172 | 0.55288 | 0.49193 | 0.39012 | 0.31007 | 0.24698 | 0.15770 | 0.10153 | 0.06588 |
| 25 | 0.77977 | 0.68921 | 0.60953 | 0.53939 | 0.47761 | 0.37512 | 0.29530 | 0.23300 | 0.14602 | 0.09230 | 0.05882 |
| 26 | 0.77205 | 0.67902 | 0.59758 | 0.52623 | 0.46369 | 0.36069 | 0.28124 | 0.21981 | 0.13520 | 0.08391 | 0.05252 |
| 27 | 0.76440 | 0.66899 | 0.58586 | 0.51340 | 0.45019 | 0.34682 | 0.26785 | 0.20737 | 0.12519 | 0.07628 | 0.04689 |
| 28 | 0.75684 | 0.65910 | 0.57437 | 0.50088 | 0.43708 | 0.33348 | 0.25509 | 0.19563 | 0.11591 | 0.06934 | 0.04187 |
| 29 | 0.74934 | 0.64936 | 0.56311 | 0.48866 | 0.42435 | 0.32065 | 0.24295 | 0.18456 | 0.10733 | 0.06304 | 0.03738 |
| 30 | 0.74192 | 0.63976 | 0.55207 | 0.47674 | 0.41199 | 0.30832 | 0.23138 | 0.17411 | 0.09938 | 0.05731 | 0.03338 |

Rate per period

The table shows the lump sum amount of money, present value (PV), that should be invested now so that the accumulated amount will be $1.00 after a specified number of periods, N, at a specified rate per period, R. Table values can be generated using the formula $PV = \dfrac{\$1.00}{(1 + R)^N}$.

---

 **STOP AND CHECK**

1. The 7th Inning needs $35,000 in four years to buy new framing equipment. How much should be invested at 4% interest compounded annually?

2. How much should be invested now to have $15,000 in two years if interest is 4% compounded quarterly?

3. How much should be invested now to have $15,000 in four years if interest is 4% compounded quarterly?

4. How much should be invested now to have $15,000 in six years if interest is 4% compounded quarterly? Compare your results for Exercises 2–4.

---

## 3 Find the present value using a formula (optional).

A formula for finding the present value can be found by solving the future value formula for the present value.

$$FV = P(1 + R)^N$$  Divide both sides of the equations by $(1 + R)^N$.

$$\dfrac{FV}{(1 + R)^N} = \dfrac{P(1 + R)^N}{(1 + R)^N}$$  Reduce.

$$\dfrac{FV}{(1 + R)^N} = P$$  Rewrite with $P$ on the left side of the equation.

$$P = \frac{FV}{(1 + R)^N}$$

Original principal is present value.

$$PV = \frac{FV}{(1 + R)^N}$$

### HOW TO  Find the present value using a formula.

The present value formula is

$$PV = \frac{FV}{(1 + R)^N}$$

where $PV$ is the present value, $FV$ is the future value, $R$ is the interest rate per period, and $N$ is the number of periods.

### EXAMPLE 1

The Holiday Boutique would like to put away some of the holiday profits to save for a planned expansion. A total of $8,000 is needed in three years. How much money in a 5.2% three-year certificate of deposit that is compounded monthly must be invested now to have the $8,000 in three years?

Period interest rate $= \dfrac{5.2\%}{12} = \dfrac{0.052}{12} = 0.0043333333$

Number of periods $= 3(12) = 36$

$$PV = \frac{FV}{(1 + R)^N}$$
Substitute known values.

$$PV = \frac{8,000}{(1 + 0.0043333333)^{36}}$$
Mentally add inside parentheses.

$$PV = \frac{8,000}{(1.0043333333)^{36}}$$
Evaluate using a calculator.

$8000 \div ( ( ( 1.0043333333 ) \wedge 36 = \Rightarrow 6846.78069$

$PV = \$6,846.78$
Rounded

**The Holiday Boutique must invest \$6,846.78 now at 5.2% interest for three years, compounded monthly to have \$8,000 at the end of the three years.**

---

 ## STOP AND CHECK

1. Mary Kaye Keller needs $30,000 in seven years. How much must she set aside today at 4.8% compounded monthly?

2. How much should a family invest now at 10% compounded annually to have a $7,000 house down payment in four years?

3. If you were offered $700 today or $800 in two years, which would you accept if money can be invested at 12% annual interest compounded monthly?

4. Bridgett Smith inherited some money and needs $45,000 in 15 years for her child's college fund. How much of the inheritance should she invest now at 5.6% compounded quarterly?

---

## 13-2 SECTION EXERCISES

### SKILL BUILDERS

*Find the amount that should be set aside today to yield the desired future amount; use Table 13-3 or the appropriate formula.*

| | Future amount needed | Interest rate | Compounding period | Investment time |
|---|---|---|---|---|
| 1. | $4,000 | 3% | semiannually | 2 years |

| Future amount needed | Interest rate | Compounding period | Investment time |
|---|---|---|---|
| 2. $7,000 | 2.5% | annually | 20 years |
| 3. $10,000 | 6% | quarterly | 4 years |
| 4. $5,000 | 8% | semiannually | 6 years |

## APPLICATIONS

5. Compute the amount of money to be set aside today to ensure a future value of $2,500 in one year if the interest rate is 11% annually, compounded annually.

6. How much should Linda Bryan set aside now to buy equipment that costs $8,500 in one year? The current interest rate is 7.5% annually, compounded annually.

7. Ronnie Cox has just inherited $27,000. How much of this money should he set aside today to have $21,000 to pay cash for a Ventura Van, which he plans to purchase in one year? He can invest at 7.9% annually, compounded annually.

8. Shirley Riddle received a $10,000 gift from her mother and plans a minor renovation to her home. She also plans to make an investment for one year, at which time she plans to take a trip projected to cost $6,999. The current interest rate is 8.3% annually, compounded annually. How much should be set aside today for her trip?

9. Rosa Burnett needs $2,000 in three years to make the down payment on a new car. How much must she invest today if she receives 8% interest annually, compounded annually? Use Table 13-3.

10. Use Table 13-3 to calculate the amount of money that must be invested now at 6% annually, compounded quarterly, to obtain $1,500 in three years.

11. Dewey Sykes plans to open a business in four years when he retires. How much must he invest today to have $10,000 when he retires if the bank pays 10% annually, compounded quarterly?

12. Charlie Bryant has a child who will be college age in five years. How much must he set aside today to have $20,000 for college tuition in five years if he gets 8% annually, compounded annually?

## Learning Outcomes

### Section 13-1

**1** Find the future value and compound interest by compounding manually. (p. 454)

## What to Remember with Examples

**Find the period interest rate.** Divide the annual interest rate by the number of interest periods per year.

$$\text{Period interest rate} = \frac{\text{annual interest rate}}{\text{number of interest periods per year}}$$

**Find the future value using the simple interest formula method.**

1. Find the first end-of-period principal: Multiply the original principal by the sum of 1 and the period interest rate.

$$\text{First end-of-period principal} = \text{original principal} \times (1 + \text{period interest rate})$$

2. For each remaining period in turn, find the next end-of-period principal: Multiply the previous end-of-period principal by the sum of 1 and the period interest rate.

$$\text{End-of-period principal} = \text{previous end-of-period principal} \times (1 + \text{period interest rate})$$

3. Identify the last end-of-period principal as the future value.

$$\text{Future value} = \text{last end-of-period principal}$$

**Find the compound interest.** Subtract the original principal from the future value.

$$\text{Compound interest} = \text{future value} - \text{original principal}$$

Find the compound amount and compound interest on $5,000 at 7% compounded annually for two years.

($5,000)(1 + 0.07) = $5,350 end-of-first-period principal
($5,350)(1 + 0.07) = $5,724.50 end-of-last-period principal (future value)
Compound amount = $5,724.50
Compound interest = $5,724.50 − $5,000 = $724.50

Find the compound amount (future value) and compound interest on $1,500 at 8% compounded semiannually for two years.

Number of interest periods = 2(2) = 4 periods

$$\text{Period interest rate} = \frac{8\%}{2} = 4\% \text{ or } 0.04 \text{ per period}$$

$1,500(1 + 0.04) = $1,560 (first period)
$1,560(1 + 0.04) = $1,622.40 (second period)
$1,622.40(1 + 0.04) = $1,687.30 (third period)
$1,687.30(1 + 0.04) = $1,754.79 (fourth period)
Compound amount = $1,754.79
Compound interest = $1,754.79 − $1,500 = $254.79

**2** Find the future value and compound interest using a $1.00 future value table. (p. 456)

1. Find the number of interest periods: Multiply the number of years by the number of interest periods per year.

$$\text{Interest periods} = \text{number of years} \times \text{number of interest periods per year}$$

2. Find the period interest rate: Divide the annual interest rate by the number of interest periods per year.

$$\text{Period interest rate} = \frac{\text{annual interest rate}}{\text{number of interest periods per year}}$$

3. Using Table 13-1, select the periods row corresponding to the number of interest periods.
4. Select the rate-per-period column corresponding to the period interest rate.
5. Locate the value in the cell where the periods row intersects the rate-per-period column.
6. Multiply the original principal by the value from step 5 to find future value or compound amount.

**7.** To find the compound interest:

$$\text{Compound interest} = \text{future value} - \text{original principal}$$

Find the future value of $2,000 at 12% compounded semiannually for four years.

$4(2) = 8$ periods

$\dfrac{12\%}{2} = 6\%$ period interest rate.

Find periods row 8 in Table 13-1 and move across to the 6% rate column: 1.59385.

$2,000(1.59385) = \$3,187.70$ future value or compound amount

Find the compound interest on $800 at 8% compounded annually for four years. Annually indicates one period per year. Period interest rate is 8%.

Find periods row 4 in Table 13-1.

Move across to the 8% rate column and find the compound amount per dollar of principal: 1.36049.

$800(1.36049) = \$1,088.39$ compound amount

| | |
|---|---|
| $1,088.39 | compound amount or future value |
| $-800.00$ | principal |
| $288.39 | compound interest |

**3** Find the future value and compound interest using a formula (optional). (p. 459)

The future value formula is

$$FV = P(1 + R)^N$$

where $FV$ is the future value, $P$ is the principal, $R$ is the period interest rate, and $N$ is the number of periods.

Find the future value of a three-year investment of $3,500 that earns 5.4% compounded monthly.

Find the period interest rate:

$R = \dfrac{5.4\%}{12} = \dfrac{0.054}{12} = 0.0045$ — Change the annual rate to a decimal equivalent and divide by 12.

Find the number of periods:

$N = (3)(12) = 36$ — Multiply the number of years by 12.

Evaluate the future value formula:

$FV = P(1 + R)^N$ — Substitute known values.

$FV = 3,500(1 + 0.0045)^{36}$ — Mentally add inside of parentheses.

$FV = 3,500(1.0045)^{36}$ — Evaluate using a calculator or spreadsheet.

$3500\ \boxed{(}\ 1.0045\ \boxed{)}\ \boxed{\wedge}\ 36\ \boxed{=}\ \Rightarrow 4114.015498$

$FV = \$4,114.02$ — Rounded

The compound interest formula is

$$I = P(1 + R)^N - P$$

where $I$ is the compound interest, $P$ is the principal, $R$ is the period rate, and $N$ is the number of periods.

Find the compound interest earned on a four-year investment of $6,500 at 5.5% compounded monthly.

Find the period interest rate:

$R = \dfrac{5.5\%}{12} = \dfrac{0.055}{12} = 0.0045833333$ — Change the annual rate to a decimal equivalent and divide by 12.

Find the number of periods:

$N = (4)(12) = 48$ — Multiply the number of years by 12.

Evaluate the compound interest formula:

$I = P(1 + R)^N - P$ — Substitute known values.

$I = 6,500(1 + 0.0045833333)^{48} - 6,500$ — Mentally add inside of parentheses.

$I = 6,500(1.0045833333)^{48} - 6,500$ — Evaluate using a calculator or spreadsheet.

$6500\ \boxed{(}\ 1.0045833333\ \boxed{)}\ \boxed{\wedge}\ 48\ \boxed{=}\ \boxed{-}\ 6500\ \boxed{=}\ \Rightarrow 1,595.428696$

$I = \$1,595.43$ — Rounded

**4** Find the effective interest rate. (p. 461)

Using the manual compound interest method: Divide the compound interest for the first year by the principal.

$$\text{Effective annual interest rate} = \frac{\text{compound interest for first year}}{\text{principal}} \times 100\%$$

Using the table method: Use Table 13-1 to find the future value of $1.00 of the investment. Subtract $1.00 from the future value of $1.00 after one year and divide by $1.00 to remove the dollar sign.

$$\text{Effective interest rate} = \frac{\text{future value of \$1.00 after 1 year} - \$1.00}{\$1.00} \times 100\%$$

Betty Padgett earned $247.29 interest on a one-year investment of $3,000 at 8% annually, compounded quarterly. Find the effective interest rate.

Using the simple interest formula method:

$$\text{Effective interest} = \frac{\$247.29}{\$3,000}(100\%) = 0.08243(100\%) = 8.24\%$$

Using Table 13-1: Periods per year $= 4$

$$\text{Rate per period} = \frac{8\%}{4} = 2\%$$

$$\text{Table value} = 1.08243 \text{ (from Table 13-1)}$$

Effective interest rate $= 1.08243 - 1.00 = 0.08243 = 8.24\%$

**5** Find the interest compounded daily using a table. (p. 462)

1. Determine the amount of money the table uses as the principal. (A typical table principal is $1, $100, or $1,000.)
2. Divide the loan principal by the table principal.
3. Using Table 13-2, select the days row corresponding to the time period (in days) of the loan.
4. Select the interest rate column corresponding to the interest rate of the loan.
5. Locate the value in the cell where the interest column intersects the days row.
6. Multiply the quotient from step 2 by the value from step 5.

Find the interest on a $300 loan borrowed at 9% compounded daily for 21 days.

Select the 21 days row of Table 13-2; then move across to the 9% rate column. The table value is 0.519087.

$$\frac{\$300}{100}(0.519087) = \$1.56$$

The interest on $300 is $1.56.

## Section 13-2

**1** Find the present value based on annual compounding for one year. (p. 467)

Divide the future value by the sum of 1 and the decimal equivalent of the annual interest rate.

$$\text{Present value (principal)} = \frac{\text{future value}}{1 + \text{annual interest rate}}$$

Find the amount of money that must be invested to produce $4,000 in one year if the interest rate is 7% annually, compounded annually.

$$\text{Present value} = \frac{\$4,000}{1 + 0.07} = \frac{\$4,000}{1.07} = \$3,738.32$$

How much must be invested to produce $30,000 in one year if the interest rate is 6% annually, compounded annually?

$$\text{Present value} = \frac{\$30,000}{1 + 0.06} = \frac{\$30,000}{1.06} = \$28,301.89$$

**2**    Find the present value using a $1.00 present value table. (p. 469)

1. Find the number of interest periods: Multiply the time period, in years, by the number of interest periods per year.

$$\text{Interest periods} = \text{number of years} \times \text{number of interest periods per year}$$

2. Find the period interest rate: Divide the annual interest rate by the number of interest periods per year.

$$\text{Period interest rate} = \frac{\text{annual interest rate}}{\text{number of interest periods per year}}$$

3. Using Table 13-3, select the periods row corresponding to the number of interest periods.
4. Select the rate-per-period column corresponding to the period interest rate.
5. Locate the value in the cell where the periods row intersects the rate-per-period column.
6. Multiply the future value by the value from step 5.

---

Find the amount of money that must be deposited to ensure $3,000 at the end of three years if the investment earns 6% compounded semiannually.

$(3)(2) = 6$ periods

$\dfrac{6\%}{2} = 3\%$ rate per period

Find periods row 6 in Table 13-3 and move across to the 3% rate column: 0.83748.

$\$3,000(0.83748) = \$2,512.44$

The amount that must be invested now to have $3,000 in three years is $2,512.44.

---

**3**    Find the present value using a formula (optional). (p. 470)

Present Value Formula

$$PV = \frac{FV}{(1 + R)^N}$$ where $PV$ is the present value, $FV$ is the future value, $R$ is the interest rate per period, and $N$ is the number of periods.

---

Ezell Allen has saved some money that he wants to put away for a down payment on a home in five years. He can invest the money in a 5.4% five-year certificate of deposit that is compounded monthly. How much of his money should he set aside now for a down payment of $10,000 in 5 years?

$$\text{Period interest rate} = \frac{5.4\%}{12} = \frac{0.054}{12} = 0.0045$$

Number of periods $= 5(12) = 60$

$$PV = \frac{FV}{(1 + R)^N} \qquad \text{Substitute known values.}$$

$$PV = \frac{10,000}{(1 + 0.0045)^{60}} \qquad \text{Mentally add inside parentheses.}$$

$$PV = \frac{10,000}{(1.0045)^{60}} \qquad \text{Evaluate using a calculator.}$$

$10000 \boxed{\div} \boxed{(} \boxed{(} \boxed{(} 1.0045 \boxed{)} \boxed{^\wedge} 60 \boxed{=} \Rightarrow 7638.420009$

$PV = \$7,638.42 \qquad$ Rounded

**Ezell must invest $7,638.42 now at 5.4% interest for five years, compounded monthly to have $10,000 at the end of the five years.**

# EXERCISES SET A

## CHAPTER 13

*Use Table 13-1 or the appropriate formula for Exercises 1–4.*

| Principal | Term (years) | Rate of compound interest | Compounded | Compound amount | Compound interest |
|-----------|--------------|---------------------------|------------|-----------------|-------------------|
| **1.** $2,000 | 3 | 3% | semiannually | _____ | _____ |
| **2.** $5,000 | 4 | 6% | quarterly | _____ | _____ |
| **3.** $10,000 | 2 | 2.5% | annually | _____ | _____ |
| **4.** $8,000 | 4 | 8% | semiannually | _____ | _____ |

*Find the amount that should be set aside today to yield the desired future amount. Use Table 13-3 or the present value formula.*

| | Future amount needed | Interest rate | Compounding | Investment time (years) | | Future amount needed | Interest rate | Compounding | Investment time (years) |
|---|----------------------|---------------|-------------|-------------------------|---|----------------------|---------------|-------------|-------------------------|
| **CEL 5.** | $20,000 | 4% | semiannually | 5 | **EXCEL 6.** | $8,000 | 6% | quarterly | 6 |
| **CEL 7.** | $9,800 | 2% | semiannually | 12 | **EXCEL 8.** | $14,700 | 3% | annually | 20 |

**9.** Manually calculate the compound interest on a loan of $1,000 at 8%, compounded annually for two years.

**10.** Manually calculate the compound interest on a 13% loan of $1,600 for three years if the interest is compounded annually.

**11.** Use Table 13-1 or the appropriate formula to find the future value of an investment of $3,000 made by Ling Lee for five years at 12% annual interest compounded semiannually.

**12.** Use Table 13-1 or the appropriate formula to find the interest on a certificate of deposit (CD) of $10,000 for five years at 4% compounded semiannually.

**13.** Find the future value of an investment of $8,000 compounded quarterly for seven years at 8%.

**14.** Find the compound interest on $5,000 for two years if the interest is compounded quarterly at 12%.

**15.** Mario Piazza was offered $900 now for one of his salon photographs or $1,100 in one year for the same photograph. Which would give Mr. Piazza a greater yield if he could invest the $900 for one year at 16% compounded quarterly? Use Table 13-1.

**16.** Lauren McAnally invests $2,000 at 8% compounded semiannually for two years, and Inez Everett invests an equal amount at 8% compounded quarterly for 18 months. Use Table 13-1 to determine which investment yields the greater interest.

**17.** Use Table 13-2 to find the compound interest and the compound amount on an investment of $2,000 if it is invested for 21 days at 8% compounded daily.

**18.** Use Table 13-2 to find the amount of interest on $100 invested for 10 days at 8.5% compounded daily.

*In the following exercises, find the amount of money that should be invested (present value) at the stated interest rate to yield the given amount (future value) after the indicated amount of time. Use Table 13-3 or the appropriate formula.*

**19.** $1,500 in three years at 10% compounded annually

**20.** $1,000 in seven years at 8% compounded quarterly

**21.** $4,000 in two years at 12% annual interest compounded quarterly

**22.** $500 in 15 years at 8% annual interest compounded semiannually

**23.** Find the amount that should be invested today to have $1,800 in one year at 12% annual interest compounded monthly.

**24.** Myrna Lewis wishes to have $4,000 in four years to tour Europe. How much must she invest today at 8% annual interest compounded quarterly to have $4,000 in four years?

# EXERCISES SET B

*Use Table 13-1 for Exercises 1–4.*

| | Principal | Term (years) | Rate of compound interest | Compounded | Compound amount | Compound interest |
|---|---|---|---|---|---|---|
| **1.** | $5,000 | 5 | 5% | semiannually | _____ | _____ |
| **2.** | $12,000 | 7 | 4% | quarterly | _____ | _____ |
| **3.** | $7,000 | 10 | 2% | semiannually | _____ | _____ |
| **4.** | $2,985 | 8 | 3% | annually | _____ | _____ |

*Find the amount that should be set aside today to yield the desired future amount. Use Table 13-3 or the Present Value table.*

| | | Future amount needed | Interest rate | Compounding | Investment time (years) | | | Future amount needed | Interest rate | Compounding | Investment time (years) |
|---|---|---|---|---|---|---|---|---|---|---|---|
| **EXCEL** | **5.** | $3,000 | 6% | quarterly | 5 | **EXCEL** | **6.** | $46,000 | 2.5% | annually | 25 |
| **EXCEL** | **7.** | $17,000 | 3% | semiannually | 8 | **EXCEL** | **8.** | $11,200 | 4% | quarterly | 3 |

**9.** Manually calculate the compound interest on a loan of $200 at 6% compounded annually for four years.

**10.** Calculate the compound interest on a loan of $6,150 at $11\frac{1}{2}\%$ annual interest compounded annually for three years.

**11.** EZ Loan Company loaned $500 at 8% annual interest compounded quarterly for one year. Use Table 13-1 or the appropriate formula to calculate the amount the loan company will earn in interest.

**12.** Use Table 13-2 to find the daily interest on $2,500 invested for 21 days at 8.75% compounded daily.

**13.** Find the factor for compounding an amount for 25 periods at 8% per period.

**14.** Find the compound interest on $5,000 for two years if the interest is compounded semiannually at 12%.

**15.** An investment of $1,000 is made for two years and is compounded semiannually at 10%. Find the compound amount and compound interest at the end of the two years.

**16.** Carlee McNally invests $5,000 at 6% compounded semiannually for one year, and Jake McNally invests an equal amount at 6% compounded quarterly for one year. Use Table 13-1 to determine the interest for each investment. Find the effective rate to the nearest hundredth percent for each investment.

**17.** Use Table 13-2 to find the compound interest and the compound amount on an investment of $24,982 if it is invested for 28 days at 7% compounded daily.

**18.** Use Table 13-2 to find the accumulated daily interest on an investment of $5,000 invested for 30 days at 9%.

*In the following exercises, find the amount of money that should be invested (present value) at the stated interest rate to yield the given amount (future value) after the indicated amount of time. Use Table 13-3 or the appropriate formula.*

**19.** $2,000 in five years at 10% compounded semiannually

**20.** $3,500 in 12 years at 12% compounded annually

**21.** $10,000 in seven years at 16% annual interest compounded quarterly

**22.** $800 in four years at 10% annual interest compounded annually

**23.** Find the amount that should be invested today to have $700 in six years at 8% annual interest compounded quarterly

**24.** Louis Banks was offered $15,000 cash or $19,500 to be paid in two years for a resort cabin. If money can be invested in today's market for 12% annual interest compounded quarterly, which offer should Louis accept?

## PRACTICE TEST

1. Manually calculate the compound interest on a loan of $2,000 at 7% compounded annually for three years.

2. Manually calculate the compound interest on a 6.25% annual interest loan of $3,000 for four years if interest is compounded annually.

3. Use Table 13-1 or the appropriate formula to find the interest on a loan of $5,000 for six years at 10% annual interest if interest is compounded semiannually.

4. Use Table 13-1 to find the future value on an investment of $12,000 for seven years at 6% annual interest compounded quarterly.

5. An investment of $1,500 is made for two years at 12% annual interest compounded semiannually. Find the compound amount and the compound interest at the end of two years.

6. Use Table 13-1 to find the compound interest on a loan of $3,000 for one year at 12% annual interest if the interest is compounded quarterly.

7. Find the effective interest rate for the loan described in Exercise 6.

8. Use Table 13-2 to find the interest compounded on an investment of $2,000 invested at 5.75% for 28 days compounded daily.

9. Use Tables 13-1 and 13-2 to compare the interest on an investment of $3,000 that is invested at 8% annual interest compounded quarterly and daily, respectively, for one year.

*Find the amount that should be invested today (present value) at the stated interest rate to yield the given amount (future value) after the indicated amount of time.*

10. $3,400 in four years at 8% annual interest compounded annually

11. $5,000 in eight years at 8% annual interest compounded semiannually

**12.** $8,000 in 12 years at 12% annual interest compounded annually

**13.** $6,000 in six years at 12% annual interest compounded quarterly

**14.** Jamie Juarez needs $12,000 in 10 years for her daughter's college education. How much must be invested today at 8% annual interest compounded semiannually to have the needed funds?

**15.** If you were offered $600 today or $680 in one year, which would you accept if money can be invested at 12% annual interest compounded monthly?

**16.** Derek Anderson plans to buy a house in four years. He will make an $8,000 down payment on the property. How much should he invest today at 6% annual interest compounded quarterly to have the required amount in four years?

**17.** Which of the two options yields the greatest return on your investment of $2,000?
Option 1: 8% annual interest compounded quarterly for four years
Option 2: $8\frac{1}{4}$% annual interest compounded annually for four years

**18.** If you invest $2,000 today at 8% annual interest compounded quarterly, how much will you have after three years? (Table 13-1)

**19.** If you invest $1,000 today at 5% annual interest compounded daily, how much will you have after 20 days? (Table 13-2)

**20.** How much money should Bryan Trailer Sales set aside today to have $15,000 in one year to purchase a forklift if the interest rate is 10.4% compounded annually?

1. The compound amount or future value can be found using two formulas: $I = PR$ (assuming $T = 1$) and $A = P + I$. Show how these two formulas relate to the single formula $A = P(1 + R)$.

2. Since the entries in the present value table (Table 13-3) are reciprocals of the corresponding entries in the future value table (Table 13-1), how can Table 13-3 be used to find the future value of an investment?

3. In finding a future value, how will your result compare in size to your original investment?

4. In finding a present value, how will your result compare in size to your desired goal?

5. How can the future value table (Table 13-1) be used to find the present value of a desired goal?

6. Banking regulations require that the effective interest rate (APR or APY) be stated on all loan or investment contracts. Why?

7. Illustrate the procedure described in Exercise 5 to find the present value of an investment if you want to have $500 at the end of two years. The investment earns 8% compounded quarterly. Check your result using the present value table.

8. How does the effective interest rate compare with the compounded rate on a loan or investment? Illustrate your answer with an example that shows the compounded rate and the effective rate.

## Challenge Problem

One real estate sales technique is to encourage customers or clients to buy today because the value of the property will probably increase during the next few years. "Buy this lot today for $28,000. In two years, I project it will sell for $32,500." The buyer has a CD worth $30,000 now, which earns 4% compounded annually and will mature in 2 years. Cashing in the CD now requires the buyer to pay an early withdrawal penalty of $600.
a.  Should the buyer purchase the land now or in two years?

b.  What are some of the problems with waiting to buy land?

c.  What are some of the advantages of waiting?

d.  Lots in a new subdivision sell for $15,600. Assuming that the price of the lot does not increase, how much would you need to invest today at 8% compounded quarterly to buy the lot in one year?

e.  1.  You have inherited $60,000 and plan to buy a home. If you invest the $60,000 today at 5%, compounded annually, how much could you spend on the house in one year?
    2.  If you intend to spend $60,000 on a house in one year, how much of your inheritance should you invest today at 5%, compounded annually? How much do you have left to spend on a car?

# CASE STUDIES

## 13.1  How Fast Does Your Money Grow?

Barry heard in his Personal Finance class that he should start investing as soon as possible. He had always thought that it would be smart to start investing after he finishes college and when his salary is high enough to pay the bills and to have money left over. He projects that will be 5–10 years from now. Barry wants to compare the difference between investing now and investing later. A financial planner who spoke to the class suggested that a Roth IRA (Individual Retirement Account) would be a more profitable investment over the long term than a regular IRA, so Barry wants to seriously consider the Roth IRA.

When table values do not include the information you need, use the formula $FV = \$1(1 + R)^N$ where $R$ is the period rate and $N$ is the number of periods.

1. If Barry purchases a $2,000 Roth IRA when he is 25 years old and expects to earn an average of 6% per year compounded annually over 35 years (until he is 60), how much will accumulate in the investment?

2. If Barry doesn't put the money in the IRA until he is 35 years old, how much money will accumulate in the account by the time he is 60 years old? How much less will he earn because he invested 10 years later?

3. Interest rate is critical to the speed at which your investment grows. If $1 is invested at 2%, it takes approximately 34.9 years to double. If $1 is invested at 5%, it takes approximately 14.2 years to double. Use Table 13-1 to determine how many years it takes $1 to double if invested at 10%; at 12%.

4. At what interest rate would you need to invest to have your money double in 10 years?

## 13.2  Planning: The Key to Wealth

Abdol Akhim has just come from a Personal Finance class where he learned that he can determine how much his savings will be worth in the future. Abdol is completing his two-year business administration degree this semester and has been repairing computers in his spare time to pay for his tuition and books. Abdol got out his savings records and decided to apply what he had learned. He has a balance of $1,000 in a money market account at First Savings Bank, and he considers this to be an emergency fund. His instructor says that he should have 3–6 months of his total bills in an emergency fund. His bills are currently $700 a month. He also has a checking account and a regular savings account at First Savings Bank, and he will shift some of his funds from those accounts into the emergency fund. One of Abdol's future goals is to buy a house. He wants to start another money market account to save the $8,000 he needs for a down payment.

1. How much interest will Abdol receive on $1,000 in a 365-day year if he keeps it in the money market account earning 5.5% compounded daily?

2. How much money must Abdol shift from his other accounts to his emergency fund to have four times his monthly bills in the account by the end of the year?

3. Find the amount Abdol needs to invest to have the $8,000 down payment for his house in 5 years. Assume annual compounding on an account that pays 5.5% interest annually.

# 13.3 Future Value/Present Value

At 45 years of age, Seth figured he wanted to work only 10 more years. Being a full-time landlord had a lot of advantages: cash flow, free time, and being his own boss; but it was time to start thinking towards retirement. The real estate investments that he had made over the last 15 years had paid off handsomely. After selling a duplex and a four-unit and paying the associated taxes, Seth had $350,000 in the bank and was debt-free. With only 10 years before retirement, Seth wanted to make solid financial decisions that would limit his risk exposure. Fortunately, he had located another property that seemed to meet his needs—an older, but well maintained four-unit apartment. The price tag was $250,000, well within his range, and the apartment would require no remodeling. Seth figured he could invest the other $100,000, and between the two hoped to have $1 million to retire on by age 55.

1. Seth read an article in the local newspaper stating the real estate in the area was appreciating by 6% per year. Assuming the article is correct, what would the future value of the $250,000 apartment be in 10 years?

2. Seth's current bank offers a 1-year certificate of deposit account paying 5% compounded quarterly. A competitor bank is also offering 5%, but compounded daily. If Seth invests the $100,000, how much more money will he have in the second bank after one year, due to the daily compounding?

3. A friend of Seth's who is a real estate developer needs to borrow $80,000 to finish a development project. He is desperate for cash and offers Seth 18%, compounded monthly, for $2\frac{1}{2}$ years. Find the future value of the loan using the future value table. Does this loan meet Seth's goals of low risk? How could he reduce the risk associated with this loan?

4. After purchasing the apartment, Seth receives a street, sewer, and gutter assessment for $12,500 due in 2 years. How much would he have to invest today in a CD paying 6%, compounded semiannually, to fully pay the assessment in 2 years?

# Is Social Security in Crisis?

Will Social Security be there when you need it? Social Security payroll taxes currently produce more revenue than is needed to pay benefits to current retirees. Social Security projections are that benefits will begin to exceed revenues in 2017. By 2032, the trust fund will be exhausted, and will be unable to pay the full benefits that have been promised to older Americans.

So started the formal Social Security debate, which has dominated most of the past decade, and has since become largely a political fight. But what was the original purpose of Social Security? And what are the implications for you today?

Social Security provided a critical foundation of income for retired and disabled workers. For one-third of Americans over 65, Social Security benefits represent 90% of their total income. It was originally structured to resemble private-sector pensions (retirement plans). The retirement benefit was based on a worker's wages and years of service. In most plans, the monthly lifetime benefit after 35 years of service would be at least half of the income earned in the final working year.

Congress expected that company pensions would eventually replace Social Security benefits. But pension coverage peaked at 40% in the 1960s. Today, only 16% of private-sector workers are covered by defined-benefit pensions.

So how can you avoid relying on Social Security when you retire? One of the best things you can do is start a supplemental retirement program right now with an annuity. Annuities may be single- or flexible-payment; fixed or variable; deferred or immediate. No matter the type, annuities are financial contracts with an insurance company that are designed to be a source of retirement income. The very best plans are systematic and enable the investor to make regular and consistent payments into the annuity fund, which compounds interest. And these plans are not expensive; many require as little as $25 a month, or $300 annually to get started. Let's say you're age 25. By investing $300 annually for 40 years at 7%, you would end up with $59,890.50 at age 65. Not a bad investment for $25 a month—about the same price as dinner and a movie.

Will Social Security still be there when you retire? It's impossible to say. Better to get started investing with an annuity now (or soon), rather than find out later when it's too late.

## LEARNING OUTCOMES

### 14-1 Future Value of an Annuity

1. Find the future value of an ordinary annuity using the simple interest formula method.
2. Find the future value of an ordinary annuity with periodic payments using a $1.00 ordinary annuity future value table.
3. Find the future value of an annuity due with periodic payments using the simple interest formula method.
4. Find the future value of an annuity due with periodic payments using a $1.00 ordinary annuity future value table.
5. Find the future value of an ordinary annuity or an annuity due using a formula.

### 14-2 Sinking Funds and the Present Value of an Annuity

1. Find the sinking fund payment using a $1.00 sinking fund payment table.
2. Find the present value of an ordinary annuity using a $1.00 ordinary annuity present value table.
3. Find the sinking fund payment or the present value of an annuity using a formula.

So far we have discussed interest accumulated from one *lump-sum* amount of money. Another type of investment option is an annuity. An **annuity** is a contract between you (the **annuitant**) and an insurance company (the **insurer**) for receiving and disbursing money for the annuitant or the beneficiary of the annuitant. An annuity has two phases—the accumulation phase and the liquidation phase. The **accumulation phase of an annuity** is the time when you are paying money into the fund. The **liquidation or payout phase of an annuity** is the time when you are receiving money from the fund. During both phases of the annuity, the fund balance may earn compound interest. An annuity is purchased by making either a single lump-sum payment or a series of periodic payments. Under the terms of the contract the insurer agrees to make a lump-sum payment or periodic payments to you beginning at some future date. This investment option is a long-term investment option that is commonly used for retirement planning or as a college fund for small children. Penalties are normally applied if funds are withdrawn before a time specified in the agreement.

There are many options to consider when purchasing an annuity. You can choose how the money is invested (stocks, bonds, money market instruments, or a combination of these) and the level of risk of the investment. High-risk options have the potential to earn a high rate of return but the investment may be at risk. Low-risk options normally earn a lower rate of interest but the risk is also lower. A guaranteed rate of interest has no risk at all on the principal and guarantees a specific interest rate.

You can choose if the investment is made with pre-taxed money or with taxed money. If pre-taxed money is invested, the tax on the entire fund is deferred until you begin receiving payments. If taxed money is invested, only the tax on the earnings is deferred until you begin receiving payments. In our study of annuities, we will examine only some basic interest-based options. Other options can be investigated by contacting insurance agencies or brokers or the Office of Investor Education and Assistance with the U.S. Securities and Exchange Commission. (*http://www.sec.gov/investor/pubs/varannty.htm*).

## 14-1 FUTURE VALUE OF AN ANNUITY

### LEARNING OUTCOMES

1 Find the future value of an ordinary annuity using the simple interest formula method.
2 Find the future value of an ordinary annuity with periodic payments using a $1.00 ordinary annuity future value table.
3 Find the future value of an annuity due with periodic payments using the simple interest formula method.
4 Find the future value of an annuity due with periodic payments using a $1.00 ordinary annuity future value table.
5 Find the future value of an ordinary annuity or an annuity due using a formula.

An annuity paid out over a guaranteed number of periods is an **annuity certain**. An annuity paid out over an uncertain number of periods is a **contingent annuity**.

We can also categorize annuities according to when payment is made into the fund. For an **ordinary annuity**, payment is made at the *end* of the period. For an **annuity due**, payment is made at the *beginning* of the period.

### 1 Find the future value of an ordinary annuity using the simple interest formula method.

Finding the future value of an annuity into which periodic payments are made means finding the amount of the annuity at the end of the accumulation phase. This is similar to finding the future value of a lump sum. The significant difference is that for each interest period, more principal—the annuity payment—is added to the amount on which interest is earned. The simple interest formula $I = PRT$ is still the basis of calculating interest for each period of the annuity.

| HOW TO | Find the future value of an ordinary annuity in the accumulation phase with periodic payments using the simple interest formula method |
|---|---|

1. Find the first end-of-period principal.

$$\text{First end-of-period principal} = \text{annuity payment}$$

2. For each remaining period in turn, find the next end-of-period principal.
   (a) Multiply the previous end-of-period principal by the sum of 1 and the decimal equivalent of the period interest rate.

(b) Add the product from step 2a and the annuity payment.

$$\text{End-of-period principal} = \text{previous end-of-period principal}$$
$$\times (1 + \text{period interest rate}) + \text{annuity payment}$$

3. Identify the last end-of-period principal as the future value.

$$\text{Future value} = \text{last end-of-period principal}$$

For an ordinary annuity, no interest accumulates on the annuity payment during the period in which it is paid because the payment is made at the *end* of the period. For the first period, this means no interest accumulates at all.

### EXAMPLE 1

What is the future value of an ordinary annuity with annual payments of $1,000 after three years at 4% annual interest?

The period interest rate is 0.04. The annuity is $1,000.
End-of-year value = (previous end-of-year value)(1 + 0.04) + 1,000

End-of-year 1 = $1,000.00        No interest earned the first year.
End-of-year 2 = $1,000.00(1.04) + $1,000.00
       = $1,040.00 + $1,000.00
       = $2,040.00

End-of-year 3 = $2,040.00(1.04) + $1,000.00
       = $2,121.60 + $1,000.00
       = $3,121.60

**The future value is $3,121.60.**

### HOW TO    Find the total interest earned on an annuity

1. Find the total amount invested:

$$\text{Total invested} = \text{payment amount} \times \text{number of payments}$$

2. Find the total interest:

$$\text{Total interest} = \text{future value of annuity} - \text{total invested}$$

### EXAMPLE 2

Find the total interest earned on the annuity in the preceding example.

Total invested = $1,000(3)        Payment = $1,000
                         Number of payments = 3
           = $3,000
Total interest = $3,121.60 − $3,000        Future value = $3,121.60
                = $121.60

**The total interest earned is $121.60.**

A lump-sum investment earns more interest than an annuity. Compare the earnings of a $3,000 lump-sum investment (Figure 14-1) and an annuity of the same accumulated investment (Figure 14-2).

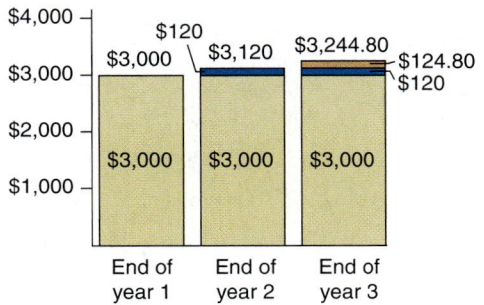

**FIGURE 14-1**
**Lump-Sum Investment of $3,000**

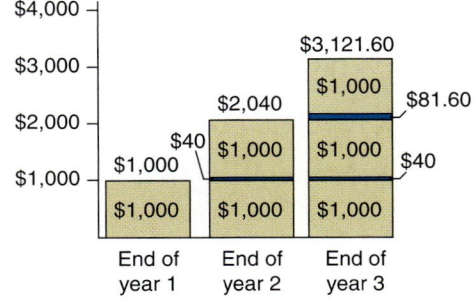

**FIGURE 14-2**
**Three-Year Ordinary Annuity of $1,000 per Year**

The advantages of the lump-sum annuity are obvious, but an annuity with periodic payments also offers some advantages. When a lump sum is not available, an annuity with periodic payments provides an alternative investment strategy.

## 2 Find the future value of an ordinary annuity with periodic payments using a $1.00 ordinary annuity future value table.

Calculating the future value of an ordinary annuity with periodic payments can become quite tedious if the number of periods is large. For example, a monthly annuity such as a monthly savings plan running for five years has 60 periods and 60 calculation sequences. For this reason, most businesspeople rely on prepared tables, calculators, or computers.

### HOW TO Find the future value of an ordinary annuity with periodic payments using a $1.00 ordinary annuity future value table

Using Table 14-1:

1. Select the periods row corresponding to the number of interest periods.
2. Select the rate-per-period column corresponding to the period interest rate.
3. Locate the value in the cell where the periods row intersects the rate-per-period column.
4. Multiply the annuity payment by the table value from step 3.

$$\text{Future value} = \text{annuity payment} \times \text{table value}$$

### EXAMPLE 1 Use Table 14-1 to find the future value of a semiannual ordinary annuity of $6,000 for five years at 6% annual interest compounded semiannually.

$$5 \text{ years} \times 2 \text{ periods per year} = 10 \text{ periods}$$
$$\frac{6\% \text{ annual interest rate}}{2 \text{ periods per year}} = 3\% \text{ period interest rate}$$

The Table 14-1 value for 10 periods at 3% is 11.464.

$$\begin{aligned}
\text{Future value of annuity} &= \text{annuity payment} \times \text{table value} \\
&= \$6,000(11.464) \\
&= \$68,784
\end{aligned}$$

**The future value of the ordinary annuity is $68,784.**

**TABLE 14-1**
Future Value of $1.00 Ordinary Annuity

**Rate per period**

| Periods | 2% | 3% | 4% | 5% | 6% | 7% | 8% | 9% | 10% | 12% |
|---|---|---|---|---|---|---|---|---|---|---|
| 1 | 1.000 | 1.000 | 1.000 | 1.000 | 1.000 | 1.000 | 1.000 | 1.000 | 1.000 | 1.000 |
| 2 | 2.020 | 2.030 | 2.040 | 2.050 | 2.060 | 2.070 | 2.080 | 2.090 | 2.100 | 2.120 |
| 3 | 3.060 | 3.091 | 3.122 | 3.153 | 3.184 | 3.215 | 3.246 | 3.278 | 3.310 | 3.374 |
| 4 | 4.122 | 4.184 | 4.246 | 4.310 | 4.375 | 4.440 | 4.506 | 4.573 | 4.641 | 4.779 |
| 5 | 5.204 | 5.309 | 5.416 | 5.526 | 5.637 | 5.751 | 5.867 | 5.985 | 6.105 | 6.353 |
| 6 | 6.308 | 6.468 | 6.633 | 6.802 | 6.975 | 7.153 | 7.336 | 7.523 | 7.716 | 8.115 |
| 7 | 7.434 | 7.662 | 7.898 | 8.142 | 8.394 | 8.654 | 8.923 | 9.200 | 9.487 | 10.089 |
| 8 | 8.583 | 8.892 | 9.214 | 9.549 | 9.897 | 10.260 | 10.637 | 11.028 | 11.436 | 12.300 |
| 9 | 9.755 | 10.159 | 10.583 | 11.027 | 11.491 | 11.978 | 12.488 | 13.021 | 13.579 | 14.776 |
| 10 | 10.950 | 11.464 | 12.006 | 12.578 | 13.181 | 13.816 | 14.487 | 15.193 | 15.937 | 17.549 |
| 11 | 12.169 | 12.808 | 13.486 | 14.207 | 14.972 | 15.784 | 16.645 | 17.560 | 18.531 | 20.655 |
| 12 | 13.412 | 14.192 | 15.026 | 15.917 | 16.870 | 17.888 | 18.977 | 20.141 | 21.384 | 24.133 |
| 13 | 14.680 | 15.618 | 16.627 | 17.713 | 18.882 | 20.141 | 21.495 | 22.523 | 24.523 | 28.029 |
| 14 | 15.974 | 17.086 | 18.292 | 19.599 | 21.015 | 22.550 | 24.215 | 26.019 | 27.975 | 32.393 |
| 15 | 17.293 | 18.599 | 20.024 | 21.579 | 23.276 | 25.129 | 27.152 | 29.361 | 31.772 | 37.280 |
| 16 | 18.639 | 20.157 | 21.825 | 23.657 | 25.673 | 27.888 | 30.324 | 33.003 | 35.950 | 42.753 |
| 17 | 20.012 | 21.762 | 23.698 | 25.840 | 28.213 | 30.840 | 33.750 | 36.974 | 40.545 | 48.884 |
| 18 | 21.412 | 23.414 | 25.645 | 28.132 | 30.906 | 33.999 | 37.450 | 41.301 | 45.599 | 55.750 |
| 19 | 22.841 | 25.117 | 27.671 | 30.539 | 33.760 | 37.379 | 41.446 | 46.018 | 51.159 | 63.440 |
| 20 | 24.297 | 26.870 | 29.778 | 33.066 | 36.786 | 40.995 | 45.762 | 51.160 | 57.275 | 72.052 |
| 21 | 25.783 | 28.676 | 31.969 | 35.719 | 39.993 | 44.865 | 50.423 | 56.765 | 64.002 | 81.699 |
| 22 | 27.299 | 30.537 | 34.248 | 38.505 | 43.392 | 49.006 | 55.457 | 62.873 | 71.403 | 92.503 |
| 23 | 28.845 | 32.453 | 36.618 | 41.430 | 46.996 | 53.436 | 60.893 | 69.532 | 79.543 | 104.603 |
| 24 | 30.422 | 34.426 | 39.083 | 44.502 | 50.816 | 58.177 | 66.765 | 76.790 | 88.497 | 118.155 |
| 25 | 32.030 | 36.459 | 41.646 | 47.727 | 54.865 | 63.249 | 73.106 | 84.701 | 98.347 | 133.334 |
| 26 | 33.671 | 38.553 | 44.312 | 51.113 | 59.156 | 68.676 | 79.954 | 93.324 | 109.182 | 150.334 |
| 27 | 35.344 | 40.710 | 47.084 | 54.669 | 63.706 | 74.484 | 87.351 | 102.723 | 121.100 | 169.374 |
| 28 | 37.051 | 42.931 | 49.968 | 58.403 | 68.528 | 80.698 | 95.339 | 112.968 | 134.210 | 190.699 |
| 29 | 38.792 | 45.219 | 52.966 | 62.323 | 73.640 | 87.347 | 103.966 | 124.135 | 148.631 | 214.583 |
| 30 | 40.568 | 47.575 | 56.085 | 66.439 | 79.058 | 94.461 | 113.283 | 136.308 | 164.494 | 241.333 |
| 35 | 49.994 | 60.462 | 73.652 | 90.320 | 111.435 | 138.237 | 172.317 | 215.711 | 271.024 | 431.663 |
| 40 | 60.402 | 75.401 | 95.026 | 120.800 | 154.762 | 199.635 | 259.057 | 337.882 | 442.593 | 767.091 |
| 45 | 71.893 | 92.720 | 121.029 | 159.700 | 212.744 | 285.749 | 386.506 | 525.859 | 718.905 | 1358.230 |
| 50 | 84.579 | 112.797 | 152.667 | 209.348 | 290.336 | 406.529 | 573.770 | 815.084 | 1163.909 | 2400.018 |
| 55 | 98.587 | 136.072 | 191.159 | 272.713 | 394.172 | 575.929 | 848.923 | 1260.092 | 1880.591 | 4236.005 |
| 60 | 114.052 | 163.053 | 237.991 | 353.584 | 533.128 | 813.520 | 1253.213 | 1944.792 | 3034.816 | 7471.641 |
| 65 | 131.126 | 194.333 | 294.968 | 456.798 | 719.083 | 1146.755 | 1847.248 | 2998.288 | 4893.707 | 13173.937 |
| 70 | 149.978 | 230.594 | 364.290 | 588.529 | 967.932 | 1614.134 | 2720.080 | 4619.223 | 7887.470 | 23223.332 |
| 75 | 170.792 | 272.631 | 448.631 | 756.654 | 1300.949 | 2269.657 | 4002.557 | 7113.232 | 12708.954 | 40933.799 |
| 80 | 193.772 | 321.363 | 551.245 | 971.229 | 1746.600 | 3189.063 | 5886.935 | 10950.574 | 20474.002 | 72145.693 |
| 85 | 219.144 | 377.857 | 676.090 | 1245.087 | 2342.982 | 4478.576 | 8655.706 | 16854.800 | 32979.690 | 127151.714 |
| 90 | 247.157 | 443.349 | 827.983 | 1594.607 | 3141.075 | 6287.185 | 12723.939 | 25939.184 | 53120.226 | 224091.119 |
| 95 | 278.085 | 519.272 | 1012.785 | 2040.694 | 4209.104 | 8823.854 | 18701.507 | 39916.635 | 85556.760 | 394931.472 |
| 100 | 312.232 | 607.288 | 1237.624 | 2610.025 | 5638.368 | 12381.662 | 27484.516 | 61422.675 | 137796.123 | 696010.548 |

Table values show the future value, or accumulated amount of the investment and interest, of a $1.00 investment for a given number of periods at a given rate per period.

Table values can be generated using the formula $FV$ of $1.00 per period $= \left( \dfrac{(1 + R)^N - 1}{R} \right)$, where $FV$ is the future value, $R$ is the interest rate per period, and $N$ is the number of periods.

---

**EXAMPLE 2**  Find the total interest earned on the annuity in Example 1.

Total invested = $6,000(10)

Payment = $6,000
Number of payments = 10

= $60,000

Total interest = $68,784 − $60,000

Future value = $68,784

= $8,784

**The total interest earned is $8,784.**

# ✓ STOP AND CHECK

1. Use Table 14-1 to find the accumulation phase future value and total interest of an ordinary annuity of $4,000 for eight years at 2% annual interest.

2. Use Table 14-1 to find the accumulated amount and total interest of an ordinary annuity with semiannual payments of $6,000 for five years at 4% annual interest.

3. John Crampton put $1,200 in an ordinary annuity account every quarter of the accumulation phase for five years at an 8% annual rate compounded quarterly. What is the future value of the annuity?

4. Tiffany Evans created an ordinary annuity with $2,500 payments made semiannually at 6% annually. Find her annuity value at the end of six years.

## 3 Find the future value of an annuity due with periodic payments using the simple interest formula method.

Because an annuity due is paid at the *beginning* of each period rather than at the end, the annuity due payment earns interest throughout the period in which it is paid. The future value of an annuity due, then, is greater than the future value of the corresponding ordinary annuity, given the same number of periods, the same period interest rate, and the same annuity payment. The difference in the future value of an ordinary annuity and an annuity due is exactly one additional period's worth of interest.

> ### HOW TO  Find the future value of an annuity due with periodic payments using the simple interest formula method
>
> 1. Find the first end-of-period principal: Multiply the annuity payment by the sum of 1 and the decimal equivalent of the period interest rate.
>
>    First end-of-period principal = annuity payment × (1 + period interest rate)
>
> 2. For each remaining period in turn, find the next end-of-period principal:
>    (a) Add the previous end-of-period principal and the annuity payment.
>    (b) Multiply the sum from step 2a by the sum of 1 and the period interest rate.
>
>    End-of-period principal = (previous end-of-period principal + annuity payment)
>    × (1 + period interest rate)
>
> 3. Identify the last end-of-period principal as the future value.
>
>    Future value = last end-of-period principal

### EXAMPLE 1

What is the future value of an annuity due with an annual payment of $1,000 for three years at 4% annual interest? Find the total investment and the total interest earned.

The annuity payment is $1,000; the period interest rate is 4%.

End-of-year value = (previous end-of-year + $1,000)(1 + 0.04)

End-of-year 1 = $1,000(1.04)  
     = $1,040    The annuity due earns interest during the first period.

End-of-year 2 = ($1,040 + $1,000)(1.04)   Second payment is made.  
     = ($2,040)(1.04)  
     = $2,121.60

End-of-year 3 = ($2,121.60 + $1,000)(1.04)   Third payment is made.  
     = ($3,121.60)(1.04)  
     = $3,246.46    Future value of annuity due

Total investment = investment per period × total periods  
     = $1,000(3)  
     = $3,000

Total interest earned = future value − total investment  
     = $3,246.46 − $3,000  
     = $246.46

**The future value of the annuity due is $3,246.46, the total investment is $3,000, and the total interest earned is $246.46.**

### TIP

**Ordinary Annuity versus Annuity Due**

The difference between an ordinary annuity and an annuity due is whether you make the first payment immediately or at the end of the first period.

If you are establishing your own annuity plan through a savings account, you begin your annuity with your first payment or deposit (annuity due).

If you are entering a payroll deduction plan, a 401(k) plan, or an annuity plan with an insurance company, you may complete the paperwork to establish the plan, and the first payment will be made at a later time.

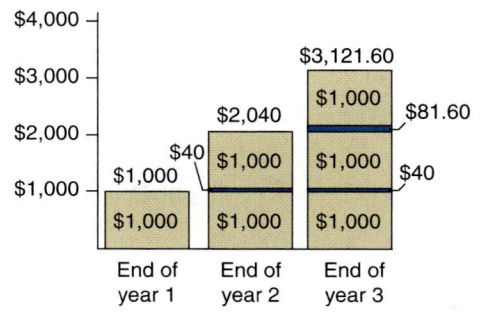

FIGURE 14-3

**Three-year ordinary annuity of $1,000 per year**

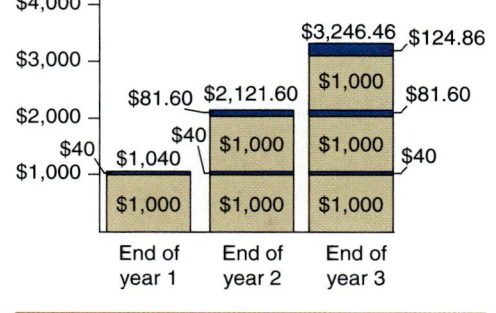

FIGURE 14-4

**Three-year annuity due of $1,000 per year**

In the three-year ordinary annuity (Figure 14-3, repeated from Figure 14-2 for comparison purposes) the final interest earned is $121.60. In the annuity due (Figure 14-4) the first $1,000 payment earns interest during the first period and then interest is earned on that interest throughout the duration of the annuity. The total interest earned is $246.46.

 **STOP AND CHECK**

1. Manually calculate the future value of an annuity due that sets aside $1,500 annually for four years at 3.75% annual interest compounded semianually. How much interest is earned?

2. Manually calculate the value of an annuity due after two years of $4,000 payments at 4.25% compounded annually.

3. DeMarco receives $5,000 semiannually from his grandmother's estate. He invests the money at 3.8%. How much will he have after two years investing as an annuity due?

4. If you make six monthly payments of $50 to an annuity due and receive 6% annual interest compounded monthly, how much will you accumulate?

## 4 Find the future value of an annuity due with periodic payments using a $1.00 ordinary annuity future value table.

Because the future value of an annuity due is so closely related to the future value of the corresponding ordinary annuity, we can also use Table 14-1 to find the future value of an annuity due. An annuity due accumulates interest one period more than does the ordinary annuity, but has the same number of payments. Thus, we adjust Table 14-1 values by multiplying by the sum of 1 and the period interest rate. This applies interest for the first payment, which is made at the beginning of the first period, for the entire time of the annuity.

> **HOW TO** Find the future value of an annuity due with a periodic payment using a $1.00 ordinary annuity future value table
>
> Use Table 14-1:
>
> 1. Select the periods row corresponding to the number of interest periods.
> 2. Select the rate-per-period column corresponding to the period interest rate.
> 3. Locate the value in the cell where the periods row intersects the rate-per-period column.
> 4. Multiply the annuity payment by the table value from step 3. This is equivalent to an *ordinary annuity*.
> 5. Multiply the amount that is equivalent to an ordinary annuity by the sum of 1 and the period interest rate to adjust for the extra interest that is earned on an annuity due.
>
> Future value = annuity payment $\times$ table value $\times$ (1 + period interest rate)

## EXAMPLE 1

Use Table 14-1 to find the future value of a quarterly annuity due of $2,800 for four years at 8% annual interest compounded quarterly.

$$4 \text{ years} \times 4 \text{ periods per year} = 16 \text{ periods}$$

$$\frac{8\% \text{ annual interest rate}}{4 \text{ periods per year}} = 2\% \text{ period interest rate}$$

The Table 14-1 value for 16 periods at 2% is 18.639.

Future value = annuity payment × table value × (1 + period interest rate)
= $2,800(18.639)(1.02)     Future value for ordinary annuity
= $52,189.20(1.02)         Adjustment for annuity due
= $53,232.98               Future value for annuity due

**The future value is $53,232.98.**

## EXAMPLE 2

What is the total interest earned on the annuity due in the previous example?

Total invested = $2,800(16)          Payment = $2,800
= $44,800                            Number of payments = 16
Total interest = $53,232.98 − $44,800
= $8,432.98

**The total interest earned is $8,432.98.**

## EXAMPLE 3

Sarah Smith wants to select the best annuity plan. She plans to invest a total of $40,000 over ten years' time at 8% annual interest. Annuity 1 is a quarterly ordinary annuity of $1,000; interest is compounded quarterly. Annuity 2 is a semiannual ordinary annuity of $2,000; interest is compounded semiannually. Annuity 3 is a quarterly annuity due of $1,000; interest is compounded quarterly. Annuity 4 is a semiannual annuity due of $2,000; interest is compounded semiannually. Which annuity yields the greatest future value?

| What You Know | What You Are Looking For | Solution Plan |
|---|---|---|
| Annuity 1: Ordinary annuity of $1,000 quarterly for ten years at 8% annual interest compounded quarterly | Which annuity yields the greatest future value? Future value of each annuity | Number of periods = years × periods per year |
| Annuity 2: Ordinary annuity of $2,000 semiannually for ten years at 8% annual interest compounded semiannually | | Period interest rate $= \dfrac{\text{annual interest rate}}{\text{periods per year}}$ |
| Annuity 3: Annuity due of $1,000 quarterly for ten years at 8% annual interest compounded quarterly | | Future value of ordinary annuity = annuity payment × Table 14-1 value |
| Annuity 4: Annuity due of $2,000 semiannually for ten years at 8% annual interest compounded semiannually. | | Future value of annuity due = annuity payment × Table 14-1 value × (1 + period interest rate) |

### Solution

*Annuity 1*

Number of periods = years × periods per year
= 10(4)
= 40

$$\text{Period interest rate} = \frac{\text{annual interest rate}}{\text{periods per year}}$$

$$= \frac{8\%}{4} = 2\%$$

Table value = 60.402
Future value = annuity payment × table value
Future value = ($1,000)(60.402)
= $60,402

*Annuity 2*
Number of periods = years × periods per year
= 10(2)
= 20

Period interest rate = $\dfrac{\text{annual interest rate}}{\text{periods per year}}$

= $\dfrac{8\%}{2}$ = 4%

Table value = 29.778
Future value = annuity payment × table value
= $2,000(29.778)
= $59,556

*Annuity 3*
The number of periods and period interest rate are the same as those for annuity 1.
Future value = annuity payment × table value × (1 + period interest rate)
= $1,000(60.402)(1.02)
= $61,610.04

*Annuity 4*
The number of periods and period interest rate are the same as those for annuity 2.
Future value = annuity payment × table value × (1 + period interest rate)
= $2,000(29.778)(1.04)
= $61,938.24

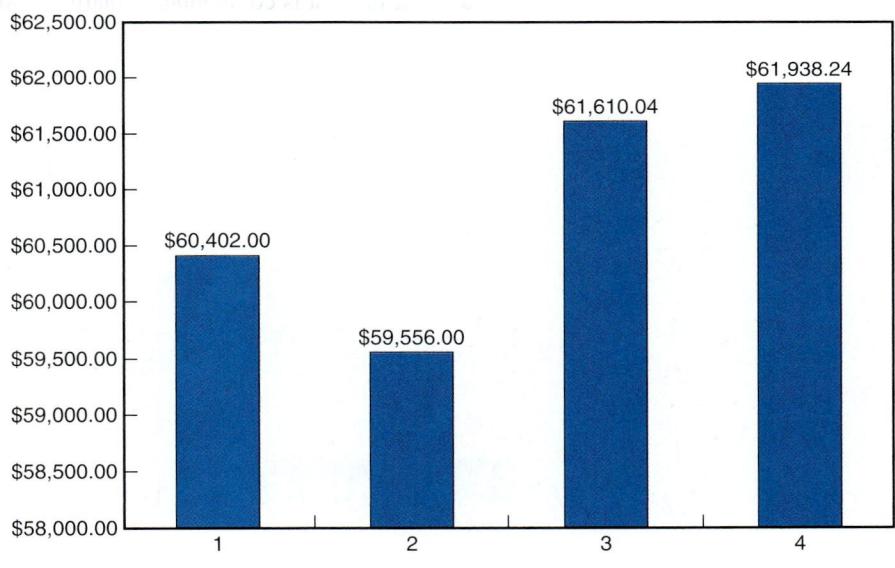

**FIGURE 14-5**
Four Two-Year Annuities at 8% Annual Interest

### Conclusion

**Annuity 4, with the larger annuity due payment, yields the greatest future value.** Notice that the ordinary annuity with fewer periods per year yields the least future value of all four annuities. If the total investment is the same, the number of years is the same, and the annual rate of interest is the same, any annuity due yields a larger future value than any corresponding ordinary annuity. The annuity due with the largest payment is the most profitable, while the ordinary annuity paid most frequently is the most profitable ordinary annuity.

1. Use Table 14-1 to find the future value of an annual annuity due of $3,000 for ten years at 5%.

2. Use Table 14-1 to find the future value of a semiannual annuity due of $1,000 for five years at 6% annually compounded semiannually.

3. Use Table 14-1 to find the future value of a quarterly annuity of $500 invested at 8% annually compounded quarterly for five years.

4. Use Table 14-1 to find the future value of a semiannual annuity of $1,000 for five years invested at 8% annually compounded semiannually. Compare the interest earned on this annuity with the interest earned on the annuity in Exercise 3.

## 5 Find the future value of an ordinary annuity or an annuity due using a formula.

Using tables to find the future value of an annuity can be limiting. Annuity rates may not be stated as whole number percents. Evaluating an annuity formula requires a business, scientific, or graphing calculator or computer software like Excel. Many of the calculator or software features can be used to facilitate these calculations. Be sure to apply the *order of operations*. For more details, review Chapter 5, Section 1, Learning Outcome 5.

---

**HOW TO** Find the future value of an ordinary annuity or an annuity due using a formula:

1. Identify the period rate $R$ as a decimal equivalent, the number of periods $N$, and the amount of the annuity payment $PMT$.
2. Substitute the values from Step 1 into the appropriate formula.

$$FV_{\text{ordinary annuity}} = PMT\left(\frac{(1 + R)^N - 1}{R}\right)$$

$$FV_{\text{annuity due}} = PMT\left(\frac{(1 + R)^N - 1}{R}\right)(1 + R)$$

3. Evaluate the formula.

---

**EXAMPLE 1** Find the future value of an ordinary annuity of $100 paid monthly at 5.25% for 10 years.

$$R = \frac{5.25\%}{12} = \frac{0.0525}{12} = 0.004375 \qquad \text{Periodic interest rate}$$

$$N = 10(12) = 120 \qquad \text{Number of payments}$$

$$PMT = \$100$$

$$FV_{\text{ordinary annuity}} = \$100\left(\frac{(1 + 0.004375)^{120} - 1}{0.004375}\right) \qquad \text{Mentally add within the innermost parentheses.}$$

$$FV_{\text{ordinary annuity}} = \$100\left(\frac{(1.004375)^{120} - 1}{0.004375}\right)$$

Calculator sequence:

$$100 \boxed{(} 1.004375 \boxed{\wedge} 120 \boxed{-} 1 \boxed{)} \boxed{\div} 0.004375 \boxed{=} \Rightarrow 15737.69632$$

**The future value of the ordinary annuity is $15,737.70.**

**EXAMPLE 2** Find the future value of an annuity due of $50 monthly at 5.75% for 5 years.

$$R = \frac{5.75\%}{12} = \frac{0.0575}{12} = 0.0047916667 \qquad \text{Periodic interest rate}$$

$$N = 5(12) = 60 \qquad \text{Number of payments}$$

$$PMT = \$50$$

$$FV_{\text{annuity due}} = \$50\left(\frac{(1 + 0.0047916667)^{60} - 1}{0.0047916667}\right)(1 + 0.0047916667) \qquad \begin{array}{l}\text{Mentally add within}\\ \text{the parentheses.}\end{array}$$

$$FV_{\text{annuity due}} = \$50\left(\frac{(1.0047916667)^{60} - 1}{0.0047916667}\right)(1.0047916667)$$

Calculator sequence:

$$50\ (\ 1.0047916667\ ^\wedge\ 60\ -\ 1\ )\ \div\ 0.0047916667\ =$$
$$\boxed{\text{ANS}}\ (\ 1.0047916667\ )\ = \Rightarrow 3482.788889$$

**The future value of the annuity due is $3,482.79.**

---

 ## STOP AND CHECK

1. Use the formula to find the future value of an ordinary annuity of $250 paid monthly at 4.62% for 25 years.

2. Use the formula to find the future value of an ordinary annuity of $30 paid weekly at 5.2% for 15 years.

3. Use the formula to find the future value of an annuity due of $200 monthly at 7.35% for 14 years.

4. Marquita is creating an annuity due of $25 every two weeks at 6% for 35 years. Find the future value of her annuity due.

---

## 14-1 SECTION EXERCISES

### SKILL BUILDERS

*Use Table 14-1 to find the future value of the annuities.*

| | Annuity type | Periodic payment | Annual interest rate | Payment paid | Years |
|---|---|---|---|---|---|
| 1. | Ordinary annuity | $1,000 | 5% | Annually | 8 |
| 2. | Ordinary annuity | $ 500 | 4% | Semiannually | 4 |
| 3. | Ordinary annuity | $2,000 | 8% | Quarterly | 3 |
| 4. | Annuity due | $3,000 | 6% | Semiannually | 3 |
| 5. | Annuity due | $5,000 | 3% | Annually | 4 |
| 6. | Annuity due | $ 800 | 7% | Annually | 5 |

7. Manually find the future value of an ordinary annuity of $300 paid annually at 5% for three years. Verify your result by using the table method.

8. Manually find the future value of an annuity due of $500 paid semiannually for two years at 6% annual interest compounded semiannually. Verify your result by using the table method.

## APPLICATIONS

*Use the simple interest formula method for Exercises 9–12.*

9. Find the future value of an ordinary annuity of $3,000 annually after two years at 3.8% annual interest. Find the total interest earned.

10. Len and Sharron Smith are saving money for their daughter Heather to attend college. They set aside an ordinary annuity of $4,000 annually for ten years at 7% annual interest. How much will Heather have for college after two years? Find the total interest earned.

11. Harry Taylor plans to pay an ordinary annuity of $5,000 annually for ten years so he can take a year's sabbatical to study for a master's degree in business. The annual rate of interest is 3.8%. How much will Harry have at the end of three years? How much interest will he earn on the investment after three years?

12. Scott Martin is planning to establish a retirement annuity. He is committed to an ordinary annuity of $3,000 annually at 3.6% annual interest. How much will Scott have accumulated after three years? How much interest will he earn?

*Use Table 14-1 or the appropriate formula for Exercises 13–17.*

**13.** Find the future value of an ordinary annuity of $6,500 semiannually for seven years at 6% annual interest compounded semiannually. How much was invested? How much interest was earned?

**14.** Pat Lechleiter pays an ordinary annuity of $2,500 quarterly at 8% annual interest compounded quarterly to establish supplemental income for retirement. How much will Pat have available at the end of five years?

**15.** Latanya Brown established an ordinary annuity of $1,000 annually at 7% annual interest. What is the future value of the annuity after 15 years? How much of her own money will Latanya have invested during this time period? By how much will her investment have grown?

**16.** You invest in an ordinary annuity of $500 annually at 8% annual interest. Find the future value of the annuity at the end of ten years. How much have you invested? How much interest has your annuity earned?

**17.** You invest in an ordinary annuity of $2,000 annually at 8% annual interest. What is the future value of the annuity at the end of five years? How much have you invested? How much interest has your annuity earned?

**18.** Make a chart comparing your results for Exercises 16 and 17. Use these headings: Years, Total Investment, Total Interest. What general conclusion might you draw about effective investment strategy?

*Use the simple interest formula method for Exercises 19–22:*

**19.** Find the future value of an annuity due of $12,000 annually for three years at 3% annual interest. How much was invested? How much interest was earned?

**20.** Bernard McGhee has decided to establish an annuity due of $2,500 annually for 15 years at 7.2% annual interest. How much is the annuity due worth after two years? How much was invested? How much interest was earned?

**21.** Find the future value of an annuity due of $7,800 annually for two years at 8.1% annual interest. Find the total amount invested. Find the interest.

**22.** Find the future value of an annuity due of $400 annually for two years at 6.8% annual interest compounded annually.

*Use Table 14-1 or the appropriate formula for Exercises 23–26.*

**23.** Find the future value of a quarterly annuity due of $4,400 for three years at 8% annual interest compounded quarterly. How much was invested? How much interest was earned?

**24.** Find the future value of an annuity due of $750 semiannually for four years at 8% annual interest compounded semiannually. What is the total investment? What is the interest?

**25.** Which annuity earns more interest: an annuity due of $300 quarterly for one year at 8% annual interest compounded quarterly, or an annuity due of $600 semiannually for one year at 8% annual interest compounded semiannually?

**26.** You have carefully examined your budget and determined that you can manage to set aside $250 per year. So you set up an annuity due of $250 annually at 7% annual interest. How much will you have contributed after 20 years? What is the future value of your annuity after 20 years? How much interest will you earn?

## 14-2 SINKING FUNDS AND THE PRESENT VALUE OF AN ANNUITY

### LEARNING OUTCOMES

1 Find the sinking fund payment using a $1.00 sinking fund payment table.
2 Find the present value of an ordinary annuity using a $1.00 ordinary annuity present value table.
3 Find the sinking fund payment or the present value of an annuity using a formula.

Businesses and individuals often use sinking funds to accumulate a desired amount of money by the end of a certain period of time to pay off a financial obligation, to use for a retirement or college fund, or to reach a specific goal such as retiring a bond issue or paying for equipment replacement and modernization. Essentially, a **sinking fund** is payment into an ordinary annuity to yield a desired future value. That is, the future value is known and the payment amount is unknown.

**Sinking fund:** payment into an ordinary annuity to yield a desired future value.

|  | Payment | Future Value |
|---|---|---|
| **Sinking Fund** | Unknown | Known |
| **Accumulation Phase of an Annuity** | Known | Unknown |

## 1 Find the sinking fund payment using a $1.00 sinking fund payment table.

A sinking fund payment is made at the *end* of each period, so a sinking fund payment is an ordinary annuity payment. These payments, along with the interest, accumulate over a period of time in order to provide the desired future value.

To calculate the *payment* required to yield a desired future value, use Table 14-2. The procedure for locating a value in Table 14-2 is similar to the procedure used for Table 14-1.

> ### HOW TO  Find the sinking fund payment using a $1.00 sinking fund payment table
>
> Use Table 14-2:
>
> 1. Select the periods row corresponding to the number of interest periods.
> 2. Select the rate-per-period column corresponding to the period interest rate.
> 3. Locate the value in the cell where the periods row intersects the rate-per-period column.
> 4. Multiply the table value from step 3 by the desired future value.
>
> Sinking fund payment = future value × Table 14-2 value

## TABLE 14-2
### $1.00 Sinking Fund Payments

| | | | | Rate per period | | | |
|---|---|---|---|---|---|---|---|
| **Periods** | **1%** | **2%** | **3%** | **4%** | **6%** | **8%** | **12%** |
| 1 | 1.0000000 | 1.0000000 | 1.0000000 | 1.0000000 | 1.0000000 | 1.0000000 | 1.0000000 |
| 2 | 0.4975124 | 0.4950495 | 0.4926108 | 0.4901961 | 0.4854369 | 0.4807692 | 0.4716981 |
| 3 | 0.3300221 | 0.3267547 | 0.3235304 | 0.3203485 | 0.3141098 | 0.3080335 | 0.2963490 |
| 4 | 0.2462811 | 0.2426238 | 0.2390270 | 0.2354900 | 0.2285915 | 0.2219208 | 0.2092344 |
| 5 | 0.1960398 | 0.1921584 | 0.1883546 | 0.1846271 | 0.1773964 | 0.1704565 | 0.1574097 |
| 6 | 0.1625484 | 0.1585258 | 0.1545975 | 0.1507619 | 0.1433626 | 0.1363154 | 0.1232257 |
| 7 | 0.1386283 | 0.1345120 | 0.1305064 | 0.1266096 | 0.1191350 | 0.1120724 | 0.0991177 |
| 8 | 0.1206903 | 0.1165098 | 0.1124564 | 0.1085278 | 0.1010359 | 0.0940148 | 0.0813028 |
| 9 | 0.1067404 | 0.1025154 | 0.0984339 | 0.0944930 | 0.0870222 | 0.0800797 | 0.0676789 |
| 10 | 0.0955821 | 0.0913265 | 0.0872305 | 0.0832909 | 0.0758680 | 0.0690295 | 0.0569842 |
| 11 | 0.0864541 | 0.0821779 | 0.0780774 | 0.0741490 | 0.0667929 | 0.0600763 | 0.0484154 |
| 12 | 0.0788488 | 0.0745596 | 0.0704621 | 0.0665522 | 0.0592770 | 0.0526950 | 0.0414368 |
| 13 | 0.0724148 | 0.0681184 | 0.0670295 | 0.0601437 | 0.0529601 | 0.0465218 | 0.0356772 |
| 14 | 0.0669012 | 0.0626020 | 0.0585263 | 0.0546690 | 0.0475849 | 0.0412969 | 0.0308712 |
| 15 | 0.0621238 | 0.0578255 | 0.0537666 | 0.0499411 | 0.0429628 | 0.0368295 | 0.0268242 |
| 16 | 0.0579446 | 0.0536501 | 0.0496108 | 0.0458200 | 0.0389521 | 0.0329769 | 0.0233900 |
| 17 | 0.0542581 | 0.0499698 | 0.0459525 | 0.0421985 | 0.0354448 | 0.0296294 | 0.0204567 |
| 18 | 0.0509820 | 0.0467021 | 0.0427087 | 0.0389933 | 0.0323565 | 0.0267021 | 0.0179373 |
| 19 | 0.0480518 | 0.0437818 | 0.0398139 | 0.0361386 | 0.0296209 | 0.0241276 | 0.0157630 |
| 20 | 0.0454153 | 0.0411567 | 0.0372157 | 0.0335818 | 0.0271846 | 0.0218522 | 0.0138788 |
| 25 | 0.0354068 | 0.0312204 | 0.0274279 | 0.0240120 | 0.0182267 | 0.0136788 | 0.0075000 |
| 30 | 0.0287481 | 0.0246499 | 0.0210193 | 0.0178301 | 0.0126489 | 0.0088274 | 0.0041437 |
| 40 | 0.0204556 | 0.0165558 | 0.0132624 | 0.0105235 | 0.0064615 | 0.0038602 | 0.0013036 |
| 50 | 0.0155127 | 0.0118232 | 0.0088655 | 0.0065502 | 0.0034443 | 0.0017429 | 0.0004167 |

Table values show the sinking fund payment earning a given rate for a given number of periods so that the accumulated amount at the end of the time will be $1.00. The formula for generating the table values is $TV = \dfrac{R}{(1+R)^N - 1}$, where $TV$ is the table value, $R$ is the rate per period, and $N$ is the number of periods or payments.

**EXAMPLE 1** Use Table 14-2 to find the annual sinking fund payment required to accumulate $140,000 in 12 years at 6% annual interest.

$$12 \text{ years} \times 1 \text{ period per year} = 12 \text{ periods}$$

$$\frac{6\% \text{ annual interest rate}}{1 \text{ period per year}} = 6\% \text{ period interest rate}$$

The Table 14-2 value for 12 periods at 6% is 0.0592770

$$\text{Sinking fund payment} = \text{desired future value} \times \text{table factor}$$
$$= \$140,000(0.0592770)$$
$$= \$8,298.78$$

**A sinking fund payment of \$8,298.78 is required at the end of each year for 12 years at 6% to yield the desired \$140,000.**

**EXAMPLE 2** Find the total interest earned on the sinking fund in the previous example.

$FV = \$140,000$     Number of payments $= 12$

Total investment $= \text{amount of payment} \times 12$
$$= \$8,298.78(12)$$
$$= \$99,585.36$$

Total interest earned $= \$140,000 - \$99,585.36$
$$= \mathbf{\$40,414.64}$$

 ## STOP AND CHECK

1. Use Table 14-2 to find the annual sinking fund payment needed to accumulate \$12,000 in six years at 4% annual interest.

2. What is the total amount paid and the interest on the sinking fund in Exercise 1?

3. Use Table 14-2 to find the quarterly sinking fund payment needed to accumulate \$25,000 in ten years at 4% annual interest compounded quarterly.

4. What is the amount paid and the interest on the sinking fund in Exercise 3?

## 2   Find the present value of an ordinary annuity using a \$1.00 ordinary annuity present value table.

In the liquidation or payout phase of an annuity, a common option is for periodic payments to be made to the annuitant or beneficiary for a certain period of time. The future value of the *accumulation phase* of the annuity becomes the present value of the *liquidated or payout phase* of the annuity. Figure 14-6 shows the accumulation phase or future value growth of an annuity. The **present value of an annuity** is the amount needed in a fund to receive a specific periodic payment over a specified period of time during the liquidation or payout phase. The balance that is in the fund continues to earn interest while payouts are being made, but the balance is steadily declining. At the end of the specified time of the liquidation phase, the balance will be zero. See Figure 14-7.

**Present value of an annuity:** the amount needed in a fund so that the fund can pay out a specified regular payment for a specified amount of time.

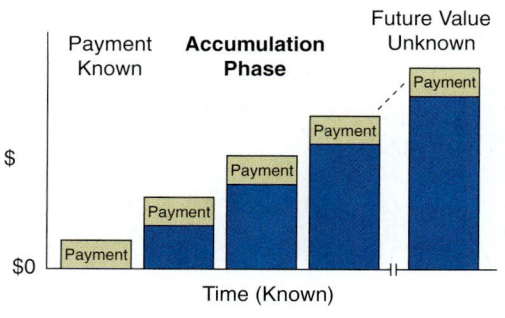

**FIGURE 14-6**
**Future Value of an Annuity**

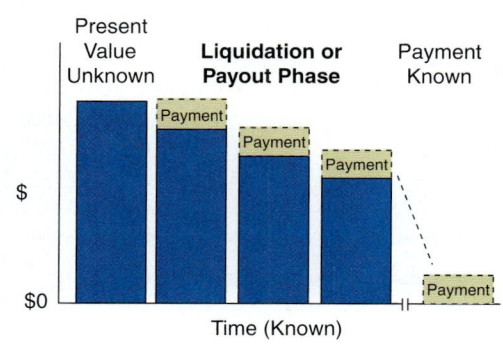

**FIGURE 14-7**
**Present Value of an Annuity**

Use Table 14-3:

1. Locate the table value for the given number of payout periods and the given rate per period.
2. Multiply the table value times the periodic annuity payment.

$$\text{Present value of annuity} = \text{periodic annuity payment} \times \text{table value}$$

**EXAMPLE 1** Use Table 14-3 to find the present value of an ordinary annuity in the payout phase with semiannual payments of $3,000 for seven years at 6% annual interest compounded semiannually.

$$7 \text{ years} \times 2 \text{ periods per year} = 14 \text{ periods}$$

$$\frac{6\% \text{ annual interest}}{2 \text{ periods per year}} = 3\% \text{ period interest rate}$$

The Table 14-3 value for 14 periods at 3% is 11.296.

$$\text{Present value of annuity} = \text{annuity payment} \times \text{table factor}$$
$$= \$3,000(11.296)$$
$$= \$33,888$$

**A fund of $33,888 is needed now at 6% interest compounded semiannually to receive an annuity payment of $3,000 twice a year for seven years.**

## TABLE 14-3
### Present Value of a $1.00 Ordinary Annuity

| Periods | 2% | 3% | 4% | 5% | 6% | 7% | 8% | 9% | 10% | 12% |
|---|---|---|---|---|---|---|---|---|---|---|
| | | | | | Rate per period | | | | | |
| 1 | 0.980 | 0.971 | 0.962 | 0.952 | 0.943 | 0.935 | 0.926 | 0.917 | 0.909 | 0.893 |
| 2 | 1.942 | 1.913 | 1.886 | 1.859 | 1.833 | 1.808 | 1.783 | 1.759 | 1.736 | 1.690 |
| 3 | 2.884 | 2.829 | 2.775 | 2.723 | 2.673 | 2.624 | 2.577 | 2.531 | 2.487 | 2.402 |
| 4 | 3.808 | 3.717 | 3.630 | 3.546 | 3.465 | 3.387 | 3.312 | 3.240 | 3.170 | 3.037 |
| 5 | 4.713 | 4.580 | 4.452 | 4.329 | 4.212 | 4.100 | 3.993 | 3.890 | 3.791 | 3.605 |
| 6 | 5.601 | 5.417 | 5.242 | 5.076 | 4.917 | 4.767 | 4.623 | 4.486 | 4.355 | 4.111 |
| 7 | 6.472 | 6.230 | 6.002 | 5.786 | 5.582 | 5.389 | 5.206 | 5.033 | 4.868 | 4.564 |
| 8 | 7.325 | 7.020 | 6.733 | 6.463 | 6.210 | 5.971 | 5.747 | 5.535 | 5.335 | 4.968 |
| 9 | 8.162 | 7.786 | 7.435 | 7.108 | 6.802 | 6.515 | 6.247 | 5.995 | 5.759 | 5.328 |
| 10 | 8.983 | 8.530 | 8.111 | 7.722 | 7.360 | 7.024 | 6.710 | 6.418 | 6.145 | 5.650 |
| 11 | 9.787 | 9.253 | 8.760 | 8.306 | 7.887 | 7.499 | 7.139 | 6.805 | 6.495 | 5.938 |
| 12 | 10.575 | 9.954 | 9.385 | 8.863 | 8.384 | 7.943 | 7.536 | 7.161 | 6.814 | 6.194 |
| 13 | 11.348 | 10.635 | 9.986 | 9.394 | 8.853 | 8.358 | 7.904 | 7.487 | 7.103 | 6.424 |
| 14 | 12.106 | 11.296 | 10.563 | 9.899 | 9.295 | 8.745 | 8.244 | 7.786 | 7.367 | 6.628 |
| 15 | 12.849 | 11.938 | 11.118 | 10.380 | 9.712 | 9.108 | 8.559 | 8.061 | 7.606 | 6.811 |
| 16 | 13.578 | 12.561 | 11.652 | 10.838 | 10.106 | 9.447 | 8.851 | 8.313 | 7.824 | 6.974 |
| 17 | 14.292 | 13.166 | 12.166 | 11.274 | 10.477 | 9.763 | 9.122 | 8.544 | 8.022 | 7.120 |
| 18 | 14.992 | 13.754 | 12.659 | 11.690 | 10.828 | 10.059 | 9.372 | 8.756 | 8.201 | 7.250 |
| 19 | 15.678 | 14.324 | 13.134 | 12.085 | 11.158 | 10.336 | 9.604 | 8.950 | 8.365 | 7.366 |
| 20 | 16.351 | 14.877 | 13.590 | 12.462 | 11.470 | 10.594 | 9.818 | 9.129 | 8.514 | 7.469 |
| 25 | 19.523 | 17.413 | 15.622 | 14.094 | 12.783 | 11.654 | 10.675 | 9.823 | 9.077 | 7.843 |
| 30 | 22.396 | 19.600 | 17.292 | 15.372 | 13.765 | 12.409 | 11.258 | 10.274 | 9.427 | 8.055 |
| 40 | 27.355 | 23.115 | 19.793 | 17.159 | 15.046 | 13.332 | 11.925 | 10.757 | 9.779 | 8.244 |
| 50 | 31.424 | 25.730 | 21.482 | 18.256 | 15.762 | 13.801 | 12.233 | 10.962 | 9.915 | 8.304 |

Table values show the present value of a $1.00 ordinary annuity, or the lump sum amount that, invested now, yields the same compounded amount as an annuity of $1.00 at a given rate per period for a given number of periods. The formula for generating the table values is $TV = \dfrac{(1 + R)^N - 1}{R(1 + R)^N}$, where $TV$ is the table value, $R$ is the rate per period, and $N$ is the number of periods.

1. Use Table 14-3 to find the present value of an ordinary annuity with an annual payout of $5,000 for five years at 4% interest compounded annually.

2. What is the present value of an ordinary annuity with an annual payout of $20,000 at 7% annual interest for 20 years?

3. What lump sum must be set aside today at 8% annual interest compounded quarterly to provide quarterly payments of $7,000 to Demetrius Ball for the next ten years?

4. Tim Warren is setting up an ordinary annuity and wants to receive $10,000 semiannually for the next 20 years. How much should he set aside at 6% annual interest compounded semiannually?

## 3  Find the sinking fund payment or the present value of an annuity using a formula.

As with future value, tables do not always have the values that you need to find a sinking fund payment or a present value of an annuity. A formula allows you the flexibility of using any interest rate or any number of periods.

> **HOW TO** Find the sinking fund payment or present value of an ordinary annuity using a formula
>
> 1. Identify the period rate $R$ as a decimal equivalent, the number of periods $N$, and the future value $FV$ of the annuity.
> 2. Substitute the values from Step 1 in the appropriate formula.
>
> $$PMT_{\text{ordinary annuity}} = FV\left(\frac{R}{(1 + R)^N - 1}\right)$$
>
> $$PV_{\text{ordinary annuity}} = PMT\left(\frac{(1 + R)^N - 1}{R(1 + R)^N}\right)$$
>
> 3. Evaluate the formula.

**EXAMPLE 1**   Debbie Bennett wants to have $100,000 in a retirement fund to supplement her retirement. She plans to work for 20 more years and has found an annuity fund that earns 5.5% annual interest. How much does she need to contribute to the fund each month to reach her goal?

$$R = \frac{5.5\%}{12} = \frac{0.055}{12} = 0.0045833333 \qquad \text{Periodic interest rate}$$

$$N = 20(12) = 240 \qquad \text{Number of payments}$$

$$FV = \$100,000$$

$$PMT_{\text{ordinary annuity}} = \$100,000\left(\frac{0.0045833333}{(1 + 0.0045833333)^{240} - 1}\right)$$

$100000 \boxed{\times} 0.0045833333 \boxed{\div} \boxed{(} 1.0045833333 \boxed{\wedge} 240 \boxed{-} 1 \boxed{)} \boxed{=} \Rightarrow$

$$PMT = 229.5539756 \text{ (round to nearest cent)}$$

**The payment that Debbie should make into the sinking fund each month is $229.55.**

**EXAMPLE 2**   At retirement Debbie Bennett will begin drawing a payment each month from her retirement fund. How much does she need in a fund that pays 5.5% interest to receive a $700 per month payment for 20 years?

$$R = \frac{5.5\%}{12} = \frac{0.055}{12} = 0.0045833333 \qquad \text{Periodic interest rate}$$

$$N = 20(12) = 240 \qquad \text{Number of payments}$$

$$P = \$700$$

$$PV_{\text{ordinary annuity}} = \$700\left(\frac{(1 + 0.0045833333)^{240} - 1}{0.0045833333(1 + 0.0045833333)^{240}}\right)$$

700 ( 1.0045833333 ^ 240 − 1 ) ÷
( 0.0045833333 × 1.0045833333 ^ 240 ) = ⇒

$PV = 101760.8545$ Round to nearest cent.

**Debbie needs to have \$101,760.85 in the fund to receive an annuity payment of \$700 each month for 20 years.**

 **STOP AND CHECK**

1. Shameka plans to have \$350,000 in a retirement fund at her retirement. She plans to work for 26 years and has found a sinking fund that earns 4.85% annual interest compounded monthly. How much does she need to contribute to the fund each month to reach her goal?

2. At retirement Mekisha will begin drawing a payment each month from her retirement fund. Use the formula to determine the amount she needs in a fund that pays 5.25% interest to receive a \$2,000 per month payment for 25 years.

## 14-2 SECTION EXERCISES

### SKILL BUILDERS

1. What semiannual sinking fund payment would be required to yield \$48,000 nine years from now? The annual interest rate is 6% compounded semiannually.

2. The Bamboo Furniture Company manufactures rattan patio furniture. It has just purchased a machine for \$13,500 to cut and glue the pieces of wood. The machine is expected to last five years. If the company establishes a sinking fund to replace this machine, what annual payments must be made if the annual interest rate is 8%?

3. Tristin and Kim Denley are establishing a college fund for their 1-year-old daughter, Chloe. They want to save enough now to pay college tuition at the time she enters college (17 years from now). If her tuition is projected to be \$35,000 for a two-year degree, what annual sinking fund payment should they establish if the annual interest is 8%?

4. Kathy and Patrick Mowers have a 12-year-old daughter and are now in a financial position to begin saving for her college education. What annual sinking fund payment should they make to have her entire college expenses paid at the time she enters college six years from now? Her college expenses are projected to be \$30,000 and the annual interest rate is 6%.

5. Matthew Bennett recognizes the value of saving part of his income. He has set a goal to have $25,000 in cash available for emergencies. How much should he invest semiannually to have $25,000 in ten years if the sinking fund he has selected pays 8% annually, compounded semiannually?

6. Stein and Company has established a sinking fund to retire a bond issue of $500,000, which is due in ten years. How much is the quarterly sinking fund payment if the account pays 8% annual interest compounded quarterly?

7. What is the present value of an ordinary annuity with annual payments of $680 at 9% annual interest for 25 years?

8. Erin Calipari plans to have a stream of $2,500 payments each year for two years at 8% annual interest. How much should she set aside today?

9. Emily Bennett is setting up an annuity for a memorial scholarship. What lump sum does she need to set aside today at 7% annual interest to have the scholarship pay $3,000 annually for 10 years?

10. Kristin Bennett, a nationally recognized philanthropist, set up an ordinary annuity of $1,600 for ten years at 9% annual interest. How much does Bennett have to deposit today to pay the stream of annual payments?

11. Ken and Debbie Bennett have agreed to pay for their granddaughter's college education and need to know how much to set aside so annual payments of $15,000 can be made for five years at 3% annual interest.

12. Janice and Terry Van Dyke have decided to establish a quarterly ordinary annuity of $3,000 for the next ten years at 8% annual interest compounded quarterly. How much should they invest in a lump sum now to provide the stream of payments?

## Learning Outcomes

## What to Remember with Examples

### Section 14-1

**1** Find the future value of an ordinary annuity using the simple interest formula method. (p. 488)

**1.** Find the first end-of-period principal.

$$\text{First end-of-period principal} = \text{annuity payment}$$

**2.** For each remaining period in turn, find the next end-of-period principal:
  **(a)** Multiply the previous end-of-period principal by the sum of 1 and the decimal equivalent of the period interest rate.
  **(b)** Add the product from step 2a and the annuity payment.

$$\text{End-of-period principal} = \text{previous end-of-period principal} \times$$
$$(1 + \text{period interest rate}) + \text{annuity payment}$$

**3.** Identify the last end-of-period principal as the future value.

$$\text{Future value} = \text{last end-of-period principal}$$

Find the future value of an annual ordinary annuity of $2,000 for two years at 4% annual interest.

$$\text{End-of-year 1} = \$2,000$$
$$\text{End-of-year 2} = \$2,000(1.04) + \$2,000$$
$$= \$2,080 + \$2,000$$
$$= \$4,080$$

The future value is $4,080.

Find the future value of a semiannual ordinary annuity of $300 for one year at 5% annual interest, compounded semiannually.

$$\frac{5\% \text{ annual interest rate}}{2 \text{ periods per year}} = 2.5\% = 0.025 \text{ period interest rate}$$
$$\text{End-of-period 1} = \$300$$
$$\text{End-of-period 2} = \$300(1.025) + \$300$$
$$= \$307.50 + \$300$$
$$= \$607.50$$

The future value is $607.50.

Find the total interest earned on an annuity:

**1.** Find the total amount invested:

$$\text{Total invested} = \text{payment amount} \times \text{number of payments}$$

**2.** Find the total interest:

$$\text{Total interest} = \text{future value of annuity} - \text{total invested}$$

Find the total interest earned on the semiannual ordinary annuity in the previous example.

| | |
|---|---|
| Total invested = $300(2) | Payment = $300 |
| = $600 | Number of payments = 2 |
| Total interest = $607.50 − $600 | Future value = $607.50 |
| = $7.50 | |

**2** Find the future value of an ordinary annuity with periodic payments using a $1.00 ordinary annuity future value table. (p. 490)

Using Table 14-1:

**1.** Select the periods row corresponding to the number of interest periods.
**2.** Select the rate-per-period column corresponding to the period interest rate.
**3.** Locate the value in the cell where the periods row intersects the rate-per-period column.
**4.** Multiply the annuity payment by the table value from step 3.

$$\text{Future value} = \text{annuity payment} \times \text{table value}$$

Find the future value of an ordinary annuity of $5,000 semiannually for four years at 4% annual interest compounded semiannually.

$$4 \text{ years} \times 2 \text{ periods per year} = 8 \text{ periods}$$

$$\frac{4\% \text{ annual interest rate}}{2 \text{ periods per year}} = 2\% \text{ period interest rate}$$

The Table 14-1 value for eight periods at 2% is 8.583.

$$\text{Future value} = \$5,000(8.583)$$
$$= \$42,915$$

The future value is $42,915.

---

**3** Find the future value of an annuity due with periodic payments using the simple interest formula method. (p. 492)

1. Find the first end-of-period principal: Multiply the annuity payment by the sum of 1 and the decimal equivalent of the period interest rate.

$$\text{First end-of-period principal} = \text{annuity payment} \times (1 + \text{period interest rate})$$

2. For each remaining period in turn, find the next end-of-period principal:
   **(a)** Add the previous end-of-period principal and the annuity payment.
   **(b)** Multiply the sum from step 2a by the sum of 1 and the period interest rate.

$$\text{End-of-period principal} = (\text{previous end-of-period principal} + \text{annuity payment}) \times (1 + \text{period interest rate})$$

3. Identify the last end-of-period principal as the future value.

$$\text{Future value} = \text{last end-of-period principal}$$

Find the future value of an annual annuity due of $3,000 for two years at 5% annual interest.

$$\text{End-of-year 1} = \$3,000(1.05)$$
$$= \$3,150$$
$$\text{End-of-year 2} = (\$3,150 + \$3,000)(1.05)$$
$$= \$6,150(1.05)$$
$$= \$6,457.50$$

Find the future value and the total interest earned of a semiannual annuity due of $400 for one year at 4% annual interest compounded semiannually.

$$\frac{4\% \text{ annual interest rate}}{2 \text{ periods per year}} = 2\% = 0.02 \text{ period interest rate}$$

$$\text{End-of-period 1} = \$400(1.02)$$
$$= \$408$$
$$\text{End-of-period 2} = (\$408 + \$400)(1.02)$$
$$= (\$808)(1.02)$$
$$= \$824.16$$

The future value is $824.16.

Find the total interest earned on the semiannual annuity:

| | |
|---|---|
| Total invested = $400(2) | Payment = $400 |
| = $800 | Number of payments = 2 |
| Total interest = $824.16 − $800 | Future value = $824.16 |
| = $24.16 | |

---

**4** Find the future value of an annuity due with periodic payments using a $1.00 ordinary annuity future value table. (p. 493)

Use Table 14-1:

1. Select the periods row corresponding to the number of interest periods.
2. Select the rate-per-period column corresponding to the period interest rate.
3. Locate the value in the cell where the periods row intersects the rate-per-period column.

4. Multiply the annuity payment by the table value from step 3. This is equivalent to an ordinary annuity.
5. Multiply the product from step 4 by the sum of 1 and the period interest rate.

$$\text{Future value} = \text{annuity payment} \times \text{table value} \times (1 + \text{period interest rate})$$

Find the future value of a quarterly annuity due of \$1,500 for three years at 8% annual interest compounded quarterly.

$$3 \text{ years} \times 4 \text{ periods per year} = 12 \text{ periods}$$

$$\frac{8\% \text{ annual interest rate}}{4 \text{ periods per year}} = 2\% \text{ period interest rate}$$

The Table 14-1 value for 12 periods at 2% is 13.412.

$$\text{Future value} = \$1,500(13.412)(1.02)$$
$$= \$20,520.36$$

The future value is \$20,520.36.

| 5 | Find the future value of an ordinary annuity or an annuity due using a formula. (p. 496) |

Find the future value of an ordinary annuity or an annuity due using the formula.

1. Identify the period rate $R$ as a decimal equivalent, the number of periods $N$, and the amount of the annuity payment $PMT$.
2. Substitute the values from Step 1 into the appropriate formula.

$$FV_{\text{ordinary annuity}} = PMT\left(\frac{(1 + R)^N - 1}{R}\right)$$

$$FV_{\text{annuity due}} = PMT\left(\frac{(1 + R)^N - 1}{R}\right)(1 + R)$$

3. Evaluate the formula.

Use the formula to find the future value of an ordinary annuity of \$50 paid monthly at 5% for 20 years.

$$R = \frac{5\%}{12} = \frac{0.05}{12} = 0.0041666667 \qquad \text{Periodic interest rate}$$

$$N = 20(12) = 240 \qquad\qquad\qquad \text{Number of payments}$$

$$PMT = \$50$$

$$FV_{\text{ordinary annuity}} = \$50\left(\frac{(1 + 0.0041666667)^{240} - 1}{0.0041666667}\right) \qquad \begin{array}{l}\text{Mentally add within innermost} \\ \text{parentheses.}\end{array}$$

$$FV_{\text{ordinary annuity}} = \$50\left(\frac{(1.0041666667)^{240} - 1}{0.0041666667}\right)$$

Calculator sequence:

$$50 \; \boxed{(} \; 1.0041666667 \; \boxed{\wedge} \; 240 \; \boxed{-} \; 1 \; \boxed{)} \; \boxed{\div} \; 0.0041666667 \; \boxed{=} \Rightarrow 20551.68352$$

The future value of the ordinary annuity is \$20,551.68.

## Section 14-2

| 1 | Find the sinking fund payment using a \$1.00 sinking fund payment table. (p. 501) |

Use Table 14-2:

1. Select the periods row corresponding to the number of interest periods.
2. Select the rate-per-period column corresponding to the period interest rate.
3. Locate the value in the cell where the periods row intersects the rate-per-period column.
4. Multiply the table value from step 3 by the desired future value.

$$\text{Sinking fund payment} = \text{future value} \times \text{table value}$$

Find the quarterly sinking fund payment required to yield $15,000 in five years if interest is 8% compounded quarterly.

$$5 \text{ years} \times 4 \text{ periods per year} = 20 \text{ periods}$$

$$\frac{8\% \text{ annual interest rate}}{4 \text{ periods per year}} = 2\% \text{ period interest rate}$$

The Table 14-2 value for 20 periods at 2% is 0.0411567.

$$\text{Sinking fund payment} = \$15,000(0.0411567)$$
$$= \$617.35$$

The required quarterly payment is $617.35.

**2** Find the present value of an ordinary annuity using a $1.00 ordinary annuity present value table. (p. 502)

Use Table 14-3:

1. Locate the table value for the given number of periods and the given rate per period.
2. Multiply the table value by the periodic annuity payment.

$$\text{Present value of annuity} = \text{periodic annuity payment} \times \text{table value}$$

Find the lump sum required today earning 6% annual interest compounded semiannually to yield a semiannual ordinary annuity payment of $2,500 for 15 years.

$$15 \text{ years} \times 2 \text{ periods per year} = 30 \text{ periods}$$

$$\frac{6\% \text{ annual interest rate}}{2 \text{ periods per year}} = 3\% \text{ period interest rate}$$

The Table 14-3 value for 30 periods at 3% is 19.600.

$$\text{Present value} = \$2,500(19.600)$$
$$= \$49,000$$

The lump sum required for deposit today is $49,000.

**3** Find the sinking fund payment or the present value of an annuity using a formula. (p. 504)

Find the sinking fund payment or present value of an ordinary annuity using a formula:

1. Identify the period rate $R$ as a decimal equivalent, the number of periods $N$, and the future value $FV$ of the annuity.
2. Substitute the values from Step 1 in the appropriate formula.

$$PMT_{\text{ordinary annuity}} = FV\left(\frac{R}{(1+R)^N - 1}\right)$$

$$PV_{\text{ordinary annuity}} = P\left(\frac{(1+R)^N - 1}{R(1+R)^N}\right)$$

3. Evaluate the formula.

Camesa plans to have $500,000 in her retirement fund when she retires in 23 years. She is investigating a sinking fund that earns 4.75% annual interest. How much does she need to contribute to the fund each month to reach her goal?

$$R = \frac{4.75\%}{12} = \frac{0.0475}{12} = 0.0039583333 \qquad \text{Periodic interest rate}$$

$$N = 23(12) = 276 \qquad \text{Number of payments}$$

$$FV = \$500,000$$

$$PMT_{\text{ordinary annuity}} = \$500,000\left(\frac{0.0039583333}{(1 + 0.0039583333)^{276} - 1}\right)$$

500000 $\boxed{\times}$ 0.0039583333 $\boxed{\div}$ $\boxed{(}$ $\boxed{(}$ 1.0039583333 $\boxed{^\wedge}$ 276 $\boxed{-}$ 1 $\boxed{)}$ $\boxed{)}$ $\boxed{=}$

$PMT = 1,001.959664$ (round to next cent)

Camesa should make monthly payments of $1,001.96 into the sinking fund.

## EXERCISES SET A

*Use Table 14-1 to complete the following table.*

| Annuity payment | Annual rate | Annual interest | Years | Type of annuity | Future value of annuity |
|---|---|---|---|---|---|
| **1.** $1,400 | 3% | Compounded annually | 5 | Ordinary | _____ |
| **2.** $2,900 | 8% | Compounded quarterly | 10 | Ordinary | _____ |
| **3.** $1,250 | 6% | Compounded semiannually | $1\frac{1}{2}$ | Annuity due | _____ |
| **4.** $800 | 5% | Compounded annually | 15 | Annuity due | _____ |

*Use Table 14-2 to find the sinking fund payment.*

| | Desired future value | Annual interest rate | Years | Frequency of payments |
|---|---|---|---|---|
| CEL | **5.** $240,000 | 6% | 15 | Annually |
| CEL | **6.** $3,000 | 4% | 10 | Semiannually |
| CEL | **7.** $50,000 | 4% | 5 | Quarterly |
| CEL | **8.** $45,000 | 3% | 8 | Annually |

*Use Table 14-3 to find the amount that needs to be invested today to provide a stream of payments in the annuity liquidation phase.*

| Payment amount | Annual interest rate | Years | Frequency of payments |
|---|---|---|---|
| **9.** $10,000 | 4% | 20 | Annually |
| **10.** $12,000 | 4% | 10 | Semiannually |
| **11.** $5,000 | 8% | 4 | Quarterly |
| **12.** $1,000 | 3% | 15 | Annually |

13. Roni Sue deposited $1,500 at the beginning of each year for three years at an annual interest rate of 9%. Find the future value manually.

*Use Table 14-1.*

14. Barry Michael plans to deposit $2,000 at the end of every six months for the next five years to save up for a boat. If the interest rate is 6% annually, compounded semiannually, how much money will Barry have in his boat fund after five years?

15. Bob Paris opens a retirement income account paying 5% annually. He deposits $3,000 at the beginning of each year.
    (a) How much will be in the account after ten years?
    (b) When Bob retires at age 65, in 19 years, how much will be in the account?

16. The Shari Joy Corporation decided to set aside $3,200 at the beginning of every six months to provide donation funds for a new Little League baseball field scheduled to be built in 18 months. If money earns 4% annual interest compounded semiannually, how much will be available as a donation for the field?

*Use Table 14-2 for Exercises 17–18.*

17. How much must be set aside at the end of each six months by the Fabulous Toy Company to replace a $155,000 piece of equipment at the end of eight years if the account pays 6% annual interest compounded semiannually?

18. Lausanne Private School System needs to set aside funds for a new computer system. What quarterly sinking fund payment would be required to amount to $45,000, the approximate cost of the system, in $1\frac{1}{2}$ years at 4% annual interest compounded quarterly?

# EXERCISES SET B

Use Table 14-1 to complete the table below.

| Annuity payment | Annual rate | Annual interest | Years | Type of annuity | Future value of annuity |
|---|---|---|---|---|---|
| 1. $1,900 | 8% | Compounded quarterly | 3 | Ordinary | _____ |
| 2. $5,000 | 5% | Compounded annually | 20 | Ordinary | _____ |
| 3. $2,150 | 7% | Compounded annually | 8 | Annuity due | _____ |
| 4. $600 | 6% | Compounded semiannually | 5 | Annuity due | _____ |

Use Table 14-2 to find the sinking fund payment.

| | Desired future value | Annual interest rate | Years | Frequency of payments | Sinking fund payment |
|---|---|---|---|---|---|
| CEL 5. | $24,000 | 6% | 10 | Semiannually | _____ |
| CEL 6. | $45,000 | 8% | 4 | Quarterly | _____ |
| CEL 7. | $8,000 | 6% | 17 | Annually | _____ |
| CEL 8. | $10,000 | 4% | 19 | Annually | _____ |

Use Table 14-3 to find the amount that needs to be invested today to receive payments for the specified length of time.

| Payment amount | Annual interest rate | Years | Frequency of payments |
|---|---|---|---|
| 9. $7,000 | 2% | 30 | Annually |
| 10. $20,000 | 6% | 15 | Semiannually |
| 11. $10,000 | 8% | 5 | Quarterly |
| 12. $6,000 | 5% | 10 | Annually |

13. Manually find the future value of an annuity due of $1,100 deposited annually for three years at 5% interest.

14. Sam and Jane Crawford had a baby in 1998. At the end of that year they began putting away $2,000 a year at 10% annual interest for a college fund. How much money will be in the account when the child is 18 years old?

15. A business deposits $4,500 at the end of each quarter in an account that earns 8% annual interest compounded quarterly. What is the value of the annuity in five years?

16. University Trailers is setting aside $800 at the beginning of every quarter to purchase a forklift in 30 months. The annual interest will be 8% compounded quarterly. How much will be available for the purchase?

*Use Table 14-2 for Exercises 17–18.*

17. Tasty Food Manufacturers, Inc., has a bond issue of $1,400,000 due in 30 years. If it wants to establish a sinking fund to meet this obligation, how much must be set aside at the end of each year if the annual interest rate is 6%?

18. Zachary Alexander owns a limousine that will need to be replaced in four years at a cost of $65,000. How much must he put aside each year in a sinking fund at 8% annual interest to purchase the new limousine?

# PRACTICE TEST

1. Manually find the future value of an ordinary annuity of $9,000 per year for two years at 3.25% annual interest.

2. Manually find the future value of an annuity due of $2,700 per year for three years at 4.5% annual interest.

3. What is the future value of an annuity due of $5,645 paid every six months for three years at 6% annual interest compounded semiannually?

4. What is the future value of an ordinary annuity of $300 every three months for four years at 8% annual interest compounded quarterly?

5. What is the sinking fund payment required at the end of each year to accumulate $125,000 in 16 years at 4% annual interest?

6. What is the present value of an ordinary annuity of $985 paid out every six months for eight years at 8% annual interest compounded semiannually?

7. Mike's Sport Shop deposited $3,400 at the end of each year for 12 years at 7% annual interest. How much will Mike have in the account at the end of the time period?

8. How much would the annuity amount to in Exercise 7 if Mike had deposited the money at the beginning of each year instead of at the end of each year?

9. How much must be set aside at the end of each year by the Caroline Cab Company to replace four taxicabs at a cost of $90,000? The current interest rate is 6% annually. The existing cabs will wear out in three years.

10. How much must Johnny Williams invest today to have an amount equivalent to investing $2,800 at the end of every six months for the next 15 years if interest is earned at 8% annually compounded semiannually?

11. Maurice Eftink owns a lawn design business. His lawnmower cost $7,800 and should last for six years. How much must he set aside each year at 6% annual interest to have enough money to buy a new mower?

12. Reed and Sondra Davis want to know how much they must deposit in a retirement savings account today to have payments of $1,500 every six months for 15 years. The retirement account is paying 8% annual interest compounded semiannually.

**13.** Morris Stocks wants to save $2,200 at the end of each year for 11 years in an account paying 7% annual interest. What is the future value of the annuity at the end of this period of time?

**14.** Maura Helba is saving for her college expenses. She sets aside $175 at the beginning of each three months in an account paying 8% annual interest compounded quarterly. How much will Maura have accumulated in the account at the end of four years?

**15.** What is the present value of a semiannual ordinary annuity of $2,500 for seven years at 6% annual interest compounded semiannually?

**16.** How much will you need to invest today to have quarterly payments of $800 for ten years? The interest rate is 8% annually, compounded quarterly.

**17.** Goldie's Department Store has a fleet of delivery trucks that will last for three years of heavy use and then need to be replaced at a cost of $75,000. How much must they set aside every three months in a sinking fund at 8% annual interest, compounded quarterly, to have enough money to replace the trucks?

**18.** Linda Zuk wants to save $25,000 for a new boat in six years. How much must be put aside in equal payments each year in an account earning 6% annual interest for Linda to be able to purchase the boat?

**19.** What is the present value of an ordinary annuity of $3,400 at 5% annual interest for seven years?

**20.** An annual ordinary annuity of $2,500 for five years at 5% annual interest requires what lump-sum payment now?

**21.** Danny Lawrence Properties, Inc., has a bond issue that will mature in 25 years for $1 million. How much must the company set aside each year in a sinking fund at 8% annual interest to meet this future obligation?

**22.** How much money needs to be set aside today at 10% annual interest compounded semiannually to pay $500 for five years?

**23.** You are starting an ordinary annuity of $680 for 25 years at 5% annual interest. What lump-sum amount would have to be set aside today for this annuity?

**24.** Your parents are retiring and want to set aside a lump sum earning 8% annual interest compounded quarterly to pay out $5,000 quarterly for ten years. What lump sum should your parents set aside today?

**25.** Ted Davis has set the goal of accumulating $80,000 for his son's college fund, which will be needed 18 years in the future. How much should he deposit each year in a sinking fund that earns 8% annual interest? How much should he deposit each year if he waits until his son starts school (at age six) to begin saving? Compare the two payment amounts.

1. Select three table values from Table 14-1 and verify them using the formula

$$FV = \frac{(1 + R)^N - 1}{R}$$

2. To find the future value of an annuity due, you multiply the future value of an ordinary annuity by the sum of $1 +$ the period interest rate. Explain why this is the same as adding the simple interest earned on the first payment for the entire length of the annuity.

3. In Example 3 on page 494, we found that the annuity due with semiannual payments had the greater future value. Also, the ordinary annuity with the quarterly payments was more than the ordinary annuity with semiannual payments. Why?

4. How are future value of a lump sum and future value of an annuity similar?

5. How are future value of a lump sum and future value of an annuity different?

6. How are the present value of a lump sum and the periodic payment of a sinking fund similar? How are they different?

7. How are annuities and sinking funds similar? How are they different?

8. Select three table values from Table 14-2 and verify them using the formula

$$TV = \frac{R}{(1 + R)^N - 1}$$

9. Select three table values from Table 14-3 and verify them using the formula

$$TV = \frac{(1 + R)^N - 1}{R(1 + R)^N}$$

10. Explain the difference in an ordinary annuity and an annuity due.

# Challenge Problem

Carolyn Ellis is setting up an annuity for her retirement. She can set aside $2,000 at the end of each year for the next 20 years and it will earn 6% annual interest. What lump sum will she need to set aside today at 6% annual interest to have the same retirement fund available 20 years from now? How much more will Carolyn need to invest in periodic payments than she will if she makes a lump sum payment if she intends to accumulate the same retirement balance?

# CASE STUDIES

## 14.1  Annuities for Retirement

Naomi Dexter is 20 years old and attends Southwest Tennessee Community College. Her Business English instructor asked her to write a report detailing her plans for retirement. Naomi decided she would investigate several ways to accumulate $1 million by the time she retires. She also thinks she would like to retire early when she is 50 years old so she can travel around the world. She has a money market account that pays 3% interest annually. She checked the rate on a 10-year certificate of deposit (CD) through her bank and found that it currently pays 6%. She also did a little research and learned that the average long-term return from stock market investments is between 10% and 12%. Now she needs to calculate how much money she will need to deposit each year to accumulate $1 million.

1. If Naomi wants to accumulate $1,000,000 by investing money every year into her savings account at 3% for 30 years until retirement, how much does she need to deposit each year?

2. If she decides to invest in certificates of deposit at 6% interest, how much will she need to deposit annually to accumulate the $1,000,000?

3. If Naomi invests in a stock portfolio, her returns for 10 or more years will average 10%–12%. Naomi realizes that the stock market has higher returns because it is a more risky investment than a savings account or a CD. She wants her calculations to be conservative so she decides to use 8% to calculate possible stock market earnings. How much will she need to invest annually to accumulate $1,000,000 in the stock market?

4. After looking at the results of her calculations, Naomi has decided to aim for $500,000 savings by the time she retires. She expects to have a starting salary after college of $25,000 to $35,000 and she has taken into account all of the living expenses that will come out of her salary. What will Naomi's annual deposits need to be to accumulate $500,000 in a CD at 6%?

5. If Naomi decides that she will invest $3,000 per year in a 6% annuity for the first ten years, $6,000 for the next ten years, and $9,000 for the next ten years, how much will she accumulate? Treat each ten-year period as a separate annuity. After the ten years of an annuity, then it will continue to grow at compound interest for the remaining years of the 30 years.

## 14.2 Accumulating Money

Joseph reads a lot about people who are success-oriented. He loves to learn about courage, risk-taking, and as he describes it, "the road less traveled." His local bookstore has a large business section where he has found biographies of entrepreneurs and maverick corporate leaders. He also finds fascinating some of the books he has seen on financial planning and ways to accumulate wealth. One interesting savings plan he read about challenges the reader to put aside one full paycheck at the end of the year as a "holiday present to yourself." Joseph had never thought about saving in that way, and wondered if it would really accumulate much savings.

1. He decided to test the numbers by seeing how much money he would accumulate by a retirement age of 65 if he put one paycheck away at the end of each year. Right now that would mean depositing $1,000 at year-end for the next 35 years. Assuming he makes one yearly deposit of $1,000 at 5% compounded annually, how much interest would he earn?

2. Joseph was surprised at how large the sum would be and then realized that he would be able to put more money away in future years because most likely, his salary would go up. He also thought that he could invest the money over the long term at a higher interest rate, so he redid the calculations with a $1,500 annual year-end deposit, at 8% for 35 years. What was his result?

3. Joseph was amazed at how much he could save in this manner and decided to design a detailed savings plan based on projected yearly increases. He realized that he could not start depositing $1,500 now, but that he would be able to deposit more than that in the future. If he were able to deposit $1,000 at the end of each year for the next 5 years at 8% compounded annually, $1,500 at the end of years 6–10 at 8% compounded annually, and $2,000 at the end of years 11–35 at 5% compounded annually, how much would he accumulate at the end of 35 years? Assume that any balances from earlier depositing periods would continue to earn the same rate of annual interest. Use the tables for future value of annuities.

4. By how much does the result differ from the amount calculated above for $1,500 deposited for 35 years? What accounts for the difference?

5. If Joseph decided that he wanted to have $300,000 accumulated in 30 years by making an annual payment at the end of each year that would earn 12% compounded annually, what would his sinking fund payment be? Use the appropriate table to determine the answer.

## 14.3 Certified Financial Planner

After completing his Certified Financial Planner designation (CFP), Andre was excited about the prospects of working with small business owners and their employees regarding retirement planning. Andre wanted to show the value of an annuity program as one of the viable investment options in a salary reduction retirement plan. In addition, he wanted to demonstrate the substantial tax benefits that annuities can provide. For instance, qualified annuities (by definition) not only reduce your current taxable salary, they also accumulate earnings on a tax deferred basis—meaning you don't pay taxes on the earnings until they are withdrawn. Andre was developing a spreadsheet to show the way that annuities could grow using various rates of return.

1. If an individual put the equivalent of $50 per month, or $600 annually into an ordinary annuity, how much money would accumulate in 20 years at 3% compounded annually? How much at 5%?

2. Using the same information from Exercise 1 and assuming a 25% tax bracket, what would be the net effect of investing in a certificate of deposit at 8% for 20 years if taxes on the earnings were paid from the investment fund each year? How would this compare if no taxes had to be paid, such as in a tax-deferred annuity at 8% for 20 years?

3. Jessica, a 25-year-old client of Andre's, wants to retire by age 65 with $1,000,000. How much would she have to invest annually assuming a 6% rate of return?

4. Jessica decides that 40 years is just too long to work, and she thinks that she can do much better than 6%. She decides that she wants to accumulate $1,000,000 by age 55 using a variable annuity earning 12%. How much will she have to invest annually to achieve this goal? Do you think that 12% is a reasonable interest rate to use? Why or why not?

# Real Estate Tax Benefits

Everyone knows that owning a home is the American dream, but did you know that borrowing to pay for one is a taxpayer's dream? Home mortgage interest is deductible on your income taxes if you itemize deductions. You can deduct the interest on up to $1 million of home mortgage debt, whether it is used to purchase a first or a second home. You can also deduct the interest on up to $100,000 of home equity debt, even if you don't use the money for home improvements. What could the home mortgage deduction mean to you? What follows is an example of the potential tax savings for Devin, age 27.

Devin rents a home at a cost of $1,200 per month. He is single with no children and takes the standard deduction on his income taxes. His adjusted gross income is $50,000. He has $3,500 in state income tax withheld from his paychecks throughout the year, but doesn't qualify for any other itemized deductions. Devin's federal income tax liability for 2007 will look something like this:

| | |
|---|---|
| Adjusted gross income: | $50,000 |
| Less standard deduction (single): | $5,350 |
| Less personal exemption: | $3,400 |
| Taxable income | $41,250 |

Devin's 2007 federal income tax is $6,736.25

However, if Devin purchases a home with a monthly mortgage payment of $1,200, his tax liability is lowered. At the end of the year Devin will receive a Form 1098 from his mortgage company that shows how much of his mortgage payments for the year went to mortgage interest. In this case, Devin's 1098 for the year 2007 shows that he paid $11,400 in mortgage interest. Devin also paid $2,500 in real estate taxes on his home in 2007. His federal income tax liability for 2007 will look something like this:

| | |
|---|---|
| Adjusted gross income: | $50,000 |
| Less itemized deduction (state taxes): | $3,500 |
| Less itemized deduction (real estate taxes): | $2,500 |
| Less itemized deduction (mortgage interest): | $11,400 |
| Less personal exemption: | $3,400 |
| Taxable income | $29,200 |

Devin's 2007 federal income tax is $3,988.75

In this example, Devin saves $2,747.50 in federal income taxes. This amount is more than enough to pay for Devin's real estate taxes of $2,500. In addition, his monthly housing cost stays the same and he owns his home rather than renting. Good deal, Devin!

## LEARNING OUTCOMES

### 15-1 Mortgage Payments

1. Find the monthly mortgage payment.
2. Find the total interest on a mortgage and the PITI.

### 15-2 Amortization Schedules and Qualifying Ratios

1. Prepare a partial amortization schedule of a mortgage.
2. Calculate qualifying ratios.

 A corresponding Business Math Case Video for this chapter, *The Real World: Video Case: Should I Buy a House?* can be found in Appendix A.

# 15-1 MORTGAGE PAYMENTS

## LEARNING OUTCOMES

1 Find the monthly mortgage payment.
2 Find the total interest on a mortgage and the PITI.

The purchase of a home is one of the most costly purchases individuals or families make in a lifetime. A home is a type of "real" property. **Real estate** or **real property** is land plus any permanent improvements to the land. The improvements can be water or sewage systems, homes, commercial buildings, or any type of structure. Most individuals must borrow money to pay for the real property. These loans are referred to as **mortgages** because the lending agency requires that the real property be held as **collateral**. If the payments are not made as scheduled, the lending agency can take possession of the property and sell it to pay against the loan.

As a home buyer makes payments on a mortgage, the home buyer builds equity in the home. The home buyer's **equity** is the difference between the expected selling price of a home or **market value** and the balance owed on the home. A home may increase in value as a result of rising prices and average prices of other homes in the neighborhood. This increase in value also increases the owner's equity in the home.

A home buyer may select from several types of first mortgages. A **first mortgage** is the primary mortgage on a home and is ordinarily made at the time of purchase of the home. The agency holding the first mortgage has the first right to the proceeds up to the amount of the mortgage and settlement fees from the sale of the home if the homeowner fails to make required payments.

One type of first mortgage is the **conventional mortgage**. Money for a conventional mortgage is usually obtained through a savings and loan institution or a bank. These loans are not insured by a government program. Two types of conventional mortgages are the *fixed-rate mortgage* (FRM) and the *adjustable-rate mortgage* (ARM). The rate of interest on the loan for a **fixed-rate mortgage** remains the same for the entire time of the loan. Fixed-rate mortgages have several payment options. The number of years of the loan may vary, but 15- and 30-year loans are the most common. The home buyer makes the same payment (principal plus interest) each month of the loan. Another option is the **biweekly mortgage**. The home buyer makes 26 equal payments each year rather than 12. This method builds equity more quickly than the monthly payment method.

Another option for fixed-rate loans is the **graduated payments mortgage**. The home buyer makes small payments at the beginning of the loan and larger payments at the end. Home buyers who expect their income to rise may choose this option.

The rate of interest on a loan for an **adjustable-rate mortgage** may escalate (increase) or de escalate (decrease) during the time of the loan. The rate of adjustable-rate mortgages depends on the prime lending rate of most banks.

Several government agencies insure the repayment of first mortgage loans. Loans with this insurance include those made under the **Federal Housing Administration (FHA)** and the **Veterans Administration (VA)**. These loans may be obtained through a savings and loan institution, a bank, or a mortgage lending company and are insured by a government program.

Interest paid on home loans is an allowable deduction on personal federal income tax under certain conditions. For this reason, many homeowners choose to borrow money for home improvements, college education, and the like by making an additional loan using the real property as collateral. This type of loan is a **second mortgage** or an **equity line of credit** and is made against the equity in the home. In the case of a loan default, the second mortgage lender has rights to the proceeds of the sale of the home *after* the first mortgage has been paid.

## 1 Find the monthly mortgage payment.

The repayment of a loan in equal installments that are applied to principal and interest over a specific period of time is called the **amortization** of the loan. To calculate the **monthly mortgage payment**, it is customary to use a table, a formula, a business or financial calculator that has the formula programmed into the calculator, or computer software. The monthly payment table gives the factor that is multiplied by the dollar amount of the loan in thousands to give the total monthly payment, including principal and interest. A portion of a monthly payment table is shown in Table 15-1.

The interest rate for first mortgages has fluctuated between 5% and 9% for the past few years. Second mortgage rates are generally higher than first mortgage rates.

---

**Real estate or real property:** land plus any permanent improvements to the land.

**Mortgage:** a loan in which real property is used to secure the debt.

**Collateral:** the property that is held as security on a mortgage.

**Equity:** the difference between the expected selling price and the balance owed on property.

**Market value:** the expected selling price of a property.

**First mortgage:** the primary mortgage on a property.

**Conventional mortgage:** mortgage that is not insured by a government program.

**Fixed-rate mortgage:** the interest rate remains the same for the entire loan.

**Biweekly mortgage:** payment made every two weeks for 26 payments per year.

**Graduated payments mortgage:** payments at the beginning of the loan are smaller and they increase during the loan.

**Adjustable-rate mortgage:** the interest rate may change during the time of the loan.

**Federal Housing Administration (FHA):** a governmental agency within the U.S. Department of Housing and Urban Development (HUD) that insures residential mortgage loans. To receive an FHA loan, specific construction standards must be met and the lender must be approved.

**Veterans Administration (VA):** a governmental agency that guarantees the repayment of a loan made to an eligible veteran. The loans are also called GI loans.

**Second mortgage:** a mortgage in addition to the first mortgage that is secured by the real property.

**Equity line of credit:** a revolving, open-end account that is secured by real property.

**Amortization:** the process for repaying a loan through equal payments at a specified rate for a specific length of time.

**Monthly mortgage payment:** the amount of the equal monthly payment that includes interest and principal.

## TABLE 15-1
Monthly Payment of Principal and Interest per $1,000 of Amount Financed

| | Annual interest rate | | | | | | | | | | | | | | | |
|---|---|---|---|---|---|---|---|---|---|---|---|---|---|---|---|---|
| **Years financed** | **5.00%** | **5.25%** | **5.50%** | **5.75%** | **6.00%** | **6.25%** | **6.50%** | **6.75%** | **7.00%** | **7.25%** | **7.50%** | **7.75%** | **8.00%** | **8.25%** | **8.50%** | **8.75%** |
| 10 | 10.61 | 10.73 | 10.85 | 10.98 | 11.10 | 11.23 | 11.35 | 11.48 | 11.61 | 11.74 | 11.87 | 12.00 | 12.13 | 12.27 | 12.40 | 12.53 |
| 12 | 9.25 | 9.37 | 9.50 | 9.63 | 9.76 | 9.89 | 10.02 | 10.15 | 10.28 | 10.42 | 10.55 | 10.69 | 10.82 | 10.96 | 11.10 | 11.24 |
| 15 | 7.91 | 8.04 | 8.17 | 8.30 | 8.44 | 8.57 | 8.71 | 8.85 | 8.99 | 9.13 | 9.27 | 9.41 | 9.56 | 9.70 | 9.85 | 9.99 |
| 17 | 7.29 | 7.42 | 7.56 | 7.69 | 7.83 | 7.97 | 8.11 | 8.25 | 8.40 | 8.54 | 8.69 | 8.83 | 8.98 | 9.13 | 9.28 | 9.43 |
| 20 | 6.60 | 6.74 | 6.88 | 7.02 | 7.16 | 7.31 | 7.46 | 7.60 | 7.75 | 7.90 | 8.06 | 8.21 | 8.36 | 8.52 | 8.68 | 8.84 |
| 22 | 6.25 | 6.39 | 6.54 | 6.68 | 6.83 | 6.98 | 7.13 | 7.28 | 7.43 | 7.59 | 7.75 | 7.90 | 8.06 | 8.22 | 8.38 | 8.55 |
| 25 | 5.85 | 5.99 | 6.14 | 6.29 | 6.44 | 6.60 | 6.75 | 6.91 | 7.07 | 7.23 | 7.39 | 7.55 | 7.72 | 7.88 | 8.05 | 8.22 |
| 30 | 5.37 | 5.52 | 5.68 | 5.84 | 6.00 | 6.16 | 6.32 | 6.49 | 6.65 | 6.82 | 6.99 | 7.16 | 7.34 | 7.51 | 7.69 | 7.87 |
| 35 | 5.05 | 5.21 | 5.37 | 5.54 | 5.70 | 5.87 | 6.04 | 6.21 | 6.39 | 6.56 | 6.74 | 6.92 | 7.10 | 7.28 | 7.47 | 7.65 |

Table values show the monthly payment of a $1,000 mortgage for the given number of years at the given annual interest rate if the interest is compounded monthly. Table values can be generated by using the formula: $M = (\$1{,}000R)/(1 - (1 + R)^\wedge(-N))$, where $M$ = Monthly payment, $R$ = the monthly interest rate, and $N$ = total number of payments of the loan.

### HOW TO Find the monthly mortgage payment of principal and interest using a per-$1,000 monthly payment table

1. Find the amount financed: Subtract the down payment from the purchase price.
2. Find the $1,000 units of amount financed: Divide the amount financed (from step 1) by $1,000.
3. Locate the table value for the number of years financed and the annual interest rate.
4. Multiply the table value from step 3 by the $1,000 units from step 2.

$$\text{Monthly mortgage payment} = \frac{\text{amount financed}}{\$1{,}000} \times \text{table value}$$

### EXAMPLE 1

Lunelle Miller is purchasing a home for $87,000. Home Federal Savings and Loan has approved her loan application for a 30-year fixed-rate loan at 7% annual interest. If Lunelle agrees to pay 20% of the purchase price as a down payment, calculate the monthly payment.

$87,000(0.20) = $17,400 — Down payment

$87,000 − $17,400 = $69,600 — Amount to be financed

$69,600 ÷ $1,000 = 69.6 — $1,000 units

Use Table 15-1 to find the factor for financing a loan for 30 years with a 7% annual interest rate. This factor is 6.65.

Multiply the number of thousands times the factor.

69.6(6.65) = $462.84

**The monthly payment of $462.84 includes the principal and interest.**

### HOW TO Find the monthly mortgage payment of principal and interest using a formula

1. Identify the monthly rate ($R$) as a decimal equivalent, the number of months ($N$) and the loan principal ($P$).
2. Substitute the values from step 1 in the formula.

$$M = P\left(\frac{R}{1 - (1 + R)^{-N}}\right)$$

3. Evaluate the formula.

## EXAMPLE 2

Use the monthly payment of principal and interest formula to find the monthly payment for Lunelle Miller's loan from Example 1.

$$R = \frac{7\%}{12} = \frac{0.07}{12} = 0.0058333333 \qquad \text{Monthly interest rate}$$

$$N = 30(12) = 360 \qquad \text{Total number of payments}$$

$$P = \$69,600 \qquad \text{Amount financed}$$

$$M = P\left(\frac{R}{1 - (1 + R)^{-N}}\right) \qquad \text{Substitute known values.}$$

$$M = 69,600\left(\frac{0.0058333333}{1 - (1 + 0.0058333333)^{-360}}\right)$$

$$M = 69,600\left(\frac{0.0058333333}{1 - (1.0058333333)^{-360}}\right)$$

$$M = 69,600\left(\frac{0.0058333333}{1 - (0.1232058536)}\right)$$

$$M = 69,600\left(\frac{0.0058333333}{0.8767941464}\right)$$

$$M = 69,600(0.0066530246)$$

$$M = \$463.0505122$$

$$M = \$463.05$$

Calculator sequence:

$69600\ (\ .0058333333\ )\ \div\ (\ 1\ -\ (\ 1\ +\ .0058333333\ )\ \wedge\ (\ (-)\ 360\ )\ )$
$\boxed{\text{ENTER}} \Rightarrow 463.0505348$

On many calculators entering a negative number like $-300$ requires using a special key $\boxed{(-)}$.

**The monthly payment of \$463.05 includes the principal and interest.**

Note that the monthly payment using the table value, using the formula in steps, compared to using the formula using a calculator sequence, varies slightly because of rounding discrepancies.

 **STOP AND CHECK**

1. Natalie Bradley is purchasing a home for \$148,500 and has been preapproved for a 30-year fixed-rate loan of 5.75% annual interest. If Natalie pays 20% of the purchase price as a down payment, what will her principal-plus-interest payment be?

2. Find the monthly payment for a home loan of \$160,000 using a 20-year fixed-rate mortgage at 5.5%.

3. Find the monthly payment for a home loan of \$160,000 using a 25-year fixed-rate mortgage at 5.5%.

4. Find the monthly payment for a home loan of \$160,000 using a 30-year fixed-rate mortgage at 5.5%.

## 2 Find the total interest on a mortgage and the PITI.

Often, a person wants to know the total amount of interest that will be paid during the entire loan.

### HOW TO   Find the total interest on a mortgage

1. Find the total of the payments: Multiply the number of payments by the amount of the payment (principal + interest).
2. Subtract the amount financed from the total of the payments.

Total interest = number of payments $\times$ amount of payment $-$ amount financed

**EXAMPLE 1** Calculate the total interest paid on the fixed-rate loan of $69,600 for 30 years at 7% interest rate.

Total interest = number of payments $\times$ amount of payment − amount financed

$$= 30(12)(\$462.84) - \$69,600$$
$$= \$166,622.40 - \$69,600$$
$$= \$97,022.40$$

**The total interest is $97,022.40.**

---

**Points:** a one-time payment to the lender made at closing that is a percentage of the total loan.

**Mortgage closing costs:** fees charged for services that must be performed to process and close a home mortgage loan.

**Good faith estimate:** an estimate of the mortgage closing costs that lenders are required to provide to the buyer in writing prior to the loan closing date.

**Escrow:** an account for holding the part of a monthly payment that is to be used to pay taxes and insurance. The amount accumulates and the lender pays the taxes and insurance from this account as they are due.

**PITI:** the adjusted monthly payment that includes the principal, interest, taxes, and insurance.

The two preceding examples show how to calculate the monthly payment and the total interest for a mortgage loan. There are other costs associated with purchasing a home. Lending companies may require the borrower to pay **points** at the time the loan is made or closed. Payment of points is a one-time payment of a percentage of the loan that is an additional cost of making the mortgage. One point is 1%, two points is 2%, and so on.

Fees charged for services that must be performed to process and close a home mortgage loan are called **mortgage closing costs**. Examples of these costs include credit reports, surveys, inspections, appraisals, legal fees, title insurance, and taxes. Even though these fees are paid when the loan is closed, lenders are required by law to disclose to the buyer in writing the estimated mortgage closing costs prior to the closing date. This estimate is known as the **good faith estimate**. Some fees are paid by the buyer and some by the seller. Average closing costs for most home purchases are about 6% of the loan amount.

Since the lending agency must be assured that the property taxes and insurance are paid on the property, the annual costs of these items may be prorated each year and added to the monthly payment for that year. These funds are held in **escrow** until the taxes or insurance payment is due, at which time the lending agency makes the payment for the home owner. These additional costs make the monthly payment more than just the principal and interest payment we found in the preceding examples. The adjusted monthly payment that includes the principal, interest, taxes, and insurance is abbreviated as **PITI**.

---

**HOW TO** Find the total PITI payment

1. Find the principal and interest portion of the monthly payment.
2. Find the monthly taxes by dividing the annual taxes by 12.
3. Find the monthly insurance by dividing the annual insurance by 12.
4. Find the sum of the monthly principal, interest, taxes, and insurance.

---

**EXAMPLE 2** Find the total PITI payment for Lunelle Miller's loan from Example 1 if her annual taxes are $985 and her annual homeowner's insurance is $560.

| | |
|---|---|
| $462.84 | Monthly principal and interest found in Example 1 |
| $985 ÷ 12 = $82.08333333 | Monthly taxes |
| $560 ÷ 12 = $46.66666667 | Monthly insurance |

PITI = $462.84 + $82.08 + $46.67
= $591.59

**The total PITI payment is $591.59.**

---

**EXAMPLE 3** Qua Wau is trying to determine whether to accept a 25-year 6.5% mortgage or a 20-year 6% mortgage on the house he is planning to buy. He needs to finance $125,700 and has planned to budget $1,000 monthly for his payment of principal and interest. Which mortgage should Qua choose?

| What You Know | What You Are Looking For |
|---|---|
| Amount financed: $125,700<br>Annual interest rate: 6.5% and 6%<br>Monthly budget<br>allowance for payment: $1,000 | Monthly payment and total cost for 25-year mortgage and monthly payment and total cost for 20-year mortgage.<br><br>Which mortgage should Qua choose? |

### Solution Plan

Total cost = monthly payment × 12 × number of years financed

Number of $1,000 units of amount financed = amount financed ÷ $1,000

Monthly payment = number of $1,000 units of amount financed × table value

### Solution

Number of $1,000 units financed = $125,700 ÷ $1,000
$$= 125.7$$

*25-Year Mortgage*
The Table 15-1 value for 25 years and 6.5% is $6.75.

Monthly payment = number of $1,000 units financed × table value
$$= 125.7\,(\$6.75)$$
$$= \$848.48$$

Total cost = monthly payment × 12 × number of years financed
$$= \$848.48(12)(25)$$
$$= \$254,544.00$$

*20-Year Mortgage*
The Table 15-1 value for 20 years and 6% is $7.16.

Monthly payment = number of $1,000 units financed × table value
$$= 125.7\,(\$7.16)$$
$$= \$900.01$$

Total cost = monthly payment × 12 × years financed
$$= \$900.01(12)(20)$$
$$= \$216,002.40$$

The monthly payment for the 25-year mortgage is $848.48 for a total cost of $254,544.00.
The monthly payment for the 20-year mortgage is $900.01 for a total cost of $216,002.40.

### Conclusion

**Qua's budget of $1,000 monthly can cover either monthly payment. He would save $38,541.60 over the 20-year period if he chooses the 20-year plan. That is the plan he should choose.** Other considerations that could impact his decision would be the return on an investment of the difference in the monthly payments ($51.53) if an annuity were started with the difference. Also, will the addition of the taxes and insurance to the monthly payment (PITI) be more than he can manage?

## ✔ STOP AND CHECK

1. Find the monthly payment on a home mortgage of $195,000 at 6.25% annual interest for 17 years.

2. How much interest is paid on the mortgage in Exercise 1?

3. The annual insurance premium on the home in Exercise 1 is $1,080 and the annual property tax is $1,252. Find the adjusted monthly payment including principal, interest, taxes, and insurance (PITI).

4. Marcella Cannon can budget $1,200 monthly for a house note (not including taxes and insurance). The home she has fallen in love with would have a $185,400 mortgage. She can finance the loan for 15 years at 5.75% or 30 years at 6.25%. Which terms should she choose to best fit her budget?

## SKILL BUILDERS

*Find the indicated amounts for the fixed-rate mortgages.*

| Purchase price of home | Down payment | Annual mortgage amount | Interest rate | Years | Monthly payment per $1,000 | Mortgage payment | Total paid for mortgage | Interest paid |
|---|---|---|---|---|---|---|---|---|
| **1.** $100,000 | $0 | | 5.75% | 30 | | | | |
| **2.** $183,000 | $13,000 | | 5.50% | 30 | | | | |
| **3.** $95,000 | $8,000 | | 5.75% | 25 | | | | |
| **4.** $125,500 | 20% | | 6.25% | 20 | | | | |
| **5.** $495,750 | 18% | | 5.00% | 35 | | | | |
| **6.** $83,750 | 15% | | 6% | 22 | | | | |

## APPLICATIONS

7. Stephen Black has just purchased a home for $155,000. Northridge Mortgage Company has approved his loan application for a 30-year fixed-rate loan at 6%. Stephen has agreed to pay 25% of the purchase price as a down payment. Find the down payment, amount of mortgage, and monthly payment.

8. Find the total interest Stephen will pay if he pays the loan on schedule.

9. If Stephen made the same loan for 20 years, how much interest would he save?

10. How much would Stephen's monthly payment increase for a 20-year mortgage over a 30-year mortgage?

## 15-2 AMORTIZATION SCHEDULES AND QUALIFYING RATIOS

### LEARNING OUTCOMES

1 Prepare a partial amortization schedule of a mortgage.
2 Calculate qualifying ratios.

### 1 Prepare a partial amortization schedule of a mortgage.

**Amortization schedule:** a table that shows the balance of principal and interest for each payment of the mortgage.

Homeowners are sometimes given an **amortization schedule** that shows the amount of principal and interest for each payment of the loan. With some loan arrangements, extra amounts paid with the monthly payment are credited against the principal, allowing for the mortgage to be paid sooner.

### HOW TO     Prepare an amortization schedule of a mortgage

1. For the first month:
   (a) Find the interest portion of the first monthly payment (principal and interest portion only):

   Interest portion of the first monthly payment = original principal
   $\times$ monthly interest rate

   (b) Find the principal portion of the monthly payment:

   Principal portion of the first monthly payment = monthly payment
   − interest portion of the first monthly payment

   (c) Find the first end-of-month principal:

   First end-of-month principal = original principal
   − principal portion of the first monthly payment

2. For the interest portion, principal portion, and end-of-month principal for each remaining month in turn:

   (a) Find the interest portion of the monthly payment:

   Interest portion of the monthly payment
   $$= \text{previous end-of-month principal} \times \text{monthly interest rate}$$

   (b) Find the principal portion of the monthly payment:

   Principal portion of the monthly payment $= \text{monthly payment}$
   $$- \text{interest portion of the monthly payment}$$

   (c) Find the end-of-month principal:

   End-of-month principal $= \text{previous end-of-month principal}$
   $$- \text{principal portion of the monthly payment}$$

## EXAMPLE 1

Complete the first two rows of the amortization schedule for Lunelle's mortgage of $69,600 at 7% annual interest for 30 years. The monthly payment for interest and principal was found to be $462.84.

*First month*

$$\text{Interest portion of monthly payment} = \text{original principal} \times \text{monthly rate}$$
$$= \$69,600\left(\frac{0.07}{12}\right) \qquad 7\% = 0.07$$
$$= \$406.00$$

$$\text{Principal portion of monthly payment} = \text{monthly payment (without insurance and taxes)} - \text{interest portion of monthly payment}$$
$$= \$462.84 - \$406.00$$
$$= \$56.84$$

$$\text{End-of-month principal} = \text{previous end-of-month principal} - \text{principal portion of monthly payment}$$
$$= \$69,600 - \$56.84$$
$$= \$69,543.16$$

*Second month*

$$\text{Interest portion of monthly payment} = \$69,543.16\left(\frac{0.07}{12}\right)$$
$$= \$405.67$$

$$\text{Principal portion of monthly payment} = \$462.84 - \$405.67$$
$$= \$57.17$$

$$\text{End-of-month principal} = \$69,543.16 - \$57.17$$
$$= \$69,485.99$$

**The first two rows of an amortization schedule for this loan are shown in the following chart.**

| | | Portion of payment applied to: | | |
|---|---|---|---|---|
| Month | Monthly payment | Interest [previous end-of-month principal × monthly rate] | Principal [monthly payment − interest portion] | End-of-month principal [previous end-of-month principal − principal portion] |
| 1 | $462.84 | $406.00 | $56.84 | $69,543.16 |
| 2 | $462.84 | $405.67 | $57.17 | $69,485.99 |

Software programs such as Excel are normally used to generate an amortization schedule that shows the interest and principal breakdown for each payment of the loan.

1. Complete two rows of an amortization schedule for Natalie's home mortgage in Exercise 1 on p. 526.

2. Complete two rows of an amortization schedule for the mortgage in Exercise 2 on p. 526.

3. Complete three rows of an amortization schedule for the mortgage in Exercise 3 on p. 526.

4. Complete rows 4–6 of an amortization schedule for the mortgage in Exercise 4 on p. 526.

## 2    Calculate qualifying ratios.

**Loan-to-value ratio:** the amount mortgaged divided by the appraised value of the property.

**Housing or front-end ratio:** monthly housing expenses (PITI) divided by the gross monthly income

**Debt-to-income or back-end ratio:** fixed monthly expenses divided by the gross monthly income

Mortgage ratios are the most important factors, after your credit report, that lending institutions examine to determine loan applicants' capacity to repay a loan. The **loan-to-value ratio (LTV)** is found by dividing the amount mortgaged by the appraised value of the property. If this ratio, when expressed as a percent, is more than 80%, the borrower may be required to purchase private mortgage insurance (PMI). The **housing ratio** or **front-end ratio** is found by dividing the monthly housing expenses (PITI) by your gross monthly income. In most cases the housing ratio should not exceed 28%.

The **debt-to-income ratio (DTI)** or **back-end ratio** is found by dividing your fixed monthly expenses by your gross monthly income. The debt-to-income ratio should be no more than 36%. Fixed monthly expenses are monthly housing expenses (PITI plus any other expenses directly associated with home ownership), monthly installment loan payments, monthly revolving credit line payments, alimony and child support, and other fixed monthly expenses. Monthly income includes income from employment, including overtime and commissions, self-employment income, alimony, child support, Social Security, retirement or VA benefits, interest and dividend income, income from trusts, partnerships, and so on.

### HOW TO    Find the qualifying ratio for a mortgage

1. Select the formula for the desired qualifying ratio.

$$\text{Loan-to-value ratio} = \frac{\text{amount mortgaged}}{\text{appraised value of property}}$$

$$\text{Housing ratio} = \frac{\text{total mortgage payment (PITI)}}{\text{gross monthly income}}$$

$$\text{Debt-to-income ratio} = \frac{\text{total fixed monthly expenses}}{\text{gross monthly income}}$$

2. Evaluate the formula.

### EXAMPLE 1    Find the loan-to-value ratio for a home appraised at $250,000 that the buyer will purchase for $248,000. The buyer plans to make a down payment of $68,000.

Amount mortgaged = $248,000 − $68,000 = $180,000
Appraised value = $250,000

$$\text{Loan-to-value ratio} = \frac{\text{Amount mortgaged}}{\text{Appraised value of property}}$$    Substitute values in the formula.

$$\text{Loan-to-value ratio} = \frac{\$180,000}{\$250,000}$$    Divide.

Loan-to-value ratio = 0.72 or 72%

**The loan-to-value ratio is 72%.**

# STOP AND CHECK

1. Reed Davis has $84,000 for a down payment on a home and has identified a property that can be purchased for $386,000. The appraised value of the property is $395,000. What is the loan-to-value ratio?

2. If Sheri Rieth has total gross monthly earnings of $5,893 and the total PITI for the loan she wants is $1,482, what is the housing ratio? How does this ratio compare with the desired acceptable ratio?

3. Emily Harrington has $1,675 total fixed monthly expenses and gross monthly income of $4,975. What is the debt-to-income ratio she would use in purchasing a home?

4. Pam Cox expects to pay monthly $1,845 in principal and interest, $74 in homeowner's insurance, and $104 in real estate tax for her home mortgage. Her gross monthly salary is $5,798 and she receives alimony of $200 per month. Find the housing ratio she would have when purchasing the home. Is her ratio favorable?

## 15-2 SECTION EXERCISES

### SKILL BUILDERS

*Make an amortization table to show the first two payments for the mortgages.*

| Amount of mortgage | Annual interest rate | Years in mortgage | Monthly payment |
|---|---|---|---|
| 1. $100,000 | 5.75% | 30 | $584 |
| 2. $180,000 | 5.5% | 30 | $1,022.40 |
| 3. $87,000 | 5.75% | 25 | $547.23 |
| 4. $100,400 | 6.25% | 20 | $733.92 |
| 5. $406,515 | 5% | 35 | $2,052.90 |
| 6. $71,187.50 | 6% | 22 | $486.21 |

| Amount of mortgage | Annual interest rate | Years | Monthly payment | Amount of mortgage | Annual interest rate | Years | Monthly payment |
|---|---|---|---|---|---|---|---|
| 1. $100,000 | 5.75% | 30 | $584 | 2. $180,000 | 5.5% | 30 | $1,022.40 |

| Amount of mortgage | Annual interest rate | Years | Monthly payment | Amount of mortgage | Annual interest rate | Years | Monthly payment |
|---|---|---|---|---|---|---|---|
| **3.** $87,000 | 5.75% | 25 | $547.23 | **4.** $100,400 | 6.25% | 20 | $733.92 |

| Amount of mortgage | Annual interest rate | Years | Monthly payment | Amount of mortgage | Annual interest rate | Years | Monthly payment |
|---|---|---|---|---|---|---|---|
| **5.** $406,515 | 5% | 35 | $2,052.90 | **6.** $71,187.50 | 6% | 22 | $486.21 |

## APPLICATIONS

**7.** Justin Wimmer is financing $69,700 for a home at 7% interest with a 20-year fixed-rate loan. Find the interest paid and principal paid for each of the first two months of the loan and find the principal owed at the end of the second month.

8. Heike Drechsler is financing $84,700 for a home in the mountains. The 17-year fixed-rate loan has an interest rate of 6%. Create an amortization schedule for the first two months of the loan.

9. Conchita Martinez has made a $210,300 loan for a home near Albany, New York. Her 20-year fixed-rate loan has an interest rate of $8\frac{1}{2}\%$. Create an amortization schedule for the first two payments.

10. Jake Drewrey is financing $142,500 for a ten-year fixed-rate mortgage at 5.75%. Create an amortization schedule for the first two payments.

11. Conchita Martinez will have a monthly interest and principal payment of $1,825.40. Her monthly real estate taxes will be $58.93 and her monthly homeowner's payments will be $84.15. If her gross monthly income is $6,793, find the housing ratio.

12. Jake Drewrey has total fixed monthly expenses of $1,340 and his gross monthly income is $3,875. What is his debt-to-income ratio? How does his ratio compare to the desired ratio?

## Learning Outcomes

### What to Remember with Examples

### Section 15-1

**1** Find the monthly mortgage payment. (p. 524)

1. Find the amount financed: Subtract the down payment from the purchase price.
2. Find the $1,000 units of amount financed: Divide the amount financed (from step 1) by $1,000.
3. Locate the table value for the number of years financed and the annual interest rate.
4. Multiply the table value from step 3 by the $1,000 units from step 2.

$$\text{Monthly mortgage payment} = \frac{\text{amount financed}}{\$1,000} \times \text{table value}$$

Find the monthly payment for a home selling for $90,000 if a 10% down payment is made, payments are made for 30 years, and the annual interest rate is 7.5%.

$$\$90,000(0.1) = \$9,000 \text{ down payment}$$
$$\$90,000 - \$9,000 = \$81,000 \text{ mortgage amount}$$
$$\$81,000 \div \$1,000 = 81 \text{ units of } \$1,000$$

The table value for 30 years and 7.5% is $6.99.
Payment = 81($6.99) = $566.19

**2** Find the total interest on a mortgage and the PITI. (p. 526)

1. Find the total of the payments: Multiply the number of payments by the payment (principal + interest).
2. Subtract the amount financed from the total of the payments.

$$\text{Total interest} = \text{number of payments} \times \text{amount of payment} - \text{amount financed}$$

Find the total interest on the mortgage in the preceding example.

$$\text{Total interest} = 30(12)(\$566.19) - \$81,000$$
$$= \$203,828.40 - \$81,000$$
$$= \$122,828.40$$

To find the total PITI payment

1. Find the principal and interest portion of the monthly payment.
2. Find the monthly taxes by dividing the annual taxes by 12.
3. Find the monthly insurance by dividing the annual insurance by 12.
4. Find the sum of the monthly principal, interest, taxes, and insurance.

Find the total PITI payment for a loan that has monthly principal and interest payments of $2,134, annual taxes of $1,085, and annual homeowners insurance of $1,062.

| | |
|---|---|
| $2,134 | Monthly principal and interest |
| $1,085 ÷ 12 = $90.41666667 | Monthly taxes |
| $1,062 ÷ 12 = $88.50 | Monthly insurance |

PITI = $2,134 + $90.42 + $88.50 = $2,312.92

The total PITI payment is $2,312.92.

### Section 15-2

**1** Prepare a partial amortization schedule of a mortgage. (p. 530)

1. For the first month:
   (a) Find the interest portion of the first monthly payment:

$$\text{Interest portion of the first monthly payment} = \text{original principal}$$
$$\times \text{monthly interest rate}$$

**(b)** Find the principal portion of the monthly payment:

Principal portion of the first monthly payment = monthly payment
− interest portion of first monthly payment

**(c)** Find the first end-of-month principal:

First end-of-month principal = original principal
− principal portion of the first monthly payment

**2.** For each remaining month in turn:
**(a)** Find the interest portion of the monthly payment:

Interest portion of the monthly payment = previous end-of-month principal
× monthly interest rate

**(b)** Find the principal portion of the monthly payment:

Principal portion of the monthly payment = monthly payment
− interest portion of the monthly payment

**(c)** Find the end-of-month principal:

End-of-month principal = previous end-of-month principal
− principal portion of the monthly payment

Complete an amortization schedule for three months of payments on a $90,000 mortgage at 8% for 30 years.

$$\text{Monthly payment} = \frac{\$90,000}{\$1,000} \times \text{table value}$$
$$= 90(7.34)$$
$$= \$660.60$$

*Month 1*

$$\text{Interest portion} = \$90,000\left(\frac{0.08}{12}\right)$$
$$= \$600$$
$$\text{Principal portion} = \$660.60 - \$600$$
$$= \$60.60$$
$$\text{End-of-month principal} = \$90,000 - \$60.60$$
$$= \$89,939.40$$

*Month 2*

$$\text{Interest portion} = \$89,939.40\left(\frac{0.08}{12}\right)$$
$$= \$599.60$$
$$\text{Principal portion} = \$660.60 - \$599.60$$
$$= \$61.00$$
$$\text{End-of-month principal} = \$89,939.40 - \$61.00$$
$$= \$89,878.40$$

*Month 3*

$$\text{Interest portion} = \$89,878.40\left(\frac{0.08}{12}\right)$$
$$= \$599.19$$
$$\text{Principal portion} = \$660.60 - \$599.19$$
$$= \$61.41$$
$$\text{End-of-month principal} = \$89,878.40 - \$61.41$$
$$= \$89,816.99$$

**Portion of payment applied to:**

| Month | Monthly payment | Interest | Principal | End-of-month principal |
|-------|-----------------|----------|-----------|------------------------|
| 1 | $660.60 | $600.00 | $60.60 | $89,939.40 |
| 2 | $660.60 | 599.60 | 61.00 | 89,878.40 |
| 3 | $660.60 | 599.19 | 61.41 | 89,816.99 |

**2** Calculate qualifying ratios. (p. 532)

**Find the qualifying ratio for a mortgage**

1. Select the formula for the desired qualifying ratio.

$$\text{Loan-to-value ratio} = \frac{\text{amount mortgaged}}{\text{appraised value of property}}$$

$$\text{Housing ratio} = \frac{\text{total mortgage payment (PITI)}}{\text{gross monthly income}}$$

$$\text{Debt-to-income ratio} = \frac{\text{total fixed monthly expenses}}{\text{gross monthly income}}$$

2. Evaluate the formula.

Find the loan-to-value ratio for a home appraised at $398,400 that the buyer will purchase for $398,000. The buyer plans to make a down payment of $100,000.

Amount mortgaged = $398,000 − $100,000 = $298,000

Appraised value = $398,400

$$\text{Loan-to-value ratio} = \frac{\text{amount mortgaged}}{\text{appraised value of property}} \qquad \text{Substitute values in the formula.}$$

$$\text{Loan-to-value ratio} = \frac{\$298,000}{\$398,400} \qquad \text{Divide.}$$

Loan-to-value ratio = 0.7479919679 or 75%

# EXERCISES SET A

*Find the monthly payment.*

| | Mortgage amount | Annual percentage rate | Years |
|---|---|---|---|
| **1.** | $287,500 | 5.75% | 20 |
| **2.** | $146,800 | 5.25% | 30 |
| **3.** | $152,300 | 6.25% | 25 |
| **4.** | $113,400 | 5% | 15 |

**XCEL 5.** Find the total interest paid for the mortgage in Exercise 1.

**EXCEL 6.** Find the total interest paid for the mortgage in Exercise 2.

**XCEL 7.** Find the total interest paid for the mortgage in Exercise 3.

**EXCEL 8.** Find the total interest paid for the mortgage in Exercise 4.

**9.** Create an amortization schedule for the first two months' payments on a mortgage of $487,700 with an interest rate of 6% and monthly payment of $2,926.20.

**10.** Louise Grantham is buying a home for $198,500 with a 20% down payment. She has a 5.75% loan for 25 years. Create an amortization schedule for the first two months of her loan.

**11.** James Author's monthly principal plus interest payment is $1,565.74 and his annual homeowner's insurance premium is $1,100. His annual real estate taxes total $1,035. Find his PITI payment.

**12.** Find the loan-to-value ratio for a home appraised at $583,620 that the buyer will purchase for $585,000. The buyer plans to make a down payment of $175,000.

**13.** Find James Author's housing ratio if his PITI is $1,743.66 and his gross monthly income is $6,310.

**14.** Find Julia Rholes' debt-to-income ratio if her fixed monthly expenses are $1,836 and her gross monthly income is $4,934.

## EXERCISES SET B

*Find the monthly payment.*

| Mortgage amount | Annual percentage rate | Years |
|---|---|---|
| **1.** $487,700 | 6% | 30 |
| **2.** $212,983 | 6.75% | 15 |
| **3.** $82,900 | 8.5% | 35 |
| **4.** $179,500 | 8% | 17 |

**5.** Find the total interest paid for the mortgage in Exercise 1.

**6.** Find the total interest paid for the mortgage in Exercise 2.

**7.** Find the total interest paid for the mortgage in Exercise 3.

**8.** Find the total interest paid for the mortgage in Exercise 4.

**9.** Create a partial amortization schedule for the first two payments on a mortgage of $152,300 at 6.25% that has a monthly payment of $1,005.18 and is financed for 25 years.

**10.** Mary Starnes is paying $14,000 down on a house that costs $138,200 and she has a 6% loan for 30 years. Create a partial amortization table for the first two months of her mortgage.

11. Jerry Corless' monthly principal plus interest payment is $2,665.45 and his annual homeowner's insurance premium is $1,320. His annual real estate taxes total $1,325. Find his PITI payment.

12. Find the loan-to-value ratio for a home appraised at $135,230 that the buyer will purchase for $135,000. The buyer plans to make a down payment of $25,000.

13. Find Jerry Corless' housing ratio if his PITI is $2,885.87 and his gross monthly income is $8,310.

14. Find Elizabeth Herrington's debt-to-income ratio if her fixed monthly expenses are $1,236 and her gross monthly income is $4,194.

## PRACTICE TEST

1. Find the table value for a 25-year mortgage at 6%.

2. Find the monthly payment on a mortgage of $230,000 for 30 years at 7.5%.

3. Find the total amount of interest that will be paid on the mortgage in Exercise 2.

4. What percent of the mortgage in Exercise 2 is the interest paid?

*Hullett Houpt is purchasing a home for $197,000. He will finance the mortgage for 15 years and pay 7% interest on the loan. He makes a down payment that is 20% of the purchase price. Use Table 15-1 as needed.*

5. Find the down payment.

6. Find the amount of the mortgage.

7. If Hullett is required to pay two points for making the loan, how much will the points cost?

8. Find the monthly payment that includes principal and interest.

9. Find the total interest Hullett will pay over the 15-year period.

10. Calculate the monthly payment and the total interest Hullett would have to pay if he decided to make the loan for 30 years instead of 15 years.

11. How much interest can be saved by paying for the home in 15 years rather than 30 years?

12. Find the interest portion and principal portion for the first payment of Hullett's 15-year loan.

13. Make an amortization schedule for the first three payments of the 15-year loan Hullett could make.

**14.** Make an amortization schedule for the first three payments of the 30-year loan Hullett could make.

**15.** Find Leshaundra's debt-to-income ratio if her fixed monthly expenses are $1,972 and her gross monthly income is $5,305.

1. How does a mortgage relate to a sinking fund?

2. For a mortgage of a given amount and rate, what happens to the total amount of interest paid if the number of years in the mortgage increases?

3. How can you reduce your monthly payment on a home mortgage?

4. Describe the process for finding the monthly payment for a mortgage of a given amount at a given rate for a given period.

## Challenge Problem

Bob Owen is closing a real estate transaction on a farm in Yocona, Mississippi, for $385,900. His mortgage holder requires a 25% down payment and he also must pay $60.00 to record the deed, $100 in attorney's fees for document preparation, and $350 for an appraisal report. Bob will also have to pay a 1.5% loan origination fee. Bob chooses a 35-year mortgage at 7%. (a) How much cash will Bob need to close on the property? (b) How much will Bob's mortgage be? (c) What is Bob's monthly payment on the property?

# CASE STUDIES

## 15.1 Home Buying: A 30-Year Commitment?

Shantel and Kwamie are planning to buy their first home. Although they are excited about the prospect of being homeowners, they are also a little frightened. A mortgage payment for the next 30 years sounds like a huge commitment. They visited a few new developments and scanned the real estate listings of preowned homes, but they really have no idea how much a mortgage payment would be on a $150,000, $175,000, or $200,000 loan. They have come to you for advice.

1. After you explain to them that they can borrow money at different rates and for different amounts of time, Shantel and Kwamie ask you to complete a chart indicating what the monthly mortgage payment would be under some possible interest rates and borrowing periods. They also want to know what their total interest would be on each if they chose a 25-year loan. Complete the chart.

| Amount borrowed | 6.25% 15 year | 6.5% 20 year | 6.75% 25 year | 7% 30 year | Total interest paid |
|---|---|---|---|---|---|
| $150,000 | | | | | |
| $175,000 | | | | | |
| $200,000 | | | | | |

2. If Shantel and Kwamie made a down payment of $20,000 on a $175,000 home, what would be their monthly mortgage payment assuming they finance for 25 years at 6.75%? How much would they save on each monthly payment by making the down payment? How much interest would they save over the life of the loan?

## 15.2 Flippin' Houses

Jacob had finally found the house that he was looking for, and was anxious to make an offer. He knew that one of the keys to success with turning over real estate profitably and quickly was to make money on the front end by buying properties for at least 30% below market value. He had done his research, and with an asking price of only $124,500, this 2-bedroom ranch-style home was a bargain and well within his price range. The house, though, needed a number of repairs including paint, carpet, appliances, and a new wall to turn an open area into another bedroom. After contacting several contractors, he felt confident that the work could be completed for $12,000. With that figure in mind, Jacob decided that the total cost of the house would be $140,000 or less, including any settlement charges. He just needed to finalize some of the payment details to make sure the house was right for him.

1. By putting 20% down on the house, Jacob can get a 30-year fixed-rate mortgage for 6.25%. Based on a purchase price of $140,000, compute the down payment, and the principal and interest payment for the loan.

2. Although Jacob hopes to have the house sold within a few months, he knows there is a possibility that it will not sell quickly. In that case, he would likely end up keeping it as a rental property. Using the information from Exercise 1, find the total amount of interest that Jacob will pay on the mortgage if he keeps it for the full 30 years.

**3.** Jacob finds a lender that will offer him 100% financing using an adjustable-rate mortgage based on a 30-year amortization, with a 5-year interest lock at 5.0%. The loan, however, would include a prepayment penalty, which is applied as follows: prepayment penalty is 80% of the balance of the first mortgage, times the interest rate, divided by 2. Compute the new mortgage payment, along with the maximum prepayment penalty. Is it a good idea for Jacob to take this loan? Why or why not?

**4.** Jacob decides that the 30-year fixed-rate mortgage in Exercise 1 is the best for him. Construct an amortization table for the first three payments of the mortgage. The monthly payment will be $689.92.

# CHAPTER
# 16 | Depreciation

## Is There a Benefit?

Depreciation is an income tax deduction that allows a taxpayer to recover the cost or other basis of certain property. It is an annual allowance or "paper loss" for the wear and tear, deterioration, or obsolescence of the property. Most types of tangible property (except land) such as buildings, machinery, vehicles, furniture, and equipment are depreciable. Likewise, certain intangible property, such as patents, copyrights, and computer software, is depreciable.

Let's consider a depreciation example from one of the most common small businesses in the United States, farming. It is the end of a very profitable year for Christaki's vegetable produce business. After expenses, his business shows a net profit of almost $30,000. The business is growing, so he is considering purchasing a new 4-wheel-drive tractor for $28,000 before the end of the year.

After some research, he consults IRS Publication 946, How to Depreciate Property. There he sees that the Modified Accelerated Cost Recovery System (MACRS) is the proper depreciation method for *most* property. In the MACRS, he sees that agricultural machinery and equipment is listed as 7-year property. Using the formula presented in the publication, he figures that he can write off $4,000 in the year of purchase.

After reading further Christaki discovers that during the year the qualifying property is purchased and placed into service, a one-time *depreciation* deduction could be taken under section 179 of the IRS tax code. In other words, the entire $28,000 could be written off in the year of purchase. The amount of the purchase would almost wipe out his profit for the year. This purchase seems like a really good idea, but he isn't sure. What would you recommend?

## LEARNING OUTCOMES

### 16-1 Depreciation Methods for Financial Statement Reporting

1. Depreciate an asset and prepare a depreciation schedule using the straight-line method.
2. Depreciate an asset and prepare a depreciation schedule using the units-of-production method.
3. Depreciate an asset and prepare a depreciation schedule using the sum-of-the-years'-digits method.
4. Depreciate an asset and prepare a depreciation schedule using the declining-balance method.

### 16-2 Depreciation Methods for IRS Reporting

1. Depreciate an asset and prepare a depreciation schedule using the modified accelerated cost-recovery system (MACRS).
2. Depreciate an asset after taking a section 179 deduction.

Buildings, machinery, equipment, furniture, and other items bought for the operation of a business are included among the **assets** of that business. The dollar value of each asset is used in figuring the value and profitability of the business and in figuring the taxable income for the business. The expense of running a business, including the purchase of assets, can be deducted from the company's taxable income before taxes are calculated, so it is important to have a way of keeping track of the value of assets.

Some assets have a useful life of one year or less, and their costs can be deducted from the business's income in the year they are purchased. The cost of items that are expected to last more than a year can be prorated and deducted over a period of years, called the **estimated life**, or **useful life**, of the item. During this time period, the asset *depreciates,* or decreases in value. At the end of an asset's estimated life, it may still have a dollar value, called the **salvage value**, or **scrap value**. The amount an asset decreases in value from its original cost is called its **depreciation**.

This chapter examines five widely used depreciation methods: straight-line, units-of-production, sum-of-the-years'-digits, declining-balance, and the modified accelerated cost-recovery system (MACRS) method. The Internal Revenue Service (IRS) regulates the methods of depreciation that are allowed for income tax purposes. In general, the same depreciation method must be used throughout the useful life of any particular asset. The IRS requires the use of the modified accelerated cost-recovery system of depreciation unless special circumstances are approved by the IRS. The IRS limits the use of many methods of depreciation, so you should consult IRS publications or an accountant before choosing a depreciation method.

## 16-1 DEPRECIATION METHODS FOR FINANCIAL STATEMENT REPORTING

### LEARNING OUTCOMES

1  Depreciate an asset and prepare a depreciation schedule using the straight-line method.
2  Depreciate an asset and prepare a depreciation schedule using the units-of-production method.
3  Depreciate an asset and prepare a depreciation schedule using the sum-of-the-years'-digits method.
4  Depreciate an asset and prepare a depreciation schedule using the declining-balance method.

### 1  Depreciate an asset and prepare a depreciation schedule using the straight-line method.

A commonly used method of depreciation for internal business purposes is the **straight-line depreciation** method. It is easy to use because the depreciation is the same for each full year the equipment is used.

If you know the original cost of an asset, its estimated useful life, and its salvage value, you can find the yearly depreciation amount. In calculating depreciation, by whatever method, the cost of an asset means the **total cost**, including shipping and installation charges if the asset is a piece of equipment. The **depreciable value** is the cost minus the salvage value.

**HOW TO**  Find the yearly depreciation using the straight-line method

1. Find the *total cost* of the asset:

$$\text{Total cost} = \text{cost} + \text{shipping} + \text{installation}$$

2. Find the *depreciable value:*

$$\text{Depreciable value} = \text{total cost} - \text{salvage value}$$

3. Find the *yearly depreciation:*

$$\text{Yearly depreciation} = \frac{\text{depreciable value}}{\text{years of expected life}}$$

**EXAMPLE 1**  Use the straight-line method to find the yearly depreciation for a plating machine that has an expected useful life of five years. The plating machine costs $27,300, its shipping costs totaled $250, its installation charges came to $450, and its salvage value is $1,000.

$$\text{Total cost} = \text{cost of asset} + \text{shipping} + \text{installation}$$
$$= \$27,300 + \$250 + \$450 = \$28,000$$

$$\text{Depreciable value} = \text{total cost} - \text{salvage value}$$
$$= \$28,000 - \$1,000$$
$$= \$27,000$$

$$\text{Yearly depreciation} = \frac{\text{depreciable value}}{\text{years of expected life}}$$
$$= \frac{\$27,000}{5} = \$5,400$$

**The depreciation is $5,400 per year.**

---

## TIP

**Total Cost Versus Depreciable Value**

A common mistake in figuring yearly depreciation using the straight-line method is to divide the total cost rather than the depreciable value by the expected life. See what happens when this is done with the preceding example:

**CORRECT**

$$\text{Yearly depreciation} = \frac{\text{depreciable value}}{\text{years of expected life}}$$
$$= \frac{\text{total cost of equipment} - \text{salvage value}}{\text{years of expected life}}$$
$$= \frac{\$28,000 - \$1,000}{5} = \frac{\$27,000}{5} = \$5,400$$

**INCORRECT**

$$\text{Yearly depreciation} = \frac{\text{total cost of equipment}}{\text{years of expected life}} = \frac{\$28,000}{5} = \$5,600$$

---

**Depreciation schedule:** a table showing the year's depreciation, the accumulated depreciation, and the end-of-year book value.

**Accumulated depreciation:** the current year's depreciation plus all previous years' depreciation.

**End-of-year book value:** total cost minus depreciation for the first year. Thereafter, it is the previous year's end-of-year book value minus the current year's depreciation.

A **depreciation schedule** is often the best way to record the depreciation of an asset over time. The depreciation schedule shows consistent information for any depreciation method. For each year of depreciation, the following values are recorded: the year's depreciation, the accumulated depreciation and the year's end-of-year book value. **Accumulated depreciation** is the year's depreciation plus the sum of all previous years' depreciation. The first year's **end-of-year book value** is the total cost minus the year's depreciation. For all other years, the year's end-of-year book value is the previous end-of-year book value minus the year's depreciation.

---

**HOW TO**　　**Prepare a Depreciation Schedule**

1. For the first year of expected life:
   (a) Find the yearly or annual depreciation.
   (b) Find the first end-of-year book value:

   $$\text{First end-of-year book value} = \text{total cost} - \text{first year's depreciation}$$

2. For each remaining year of expected life:
   (a) Find the year's annual depreciation.
   (b) Find the year's accumulated depreciation:

   $$\text{Year's accumulated depreciation} = \text{annual depreciation} + \text{sum of all the previous years' depreciation}$$

   (c) Find the year's end-of-year book value:

   $$\text{Year's end-of-year book value} = \text{previous end-of-year book value} - \text{annual depreciation}$$

3. Make a table with the following column headings and fill in the data: year, annual depreciation, accumulated depreciation, end-of-year book value.

Table 16-1 shows the depreciation schedule for the plating machine of the preceding example.

**TABLE 16-1**
Straight-Line Depreciation Schedule for Plating Machine

| Total cost: $28,000 | Year | Annual depreciation | Accumulated depreciation | End-of-year book value |
|---|---|---|---|---|
| Depreciable | 1 | $5,400 | $ 5,400 | $22,600 |
| value: | 2 | 5,400 | 10,800 | 17,200 |
| $27,000 | 3 | 5,400 | 16,200 | 11,800 |
| | 4 | 5,400 | 21,600 | 6,400 |
| | 5 | $5,400 | $27,000 | $ 1,000 |

**TIP**

**The Final End-of-Year Book Value Is the Salvage Value**

The straight-line depreciation of the end-of-year book value cannot be less than the salvage value. The final accumulated depreciation plus the salvage value must equal the total cost.

 **STOP AND CHECK**

1. Find the depreciable value of an asset that costs $5,323 and has a scrap value of $500.

2. Use the straight-line method to find the yearly depreciation for a van that costs $18,000, has an expected life of three years, and has a residual value of $3,000.

3. Find the yearly depreciation for a computer network system that costs $21,500, has an expected life of four years, and has a salvage value of $4,000. Use straight-line depreciation.

4. Find the straight-line depreciation for a security system that costs $5,800, has an expected life of three years, and has a residual value of $1,500.

## 2 Depreciate an asset and prepare a depreciation schedule using the units-of-production method.

**Units-of-production depreciation:** a method of depreciation that is based on the expected number of units produced by an asset.

Machines and other types of equipment that are used heavily for a period of time and then left to sit idle for another period of time, sometimes months, are often depreciated using the **units-of-production depreciation** method. For example, earth-moving equipment and farm equipment are often idle during the winter months. Instead of basing depreciation on the expected lifetime of a piece of equipment in years, this method takes into account how the equipment is used—for example, how many items it has produced, how many miles it has been driven, how many hours it has operated, or how many times it has performed some particular operation.

The units-of-production method of depreciation is used for internal accounting purposes. Special written permission from the IRS is required for this method to be used on tax returns. Companies that use this method internally often adjust to a method acceptable by the IRS for tax-reporting purposes.

**Unit depreciation:** the amount the asset depreciates with each unit produced or mile driven.

To use the units-of-production method, you must find the **unit depreciation**—how much the asset depreciates with each unit produced, each mile driven, or each hour of operation.

**HOW TO** — Find the depreciation for units produced using the units-of-production method

1. Find the *unit depreciation*.

$$\text{Unit depreciation} = \frac{\text{depreciable value}}{\text{units produced during expected life}}$$

Keep the full calculator value of the quotient.

2. Multiply the unit depreciation by the number of units produced.

$$\text{Depreciation for units produced} = \text{unit depreciation} \times \text{number of units produced}$$

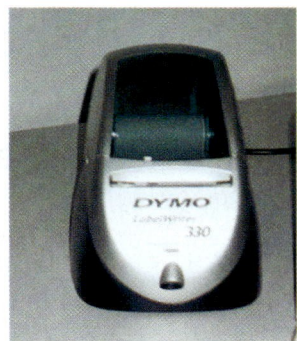

**EXAMPLE 1** A label-making machine that costs $28,000 after shipping and installation is expected to print 50,000,000 labels during its useful life. If the salvage value of the machine is $1,000, find the unit depreciation and depreciation for printing 2,125,000 labels.

$$\begin{aligned}
\text{Unit depreciation} &= \frac{\text{depreciable value}}{\text{unit produced during expected life}} \\
&= \frac{\$28,000 - \$1,000}{50,000,000} \\
&= \$0.00054
\end{aligned}$$

Use the full calculator value of the unit depreciation.

$$\begin{aligned}
\text{Depreciation} &= \text{unit depreciation} \times \text{units produced} \\
&= \$0.00054(2,125,000) = \$1,147.50
\end{aligned}$$

**The depreciation is $1,147.50.**

The depreciation of the label maker for its entire useful life is recorded in the depreciation schedule shown in Table 16-2. Note that the table shows the number of labels made each year and that the number differs from year to year. This pattern of use is typical of equipment that is depreciated by the units-of-production method.

**TABLE 16-2**
**Units-of-Production Depreciation Schedule for the Label Maker**

| Total cost $28,000 | Year | Labels printed | Annual depreciation | Accumulated depreciation | End-of-year book value |
|---|---|---|---|---|---|
| Depreciable | 1 | 2,125,000 | $ 1,147.50 | $ 1,147.50 | $26,852.50 |
| value: | 2 | 11,830,000 | 6,388.20 | 7,535.70 | 20,464.30 |
| $27,000 | 3 | 12,765,000 | 6,893.10 | 14,428.80 | 13,571.20 |
| Unit | 4 | 12,210,000 | 6,593.40 | 21,022.20 | 6,977.80 |
| depreciation: | 5 | 11,070,000 | $ 5,977.80 | $27,000.00 | $ 1,000.00 |
| $0.00054 | | | | | |
| Totals | | 50,000,000 | $27,000.00 | | |

**TIP**

**Check Your Schedule Calculations**

One way to check your schedule calculations is to find the totals of the labels printed and the yearly depreciation amounts. The total labels printed should equal the useful life. The total of the yearly depreciations should equal the depreciable value and the last entry in the accumulated depreciation column.

*Use full calculator value of the unit depreciation.*

1. A van that costs $18,000 is expected to be driven 75,000 miles during its useful life. If the salvage value of the van is $3,000, find the unit depreciation and the depreciation for 56,000 miles.

2. A company car is purchased for $23,580 and is expected to be driven 95,000 miles before being sold. The expected salvage value for the car is $2,300. Find the unit depreciation for the car.

3. An engraving machine that costs $28,700 is being set up on a unit depreciation schedule. The scrap value of the machine is anticipated to be $2,500. If the machine will engrave 300,000 objects during its useful life, find the unit depreciation. What is the first year's depreciation if 28,452 objects are engraved?

4. Chou's Meat Processing Company purchased a meat cutting machine for $7,500. Its expected life is 60,000 hours, and it will have a salvage value of $600. Use units-of-production depreciation to find the year's depreciation on the machine if it is used 8,500 hours during the first year.

## 3 Depreciate an asset and prepare a depreciation schedule using the sum-of-the-years'-digits method.

The straight-line depreciation method of depreciating an asset is the simplest way to depreciate the asset, but it is not always the most realistic method of depreciation to use. Most equipment depreciates more during its first year of operation than during any subsequent year. Many businesses prefer to use a method that shows the largest depreciation during the first year or two. One such method is the **sum-of-the-years'-digits depreciation** method.

**Sum-of-the-years'-digits depreciation:** a depreciation method that allows the greatest depreciation the first year and a decreasing amount each year thereafter.

**Year's depreciation rate:** the depreciation rate for any given year of a depreciation schedule.

To find a year's depreciation, we find the **year's depreciation rate** and multiply it by the depreciable value. The numerator of the year's depreciation rate is the number of years of expected life *remaining*. The denominator of the year's depreciation rate is the sum of the numbers from 1 to the number of years of expected life. We can use the shortcut formula for finding such a sum. If, for example, the expected life is five years, the sum from 1 to 5 is

$$\frac{n(n + 1)}{2} = \frac{5(5 + 1)}{2} = \frac{5(6)}{2} = \frac{30}{2} = 15$$

If the number of years of expected life is five years, the denominator of each year's depreciation rate is 15.

| Year | 1 | 2 | 3 | 4 | 5 |
|---|---|---|---|---|---|
| Year's depreciation rate | $\frac{5}{15}$ | $\frac{4}{15}$ | $\frac{3}{15}$ | $\frac{2}{15}$ | $\frac{1}{15}$ |

### HOW TO   Find the year's depreciation using the sum-of-the-years'-digits method

1. Find the year's depreciation rate:

   (a) Use the $\dfrac{n(n + 1)}{2}$ shortcut formula to find the sum from 1 to the number of years of expected life.

   Sum from 1 to the number of years of expected life

   $$= \frac{(\text{number of years of expected life})(1 + \text{number of years of expected life})}{2}$$

   (b) Divide the number of years remaining of expected life by the value from step 1a.

   $$\text{Year's sum-of-the-years' depreciation rate} = \frac{\text{number of years remaining of expected life}}{\text{sum from 1 to the years of expected life}}$$

2. Find the depreciable value:

   $$\text{Depreciable value} = \text{total cost} - \text{salvage value}$$

3. Multiply the depreciable value by the year's depreciation rate:

   $$\text{Year's depreciation} = \text{depreciable value} \times \text{year's depreciation rate}$$

**EXAMPLE 1** Find the depreciation for each of the five years of expected life of a bottle capping machine that costs $27,300 and has a shipping cost of $250, an installation cost of $450, and a salvage value of $1,000. Make a depreciation schedule.

$$\text{Denominator of depreciation rate} = \frac{5(6)}{2} = 15 \qquad \text{Sum of 1 to 5}$$

Write the depreciation rate for each year.

Depreciation rate for each year $\qquad \dfrac{5}{15}, \quad \dfrac{4}{15}, \quad \dfrac{3}{15}, \quad \dfrac{2}{15}, \quad \dfrac{1}{15},$ Years remaining

$$\qquad\qquad\qquad \uparrow \qquad \uparrow \qquad \uparrow \qquad \uparrow \qquad \uparrow$$

Year $\quad 1 \qquad 2 \qquad 3 \qquad 4 \qquad 5$

Depreciable value = total cost − salvage value

($27,300 + $250 + $450) − $1,000 = $27,000

Year 1 depreciation = depreciable value × depreciation rate

$$= \frac{\$27,000}{1}\left(\frac{5}{15}\right)$$

$$= \$9,000$$

Year 1 end-of-year book value = total cost − depreciation

$$= \$28,000 - \$9,000$$

$$= \$19,000$$

The results of the calculations for the remaining years can be organized in a depreciation schedule (Table 16-3).

**TABLE 16-3**
**Sum-of-the-Years'-Digits Depreciation Schedule for Bottle-Capping Machine**

| Total cost $28,000 | Year | Depreciation rate | Annual depreciation | Accumulated depreciation | End-of-year book value |
|---|---|---|---|---|---|
| **Depreciable value:** **$27,000** | 1 | $\dfrac{5}{15}$ | $ 9,000 | $ 9,000 | $19,000 |
| | 2 | $\dfrac{4}{15}$ | 7,200 | 16,200 | 11,800 |
| | 3 | $\dfrac{3}{15}$ | 5,400 | 21,600 | 6,400 |
| | 4 | $\dfrac{2}{15}$ | 3,600 | 25,200 | 2,800 |
| | 5 | $\dfrac{1}{15}$ | $ 1,800 | $27,000 | $ 1,000 |
| | Check: | $\dfrac{15}{15} = 1$ | $27,000 | | |

**TIP**

**Built-In Checks**

One way to check your calculations in the depreciation schedule in Table 16-3 is to add the columns for the depreciation rate and annual depreciation.

• The sum of the depreciation rates should equal 1.
• The sum of the annual depreciation amounts should equal the depreciable value.
• The last entry in the accumulated depreciation column is the depreciable value.
• The last entry in the end-of-year book-value column is the salvage value.

##  STOP AND CHECK

1. Find the denominator of the depreciation rate if the expected life is (a) 8 years and (b) 12 years.

2. Use the sum-of-the-years'-digits method to find the depreciation for each of the three years of the expected life of a van that has a total cost of $18,000 and a salvage value of $3,000.

3. Use the sum-of-the-years'-digits method to make a depreciation schedule for an asset that has a total cost of $9,000 and a scrap value of $1,500 after four years.

4. Brown Shipping Company is making a depreciation schedule for one of its new tractor/trailer rigs by using the sum-of-the-years'-digits method of depreciation. The rig has a total cost of $45,000 and is expected to be in service for ten years. The scrap value is approximated to be $3,500. Find the depreciation rate for each of the ten years. Make a sum-of-the-years'-digits depreciation schedule for the first four years' depreciation of the rig.

## 4 Depreciate an asset and prepare a depreciation schedule using the declining-balance method.

**Declining-balance method:** a depreciation method that provides for large depreciation in the early years of the life of an asset.

Another way to calculate depreciation so that the depreciation is large in the early years of the asset's life and becomes smaller in the later years is by using the **declining-balance method**.

**Double-declining rate:** a declining-balance depreciation rate that is twice the straight-line depreciation rate.

**200%-declining-balance method:** another name for the double-declining-balance method of depreciation.

**150%-declining rate:** a common declining-balance rate that is one and one-half times the straight-line rate.

The *straight-line rate* of depreciation is a fraction with a numerator of 1 and a denominator equal to the number of useful years of an asset. The **double-declining rate** is twice the straight-line rate. The double-declining-balance method is also referred to as the **200%-declining-balance method.** Other declining-balance rates are possible, too, and each rate is some factor times the straight-line rate. The **150%-declining rate** is a common declining-balance rate.

---

### HOW TO  Find the year's depreciation using the declining-balance method

1. Find the yearly depreciation rate.
   (a) Using *straight-line declining balance:* Divide 1 by the years of expected life.

$$\text{Yearly straight-line depreciation rate} = \frac{1}{\text{years of expected life}}$$

   (b) Using other declining-balance depreciation rates, such as *double-declining-balance* or *150%-declining-balance:* Multiply the yearly straight-line depreciation rate by the appropriate factor.

   Yearly double-declining depreciation rate = yearly straight-line depreciation rate $\times$ 2
   Yearly 150%-declining depreciation rate = yearly straight-line depreciation rate $\times$ 1.5

2. Find the depreciation for the first year.

   First year's depreciation = total cost $\times$ yearly depreciation rate

3. Find the depreciation for all other years. Do not depreciate below the salvage value.

   Year's depreciation = previous end-of-year book value $\times$ yearly depreciation rate

---

### EXAMPLE 1
An ice cream freezer has a useful life of six years. Find the yearly (a) straight-line rate expressed as a decimal and percent, (b) double-declining rate expressed as a decimal and percent, and (c) 150%-declining rate expressed as a decimal and percent.

(a) Yearly straight-line rate $= \dfrac{1}{\text{years of expected life}} = \dfrac{1}{6}$

$\dfrac{1}{6} = 0.16666$ (decimal equivalent)

$= 16.67\%$ (percent equivalent)

**The yearly straight-line rate is 0.1667 or 16.67%.**

(b) Yearly double-declining rate = straight-line rate $\times$ 2 $= \dfrac{1}{6}(2) = \dfrac{2}{6} = \dfrac{1}{3}$

$\dfrac{1}{3} = 0.33333$ (decimal equivalent)

$= 33.33\%$ (percent equivalent)

**The yearly double-declining rate is 0.3333 or 33.33%.**

(c) 150%-declining rate = straight-line rate $\times$ 1.5

$= \dfrac{1}{6}(1.5) = 0.16666(1.5)$

$= 0.25$ (decimal equivalent)
$= 25\%$ (percent equivalent)

**The yearly 150%-declining rate is 0.25 or 25%.**

---

### TIP

**Declining-Balance Methods and the Salvage Value**

In declining-balance depreciation, the depreciation for the first year **is based on the total cost of the asset**. Do *not* subtract the salvage value from the total cost to find the depreciation for the first year. At the end of the year, subtract the year's depreciation from the total cost of the asset, not the depreciable value, to get the end-of-year book value.

The end-of-year book value for any year *cannot* **drop below the salvage value of the asset.** In such cases when calculations would cause the end-of-year book value to be less than the salvage value, the year's ending value will be the salvage value, and the year's depreciation is adjusted. There will then be no further depreciation in future years.

**EXAMPLE 2** A packaging machine costing $28,000 with an expected life of five years and a resale value of $1,000 is depreciated by the declining-balance method at twice the straight-line rate. Prepare a depreciation schedule.

$$\text{Double-declining rate} = \text{straight-line rate} \times 2$$

$$= \frac{1}{\text{years of expected life}} \times 2$$

$$= \frac{1}{5}(2) = \frac{2}{5} = 0.4 = 40\%$$

$$\text{Year 1 depreciation} = \text{total cost} \times \text{double-declining rate}$$
$$= \$28,000(0.4)$$
$$= \$11,200$$

$$\text{End-of-year 1 book value} = \text{total cost} - \text{depreciation}$$
$$= \$28,000 - \$11,200$$
$$= \$16,800$$

$$\text{Year 2 depreciation} = \text{previous end-of-year book value} \times \text{double-declining rate}$$
$$= \$16,800(0.4)$$
$$= \$6,720$$

$$\text{End-of-year 2 book value} = \text{previous end-of-year book value} - \text{depreciation}$$
$$= \$16,800 - \$6,720$$
$$= \$10,080$$

$$\text{Year 3 depreciation} = \$10,080(0.4)$$
$$= \$4,032$$

$$\text{End-of-year 3 book value} = \$10,080 - \$4,032$$
$$= \$6,048$$

$$\text{Year 4 depreciation} = \$6,048(0.4)$$
$$= \$2,419.20$$

$$\text{End-of-year 4 book value} = \$6,048 - \$2,419.20$$
$$= \$3,628.80$$

$$\text{Year 5 depreciation} = \$3,628.80(0.4)$$
$$= \$1,451.52$$

$$\text{End-of-year 5 book value} = \$3,628.80 - \$1,451.52$$
$$= \$2,177.28$$

Table 16-4 shows the depreciation schedule for the packaging machine.

**TABLE 16-4**
Double-Declining Balance Depreciation Schedule for Packaging Machine

| Total cost: $28,000 | Year | Annual depreciation | Accumulated depreciation | End-of-year book value |
|---|---|---|---|---|
| | 1 | $11,200.00 | $11,200.00 | $16,800.00 |
| | 2 | 6,720.00 | 17,920.00 | 10,080.00 |
| | 3 | 4,032.00 | 21,952.00 | 6,048.00 |
| | 4 | 2,419.20 | 24,371.20 | 3,628.80 |
| | 5 | 1,451.52 | 25,822.72 | 2,177.28 |

**TIP**

**Which Amount Do I Start With?**

Be sure to *start with the total cost of the asset* when using the declining-balance method. A common error is to use total cost minus salvage value, rather than total cost. That is, in the previous example,

$$\text{Depreciation for year 1} = \text{total cost} \times \text{declining balance rate}$$
$$\$28,000(0.4) = \$11,200$$

**CORRECT**

$$\text{Total cost} - \text{salvage value} = \$28,000 - \$1,000 = \$27,000$$
$$\text{Depreciation for year 1} = \$27,000(0.4) = \$10,800$$

**INCORRECT**

## STOP AND CHECK

1. An acid disposal tank has a useful life of three years. Find (a) the straight-line rate of depreciation expressed as a decimal and percent and (b) the double-declining rate expressed as a decimal and percent. Round to hundredths.

2. A van costing $18,000 with an expected life of four years and a salvage value of $1,000 is depreciated by the declining-balance method at twice the straight-line rate. Determine the depreciation and the year-end book value for each of the four years.

3. Use the double-declining-balance method to make a depreciation schedule for equipment that cost $4,500 and has a salvage value of $300. The equipment is expected to last five years.

4. A robot designed to paint cars costs $25,000 and is expected to last eight years. It will have a scrap value of $2,500. Use the 200%-declining-balance method to make a depreciation schedule for the robot.

## 16-1 SECTION EXERCISES

### SKILL BUILDERS

*Use the straight-line method to complete the depreciation table for an SUV that costs $44,000, has a residual value of $8,000 and an estimated life of six years.*

| Total cost = $44,000 | Year | Annual depreciation | Accumulated depreciation | End-of-year book value |
|---|---|---|---|---|
| 1. | —— | ———— | ———— | ———— |
| 2. | —— | ———— | ———— | ———— |
| 3. | —— | ———— | ———— | ———— |
| 4. | —— | ———— | ———— | ———— |
| 5. | —— | ———— | ———— | ———— |
| 6. | —— | ———— | ———— | ———— |

*Make a partial depreciation schedule for the first three years using the units-of-production depreciation for a laser engraver that costs $38,000 and has a scrap value of $2,000. The engraver has an expected life of 500,000 hours and is expected to last 15 years.*

| Total cost $38,000 | Year | Hours used | Annual depreciation | Accumulated depreciation | End-of-year book value |
|---|---|---|---|---|---|
| 7. | 1 | 24,848 | ———— | ———— | ———— |
| 8. | 2 | 20,040 | ———— | ———— | ———— |
| 9. | 3 | 20,860 | ———— | ———— | ———— |

*Use the sum-of-the-years'-digits depreciation method to make a depreciation schedule (first three years) for a forklift that cost $28,000, has an expected useful life of ten years, and has a residual value of $2,500.*

| Total cost $28,000 | Year | Depreciation rate | Annual depreciation | Accumulated depreciation | End-of-year book value |
|---|---|---|---|---|---|
| **10.** | 1 | _____ | _____ | _____ | _____ |
| **11.** | 2 | _____ | _____ | _____ | _____ |
| **12.** | 3 | _____ | _____ | _____ | _____ |

*A printing press that costs $285,900 is depreciated using the 1.5 declining-balance method. The scrap value of the press is estimated to be $3,000 and the press has an expected life of 20 years. Prepare the first four years of a depreciation schedule.*

| Total cost $285,900 | Year | Annual depreciation | Accumulated depreciation | End-of-year book value |
|---|---|---|---|---|
| **13.** | 1 | _____ | _____ | _____ |
| **14.** | 2 | _____ | _____ | _____ |
| **15.** | 3 | _____ | _____ | _____ |
| **16.** | 4 | _____ | _____ | _____ |

## APPLICATIONS

**17.** A tractor costs $25,000, has an expected life of 12 years, and has a salvage value of $2,500. Use straight-line depreciation to find the yearly depreciation. Make a depreciation schedule for the first three years' depreciation.

**18.** Prepare a straight-line depreciation schedule for the first four years of depreciation of a forklift that costs $9,450, is expected to be used for 12 years, and is projected to be scrapped for $500.

**19.** Find the yearly straight-line depreciation of a notebook computer system including the computer and monitor, the networking equipment, and a postscript printer that costs $6,300 and has a scrap value of $600 after an expected life of five years in a college engineering lab.

**20.** Make a straight-line depreciation schedule for an asset that costs $7,500 and has a scrap value of $1,200. The useful life of the asset is eight years.

**21.** A printing machine is expected to be operational for 90,000 hours. If the machine costs $84,500 and has a projected salvage value of $2,900, find the unit depreciation. The machine is used for 3,853 hours the first year. What is the first year's depreciation? Use the full calculator value of the unit depreciation.

**22.** Stuart Dybeck purchased an asphalt packing machine for $56,900 and is using sum-of-the-years' digits depreciation to schedule depreciation over six years. If the residual value is $4,000, make the depreciation schedule.

**23.** Ron Tibbett is depreciating a panel truck purchased for $37,290. He will use double-declining-balance and depreciate over seven years. What is the yearly double-declining-balance rate rounded to the nearest ten-thousandth and the first year's depreciation?

## LEARNING OUTCOMES

1 Depreciate an asset and prepare a depreciation schedule using the modified accelerated cost-recovery system (MACRS).
2 Depreciate an asset after taking a section 179 deduction.

## 1 Depreciate an asset and prepare a depreciation schedule using the modified accelerated cost-recovery system (MACRS).

**Modified accelerated cost-recovery system (MACRS):** a modified depreciation method implemented by the IRS for property placed in service after 1986.

The Tax Reform Act of 1986 introduced some changes in the depreciation rates for property put in use after 1986 (but not affecting property in use before 1986). These changes comprise the **modified accelerated cost-recovery system** or **MACRS**. MACRS consists of two systems that determine how you depreciate your property—the General Depreciation System (GDS) and the Alternative Depreciation System (ADS). Your use of either the GDS or the ADS to depreciate property under MACRS determines what depreciation method and recovery period you use. You should use GDS unless you are specifically required by law to use ADS or you elect to use ADS. To figure your MACRS deduction, you need to know the recovery period, placed-in-service date, and depreciable basis for the property. This method of depreciation, which is used in figuring depreciation for federal income tax purposes, allows businesses to write off the cost of assets more quickly than in the past. The other methods of depreciation are used for accounting purposes. The faster depreciation was meant to encourage businesses to invest in more assets despite an economic slowdown at the time. The following is a list of property classes with examples that can be depreciated under the MACRS. The list is provided by an IRS publication.

1. 3-year property.
   a. Tractor units for over-the-road use.
   b. Any race horse over 2 years old when placed in service.
   c. Any other horse over 12 years old when placed in service.
   d. Qualified rent-to-own property (defined later).
2. 5-year property.
   a. Automobiles, taxis, buses, and trucks.
   b. Computers and peripheral equipment.
   c. Office machinery (such as typewriters, calculators, and copiers).
   d. Any property used in research and experimentation.
   e. Breeding cattle and dairy cattle.
   f. Appliances, carpets, furniture, etc., used in a residential rental real estate activity.
   g. Any qualified Liberty Zone leasehold improvement property (see *Qualified New York Liberty Zone leasehold improvement property* under *Excepted Property* in chapter 3).
3. 7-year property.
   a. Office furniture and fixtures (such as desks, files, and safes).
   b. Agricultural machinery and equipment.
   c. Any property that does not have a class life and has not been designated by law as being in any other class.
4. 10-year property.
   a. Vessels, barges, tugs, and similar water transportation equipment.
   b. Any single purpose agricultural or horticultural structure.
   c. Any tree or vine bearing fruits or nuts.
5. 15-year property.
   a. Certain improvements made directly to land or added to it (such as shrubbery, fences, roads, and bridges).
   b. Any retail motor fuels outlet (defined later), such as a convenience store.
   c. Any municipal wastewater treatment plant.
6. 20-year property. This class includes farm buildings (other than single purpose agricultural or horticultural structures).
7. 25-year property. This class is water utility property, which is either of the following.
   a. Property that is an integral part of the gathering, treatment, or commercial distribution of water, and that, without regard to this provision, would be 20-year property.
   b. Any municipal sewer.
8. Residential rental property. This is any building or structure, such as a rental home (including a mobile home), if 80% or more of its gross rental income for the tax year is from dwelling units. A dwelling unit is a house or apartment used to provide living accommodations in a building or

structure. It does not include a unit in a hotel, motel, or other establishment where more than half the units are used on a transient basis. If you occupy any part of the building or structure for personal use, its gross rental income includes the fair rental value of the part you occupy.

9. Nonresidential real property. This is section 1250 property, such as an office building, store, or warehouse, that is neither residential rental property nor property with a class life of less than 27.5 years.

(Source: http://www.irs.gov/publications/p946/ch04.html)

**TABLE 16-5**
MACRS Cost-Recovery Rates, Half-Year Convention, in Percents

| Year | Depreciation rate for recovery period | | | | | |
|---|---|---|---|---|---|---|
| | 3-Year | 5-Year | 7-Year | 10-Year | 15-Year | 20-Year |
| 1 | 33.33% | 20.00% | 14.29% | 10.00% | 5.00% | 3.750% |
| 2 | 44.45 | 32.00 | 24.49 | 18.00 | 9.50 | 7.219 |
| 3 | 14.81 | 19.20 | 17.49 | 14.40 | 8.55 | 6.677 |
| 4 | 7.41 | 11.52 | 12.49 | 11.52 | 7.70 | 6.177 |
| 5 | | 11.52 | 8.93 | 9.22 | 6.93 | 5.713 |
| 6 | | 5.76 | 8.92 | 7.37 | 6.23 | 5.285 |
| 7 | | | 8.93 | 6.55 | 5.90 | 4.888 |
| 8 | | | 4.46 | 6.55 | 5.90 | 4.522 |
| 9 | | | | 6.56 | 5.91 | 4.462 |
| 10 | | | | 6.55 | 5.90 | 4.461 |
| 11 | | | | 3.28 | 5.91 | 4.462 |
| 12 | | | | | 5.90 | 4.461 |
| 13 | | | | | 5.91 | 4.462 |
| 14 | | | | | 5.90 | 4.461 |
| 15 | | | | | 5.91 | 4.462 |
| 16 | | | | | 2.95 | 4.461 |
| 17 | | | | | | 4.462 |
| 18 | | | | | | 4.461 |
| 19 | | | | | | 4.462 |
| 20 | | | | | | 4.461 |
| 21 | | | | | | 2.231 |

Source: IRS Publications (www.irs.gov/publications).

IRS publications outline all the options that may be used in calculating depreciation with MACRS. Some of the options involve placing properties in service at various times during the year. Several tables of rates are provided in IRS publications. MACRS rates when property is placed in service midyear are shown in Table 16-5.

In Table 16-5 each recovery period has a depreciation rate for one year more than the recovery period indicates. The first and last years in the recovery period are partial years because the property is placed in service at midyear. The largest amount of depreciation is realized in the second year, which is the first full year.

**HOW TO** Find the year's depreciation using the MACRS method

1. According to IRS publications, determine the asset's recovery period (expected life) and the appropriate table based on the time of year the property is placed in service.
2. Find the year's MACRS rate: Using Table 16-5, locate the MACRS rate for the year and recovery period.
3. Multiply the year's MACRS rate by the total cost of the asset.

Year's depreciation = year's MACRS rate × total cost

**TIP**

**What Makes MACRS Easier?**

Three major differences in the MACRS method of depreciation from the other methods are:

1. You do not have to find a depreciable value.
2. You do not have to determine a salvage value.
3. The useful life is determined by the property classes.

**EXAMPLE 1** Find the depreciation for each year for a boiler that was purchased for $28,000 and placed in service at midyear under the MACRS method of depreciation as a five-year property.

$$
\begin{aligned}
\text{Year 1 depreciation} &= \text{MACRS rate} \times \text{total cost} \\
&= 20\%(\$28,000) \\
&= 0.2(\$28,000) \\
&= \$5,600
\end{aligned}
$$

Year 2 depreciation $= 0.32(\$28,000) = \$8,960$
Year 3 depreciation $= 0.192(\$28,000) = \$5,376$
Year 4 depreciation $= 0.1152(\$28,000) = \$3,225.60$
Year 5 depreciation $= 0.1152(\$28,000) = \$3,225.60$
Year 6 depreciation $= 0.0576(\$28,000) = \$1,612.80$

The sum of the yearly depreciations should equal the total cost.

$$\$5,600 + \$8,960 + \$5,376 + \$3,225.60 + \$3,225.60 + \$1,612.80 = \$28,000$$

These calculations are most useful if they are organized into a depreciation schedule such as the one shown in Table 16-6.

**TABLE 16-6**
MACRS Depreciation Schedule for Boiler

| Total cost: $28,000 | Year | MACRS rate | Depreciation | Accumulated depreciation | End-of-year book value |
|---|---|---|---|---|---|
| | 1 | 20.00% | $5,600.00 | $ 5,600.00 | $22,400.00 |
| | 2 | 32.00% | $8,960.00 | $14,560.00 | $13,440.00 |
| | 3 | 19.20% | $5,376.00 | $19,936.00 | $ 8,064.00 |
| | 4 | 11.52% | $3,225.60 | $23,161.60 | $ 4,838.40 |
| | 5 | 11.52% | $3,225.60 | $26,387.20 | $ 1,612.80 |
| | 6 | 5.76% | $1,612.80 | $28,000.00 | $ 0 |

## TIP

**What Happens to the Salvage Value?**

MACRS allows for 100% of the total cost of a property to be depreciated. Add the percents in any recovery period column of Table 16-5. The sum is 100% for every recovery period. Other methods of depreciation do not allow an asset to be depreciated below its salvage value. When MACRS is used to depreciate an asset, the salvage value is treated as income when the asset is sold.

 ## STOP AND CHECK

*Assume all property is placed in service using the midyear convention.*

1. Find the depreciation for the ninth year for a vineyard that was purchased for $58,000 and placed in service under the MACRS method of depreciation as a ten-year property.

2. Use the MACRS table to find the eighth year's depreciation for a property that cost $45,000 and is depreciated over a ten-year period.

3. Find the depreciation for the 14th year of a property that cost $83,500 and is placed in service as a 15-year property under the MACRS method of depreciation.

4. Complete a depreciation schedule for the vineyard in Exercise 1.

## 2 Depreciate an asset after taking a section 179 deduction.

The purchase of certain qualifying property can be treated for tax purposes as a one-time expense rather than as a capital expenditure that is depreciated over several years. During the first year that a qualifying property is purchased and placed in service, a deduction under **section 179** of the IRS Tax Code can be taken.

The IRS section 179 limit was increased to $112,000 for 2007. For 2008 and 2009 the federal maximum will be $112,000 plus a cost of living allowance to be determined. For each dollar of newly acquired qualifying property a business purchases in a tax year that exceeds $450,000 in 2007, the section 179 deduction is reduced by one dollar, but the reduction does not go below zero. These excess amounts have been increasing since 2003. The IRS will begin severely reducing the section 179 deduction in 2010. In 2010 the maximum amount of a section 179 deduction will be only $25,000. This deduction can be taken in the tax year of the purchase for machinery and equipment, furniture and fixtures, most storage facilities, single-purpose agricultural and horticultural structures, and off-the-shelf computer software. The deduction is limited to the taxable income of the business (including spouse's income for sole proprietorships). The taxpayer must decide to take the section 179 deduction or to depreciate the property over several years. This choice is only allowed in the year the purchase is made.

The amount that is claimed under section 179 is subtracted from the original price of the property, and the balance can be depreciated using any of the approved methods of depreciation. The deduction can be claimed on one property or spread to more than one property. However, this deduction is only available the first year that a property or properties are purchased and placed in service, except under special circumstances. As with other IRS regulations, the maximum amount of the deduction, the circumstances under which the deduction is allowed, and the circumstances under which the deduction can be carried over to a future year are subject to change annually. It is necessary to consult IRS publications regularly for current requirements. These can be viewed on the Internet at www.irs.gov.

Certain conditions must be met before you can elect to take a section 179 deduction. One is that the property is placed in service *for business purposes* in the first year it is purchased. For instance, if a car is purchased for personal use and in a future year placed in service for business use, the section 179 deduction is not allowed. In general, eligible property is tangible, depreciable personal property that is used for the production of income. Finally, a section 179 deduction can only be used to reduce taxable income and not to create a net loss. Under certain conditions, a section 179 deduction can be carried over to future years when the taxable income for a given year has already been reduced to zero by other deductions. Estates and trusts cannot elect the section 179 deduction.

---

**HOW TO** | Depreciate an asset after taking a section 179 deduction

1. Decide how much of the maximum section 179 deduction allowance—$112,000 for 2007—to apply to the asset.
2. Subtract the elected section 179 deduction from the total cost of the asset.
3. Apply an approved depreciation method to the value from step 2, instead of to the actual total cost.

---

**EXAMPLE 1** The 7th Inning is renovating the kitchen equipment for the restaurant portion of the business. Find the first-year depreciation using MACRS on the kitchen equipment (seven-year eligible property) that is purchased and placed in service at midyear. The price of the property is $125,250 and the maximum $112,000 section 179 deduction is elected.

$$\text{Depreciation} = (\text{total cost} - \text{section 179 deduction}) \times \text{MACRS rate}$$
$$= (\$125,250 - \$112,000)(14.29\%)$$
$$= \$13,250(0.1429)$$
$$= \$1,893.43$$

**The first-year depreciation is $1,893.43**

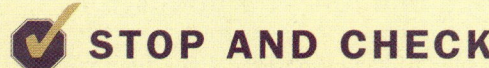

1. Find the third-year depreciation for a tractor/trailer rig that costs $160,980 and is purchased and placed in service at midyear. The maximum $112,000 section 179 deduction is elected for this three-year property.

2. A barge costing $154,840 is purchased and placed in service at midyear. The maximum $112,000 section 179 deduction is elected for this ten-year property. Find the eighth-year depreciation amount for the barge.

3. The Circle B Farm placed a storage facility (farm building) into service using the MACRS cost-recovery, half-year convention rates. What is the amount of depreciation for year 2 if the cost was $143,300 and a section 179 deduction of $112,000 was elected?

4. The Genesceo Citrus Farm placed 2,800 tangerine trees into service at a cost of $50 per tree. What is the first year's depreciation if MACRS cost-recovery, half-year convention rates are used with a section 179 deduction of $112,000?

## 16-2 SECTION EXERCISES

### SKILL BUILDERS

*Find the depreciation for the indicated year using MACRS cost-recovery rates for the properties placed in service at midyear.*

| | Property class | Depreciation year | Cost of property |
|---|---|---|---|
| 1. | 3-year | 2 | $ 82,500 |
| 2. | 5-year | 4 | $ 46,250 |
| 3. | 10-year | 1 | $127,900 |
| 4. | 20-year | 8 | $ 42,500 |

*A section 179 maximum deduction is taken for the properties placed in service in 2007. How much can be depreciated for the properties listed in Exercises 5 and 6?*

5. Property cost $282,900

6. Property cost $345,800

7. Find the depreciation each year for a tractor that was purchased for $18,000 and placed in service midyear under the MACRS method of depreciation as a three-year property.

8. Use the MACRS method to find the depreciation for the 17th year of a municipal sewer that is placed in service at midyear as a 20-year property with a cost of $385,400.

9. A barn that cost $45,000 to construct is placed in service midyear as a 20-year property. What is the MACRS depreciation for year 7?

10. Kentucky Thoroughbred Farms has a racehorse that is just over two years old. The racehorse, a three-year property, is being placed in service midyear with a total cost of $83,500. Use the MACRS to find the depreciation that can be taken for the horse for each year of its service.

11. Jones' Automotive purchased equipment for $182,000 and takes the maximum section 179 deduction. What is the first year's depreciation on the seven-year property if the property is placed in service in July 2007?

12. Find the third-year depreciation using MACRS for a fleet of taxis (five-year property) that is purchased and placed in service at midyear. The price of the fleet is $141,971 and the maximum $112,000 section 179 deduction was elected when the fleet was placed in service.

## APPLICATIONS

**13.** A Western Star over-the-road tractor is purchased for $132,895 and placed in service in July 2009. The owner elects to depreciate this three-year property using MACRS. Make a depreciation schedule showing each year's depreciation, accumulated depreciation, and end-of-year book value for the property.

**14.** Use the MACRS method to make a depreciation schedule for property that cost $4,800 and was placed in service midyear with a three-year recovery period. No section 179 deduction was taken.

**15.** A five-year property costing $398,000 is placed in service at midyear in 2007. A section 179 deduction of $112,000 is taken for this property and the remaining value is depreciated using MACRS. Prepare a depreciation schedule for the property.

## Learning Outcomes

### Section 16-1

**1** Depreciate an asset and prepare a depreciation schedule using the straight-line method (p. 550)

## What to Remember with Examples

**Find the yearly depreciation using the straight-line method.**

1. Find the *total cost* of the asset.

$$\text{Total cost} = \text{cost} + \text{shipping} + \text{installation}$$

2. Find the *depreciable value*.

$$\text{Depreciable value} = \text{total cost} - \text{salvage value}$$

3. Find the yearly depreciation.

$$\text{Yearly depreciation} = \frac{\text{depreciable value}}{\text{years of expected life}}$$

**Prepare a depreciation schedule.**

1. For the first year of expected life:
   (a) Find the yearly or annual depreciation.
   (b) Find the *first end-of-year book value.*

   $$\text{First end-of-year book value} = \text{total cost} - \text{first year's depreciation}$$

2. For each remaining year of expected life:
   (a) Find the annual depreciation.
   (b) Find the *year's accumulated depreciation.*

   $$\text{Year's accumulated depreciation} = \text{annual depreciation} + \text{sum of all the previous years' depreciation}$$

   (c) Find the *year's end-of-year book value.*

   $$\text{Year's end-of-year book value} = \text{previous end-of-year book value} - \text{annual depreciation}$$

3. Make a table with the following column headings and fill in the data: year, annual depreciation, accumulated depreciation, end-of-year book value.

> Make a straight-line depreciation schedule for a property that costs $3,700 and has a salvage value of $400 at the end of three years.
>
> $$\text{Depreciable value} = \$3,700 - \$400$$
> $$= \$3,300$$
> $$\text{Yearly depreciation} = \frac{\$3,300}{3}$$
> $$= \$1,100$$
>
> | Total cost: $3,700 | Year | Depreciation | Accumulated depreciation | End-of-year book value |
> |---|---|---|---|---|
> | Depreciable | 1 | $1,100 | $1,100 | $2,600 |
> | value: $3,300 | 2 | 1,100 | 2,200 | 1,500 |
> | | 3 | 1,100 | 3,300 | 400 |

**2** Depreciate an asset and prepare a depreciation schedule using the units-of-production method. (p. 552)

**Find the depreciation for units produced using the units-of-production method.**

1. Find the *unit depreciation*.

$$\text{Unit depreciation} = \frac{\text{depreciable value}}{\text{units produced during expected life}}$$

Keep the full calculator value of the quotient.

2. Multiply the unit depreciation by the units produced.

$$\text{Depreciation for units produced} = \text{unit depreciation} \times \text{units produced}$$

Make a units-of-production depreciation schedule for a vehicle that costs $18,900 and has a resale value of $3,000 after 150,000 miles. The vehicle is driven 39,270 miles the first year, 37,960 miles the second year, 38,520 miles the third year, and 34,250 miles the fourth year.

$$\text{Depreciable value} = \$18,900 - \$3,000$$
$$= \$15,900$$
$$\text{Unit depreciation} = \frac{\$15,900}{\$150,000} = 0.106$$

| Total cost: $18,900 Depreciable value: $15,900 | Year | Miles driven | Depreciation | Accumulated depreciation | End-of-year book value |
|---|---|---|---|---|---|
| | 1 | 39,270 | $4,162.62 | $4,162.62 | $14,737.38 |
| | 2 | 37,960 | 4,023.76 | 8,186.38 | 10,713.62 |
| | 3 | 38,520 | 4,083.12 | 12,269.50 | 6,630.50 |
| | 4 | 34,250 | 3,630.50 | 15,900.00 | 3,000.00 |

**3** Depreciate an asset and prepare a depreciation schedule using the sum-of-the-years'-digits method. (p. 554)

**Find the year's depreciation using the sum-of-the-years'-digits method.**

1. Find the *year's depreciation rate:*

   (a) Use the $\dfrac{n(n+1)}{2}$ shortcut to find the sum from 1 to the number of years of expected life.

   Sum from 1 to the number of years of expected life
   $$= \frac{(\text{years of expected life})(1 + \text{years of expected life})}{2}$$

   (b) Divide the number of years remaining of expected life by the sum from step 1a.

   $$\text{Year's sum-of-the-years' depreciation rate} = \frac{\text{number of years remaining of expected life}}{\text{sum from 1 to the years of expected life}}$$

2. Find the depreciable value:

   $$\text{Depreciable value} = \text{total cost} - \text{salvage value}$$

3. Multiply the year's depreciable value by the year's depreciation rate.

   $$\text{Year's depreciation} = \text{depreciable value} \times \text{year's depreciation rate}$$

Make a sum-of-the-years'-digits schedule for a property that costs $3,700 and has a salvage value of $400 at the end of three years.

$$\text{Depreciable value} = \text{cost} - \text{salvage value}$$
$$= \$3,700 - \$400$$
$$= \$3,300$$

$$\text{Sum of the years' digits} = \frac{n(n+1)}{2}$$
$$= \frac{3(3+1)}{2}$$
$$= 6$$

$$\text{Depreciation rate} = \frac{\text{number of years remaining}}{\text{sum of the years of expected life}}$$
$$= \frac{\text{number of years remaining}}{6}$$

| Total cost: $3,700 Depreciable value: $3,300 | Year | Depreciation rate | Depreciation | Accumulated depreciation | End-of-year book value |
|---|---|---|---|---|---|
| | 1 | $\frac{3}{6}$ | $1,650 | $1,650 | $2,050 |
| | 2 | $\frac{2}{6}$ | 1,100 | 2,750 | 950 |
| | 3 | $\frac{1}{6}$ | 550 | 3,300 | 400 |

## 4 Depreciate an asset and prepare a depreciation schedule using the declining-balance method. (p. 556)

**Find the year's depreciation using the declining-balance method.**

1. Find the yearly depreciation rate:
   (a) Using *straight-line declining balance,* divide 1 by the number of years of expected life.

$$\text{Yearly straight-line depreciation rate} = \frac{1}{\text{years of expected life}}$$

   (b) Using other declining-balance depreciation rates, such as *double-declining-balance* or *150%-declining-balance,* multiply the yearly straight-line depreciation rate by the appropriate factor.

   Yearly double-declining depreciation rate = yearly straight-line depreciation rate $\times$ 2
   Yearly 150%-declining depreciation rate = yearly straight-line depreciation rate $\times$ 1.5

2. Find the depreciation for the first year.

   First year's depreciation = total cost $\times$ yearly depreciation rate

3. Find the depreciation for all other years.

   Year's depreciation = previous end-of-year book value $\times$ yearly depreciation rate

Make a double-declining-balance schedule of depreciation for a property that costs $3,700 and has a salvage value of $400 after three years' use.

$$\text{Yearly double-declining rate} = \frac{1}{3}(2) = \frac{2}{3} = 0.666667$$

| Total cost: $3,700 | Year | Depreciation | Accumulated depreciation | End-of-year book value |
|---|---|---|---|---|
| | 1 | $2,466.67 | $2,466.67 | $1,233.33 |
| | 2 | 822.22 | 3,288.89 | 411.11 |
| | 3 | 11.11* | 3,300.00 | 400.00 |

*An asset *cannot* be depreciated below its salvage value. So the depreciation for year 3 is $411.11 − $400 = $11.11.

## Section 16-2

## 1 Depreciate an asset and prepare a depreciation schedule using the modified accelerated cost-recovery system (MACRS). (p. 562)

**Find the year's depreciation using the MACRS method.**

1. According to IRS publications, determine the asset's recovery period (expected life) and the appropriate table.
2. Find the year's MACRS rate: Using Table 16-5, locate the MACRS rate for the year and recovery period.
3. Multiply the year's MACRS rate by the total cost of the asset. (*Note:* 100% of the asset's value is depreciated.)

   Year's depreciation = year's MACRS rate $\times$ total cost

Make a MACRS depreciation schedule for a property that costs $3,700, is put into service at midyear, and is to be depreciated over a three-year recovery period. The salvage value is $200.

| Total cost: $3,700 | Year | MACRS rate | Depreciation | Accumulated depreciation | End-of-year book value |
|---|---|---|---|---|---|
| | 1 | 33.33% | $1,233.21 | $1,233.21 | $2,466.79 |
| | 2 | 44.45% | 1,644.65 | 2,877.86 | 822.14 |
| | 3 | 14.81% | 547.97 | 3,425.83 | 274.17 |
| | 4 | 7.41% | 274.17 | 3,700.00 | 0 |

**2** Depreciate an asset after taking a section 179 deduction. (p. 565)

1. Decide how much of the maximum section 179 deduction allowance—$112,000 for 2007—to apply to the asset.
2. Subtract the elected section 179 deduction from the total cost of the asset.
3. Apply an approved depreciation method to the value from step 2, instead of to the actual total cost.

Trip's Nursery constructs a greenhouse for $114,000 and places it in service at midyear as a ten-year property under the MACRS. If the maximum section 179 deduction of $112,000 is taken the first year, what is the first-year depreciation?

$$\text{Depreciable amount} = \$114,000 - \$112,000$$
$$= \$2,000$$
$$\text{Year 1 depreciation} = 0.1(\$2,000) \qquad \text{From Table 16-5}$$
$$= \$200$$

# EXERCISES SET A

*Use straight-line depreciation to complete the yearly depreciation column of a depreciation schedule. Round answers to the nearest cent.*

| | Total cost | Salvage value | Expected life | Yearly depreciation |
|---|---|---|---|---|
| **1.** | $7,200 | $300 | 3 years | |
| **2.** | $12,000 | $2,500 | 5 years | |
| **3.** | $100,000 | $10,000 | 20 years | |

**4.** A machine was purchased by the Wabash Company for $5,900. Its normal life expectancy is four years. If it can be traded in for $900 at the end of this time, determine the yearly depreciation by the straight-line method.

**5.** Station WMAT spent $5,000 for a new television camera. This camera will be replaced in five years. If the scrap value will be $500, determine the annual depreciation by the straight-line method.

**6.** The Acme Management Corporation purchased a computer for $5,400. Its life expectancy is projected to be four years, and the salvage value will be $800. Make a straight-line depreciation schedule like Table 16-1.

*Find the unit depreciation and year's depreciation columns.*

| | Cost | Scrap value | Expected life | Hours operated this year |
|---|---|---|---|---|
| **7.** | $42,000 | $2,000 | 80,000 (hours) | 6,700 |
| **8.** | $4,340 | $340 | 16,000 | 2,580 |
| **9.** | $2,370 | $420 | 7,800 | 1,520 |

**10.** A tractor for trailers was purchased for $58,000 and has a resale value of $8,000. The tractor is expected to be used for 250,000 miles and is driven 19,740 miles the first year. Find the depreciation for the year.

**11.** Find the unit depreciation for an air conditioning–heating unit that costs $7,800 and has a scrap value of $600 if it is expected to operate 40,000 hours.

**12.** Make a depreciation schedule for the first two years like Table 16-2 for a truck driven 28,580 miles the first year, 32,140 miles the second year, 29,760 miles the third year, 31,810 miles the fourth year, and 27,710 miles the fifth year. The expected life of the truck is 150,000 miles and it costs $18,500. The salvage value is $2,000.

EXCEL

**13.** Using the sum-of-the-years'-digits method, make a depreciation schedule for the first two years for a machine that costs $4,200 and will be worth $750 at the end of five years.

**14.** Make a depreciation schedule using the double-declining rate for three years for a computer system costing $21,000 with an estimated life of three years and a resale value of $1,000.

*Round answers to the nearest cent.*

**15.** Find the depreciation for the tenth year for a theme park structure that was purchased for $14,489 and placed in service under the MACRS as a ten-year property.

**16.** Find the depreciation for the ninth year for a property that was purchased for $302,588 and placed in service under the MACRS as a ten-year property.

**17.** Find the depreciation for the first three years for a laser printer that costs $5,800 and was placed in service midyear under the MACRS as a five-year property.

**18.** Find the MACRS depreciation for year 4 for office furniture that costs $131,000 and is placed in service at midyear as a seven-year property. The maximum $112,000 section 179 deduction is elected for this property.

**19.** Make a depreciation schedule like Table 16–6 for an asset that costs $3,270 and was placed in service midyear under the MACRS as a three-year property.

# EXERCISES SET B

*Use straight-line depreciation to fill in the yearly depreciation column. Round answers to the nearest cent.*

| | Total cost | Salvage value | Expected life | Yearly depreciation |
|---|---|---|---|---|
| 1. | $6,000 | $50 | 11 years | |
| 2. | $50,000 | $5,000 | 10 years | |
| 3. | $82,500 | $12,000 | 12 years | |

**4.** A stamping machine was purchased by Deskin Glass Company for $8,595. Freight and installation costs were $405. If it will be worth $2,000 after seven years, find the annual depreciation using the straight-line method.

**5.** A dress factory paid $14,000 for an assembly-line system. If the used equipment will be worth $2,000 at the end of 15 years, find the annual depreciation by the straight-line method.

**6.** Make a depreciation schedule for Exercise 5 showing the first four years.

| Total cost: $14,000 | Year | Depreciation | Accumulated depreciation | End-of-year book value |
|---|---|---|---|---|

*Fill in the unit depreciation and year's depreciation columns.*

| | Cost | Scrap value | Expected life | Hours operated this year | Unit depreciation | Year's depreciation |
|---|---|---|---|---|---|---|
| 7. | $25,000 | $2,500 | 90,000 hours | 7,000 | | |
| 8. | $19,000 | $1,000 | 45,000 | 8,000 | | |

**9.** SERV-U Computer Service Company bought a laser printer for $15,000. The machine is expected to operate for 28,000 hours, after which its trade-in value will be $1,000. Find the unit depreciation for the printer. The first year the machine was operated 4,160 hours. Find the depreciation for the year.

**10.** BEST Delivery Service purchased a delivery truck for $18,500 and expected to resell it for $2,000 after driving it 150,000 miles. Find the unit depreciation for the truck.

**11.** Make a depreciation schedule for the printer in Exercise 9 to show the depreciation for three years if it was operated 3,140 hours the second year and 6,820 hours the third year.

| Total cost: $15,000 | Year | Hours used | Depreciation | Accumulated depreciation | End-of-year book value |
|---|---|---|---|---|---|

**12.** If the unit in Exercise 7 operates 6,190 hours the second year, what is the depreciation for the year?

**13.** Wee-Kare purchased a van for $21,500 and will drive it 75,000 miles. If the resale value of the van is projected to be $6,500, find the unit depreciation. Wee-Kare drove the van 2,584 miles the second year. Find the year's depreciation.

**14.** Make a sum-of-the-years'-digits depreciation schedule for the first two years for an asset that costs $21,500 and will be worth $5,000 at the end of four years.

| Total cost: $21,500 | Year | Depreciation rate | Depreciation | Accumulated depreciation | End-of-year book value |
|---|---|---|---|---|---|
| | | | | | |

**15.** Concon Corp. bought office equipment for $6,000. At the end of three years, its scrap value is $750. Use a double-declining rate to make a depreciation schedule. Note that an asset *cannot* be depreciated below its scrap value.

| Total cost: $6,000 | Year | Depreciation | Accumulated depreciation | End-of-year book value |
|---|---|---|---|---|
| | | | | |

**16.** Make a depreciation schedule using a 150%-declining-balance for three years for furniture that costs $15,000 and has a salvage value of $500.

| Total cost: $15,000 | Year | Depreciation | Accumulated depreciation | End-of-year book value |
|---|---|---|---|---|
| | | | | |

**17.** Find the depreciation for each of the final two years for property purchased for $113,984 and placed in service under the MACRS as a 15-year property.

**18.** Find the depreciation for the 15th year of a 15-year rental property purchased for $182,500 and placed in service before March 15, 2008, under the MACRS.

**19.** Make a depreciation schedule like Table 16-6 for the first three years for an asset that costs $16,250 and was placed in service midyear under the MACRS as a five-year property.

| Total cost: $16,250 | Year | MACRS rate | Depreciation | Accumulated depreciation | End-of-year book value |
|---|---|---|---|---|---|
| | | | | | |

# PRACTICE TEST

**CHAPTER 16**

1. Using the sum-of-the-years'-digits method, find the denominator of the depreciation rates for assets with an expected life of seven years.

2. Find the depreciable value of an asset that costs $38,490 and has a scrap value of $4,800 if the straight-line method of depreciation is used.

3. Make a depreciation schedule to show the annual straight-line depreciation, accumulated depreciation, and end-of-year book value for furniture that costs $4,500 and has a scrap value of $700. The useful life of the furniture is five years.

| Total cost: $4,500 | Year | Depreciation | Accumulated depreciation | End-of-year book value |
|---|---|---|---|---|
|  |  |  |  |  |

4. A pizza delivery car was purchased for $19,580. The car is expected to be driven 125,000 miles before being sold for $500. What is the unit depreciation on the car (depreciation per mile)?

5. Using the sum-of-the-years'-digits method, find the denominator of the depreciation rates for an asset with an expected life of 24 years.

6. Use the sum-of-the-years'-digits method to make a depreciation schedule for an asset that costs $7,500 and has a salvage value of $1,500. The asset is to be used for three years.

| Total cost: $7,500 | Year | Depreciation rate | Depreciation | Accumulated depreciation | End-of-year book value |
|---|---|---|---|---|---|
|  |  |  |  |  |  |

**7.** Use the double-declining-balance method to make a depreciation schedule for a piece of equipment that costs $2,780 and has a salvage value of $300. The equipment is expected to be used for four years.

| Total cost: $2,780 | Year | Depreciation | Accumulated depreciation | End-of-year book value |
|---|---|---|---|---|

**8.** Use the MACRS to make a depreciation schedule for a vehicle that was placed in service at midyear and cost $13,580. The vehicle is to be depreciated over a three-year period.

| Total cost: $13,580 | Year | MACRS rate | Depreciation | Accumulated depreciation | End-of-year book value |
|---|---|---|---|---|---|

**9.** Use the MACRS to find the first year's depreciation on an asset that costs $8,580 if the asset is placed in service at midyear to be depreciated over a three-year period.

**10.** Use the MACRS to find the depreciation for the fourth year for office furniture that costs $17,872. A recovery period of seven years is used.

**11.** Capital equipment for a marine biological research lab costing $127,800 is placed in service at midyear as a five-year property under the MACRS. A section 179 deduction of $112,000 is taken the first year. What is the first-year depreciation?

**12.** For Exercise 11, what was the total deduction for the lab equipment claimed by the research company on its federal income tax form the first year the equipment was purchased?

1. Using the three formulas in the How To on page 550, find the yearly depreciation using the straight-line method to write one formula to find the yearly depreciation.

2. Observing patterns in business formulas and calculations enables the businessperson to better estimate or predict results and trends. Examine Table 16-3 on page 555 and explain the pattern found in the Annual depreciation column. Explain how each subsequent year's depreciation can be found without using the depreciation rate fraction.

3. In Table 16-3, compare the pattern identified in the Accumulated Depreciation column with the pattern formed by the data in the End-of-Year Book Value column.

4. Examine Table 16-5 and explain why the second year's depreciation percent is larger than any of the other years' percents.

5. Make a chart that shows the depreciation method and the value that is used as the basis for depreciation for the five depreciation methods described in this chapter.

6. Both declining-balance depreciation and MACRS depreciation use the total cost of an asset as the basis for depreciation. Explain the difference in the way the ending book value is handled in the two methods.

7. Explain how you could use only the data in Table 16-5 to verify that any asset depreciated using the MACRS method can be depreciated for its entire cost.

8. Give at least two circumstances in which a section 179 deduction is not permitted on a company's asset.

## Challenge Problem

A new minivan was purchased for $24,400 and currently has an end-of-year book value of $20,081.20 after one year of operation. Find the year's rate of depreciation. What will be the end-of-year book value of this minivan after two years if the rate of depreciation remains the same and depreciation is based on the purchase price?

# CASE STUDIES

## 16.1 O'Brien Nursery

"With the Luck of the Irish, May All of Your Plants Stay Green." So reads the slogan of O'Brien Nursery, a family-owned nursery business located in west-central Illinois. Started as a small greenhouse, the business has evolved into a full-scale nursery, including landscape services. The primary assets of the business include the following: 54 acres of land including a 4-acre active vineyard of grape vines; 4 trucks, 2 vans, and 4 tractors; a greenhouse, a storage building, a building housing the retail space and offices; and office equipment. Due to substantial residential growth in the area, there is more demand than ever for landscaping services and nursery stock. One of the hottest selling items has been small ornamental trees, which are typically priced from $40 to $200 each. In order to meet this demand, the nursery is considering the purchase of additional land and a state-of-the-art tree planter, which sells for $17,500.

1. Using the MACRS classification guide, determine the property classification for all of the current assets owned by the nursery.

2. After one of the cargo vans breaks down, Mike O'Brien decides to convert his personal family van, purchased two years ago, to a business vehicle by having some paint detailing done. The original cost of the van was $21,400, and the custom painting cost $350. What portion of the cost of the van and/or painting would be eligible for a current year IRS section 179 deduction?

3. Create a depreciation schedule for the tree planter costing $17,500 using the MACRS method of depreciation as a 7-year property, and placed in service at midyear.

4. The tree planter is expected to plant 92,000 trees during its useful life. If the salvage value is $1,500, find the unit depreciation and depreciation for planting 8,700 trees in a year. Would this be a better depreciation method than the MACRS? Why or why not?

# 16.2 The Life of a Mower

Carl has decided to fund his college expenses by mowing lawns and doing landscape maintenance during his free time. He already has some of the equipment he will need, but still needs to purchase a riding mower. Because he will be mowing fairly small residential lots, he decides that the John Deere LT150 with a grass bagging mechanism would be his best choice. The mower will cost $2,800. Carl lives in an area where grass needs to be mowed year-round, and he hopes to have 25 to 30 weekly clients. Carl thinks the estimated useful life of the mower will be four years at which time he thinks he will be able to sell it for $800.

1. If Carl uses the straight-line method of depreciation, how much depreciation will he record for each of the next four years? Complete the following chart.

Total cost: $2,800    Depreciable value: $2,000    Annual depreciation: $\dfrac{\$2,000}{4} = \$500$

| Year | Annual depreciation | Accumulated depreciation | End-of-year book value |
|---|---|---|---|
| 1 | | | |
| 2 | | | |
| 3 | | | |
| 4 | | | |

2. If Carl uses the sum-of-the-years'-digits method, how much depreciation will he record for each of the next four years? Complete the following chart:

Total cost: $2,800        Depreciable value: $2,000

| Year | Depreciation rate | Annual depreciation | Accumulated depreciation | End-of-year book value |
|---|---|---|---|---|
| 1 | $\frac{4}{10}$ | | | |
| 2 | $\frac{3}{10}$ | | | |
| 3 | $\frac{2}{10}$ | | | |
| 4 | $\frac{1}{10}$ | | | |

3. Carl thinks that his riding mower will fall under the 7-year agricultural machinery and equipment category for MACRS tax depreciation purposes. How much depreciation will he record each year on his tax return? Complete the chart for the full 7 years.

Total cost: $2,800

| Year | MACRS rate | Depreciation | Accumulated depreciation | End-of-year book value |
|---|---|---|---|---|
| 1 | | | | |
| 2 | | | | |
| 3 | | | | |
| 4 | | | | |
| 5 | | | | |
| 6 | | | | |
| 7 | | | | |
| 8 | | | | |

## Controlling Employee Theft

Employees and customers in nearly every type of business steal over a billion dollars a week. Theft of goods is on the rise in retail establishments nationwide. The University of Florida's 2002 National Retail Security Survey reported that total inventory shrinkage (the reduction in physical inventory) approached $32 billion. Amazingly, the number one cause was employee theft, which totaled $15 billion, while shoplifting was $10 billion. Administrative errors totaled $5 billion and vendor fraud $2 billion.

In the retail industry, businesses recover an average of $1,350 from each employee apprehended for stealing, compared to $196 recovered from shoplifters. So who pays for this reduction in physical inventory through employee theft and shoplifting? Unfortunately, we all do—through higher prices.

There are proven ways to detect and prevent theft-related losses within your business. A comprehensive program to eliminate employee theft can be simple and inexpensive, or elaborate and expensive.

1. **Keep a closer eye.** It is possible to install physical obstacles to theft, such as alarm systems and secured, restricted areas. Electronic security systems can protect your building when it is unoccupied. These systems include window and door monitors, movement sensors, alarms, and video cameras. However, be aware that while these devices deter theft and help prevent losses, they also convey clearly to employees that they are not trusted.

2. **Hire people you can trust.** Perform thorough background checks on all new hire prospects, particularly for sensitive positions involving the flow of money. Call previous employers to verify resume and application information. Make sure applicants do not have a history of stealing from previous employers, and that all credentials and references are valid. Personal interviews, drug screening, reference checks, and criminal background reviews all have merit—and should be used prior to hiring employees.

3. **Occasionally inspect or audit inventory.** Monitoring activities, especially in receiving, can prevent theft. Keep records of any problems such as overages, shortages, and damage discrepancies. Cycle counting and periodic inventories are essential to verify the physical inventory levels on hand. Try to have a management-level supervisor oversee inventory.

Although there are many different ways to value inventory, as you will see in Chapter 17, inventory has no value to a business if it has been stolen. By paying attention to the basics of inventory management, you can help ensure that your inventory leaves in the hands of paying customers, not with employees or shoplifters.

## LEARNING OUTCOMES

### 17-1 Inventory

1. Use the specific identification inventory method to find the ending inventory and the cost of goods sold.
2. Use the weighted-average inventory method to find the ending inventory and the cost of goods sold.
3. Use the first-in, first-out (FIFO) inventory method to find the ending inventory and the cost of goods sold.
4. Use the last-in, first-out (LIFO) inventory method to find the ending inventory and the cost of goods sold.
5. Use the retail inventory method to estimate the ending inventory and the cost of goods sold.
6. Use the gross profit inventory method to estimate the ending inventory and the cost of goods sold.

### 17-2 Turnover and Overhead

1. Find the inventory turnover rate.
2. Find the department overhead based on sales or floor space.

Any business needs to know the value of goods on hand that are available for sale or for use in manufacturing items for sale. Any business also needs to know how often all merchandise is sold or used and replaced with new merchandise. The expenses incurred in operating the business are also other critical pieces of information needed to run a successful business. A knowledge of these concepts—inventory, turnover, and overhead—is important for making wise business decisions and for preparing required tax documents.

## 17-1 INVENTORY

### LEARNING OUTCOMES

1 Use the specific identification inventory method to find the ending inventory and the cost of goods sold.
2 Use the weighted-average inventory method to find the ending inventory and the cost of goods sold.
3 Use the first-in, first-out (FIFO) inventory method to find the ending inventory and the cost of goods sold.
4 Use the last-in, first-out (LIFO) inventory method to find the ending inventory and the cost of goods sold.
5 Use the retail inventory method to estimate the ending inventory and the cost of goods sold.
6 Use the gross profit inventory method to estimate the ending inventory and the cost of goods sold.

**Inventory:** merchandise available for sale or goods available for the production of products.

**Periodic or physical inventory:** a physical count of goods or merchandise made at a specific time.

**Perpetual inventory:** an inventory process that adjusts the inventory count after each sale or purchase of goods.

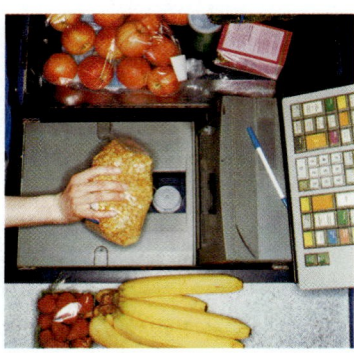

**Cost of goods sold (COGS):** the difference between the cost of goods available for sale and the cost of the ending inventory.

Merchandise available for sale or goods available for the production of products on a certain date are called **inventory**. The value of inventory is important for a number of reasons. Two of the financial statements covered in Chapter 20 require inventory values, as do various tax documents. Inventory may be checked weekly, monthly, quarterly, semiannually, annually, or at any other specific interval of time. At the end of the specified time, a physical count is made of the merchandise on hand. This type of inventory is called a **periodic inventory** or **physical inventory**.

Many stores have computerized the inventory process so that the inventory is adjusted with each sale or purchase of additional goods. That is, a count of merchandise on hand is available at any time. This continual inventory method is called **perpetual inventory**. Even with a perpetual inventory system, a physical count is made periodically to verify and adjust the inventory records. A discrepancy between the perpetual inventory and the actual inventory is sometimes a result of theft or loss due to damage.

Once a count of merchandise has been made, the merchandise is given a value according to various accounting methods. What makes this process time-consuming is that the cost of the goods purchased during a specific period often varies. For example, at one point in a month, coffee may be purchased at $2.79 a pound. The next time coffee is ordered, the cost may be $2.93 a pound. This section discusses six methods commonly used by accountants to assign a value to an inventory: specific identification; weighted-average; first-in, first-out (FIFO); last-in, first-out (LIFO); retail; and gross profit.

For the purpose of examining the various methods of assigning the value to inventory, we use an overly simplified set of circumstances. In actual practice, the process involves many different items. For our example we use the inventory records for 12-inch battery clocks. Table 17-1 gives these records.

Throughout this discussion, the same formula is used. It shows how to find the **cost of goods sold (COGS)**:

$$\text{Cost of goods sold} = \text{cost of goods available for sale} - \text{cost of ending inventory}$$

The data in Table 17-1 are used to find the cost of goods available for sale. This amount remains the same throughout the discussion. The cost of the ending inventory and the cost of goods sold vary with each method.

**TABLE 17-1**
Inventory Report for Battery Wall Clocks

| Date of purchase | Units purchased | Cost per unit |
| --- | --- | --- |
| Beginning inventory | 29 | $ 8 |
| January 15 | 18 | 7 |
| February 4 | 9 | 10 |
| March 3 | 14 | 8 |

## 1 Use the specific identification inventory method to find the ending inventory and the cost of goods sold.

Many companies code their incoming merchandise with the purchase price or cost. Their inventory values are based on the actual cost of each item available for sale. This system of evaluating inventory is the **specific identification inventory method**. This method is best for low-volume, high-cost items, such as automobiles or fine jewelry, since a company must be able to identify the actual cost of the specific individual items bought. The name of this method is derived from the fact that in each case, when calculating the cost of goods available for sale and the cost of ending inventory, an *exact price per unit* is available.

**Specific identification inventory method:** an inventory valuation method that is based on the actual cost of each item available for sale.

---

**HOW TO** Find the ending inventory and the cost of goods sold (COGS) using the specific identification inventory method

1. Find the cost of goods available for sale:

   Cost of goods available for sale = number of units purchased × cost per unit

2. Find the cost of ending inventory:

   Cost of ending inventory = number of units in ending inventory × cost per unit

3. Find the cost of goods sold (COGS):

   Cost of goods sold = cost of goods available for sale − cost of ending inventory

---

**EXAMPLE 1** Use the ending inventory information in Table 17-2 to calculate the cost of goods available for sale using the specific identification method. Then determine the cost of goods sold.

Find the cost of goods available for sale:

$$29(\$8) = \$232 \qquad 18(\$7) = \$126$$
$$9(\$10) = \$\ 90 \qquad 14(\$8) = \$112$$
$$\$232 + \$126 + \$90 + \$112 = \$560$$

**Ending inventory** = 14 + 5 + 3 = **22 items**

Find the cost of ending inventory:

$$14(\$8) = \$112 \qquad 5(\$7) = \$35 \qquad 3(\$10) = \$30$$
$$\$112 + \$35 + \$30 = \$177$$

$$\text{Cost of goods sold} = \text{cost of goods available for sale} - \text{cost of ending inventory}$$
$$= \$560 - \$177$$
$$= \$383$$

**The cost of goods sold is \$383.**

---

### TABLE 17-2
Cost of Goods Available for Sale and the Ending Inventory for 12-inch Battery Clocks

| Date of purchase | Units purchased | Cost per unit | Total cost | Ending inventory |
|---|---|---|---|---|
| Beginning inventory | 29 | $8 | $232 | 14 |
| January 15 | 18 | 7 | 126 | 5 |
| February 4 | 9 | 10 | 90 | 3 |
| March 3 | +14 | 8 | 112 | — |
| **Goods available for sale** | 70 | | $560 | 22 |

## STOP AND CHECK

**1.** Complete the inventory table for the total cost of goods available for sale, cost of ending inventory, and cost of goods sold.

Inventory Table for Gadgets by Marqueta

| Date of purchase | Number of bottle coolers purchased | Cost per unit | Total cost | Ending inventory |
|---|---|---|---|---|
| January 1 inventory | 314 | $ 9 | | 128 |
| February 1 | 200 | $ 8 | | 79 |
| March 1 | 300 | $11 | | 183 |

**2.** Complete the inventory table and find the cost of goods available for sale, cost of ending inventory, and cost of goods sold.

| Date of purchase | Number of plate stands purchased | Cost per unit | Total cost | Ending inventory |
|---|---|---|---|---|
| January 1 inventory | 538 | $2 | | 317 |
| April 1 | 400 | $1.90 | | 17 |
| July 1 | 200 | $2.10 | | 123 |
| October 1 | 500 | $1.90 | | 47 |

**3.** Use the specific inventory method to find the cost of goods available for sale, cost of ending inventory, and cost of goods sold.

| Date of purchase | Number of book bags purchased | Cost per unit | Total cost | Ending inventory |
|---|---|---|---|---|
| February 1 | 389 | $7 | | 117 |
| February 12 | 400 | $6 | | 89 |
| February 25 | 200 | $9 | | 36 |

**4.** Find the cost of ending inventory, cost of goods available for sale, and cost of goods sold using the specific inventory method.

| Date of purchase | Number of pencils purchased | Cost per unit | Total cost | Ending inventory |
|---|---|---|---|---|
| January 1 | 538 | $0.86 | | 115 |
| April 1 | 576 | $0.93 | | 219 |
| July 1 | 360 | $0.95 | | 28 |
| October 1 | 624 | $0.90 | | 107 |

## 2 Use the weighted-average inventory method to find the ending inventory and the cost of goods sold.

**Weighted-average inventory method:** an inventory valuation method that is based on the average unit cost of the goods available for sale.

Another way to place a value on the ending inventory is the **weighted-average inventory method**. The cost of goods available for sale is divided by the number of units available for sale to get the average unit cost. This method takes less time than finding the exact price for each unit. It often is used with goods that are similar in cost and have a relatively stable cost.

> **HOW TO** Find the ending inventory and the cost of goods sold (COGS) using the weighted-average inventory method
>
> 1. Find the cost of goods available for sale:
>
>    Cost of goods available for sale = number of units purchased × cost per unit
>
> 2. Find the average unit cost:
>
>    $$\text{Average unit cost} = \frac{\text{cost of goods available for sale}}{\text{number of units available for sale}}$$
>
> 3. Find the cost of ending inventory:
>
>    Cost of ending inventory = number of units in ending inventory × average unit cost
>
> 4. Find the cost of goods sold (COGS):
>
>    COGS = cost of goods available for sale − cost of ending inventory

**STOP AND CHECK**

1. Use the weighted-average method to complete the inventory table and find the total cost of goods available for sale, cost of ending inventory, and cost of goods sold.

Inventory Table for Gadgets by Marqueta

| Date of purchase | Number of bottle coolers purchased | Cost per unit | Total cost | Ending inventory |
|---|---|---|---|---|
| January 1 inventory | 314 | $ 9 | | 128 |
| February 1 | 200 | $ 8 | | 79 |
| March 1 | 300 | $11 | | 183 |

2. Use the weighted-average method to complete the inventory table and find the cost of goods available for sale, cost of ending inventory, and cost of goods sold.

| Date of purchase | Number of plate stands purchased | Cost per unit | Total cost | Ending inventory |
|---|---|---|---|---|
| January 1 inventory | 538 | $2 | | 317 |
| April 1 | 400 | $1.90 | | 17 |
| July 1 | 200 | $2.10 | | 123 |
| October 1 | 500 | $1.90 | | 47 |

3. Use the weighted-average method to find the cost of goods available for sale, cost of ending inventory, and cost of goods sold.

| Date of purchase | Number of book bags purchased | Cost per unit | Total cost | Ending inventory |
|---|---|---|---|---|
| February 1 | 389 | $7 | | 117 |
| February 12 | 400 | $6 | | 89 |
| February 25 | 200 | $9 | | 36 |

4. Find the cost of ending inventory, cost of goods available for sale, and cost of goods sold using the weighted-average method.

| Date of purchase | Number of pencils purchased | Cost per unit | Total cost | Ending inventory |
|---|---|---|---|---|
| January 1 | 538 | $0.86 | | 115 |
| April 1 | 576 | $0.93 | | 219 |
| July 1 | 360 | $0.95 | | 28 |
| October 1 | 624 | $0.90 | | 107 |

## 3 Use the first-in, first-out (FIFO) inventory method to find the ending inventory and the cost of goods sold.

**FIFO (first-in, first-out) inventory method:** an inventory valuation method in which items sold are assumed to be the oldest items in inventory and the most recently purchased goods are those remaining in the ending inventory.

Many companies, especially those who want the cost of inventory to match replacement costs as closely as possible, use the **FIFO (first-in, first-out) inventory method**. In the FIFO method, the earliest units purchased (the first in) are assumed to be the first units sold (the first out). In this method, the ending inventory is assumed to consist of the latest units purchased. Thus, the cost of the goods available for sale is relatively close to the current cost for purchasing additional items.

---

**HOW TO** Find the ending inventory and the cost of goods sold (COGS) using the first-in, first-out (FIFO) inventory method

1. Find the cost of goods available for sale:

$$\text{Cost of goods available for sale} = \text{number of units purchased} \times \text{cost per unit}$$

2. Find the assigned cost per unit: Assign a cost per unit in the ending inventory by assuming these units were the latest units purchased.
3. Find the cost of ending inventory:

$$\text{Cost of ending inventory} = \text{number of units in ending inventory} \times \text{assigned cost per unit}$$

4. Find the cost of goods sold (COGS):

$$\text{Cost of goods sold} = \text{cost of goods available for sale} - \text{cost of ending inventory}$$

---

**EXAMPLE 1** Use the information from Table 17-2 to find the cost of goods sold using the FIFO method.

Assign a cost per unit in the ending inventory by assuming that these units were the latest units purchased.

There are 22 units in the ending inventory, and by this method they must be the latest units purchased. Count back in the table from the most recently purchased units until you have 22 units.

March 3    14 units at $8 per unit
$22 - 14 = 8$ units left to be assigned

Multiply the cost per unit by the number of units. Add to get the cost of ending inventory.

| | | |
|---|---|---|
| March 3 | 14 units ($8) | = $112 |
| February 4 | 8 units ($10) | = $80 |
| | 22 units | $192 |

$$\text{Cost of goods sold} = \text{cost of goods available for sale} - \text{cost of ending inventory}$$
$$= \$560 - \$192$$
$$= \$368$$

**The cost of goods sold is $368.**

---

 **STOP AND CHECK**

1. Use the FIFO inventory method to complete the inventory table and find the total cost of goods available for sale, cost of ending inventory, and cost of goods sold.

Inventory Table for Gadgets by Marqueta

| Date of purchase | Number of bottle coolers purchased | Cost per unit | Total cost | Ending inventory |
|---|---|---|---|---|
| January 1 inventory | 314 | $9 | | 128 |
| February 1 | 200 | $8 | | 79 |
| March 1 | 300 | $11 | | 183 |

**2.** Use the FIFO inventory method to complete the inventory table and find the cost of goods available for sale, cost of ending inventory, and cost of goods sold.

| Date of purchase | Number of plate stands purchased | Cost per unit | Total cost | Ending inventory |
|---|---|---|---|---|
| January 1 inventory | 538 | $2 | | 317 |
| April 1 | 400 | $1.90 | | 17 |
| July 1 | 200 | $2.10 | | 123 |
| October 1 | 500 | $1.90 | | 47 |

**3.** Use the FIFO inventory method to find the cost of goods available for sale, cost of ending inventory, and cost of goods sold.

| Date of purchase | Number of book bags purchased | Cost per unit | Total cost | Ending inventory |
|---|---|---|---|---|
| February 1 | 389 | $7 | | 117 |
| February 12 | 400 | $6 | | 89 |
| February 25 | 200 | $9 | | 36 |

**4.** Find the cost of ending inventory, cost of goods available for sale, and cost of goods sold using the FIFO inventory method.

| Date of purchase | Number of pencils purchased | Cost per unit | Total cost | Ending inventory |
|---|---|---|---|---|
| January 1 | 538 | $0.86 | | 115 |
| April 1 | 576 | $0.93 | | 219 |
| July 1 | 360 | $0.95 | | 28 |
| October 1 | 624 | $0.90 | | 107 |

## 4 Use the last-in, first-out (LIFO) inventory method to find the ending inventory and the cost of goods sold.

A fourth method for determining the cost of the ending inventory and the cost of goods sold is the **LIFO (last-in, first-out) inventory method**. In this method, the latest units purchased (the last in) are assumed to be the first units sold (the first out). The ending inventory is assumed to consist of the earliest units purchased. The cost of the ending inventory is figured on the cost of the oldest stock. Thus, the difference between the cost of the goods available for sale and the replacement cost for new goods could be significant. Also, the short-term profit on goods sold would be less since the newer, higher-priced goods were sold first. At some later point, when the low-priced goods are sold, the profits will be high.

Even though this method does not follow natural business practices of rotating stock to maintain freshness or quality, there are some economic advantages to using this method under certain conditions.

---

**HOW TO** Find the ending inventory and the cost of goods sold (COGS) using the last-in, first-out (LIFO) inventory method

1. Find the cost of goods available for sale:

    Cost of goods available for sale = number of units purchased × cost per unit

2. Find the assigned cost per unit: Assign a cost per unit in the ending inventory by assuming these units were the earliest units purchased.

3. Find the cost of ending inventory:

    Cost of ending inventory = number of units in ending inventory × assigned cost per unit

4. Find the cost of goods sold (COGS):

    Cost of goods sold = cost of goods available for sale − cost of ending inventory

**EXAMPLE 1** Use the information from Table 17-2 to find the cost of goods sold using the LIFO method.

Assign a cost for each unit in the ending inventory by assuming these units were the earliest units purchased.

There are 22 items in the ending inventory, and by this method they must be the earliest units purchased. Count from the top of the table until you have 22 items. These items are all from beginning inventory.

$$\text{Beginning inventory: 22 items at \$8 per unit}$$

Multiply the cost per unit by the number of units.

$$\text{Cost of ending inventory: } \$8(22) \text{ items} = \$176$$
$$\text{Cost of goods sold} = \text{cost of goods available for sale} - \text{cost of ending inventory}$$
$$= \$560 - \$176$$
$$= \$384$$

**The cost of goods sold is $384.**

Certain types of businesses may experience a severe decline in the value of inventory based on market conditions. For example, over the past decade in some parts of the country, the market value of sports trading cards has declined. In cases such as this, companies that use the weighted average, FIFO, or LIFO methods for valuing inventory may use a method known as the **lower-of-cost-or-market (LCM) rule** to evaluate inventory. The LCM rule compares the market value (current replacement cost) with the cost of each item on hand and the lower amount is used as the inventory value of that item.

 **STOP AND CHECK**

1. Use the LIFO method to complete the inventory table and find the total cost of goods available for sale, cost of ending inventory, and cost of goods sold.

Inventory Table for Gadgets by Marqueta

| Date of purchase | Number of bottle coolers purchased | Cost per unit | Total cost | Ending inventory |
|---|---|---|---|---|
| January 1 inventory | 314 | $9 | | 128 |
| February 1 | 200 | $8 | | 79 |
| March 1 | 300 | $11 | | 183 |

2. Use the LIFO method to complete the inventory table and find the cost of goods available for sale, cost of ending inventory, and cost of goods sold.

| Date of purchase | Number of plate stands purchased | Cost per unit | Total cost | Ending inventory |
|---|---|---|---|---|
| January 1 inventory | 538 | $2 | | 317 |
| April 1 | 400 | $1.90 | | 17 |
| July 1 | 200 | $2.10 | | 123 |
| October 1 | 500 | $1.90 | | 47 |

3. Use the LIFO method to find the cost of goods available for sale, cost of ending inventory, and cost of goods sold.

| Date of purchase | Number of book bags purchased | Cost per unit | Total cost | Ending inventory |
|---|---|---|---|---|
| February 1 | 389 | $7 | | 117 |
| February 12 | 400 | $6 | | 89 |
| February 25 | 200 | $9 | | 36 |

4. Find the cost of ending inventory, cost of goods available for sale, and cost of goods sold using the LIFO method.

| Date of purchase | Number of pencils purchased | Cost per unit | Total cost | Ending inventory |
|---|---|---|---|---|
| January 1 | 538 | $0.86 | | 115 |
| April 1 | 576 | $0.93 | | 219 |
| July 1 | 360 | $0.95 | | 28 |
| October 1 | 624 | $0.90 | | 107 |

## 5 Use the retail inventory method to estimate the ending inventory and the cost of goods sold.

Sometimes businesses do not make monthly or periodic inventories. Instead, they *estimate* the cost of inventory rather than counting goods individually. One method used to estimate inventory is called the **retail inventory method**.

The retail method uses a ratio that compares the cost of goods available for sale to the retail value of those goods. That is, it compares what it costs to buy the goods with what the goods sell for. To use this method to find the cost of goods sold, you also need to know the dollar value of sales. Take note that we refer to the cost of ending inventory as the **ending inventory at cost**, and we refer to the retail value of ending inventory as the **ending inventory at retail**.

### HOW TO Estimate the ending inventory and the cost of goods sold (COGS) using the retail inventory method

1. Find the cost of goods available for sale:

$$\text{Cost of goods available for sale} = \text{number of units purchased} \times \text{cost per unit}$$

2. Find the retail value of goods available for sale.
3. Find the cost ratio:

$$\text{Cost ratio} = \frac{\text{cost of goods available for sale}}{\text{retail value of goods available for sale}}$$

4. Find the ending inventory at retail:

$$\text{Ending inventory at retail} = \text{retail value of goods available for sale} - \text{sales}$$

5. Find the ending inventory at cost:

$$\text{Ending inventory at cost} = \text{ending inventory at retail} \times \text{cost ratio}$$

6. Find the cost of goods sold:

$$\text{Cost of goods sold} = \text{cost of goods available for sale} - \text{ending inventory at cost}$$

or

$$\text{Cost of goods sold} = \text{dollar value of sales} \times \text{cost ratio}$$

The retail inventory method is popular among small businesses, especially businesses that have limited human resources and technology for handling the more complex methods. Another reason for the popularity of this method is that it uses information already being collected for other purposes and does not greatly increase the inventory maintenance workload.

### EXAMPLE 1 Use the information from Table 17-2 and the following retail value information to find the cost of the ending inventory and the cost of goods sold using the retail method.

| Date of purchase | Retail value |
|---|---|
| Beginning inventory | $331 |
| January 15 | 180 |
| February 4 | 129 |
| March 3 | 160 |
| **Goods available for sale** | $800 |
| **Sales** | $487 |

According to Table 17-2, the cost of goods available for sale is $560. Their retail price is $800.

$$\text{Cost ratio} = \frac{\text{cost of goods available for sale}}{\text{retail value of goods available for sale}} = \frac{\$560}{\$800} = 0.7$$

$$\text{Ending inventory at retail} = \text{retail value of goods available for sale} - \text{retail value of sales}$$
$$= \$800 - \$487 = \$313$$
$$\text{Ending inventory at cost} = \text{ending inventory at retail} \times \text{cost ratio}$$
$$= \$313(0.7) = \$219.10$$

$$\text{Cost of goods sold} = \text{dollar value of sales} \times \text{cost ratio}$$
$$= \$487(0.7) = \$340.90$$
$$\text{or}$$

$$= \text{cost of goods available for sale} - \text{ending inventory at cost}$$
$$= \$560.00 - \$219.10$$
$$= \$340.90$$

**The ending inventory at cost is $219.10 and the cost of goods sold is $340.90.**

 **STOP AND CHECK**

1. Use the information in the table to find the cost of ending inventory and the cost of goods sold using the retail inventory method if sales total $5,029.12.

Inventory Table for Gadgets by Marqueta

| Date of purchase | Number of bottle coolers purchased | Cost per unit | Total cost | Ending inventory | Retail value of goods available for sale |
|---|---|---|---|---|---|
| January 1 inventory | 314 | $9 | | 128 | $3,617.28 |
| February 1 | 200 | $8 | | 79 | $2,048 |
| March 1 | 300 | $11 | | 183 | $4,224 |

2. Use the retail inventory method to find the cost of ending inventory and the cost of goods sold for the inventory data in the table if sales for the period total $3,171.32.

| Date of purchase | Number of plate stands purchased | Cost per unit | Total cost | Ending inventory | Retail value of goods available for sale |
|---|---|---|---|---|---|
| January 1 inventory | 538 | $2 | | 317 | $1,554.37 |
| April 1 | 400 | $1.90 | | 17 | $1,100 |
| July 1 | 200 | $2.10 | | 123 | $ 608 |
| October 1 | 500 | $1.90 | | 47 | $1,375 |

3. Use the retail inventory method to find the cost of ending inventory and the cost of goods sold for the inventory data in the table if sales for the period total $7,606.70.

| Date of purchase | Book bags purchased | Cost per unit | Total cost | Ending inventory | Retail value of goods available for sale |
|---|---|---|---|---|---|
| February 1 inventory | 389 | $7 | | 117 | $3,948.35 |
| February 12 | 400 | $6 | | 89 | $3,480 |
| February 25 | 200 | $9 | | 36 | $2,610 |

4. Use the retail inventory method to find the cost of ending inventory and the cost of goods sold for the inventory data in the table if retail sales total $2,436.22.

| Date of purchase | Pencils purchased | Cost per unit | Total cost | Ending inventory | Retail value of goods available for sale |
|---|---|---|---|---|---|
| January 1 inventory | 538 | $0.86 | | 115 | $763.42 |
| April 1 | 576 | $0.93 | | 219 | $883.87 |
| July 1 | 360 | $0.95 | | 28 | $564.30 |
| October 1 | 624 | $0.90 | | 107 | $926.64 |

## 6   Use the gross profit inventory method to estimate the ending inventory and the cost of goods sold.

**Gross profit (margin) inventory method:** a method for estimating the value of inventory that is based on a constant gross profit (margin) rate and net sales.

Another method for estimating inventory for interim reports or for insurance claims is the **gross profit (margin) inventory method**. This method assumes that a company maintains approximately the same gross profit rate from year to year. This method is not used for preparing annual financial statements or calculating income taxes.

1. Find the goods available for sale:

$$\text{Goods available for sale} = \text{beginning inventory} + \text{net purchases}$$

2. Find the estimated cost of goods sold:

$$\text{Estimated cost of goods sold} = \text{net sales} \times \text{complement of percent of gross profit}$$

3. Find the estimated ending inventory:

$$\text{Estimated ending inventory} = \text{goods available for sale} - \text{estimated cost of goods sold}$$

**EXAMPLE 1** Use the inventory report in Table 17-1 and net sales of $487 to estimate inventory with the gross profit method if gross profit on sales is 28%.

$$\text{Beginning inventory} = 29(\$8) = \$232$$
$$\text{Net purchases} = 18(\$7) + 9(\$10) + 14(\$8) = \$328$$

$$\text{Cost of goods available for sale} = \$232 + \$328 = \$560$$

$$\text{Estimated cost of goods sold} = \$487(1 - 0.28)$$
$$= \$487(0.72)$$
$$= \$350.64$$
$$\text{Estimated ending inventory} = \$560 - \$350.64$$
$$= \$209.36$$

Each of the different methods of figuring the value of inventory has advantages and disadvantages, depending on current economic conditions, tax regulations, and so on. However, it is important to know that once a business has selected a method, it must get approval from the Internal Revenue Service to change methods.

This section shows the result of calculating the value of the same inventory by each of the six different methods. Table 17-3 compares the six methods and their results.

**TABLE 17-3**
Summary of Inventory Methods Based on Table 17-2 Data

| Method | Cost of ending inventory | Cost of goods sold | Comment |
|---|---|---|---|
| Specific identification | $177 | $383 | The most accurate method, but also the most time-consuming. |
| Weighted-average | $176 | $384 | Perhaps the easiest to use, but appropriate only when the economy is relatively stable. Radical changes in prices may result in a distorted inventory value. |
| First-in, first-out (FIFO) | $192 | $368 | The value of ending inventory is closely related to the current market price of the goods. During high inflation, this method produces the highest income. |
| Last-in, first-out (LIFO) | $176 | $384 | The value of ending inventory may vary significantly from the current market price of the goods. During high inflation, this method produces lower income, which results in a lower income tax for the company. |
| Retail | $219.10 | $340.90 | Cost of ending inventory is based on the retail value and the net sales. Since the information needed for using this method is easily accessible, this is one of the most efficient methods. |
| Gross profit | $209.36 | $350.64 | Cost of ending inventory is based on estimating the cost of goods sold using the gross profit percentage. |

**EXAMPLE 2** The Sports Card Department of The 7th Inning bases its prices for vintage cards on the most recent edition of an appropriate pricing guide, such as *Beckett's Almanac of Baseball Cards and Collectibles*. These guides are distributed annually and prices vary significantly from year to year. What method of inventory valuation should be used?

| What You Know | What You Are Looking For | Solution Plan |
|---|---|---|
| Prices change as a new pricing guide is available | An appropriate method for determining the value of inventory | Examine the advantages and disadvantages of each method |

**Solution**

| | |
|---|---|
| Specific identification: | too many individual cards to keep up with |
| Weighted-average: | cost of cards very unstable |
| FIFO and LIFO: | decrease in quality not an issue, some cards increase in value while others decrease, inflation not an issue |
| Retail: | a good choice for annual financial statements |
| Gross profit: | not acceptable for official reporting, but a good choice for interim reports and insurance claims |

**Conclusion**

**The retail inventory method is the most practical for the official records of the business.**

---

## TIP

**Let the Title Be Your Guide**

The title of each method for finding the cost of goods sold contains key words to help you remember the procedures.

| Method | Clue |
|---|---|
| • Specific identification | *Specific* cost to be determined. |
| • Weighted-average | Varying costs to be *averaged.* |
| • FIFO | Cost of *oldest* merchandise is used. |
| • LIFO | Cost of *most recently purchased* merchandise is used. |
| • Retail | COGS is calculated from *retail value,* and the ratio of retail value to cost is shown. |
| • Gross profit | Percentage of *profit* is used. |

---

 **STOP AND CHECK**

1. Use the information in the table to estimate ending inventory value using the gross profit method if gross profit on sales is 36% and net sales are $5,815.

   Inventory Table for Gadgets by Marqueta

   | Date of purchase | Number of bottle coolers purchased | Cost per unit |
   |---|---|---|
   | January 1 inventory | 314 | $9 |
   | February 1 | 200 | $8 |
   | March 1 | 300 | $11 |

2. Use the gross profit method to estimate the ending inventory for the inventory data in the table if gross profit on sales is 42% and net sales are $2,058.

   | Date of purchase | Number of plate stands purchased | Cost per unit |
   |---|---|---|
   | January 1 inventory | 538 | $2 |
   | April 1 | 400 | $1.90 |
   | July 1 | 200 | $2.10 |
   | October 1 | 500 | $1.90 |

**3.** Use the gross profit method to estimate the cost of ending inventory for the inventory data in the table if the gross profit is 40% on sales and net sales is $4,283.

| Date of purchase | Number of book bags purchased | Cost per unit |
|---|---|---|
| February 1 inventory | 389 | $7 |
| February 12 | 400 | $6 |
| February 25 | 200 | $9 |

**4.** Use the gross profit method to estimate the cost of ending inventory for the inventory data in the table if gross profit is 56% on sales and net sales is $2,048.

| Date of purchase | Number of pencils purchased | Cost per unit |
|---|---|---|
| January 1 inventory | 538 | $0.86 |
| April 1 | 576 | $0.93 |
| July 1 | 360 | $0.95 |
| October 1 | 624 | $0.90 |

## 17-1 SECTION EXERCISES

### SKILL BUILDERS

*Use the specific identification inventory method for Exercises 1–6.*

**1.** Complete Inventory Table A for total cost of purchases, goods available for sale, cost of goods available for sale, and ending inventory. Total retail value is calculated in Exercise 21.

Inventory Table A

| Date of purchase | Units purchased | Cost per unit | Total cost | Retail price per unit | Total retail value |
|---|---|---|---|---|---|
| Beginning inventory | 42 | $850 | | $975 | |
| February 5 | 21 | $1,760 | | $2,115 | |
| February 19 | 17 | $965 | | $1,206 | |
| March 3 | 28 | $480 | | $600 | |
| **Goods available for sale** | | | | | |
| **Units sold** | 74 | | | | |
| **Ending inventory** | | | | | |

**2.** Cost Table A shows a breakdown of the ending inventory from Inventory Table A according to various costs per unit. Complete Cost Table A.

Cost Table A

| Cost per unit | Number of units on hand | Total cost |
|---|---|---|
| $850 | 9 | |
| $1,760 | 11 | |
| $965 | 8 | |
| $480 | 6 | |
| **Ending inventory** | | |

**3.** Use Inventory Table A and Cost Table A to calculate the cost of goods sold.

**4.** Complete Inventory Table B for total cost of purchases, goods available for sale, cost of goods available for sale, and ending inventory. Total retail value is calculated in Exercise 24.

Inventory Table B

| Date of purchase | Units purchased | Cost per unit | Total cost | Retail price per unit | Total retail value |
|---|---|---|---|---|---|
| Beginning inventory | 96 | $12 | | $18 | |
| April 12 | 23 | $9 | | $13 | |
| May 8 | 15 | $11 | | $17 | |
| June 2 | 37 | $15 | | $21 | |
| **Goods available for sale** | | | | | |
| **Units sold** | 89 | | | | |
| **Ending inventory** | | | | | |

**5.** Cost Table B breaks down the ending inventory from Inventory Table B. Complete Cost Table B.

Cost Table B

| Cost per unit | Number of units on hand | Total cost |
|---|---|---|
| $12 | 43 | |
| $9 | 11 | |
| $11 | 7 | |
| $15 | 21 | |
| **Ending inventory** | | |

**6.** Use Inventory Table B and Cost Table B to calculate the cost of goods sold.

*Use the weighted-average inventory method for Exercises 7–12.*

**7.** Calculate the average unit cost for Inventory Table A.

**8.** Calculate the cost of ending inventory for Inventory Table A.

**9.** Calculate the cost of goods sold for Inventory Table A.

**10.** Calculate the average unit cost for Inventory Table B.

**11.** Calculate the cost of ending inventory for Inventory Table B.

**12.** Calculate the cost of goods sold for Inventory Table B.

*Use the first-in, first-out inventory method for Exercises 13–16.*

**13.** Determine the unit cost and cost of ending inventory for units in ending inventory for Inventory Table A.

**14.** Find the cost of goods sold for Inventory Table A.

**15.** Determine the unit costs for units in ending inventory for Inventory Table B.

**16.** Find the cost of goods sold for Inventory Table B.

*Use the last-in, first-out inventory method for Exercises 17–20.*

**17.** Determine the unit costs for units in ending inventory for Inventory Table A.

**18.** Find the cost of goods sold for Inventory Table A.

**19.** Determine the unit cost for units in ending inventory for Inventory Table B.

**20.** Find the cost of goods sold for Inventory Table B.

## APPLICATIONS

*Use the retail inventory method for Exercises 21–26.*

**21.** Complete Inventory Table A for total retail price of purchases and retail price of goods available for sale.

**22.** Find the cost ratio for Inventory Table A.

**23.** Find the cost of goods sold if sales total $78,982 for Table A.

**24.** Complete Inventory Table B for total retail price of purchases and retail price of goods available for sale.

**25.** Find the cost ratio for Inventory Table B.

**26.** Find the cost of goods sold if sales total $1,691 for Table B.

**27.** Use Inventory Table A and the gross profit inventory method to estimate the ending inventory and cost of goods sold if a 30% gross profit is realized on sales and net sales are $115,440.

**28.** Use Inventory Table B and the gross profit inventory method to estimate the ending inventory and cost of goods sold if a 54% gross profit on sales is realized and net sales are $1,644.72.

## LEARNING OUTCOMES

1 Find the inventory turnover rate.
2 Find the department overhead based on sales or floor space.

**Inventory turnover:** the frequency with which the inventory is sold and replaced.

Businesses keep careful records of their **inventory turnover**, which is how often the inventory of merchandise is sold and replaced. The rate of inventory turnover varies greatly according to the type of business. A restaurant, for example, should have a high turnover rate but probably carries a small inventory of goods. A furniture company, on the other hand, normally keeps a larger inventory but has a relatively low turnover. Another term that retailers use is *sell through* to discuss the rate inventory is turned over.

Knowing the turnover of a business can be useful in making future decisions and in analyzing business practices. For example, a low turnover rate may indicate some or all of the following:

1. Too much capital (company's money) is tied up in inventory.
2. Customers are dissatisfied with merchandise choice, quality, or price.
3. Merchandise is not properly marketed.

On the other hand, a high turnover rate may indicate some or all of the following:

1. Inventory is too small for the demand, resulting in a loss in sales because merchandise is "out of stock."
2. Merchandise is highly desirable.
3. Merchandise prices may be significantly lower than the competition's prices.

## 1 Find the inventory turnover rate.

Lending institutions use the turnover rate as one of the factors considered in making business loans. There are two ways to calculate turnover rate: *at cost* and *at retail*. Cost means the price at which the company buys the merchandise. Retail means the price at which the company sells the merchandise. Turnover rate can cover any period of time, but is usually calculated monthly, semiannually (twice a year), or yearly.

---

### HOW TO  Find the turnover rate at cost

1. Find the average inventory at cost:

$$\text{Average inventory at cost} = \frac{\text{beginning inventory at cost} + \text{ending inventory at cost}}{2}$$

2. Divide the cost of goods sold by the average inventory at cost:

$$\text{Turnover rate at cost} = \frac{\text{cost of goods sold}}{\text{average inventory at cost}}$$

---

**Inventory turnover ratio:** another term for the inventory turnover rate.

The formula for finding inventory turnover rate is often referred to as the **inventory turnover ratio**. The ratio shows the number of times a business's inventory has been sold during a specified period. For example, an inventory turnover of 3 to 1 for one year means that a store sold three times the value of the average inventory during the year. Its "sell through" rate is 3 to 1. Another way of saying this is that the merchandise has been sold and replaced three times during the year.

**EXAMPLE 1**   Ann's Dress Shop had net sales of $52,500 at cost for the month of September. The cost of inventory at the beginning of September was $15,980 and at the end of September was $18,000. Find the average inventory at cost and the turnover rate at cost for September.

$$\text{Average inventory at cost} = \frac{\text{beginning inventory at cost} + \text{ending inventory at cost}}{2}$$
$$= \frac{\$15,980 + \$18,000}{2}$$
$$= \frac{\$33,980}{2}$$
$$= \$16,990$$

$$\text{Turnover rate at cost} = \frac{\text{cost of goods sold}}{\text{average inventory at cost}}$$

$$= \frac{\$52,500}{\$16,990}$$

$$\text{Turnover rate at cost} = 3 \text{ (rounded)}$$

**The average inventory at cost is \$16,990 and the turnover rate at cost is three times.**

---

## HOW TO    Find the turnover rate at retail

1. Find the average inventory at retail:

$$\text{Average inventory at retail} = \frac{\text{beginning inventory at retail} + \text{ending inventory at retail}}{2}$$

2. Divide the sales by the average inventory at retail:

$$\text{Turnover rate at retail} = \frac{\text{sales}}{\text{average inventory at retail}}$$

---

## EXAMPLE 2

A local Hungarian restaurant had net sales of \$32,000 for the month of June. The retail price of inventory at the beginning of June was \$7,000, and at the end of June was \$9,000. Find the average inventory at retail and the turnover rate at retail for June.

$$\text{Average inventory at retail} = \frac{\text{beginning inventory at retail} + \text{ending inventory at retail}}{2}$$

$$= \frac{\$7,000 + \$9,000}{2} = \frac{\$16,000}{2} = \$8,000$$

$$\text{Turnover rate at retail} = \frac{\text{net sales}}{\text{average inventory at retail}}$$

$$= \frac{\$32,000}{\$8,000}$$

$$= 4$$

**The turnover rate at retail is four times in the month of June.**

Lending institutions examine the turnover rate when determining the risk of a business repaying a loan. An acceptable turnover rate varies based on the type of merchandise and whether the business is expanding. A high turnover rate indicates a good cash flow and is desirable unless sales are lost due to out-of-stock merchandise.

In general, a rate of less than two to three times per year is a reason for concern unless the company is undergoing extensive expansion that involves expanding its inventory. Three to four times per year is usually judged to be a good turnover rate for nonperishable or nonseasonal inventory goods unless the average turnover for the particular industry is higher.

---

## TIP

**What Does the Inventory Turnover Ratio Really Mean?**

The ratio has little meaning if it is not compared to another ratio. Most companies compare it to industry figures for similar businesses. Using this comparison, a business can determine how well it is doing. Comparing a company's inventory turnover ratio with industry ratios is sometimes called **benchmarking.**

**Benchmarking:** comparing a company's performance, such as inventory turnover ratio, with industry standards or with a similar company's performance.

1. Brubaker's in the 7th Inning had net sales of $71,817 at cost for November. The cost of inventory on November 1 was $13,217, and on November 30, the inventory was $14,067. Find the average inventory at cost and the turnover rate at cost for September.

2. The Frame Shop in the 7th Inning had net sales of $48,206 at cost for June. The cost of inventory on June 1 was $8,915, and on June 30, the inventory was $9,205. Find the average inventory at cost and the turnover rate at cost for June.

3. The Indian Restaurant had net sales of $74,508 for June. The retail inventory on June 1 was $5,972, and on June 30, the retail inventory was $7,291. Find the average inventory at retail and the turnover rate at retail for June.

4. Square Books Jr had net sales of $107,582 for August. On August 1, the inventory at retail was $35,169, and on August 31, the inventory at retail was $28,437. Find the average inventory at retail and the turnover rate at retail for August.

## 2 Find the department overhead based on sales or floor space.

A business encounters many expenses other than buying stock (merchandise to sell) and equipment. It must pay salaries, rent or mortgages, utilities, taxes, and insurance fees. It must buy office supplies and keep up equipment. These expenses, along with depreciation, are called **overhead**. The ratio between overhead and sales can say much about a firm's efficiency. Overhead is another factor that lending institutions use in making decisions about business loans.

In addition, companies sometimes need to know not only how much total overhead expenses are but also the overhead expense of each department so that excessive overhead expenses of certain departments can be reduced to increase profits. There are many methods of calculating overhead by department. Two of the most widely used methods are according to sales and according to floor space. Other ways of calculating overhead are similar to these and apply a similar problem-solving approach.

Using the sales method, the company determines what fraction of the total sales was made by each department. This department sales fraction is multiplied by the total overhead to find the overhead for each department.

> **Overhead:** depreciation and expenses required for the operation of a business, such as salaries, rent or mortgages, utilities, office supplies, taxes, insurance, and maintenance of equipment.

> **HOW TO** Find the department overhead based on sales
>
> 1. Find the total sales: Add the sales of individual departments.
> 2. Find the department sales rate:
>
> $$\text{Department sales rate} = \frac{\text{department sales}}{\text{total sales}}$$
>
> 3. Find the overhead assigned to the department by sales:
>
> $$\text{Department overhead} = \text{department sales rate} \times \text{total overhead}$$

**EXAMPLE 1** Just For Fun's overhead totaled $8,000 during one month. Find the overhead for each department, based on total sales, if the store had the following monthly sales by department: cameras, $5,000; jewelry, $8,200; sporting goods, $6,700; silver, $9,200; and toys, $12,000.

Organize the facts and results of calculations in a table.

| Department | Sales | Sales rate[*] | Overhead[*] |
|---|---|---|---|
| Cameras | $5,000 | $\dfrac{\$5,000}{\$41,100}$ or 0.1216545 | 0.1216545($8,000) or $ 973.24 |
| Jewelry | $8,200 | $\dfrac{\$8,200}{\$41,100}$ or 0.1995134 | 0.1995134($8,000) or $1,596.11 |
| Sporting goods | $6,700 | $\dfrac{\$6,700}{\$41,100}$ or 0.1630170 | 0.1630170($8,000) or $1,304.14 |
| Silver | $9,200 | $\dfrac{\$9,200}{\$41,100}$ or 0.2238443 | 0.2238443($8,000) or $1,790.75 |
| Toys | $12,000 | $\dfrac{\$12,000}{\$41,100}$ or 0.2919708 | 0.2919708($8,000) or $2,335.77 |
| Total | $41,100 | $\dfrac{\$41,100}{\$41,100}$ or 1.000000 | $8,000.01 |

*Full calculator values are not shown but are used for all calculations.

---

**TIP**

**Making Periodic Checks of Calculations**

When an example requires several calculations, it is helpful to periodically check your work rather than checking only the final result.

*Interim Check:* The total of the sales rates should be 1 or very close to 1.
*Final Check:* The sum of the amounts of overhead for each department should be the total overhead or very close to the total overhead.

In the preceding example, the interim check is exactly 1 and the final check is 1 cent more than the total overhead as a result of rounding.

---

**TIP**

**Using Conversion Factors**

In both methods for allocating overhead by department, a value by department is divided by a total value and multiplied by the total overhead. A conversion factor can be determined by making the calculations with the values that stay the same. The total sales and overhead are the same for all departments.

$$\frac{\text{Department sales}}{\text{Total sales}} = \text{department sales} \times \frac{1}{\text{total sales}}$$

In the series of calculations,

$$\text{Department sales} \times \frac{1}{\text{total sales}} \times \text{overhead}$$

the one value that changes is department sales. A conversion factor can be made by finding

$$\frac{1}{\text{total sales}} \times \text{overhead}$$

In Example 1, the conversion factor would be

$$\frac{1}{\$41,100}(\$8,000) = \frac{\$8,000}{\$41,100} = 0.1946472019$$

Use this conversion factor and the calculator memory function to recalculate the overhead by department in the example.

A computer spreadsheet can also be used to generate the table.

| Department | Sales | Conversion factor | Overhead |
|---|---|---|---|
| Cameras | $5,000 | 0.1946472019 | $973.24 |
| Jewelry | $8,200 | 0.1946472019 | $1,596.11 |
| Sporting goods | $6,700 | 0.1946472019 | $1,304.14 |
| Silver | $9,200 | 0.1946472019 | $1,790.75 |
| Toys | $12,000 | 0.1946472019 | $2,335.77 |
| Total | $41,100 | 0.1946472019 | $8,000.01 |

Another way to distribute overhead is according to the amount of floor space each department occupies. This method is similar to the sales method. A rate for each department is calculated, this time by dividing the department's floor space by the total floor space. To find the overhead for the department, multiply the department floor-space rate by the total overhead.

## HOW TO  Find department overhead based on floor space

1. Find the total floor space: Add the square feet of floor space in each department.
2. Find the department floor space rate:

$$\text{Department floor space rate} = \frac{\text{floor space in department}}{\text{total floor space}}$$

3. Find the overhead assigned to the department by floor space:

$$\text{Department overhead by floor space} = \text{department floor space rate} \times \text{total overhead}$$

## EXAMPLE 2

The Super Store assigns overhead to its various departments according to the floor space used by each department. The store's total overhead is $25,000. Find the overhead for each department if each department occupies the following square feet: junior department, 3,000; women's wear, 4,000; men's wear, 3,500; children's wear, 3,000; china and silver, 2,500; housewares, 2,500; linens, 2,000; toys, 1,500; carpets, 3,500; and cosmetics, 500. Round the *final* answers to the nearest cent if necessary.

Calculator steps for Junior department:

3000 ÷ 26000 × 25000 ⟹ 2884.615385

Use similar calculator steps for all departments.

Organize the information and results in a table. This table could also be generated using a spreadsheet.

| Department | Floor space in square feet | Floor space rate* | Overhead* |
|---|---|---|---|
| Junior department | 3,000 | $\frac{3,000}{26,000}$ or 0.115385 | 0.115385($25,000) or $2,884.62 |
| Women's wear | 4,000 | $\frac{4,000}{26,000}$ or 0.153846 | 0.153846($25,000) or $3,846.15 |
| Men's wear | 3,500 | $\frac{3,500}{26,000}$ or 0.134615 | 0.134615($25,000) or $3,365.38 |
| Children's wear | 3,000 | $\frac{3,000}{26,000}$ or 0.115385 | 0.115385($25,000) or $2,884.62 |
| China and silver | 2,500 | $\frac{2,500}{26,000}$ or 0.096154 | 0.096154($25,000) or $2,403.85 |
| Housewares | 2,500 | $\frac{2,500}{26,000}$ or 0.096154 | 0.096154($25,000) or $2,403.85 |
| Linens | 2,000 | $\frac{2,000}{26,000}$ or 0.076923 | 0.076923($25,000) or $1,923.08 |
| Toys | 1,500 | $\frac{1,500}{26,000}$ or 0.057692 | 0.057692($25,000) or $1,442.31 |

| | | | |
|---|---|---|---|
| Carpets | 3,500 | $\dfrac{3,500}{26,000}$ or 0.134615 | 0.134615($25,000) or $3,365.38 |
| Cosmetics | 500 | $\dfrac{500}{26,000}$ or 0.019231 | 0.019231($25,000) or $480.77 |
| **Total** | 26,000 | $\dfrac{26,000}{26,000}$ or 1.000000 | $25,000.01 |

*Full calculator values are not shown but are used for all calculations.

The conversion-factor method could also be used in the preceding example. The conversion factor would be

$$\frac{1}{26,000}(\$25,000) = \frac{\$25,000}{26,000} = \$0.9615384615$$

 **STOP AND CHECK**

1. The 7th Inning paid $12,516 in total overhead for May. Find the overhead for each department based on each department's sales: Memorabilia, $3,816; Brubaker's Restaurant, $32,167; Engraving, $67,015; and Frame Shop, $17,816.

2. Home Depot had $25,116 in total overhead for March. Find the overhead for each department based on sales: Paint, $17,815; Lighting, $19,583; Lumber, $58,982; Plumbing, $38,917; Tiles and Flooring, $27,895; Chemicals, $32,518; Home and Garden, $62,906.

3. Square Books assigned overhead of $12,196 based on floor space. Textbooks uses 100 square feet, casebound travel and fiction uses 120 square feet, paperbacks uses 80 square feet, children's books uses 130 square feet, electronic media uses 140 square feet, and the coffee shop uses 300 square feet. Allocate the overhead by floor space.

4. Oxford Floral allocated overhead of $7,815 by floor space. What is the overhead for each department? Floor space: fresh flowers, 1,000 square feet; pottery, 300 square feet; fine china, 700 square feet; gifts, 800 square feet.

## 17-2 EXERCISES

### SKILL BUILDERS

1. Rutledge Equipment Company had net sales of $335,000. The beginning inventory at retail was $122,000 and the ending inventory at retail was $155,000. Find the turnover rate at retail.

2. The 7th Inning Baseball Card Shop had a beginning inventory cost of $59,800. The ending inventory cost was $48,500. If the cost of the goods sold during the period was $117,500, find the turnover rate at cost.

3. University Trailer Sales had a beginning inventory cost of $38,440. The ending inventory cost was $52,833. The cost of merchandise sold during the period was $184,302. Find the turnover rate based on cost.

4. Jeremiah Williams, owner of The Lamb Shop, needed to calculate the turnover rate based on retail prices. Net sales of $225,294 were recorded for a recent year. The retail price of inventory at the beginning of the year was $89,023 and was $68,392 at the end of the year. Find the turnover rate at retail for the year.

## APPLICATIONS

**5.** Overhead for one month at the Allimore Department Store totaled $6,000. Find the overhead for each department, based on sales, if the store had the following monthly sales by department: toys, $4,000; appliances, $6,600; children's clothing, $6,800; books, $4,600; and furniture, $8,400.

**6.** Carlisle's Stock Trailer Sales had overhead expenses that totaled $4,932 during one month. The business had the following departmental sales for the month: cattle trailers, $8,523; utility trailers, $6,201; boat trailers, $2,932; parts, $1,392. Find the overhead for each department, based on sales.

**7.** Dale Crosby's Gift Shop had overhead expenses totaling $2,732 during the month of August. The business recorded departmental sales for the month of August as follows: china, $3,923; silver, $8,923; crystal, $2,932; linens, $1,923; new gifts, $6,291; antiques, $8,923. Use this information to find the overhead for each department based on sales.

8. Savemore Discount Clothing Store assigns overhead to its various departments according to the floor space used by each department. The store's total monthly overhead is $15,800. Find the overhead for each department using the following square feet for each department: women's clothing, 2,000; men's clothing, 1,200; children's clothing, 2,500. Round *final* answers to the nearest cent if necessary.

9. Hughes' Trailer Manufacturer assigns overhead to its departments according to the floor space used by each department. The company's total monthly overhead for the month of April is $7,832. Find the overhead for each department using the following square feet for each department: welding bay, 2,100; paint shop, 1,950; axles and steel storage, 780; flooring lumber, 380; office space, 500.

10. Make a conversion factor for the data in Example 2 (p. 602) and use the conversion factor to calculate the overhead for each department.

## Learning Outcomes

### Section 17-1

**1** Use the specific identification inventory method to find the ending inventory and the cost of goods sold. (p. 585)

## What to Remember with Examples

1.  Find the cost of goods available for sale:

    Cost of goods available for sale = number of units purchased × cost per unit

2.  Find the cost of ending inventory:

    Cost of ending inventory = number of units in ending inventory × cost per unit

3.  Find the cost of goods sold (COGS):

    Cost of goods sold = cost of goods available for sale − cost of ending inventory

Use the specific identification method to find the cost of goods available for sale, the cost of ending inventory, and the cost of goods sold.

| Date of purchase | Units purchased | Cost per unit | Total cost |
|---|---|---|---|
| Beginning inventory | 17 | $10 | $170 |
| January 8 | 25 | $8 | $200 |
| February 3 | 22 | $12 | $264 |
| March 5 | 20 | $8 | $160 |
| **Goods available for sale** | | | $794 |

| Cost per unit | Units | Total cost |
|---|---|---|
| $10 | 12 | $120 |
| $8 | 19 | $152 |
| $12 | 11 | $132 |
| $8 | 16 | $128 |
| **Ending inventory** | | $532 |

Cost of goods sold = cost of goods available for sale
− cost of ending inventory = $794 − $532 = $262

**2** Use the weighted-average inventory method to find the ending inventory and the cost of goods sold. (p. 586).

1.  Find the cost of goods available for sale:

    Cost of goods available for sale = number of units purchased × cost per unit

2.  Find the average unit cost:

    $$\text{Average unit cost} = \frac{\text{cost of goods available for sale}}{\text{number of units available for sale}}$$

3.  Find the cost of ending inventory:

    Cost of ending inventory = number of units in ending inventory × average unit cost

4.  Find the cost of goods sold:

    Cost of goods sold = cost of goods available for sale − cost of ending inventory

Find the average unit cost using the following table:

| Date of purchase | Units purchased | Cost per unit | Total cost |
|---|---|---|---|
| Beginning inventory | 18 | $18 | $324 |
| April 6 | 25 | $19 | $475 |
| May 4 | 26 | $12 | $312 |
| June 9 | 22 | $8 | $176 |
| **Goods available for sale** | 91 | | $1,287 |

$$\text{Average unit cost} = \frac{\$1,287}{91} = \$14.14$$

Now find the cost of ending inventory and the cost of goods sold if the ending inventory is 50 units.

$$\text{Cost of ending inventory} = 50(\$14.14) = \$707$$
$$\text{Cost of goods sold} = \$1,287 - \$707 = \$580$$

**3** Use the first-in, first-out (FIFO) inventory method to find the ending inventory and the cost of goods sold. (p. 588)

1. Find the cost of goods available for sale:

   $$\text{Cost of goods available for sale} = \text{number of units purchased} \times \text{cost per unit}$$

2. Find the assigned cost per unit: Assign a cost per unit in the ending inventory by assuming these units were the latest units purchased.

3. Find the cost of ending inventory:

   $$\text{Cost of ending inventory} = \text{number of units in ending inventory} \times \text{assigned cost per unit}$$

4. Find the cost of goods sold:

   $$\text{Cost of goods sold} = \text{cost of goods available for sale} - \text{cost of ending inventory}$$

Find the cost of goods sold and the cost of ending inventory if 465 units are in ending inventory.

| Date of purchase | Units purchased | Cost per unit | Total cost |
|---|---|---|---|
| Beginning inventory | 222 | $10 | $2,220 |
| January 15 | 142 | $12 | $1,704 |
| February 5 | 134 | $15 | $2,010 |
| March 2 | 141 | $24 | $3,384 |
| **Goods available for sale** | 639 | | $9,318 |

Units sold = 639 − 465 = 174

| Date of purchase | Number of units in ending inventory | Cost per unit | Total cost |
|---|---|---|---|
| Beginning inventory | 48 (222 − 174) | $10 | $480 |
| January 15 | 142 | $12 | $1,704 |
| February 5 | 134 | $15 | $2,010 |
| March 2 | 141 | $24 | $3,384 |
| **Ending inventory** | 465 | | $7,578 |

Cost of goods sold = $9,318 − $7,578 = $1,740

**4** Use the last-in, first-out (LIFO) inventory method to find the ending inventory and the cost of goods sold. (p. 589)

1. Find the cost of goods available for sale:

   $$\text{Cost of goods available for sale} = \text{number of units purchased} \times \text{cost per unit}$$

2. Find the assigned cost per unit: Assign a cost per unit in the ending inventory by assuming these units were the earliest units purchased.

3. Find the cost of ending inventory:

   $$\text{Cost of ending inventory} = \text{number of units in ending inventory} \times \text{assigned cost per unit}$$

4. Find the cost of goods sold:

   $$\text{Cost of goods sold} = \text{cost of goods available for sale} - \text{cost of ending inventory}$$

Find the cost of goods sold and the cost of ending inventory if 282 units are in ending inventory.

| Date of purchase | Units purchased | Cost per unit | Total cost |
|---|---|---|---|
| Beginning inventory | 111 | $10 | $1,110 |
| April 12 | 343 | $12 | $4,116 |
| May 8 | 191 | $9 | $1,719 |
| June 10 | 106 | $24 | $2,544 |
| **Goods available for sale** | 751 | | $9,489 |

Units sold = 751 − 282 = 469

Units purchased: May 8 + June 10 = 191 + 106 = 297 units

469 − 297 = 172 units from April 12

| Date of purchase | Units in ending inventory | Cost per unit | Total cost |
|---|---|---|---|
| Beginning inventory | 111 | $10 | $1,110 |
| April 12 | 171 (343 − 172) | $12 | $2,052 |
| **Ending inventory** | 282 | | $3,162 |

Cost of goods sold = $9,489 − $3,162 = $6,327

**5** Use the retail inventory method to estimate the ending inventory and the cost of goods sold. (p. 591)

**1.** Find the cost of goods available for sale:

Cost of goods available for sale = number of units purchased × cost per unit

**2.** Find the retail value of goods available for sale.
**3.** Find the cost ratio:

$$\text{Cost ratio} = \frac{\text{cost of goods available for sale}}{\text{retail value of goods available for sale}}$$

**4.** Find the ending inventory at retail:

Ending inventory at retail = retail value of goods available for sale − sales

**5.** Find the ending inventory at cost:

Ending inventory at cost = ending inventory at retail × cost ratio

**6.** Find the cost of goods sold:

Cost of goods sold = cost of goods available for sale − ending inventory at cost

OR

Cost of goods sold = dollar value of sales × cost ratio

Find the cost of goods sold and the cost of ending inventory.

| | Cost | Retail |
|---|---|---|
| Beginning inventory | $4,824 | $6,030 |
| Purchases | $872 | $1,090 |
| **Goods available for sale** | $5,696 | $7,120 |
| **Sales** | | $2,464 |
| Ending inventory | | $4,656 |

$$\text{Cost ratio} = \frac{\$5,696}{\$7,120} = 0.8$$

Ending inventory at cost = $4,656(0.8) = $3,724.80
Cost of goods sold = $5,696 − $3,724.80 = $1,971.20

**6** Use the gross profit inventory method to estimate the ending inventory and the cost of goods sold. (p. 592)

**1.** Find the goods available for sale:

Goods available for sale = beginning inventory + net purchases

**2.** Find the estimated cost of goods sold:

Estimated cost of goods sold = net sales × complement of percent of gross profit

**3.** Find the estimated ending inventory:

Estimated ending inventory = goods available for sale − estimated cost of goods sold

Estimate the cost of goods sold and the cost of ending inventory. Net sales for the period are $4,395 and gross profit on sales is 30%.

| Date of purchase | Units purchased | Cost per unit |
|---|---|---|
| Beginning inventory | 47 | $12 |
| March 1 | 216 | $12 |
| March 12 | 288 | $10 |
| March 31 | 360 | $9 |

Beginning inventory $= 47(\$12) = \$564$
Net purchases $= 216(\$12) + 288(\$10) + 360(\$9) = \$8,712$
Cost of goods available for sale $= \$564 + \$8,712 = \$9,276$

$$\begin{aligned} \text{Estimated cost of goods sold} &= \$4,395(1 - 0.30) \\ &= \$4,395(0.7) \\ &= \$3,076.50 \end{aligned}$$

$$\begin{aligned} \text{Estimated ending inventory} &= \$9,276 - \$3,076.50 \\ &= \$6,199.50 \end{aligned}$$

## Section 17-2

**1** Find the inventory turnover rate. (p. 598)

**Find the turnover rate at cost.**

1. Find the average inventory at cost:

$$\text{Average inventory at cost} = \frac{\text{beginning inventory at cost} + \text{ending inventory at cost}}{2}$$

2. Divide the cost of goods sold by the average inventory at cost:

$$\text{Turnover rate at cost} = \frac{\text{cost of goods sold}}{\text{average inventory at cost}}$$

**Find the turnover rate at retail.**

1. Find the average inventory at retail:

$$\text{Average inventory at retail} = \frac{\text{beginning inventory at retail} + \text{ending inventory at retail}}{2}$$

2. Divide the sales by the average inventory at retail:

$$\text{Turnover rate at retail} = \frac{\text{sales}}{\text{average inventory at retail}}$$

A store had net sales of $10,000 ($5,000 cost) with a beginning inventory of $5,000 retail ($2,500 cost) and an ending inventory of $6,000 retail ($3,000 cost). Find the turnover rate at cost and at retail.

$$\text{Average inventory at cost} = \frac{\$2,500 + \$3,000}{2} = \$2,750$$

$$\text{Turnover rate at cost} = \frac{\$5,000}{\$2,750} = 1.818182$$

$$\text{Average inventory at retail} = \frac{\$5,000 + \$6,000}{2} = \$5,500$$

$$\text{Turnover at retail} = \frac{\$10,000}{\$5,500} = 1.818182$$

**2** Find the department overhead based on sales or floor space. (p. 600)

**Find the department overhead based on sales:**

1. Find the total sales: Add the sales of individual departments.
2. Find the department sales rate:

$$\text{Department sales rate} = \frac{\text{department sales}}{\text{total sales}}$$

3. Find the overhead assigned to the department by sales:

$$\text{Department overhead} = \text{department sales rate} \times \text{total overhead}$$

Make a table to show the overhead by departments if overhead is assigned based on total sales and the store had the following monthly sales by department: paint, $5,000; lumber, $6,200; wall coverings, $3,200; plumbing, $3,200; and electrical, $1,500. Overhead expenses during the month are $1,780.

Multiply each department's sales rate by the total overhead to find the overhead for each department.

| Department | Sales | Sales rate | Overhead |
|---|---|---|---|
| Paint | $ 5,000 | $\dfrac{\$5,000}{\$19,100}$ or 0.2617801047 | 0.2617801047($1,780) = $465.97 |
| Lumber | $ 6,200 | $\dfrac{\$6,200}{\$19,100}$ or 0.3246073298 | 0.3246073298($1,780) = $577.80 |
| Wall coverings | $ 3,200 | $\dfrac{\$3,200}{\$19,100}$ or 0.167539267 | 0.167539267($1,780) = $298.22 |
| Plumbing | $ 3,200 | $\dfrac{\$3,200}{\$19,100}$ or 0.167539267 | 0.167539267($1,780) = $298.22 |
| Electrical | $ 1,500 | $\dfrac{\$1,500}{\$19,100}$ or 0.0785340314 | 0.0785340314($1,780) = $139.79 |
| Total | $19,100 | $\dfrac{\$19,100}{\$19,100}$ or 0.9999999999* | $1,780.00 |

*Sum of rounded decimal equivalents.

### Find department overhead based on floor space:

1. Find the total floor space: Add the square feet of floor space in each department.
2. Find the department floor space rate:

$$\text{Department floor space rate} = \frac{\text{floor space in department}}{\text{total floor space}}$$

3. Find the overhead assigned to the department by floor space:

$$\text{Department overhead by floor space} = \text{department floor space rate} \times \text{total overhead}$$

Make a table to show the overhead for a store that had $25,000 in overhead if overhead is calculated based on number of square feet a department uses: department 1: 5,100; department 2: 4,120; department 3: 1,200; department 4: 2,500.

| Department | Floor space in square feet | Floor space rate | Overhead |
|---|---|---|---|
| 1 | 5,100 | $\dfrac{5,100}{12,920}$ or 0.3947368421 | 0.3947368421($25,000) = $9,868.42 |
| 2 | 4,120 | $\dfrac{4,120}{12,920}$ or 0.3188854489 | 0.3188854489($25,000) = $7,972.14 |
| 3 | 1,200 | $\dfrac{1,200}{12,920}$ or 0.092879257 | 0.092879257($25,000) = $2,321.98 |
| 4 | 2,500 | $\dfrac{2,500}{12,920}$ or 0.193498452 | 0.193498452($25,000) = $4,837.46 |
| Total | 12,920 | $\dfrac{12,920}{12,920}$ or 1 | $25,000.00 |

*Sum of rounded decimal equivalents.

# EXERCISES SET A

*Use the specific identification method for Exercises 2–3.*

**1.** Find the cost of goods available for sale using the following table:

| Date of purchase | Units purchased | Cost per unit | Total cost |
|---|---|---|---|
| Beginning inventory | 182 | $21 | |
| August 20 | 78 | $27 | |
| September 12 | 39 | $28 | |
| October 2 | 52 | $21 | _____ |
| Cost of goods available for sale | | | |

**2.** Find the cost of ending inventory using the following table showing a breakdown of unit costs for ending inventory:

| Cost per unit | Units | Total cost |
|---|---|---|
| $21 | 13 | |
| $27 | 64 | |
| $28 | 29 | |
| $21 | 48 | _____ |

**3.** Find the cost of goods sold using the tables in Exercises 1 and 2.

*Use the weighted-average method for Exercises 4–5.*

**4.** Find the average unit cost using the table in Exercise 1.

**5.** Find the cost of ending inventory and the cost of goods sold using the tables in Exercises 1 and 2.

**6.** Use the first-in, first-out method to find the cost of goods sold and the cost of ending inventory using the table from Exercise 1 and the fact that the ending inventory is 96 units.

**7.** Use the last-in, first-out method to find the cost of goods sold and the cost of ending inventory using the table from Exercise 1 and the fact that the ending inventory is 200 units.

**8.** Use the retail method to find the cost of goods sold and the cost of ending inventory using the table in Exercise 1, the following table, and the fact that sales are $5,000:

| Date of purchase | Retail price per unit |
|---|---|
| Beginning inventory | $26 |
| August 20 | $32 |
| September 12 | $35 |
| October 2 | $26 |

*Complete the tables for Exercises 9–10. Round to the nearest tenth.*

| | Beginning inventory at retail | Ending inventory at retail | Sales | Turnover rate at retail |
|---|---|---|---|---|
| **9.** | $8,920 | $7,460 | $19,270 | ____ |
| **10.** | $8,000 | $10,000 | $36,000 | ____ |

**11.** Find the turnover rate at retail for a business with sales of $75,000 and an average inventory at retail of $15,000.

*Decimal equivalents are given to six decimal digits but the entire calculator value is used to calculate the overhead in Exercises 12–13.*

**12.** Department 1 had $5,200 in sales for the month, department 2 had $4,700, department 3 had $6,520, department 4 had $4,870, and department 5 had $2,010. The total overhead was $10,000. Find each department's overhead based on sales.

**13.** Tyson's Fixit Store has a monthly overhead of $9,200. Find each department's monthly overhead based on floor space using the following square feet for each department: hardware, 800; plumbing, 600; tools, 400; supplies, 600.

# EXERCISES SET B

**1.** Find the cost of goods available for sale using the following table:

| Date of purchase | Units purchased | Cost per unit |
|---|---|---|
| Beginning inventory | 25 | $18 |
| June 8 | 10 | $19 |
| July 7 | 18 | $20 |
| August 3 | 22 | $17 |

*Use the specific identification method for Exercises 2–3.*

**2.** Find the cost of ending inventory using the following table showing a breakdown of unit costs for ending inventory:

| Date of purchase | Cost per unit | Units |
|---|---|---|
| January 1 | $18 | 17 |
| February 9 | $19 | 12 |
| March 5 | $20 | 7 |
| April 7 | $17 | 14 |

**3.** Use the weighted-average method to find the average unit cost using the following table:

| Date of purchase | Units purchased | Cost per unit |
|---|---|---|
| Beginning inventory | 21 | $12 |
| May 12 | 10 | $10 |
| June 9 | 16 | $11 |
| July 5 | 20 | $13 |
| Units sold | 46 | |

**4.** Find the cost of goods sold using the tables in Exercises 1 and 2.

**5.** Find the cost of ending inventory and the cost of goods sold using the results of Exercises 3 and 4.

**6.** Use the first-in, first-out method to find the cost of goods sold and the cost of ending inventory using the following table and the fact that the ending inventory is 500 units:

| Date of purchase | Number of units purchased | Cost per unit |
|---|---|---|
| Beginning inventory | 221 | $16 |
| April 15 | 328 | $15 |
| May 12 | 167 | $12 |
| June 5 | 201 | $9 |

**7.** Use the last-in, first-out method to find the cost of goods sold and the cost of ending inventory using the following table and the table in Exercise 6:

| Date of purchase | Units purchased | Number of units in ending inventory | Cost per unit |
|---|---|---|---|
| Beginning inventory | 315 | 221 | $16 |
| April 15 | 180 | 4 | $15 |
| May 12 | 200 | 0 | $12 |
| June 5 | 280 | 0 | $9 |
| | | 225 | |

**8.** Use the following inventory costs to find the average inventory cost: $2,596; $3,872.

*Complete the tables for Exercises 9–10. Round to the nearest tenth.*

| Beginning inventory at cost | Ending inventory at cost | Cost of goods sold | Turnover rate at cost |
|---|---|---|---|
| 9. $51,266 | $42,780 | $25,000 | ____ |
| 10. $26,108 | $5,892 | $73,600 | ____ |

11. At Best Buy Hardware, the nuts and bolts department had $1,500 in sales for the month, the electrical department had $4,000, and the paint department had $2,300. The total overhead was $3,800. Find each department's overhead based on sales.

12. A corner grocery store has a monthly overhead of $1,500. Find each department's monthly overhead based on sales if department sales were as follows: meats, $1,200; groceries, $2,400; dairy, $600; and housewares, $800.

1. Find the cost of goods available for sale using the following table:

| Date of purchase | Units purchased | Cost per unit |
|---|---|---|
| Beginning inventory | 26 | $10 |
| March 12 | 32 | $13 |
| April 3 | 29 | $9 |
| May 5 | 25 | $12 |

2. Find the cost of ending inventory using the specific identification method and the following table showing a breakdown of units' costs for ending inventory:

| Cost per unit | Units |
|---|---|
| $10 | 17 |
| $13 | 12 |
| $9 | 15 |
| $12 | 25 |

3. Find the cost of goods sold using the specific identification method and the tables in Exercises 1 and 2.

4. Find the average unit cost using the table in Exercise 1.

5. Find the cost of ending inventory and the cost of goods sold using the weighted-average method and the tables in Exercises 1 and 2.

6. Find the cost of goods sold and the cost of ending inventory using the FIFO method, the table in Exercise 1, and the fact that the ending inventory is 32 units.

7. Find the cost of goods sold and the cost of ending inventory using the LIFO method, the table in Exercise 1, and the fact that the ending inventory is 82 units.

8. AMX Department Store's overhead totaled $12,000 during one month. The sales by department for the month were as follows: cameras, $12,000; toys, $14,000; hardware, $13,500; garden supplies, $8,400; sporting goods, $9,500; and clothing, $28,600. Find the monthly overhead for all departments. Use the full calculator value of the decimal equivalent to find overhead.

9. Office Supply World assigns overhead to a department based on the square feet of office space it occupies. The overhead for a month totaled $9,000 and each department occupies the following number of square feet: furniture, 2,000; computer supplies, 1,600; consumable office supplies, 2,500; leather goods, 1,200; and administrative services, 800. Find each department's overhead. Use the full calculator value of the decimal equivalent to find overhead.

**10.** A restaurant had a beginning inventory at retail of $13,900 and an ending inventory at retail of $10,000. If the sales were $47,800, find the turnover rate at retail.

**11.** A retail parts business had an average inventory at retail of $258,968 and sales of $756,893. Find the rate of turnover at retail to the nearest hundredth.

**12.** A plant had an average inventory at cost of $13,000 and sales of $26,000. Find the rate of turnover at cost.

**13.** The office photocopy machine is on the blink again. You are responsible for replacing the photocopier with a more powerful model and equitably charging each department its share of the cost of the new copier. The new copier costs $7,580 and is expected to produce 500,000 copies in its lifetime. You decide that each department's share should be based on the number of copies the department makes. The following record of use was recorded at the end of the first year. How much do you charge the four departments for the first year?

| Department | Number of copies made |
|---|---|
| Purchasing | 8,711 |
| Personnel | 30,872 |
| Payroll | 32,521 |
| Secretarial pool | 52,896 |

**14.** Department A uses 5,000 square feet of floor space, department B uses 2,500, department C uses 4,300, and department D uses 2,700. The total overhead is $8,200. Find each department's overhead based on floor space.

1. Combine the formulas in steps 1 and 2 of the How To box: Find the Cost of Goods Sold Using the Specific Identification Inventory Method (p. 585) to rewrite the formula in step 3 to find the cost of goods sold.

2. Combine the formulas in steps 1 and 2 of the How To box: Find the Cost of Goods Sold Using the Weighted-Average Inventory Method (p. 586) to rewrite the formula in step 3 to find the cost of ending inventory.

3. Combine the formulas in steps 1, 3, and 4 of the How To box: Find the Cost of Goods Sold Using the First-In, First-Out Inventory Method (p. 588) to find the cost of goods sold.

4. Explain the difference between a turnover rate at retail and a turnover rate at cost.

5. Discuss the difference in finding the cost of goods sold using the specific inventory method and using the retail method.

6. Explain the difference in the assumptions made in using the FIFO inventory method versus the LIFO inventory method.

7. Combine the formulas in steps 1 and 3 of the How To box: Find the Cost of Goods Sold Using Retail Inventory Method (p. 591) to find the cost ratio.

8. Combine and simplify the formulas in steps 1 and 2 in the How To box: Find the Turnover Rate at Cost (p. 598) to solve for turnover rate at cost.

# Challenge Problem

The 7th Inning Memorabilia Shop has five departments and allocates its monthly overhead by floor space. The Gallery has 4,250 square feet, Engraving has 2,675 square feet, Framing has 3,500 square feet, Brubaker's Restaurant has 5,000 square feet, and Sports Cards and Memorabilia has 4,700 square feet. In June, rent was $2,900, telephone was $289.46, utilities were $512.72, parking lot and grounds maintenance was $195, and salaries were $1,980. How much overhead should Charlie assign to Brubaker's Restaurant? If the shop had a total revenue of $27,984 for June and each department was expected to produce revenue in proportion to its space, how much of the revenue should be produced by Brubaker's Restaurant?

## 17.1 Decorah Custom Canoes

In the tradition of their Native American ancestors, Decorah Custom Canoes specializes in creating hand-crafted canoes using only the finest natural materials. Whether they are from birch bark or cedar, all canoes are custom-built from native wood. Each piece is a work of art, and normal construction time varies from one to two months. Once completed, the canoes are purchased by and sold through a retail outlet under the same name. Only three canoes are offered, the Iroquois, Chippewa, and Winnebago, which cost $1,100, $1,400, and $2,100, respectively. Each canoe also comes as a kit and costs $450, $550, and $800, respectively. Custom paddles are also available and cost $45 and $75, for medium and large sizes. The beginning inventory on April 1 is as follows: Iroquois—1 canoe/2 kits; Chippewa—2 canoes/2 kits; Winnebago—0 canoes/3 kits; and paddles—4 medium/6 large. The ending inventory on June 30 is as follows: Iroquois—2 canoes/1 kit; Chippewa—0 canoes/1 kit; Winnebago—2 canoes/1 kit; and paddles—6 medium/4 large. The following information is a summary of inventory purchased by the retail outlet during the past three months (April through June):

| Date of purchase | Units | Item | Cost per unit |
|---|---|---|---|
| April 5 | 3 | Iroquois canoe | $1,100 |
| | 3 | Chippewa canoe | $1,400 |
| | 3 | Winnebago canoe | $2,100 |
| May 1 | 3 | Iroquois kit | $450 |
| | 2 | Chippewa kit | $550 |
| | 1 | Winnebago kit | $800 |
| | 8 | Paddle medium | $45 |
| | 6 | Paddle large | $75 |
| June 10 | 2 | Chippewa kit | $550 |
| | 1 | Winnebago kit | $800 |

1. Find the cost of goods sold using the specific identification inventory method.

2. Find the cost of goods sold using the weighted-average inventory method.

**3.** Decorah Custom Canoes had net sales of $8,085 at cost for the month of April, and the ending inventory on April 30 was $14,645. Compute the beginning inventory on April 1 (hint: based on what is listed in the case), and then find the average inventory at cost and the turnover rate at cost for April.

# 17.2  PBC Office Supplies

James has recently accepted a position as assistant inventory clerk at PBC Office Supplies. His main responsibilities will focus on tracking inventory costs, calculating cost of goods sold, determining turnover rates, and other aspects of ensuring good inventory control procedures.

Today he wants to determine how the cost of goods sold would differ under three possible methods. He will focus on three-subject notebooks, because those are hot sellers with school starting in just a few weeks. A review of accounting records indicates the following purchases of notebooks from their suppliers:

| June 1 | 200 notebooks | $0.75 each | $150 total cost |
| June 10 | 250 notebooks | $0.80 each | $200 total cost |
| June 25 | 500 notebooks | $0.70 each | $350 total cost |
| June 30 | 200 notebooks | $0.75 each | $150 total cost |
| Total | 1,150 notebooks | | $850 |

**1.** At their Fourth of July Back-to-School Sale, PBC sold 700 notebooks. What are the cost of goods sold and ending inventory under the LIFO, FIFO, and Weighted Average methods?

**2.** On occasion, James will sometimes use the gross profit method for estimating ending inventory and cost of goods sold. If PBC generally has a profit margin of 33% on the sale of notebooks and they sold $700 worth of notebooks, what is the estimated cost of goods sold and estimated ending inventory?

**3.** James also wants to calculate the inventory turnover rate for the entire stationery section for the last six-month period. His beginning inventory was $400,000, his ending inventory was $350,000, and net sales at cost were $800,000. What were the average inventory and turnover rate at cost?

# The Price of Disaster

Until now, it had been a beautiful summer day. Angela finished work, did some shopping, and was returning from daycare with her two young children when she noticed storm clouds approaching. These clouds looked more ominous and threatening than usual. She pulled her car into the garage, and the children (Jacob, 10, and Emily, 8) scrambled out and into the house. Angela heard the faint sound of a siren. Straining to hear better, she headed back outside and saw the unimaginable—a massive tornado had formed and was heading straight toward her neighborhood. Dropping her groceries, Angela rushed into the house and had both her children in the shelter of the basement in less than a minute.

The tornado wasn't far behind. Smashing into the house with full force, the F-3 twister demolished the house in a matter of seconds, leaving their overturned car in the rubble. The twister was gone as quickly as it came. Angela and the children were unharmed, and were able to walk out a lower-level door with little difficulty. It wasn't until they were outside that they realized the devastation to their neighborhood and how truly fortunate they were to be alive!

After the immediate shock subsided, Angela's first thought was about insurance, or more appropriately, her lack of insurance. Money had always been tight and paying for insurance just had not been a priority. Now, it seemed like the most important thing in the world. Angela had property insurance on the house, but had no idea for how much or whether it covered tornadoes. She had liability coverage on the car, but had dropped the collision/comprehensive coverage. And life insurance? She had only the $10,000 policy provided by her employer. Angela knew that she was lucky to be alive. Who would provide for her children if she died? Could she afford to repair her house? Could she replace her car? What should she do next?

## LEARNING OUTCOMES

### 18-1 Life Insurance

1. Estimate life insurance premiums using a rate table.
2. Apply the extended term nonforfeiture option to a cancelled straight-life policy.

### 18-2 Property Insurance

1. Estimate property insurance premiums using a rate table.
2. Find the refund for a cancelled policy.
3. Find the compensation with a coinsurance clause.

### 18-3 Motor Vehicle Insurance

1. Find automobile insurance premiums using rate tables.

**Insurance:** a form of protection against unexpected financial loss.

**Comprehensive policy:** insurance policy that protects the insured against several risks—for example, fire, flood, and earthquake.

**Insured (policyholder):** the individual, organization, or business that carries the insurance or financial protection against loss.

**Insurer (underwriter):** the insurance company that insures for a specific loss according to contract provisions.

**Policy:** the contract between the insurer and the insured.

**Premium:** the amount paid by the insured for the protection provided by the policy.

**Face value:** the maximum amount of insurance provided by the policy.

**Beneficiary:** the individual, organization, or business to whom the proceeds of the policy are payable.

**Life insurance:** an insurance policy that pays a specified amount to the beneficiary of the policy upon the death of the insured.

**Income shortfall:** the difference in the total living expenses of a family and the amount of income a family would have after the death of the insured. This shortfall can be used to project the amount of insurance needed by the family.

**Term insurance:** insurance purchased for a certain period of time. At the end of the time period, the policy has no cash value and the insurance ends.

**Straight-life (ordinary life) insurance:** the insured pays premiums for his or her entire life. At the death of the insured, the beneficiary receives the face value of the policy. If the policy is cancelled, the insured is paid the cash value of the policy.

**Insurance** is a form of protection against unexpected financial loss. Businesses and individuals need insurance to help bear the burden of accidents, acts of God that result in large financial losses, and loss of life. Insurance helps distribute the burden of financial loss among those who share the same type of risk. Many types of insurance are available, such as fire, life, homeowner's, health, accident, and automobile. Many insurance companies offer a **comprehensive policy** that protects the insured against several risks. It is common, for example, to purchase fire, flood, and earthquake insurance in one comprehensive policy. The combined rate for a comprehensive policy is usually lower than if each type of protection is purchased separately.

Before we can discuss specific types of insurance, we need to understand some important terms used in the insurance field.

| | |
|---|---|
| **Insured (policyholder)** | The individual, organization, or business that carries the insurance or financial protection against loss |
| **Insurer (underwriter)** | The insurance company that assures payment for a specific loss according to contract provisions |
| **Policy** | The contract between the insurer and the insured |
| **Premium** | The amount paid by the insured for the protection provided by the policy |
| **Face value** | The maximum amount of insurance provided by the policy |
| **Beneficiary** | The individual, organization, or business to whom the proceeds of the policy are payable |

## 18-1 LIFE INSURANCE

### LEARNING OUTCOMES

1 Estimate life insurance premiums using a rate table.
2 Apply the extended term nonforfeiture option to a cancelled straight-life policy.

**Life insurance** provides financial assistance to the designated beneficiary, surviving spouse, or dependents of the insured in the event of the insured person's death. Knowing the right amount of life insurance to carry is as important as understanding the type of insurance to carry. Life insurance is usually purchased for the purpose of providing income for a family upon the death or disability of the insured person. Some financial planners suggest life insurance coverage should be seven to ten times annual income. Another way to determine the amount of life insurance needed by a family is to determine the difference in the total expenses of a family and the amount of income the family would have after the death of the insured. This difference is sometimes called **income shortfall.**

Although anyone may purchase life insurance, companies often insure the lives of their employees as a fringe benefit of employment. In partnerships, the beneficiary is often the surviving partner. Several types of life insurance policies are available, some of which even function as savings programs. In this section, we look at two types of life insurance policies in common use: *term* and *straight-life*.

**Term insurance** is purchased for a certain period of time such as 5, 10, or 20 years. For example, those insured under a 10-year term policy pay premiums for 10 years or until they die, whichever occurs first. If the insured dies during the 10-year period, the beneficiary of the policy receives the face value of the policy. If the insured is still living at the end of the 10-year period, the insurance ends and the policy has no cash value. The insured can then renew the policy, but at a higher rate than paid before. Term insurance is the least expensive type of life insurance.

People who take out **straight-life (ordinary life) insurance** policies agree to pay premiums for their entire lives. At the time of the insured's death, a beneficiary receives the face value of the policy. This type of policy also builds up a cash value. Policyholders who cancel their policy are entitled to a certain sum of money back, depending on the amount that was paid in.

## 1 Estimate life insurance premiums using a rate table.

Life insurance rates are typically determined by the age, gender, and health of the insured and the type of policy. Therefore, rate quotes are generally made on an individual basis. Many rate calculators are available on the Internet that can be used for personalized rate quotes. Table 18-1 gives some typical annual premiums for fixed-rate term or straight-life insurance that can be used to estimate an annual premium.

## TABLE 18-1
### Estimated Annual Life Insurance Premium Rates per $1,000 of Face Value

| Age | 10-Year fixed rate Male | 10-Year fixed rate Female | 20-Year fixed rate Male | 20-Year fixed rate Female | Straight-life Male | Straight-life Female |
|-----|------|--------|------|--------|------|--------|
| 20 | 1.21 | 1.17 | 1.82 | 1.76 | 2.72 | 2.63 |
| 30 | 1.27 | 1.23 | 1.91 | 1.85 | 3.49 | 3.38 |
| 40 | 1.46 | 1.41 | 2.20 | 2.13 | 4.02 | 3.88 |
| 50 | 2.41 | 2.33 | 3.63 | 3.51 | 5.18 | 5.01 |
| 60 | 4.72 | 4.56 | 7.11 | 6.88 | 8.21 | 7.93 |

## HOW TO  Estimate an annual life insurance premium using a table

1. Locate the estimated annual rate in Table 18-1 according to type of policy, age, and sex.
2. Divide the policy face value by $1,000 and multiply the quotient by the rate from step 1.

$$\text{Estimated annual premium} = \frac{\text{face value}}{\$1,000} \times \text{rate}$$

## EXAMPLE 1  Estimate the annual premium of an insurance policy with a face value of $100,000 for a 30-year-old male for (a) a 20-year fixed-rate policy; (b) a straight-life policy.

$$\begin{aligned}
\text{Estimated annual premium} &= \frac{\text{face value}}{\$1,000} \times \text{rate} \\
&= \frac{\$100,000}{\$1,000} \times \text{rate} \qquad \text{The face value is } \$100,000. \\
&= 100 \times \text{rate}
\end{aligned}$$

Look at Table 18-1 to find the rate for each type of policy.

(a) 20-year term policy: 100($1.91) = $191
(b) Straight-life policy: 100($3.49) = $349

**The estimated annual premium for a $100,000 20-year term policy is $191 and for a $100,000 straight-life policy is $349.**

Since it is often inconvenient to make lump-sum annual payments, most companies allow payments to be made semiannually (twice a year), quarterly (every three months), or monthly for slightly higher rates than would apply on an annual basis. Table 18-2 shows some typical rates for periods of less than one year.

## EXAMPLE 2  Use Tables 18-1 and 18-2 to estimate the (a) semiannual, (b) quarterly, and (c) monthly premiums for a $250,000 straight-life policy on a 40-year-old female.

$$\begin{aligned}
\text{Annual premium} &= \frac{\text{amount of coverage}}{\$1,000} \times \text{rate} \\
&= \left(\frac{\$250,000}{\$1,000}\right)(\$3.88) \qquad \text{The face value is } \$250,000. \text{ The rate, according to Table 18-1, is } \$3.88. \\
&= 250(\$3.88) = \$970
\end{aligned}$$

Find the period rates using Table 18-2.

(a) Semiannual premium:  Annual premium × semiannual rate = semiannual premium
$970 (51%)
= $970 (0.51) = $494.70

(b) Quarterly premium:  Annual premium × quarterly rate = quarterly premium
$970 (26%)
= $970 (0.26) = $252.20

(c) Monthly premium  Annual premium × monthly rate = monthly premium
$970 (8.75%)
= $970 (0.0875) = $84.88

**The semiannual premium is $494.70, quarterly is $252.20, and monthly is $84.88.**

## TABLE 18-2
### Premium Rates for Periods Less than One Year

| Period | Percent of annual premium |
|--------|------|
| Semiannually | 51.00 |
| Quarterly | 26.00 |
| Monthly | 8.75 |

**Fixed-time payment insurance:** a policy with a specified face value for the insured's entire life with payment made for a fixed period of time.

**Paid-up insurance:** insurance that continues after premiums are no longer paid.

**Fixed-time endowment insurance:** a policy that is a combination insurance and savings plan that is paid for a fixed period of time.

**Universal life insurance:** a policy with a flexible premium rate and death benefits.

Other types of life insurance are fixed-time payment insurance, fixed-time endowment, and universal life policies. A **fixed-time payment insurance** policy gives a specified face value for the insured's entire life, but payments are made only for a fixed period of time. At the end of the fixed time, the insured has **paid-up insurance**, that is, the insurance continues after premiums are no longer paid. A **fixed-time endowment insurance** policy is a combination insurance and savings plan. The insured has term insurance protection for the face value of the policy for the fixed time of the policy. At the end of the fixed time, the insured receives the face value of the policy and the insurance ends. The premiums for fixed-term payment and fixed-term endowment policies are significantly higher than the premiums for term or straight-life policies.

A **universal life insurance** policy has flexible premium rates and death benefits. That is, as interest rates or mortality rates change, the premiums may increase or the death benefits may be decreased. The rates may also increase as the insured becomes older.

 **STOP AND CHECK**

1. Estimate the annual premium of a 10-year fixed-rate insurance policy with a face value of $200,000 for a 20-year-old female.

2. Use Tables 18-1 and 18-2 to estimate the (a) semiannual, (b) quarterly, and (c) monthly premiums for a $500,000 straight-life insurance policy on a 50-year-old male.

3. Estimate the monthly premium on a 20-year fixed-rate insurance policy of $300,000 for a 60-year-old male.

4. Estimate the quarterly premium on a straight-life insurance policy for a 30-year-old female. The face value of the policy is $600,000.

## 2 Apply the extended term nonforfeiture option to a cancelled straight-life policy.

**Lapse:** the loss of insurance coverage due to nonpayment of premiums.

**Nonforfeiture options:** the options that are available to a policyholder when payments are discontinued.

Most types of life insurance policies except term insurance build up cash value. If a policy holder decides to cancel a policy or to allow it to **lapse** by not making the required payments, the insured normally has three choices, called **nonforfeiture options**:

1. **Cash Value or Surrender Option.** A policyholder can choose to surrender (give up) a policy and receive its cash value. If the insured wants to maintain the insurance coverage but use the cash value, a loan can be made for the amount of the cash value. The loan must be repaid with interest, or the amount of the loan and interest is deducted from the face value of the policy.

2. **Paid-Up Insurance.** The cash value of the policy is applied to a reduced amount of paid-up insurance. The reduced insurance continues for the entire life of the insured and no additional premiums are paid.

3. **Extended Term Insurance.** The cash value of the policy is applied to a term policy for the same face value as the original policy. The term policy will last as long a time period as the cash value will purchase. If the insured stops paying a policy and does not choose a nonforfeiture option, in most cases this option will be automatically implemented.

---

**HOW TO**    **Apply the extended term nonforfeiture option to a cancelled straight-life policy.**

1. Identify the cash value of the cancelled policy.
2. Estimate the annual premium for a term policy of the same face value. Use a fixed rate in Table 18-1.
3. Determine the number of years of paid-up insurance.

$$\text{Years of paid-up insurance} = \frac{\text{cash value of surrendered policy}}{\text{annual premium of term policy}}$$

**EXAMPLE 1** Lisa Loden started a $100,000 straight-life insurance policy when she was 30 years old. At age 50, she determines that she has a cash value of $3,857 and wants to convert to extended term for the same face value. Using the 20-year fixed rates, estimate how long her extended term insurance will last.

Estimated annual term premium: $3.51 per $1,000    50-year-old female. 20-year fixed rate

$$\frac{\$100,000}{\$1,000} = 100 \text{ units}$$    Number of insurance units

$$\$3.51(100) = \$351$$    Annual term rate

Years of term insurance: $\dfrac{\text{cash value}}{\text{annual premium}}$

$$\frac{\$3,857}{\$351} = 10.99 \text{ years}$$

**The paid-up term insurance will extend for approximately 11 years.**

## STOP AND CHECK

1. Juanna Makhloufi started a straight-life insurance policy for $300,000 when she was 20 years old. At age 50, the policy has a cash value of $12,594 and Juanna decides to convert the policy to extended term for the same face value. Using 20-year fixed rates, estimate the number of years her extended term insurance will last.

2. Byron Johnson started a straight-life insurance policy for $500,000 when he was 38 years old. At age 60, the policy has a cash value of $13,512 and Bryon plans to convert the policy to extended term for the same face value. Use 10-year fixed rates to estimate the number of years of extended coverage he will have.

3. Frances Johnson started a $250,000 straight-life insurance policy at age 32. Her policy has a cash value of $4,052 at age 50. Use 10-year fixed rates to estimate the number of years of extended term coverage she can expect.

4. At age 60, Irene Doo wants to convert a $300,000 straight-life insurance policy to extended term with the same face value. Use 20-year fixed rates to estimate the number of years of extended term coverage her cash value of $12,892 will buy.

## 18-1 SECTION EXERCISES

### SKILL BUILDERS

*Use Tables 18-1 and 18-2.*

1. Find the annual premium for a 10-year fixed-rate insurance policy with a face value of $45,000 for a 20-year-old female.

2. Find the annual premium for a straight-life insurance policy with a face value of $45,000 for a 20-year-old female.

3. What are the quarterly payments on a $100,000 straight-life insurance policy for a 30-year-old male?

4. What are the monthly payments on a $200,000 straight-life insurance policy for a 50-year-old male?

5. Compare a 10-year fixed-rate policy for $75,000 for a 40-year-old male to the same policy for a 40-year-old female.

6. Compare a 20-year fixed-rate policy for $500,000 for a 60-year-old male to the same policy for a 60-year-old female.

7. Cindy Franklin started a straight-life insurance policy for $250,000 when she was 23 years old. At age 50, the policy has a cash value of $10,058 and Cindy converts the policy to extended term insurance for the same face value. Use 20-year fixed rates to estimate the number of years of extended term insurance she has.

8. Candice Weppner's $200,000 straight-life insurance policy has a cash value of $4,099. Candice is 60 years old and is converting to an extended term policy for the same face value. Use 10-year fixed rates to estimate the number of years of extended term insurance she has.

## 18-2 PROPERTY INSURANCE

### LEARNING OUTCOMES

1 Estimate property insurance premiums using a rate table.
2 Find the refund for a cancelled policy.
3 Find the compensation with a coinsurance clause.

Businesses and homeowners need insurance to protect them from financial loss if their property is damaged or destroyed. Some types of perils that might cause damage or loss to property are fire, storms, burglary, and vandalism. Many types of comprehensive policies are available to cover property damage or loss, medical expenses for injuries on the property, loss of income when damage peril causes a business to be closed for a period of time, or rental expense when a peril causes a home to be unlivable. Since premiums for a comprehensive policy are based on numerous factors, we will illustrate property insurance by focusing on fire insurance.

### 1 Estimate property insurance premiums using a rate table.

**Fire insurance:** an insurance that protects against fire losses or losses that may result directly from attempts to extinguish a fire.

**Fire insurance** provides protection against fire losses or losses that may result directly from attempts to extinguish a fire, such as damage caused by water and chemical extinguishers and damage to property by firefighters.

Rates for fire insurance vary according to several factors, such as type of structure, location, proximity to the fire department, rating of the fire department, water supply, and fire hazards. Most states have developed a system for classifying rates according to these factors. For example, a class A building might be made of brick instead of wood. Or the contents of the building might be classed as resistant to fire damage, such as bags of cement, rather than fabric, which would be much more flammable (easily burned). Table 18-3 shows a sample classification system. The area rankings in the left column are based on how close the buildings are to a fire station and how easy access is to the building and its contents.

As you can see from Table 18-3, insurance rates are expressed as an annual amount per $100 of coverage. To find the annual premium, divide the amount of coverage by $100 and multiply by the rate in the table. Do this for both building and contents.

---

**HOW TO** Estimate an annual fire insurance premium amount using a table

1. Locate the annual rate for the building (or contents) being insured according to the building's area rank and its class.
2. Find the annual premium for both the building and the contents.

$$\text{Annual premium} = \frac{\text{face value}}{\$100} \times \text{rate}$$

3. Add the two premiums.

---

**EXAMPLE 1** The building owned and occupied by O'Toole's Hardware is insured for $85,000. Its contents are insured for $50,000. If it is a class B building located in area 2, find the annual premium for the building and contents.

Annual premium for building

$$= \frac{\text{face value}}{\$100} \times \text{rate}$$

$$= \left(\frac{\$85,000}{\$100}\right)(\$0.54) = \$459$$

Look up the annual rate for a building classified as class B in area 2. The rate is $0.54. Multiply $85,000 divided by $100 times the rate.

Annual premium for contents

$$= \frac{\text{face value}}{\$100} \times \text{rate}$$

$$= \left(\frac{\$50,000}{\$100}\right)(\$0.62) = \$310$$

Look up the annual rate for contents classified as class B in area 2. The rate is $0.62. Multiply $0.62 times $50,000 divided by $100.

Total annual premium = $459 + $310 = $769

**The annual premium for the building is $459 and the premium for its contents is $310, for a total premium of $769.**

### TABLE 18-3
Annual Fire Insurance Rates per $100 of Face Value

| | Building classification | | | | | |
|---|---|---|---|---|---|---|
| | Class A | | Class B | | Class C | |
| Area rank | Building | Contents | Building | Contents | Building | Contents |
| 1 | $0.23 | $0.28 | $0.35 | $0.39 | $0.45 | $0.51 |
| 2 | 0.41 | 0.52 | 0.54 | 0.62 | 0.68 | 0.74 |
| 3 | 0.62 | 0.67 | 0.78 | 0.93 | 0.98 | 1.16 |

 ## STOP AND CHECK

1. The 7th Inning has its building insured for $600,000. Its contents are insured for $188,000. The building is a class A building located in area 3. Find the annual premium for the building and contents.

2. The Downtown Grill insures its building for $350,000 and the contents for $200,000. The building is class C located in area 1. Find the annual combined building and contents premium.

3. Proud Larry's Pizza insures its building for $265,000 and the contents for $190,000. What is the annual premium for building and contents that are class B and located in area 2?

4. Kiser Floor Covering's building is insured for $328,000 and has contents insurance for $185,000. The building is located in area 1 and is class A. Find the annual premium.

## 2 Find the refund for a cancelled policy.

**Short-term policy:** an insurance policy for less than one year.

**Short-rate premium:** the premium for a short-term policy.

A business or individual may need insurance for less than a year or they may need to cancel a policy before the policy has expired. A policy for less than one year is a **short-term policy**. The premium for a short-term policy is called a **short-rate premium**. Short rates are also used in calculating the refund when the insured cancels a policy before it expires. Short rates produce a higher premium or a lower refund than prorating the actual portion of the year that a policy is in force. If the insurer cancels the policy, it is required to refund at the prorated amount rather than the short rate. Table 18-4 shows short-rate percents for days of a month in five-day increments and for months the policy is in effect.

For a time period between two increments, use the higher percent.

### HOW TO    Find the refund for a cancelled policy

1. Identify the annual premium.
2. Identify the time the policy is in force.
3. Use Table 18-4 to find the short rate for the time the policy is in force.
4. Find the short-rate premium:

$$\text{Short-rate premium} = \text{annual premium} \times \text{short rate}$$

5. Find the refund:

$$\text{Refund} = \text{annual premium} - \text{short-rate premium}$$

## TABLE 18-4
### Short-Rate Property Insurance Schedule

| Time policy in force | Percent of annual premium |
|---|---|
| 5 days | 8 |
| 10 days | 10 |
| 15 days | 12 |
| 20 days | 15 |
| 25 days | 18 |
| 1 month | 20 |
| 2 months | 30 |
| 3 months | 40 |
| 4 months | 50 |
| 5 months | 60 |
| 6 months | 70 |
| 7 months | 75 |
| 8 months | 80 |
| 9 months | 85 |
| 10 months | 90 |
| 11 months | 95 |

### EXAMPLE 1

Sheldon Dan paid an annual premium of $5,285 for the building and contents for his business. He sold his business seven months after the policy was in force and cancelled the policy. What was his refund?

Annual premium = $5,285  
Time policy is in force = 7 months  
Short-rate percent = 75%  
Short-rate premium = annual premium × short-rate percent  
= $5,285(0.75)  
= $3,963.75  
Refund = annual premium − short-rate premium  
= $5,285 − $3,963.75  
= $1,321.25

*Use Table 18-4.*

**Sheldon Dan's refund was $1,321.25.**

### EXAMPLE 2

If the closing could not be scheduled until 12 days after the policy was cancelled, how much must Sheldon pay to insure the property for the additional 12 days?

Short-rate premium = annual premium × short-rate premium  
= $5,285(0.12)  
= $634.20

*Rate for 15 days from Table 18-4.*

**The premium for the 12 days is $634.20.**

## STOP AND CHECK

1. Raymond Davis paid a $3,086 annual premium for building and contents for his business property. He sold the property five months into the policy year and cancelled the policy. What was his refund?

2. Antoine Brady sold his business eight months after he paid his annual property insurance premium for building and contents. What is his refund on the annual premium of $3,972 if he cancelled?

3. Quesha Lane closed her business and cancelled her property insurance 22 days after her policy year began. How much refund should she receive on a premium of $2,805?

4. The Fabric Shop paid $4,985 annually for property insurance. When the business was sold three months after the insurance effective date, the insurance was cancelled. What is the refund?

## 3  Find the compensation with a coinsurance clause.

Because a fire rarely destroys a whole building or all of its contents, many businesses take out policies that cover only a portion of the value of the building or its contents. Thus, they save money on premiums by covering only 40% of their property's value, for example. To encourage businesses to take out full insurance, insurance companies offer plans that include a **coinsurance clause**. Such a clause means that the insured gets full protection or compensation up to the value of the policy from the insurance company only if the property is insured for 80% of its replacement value. If the policy covers only 40% of the value, then the insurance company pays only a portion of the loss.

**Coinsurance clause:** property must be insured for at least 80% of the replacement cost for full compensation for a loss.

### HOW TO  Find the compensation with a coinsurance clause

1. Find the face value required by the 80% coinsurance clause for full compensation: Multiply 0.8 by the replacement value of the property.
2. Find the compensation for the loss if the insurance is less than 80% of the replacement value:

Compensation (up to amount of loss)

$$= \text{amount of loss (up to the face value)} \times \frac{\text{face value of policy}}{80\% \text{ of replacement value of property}}$$

## EXAMPLE 1

Budget Construction owns a building with a replacement value of $200,000. It has a fire insurance policy with an 80% coinsurance clause and a face value of $130,000. There is a fire, and the building damage is figured to be $50,000. What will the insurance company pay as compensation?

Does Budget carry as much insurance as its coinsurance clause requires for full protection?

$$0.8(\$200,000) = \$160,000 \qquad \text{80\% of replacement value}$$

Budget has a policy worth only $130,000, so it does *not* get full compensation for the loss. Find the compensation:

$$\text{Compensation} = \text{loss} \times \frac{\text{face value of policy}}{\text{80\% of replacement value}}$$

$$\text{Compensation} = \$50,000\left(\frac{\$130,000}{\$160,000}\right) = \$40,625$$

**Budget receives $40,625 compensation for its loss of $50,000.**

If Budget had carried a policy for 80% of the replacement value of its property, it would have gotten the full $50,000 compensation for the loss.

### TIP

**Maximum Compensation for a Loss**

When calculating the compensation an insurance company will pay, if the policy has a coinsurance clause, the compensation for the amount of loss can be *no more than the face value of the policy,* regardless of the actual dollar value of the loss.

## EXAMPLE 2

McLean's Machine Shop is insured for 80% of the replacement value. The replacement value of the shop is $105,000. A fire causes $90,000 worth of damage to the property. How much compensation will McLean's receive from the insurance company?

$$0.8(\$105,000) = \$84,000 \text{ face value of policy} \qquad \text{Compensation cannot exceed the face value of the policy.}$$

$$\text{Compensation} = \$84,000$$

**The loss compensation is $84,000.**

In the preceding example, the $90,000 loss can only be compensated at $84,000 because the face value of the policy is only $84,000.

Some businesses have multiple locations, have expanded over time, or find that one insurance company is not willing to assume the entire liability. A property may have fire insurance policies with more than one company. Such insurance companies are known as **multiple carriers**. When multiple carriers insure the same property, each carrier assumes its portion of the total coverage. For example, if a business has a policy of $100,000 with one company and a policy of $250,000 with another company, the first company is responsible for its portion of the total amount of insurance coverage on the property. $\frac{\$100,000}{\$350,000} = 0.2857142857$ or 29% of a claim.

**Multiple carriers:** two or more insurance companies that provide fire coverage on the same property at the same time. Each insurance company is responsible for paying its portion of a loss based on the total dollar amount of insurance coverage on the property.

 **STOP AND CHECK**

1. Wendy's owns a building with a replacement value of $650,000. Its fire insurance policy has an 80% coinsurance clause and a face value of $400,000. Damage from a fire is estimated to be $82,000. What compensation will the insurance company pay?

2. Laverne's Shoes owns a building with a replacement value of $492,000. The fire insurance policy has an 80% coinsurance clause and a face value of $350,000. Damage caused by a fire costs $43,790 to repair. What compensation will the insurance company pay?

3. Larry Siler owns an office building with a replacement value of $798,500. His fire insurance policy has an 80% coinsurance clause and a face value of $600,000. Damage caused by a hurricane costs $590,000. How much will Larry's insurance company pay?

4. Memphis Ballet has insured its building for $550,000. The replacement value of the building is $690,000 with an 80% coinsurance clause. Repairs from a fire cost $38,588. How much will the insurance company pay?

## SKILL BUILDERS

**1.** Find the annual fire insurance premium on a class A building located in area 3 if the building is insured for $120,000 and its contents are insured for $75,000.

**2.** A class C building and its contents are located in area 1 and are insured for $150,000 and $68,000, respectively. Find the total annual insurance premium.

**3.** If a 2% charge is added to the annual premium of $1,021.80 when payments are made semiannually, how much would semiannual payments be?

**4.** Chandler Burford owns a class B office building located in area 2. What is the annual fire insurance premium if the building is insured for $350,000 and the contents are insured for $100,000?

**5.** Alice Lee owns a class A building in area 1. The building is insured for $200,000 and contents are insured for $85,000. A 3% charge is added to the annual premium because she pays quarterly. Find her quarterly payment.

## APPLICATIONS

**6.** The market value of a building is $255,000. It has been insured for $204,000 in a fire insurance policy with an 80% coinsurance clause. What part of a loss due to fire will the insurance company pay?

**7.** If a fire causes damage valued at $75,000, what is the amount of compensation to the owner of the building in Exercise 6?

**8.** A building valued at $295,000 is insured in a policy that contains an 80% coinsurance clause. The face value of the policy is $100,000. If the building is a total loss, what is the amount of compensation?

**9.** Mays Jewelry Store owns a property that has a replacement value of $395,000. How much insurance is required on the property for coverage up to the face value of the policy if an 80% coinsurance clause exists?

**10.** Mays Jewelry Store (Exercise 9) had a fire that resulted in a loss valued at $83,000. How much compensation is the insurance company obligated to pay if the property is insured for $220,000?

**11.** How much compensation is the insurance company obligated to pay Mays Jewelry Store if they have the $83,000 loss shown in Exercise 10 but the property is insured for $300,000?

**12.** Dewell Gandy sold his business eight months after his insurance annual effective date, so he cancelled the insurance. If the annual premium paid was $6,815, how much was the refund?

**13.** Dionte Hall sold his business and cancelled his policy three months and 20 days after the effective date of his property insurance policy of $2,817. How much was his refund?

**14.** Armie Gustafson paid an annual premium of $7,098 for property insurance and cancelled the policy 22 days after the effective policy date. How much was the refund?

### LEARNING OUTCOME

1 Find automobile insurance premiums using rate tables.

**Motor vehicle insurance:** liability, comprehensive, and collision insurance for a motor vehicle.

**Liability insurance:** protection for the owner of a vehicle if an accident causes personal injury or damage to someone else's property and is the fault of the driver of the insured vehicle.

**Comprehensive insurance:** protection for the owner of a vehicle for damage caused by a nonaccident incident such as fire, water, theft, or vandalism.

**Collision insurance:** protection for the owner of a vehicle for damages (both personal and property) from an accident that is the insured driver's fault.

**No-fault insurance:** protection for the owner of a vehicle for damage to the insured vehicle when the amount of damage is within the no-fault limits imposed by state law.

**Deductible:** the dollar amount the insured pays for each automobile insurance claim. The insurance company pays the remainder of the cost of each covered loss up to the limits of the policy.

**Uninsured motorist coverage:** protection for the owner of a vehicle when damages are incurred in an accident that is not the owner's fault but the other driver has no insurance. This coverage only applies to the owner's vehicle.

**Motor vehicle insurance** is a major expense item for individuals and businesses because of the high risk of personal injury or death and damage to property. Insurance for motor vehicles may be purchased to protect the individual or business from several risks. These include liability for personal injury and property damage; damage or loss to the insured vehicle and its occupants caused by a collision; and damage or loss to the insured vehicle caused by theft, fire, flood, storms, and other incidents that may not be related to a collision. These types of insurance generally fall into three types: liability, comprehensive, and collision.

**Liability insurance** protects the insured from losses incurred in a vehicle accident resulting in personal injury or damage to someone else's property if the accident is the fault of the insured or a designated driver.

**Comprehensive insurance** protects the insured's vehicle from damage caused by fire, theft, vandalism, and other risks, such as falling debris, storm damage, or road hazards such as rocks.

**Collision insurance** protects the insured's vehicle from damage (both personal and property) caused by an automobile accident in which the driver of the insured vehicle is *also* at fault. This type of insurance is also used when the driver of the vehicle who is at fault does not have insurance coverage.

Some states have **no-fault insurance** programs. In these states, all parties involved in an accident submit a claim for personal and property damages to their own insurance company if the amount is under a certain stated maximum. However, a person can still pursue legal action for additional compensation if the damage is above the stated maximum.

All auto insurance policies have a deductible. The **deductible** is the portion of the policy the policyholder is responsible for paying if a claim is filed. The amount the insured is required to pay for damages depends on the policy. Deductibles vary, but they are most often amounts of $100, $250, $500, or $1,000. For example, if you are in a vehicle crash that causes $3,500 worth of damage and your deductible is $1,000, you are required to pay the first $1,000 and the insurance company will pay the remaining amount up to the amount of the policy, or $2,500 in this example. Deductibles are paid each and every time the insured requires the insurance company to cover damages. The insurance premium you pay, or the price of your total annual coverage, can be reduced by choosing a higher deductible. In other words, if you are willing to pay a larger amount of each and every claim, you can reduce the total cost of your insurance.

### 1 Find automobile insurance premiums using rate tables.

Factors that affect the cost of automobile insurance include the primary location of the vehicle (large city, small town, rural area); the total distance traveled per year and the distance traveled to work each day; the types of use (such as pleasure, traveling to and from work, strictly business); the driving record and training of the insured driver(s); the academic grades of drivers who are still in school; the age, sex, and marital status of the insured driver(s); the type and age of the vehicle; and the amount of coverage desired. Accident statistics and probabilities involving these factors are used in determining appropriate insurance rates. Many companies offer **uninsured motorist coverage**, which compensates the insured person when the accident is the fault of a motorist who has no insurance.

**TABLE 18-5**
Annual Automobile Liability Insurance Premiums

| Territory | Driver class | Bodily injury coverage | | | Property damage coverage | | | |
|---|---|---|---|---|---|---|---|---|
| | | 25/50 | 50/100 | 100/300 | 10 | 25 | 50 | 100 |
| 1 | A | $187 | $230 | $278 | $105 | $128 | $144 | $178 |
| | B | 217 | 280 | 351 | 125 | 158 | 197 | 232 |
| | C | 332 | 381 | 421 | 194 | 253 | 319 | 341 |
| 2 | A | 124 | 188 | 204 | 82 | 96 | 112 | 136 |
| | B | 181 | 218 | 263 | 104 | 122 | 153 | 175 |
| | C | 251 | 289 | 333 | 128 | 153 | 182 | 196 |

**TABLE 18-6**
Annual Automobile Comprehensive and Collision Insurance

| Model class | Vehicle age | Territory 1 | | | | Territory 2 | | | |
|---|---|---|---|---|---|---|---|---|---|
| | | Comprehensive | | Collision | | Comprehensive | | Collision | |
| | | $250 Ded. | $500 Ded. | $100 Ded. | $250 Ded. | $250 Ded. | $500 Ded. | $100 Ded. | $250 Ded. |
| 1 | 0–1 | 157 | 133 | 255 | 201 | 117 | 104 | 199 | 188 |
| | 2–3 | 124 | 100 | 232 | 180 | 106 | 92 | 190 | 158 |
| | 4–5 | 106 | 84 | 187 | 158 | 98 | 90 | 154 | 140 |
| | 6+ | 100 | 80 | 157 | 132 | 86 | 81 | 137 | 116 |
| 2 | 0–1 | 135 | 121 | 243 | 189 | 105 | 92 | 187 | 176 |
| | 2–3 | 112 | 88 | 210 | 168 | 94 | 80 | 178 | 146 |
| | 4–5 | 94 | 72 | 175 | 136 | 86 | 78 | 142 | 128 |
| | 6+ | 88 | 68 | 145 | 120 | 74 | 69 | 125 | 104 |
| 3 | 0–1 | 127 | 113 | 235 | 181 | 97 | 84 | 179 | 168 |
| | 2–3 | 104 | 80 | 202 | 160 | 86 | 74 | 170 | 138 |
| | 4–5 | 86 | 64 | 167 | 148 | 78 | 70 | 134 | 120 |
| | 6+ | 80 | 60 | 137 | 112 | 66 | 61 | 117 | 96 |

**Territory:** the primary location where the vehicle is driven.

**Driver class:** the class for the primary driver based on factors such as age, sex, marital status, and driving history.

**Bodily injury:** personal injury sustained in an accident.

**Property damage:** damage to the property of others in an accident.

Table 18-5 shows a hypothetical annual rate schedule for liability insurance. Notice that there are several columns of information. The **territory** refers to the type of area in which the car is kept and driven. The **driver class** refers to such personal information about the driver as age, sex, or marital status. The 25/50 under the **bodily injury** heading means the insurance company will pay up to $25,000 for bodily injury of one individual in an accident and no more than a total of $50,000 per accident for bodily injury, regardless of the number of individuals injured in the accident. The 10, 25, 50, and 100 under the **property damage** heading indicates the limit for coverage of $10,000, $25,000, $50,000, or $100,000 for damage to the property of others, including other vehicles or property such as fences, buildings, utility poles, and so on that are involved in the accident.

Two other components of the motor vehicle insurance premium are premiums for comprehensive and collision coverage. Comprehensive and collision premiums are based on the *model class* (compact, luxury, SUV, truck, etc.), the *vehicle age*, the *territory* where the vehicle is primarily driven, and the amount of the *deductible*. Table 18-6 gives sample rates for comprehensive and collision premiums.

**HOW TO** Find an annual automobile insurance premium using table values

1. Locate the bodily injury premium according to territory, driver class, and per person/per accident bodily injury coverage.
2. Locate the property damage premium according to territory, driver class, and property damage coverage.
3. Locate the comprehensive premium according to model class, vehicle age, territory, and deductible.
4. Locate the collision premium according to model class, vehicle age, territory, and deductible.
5. Add the premiums from steps 1 to 4.

Total annual premium = bodily injury premium + property damage premium + comprehensive premium + collision premium

## EXAMPLE 1

Use Tables 18-5 and 18-6 to find the annual premium for an automobile liability insurance policy in which the insured lives in territory 1, is class A, and wishes to have 50/100/10 coverage. The vehicle is a three-year-old, model class 2 vehicle and both comprehensive and collision are carried with a $250 deductible.

| | |
|---|---|
| Bodily injury premium = $230 | Territory 1, class A, 50/100. |
| Property damage premium = $105 | Territory 1, class A, 10. |
| Comprehensive premium = $112 | Model class 2, age 3, $250 deductible. |
| Collision premium = $168 | Model class 2, age 3, $250 deductible. |
| Total annual premium = $615 | Sum. |

**The total annual premium is $615.**

## TIP

**What If Damages Exceed the Book Value of the Vehicle?**

As vehicles age, they generally decrease in value. The value of a particular year, make, and model of a vehicle is published for car dealers and insurance companies. This value is referred to as the **book value** of a vehicle. If the damages resulting from an accident exceed the book value, the insurance company will only pay for the book value. When this situation occurs, the vehicle is commonly said to be **totaled**.

In the preceding example, if the vehicle *books* for $14,500 and the damages to the vehicle are $16,000, the vehicle is *totaled* and the vehicle owner receives $14,500.

**Book value:** the value of a specific model and year of a used vehicle that is based on the estimated resale value of the vehicle.

**Totaled:** when damages to a vehicle exceed the book value, the insurance covers the damages up to the book value.

While the insured pays insurance premiums, the insurance company must pay when the insured is involved in an automobile crash or if something happens to the insured automobile. These payments or claims are called **compensation**.

**Claim compensation:** money paid by the insurance company to persons as a result of an automobile crash when the insured is at fault. The money may be for bodily injury or for property damage. The insured must pay any amounts that exceed the amount of coverage of the policy.

## EXAMPLE 2

Margo Mahler has 50/100/250 insurance. She has $500 deductible collision and $250 deductible comprehensive. Margo crashed into a vehicle (failed to yield) and three persons, Leslie, Jim, and Ursala, were injured. Leslie's medical care was $21,000, Jim's medical care was $68,754, Ursala had no injuries, and their car required $3,895 to repair. Margo's vehicle damage amounted to $5,093 but she had no injuries. How much will the insurance company need to pay and to whom? Will Margo need to pay anything? If so, how much?

Liability: Margo's insurance pays up to $50,000 per person. Leslie's $21,000 medical care will be paid by the insurance company. The insurance company will pay the limit, $50,000, for Jim's medical care. Margo will need to pay the difference $68,754 − $50,000 = $18,754. The insurance company will pay $3,895 to Ursala for vehicle repair and $5,093 − $500 = $4,593 to Margo for vehicle repairs.

## ✓ STOP AND CHECK

1. Use Tables 18-5 and 18-6 to find the annual premium for an automobile insurance policy in which the insured lives in territory 1, is class A, and buys 100/300/50 coverage. The vehicle is a 5-year-old, model class 3 vehicle and both comprehensive and collision are carried with a $100 deductible on collision and a $250 deductible on comprehensive.

2. Use Tables 18-5 and 18-6 to find the annual premium for an automobile insurance policy for Megan Anders, who lives in territory 2, is class C, and buys 50/100/100 coverage. The vehicle is 7 years old, model class 2, and both comprehensive and collision are carried with a $500 deductible on comprehensive and a $250 deductible on collision.

3. Margaret Davis has an automobile insurance policy in driver class B and she lives in territory 2. She buys 100/300/100 coverage. Her vehicle is new, in model class 1, and she elects a $500 deductible on comprehensive and a $250 deductible on collision. What is her annual premium?

4. Find the annual auto insurance premium for Reed Davis if he is in driver class A and lives in territory 1. Reed buys 50/100/50 liability coverage and $250 deductible comprehensive and $250 deductible collision coverage. Reed's truck is 2 years old and falls in model class 2.

## SKILL BUILDERS

*Find the total annual insurance premium.*

| | Territory | Driver class | Model class | Vehicle age | Liability coverage | Comprehensive deductible | Collision deductible |
|---|---|---|---|---|---|---|---|
| **1.** | 1 | A | 1 | New | 25/50/50 | $250 | $100 |
| **2.** | 1 | B | 2 | 3 years | 50/100/100 | $500 | $250 |
| **3.** | 2 | C | 3 | 4 years | 100/300/100 | $500 | $100 |
| **4.** | 2 | A | 2 | 6 years | 100/300/50 | $250 | $250 |
| **5.** | 1 | C | 1 | 1 year | 25/50/50 | $250 | $100 |
| **6.** | 2 | B | 3 | 2 years | 50/100/50 | $500 | $250 |

**7.** Find the annual auto insurance premium for Dontae Knight if he is in driver class B and lives in territory 2. Dontae has 50/100/100 liability coverage and a $250 comprehensive deductible and a $100 collision deductible. His vehicle is new and is in model class 1.

**8.** What is the annual vehicle insurance premium for Shanté Banks if she is a class B driver and lives in territory 1? Shanté has 100/300/100 liability coverage and a $250 deductible on both comprehensive and collision coverage. Her vehicle is 30 months old and is in model class 1.

## APPLICATIONS

**9.** Find the annual premium for an automobile insurance policy if the insured lives in territory 2 and is classified as a class C driver. The policy contains 25/50/10 coverage.

The vehicle is 3 years old and in model class 3, the deductible for collision is $100, and the deductible for comprehensive is $250.

**10.** Find the annual premium on a 50/100/50 policy for a class C driver in territory 1 if the vehicle is 4.5 years old and in model class 2. The insured selects a comprehensive deductible of $500 and a collision deductible of $250.

11. What are the monthly payments on an automobile insurance policy for a class B driver in territory 1 with 50/100/25 coverage? The 8-year-old vehicle is in model class 1; the comprehensive deductible is $250 and the collision deductible is $100. Assume no additional fee is required for the monthly payment option.

12. How much will an automobile liability insurance policy pay an injured person with medical expenses of $8,362 if the insured has a policy with 25/50/10 coverage?

## Learning Outcomes

## What to Remember with Examples

### Section 18-1

**1** Estimate life insurance premiums using a rate table. (p. 622)

1. Locate the estimated annual rate in Table 18-1 according to type of policy, age, and sex.
2. Divide the policy face value by $1,000 and multiply this quotient by the rate from step 1.

$$\text{Estimated annual premium} = \frac{\text{face value}}{\$1,000} \times \text{rate}$$

Use Table 18-1 to find the annual premium for a 40-year-old male for a $50,000 (a) 10-year fixed-rate policy and (b) straight-life policy.

(a) 10-year fixed rate policy: $\left(\dfrac{\$50,000}{\$1,000}\right)(\$1.46) = \$73$

(b) Straight-life policy: $\left(\dfrac{\$50,000}{\$1,000}\right)(\$4.02) = \$201$

Use Tables 18-1 and 18-2 to find the quarterly premium for a $50,000 straight-life policy on a 30-year-old female.

$$\begin{pmatrix}\text{Monthly, quarterly,} \\ \text{or semiannual} \\ \text{premium}\end{pmatrix} = \begin{pmatrix}\text{annual} \\ \text{premium}\end{pmatrix} \times \begin{pmatrix}\text{rate from} \\ \text{Table 18-2}\end{pmatrix}$$

$$\text{Annual premium} = \left(\frac{\$50,000}{\$1,000}\right)(\$3.38) = \$169$$

$$\text{Quarterly premium} = (\$169)(0.26) = \$43.94$$

**2** Apply the extended term nonforfeiture option to a cancelled straight-life policy. (p. 624)

1. Identify the cash value of the cancelled policy.
2. Estimate the annual premium for a term policy of the same face value. Use a fixed rate in Table 18-1.
3. Determine the years of paid-up insurance.

$$\text{Years of paid-up insurance} = \frac{\text{cash value of surrendered policy}}{\text{annual premium of term policy}}$$

Craig Schmaling started a $200,000 straight-life insurance policy at age 45. At age 60, he decides to use the $6,910 cash value for paid-up 10-year term insurance for the same face value. How many years of paid-up insurance will he have?

Estimated annual term premium:

$$\$4.72 \text{ per } \$1,000$$
$$\frac{\$200,000}{\$1,000} = 200 \text{ units}$$
$$200(\$4.72) = \$944$$

Years of term insurance:

$$\frac{\text{Cash value}}{\text{Annual premium}}$$
$$\frac{\$6,910}{\$944} = 7.32 \text{ years}$$

### Section 18-2

**1** Estimate property insurance premiums using a rate table. (p. 626)

1. Locate the annual rate for the building (or contents) being insured according to the building's area rank and its class.
2. Find the annual premium for both the building and the contents.

$$\text{Annual premium} = \frac{\text{face value}}{\$100} \times \text{rate}$$

**3.** Add the two premiums.

Use Table 18-3 to find the annual premium for building and contents if a building is insured for $120,000 and its contents are insured for $350,000. The building is a class C building in area 3.

Annual premium for building:

$$\left(\frac{\$120,000}{\$100}\right)(\$0.98) = \$1,176$$

Annual premium for contents:

$$\left(\frac{\$350,000}{\$100}\right)(\$1.16) = \$4,060$$

Total premium:

$$\$1,176 + \$4,060 = \$5,236$$

---

**2** Find the refund for a cancelled policy. (p. 627)

1. Identify the annual premium.
2. Identify the time the policy is in force.
3. Use Table 18-4 to find the short rate for the time the policy is in force.
4. Find the short-rate premium:

$$\text{Short-rate premium} = \text{annual premium} \times \text{short rate}$$

5. Find the refund:

$$\text{Refund} = \text{annual premium} - \text{short-rate premium}$$

The building insurance in the preceding example was cancelled after nine months. What was the refund due on the insurance policy?

$$\text{Annual premium} = \$5,236$$
$$\text{Time policy in force} = 9 \text{ months}$$
$$\text{Short-rate percent} = 85\%$$
$$\text{Short-rate premium} = \$5,236(0.85)$$
$$= \$4,450.60$$
$$\text{Refund} = \$5,236 - \$4,450.60$$
$$= \$785.40$$

**The refund due is $785.40**

---

**3** Find the compensation with a coinsurance clause. (p. 628)

1. Find the face value required by the 80% coinsurance clause for full compensation: Multiply 0.8 by the replacement value of the property.
2. Find the compensation for the loss if the insurance is less than 80% of the replacement value.

$$\begin{array}{l}\text{Compensation (up to} \\ \text{amount of loss)}\end{array} = \begin{array}{c}\text{amount of loss} \\ \text{(up to face value)}\end{array} \times \frac{\text{face value of policy}}{80\% \text{ of replacement value of property}}$$

A property valued at $325,000 is insured in a policy that contains an 80% coinsurance clause. The face value of the policy is $200,000. What is the amount of compensation if a fire results in a total loss of the property?

$$\text{Compensation} = \$200,000\left(\frac{\$200,000}{0.8 \times \$325,000}\right)$$
$$= \$200,000\left(\frac{\$200,000}{\$260,000}\right)$$
$$\text{Compensation} = \$200,000(0.769230769) = \$153,846.15$$

Even though the fire caused damages valued at $325,000, the insured receives only $153,846.15 in compensation.

## Section 18-3

**1** Find automobile insurance premiums using rate tables. (p. 631)

1. Locate the bodily injury premium according to territory, driver class, and per person/per accident bodily injury coverage.
2. Locate the property damage premium according to territory, driver class, and property damage coverage.
3. Locate the comprehensive premium according to model class, vehicle age, territory, and deductible.
4. Locate the collision premium according to model class, vehicle age, territory, and deductible.
5. Add the premiums from steps 1 through 4.

$$\text{Total annual premium} = \text{bodily injury premium} + \text{property damage}$$
$$\text{premium} + \text{comprehensive premium} + \text{collision premium}$$

Use Tables 18-5 and 18-6 to find the annual premium for an automobile insurance policy in which the insured lives in territory 2, is in class C, model class 2, has a vehicle age of 4 years, and wishes to have 25/50/10 liability coverage and comprehensive and collision coverage with a $250 deductible.

The cost of 25/50 bodily injury coverage for territory 2 and class C is $251.
The cost of $10,000 property damage is $128.
The cost of comprehensive coverage with a $250 deductible is $86.
The cost of collision coverage with a $250 deductible is $128.
Total annual premium = $251 + $128 + $86 + $128 = $593.

# EXERCISES SET A

*Using Table 18-3, find the annual fire insurance premium for each of the following.*

| Area rank | Class | Face value of policy Building | Face value of policy Contents | Annual premium Building | Annual premium Contents | Total |
|---|---|---|---|---|---|---|
| **CEL 1.** 3 | A | $372,000 | $226,000 | | | |
| **2.** 2 | B | $416,000 | $241,700 | | | |
| **3.** 3 | C | $105,000 | $63,500 | | | |

*Use Tables 18-3 and 18-4 when necessary to solve the following problems.*

**4.** A sign company owns a class A building in area 2 valued at $95,000. The building is insured for $60,000 and the policy has an 80% coinsurance clause. How much will the owner of the sign company receive from his policy if a fire causes $38,000 in damages?

**5.** Robyn Presley insures her class B building located in area 3 for $260,000 and the contents for $135,000. Find the total annual insurance premium.

**6.** Trent Sweebe cancelled his property insurance 11 months after the effective date because he went out of business. He had paid a $4,917 annual premium. What is his refund?

*Use Tables 18-5 and 18-6 to find the total annual premium for each of the following automobile liability insurance policies.*

| | Territory | Driver class | Liability coverage | Model class | Vehicle age | Comprehensive deductible | Collision deductible |
|---|---|---|---|---|---|---|---|
| **7.** | 1 | B | 25/50/25 | 3 | New | $250 | $100 |
| **8.** | 1 | C | 100/300/100 | 2 | 4 years | $500 | $250 |
| **9.** | 2 | A | 50/100/50 | 1 | 3 years | $250 | $250 |

**10.** The company car for the Greenwood Rental Agency in territory 2 for a class C driver is insured with 50/100/25 coverage. The car is model class 1, is 3 years old, and has a comprehensive deductible of $500 and a collision deductible of $250. What is the annual insurance premium?

**11.** Sally Greenspan has 100/300/100 liability coverage and lives in territory 2. She is a class B driver and carries a comprehensive deductible of $250 and a collision deductible of $100. Her 4-year-old vehicle falls in model class 3. Find her annual insurance premium.

**12.** As a class A driver in territory 1, Laura Jansky is buying an auto insurance policy with 100/300/100 coverage. She has a comprehensive deductible of $250 and a collision deductible of $250. Her new vehicle is in model class 2. Find her annual premium.

**13.** Cheuk NamLam is a class A driver living in territory 1. He has auto liability insurance with 50/100/25 coverage. He has a $250 deductible for both comprehensive and collision. His 8-year-old vehicle is in model class 2. Find his annual premium.

*Use Table 18-1 to find the annual premium of each of the following life insurance policies:*

| | Sex | Age | Policy type | Face value | Annual premium |
|---|---|---|---|---|---|
| **14.** | Male | 20 | 20-year fixed rate | $150,000 | |
| **15.** | Female | 30 | Straight-life | $200,000 | |

*Use Tables 18-1 and 18-2 to find the following premiums:*

| | Sex | Age | Policy type | Face value | Annual premium | Monthly premium | Quarterly premium |
|---|---|---|---|---|---|---|---|
| **16.** | Female | 60 | Straight-life | $350,000 | | | |
| **17.** | Female | 30 | 10-year fixed rate | $480,000 | | | |

**18.** (a) Find the annual premium paid by Sara Cushion, age 40, on a straight-life insurance policy for $500,000.
(b) Find the semiannual premium Sara would pay on the straight-life policy.

**19.** A straight-life policy purchased at age 50 by Thomas Wimberly costs how much more per $1,000 than the same policy for a male age 60?

**20.** How much are the total quarterly payments paid by Erich Shultz, age 40, and his wife Demetria, age 30, if each has a 20-year fixed-rate insurance policy for $300,000?

**21.** Marguerite Jones is 40 years old and decides to convert her $500,000 straight-life insurance policy to extended term insurance. Use 20-year fixed rates to estimate the number of years of extended term life insurance her cash value of $15,748 will buy.

**22.** Marquesha Long at age 60 wants to convert her $200,000 straight-life insurance policy to extended term insurance with the same face value. Use 20-year fixed rates to estimate the number of years of coverage her cash value of $14,513 will buy.

## EXERCISES SET B

*Using Table 18-3, find the annual fire insurance premium for each of the following:*

| | Area rank | Class | Face value of policy Building | Contents | Annual premium Building | Contents | Total |
|---|---|---|---|---|---|---|---|
| 1. | 1 | C | $538,000 | $221,000 | | | |
| 2. | 2 | A | $878,500 | $232,300 | | | |
| 3. | 3 | B | $258,000 | $179,000 | | | |

*Use Table 18-3 and Table 18-4 when necessary to solve the following.*

**4.** What part of the damages will Hampton Insurance Company pay on a building with $18,000 damage by fire if the market value is $86,000 and it is insured for $65,000? The policy contains an 80% coinsurance clause.

**5.** In area 1, a class C building is insured for $305,000 and its contents for $95,000. If no extra charge is added for semiannual payments, find the premium paid every six months.

**6.** Hannah Ricker closed her consulting business and cancelled her property insurance nine months after the effective date. Hannah had paid a $3,040 annual premium. How much refund is she due?

*Use Tables 18-5 and 18-6 to find the total annual premium for each of the following automobile liability insurance policies.*

| | Territory | Driver class | Total coverage | Model class | Vehicle age | Comprehensive deductible | Collision deductible |
|---|---|---|---|---|---|---|---|
| 7. | 2 | A | 50/100/10 | 1 | 1 year | $500 | $250 |
| 8. | 2 | B | 50/100/25 | 3 | 4 years | $500 | $250 |
| 9. | 1 | C | 100/300/100 | 1 | New | $250 | $100 |

10. Aggawal Montoya is a class B driver who lives in territory 1. He has automobile insurance on his 3-year-old vehicle with 100/300/50 coverage. The vehicle is in model class 1 and has a $250 deductible for both comprehensive and collision. Find his annual premium.

11. Larry Tremont has an insurance policy with a $100 deductible clause for collision and a $500 deductible clause for comprehensive. Larry's liability coverage on his 5-year-old, model class 2 vehicle is 50/100/100. Find his annual premium if he is a class C driver in territory 2.

12. Fred Case has an auto insurance policy with 25/50/10 liability coverage. He lives in territory 2 and is a class C driver. His vehicle is in model class 3 and is 26 months old. His deductible for comprehensive and collision is $250. Find his annual premium.

13. John Malinowsky has auto insurance with 25/50/25 liability coverage. His vehicle is 12 years old and is in model class 2. John lives in territory 1. Find his annual premium if he has a $500 deductible on comprehensive and a $250 deductible on collision and is a class B driver.

*Use Table 18-1 to find the annual premium of the following life insurance policies:*

| | Sex | Age | Policy type | Face value | Annual premium |
|---|---|---|---|---|---|
| 14. | Male | 30 | 10-year fixed rate | $300,000 | |
| 15. | Female | 50 | Straight-life | $100,000 | |

*Use Tables 18-1 and 18-2 to find the premiums.*

| | Sex | Age | Policy type | Face value | Annual premium | Monthly premium | Quarterly premium |
|---|---|---|---|---|---|---|---|
| 16. | Female | 20 | Straight-life | $350,000 | | | |
| 17. | Male | 40 | 20-year fixed rate | $100,000 | | | |

18. Sam Molla has a 10-year fixed-rate life insurance policy with a value of $250,000. How much is his semiannual premium if he is 40 years old?

19. Find the annual premium paid on a straight-life insurance policy for $375,000 taken out at age 30 by a male.

20. Find the monthly premium of a $450,000 straight-life insurance policy purchased by a 20-year-old female.

21. At 30 years old Jaime Dawson finds the need to convert his straight-life insurance policy of $500,000 to extended term coverage with the same face value. Use 10-year fixed rates to estimate the number of years of extended term coverage his cash value of $1,023 will provide.

22. Tancia Brown is 50 years old and is converting her $450,000 straight-life insurance policy to extended term insurance with the same face value. Use 10-year fixed rates to estimate the number of years of coverage her cash value of $7,252 will buy.

# PRACTICE TEST

1. Find the annual premium on a $300,000 straight-life insurance policy for a 40-year-old male.

2. Find the annual premium on a 50/100/50 automobile insurance policy for a class C driver in territory 2 who has a 2-year-old car in model class 1. The comprehensive deductible is $250 and the collision deductible is $100.

3. Find the annual premium for a fire-protection policy on a building insured at $287,500 in class B, area 2. The contents are insured for $68,000.

4. Find the annual premium on a 100/300/100 automobile insurance policy for a class A driver in territory 2. The vehicle is 5 years old, in model class 2, and the comprehensive and collision deductible is $250.

5. Find the annual premium on a 10-year fixed-rate insurance policy for $150,000 for a 30-year-old male.

6. Find the annual premium on a 50/100/25 automobile insurance policy for a class B driver in territory 1. The new car is in model class 3 and has a $500 comprehensive deductible and a $250 collision deductible.

7. A building and its contents are insured for $178,000 and $42,760, respectively. Find the total annual premium if the building is a class C building in area 3.

8. Compare the cost per year of a straight-life insurance policy for $200,000 to a 20-year fixed-rate policy for a 60-year-old male.

**9.** How much does a 30-year-old female pay in monthly premiums for a $250,000 straight-life insurance policy?

**10.** Find the quarterly payments on a 10-year fixed-rate life insurance policy for $150,000 on a 40-year-old male.

**11.** The market value of a building is $72,500. It is insured for $50,000 with an 80% coinsurance clause. If a fire causes $62,000 in damages, how much of the damages will the policy cover?

**12.** Find the annual premium for a 50/100/25 automobile liability insurance policy for a class A driver in territory 2 with a 12-year-old car in model class 3. Comprehensive has a $500 deductible and collision has a $250 deductible.

**13.** Mary Lynne Winston is 50 years old and decides to convert her $100,000 straight-life insurance policy to extended term coverage with the same face value. How many years of 10-year fixed-rate term insurance will she have if her cash value is $973?

**14.** Paige Duvall paid a $6,803 annual property insurance premium but cancelled the policy two months after the effective date. How much refund should she receive?

1. The formula for finding an annual fire insurance premium using a table with rates per $100 of face value (Table 18-3) is given on page 626. Another source may have a table giving rates per $1,000 of face value. How will the formula change when using this table?

2. If the new rates for the table described in Exercise 1 are equivalent to the rates in Table 18-3, what would the new rates be? Revise Table 18-3 to show the equivalent rates per $1,000.

3. If a business had fire insurance to cover 60% of the property's value, and fire damages were 40% of the property value, what percent will the insurance company with an 80% coinsurance clause pay for the loss?

4. If a business had fire insurance to cover 80% of the property's value, and fire damages were 90% of the total value, what percent will the insurance company with an 80% coinsurance clause pay for the loss?

5. If a car rental agency charges $8.50 per day for a liability, comprehensive, and collision waiver, this would be equivalent to what annual premium? Why do you suppose no difference is made for territory or driver class?

6. Why is straight-life insurance more expensive than term life insurance?

7. Justify why life insurance premiums are higher for males than females who are in the same age category.

8. The formula given for using Table 18-1 is

$$\text{Annual premium} = \frac{\text{face value}}{\$1,000} \times \text{rate}.$$

Is the formula

$$\text{Annual premium} = \text{face value} \times \frac{\text{rate}}{\$1,000}$$

equivalent? Why or why not?

## Challenge Problem

Manny Bober has a property insurance policy with a value of $500,000. His annual premium is $0.95 per $100 of coverage. If Manny cancels the policy after 300 days, what is his refund if the refund is prorated based on a 360-day year?

# CASE STUDIES

## 18.1  How Much Is Enough?

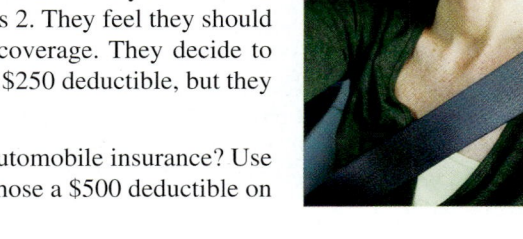

Alex and Christa have been married for several years. They have two young children, both under the age of 5. Alex works full-time as an electrical engineer and Christa works part-time as a floral designer. They own a modest 3-bedroom, 2-bath home on a ¼-acre lot and have two cars. They recently attended a financial planning seminar that highlighted a number of issues, such as saving, investing, insuring, and tax and estate planning. Alex and Christa have decided to reassess their insurance needs to determine what portion of their budget should be designated for insurance premiums.

They decide to review their auto insurance first. According to the literature they picked up, they live in Territory 1 and are considered Class A drivers. They own two cars, one of which is 2 years old and considered Model Class 1; the other is 6 years old and considered Model Class 2. They feel they should have $100/$300 bodily injury coverage, and $100,000 of property damage coverage. They decide to purchase comprehensive and collision coverage on their newer vehicle with a $250 deductible, but they decide to forego comprehensive and collision coverage on their older vehicle.

1. What amount should Alex and Christa plan to spend annually on their automobile insurance? Use the tables provided in this chapter. How much would they save if they chose a $500 deductible on the comprehensive coverage?

   | Coverage | Car 1: 2 years old | Car 2: 6 years old |
   |---|---|---|
   | Bodily injury | | |
   | Property damage | | |
   | Comprehensive | | |
   | Collision | | |

2. The market value of their home is approximately $180,000. Their insurance policy contains a coinsurance clause. How much insurance should Alex and Christa carry to meet the coinsurance requirement and how much should they anticipate for an annual insurance premium for building and contents if their home is considered Class B and is located in an area considered Area rank 1? Assume they want contents coverage of $100,000.

3. Alex is also thinking about purchasing additional life insurance. His employer provides some life insurance coverage, but the financial planner at the seminar they attended suggested he carry insurance to represent an amount 5 to 15 times his annual earnings. Alex earns $75,000 a year and his employer provides $75,000 of life insurance. If Alex decides to purchase enough insurance to cover 10 times his earnings, how much more insurance should he purchase? If he falls in the 30-year-old male category and selects 20-year fixed-rate insurance, how much should he plan to spend annually on life insurance?

4. Considering the auto insurance, the property insurance, and the life insurance, how much should Alex and Christa plan to pay each year in premiums? Assume a $250 deductible for the auto insurance. What percentage of Alex's gross pay do these premiums represent?

# 18.2 Divine Soul Food Catering

Amaya left the doctor's office with a strange feeling that seemed to be a combination of euphoria and apprehension. As if moving her catering business to a new location wasn't enough. Now she felt apprehension at being a first-time mom at age 30 while running a successful business. And she felt euphoria about the new addition to the family. Amaya couldn't wait to tell her husband that they were expecting a baby. This was going to mean big changes. Her first thought was childcare—but for now, that could wait. Her most pressing concern was insurance. With the move to a new and larger building valued at $250,000, certainly the cost for property insurance was going up. By adding two more delivery vans at $17,500 each, the cost for automobile insurance would, at minimum, double. And now with a baby on the way, life insurance was more important than ever. After her husband, the next call was going to be to their insurance agent. There was a lot of planning to do.

1. Amaya's agent states that a good rule of thumb for life insurance is to purchase 5 to 7 times your annual income. Amaya's income averages $50,000 annually, but she would like to have the building paid off as well in the event of her death, so she decides $600,000 is the face amount she would like to have. Using the life insurance table, make a comparison of 10-year, 20-year, and straight-life annual rates for $600,000 of face amount.

2. Given your answers to question 1, which coverage would you recommend that Amaya take? What incentive does she have to take a higher-priced premium? Explain.

3. Due to a higher replacement cost, Amaya's agent recommends insuring the new building at $275,000, and the contents at 70% of the building. The building is a class C building located in Area 2. Using the fire insurance rates per $100 of face value in your text, find the annual premium for the building and contents.

4. Amaya is very concerned about the liability of having her employees driving the new vans, so she decides to go with 100/300/100 liability coverage. Use Table 18-5 to find the annual premium for automobile liability insurance using Territory 2, Class B; and Table 18-6 to find the comprehensive and collision rates using Territory 2, Class 3, with a $250 deductible for comprehensive and a $100 deductible for collision.

# Preparing Your Own Tax Return

Preparing your own tax return for the first time can be intimidating, but it has several advantages. You are in full control of your tax return, you can work on your taxes at your own pace, and you get to see first hand how various parts of your financial situation come together to impact your tax bill. Software packages for preparing your own tax return have improved, and it is often just as easy to use tax software as it is to go to a professional tax preparer.

Before preparing your taxes, take the time to organize all the documents you will need. These documents include all W-2 forms sent from your employers and tax statements relating to your bank accounts and investment holdings. You can find Web-based versions of powerful tax software, such as SecureTax or TurboTax, that help you prepare and file your taxes. These sites are still best suited to simple returns, but they are becoming more sophisticated. And most individuals preparing their returns for the first time qualify for IRS Form 1040-EZ (EZ stands for easy), the simplest of the IRS returns.

You qualify to use the 1040-EZ* if:

- Your total income is under $100,000.
- Your interest income is under $1,500.
- You have income only from wages, interest, unemployment compensation, and Alaska Permanent Fund dividends.
- You and your spouse are under 65 years old.
- You do not have any adjustments to income.
- You are claiming only the standard deduction.
- You may claim the Earned Income Credit.
- You may claim the Telephone Excise Tax Refund.
- You are not claiming any other tax credit.

If you plan to prepare your taxes, you may want to file electronically instead of sending your tax documents via U.S. Mail. E-filing or electronic filing is a quick, easy, and accurate alternative to traditional paper returns with many advantages:

- You receive your refund in about 3 weeks instead of the usual 10 weeks.
- Your chance of getting an error notice from the IRS is decreased because it is more accurate than mailing a paper return. The error rate for electronic returns is less than 1 percent versus 20 to 21 percent for paper returns.
- You get proof that the IRS has accepted your return within 48 hours.
- Your privacy and security are assured.

*Always check with the IRS at www.irs.gov for the current tax year requirements.

## LEARNING OUTCOMES

### 19-1 Sales Tax and Excise Tax

1. Use the percent method to find the sales tax and excise tax.
2. Find the marked price and the sales tax from the total price.

### 19-2 Property Tax

1. Find the assessed value.
2. Calculate property tax.
3. Determine the property tax rate.

### 19-3 Income Taxes

1. Find taxable income.
2. Use the tax tables to calculate income tax.
3. Use the tax rate schedules to calculate income tax.

**Tax:** money collected by a government for its support and for providing services to the populace.

Taxes affect everyone in one way or another. A **tax** is money collected by a government for its support and for providing services to the populace. Governments use tax money to pay the salaries of government officials and employees. Tax monies run and staff public schools, parks, and playgrounds; build and maintain roads and highways; and provide police and fire protection, health services, unemployment compensation, and numerous other benefits.

To meet these many needs, governments have a variety of tax types from which to choose. Among the most common are sales taxes, property taxes, and income taxes.

## 19-1 SALES TAX AND EXCISE TAX

### LEARNING OUTCOMES

1 Use the percent method to find the sales tax and excise tax.
2 Find the marked price and the sales tax from the total price.

**Sales tax:** a tax that is based on the price of a purchase. The tax is collected at the time of purchase and the business periodically sends the collected tax to a governmental agency.

The sales tax is probably the first type of tax that most people encounter since most states have sales taxes. Sales taxes are determined by state and local governments. At the time of a purchase, a store collects an extra amount, called a **sales tax**, and later pays it to the state. In some states, county or city governments charge a local sales tax in addition to the state sales tax. Many states charge no sales tax on food or medicine, and some states make other exceptions. New Jersey, for example, does not charge tax on clothing. By a recent count, thirteen states and Washington, DC have sales tax holidays. These are days when the shoppers get a break on back-to-school shopping. Most holidays fall on the first weekend in August and apply to school-related items. In Texas, for example, these dates are August 3, 4, and 5. Tennessee observes the first Monday in August as tax-free day, and in 2007 there was a special one-time tax-free holiday from April 27 through 29.

In some areas a sales tax is charged only on purchases made and delivered within the tax area. For instance, if an item is purchased in one state and delivered to another, the sales tax is not always charged. This also applies to many catalog and Internet purchases. State laws vary and change often, and it is the responsibility of the seller to determine if tax is exempt on a sale. However, the state to which large purchases are delivered may impose its sales tax. For instance, if an automobile is purchased in one state and delivered to another, the state into which it is delivered may require that sales tax be paid before the automobile can be registered.

### 1 Use the percent method to find the sales tax or excise tax.

In most states the sales tax is a specified percent of the selling price. Most businesses use computerized cash registers that allow the current tax rate to be programmed into the cash register. Then the register automatically figures sales tax.

**Excise tax:** a tax or duty levied on the sale or importation of goods for the purpose of raising revenue or discouraging a particular behavior.

**Excise tax** is usually a tax or duty levied on the sale or importation of particular goods. These taxes usually are imposed to raise revenue or to discourage a particular behavior. Most states impose excise tax on sales of fuel, alcohol, and tobacco to accomplish both aims. Portions of excise tax from alcohol and tobacco are used to pay for the treatment of diseases caused by these substances. Excise tax on motor fuel ranges from a low of 4.0% on gasoline in Florida to a high of 30.0% on gasoline, diesel fuel, and gasohol in Rhode Island. Excise tax rates for cigarettes range from a low of $0.07 per pack in South Carolina to a high of $2.58 per pack in New Jersey.

| HOW TO | Use the percent method to find the sales tax or excise tax |
|---|---|

1. Write the given percent as a decimal.
2. Find the sales tax:

$$\text{Sales tax} = \text{purchase price} \times \text{sales tax rate}$$

where sales tax rate = tax per $1.00 of the purchase price or a percent of the purchase price.

**EXAMPLE 1**    Find the state sales tax on $128.72 at six cents per $1.00, or 6%.

$128.72(6\%) = \$128.72(0.06)$    Multiply the purchase price by 6%.
Change the percent to a decimal (0.06).
$= \$7.72$ (rounded)    Round the answer to the nearest cent.

**The state sales tax is $7.72.**

**EXAMPLE 2** Find the excise tax on a purchase of $45.93 in gasoline in Nebraska where the excise tax rate is 27.1%.

$45.93(27.1\%) =$      Multiply the purchase price by the excise tax rate. Change the percent to a decimal.

$45.93(0.271) = \$12.44703$      Round to the nearest cent.

**The excise tax on the purchase is $12.45.**

---

## ✔ STOP AND CHECK

**1.** California's state sales tax rate is 7.25%. What is the sales tax on a CD that costs $19.95 and is purchased in California?

**2.** Colorado's state sales tax rate is 2.9%. Find the sales tax on a DVD player purchased in Colorado for $298.99.

**3.** The state sales tax rate in Utah is 4.75%. How much sales tax is paid on a skateboard that costs $49.99?

**4.** Maine has a 5% general, service provider, and use state sales tax rate. How much tax is paid on a pair of boots purchased in Maine for $149.95?

---

## 2   Find the marked price and the sales tax from the total price.

Some circumstances make it more convenient to include the sales tax in the quoted price. These circumstances may include sporting events, amusement parks, flea markets, or other places where making change can be difficult and time-consuming. In these instances, the sales tax eventually must be calculated so that the proper tax is turned over to the tax agency. When the sales tax is not itemized, you may want to know how much the sales tax was or what the *marked price* of the item was. The **marked price** is the purchase price or the price before sales tax is added. The **total price** is the marked price plus the sales tax.

**Marked price:** the purchase price before sales tax is added.

**Total price:** the marked price plus the sales tax.

---

**HOW TO**   Find the marked price and the sales tax from the total price

1. Find the marked price:
   (a) Write the sales tax rate as a decimal equivalent.
   (b) Add 1 to the decimal equivalent of the sales tax rate from step 1a.
   (c) Divide the total price by the sum from step 1b.

$$\text{Marked price} = \frac{\text{total price}}{1 + \text{sales tax rate}}$$

2. Find the sales tax:

$$\text{Sales tax} = \text{total price} - \text{marked price}$$

---

**EXAMPLE 1** At an amusement park concession, the items are priced to include tax. Find the marked price and the sales tax. The sales tax rate is 7%.

Popcorn: $3.00; soft drink: $3.50; hot dog: $4.00

$$\text{Marked price} = \frac{\text{total price}}{1 + \text{sales tax rate (as a decimal)}}$$

$$\text{Popcorn marked price} = \frac{\$3.00}{1 + 0.07} = \frac{\$3.00}{1.07} = \$2.80$$

$$\text{Soft drink marked price} = \frac{\$3.50}{1 + 0.07} = \frac{\$3.50}{1.07} = \$3.27$$

$$\text{Hot dog marked price} = \frac{\$4.00}{1 + 0.07} = \frac{\$4.00}{1.07} = \$3.74$$

$$\text{Sales tax} = \text{total price} - \text{marked price}$$

$$\text{Popcorn sales tax} = \$3.00 - \$2.80 = \$0.20$$

$$\text{Soft drink sales tax} = \$3.50 - \$3.27 = \$0.23$$

$$\text{Hot dog sales tax} = \$4.00 - \$3.74 = \$0.26$$

**The marked prices for the popcorn, soft drink, and hot dog are \$2.80, \$3.27, and \$3.74. The sales taxes for the popcorn, soft drink, and hot dog are \$0.20, \$0.23, and \$0.26.**

---

## TIP

**Why Not Just Multiply the Sales Tax Rate Times the Total Price and Subtract?**

A common mistake when determining the marked price from the total price is to apply the sales tax rate to the total price and then subtract. Let's try that with the \$3 popcorn.

$$\text{Popcorn} = \frac{\$3.00}{1 + 0.07}$$
$$= \frac{\$3.00}{1.07}$$
$$= \$2.80 \text{ (marked price)}$$

**CORRECT**

$$\text{Popcorn} = \$3.00 \times 0.07$$
$$= 0.21$$
$$\$3.00 - \$0.21 = \$2.79 \text{ (marked price)}$$

**INCORRECT**

What happened? Sales tax is applied to the marked or purchase price. That is, the marked price is the base. To find a percent of the total price, the total price is the base.

As the marked price increases, the difference would be more dramatic. Look at a painting sold at a flea market for \$200 with a sales tax rate of 7%.

$$\text{Marked price} = \frac{\$200}{1 + 0.07}$$
$$= \frac{\$200}{1.07}$$
$$= \$186.92 \text{ (rounded)}$$

$$\text{Sales tax} = \$200 - \$186.92$$
$$= \$13.08$$

**CORRECT**

$$\text{Sales tax} = \$200 \times 0.07$$
$$= \$14$$
$$\text{Marked price} = \$200 - \$14$$
$$= \$186$$

**INCORRECT**

Here the correct sales tax is \$0.92 less than the incorrect calculations.

---

## ✔ STOP AND CHECK

1. Susan Riddle includes state sales tax in the cost of her photos. One client paid \$790 for family photos. Susan lives in Tennessee where the state sales tax rate is 7%. How much sales tax does Susan send to the state for this sale?

2. First Serve Vending had \$5,852.25 in sales from its vending machines. These sales include taxes at 6.25%. Find the marked price and the sales tax for these items.

3. A sports team sold \$380,926 in admission tickets, all subject to a 5.75% state sales tax. Find the total marked price of admission tickets and the sales tax.

4. A flea market vendor who sells all his items "including tax" reported a total of \$12,583 in weekend sales. Find the marked price total and the sales tax if the tax rate is 7%.

## SKILL BUILDERS

*Find the sales tax and total sale.*

| Item marked price | Sales tax rate | Sales tax | Total sale |
|---|---|---|---|
| **1.** $592.36 | 5.125% | | |

| Item marked price | Sales tax rate | Sales tax | Total sale |
|---|---|---|---|
| **2.** $38.56 | 4.225% | | |

| Item marked price | Sales tax rate | Sales tax | Total sale |
|---|---|---|---|
| **3.** $3,296 | 4.5% | | |

| Item marked price | Sales tax rate | Sales tax | Total sale |
|---|---|---|---|
| **4.** $738.47 | 6% | | |

*Find the marked price and sales tax.*

| Total price | Sales tax rate | Marked price | Sales tax |
|---|---|---|---|
| **5.** $681.42 | 4% | | |

| Total price | Sales tax rate | Marked price | Sales tax |
|---|---|---|---|
| **6.** $48.97 | 1.225% | | |

| Total price | Sales tax rate | Marked price | Sales tax |
|---|---|---|---|
| **7.** $395.17 | 6.5% | | |

| Total price | Sales tax rate | Marked price | Sales tax |
|---|---|---|---|
| **8.** $1,382.56 | 5.2% | | |

**9.** Find the sales tax on an appliance costing $288.63 if the tax rate is 5.5%.

**10.** Find the sales tax on a ring that costs $2,860 in a state with a 6.5% sales tax rate.

**11.** Barbara Montgomery purchased 100 azaleas at a cost of $283. Find the sales tax on the purchase if the rate is 7.25%.

**12.** Larry Burton paid $195.95 for a new television. He paid sales tax at a rate of 6.75%. How much tax did he pay?

**13.** What is the marked price if a total bill is $182.38 and the sales tax rate is 6%?

**14.** Clifford Shropshire has a flea market booth and marks all his items so that the price includes state sales tax at a rate of 6.5%. He sold a set of china for $285. How much sales tax should he send to the state?

**15.** You have agreed to pay $850 for a used utility trailer. The price includes sales tax at a rate of 7.75%. What was the marked price of the trailer and how much tax was paid?

**16.** You have a receipt for a purchase that shows the total amount of the purchase to be $318.97. The sales tax rate is 8.25%. How much of the $318.97 is the cost of the item and how much is sales tax?

## LEARNING OUTCOMES

1 Find the assessed value.
2 Calculate property tax.
3 Determine the property tax rate.

**Property tax:** tax collected by county, municipality, or local governments from property owners. The tax is based on the type of property and the value of the property.

Most states allow cities and counties to collect money by charging a **property tax** on land, houses, buildings, and improvements and on such personal property as automobiles, jewelry, and furniture.

## 1 Find the assessed value.

**Market value:** the expected selling price of a property.

**Assessed value:** a specified percent of the estimated market value of the property.

Property tax is usually calculated using the assessed value of the property rather than using the **market value** (the expected selling price of the property). The **assessed value** is a specified percent of the estimated market value of the property. This percent, which may vary according to the type of property, is set by the city or county that charges the tax. For example, your city or county may assess farm property and single-family dwellings at 25% of the market value, businesses and multifamily dwellings (duplexes, apartments) at 40% of the market value, and utilities (power companies, telephone companies) at 50% of the market value.

### HOW TO Find the assessed value

1. Write the assessment rate as the decimal equivalent of the percent.
2. Find the assessed value:

$$\text{Assessed value} = \text{market value} \times \text{assessment rate}$$

### EXAMPLE 1
Find the assessed value of a farm with a market value of $175,000 if the assessed valuation is 25% of the market value.

$175,000(0.25) = $43,750     Find 25% of $175,000.

**The assessed value is $43,750.**

---

## STOP AND CHECK

1. Find the assessed value of a single-family dwelling with a market value of $338,500 if the assessed valuation is 25% of the market value.

2. What is the assessed value of an apartment building with a market value of $2,580,000 if the assessed valuation is 40% of market value?

3. Lafayette Water Company has a market value of $2,839,800 and utilities are assessed at 50% of market value. Find the assessed value of the utility company.

4. The 7th Inning Sports Memorabilia Shop has a market value of $1,800,000 and is assessed at 40% of its market value. Find the assessed value of the shop.

---

## 2 Calculate property tax.

**Property tax rate:** the rate of tax that is paid for owning property.

**Mill:** one-thousandth of a dollar.

The city or county government imposes a property tax that might express the **property tax rate,** the rate of tax that must be paid on a piece of property, in one of several ways. The rate could be stated as a percent of the assessed value, as an amount of tax per $1.00 of assessed value, as an amount of tax per $100 of assessed value, as an amount of tax per $1,000 of assessed value, or in mills. A **mill** is one-thousandth $(\frac{1}{1000}, \text{ or } 0.001)$ of a dollar.

**Calculate the property tax**

1. Express the given property tax rate as tax per $1.00 of assessed value:
   (a) If the given rate is a percent of assessed value, write the percent in decimal form.

$$\text{Tax per } \$1.00 = \text{decimal form of the percent of assessed value}$$

   (b) If the given rate is tax per $100 of assessed value, divide the tax on $100 by $100.

$$\text{Tax per } \$1.00 = \frac{\text{tax on } \$100}{\$100}$$

   (c) If the given rate is tax per $1,000 of assessed value, divide the tax on $1,000 by $1,000.

$$\text{Tax per } \$1.00 = \frac{\text{tax on } \$1,000}{\$1,000}$$

   (d) If the given rate is a number of mills per $1.00 of assessed value, divide the number of mills by $1,000.

$$\text{Tax per } \$1.00 = \frac{\text{mills per } \$1.00}{\$1,000}$$

2. Find the property tax:

$$\text{Property tax} = \text{assessed value} \times \text{property tax rate per } \$1.00$$

**EXAMPLE 1** Find the property tax on a home with an assessed value of $90,000 if the property tax rate is (a) 11.08% of the assessed value, (b) $11.08 per $100 of the assessed value, (c) $110.80 per $1,000 of the assessed value, (d) 110.8 mills per $1.00 of assessed value.

(a) Property tax = assessed value × tax rate
$$= \$90,000\,(0.1108) = \$9,972$$

Write the percent in decimal form as a tax per $1.00 of assessed value. Multiply.

**The property tax is $9,972.**

(b) Property tax = assessed value × $\dfrac{\text{tax on } \$100}{\$100}$

Write the tax rate as an equivalent amount per $1.00 of assessed value.

$$= \$90,000\left(\frac{\$11.08}{\$100}\right)$$

Divide.

$$= \$90,000\,(0.1108) = \$9,972$$

Multiply the assessed value by the property tax rate per $1.00.

**The property tax is $9,972.**

(c) Property tax = assessed value × $\dfrac{\text{tax on } \$1,000}{\$1,000}$

Write the tax rate as an equivalent amount per $1.00 of assessed value.

$$= \$90,000\left(\frac{\$110.80}{\$1,000}\right)$$

Divide.

$$= \$90,000\,(0.1108) = \$9,972$$

Multiply the assessed value by the property tax rate per $1.00.

**The property tax is $9,972.**

(d) Property tax = assessed value × $\dfrac{\text{mills per } \$1.00}{\$1,000}$

Write the tax rate as an equivalent amount per $1.00 of assessed value.

$$= \$90,000\left(\frac{110.8 \text{ mills}}{\$1,000}\right)$$

Divide.

$$= \$90,000\,(0.1108) = \$9,972$$

Multiply the assessed value by the property tax rate per $1.00.

**The property tax is $9,972.**

 **STOP AND CHECK**

1. Find the property tax on a home with an assessed value of $85,250 if the property tax rate is 9.58% of the assessed value.

2. What is the property tax on the 7th Inning Sports Memorabilia Shop, which has an assessed value of $720,000, if the property tax rate is $3.45 per $100 of assessed value?

*(continued)*

3. Reggie Howard owns property assessed at $125,300 and the property tax rate is $78.45 per $1,000 of assessed value. How much tax does Reggie pay?

4. Antonio Burks's home has an assessed value of $72,520. The property tax rate is 72.5 mills per $1.00 of assessed value. How much tax does Antonio pay?

## 3 Determine the property tax rate.

**Total assessed value:** the total of all assessed values of property in a municipality or tax jurisdiction.

How does the city or county decide what the tax rate should be? The local government uses its estimated budget to determine how much money it will need in the year ahead. That amount is then divided by the **total assessed value** of *all* the property in its area. This calculation tells how much tax must be collected for each dollar of assessed property value. The tax rate can be written as a tax per $100 or $1,000 of assessed value by multiplying the tax on $1.00 by 100 or 1,000. Whenever you calculate the tax rate, if the division does not come out even, *round* the digit in the hundredths position *up* to the next digit.

---

### TIP

**Why Is the Tax Rate Always Rounded Up?**

Find the tax rate per $1.00 if the total estimated budget is $18,000,000 and the total assessed property value is $118,400,000. Round using ordinary methods.

$$\text{Tax per } \$1.00 = \frac{\$18,000,000}{\$118,400,000} = \$0.152027027 = \$0.15$$

Now, calculate the amount of tax that will be collected.

$$\text{Total tax} = \text{assessed value} \times \text{tax rate per } \$1.00 = \$118,400,000(\$0.15) = \$17,760,000$$

The amount of money needed for the estimated budget would be short by $240,000. ($18,000,000 − $17,760,000 = $240,000)

---

### HOW TO    Determine a property tax rate

1. Select the appropriate formula according to the desired tax rate type.

$$(\text{Tax per } \$1.00 \text{ of assessed value}) = \frac{\text{total estimated budget}}{\text{total assessed property value}}$$

$$(\text{Tax per } \$100 \text{ of assessed value}) = \frac{\text{total estimated budget}}{\text{total assessed property value}} \times \$100$$

$$(\text{Tax per } \$1,000 \text{ of assessed value}) = \frac{\text{total estimated budget}}{\text{total assessed property value}} \times \$1,000$$

$$(\text{Tax, in mills, per } \$1.00 \text{ of assessed value}) = \frac{\text{total estimated budget}}{\text{total assessed property value}} \times \$1,000$$

2. Make calculations using the selected formula. Always round up.

---

### EXAMPLE 1    Find the tax rate expressed as tax per $100 of assessed value for Harbortown, which anticipates expenses of $95,590,000 and has property assessed at $3,868,758,500.

$$(\text{Tax per } \$100 \text{ of assessed value}) = \left(\frac{\$95,590,000}{\$3,868,758,500}\right)(\$100)$$
$$= \$0.024708184(\$100)$$
$$= \$2.4708184$$
$$= \$2.48 \text{ (rounded up)}$$

**The tax rate is $2.48 per $100 of assessed value.**

## EXAMPLE 2

Harbortown (see the previous example) expects an increase in expenses of $5,000,000. To cover these expenses, the city has to increase the tax rate or to reassess property values. The city assessor's office predicts that the reassessment would cost $100,000 and increase the city's assessment value of property to $4,300,000,000. The city leaders prefer the reassessment choice but do not want to reassess property value and increase the tax rate in the same year. Which choice should the city leaders make?

### What You Know

Current expenses: $95,590,000
Expected increase in expenses: $5,000,000
Current assessed property: $3,868,758,500
Current tax rate: $2.48 per $100 of assessed value

Expected reassessment value:
$4,300,000,000
Cost of reassessment: $100,000

### What You Are Looking For

Total revenue from property taxes if property is reassessed
Should property be reassessed or should the tax rate be increased?

### Solution Plan

Total property taxes from reassessed property values = expected reassessed values $\times \dfrac{\$2.48}{\$100}$

Expected total expenses if property is reassessed =
current expenses + expected increase + cost of reassessment

### Solution

Total property taxes from reassessment = $\$4,300,000,000 \left( \dfrac{\$2.48}{\$100} \right)$

$= \$106,640,000$

Expected total expenses = $\$95,590,000 + \$5,000,000 + \$100,000$
$= \$100,690,000$

### Conclusion

**Property taxes from the reassessment ($106,640,000) are more than expected total expenses ($100,690,000). Since a reassessment will cover the increase in expenses without a tax increase, property will be reassessed.**

---

## ✓ STOP AND CHECK

1. Find the tax rate expressed as tax per $100 of assessed value for Suffolk County, which anticipates tax-funded expenses of $109,047,773 and has property assessed at $4,098,530,000.

2. Find the tax rate expressed as a percent of assessed value for the town of Tuxedo, which anticipates property tax funded expenses of $5,347,364 and has property assessed at $218,560,000.

3. Ithaca has property tax funded expenses of $6,344,549.65 and assessed real property valued at $544,029,090. Find the tax rate in mills.

4. Northhaven anticipates expenses of $68,914,808 and has real estate with a total assessed value of $2,856,919,000. Find the tax rate per $1,000 for the year.

## SKILL BUILDERS

*Find the property tax for each property.*

| | Assessed value | Tax rate | Property tax | | Assessed value | Tax rate | Property tax |
|---|---|---|---|---|---|---|---|
| **1.** | $78,920 | 5.75% | | **2.** | $125,035 | $3.07 per $100 | |
| **3.** | $682,500 | $19.86 per $1,000 | | **4.** | $12,800 | 15.46 mills | |

*Determine the tax rate for each city or county. For Exercises 5–10, an equal number of zeros in the numerator and denominator can be reduced to facilitate calculator entry.*

| | Assessed property value | Expenses to be funded by property tax | Tax per amount of assessed value | Tax rate |
|---|---|---|---|---|
| **5.** | $1,549,465,000 | $125,807,560 | $1.00 | |
| **6.** | $2,252,136,000 | $86,987,037 | $100 | |
| **7.** | $7,063,274,000 | $188,942,580 | $1,000 | |
| **8.** | $17,881,455,000 | $376,583,460 | mill | |
| **9.** | $2,412,500,000 | $86,529,807 | $100 | |
| **10.** | $1,950,000,000 | $48,957,840 | $1,000 | |

**11.** Find the assessed value of a store with a market value of $150,000 if the rate for assessed value is 35% of market value.

**12.** Donna McAnally owns an apartment building that has a market value of $583,000. If apartments are assessed at 40% of market value, find the assessed value of Donna's apartment building.

**13.** Tim Warner's farm has a market value of $385,000. Find the assessed value of the farm if farms are assessed at 25% of the market value.

**14.** Rebecca Drewrey owns a small telephone company that has a market value of $1,895,000. If the phone company is assessed at 50% of market value, what is the assessed value of the property?

**15.** What is the tax on a property with an assessed value of $88,500 if the tax rate is 4.5% of the assessed value?

**16.** Find the property tax on a vacant lot with an assessed value of $32,350 and a tax rate of $4.37 per $100 of assessed value.

**17.** Find the property tax on a home with an assessed value of $75,000 in a community with a tax rate of $12.75 per $1,000 of assessed value.

**18.** Calculate the property tax on a store with an assessed value of $150,250 if the tax rate is 58 mills per $1.00 of assessed value.

**19.** Find the tax rate expressed as tax per $1.00 of assessed value in a municipality that has budgeted expenses of $5,985,500 and has property assessed at $230,211,500.

**20.** Find the tax rate expressed as tax per $100 of assessed value for a town that anticipates expenses of $55,800 and has property assessed at $9,830,000.

**21.** What is the tax rate expressed as tax per $1,000 of assessed property value in a county that has property assessed at $185,910,000 and has budgeted expenses of $5,810,000?

**22.** What is the tax rate expressed in mills per $1.00 of assessed value if an incorporated town has a budget of $497,000 and has property assessed at $11,045,000?

## 19-3 INCOME TAXES

### LEARNING OUTCOMES

1  Find taxable income.
2  Use the tax tables to calculate income tax.
3  Use the tax rate schedules to calculate income tax.

**Income tax:** a tax collected by the federal government, many states, and some cities that is based on a person's income.

**Gross income:** all income received in the form of money, goods, property, and services that is not exempt from tax.

**Adjusted gross income:** total or gross income minus certain educator or moving expenses and specific deductions such as IRAs, student loan interest, tuition and fees, alimony paid, and so on.

**Taxable income:** adjusted gross income minus exemptions and either the standard or the itemized deductions.

**Exemption or allowance:** an amount of money that a taxpayer is allowed to subtract from the adjusted gross income for himself or herself, a spouse, and each dependent.

**Deductions:** certain expenses the taxpayer is allowed to subtract from income to reduce the amount of taxable income.

**Itemized deductions:** a listing of deductions that can be used by certain taxpayers to reduce taxable income. Normally, taxpayers use itemized deductions when the total of their itemized deductions is greater than the standard deduction.

**Standard deduction:** a specified reduction of taxable income. The standard deduction amount is based on filing status and is adjusted yearly for inflation. Normally, taxpayers who do not use the standard deduction have eligible itemized deductions that exceed the standard deduction.

Many state governments and the federal government collect much of their revenue through individual and business **income taxes**. Federal income tax regulations are enacted by the Congress of the United States, and the tax laws change frequently.

Although the laws and forms change from year to year, the *procedures* for computing income tax remain basically the same. Each year an instruction booklet accompanies the current income tax forms. This booklet explains any recent changes in the tax laws, provides instructions for computing tax and filling out the forms, and contains various tax tables needed for filing an income tax return.

To calculate income tax owed, begin with a business's or individual's **gross income**, which is the money, goods, and property received during the year. From this subtract any adjustments allowed, such as credit for employee expenses that are not reimbursed by the employer; this gives you the **adjusted gross income**. Next, arrive at the **taxable income**, which is the adjusted gross income minus exemptions and deductions. The taxable income is the amount that is used to calculate the taxes owed.

Exemptions provide one of the ways of reducing taxable income. One personal **exemption** or **allowance** is allowed for the taxpayer, and additional exemptions are allowed for the taxpayer's spouse and other dependents if the adjusted gross income is below a certain level. Other exemptions are allowed if the taxpayer or the spouse is over 65 or blind. The deduction for personal exemptions was $3,300 in 2006.

A taxpayer is allowed to take **deductions**, or to deduct certain expenses such as charitable contributions, interest paid on certain loans, certain taxes, certain losses, excessive medical expenses, and certain miscellaneous expenses, to name a few. Rather than listing these expenses (called **itemized deductions**), the taxpayer may choose to take the **standard deduction**. The standard deduction changes from year to year, but in a recent year for most people it was $10,300 for married taxpayers filing jointly (if both were under 65) or a qualifying widow (widower) with a dependent child; $5,150 for married taxpayers filing separately or for single taxpayers; and $7,550 for taxpayers who were the head of a household.

Filing status: category of taxpayer: single,
married filing jointly, married filing separately,
or head of household.

The tax due on taxable personal income depends also on the **filing status** of the taxpayer. Filing status is the marital status of the taxpayer. The individual taxpayer must select the filing status from four categories. The *single* category is for a person who has never married, is legally separated, is widowed, or is divorced. A husband and wife filing a return together, even if only one had income, are classified as *married filing jointly*. This filing status sometimes results in married persons paying a different tax than single persons with a comparable income. When a husband and wife each file a separate return, they are classified as *married filing separately*, and this status may result in a different tax liability than the married filing jointly status. The filing status *head of household* should be selected by individuals who provide a home for certain other persons.

## 1 Find taxable income.

Whether you choose to itemize deductions or use the standard deduction, you must determine your *taxable income* before you can compute the tax. An employer is required to issue each employee a **W-2 form**, which shows the income earned, income tax withheld, Social Security tax withheld, and Medicare tax withheld for the employee for the calendar year. If a person works for more than one employer in a year, he or she will receive a W-2 form from each employer. Under some circumstances a form 1099 is used to report income to an individual.

**W-2 form:** a form an employer must provide each employee that shows the earned income, income tax withheld, and Social Security and Medicare taxes withheld.

### TIP

**When Do You Expect Your W-2 Form?**

The IRS requires employers to deliver or have postmarked W-2 forms by midnight on January 31 following the year the income was earned. Employees who do not receive a W-2 from an employer because of address changes or other changes should contact the employer soon after January 31.

### HOW TO    Find the taxable income

1. Find the adjusted gross income:

   Adjusted gross income = total income − allowable expenses and deductions

2. Total the deductions or choose the standard deduction and total the exemptions.
3. Find the taxable income:

   Taxable income = adjusted gross income − itemized or standard deductions − exemptions

### EXAMPLE 1    Find the taxable income for a family of four (husband, wife, two children) if their adjusted gross income is $67,754 and their itemized deductions are $11,345. Use $3,300 as the amount of each personal exemption.

Taxable income = adjusted gross income − deductions − exemptions
= $67,754 − $11,345 − ($3,300)(4)
= $67,754 − $11,345 − $13,200 = $43,209

**The taxable income is $43,209.**

## ✓ STOP AND CHECK

**1.** Find the taxable income for a married couple filing a joint return with one additional dependent if their adjusted gross income is $62,596 and itemized deductions are $10,109. Use $3,300 for each personal exemption.

**2.** Find the taxable income for a single person if her adjusted gross income is $105,896 and her itemized deductions are $12,057. Use $3,300 for her personal exemption.

3. Corey Wells's family of five has an adjusted gross income of $115,993 and $18,930 in itemized deductions. Use $3,300 for each personal exemption and find the Wells's taxable income.

4. Bonzi McFagdon is single, has an adjusted gross income of $68,929, and takes the standard deduction of $5,150. He claims only one personal exemption of $3,300. Find his taxable income.

## 2 Use the tax tables to calculate income tax.

Income tax tables: tax tables found in the IRS 1040 Instructions publication for finding the amount of tax liability.

Once you know your taxable income and filing status, you can determine the taxes owed. **Income tax tables** like those in Table 19-1 are used to find the tax liability for taxable incomes of *less than* $100,000.

### HOW TO — Use the tax tables to calculate income tax

1. Locate the taxable income under the column headed "If line 40 (taxable income) is—."
2. Move across to the column headed "And you are—," which has the four filing status categories listed under it. The tax owed appears under the appropriate category.

### TIP

**Other Tax Tables**

If a taxpayer files a 1040 or 1040EZ form, the instructions and corresponding tax tables reference lines 43 and 6 respectively for taxable income.

**EXAMPLE 1**  Find the tax owed by a married taxpayer (a) filing separately on a taxable income of $39,478; (b) filing jointly on a taxable income of $39,478.

First, locate the income range in which $39,478 falls. Because $39,478 is *at least* $39,450 *but less than* $39,500, it falls within the range of $39,450–$39,500.
(a) Locate the tax in the column to the right headed *married filing separately*. **The tax is $6,426.**
(b) For the taxable income range $39,450–$39,500, the tax for a taxpayer *married filing jointly* **is $5,166.**

### TIP

**Settling Up on Income Tax**

Most taxpayers have taxes withheld from their paychecks throughout the year. By April 15 of the following year, taxpayers are required to file a report that will determine if additional taxes are owed or if a refund is due.

The taxpayer refers to his or her W-2 form to determine the income tax that has been withheld during the year. This tax withheld is subtracted from the tax owed to determine the remaining tax that must be paid. If more tax has been withheld than the taxpayer owes, subtraction will show the tax refund due the taxpayer.

## ✔ STOP AND CHECK

1. Find the tax owed by a married taxpayer filing jointly on a total taxable income of $37,519.

2. Find the tax for a single taxpayer who has a taxable income of $31,795.

3. Find the tax for a married person filing separately if her taxable income is $30,650.

4. Find the tax owed by Sean Banks, whose taxable income is $38,456, if his filing status is "Head of household."

TABLE 19-1
Portion of Tax Table

## 2006 Tax Table – Continued

| If line 43 (taxable income) is— At least | But less than | Single | Married filing jointly * | Married filing separately | Head of a household |
|---|---|---|---|---|---|
| **23,000** | | | | | |
| 23,000 | 23,050 | 3,076 | 2,699 | 3,076 | 2,916 |
| 23,050 | 23,100 | 3,084 | 2,706 | 3,084 | 2,924 |
| 23,100 | 23,150 | 3,091 | 2,714 | 3,091 | 2,931 |
| 23,150 | 23,200 | 3,099 | 2,721 | 3,099 | 2,939 |
| 23,200 | 23,250 | 3,106 | 2,729 | 3,106 | 2,946 |
| 23,250 | 23,300 | 3,114 | 2,736 | 3,114 | 2,954 |
| 23,300 | 23,350 | 3,121 | 2,744 | 3,121 | 2,961 |
| 23,350 | 23,400 | 3,129 | 2,751 | 3,129 | 2,969 |
| 23,400 | 23,450 | 3,136 | 2,759 | 3,136 | 2,976 |
| 23,450 | 23,500 | 3,144 | 2,766 | 3,144 | 2,984 |
| 23,500 | 23,550 | 3,151 | 2,774 | 3,151 | 2,991 |
| 23,550 | 23,600 | 3,159 | 2,781 | 3,159 | 2,999 |
| 23,600 | 23,650 | 3,166 | 2,789 | 3,166 | 3,006 |
| 23,650 | 23,700 | 3,174 | 2,796 | 3,174 | 3,014 |
| 23,700 | 23,750 | 3,181 | 2,804 | 3,181 | 3,021 |
| 23,750 | 23,800 | 3,189 | 2,811 | 3,189 | 3,029 |
| 23,800 | 23,850 | 3,196 | 2,819 | 3,196 | 3,036 |
| 23,850 | 23,900 | 3,204 | 2,826 | 3,204 | 3,044 |
| 23,900 | 23,950 | 3,211 | 2,834 | 3,211 | 3,051 |
| 23,950 | 24,000 | 3,219 | 2,841 | 3,219 | 3,059 |
| **24,000** | | | | | |
| 24,000 | 24,050 | 3,226 | 2,849 | 3,226 | 3,066 |
| 24,050 | 24,100 | 3,234 | 2,856 | 3,234 | 3,074 |
| 24,100 | 24,150 | 3,241 | 2,864 | 3,241 | 3,081 |
| 24,150 | 24,200 | 3,249 | 2,871 | 3,249 | 3,089 |
| 24,200 | 24,250 | 3,256 | 2,879 | 3,256 | 3,096 |
| 24,250 | 24,300 | 3,264 | 2,886 | 3,264 | 3,104 |
| 24,300 | 24,350 | 3,271 | 2,894 | 3,271 | 3,111 |
| 24,350 | 24,400 | 3,279 | 2,901 | 3,279 | 3,119 |
| 24,400 | 24,450 | 3,286 | 2,909 | 3,286 | 3,126 |
| 24,450 | 24,500 | 3,294 | 2,916 | 3,294 | 3,134 |
| 24,500 | 24,550 | 3,301 | 2,924 | 3,301 | 3,141 |
| 24,550 | 24,600 | 3,309 | 2,931 | 3,309 | 3,149 |
| 24,600 | 24,650 | 3,316 | 2,939 | 3,316 | 3,156 |
| 24,650 | 24,700 | 3,324 | 2,946 | 3,324 | 3,164 |
| 24,700 | 24,750 | 3,331 | 2,954 | 3,331 | 3,171 |
| 24,750 | 24,800 | 3,339 | 2,961 | 3,339 | 3,179 |
| 24,800 | 24,850 | 3,346 | 2,969 | 3,346 | 3,186 |
| 24,850 | 24,900 | 3,354 | 2,976 | 3,354 | 3,194 |
| 24,900 | 24,950 | 3,361 | 2,984 | 3,361 | 3,201 |
| 24,950 | 25,000 | 3,369 | 2,991 | 3,369 | 3,209 |
| **25,000** | | | | | |
| 25,000 | 25,050 | 3,376 | 2,999 | 3,376 | 3,216 |
| 25,050 | 25,100 | 3,384 | 3,006 | 3,384 | 3,224 |
| 25,100 | 25,150 | 3,391 | 3,014 | 3,391 | 3,231 |
| 25,150 | 25,200 | 3,399 | 3,021 | 3,399 | 3,239 |
| 25,200 | 25,250 | 3,406 | 3,029 | 3,406 | 3,246 |
| 25,250 | 25,300 | 3,414 | 3,036 | 3,414 | 3,254 |
| 25,300 | 25,350 | 3,421 | 3,044 | 3,421 | 3,261 |
| 25,350 | 25,400 | 3,429 | 3,051 | 3,429 | 3,269 |
| 25,400 | 25,450 | 3,436 | 3,059 | 3,436 | 3,276 |
| 25,450 | 25,500 | 3,444 | 3,066 | 3,444 | 3,284 |
| 25,500 | 25,550 | 3,451 | 3,074 | 3,451 | 3,291 |
| 25,550 | 25,600 | 3,459 | 3,081 | 3,459 | 3,299 |
| 25,600 | 25,650 | 3,466 | 3,089 | 3,466 | 3,306 |
| 25,650 | 25,700 | 3,474 | 3,096 | 3,474 | 3,314 |
| 25,700 | 25,750 | 3,481 | 3,104 | 3,481 | 3,321 |
| 25,750 | 25,800 | 3,489 | 3,111 | 3,489 | 3,329 |
| 25,800 | 25,850 | 3,496 | 3,119 | 3,496 | 3,336 |
| 25,850 | 25,900 | 3,504 | 3,126 | 3,504 | 3,344 |
| 25,900 | 25,950 | 3,511 | 3,134 | 3,511 | 3,351 |
| 25,950 | 26,000 | 3,519 | 3,141 | 3,519 | 3,359 |

| If line 43 (taxable income) is— At least | But less than | Single | Married filing jointly * | Married filing separately | Head of a household |
|---|---|---|---|---|---|
| **26,000** | | | | | |
| 26,000 | 26,050 | 3,526 | 3,149 | 3,526 | 3,366 |
| 26,050 | 26,100 | 3,534 | 3,156 | 3,534 | 3,374 |
| 26,100 | 26,150 | 3,541 | 3,164 | 3,541 | 3,381 |
| 26,150 | 26,200 | 3,549 | 3,171 | 3,549 | 3,389 |
| 26,200 | 26,250 | 3,556 | 3,179 | 3,556 | 3,396 |
| 26,250 | 26,300 | 3,564 | 3,186 | 3,564 | 3,404 |
| 26,300 | 26,350 | 3,571 | 3,194 | 3,571 | 3,411 |
| 26,350 | 26,400 | 3,579 | 3,201 | 3,579 | 3,419 |
| 26,400 | 26,450 | 3,586 | 3,209 | 3,586 | 3,426 |
| 26,450 | 26,500 | 3,594 | 3,216 | 3,594 | 3,434 |
| 26,500 | 26,550 | 3,601 | 3,224 | 3,601 | 3,441 |
| 26,550 | 26,600 | 3,609 | 3,231 | 3,609 | 3,449 |
| 26,600 | 26,650 | 3,616 | 3,239 | 3,616 | 3,456 |
| 26,650 | 26,700 | 3,624 | 3,246 | 3,624 | 3,464 |
| 26,700 | 26,750 | 3,631 | 3,254 | 3,631 | 3,471 |
| 26,750 | 26,800 | 3,639 | 3,261 | 3,639 | 3,479 |
| 26,800 | 26,850 | 3,646 | 3,269 | 3,646 | 3,486 |
| 26,850 | 26,900 | 3,654 | 3,276 | 3,654 | 3,494 |
| 26,900 | 26,950 | 3,661 | 3,284 | 3,661 | 3,501 |
| 26,950 | 27,000 | 3,669 | 3,291 | 3,669 | 3,509 |
| **27,000** | | | | | |
| 27,000 | 27,050 | 3,676 | 3,299 | 3,676 | 3,516 |
| 27,050 | 27,100 | 3,684 | 3,306 | 3,684 | 3,524 |
| 27,100 | 27,150 | 3,691 | 3,314 | 3,691 | 3,531 |
| 27,150 | 27,200 | 3,699 | 3,321 | 3,699 | 3,539 |
| 27,200 | 27,250 | 3,706 | 3,329 | 3,706 | 3,546 |
| 27,250 | 27,300 | 3,714 | 3,336 | 3,714 | 3,554 |
| 27,300 | 27,350 | 3,721 | 3,344 | 3,721 | 3,561 |
| 27,350 | 27,400 | 3,729 | 3,351 | 3,729 | 3,569 |
| 27,400 | 27,450 | 3,736 | 3,359 | 3,736 | 3,576 |
| 27,450 | 27,500 | 3,744 | 3,366 | 3,744 | 3,584 |
| 27,500 | 27,550 | 3,751 | 3,374 | 3,751 | 3,591 |
| 27,550 | 27,600 | 3,759 | 3,381 | 3,759 | 3,599 |
| 27,600 | 27,650 | 3,766 | 3,389 | 3,766 | 3,606 |
| 27,650 | 27,700 | 3,774 | 3,396 | 3,774 | 3,614 |
| 27,700 | 27,750 | 3,781 | 3,404 | 3,781 | 3,621 |
| 27,750 | 27,800 | 3,789 | 3,411 | 3,789 | 3,629 |
| 27,800 | 27,850 | 3,796 | 3,419 | 3,796 | 3,636 |
| 27,850 | 27,900 | 3,804 | 3,426 | 3,804 | 3,644 |
| 27,900 | 27,950 | 3,811 | 3,434 | 3,811 | 3,651 |
| 27,950 | 28,000 | 3,819 | 3,441 | 3,819 | 3,659 |
| **28,000** | | | | | |
| 28,000 | 28,050 | 3,826 | 3,449 | 3,826 | 3,666 |
| 28,050 | 28,100 | 3,834 | 3,456 | 3,834 | 3,674 |
| 28,100 | 28,150 | 3,841 | 3,464 | 3,841 | 3,681 |
| 28,150 | 28,200 | 3,849 | 3,471 | 3,849 | 3,689 |
| 28,200 | 28,250 | 3,856 | 3,479 | 3,856 | 3,696 |
| 28,250 | 28,300 | 3,864 | 3,486 | 3,864 | 3,704 |
| 28,300 | 28,350 | 3,871 | 3,494 | 3,871 | 3,711 |
| 28,350 | 28,400 | 3,879 | 3,501 | 3,879 | 3,719 |
| 28,400 | 28,450 | 3,886 | 3,509 | 3,886 | 3,726 |
| 28,450 | 28,500 | 3,894 | 3,516 | 3,894 | 3,734 |
| 28,500 | 28,550 | 3,901 | 3,524 | 3,901 | 3,741 |
| 28,550 | 28,600 | 3,909 | 3,531 | 3,909 | 3,749 |
| 28,600 | 28,650 | 3,916 | 3,539 | 3,916 | 3,756 |
| 28,650 | 28,700 | 3,924 | 3,546 | 3,924 | 3,764 |
| 28,700 | 28,750 | 3,931 | 3,554 | 3,931 | 3,771 |
| 28,750 | 28,800 | 3,939 | 3,561 | 3,939 | 3,779 |
| 28,800 | 28,850 | 3,946 | 3,569 | 3,946 | 3,786 |
| 28,850 | 28,900 | 3,954 | 3,576 | 3,954 | 3,794 |
| 28,900 | 28,950 | 3,961 | 3,584 | 3,961 | 3,801 |
| 28,950 | 29,000 | 3,969 | 3,591 | 3,969 | 3,809 |

| If line 43 (taxable income) is— At least | But less than | Single | Married filing jointly * | Married filing separately | Head of a household |
|---|---|---|---|---|---|
| **29,000** | | | | | |
| 29,000 | 29,050 | 3,976 | 3,599 | 3,976 | 3,816 |
| 29,050 | 29,100 | 3,984 | 3,606 | 3,984 | 3,824 |
| 29,100 | 29,150 | 3,991 | 3,614 | 3,991 | 3,831 |
| 29,150 | 29,200 | 3,999 | 3,621 | 3,999 | 3,839 |
| 29,200 | 29,250 | 4,006 | 3,629 | 4,006 | 3,846 |
| 29,250 | 29,300 | 4,014 | 3,636 | 4,014 | 3,854 |
| 29,300 | 29,350 | 4,021 | 3,644 | 4,021 | 3,861 |
| 29,350 | 29,400 | 4,029 | 3,651 | 4,029 | 3,869 |
| 29,400 | 29,450 | 4,036 | 3,659 | 4,036 | 3,876 |
| 29,450 | 29,500 | 4,044 | 3,666 | 4,044 | 3,884 |
| 29,500 | 29,550 | 4,051 | 3,674 | 4,051 | 3,891 |
| 29,550 | 29,600 | 4,059 | 3,681 | 4,059 | 3,899 |
| 29,600 | 29,650 | 4,066 | 3,689 | 4,066 | 3,906 |
| 29,650 | 29,700 | 4,074 | 3,696 | 4,074 | 3,914 |
| 29,700 | 29,750 | 4,081 | 3,704 | 4,081 | 3,921 |
| 29,750 | 29,800 | 4,089 | 3,711 | 4,089 | 3,929 |
| 29,800 | 29,850 | 4,096 | 3,719 | 4,096 | 3,936 |
| 29,850 | 29,900 | 4,104 | 3,726 | 4,104 | 3,944 |
| 29,900 | 29,950 | 4,111 | 3,734 | 4,111 | 3,951 |
| 29,950 | 30,000 | 4,119 | 3,741 | 4,119 | 3,959 |
| **30,000** | | | | | |
| 30,000 | 30,050 | 4,126 | 3,749 | 4,126 | 3,966 |
| 30,050 | 30,100 | 4,134 | 3,756 | 4,134 | 3,974 |
| 30,100 | 30,150 | 4,141 | 3,764 | 4,141 | 3,981 |
| 30,150 | 30,200 | 4,149 | 3,771 | 4,149 | 3,989 |
| 30,200 | 30,250 | 4,156 | 3,779 | 4,156 | 3,996 |
| 30,250 | 30,300 | 4,164 | 3,786 | 4,164 | 4,004 |
| 30,300 | 30,350 | 4,171 | 3,794 | 4,171 | 4,011 |
| 30,350 | 30,400 | 4,179 | 3,801 | 4,179 | 4,019 |
| 30,400 | 30,450 | 4,186 | 3,809 | 4,186 | 4,026 |
| 30,450 | 30,500 | 4,194 | 3,816 | 4,194 | 4,034 |
| 30,500 | 30,550 | 4,201 | 3,824 | 4,201 | 4,041 |
| 30,550 | 30,600 | 4,209 | 3,831 | 4,209 | 4,049 |
| 30,600 | 30,650 | 4,216 | 3,839 | 4,216 | 4,056 |
| 30,650 | 30,700 | 4,226 | 3,846 | 4,226 | 4,064 |
| 30,700 | 30,750 | 4,239 | 3,854 | 4,239 | 4,071 |
| 30,750 | 30,800 | 4,251 | 3,861 | 4,251 | 4,079 |
| 30,800 | 30,850 | 4,264 | 3,869 | 4,264 | 4,086 |
| 30,850 | 30,900 | 4,276 | 3,876 | 4,276 | 4,094 |
| 30,900 | 30,950 | 4,289 | 3,884 | 4,289 | 4,101 |
| 30,950 | 31,000 | 4,301 | 3,891 | 4,301 | 4,109 |
| **31,000** | | | | | |
| 31,000 | 31,050 | 4,314 | 3,899 | 4,314 | 4,116 |
| 31,050 | 31,100 | 4,326 | 3,906 | 4,326 | 4,124 |
| 31,100 | 31,150 | 4,339 | 3,914 | 4,339 | 4,131 |
| 31,150 | 31,200 | 4,351 | 3,921 | 4,351 | 4,139 |
| 31,200 | 31,250 | 4,364 | 3,929 | 4,364 | 4,146 |
| 31,250 | 31,300 | 4,376 | 3,936 | 4,376 | 4,154 |
| 31,300 | 31,350 | 4,389 | 3,944 | 4,389 | 4,161 |
| 31,350 | 31,400 | 4,401 | 3,951 | 4,401 | 4,169 |
| 31,400 | 31,450 | 4,414 | 3,959 | 4,414 | 4,176 |
| 31,450 | 31,500 | 4,426 | 3,966 | 4,426 | 4,184 |
| 31,500 | 31,550 | 4,439 | 3,974 | 4,439 | 4,191 |
| 31,550 | 31,600 | 4,451 | 3,981 | 4,451 | 4,199 |
| 31,600 | 31,650 | 4,464 | 3,989 | 4,464 | 4,206 |
| 31,650 | 31,700 | 4,476 | 3,996 | 4,476 | 4,214 |
| 31,700 | 31,750 | 4,489 | 4,004 | 4,489 | 4,221 |
| 31,750 | 31,800 | 4,501 | 4,011 | 4,501 | 4,229 |
| 31,800 | 31,850 | 4,514 | 4,019 | 4,514 | 4,236 |
| 31,850 | 31,900 | 4,526 | 4,026 | 4,526 | 4,244 |
| 31,900 | 31,950 | 4,539 | 4,034 | 4,539 | 4,251 |
| 31,950 | 32,000 | 4,551 | 4,041 | 4,551 | 4,259 |

* This column must also be used by a qualifying widow(er).

Source: IRS Publication 2006 1040 Instructions.

TABLE 19-1
Portion of Tax Table—*Continued*

| If line 43 (taxable income) is— | | And you are— | | | |
|---|---|---|---|---|---|
| At least | But less than | Single | Married filing jointly * | Married filing separately | Head of a household |
| | | Your tax is— | | | |

**32,000**

| At least | But less than | Single | MFJ * | MFS | HoH |
|---|---|---|---|---|---|
| 32,000 | 32,050 | 4,564 | 4,049 | 4,564 | 4,266 |
| 32,050 | 32,100 | 4,576 | 4,056 | 4,576 | 4,274 |
| 32,100 | 32,150 | 4,589 | 4,064 | 4,589 | 4,281 |
| 32,150 | 32,200 | 4,601 | 4,071 | 4,601 | 4,289 |
| 32,200 | 32,250 | 4,614 | 4,079 | 4,614 | 4,296 |
| 32,250 | 32,300 | 4,626 | 4,086 | 4,626 | 4,304 |
| 32,300 | 32,350 | 4,639 | 4,094 | 4,639 | 4,311 |
| 32,350 | 32,400 | 4,651 | 4,101 | 4,651 | 4,319 |
| 32,400 | 32,450 | 4,664 | 4,109 | 4,664 | 4,326 |
| 32,450 | 32,500 | 4,676 | 4,116 | 4,676 | 4,334 |
| 32,500 | 32,550 | 4,689 | 4,124 | 4,689 | 4,341 |
| 32,550 | 32,600 | 4,701 | 4,131 | 4,701 | 4,349 |
| 32,600 | 32,650 | 4,714 | 4,139 | 4,714 | 4,356 |
| 32,650 | 32,700 | 4,726 | 4,146 | 4,726 | 4,364 |
| 32,700 | 32,750 | 4,739 | 4,154 | 4,739 | 4,371 |
| 32,750 | 32,800 | 4,751 | 4,161 | 4,751 | 4,379 |
| 32,800 | 32,850 | 4,764 | 4,169 | 4,764 | 4,386 |
| 32,850 | 32,900 | 4,776 | 4,176 | 4,776 | 4,394 |
| 32,900 | 32,950 | 4,789 | 4,184 | 4,789 | 4,401 |
| 32,950 | 33,000 | 4,801 | 4,191 | 4,801 | 4,409 |

**33,000**

| At least | But less than | Single | MFJ * | MFS | HoH |
|---|---|---|---|---|---|
| 33,000 | 33,050 | 4,814 | 4,199 | 4,814 | 4,416 |
| 33,050 | 33,100 | 4,826 | 4,206 | 4,826 | 4,424 |
| 33,100 | 33,150 | 4,839 | 4,214 | 4,839 | 4,431 |
| 33,150 | 33,200 | 4,851 | 4,221 | 4,851 | 4,439 |
| 33,200 | 33,250 | 4,864 | 4,229 | 4,864 | 4,446 |
| 33,250 | 33,300 | 4,876 | 4,236 | 4,876 | 4,454 |
| 33,300 | 33,350 | 4,889 | 4,244 | 4,889 | 4,461 |
| 33,350 | 33,400 | 4,901 | 4,251 | 4,901 | 4,469 |
| 33,400 | 33,450 | 4,914 | 4,259 | 4,914 | 4,476 |
| 33,450 | 33,500 | 4,926 | 4,266 | 4,926 | 4,484 |
| 33,500 | 33,550 | 4,939 | 4,274 | 4,939 | 4,491 |
| 33,550 | 33,600 | 4,951 | 4,281 | 4,951 | 4,499 |
| 33,600 | 33,650 | 4,964 | 4,289 | 4,964 | 4,506 |
| 33,650 | 33,700 | 4,976 | 4,296 | 4,976 | 4,514 |
| 33,700 | 33,750 | 4,989 | 4,304 | 4,989 | 4,521 |
| 33,750 | 33,800 | 5,001 | 4,311 | 5,001 | 4,529 |
| 33,800 | 33,850 | 5,014 | 4,319 | 5,014 | 4,536 |
| 33,850 | 33,900 | 5,026 | 4,326 | 5,026 | 4,544 |
| 33,900 | 33,950 | 5,039 | 4,334 | 5,039 | 4,551 |
| 33,950 | 34,000 | 5,051 | 4,341 | 5,051 | 4,559 |

**34,000**

| At least | But less than | Single | MFJ * | MFS | HoH |
|---|---|---|---|---|---|
| 34,000 | 34,050 | 5,064 | 4,349 | 5,064 | 4,566 |
| 34,050 | 34,100 | 5,076 | 4,356 | 5,076 | 4,574 |
| 34,100 | 34,150 | 5,089 | 4,364 | 5,089 | 4,581 |
| 34,150 | 34,200 | 5,101 | 4,371 | 5,101 | 4,589 |
| 34,200 | 34,250 | 5,114 | 4,379 | 5,114 | 4,596 |
| 34,250 | 34,300 | 5,126 | 4,386 | 5,126 | 4,604 |
| 34,300 | 34,350 | 5,139 | 4,394 | 5,139 | 4,611 |
| 34,350 | 34,400 | 5,151 | 4,401 | 5,151 | 4,619 |
| 34,400 | 34,450 | 5,164 | 4,409 | 5,164 | 4,626 |
| 34,450 | 34,500 | 5,176 | 4,416 | 5,176 | 4,634 |
| 34,500 | 34,550 | 5,189 | 4,424 | 5,189 | 4,641 |
| 34,550 | 34,600 | 5,201 | 4,431 | 5,201 | 4,649 |
| 34,600 | 34,650 | 5,214 | 4,439 | 5,214 | 4,656 |
| 34,650 | 34,700 | 5,226 | 4,446 | 5,226 | 4,664 |
| 34,700 | 34,750 | 5,239 | 4,454 | 5,239 | 4,671 |
| 34,750 | 34,800 | 5,251 | 4,461 | 5,251 | 4,679 |
| 34,800 | 34,850 | 5,264 | 4,469 | 5,264 | 4,686 |
| 34,850 | 34,900 | 5,276 | 4,476 | 5,276 | 4,694 |
| 34,900 | 34,950 | 5,289 | 4,484 | 5,289 | 4,701 |
| 34,950 | 35,000 | 5,301 | 4,491 | 5,301 | 4,709 |

**35,000**

| At least | But less than | Single | MFJ * | MFS | HoH |
|---|---|---|---|---|---|
| 35,000 | 35,050 | 5,314 | 4,499 | 5,314 | 4,716 |
| 35,050 | 35,100 | 5,326 | 4,506 | 5,326 | 4,724 |
| 35,100 | 35,150 | 5,339 | 4,514 | 5,339 | 4,731 |
| 35,150 | 35,200 | 5,351 | 4,521 | 5,351 | 4,739 |
| 35,200 | 35,250 | 5,364 | 4,529 | 5,364 | 4,746 |
| 35,250 | 35,300 | 5,376 | 4,536 | 5,376 | 4,754 |
| 35,300 | 35,350 | 5,389 | 4,544 | 5,389 | 4,761 |
| 35,350 | 35,400 | 5,401 | 4,551 | 5,401 | 4,769 |
| 35,400 | 35,450 | 5,414 | 4,559 | 5,414 | 4,776 |
| 35,450 | 35,500 | 5,426 | 4,566 | 5,426 | 4,784 |
| 35,500 | 35,550 | 5,439 | 4,574 | 5,439 | 4,791 |
| 35,550 | 35,600 | 5,451 | 4,581 | 5,451 | 4,799 |
| 35,600 | 35,650 | 5,464 | 4,589 | 5,464 | 4,806 |
| 35,650 | 35,700 | 5,476 | 4,596 | 5,476 | 4,814 |
| 35,700 | 35,750 | 5,489 | 4,604 | 5,489 | 4,821 |
| 35,750 | 35,800 | 5,501 | 4,611 | 5,501 | 4,829 |
| 35,800 | 35,850 | 5,514 | 4,619 | 5,514 | 4,836 |
| 35,850 | 35,900 | 5,526 | 4,626 | 5,526 | 4,844 |
| 35,900 | 35,950 | 5,539 | 4,634 | 5,539 | 4,851 |
| 35,950 | 36,000 | 5,551 | 4,641 | 5,551 | 4,859 |

**36,000**

| At least | But less than | Single | MFJ * | MFS | HoH |
|---|---|---|---|---|---|
| 36,000 | 36,050 | 5,564 | 4,649 | 5,564 | 4,866 |
| 36,050 | 36,100 | 5,576 | 4,656 | 5,576 | 4,874 |
| 36,100 | 36,150 | 5,589 | 4,664 | 5,589 | 4,881 |
| 36,150 | 36,200 | 5,601 | 4,671 | 5,601 | 4,889 |
| 36,200 | 36,250 | 5,614 | 4,679 | 5,614 | 4,896 |
| 36,250 | 36,300 | 5,626 | 4,686 | 5,626 | 4,904 |
| 36,300 | 36,350 | 5,639 | 4,694 | 5,639 | 4,911 |
| 36,350 | 36,400 | 5,651 | 4,701 | 5,651 | 4,919 |
| 36,400 | 36,450 | 5,664 | 4,709 | 5,664 | 4,926 |
| 36,450 | 36,500 | 5,676 | 4,716 | 5,676 | 4,934 |
| 36,500 | 36,550 | 5,689 | 4,724 | 5,689 | 4,941 |
| 36,550 | 36,600 | 5,701 | 4,731 | 5,701 | 4,949 |
| 36,600 | 36,650 | 5,714 | 4,739 | 5,714 | 4,956 |
| 36,650 | 36,700 | 5,726 | 4,746 | 5,726 | 4,964 |
| 36,700 | 36,750 | 5,739 | 4,754 | 5,739 | 4,971 |
| 36,750 | 36,800 | 5,751 | 4,761 | 5,751 | 4,979 |
| 36,800 | 36,850 | 5,764 | 4,769 | 5,764 | 4,986 |
| 36,850 | 36,900 | 5,776 | 4,776 | 5,776 | 4,994 |
| 36,900 | 36,950 | 5,789 | 4,784 | 5,789 | 5,001 |
| 36,950 | 37,000 | 5,801 | 4,791 | 5,801 | 5,009 |

**37,000**

| At least | But less than | Single | MFJ * | MFS | HoH |
|---|---|---|---|---|---|
| 37,000 | 37,050 | 5,814 | 4,799 | 5,814 | 5,016 |
| 37,050 | 37,100 | 5,826 | 4,806 | 5,826 | 5,024 |
| 37,100 | 37,150 | 5,839 | 4,814 | 5,839 | 5,031 |
| 37,150 | 37,200 | 5,851 | 4,821 | 5,851 | 5,039 |
| 37,200 | 37,250 | 5,864 | 4,829 | 5,864 | 5,046 |
| 37,250 | 37,300 | 5,876 | 4,836 | 5,876 | 5,054 |
| 37,300 | 37,350 | 5,889 | 4,844 | 5,889 | 5,061 |
| 37,350 | 37,400 | 5,901 | 4,851 | 5,901 | 5,069 |
| 37,400 | 37,450 | 5,914 | 4,859 | 5,914 | 5,076 |
| 37,450 | 37,500 | 5,926 | 4,866 | 5,926 | 5,084 |
| 37,500 | 37,550 | 5,939 | 4,874 | 5,939 | 5,091 |
| 37,550 | 37,600 | 5,951 | 4,881 | 5,951 | 5,099 |
| 37,600 | 37,650 | 5,964 | 4,889 | 5,964 | 5,106 |
| 37,650 | 37,700 | 5,976 | 4,896 | 5,976 | 5,114 |
| 37,700 | 37,750 | 5,989 | 4,904 | 5,989 | 5,121 |
| 37,750 | 37,800 | 6,001 | 4,911 | 6,001 | 5,129 |
| 37,800 | 37,850 | 6,014 | 4,919 | 6,014 | 5,136 |
| 37,850 | 37,900 | 6,026 | 4,926 | 6,026 | 5,144 |
| 37,900 | 37,950 | 6,039 | 4,934 | 6,039 | 5,151 |
| 37,950 | 38,000 | 6,051 | 4,941 | 6,051 | 5,159 |

**38,000**

| At least | But less than | Single | MFJ * | MFS | HoH |
|---|---|---|---|---|---|
| 38,000 | 38,050 | 6,064 | 4,949 | 6,064 | 5,166 |
| 38,050 | 38,100 | 6,076 | 4,956 | 6,076 | 5,174 |
| 38,100 | 38,150 | 6,089 | 4,964 | 6,089 | 5,181 |
| 38,150 | 38,200 | 6,101 | 4,971 | 6,101 | 5,189 |
| 38,200 | 38,250 | 6,114 | 4,979 | 6,114 | 5,196 |
| 38,250 | 38,300 | 6,126 | 4,986 | 6,126 | 5,204 |
| 38,300 | 38,350 | 6,139 | 4,994 | 6,139 | 5,211 |
| 38,350 | 38,400 | 6,151 | 5,001 | 6,151 | 5,219 |
| 38,400 | 38,450 | 6,164 | 5,009 | 6,164 | 5,226 |
| 38,450 | 38,500 | 6,176 | 5,016 | 6,176 | 5,234 |
| 38,500 | 38,550 | 6,189 | 5,024 | 6,189 | 5,241 |
| 38,550 | 38,600 | 6,201 | 5,031 | 6,201 | 5,249 |
| 38,600 | 38,650 | 6,214 | 5,039 | 6,214 | 5,256 |
| 38,650 | 38,700 | 6,226 | 5,046 | 6,226 | 5,264 |
| 38,700 | 38,750 | 6,239 | 5,054 | 6,239 | 5,271 |
| 38,750 | 38,800 | 6,251 | 5,061 | 6,251 | 5,279 |
| 38,800 | 38,850 | 6,264 | 5,069 | 6,264 | 5,286 |
| 38,850 | 38,900 | 6,276 | 5,076 | 6,276 | 5,294 |
| 38,900 | 38,950 | 6,289 | 5,084 | 6,289 | 5,301 |
| 38,950 | 39,000 | 6,301 | 5,091 | 6,301 | 5,309 |

**39,000**

| At least | But less than | Single | MFJ * | MFS | HoH |
|---|---|---|---|---|---|
| 39,000 | 39,050 | 6,314 | 5,099 | 6,314 | 5,316 |
| 39,050 | 39,100 | 6,326 | 5,106 | 6,326 | 5,324 |
| 39,100 | 39,150 | 6,339 | 5,114 | 6,339 | 5,331 |
| 39,150 | 39,200 | 6,351 | 5,121 | 6,351 | 5,339 |
| 39,200 | 39,250 | 6,364 | 5,129 | 6,364 | 5,346 |
| 39,250 | 39,300 | 6,376 | 5,136 | 6,376 | 5,354 |
| 39,300 | 39,350 | 6,389 | 5,144 | 6,389 | 5,361 |
| 39,350 | 39,400 | 6,401 | 5,151 | 6,401 | 5,369 |
| 39,400 | 39,450 | 6,414 | 5,159 | 6,414 | 5,376 |
| 39,450 | 39,500 | 6,426 | 5,166 | 6,426 | 5,384 |
| 39,500 | 39,550 | 6,439 | 5,174 | 6,439 | 5,391 |
| 39,550 | 39,600 | 6,451 | 5,181 | 6,451 | 5,399 |
| 39,600 | 39,650 | 6,464 | 5,189 | 6,464 | 5,406 |
| 39,650 | 39,700 | 6,476 | 5,196 | 6,476 | 5,414 |
| 39,700 | 39,750 | 6,489 | 5,204 | 6,489 | 5,421 |
| 39,750 | 39,800 | 6,501 | 5,211 | 6,501 | 5,429 |
| 39,800 | 39,850 | 6,514 | 5,219 | 6,514 | 5,436 |
| 39,850 | 39,900 | 6,526 | 5,226 | 6,526 | 5,444 |
| 39,900 | 39,950 | 6,539 | 5,234 | 6,539 | 5,451 |
| 39,950 | 40,000 | 6,551 | 5,241 | 6,551 | 5,459 |

**40,000**

| At least | But less than | Single | MFJ * | MFS | HoH |
|---|---|---|---|---|---|
| 40,000 | 40,050 | 6,564 | 5,249 | 6,564 | 5,466 |
| 40,050 | 40,100 | 6,576 | 5,256 | 6,576 | 5,474 |
| 40,100 | 40,150 | 6,589 | 5,264 | 6,589 | 5,481 |
| 40,150 | 40,200 | 6,601 | 5,271 | 6,601 | 5,489 |
| 40,200 | 40,250 | 6,614 | 5,279 | 6,614 | 5,496 |
| 40,250 | 40,300 | 6,626 | 5,286 | 6,626 | 5,504 |
| 40,300 | 40,350 | 6,639 | 5,294 | 6,639 | 5,511 |
| 40,350 | 40,400 | 6,651 | 5,301 | 6,651 | 5,519 |
| 40,400 | 40,450 | 6,664 | 5,309 | 6,664 | 5,526 |
| 40,450 | 40,500 | 6,676 | 5,316 | 6,676 | 5,534 |
| 40,500 | 40,550 | 6,689 | 5,324 | 6,689 | 5,541 |
| 40,550 | 40,600 | 6,701 | 5,331 | 6,701 | 5,549 |
| 40,600 | 40,650 | 6,714 | 5,339 | 6,714 | 5,556 |
| 40,650 | 40,700 | 6,726 | 5,346 | 6,726 | 5,564 |
| 40,700 | 40,750 | 6,739 | 5,354 | 6,739 | 5,571 |
| 40,750 | 40,800 | 6,751 | 5,361 | 6,751 | 5,579 |
| 40,800 | 40,850 | 6,764 | 5,369 | 6,764 | 5,586 |
| 40,850 | 40,900 | 6,776 | 5,376 | 6,776 | 5,594 |
| 40,900 | 40,950 | 6,789 | 5,384 | 6,789 | 5,601 |
| 40,950 | 41,000 | 6,801 | 5,391 | 6,801 | 5,609 |

* This column must also be used by a qualifying widow(er).

## 3 Use the tax rate schedules to calculate income tax.

**Tax rate schedules:** directions for calculating the tax on taxable incomes of $100,000 or more.

The **tax rate schedules** are used to compute tax on taxable incomes of $100,000 *or more*. There are separate tax rate schedules for single taxpayers, heads of households, and married taxpayers (and certain qualifying widows and widowers).

The Tax Reform Act of 1986 changed the tax rate to the structure that is currently used. An individual's income is taxed at different rates depending on how much of his or her income falls into each of various income brackets. Table 19-2 shows the tax rates for 2006.

**TABLE 19-2**
2006 Tax Rate Schedules

# 2006 Tax Rate Schedules

*The Tax Rate Schedules are shown so you can see the tax rate that applies to all levels of taxable income. Do not use them to figure your tax. Instead, see the instructions for line 44 that begin on page 36.*

**Schedule X—If your filing status is Single**

| If your taxable income is: Over— | But not over— | The tax is: | of the amount over— |
|---|---|---|---|
| $0 | $7,550 | ......... 10% | $0 |
| 7,550 | 30,650 | $755.00 + 15% | 7,550 |
| 30,650 | 74,200 | 4,220.00 + 25% | 30,650 |
| 74,200 | 154,800 | 15,107.50 + 28% | 74,200 |
| 154,800 | 336,550 | 37,675.50 + 33% | 154,800 |
| 336,550 | ........ | 97,653.00 + 35% | 336,550 |

**Schedule Y-1—If your filing status is Married filing jointly or Qualifying widow(er)**

| If your taxable income is: Over— | But not over— | The tax is: | of the amount over— |
|---|---|---|---|
| $0 | $15,100 | ......... 10% | $0 |
| 15,100 | 61,300 | $1,510.00 + 15% | 15,100 |
| 61,300 | 123,700 | 8,440.00 + 25% | 61,300 |
| 123,700 | 188,450 | 24,040.00 + 28% | 123,700 |
| 188,450 | 336,550 | 42,170.00 + 33% | 188,450 |
| 336,550 | ......... | 91,043.00 + 35% | 336,550 |

**Schedule Y-2—If your filing status is Married filing separately**

| If your taxable income is: Over— | But not over— | The tax is: | of the amount over— |
|---|---|---|---|
| $0 | $7,550 | ......... 10% | $0 |
| 7,550 | 30,650 | $755.00 + 15% | 7,550 |
| 30,650 | 61,850 | 4,220.00 + 25% | 30,650 |
| 61,850 | 94,225 | 12,020.00 + 28% | 61,850 |
| 94,225 | 168,275 | 21,085.00 + 33% | 94,225 |
| 168,275 | ......... | 45,521.50 + 35% | 168,275 |

**Schedule Z—If your filing status is Head of household**

| If your taxable income is: Over— | But not over— | The tax is: | of the amount over— |
|---|---|---|---|
| $0 | $10,750 | ......... 10% | $0 |
| 10,750 | 41,050 | $1,075.00 + 15% | 10,750 |
| 41,050 | 106,000 | 5,620.00 + 25% | 41,050 |
| 106,000 | 171,650 | 21,857.50 + 28% | 106,000 |
| 171,650 | 336,550 | 40,239.50 + 33% | 171,650 |
| 336,550 | ......... | 94,656.50 + 35% | 336,550 |

Source: IRS Publication 2006 1040 Instructions.

**HOW TO**   Use the tax rate schedules to calculate income tax

1. Locate the correct schedule according to filing status.
2. Locate the range in which the taxable income falls.
3. Subtract the low end of the range from the taxable income.
4. Multiply the difference from step 3 by the given percent for the range.
5. Add the tax from step 4 to the given tax for the range.

**EXAMPLE 1**   Find the tax on a taxable income of (a) $112,418 for a married taxpayer filing jointly using Table 19-2; (b) $128,382 for a married taxpayer filing separately using Table 19-2.

(a)  The taxpayer would use Schedule Y-1. Schedule Y-1 shows that the taxable income falls in the range $61,300–$123,700.

$$\$112,418 - \$61,300 = \$51,118$$
$$\$51,118(0.25) = \$12,779.50$$
$$\$12,779.50 + \$8,440.00 = \$21,219.50$$

**The tax is $21,219.50.**

(b)  The taxpayer is married filing separately, so use Schedule Y-2. The taxable income, $128,382, falls in the range over $94,225 but not over $168,275.

$$\$128,382 - \$94,225 = \$34,157$$
$$\$34,157(0.33) = \$11,271.81$$
$$\$11,271.81 + \$21,085.00 = \$32,356.81$$

**The tax is $32,356.81.**

**Tax credit:** an amount that is subtracted from the *tax owed*, in contrast to a deduction, which is subtracted from the gross income.

**Tax refund:** the amount of income tax a taxpayer gets back when filing an income tax return. It is the difference in the amount of tax the taxpayer has paid during the year and the amount of tax owed for a tax year.

**Tax owed:** the amount of income tax a taxpayer must pay when filing an income tax return. It is the difference in the amount of tax already paid and the total amount of tax that should be paid.

**Electronic filing:** a paperless way to file income tax with the IRS. The tax forms are submitted electronically to the IRS.

Taxpayers can take a **tax credit** in certain cases. A tax credit is an amount that is subtracted from the amount of tax owed rather than the gross income. The subtraction is made after the amount of tax owed has been calculated.

If a taxpayer pays in more income tax during the year than is owed when the income tax is filed, the difference is a **tax refund**. If the taxpayer has not paid as much income tax during the year as is owed when the income tax is filed, the taxpayer must pay the difference, which is called **tax owed.**

Taxpayers may file their income tax return electronically, known as **electronic filing**. More than 72 million taxpayers filed electronically in a recent year. The IRS web site www.irs.gov/efile provides all the details and latest information. Taxpayers who elect to *e-file* receive refunds in half the time as paper filers. The IRS provides electronic proof of receipt of all electronic filed tax returns within 48 hours after the IRS receives the return. Persons who file electronically can also authorize an electronic funds withdrawal from a bank account or pay by credit card. Computer software programs such as TurboTax can be used to calculate income tax and make electronic filing easier than ever before.

Taxpayers can also use TeleTax to receive recorded tax information about many tax return preparation topics. This service is available 24 hours a day, seven days a week. The toll-free number is 1-800-829-4477.

## STOP AND CHECK

1. Find the tax on a taxable income of $152,783 for a married taxpayer filing jointly.

2. Find the tax on a taxable income of $172,500 for a married taxpayer filing separately.

3. What is the tax on a taxable income of $117,832 for a single taxpayer?

4. Rodney Carney has a taxable income of $456,987 and his filing status is head of household. What is his tax?

## 19-3 SECTION EXERCISES

### SKILL BUILDERS

*Find the taxable income. Use $3,300 for each exemption.*

|  | Number of exemptions | Adjusted gross income | Itemized deductions |
|---|---|---|---|
| 1. | 4 | $49,071 | $12,019 |
| 2. | 1 | $138,503 | $32,167 |
| 3. | 5 | $167,413 | $27,534 |
| 4. | 2 | $75,013 | $16,532 |

*Use Table 19-1 to find the federal income tax.*

|  | Taxable income | Filing status |
|---|---|---|
| 5. | $40,317 | Single |
| 6. | $32,417 | Married, filing jointly |
| 7. | $30,307 | Married, filing separately |
| 8. | $29,553 | Head of household |

*Use Table 19-2 to find the federal income tax.*

|  | Taxable income | Filing status |
|---|---|---|
| 9. | $172,518 | Single |

|  | Taxable income | Filing status |
|---|---|---|
| 10. | $198,846 | Married, filing jointly |

11. Find the taxable income for a family of six (husband, wife, four children) whose adjusted gross income is $43,873 and itemized deductions are $9,582. (One exemption = $3,300.)

12. Find the taxable income for a single person whose adjusted gross income is $28,932 and itemized deductions are $4,915. (One exemption = $3,300.)

13. Canty O'Neal has an adjusted gross income of $68,917 and itemized deductions that total $18,473. Canty can claim three exemptions. What is her taxable income? (One exemption = $3,300.)

14. Noel Womack is single and calculates his taxable income to be $30,175. How much tax does he owe? Use Table 19-1.

15. Tommy and Michelle Fernandez have a combined taxable income of $23,300. How much tax should they pay if they file jointly? Use Table 19-1.

16. Vladimir Bozin is a head of household and has a taxable income of $26,873. Use Table 19-1 to find his tax.

17. Donna Shroyer is single and has a taxable income of $29,897. If her W-2 form shows that she has already paid $5,647 in income taxes for the year, use Table 19-1 to determine if she is due a refund or if she must pay more taxes. How much is the refund or how much more must she pay?

18. Paul Smith is married and filing his tax jointly with his wife, Anna. Their combined taxable income is $167,983. Use the tax rate schedules (Table 19-2) to calculate the tax they must pay.

19. Dr. Steven Katz is single and has a taxable income of $160,842. Use the tax rate schedules (Table 19-2) to calculate his income tax liability.

20. Jack Falcinelli is filing his tax as a head of household. His taxable income is $133,896 and his W-2 form shows he has already paid $34,197.00. Calculate his tax refund or payment.

## Learning Outcomes

## What to Remember with Examples

### Section 19-1

**1** Use the percent method to find the sales tax and excise tax. (p. 650)

1. Write the given percent as a decimal.
2. Find the sales tax:

$$\text{Sales tax} = \text{purchase price} \times \text{sales tax rate}$$

where sales tax rate = tax per \$1.00 of purchase price or a percent of the purchase price.

> Use the percent method to find the sales tax on a \$685 fax machine taxed at 6.6%.
>
> $$6.6\% = 0.066$$
> $$\text{Tax} = \$685(0.066)$$
> $$= \$45.21$$

**2** Find the marked price and the sales tax from the total price. (p. 651)

1. Find the marked price:
   (a) Write the sales tax rate as a decimal equivalent.
   (b) Add 1 to the decimal equivalent of the sales tax rate from step 1a.
   (c) Divide the total price by the sum from step 1b.

$$\text{Marked price} = \frac{\text{total price}}{1 + \text{sales tax rate (in decimal form)}}$$

2. Find the sales tax:

$$\text{Sales tax} = \text{total price} - \text{marked price}$$

> Homer Ray sells handcrafted furniture at prices that include the state sales tax. One inlaid table sold for \$3,950. Calculate the marked price and the sales tax Homer must send to the state if the tax rate is 8%.
>
> $$\begin{aligned} \text{Marked price} &= \frac{\text{total price}}{1 + \text{sales tax rate}} \\ &= \frac{\$3,950}{1 + 0.08} \\ &= \frac{\$3,950}{1.08} \\ &= \$3,657.41 \end{aligned}$$
>
> $$\begin{aligned} \text{Sales tax} &= \text{total price} - \text{marked price} \\ &= \$3,950 - \$3,657.41 \\ &= \$292.59 \\ &\quad\text{or} \\ &\quad \$3,657.41(0.08) \\ &= \$292.59 \end{aligned}$$

### Section 19-2

**1** Find the assessed value. (p. 654)

1. Write the assessment rate as the decimal equivalent of the percent.
2. Find the assessed value:

$$\text{Assessed value} = \text{market value} \times \text{assessment rate}$$

> Find the assessed value of a home with a market value of \$106,000 if the assessed value is 30% of the market value.
>
> $$30\% = 0.3$$
> $$\$106,000(0.3) = \$31,800$$

**2** Calculate the property tax. (p. 654)

1. Express the given property tax rate as tax per \$1.00 of assessed value.
   (a) Percent of assessed value:

$$\text{Tax per } \$1.00 = \text{decimal form of percent of assessed value}$$

   (b) Tax per \$100 of assessed value:

$$\text{Tax per } \$1.00 = \frac{\text{tax on } \$100}{\$100}$$

**(c)** Tax per $1,000 of assessed value:

$$\text{Tax per } \$1.00 = \frac{\text{tax on } \$1,000}{\$1,000}$$

**(d)** Tax in mills times assessed value:

$$\text{Tax per } \$1.00 = \frac{\text{mills per } \$1.00}{\$1,000}$$

**2.** Find the property tax:

$$\text{Property tax } = \text{ assessed value } \times \text{ property tax rate per } \$1.00$$

Find the property tax on a farm with an assessed value of $430,000 for each given tax rate.

The tax rate is 8.05% of the assessed value:

$$\text{Property tax } = 8.05\% = 0.0805 = \$430,000(0.0805)$$
$$= \$34,615$$

The tax rate is $8.05 per $100 of assessed value:

$$\text{Property tax } = \$430,000\left(\frac{\$8.05}{\$100}\right) = \$34,615$$

The tax rate is $80.50 per $1,000 of assessed value:

$$\text{Property tax } = \$430,000\left(\frac{\$80.50}{\$1,000}\right) = \$34,615$$

The tax rate is 80.5 mills per $1.00 of assessed value:

$$80.5 \text{ mills } = \frac{80.5}{1,000}$$
$$\text{Property tax } = \$430,000\left(\frac{80.5}{1,000}\right) = \$34,615$$

**3** Determine the property tax rate.
(p. 656)

**1.** Select the appropriate formula according to the desired tax rate type.

$$\text{Tax per } \$1.00 \text{ of assessed value } = \frac{\text{total estimated budget}}{\text{total assessed property value}}$$

$$\text{Tax per } \$100 \text{ of assessed value } = \frac{\text{total estimated budget}}{\text{total assessed property value}} \times \$100$$

$$\text{Tax per } \$1,000 \text{ of assessed value } = \frac{\text{total estimated budget}}{\text{total assessed property value}} \times \$1,000$$

$$\text{Tax, in mills, per } \$1.00 \text{ of assessed value } = \frac{\text{total estimated budget}}{\text{total assessed property value}} \times \$1,000$$

**2.** Make calculations using the selected formula. Always round up.

Find the tax expressed as tax per $1,000 of assessed value for Piperton if $15,872,000 is anticipated for expenses and the town has property assessed at $651,375,000.

$$\text{Tax per } \$1,000 \text{ of assessed value } = \left(\frac{\$15,872,000}{\$651,375,000}\right)(\$1,000)$$
$$= \$24.36691614 = \$24.37$$

## Section 19-3

**1** Find taxable income.
(p. 660)

**1.** Find the adjusted gross income:

$$\text{Adjusted gross income } = \text{ total income } - \text{ specific expenses and deductions}$$

**2.** Total the deductions or choose the standard deduction and total the exemptions.
**3.** Find the taxable income:

$$\text{Taxable income } = \text{ adjusted gross income } - \text{ itemized or standard deductions } - \text{ exemptions}$$

Toni Wilson and her spouse earned $53,950 gross income and had itemized deductions of $10,700. They have a seven-year-old daughter. Find the taxable income, using $3,300 for each exemption.

$$\text{Taxable income} = \$53,950 - \$10,700 - (3)(\$3,300)$$
$$= \$53,950 - \$10,700 - \$9,900 = \$33,350$$

**2** Use the tax tables to calculate income tax. (p. 661)

1. Locate the taxable income under the column headed "If line 40 (taxable income) is—."
2. Move across to the column headed "And you are—," which has the four filing status categories listed under it. The tax owed appears under the appropriate category.

Use Table 19-1 to find Toni's tax if she and her husband file jointly.

Find the range of $33,350–$33,400. Move across to the tax in the column "Married filing jointly," which is $4,251.

**3** Use the tax rate schedules to calculate income tax. (p. 664)

1. Locate the correct schedule according to filing status.
2. Locate the range in which the taxable income falls.
3. Subtract the low end of the range from the taxable income.
4. Multiply the difference from step 3 by the given percent for the range.
5. Add the tax from step 4 to the given tax for the range.

Sue Wilson has a taxable income of $153,897. Her filing status is single. Find the income tax she owes, using Schedule X in Table 19-2. $153,897 falls in the range "over $74,200 but not over $154,800."

$$\$153,897 - \$74,200 = \$79,697$$
$$\$79,697(0.28) = \$22,315.16$$
$$\text{Income tax} = \$22,315.16 + \$15,107.50$$
$$= \$37,422.66$$

# EXERCISES SET A

*Calculate the sales tax on the given purchase using the given sales tax rate. (Round to the nearest cent.)*

**1.** $237.42; 6%  

**2.** $1,294.26; 4.5%  

**3.** $675.93; 5%

*Find the marked price if the given total bill includes sales tax at the given rate. (Round to the nearest cent.)*

**4.** $27.45; 5%  

**5.** $347.28; 4.5%  

**6.** $87.26; 3.5%

*Find the assessed value of each property using the following rates.*

Farm property or single-family dwellings: 25% of market value
Commercial property or multi-family dwellings: 40% of market value
Utilities: 50% of market value

**7.** Single-family dwelling with market value of $55,000  

**8.** Grocery store with market value of $115,000

**9.** Power company with market value of $5,175,000

*Find the tax on the given assessed value using the given rate.*

**10.** $37,000; 1.5% of assessed value  

**11.** $12,500; 2% of assessed value

**12.** If the county tax rate is $3.74 per $100 of assessed value, find the tax on a property that is assessed at $35,000.  

**13.** The tax rate for a city is $3.25 per $100 of assessed value. Find the tax on a property that is assessed at $125,000.

**14.** A home has a market value of $50,000 (assessed value = 25% of market value). Find the amount of county taxes to be paid on the home if the county tax rate is $4.00 per $100 of assessed value.

*Find the tax on the given assessed value using the given rate.*

**15.** $37,000; $14.25 per $1,000 of assessed value  

**16.** $172,500; $16.23 per $1,000 of assessed value

**17.** $87,500; $12.67 per $1,000 of assessed value

*Express the mills as dollars to the nearest thousandth.*

**18.** 63 mills  

**19.** 72 mills

*Find the tax on each property at the given assessed valuation using the given tax rate.*

**20.** $23,275; 55 mills per $1.00 of assessed value

**21.** $28,750; 64 mills per $1.00 of assessed value

*Complete the following table. (Express the tax on the given assessed valuation in cents or dollars and cents. Round up any remainder.)*

| EXCEL | Total assessed value | Total expenses | Tax on | | |
|---|---|---|---|---|---|
| | | | $1.00 | $100 | $1,000 |
| **22.** | $87,460,000 | $4,348,800 | | | |
| **23.** | $528,739,000 | $17,205,160 | | | |

*Use $3,300 for each allowed personal exemption in Exercises 24–26.*

**24.** Find the taxable income for the Zuckmans, a family of four (husband, wife, two children), if the adjusted gross income is $34,728, and the itemized deductions are $10,246.

**25.** Find the taxable income for Mario Gravez, a single person whose adjusted gross income is $37,486 and whose itemized deductions are $5,412.

**26.** Find the taxable income for Lorenda and James Atlas, a husband and wife with no children who have an adjusted gross income of $56,000 and are filing jointly. Their total itemized deductions are $13,589.

*Use Table 19-1 (pp. 662–663) to find the tax owed by taxpayers with the following taxable incomes:*

**27.** $39,678 (single)

**28.** $40,876 (single)

**29.** $38,979 (married, filing jointly)

**30.** $40,987 (married, filing separately)

*Use Table 19-2 (p. 664) to find the tax on the following taxable incomes:*

**31.** $172,478 (married, filing separately)

**32.** $188,342 (single)

# EXERCISES SET B

*Calculate the sales tax on the given purchase using the given sales tax rate. (Round to the nearest cent.)*

**1.** $523.85; 5%

**2.** $482.12; 6%

**3.** $2,998.97; 4.5%

*Find the marked price if the given total bill includes sales tax at the given rate. (Round to the nearest cent.)*

**4.** $139.53; 6%

**5.** $53.92; 5%

**6.** $3,580.53; 7.25%

*Find the assessed value of each property using the following rates:*

Farm property or single-family dwellings: 25% of market value
Commercial property or multi-family dwellings: 40% of market value
Utilities: 50% of market value

**7.** Apartment with market value of $235,000

**8.** Farmland with market value of $150,000

**9.** Thomas Richardson owns a home on 2 acres of land. The property has a market value of $215,000. What is the assessed value?

*Find the tax on the given assessed value using the given rate.*

**10.** $45,000; 1.75% of assessed value

**11.** $575,000; 1.8% of assessed value

**12.** If the county tax rate is increased to $4.25 from $3.74 per $100 of assessed value, how much is the tax increase on a $35,000 piece of property?

**13.** Vicki Froehlich lives in a city where the tax rate is $21.50 per $1,000 of assessed value. Vicki's home has an assessed value of $31,820. How much city tax must Vicki pay?

**14.** What is the city property tax on a house assessed at $12,500 if the city tax rate is $3.06 per $100 of assessed valuation?

*Find the tax on the given assessed value using the given rate.*

**15.** $150,000; $15.50 per $1,000 of assessed value

**16.** $32,250; $13.78 per $1,000 of assessed value

*Express the mills as dollars to the nearest thousandth.*

**17.** 34 mills

**18.** 51 mills

*Find the tax on each property at the given assessed valuation using the given tax rate.*

**19.** $12,500; 65 mills per $1.00 of assessed value

**20.** $52,575; 71 mills per $1.00 of assessed value

*Complete the following table. (Express the tax on the given assessed valuation in cents or dollars and cents. Round up any remainder.)*

| Total assessed value | Total expenses | Tax on | | |
|---|---|---|---|---|
| | | **$1.00** | **$100** | **$1,000** |
| **21.** $11,370,000 | $386,450 | | | |
| **22.** $5,718,000 | $374,740 | | | |

*Use $3,300 for each allowed personal exemption in Exercises 23–25.*

**23.** Find the taxable income for Sam and Delois Johns, a husband and wife without children, whose adjusted gross income is $48,378 and itemized deductions are $10,023.

**24.** Find the taxable income for the Shotwells, a family of three (husband, wife, one child), if their adjusted gross income is $72,376 and itemized deductions are $24,375.

**25.** Find the taxable income for the Thungs, a family of three (husband, wife, one child), if their adjusted gross income is $66,833 and itemized deductions are $12,583.

*Use Table 19-1 (pp. 662–663) to find the tax owed by taxpayers with the following taxable incomes:*

**26.** $36,057 (single)

**27.** $39,512 (single)

**28.** $40,095 (married, filing jointly)

**29.** $40,002 (head of household)

*Use Table 19-2 (p. 664) to find the tax on the following taxable incomes:*

**30.** $154,456 (married, filing jointly)

**31.** $161,200 (head of household)

**32.** $458,919 (single)

# PRACTICE TEST

## CHAPTER 19

*Find the sales tax on the given marked price using the given sales tax rate.*

**1.** $15.17; 5%

**2.** $18.26; 6.25%

**3.** $287.52; 7.75%

**4.** $2.98; 6.5%

*What is the total price if the given sales tax rate is applied to the given marked price?*

**5.** $187.21; 6%

**6.** $4.25; 5.25%

*Find the marked price if the given total price includes sales tax at the given rate.*

**7.** $18.84; 7%

**8.** $7.87; 6.5%

**9.** $52.63; 5.25%

**10.** A telephone bill of $84.15 is assessed state sales tax at a rate of 6%. Find the tax on the telephone bill.

**11.** Find the total telephone bill in Exercise 10.

**12.** Find the assessed value of an apartment building (assessed at 40% of the market value) if the market value is $485,298.

**13.** Find the tax on a business property if the assessed value of the property is $176,297 and the tax rate is $7.56 per $100 of assessed value.

**14.** Find the tax on a home if the assessed value is $24,375 and the tax rate is $43.97 per $1,000.

**15.** A property has an assessed value of $72,000. The city tax rate for this property is $4.12 per $100 of assessed valuation. Find the city tax on the property.

**16.** The property in Exercise 15 is located in a county that has set a property tax rate of $2.57 per $100 of assessed value. What is the county tax on the property?

**17.** Find the tax rate per $100 of assessed value that a county should set if the total assessed property value in the county is $31,800,000 and the total expenses are $957,300.

**18.** Use Table 19-2 (p. 664) to calculate the amount of tax owed by Erma Thornton Braddy if her taxable income is $182,817 and her filing status is single.

**19.** Charles Wossum and his wife Ruby are filing their income tax jointly. Their combined taxable income is $39,872. How much tax must they pay? Use Table 19-1 (p. 662–663).

**20.** Juanita and Robert Gray have a gross income of $68,521, all of which is subject to income tax. They have two children and plan to file a joint income tax return. If each exemption is $3,300 and they have itemized deductions of $14,521, what is their taxable income?

1. Explain why the following formulas are equivalent.

$$\text{Tax per } \$1.00 = \frac{\text{tax on } \$1.00}{\$100}$$

$$\text{Tax per } \$1.00 = \frac{\text{tax on } \$1,000}{\$1,000}$$

2. Examine Table 19-1 to find the relationship between income tax for a single person and a married person filing jointly for incomes more than $23,000 and less than $41,000.

3. Examine Table 19-1 to identify the tax relationship between single persons and married persons filing separately.

4. Compare Schedules X, Y-1, Y-2, and Z in Table 19-2 to determine which type of taxpayer that earns $112,000 would pay the most income tax. Which pays the least?

5. Use Schedule X in Table 19-2 to find the income tax on an income of $40,000. Compare this tax to the amount of tax required for a single person earning $40,000 in the tax table (Table 19-1).

6. Examine Schedule X in Table 19-2. Explain how a single person with a taxable income of $85,000 pays less tax than a single person with an income of $105,000, even though both incomes are in the same range.

7. Schedule X in Table 19-2 indicates that the maximum percent of income tax is 35% of the taxable income. Calculate the income tax for a single person whose taxable income is $400,000. Calculate the tax rate across the entire $400,000. Explain why the overall rate is less than 35%.

## Challenge Problem

Before purchasing investment property, an interested buyer can go to the tax assessor's office to find the taxes to be paid on the property. Using a computer provided for this purpose, the assessor can find the assessed value of the property, the tax rate, and the tax. If the property is purchased before the end of the tax year, the seller will pay the taxes only for the number of days the seller owns the land. This amount is called the seller's *pro rata* share of the annual taxes and can be found by dividing the annual taxes by 365 days to get the taxes due per day and then multiplying by the number of days the land is owned during that tax year by the seller. The buyer also pays a *pro rata* share.

Dan is interested in buying a piece of investment property. The market value is $30,500 and the assessment rate is 18% of the market value. Dan found the city tax rate to be 92.7 mills per $1.00 of assessed value and the county rate to be 138.4 mills per $1.00 of assessed value. Dan buys the land on April 13. What is Dan's *pro rata* share of the property taxes? The tax years for both the city and the county start and stop at the same time.

# CASE STUDIES

## 19.1 Paying Sales Tax

It was the end of a very busy and successful year for Lou Vang's environmental consulting business, and the paperwork had been piling up. Most of it seemingly had to do with taxes. Lou had an inquiry from his home state of Colorado regarding sales tax due on some environmental testing equipment he had purchased out of state. The equipment totaled $11,884.76, and the 2.9% sales tax apparently had not been paid. Lou made a mental note to send in payment with the return envelope. The sales tax inquiry reminded him that he still hadn't calculated the sales tax for the radon testing units that he was going to market online. Each unit sold for $9.95, but he knew a portion would have to be paid to the state for sales tax. Another letter contained the new assessment from the county for his small office building. The letter indicated that the market value of the building had increased to $350,000, and the assessed valuation had increased to 60%. And finally, Lou received his last outstanding 1099 form (which shows income for independent contractors) and was finally able to calculate the adjusted gross income for his family of five (husband, wife, three children) as $122,214. Lou knew that he would end up paying a lot of money in taxes, but at least he had all of the information he needed to do so.

1. Based on Lou's equipment purchase of $11,884.76, how much does he owe the state of Colorado in sales tax? Is state sales tax the only sales tax that Lou needs to be concerned with?

2. Lou plans to sell radon testing units for $9.95 each, or at $9.00 apiece for quantities of 20 or more, sales tax included. Find the marked price and the sales tax for each unit price using a sales tax rate of 2.9%.

3. Calculate the property tax due on Lou's building if the property tax rate is $3.57 per $100 of assessed value.

4. Using the Vangs' adjusted gross income, find the taxable income and income tax due as a married couple filing a joint return. The Vangs have itemized deductions totaling $26,457. Use $3,400 for each personal exemption.

## 19.2 A Tax Dilemma

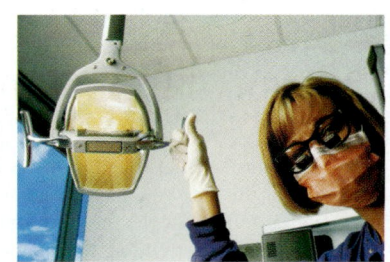

Rita just finished completing her educational requirements to become a dental hygienist. She has been offered jobs in two different cities and is trying to determine which one she should accept. Both employers offer similar benefits and working conditions, but the jobs are in two different states. Rita will move to the state in which she accepts a position.

The first position is in Pennsylvania. Rita would earn $50,000 a year, and she could purchase a starter duplex in the older part of the city for about $75,000. Property taxes equal about 3.5% of assessed value. Assessed value is normally 85% of market value. The state sales tax rate is 6% but does not apply to clothing or food. State income taxes average 3%.

The other position is in Maryland. Rita would earn $65,000 a year, but a starter duplex would cost her $135,000. In that area, property taxes average about 4% of assessed value, and values are assessed at 60% of market value. The state sales tax is generally considered to be about 1% higher because it applies to clothing as well as other purchases. Additionally, state income taxes average 1.5% higher in Maryland than in Pennsylvania.

1. What would be the difference in cost of living between the two locations based only on the differences in sales tax, income tax, and property tax?

| Tax | Pennsylvania | Maryland | Difference |
|---|---|---|---|
| Property | | | |
| Sales | | | |
| State Income | | | |

2. What percentage of the difference in annual salaries does this additional cost represent? Assume $24,000 of taxable purchases for this exercise.

# Financial Statements

## Collapse of Enron

Enron, formed in 1985, was admired on Wall Street as a technological innovator. The company enjoyed dramatic growth with annual revenue hitting $100 billion in 2000, making it the seventh-largest company on the Fortune 500. The company's stock reached a high of $90 per share.

However, Enron lied about its profits and stands accused of a range of shady dealings, including concealing debts so they didn't show up in the company's accounts. It used complex partnerships to mask its financial problems so it could continue to get cash and credit to run its trading business. When these suspicious accounting tactics were discovered, Enron collapsed. Shareholders, including Enron employees who held stock in 401(k) retirement accounts, lost tens of billions of dollars.

Outraged investors, employees, pension holders, and politicians are demanding to know why Enron's failings were not spotted earlier. Its collapse has prompted the accounting industry to take a hard look at itself, and the U.S. Securities and Exchange Commission launched an investigation. As the depth of the deception unfolded, investors and creditors retreated, forcing the firm into Chapter 11 bankruptcy. Enron officials have acknowledged that the company has overstated its profits by more than $580 million since 1997.

Since the collapse of Enron, approximately 30 of the company's executives have been criminally charged. If you were on the jury of one of those cases, what would your verdict be? Should the company executives face jail time for falsifying financial statements? These individuals were able to sell their company stock before Enron collapsed, many making millions of dollars at the expense of other stockholders, including Enron employees, who lost everything. Or should Enron's accounting firm be held responsible? In any case, the Enron collapse taught us one very simple lesson: The incredible importance of keeping accurate and reliable financial statements.

## LEARNING OUTCOMES

### 20-1 The Balance Sheet

1. Prepare a balance sheet.
2. Prepare a vertical analysis of a balance sheet.
3. Prepare a horizontal analysis of a balance sheet.

### 20-2 Income Statements

1. Prepare an income statement.
2. Prepare a vertical analysis of an income statement.
3. Prepare a horizontal analysis of an income statement.

### 20-3 Financial Statement Ratios

1. Find and use financial ratios.

The financial condition of a business must be monitored all the time. The owner of a business, investors, and creditors need to know the financial condition of the business before they can make decisions and plans. Lending institutions consider the overall financial health of a business before lending money. The stockholders of incorporated businesses expect to receive periodic reports on the financial condition of the corporation. Many companies or organizations hire an auditor once a year to determine this condition. Two financial statements, the *balance sheet* and the *income statement,* are normally prepared as part of this analysis. The balance sheet describes the condition of a business at some exact point in time, whereas the income statement shows what the business did over a period of time.

## 20-1 THE BALANCE SHEET

### LEARNING OUTCOMES

1 Prepare a balance sheet.
2 Prepare a vertical analysis of a balance sheet.
3 Prepare a horizontal analysis of a balance sheet.

### 1 Prepare a balance sheet.

The **balance sheet** is a type of financial statement that indicates the worth or financial condition of a business *as of a certain date*. It does not give any historical background about the company or make future projections, but rather shows the status of the company on a given date. On that date, it answers these questions:

How much does the business own? What are its *assets?*
How much does the business owe? What are its *liabilities?*
How much is the business worth? What is its *equity?*

Assets are properties owned by the business. They include anything of monetary value and things that could be exchanged for cash or other property. **Current assets** are assets that are normally turned into cash within a year. **Plant and equipment** are assets that are used in transacting business and are more long-term in nature. These types of assets can be further subdivided as follows:

| | |
|---|---|
| **Current assets** | |
| **Cash** | Money in the bank as well as cash on hand |
| **Accounts receivable** | Money that customers owe the business for merchandise or services they have received but have not yet paid for |
| **Notes receivable** | Promissory notes owed to the business |
| **Merchandise inventory** | Value of merchandise on hand |
| **Office supplies** | Value of supplies such as stationery, pens, file folders, and computer storage devices |
| | |
| **Plant and equipment** | |
| **Business equipment** | Value of equipment (tools, display cases, machinery, and so on) that the business owns |
| **Office furniture and equipment** | Value of office furniture (desks, chairs, filing cabinets, and so on) and equipment (computers, printers, copiers, calculators, postage meters, fax machines, and the like) that the business owns |
| **Buildings** | Value of the buildings the business owns |
| **Land** | Value of the property and grounds on which the buildings stand and other land the business owns |

Liabilities are amounts that the business owes. **Current liabilities** are those that must be paid shortly. **Long-term liabilities** are those that will be paid over a long period of time—a year or more. These types of liabilities can be further subdivided as follows:

| | |
|---|---|
| **Current liabilities** | |
| **Accounts payable** | Money owed for merchandise or services that the business has received but has not yet paid for |
| **Notes payable** | Promissory notes that the business owes |
| **Wages payable** | Salaries that a business owes its employees |
| **Long-term liabilities** | |
| **Mortgage payable** | The debt owed on buildings and land that the business owns |

---

**Balance sheet:** financial statement that indicates the worth or financial condition of a business as of a certain date.

**Assets:** properties or anything of monetary value owned by the business.

**Current assets:** assets that are normally turned into cash within a year.

**Plant and equipment:** assets used in transacting business.

**Cash:** a current asset of money in the bank or cash on hand.

**Accounts receivable:** a current asset that is the money owed by customers.

**Notes receivable:** a current asset that is a promissory note owed to the business.

**Merchandise inventory:** a current asset that is the value of merchandise on hand.

**Business equipment:** value of equipment such as tools, display cases, and machinery owned by the business.

**Office furniture and equipment:** value of office furniture and equipment such as computers, printers, and copiers owned by the business.

**Buildings:** value of buildings and structures owned by the business.

**Land:** value of the grounds or land owned by the business.

**Liabilities:** amounts that the business owes.

**Current liabilities:** debts that must be paid within a short amount of time.

**Long-term liabilities:** liabilities that are paid over a long period of time.

**Accounts payable:** a current liability for merchandise or services that have not been paid for.

**Note payable:** promissory notes that are owed.

**Wages payable:** salaries a business owes its employees.

**Mortgage payable:** a long-term liability for the building and land the business owns.

**Owner's equity** or **stockholder's equity:** the difference between the company's assets and the liabilities.

**Capital, proprietorship,** or **net worth:** other terms for owner's equity.

In addition to its debts to creditors, a firm is considered to owe its investors. This "debt", expressed as **owner's equity,** also called **stockholder's equity,** is the amount of clear ownership or the owner's rights to the properties. It is the difference between assets and liabilities. For instance, if a business has assets of \$175,000 and liabilities of \$100,000, the owner's equity is \$175,000 − \$100,000, or \$75,000. Other words used to mean the same thing as owner's equity are **capital, proprietorship,** and **net worth.**

A balance sheet (see Figure 20-1) lists the assets, liabilities, and owner's equity of a business on a specific date, using the basic accounting equation of business:

Basic Accounting Equation

$$\text{Assets} = \text{liabilities} + \text{owner's equity}$$

$$A = L + OE$$

| Sander's Woodworks<br>Balance Sheet<br>December 31, 2007 |
|---|
| **Assets** |
| *Current assets* |
| Cash |
| Accounts receivable |
| Merchandise inventory |
| Total current assets |
| *Plant and equipment* |
| Equipment |
| Total plant and equipment |
| Total assets |
| **Liabilities** |
| *Current liabilities* |
| Accounts payable |
| Wages payable |
| Total current liabilities |
| *Long-term liabilities* |
| Mortgage note payable |
| Total long-term liabilities |
| Total liabilities |
| **Owner's Equity** |
| J. Sander's capital |
| Total liabilities and owner's equity |

**FIGURE 20-1**
**Sander's Woodworks Balance Sheet Template**

## HOW TO **Prepare a balance sheet**

1. Find and record the *total assets,* working by asset category.
   (a) List the *current assets* and draw a single line underneath the last entry.
   (b) Add the entries and record the *total current assets,* drawing a single line underneath the total.
   (c) Repeat step 1a for *plant and equipment assets* and step 1b for *total plant and equipment assets*.
   (d) Add the category totals and draw a double line underneath the grand total.

$$\text{Total assets} = \text{total current assets} + \text{total plant and equipment}$$

2. Find and record the *total liabilities,* working by liability category.
   (a) Repeat step 1a for *current liabilities* and step 1b for *total current liabilities*.
   (b) Repeat step 1a for *long-term liabilities* and step 1b for *total long-term liabilities*.
   (c) Add the category totals and draw a single line underneath the total.

$$\text{Total liabilities} = \text{total current liabilities} + \text{total long-term liabilities}$$

3. Find and record the *total owner's equity*.
   (a) List the equity entries and draw a single line underneath the last entry.
   (b) Add the entries and draw a single line underneath the total.
4. Find and record the *total liabilities and owner's equity:* Add the total liabilities to the total owner's equity and draw a double line underneath the grand total.

$$\text{Total liabilities and owner's equity} = \text{total liabilities} + \text{total owner's equity}$$

5. Confirm that the double line grand totals from step 1 and step 4 are the same.

$$\text{Total assets} = \text{total liabilities} + \text{owner's equity}$$

## TIP

**Single Underline versus Double Underline**

One way of distinguishing totals and subtotals on financial statements is by the type of underline used. A single underline indicates the result of addition or subtraction that is a subtotal. The double underline indicates the result of addition or subtraction that is a grand total.

**EXAMPLE 1** Prepare a balance sheet, using Figure 20-1 as a guide, for Sander's Woodworks for December 31, 2007. The company assets are: cash, $1,973; accounts receivable, $2,118; merchandise inventory, $18,476; equipment, $18,591. The liabilities are: accounts payable, $2,317; wages payable, $684; mortgage note payable, $15,286. The owner's capital is $22,871.

The completed balance sheet is shown in Figure 20-2.

| | | |
|---|---|---|
| | Sander's Woodworks | |
| | Balance Sheet | |
| | December 31, 2007 ← Specific date | |
| **Assets** | | |
| *Current assets* | | |
| Cash | $1,973 | |
| Accounts receivable | 2,118 | |
| Merchandise inventory | 18,476 | |
| Total current assets | 22,567 ← Subtotal | |
| *Plant and equipment* | | |
| Equipment | 18,591 | |
| Total plant and equipment | 18,591 | |
| Total assets | $41,158 ← Total | |
| **Liabilities** | | |
| *Current liabilities* | | |
| Accounts payable | 2,317 | |
| Wages payable | 684 | |
| Total current liabilities | 3,001 ← Subtotal | |
| *Long-term liabilities* | | |
| Mortgage note payable | 15,286 | |
| Total long-term liabilities | 15,286 ← Subtotal | |
| Total liabilities | 18,287 ← Subtotal | |
| **Owner's Equity** | | |
| J. Sander's capital | 22,871 | |
| Total liabilities and owner's equity | $41,158 ← Total | |

**FIGURE 20-2**
**Completed Balance Sheet**

**STOP AND CHECK**

1. Find total current assets if the 7th Inning has $43,518 in cash; $3,988 in accounts receivable; and $96,532 in merchandise inventory.

2. Datatech, Inc., has $15,817 in accounts payable; $9,892 in wages payable; and $418,250 for its mortgage note. If owner's equity totals $45,986, find total liabilities and owner's equity.

3. Prepare a balance sheet for Rayco, Inc., for December 31, 2007. The company assets are: cash, $105,095; accounts receivable, $6,503; merchandise inventory, $190,014; equipment, $32,507. The liabilities are: accounts payable, $6,007; wages payable, $4,761; mortgage note payable, $281,017. The owner's capital is $42,334.

4. Prepare a balance sheet for Rayco, Inc., for December 31, 2008. The company assets are: cash, $114,975; accounts receivable, $8,918; merchandise inventory, $187,915; equipment, $29,719. The liabilities are: accounts payable, $6,832; wages payable, $5,215; mortgage note payable, $279,409. The owner's capital is $50,071.

## 2 Prepare a vertical analysis of a balance sheet.

**Vertical analysis:** the ratio of each item on the balance sheet to total assets.

A **vertical analysis** of a balance sheet shows the ratio of each item on the balance sheet to the *total assets*. To find these ratios, we use the percentage formula $R = \frac{P}{B}$. Each item on the balance sheet is a portion $P$ and the total assets amount is the base $B$. Their ratio $R$ is expressed as a percent.

For instance, if total assets are $50,000, a liability of $5,000 is 10% of total assets.

$$R = \frac{P}{B} = \frac{\text{liability}}{\text{total assets}} = \frac{\$5,000}{\$50,000} = 0.1 = 10\%$$

### HOW TO   Prepare a vertical analysis of a balance sheet

1. Prepare a balance sheet of assets, liabilities, and owner's equity.
2. Create an additional column labeled *percent*: For each item, divide the amount of the item by the total assets then multiply by 100% to record the result as a percent.

$$\text{Percent of total assets} = \frac{\text{amount of item}}{\text{total assets}} \times 100\%$$

### EXAMPLE 1   Prepare a vertical analysis of the balance sheet for Sander's Woodworks shown in Figure 20-2.

For each item, divide the amount of the item by the total assets.

Cash: $\dfrac{\$1,973}{\$41,158}(100\%) = 0.0479372(100\%) = $ **4.8%** (nearest tenth of a percent)

Accounts receivable: $\dfrac{\$2,118}{\$41,158}(100\%) = 0.0514602(100\%) = $ **5.1%**

Merchandise inventory: $\dfrac{\$18,476}{\$41,158}(100\%) = 0.4489042(100\%) = $ **44.9%**

$$\text{Total current assets: } \frac{\$22{,}567}{\$41{,}158}(100\%) = 0.5483017(100\%) = 54.8\%$$

$$\text{Equipment: } \frac{\$18{,}591}{\$41{,}158}(100\%) = 0.4516983(100\%) = 45.2\%$$

$$\text{Total assets: } \frac{\$41{,}158}{\$41{,}158}(100\%) = 1(100\%) = 100\%$$

$$\text{Accounts payable: } \frac{\$2{,}317}{\$41{,}158}(100\%) = 0.0562953(100\%) = 5.6\%$$

$$\text{Wages payable: } \frac{\$684}{\$41{,}158}(100\%) = 0.0166189(100\%) = 1.7\%$$

$$\text{Total current liabilities: } \frac{\$3{,}001}{\$41{,}158}(100\%) = 0.0729141(100\%) = 7.3\%$$

$$\text{Mortgage note payable: } \frac{\$15{,}286}{\$41{,}158}(100\%) = 0.3713980(100\%) = 37.1\%$$

$$\text{Total liabilities: } \frac{\$18{,}287}{\$41{,}158}(100\%) = 0.4443122(100\%) = 44.4\%$$

$$\text{J. Sander's capital: } \frac{\$22{,}871}{\$41{,}158}(100\%) = 0.5556878(100\%) = 55.6\%$$

$$\text{Total liabilities and owner's equity: } \frac{\$41{,}158}{\$41{,}158}(100\%) = 1(100\%) = 100\%$$

The percent both for total assets and for total liabilities and owner's equity is 100%. Minor discrepancies may occur due to rounding. The completed balance sheet is shown in Figure 20-3.

| Sander's Woodworks Balance Sheet December 31, 2007 | Amount | Percent |
|---|---|---|
| **Assets** | | |
| *Current assets* | | |
| Cash | $1,973 | 4.8 |
| Accounts receivable | 2,118 | 5.1 |
| Merchandise inventory | 18,476 | 44.9 |
| Total current assets | 22,567 | 54.8 |
| *Plant and equipment* | | |
| Equipment | 18,591 | 45.2 |
| Total plant and equipment | 18,591 | 45.2 |
| Total assets | $41,158 ←Total→ | 100.0 |
| **Liabilities** | | |
| *Current liabilities* | | |
| Accounts payable | $ 2,317 | 5.6 |
| Wages payable | 684 | 1.7 |
| Total current liabilities | 3,001 | 7.3 |
| *Long-term liabilities* | | |
| Mortgage note payable | 15,286 | 37.1 |
| Total long-term liabilities | 15,286 | 37.1 |
| Total liabilities | 18,287 | 44.4 |
| **Owner's Equity** | | |
| J. Sander's capital | 22,871 | 55.6 |
| Total liabilities and owner's equity | $41,158 ←Total→ | 100.0 |

**FIGURE 20-3**
Vertical Analysis of Sander's Woodworks Balance Sheet

**Comparative balance sheet:** a balance sheet that includes data from two or more years.

Comparing balance sheets from two years may reveal important trends in a business's operations. Such a **comparative balance sheet** can be seen in Figure 20-4. Note that data for the most recent year are entered in the first columns.

**FIGURE 20-4**
**Vertical Analysis of Sander's Woodworks Comparative Balance Sheet**

Sander's Woodworks
Comparative Balance Sheet
December 31, 2007 and 2008

Most recent year first → 2008

| | 2008 | | 2007 | |
|---|---|---|---|---|
| | **Amount** | **Percent** | **Amount** | **Percent** |
| **Assets** | | | | |
| *Current assets* | | | | |
| Cash | $2,184 | 5.7 | $1,973 | 4.8 |
| Accounts receivable | 4,308 | 11.3 | 2,118 | 5.1 |
| Merchandise inventory | 17,317 | 45.6 | 18,476 | 44.9 |
| Total current assets | 23,809 | 62.6 | 22,567 | 54.8 |
| *Plant and equipment* | | | | |
| Equipment | 14,203 | 37.4 | 18,591 | 45.2 |
| Total plant and equipment | 14,203 | 37.4 | 18,591 | 45.2 |
| Total assets | $38,012 | 100.0 | $41,158 | 100.0 |
| **Liabilities** | | | | |
| *Current liabilities* | | | | |
| Accounts payable | $ 1,647 | 4.3 | $ 2,317 | 5.6 |
| Wages payable | 894 | 2.4 | 684 | 1.7 |
| Total current liabilities | 2,541 | 6.7 | 3,001 | 7.3 |
| *Long-term liabilities* | | | | |
| Mortgage note payable | 12,715 | 33.4 | 15,286 | 37.1 |
| Total long-term liabilities | 12,715 | 33.4 | 15,286 | 37.1 |
| Total liabilities | 15,256 | 40.1 | 18,287 | 44.4 |
| **Owner's Equity** | | | | |
| J. Sander's capital | 22,756 | 59.9 | 22,871 | 55.6 |
| Total liabilities and owner's equity | $38,012 | 100.0 | $41,158 | 100.0 |

 **STOP AND CHECK**

1. Prepare a vertical analysis of the Rayco, Inc., balance sheet for December 31, 2007, from Exercise 3 in the Stop and Check on page 685.

2. Prepare a vertical analysis of the Rayco, Inc., balance sheet for December 31, 2008, from Exercise 4 in the Stop and Check on page 685.

3. Prepare a comparative balance sheet for Rayco for December 2007 and 2008 using information from Exercises 3 and 4 on pages 685.

4. From the comparative balance sheet for Rayco, Inc., in Exercise 3, in which year did Rayco have the greater total assets?

## 3 Prepare a horizontal analysis of a balance sheet.

**Horizontal analysis:** a balance sheet analysis that compares the same item for two different years.

Another way to analyze information on a comparative balance sheet is to compare item by item in a **horizontal analysis**. While a vertical analysis compares each item to total assets, a horizontal analysis compares the same item for two different years, recording both the amount of increase (or decrease) and the increase (or decrease) as a percent of the earlier year's amount.

---

### HOW TO   Prepare a horizontal analysis of a comparative balance sheet

1. Prepare a balance sheet for two or more years: Record each year's amounts in separate columns.
2. Create an additional column labeled *amount of increase (decrease)*: For each yearly item,
   (a) Subtract the smaller amount from the larger amount and record the difference.
   (b) If the earlier year's amount is larger than the more recent year's amount, record the difference from step 2a as a decrease by using parentheses or a negative (minus) sign.
3. Create an additional column labeled *percent increase (decrease)*: For each yearly item, divide the amount of increase (decrease) by the earlier year's amount, multiply by 100%, and record the difference as a percent.

$$\text{Percent increase (decrease)} = \frac{\text{amount of increase (decrease)}}{\text{earlier year's amount}} \times 100\%$$

---

### EXAMPLE 1
Prepare a horizontal analysis for Sander's Woodworks using the yearly amounts in Figure 20-5.

Cash: $2,184 − $1,973 = $211 (increase)
$211 ÷ $1,973 = 0.106944(100%) = 10.7% (increase)

Accounts receivable: $4,308 − $2,118 = $2,190 (increase)
$2,190 ÷ $2,118 = 1.033994 = 103.4% (increase)

Inventory: $18,476 − $17,317 = $1,159 (decrease)
1,159 ÷ $18,476 = 0.062730 = 6.3% (decrease)

Equipment: $18,591 − $14,203 = $4,388 (decrease)
$4,388 ÷ $18,591 = 0.236028 = 23.6% (decrease)

Total assets: $41,158 − $38,012 = $3,146 (decrease)
$3,146 ÷ $41,158 = 0.076437 = 7.6% (decrease)

Accounts payable: $2,317 − $1,647 = $670 (decrease)
$670 ÷ $2,317 = 0.289167 = 28.9% (decrease)

Salaries payable: $894 − $684 = $210 (increase)
$210 ÷ $684 = 0.307018 = 30.7% (increase)

Mortgage note payable: $15,286 − $12,715 = $2,571 (decrease)
$2,571 ÷ $15,286 = 0.168193 = 16.8% (decrease)

Total liabilities: $18,287 − $15,256 = $3,031 (decrease)
$3,031 ÷ $18,287 = 0.165746 = 16.6% (decrease)

J. Sander's capital: $22,871 − $22,756 = $115 (decrease)
$115 ÷ $22,871 = 0.005028 = 0.5% (decrease)

Total liabilities and owner's equity:

$41,158 − $38,012 = $3,146 (decrease)
$3,146 ÷ $41,158 = 0.0764371 = 7.6% (decrease)

---

If the horizontal analysis has been made properly, the amount of change for any *total* should equal the sum of the increases minus all decreases in the category. Also, the total liabilities and owner's equity amount of change should equal the total assets amount of change. The percent of change for the total is *not* the sum of the percents of increases and the difference of percents of decreases. This is because the base is different for each entry.

| | | Sander's Woodworks<br>Comparative Balance Sheet<br>December 31, 2007, and 2008 | | | |
|---|---|---|---|---|---|
| | | | | Increase<br>(Decrease)* | |
| | | **2008** | **2007** | **Amount** | **Percent** |
| **Assets** | | | | | |
| Cash | | $2,184 | $1,973 | **$ 211** | 10.7 |
| Accounts receivable | | 4,308 | 2,118 | **2,190** | 103.4 |
| Inventory | | 17,317 | 18,476 | **(1,159)** | (6.3) |
| Equipment | | 14,203 | 18,591 | **(4,388)** | (23.6) |
| Total assets | | $38,012 | $41,158 | **($3,146)** | (7.6) |
| **Liabilities** | | | | | |
| Accounts payable | | $ 1,647 | $ 2,317 | **$ (670)** | (28.9) |
| Wages payable | | 894 | 684 | **210** | 30.7 |
| Mortgage note payable | | 12,715 | 15,286 | **(2,571)** | (16.8) |
| Total liabilities | | 15,256 | 18,287 | **(3,031)** | (16.6) |
| **Owner's Equity** | | | | | |
| J. Sander's capital | | 22,756 | 22,871 | **(115)** | (0.5) |
| Total liabilities and owner's equity | | $38,012 | $41,158 | **($3,146)** | (7.6) |

*Parentheses indicate decrease.*

---

**FIGURE 20-5**
**Horizontal Analysis of Sander's Woodworks Comparative Balance Sheet**

**TIP**

**Which Year Is the Base in the Percent of Increase?**

In a horizontal analysis, the *earlier* year is always the base year in calculating percent increase or decrease. It is possible to have a 0% change if there is no dollar change in the amounts.

**TIP**

**Working with Decreases and Negative Values**

If the most recent year is *always* entered first, a decrease is indicated in the calculator display with a minus sign.

$$17317 \boxed{-} 18476 \boxed{=} \Rightarrow -1159$$

To find percent decrease, do not clear the calculator. The percent decrease will also be a negative value.

$$\boxed{\div} 18476 \boxed{=} \boxed{\times} 100 \boxed{=} \Rightarrow -6.2730 \text{ or } -6.3\%$$

 **STOP AND CHECK**

1. Use the 2007 and 2008 data on the comparative balance sheet prepared for Rayco, Inc., in Stop and Check Exercise 3 on p. 687 and calculate the amount of increase (or decrease) for each category in the sheet.

2. Use the 2007 and 2008 increases or decreases in Exercise 1 to compute the percent of increase (or decrease) based on total assets.

*(continued)*

# STOP AND CHECK—continued

**3.** Use the information from Exercises 2 and 3 on page 687 to create a horizontal analysis of the balance sheet for 2007 and 2008.

**4.** What was Rayco's percentage growth in total assets from 2007 to 2008?

## 20-1 SECTION EXERCISES

### SKILL BUILDERS

**1.** Prepare a balance sheet for Miss Muffins' Bakery for December 31, 2009. The company assets are: cash, $1,985; accounts receivable, $4,219; merchandise inventory, $2,512. The liabilities are: accounts payable, $3,483; wages payable, $1,696. The owner's capital is $3,537.

**2.** Expand the balance sheet for Exercise 1 to include figures for 2008. The company assets are: cash, $1,762; accounts receivable, $3,785; merchandise inventory, $2,036. The liabilities are: accounts payable, $3,631; wages payable, $1,421. The owner's capital is $2,531.

**3.** Prepare the balance sheet for O'Dell's Nursery for December 31, 2009. The company assets are: cash, $8,917; accounts receivable, $7,521; merchandise inventory, $17,826. The liabilities are: accounts payable, $10,215; wages payable, $3,716. The owner's capital is $20,333.

**4.** Expand the balance sheet for Exercise 3 for 2008. The company assets are: cash, $12,842; accounts receivable, $5,836; merchandise inventory, $18,917. The liabilities are: accounts payable, $8,968; wages payable, $2,582. The owner's capital is $26,045.

**5.** Complete the vertical analyses on the comparative balance sheet for Miss Muffins' Bakery for 2009. (Use parentheses to indicate decreases.)

**6.** Complete the vertical analyses on the comparative balance sheet for Miss Muffins' Bakery for 2008.

7. Complete the vertical analyses on the comparative balance sheet for O'Dell's Nursery for 2009.

8. Complete the vertical analyses on the comparative balance sheet for O'Dell's Nursery for 2008.

9. Complete the horizontal analyses showing differences in dollar amounts and percents on the comparative balance sheet for Miss Muffins' Bakery.

**10.** Complete the horizontal analyses showing differences in dollar amounts and percent increases (decreases) on the comparative balance sheet for O'Dell's Nursery.

**11.** To find the percent of total debt compared to total assets, divide the total liabilities by the total assets and write in percent form. Find the total debt to total assets for Miss Muffins' Bakery for 2009.

**12.** Use the formula in Exercise 11 to find the percent of total debt compared to total assets for Miss Muffins' Bakery for 2008.

## 20-2 INCOME STATEMENTS

### LEARNING OUTCOMES

1 Prepare an income statement.
2 Prepare a vertical analysis of an income statement.
3 Prepare a horizontal analysis of an income statement.

**Income statement:** a financial statement of the net income of a business over a period of time.

Another important financial statement, the **income statement,** shows the net income of a business *over a period of time.* (Remember, the balance sheet shows the financial condition of a business at a specific time.)

Among the many terms on an income statement are the following:

**Total sales:** earnings from the sale of goods or the performance of services.

**Sales returns or allowances:** refunds or adjustments for unsatisfactory merchandise or services.

**Net sales:** total sales minus sales returns or allowances.

**Cost of goods sold:** cost to the business for merchandise or goods sold.

**Gross profit or gross margin:** net sales minus the cost of goods sold.

**Operating expenses:** overhead or cost incurred in operating a business.

**Net income or net profit:** gross profit or gross margin minus the operating expenses.

| | |
|---|---|
| **Total sales** | Earnings from the sale of goods or the performance of services |
| **Sales returns or allowances** | Refunds or adjustments for unsatisfactory merchandise or services |
| **Net sales** | The difference between the total sales and the sales returns or allowances |
| **Cost of goods sold** | Cost to the business for merchandise or goods sold |
| **Gross profit or gross margin** | The difference between the net sales and the cost of goods sold |
| **Operating expenses** | The overhead or cost incurred in operating the business; examples of operating expenses are utilities, rent, insurance, permits, taxes, and employees' salaries |
| **Net income or net profit** | The difference between the gross profit (gross margin) and the operating expenses |

### 1 Prepare an income statement.

Calculating the cost of goods sold is an important part of preparing an income statement. Reviewing some of the concepts in Chapter 17, the cost of goods sold is the difference between the cost of goods available for sale and the cost of ending inventory. The cost of goods available for sale is the cost of the beginning inventory plus the cost of purchases. There are various ways to find the cost of ending inventory.

> **HOW TO** Prepare an income statement
>
> 1. Find and record *net sales.*
>    (a) Record *gross sales.*
>    (b) Record *sales returns and allowances.*
>    (c) Subtract sales returns and allowances from gross sales.
>
> $$\text{Net sales} = \text{gross sales} - \text{sales returns and allowances}$$
>
> 2. Find and record *cost of goods sold.*
>    (a) Record cost of beginning inventory.
>    (b) Record cost of purchases.
>    (c) Record cost of ending inventory.
>    (d) Add cost of beginning inventory and cost of purchases and subtract cost of ending inventory.
>
> $$\text{Cost of goods sold} = \text{cost of beginning inventory} + \text{cost of purchases} - \text{cost of ending inventory}$$
>
> 3. Find and record *gross profit from sales.*
>
> $$\text{Gross profit from sales} = \text{net sales} - \text{cost of goods sold}$$

4. Find and record *total operating expenses*. List the operating expenses and add the entries.
5. Find and record *net income*.

$$\text{Net income} = \text{gross profit from sales} - \text{operating expenses}$$

**EXAMPLE 1** Complete the portion of the income statement shown for the Corner Grocery using the information given.

Gross sales: $25,283; returns and allowances: $492; cost of beginning inventory: $5,384; cost of purchases: $18,923; cost of ending inventory: $5,557; total operating expenses: $3,750

Net sales = gross sales − returns and allowances
= $25,283 − $492
= $24,791

Cost of goods sold = cost of beginning inventory + cost of purchases − cost of ending inventory
= $5,384 + $18,923 − $5,557
= $18,750

Gross profit = net sales − cost of goods sold
= $24,791 − $18,750
= $6,041

Net income = gross profit − operating expenses
= $6,041 − $3,750
= $2,291

The completed income statement is shown in Figure 20-6.

---

**Corner Grocery**
**Income Statement**
**for the Month Ending**
**June 30, 2008**

| | | |
|---|---|---|
| Net sales | | $24,791 |
| Cost of goods sold | Subtract → | 18,750 |
| Gross profit | | 6,041 |
| Operating expenses | Subtract → | 3,750 |
| Net income | | $ 2,291 |

**FIGURE 20-6**
**Income Statement for Corner Grocery**

---

 **STOP AND CHECK**

1. Find the gross profit and net income for Cedar Rapids Auto for the year ending December 31, 2008, if the company had net sales of $5,385,920; cost of goods sold of $2,073,587; and operating expenses of $498,507.

2. Prepare an income statement for Cedar Rapids Auto for 2008.

3. For 2008 Cassandra's DVD Shop had gross sales of $597,341; sales returns and allowances of $10,514; beginning inventory cost of $38,917; cost of purchases, $261,053; and year-end inventory of $42,013. Find the net sales, cost of goods sold, and gross profit from sales.

4. Cassandra's DVD Shop had the following 2008 expenses: salary, $90,500; insurance, $12,200; utilities, $7,582; maintenance, $1,077; rent, $18,400; and depreciation, $2,700. Find the total operating expenses and net income using the data from Exercise 3. Prepare an income statement to show financial information for 2008.

## 2 Prepare a vertical analysis of an income statement.

**Vertical analysis of an income statement:** comparison of each entry in an income statement to net sales.

Just as you do with a vertical analysis of a balance sheet, to make a **vertical analysis of an income statement** you use the percentage formula $R = \frac{P}{B}$, in which each entry on the income statement is a portion or percentage $P$, net sales is the base $B$, and their ratio $R$ is expressed as a percent.

### HOW TO  Prepare a vertical analysis of an income statement

1. Prepare an income statement.
2. Create an additional column labeled *percent of net sales*: For each item, divide the amount of the item by the net sales and record the result as a percent.

$$\text{Percent of net sales} = \frac{\text{amount of item}}{\text{net sales}} \times 100\%$$

### EXAMPLE 1
Figure 20-7 is an income statement for The 7th Inning. Complete a vertical analysis of the statement.

The 7<sup>th</sup> Inning
Income Statement
For the Year Ending December 31, 2008

| | |
|---|---|
| Gross sales | $846,891 |
| Sales returns and allowances | 7,835 |
| **Net sales** | 839,056 |
| | |
| Cost of beginning inventory, January 1, 2008 | 28,527 |
| Cost of purchases | 521,054 |
| Less: cost of ending inventory, December 31, 2008 | 33,562 |
| **Cost of goods sold** | 516,019 |
| | |
| **Gross profit from sales** | 323,037 |
| | |
| Salary | 64,607 |
| Insurance | 10,137 |
| Utilities | 11,712 |
| Maintenance | 3,839 |
| Rent | 30,976 |
| Depreciation | 5,034 |
| **Total operating expenses** | 126,305 |
| | |
| **Net income** | $196,732 |

**FIGURE 20-7**
**7th Inning Income Statement**

For each item, divide the amount by the net sales and record the result as a percent. For instance,

$$\text{Gross sales: } \frac{\text{gross sales}}{\text{net sales}} \times 100\% = \frac{\$846,891}{\$839,056}(100\%) = 1.009337875(100\%) = 100.9\%$$

The completed vertical analysis is shown in Figure 20-8.

### TIP

**Use the Memory Function and the Percent Key.**

Enter the net sales into memory.

$$\boxed{\text{AC}}\ 839056\ \boxed{\text{M}^+}$$

Divide each entry by net sales and use the percent key.

$$\boxed{\text{CE/C}}\ 846891\ \boxed{\div}\ \boxed{\text{MRC}}\ \boxed{\%} \Rightarrow 100.9337875$$

$$\boxed{\text{CE/C}}\ 7835\ \boxed{\div}\ \boxed{\text{MRC}}\ \boxed{\%} \Rightarrow 0.93378749$$

Continue by dividing each item by the net sales, which is stored in memory.

**What Is the Base on a Vertical Analysis of an Income Statement?**

As with balance sheets, each item on the income statement is expressed as a percent of a base figure. For income statements, *net sales is the base.*

| The 7th Inning Income Statement For the Year Ending December 31, 2008 | Amount | Percent of Net Sales |
|---|---|---|
| **Revenue** | | |
| Gross sales | $846,891 | 100.9 |
| Sales returns and allowances | 7,835 | 0.9 |
| Net sales | 839,056 | 100.0 |
| **Cost of goods sold** | | |
| Beginning inventory, January 1, 2008 | 28,527 | 3.4 |
| Purchases | 521,054 | 62.1 |
| Less: ending inventory, December 31, 2008 | 33,562 | 4.0 |
| Cost of goods sold | 516,019 | 61.5 |
| **Gross profit from sales** | 323,037 | 38.5 |
| **Operating expenses** | | |
| Salary | 64,607 | 7.7 |
| Insurance | 10,137 | 1.2 |
| Utilities | 11,712 | 1.4 |
| Maintenance | 3,839 | 0.5 |
| Rent | 30,976 | 3.7 |
| Depreciation | 5,034 | 0.6 |
| **Total operating expenses** | 126,305 | 15.1 |
| **Net income** | $196,732 | 23.4 |

**FIGURE 20-8**
Vertical Analysis of The 7th Inning's Income Statement

An income statement can also contain information for more than one year. Figure 20-9 shows a vertical analysis of a comparative income statement.

| Davis Company Comparative Income Statement for the Years Ending June 30, 2008 and 2009 | 2009 | | 2008 | |
|---|---|---|---|---|
| | Amount | Percent of Net Sales | Amount | Percent of Net Sales |
| Net sales | $242,897 | 100.0 | $239,528 | 100.0 |
| Cost of goods sold | 116,582 | 48.0 | 115,351 | 48.2 |
| Gross profit | 126,315 | 52.0 | 124,177 | 51.8 |
| Operating expenses | 38,725 | 15.9 | 37,982 | 15.9 |
| Net income | $87,590 | 36.1 | $86,195 | 36.0 |

**FIGURE 20-9**
Vertical Analysis of the Davis Company's Comparative Income Statement

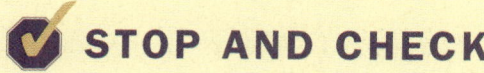

## STOP AND CHECK

1. Complete a vertical analysis of the income statement for Cedar Rapids Auto found in Exercise 1 on page 694.

2. In 2007, Cedar Rapids Auto had net sales of $4,103,370; cost of goods sold totaled $1,992,500; and total operating expenses were $503,719. Prepare a comparative income statement with a vertical analysis of 2007 and 2008.

3. Complete a vertical analysis of the income statement for Cassandra's DVD Shop found in Exercises 3 and 4 on page 694.

4. In 2007, Cassandra's DVD Shop had gross sales of $435,913; sales returns and allowances of $8,019; beginning inventory cost of $36,992; cost of purchases of $248,504; and ending inventory of $41,007. Expenses were salaries, $82,450; insurance, $12,200; utilities, $6,097; maintenance, $817; rent, $17,800; and depreciation, $2,300. Prepare a comparative income statement with a vertical analysis of 2007 and 2008.

## 3  Prepare a horizontal analysis of an income statement.

**Comparative income statement:** an income statement that includes data from two or more years.

**Horizontal analysis of an income statement:** comparison of like entries for two years. The amount of increase or decrease and the percent of increase or decrease are determined.

The horizontal analysis of an income statement is similar to the horizontal analysis of a balance sheet. Items on the statement are compared for more than one period. A **comparative income statement** is used for displaying more than one income period. The **horizontal analysis of an income statement** examines the increase or decrease of an item from one period to another.

| **HOW TO** | **Prepare a horizontal analysis of a comparative income statement** |

1. Prepare an income statement for two or more years: Record each year's amounts in separate columns.
2. Create an additional column labeled *amount of increase (decrease)*.
   For each yearly item,
   (a) Subtract the smaller amount from the larger amount and record the difference.
   (b) If the earlier year's amount is larger than the later year's amount, record the difference from step 2a as a decrease by using parentheses.
3. Create an additional column labeled *percent increase (decrease)*. For each yearly item:

$$\text{Percent increase (decrease)} = \frac{\text{amount of increase (decrease)}}{\text{earlier year's amount}} \times 100\%$$

**EXAMPLE 1**  Prepare a horizontal analysis for the Davis Company using the yearly amounts in Figure 20-9.

For each item, find the amount of increase or decrease by subtracting the smaller amount from the larger amount. For the Davis Company, the later year's amounts are all larger than the earlier year's amounts, so the difference of each amount is recorded as an increase in every case.

Next, find the percent increase by dividing the amount of increase by the earlier year's amount. For instance,

$$\text{Percent increase in net sales} = \frac{\text{amount of increase}}{2008 \text{ amount}} \times 100\%$$
$$= \frac{\$242,897 - \$239,528}{\$239,528} (100\%)$$
$$= \frac{\$3,369}{\$239,528} (100\%)$$
$$= 1.4\%$$

The completed analysis is shown in Figure 20-10.

| Davis Company Comparative Income Statement for the Years Ending June 30, 2008 and 2009 | | | Increase (Decrease) | |
|---|---|---|---|---|
| | 2009 | 2008 | Amount | Percent of net sales |
| Net sales | $242,897 | $239,528 | $3,369 | 1.4 |
| Cost of goods sold | 116,582 | 115,351 | 1,231 | 1.1 |
| Gross profit | 126,315 | 124,177 | 2,138 | 1.7 |
| Operating expenses | 38,725 | 37,982 | 743 | 2.0 |
| Net income | $87,590 | $86,195 | $1,395 | 1.6 |

**FIGURE 20-10**

**Horizontal Analysis of the Davis Company's Comparative Income Statement**

 STOP AND CHECK

1. Prepare a horizontal analysis of Cedar Rapids Auto's comparative income statement for 2007 and 2008. See pages 694 and 697.

2. Prepare a horizontal analysis of Cassandra's DVD Shop's comparative income statement for 2007 and 2008. See pages 694 and 697.

3. What number is used as the base when calculating percentages on a vertical analysis of an income statement?

4. What number is used as the base when calculating percentages on a horizontal analysis of an income statement?

## 20-2 SECTION EXERCISES

### SKILL BUILDERS

1. Complete the income statement for Sitha Ros's Oriental Groceries for the years 2008 and 2009.

| Sitha Ros's Oriental Groceries Income Statement for the Years Ending June 30, 2008 and 2009 | | |
|---|---|---|
| | 2009 | 2008 |
| Net sales | $97,384 | $92,196 |
| Cost of goods sold | 82,157 | 72,894 |
| Gross profit | | |
| Operating expenses | 4,783 | 3,951 |
| Net income | | |

2. Complete the portion for July 31, 2007, of the income statement shown for Miss Muffins' Bakery using the given information: gross sales, $32,596; returns and allowances, $296; cost of beginning inventory, $16,872; cost of purchases, $33,596; cost of ending inventory, $21,843; total operating expenses, $1,894. Compute net sales, cost of goods sold, gross profit, and net income.

3. Use the information recorded for Miss Muffins' Bakery for the month ending July 31, 2008, to extend the income statement for Exercise 2: gross sales, $35,403; returns and allowances, $342; cost of beginning inventory, $17,403; cost of purchases, $27,983; cost of ending inventory, $22,583; total operating expenses, $3,053. Compute net sales, cost of goods sold, gross profit, and net income.

### Miss Muffins' Bakery
Comparative Income Statement for the Months Ending
July 31, 2007 and July 31, 2008

|  | 2008 | 2007 |
|---|---|---|
| Gross sales |  |  |
| Returns and allowances | _____ | _____ |
| Net sales | _____ | _____ |
| Cost of beginning inventory |  |  |
| Cost of purchases |  |  |
| Cost of ending inventory | _____ | _____ |
| Cost of goods sold | _____ | _____ |
| Gross profit | _____ | _____ |
| Total operating expenses | _____ | _____ |
| Net income | _____ | _____ |

## APPLICATIONS

**4.** Extend the income statement for Sitha Ros's Oriental Groceries to include a vertical analysis for 2008 and for 2009.

### Sitha Ros' Oriental Groceries
Income Statement for Years Ending
June 30, 2008 and 2009

|  | 2009 | Percent of Net Sales | 2008 | Percent of Net Sales |
|---|---|---|---|---|
| Net sales |  |  |  |  |
| Cost of goods sold | _____ |  | _____ |  |
| Gross profit | _____ |  | _____ |  |
| Operating expenses | _____ |  | _____ |  |
| Net income | _____ |  | _____ |  |

**5.** Extend the income statement for Miss Muffins' Bakery to include a vertical analysis for 2007 and 2008.

### Miss Muffins' Bakery
Vertical Analysis of Income Statement for the Months Ending
July 31, 2007 and July 31, 2008

|  | 2008 | Percent of Net Sales | 2007 | Percent of Net Sales |
|---|---|---|---|---|
| Gross sales |  |  |  |  |
| Returns and allowances | _____ |  | _____ |  |
| Net sales | _____ |  | _____ |  |
| Cost of beginning inventory |  |  |  |  |
| Cost of purchases |  |  |  |  |
| Cost of ending inventory | _____ |  | _____ |  |
| Cost of goods sold | _____ |  | _____ |  |
| Gross profit | _____ |  | _____ |  |
| Total operating expenses | _____ |  | _____ |  |
| Net income | _____ |  | _____ |  |

**6.** Extend the income statements for Sitha Ros's Oriental Groceries to include the amounts of increase or decrease and the percents of increase or decrease for a horizontal analysis.

**7.** Extend the income statement for Miss Muffins' Bakery to include the amounts of increase or decrease and the percents of increase or decrease for a horizontal analysis.

| Miss Muffins' Bakery Horizontal Analysis of Income Statement for the Months Ending July 31, 2007 and July 31, 2008 | | | | |
|---|---|---|---|---|
| | **2008** | **2007** | **Increase (Decrease) Amount** | **Percent** |
| Gross sales | | | | |
| Returns and allowances | _____ | _____ | | |
| Net sales | _____ | _____ | | |
| Cost of beginning inventory | | | | |
| Cost of purchases | | | | |
| Cost of ending inventory | _____ | _____ | | |
| Cost of goods sold | _____ | _____ | | |
| Gross profit | _____ | _____ | | |
| Total operating expenses | _____ | _____ | | |
| Net income | ══════ | ══════ | | |

## 20-3 FINANCIAL STATEMENT RATIOS

### LEARNING OUTCOME

1 Find and use financial ratios.

**Financial ratio:** an analysis of financial data to compare a business's performance with past performance or with other similar businesses.

Financial statements organize and summarize information about the financial condition of a business. Using data from financial statements, **financial ratios** give businesses a way to evaluate their business compared to its past performance and compared to other similar businesses. Financial ratios are used by lending institutions and stockholders to determine the financial well-being of a business.

# 1  Find and use financial ratios.

Cash flow is an aspect of a business's operation. A business must know if it has enough cash on hand or cash coming in to pay its bills as they come due. Financial ratios that show a comparison between a business's cash on hand to its financial obligations that are due within the next few months are called **liquidity ratios**. These ratios are of interest to short-term creditors.

**Current Ratio**

It is important to know whether a business has enough assets to cover its liabilities. The **working capital** of a business is the current assets minus current liabilities. But that amount alone does not tell much about the relative financial condition of the business. Look at the following information about Aaron's Air Conditioning and Zelda's Zeppelins:

|  | Aaron's Air Conditioning | Zelda's Zeppelins |
|---|---|---|
| Current assets | $11,000 | $615,000 |
| Current liabilities | − 5,000 | − 609,000 |
| Working capital | $6,000 | $6,000 |

$$\text{Working capital} = \text{current assets} - \text{current liabilities}$$

Both companies have the same working capital, but Zelda's *owes* almost as much as it *owns*. To compare these companies, we need to use ratios. A commonly used ratio in business is the **current ratio** (also called the **working capital ratio**), which is the ratio of current assets to current liabilities.

$$\text{Current ratio} = \frac{\text{current assets}}{\text{current liabilities}}$$

The current ratio for Aaron's Air Conditioning, for example, is the ratio of $11,000 to $5,000.

$$\text{Aaron's current ratio} = \frac{\text{Aaron's current assets}}{\text{Aaron's current liabilities}} = \frac{\$11,000}{\$5,000}$$

This ratio expresses the fact that Aaron's has $11,000 in current assets for $5,000 of current liabilities. If we write this ratio in decimal form, we have an equivalent ratio whose denominator is 1:

$$\frac{\$11,000}{\$5,000} = 2.2 = \frac{2.2}{1}$$

Thus, Aaron's current ratio is 2.2 to 1, telling us that Aaron's has $2.20 in current assets for every $1 in current liabilities.

The current ratio for Zelda's Zeppelins is the ratio of $615,000 to $609,000. Writing Zelda's current ratio in decimal form, we are able to see the usefulness of current ratio as a way of comparing businesses.

$$\text{Zelda's current ratio} = \frac{\text{Zelda's current assets}}{\text{Zelda's current liabilities}} = \frac{\$615,000}{\$609,000} = 1.01 = \frac{1.01}{1}$$

This ratio tells us that Zelda's has $1.01 in current assets for every $1 in current liabilities. Since Aaron's ratio is 2.2 to 1, we see that for every $1 of current liability, Aaron's has more than twice as much in current assets as does Zelda's. There are many financial ratios we might calculate, but the basic process is the same for all.

## HOW TO  Find a financial ratio

1. Write one amount as the numerator of a fraction and a second amount as the denominator.
2. Write the fraction in decimal form (or, for some ratios, in percent form).

## EXAMPLE 1
Find the current ratio of a business whose current assets are $18,000 and whose current liabilities are $12,000.

Write the ratio of current assets to current liabilities in decimal form.

$$\text{Current ratio} = \frac{\text{current assets}}{\text{current liabilities}} = \frac{\$18,000}{\$12,000} = 1.5$$

**The current ratio is 1.5, or 1.5 to 1.**

---

**Liquidity ratio:** a financial ratio that shows how well a business can be expected to meet its short-term financial obligations.

**Working capital:** current assets minus current liabilities.

**Current ratio or working capital ratio:** the ratio of current assets to the current liabilities. It indicates a company's ability to meet its obligations when they are due.

Many lending companies consider a current ratio of 2 to 1 ($\frac{2}{1}$) to be the minimum acceptable current ratio for approving a loan to a business. The business in the preceding example, for instance, may find it difficult to get a loan because its current ratio is 1.5 to 1.

### Acid-Test Ratio

**Acid-test ratio or quick ratio:** the ratio of quick current assets to current liabilities.

Another ratio used to evaluate the financial condition of a business is the **acid-test ratio,** sometimes called the **quick ratio**. Instead of using all of the current assets of a business, the acid-test ratio uses only the **quick current assets**, those assets that can be readily exchanged for cash: marketable securities, accounts receivable, and notes receivable. Merchandise inventory is a current asset, but it is not included because a loss would probably occur if a business were to make a quick sale of all merchandise.

**Quick current assets:** assets that can be readily exchanged for cash, such as marketable securities, accounts receivable, or notes receivable.

$$\text{Acid-test ratio (quick ratio)} = \frac{\text{quick current assets}}{\text{current liabilities}}$$

**EXAMPLE 2** Find the acid-test ratio if the balance sheet shows the following amounts:

Cash = $17,342

Marketable securities = $0

Receivables = $10,345

Current liabilities = $26,345

$$\text{Acid-test ratio} = \frac{\$17,342 + \$10,345}{\$26,345} = \frac{\$27,687}{\$26,345} = 1.05 \text{ (nearest hundredth)}$$

**The acid-test ratio is 1.05 to 1.**

---

### TIP

**What's a Good Acid-Test Ratio?**

If the acid-test ratio is 1:1, the business is in a satisfactory financial condition and has the ability to meet its obligations. If the ratio is significantly *less* than 1:1 (such as 0.85:1), the business is in poor financial condition; and if the ratio is significantly *more* than 1:1 (such as 1.15:1), the business is in good financial condition.

---

### Ratios to Net Sales

**Ratios to net sales:** ratios that make comparisons to net sales.

Other useful ratios can be determined from an income statement. Two of the most important are the *operating ratio* and the *gross profit margin ratio*. These two are also called **ratios to net sales.** These ratios make comparisons possible between the major elements of the statement and net sales. These ratios are usually expressed in percent form, rather than decimal form, and they usually (but do not necessarily) cover one year.

Remember, the first amount in a ratio appears in the numerator and the second amount appears in the denominator. In both of the ratios to net sales, the denominator is the net sales.

**Operating ratio:** the cost of goods sold plus the operating expenses divided by net sales.

The **operating ratio** indicates the amount of sales dollars that are used to pay for the cost of goods and administrative expenses. A ratio of *less* than 1:1 is desirable. The lower the operating ratio, the more income there is to meet financial obligations.

$$\text{Operating ratio} = \frac{\text{cost of goods sold} + \text{operating expenses}}{\text{net sales}}$$

**Profitability ratio:** a ratio comparing profits and sales.

Another important category of financial ratios is **profitability ratios**. A profitability ratio shows the relationship between the sales and the gross and net profit. Stockholders and investors have a keen interest in these ratios.

**Gross profit margin ratio:** the ratio of the gross profit from sales to the net sales.

The **gross profit margin ratio** shows the average spread between cost of goods sold and the selling price. The desirable gross profit margin ratio varies with the type of business. For example, a jewelry store might expect to have a ratio of 0.6 to 1 because there is a high rate of markup in jewelry. An auto parts store may, however, have a ratio of 0.25 to 1.

$$\text{Gross profit margin ratio} = \frac{\text{gross profit from sales}}{\text{net sales}} = \frac{\text{net sales} - \text{cost of goods sold}}{\text{net sales}}$$

**EXAMPLE 3** Based on the income statement in Figure 20-11, find the operating ratio and the gross profit margin ratio for Vincent's Gift Shop. Express results in percent form, rounded to the nearest tenth of a percent.

| Vincent's Gift Shop<br>Income Statement<br>for the Year Ending December 31, 2007 | |
| --- | ---: |
| Net sales | $173,157 |
| Cost of beginning inventory | 37,376 |
| Cost of purchases | 123,574 |
| Cost of goods available for sale | 160,950 |
| Cost of ending inventory | 34,579 |
| Cost of goods sold | 126,371 |
| Gross profit | 46,786 |
| Operating expenses | 17,643 |
| Net income | $29,143 |

**FIGURE 20-11**
Income Statement for Vincent's Gift Shop

$$\text{Operating ratio} = \frac{\text{cost of goods sold} + \text{operating expenses}}{\text{net sales}}$$

$$= \frac{\$126,371 + \$17,643}{\$173,157}$$

$$= 0.831696 \text{ or } 83.2\%$$

**The operating ratio is 0.832 to 1 or 83.2%.**

$$\text{Gross profit margin ratio} = \frac{\text{net sales} - \text{cost of goods sold}}{\text{net sales}}$$

$$= \frac{\$173,157 - \$126,371}{\$173,157}$$

$$= 0.270194 \text{ or } 27.0\%.$$

**The gross profit margin ratio is 0.270 to 1 or 27.0%.**

### Other Financial Ratios

**Asset turnover ratio:** the ratio of the net sales to the average total assets.

**Efficiency ratio:** a financial ratio that measures a business's ability to effectively use its assets to generate sales.

**Total debt to total assets ratio:** the ratio of the total liabilities to the total assets.

**Leverage ratio:** a financial ratio that examines a business's indebtedness.

Many other comparisons of data are found on the balance sheet, income statement, and other financial documents that are useful in analyzing various aspects of the business. For instance, the **asset turnover ratio** compares the net sales to the average total assets. This comparison shows the average return in sales for each $1 invested in assets. The asset turnover ratio and the inventory turnover ratios that were introduced in Chapter 17 are examples of **efficiency ratios**. An efficiency ratio is a measure of how effectively a business uses its assets to generate sales. The **total debt to total assets ratio** compares the total liabilities to the total assets. This comparison shows total indebtedness of the company for each $1 in assets and is an example of a **leverage ratio**. A leverage ratio examines the debts of a business.

The calculations for determining these ratios are the same as for determining any ratio. The amount in the numerator is divided by the amount in the denominator to give a decimal equivalent. This decimal equivalent can be interpreted as a comparison of the decimal equivalent to 1, or it can be interpreted as a percent by multiplying the decimal equivalent by 100%.

$$\text{Asset turnover ratio} = \frac{\text{net sales}}{\text{average total assets}}$$

$$\text{Total debt to total assets ratio} = \frac{\text{total liabilities}}{\text{total assets}}$$

### Interpreting Financial Ratios

A business needs to track its own progress over several periods of time to compare its results to industry standards. A business uses financial ratios to make internal decisions or to distribute to stockholders, banks, and prospective investors or buyers to show the financial status of the business. In Table 20-1 you will see some possible interpretations of financial ratios. Keep in mind, just as one statistic does not give a total picture, one ratio does not give a complete profile of a business's financial status.

**TABLE 20-1**
Financial Ratio Analysis

| Ratio | Value less than 1 | Value = 1 | Value more than 1 |
|---|---|---|---|
| Current ratio $= \dfrac{\text{current assets}}{\text{current liabilities}}$ | Debts greater than assets; potentially major problems | Debts and assets are equal | Assets greater than debts; current ratio of 2 is desirable |
| Acid-test ratio $= \dfrac{\text{quick current assets}}{\text{current liabilities}}$ | Cash flow could be a problem | Business is in satisfactory condition | Business is in good financial condition |
| Operating ratio $= \dfrac{\text{COGS} + \text{operating expenses}}{\text{net sales}}$ | Desirable | Marginal | Undesirable |
| Gross profit margin ratio $= \dfrac{\text{gross profit from sales}}{\text{net sales}}$ | 0.25 to 0.40 is industry average | Uncommon except for businesses with low turnover and high investment | Undesirable |
| Asset turnover ratio $= \dfrac{\text{net sales}}{\text{average total assets}}$ | 0.40 to 1.0 is industry average | Uncommon | Uncommon |
| Total debt to total assets ratio $= \dfrac{\text{total liabilities}}{\text{total assets}}$ | 0.05 to 0.75 is industry average | Debt ratio is too high | Debt ratio is dangerously high |

**EXAMPLE 4**  Arsella would like to apply for a loan to expand Vincent's Gift Shop. The business's current assets are $58,482, its total assets are $210,580, and total (current) liabilities are $32,289. Other information about the business can be found in the preceding example. Analyze the financial condition of the business using information given in Table 20-1. Should Arsella plan to expand the business at this time?

| What You Know | What You Are Looking For | Solution Plan |
|---|---|---|
| Current assets: $58,482<br>Total assets: $210,580<br>Current liabilities: $32,289<br>Ending inventory: $34,579<br>Net sales: $173,157<br>Operating expenses: $17,643<br>Cost of goods sold: $126,371 | Current ratio<br>Acid-test ratio<br>Operating ratio<br>Gross profit margin ratio<br>Asset turnover ratio<br>Total debt to total assets ratio<br>Should Arsella expand the business at this time? | Find the financial ratios and use Table 20-1 to analyze the results. |

**Solution**

$$\text{Current ratio} = \frac{\text{current assets}}{\text{current liabilities}} = \frac{\$58,482}{\$32,289} = 1.81$$

$$\text{Acid-test ratio} = \frac{\text{quick current assets}}{\text{current liabilities}} = \frac{\$58,482 - \$34,579}{\$32,289} = 0.74$$

$$\text{Operating ratio} = \frac{\text{COGS} + \text{operating expenses}}{\text{net sales}} = \frac{\$126,371 + \$17,643}{\$173,157} = 0.83$$

$$\text{Gross profit margin ratio} = \frac{\text{gross profit from sales}}{\text{net sales}} = \frac{\text{net sales} - \text{COGS}}{\text{net sales}}$$
$$= \frac{\$173,157 - \$126,371}{\$173,157} = 0.27$$

$$\text{Asset turnover ratio} = \frac{\text{net sales}}{\text{average total assets}} = \frac{\$173,157}{\$210,580} = 0.82$$

$$\text{Total debt to total assets ratio} = \frac{\text{total liabilities}}{\text{total assets}} = \frac{\$32,289}{\$210,580} = 0.15$$

**TIP**

**Total Assets and Average Total Assets**

In the asset turnover ratio, the divisor is average total assets. This is not necessarily the same as the total assets.

**Conclusion**

The current ratio, operating ratio, gross profit margin ratio, and total debt to total assets ratio demonstrate a business with a healthy financial status. The acid-test ratio may indicate a potential cash flow problem, but the extremely high asset turnover ratio shows that inventory can be quickly turned into cash.

**This is an acceptable time to expand the business with the understanding that the amount of cash is marginal and if receivables come in slower than expected.**

**Trend analysis:** an analysis of business trends over an extended period of time.

**Index numbers:** numbers that represent percent of change for several successive operating time periods (usually years) while keeping one selected year (base year) to represent the base or 100%.

It is important to both internal and external decisions for a business to look at business trends over an extended period of time. The most common type of analysis is to examine the percent of change for several successive operating time periods (normally years). This process is often referred to as a **trend analysis**. One way to analyze trends is to select one particular period (year) to be the reference or base in the percentage formula. The selected year (base year) is considered to be 100%. All other years are a percent of the base year. These percents are referred to as **index numbers**.

## HOW TO  Prepare a trend analysis

1. Select a base year to be represented by 100%.
2. Calculate the index number for each successive year using the variation of the percentage formula.

$$\text{Index number (rate)} = \frac{\text{yearly amount (portion)}}{\text{base year amount (base)}}$$

3. Express the index number to the nearest tenth of a percent.
4. Prepare a table of the base and index numbers.
5. Prepare a graph of the base and index numbers.

## EXAMPLE 1

The following data were collected by Stein Enterprises, Inc. Prepare a trend analysis of the net sales, the net income, and the total assets.

Stein Enterprises, Inc.
Financial Data for 2004 – 2008

|  | 2008 | 2007 | 2006 | 2005 | 2004 |
|---|---|---|---|---|---|
| Net Sales | 594,398 | 507,287 | 572,103 | 550,524 | 512,854 |
| Net Income | 84,312 | 65,214 | 78,513 | 72,998 | 68,415 |
| Total Assets | 218,345 | 215,997 | 205,143 | 201,445 | 195,295 |

|  | 2008 | 2007 | 2006 | 2005 | 2004 |
|---|---|---|---|---|---|
| Net Sales | 115.9 | 98.9 | 111.6 | 107.3 | 100.0 |
| Net Income | 123.2 | 95.3 | 114.8 | 106.7 | 100.0 |
| Total Assets | 111.8 | 110.6 | 105.0 | 103.1 | 100.0 |

Figure 20-12 plots the trend analysis of net sales, net income, and total assets.

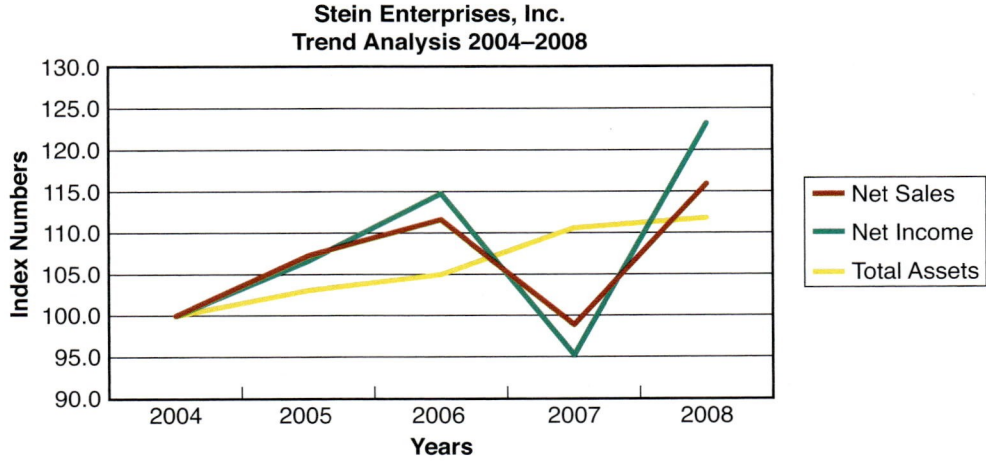

**FIGURE 20-12**
Trend Analysis of Net Sales, Net Income, and Total Assets.

 **STOP AND CHECK**

1. Find the operating ratio for Cedar Rapids Auto, Inc., for 2008. This income statement was prepared as Exercise 2 on page 696.

2. Interpret the ratio found for Cedar Rapids Auto, Inc.

3. Find the debt ratio at the end of 2007 for Rayco, Inc. This balance sheet was prepared as Exercise 3 on page 698.

4. Interpret the ratio found for Rayco, Inc.

## 20-3 SECTION EXERCISES

### SKILL BUILDERS

1. What is the current ratio for Denmark, Inc., which has current assets of $148,947 and current liabilities of $103,537?

2. Find the operating ratio for Chaney's Pharmacy if the annual cost of goods sold is $315,842, the operating expenses are $62,917, and net sales are $597,064.

3. Find the gross profit margin ratio if The Premier Eatery had net sales of $392,054 and its cost of goods sold was $179,515.

4. Proud Larry's Grill reported net sales of $289,512 and had average total assets of $145,753. Find its asset turnover ratio.

### APPLICATIONS

5. Find the current ratio for George's business and the current ratio for José's business, given the following information:

|  | George | José |
|---|---|---|
| Current assets | $28,000 | $840,000 |
| Current liabilities | − 7,000 | −819,000 |
| Working capital | $21,000 | $21,000 |

6. Find the acid-test ratio for Carley's business if the balance sheet shows the following amounts: cash, $32,981; receivables, $12,045; marketable securities, $0; current liabilities, $22,178.

7. Find the operating ratio for Sol's Dry Goods if the income statement for the month shows net sales, $15,500; cost of goods sold, $7,500; gross profit, $8,000; operating expenses, $3,500; net income, $4,500. Express results to the nearest tenth of a percent.

8. Find the gross profit margin ratio for Sol's Dry Goods in Exercise 7 to the nearest tenth of a percent.

## Learning Outcome

**Section 20-1**

## What to Remember with Examples

**1** Prepare a balance sheet. (p. 682)

1. Find and record the *total assets*. Balance sheets may be prepared by asset category.
   **(a)** List the *current assets* and draw a single line underneath the last entry.
   **(b)** Add the entries and record the *total current assets*, drawing a single line underneath the total.
   **(c)** Repeat step 1a for *plant and equipment assets* and step 1b for *total plant and equipment assets*.
   **(d)** Add the category totals and draw a double line underneath the grand total.

   Total assets = total current assets + total plant and equipment

2. Find and record the *total liabilities*. Balance sheets may be prepared by liability category.
   **(a)** Repeat step 1a for *current liabilities* and step 1b for *total current liabilities*.
   **(b)** Repeat step 1a for *long-term liabilities* and step 1b for *total long-term liabilities*.
   **(c)** Add the category totals and draw a single line underneath the total.

   Total liabilities = total current liabilities + total long-term liabilities

3. Find and record the *total owner's equity*.
   **(a)** List the equity entries and draw a single line underneath the last entry.
   **(b)** Add the entries and draw a single line underneath the total.
4. Find and record the *total liabilities and owner's equity*: Add the total liabilities to the total owner's equity and draw a double line underneath the grand total.

   Total liabilities and owner's equity = total liabilities + total owner's equity

5. Confirm that the double line grand total from step 1 and step 4 are the same.

   Total assets = total liabilities + owner's equity

| Roy Russell's Security Service Balance Sheet | |
|---|---|
| | **2008** |
| **Assets** | |
| Cash | $8,000 |
| Accounts receivable | 4,860 |
| Inventory | 19,823 |
| Equipment | 8,925 |
| Total assets | $41,608 |
| **Liabilities** | |
| Accounts payable | $11,281 |
| Wages payable | 11,185 |
| Total liabilities | 22,466 |
| Owner's equity | 19,142 |
| Total liabilities and owner's equity | $41,608 |

**2** Prepare a vertical analysis of a balance sheet. (p. 685)

1. Prepare a balance sheet of assets, liabilities, and owner's equity.
2. Create an additional column labeled *percent*: For each item, divide the amount of the item by the total assets then multiply by 100% to record the result as a percent.

$$\text{Percent of total assets} = \frac{\text{amount of item}}{\text{total assets}} \times 100\%$$

Following is a vertical analysis of the balance sheet above. Each entry in the percent column is a percent of total assets. For example, for the item *cash*, the percent is

$$\frac{\text{Cash}}{\text{Total assets}} = \frac{\$8,000}{\$41,608}(100\%) = 0.192271(100\%) = 19.2\%$$

### Roy Russell's Security Service
### Balance Sheet

| | 2008 | Percent of total assets |
|---|---|---|
| **Assets** | | |
| Cash | $8,000 | 19.2 |
| Accounts receivable | 4,860 | 11.7 |
| Inventory | 19,823 | 47.6 |
| Equipment | 8,925 | 21.5 |
| Total assets | $41,608 | 100.0 |
| **Liabilities** | | |
| Accounts payable | $11,281 | 27.1 |
| Wages payable | 11,185 | 26.9 |
| Total liabilities | 22,466 | 54.0 |
| Owner's equity | 19,142 | 46.0 |
| Total liabilities and owner's equity | $41,608 | 100.0 |

**3** Prepare a horizontal analysis of a balance sheet. (p. 688)

1. Prepare a balance sheet for two or more years: Record each year's amounts in separate columns.
2. Create an additional column labeled *amount of increase (decrease)*: For each yearly item,
   (a) Subtract the smaller amount from the larger amount and record the difference.
   (b) If the earlier year's amount is larger than the later year's amount, record the difference from step 2a as a decrease by using parentheses or a negative (minus) sign.
3. Create an additional column labeled *percent increase (decrease)*: For each yearly item, divide the amount of increase (decrease) by the earlier year's amount and record the difference as a percent.

$$\text{Percent increase (decrease)} = \frac{\text{amount of increase (decrease)}}{\text{earlier year's amount}} \times 100\%$$

Following is a horizontal analysis of the corporation balance sheet that extends the balance sheet for Russell's Security Service. Notice that an additional year's data are given and two *increase (decrease)* columns, one for *amount* and one for *percent*, are given as well. Notice that parentheses indicate that an item decreased from the earlier year to the later year.

### Roy Russell's Security Service
### Balance Sheet

| | 2009 | 2008 | Increase (decrease) | Percent increase (decrease) |
|---|---|---|---|---|
| **Assets** | | | | |
| Cash | $8,983 | $8,000 | $983 | 12.3 |
| Accounts receivable | 3,952 | 4,860 | (908) | (18.7) |
| Inventory | 22,507 | 19,823 | 2,684 | 13.5 |
| Equipment | 12,784 | 8,925 | 3,859 | 43.2 |
| Total assets | $48,226 | $41,608 | 6,618 | 15.9 |
| **Liabilities** | | | | |
| Accounts payable | $12,197 | $11,281 | $916 | 8.1 |
| Wages payable | 5,872 | 11,185 | (5,313) | (47.5) |
| Total liabilities | 18,069 | 22,466 | (4,397) | (19.6) |
| Owner's equity | 30,157 | 19,142 | 11,015 | 57.5 |
| Total liabilities and owner's equity | $48,226 | $41,608 | $6,618 | 15.9 |

## Section 20-2

**1** Prepare an income statement. (p. 693)

1. Find and record *net sales*.
   (a) Record *gross sales*.
   (b) Record *sales returns and allowances*.
   (c) Subtract sales returns and allowances from gross sales.

$$\text{Net sales} = \text{gross sales} - \text{sales returns and allowances}$$

2. Find and record *cost of goods sold*.
   (a) Record cost of beginning inventory.
   (b) Record cost of purchases.
   (c) Record cost of ending inventory.
   (d) Add cost of beginning inventory and cost of purchases and subtract cost of ending inventory.

$$\text{Cost of goods sold} = \text{cost of beginning inventory} + \text{cost} \\ \text{of purchases} - \text{cost of ending inventory}$$

3. Find and record *gross profit from sales*.

$$\text{Gross profit from sales} = \text{net sales} - \text{cost of goods sold}$$

4. Find and record *total operating expenses*. List the operating expenses and add the entries.
5. Find and record *net income*.

$$\text{Net income} = \text{gross profit from sales} - \text{operating expenses}$$

The Triple X Corporation records the following data for the year 2008: gross sales, $187,700; sales returns and allowances, $8,200; cost of beginning inventory, $83,540; cost of purchases, $127,386; cost of ending inventory, $64,126; operating expenses, $18,500. Using this data, prepare an income statement.

$$\begin{aligned} \text{Net sales} &= \text{gross sales} - \text{sales returns and allowances} \\ &= \$187,700 - \$8,200 \\ &= \$179,500 \end{aligned}$$

$$\begin{aligned} \text{Cost of goods sold} &= \text{cost of beginning inventory} + \text{cost of purchases} \\ &\quad - \text{cost of ending inventory} \\ &= \$83,540 + \$127,386 - \$64,126 \\ &= \$146,800 \end{aligned}$$

$$\begin{aligned} \text{Gross profit from sales} &= \text{net sales} - \text{cost of goods sold} \\ &= \$179,500 - \$146,800 \\ &= \$32,700 \end{aligned}$$

$$\begin{aligned} \text{Net income} &= \text{gross profit from sales} - \text{operating expenses} \\ &= \$32,700 - \$18,500 \\ &= \$14,200 \end{aligned}$$

**Triple X Corporation**
**Income Statement for 2008**

| | | |
|---|---:|---|
| **Gross sales** | $187,700 | |
| Sales returns and allowances | 8,200 | |
| **Net sales** | $179,500 | |
| **Cost of goods sold** | | |
| Beginning inventory | 83,540 | |
| Purchases | 127,386 | Add. |
| Goods available for sale | 210,926 | |
| Less: ending inventory | 64,126 | Subtract. |
| **Cost of goods sold** | 146,800 | |
| Gross profit from sales | 32,700 | Net sales − COGS |
| **Operating expenses** | 18,500 | Subtract. |
| **Net income** | $14,200 | |

**2** Prepare a vertical analysis of an income statement. (p. 695)

1. Prepare an income statement.
2. Create an additional column labeled *percent of net sales*: For each item, divide the amount of the item by the net sales and record the result as a percent.

$$\text{Percent of net sales} = \frac{\text{amount of item}}{\text{net sales}} \times 100\%$$

Following is a vertical analysis of the income statement for Triple X Corporation. Each entry in the percent column is a percent of net sales. For example, for the item *net income,* the percent is

$$\frac{\text{Net income}}{\text{Net sales}} = \frac{\$14,200}{\$179,500}(100\%) = 0.079109(100\%) = 7.9\%$$

**Triple X Corporation**
**Income Statement**

| | 2008 | Percent of net sales |
|---|---|---|
| **Net sales** | $179,500 | 100.0 |
| **Cost of goods sold** | | |
| Beginning inventory | 83,540 | 46.5 |
| Purchases | 127,386 | 71.0 |
| Goods available for sale | 210,926 | 117.5 |
| Less: ending inventory | 64,126 | 35.7 |
| **Cost of goods sold** | 146,800 | 81.8 |
| Gross profit from sales | 32,700 | 18.2 |
| **Operating expenses** | 18,500 | 10.3 |
| **Net income** | $14,200 | 7.9 |

**3** Prepare a horizontal analysis of an income statement. (p. 697)

1. Prepare an income statement for two or more years: Record each year's amounts in separate columns.
2. Create an additional column labeled *amount of increase (decrease).*
   For each yearly item,
   (a) Subtract the smaller amount from the larger amount and record the difference.
   (b) If the earlier year's amount is larger than the later year's amount, record the difference from step 2a as a decrease by using parentheses.
3. Create an additional column labeled *percent increase (decrease).* For each yearly item,

$$\text{Percent increase (decrease)} = \frac{\text{amount of increase (decrease)}}{\text{earlier year's amount}} \times 100\%$$

Following is a horizontal analysis of the Triple X Corporation income statement that extends the income statement in the previous section. Notice that an additional year's data are given and two *increase (decrease)* columns, one for *amount* and one for *percent,* are given as well. Notice that parentheses indicate that an item decreased from the earlier year to the later year.

**Triple X Corporation**
**Comparative**
**Income Statement**

| | 2009 | 2008 | Increase (decrease) | Percent increase (decrease) |
|---|---|---|---|---|
| **Net sales** | $215,832 | $179,500 | $36,332 | 20.2 |
| **Cost of goods sold** | | | | |
| Beginning inventory | 95,843 | 83,540 | 12,303 | 14.7 |
| Purchases | 107,395 | 127,386 | (19,991) | (15.7) |
| Goods available for sale | 203,238 | 210,926 | (7,688) | (3.6) |
| Less: ending inventory | 79,583 | 64,126 | 15,457 | 24.1 |
| **Cost of goods sold** | 123,655 | 146,800 | (23,145) | (15.8) |
| Gross profit from sales | 92,177 | 32,700 | 59,477 | 181.9 |
| **Operating expenses** | 25,713 | 18,500 | 7,213 | 39.0 |
| **Net income** | $66,464 | $14,200 | $52,264 | 368.1 |

**1** Find and use financial ratios.
(p. 701)

1. Write one amount as the numerator of a fraction and a second amount as the denominator.
2. Write the fraction in decimal form (or, for some ratios, in percent form).

$$\text{Working capital} = \text{current assets} - \text{current liabilities}$$

$$\text{Current ratio} = \frac{\text{current assets}}{\text{current liabilities}}$$

$$\text{Acid-test ratio (quick ratio)} = \frac{\text{quick current assets}}{\text{current liabilities}}$$

$$\text{Operating ratio} = \frac{\text{cost of goods sold} + \text{operating expenses}}{\text{net sales}}$$

$$\text{Gross profit margin ratio} = \frac{\text{gross profit from sales}}{\text{net sales}} = \frac{\text{net sales} - \text{cost of goods sold}}{\text{net sales}}$$

$$\text{Asset turnover ratio} = \frac{\text{net sales}}{\text{average total assets}}$$

$$\text{Total debt to total assets ratio} = \frac{\text{total liabilities}}{\text{total assets}}$$

Use the income statement amounts for 2008 for the Triple X Corporation (p. 709) to find the financial ratios. Additional information needed from the balance sheet is total assets, $108,000; current assets, $40,000; quick current assets: cash, $15,892; marketable securities, $10,000; and receivables, $7,486; total liabilities, $57,000; current liabilities, $28,000.

$$\text{Working capital} = \text{current assets} - \text{current liabilities}$$
$$= \$40,000 - \$28,000 = \$12,000$$

$$\text{Current ratio} = \frac{\text{current assets}}{\text{current liabilities}} = \frac{\$40,000}{\$28,000} = 1.43 \text{ to } 1$$

$$\text{Acid-test ratio} = \frac{\text{quick current assets}}{\text{current liabilities}}$$
$$= \frac{\$15,892 + \$10,000 + \$7,486}{\$28,000} = 1.19 \text{ to } 1$$

$$\text{Operating ratio} = \frac{\text{cost of goods sold} + \text{operating expenses}}{\text{net sales}}$$
$$= \frac{\$146,800 + \$18,500}{\$179,500} = 0.921 \text{ or } 92.1\%$$

$$\text{Gross profit margin ratio} = \frac{\text{gross profit from sales}}{\text{net sales}} = \frac{\text{net sales} - \text{cost of goods sold}}{\text{net sales}}$$
$$= \frac{\$179,500 - \$146,800}{\$179,500}$$
$$= 0.182 \text{ or } 18.2\%$$

$$\text{Asset turnover ratio} = \frac{\text{net sales}}{\text{average total assets}} = \frac{\$179,500}{\$108,000} = 1.66 \text{ to } 1$$

$$\text{Total debt to total ratio} = \frac{\text{total liabilities}}{\text{total assets}} = \frac{\$57,000}{\$108,000} = 0.528 \text{ to } 1$$

# EXERCISES SET A

1. Complete the following balance sheet for Fawcett's Plumbing Supplies.

Fawcett's Plumbing Supplies
Balance Sheet
March 31, 2008

**Assets**
*Current assets*
| | |
|---|---|
| Cash | $1,724.00 |
| Office supplies | 173.00 |
| Accounts receivable | 9,374.00 |
| Total current assets | |

*Plant and equipment*
| | |
|---|---|
| Equipment | 12,187.00 |
| Total plant and equipment | 12,187.00 |
| Total assets | |

**Liabilities**
*Current liabilities*
| | |
|---|---|
| Accounts payable | $2,174.00 |
| Wages payable | 674.00 |
| Property and taxes payable | 250.00 |
| Total current liabilities | |
| Total liabilities | |

**Owner's equity**
| | |
|---|---|
| D. W. Fawcett, capital | 20,360.00 |
| Total liabilities and owner's equity | |

CEL 2. Complete the vertical analysis and horizontal analysis of the comparative balance sheet for Seymour's Videos, Inc. Express percents to the nearest tenth of a percent.

Seymour's Videos, Inc.
Comparative Balance Sheet
December 31, 2007 and 2008

| | 2008 | 2007 | Increase (decrease) Amount | Increase (decrease) Percent | Percent of total assets 2008 | Percent of total assets 2007 |
|---|---|---|---|---|---|---|
| **Assets** | | | | | | |
| *Current assets* | | | | | | |
| Cash | $2,374 | $2,184 | | | | |
| Accounts receivable | 5,374 | 4,286 | | | | |
| Merchandise inventory | 15,589 | 16,107 | | | | |
| Total assets | | | | | | |
| **Liabilities** | | | | | | |
| *Current liabilities* | | | | | | |
| Accounts payable | $7,384 | $6,118 | | | | |
| Wages payable | 1,024 | 964 | | | | |
| Total liabilities | | | | | | |
| **Owner's equity** | | | | | | |
| James Seymour, capital | 14,929 | 15,495 | | | | |
| Total liabilities and owner's equity | | | | | | |

**3.** Complete the following income statement and vertical analysis.

Marten's Family Store
Income Statement
For Year Ending December 31, 2008

|  |  | **Percent of net sales** |
|---|---|---|
| **Revenue** | | |
| Gross sales | $238,923 | |
| Sales returns and allowances | 13,815 | |
| Net sales | | |
| **Cost of goods sold** | | |
| Beginning inventory, January 1, 2008 | 25,814 | |
| Purchases | 109,838 | |
| Ending inventory, December 31, 2008 | 23,423 | |
| Cost of goods sold | _____ | |
| **Gross profit from sales** | _____ | |
| **Operating expenses** | | |
| Salary | $42,523 | |
| Rent | 8,640 | |
| Utilities | 1,484 | |
| Insurance | 2,842 | |
| Fees | 860 | |
| Depreciation | 1,920 | |
| Miscellaneous | 3,420 | |
| **Total operating expenses** | 61,689 | |
| **Net income** | | |

**4.** Complete the following horizontal analysis of a comparative income statement.

**Alonzo's Auto Parts**
**Comparative Income Statement**
**For years ending June 30, 2008 and 2009**

| | 2009 | 2008 | Increase (decrease) | |
| | | | Amount | Percent |
|---|---|---|---|---|
| **Revenue** | | | | |
| Gross sales | $291,707 | $275,873 | | |
| Sales returns and allowances | 5,895 | 6,821 | | |
| Net sales | | | | |
| **Cost of goods sold** | | | | |
| Beginning inventory, July 1 | 35,892 | 32,587 | | |
| Purchases | 157,213 | 146,999 | | |
| Ending inventory, June 30 | 32,516 | 30,013 | | |
| Cost of goods sold | | | | |
| **Gross profit from sales** | | | | |
| **Operating expenses** | | | | |
| Salary | 42,000 | 40,000 | | |
| Insurance | 3,800 | 3,800 | | |
| Utilities | 1,986 | 2,097 | | |
| Rent | 3,600 | 3,300 | | |
| Depreciation | 4,000 | 4,500 | | |
| **Total operating expenses** | | | | |
| **Net income** | | | | |

*Find the current ratio for each of the following businesses. Round answers to the nearest hundredth.*

| | **Current assets** | **Current liabilities** | | | **Current assets** | **Current liabilities** |
|---|---|---|---|---|---|---|
| **5.** | $1,231,704 | $784,184 | | **6.** | $174,316 | $125,342 |

**7.** Stevens Gift Shop: cash, $2,345; accounts receivable, $5,450; government securities, $4,500; accounts payable, $6,748; notes payable, $7,457. Find the acid-test ratio. Round to the nearest hundredth.

**8.** Find the acid-test ratio for Edna Nunez and Company if the balance sheet shows cash, $23,500; marketable securities, $0; receivables, $12,300; current liabilities, $27,800. Round to the nearest hundredth.

**9.** Find the operating ratio and gross profit margin ratio for the following income statement:

Corner Grocery
Income Statement
For the Month Ending June 30, 2008

| | |
|---|---|
| Net sales | $25,000 |
| Cost of goods sold | $18,750 |
| Gross profit | $6,250 |
| Operating expenses | $3,750 |
| Net income | $2,500 |

**10.** Find the operating ratio for A to Z Sales if the income statement for the month shows net sales, $173,200; cost of goods sold, $138,400; gross profit, $34,800; operating expenses, $16,300; net income, $18,500. Express answer to the nearest tenth of a percent.

**11.** Find the gross profit margin ratio for the business in Exercise 10 to the nearest tenth of a percent.

**12.** Find the operating ratio and the gross profit margin ratio for Molene Internet Store if the month's income statement shows net sales, $285,832; cost of goods sold, $198,530; gross profit, $87,302; operating expenses, $36,593; net income, $50,709. Round to the nearest tenth.

1. Complete the following balance sheet for Rooter Company.

**Rooter Company**
**Balance Sheet**
**June 30, 2009**

**Assets**

*Current assets*

| | |
|---|---|
| Cash | $2,350.00 |
| Supplies | 175.00 |
| Accounts receivable | 8,956.00 |
| Total current assets | _____ |

*Plant and equipment*

| | |
|---|---|
| Equipment | 11,375.00 |
| Total plant and equipment | 11,375.00 |
| Total assets | _____ |

**Liabilities**

*Current liabilities*

| | |
|---|---|
| Accounts payable | $1,940.00 |
| Wages payable | 855.00 |
| Rent payable | 775.00 |
| Total current liabilities | _____ |
| Total liabilities | _____ |

**Owner's equity**

| | |
|---|---|
| Wilson Rooter, capital | 19,286.00 |
| Total liabilities and owner's equity | _____ |

2. Complete the vertical analysis and the horizontal analysis of the comparative balance sheet for Miller's Model Ships. Express percents to the nearest tenth of a percent.

**Miller's Model Ships**
**Comparative Balance Sheet**
**December 31, 2007 and 2008**

| | 2008 | 2007 | Increase (decrease) Amount | Increase (decrease) Percent | Percent of total assets 2008 | Percent of total assets 2007 |
|---|---|---|---|---|---|---|
| **Assets** | | | | | | |
| *Current assets* | | | | | | |
| Cash | $2,176 | $1,948 | | | | |
| Accounts receivable | 2,789 | 1,742 | | | | |
| Merchandise inventory | 4,985 | 5,450 | | | ____ | ____ |
| Total assets | | | | | | |
| **Liabilities** | | | | | | |
| *Current liabilities* | | | | | | |
| Accounts payable | $901 | $872 | | | | |
| Wages payable | 1,342 | 1,224 | | | | |
| Insurance payable | 690 | 680 | ____ | | ____ | ____ |
| Total liabilities | | | | | ____ | ____ |
| **Owner's equity** | | | | | | |
| Kathy Miller, capital | 7,017 | 6,364 | ____ | | ____ | ____ |
| Total liabilities and owner's equity | | | | | | |

**3.** Complete the following income statement and vertical analysis. Express percents to the nearest tenth of a percent.

Serpa's Gifts
Income Statement
For Year Ending December 31, 2007

|  |  | **Percent of net sales** |
|---|---|---|
| **Revenue** | | |
| Gross sales | $148,645 | |
| Sales returns and allowances | 8,892 | |
| Net sales | | |
| **Cost of goods sold** | | |
| Beginning inventory, January 1, 2007 | 12,100 | |
| Purchases | 47,800 | |
| Ending inventory, December 31, 2007 | 11,950 | |
| Cost of goods sold | ____ | |
| **Gross profit from sales** | ____ | |
| **Operating expenses** | | |
| Salary | 25,500 | |
| Rent | 4,500 | |
| Utilities | 1,445 | |
| Insurance | 2,100 | |
| Fees | 225 | |
| Depreciation | 1,240 | |
| Miscellaneous | 750 | |
| **Total operating expenses** | ____ | |
| **Net income** | ____ | |

**4.** Complete the following horizontal analysis of a comparative income statement. Express percents to the nearest tenth of a percent.

**Designer Crafts**
**Comparative Income Statement**
**For Years Ending December 31, 2008 and 2009**

| | 2009 | 2008 | Increase (decrease) Amount | Percent |
|---|---|---|---|---|
| **Revenue** | | | | |
| Gross sales | $239,873 | $236,941 | | |
| Sales returns and allowances | 12,815 | 13,895 | | |
| Net sales | | | | |
| **Cost of goods sold** | | | | |
| Beginning inventory, January 1 | 27,814 | 25,887 | | |
| Purchases | 123,213 | 112,604 | | |
| Ending inventory, December 31 | 24,482 | 23,838 | | |
| Cost of goods sold | | | | |
| **Gross profit from sales** | | | | |
| **Operating expenses** | | | | |
| Salary | 44,772 | 42,640 | | |
| Insurance | 3,006 | 2,863 | | |
| Utilities | 1,597 | 1,521 | | |
| Rent | 3,600 | 3,600 | | |
| Depreciation | 4,100 | 3,400 | | |
| **Total operating expenses** | | | | |
| **Net income** | | | | |

*Find the current ratio for each of the following businesses. Round answers to the nearest hundredth.*

| | **Current assets** | **Current liabilities** | | | **Current assets** | **Current liabilities** |
|---|---|---|---|---|---|---|
| **5.** | $32,194 | $38,714 | | **6.** | $724,987 | $334,169 |

**7.** Find the acid-test ratio for Central Office Supply: cash, $5,745; accounts receivable, $12,496; accounts payable, $10,475. Round to the nearest hundredth.

**8.** Find the acid-test ratio for Jefferson's Photo if the balance sheet shows cash, $6,700; marketable securities, $0; receivables, $12,756; current liabilities, $18,345.

9. Find the operating ratio for M. Ng's Grocery if the income statement for the month shows net sales, $23,500; cost of goods sold, $16,435; gross profit, $7,065; operating expenses, $3,100; net income, $3,965. Round to the nearest tenth of a percent.

10. Find the gross profit margin ratio for the business in Exercise 9 to the nearest tenth of a percent.

# PRACTICE TEST

### CHAPTER 20

1. Complete the horizontal analysis of the following comparative balance sheet. Express percents to the nearest tenth of a percent.

**O'Toole's Hardware Store**
**Comparative Balance Sheet**
**December 31, 2008 and 2009**

|  | 2009 | 2008 | Increase (Decrease) Amount | Percent |
|---|---|---|---|---|
| **Assets** | | | | |
| *Current assets* | | | | |
| Cash | $7,318 | $5,283 | | |
| Accounts receivable | 3,147 | 3,008 | | |
| Merchandise inventory | 63,594 | 60,187 | | |
| Total current assets | | | | |
| *Plant and equipment* | | | | |
| Building | 36,561 | 37,531 | | |
| Equipment | 8,256 | 4,386 | | |
| Total plant and equipment | | | | |
| Total assets | | | | |
| **Liabilities** | | | | |
| *Current liabilities* | | | | |
| Accounts payable | $5,174 | $4,563 | | |
| Wages payable | 780 | 624 | | |
| Total current liabilities | | | | |
| *Long-term liabilities* | | | | |
| Mortgage note payable | 34,917 | 36,510 | | |
| Total long-term liabilities | | | | |
| Total liabilities | | | | |
| **Owner's Equity** | | | | |
| James O'Toole, capital | 78,005 | 68,698 | | |
| Total liabilities and owner's equity | | | | |

2. Find the current ratio to the nearest hundredth for 2009 for O'Toole's Hardware Store.

3. Find the acid-test ratio to the nearest hundredth for 2009 for O'Toole's Hardware Store.

4. Find the current ratio to the nearest hundredth for 2008 for O'Toole's Hardware Store.

5. Find the acid-test ratio to the nearest hundredth for 2008 for O'Toole's Hardware Store.

**6.** Complete the horizontal analysis of the following comparative income statement.

**Mile Wide Woolens, Inc.**
**Comparative Income Statement**
**For Years Ending December 31, 2007 and 2008**

| | 2008 | 2007 | Increase (decrease) Amount | Percent |
|---|---|---|---|---|
| **Revenue** | | | | |
| Gross sales | $219,827 | $205,852 | | |
| Sales returns and allowances | 8,512 | 7,983 | | |
| Net sales | | | | |
| **Cost of goods sold** | | | | |
| Beginning inventory, January 1 | 42,816 | 40,512 | | |
| Purchases | 97,523 | 94,812 | | |
| Ending inventory, December 31 | 43,182 | 42,521 | | |
| Cost of goods sold | | | | |
| **Gross profit from sales** | | | | |
| **Operating expenses** | | | | |
| Salary | 28,940 | 27,000 | | |
| Insurance | 800 | 750 | | |
| Utilities | 1,700 | 1,580 | | |
| Rent | 3,600 | 3,000 | | |
| Depreciation | 2,000 | 2,400 | | |
| **Total operating expenses** | | | | |
| **Net income** | | | | |

**7.** Find the operating ratio for Mile Wide for 2007 and 2008.

**8.** Find the gross profit margin ratio for Mile Wide for 2007 and 2008.

**9.** Find the asset turnover ratio for Mile Wide for 2007 if its average total assets were $126,432.

**10.** Find the asset turnover ratio for Mile Wide for 2008 if its average total assets were $138,057.

1. Use the formulas in the How To box: Prepare a Balance Sheet (p. 683) to explain the formula: Total current assets + total plant and equipment = total liabilities + total owner's equity.

2. Explain how the formula
Gross profit = net sales − cost of goods sold
can be rearranged to find net sales.

3. If you have the formula:
Net profit = gross profit − operating expenses,
and the net profit is $25,982 and operating expenses are $150,986, write an equation to find gross profit.

4. Explain how the formula
$$\text{Percent of net sales} = \frac{\text{amount of item}}{\text{net sales}}$$
can be rearranged to find the amount of the item.

5. Compare the formula in step 3 of the How To box: Prepare a Horizontal Analysis of a Comparative Income Statement (p. 697) with the formula you would use to find the percent of sales tax if you know the amount of tax and the amount (price) of the item.

6. How do the two formulas in Exercise 5 compare to the basic percentage formula $P = RB$?

7. Explain why the same formula $P = RB$ can be used to calculate an increase or a decrease.

8. If a current ratio for a company equals 1, what is the relationship of the current assets to the current liabilities?

9. If the current ratio is less than 1, what is the relationship of the current assets to the current liabilities?

10. If a company has an acid-test ratio that is greater than 1, what is the relationship of the quick current assets to current liabilities?

## Challenge Problem

Cedar-Crest Greeting Card Company ended the year 2007 with assets that totaled $120,000. The assets for 2008 increased to $580,000. What was the rate of growth for Cedar-Crest?

## 20.1  Contemporary Wood Furniture

Charles Royston was checking the year-end balances for his wood furniture manufacturing and retail business and was concerned about the numbers. From what he remembered, his debts and accounts receivable were higher than the previous year. Rather than get worked up over nothing, he decided he would gather the information and make a comparison. For December 31, 2008, the business had current assets of: $1,844 cash, $11,807 accounts receivable, and $9,628 inventory. Plant and equipment totaled $158,700. Current liabilities were: accounts payable $13,446; wages payable $650; and property and taxes payable $4,124. Long-term debt totaled $92,800; and owner's equity $70,959. By comparison, for December 31, 2007, the business had current assets of: $3,278 cash; $6,954 accounts receivable; $17,417 inventory. Plant and equipment totaled $144,500. Current liabilities were: accounts payable $9,250; wages payable $1,110; property and taxes payable $3,650. Long-term debt totaled $75,800; and owner's equity $82,339.

1. Construct a comparative balance sheet for Contemporary Wood Furniture for year-end 2007 and 2008, including a vertical and horizontal analysis of the comparative balance sheet. Express percents to the nearest tenth of a percent.

2. Calculate the current ratio and the total debt to total assets ratio for 2007 and 2008.

**3.** Overall, what does your analysis mean? Is Charles correct to be concerned about these numbers? Explain.

## 20.2  Balanced Books Bookkeeping

Jessica and David are student interns at Balanced Books Bookkeeping. They have taken several business math and accounting classes and are now applying what they have learned to real-life situations. They enjoy their internship, but they are sometimes surprised by the assignments they are given. Luckily, they work together, so they share the assignments and learn from each other. Their most recent assignment is to take a listing of accounts provided by one of Balanced Books' clients and turn them into a balance sheet and income statement. David suggests that their client might appreciate it if they also performed a vertical analysis of each statement. Jessica suggests that they should also compute the current ratio and the acid-test ratio.

**1.** Create the financial statements, depict them in vertical format, and compute the current and acid test ratios.

# Investments

# Getting Started Investing

Have you been putting off investing because you don't know where to start? Getting started can be the most difficult step. Let's face it, there is an incredible amount of investment information available, and just beginning your research can be overwhelming. Fortunately, there are tools available that can point you in the right direction. One of the most valuable is the investment pyramid.

The investment pyramid is very similar to the food pyramid. At the base of the pyramid are low-risk investments with lower returns. These investments should make up a foundation percentage of your portfolio. As you move up the pyramid, the risk and possible returns increase.

The basic principle of the investment pyramid is to build a solid foundation in lower-risk investments such as money markets, before moving to higher-risk investments such as stocks. That way, your investment choices will be able to withstand the ups and downs in the marketplace.

This chapter covers stocks, bonds, and mutual funds. In what section of the investment pyramid would each of these fit? Would a corporate bond be more risky than a treasury bond, which is backed by the government?

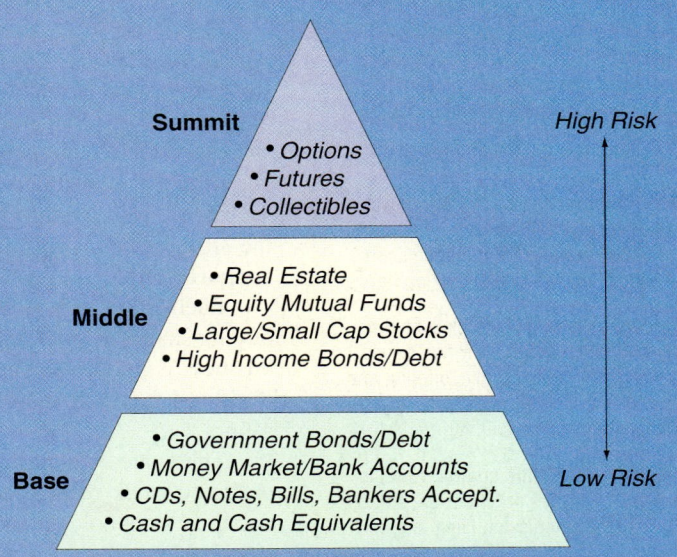

Which is more risky, an individual stock or a mutual fund? And if you could pick only one investment to get started with, what would it be? What would your investment pyramid look like? Read on; your investment in studying Chapter 21 will answer many of these questions.

## LEARNING OUTCOMES

### 21-1 Stocks

1. Read stock listings.
2. Calculate and distribute dividends.

### 21-2 Bonds and Mutual Funds

1. Read bond listings.
2. Calculate the price of bonds.
3. Read mutual fund listings.

"The Dow Zips Past 13,000 and Doesn't Stop," "Dow 14,000?" "Blue Chips Claw Their Way Back"—these and other headlines in your daily paper underscore the important role of stocks and bonds.

But just what are stocks, bonds, and mutual funds? How are stocks different from bonds? Both stocks and bonds are sold by companies to raise money and are bought by investors in the hopes of realizing a profit. But these financial instruments work in quite different ways, and we explore stocks, bonds, and mutual funds in this chapter.

## 21-1 STOCKS

### LEARNING OUTCOMES

1 Read stock listings.
2 Calculate and distribute dividends.

**Stock or equity:** the distribution of ownership of a corporation. Partial ownership can be purchased through various stock markets.

**Share:** one unit of ownership of a corporation.

**Publicly held corporation:** a company that has issued and sells shares of stock or securities through an initial public offering. These shares are traded through at least one stock exchange.

**Publicly traded:** a company's stock is said to be publicly traded if the company has issued securities through an initial public offering and these securities are traded on at least one stock exchange or over-the-counter market.

**Privately held corporation:** a company that is privately owned and does not meet the strict Security Exchange Commission filing required of publicly held corporations. Private corporations may issue stock and the owners are shareholders.

**Face value (par value):** the value of one share of stock.

**Stock certificate:** a certificate of ownership of stock issued to the buyer.

**Dividend:** a portion of the profit of a company that is periodically distributed to the stockholders of a company.

**Preferred stock:** a type of stock that guarantees a specific dividend to the stockholder. The preferred stockholder does not have voting rights.

**Common stock:** a type of stock that gives the stockholder voting rights. After dividends are paid to preferred stockholders, the remaining dividends are distributed among the common stockholders.

**Stock market:** the structure for buying and selling stock.

**Trade:** either the buying or the selling of a stock.

**Stockbroker:** the person who handles the trading of stock. A stockbroker receives a commission for these services.

**Stock listings:** information about the price of a share of stock and some historical information that is published in newspapers and on the Internet.

Any incorporated business can issue **stocks**, also known as equities or securities. Each **share** of stock represents partial ownership of the corporation. Thus, if a company issues 2 million shares of stock and you own 1 million of them, you own one-half of the company. Corporations that sell shares of stock to the public are known as **publicly held corporations**. Shares of stock in these corporations are **publicly traded**. That is, the stock is bought and sold through a stock exchange such as the New York Stock Exchange or the American Stock Exchange. Companies in which all the stock is held privately by individuals or groups of individuals are called **privately held corporations**.

Each share of a stock has a specific value, called the **face value (par value)**. A person buying shares of stock may receive a certificate of ownership, called a **stock certificate**. If the business is good, stockholders may receive a portion of the company profits in the form of a **dividend** for each share they hold. Some stockholders also have voting rights in corporate affairs.

There are two basic types of stock: **preferred stock** and **common stock**. Holders of preferred stock receive certain preferential financial benefits over common stockholders. But common stockholders have voting rights in the company—one vote per share—that preferred stockholders do not have.

After the stock is issued, people buy and sell their shares in the **stock market** for prices that vary from day to day and within a day. The price of a given company's shares is affected by supply and demand: When more people want to buy than want to sell, the price tends to rise; when more people want to sell than want to buy, the price tends to fall. Keep in mind that for each sale (called a **trade**) there is both a buyer and a seller at a given price, but supply and demand exert a pressure on the price to go up or down. Factors that affect demand include good news about a company's product, bad news of higher-than-expected business expenses, international events, or what people think the trend of the national economy or of the business is.

The actual buying and selling of shares is done by a person called a **stockbroker**, who specializes in work in the stock market. Usually a person who wishes to buy or sell stock contacts a broker in person, by phone or fax, or on the Internet. The broker's representative at the actual trading location (such as at the New York Stock Exchange on Wall Street in New York or at the American Stock Exchange in Chicago) performs the transaction. The broker receives a *commission* for the services of both buying and selling stocks.

## 1 Read stock listings.

The daily prices of stocks, along with other information about the companies, are reported on the Internet and in some newspapers. Most print media are migrating to the Internet. *The Wall Street Journal* reports only selected information about selected stocks and *The New York Times* includes stock listings only in its Sunday paper. *Barron's the Dow Jones Business and Financial Weekly* includes composite stock listings as well as listings of corporate bonds and mutual funds. *Barron's* provides the most comprehensive information in its listings. In Table 21-1, we look at listings from the *New York Times* to see how to read **stock listings**. Stock prices are listed in dollars and cents. Positive and negative signs show the direction of change. Thus $+0.13$ is read "up thirteen cents" and means the price of each share has gone up by 13 cents over the previous day's price. Similarly, $-1.75$ means the price of one share of stock has gone down by $1.75.

# TABLE 21-1
Portion of New York Stock Exchange Listing

| ① Name | ② Symbol | ③ Open | ④ High | ⑤ Low | ⑥ Close | ⑦ Net Chg | ⑧ % Chg | ⑨ Volume | ⑩ 52 Wk High | ⑪ 52 Wk Low | ⑫ Div | ⑬ Yield | ⑭ P/E | ⑮ YTD % Chg |
|---|---|---|---|---|---|---|---|---|---|---|---|---|---|---|
| AAR CORP. | AIR | 30.6 | 31.24 | 30.5 | 31.12 | 0.58 | 1.9 | 994,770 | 32.9 | 19.4 | … | … | 24 | 6.6 |
| ABM INDUSTRIES INC. | ABM | 28.14 | 28.57 | 27.67 | 28.42 | 0.28 | 1 | 270,400 | 28.87 | 16.11 | 0.48 | 1.7 | 14 | 25.1 |
| ABN AMRO HOLDING N.V. ADS | ABN | 48.6 | 49.07 | 48.52 | 48.74 | 0.29 | 0.6 | 1,598,100 | 50.33 | 25.43 | 1.48e | 3 | … | 52.1 |
| ACA CAPITAL HOLDINGS INC. | ACA | 14.35 | 14.58 | 13.92 | 14.51 | 0.16 | 1.11 | 54,900 | 16.55 | 12.6 | … | … | … | −6.1 |
| ACCO BRANDS CORP. | ABD | 23.76 | 24.3 | 23.62 | 24.03 | 0.23 | 0.97 | 570,711 | 27.45 | 17.95 | … | … | 172 | −9.2 |
| ACE LTD. | ACE | 59.7 | 59.98 | 59.27 | 59.85 | 0.39 | 0.66 | 755,400 | 61.9 | 47.81 | 1 | 1.7 | 8 | −1.2 |
| AES CORP. | AES | 22.14 | 22.28 | 21.85 | 22.25 | 0.26 | 1.18 | 2,577,840 | 23.85 | 16.5 | … | … | 45 | 1 |
| AFLAC INC. | AFL | 51.45 | 51.56 | 51.08 | 51.46 | 0.12 | 0.23 | 1,973,900 | 54 | 41.63 | .82f | 1.6 | 17 | 11.9 |
| AGCO CORP. | AG | 41.88 | 42.3 | 41 | 41.79 | 0.06 | 0.14 | 1,484,300 | 43.98 | 20.76 | … | … | dd | 35.1 |
| AGL RESOURCES INC. | ATG | 43.54 | 44.01 | 43.33 | 43.85 | 0.31 | 0.71 | 329,900 | 44.67 | 34.63 | 1.64f | 3.7 | 16 | 12.7 |
| AK STEEL HOLDING CORP. | AKS | 30.65 | 31.22 | 29.7 | 30.48 | −0.04 | −0.13 | 5,626,775 | 32.25 | 11.11 | … | … | 50 | 80.4 |
| AMB PROPERTY CORP. | AMB | 61 | 61.06 | 60.09 | 60.64 | −0.27 | −0.44 | 823,342 | 65.38 | 46.26 | 2.00f | 3.3 | 26 | 3.5 |
| AMCOL INTERNATIONAL CORP. | ACO | 24.09 | 24.16 | 23.75 | 23.9 | −0.13 | −0.54 | 224,200 | 33.5 | 18.54 | 0.56 | 2.3 | 16 | −13.8 |
| AMR CORP. | AMR | 25.75 | 26.49 | 25.3 | 26.38 | 0.29 | 1.11 | 12,735,676 | 41 | 18.78 | … | … | 17 | −12.7 |
| APT SATELLITE HOLDINGS LTD | ATS | 1.91 | 1.95 | 1.9 | 1.9 | −0.01 | −0.52 | 1,300 | 2.6 | 1.2 | … | … | … | 22.6 |
| AT&T INC. | ATT | 38.93 | 39.17 | 38.7 | 38.84 | 0.12 | 0.31 | 25,165,303 | 40.14 | 24.72 | 1.42 | 3.7 | 20 | 8.6 |
| AVX CORP. | AVX | 16.82 | 16.87 | 16.51 | 16.66 | 0.02 | 0.12 | 479,400 | 19.31 | 13.09 | 0.15 | 0.9 | 19 | 12.6 |
| AXA S.A. ADS | AXA | 46.13 | 46.27 | 45.79 | 46.06 | … | … | 260,300 | 46.56 | 29.25 | 1.42e | 3.1 | … | 14.2 |
| AZZ INCORPORATED | AZZ | 57.55 | 57.98 | 53.02 | 55.66 | −1.44 | −2.52 | 117,200 | 58.1 | 21.33 | … | … | 15 | 8.7 |
| AARON RENTS INC. | RNT | 28.36 | 28.52 | 28.09 | 28.42 | 0.05 | 0.18 | 452,600 | 30.56 | 21.8 | 0.06 | 0.2 | 18 | −1.3 |
| ABB LTD. ADS | ABB | 20.03 | 20.2 | 19.85 | 20 | 0.04 | 0.2 | 3,291,900 | 20.45 | 10.11 | .20e | … | 26 | 11.2 |
| ABBOTT LABORATORIES | ABT | 56.56 | 57.19 | 56.43 | 57.01 | 0.39 | 0.69 | 4,588,425 | 59.4 | 41.13 | 1.30f | 2.3 | 57 | 17 |
| ABERCROMBIE & FITCH CO. CL | ANF | 81.44 | 81.66 | 79.61 | 80.99 | −0.67 | −0.82 | 1,968,800 | 84.92 | 49.98 | 0.7 | 0.9 | 18 | 16.3 |

Source: Wall Street Journal Online http://online.wsj.com

**Read stock listings**

1. Column 1 (Name) shows the name of the corporation in abbreviated form.

   Read the stock listing in Table 21-1 for **ABN Amro.**

2. Column 2 (Symbol) shows the company symbol used in stock listings.

   Stock symbol is ABN.

3. Column 3 (Open) shows the share price when the market opens for this day.

   Open price is $48.60.

4. Columns 4 (High), 5 (Low), and 6 (Close) show the highest and lowest prices at which the stock sold this day and the price of the stock at market closing time.

   High is $49.07; low is $48.52; close is $48.74.

5. Column 7 (Net Chg) shows how much this day's closing price per share differs from the previous day's closing price per share for that stock.

   Net change is $0.29.

6. Column 8 (% Chg) shows the percentage of increase or decrease of the day's closing price over the day's opening price of a stock.

   Percent change is 0.6%.

7. Column 9 (Volume) shows the total number of shares of the stock that are traded on this day.

   Number of shares sold on this day is 1,598,100.

8. Columns 10 (52 Wk High) and 11 (52 Wk Low) show the highest and lowest prices at which the stock has sold in the last year (52 weeks), not including this day.

   52 Wk High is $50.83; 52 Wk Low is $25.43.

9. Column 12 (Div) shows the dividend paid per share of stock the previous year. An *e* following the dividend indicates that the dividend is an irregular cash dividend.

   This stock paid an irregular cash dividend of $1.48 per share in the previous year.

10. Column 13 (Yield) shows the previous year's dividend as a percent of the current price per share. If no dividend was paid the previous year, the entry is "…"

    Yield is 3%.

11. Column 14 (P/E) shows the stock's price/earnings ratio.

    The P/E ratio is unchanged.

12. Column 15 (YTD% Chg) shows the percentage by which this day's closing price per share differs from the closing price per share on the first day of business of the current year.

    The price per share rose 52.1% from the beginning of the year.

**Explanation of Additional Symbols**

Additional symbols in the stock listings are defined or explained in most stock listings. For example, in the *Wall Street Journal Online,* colored type marks stocks that have gained (green) or lost (red) value from close of the previous day to close of this day. An <u>underscore</u> means the stock traded more than 1 percent of its total shares outstanding. An *n* following the name of a stock indicates a new issue. An *e* following the dividend payment indicates the sum of dividends paid per share during the last year. This may also be called an *irregular dividend.* An *f* following the dividend payment indicates the annual dividend rate increased over the previous year.

**EXAMPLE 1** Refer to Table 21-1.

(a) How many shares of AFL were traded this day?

(b) What is the difference between the high price and low price of the day?

(c) What was the closing price the previous day?

(a) From column 9, we see that the day's traded shares are 1,973,900 shares.

(b) From columns 4 and 5, we see the difference in high and low is

$$
\begin{array}{r}
\text{High } 51.56 \\
-\text{ Low } \underline{51.08} \\
\$0.48 \text{ difference per share}
\end{array}
$$

(c) From column 7, we see the change in price is +$0.12. Since the change is up, the price the previous day was less.

$$\text{Previous day's closing price} = \text{this day's closing price} - \text{change}$$
$$\$51.46 - \$0.12 = \$51.34$$

**Thus, 1,973,900 shares were traded, with a difference between the high and low of $0.48 and a closing price the previous day of $51.34.**

Important historical information is given by the percent yield of a stock. A large yield would ordinarily be more desirable than a small one, but if a company is putting its profits into redevelopment instead of dividends, there may be a small yield now. However, if the company becomes a stronger business, the stock price itself might rise. If an investor sold the stock at that later time, the return on the investment then could be high, even though the yield figure now is low.

A company's **price-earnings (P/E) ratio** is the current market price (at the close of business) of one share of stock divided by the company's per-share earnings (net income). The company's earnings-per-share is found by dividing the company's after-tax profit by the number of outstanding shares. P/E ratios are usually expressed as whole numbers and are usually computed with trailing earnings. **Trailing earnings** are earnings for the past 12 months. This is called the **trailing P/E**. If the P/E ratio is computed with **leading earnings**, earnings that are projected for the upcoming 12-month period, the ratio is called a **leading P/E**.

## HOW TO   Calculate the price-earnings ratio of a stock

1. Divide the current stock price by the annual net income per share for the past 12 months.

$$\text{Price-earnings (P/E) ratio} = \frac{\text{current price per share}}{\text{net income per share (past 12 months)}}$$

2. Round quotient to the nearest whole number.

## EXAMPLE 1

Find the P/E ratio of a corporation that reported last year's net income as $6.16 per share if the company's stock sells for $58 per share.

Current price per share = $58

Net income per share = $6.16

$$\text{Price-earnings (P/E) ratio} = \frac{\text{current price per share}}{\text{net income per share (past 12 months)}}$$

$$\text{Price-earnings (P/E) ratio} = \frac{\$58}{\$6.16} \qquad \text{Divide.}$$

$$\text{P/E ratio} = 9.415584416 \qquad \text{Round.}$$

**The P/E ratio is 9. Stated differently, investors are willing to pay $9 for every $1 of last year's earnings for this stock at the price of $58.**

While P/E ratios change every day as the stock price fluctuates, the P/E ratio for a company is best viewed over time. Companies with steadily increasing P/E ratios may be viewed by the investment community as becoming increasingly speculative. Companies that are expected to grow and have higher future earnings should have a higher P/E than companies in decline. The P/E ratio is a better indicator of the value of a stock than its share price. As a general rule the P/E ratio of a company should be comparable to the company's growth rate. It is also important to consider the P/E ratio in context with other companies for the industry sector. If a P/E ratio is not given in the stock listings, the company probably has lost money during the past year.

Stocks cannot be judged on any one aspect. One stock may have a high dividend, a high yield, and yet a high P/E ratio. A cautious investor "follows the stock market" and seeks advice from knowledgeable persons, such as stockbrokers, in order to determine if a particular company meets his or her investment needs.

## STOP AND CHECK

1. How many shares of AMR stock traded on the day shown in Table 21-1?

2. What is the difference in the high price and low price for AMR on the day shown in Table 21-1?

3. AMR closed at $26.38. What was its closing price on the previous day shown in Table 21-1?

4. Which stock listed in Table 21-1 had the highest percentage yield change?

5. Find the P/E ratio of a corporation that reported last year's net income as $4.32 per share if the company's stock sells for $54 per share.

6. Find the trailing P/E ratio of AVX Corporation if the closing share price is $25.38 and the trailing net income was $1.49 per share.

## 2 Calculate and distribute dividends.

A corporation's board of directors can vote to reinvest any profits into the business or can declare a dividend with some or all of the profits. The dividend is expressed as a dollar amount per share. It is usually declared quarterly (every three months), but if a business is in poor financial condition or if the directors so decide, there may be no dividends at all.

Sometimes dividends vary according to whether the stock is preferred stock or common stock. Holders of preferred stock (which has the letters "pf" after its name in a stock listing) are entitled to first claim on the corporation's profits and assets. Thus, if a company has limited profits, it must pay all its preferred shareholders dividends before it can pay any of its common stock shareholders. Similarly, in case of bankruptcy, preferred stockholders must be paid before common stockholders. However, only holders of common stock are entitled to a vote in corporate affairs (one vote per share).

Dividends on various kinds of preferred stock are usually fixed, though owners of **participating preferred stock** can receive additional dividends if the company decides to do so. This sometimes occurs after a hostile takeover attempt. **Convertible preferred stock** allows the stock to be exchanged for a certain number of shares of common stock later. And with **cumulative preferred stock**, dividends are earned every year. If no dividends are paid one year, the amounts not paid are recorded. These **dividends in arrears** must be paid when money becomes available before other preferred or common stock dividends are paid.

**Participating preferred stock:** a type of preferred stock that allows stockholders to receive additional dividends if the company decides to do so.

**Convertible preferred stock:** a stock option that allows the stockholder to exchange the stock for a certain number of shares of common stock.

**Cumulative preferred stock:** preferred stock that earns dividends every year.

**Dividends in arrears:** dividends that were not paid in a previous year and must be paid to cumulative preferred stockholders before dividends can be distributed to other stockholders.

### HOW TO  Calculate and distribute dividends from an available amount of money

1. First pay dividends in arrears:
   (a) Multiply the number of shares held by preferred stockholders by the given rate, expressed as dollars per share.
   (b) Subtract these dividends in arrears from the available amount of money.
2. Pay the present year's preferred stock dividends:
   (a) Multiply the number of preferred shares held by stockholders by the given rate.
   (b) Subtract these preferred stock dividends from the difference from step 1b.
3. Pay the common stock dividend: Divide the difference from step 2b by the number of common shares held by stockholders. This is the dividend per share paid to common stockholders.

### EXAMPLE 1
Your company has issued 20,000 shares of cumulative preferred stock that will earn dividends at $0.60 per share and has issued 100,000 shares of common stock. Last year you paid no dividends. This year $250,000 is available for dividends. How are the dividends to be distributed?

Preferred stockholders received no dividends last year, so this year's dividends in arrears must be paid:

Dividends in arrears: 20,000($0.60) = $12,000    To preferred stockholders

The remaining money ($250,000 − $12,000 = $238,000) is distributed to the preferred and common stockholders for this year as follows:

To preferred stockholders: 20,000($0.60) = $12,000

The amount left for common stockholders ($238,000 − $12,000 = $226,000) is divided among all the common stockholders:

$$\text{To common stockholders: } \frac{\$226,000}{100,000} = \$2.26 \text{ per share}$$

**Preferred stockholders receive $24,000 and common stockholders receive $226,000.**

Notice that the $0.60 dividend per share for the preferred stock is a guaranteed but fixed rate, whereas the dividend per share of common stock has the *potential* to be higher (or lower) than that, but with no guarantee. Last year's common stock owners received no dividends, but this year they received more than did the preferred stockholders in two years. Since dividends are income to the stockholder and now receive preferential income tax treatement, they are one measure of the desirability of owning a particular stock.

## ✔ STOP AND CHECK

1. American Transit Company has 100,000 shares of common stock held by stockholders and paid $0.32 per share in dividends. How much was paid out in dividends?

2. A publicly traded corporation has issued 10,000 shares of cumulative preferred stock that will earn $0.73 per share and 1,000,000 shares of common stock. No dividends were paid last year. This year the corporation's board of directors has voted to pay out $2,800,000 in dividends. How are the dividends distributed?

3. What is the dividend per share of the common stock for the corporation in Exercise 2?

4. AVX, a stock in Table 21-1, has 6,684,582 outstanding shares of common stock. How much was paid in dividends for last year?

## 21-1 SECTION EXERCISES

*Use information about the common stock for AK Steel (Table 21-1) for Exercises 1–5.*

1. What was the closing price in dollars and cents?

2. During the previous year, what was its high price? Its low price?

3. What is the difference between this day's high price and low price?

4. What was the previous day's closing price?

5. How many shares of AK Steel stock were sold?

6. AFL stock had what P/E ratio?

7. If AFL had 3,500,000 shares of common stock outstanding when it paid dividends last year, how much did it pay in dividends?

8. What was the value of AFL's outstanding stock at the close of business according to the stock listing in Table 21-1 if it had 3,500,000 shares outstanding?

*Your company has $200,000 to distribute in dividends. There are 20,000 shares of preferred stock that earn dividends at $0.50 per share and 80,000 shares of common stock.*

**9.** How much money goes to preferred stockholders?

**10.** How much money goes to common stockholders?

**11.** How much per share does a common stockholder receive in dividends to the nearest cent?

*The ARMMO Corporation has $1,550,000 to distribute in dividends and did not distribute dividends the previous year. There are 100,000 shares of cumulative preferred stock that earn dividends at $0.78 per share and 800,000 shares of common stock.*

**12.** How much money goes to preferred stockholders?

**13.** How much money goes to common stockholders?

**14.** How much per share does a common stockholder receive in dividends to the nearest cent?

# 21-2 BONDS AND MUTUAL FUNDS

## LEARNING OUTCOMES

1  Read bond listings.
2  Calculate the price of bonds.
3  Read mutual fund listings.

**Bond:** a type of loan to the issuer to raise money for a company or municipality. The investor or bondholder will be paid a specified rate of interest each year and will be paid the entire value of the bond at maturity.

**Issuer:** a company, state, or municipality that issues bonds to raise money.

**Coupon:** the annual interest paid by the issuer to the lender on a bond.

**Coupon rate:** the annual payout percentage based on the bond's par value (original value of the bond).

**Face value (par value):** the original value of a bond, usually $1,000.

**Maturity date:** the date at which the face value of the bond is paid to the bondholder.

**Junk bonds:** high-risk bonds that are usually from companies in bankruptcy or in financial difficulty.

**Corporate bonds:** bonds issued by businesses.

**Municipal bonds:** bonds issued by local and state governments.

**Treasury bonds:** bonds issued by the federal government.

**Registered bonds:** bonds for which investors receive interest automatically by being listed with the company.

**Convertible bonds:** bonds with a provision for being converted to stock.

**Recallable bonds:** bonds that can be repurchased by the company before the maturity date.

After time passes, a corporation may need to raise more money than its initial offering of stock produced. It can then issue more stock, thereby creating more shares of ownership. However, the company management may be reluctant to do so because additional shares lessen the ownership power (dilute the rights) of the existing stockholders. To raise the needed money, the company may decide to borrow it for a short term from a bank or for a longer term (five years or more) from the public, by selling bonds. In exchange for money from the sale, the company issues a **bond**, a promise to repay the money at a specific later date and in the meantime to pay interest annually. The company, state, or municipality that issues the bond is called the **issuer**. The annual interest paid by the issuer to the lender on the bond is referred to as the **coupon**. The **coupon rate** is the annual payout as a percentage of the bond's par value.

A bond has a **face value (par value)**, usually $1,000 or a multiple of $1,000, a date of repayment (**maturity date**), and a fixed *rate of interest* per year. Since a bond obligates the company to future repayment, the public's judgment of the company's future will affect sales of a bond. Investors also look closely at the interest to be paid.

Since bonds are a legal debt of the corporation, if the company goes bankrupt, the bondholder's claims have priority over those of the stockholders. Bonds of businesses that are bankrupt or in financial difficulty, called **junk bonds**, can thus yield a high return—or be next to worthless—making them a risky and speculative investment.

In addition to these **corporate bonds** issued by businesses, state and local governments sell **municipal bonds** and the federal government sells **treasury bonds**. Government bonds are often attractive to investors because the interest payments on them may be exempt from federal income tax. In this text, however, we deal only with corporate bonds.

Corporate bonds come in various types. **Registered bonds** allow the investor to receive interest automatically by being listed with the corporation. **Convertible bonds** have a provision that allows them to be converted to stock. **Recallable bonds** allow the corporation to repurchase the bonds before the maturity date.

Once bonds are issued, they may be bought and sold at varying prices in the **bond market**. Here, as in the stock market, "market conditions" prevail: A bond with high interest payments may be attractive to investors, so its price may rise, causing the bond to *sell at a premium* (a **premium bond**). Or, if interest payments are low, a bond price may tend to drop in order to attract investors, causing the bond to *sell at a discount* (a **discount bond**).

## TIP

**How Much Do I Get at Maturity of a Bond?**

Keep in mind that no matter what the market price of a bond, the corporation pays interest on the face value of $1,000 per bond and repays the face or par value of the bond at maturity.

## 1   Read bond listings.

Table 21-2 shows how bonds are listed in the *Barrons Online* bonds listing. While bond prices, like stock prices, change during business hours, *Barrons* lists bond prices weekly. A quick look at the closing price (Weekly Last) column in Table 21-2 reveals two bonds selling at exactly par value (100%). The discount bonds have a listing less than 100%; the premium bonds have a listing greater than 100%. NoPac is selling at a discount, whereas the OcciP bond is selling at a premium.

**TABLE 21-2**
Portion of NYSE Bonds Listing

| ① | ② | ③ | ④ | ⑤ | ⑥ | ⑦ | ⑧ | ⑨ |
|---|---|---|---|---|---|---|---|---|
| 52-Weeks | | Name and | Cur | Sales | Weekly | Weekly | Weekly | Net |
| **High** | **Low** | **Coupon** | **Yld** | **$1,000** | **High** | **Low** | **Last** | **Change** |
| 110 | 93 | AMR 9s16 | 8.7 | 6 | 104.25 | 103.5 | 103.5 | −0.75 |
| 133.38 | 122.88 | ATTBdb 9.45s22 | 7.3 | 10 | 130.13 | 130.13 | 130.13 | 0.38 |
| 104.13 | 99 | BurN 6.55s20 O | 6.5 | 1 | 100 | 100 | 100 | −4.13 |
| 146 | 112 | DevonE 4.95s08 | cv | 25 | 146 | 146 | 146 | — |
| 100.41 | 95.25 | GMAC $6\frac{1}{8}$08 | 6.1 | 1 | 100.25 | 100.25 | 100.25 | 0.25 |
| 108 | 102.25 | GMAC $8\frac{7}{8}$10 | 8.5 | 29 | 105 | 105 | 105 | −0.75 |
| 99.5 | 88.75 | GMAC dc6s11 | 6.2 | 50 | 97.13 | 96.26 | 96.26 | −0.73 |
| 67.75 | 63.75 | GMAC zr12 | — | 112 | 65.5 | 63.75 | 65.5 | 0.88 |
| 58.88 | 44.5 | GMAC zr15 | — | 17 | 55 | 54 | 54 | 1 |
| 101.13 | 99.25 | IBM $5\frac{3}{8}$09 | 5.3 | 5 | 100.75 | 100.75 | 100.75 | — |
| 114 | 108.5 | IBM $7\frac{1}{2}$13 | 6.7 | 20 | 111.51 | 111.51 | 111.51 | 0.01 |
| 126.75 | 120.13 | IBM$8\frac{3}{8}$19 | 6.7 | 50 | 124.82 | 124.82 | 124.82 | 0.45 |
| 102.63 | 101.13 | IntLseFn $6\frac{3}{8}$09 | 6.3 | 5 | 101.25 | 101.25 | 101.25 | 0.13 |
| 101.75 | 99.13 | JCPL $6\frac{3}{4}$25 | 6.8 | 5 | 100 | 100 | 100 | −0.38 |
| 105.88 | 101.13 | Leucadia $7\frac{3}{4}$13 | 7.4 | 15 | 104.63 | 104.63 | 104.63 | −0.13 |
| 102 | 100 | McDnl 7.31s27 | 7.3 | 10 | 100.25 | 100.25 | 100.25 | −0.13 |
| 105 | 103.38 | NatwFS 8s27 | 7.7 | 23 | 103.63 | 103.63 | 103.63 | — |
| 62 | 50.5 | NoPac 3s47str | 4.8 | 8 | 62 | 62 | 62 | 4.63 |
| 114.88 | 108.75 | OcciP $10\frac{1}{8}$09 | 9.3 | 26 | 110 | 108.75 | 108.75 | −1.5 |
| 103.25 | 102 | PhilPt $6\frac{3}{8}$09 | 6.2 | 15 | 103.13 | 103.13 | 103.13 | −0.13 |
| 101.88 | 100.13 | Safway 7s07 | 7 | 10 | 100.13 | 100.13 | 100.13 | — |
| 118 | 112.75 | TVA $8\frac{1}{4}$42 | 7.1 | 3 | 116.13 | 116.13 | 116.13 | 0.5 |
| 79.75 | 79.75 | TechOly $10\frac{3}{8}$12 | 13 | 100 | 79.75 | 79.75 | 79.75 | — |
| 93.25 | 84 | Tenet $6\frac{3}{4}$12 | 7.3 | 10 | 93 | 93 | 93 | 1 |
| 101.75 | 97.25 | XeroxCr 7.2s12 | 7.1 | 10 | 101 | 100.75 | 100.75 | −0.25 |

Source: www.onlinebarrons.com

**HOW TO**     Read bond listings

1. Columns 1 and 2 give the high and low values over the past 52 weeks.
2. Column 3 (Name and Coupon) tells the name of the issuing company and the annual interest rate (expressed as a percent of face value), and the last two digits of the year of maturity.
3. Column 4 (Cur Yld) tells the current yield, which is the ratio of the annual interest earned per bond and the current price per bond.
4. Column 5 (Sales) tells the volume (number) of bonds traded; so if the entry is 10, it means that 10 bonds have been traded this week.
5. Columns 6 and 7 give the weekly high and low values.
6. Column 8 (Weekly Last) tells the closing price per bond as a percent of the face value per bond; an entry of 101.25 means the bond sold for 101.25% of $1,000 per bond, or 1.0125 times $1,000 per bond, or $1,012.50 per bond.
7. Column 9 (Net Change) tells how much this week's closing price per bond differs from the previous week's closing price per bond, as a percent of the face value per bond.

**EXAMPLE 1**     Refer to Table 21-2.

(a) What are the interest rate and the year of maturity for McDnl 7.31s27?
(b) How many bonds were sold during this week?
(c) What was the net change for the week?

(a) From column 3, we see the interest rate is 7.31%, and the year of maturity is 2027. See the Tip for explanation of the *s*.
(b) From column 5, we see the number of bonds sold this week is 10.
(c) From column 9, we see the change is −0.13, or down 0.13% of $1,000, or down $1.30.

**TIP**

**Bond Symbols**

What does *s* mean in between the rate and maturity date?

For an interest rate that is a whole percent, the letter *s* (for *space*) is inserted to separate the rate and the maturity date. A listing of 8s08 means 8% maturing in 2008. Other symbols are normally explained in an explanatory note in a listing.

 **STOP AND CHECK**

1. From Table 21-2 find the interest rate and the year of maturity for JCPL.

2. How many JCPL bonds were sold this week?

3. What was the net change in the JCPL bond price for the week?

4. What is the current yield for the JCPL bond?

## 2   Calculate the price of bonds.

Even though a bond has a face value of $1,000, bonds on the bond market are bought and sold for more or less than $1,000. Column 8 in Table 21-2 gives the closing price per bond as a percent of $1,000.

## EXAMPLE 1   Calculate the closing price of the PhilPt bond.

From column 8, the closing price as a percent of face value was 103.13%.

$$103.13\% = 1.0313$$
$$\text{Closing bond price} = \$1.000 \times \text{percent in column 8}$$
$$= 1,000\,(1.0313)$$
$$= \$1,031.30$$

**The closing bond price is $1,031.30**

## EXAMPLE 2   Calculate the previous week's closing price per bond for ATTBdb (Table 21-2).

The bond closed at 130.13% of its face value, up 0.38% of its face value from the previous week's closing price. The previous week's closing price was this week's closing price minus 0.38% of the face value.

$$\text{Previous week's closing listing} = 130.13\% - 0.38\% = 129.75\%$$
$$129.75\% = 1.2975$$
$$\text{Previous week's bond price} = \$1,000(1.2975) = \$1,297.50.$$

**The previous week's bond price is $1,297.50.**

**Yield:** a measure of the profitability of the investment.

**Current bond yield or average annual yield:** the ratio of the annual interest per bond to the current price per bond.

Investors in bonds, like investors in stocks, want to know the **yield** of their investments. In Table 21-2 the "Cur Yld" (current yield) column gives a measure of how profitable the investment is. **Current bond yield**, sometimes called **average annual yield**, compares annual earnings (interest) with the closing price of a bond. It is expressed as a percent of face value.

Interest is paid on the $1,000 face value of the bond. For example, the stated interest rate for the NatwFS bond is 8%. The interest per year is 8% of $1,000 or $80. The current price is 103.63% of $1,000 or $1,036.30. Then, the current yield is $\frac{\$80}{\$1,036.30}$ (100%) or 7.7%.

## ✔ STOP AND CHECK

1. What was the closing price of the AMR bond?

2. Find the closing price of the ATTBdb bond.

3. What was the closing price of the AMR bond in the previous week?

4. Find the closing price of the ATTBdb bond in the previous week.

## 3 Read mutual fund listings.

**Portfolio:** a variety of types of investments.

**Mutual fund:** a collection of stocks, bonds, and other securities that is managed by a mutual fund company.

**Net asset value:** the value of one share of a mutual fund.

**Fund family:** the mutual fund company that offers more than one type of fund.

**Front-end load mutual fund:** a mutual fund for which the sales charge is included in the selling price of the shares.

**No load mutual fund:** a mutual fund that does not charge a sales charge for buying and selling its shares.

Many individual investors do not have the time or expertise to research all of the many investment options, and investors are advised to maintain a variety of investments called a **portfolio**. To accomplish these goals, many investors choose a **mutual fund**. A mutual fund or investment trust is a collection of stocks, bonds, and other securities that is managed by a mutual fund company. Individual investors purchase shares in the mutual fund and own a small portion of each holding in the fund. The value of one share of the fund is called the **net asset value**. The net asset value is the amount of money you would get per share if you sold shares of your mutual fund stock. This value fluctuates just as the value of stocks and bonds fluctuates.

Mutual fund listings can be found on the Internet just like listings for stocks and bonds. The information given varies with the source of the listing. Table 21-3 is a portion of a listing from the *Wall Street Journal Online*. A mutual fund corporation may offer more than one type of fund to satisfy a variety of investors. Some funds may be high-risk aggressive funds while others have a moderate risk. The mutual fund company is listed as the **fund family** and the various funds that are offered are listed under the fund family.

The selling price of a share of a mutual fund usually includes a sales charge. The sales charge is found by subtracting the net asset value from the selling price of a share of stock in a mutual fund. This sales charge is sometimes called a **front-end load**. Some mutual funds do not charge a load and are known as **no load funds**.

---

**HOW TO**    Find the mutual fund sales charge and the sales charge percent

1. Subtract net asset value from selling (offer) price

$$\text{Mutual fund sales charge} = \text{selling (offer) price} - \text{net asset value}$$

2. $\text{Sales charge percent} = \dfrac{\text{sales charge}}{\text{net asset value}} \times 100\%$

---

**TABLE 21-3**
Portion of Mutual Fund Listing

**Mutual Funds: Closing Quotes**

| Family/ Fund | Symbol | NAV | Chg | YTD % return | 3-yr % chg |
|---|---|---|---|---|---|
| **AARPAggr p** | | | | | |
| AARPAggr p | AAGSX | 11.67 | 0.01 | 5.1 | NS |
| **AARPMod p** | | | | | |
| AARPMod p | AAMDX | 11.17 | — | 4 | NS |
| **AFBA 5Star Funds** | | | | | |
| Balancedl r | AFBAX | 14.47 | 0.02 | 4.1 | 12 |
| LgCapl | AFBEX | 16.4 | 0.01 | 10.4 | 10.3 |
| SmCapA t | AFCAX | 19.39 | 0.03 | 6.3 | 11.3 |
| SmCapC t | AFCCX | 18.59 | 0.02 | 6 | 10.4 |
| USA Gbl lr | AFGLX | 18.32 | 0.05 | 8.9 | 9.4 |
| **AIM Funds A** | | | | | |
| GrowAlloc p | AADAX | 14.58 | 0.01 | 6.2 | 15.6 |
| LimMA p | LMTAX | 10.02 | — | 1.4 | 2 |
| **AIM Funds B** | | | | | |
| DivrsDiv t | LCEDX | 14.09 | 0.05 | 4.4 | 11.6 |
| EuroSmCo | ESMBX | 30.99 | −0.03 | 15.9 | 45 |
| GlEqty | GNDBX | 16.87 | 0.02 | 7.2 | 17.3 |
| GlValue | AWSBX | 16.48 | 0.08 | 4.8 | 17.6 |
| GrowAlloc t | AAEBX | 14.45 | 0.01 | 5.9 | 14.8 |
| IntlSmall t | IEGBX | 26.45 | — | 13.2 | 37.2 |
| **AIM Funds C** | | | | | |
| BasicBal t | BBLCX | 13.75 | 0.02 | 4.2 | 7.8 |
| EuroSmCo | ESMCX | 30.99 | −0.03 | 15.9 | 45 |

Source: Wall Street Journal Online

Find the sales charge and the sales charge percent for one share of AAMDX mutual fund stock if the stock was offered at $11.59.

The NAV is 11.17 and the offering (selling) price of the stock is $11.59.

Mutual fund sales charge = offer price − net asset value

Mutual fund sales charge = $11.59 − $11.17 = 0.42

$$\text{Sales charge percent} = \frac{\text{sales charge}}{\text{net asset value}} \times 100\%$$

$$\text{Sales charge percent} = \left(\frac{\$0.42}{\$11.17}\right)(100\%)$$

**Sales charge percent = 0.0376007162(100%) = 3.7% sales charge.**

---

**HOW TO**    Read mutual fund listings

In Table 21-3,

1. Find the appropriate fund family (bold entry in column 1).
2. Find the appropriate fund name (indented entry in column 1).
3. Find the stock symbol in column 2.
4. Find the net asset value (NAV) in column 3.
5. Identify the one-day total change (Chg) from column 4.
6. Identify the total return for the year to date (YTD % Ret) from column 5.

---

**EXAMPLE 2**    (a) Find the current price per share of LCEDX fund. (b) What was the price per share yesterday?

(a) Current price per share (NAV) = $14.09
(b) Change = +0.05
    Yesterday's price = $14.09 − $0.05
    Yesterday's price = $14.04

---

**HOW TO**    Find the net asset value at the beginning of the year for one share of a mutual fund

1. Divide the Current NAV by the sum of 100% and YTD % return

$$\text{Beginning of year NAV} = \frac{\text{current NAV}}{100\% + \text{YTD \% return}}$$

2. Round the quotient to the nearest cent.

---

**EXAMPLE 3**    Find the beginning of year NAV for AWSBX.

$$\text{Beginning of year NAV} = \frac{\text{current NAV}}{100\% + \text{YTD \% return}}$$

$$\text{Beginning of year NAV} = \frac{16.48}{1 + .048} = \frac{16.48}{1.048} = 15.72519084$$

**The beginning of year NAV = $15.73.**

##  STOP AND CHECK

1. Find the current price per share of AAMDX fund.

2. What was yesterday's price per share of AAMDX fund?

3. What was the price per share (NAV) of AAMDX at the beginning of the year?

4. What was the price per share (NAV) of AFBEX at the beginning of the year?

## 21-2 SECTION EXERCISES

### SKILL BUILDERS

1. Refer to Table 21-2 to determine the interest rate and maturity of a bond issued by Leucadia.

2. What is the current yield for the bond issue of IBM that has an interest rate of $7\frac{1}{2}\%$ and matures in 2013?

3. How many bonds for the GMAC issue maturing in 2015 were traded in the week shown in the bond listing in Table 21-2?

4. AMR closed at 103.5 in Table 21-2. What does this mean?

5. Which of the first two GMAC bonds (Table 21-2) is producing the greater current yield?

6. How many GMAC bonds maturing in 2012 sold during the week as shown in Table 21-2?

7. Use Table 21-2 to find the selling price at the close of the selling week of the bond issue for BurN that matures in 2020.

8. Give the closing price of an IBM bond that matures in 2019.

9. What is the weekly high of the IBM bond listed as 0.45%?

10. From Table 21-2, what was the previous week's closing bond price for an ATTBdb bond that matures in 2022?

11. What is the current price per share of the AFGLX mutual fund (Table 21-3)?

## APPLICATIONS

**12.** What was yesterday's price per share for the AFGLX mutual fund?

**13.** What was the price per share for the AFGLX mutual fund at the beginning of the year?

**14.** What was the change for the ESMBX mutual fund? What was yesterday's price?

## Learning Outcomes

## What to Remember with Examples

### Section 21-1

**1** Read stock listings. (p. 728)

1. Column 1 (Name) shows the name of the corporation in abbreviated form.
2. Column 2 (Symbol) shows the company symbol used in stock listings.
3. Column 3 (Open) shows the share price when the market opens for this day.
4. Columns 4 (High), 5 (Low), and 6 (Close) show the highest and lowest prices at which the stock sold this day and the price of the stock at market closing time.
5. Column 7 (Net Chg) shows how much this day's closing price per share differs from the previous day's closing price per share for that stock.
6. Column 8 (% Chg) shows the percentage of increase or decrease of the day's closing price over the day's opening price of a stock.
7. Column 9 (Volume) shows the total number of shares of the stock that are traded on this day.
8. Columns 10 (52 Wk High) and 11 (52 Wk Low) show the highest and lowest prices at which the stock has sold in the last year (52 weeks), not including this day.
9. Column 12 (Div) shows the dividend paid per share of stock the previous year. An *e* following the dividend indicates that the dividend is an irregular cash dividend.
10. Column 13 (Yield) shows the previous year's dividend as a percent of the current price per share. If no dividend was paid the previous year, the entry is "…"
11. Column 14 (P/E) shows the stock's price/earnings ratio.
12. Column 15 (YTD% Chg) shows the percentage by which this day's closing price per share differs from the closing price per share on the first day of business of the current year.

Refer to Table 21-1:

How many shares of ABN Amro were traded this day?

From column 9:
1,598,100 shares traded this day

What is the difference between the highest and lowest prices of ABN Amro stock for the year?

From columns 10 and 11:
$50.33 − $25.43 = $24.90

**2** Calculate and distribute dividends. (p. 732)

1. First pay dividends in arrears:
   (a) Multiply the number of shares held by preferred stockholders by the given dividend rate, expressed as dollars per share.
   (b) Subtract the dividends in arrears from the available amount of money.
2. Pay the present year's preferred stock dividends:
   (a) Multiply the number of preferred shares held by stockholders by the given dividend rate.
   (b) Subtract these preferred stock dividends from the difference from step 1b.
3. Pay the common stock dividend: Divide the difference from step 2b by the number of common shares held by stockholders. This is the dividend per share for common stockholders.

$500,000 is available for dividends, including $20,000 for dividends in arrears and $20,000 for current preferred stock dividends. How much will be given for common stock dividends?

$500,000 − $40,000 = $460,000

$460,000 is available for common stock dividends. There are 300,000 shares of common stock. What is the dividend per share?

$$\frac{\$460,000}{300,000} = \$1.533333333 = \$1.53 \text{ per share}$$

**1** Read bond listings. (p. 735)

1. Columns 1 and 2 give the high and low values over the past 52 weeks.
2. Column 3 (Name and Coupon) tells the name of the issuing company, the annual interest rate (expressed as a percent of the face value), and the last two digits of the year of maturity.
3. Column 4 (Cur Yld) tells the current yield, which is the ratio of the annual interest earned per bond and the current price per bond.
4. Column 5 (Sales) tells the volume (number) of bonds traded. If the entry is 10, it means that 10 bonds have been traded this week.
5. Columns 6 and 7 give the weekly high and low values.
6. Column 8 (Weekly Last) tells the closing price per bond as a percent of the face value per bond; an entry of 101.25 means the bond sold for 101.25 of $1,000 per bond, or 1.0125 times $1,000 per bond, or $1,012.50 per bond.
7. Column 9 (Net Change) tells how much this week's closing price per bond differs from the previous week's closing price per bond, as a percent of the face value per bond.

A bond is listed as having a closing price of $80\frac{3}{8}$, up $\frac{1}{8}$ from last week's close. What is the price today? What was it last week?

$$80\frac{3}{8}\% \text{ of face value is } 0.80375(\$1,000) \text{ or } \$803.75 \text{ per bond today.}$$

$$80\frac{3}{8}\% - \frac{1}{8}\% = 80\frac{1}{4}\% \text{ or } 0.8025(\$1,000) = \$802.50 \text{ per bond last week.}$$

Bond A has 15 listed in the "volume" column. How many bonds were traded for the week? 15 in the "volume" column means 15 bonds were traded.

A bond is listed at $6\frac{5}{8}15$. How much interest is paid annually?

$$\text{The interest rate is } 6\frac{5}{8}\%. \ 6\frac{5}{8}\% \text{ of } \$1,000 = 0.06625(\$1,000) = \$66.25.$$

What is the maturity date of the bond?

The bond matures in 2015, as indicated by 15 after the interest rate of $6\frac{5}{8}$.

**2** Calculate the price of bonds. (p. 736)

1. Locate the percent of $1,000 that the bond was selling for at the close of the week (column 8).
2. Multiply the decimal equivalent of the percent by $1,000.
3. Round the product to the nearest cent.

You purchase five bonds listed at $98\frac{1}{2}$. What is the cost of one bond? five bonds?

$$\text{For one bond: } 98\frac{1}{2}\% \text{ of } \$1,000 = 0.985(\$1,000) = \$985$$

$$\text{For five bonds: } 5(\$985) = \$4,925$$
$$\text{Cost of bonds: } \$4,925$$

**3** Read mutual fund listings. (p. 738)

1. Find the appropriate fund family (bold entry in column 1, Table 21-3).
2. Find the appropriate fund name (indented entry in column 1).
3. Find the mutual fund symbol in column 2.
4. Find the net asset value (NAV) in column 3.
5. Identify the one-day total change (Chg) from column 4.
6. Identify the total return for the year to date (YTD % Return) from column 5.

Use Table 21-3 to find the current price per share (NAV), the percent change from yesterday's NAV (Chg), and the percent change in the NAV from the beginning of the year (YTD % Ret) for BBLCX.

NAV = $13.75     Current price per share
Chg = +0.02     Percent change from yesterday's price per share

YTD % Ret = 4.2%    Percent change from the price per share at the beginning of the year

# EXERCISES SET A

*For Exercises 1–6, refer to Table 21-1.*

**1.** How many shares of ACE LTD. were traded?

**2.** What is the difference between the high and low prices of ACE LTD. for the last 52 weeks?

**3.** What was the difference between the day's high and low trading prices for one share of ACE LTD. stock?

**4.** What was the previous day's closing price of ACE LTD. stock?

**5.** How much money was paid in dividends for one share of Abercrombie stock? For 50 shares? For 100 shares?

**6.** What is this day's closing price for one share of AFLAC Inc. stock?

*Your company has 120,000 shares of cumulative preferred stock that pays dividends at $0.25 per share and 200,000 shares of common stock. This year, $500,000 is to be distributed. The preferred stockholders are also due to receive dividends in arrears for one year.*

**7.** What is the amount of the dividends in arrears?

**8.** How much will go to the preferred stockholders for this year?

**9.** How much money will be distributed in all to common stockholders?

**10.** What is the dividend per share for the common stockholders?

*For Exercises 11–15, refer to Table 21-2.*

**11.** How many ATTB bonds were traded this week?

**12.** What is the current yield for the ATTB bond?

**13.** What is the date of maturity of the ATTB bond?

**14.** Find the previous week's closing price for an ATTB bond.

**15.** Calculate the previous week's closing price for an McDnl bond.

**16.** Use Table 21-3 to find the current price per share of IEGBX mutual fund.

**17.** Find yesterday's NAV for AAEBX mutual fund.

**EXCEL** **18.** Find the beginning-of-the-year NAV for the AAEBX mutual fund.

# EXERCISES SET B

*For Exercises 1–6, refer to Table 21-1.*

**1.** What was the annual dividend paid for one share of AT&T INC. stock.?

**2.** What is this day's closing price of AT&T INC. stock?

**3.** What is the current yield on AT&T INC. stock?

**4.** Find the current yield for ABBOT Laboratories.

**5.** Which of the two companies, AMB Property or AT&T INC., has the greater dividend per share?

**6.** Which of the two companies, AT&T INC. or AVX CORP, has the greater yield?

*Aetna has 400,000 shares of cumulative preferred stock that pays dividends at $2.13 per share and 1,500,000 shares of common stock. This year, $4,250,000 is to be distributed, and preferred stockholders are due to receive dividends in arrears for one year.*

**7.** What is the amount of dividends in arrears?

**8.** What are this year's preferred stockholder dividends?

**9.** Find the dividends distributed to common stockholders.

**10.** What is the dividend per share for common stockholders?

*For Exercises 11–15, refer to Table 21-2.*

**11.** What is the coupon rate of an NatwFS bond that is listed at closing at 103.63%?

**12.** What is the dollar price of an NatwFS bond listed at closing?

**13.** Which of the bonds GMAC $6\frac{1}{8}$08 or GMAC dc6s11 is selling at a discount? At a premium?

**14.** Find the previous week's closing price for an IBM $8\frac{3}{8}$19 bond.

**15.** Find the previous week's closing price for a DevonE bond.

**16.** Use Table 21-3 to find the current price per share of GNDBX mutual fund.

**17.** Find the closing NAV for BBLCX mutual fund.

**18.** Find the beginning-of-the-year NAV for the BBLCX mutual fund.

# PRACTICE TEST

## CHAPTER 21

Use the following stock listing for McDonaldsCorp for Exercises 1–7.

| 52 Weeks | | | | Yld | | Sales | | | | |
| High | Low | Stock | Div | % | P/E | 100s | High | Low | Last | Chg |
| --- | --- | --- | --- | --- | --- | --- | --- | --- | --- | --- |
| 43.63 | 26.38 | MCD | .20 | 0.6 | 21 | 45,905 | 32.25 | 31.44 | 31.50 | −0.06 |

**1.** What is the difference between this day's high and low?

**2.** What is the current yield?

**3.** What is this day's closing price, in dollars?

**4.** What was the previous day's closing price, in dollars?

**5.** How many shares were traded this day?

**6.** Last year you bought 120 shares of McDonaldsCorp at $50.50. Calculate the amount the shares cost when purchased.

**7.** Calculate the value of your stock at the close of business this day.

Use the following information to answer Exercises 8–11.

Your company has $200,000 to distribute in dividends to three groups:
A: One year's dividends in arrears for 5,000 shares of cumulative preferred stock ($0.40 per share)
B: The current year's dividends for those 5,000 shares of cumulative preferred stock ($0.40 per share)
C: Dividends on 75,000 shares of common stock

**8.** How much is distributed to group A?

**9.** How much is distributed to group B?

**10.** How much is distributed to group C?

**11.** What is the dividend per share of common stock?

Use the following stock listing for Exercises 12 and 13.

| 52 Weeks | | | | Yld | | Sales | | | | |
| High | Low | Stock | Div | % | P/E | 100s | High | Low | Last | Chg |
| --- | --- | --- | --- | --- | --- | --- | --- | --- | --- | --- |
| $9.75 | $6.63 | PennAM | .21 | 2.7 | dd | 11 | 7.69 | 7.56 | 7.69 | + 0.13 |
| $34.31 | $20.00 | PennEMA | .56 | 1.9 | 12 | 5 | 29.81 | 21.81 | 29.81 | − 0.06 |

**12.** What is the PE ratio of PennEMA?

**13.** You own 1,000 shares of PennAM. How much do you receive in annual dividends?

Use the following bond listing for Exercises 14–17.

| 12 Mo | | | Cur | | Weekly | | | | |
| Hi | Lo | Name | Yld | Vol | Hi | Lo | Cls | Chg | |
| --- | --- | --- | --- | --- | --- | --- | --- | --- | --- |
| $106\frac{7}{8}$ | 60 | Polaroid $11\frac{1}{2}$ 09 | 18.0 | 2211 | $73\frac{7}{8}$ | 60 | 64 | $-8\frac{3}{8}$ | |

**14.** What is the date of maturity of the bond?

**15.** What is the closing price of the bond, in dollars?

**16.** What was the previous week's closing price, in dollars?

**17.** Is the Polaroid bond selling at a premium or a discount?

**18.** Use Table 21-3 to find the current price per share of GNDBX mutual fund.

**19.** Find yesterday's price per share of AADAX mutual fund in Table 21-3.

**20.** What is the price per share of LMTAX mutual fund at the beginning of the year from Table 21-3?

1. In the columns for listing stock information, some columns give necessary information for finding additional information, and other columns give convenience information that could have been generated by information in other columns. Give an example of a column giving convenience information.

2. To find the previous day's price of a stock, you use the current day's price and the amount of change. When do you add and when do you subtract? Give a strategy for predicting the result that will help you to avoid performing the wrong operation.

3. Using the formula

$$\text{P/E ratio} = \frac{\text{closing price per share}}{\text{annual earnings per share}}$$

write a formula and explain your rationale for finding the annual earnings per share for the stock listing information.

4. How are bonds different from stocks?

5. How are bonds different from certificates of deposit or savings accounts?

6. Does column 4 in Table 21-2 give convenience information or new information that could not be calculated from other table information? Explain your answer.

7. In Table 21-2, select three bonds that are discounted bonds. How can you tell the difference?

8. When are premium bonds a wise investment? When are discounted bonds a wise investment?

## Challenge Problem

Column 13 of Table 21-1 shows the Yield in percent form. The notes on reading stock listings indicate the yield is the previous year's dividends as a percent of the current price per share. Use this explanation to verify the yield of ABM stock that has a closing price of $28.42 and paid dividends of $0.48 last year.

# CASE STUDIES

## 21.1 Dynamic Thermoforming, Inc.

With the upcoming annual shareholders' meeting only a week away, Chief Executive Officer Christopher Lee had a great deal of information to prepare. There was some very good news to communicate: Profits for the five-year-old plastics company were at record levels and $275,000 was available for dividends to be paid, unlike last-year when no dividends were paid. But the business was at a crossroads as well. Technological advancements in the thermoforming industry were forcing individual companies to make substantial investments in advanced production capacity to remain viable. Christopher would be recommending to the Board of Directors a $2.4 million corporate bond issue to pay for the improved production capabilities. In addition, employee retention was also a major goal for the company. Feedback from the employees had focused on the need for a company-sanctioned retirement program. In response, Dynamic Thermoforming, Inc. would be offering a 401(k) retirement program complete with a number of different investment choices, including some of the top mutual fund families. In addition, the first 3% contributed by an employee would be fully matched by the company. Together, these three topics would set the tone for continued success in the marketplace, and surely give a boost to the already favorable employee morale.

1. Dynamic Thermoforming, Inc. has previously issued 25,000 shares of cumulative preferred stock that will earn dividends at $0.70 per share, and 75,000 shares of common stock. Since no dividends were paid last year, how will the $275,000 declared for dividends be distributed?

2. A Dynamic Thermoforming $1,000 corporate bond is issued, and has a stated interest rate of 4.5% with a current price of $55\frac{3}{4}$. What is the current yield? Round your answer to the nearest 0.01%.

3. Quentin Avery, a sales manager with Dynamic Thermoforming, decides to put 3% of his $72,000 salary into an international growth fund offered through the new 401(k) plan. The current net asset value is 17.94, daily percent return is −0.3%, and the year-to-date return is +4.9%. How many shares will Quentin be able to purchase each month, and what was the net asset value of the fund at the beginning of the year?

## 21.2 Paying Dividends

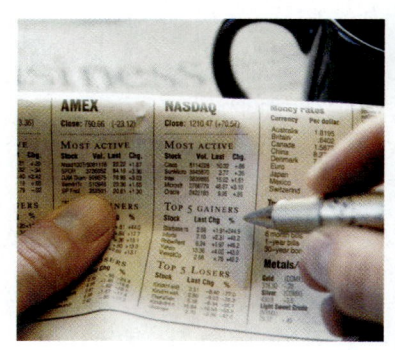

Jason is the supervisor of his company's accounting department and reports to the company's assistant controller. Jason's duties vary, but two things he is responsible for include determining how much money must be on hand to pay dividends when the Board of Directors declares them, and recommending investments when his company has extra cash to invest.

Earnings have been strong and recently the Board of Directors declared a dividend. The 500,000 shares of cumulative preferred stock are entitled to 30 cents a share each year and the 1,000,000 common shares are to be given 40 cents a share. Because earnings were less than expected for the last two years, dividends were not paid to any of the shareholders last year. Because the preferred shares are cumulative, Jason knows the preferred shareholders must be paid their contractual amount along with this year's dividend.

1. How much money should Jason plan to have available for the dividend distribution that is to occur in two weeks?

Jason knows this amount of cash will be available. In fact, in addition to this amount, he feels that the company could invest another $1,000,000 in the stock and bond market. He feels that it would be appropriate to put half in the bond market and half in the stock market and intends to make that suggestion to the assistant controller. He would also like to make some specific recommendations for the assistant controller to consider. He only suggests investments that are actively traded, do not fluctuate widely in their prices, and have moderate yields.

Jason read the investment pages of last night's newspaper. In the bond section he studied the differences between the bonds' high and low prices, their current yields, and the volume traded. In the stock section, he focused on high and low prices, 100s, and yield. He has identified the following three bonds and three stocks with their respective closing prices and PE ratios as possible candidates for his company to buy:

| Bonds | | Stocks | | |
|-------|------|--------|-------|--------|
| Carlsa | $97\frac{3}{4}$ | AGCO | 9.25 | PE = 5 |
| Flenx | 103 | Glesma | 12.5 | PE = 15 |
| Jayco | $92\frac{1}{2}$ | Layco | 14.75 | PE = 10 |

2. Based on the above information, at what price is each bond currently selling?

3. Based on the information you used for Exercise 2, how much would 100 shares of each stock cost? Ignore commission costs. What were the earnings per share over the last year for each stock?

4. Based on upcoming cash needs, the assistant controller feels that the company should invest only $750,000 and should put the full amount into stocks. If she distributes the money evenly among the three stocks, how much money will she spend on each purchase? How many shares will she be able to buy of each stock?

## 1. Introduction to the 7th Inning Business and Personnel

### Business Math Topics Covered

1. Whole Numbers
2. Fractions

### Learning Outcomes

After viewing this video, you should be able to:

1. Identify the different departments of The 7th Inning business.
2. Identify the gross revenue of The 7th Inning business.
3. Identify the fraction of revenue each department contributes to the gross revenue.
4. Calculate the value of each department based upon the fraction of gross revenue.

### Synopsis

The 7th Inning Sports Memorabilia Company is a small business located in Memphis, Tennessee, owned and operated by Charlie Cleaves. Charlie got his start in the memorabilia business collecting, trading, and selling sports cards. He also collected autographs and other historically interesting items. At some point during the 1990s Charlie realized that his hobby could become his career. He opened a small store, which he rapidly outgrew. Now, he owns his own building and his business has grown to include several departments: a sports and historical memorabilia department where he sells sports, music, political, and general interest historical memorabilia; a card and collectible supplies department where he sells a variety of sports, entertainment, and fantasy game cards, caps, buttons, pennants, and collecting supplies; a custom framing department; a trophy and engraving department; and a barbecue restaurant.

Charlie has recently hired an assistant manager, Joe, and a clerk, Sharese. Today is Joe and Sharese's first day on the job, so Charlie takes them on a tour of the business. As they move from department to department, Charlie introduces the other 7th Inning employees and gives them an overview of how much each business contributes to overall revenue.

### Worksheet and Discussion Questions

1. Download the worksheet for this video and then watch the video. Work through the calculations to figure out the dollar revenue generated by each department.
2. Why would Charlie have five different departments under one roof? How are the departments related?

### Extension Activity

1. At the very end of the video, Joe asked Charlie where they can make the most money. Even though you do not know all of the cost factors involved in each department, consider each of the following questions and try to figure out which department can generate the greatest profit.
   (a) Which department(s) involve the most money (capital) in inventory?
   (b) Which department(s) involve the highest costs for labor?
   (c) Which items or services are the most expensive and likely to generate the most money per sale?
   (d) Which department(s) pose the greatest risk of losing money?

## 2. Which Bank Account Is Best?

### Business Math Topics Covered

1. Banking
   (a) Checking Accounts
   (b) Savings Accounts

## Learning Outcomes

After viewing this video, you should be able to:

1. Understand the terminology of opening a checking account.
2. Compare different types of checking accounts.
3. Understand the terminology of opening a savings account.
4. Compare the different types of savings accounts.

## Synopsis

Sharese has realized that she can't keep her entire paycheck in cash at her apartment or carry it around with her in her purse. She has also discovered that it is costly to get her check cashed at a check-cashing shop. She has decided that she needs to open a checking account. After work on payday, Sharese takes the bus to the local branch of InSouth. She talks to a bank officer about the various checking account options. While at the bank, the bank officer also brings up the idea of opening a savings account and explains why it is beneficial to start saving early in life.

## Worksheet and Discussion Questions

1. Download the worksheet for this video and after viewing the video, utilize the worksheet to figure out which checking account and savings account might be best for Sharese.
2. Now look at your own situation. Which checking or savings account is best for your personal situation?
3. Why is it important for most people to have a relationship with a bank?
4. What are the benefits of starting to save early in your life?

## Extension Activities

1. Visit a local bank and ask for a summary of checking and savings account options. Which one is best for your situation?
2. Investigate *www.ofac.gov* for questions and answers regarding banking issues.
3. Use *www.google.com* to investigate the Patriot Act of 2003. Why is this act important to consumers?

# 3. How Many Hamburgers?

## Business Math Topics Covered

1. Decimals
2. Basic Equations
3. Percents

## Learning Outcomes

After viewing this video, you should be able to:

1. Calculate and compare order quantities based upon historical information.
2. Identify a variety of business variables involved in making purchasing decisions.

## Synopsis

While Charlie is out of the shop, a local meat vendor calls and asks to speak to the manager of Brubaker's Grill regarding an attractive deal he can offer on hamburger meat. Joe is excited to talk with the vendor. He is anxious to prove to Charlie that he can be a manager, so he arranges a meeting with the vendor to explore the offer. The deal, as proposed by the vendor, would require Brubaker's to buy a lot of hamburgers, but the price per patty sounds very attractive. Joe listens to the proposal and wonders if this offer is worth pursuing, given their historical rate of hamburger usage and the prices per patty that they are currently paying.

## Worksheet and Discussion Questions

1. Download the worksheet for this video and after viewing the video, utilize the worksheet to compare the new deal and the existing deal. What is positive about the new deal? What is negative about the new deal?
2. What factors should Joe consider, beyond the price per patty, before making a recommendation to Charlie?

# 4. How Many Baseball Cards?

## Business Math Topics Covered

1. Basic Equations
2. Percentages

## Learning Outcomes

After viewing this video, you should be able to:

1. Calculate ordering quantities based on historical data.
2. Calculate gross revenue and net revenue.
3. Calculate net profit on gross revenue.

## Synopsis

It is time for Joe to start learning about the trading card business. The 7th Inning maintains around ten million cards in-stock year round, though the number is highest early each year following the release of the new professional sports team cards. In addition to major professional sports cards, Charlie also carries cards that feature movies, military hardware, and fantasy game-related cards. The trading card industry has grown so much over the past several years that ordering cards is a complicated business that requires market savvy and hands-on experience. Charlie has decided to let Joe try to figure out what quantity they should order of two of his most popular selling sports trading cards, the *Topps* cards and the *Fleer EX* cards. He gives Joe a budget of $18,500 to spend and provides him with the basic cost, pricing, and other data he will need to arrive at a recommended purchase quantity.

## Worksheet and Discussion Questions

1. Download the worksheet for this video and after viewing the video, utilize the worksheet to work through the process of figuring out how many of each card to order, how much the inventory will cost, and what the likely net revenue and net profit will be for each card order and for the total order of both cards.
2. Why is it important to know the historical sales pattern of each brand before ordering cards for the next year?
3. Make a list of the factors that influence the business of selling trading cards.

## Extension Activity

1. Obtain a professional sports player card. Go to *www.beckett.com* to find the current estimated market value of the card. In the "Your Card" box, enter the name of the player you want to investigate and, when prompted, enter the name of the card manufacturer. Keep in mind that the values you see reflect prices that other cards in mint condition have recently sold for at auction. If there is any damage to your card whatsoever, the value of your card will likely be substantially less.

# 5. An All-Star Signing!

## Business Math Topics Covered

1. Basic Equations
2. Markup

## Learning Outcomes

After viewing this video, you should be able to:

1. Calculate selling price based on markup.
2. Calculate gross profit.
3. Calculate net profit.

## Synopsis

One of Charlie's earliest business ventures in the trading card business involved organizing local signing events for popular pro athletes. In the past he has hosted signing events by many of the big names in sports including baseball players like Yogi Berra, Ted Williams, and Hank Aaron and he even hosted prizefighter Joe Frazier. Some of the signings made a good return, while others did not cover the costs involved in hosting the signing. Charlie and The 7th Inning try to host at least one autograph session with a major sports figure each year. This year, he wants to bring Derek Jeter of the New York Yankees to Memphis for an autograph session. The going rate to bring a player of Derek's stature to a signing is $40,000 plus travel costs. For this fee, the athlete will spend around 4–6 hours at The 7th Inning and sign 1,000 items including photographs, baseballs, and reproduction jerseys. There is a bit of a hitch—the athlete usually specifies the maximum number of each item he will sign. In this case, Derek will agree to sign up to 650 photos, 400 baseballs, and 100 jerseys. Charlie wants Joe and Sharese to help him figure out how many of each item they should have Derek sign in order to make the greatest potential profit overall and how much net profit they can make on the signing over costs, if they sell all of the items.

## Worksheet and Discussion Questions

1. Download the worksheet for this video and after viewing the video, utilize the worksheet to work through the process of figuring out which combination of signed items will generate the most revenue and net profit and how much net profit they will make if they sell all items the day of the signing.
2. Why would Derek Jeter be willing to sign more photographs than baseballs or jerseys?
3. Why do you think that there can be a larger markup on the jerseys than on the photographs?
4. If Charlie sells 427 photographs, 315 baseballs, and 68 jerseys the day of the signing, figure out what his total revenue from the signing is at that time and calculate the profit.

## Extension Activity

1. To investigate the current retail price of any athlete's signature on various items, go to *www.prosportsmemorabilia.com* and type in the athlete's name in the "Search Our Products" box. If you type in Derek Jeter's name and look at posted prices for items such as signed baseballs, you will see higher prices than those discussed in the video. Why do you think that the prices offered through this online company are so much higher than Charlie's prices?

# 6. Should I Buy New Equipment Now?

## Business Math Topics Covered

1. Simple Interest
2. Margins and Profitability

## Learning Outcomes

After viewing this video, you should be able to:

1. Understand and calculate a net profit margin.
2. Calculate simple interest on a 1-year loan.
3. Calculate a simple break-even period for a capital purchase.

## Synopsis

The engraving department uses an aging rotary engraver to engrave plaques and trophies. The machine has been reliable, but does require regular maintenance and periodic replacement of parts. Charlie has just found out that this engraver will no longer be supported by the manufacturer. This means that service and parts will be hard to get in the future and if it breaks it could take up to three weeks to get a new one up and running. They keep this machine running almost 8 hours a day, every day. Every day that the engraver is down will cost around $975 in lost income. If he has to buy a new engraver, it would cost around $25,000. He can get a 1 year loan at 12% to buy a new engraver, but he worries that this is a lot of money to spend, especially since the old engraver is still working fine. He has to make a decision. Should he purchase a new engraver now or wait until the old engraver breaks before ordering a new engraver?

## Worksheet and Discussion Questions

1. Download the worksheet for this video and after viewing the video, utilize the worksheet to figure out what the total cost of the engraver will be and how much revenue will be lost if the engraver is down for 18 business days.
2. If Charlie makes a 25% net profit margin on the engraving revenue, calculate the number of days it will take to pay for the engraver if all of the net profit is applied to the purchase cost.
3. Why is it important to calculate the number of days it will take for a capital purchase to break even?
4. Besides the lost income, what other business costs would be associated with the failure of the rotary engraver?

# 7. Which Credit Card Deal Is Best?

## Business Math Topics Covered

1. Consumer Credit
2. Interest Rates
3. Calculating Interest

## Learning Outcomes

After viewing this video, you should be able to:

1. Evaluate credit card offers based upon features, interest rates, fees, and other important criteria.
2. Identify the appropriate credit card offer based upon need.
3. Understand credit terms.

## Synopsis

Sharese thinks that it is about time for her to get a credit card. She would like to buy a car in the not-too-distant future and knows that she needs to establish a credit history. She has received several offers in the mail and has downloaded offers from several card companies from card websites. As she reviews the various offers, she finds that the process of evaluating cards is more complicated than she expected.

## Worksheet and Discussion Questions

1. Download the worksheet for this video and after viewing the video, utilize the worksheet to evaluate the four credit card offers and choose a card that would be good for Sharese.
2. Which card is best for your personal situation?
3. What questions should a consumer ask before accepting a credit card?
4. What are the advantages of building a good credit history?
5. What are the disadvantages of having access to credit?

## Extension Activities

1. Review the Federal Trade Commission website discussed in the video: *http://www.ftc.gov/bcp/conline/pubs/credit/gettingcredit.pdf*
2. Credit card offers change often. Use an Internet search engine, such as *www.google.com* to find current credit card offers for young adults. Type "Student Credit Card Offers" into the search box and press the Enter key.
3. Find other websites that discuss the advantages and disadvantages of credit cards.

# 8. Should I Buy or Lease a Car?

## Business Math Topics Covered

1. Consumer Credit
2. Purchasing versus Leasing a Car

## Learning Outcomes

After viewing this video, you should be able to:

1. Understand basic leasing and buying terminology.
2. Understand the difference between leasing and buying a car.
3. Evaluate different financial purchasing options.

## Synopsis

Sharese is tired of riding the bus. She has been saving since she began working at The 7th Inning and she thinks that she has saved up enough to buy a car. After doing her homework and investigating the possibilities, she has settled on a cute, red Honda Civic. She does not have a lot of money to put down on the car and she wants her payments to be as low as possible. When she talks with the salesman about financing, she discovers that she has several financing options to consider.

## Worksheet and Discussion Questions

1. Download the worksheet for this video and after viewing the video, utilize the worksheet to analyze different financial options.
2. List the advantages and disadvantages of leasing versus buying.
3. What are your driving habits and why should they matter in the decision to lease or purchase?
4. What is the reason that many dealerships will provide a leasing option to a recent college graduate, but not to a high school graduate?

## Extension Activities

1. Pick a new car that you would like to own and that you might be able to afford. Call up a local dealership and ask them for the actual costs of buying or leasing a car in your area.
2. For the same car, go to the following two popular auto websites that collect and publish basic information about new car sticker prices, dealer costs, and average selling prices. How does dealer cost compare to the sticker price?
   (a) *http://www.edmnds.com*
   (b) *http://www.kbb.com*
3. In most cases, your car will be worth less than you paid for it the moment that you drive it off of the lot. Almost all cars' values depreciate over time, some more than others. Search on the web for information on depreciation rates for new cars. See if you can find the actual rate of depreciation for the car that you might want to buy. One good way to check this out is to figure out the used value—the trade-in and private resale values of a 2-year-old model of the car that you like—using the two websites listed above.

# 9.  Should I Invest in Elvis?

## Business Math Topics Covered

1. Compound Interest
2. Percents
3. Basic Equations
4. Future and Present Value

## Learning Outcomes

After viewing this video, you should be able to:

1. Calculate the future value of an item based upon historical and projected rates of appreciation over time.
2. Consider risk issues related to buying and selling memorabilia.

## Synopsis

One day, a man looking something like a famous entertainer from the 1970s enters The 7th Inning memorabilia department and begins examining the items in the showroom. Charlie, intrigued by the stranger's appearance, greets him and asks him if he is interested in anything in particular. The stranger is particularly interested in Elvis memorabilia. Now, Charlie is a lifelong fan of Elvis and he actually met and talked with Elvis on many occasions. He enjoys collecting, displaying, and talking about Elvis merchandise with other fans and collectors. It is amazing, but Elvis gear does appreciate at a pretty consistent rate and the supply of items is limited enough to withstand the ups and downs in the economy. There always seems to be enough money in the hands of collectors to continue to bid up items from year to year, especially any item that had a personal association with Elvis, like his clothes, jewelry, or other personal possessions. The stranger wants to know what he can expect in terms of a return on his investment, should he buy several of the items in the shop.

## Worksheet and Discussion Questions

1. Download the worksheet for this video and after viewing the video, utilize the worksheet to calculate the possible future value of selected Elvis memorabilia.
2. Keep in mind that the increase in value is not guaranteed for a variety of reasons. Make a list of the factors that could cause the value of Elvis memorabilia to drop in the future.
3. What questions should an investor ask before investing in anything?
4. Charlie indicated that since Elvis is dead, no new memorabilia can be created with his autograph. How does the idea of scarcity increase the value of an item?
5. Why would the autograph by a contemporary artist like Justin Timberlake not appreciate in value as much as an Elvis autograph over the next 10 years?

# 10. Should I Buy a House?

## Business Math Topics Covered

1. Consumer Credit
2. Home Mortgages
3. Basic Equations
4. Percents

## Learning Outcomes

After viewing this video, you should be able to:

1. Understand the basic terminology of buying a home.
2. Understand and evaluate basic loan types for purchasing a home.
3. Understand ownership and closing costs.

## Synopsis

Joe has decided that he is tired of paying rent and not building equity of his own. He thinks that he is ready to assume the responsibility of owning a home and has found what he believes is the perfect first home. Joe meets with the loan officer at his bank where the process of buying a home is started. The loan officer provides Joe with a great deal of information, leaving him excited and apprehensive at the same time.

## Worksheet and Discussion Questions

1. Download the worksheet for this video and after viewing the video, utilize the worksheet to familiarize yourself with terminology used in buying a home, and then evaluate different financing alternatives.
2. What is a credit score?
3. How do you determine your personal credit score?
4. How do you determine how much you can afford for a down payment?
5. How do you determine how much you can afford for a monthly payment?
6. Why is it important to have an idea about how long you intend to live in the house?
7. Why is closing on a house so complicated?

## Extension Activities

1. Interview a real estate agent, mortgage officer, and home owner's insurance agent to find out what is involved in buying a house or condominium in your local area.
2. Using an Internet search engine, type the words "Mortgage Rates" and the name of your city or area and state (e.g., "Mortgage Rates Atlanta Georgia"). Visit at least two of the many mortgage sites available and note the differences in the rates quoted and the terms that are given. Call one of the sites with a higher-than-average rate. Ask them why their rates are higher than the other mortgage brokers. Be sure to ask them about points and closing costs. Call the broker with the lowest rates and ask the same questions. Following the conversations, summarize what they tell you about how rates are set.
3. Why not just pick the broker with the lowest rate and finance with that broker? What do you need to know to make an informed choice?

# Stop and Check Solutions

# CHAPTER 1

## Section 1-1

### 1

1. Seven million, three hundred fifty-two thousand, four hundred ninety-six
2. Four million, twenty-three thousand, five hundred eight
3. Sixty-two billion, eight hundred five million, nine hundred twenty-seven
4. Five hundred eighty-seven billion, nine hundred twelve

### 2

1. 18,078,397,203
2. 36,017
3. $932,806
4. 52,896

### 3

1. 3,785,000
2. 6,100
3. 53,000
4. 20,000
5. 600,000 tickets
6. $57,000

## Section 1-2

### 1

1. 
| 372 | 400 | 372 |
|---|---|---|
| 583 | 600 | 583 |
| 697 | 700 | 697 |
| | 1,700 | 1,652 |

2. 
| 9,823 | 10,000 | 9,823 |
|---|---|---|
| 7,516 | 8,000 | 7,516 |
| 8,205 | 8,000 | 8,205 |
| | 26,000 | 25,544 |

3. 
| $618 | 600 | $618 |
|---|---|---|
| 736 | 700 | 736 |
| 107 | 100 | 107 |
| | $1,400 | $1,461 |

4. 
| $1,809 | 2,000 | $1,809 |
|---|---|---|
| 3,521 | 4,000 | 3,521 |
| | $6,000 | $5,330 |

5.

| What You Know | What You Are Looking For | Solution Plan |
|---|---|---|
| Projected total revenue = $1,200,000 | Total revenue | Add and compare total revenue with projected revenue. |
| Revenue from 10 largest = $789,000 | Did the company reach its projection? | |
| Revenue from others = $342,000 | | |

**Solution**

| $ 789,000 | revenue from 10 largest clients |
|---|---|
| 342,000 | revenue from other clients |
| $1,131,000 | total revenue |

**Conclusion**

The total revenue of $1,131,000 is less than $1,200,000 so the company did not reach its projection.

**6.**

| What You Know | What You Are Looking For | Solution Plan |
|---|---|---|
| Projected total revenue = $2,500,000<br>Revenue from Quarter 1 = $492,568<br>Revenue from Quarter 2 = $648,942<br>Revenue from Quarter 3 = $703,840<br>Revenue from Quarter 4 = $683,491 | Total revenue<br><br>Did the shop reach its projected revenue? | Add and compare total revenue with projected revenue. |

**Solution**

492568 + 648942 + 703840 + 683491 ⟹ 2528841    Calculator steps for the sum.

**Conclusion**

**The shop exceeded its revenue goal of $2,500,000 since $2,528,841 is more than $2,500,000.**

# 2

1.
$$\begin{array}{r} 138 \\ -\ 96 \\ \hline \end{array} \quad \begin{array}{r} 100 \\ -100 \\ \hline 0 \end{array} \quad \begin{array}{r} 138 \\ -\ 96 \\ \hline 42 \end{array}$$

2.
$$\begin{array}{r} 1,352 \\ -\ 787 \\ \hline \end{array} \quad \begin{array}{r} 1,000 \\ -\ 800 \\ \hline 200 \end{array} \quad \begin{array}{r} 1,352 \\ -\ 787 \\ \hline 565 \end{array}$$

3.
$$\begin{array}{r} \$3,807 \\ -\ 2,689 \\ \hline \end{array} \quad \begin{array}{r} \$4,000 \\ -\ 3,000 \\ \hline \$1,000 \end{array} \quad \begin{array}{r} \$3,807 \\ -\ 2,689 \\ \hline \$1,118 \end{array}$$

4.
$$\begin{array}{r} 10,523 \\ -\ 5,897 \\ \hline \end{array} \quad \begin{array}{r} 10,000 \\ -\ 6,000 \\ \hline 4,000 \end{array} \quad \begin{array}{r} 10,523 \\ -\ 5,897 \\ \hline 4,626 \end{array}$$

5.

| What You Know | What You Are Looking For | Solution Plan |
|---|---|---|
| Jet Blue sold 2,196,512 tickets Southwest sold 1,993,813 tickets | Difference in number of tickets sold by two airlines | Difference = Jet Blue tickets minus Southwest tickets |

**Solution**

$$\begin{array}{r} 2,196,512 \\ -\ 1,993,813 \\ \hline 202,699 \end{array} \quad \begin{array}{l} \text{Jet Blue tickets} \\ \text{Southwest tickets} \\ \text{difference} \end{array}$$

**Conclusion**

**Jet Blue sold 202,699 more tickets than Southwest.**

6.

| What You Know | What You Are Looking For | Solution Plan |
|---|---|---|
| Number of firms with 1 to 4 employees = 2,734,133.<br>Number of firms with 5 to 9 employees = 1,025,497. | Difference in number of employees by size of firm. | Difference = number of firms with 1 to 4 employees minus number of firms with 5 to 9 employees. |

**Solution**

2734133 − 1025497 ⟹ 1708636    Calculator steps for the difference.

**Conclusion**

**There are 1,708,636 more firms with 1 to 4 employees than there are firms with 5 to 9 employees.**

# 3

1.
$$\begin{array}{r} 317 \\ \times\ 52 \\ \hline \end{array} \quad \begin{array}{r} 300 \\ \times\ 50 \\ \hline 15,000 \end{array} \quad \begin{array}{r} 317 \\ \times\ 52 \\ \hline 634 \\ 15\ 85 \\ \hline 16,484 \end{array}$$

2.
$$\begin{array}{r} 6,723 \\ \times\ 87 \\ \hline \end{array} \quad \begin{array}{r} 7,000 \\ \times\ 90 \\ \hline 630,000 \end{array} \quad \begin{array}{r} 6,723 \\ \times\ 87 \\ \hline 47\ 061 \\ 537\ 84 \\ \hline 584,901 \end{array}$$

3.
$$\begin{array}{r} 4,600 \\ \times\ 70 \\ \hline \end{array} \quad \begin{array}{r} 5,000 \\ \times\ 70 \\ \hline 350,000 \end{array} \quad \begin{array}{r} 4,600 \\ \times\ 70 \\ \hline 322,000 \end{array}$$

4.
$$\begin{array}{r} 538,000 \\ \times\ 420 \\ \hline \end{array} \quad \begin{array}{r} 500,000 \\ \times\ 400 \\ \hline 200,000,000 \end{array} \quad \begin{array}{r} 538,000 \\ \times\ 42\ 0 \\ \hline 10\ 76\ 0\ 000 \\ 215\ 2 \\ \hline 225,96\ 0,000 \end{array}$$

**5.**

| What You Know | What You Are Looking For | Solution Plan |
|---|---|---|
| One machine produces 75 rolls per hour. There are 15 machines. | Number of rolls produced in 24 hours by 1 machine; by 15 machines. | Multiply production per hour times number of hours times number of machines. |

**Solution**

75 rolls $\times$ 24 hours = 1,800 rolls per machine
1,800 rolls $\times$ 15 machines = 27,000 rolls

**Conclusion**

**1,800 rolls can be produced by 1 machine in 24 hours. 27,000 rolls can be produced by 15 machines in 24 hours.**

**6.**

| What You Know | What You Are Looking For | Solution Plan |
|---|---|---|
| Number of coffee cups produced in a day = 48. Number of bowls produced in a day = 72. Number of coffee cups and number of bowls sold in the 22-day month. | Number of coffee cups and number of bowls that can be produced in a 22-day month and number of each item left in inventory at the end of the month. | Multiply the number of items produced in one day by the number of days of production, which is 22 days. Subtract the number of each item sold from the number produced in the month. |

**Solution**

48 $\boxed{\times}$ 22 $\Rightarrow$ 1056          Calculator steps for the product.

72 $\boxed{\times}$ 22 $\Rightarrow$ 1584

1056 $\boxed{-}$ 809 $\Rightarrow$ 247          Calculator steps for the difference.

1584 $\boxed{-}$ 1242 $\Rightarrow$ 342

**Conclusion**

**At the end of the month 247 coffee cups and 342 bowls remained in inventory.**

# 4

1.
$$\begin{array}{r} 462 \\ 6\overline{)2,772} \\ \underline{2\ 4} \\ 37 \\ \underline{36} \\ 12 \\ \underline{12} \end{array}$$

2.
$$\begin{array}{r} 281 \\ 24\overline{)6,744} \\ \underline{4\ 8} \\ 1\ 94 \\ \underline{1\ 92} \\ 24 \\ \underline{24} \end{array}$$

3.
$$\begin{array}{r} 305 \\ 47\overline{)14,335} \\ \underline{14\ 1} \\ 235 \\ \underline{235} \end{array}$$

4.
$$\begin{array}{r} 84\ R3 \\ 15\overline{)1,263} \\ \underline{1\ 20} \\ 63 \\ \underline{60} \\ 3 \end{array}$$

**5.**

| What You Know | What You Are Looking For | Solution Plan |
|---|---|---|
| The Gap purchases 5,184 pairs of jeans and divides them among 324 stores. | How many pairs are sent to each store? | Divide the number of pairs of jeans by the number of stores. |

**Solution**

$$\begin{array}{r} 16 \\ 324\overline{)5,184} \\ \underline{3\ 24} \\ 1\ 944 \\ \underline{1\ 944} \end{array}$$

**Conclusion**

**Each store should be sent 16 pairs of jeans.**

6.

| What You Know | What You Are Looking For | Solution Plan |
|---|---|---|
| Auto Zone purchases 26,560 cans of car wax in cases of 64 cans per case. | How many stores can get 1 case of the wax? | Divide the total number of cans purchased by the number of cans in each case. |

**Solution**

$$
\begin{array}{r}
415 \\
64)\overline{26{,}560} \\
\underline{25\ 6} \\
96 \\
\underline{64} \\
320 \\
\underline{320}
\end{array}
$$

**Conclusion**

**One case of 64 cans of wax can be shipped to each of 415 stores.**

# CHAPTER 2

## Section 2-1

# 1

1. $\frac{3}{7}$; the numerator is less than the denominator so the fraction is proper.

2. $\frac{4}{3}$; the numerator is greater than the denominator so the fraction is improper.

3. $\frac{3}{7}$ is a proper fraction since the numerator is smaller than the denominator.

4. $\frac{12}{5}$ is an improper fraction since the numerator is larger than the denominator.

5. $\frac{16}{16}$ is an improper fraction since the numerator is equal to the denominator.

6. $\frac{5}{9}$ is a proper fraction since the numerator is smaller than the denominator.

# 2

1.
$$
\begin{array}{r}
5\frac{5}{28} \\
28)\overline{145} \\
\underline{140} \\
5
\end{array}
$$

2.
$$
\begin{array}{r}
11 \\
12)\overline{132} \\
\underline{12} \\
12 \\
\underline{12}
\end{array}
$$

3.
$$
\begin{array}{r}
4 \\
12)\overline{48} \\
\underline{48}
\end{array}
$$

4.
$$
\begin{array}{r}
2\frac{4}{7} \\
7)\overline{18} \\
\underline{14} \\
4
\end{array}
$$

5.
$$
\begin{array}{r}
2 \\
17)\overline{34} \\
\underline{34}
\end{array}
$$

$$\frac{145}{28} = 5\frac{5}{28}$$

$$\frac{132}{12} = 11$$

$$\frac{48}{12} = 4$$

$$\frac{18}{7} = 2\frac{4}{7}$$

$$\frac{34}{17} = 2$$

# 3

1. $(4 \times 3) + 1 = 12 + 1 = 13;\ 3\frac{1}{4} = \frac{13}{4}$

2. $(3 \times 7) + 2 = 21 + 2 = 23;\ 7\frac{2}{3} = \frac{23}{3}$

3. $(8 \times 5) + 7 = 40 + 7 = 47;\ 5\frac{7}{8} = \frac{47}{8}$

4. $3 = \frac{3}{1}$

5. $2 = \frac{2}{1}$

# 4

1. $\dfrac{18 \div 6}{24 \div 6} = \dfrac{3}{4}$

2. $\dfrac{12 \div 12}{36 \div 12} = \dfrac{1}{3}$

3. $16\overline{)24}^{\ 1} \quad 8\overline{)16}^{\ 2}$
   $\phantom{16)}\dfrac{16}{8} \quad \phantom{8)}\dfrac{16}{0}$

   8 is the GCD.

   $\dfrac{16 \div 8}{24 \div 8} = \dfrac{2}{3}$

4. $39\overline{)51}^{\ 1} \quad 12\overline{)39}^{\ 3} \quad 3\overline{)12}^{\ 4}$
   $\phantom{39)}\dfrac{39}{12} \quad \phantom{12)}\dfrac{36}{3} \quad \phantom{3)}\dfrac{12}{0}$

   3 is the GCD.

   $\dfrac{39 \div 3}{51 \div 3} = \dfrac{13}{17}$

5. $12\overline{)28}^{\ 2} \quad 4\overline{)12}^{\ 3}$
   $\phantom{12)}\dfrac{24}{4} \quad \phantom{4)}\dfrac{12}{0}$

   4 is the GCD.

   $\dfrac{12 \div 4}{28 \div 4} = \dfrac{3}{7}$

6. $18\overline{)24}^{\ 1} \quad 6\overline{)18}^{\ 3}$
   $\phantom{18)}\dfrac{18}{6} \quad \phantom{6)}\dfrac{18}{0}$

   6 is the GCD.

   $\dfrac{18 \div 6}{24 \div 6} = \dfrac{3}{4}$

# 5

1. $36 \div 12 = 3$;

   $\dfrac{7}{12} = \dfrac{7 \times 3}{12 \times 3} = \dfrac{21}{36}$

2. $32 \div 4 = 8$;

   $\dfrac{3}{4} = \dfrac{3 \times 8}{4 \times 8} = \dfrac{24}{32}$

3. $18 \div 2 = 9$;

   $\dfrac{1}{2} = \dfrac{1 \times 9}{2 \times 9} = \dfrac{9}{18}$

4. $25 \div 5 = 5$;

   $\dfrac{3}{5} = \dfrac{3 \times 5}{5 \times 5} = \dfrac{15}{25}$

5. $36 \div 12 = 3$;

   $\dfrac{5 \times 3}{12 \times 3} = \dfrac{15}{36}$

6. $24 \div 8 = 3$;

   $\dfrac{7}{8} = \dfrac{7 \times 3}{8 \times 3} = \dfrac{21}{24}$

# Section 2-2

## 1

1. $\dfrac{3}{4}$
   $\dfrac{1}{4}$
   $\dfrac{1}{4}$
   $\dfrac{5}{4} = 1\dfrac{1}{4}$

2. $\dfrac{3}{8}$
   $\dfrac{7}{8}$
   $\dfrac{1}{8}$
   $\dfrac{11}{8} = 1\dfrac{3}{8}$

3. $\dfrac{1}{5}$
   $\dfrac{2}{5}$
   $\dfrac{2}{5}$
   $\dfrac{5}{5} = 1$

4. $\dfrac{5}{8}$
   $\dfrac{3}{8}$
   $\dfrac{1}{8}$
   $\dfrac{9}{8} = 1\dfrac{1}{8}$

5. $\dfrac{5}{12}$
   $\dfrac{7}{12}$
   $\dfrac{11}{12}$
   $\dfrac{23}{12} = 1\dfrac{11}{12}$

## 2

1. $2\overline{)6\quad 12}$
   $2\overline{)3\quad 6}$
   $3\overline{)3\quad 3}$
   $\phantom{3)}1\quad 1$
   LCD =
   $2 \times 2 \times 3 = 12$

2. $2\overline{)24\quad 48}$
   $2\overline{)12\quad 24}$
   $2\overline{)6\quad 12}$
   $2\overline{)3\quad 6}$
   $3\overline{)3\quad 3}$
   $\phantom{3)}1\quad 1$
   LCD =
   $2 \times 2 \times 2 \times 2 \times 3 = 48$

3. $2\overline{)2\quad 8}$
   $2\overline{)1\quad 4}$
   $2\overline{)1\quad 2}$
   $\phantom{2)}1\quad 1$
   LCD =
   $2 \times 2 \times 2 = 8$

4. $7\overline{)11\quad 7}$
   $11\overline{)11\quad 1}$
   $\phantom{11)}1\quad 1$
   LCD $= 7 \times 11 = 77$

5. $2\overline{)42\quad 30\quad 35}$
   $3\overline{)21\quad 15\quad 35}$
   $5\overline{)7\quad 5\quad 35}$
   $7\overline{)7\quad 1\quad 7}$
   $\phantom{7)}1\quad 1\quad 1$
   LCD =
   $2 \times 3 \times 5 \times 7 = 210$

# 3

1. $4\frac{3}{8}$

   $5\frac{5}{8}$

   $3\frac{7}{8}$

   $12\frac{15}{8} = 12 + \frac{8}{8} + \frac{7}{8} = 13\frac{7}{8}$

2. $\frac{5}{12} = \frac{5}{12}$

   $\frac{3}{4} = \frac{9}{12}$

   $\frac{2}{3} = \frac{8}{12}$

   $\frac{22}{12} = 1\frac{10}{12} = 1\frac{5}{6}$

3. $4\frac{3}{5} = 4\frac{18}{30}$

   $5\frac{7}{10} = 5\frac{21}{30}$

   $3\frac{4}{15} = 3\frac{8}{30}$

   $12\frac{47}{30} = 12 + \frac{30}{30} + \frac{17}{30} = 13\frac{17}{30}$

4. $23\frac{5}{14} = 23\frac{25}{70}$

   $37\frac{9}{10} = 37\frac{63}{70}$

   $60\frac{88}{70} = 60 + \frac{70}{70} + \frac{18}{70}$

   $\quad = 61\frac{18}{70} = 61\frac{9}{35}$

5. $25\frac{3}{8} = 25\frac{3}{8}$

   $+\ 6\frac{3}{4} = +\ 6\frac{6}{8}$

   $\quad = 31\frac{9}{8}$

   $\quad = 32\frac{1}{8}$

   **$32\frac{1}{8}$ yards of fabric are needed.**

6. $32\frac{5}{8} = \quad 32\frac{5}{8}$

   $+\ 8\frac{3}{4} = +\ 8\frac{6}{8}$

   $\quad = 40\frac{11}{8}$

   $\quad = 41\frac{3}{8}$

   **$41\frac{3}{8}$ yards of fabric were used.**

# 4

1. $\frac{7}{8}$

   $-\frac{3}{8}$

   $\frac{4}{8} = \frac{1}{2}$

2. $\frac{5}{8} = \frac{5 \times 3}{8 \times 3} = \frac{15}{24}$

   $-\frac{1}{12} = -\frac{1 \times 2}{12 \times 2} = -\frac{2}{24}$

   $\frac{13}{24}$

3. $12\frac{5}{8} = 11 + \frac{8}{8} + \frac{5}{8} = 11\frac{13}{8}$

   $-\ 3\frac{7}{8} \qquad\qquad\qquad = -\ 3\frac{7}{8}$

   $\qquad\qquad\qquad\qquad 8\frac{6}{8} = 8\frac{3}{4}$

4. $15\frac{11}{12} = 15\frac{11 \times 3}{12 \times 3} = 15\frac{33}{36}$

   $-7\frac{5}{18} = -7\frac{5 \times 2}{18 \times 2} = -7\frac{10}{36}$

   $\qquad\qquad\qquad\qquad\qquad 8\frac{23}{36}$

   2)12  18
   2) 6  9
   3) 3  9
   3) 1  3
   $\quad$ 1  1

   LCD $= 2 \times 2 \times 3 \times 3 = 36$

5. $32 \quad = 31\frac{12}{12}$

   $-14\frac{5}{12} = -14\frac{5}{12}$

   $\qquad\qquad 17\frac{7}{12}$

6. $27\frac{4}{15} = 27\frac{4 \times 4}{15 \times 4} = 27\frac{16}{60} = 26\frac{60}{60} + \frac{16}{60} = 26\frac{76}{60}$

   $-14\frac{7}{12} = -14\frac{7 \times 5}{12 \times 5} = -14\frac{35}{60} = -14\frac{35}{60} \qquad = -14\frac{35}{60}$

   $\qquad\qquad\qquad\qquad\qquad\qquad\qquad\qquad\qquad\qquad\qquad 12\frac{41}{60}$

   2)15  12
   2)15  6
   3)15  3
   5) 5  1
   $\quad$ 1  1

   LCD $= 2 \times 2 \times 3 \times 5 = 60$

7.

| What You Know | What You Are Looking For | Solution Plan |
|---|---|---|
| Amount of land originally owned = 100 acres<br><br>Acreage of 3 additional purchases = $12\frac{3}{4} + 23\frac{2}{3} + 5\frac{1}{8}$<br><br>Acreage that was sold during the year = $65\frac{2}{3}$ | Acres that Marcus still owns | Acreage originally owned plus acreage purchased minus acreage sold equals acreage still owned |

## Solution

$$100 = 100$$

$$12\frac{3}{4} = 12\frac{18}{24}$$

$$23\frac{2}{3} = 23\frac{16}{24}$$

$$5\frac{1}{8} = 5\frac{3}{24}$$

$$140\frac{37}{24} =$$

$$141\frac{13}{24} \quad \text{Acres owned before sale.}$$

LCD = 24

$$141\frac{13}{24} = 141\frac{13}{24} = 140\frac{37}{24}$$

$$-65\frac{2}{3} = -65\frac{16}{24} = -65\frac{16}{24}$$

$$= 75\frac{21}{24}$$

$$= 75\frac{7}{8} \quad \text{Acres owned after sale.}$$

## Conclusion

There are $75\frac{7}{8}$ acres remaining after the purchases and sale.

8.

| What You Know | What You Are Looking For | Solution Plan |
|---|---|---|
| Amount of frame material = 60 inches. Frame material needed = $10\frac{3}{4} + 10\frac{3}{4} + 12\frac{5}{8} + 12\frac{5}{8}$ | Length of frame material remaining. | Total frame length minus amount used equals frame material remaining. |

### Solution

$$10\frac{3}{4} + 10\frac{3}{4} + 12\frac{5}{8} + 12\frac{5}{8} =$$

$$10\frac{6}{8} + 10\frac{6}{8} + 12\frac{5}{8} + 12\frac{5}{8} =$$

$$44\frac{22}{8} = 46\frac{3}{4} \text{ inches used}$$

$$60 - 46\frac{3}{4} = 59\frac{4}{4} - 46\frac{3}{4} = 13\frac{1}{4}$$

### Conclusion

There are $13\frac{1}{4}$ inches of frame material remaining.

# Section 2-3

# 1

1. $\dfrac{3}{7} \times \dfrac{5}{8} = \dfrac{15}{56}$

2. $\dfrac{\overset{1}{\cancel{4}}}{\underset{3}{\cancel{9}}} \times \dfrac{\overset{1}{\cancel{3}}}{\underset{2}{\cancel{8}}} = \dfrac{1}{6}$

3. $3\dfrac{1}{4} \times \dfrac{5}{13} = \dfrac{\overset{1}{\cancel{13}}}{4} \times \dfrac{5}{\underset{1}{\cancel{13}}} = \dfrac{5}{4} = 1\dfrac{1}{4}$

4. $1\dfrac{1}{9} \times 3 = \dfrac{10}{\underset{3}{\cancel{9}}} \times \dfrac{\overset{1}{\cancel{3}}}{1} = \dfrac{10}{3} = 3\dfrac{1}{3}$

5. $2\dfrac{2}{5} \times \dfrac{15}{21} = \dfrac{\overset{4}{\cancel{12}}}{\underset{1}{\cancel{5}}} \times \dfrac{\overset{3}{\cancel{15}}}{\underset{7}{\cancel{21}}} = \dfrac{12}{7} = 1\dfrac{5}{7}$

6. $2\dfrac{3}{8} \times 16 = \dfrac{19}{8} \times \dfrac{\overset{2}{\cancel{16}}}{1} = 38 \text{ feet}$

7. $2\dfrac{1}{3} \times 14 = \dfrac{7}{3} \times \dfrac{14}{1} = \dfrac{98}{3} = 32\dfrac{2}{3} \text{ feet}$

# 2

1. $\dfrac{5}{12}$; reciprocal $\dfrac{12}{5}$

2. $32 = \dfrac{32}{1}$; reciprocal $\dfrac{1}{32}$

3. $7\dfrac{1}{8} = \dfrac{57}{8}$; reciprocal $\dfrac{8}{57}$

4. $\dfrac{7}{8} \div \dfrac{3}{4} = \dfrac{7}{\underset{2}{\cancel{8}}} \times \dfrac{\overset{1}{\cancel{4}}}{3} = \dfrac{7}{6} = 1\dfrac{1}{6}$

5. $2\dfrac{2}{5} \div 2\dfrac{1}{10} = \dfrac{12}{5} \div \dfrac{21}{10} = \dfrac{\overset{4}{\cancel{12}}}{\underset{1}{\cancel{5}}} \times \dfrac{\overset{2}{\cancel{10}}}{\underset{7}{\cancel{21}}} = \dfrac{8}{7} = 1\dfrac{1}{7}$

6. $3\dfrac{3}{8} \div 9 = \dfrac{27}{8} \div \dfrac{9}{1} = \dfrac{\overset{3}{\cancel{27}}}{8} \cdot \dfrac{1}{\underset{1}{\cancel{9}}} = \dfrac{3}{8}$

7. $72 \div \dfrac{3}{4} = \dfrac{\overset{24}{\cancel{72}}}{1} \times \dfrac{4}{\underset{1}{\cancel{3}}} = 96 \text{ pieces of plywood}$

# CHAPTER 3

## Section 3-1

### 1

1. Five and eight-tenths
2. Seven hundred twenty-one thousandths
3. Thirty-eight dollars and fifteen cents
4. 434.76
5. 0.3548
6. $4.87

### 2

1. 14.342   3 is in the tenths place and 4 is less than 5. Round down by leaving 3 as it is and dropping the 4 and 2.

   14.3

2. 48.7965   9 is in the hundredths place and 6 is 5 or more. Round up by adding 1 to 9.

   48.80

3. $768.57   Round to the ones place. 5 is in the tenths place and is 5 or more. Round up by adding 1 to 8.

   $769

4. $54.834   Round to the hundredths place. 4 is in the thousandths place and is less than 5. Round down.

   $54.83

## Section 3-2

### 1

1. 
$$
\begin{array}{r}
67. \\
4.38 \\
+\ 0.291 \\
\hline
71.671
\end{array}
$$

2. 
$$
\begin{array}{r}
57.5 \\
13.4 \\
+\ 5.238 \\
\hline
76.138
\end{array}
$$

3. 
$$
\begin{array}{r}
17.53 \\
-\ 12.17 \\
\hline
5.36
\end{array}
$$

4. 
$$
\begin{array}{r}
542.830 \\
-\ 219.593 \\
\hline
323.237
\end{array}
$$

5. 
$$
\begin{array}{r}
\$\ 20.00 \\
-\ 18.97 \\
\hline
\$\ \ 1.03
\end{array}
$$

6. $120.01 − $95.79 = $24.22

### 2

1. 
$$
\begin{array}{r}
4.35 \\
\times\ 0.27 \\
\hline
30\,45 \\
87\,0 \\
\hline
1.17\,45
\end{array}
$$

2. 
$$
\begin{array}{r}
7.03 \\
\times\ 0.0\,35 \\
\hline
3515 \\
2109 \\
\hline
0.24605
\end{array}
$$

3. 
$$
\begin{array}{r}
5.32 \\
\times\ 15 \\
\hline
26\,60 \\
53\,2 \\
\hline
79.8\cancel{0}
\end{array}
$$

4. 
$$
\begin{array}{r}
\$8.31 \\
\times\ \ \ 4 \\
\hline
\$33.24
\end{array}
$$

5. 
$$
\begin{array}{r}
\$27.42 \\
\times\ \ \ \ 500 \\
\hline
\$13,710.00
\end{array}
$$

The dinner costs $13,710.

6. $94.05 × 1,000 = $94,050

### 3

1. 
$$
\begin{array}{r}
6.72 \\
15\overline{)100.80} \\
90 \\
\hline
10\,8 \\
10\,5 \\
\hline
30 \\
30 \\
\hline
\end{array}
$$

2. 
$$
\begin{array}{r}
17.06 \\
21\overline{)358.26} \\
21 \\
\hline
148 \\
147 \\
\hline
1\,2 \\
0 \\
\hline
1\,26 \\
1\,26 \\
\hline
\end{array}
$$

3. 
$$
\begin{array}{r}
3.41 \approx 3.4 \\
3.8\overline{)12.970} \\
114 \\
\hline
15\,7 \\
15\,2 \\
\hline
50 \\
38 \\
\hline
12 \\
\end{array}
$$

4. 
$$
\begin{array}{r}
1\,7.469 \approx 17.47 \\
5.9\overline{)103.0\,700} \\
59 \\
\hline
44\,0 \\
41\,3 \\
\hline
2\,7\,7 \\
2\,3\,6 \\
\hline
4\,10 \\
3\,54 \\
\hline
560 \\
531 \\
\hline
29 \\
\end{array}
$$

5. 
$$
\begin{array}{r}
37 \\
19.36\overline{)716.32} \\
580\,8 \\
\hline
135\,52 \\
135\,52 \\
\hline
\end{array}
$$

Gwen worked 37 hours.

6. $648,000,000 ÷ 1,000,000 = $648

## Section 3-3

### 1

1. $\dfrac{7}{10}$

2. $\dfrac{32}{100} = \dfrac{8}{25}$

3. $2\dfrac{87}{1,000}$

4. $23\dfrac{41}{100}$

5. $\dfrac{7}{100}$

### 2

1. $\dfrac{3}{5} = 0.6$  $5\overline{)3.0}^{\,0.6}$

2. $\dfrac{7}{8} = 0.88$

$$\begin{array}{r} 0.875 \approx 0.88 \\ 8\overline{)7.000} \\ \underline{6\,4}\phantom{00} \\ 60\phantom{0} \\ \underline{56}\phantom{0} \\ 40 \\ \underline{40} \end{array}$$

3. $\dfrac{5}{12} = 0.42$

$$\begin{array}{r} 0.416 \approx 0.42 \\ 12\overline{)5.000} \\ \underline{4\,8}\phantom{00} \\ 20\phantom{0} \\ \underline{12}\phantom{0} \\ 80 \\ \underline{72} \\ 8 \end{array}$$

4. $7\dfrac{4}{5} = 7.8$

$$\begin{array}{r} 0.8 \\ 5\overline{)4.0} \end{array}$$

5. $8\dfrac{4}{7} = 8.57$

$$\begin{array}{r} 0.571 \approx 0.57 \\ 7\overline{)4.000} \\ \underline{3\,5}\phantom{00} \\ 50\phantom{0} \\ \underline{49}\phantom{0} \\ 10 \\ \underline{7} \\ 3 \end{array}$$

## CHAPTER 4

## Section 4-1

### 1

1.

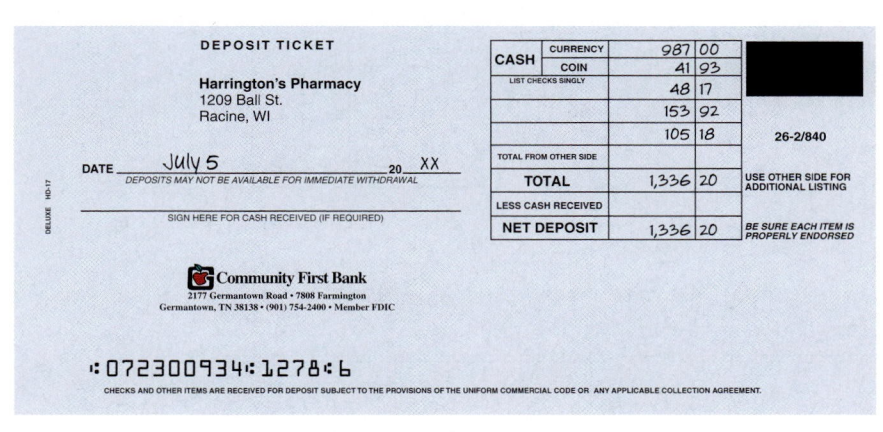

**2.**

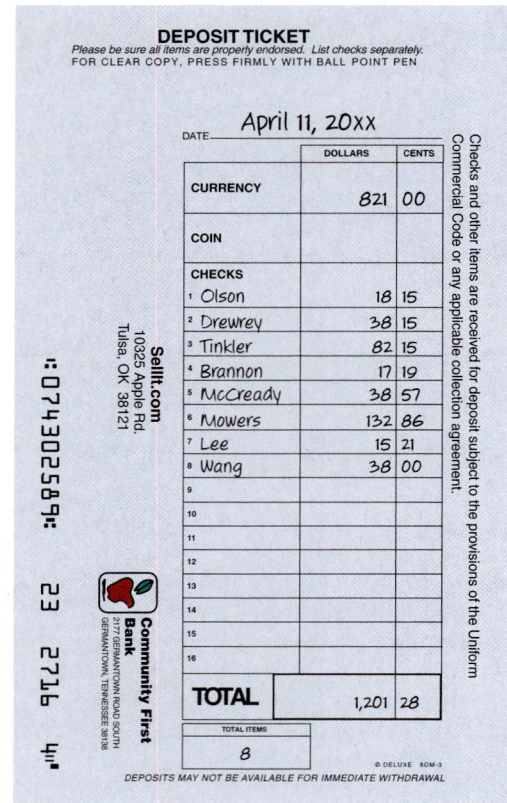

**DEPOSIT TICKET**
Please be sure all items are properly endorsed. List checks separately.
FOR CLEAR COPY, PRESS FIRMLY WITH BALL POINT PEN

DATE _April 11, 20xx_

|  | DOLLARS | CENTS |
|---|---|---|
| CURRENCY | 821 | 00 |
| COIN |  |  |
| CHECKS |  |  |
| 1 Olson | 18 | 15 |
| 2 Drewrey | 38 | 15 |
| 3 Tinkler | 82 | 15 |
| 4 Brannon | 17 | 19 |
| 5 McCready | 38 | 57 |
| 6 Mowers | 132 | 86 |
| 7 Lee | 15 | 21 |
| 8 Wang | 38 | 00 |
| 9 |  |  |
| 10 |  |  |
| 11 |  |  |
| 12 |  |  |
| 13 |  |  |
| 14 |  |  |
| 15 |  |  |
| 16 |  |  |
| **TOTAL** | 1,201 | 28 |
| TOTAL ITEMS | 8 | |

Checks and other items are received for deposit subject to the provisions of the Uniform Commercial Code or any applicable collection agreement.

**SellIt.com**
10325 Apple Rd.
Tulsa, OK 38121

**Community First Bank**
2177 GERMANTOWN ROAD SOUTH
GERMANTOWN, TENNESSEE 38138

|: 0743025B9|:  23  2716  4||"

© DELUXE 8DM-3
DEPOSITS MAY NOT BE AVAILABLE FOR IMMEDIATE WITHDRAWAL

**3.**

| ABC Plumbing | | 4359 |
|---|---|---|
| 408 Jefferson | | |
| Rexburg, ID 00000 | October 18 20 XX | 87-278/840 |

PAY TO THE ORDER OF   Frances Johnson   $ 583.17

Five hundred eighty-three and 17/100   DOLLARS

**First National Bank**
400 Washington
Rexburg, ID 00000

MEMO   tool chest   _Albert Adkins_

|: 044503279|:

**4.**

| Max's Motorcycle Shop | | 5887 |
|---|---|---|
| 1280 State Street | | |
| Tulsa, OK 00000 | August 18 20 XX | 87-278/840 |

PAY TO THE ORDER OF   Harley Davidson, Inc.   $ 2,872.15

Two thousand eight hundred seventy-two and 15/100   DOLLARS

**Tulsa State Bank**
295 Adams Street
Tulsa, OK 00000

MEMO   motorcycle parts   _Max Murphy_

|: 584325911|:

**5.** Answers will vary. Bank statements are available online. Bills can be paid online. Accounts are accessible 24 hours a day. Bank statements can be reconciled online. Bank records can be stored electronically.

# 2

**1.** a. $152.87
   b. $2,896.15
   c. $3,543.28

**2.**

| 4359 | Date _Oct 18_ 20 _XX_ |
|---|---|
| Amount _583.17_ | |
| To _Frances Johnson_ | |
| For _tool chest_ | |

| Balance Forward | 5,902 | 08 |
|---|---|---|
| Deposits | | |
| Total | 5,902 | 08 |
| Amount This Check | 583 | 17 |
| Balance | 5,318 | 91 |

**3.**

**RECORD ALL TRANSACTIONS THAT AFFECT YOUR ACCOUNT**

| NUMBER | DATE | DESCRIPTION OF TRANSACTION | DEBIT (−) | √T | FEE (IF ANY) (−) | CREDIT (+) | BALANCE | |
|---|---|---|---|---|---|---|---|---|
| | | | | | | | 6,007 | 82 |
| 5887 | 8/18 | Harley Davidson, Inc. | 2,872 15 | | | | −2,872 | 15 |
| | | motorcycle parts | | | | | 3,135 | 67 |
| Debit | 8/20 | Remmie Raynor | 498 31 | | | | −498 | 31 |
| | | pool services | | | | | 2,637 | 36 |

**4.**

| | | RECORD ALL TRANSACTIONS THAT AFFECT YOUR ACCOUNT | | | | | | |
|---|---|---|---|---|---|---|---|---|
| NUMBER | DATE | DESCRIPTION OF TRANSACTION | DEBIT (−) | √ T | FEE (IF ANY) (−) | CREDIT (+) | BALANCE | |
| | | | | | | | 5,108 | 31 |
| 4358 | 10/6 | Quesha Blunt | 49 80 | | | | −49 | 80 |
| | | Cleaning Service | | | | | 5,058 | 51 |
| Dep | 10/6 | Deposit | | | | 843 57 | +843 | 57 |
| | | travel reimb. | | | | | 5,902 | 08 |
| 4359 | 10/8 | Frances Johnson | 583 17 | | | | −583 | 17 |
| | | **tool chest** | | | | | **5,318** | **91** |
| ATM | 10/8 | Cash | 250 00 | | | | −250 | 00 |
| | | | | | | | **5,068** | **91** |
| | | | | | | | | |

# Section 4-2

# 1

1. four
2. $5.00
3. $8,218.00
4. five
5. $700.81
6. $3,485.73
7. $490.00
8. 6/20
9. Answers will vary. Yes, provided the amount requested does not exceed the limit set by the Kroger company nor the limit set by Lindy's bank.

**10.**

| | | RECORD ALL TRANSACTIONS THAT AFFECT YOUR ACCOUNT | | | | | | |
|---|---|---|---|---|---|---|---|---|
| NUMBER | DATE | DESCRIPTION OF TRANSACTION | DEBIT (−) | √ T | FEE (IF ANY) (−) | CREDIT (+) | BALANCE | |
| | | | | | | | 700 | 81 |
| 8213 | 5/28 | Lands End | 647 93 | √ | | | −647 | 93 |
| | | | | | | | 52 | 88 |
| Deposit | 6/1 | Receipts | | √ | | 1,830 00 | +1,830 | 00 |
| | | | | | | | 1,882 | 88 |
| 8214 | 6/1 | Collier Management Co. | 490 00 | √ | | | −490 | 00 |
| | | | | | | | 1,392 | 88 |
| 8215 | 6/3 | Jinkins Wholesale | 728 32 | √ | | | −728 | 32 |
| | | | | | | | 664 | 56 |
| Deposit | 6/5 | Receipts | | √ | | 2583 00 | +2,583 | 00 |
| | | | | | | | 3,247 | 56 |
| 8216 | 6/5 | Minneapolis Utility Co. | 257 13 | | | | −257 | 13 |
| | | | | | | | 2,990 | 43 |
| 8217 | 6/10 | State of MN | 416 83 | √ | | | −416 | 83 |
| | | | | | | | 2,573 | 60 |
| Deposit | 6/15 | Receipts | | √ | | 3,800 00 | +3,800 | 00 |
| | | | | | | | 6,373 | 60 |
| 8218 | 6/15 | Tracie Burke salary | 2,000 00 | | | | −2,000 | 00 |
| | | | | | | | 4,373 | 60 |
| 8219 | 6/20 | Brown's Wholesale | 3,150 00 | √ | | | −3,150 | 00 |
| | | | | | | | 1,223 | 60 |
| Deposit | 7/2 | Receipts | | | | 1,720 00 | +1,720 | 00 |
| | | | | | | | 2,943 | 60 |
| | 6/30 | Interest Earned | | √ | | 5 00 | +5 | 00 |
| | | | | | | | 2,948 | 60 |
| | 6/30 | Statement Reconciled | | | | | | |

| $ 3,485.73 | BALANCE AS SHOWN ON BANK STATEMENT | | BALANCE AS SHOWN IN YOUR REGISTER | $ 2,943.60 |
|---|---|---|---|---|
| +1,720.00 | TOTAL OF OUTSTANDING DEPOSITS | | SUBTRACT AMOUNT OF SERVICE CHARGE | 0 |
| 5,205.73 | NEW TOTAL | | NEW TOTAL | 2,943.60 |
| −2,257.13 | SUBTRACT TOTAL OF OUTSTANDING CHECKS | | ADJUSTMENTS IF ANY   Interest | + 5.00 |
| $2,948.60 | YOUR ADJUSTED STATEMENT BALANCE | SHOULD EQUAL | YOUR ADJUSTED REGISTER BALANCE | $2,948.60 |

| Outstanding Deposits (Credits) | |
|---|---|
| Date | Amount |
| 7/2 | $ 1,720.00 |
| | |
| | |
| | |
| | |
| | |
| Total | $ 1,720.00 |

| Outstanding Checks (Debits) | | |
|---|---|---|
| Check Number | Date | Amount |
| 8216 | 6/5 | $ 257.13 |
| 8218 | 6/20 | 2,000.00 |
| | | |
| | | |
| | | |
| | | |
| Total | | $ 2,257.13 |

# CHAPTER 5

## Section 5-1

## 1

1. $3A = 24$
$\dfrac{3A}{3} = \dfrac{24}{3}$
$A = 8$

2. $5N = 30$
$\dfrac{5N}{5} = \dfrac{30}{5}$
$N = 6$

3. $8 = \dfrac{B}{6}$
$(6)8 = \dfrac{B}{6}(6)$
$48 = B$
$B = 48$

4. $\dfrac{M}{5} = 7$
$5\left(\dfrac{M}{5}\right) = 7(5)$
$M = 35$

5. $\dfrac{K}{2} = 3$
$(2)\dfrac{K}{2} = 3(2)$
$K = 6$

6. $7 = \dfrac{A}{3}$
$(3)7 = \dfrac{A}{3}(3)$
$21 = A$
or
$A = 21$

## 2

1. $A + 12 = 20$
$\underline{\quad -12 \quad -12}$
$A \quad = \quad 8$

2. $A + 5 = 28$
$\underline{\quad -5 \quad -5}$
$A \quad = \quad 23$

3. $N - 7 = 10$
$\underline{\quad +7 \quad +7}$
$N \quad = \quad 17$

4. $N - 5 = 11$
$\underline{\quad +5 \quad +5}$
$N \quad = \quad 16$

5. $15 = A + 3$
$\underline{-3 \quad -3}$
$12 = A$
or
$A = 12$

6. $28 = M - 5$
$\underline{+5 \quad +5}$
$33 = M$
or
$M = 33$

## 3

1. $3N + 4 = 16$
$\underline{\quad -4 \quad -4}$
$3N \quad = 12$
$\dfrac{3N}{3} = \dfrac{12}{3}$
$N = 4$

2. $5N - 7 = 13$
$\underline{\quad +7 \quad +7}$
$5N \quad = 20$
$\dfrac{5N}{5} = \dfrac{20}{5}$
$N = 4$

3. $\dfrac{B}{8} - 2 = 2$
$\underline{\quad +2 \quad +2}$
$\dfrac{B}{8} \quad = 4$
$(8)\dfrac{B}{8} = 4(8)$
$B = 32$

4. $\dfrac{M}{3} + 2 = 5$
$\underline{\quad -2 \quad -2}$
$\dfrac{M}{3} \quad = 3$
$(3)\dfrac{M}{3} = 3(3)$
$M = 9$

5. $\dfrac{S}{6} - 3 = 4$
$\underline{\quad +3 \quad +3}$
$\dfrac{S}{6} \quad = 7$
$(6)\dfrac{S}{6} = 7(6)$
$S = 42$

6. $12 = \dfrac{A}{5} - 8$
$\underline{+8 = \quad +8}$
$20 = \dfrac{A}{5}$
$(5)20 = \dfrac{A}{5}(5)$
$100 = A$
or
$A = 100$

# 4

1. $B + 3B - 5 = 19$
$4B - 5 = 19$
$\underline{\phantom{4B} +5 \quad +5}$
$4B \phantom{-5} = 24$
$\dfrac{4B}{4} = \dfrac{24}{4}$
$B = 6$

2. $4B - 7 = 13$
$\underline{\phantom{4B} +7 \quad +7}$
$4B \phantom{-7} = 20$
$\dfrac{4B}{4} = \dfrac{20}{4}$
$B = 5$

3. $7 + 3B + 2B = 17$
$7 + 5B = 17$
$\underline{-7 \qquad -7}$
$5B = 10$
$\dfrac{5B}{5} = \dfrac{10}{5}$
$B = 2$

4. $5A - 3 + 2A = 18$
$7A - 3 = 18$
$\underline{\phantom{7A} +3 \quad +3}$
$7A \phantom{-3} = 21$
$\dfrac{7A}{7} = \dfrac{21}{7}$
$A = 3$

5. $3C - C = 16$
$2C = 16$
$\dfrac{2C}{2} = \dfrac{16}{2}$
$C = 8$

6. $12 = 8C - 5C$
$12 = 3C$
$\dfrac{12}{3} = \dfrac{3C}{3}$
$4 = C$
or
$C = 4$

# 5

1. $2(N + 4) = 26$
$2N + 2(4) = 26$
$2N + 8 = 26$
$\underline{\phantom{2N} -8 \quad -8}$
$2N \phantom{+8} = 18$
$\dfrac{2N}{2} = \dfrac{18}{2}$
$N = 9$

2. $3(N - 30) = 45$
$3N - 90 = 45$
$\underline{\phantom{3N} +90 \quad +90}$
$3N \phantom{-90} = 135$
$\dfrac{3N}{3} = \dfrac{135}{3}$
$N = 45$

3. $4(R - 3) = 8$
$4R - 12 = 8$
$\underline{\phantom{4R} +12 \quad +12}$
$4R \phantom{-12} = 20$
$\dfrac{4R}{4} = \dfrac{20}{4}$
$R = 5$

4. $7(2R - 3) = 21$
$14R - 21 = 21$
$\underline{\phantom{14R} +21 \quad +21}$
$14R \phantom{-21} = 42$
$\dfrac{14R}{14} = \dfrac{42}{14}$
$R = 3$

5. $5(3R + 2) = 40$
$15R + 10 = 40$
$\underline{\phantom{15R} -10 \quad -10}$
$15R \phantom{+10} = 30$
$\dfrac{15R}{15} = \dfrac{30}{15}$
$R = 2$

6. $30 = 6(2A + 3)$
$30 = 12A + 18$
$\underline{-18 = \phantom{12A} -18}$
$12 = 12A$
$\dfrac{12}{12} = \dfrac{12A}{12}$
$1 = A$
or
$A = 1$

# 6

1. $\dfrac{5}{7} \overset{?}{=} \dfrac{20}{28}$
$5(28) = 7(20)$
$140 = 140$
$\dfrac{5}{7}$ is proportional to $\dfrac{20}{28}$.

$\dfrac{3}{4} \overset{?}{=} \dfrac{20}{28}$
$3(28) \overset{?}{=} 4(20)$
$84 \overset{?}{=} 80$
$\dfrac{3}{4}$ is not proportional to $\dfrac{20}{28}$.

2. $\dfrac{1}{2} \overset{?}{=} \dfrac{12}{18}$
$1(18) \overset{?}{=} 2(12)$
$18 \overset{?}{=} 24$
$\dfrac{1}{2}$ is not proportional to $\dfrac{12}{18}$.

$\dfrac{2}{3} \overset{?}{=} \dfrac{12}{18}$
$2(18) = 3(12)$
$36 = 36$
$\dfrac{2}{3}$ is proportional to $\dfrac{12}{18}$.

3. $\dfrac{3}{4} = \dfrac{N}{8}$
$4N = 3(8)$
$4N = 24$
$\left(\dfrac{1}{4}\right)4N = 24\left(\dfrac{1}{4}\right)$
$N = \dfrac{24}{4} = 6$

4. $\dfrac{5}{N} = \dfrac{4}{12}$
$4N = 5(12)$
$4N = 60$
$\dfrac{4N}{4} = \dfrac{60}{4}$
$N = 15$

5. $\dfrac{N}{4} = \dfrac{9}{6}$
$6N = 4(9)$
$6N = 36$
$\dfrac{6N}{6} = \dfrac{36}{6}$
$N = 6$

6. $\dfrac{5}{12} = \dfrac{15}{N}$
$5N = 12(15)$
$5N = 180$
$\dfrac{5N}{5} = \dfrac{180}{5}$
$N = 36$

# 1

### 1.

| What You Know | What You Are Looking For | Solution Plan |
|---|---|---|
| $\frac{1}{6}$ of earnings spent on groceries <br> $117.50 spent on groceries each week | The amount of weekly earnings $= N$ | One sixth times weekly earnings $=$ amount spent on groceries |

**Solution**

$$\frac{1}{6}N = \$117.50$$

$$(6)\frac{N}{6} = 117.50(6)$$

$$N = \$705$$

**Conclusion**

**Carrie earns $705 weekly.**

### 2.

| What You Know | What You Are Looking For | Solution Plan |
|---|---|---|
| Total pounds of produce $= 2,500$ <br> potatoes $= 800$ pounds <br> broccoli $= 150$ pounds <br> tomatoes $= 390$ pounds | Number of pounds of apples $= N$ | Number of pounds of potatoes $+$ pounds of broccoli $+$ pounds of tomatoes $+$ pounds of apples $= 2,500$ |

**Solution**

$$
\begin{aligned}
800 + 150 + 390 + N &= 2,500 \\
1,340 + N &= 2,500 \\
-1,340 \qquad\quad &\;\; -1,340 \\
N &= 1,160
\end{aligned}
$$

**Conclusion**

**Marcus purchased 1,160 pounds of apples.**

### 3.

| What You Know | What You Are Looking For | Solution Plan |
|---|---|---|
| Total rooms $= 873$ <br> 8 times as many nonsmoking as there are smoking rooms. | Number of smoking rooms $= N$ <br><br> Number of nonsmoking rooms $= 8N$ | The number of smoking rooms plus the number of nonsmoking rooms $= 873$. |

**Solution**

$$
\begin{aligned}
N + 8N &= 873 \\
9N &= 873 \\
\frac{9N}{9} &= \frac{873}{9} \\
N &= 97
\end{aligned}
$$

**Conclusion**

**The hotel has 97 rooms designated as smoking rooms.**

**4.**

| What You Know | What You Are Looking For | Solution Plan |
|---|---|---|
| 480 notebooks cost $1,656. | The number of notebooks that can be purchased for $2,242.50 = N$ | Pair 1: 480 notebooks; $1,656<br><br>Pair 2: $N$ notebooks; $2,242.50 |

**Solution**

$$\frac{480}{\$1,656} = \frac{N}{\$2,242.50}$$

Pair 1    Pair 2

$$1,656N = 480(2,242.50)$$
$$1,656N = 1,076,400$$
$$\frac{1,656N}{1,656} = \frac{1,076,400}{1,656}$$
$$N = 650$$

**Conclusion**

**650 notebooks can be purchased for $2,242.50.**

# Section 5-3

## 1

**1.** $S = C + M$
$S = 317 + 250$
$S = \$567$

**2.** $S = C + M$
$629 = 463 + M$
$\underline{-463 \quad -463}$
$166 = M$
$M = \$166$

**3.** $P = RH$
$P = 19.26(40)$
$P = \$770.40$

**4.** $P = RH$
$612 = R(40)$
$\dfrac{612}{40} = \dfrac{R(40)}{40}$
$15.30 = R$
$R = \$15.30$

## 2

**1.** $S = C + M$
$\underline{-C \quad -C}$
$S - C = M$
$M = S - C$

**2.** $M = S - N$
$\underline{+N \quad +N}$
$M + N = S$
$S = M + N$

**3.** $U = \dfrac{P}{N}$
$(N)U = \dfrac{P}{N}(N)$
$NU = P$
$\dfrac{NU}{U} = \dfrac{P}{U}$
$N = \dfrac{P}{U}$

**4.** $U = \dfrac{V}{P}$
$U(P) = \dfrac{V}{P}(P)$
$UP = V$
$V = UP$

# CHAPTER 6

## Section 6-1

## 1

**1.** $0.82 = 0.82(100\%) = 0\underset{\frown}{82}.\% = 82\%$

**2.** $3.45 = 3.45(100\%) = 345\underset{\frown}{.}\% = 345\%$

**3.** $0.0007 = 0.0007(100\%) = 000\underset{\frown}{.}07\% = 0.07\%$

**4.** $5 = 5(100\%) = 500\%$

**5.** $\dfrac{43}{100} = \dfrac{43}{\underset{1}{\cancel{100}}}\left(\dfrac{\overset{1}{\cancel{100}\%}}{1}\right) = 43\%$

**6.** $\dfrac{3}{10} = \dfrac{3}{\underset{1}{\cancel{10}}}\left(\dfrac{\overset{10}{\cancel{100}\%}}{1}\right) = 30\%$

**7.** $8\dfrac{1}{4} = 8\dfrac{1}{4}(100\%) = \dfrac{33}{\underset{1}{\cancel{4}}}\left(\dfrac{\overset{25}{\cancel{100}\%}}{1}\right) = 825\%$

**8.** $\dfrac{1}{6} = \dfrac{1}{\underset{3}{\cancel{6}}}\left(\dfrac{\overset{50}{\cancel{100}\%}}{1}\right) = \dfrac{50}{3}\% = 16\dfrac{2}{3}\%$

## 2

1. $52\% = 52\% \div 100\% = 0.52 = 0.52$

2. $38.5\% = 38.5\% \div 100\% = 0.385 = 0.385$

3. $143\% = 143\% \div 100\% = 1.43 = 1.43$

4. $0.72\% = 0.72\% \div 100\% = 0.0072 = 0.0072$

5. $72\% = 72\% \div 100\% = \dfrac{\overset{18}{\cancel{72\%}}}{1}\left(\dfrac{1}{\underset{25}{\cancel{100\%}}}\right) = \dfrac{18}{25}$

6. $\dfrac{1}{8}\% = \dfrac{1}{8}\% \div 100\% = \dfrac{1}{8}\%\left(\dfrac{1}{100\%}\right) = \dfrac{1}{800}$

7. $325\% = 325\% \div 100\% = \dfrac{325\%}{1}\left(\dfrac{1}{100\%}\right) = \dfrac{325}{100} = 3\dfrac{1}{4}$

8. $16\dfrac{2}{3}\% = 16\dfrac{2}{3}\% \div 100\% = \dfrac{\overset{1}{\cancel{50\%}}}{3}\left(\dfrac{1}{\underset{2}{\cancel{100\%}}}\right) = \dfrac{1}{6}$

## Section 6-2

### 1

1. Base (of), 85; rate (%), 42%; portion (part), not known

2. Base (of), not know; rate (%), 15%; portion (part) 50

3. Base (of), 80; rate (%), not known; portion (part), 20

4. Base (of), not known; rate (%), 20%; portion (part), 17

5. Base (of), 72; rate (%), 125%; portion (part), not known

6. Base (of), 160; rate (%), not known; portion (part), 32

### 2

1. $P = RB$      $R = 15\% = 0.15$
   $P = 0.15(200)$      $B = 200$
   $P = 30$

2. $B = \dfrac{P}{R}$      $P = 120$
   $B = \dfrac{120}{0.25}$      $R = 25\% = 0.25$
   $B = 480$

3. $R = \dfrac{P}{B}$      $P = 150$
   $R = \dfrac{150}{750}$      $B = 750$
   $R = 0.2$
   $R = 20\%$

4. $P = RB$      $R = 12\dfrac{1}{2}\% = 12.5\% = 0.125$
   $P = 0.125(64)$      $B = 64$
   $P = 8$

5.

| What You Know | What You Are Looking For | Solution Plan |
|---|---|---|
| Total students or the base: 40 % of students who passed: 75% | Number of students who passed | $P = RB$, where $R = 0.75$ and $B = 40$ |

| Solution |
|---|
| $P = RB$ $P = 0.75(40)$ $P = 30$ |

| Conclusion |
|---|
| **30 students passed the test.** |

6. $R = \dfrac{P}{B}$
   $R = \dfrac{150}{500}$
   $R = 0.30$
   $R = 0.30(100\%)$
   $R = 30\%$

**1**

1.

| What You Know | What You Are Looking For | Solution Plan |
|---|---|---|
| New Lexus = $53,444<br>Previous model = $51,989 | Amount of increase | Amount of increase =<br>new price − previous price |

**Solution**

$53,444 − 51,989

53,444
−51,989
$ 1,455

**Conclusion**

**The Lexus increased by $1,455.**

2.

| What You Know | What You Are Looking For | Solution Plan |
|---|---|---|
| Ending price of $73.57<br>Beginning price $81.99 | Amount of decrease | Amount of decrease =<br>beginning price − ending price |

**Solution**

$81.99 − $73.57 = $8.42

**Conclusion**

**The stock price fell $8.42**

3.

| What You Know | What You Are Looking For | Solution Plan |
|---|---|---|
| Current earnings: $62,870<br>4.3% raise | Amount of her raise | Amount of raise = current<br>earnings × percent raise |

**Solution**

$62,870 × 4.3% = $62,870(0.043) = $2,703.41

**Conclusion**

**Her raise was $2,703.41.**

4.

| What You Know | What You Are Looking For | Solution Plan |
|---|---|---|
| Original cost of stock = $145 million | Amount of decrease of stock | $P = RB$ |
| Percent of decrease = 16% | | Decrease = percent of<br>decrease × original cost |

**Solution**

Decrease = 16%($145) = 0.16($145)
= $23.2 million or $23,200,000

**Conclusion**

**The stock decreased $23.2 million, or $23,200,000.**

5.

| What You Know | What You Are Looking For | Solution Plan |
|---|---|---|
| Zack's original weight = 230 pounds<br><br>Zack's percent of weight loss = 12% | The number of pounds Zack lost | $P = RB$<br>Decrease = percent of<br>weight loss × original weight |

### Solution

Decrease = 0.12(230)
Decrease = 27.6

### Conclusion

**Zack lost 27.6 pounds**

6.

| What You Know | What You Are Looking For | Solution Plan |
|---|---|---|
| Number of active nurses = 2,249,000<br><br>Percent of nurses added by 2020 = 20.3% | Number of new nurses to be added by 2020 | $P = RB$<br>Increase = percent of nurses needed $\times$ original number of nurses |

### Solution

Increase = 20.3%(2,249,000)
= 0.203(2,249,000)
= 456,547

### Conclusion

**The number of additional nurses needed in 2020 is 456,547.**

## 2

1. 100% + 4.3% = 104.3%
$62,870(1.043) = $65,573.41

2. 100% − 16% = 84%
$145 million (0.84) = $121.8 million, or $121,800,000

3. 100% − 12% = 88%
230(0.88) = 202.4 pounds

4. 100% + 250% = 350%
$9,500(3.5) = $33,250

5. 100% + 51% = 151%
$24.25(1.51) = $36.62

6. 100% + 20.3% = 120.3%
2,249,000(1.203) = 2,705,547

## 3

1.

| What You Know | What You Are Looking For | Solution Plan |
|---|---|---|
| Third quarter sales (original amount) = $23,583,000<br><br>Fourth quarter sales (new amount) = $38,792,000 | Percent of increase | Amount of increase = new amount − original amount<br><br>Percent of increase = $\dfrac{\text{amount of increase}}{\text{original amount}}$ |

### Solution

Amount of increase = $38,792,000 − $23,583,000
= $15,209,000

Percent of increase = $\dfrac{\$15,209,000}{\$23,583,000}$
= 0.644913709
= 64.5% (rounded)

### Conclusion

**The percent of increase in sales is 64.5%.**

2.

| What You Know | What You Are Looking For | Solution Plan |
|---|---|---|
| Fall semester spending = $9,524 (original amount)<br><br>Spring semester spending = $8,756 (original amount) | Percent of decrease in spending | Amount of decrease = original amount − new amount<br><br>Percent of decrease = $\dfrac{\text{amount of decrease}}{\text{original amount}}$ |

Amount of decrease $= \$9{,}524 - \$8{,}756 = \$768$

$$\text{Percent of decrease} = \frac{\$768}{\$9{,}524}$$
$$= 0.08063838723$$
$$= 8\% \text{ (rounded)}$$

### Conclusion

**Stephen's spending decreased 8%.**

**3.**

| What You Know | What You Are Looking For | Solution Plan |
|---|---|---|
| Sale (reduced) price = $148,500<br><br>Percent decrease = 10% | Original price | Percent representing sale price = 100% − percent decrease<br><br>$B = \dfrac{P}{R}$<br><br>Original price = $\dfrac{\text{sale price}}{\text{percent representing sale price}}$ |

### Solution

Percent representing sale price $= 100\% - 10\% = 90\%$

$$\text{Original price} = \frac{\$148{,}500}{0.9}$$

Original price $= \$165{,}000$

### Conclusion

**The house was originally priced at $165,000.**

**4.**

| What You Know | What You Are Looking For | Solution Plan |
|---|---|---|
| Amount DVD is reduced = $6.25<br><br>Percent DVD is reduced = 25% | Original price of DVD<br>Discounted price of DVD | $B = \dfrac{P}{R}$; Original price $= \dfrac{\text{amount of reduction}}{\text{percent of reduction}}$<br><br>Discounted price = original price − amount of reduction |

### Solution

$$\text{Original price} = \frac{\$6.25}{0.25}$$
$$= \$25$$
$$\text{Discounted price} = \$25 - \$6.25$$
$$= \$18.75$$

### Conclusion

**The DVD originally cost $25 and was reduced to sell for $18.75.**

**5.**

| What You Know | What You Are Looking For | Solution Plan |
|---|---|---|
| Used price (reduced price) = $14,799<br><br>Percent of reduction = 48% | "New" price (original price) | Percent representing the used or reduced price = 100% − percent of reduction<br><br>"New" price (original price) $= \dfrac{\text{used price}}{\text{percent representing used price}}$ |

### Solution

Percent representing the used or reduced price $= 100\% - 48\% = 52\%$

$$\text{"New" price} = \frac{\$14{,}799}{0.52} = \$28{,}459.61538$$
$$= \$28{,}460 \text{ rounded}$$

### Conclusion

**The "new" price is $28,460.**

6.

| What You Know | What You Are Looking For | Solution Plan |
|---|---|---|
| Average ticket price for 2006 = \$62.38 | Percent of increase in ticket price | Increase in ticket price = 2006 ticket price − 2005 ticket price |
| Average ticket price for 2005 = \$58.95 | | Percent increase in ticket price = $\dfrac{\text{Amount of increase}}{\text{Original amount}}$ |

**Solution**

Increase = \$62.38 − \$58.95
= \$3.43

Percent of increase = $\dfrac{\$3.43}{\$58.95}$      $3.43 \div 58.95 = \Rightarrow .0581849025$

Percent of increase = 0.058(100%)     rounded

Percent of increase = 5.8%

**Conclusion**

**The average NFL ticket price increased by 5.8%.**

# CHAPTER 7

## Section 7-1

# 1

1. $\dfrac{\$37{,}500 + \$32{,}000 + \$28{,}800 + \$35{,}750 + \$29{,}500 + \$47{,}300}{6} = \dfrac{\$210{,}850}{6} = \$35{,}142$

2. $\dfrac{2{,}400 + 2{,}100 + 1{,}800 + 2{,}800 + 3{,}450}{5} = \dfrac{12{,}550}{5} = 2{,}510 \text{ hours}$

3. $\dfrac{2 + 15 + 7 + 3 + 1 + 3 + 5 + 2 + 4 + 1 + 2 + 6 + 4 + 2}{14} = \dfrac{57}{14} = 4.07 \text{ or 4 days}$

4. $\dfrac{12 + 7 + 5 + 2 + 1 + 8 + 0 + 3 + 1 + 2 + 7 + 5 + 30 + 5 + 2}{15} = \dfrac{90}{15} = 6 \text{ CDs per months}$

5. (\$9,633,736,000 + \$10,237,247,000 + \$10,411,450,000 + \$11,433,495,000 + \$13,500,126,000 + \$13,326,051,000 + \$15,350,591,000 + \$17,595,484,000 + \$21,314,933,000 + \$23,627,320,000) ÷ 10 = \$14,643,043,300

# 2

1. Arrange in order by size: \$28,800; \$29,500; \$32,000; \$35,750; \$37,500; \$47,300. Since the number of scores is even, average the two middle scores.

 Median = $\dfrac{\$32{,}000 + \$35{,}750}{2} = \dfrac{\$67{,}750}{2} = \$33{,}875$

2. Arrange in order by size: 1,800; 2,100; 2,400; 2,800; 3,450. Since the number of scores is odd, select the middle score.

 Median = 2,400 hours

3. Arrange in order by size: 1 day, 1 day, 2 days, 2 days, 2 days, 2 days, 3 days, 3 days, 4 days, 4 days, 5 days, 6 days, 7 days, 15 days. The number of scores is even so average the middle 2.

 Median = $\dfrac{3 \text{ days} + 3 \text{ days}}{2} = \dfrac{6 \text{ days}}{2} = 3 \text{ days}$

4. Arrange in order from smallest to largest: 0, 1, 1, 2, 2, 2, 3, 5, 5, 5, 7, 7, 8, 12, 30.

 Median = middle scores = 5 CDs per month

5. The data are shown in order from smallest to largest. Average the 5th and 6th scores.

 Median = $\dfrac{\$13{,}500{,}126{,}000 + \$13{,}326{,}051{,}000}{2} = \$13{,}413{,}088{,}500$

# 3

1. Arrange scores from smallest to largest: 0, 2, 6, 7, 9, 12, 17, 17, 18, 18, 19, 21, 23, 23, 32, 32, 32, 32, 32, 32, 32, 32, 38, 48, 48, 48, 48, 56, 62, 62, 66, 73, 74, 83, 86, 92. The mode is 32 since it is listed 8 times.

2. Arrange scores from smallest to largest: 0, 0, 0, 0, 0, 2.9, 4, 4, 4, 4, 4, 4, 4, 4.225, 4.5, 4.5, 4.5, 4.75, 5, 5, 5, 5, 5, 5, 5, 5, 5, 5, 5, 5, 5.125, 5.3, 5.5, 5.6, 6, 6, 6, 6, 6, 6, 6, 6, 6.25, 6.25, 6.5, 6.5, 6.5, 7, 7, 7, 7.25. The mode is 5% since 11 states have a rate of 5%.

3. Arrange scores from smallest to largest: 42, 48, 76, 79, 83, 86, 92, 97, 98, 100. There is no mode since no score is reported more than once.

4. Arrange the scores from smallest to largest: 0, 2, 7, 8, 11, 11, 12, 22. The mode is 11.

5. Arrange the scores from smallest to largest: 148, 155, 158, 158, 160, 161, 162, 165, 170, 170, 172, 173. The modes are 158 and 170. Each mode is listed twice.

# 4

1.

| Class Intervals | Tally | Class Frequency |
|---|---|---|
| 0–19 | 𝍷𝍷𝍷𝍷 𝍷𝍷𝍷𝍷 𝍷 | 11 |
| 20–39 | 𝍷𝍷𝍷𝍷 𝍷𝍷𝍷𝍷 𝍷𝍷 | 12 |
| 40–59 | 𝍷𝍷𝍷𝍷 | 5 |
| 60–79 | 𝍷𝍷𝍷𝍷 | 5 |
| 80–99 | 𝍷𝍷𝍷 | 3 |
| | | 36 |

2. $5 + 5 + 3 = 13$ staff have more than 13 days vacation.

3. $12 + 11 = 23$ staff have fewer than 40 days vacation.

4. $\dfrac{3}{36}(100\%) = 8.3\%$

5. $\dfrac{(12 + 5)}{36}(100\%) = \dfrac{17}{36}(100\%) = 47.2\%$

6.

| Class interval | Class frequency | Calculations | Relative frequency |
|---|---|---|---|
| 0–19 | 11 | $\dfrac{11}{36}(100\%) = \dfrac{1100\%}{36} = 30.6\%$ | 30.6% |
| 20–39 | 12 | $\dfrac{12}{36}(100\%) = \dfrac{1200\%}{36} = 33.3\%$ | 33.3% |
| 40–59 | 5 | $\dfrac{5}{36}(100\%) = \dfrac{500\%}{36} = 13.9\%$ | 13.9% |
| 60–79 | 5 | $\dfrac{5}{36}(100\%) = \dfrac{500\%}{36} = 13.9\%$ | 13.9% |
| 80–99 | 3 | $\dfrac{3}{36}(100\%) = \dfrac{300\%}{36} = 8.3\%$ | 8.3% |
| Total | 36 | | 100% |

# 5

1. Find the midpoint of each class interval:

$$\frac{0 + 19}{2} = \frac{19}{2} = 9.5 \qquad \frac{20 + 39}{2} = \frac{59}{2} = 29.5 \qquad \frac{40 + 59}{2} = \frac{99}{2} = 49.5$$

$$\frac{60 + 79}{2} = \frac{139}{2} = 69.5 \qquad \frac{80 + 99}{2} = \frac{179}{2} = 89.5$$

| Class interval | Class frequency | Midpoint | Product of midpoint and frequency |
|---|---|---|---|
| 0–19 | 11 | 9.5 | 104.5 |
| 20–39 | 12 | 29.5 | 354 |
| 40–59 | 5 | 49.5 | 247.5 |
| 60–79 | 5 | 69.5 | 247.5 |
| 80–99 | 3 | 89.5 | 268.5 |
| Total | 36 | | 1,322 |

$$\text{Mean of grouped data} = \frac{1,322}{36} = 36.7$$

2. 
$$\frac{60 + 64}{2} = \frac{124}{2} = 62 \qquad \frac{65 + 69}{2} = \frac{134}{2} = 67 \qquad \frac{70 + 74}{2} = \frac{144}{2} = 72$$

$$\frac{75 + 79}{2} = \frac{154}{2} = 77 \qquad \frac{80 + 84}{2} = \frac{164}{2} = 82 \qquad \frac{85 + 89}{2} = \frac{174}{2} = 87$$

| Class interval | Class frequency | Midpoint | Product of midpoint and frequency |
|---|---|---|---|
| 60–64 | 6 | 62 | 372 |
| 65–69 | 8 | 67 | 536 |
| 70–74 | 12 | 72 | 864 |
| 75–79 | 22 | 77 | 1,694 |
| 80–84 | 18 | 82 | 1,476 |
| 85–89 | 9 | 87 | 783 |
| Total | 75 | | 5,725 |

Mean of grouped data $= \dfrac{5,725}{75} = 76.33333333$ or 76.33 rounded

3. 
$$\frac{0 + 19}{2} = \frac{19}{2} = 9.5 \qquad \frac{20 + 39}{2} = \frac{59}{2} = 29.5 \qquad \frac{40 + 59}{2} = \frac{99}{2} = 49.5$$

$$\frac{60 + 79}{2} = \frac{139}{2} = 69.5 \qquad \frac{80 + 99}{2} = \frac{179}{2} = 89.5$$

| Class interval | Class frequency | Midpoint | Product of midpoint and frequency |
|---|---|---|---|
| 0–4 | 3 | 2 | 6 |
| 5–9 | 7 | 7 | 49 |
| 10–14 | 4 | 12 | 48 |
| 15–19 | 2 | 17 | 34 |
| Total | 16 | | 137 |

Mean of grouped data $= \dfrac{137}{16} = 8.5625$ or 8.56

## Section 7-2

### 1

1.
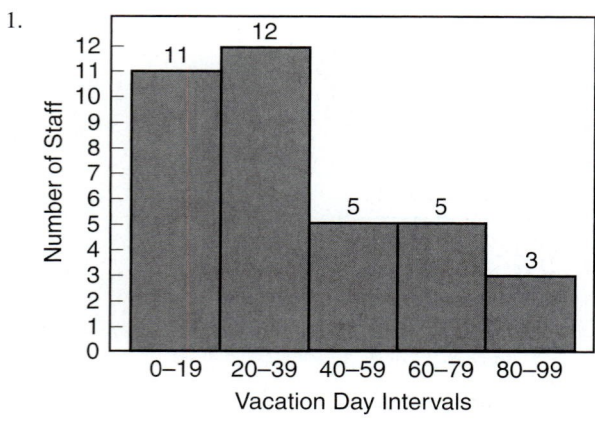

2. 20–39 interval

3. 5 students

4. $5 + 15 + 15 = 35$ students

5. $\dfrac{35}{50}(100\%) = 0.7(100\%) = 70\%$

# 2

1.

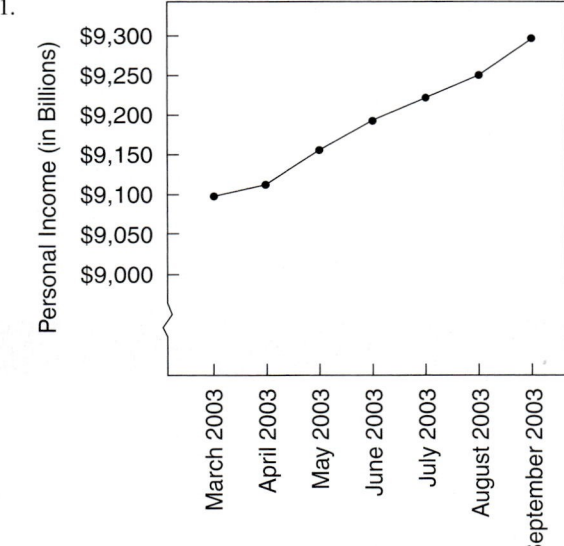

Personal Income for U.S. Workers

2. Increasing
3. September 2003
4. Fluctuating
5. $\dfrac{100 + 250 + 150 + 200 + 200 + 300}{6} = \dfrac{1,200}{6} = 200$ CDs

# 3

1. $0.35(360°) = 126°$
$0.32(360°) = 115.2°$
$0.05(360°) = 18°$
$0.04(360°) = 14.4°$
$0.04(360°) = 14.4°$
$0.2(360°) = 72°$

Marvel Comics 35%
DC Comics 32%
All others 20%
Image Comics 5%
Dark Horse Comics 4%
Dreamweave Productions 4%

2. $35\% + 32\% + 5\% = 72\%$
3. $\$80,000,000(0.35) = \$28,000,000$
4. $\$80,000,000(0.05) = \$4,000,000$

# Section 7-3

# 1

1. $\$47,300 - \$28,800 = \$18,500$
2. $3,450 - 1,800 = 1,650$ hours
3. $15 - 1 = 14$ days
4. $30 - 0 = 30$ CDs
5. $\$23,627,320,000 - \$9,633,736,000 = \$13,993,584,000$

# 2

1. Mean $= \dfrac{72 + 75 + 68 + 73 + 69}{5} = \dfrac{357}{5} = 71.4$

| Value | Mean | Deviation from the Mean |
|---|---|---|
| 72 | 71.4 | 0.6 |
| 75 | 71.4 | 3.6 |
| 68 | 71.4 | −3.4 |
| 73 | 71.4 | 1.6 |
| 69 | 71.4 | −2.4 |

2. $0.6 + 3.6 + 1.6 = 5.8$
$(-3.4) + (-2.4) = -5.8$
$5.8 + (-5.8) = 0$

3.

| Deviation from the Mean | Square of Deviation |
|---|---|
| 0.6 | 0.36 |
| 3.6 | 12.96 |
| −3.4 | 11.56 |
| 1.6 | 2.56 |
| −2.4 | 5.76 |

$0.36 + 12.96 + 11.56 + 2.56 + 5.76 = 33.2$

4. $\dfrac{33.2}{5 - 1} = \dfrac{33.2}{4} = 8.3$

5. $\sqrt{8.3} = 2.880972058$ or 2.88 (rounded)

6.

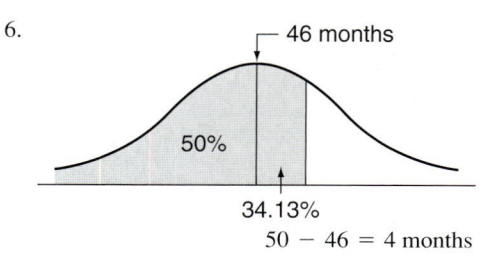

46 months

50%

34.13%

$50 - 46 = 4$ months

$$\frac{4 \text{ months}}{4 \text{ months per standard deviation}} = 1 \text{ standard deviation above the mean}$$

$50\% + 34.13\% = 84.13\%$

$0.8413(100) = 84.13$ batteries or 84 batteries

# CHAPTER 8

## Section 8-1

### 1

1. a. Trade discount $= 12\%(\$89,765) = 0.12(\$89,765)$
$= \$10,771.80$

 b. Net price $= \$89,765 - \$10,771.80$
   Net price $= \$78,993.20$

3. Trade discount $= 8\%(\$425) = 0.08(\$425) = \$34$
  Net price $= \$425 - \$34 = \$391$

5. Trade discount $= 24\%(\$21) = 0.24(\$21) = \$5.04$
  Net price $= \$21 - \$5.04 = \$15.96$

2. Trade discount $= 32\%(\$124) = 0.32(\$124)$
$= \$39.68$

 Net price $= \$124 - \$39.68 = \$84.32$

4. Trade discount $= 18\%(\$395) = 0.18(\$395) = \$71.10$
  Net price $= \$395 - \$71.10 = \$323.90$

6. Trade discount $= 15\%(\$20,588.24)$
$= 0.15(\$20,588.24)$
$= \$3,088.24$

 Net price $= \$20,588.24 - \$3,088.24$
$= \$17,500.00$

### 2

1. Net percent $= 100\% - 12\% = 88\%$
  Net price $= 88\%(\$70)$
$= 0.88(\$70)$
$= \$61.60$

3. Net percent $= 100\% - 18\% = 82\%$
  Net price $= 82\%(\$1,299)$
$= 0.82(\$1,299)$
$= \$1,065.18$

2. Net percent $= 100\% - 15\% = 85\%$
  Net price $= 85\%(\$3,200)$
$= 0.85(\$3,200)$
$= \$2,720$

4. Total list price $= 100(\$3.99) + 40(\$1.89) + 20(\$3.99)$
$= \$399 + \$75.60 + \$79.80$
$= \$554.40$

 Net percent $= 100\% - 22\% = 78\%$
  Net price $= 78\%(\$554.40)$
$= 0.78(\$554.40)$
$= \$432.43$

## Section 8-2

### 1

1. Discount complements: $100\% - 10\% = 90\% = 0.9$
$100\% - 5\% = 95\% = 0.95$

 Net decimal equivalent $= 0.9(0.95)$
$= 0.855$

 Net price $= 0.855(\$4,800) = \$4,104$

3. Discount complements: $100\% - 15\% = 85\% = 0.85$
$100\% - 10\% = 90\% = 0.9$

 Net decimal equivalent $= 0.85(0.9) = 0.765$

 Net price $= 0.765(\$600) = \$459$

2. Discount complements: $100\% - 12\% = 88\% = 0.88$
$100\% - 6\% = 94\% = 0.94$

 Net decimal equivalent $= 0.88(0.94) = 0.8272$

 Net price $= 0.8272(\$535) = \$442.55$

4. Discount complements: $100\% - 10\% = 90\% = 0.9$
$100\% - 6\% = 94\% = 0.94$
$100\% - 5\% = 95\% = 0.95$

 Net decimal equivalent $= 0.9(0.94)(0.95) = 0.8037$

 Net price $= 0.8037(\$219) = \$176.01$

5. *First manufacturer:*

Discount complements: $100\% - 10\% = 90\% = 0.9$
$\phantom{\text{Discount complements: }}100\% - \phantom{0}6\% = 94\% = 0.94$
$\phantom{\text{Discount complements: }}100\% - \phantom{0}4\% = 96\% = 0.96$

Net decimal equivalent $= 0.9(0.94)(0.96) = 0.81216$

Net price $= 0.81216(\$448) = \$363.85$

*Second manufacturer:*

Discount complements: $100\% - 15\% = 85\% = 0.85$
$\phantom{\text{Discount complements: }}100\% - 10\% = 90\% = 0.9$
$\phantom{\text{Discount complements: }}100\% - 10\% = 90\% = 0.9$

Net decimal equivalent $= 0.85(0.9)(0.9) = 0.6885$

Net price $= 0.6885(\$550) = \$378.68$

The first manufacturer has the lower price (better deal).

6. *First manufacturer:*

Discount complements: $100\% - 5\% = 95\% = 0.95$
$\phantom{\text{Discount complements: }}100\% - 10\% = 90\% = 0.9$
$\phantom{\text{Discount complements: }}100\% - 10\% = 90\% = 0.9$

Net decimal equivalent $= 0.95(0.9)(0.9) = 0.7695$

Net price $= 0.7695(\$695)$
$\phantom{\text{Net price }} = \$534.80$

The second manufacturer has the lower net price (better deal).

*Second manufacturer:*

Discount complements: $100\% - \phantom{0}6\% = 94\% = 0.94$
$\phantom{\text{Discount complements: }}100\% - 10\% = 90\% = 0.9$
$\phantom{\text{Discount complements: }}100\% - 12\% = 88\% = 0.88$

Net decimal equivalent $= 0.94(0.9)(0.88) = 0.74448$

Net price $= 0.74448(\$705)$
$\phantom{\text{Net price }} = \$524.86$

# 2

1. Complements of discounts: $100\% - 12\% = 88\% = 0.88$
$\phantom{\text{Complements of discounts: }}100\% - 10\% = 90\% = 0.9$
$\phantom{\text{Complements of discounts: }}100\% - \phantom{0}5\% = 95\% = 0.95$

Net decimal equivalent $= 0.88(0.9)(0.95) = 0.7524$

Single discount equivalent $= 1 - 0.7524 = 0.2476$

Trade discount $= 0.2476(\$504) = \$124.79$

2. Complements of discounts: $100\% - 10\% = 90\% = 0.9$
$\phantom{\text{Complements of discounts: }}100\% - \phantom{0}5\% = 95\% = 0.95$

Net decimal equivalent $= 0.9(0.95) = 0.855$

Single discount equivalent $= 1 - 0.855 = 0.145$

Trade discount $= 0.145(\$317) = \$45.97$

3. Complements of discounts: $100\% - 10\% = 90\% = 0.9$
$\phantom{\text{Complements of discounts: }}100\% - \phantom{0}5\% = 95\% = 0.95$
$\phantom{\text{Complements of discounts: }}100\% - \phantom{0}3\% = 97\% = 0.97$

Net decimal equivalent $= 0.9(0.95)(0.97) = 0.82935$

Single discount equivalent $= 1 - 0.82935 = 0.17065$

Trade discount $= 0.17065(\$24) = \$4.10$

4. Complements of discounts: $100\% - 12\% = 88\% = 0.88$
$\phantom{\text{Complements of discounts: }}100\% - \phantom{0}8\% = 92\% = 0.92$
$\phantom{\text{Complements of discounts: }}100\% - \phantom{0}6\% = 94\% = 0.94$

Net decimal equivalent $= 0.88(0.92)(0.94) = 0.761024$

Single discount equivalent $= 1 - 0.761024 = 0.238976$

Trade discount $= 0.238976(\$74) = \$17.68$

5. Complements of discounts: $100\% - \phantom{0}8\% = 92\% = 0.92$
$\phantom{\text{Complements of discounts: }}100\% - \phantom{0}6\% = 94\% = 0.94$
$\phantom{\text{Complements of discounts: }}100\% - \phantom{0}5\% = 95\% = 0.95$

Net decimal equivalent $= 0.92(0.94)(0.95) = 0.82156$

Single discount equivalent $= 1 - 0.82156 = 0.17844$

Trade discount $= 0.17844(\$289.95) = \$51.74$

6. Answers will vary. The single discount equivalent, when multiplied by the list price, gives the discount amount directly and would normally be the preferred method.

## Section 8-3

# 1

1. Latest day to pay and get discount: March 15 + 15 days = March 30.

Cash discount $= 0.02(\$985) = \$19.70$

Net amount $= \$985 - \$19.70 = \$965.30$

2. Cash discount $= 0.01(\$3,848.96)$
$\phantom{\text{Cash discount }} = \$38.49$

Net amount $= \$3,848.96 - \$38.49$
$\phantom{\text{Net amount }} = \$3,810.47$

3. August has 31 days.

$$\begin{array}{r} \text{August} + 20 \\ + 15 \text{ days} \\ \hline \text{"August 35"} \\ -31 \\ \hline \text{September 4} \end{array}$$

The invoice must be paid by September 4 to get the discount.

4. a. 3% discount; $0.97(\$3,814) = \$3,699.58$

b. No discount because payment date is after the discount period. Amount due is $3,814

c. Since May has 31 days, June 7 is 30 days from billing, so invoice amount of $3,814 must be paid.

d. A penalty of 1% is assessed.
$0.01(\$3,814) = \$38.14$
Amount to be paid $= \$3,814 + \$38.14 = \$3,852.14$

## 2

1. The discount applies since the invoice was paid before December 15.
   Amount paid $= 0.97(\$2,697) = \$2,616.09$

2. The invoice must be paid by January 10 to get a discount of $11.97.
   $0.02(\$598.46) = \$11.97$

3. The invoice must be paid by June 10.
   $100\% - 2\% = 98\%$ of the invoice amount must be paid.

4. The discount applies:
   $$100\% - 1\% = 99\%$$
   $$99\% = 0.99$$
   $$0.99(\$1,096.82) = \$1,085.85$$

5. The entire amount of the invoice, $187.17, must be paid because the discount terms require the invoice to be paid within the first 10 days of the next month.

6. The discount applies:
   $$100\% - 3\% = 97\%$$
   $$97\% = 0.97$$
   $$0.97(\$84,896) = \$82,349.12$$

## 3

1. The invoice must be paid by September 27 for the discount.
   September $12 + 15 =$ September 27.
   $0.97(\$3,097.15) = \$3,004.24$ must be paid.

2. The invoice must be paid within 10 days of receipt of goods to get a 2% discount. The full invoice amount must be paid after 10 days and within 30 days of receipt of goods.

   March 20 is within 10 days of receipt of goods so the discount applies. Amount to be paid $= 0.98(\$8,917.48) = \$8,739.13$

3. Pay on May 28, $0.98(\$1,215) = \$1,190.70$; pay on June 14, $1,215

4. The full invoice of $797 must be paid since July 12 is more than 15 days from June 17, the date the dryers arrived.

## 4

1. Amount credited $= \dfrac{\$200,000}{0.97} = \$206,185.57$

2. Amount credited $= \dfrac{\$1,900,000}{0.98} = \$1,938,775.51$

3. Amount credited $= \dfrac{\$50,000}{0.98} = \$51,020.41$

4. Amount credited $= \dfrac{\$400,000}{0.97} = \$412,371.13$

   Amount of invoice (no discount) $= 6,000(\$79) = \$474,000$
   Amount still to be paid: $\$474,000 - \$412,371.13 = \$61,628.87$

## 5

1. Cash discount $= 0.02(\$2,896) = \$57.92$
   Net amount $= 0.98(\$2,896) = \$2,838.08$
   Total amount $= \$2,838.08 + \$72 = \$2,910.08$

2. Nortex Mills

3. Net amount $= 0.98(\$7,925) = \$7,766.50$
   Total amount $= \$7,766.50 + \$215 = \$7,981.50$

4. Cost of teak boards $= 10(\$26.50) = \$265.00$
   Cost of mahogany boards $= 25(\$7.95) = \$198.75$
   Total cost of merchandise $= \$265 + \$198.75 = \$463.75$
   Net amount $= 0.97(\$463.75) = \$449.84$
   Total $= \$449.84 + \$65 = \$514.84$

## CHAPTER 9

### Section 9-1

## 1

1. $\$32 + \$40 = \$72$

2. $\$12.95 - \$7 = \$5.95$

3. $\$34.95 - \$18 = \$16.95$

4. Markup $= \$5.25 - \$3 = \$2.25$

# 2

1. Markup = \$599 − \$220 = \$379

   $M\% = \dfrac{\$379}{\$220}(100\%) = 172.3\%$

2. Markup = \$197.20 − \$145 = \$52.20

   $M\% = \dfrac{\$52.20}{\$145}(100\%) = 36\%$

3. Markup = \$395 − \$245 = \$150

   $M\% = \dfrac{\$150}{\$245}(100\%) = 61.2\%$

4. Markup = \$1,420 − \$690 = \$730

   $M\% = \dfrac{\$730}{\$690}(100\%) = 105.8\%$

5. Markup = \$249 − \$89 = \$160

   $M\% = \dfrac{\$160}{\$89}(100\%) = 179.8\%$

6. Markup = \$1,048 − \$738

   Markup = \$310

   $M\% = \dfrac{\$310}{\$738}(100\%)$

   $M\% = 42.0\%$

   Calculator steps: $\boxed{(}\;1048\;\boxed{-}\;738\;\boxed{)}\;\boxed{\div}\;738\;\boxed{\times}\;100\;\boxed{=}$
   $\Rightarrow 0.4200542005$

   Multiply the decimal by 100% to get 42.0%.

# 3

1. $S\% = 100\% + 78\%$
   $S\% = 178\%$
   $S = 178\%(\$218)$
   $S = 1.78(\$218)$
   $S = \$388.04$

2. $S\% = 100\% + 95\%$
   $S\% = 195\%$
   $S = 195\%(\$87.50)$
   $S = 1.95(\$87.50)$
   $S = \$170.63$

3. $S\% = 100\% + 80\%$
   $S\% = 180\%$
   $S = 180\%(\$465)$
   $S = 1.8(\$465)$
   $S = \$837$

4. $S\% = 100\% + 365\%$
   $S\% = 465\%$
   $S = 465\%(\$0.86)$
   $S = 4.65(\$0.86)$
   $S = \$4.00$

5. $S\% = 100\% + 110\%$
   $S\% = 210\%$
   $S = 210\%(\$0.45)$
   $S = 2.1(\$0.45)$
   $S = \$0.95$

6. $S\% = 100\% + C\%$
   $S\% = 100\% + 70\%$
   $S\% = 170\%$
   $S = 170\%(\$58.82)$
   $S = 1.7(\$58.82)$
   $S = \$99.99$

# 4

1. $C = \dfrac{M}{M\%}$
   $C = \dfrac{\$38}{62\%}$
   $C = \dfrac{\$38}{0.62}$
   $C = \$61.29$

2. $C = \dfrac{M}{M\%}$
   $C = \dfrac{\$650}{92\%}$
   $C = \dfrac{\$650}{0.92}$
   $C = \$706.52$

3. $C = \dfrac{M}{M\%}$
   $C = \dfrac{\$358}{65\%}$
   $C = \dfrac{\$358}{0.65}$
   $C = \$550.77$

4. $C = \dfrac{M}{M\%}$
   $C = \dfrac{\$4.14}{125\%}$
   $C = \dfrac{\$4.14}{1.25}$
   $C = \$3.31$

5. $C = \dfrac{M}{M\%}$
   $C = \dfrac{\$7.82}{80\%}$
   $C = \dfrac{\$7.82}{0.8}$
   $C = \$9.78$

6. $C = \dfrac{M}{M\%}$
   $C = \dfrac{0.24}{32\%}$
   $C = \dfrac{0.24}{0.32}$
   $C = \$0.75$

# 5

1. $S\% = 100\% + M\%$
   $S\% = 100\% + 60\% = 160\%$
   $C = \dfrac{S}{S\%}$
   $C = \dfrac{\$39}{160\%}$
   $C = \dfrac{\$39}{1.6}$
   $C = \$24.38$
   $M = S - C$
   $M = \$39 - \$24.38$
   $M = \$14.62$

2. $S\% = 100\% + M\%$
   $S\% = 100\% + 110\%$
   $S\% = 210\%$
   $C = \dfrac{S}{S\%}$
   $C = \dfrac{\$149}{210\%}$
   $C = \dfrac{\$149}{2.1}$
   $C = \$70.95$
   $M = S - C$
   $M = \$149 - \$70.95$
   $M = \$78.05$

3. $S\% = 100\% + M\%$
   $S\% = 100\% + 85\%$
   $S\% = 185\%$
   $C = \dfrac{\$4.65}{185\%}$
   $C = \dfrac{\$4.65}{1.85}$
   $C = \$2.51$
   $M = S - C$
   $M = \$4.65 - \$2.51$
   $M = \$2.14$

4. $S\% = 100\% + 165\%$
   $S\% = 265\%$
   $C = \dfrac{\$595}{265\%}$
   $C = \dfrac{\$595}{2.65}$
   $C = \$224.53$
   $M = S - C$
   $M = \$595 - \$224.53$
   $M = \$370.47$

5. $S\% = 100\% + 45\%$
   $S\% = 145\%$
   $C = \dfrac{\$65}{145\%}$
   $C = \dfrac{\$65}{1.45}$
   $C = \$44.83$
   $M = S - C$
   $M = \$65 - \$44.83$
   $M = \$20.17$

6. $S\% = 100 + M\%$
   $S\% = 100\% + 62\%$
   $S\% = 162\%$
   $C = \dfrac{S}{S\%}$
   $C = \dfrac{\$9.99}{162\%}$
   $C = \dfrac{\$9.99}{1.62}$
   $C = \$6.17$
   $M = S - C$
   $M = \$9.99 - \$6.17$
   $M = \$3.82$

## Section 9-2

# 1

1. $M = \$70 - \$58$
   $M = \$12$
   $M\% = \dfrac{\$12}{\$70}(100\%)$
   $M\% = 17.1\%$

2. $M = \$1{,}499 - \$385$
   $M = \$1{,}114$
   $M\% = \dfrac{\$1{,}114}{\$1{,}499}(100\%)$
   $M\% = 74.3\%$

3. $M = \$795 - \$395$
   $M = \$400$
   $M\% = \dfrac{\$400}{\$795}(100\%)$
   $M\% = 50.3\%$

4. $M = \$6.00 - \$2.40$
   $M = \$3.60$
   $M\% = \dfrac{\$3.60}{\$6.00}(100\%)$
   $M\% = 60\%$

5. $M = \$2.39 - \$0.84$
   $M = \$1.55$
   $M\% = \dfrac{\$1.55}{\$2.39}(100\%)$
   $M\% = 64.9\%$

6. $M = \$229 - \$132$
   $M = \$97$
   $M\% = \dfrac{\$97}{\$229}(100\%)$
   $M\% = 42.4\%$

# 2

1. $S = \dfrac{\$195}{60\%}$
   $S = \dfrac{\$195}{0.6}$
   $S = \$325$
   $C = \$325 - \$195$
   $C = \$130$

2. $S = \dfrac{\$21}{80\%}$
   $S = \dfrac{\$21}{0.8}$
   $S = \$26.25$
   $C = \$26.25 - \$21$
   $C = \$5.25$

3. $S = \dfrac{\$14}{75\%}$
   $S = \dfrac{\$14}{0.75}$
   $S = \$18.67$
   $C = \$18.67 - \$14$
   $C = \$4.67$

4. $S = \dfrac{\$145}{25\%}$
   $S = \dfrac{\$145}{0.25}$
   $S = \$580$
   $C = \$580 - \$145$
   $C = \$435$

5. $S = \dfrac{\$38}{70\%}$
   $S = \dfrac{\$38}{0.7}$
   $S = \$54.29$
   $C = \$54.29 - \$38$
   $C = \$16.29$

6. $S = \dfrac{\$70.08}{32\%}$
   $S = \dfrac{\$70.08}{0.32}$
   $S = \$219$
   $C = \$219 - \$70.08$
   $C = \$148.92$

# 3

1. $C\% = 100\% - 25\%$
   $C\% = 75\%$
   $S = \dfrac{\$2.99}{75\%}$
   $S = \$3.99$
   $M = \$3.99 - \$2.99$
   $M = \$1.00$

2. $C\% = 100\% - 38\%$
   $C\% = 62\%$
   $S = \dfrac{\$187}{62\%}$
   $S = \$301.61$
   $M = \$301.61 - \$187$
   $M = \$114.61$

3. $C\% = 100\% - 27\%$
   $C\% = 73\%$
   $S = \dfrac{\$3.84}{73\%}$
   $S = \$5.26$
   $M = \$5.26 - \$3.84$
   $M = \$1.42$

4\. $C\% = 100\% - 23\%$
$C\% = 77\%$
$S = \dfrac{\$127.59}{77\%}$
$S = \$165.70$
$M = \$165.70 - \$127.59$
$M = \$38.11$

5\. $C\% = 100\% - 65\%$
$C\% = 35\%$
$S = \dfrac{\$1.92}{35\%}$
$S = \$5.49$
$M = \$5.49 - \$1.92$
$M = \$3.57$

6\. $C\% = 100\% - 35\%$
$C\% = 65\%$
$S = \dfrac{\$32.49}{65\%}$
$S = \$49.98$
$M = \$49.98 - \$32.49$
$M = \$17.49$

## 4

1\. $C\% = 100\% - M\%$
$C\% = 100\% - 38\%$
$C\% = 62\%$
$C = 62\%(\$18.99)$
$C = 0.62(\$18.99)$
$C = \$11.77$
$M = \$18.99 - \$11.77$
$M = \$7.22$

2\. $C\% = 100\%$
$M\% = 60\%$
$C = \dfrac{M}{M\%}$
$C = \dfrac{\$135}{0.6}$
$C = \$225$
$S = C + M$
$S = \$225 + \$135$
$S = \$360$

3\. $C\% = 100\% - 58\%$
$C\% = 42\%$
$C = 42\%(\$349)$
$C = \$146.58$
$M = \$349 - \$146.58$
$M = \$202.42$

4\. $C\% = 100\% - 80\%$
$C\% = 20\%$
$C = 20\%(\$49)$
$C = \$9.80$
$M = \$49 - \$9.80$
$M = \$39.20$

5\. $C\% = 100\% - 46\%$
$C\% = 54\%$
$C = 54\%(\$675)$
$C = \$364.50$
$M = \$675 - \$364.50$
$M = \$310.50$

6\. $C\% = 100\% - M\%$
$C\% = 100\% - 38\%$
$C\% = 62\%$
$S = \dfrac{\$3,034.90}{62\%}$
$S = \dfrac{\$3,034.90}{0.62}$
$S = \$4,895$
$M = \$4,895 - \$3,034.90$
$M = \$1,860.10$

## 5

1\. $M = S - C$
$M = \$38 - \$12.50$
$M = \$25.50$
$M\%_{\text{cost}} = \dfrac{M}{C} \times 100\%$
$M\%_{\text{cost}} = \dfrac{\$25.50}{\$12.50}(100\%)$
$M\%_{\text{cost}} = 204\%$
$M\%_{\text{selling price}} = \dfrac{M}{S} \times 100\%$
$M\%_{\text{selling price}} = \dfrac{\$25.50}{\$38}(100\%)$
$M\%_{\text{selling price}} = 67.1\%$

2\. $M = S - C$
$M = \$18,900 - \$12.500$
$M = \$6,400$
$M\%_{\text{cost}} = \dfrac{M}{C} \times 100\%$
$M\%_{\text{cost}} = \dfrac{\$6,400}{\$12,500}(100\%)$
$M\%_{\text{cost}} = 51.2\%$
$M\%_{\text{selling price}} = \dfrac{M}{S} \times 100\%$
$M\%_{\text{selling price}} = \dfrac{\$6,400}{\$18,900}(100\%)$
$M\%_{\text{selling price}} = 33.9\%$

3\. $M = S - C$
$M = \$535 - \$375$
$M = \$160$
$M\%_{\text{cost}} = \dfrac{M}{C} \times 100\%$
$M\%_{\text{cost}} = \dfrac{\$160}{\$375}(100\%)$
$M\%_{\text{cost}} = 42.7\%$
$M\%_{\text{selling price}} = \dfrac{M}{S} \times 100\%$
$M\%_{\text{selling price}} = \dfrac{\$160}{\$535}(100\%)$
$M\%_{\text{selling price}} = 29.9\%$

4\. $M\%_{\text{cost}} = \dfrac{M\%_{\text{selling price}}}{100 - M\%_{\text{selling price}}} \times 100\%$
$M\%_{\text{cost}} = \dfrac{40\%}{100\% - 40\%}(100\%)$
$M\%_{\text{cost}} = 66.7\%$

5\. $M\%_{\text{selling price}} = \dfrac{M\%_{\text{cost}}}{100\% + M\%_{\text{cost}}} \times 100\%$
$M\%_{\text{selling price}} = \dfrac{120\%}{100\% + 120\%}(100\%)$
$M\%_{\text{selling price}} = \dfrac{120\%}{220\%}(100\%)$
$M\%_{\text{selling price}} = 54.5\%$

6\. $M\%_{\text{cost}} = \dfrac{M\%_{\text{selling price}}}{100\% - M\%_{\text{selling price}}} \times 100\%$
$M\%_{\text{cost}} = \dfrac{75\%}{100\% - 75\%}(100\%)$
$M\%_{\text{cost}} = \dfrac{75\%}{25\%}(100\%)$
$M\%_{\text{cost}} = 3(100\%)$
$M\%_{\text{cost}} = 300\%$

## Section 9-3

### 1

1. Markdown = \$135 − \$75
   Markdown = \$60
   $$M\% = \frac{\$60}{\$135}(100\%)$$
   $M\% = 44.4\%$

2. Markdown = \$15 − \$8
   Markdown = \$7
   $$M\% = \frac{\$7}{\$15}(100\%)$$
   $M\% = 46.7\%$

3. Markdown = \$249 × 35%
   Markdown = \$249(0.35)
   Markdown = \$87.15
   New price = \$249 − \$87.15
   New price = \$161.85

4. Markdown = \$38.99(25%)
   Markdown = \$38.99(0.25)
   Markdown = \$9.75
   Reduced price = \$38.99 − \$9.75
   Reduced price = \$29.24

5. Markdown = \$85(40%)
   Markdown = \$85(0.4)
   Markdown = \$34
   Sale price = \$85 − \$34
   Sale price = \$51

6. Markdown = 12.563%(\$398)
   Markdown = 0.12563(\$398)
   Markdown = \$50.00
   Reduced price = \$398.00 − \$50.00
   Reduced price = \$348.00

### 2

1. $S\% = C\% + M\%$
   $S\% = 100\% + 60\%$
   $S\% = 160\%$
   $S = 160\%(\$189)$
   $S = \$302.40$
   $N\% = 100\% - 30\%$
   $N\% = 70\%$
   $N = 70\%(\$302.40)$
   $N = \$211.68$
   Final% = $100\% - 40\%$
   Final% = $60\%$
   Final price = $60\%(\$211.68)$
   Final price = \$127.01

2. Net decimal equivalent = 0.9(0.7) = 0.63
   Final reduced price = 0.63(\$128) = \$80.64
   Final rate of reduction = 1 − 0.63 = 0.37
   Percent equivalent = 0.37(100%) = 37%

3. $S\% = 100\% + 85\%$
   $S\% = 185\%$
   $S = 185\%(\$262)$
   $S = \$484.70$
   $N\% = 100\% - 25\%$
   $N\% = 75\%$
   $N = 75\%(\$484.70)$
   $N = \$363.53$
   Final% = $100\% - 30\%$
   Final% = $70\%$
   Final price = $70\%(\$363.53)$
   Final price = \$254.47

4. Net decimal equivalent = 0.85(0.6) = 0.51
   Final reduced price = 0.51(\$249) = \$126.99

### 3

1. $C = \$0.30(300) = \$90$
   $M = 1.8(\$90) = \$162$
   $S = C + M = \$90 + \$162 = \$252$
   $100\% - 5\% = 95\%$ will sell
   $0.95(300) = 285$ pounds will sell
   $$\text{Selling price per pound} = \frac{\$252}{285} = \$0.88$$

2. $C = \$0.35(500) = \$175$
   $M = 1.75(\$175) = \$306.25$
   $S = C + M = \$175 + \$306.25$
   $S = \$481.25$
   Pounds that will sell = 0.92(500)
   = 460 pounds
   $$\text{Selling price per pound} = \frac{\$481.25}{460}$$
   Selling price per pound = \$1.05

3. $C = \$0.27(2,000) = \$540$
   $M = 1.6(\$540) = \$864$
   $S = C + M = \$540 + \$864 = \$1,404$
   Pounds that will sell = 0.96(2,000)
   = 1,920 pounds
   $$\text{Selling price per pound} = \frac{\$1,404}{1,920}$$
   Selling price per pound = \$0.73

4. $C = \$0.92(1,000) = \$920$
   $M = 1.8(\$920) = \$1,656$
   $S = C + M = \$920 + \$1,656 = \$2,576$
   Pounds that will sell = 0.9(1,000) = 900 pounds
   $$\text{Selling price per pound} = \frac{2,576}{900} = \$2.86$$

## CHAPTER 10

## Section 10-1

### 1

1. \$42,822 ÷ 26 = \$1,647
2. \$32,928 ÷ 24 = \$1,372
3. \$1,872(52) = \$97,344
4. \$3,315(12) = \$39,780

# 2

1.  $48 - 40 = 8$ hours overtime
    $40(\$15.83) = \$633.20$
    $8(\$15.83)(1.5) = \$189.96$
    Gross pay $= \$633.20 + \$189.96 = \$823.16$
3.  $55 - 40 = 15$ hours overtime
    $40(\$14.27) = \$570.80$
    $15(\$14.27)(1.5) = \$321.08$
    Gross pay $= \$570.80 + \$321.08 = \$891.88$

2.  $52 - 40 = 12$ hours overtime
    $40(\$13.56) = \$542.40$
    $12(\$13.56)(1.5) = \$244.08$
    Gross pay $= \$542.40 + \$244.08 = \$786.48$
4.  $62 - 40 = 22$ hours overtime
    $22 - 8 = 14$ hours overtime at time and a half
    $40(\$22.75) = \$910$
    $14(\$22.75)(1.5) = \$477.75$
    $8(\$22.75)(2) = \$364$
    Gross pay $= \$910 + \$477.75 + \$364 = \$1,751.75$

# 3

1.  $12(\$70) = \$840$

2.  $21 + 27 + 18 + 29 + 24 = 119$ tires
    $119(\$5.50) = \$654.50$

3.  First 200 units: $200(\$1.18) = \$236$
    Next 200 units: $200(\$1.35) = \$270$
    Next 135 units: $135(\$1.55) = \$209.25$
    Gross pay $= \$236 + \$270 + \$209.25 = \$715.25$

4.  Total units $= 37 + 42 + 40 + 46 + 52 = 217$
    First 50 units $= 50(\$2.95) = \$147.50$
    units 51–150 $= 100(\$3.10) = \$310.00$
    Last 67 units $= 67(\$3.35) = \$224.45$
    Gross pay $= \$147.50 + \$310.00 + \$224.45 = \$681.95$

# 4

1.  Gross earnings $= 0.06(\$17,945) =$
    $\$1,076.70$

2.  Earnings for listings $= \$4.00(547) =$
    $\$2,188$
    Earnings for commission $=$
    $0.01(\$30,248) = \$302.48$
    Gross earnings $= \$2,188 + \$302.48 =$
    $\$2,490.48$

3.  Amount on which commission is paid $=$
    $\$26,572 - \$3,000 = \$23,572$
    Commission $= 0.02(\$23,572) = \$471.44$
    Gross earnings $= \$471.44 + \$200 =$
    $\$671.44$
    Annual gross earnings $= \$671.44(52) =$
    $\$34,914.88$

4.  Commission $= 0.04(\$32,017) = \$1,280.68$
    Gross earnings $= \$1,280.68 + \$275 = \$1,555.68$
    Annual gross earnings $= \$1,555.68(26) = \$40,447.68$

## Section 10-2

# 1

1.  Use Figure 10-2. Select row for interval "At least 1,680 but less than 1,700." Move across to the column for two withholding allowances. The withholding tax is $180.

2.  Use Figure 10-3. Select row for interval "At least 700 but less than 710." Move across to the column for four withholding allowances. The withholding tax is $29.

3.  Use Figure 10-2. Select row for interval "At least 2,020 but less than 2,040." Move across to the column for one withholding allowance. The withholding tax is $300.

4.  Find taxable earnings: $640 − $30 = $610.
    Use Figure 10-3. Select row for interval "At least 610 but less than 620." Move across to the column for seven withholding allowances. The withholding tax is $0.

# 2

1.  $3(\$65.38) = \$196.14$

2.  $\$850 - \$196.14 = \$653.86$

3.  $\$653.86 - \$645 = \$8.86$
    $\$8.86(0.25) = \$2.22$
    Total withholding tax $=$
    $\$81.90 + \$2.22 = \$84.12$

4. Withholding allowance = 4($141.67) = $566.68

   Adjusted gross income = $1,700 − $566.68 = $1,133.32

   Use Table 3b.

   $1,133.32 − $973 = $160.32

   $160.32(0.15) = $24.05

   Total withholding tax = $64 + $24.05 = $88.05

## 3

1. Maximum annual income = $1,730(26) = $44,980

   All earnings will be taxed.

   Social Security tax = $1,730(0.062) = $107.26

   Medicare tax = $1,730(0.0145) = $25.09

2. Maximum annual income = $6,230(12) = $74,760

   All earnings will be taxed.

   Social Security tax = $6,230(0.062) = $386.26

   Medicare tax = $6,230(0.0145) = $90.34

3. Accumulated pay for 23 pay periods = $4,135(23) = $95,105

   Maximum amount subject to Social Security = $97,500.

   $97,500 − $95,105 = $2,395

   Social Security tax = $2,395(0.062) = $148.49

   Medicare tax = $4,135(0.0145) = $59.96

4. Accumulated pay for 46 weeks = $1,892(46) = $87,032

   $97,500 − $87,032 = $10,468 earnings subject to Social Security tax in 47th week.

   Social security tax = $1,892(0.062) = $117.30

   Medicare tax = $1,892(0.0145) = $27.43

## 4

1. Retirement = $732(0.06) = $43.92
   Social Security tax = $732(0.062) = $45.38
   Medicare tax = $732(0.0145) = $10.61

2. Use the table in Figure 10-3. Use the "At least 730 but less than 740" row and move across to the column with three deductions. The amount is $43.

3. Total deductions = $110.15 + $43.92 + $45.38 + $10.61 + $43.00 = $253.06

4. Net pay = $732 − $253.06 = $478.94

## Section 10-3

## 1

1. $63 + $88.37 + $29 + $57 = $237.37

2. $45.88 + $53.74 + $39.06 + $43.09 = $181.78

3. $10.73 + $12.57 + $9.14 + $10.08 = $42.52

4. Employer's share of Social Security and Medicare taxes = $181.77 + $42.62 = $224.39

   Employer's deposit = $237.37 + $181.78 + $42.52 + $224.30 = $685.97

## 2

1. SUTA = 5.4%($7,000)
          = 0.054($7,000) = $378

2. FUTA = 0.8%($7,000)
          = 0.008($7,000)
          = $56

3.

| Pay period | Employee 1 salary | Accumulated salary subject to FUTA tax | FUTA tax | Employee 2 salary | Accumulated salary subject to FUTA tax | FUTA tax |
|---|---|---|---|---|---|---|
| Jan 15 | $1,320 | $1,320 | $10.56 | $1,275 | $1,275 | $10.20 |
| Jan 31 | $1,320 | $2,640 | $10.56 | $1,275 | $2,550 | $10.20 |
| Feb 15 | $1,320 | $3,960 | $10.56 | $1,275 | $3,825 | $10.20 |
| Feb 28 | $1,320 | $5,280 | $10.56 | $1,275 | $5,100 | $10.20 |
| Mar 15 | $1,320 | $6,600 | $10.56 | $1,275 | $6,375 | $10.20 |
| Mar 31 | $1,320 | $7,920 | $3.20 | $1,275 | $7,650 | $5.00 |

For Employee 1 on March 31: $7,000 − $6,600 = $400

FUTA = $400(0.008) = $3.20

For Employee 2 on March 31: $7,000 − $6,375 = $625

FUTA = $625(0.008) = $5.00

First quarter FUTA tax = ($10.56(5) + $3.20) + ($10.20(5) + $5.00) = $56 + $56 = $112

The deposit should be made at the end of the first quarter since the total is more than $100.

4. The first quarter payment of FUTA tax is $112.

# CHAPTER 11

## Section 11-1

### 1

1. $38,000(0.105)(1) = \$3,990$
2. $17,500(0.0775)(6) = \$8,137.50$
3. $6,700(0.095)(3) = \$1,909.50$
4. $38,500(0.123)(5) = \$23,677.50$

### 2

1. $MV = \$8,000 + \$660 = \$8,660$

2. $I = \$7,250(0.12)(3) = \$2,610$
   $MV = \$7,250 + \$2,610 = \$9,860$

3. $MV = P(I + RT)$
   $MV = \$1,800(1 + 0.0975(2))$
   $MV = \$1,800(1 + 0.195)$
   $MV = \$1,800(1.195)$
   $MV = \$2,151$

4. $MV = P(I + RT)$
   $MV = \$7,275(1 + 0.11(3))$
   $MV = \$7,275(1 + 0.33)$
   $MV = \$7,275(1.33)$
   $MV = \$9,675.75$

### 3

1. $\dfrac{8}{12} = \dfrac{2}{3}; 8 \div 12 = 0.666667$

2. $\dfrac{15}{12} = 1\dfrac{3}{12} = 1\dfrac{1}{4}; 15 \div 12 = 1.25$

3. 18 months $= 18 \div 12 = 1.5$ years
   $I = \$1,200(0.095)(1.5)$
   $I = \$171$

4. $28 \div 12 = 2.333\overline{3}$
   $MV = \$1,750(1 + 0.098(2.3333))$
   $MV = \$1,750(1.22867)$
   $MV = \$2,150.17$

### 4

1. $\dfrac{\$636.50}{\$2,680(2.5)} = \dfrac{\$636.50}{\$6,700} = 0.095 = 9.5\%$

2. $\dfrac{\$1,762.50}{\$5,000(3)} = \dfrac{\$1,762.50}{\$15,000} = 0.1175 = 11.75\%$

3. $\dfrac{\$904.88}{3.5(0.0925)} = \dfrac{\$904.88}{0.32375} = \$2,795$

4. $\dfrac{\$4,167.90}{\$16,840(0.09)} = \dfrac{\$4,167.90}{\$1,515.60} = 2.75$ years, or $2\dfrac{3}{4}$ years

## Section 11-2

### 1

1. April 15: 105th day
   October 15: 288th day
   $288 - 105 = 183$ days

2. Days in March: $31 - 20 = 11$
   Days in April:        $= 30$
   Days in May:          $= 31$
   Days in June:         $= 30$
   Days in July:         $= 31$
   Days in August:       $= 31$
   Days in September:    $= 20$
   $\underline{\phantom{= 20}}$
   184 days
   or $263 - 79 = 184$ days

3. December 21: 355th day
   October 14: 287th day
   $355 - 287 = 68$ days

4. December 31: 365th day
   November 1: 305th day
   $365 - 305 = 60$ days
   March 1: 60th day
   $60 + 60 = 120$ days
   In a leap year: $120 + 1 = 121$ days

## 2

1. June 12 is day number 163.

   $163 + 120 = 283$

   October 10 is day number 283.

4. November 22 is day number 326.

   $326 + 120 = 446$

   $446 - 365 = 81$ days in the next year

   March 22 is the 81st day in the next year.

2. July 17 is day number 198.

   $198 + 150 = 348$

   December 14 is day number 348.

3. January 29 is the 29th day of the year.

   $29 + 90 = 119$

   The 119th day of the year is April 29.

## 3

1. March 3: 62nd day

   September 3: 246th day

   $246 - 62 = 184$ days

   $I = \$1{,}350(0.065)\left(\dfrac{184}{360}\right) = \$44.85$

4. April 12: 102nd day

   October 12: 285th day

   $285 - 102 = 183$ days

   $I = \$4{,}250(0.072)\left(\dfrac{183}{360}\right) = \$155.55$

   $MV = \$4{,}250 + \$155.55 = \$4{,}405.55$

2. $I = \$1{,}350(0.065)\left(\dfrac{184}{365}\right) = \$44.24$

3. $\$44.85 - \$44.24 = \$0.61$

   Ordinary interest is $0.61 more than exact interest. Bankers offer borrowers ordinary interest.

## 4

1. $\$10{,}000(0.09)\left(\dfrac{60}{360}\right) = \$150.00$

   $\$3{,}000 - \$150 = \$2{,}850$

   $\$10{,}000 - \$2{,}850 = \$7{,}150$

   $\$7{,}150(0.09)\left(\dfrac{210}{360}\right) = \$375.38$

   $\$7{,}150 + \$375.38 = \$7{,}525.38$

2. $\$5{,}800(0.075)\left(\dfrac{30}{360}\right) = \$36.25$

   $\$2{,}500 - \$36.25 = \$2{,}463.75$

   $\$5{,}800 - \$2{,}463.75 = \$3{,}336.25$

   $\$3{,}336.25(0.075)\left(\dfrac{90}{360}\right) = \$62.55$

   $\$3{,}336.25 + \$62.55 = \$3{,}398.80$

   Total interest $= \$36.25 + \$62.55 = \$98.80$

   $\$5{,}800(0.075)\left(\dfrac{120}{360}\right) = \$145$

   $\$145 - \$98.80 = \$46.20$

## Section 11-3

### 1

1. Exact days $= 312 - 220 = 92$ days

   Bank discount $= \$7{,}200(0.0825)\left(\dfrac{92}{360}\right) = \$151.80$

   Proceeds $= \$7{,}200 - \$151.80 = \$7{,}048.20$

3. Exact days $= 327 - 54 = 273$ days

   Bank discount $= \$3{,}250(0.0875)\left(\dfrac{273}{360}\right) = \$215.65$

   Proceeds $= \$3{,}250 - \$215.65 = \$3{,}034.35$

2. Exact days $= 198 - 17 = 181$ days

   Bank discount $= \$9{,}250(0.0775)\left(\dfrac{181}{360}\right) = \$360.43$

   Proceeds $= \$9{,}250 - \$360.43 = \$8{,}889.57$

4. Exact days $= 191 - 130 = 61$ days

   Bank discount $= \$32{,}800(0.075)\left(\dfrac{61}{360}\right) = \$416.83$

   Proceeds $= \$32{,}800 - \$416.83 = \$32{,}383.17$

## 2

1. $I = PRT$

$I = \$8{,}000(0.11)\left(\dfrac{120}{360}\right)$

$I = \$293.33$

Proceeds = principal − bank discount

Proceeds = \$8,000 − \$293.33

Proceeds = \$7,706.67

Find the effective interest rate:

$R = \dfrac{I}{PT}$

$R = \dfrac{\$293.33}{\$7{,}706.67\left(\dfrac{120}{360}\right)}$

$R = \dfrac{\$293.33}{\$2{,}568.89}$

$R = 0.1141855042$

$R = 11.4\%$

The effective interest rate for a simple discount note of \$8,000 for 120 days is 11.4%.

2. $I = PRT$

$I = \$22{,}000(0.0836)\left(\dfrac{90}{360}\right)$

$I = \$459.80$

Proceeds = principal − bank discount

Proceeds = \$22,000 − \$459.80

Proceeds = \$21,540.20

Find the effective interest rate:

$R = \dfrac{I}{PT}$        Substitute proceeds for principal.

$R = \dfrac{\$459.80}{\$21{,}540.20\left(\dfrac{90}{360}\right)}$

$R = \dfrac{\$459.80}{\$5{,}385.05}$

$R = 0.0853845368$

$R = 8.5\%$        Effective interest rate

The effective interest rate for a simple discount note of \$22,000 for 120 days is 8.5%.

## 3

1. 
```
  201    July 20
−  46    February 15
 155 days
```

2. Interest $= \$19{,}500(0.0825)\left(\dfrac{155}{365}\right)$

$\qquad\qquad = \$683.17$

Maturity value $= \$19{,}500 + \$683.17$

$\qquad\qquad\qquad\quad = \$20{,}183.17$

3. 
```
  201    July 20
−125    May 5
  76 days
```

Third-party discount $= \$20{,}183.17(0.1)\left(\dfrac{76}{360}\right)$

$\qquad\qquad\qquad\qquad = \$426.09$

4. Proceeds to Hugh's Trailers $= \$20{,}183.17 − \$426.09$

$\qquad\qquad\qquad\qquad\qquad = \$19{,}757.08$

# CHAPTER 12

## Section 12-1

## 1

1. Amount financed = \$1,095 − \$100 = \$995
   Total of payments = 18(\$62.50) = \$1,125
   Installment price = \$1,125 + \$100 = \$1,225
   Finance charge = \$1,225 − \$1,095 = \$130

2. Amount financed = \$2,695 − \$200 = \$2,495
   Total of payments = 24(\$118.50) = \$2,844
   Installment price = \$2,844 + \$200 = \$3,044
   Finance charge = \$3,044 − \$2,695 = \$349

3. Amount financed = \$2,295 − \$275 = \$2,020
   Total of payments = 30(\$78.98) = \$2,369.40
   Installment price = \$2,369.40 + \$275 = \$2,644.40
   Finance charge = \$2,644.40 − \$2,295 = \$349.40

4. Finance charge = \$3,115.35 − \$2,859 = \$256.35

## 2

1. Total of installment payments $= \$2{,}087 - \$150$
$= \$1{,}937$
$$\text{Installment payment} = \frac{\$1{,}937}{24}$$
$= \$80.71$

2. Total of installment payments $= \$8{,}997.40 - \$1{,}000$
$= \$7{,}997.40$
$$\text{Installment payment} = \frac{\$7{,}997.40}{36}$$
$= \$222.15$

3. Total of installment payments $= \$2{,}795.28 - \$600$
$= \$2{,}195.28$
$$\text{Installment payment} = \frac{\$2{,}195.28}{36}$$
$= \$60.98$

4. Total of installment payments $= \$3{,}296.96 - \$800$
$= \$2{,}496.96$
$$\text{Installment payment} = \frac{\$2{,}496.96}{30}$$
$= \$83.23$

## 3

1.
$$\text{Installment price} = \$347.49(36) + \$1{,}500$$
$$= \$12{,}509.64 + \$1{,}500$$
$$= \$14{,}009.64$$
$$\text{Amount financed} = \$11{,}935 - \$1{,}500$$
$$= \$10{,}435$$
$$\text{Finance charge (Interest)} = \$14{,}009.64 - \$11{,}935$$
$$= \$2{,}074.64$$
$$\text{Interest per } \$100 = \frac{\$2{,}074.64}{\$10{,}435}(\$100) = \$19.88$$

In Table 12-1, move down the Monthly Payments column to 36. Move across to 20.00 (nearest to 19.88). Move to the top of the column to find 12.25%. APR = 12.25%.

3. Installment price $= \$295.34(36) + \$2{,}000$
$= \$10{,}632.24 + \$2{,}000$
$= \$12{,}632.24$
Amount financed $= \$9{,}995 - \$2{,}000 = \$7{,}995$
Finance charge $= \$12{,}632.24 - \$9{,}995$
$= \$2{,}637.24$
$$\text{Interest per } \$100 = \frac{\$2{,}637.24}{\$7{,}995}(\$100) = \$32.99$$

In Table 12-1, move down the Monthly Payments column to 36. Move across to 32.87 (nearest to 32.99). Move to the top of the column to find 19.5% APR.

2.
$$\text{Installment price} = \$279.65(24) + \$900$$
$$= \$6{,}711.60 + \$900$$
$$= \$7{,}611.60$$
$$\text{Amount financed} = \$6{,}800 - \$900$$
$$= \$5{,}900$$
$$\text{Finance charge (interest)} = \$7{,}611.60 - \$6{,}800$$
$$= \$811.60$$
$$\text{Interest per } \$100 = \frac{\$811.60}{\$5{,}900}(\$100) = \$13.76$$

In Table 12-1, move down the Monthly Payments column to 24. Move across to 13.82 (nearest to 13.76). Move to the top of the column to find 12.75%. APR = 12.75%.

4. Installment price $= \$296.37(48) + \$2{,}500$
$= \$14{,}225.76 + \$2{,}500$
$= \$16{,}725.76$
Amount financed $= \$12{,}799 - \$2{,}500 = \$10{,}299$
Finance charge $= \$16{,}725.76 - \$12{,}799$
$= \$3{,}926.76$
$$\text{Interest per } \$100 = \frac{\$3{,}926.76}{\$10{,}299}(\$100) = \$38.13$$

In Table 12-1, move down the Monthly Payments column to 48. Move across to 37.88 (nearest to 38.13). Move to the top of the column to find 16.75% APR.

## Section 12-2

## 1

1.
$$\text{numerator} = \frac{5(6)}{2} = 15$$
$$\text{denominator} = \frac{12(13)}{2} = 78$$
$$\text{refund fraction} = \frac{15}{78} = \frac{5}{26}$$

2.
$$\text{numerator} = \frac{18(19)}{2} = 171$$
$$\text{denominator} = \frac{48(49)}{2} = 1{,}176$$
$$\text{refund fraction} = \frac{171}{1{,}176} = \frac{57}{392}$$

3. refund fraction $= \dfrac{21}{666}$

refund $= \dfrac{21}{666}(\$1{,}798) = \$56.69$

4. number of months remaining $= 60 - 50$
$= 10$ months
$$\text{refund fraction} = \frac{55}{1{,}830} = \frac{11}{366}$$
$$\text{refund} = \frac{11}{366}(\$4{,}917) = \$147.78$$

### 1

1.

| Day | Balance | Day | Balance | Day | Balance |
|-----|---------|-----|---------|-----|---------|
| 25 | $1,406.54 | 5 | $1,418.47 | 15 | $706.02 |
| 26 | $1,418.47 | 6 | $1,433.71 | 16 | $706.02 |
| 27 | $1,418.47 | 7 | $1,433.71 | 17 | $706.02 |
| 28 | $1,418.47 | 8 | $1,520.69 | 18 | $706.02 |
| 29 | $1,418.47 | 9 | $1,520.69 | 19 | $706.02 |
| 30 | $1,418.47 | 10 | $592.83 | 20 | $776.26 |
| 1 | $1,418.47 | 11 | $592.83 | 21 | $776.26 |
| 2 | $1,418.47 | 12 | $592.83 | 22 | $776.26 |
| 3 | $1,418.47 | 13 | $592.83 | 23 | $776.26 |
| 4 | $1,418.47 | 14 | $706.02 | 24 | $776.26 |

2. [$1,406.54 + 10($1,418.47) + 2($1,433.71) + 2($1,520.69) + 4($592.83) + 6($706.02) + 5($776.26)] ÷ 30 = ($1,406.54 + $14,184.70 + $2,867.42 + $3,041.38 + $2,371.32 + $4,236.12 + $3,881.30) ÷ 30 = $31,988.78 ÷ 30 = $1,066.29

3. $1,066.29(0.01075) = $11.46

4. $1,406.54 + $297.58 − $927.86 + $11.46 = $787.72

### 2

1. Monthly rate $= \dfrac{18\%}{12} = \dfrac{0.18}{12} = 0.015$

   Finance charge $= \$1,285.96(0.015) = \$19.29$

   Total purchases and cash advances $= \$98.76 + \$50 + \$46.98 = \$195.74$

   Total payments and credits $= \$135$

   New balance $= \$1,285.96 + \$19.29 + \$195.74 − \$135 = \$1,365.99$

2. Monthly rate $= \dfrac{15\%}{12} = \dfrac{0.15}{12} = 0.0125$

   Finance charge $= \$2,531.77(0.0125) = \$31.65$

   Total purchases and cash advances $= \$58.63 + \$70 + \$562.78 = \$691.41$

   Total payments and credits $= \$455 + \$85.46 = \$540.46$

   New balance $= \$2,531.77 + \$31.65 + \$691.41 − \$540.46 = \$2,714.37$

3. Monthly rate $= \dfrac{24\%}{12} = 2\% = 0.02$

   Finance charge $= \$2,094.54(0.02)$
   $= \$41.89$

   Total purchases $= \$65.82 + \$83.92 + \$12.73 + \$29.12 + \$28.87$
   $= \$220.46$

   Payments $= \$400$

   New balance $= \$2,094.54 + \$41.89 + \$220.46 − \$400$
   $= \$1,956.89$

4. Monthly rate $= \dfrac{9\%}{12} = 0.75\% = 0.0075$

   Finance charge $= \$245.18(0.0075) = \$1.84$

   Total purchases $= \$45.00 + \$22.38 + \$36.53 = \$103.91$

   Total payments and credits $= \$100 + \$74.93 = \$174.93$

   New balance $= \$245.18 + \$1.84 + \$103.91 − \$174.93 = \$176.00$

## CHAPTER 13

## Section 13-1

### 1

1. Monthly rate $= \dfrac{9.2}{12} = 0.767\%$

2. Period interest rate $= 8\% = 0.08$

   First end-of-period principal $= \$2,950(1 + 0.08)$
   $= \$3,186$

   Second end-of-period principal $= \$3,186(1 + 0.08)$
   $= \$3,440.88$

   The future value is $3,440.88.

   Compound interest $= \$3,440.88 − \$2,950$
   $= \$490.88$

**3.**

$$\text{Period interest rate} = \frac{3.5\%}{2 \text{ periods annually}} = 1.75\%$$

$$\text{Number of periods} = 2 \text{ periods annually}(2 \text{ years})$$
$$= 4 \text{ periods}$$
$$\text{First end-of-period principal} = \$20{,}000(1 + 0.0175)$$
$$= \$20{,}350$$
$$\text{Second end-of-period principal} = \$20{,}350(1 + 0.0175)$$
$$= \$20{,}706.13$$
$$\text{Third end-of-period principal} = \$20{,}706.13(1 + 0.0175)$$
$$= \$21{,}068.49$$
$$\text{Fourth end-of-period principal} = \$21{,}068.49(1 + 0.0175)$$
$$= \$21{,}437.19$$

The future value is \$21,437.19.

**4.**

$$\text{Period interest rate} = \frac{2.8\%}{2 \text{ periods annually}} = 1.4\%$$

$$\text{Number of periods} = 2 \text{ periods annually}(3 \text{ years}) = 6 \text{ periods}$$
$$\text{First end-of-period principal} = \$15{,}000(1 + 0.014)$$
$$= \$15{,}210$$
$$\text{Second end-of-period principal} = \$15{,}210(1 + 0.014)$$
$$= \$15{,}422.94$$
$$\text{Third end-of-period principal} = \$15{,}422.94(1 + 0.014)$$
$$= \$15{,}638.86$$
$$\text{Fourth end-of-period principal} = \$15{,}638.86(1 + 0.014)$$
$$= \$15{,}857.80$$
$$\text{Fifth end-of-period principal} = \$15{,}857.80(1 + 0.014)$$
$$= \$16{,}079.81$$
$$\text{Sixth end-of-period principal} = \$16{,}079.81(1 + 0.014)$$
$$= \$16{,}304.93$$

The future value is \$16,304.93.

## 2

**1.** Number of interest periods $= 5(1) = 5$ periods

$$\text{Period interest rate} = \frac{4\%}{1} = 4\%$$

Move down the Periods column to row 5. Move across to the column with 4% at the top. Read 1.21665.
$2{,}890(1.21665) = \$3{,}516.12$
The compound amount is \$3,516.12.
The compound interest $= \$3{,}516.12 - \$2{,}890$
$$= \$626.12$$

**3.** Number of periods $= 5(1) = 5$ periods

$$\text{Period interest rate} = \frac{2.5\%}{1} = 2.5\%$$

From Table 13-1, find the intersection of the 5-periods row and the 2.5% column. The future value of \$1.00 is 1.13141.
Compound amount $= \$7{,}598.42(1.13141)$
$$= \$8{,}596.93$$
Compound interest $= \$8{,}596.93 - \$7{,}598.42$
$$= \$998.51$$

**2.** Number of interest periods $= 3(4) = 12$ periods

$$\text{Period interest rate} = \frac{10\%}{4} = 2.5\%$$

From Table 13-1, find the intersection of 12 periods and 2.5%. The future value of \$1.00 is 1.34489.
Compound amount $= \$2{,}982(1.34489)$
$$= \$4{,}010.46$$
Compound interest $= \$4{,}010.46 - \$2{,}982$
$$= \$1{,}028.46$$

**4.** Number of interest periods $= 3(2) = 6$

$$\text{Period interest rate} = \frac{5\%}{2} = 2.5\%$$

From Table 13-1, find the intersection of the 6-periods row and the 2.5% column. The future value of \$1.00 is 1.15969.
Compound amount $= \$25{,}000(1.15969) = \$28{,}992.25$

## 3

**1.** Number of interest periods $= 4(12) = 48$

$$\text{Period interest rate} = \frac{4.68\%}{12} = 0.39\% = 0.0039$$

$$FV = P(1 + R)^N$$
$$FV = \$20{,}000(1 + 0.0039)^{48}$$
$$FV = \$24{,}108.59$$

**2.** Number of interest periods $= 10(2) = 20$

$$\text{Period interest rate} = \frac{5.2\%}{2} = 2.6\% = 0.026$$

$$FV = P(1 + R)^N$$
$$FV = \$17{,}500(1 + 0.026)^{20}$$
$$FV = \$29{,}240.53$$

3. Number of interest periods $= 5(4) = 20$

$$\text{Period interest rate} = \frac{4.8\%}{4} = 1.2\% = 0.012$$

$FV = P(1 + R)^N$
$FV = \$18,200(1 + 0.012)^{20}$
$FV = \$23,103.71$
Compound interest $= \$23,103.71 - \$18,200 = \$4,903.71$

4. For twice a year compounding:
Number of periods $= 5 \times 2 = 10$ periods

$$\text{Period interest rate} = \frac{4\%}{2} = 2\%$$

Compound amount $= \$12,000(1.02)^{10} = \$14,627.93$
Compound interest $= \$14,627.93 - \$12,000 = \$2,627.93$

For quarterly compounding:

Number of periods $= 5 \times 4 = 20$ periods

$$\text{Period interest rate} = \frac{4\%}{4} = 1\%$$

Compound amount $= \$12,000(1.01)^{20} = \$14,642.28$
Compound interest $= \$14,642.28 - \$12,000$
$= \$2,642.28$

Compounding quarterly yields more interest than compounding semiannually.

$\$2,642.28 - \$2,627.93 = \$14.35$

The quarterly compounding yields \$14.35 more interest than semiannual compounding.

# 4

1. Period interest rate $= \dfrac{8\%}{2} = 4\%$

First end-of-period principal $= \$2,800(1 + 0.04)$
$= \$2,912$
Second end-of-period principal $= \$2,912(1 + 0.04)$
$= \$3,028.48$
Compound interest after first year $= \$3,028.48 - \$2,800$
$= \$228.48$
Effective annual interest rate $= \dfrac{\$228.48}{\$2,800}(100\%)$
$= 8.16\%$

3. Number of periods per year $= 4$

$$\text{Period interest rate} = \frac{4\%}{4} = 1\%$$

From Table 13-1, find the intersection of the 4-period row and the 1% column. The table value is 1.04060.
Effective annual interest rate $= (1.04060 - 1.00)(100\%)$
$= 0.0406(100\%)$
$= 4.06\%$

2. Number of periods per year $= 2$ (semiannually)

$$\text{Period interest rate} = \frac{8\%}{2} = 4\%$$

From Table 13-1, find the intersection of the 2-period row and the 4% column. The table value is 1.08160.
Effective annual interest rate $= (1.08160 - 1.00)(100\%)$
$= 0.08160(100\%)$
$= 8.16\%$

The manual rate is the same as the table rate.

4. Number of periods per year $= 2$

$$\text{Period interest rate} = \frac{3\%}{2} = 1.5\%$$

From Table 13-1, find the intersection of the 2-period row and the 1.5% column. The table value is 1.03023.
Effective annual interest rate $= (1.03023 - 1.00)(100\%)$
$= 0.03023(100\%)$
$= 3.023\%$

# 5

1. $\$1,850 \div \$100 = 18.5$

Find the table value at the intersection of the 60-day row and the 7.25% column.

Table value $= 1.198791$

Compound interest $= 18.5(\$1.198791)$
$= \$22.18$

3. $\$10,000 \div \$100 = 100$

Find the table value at the intersection of the 730-day row and the 6.75% column. Table value $= 14.452250$.
Compound interest $= 100(\$14.452250)$
$= \$1,445.23$

2. $\$3,050 \div \$100 = 30.5$

Find the table value at the intersection of the 365-day row and the 6% column.

Table value $= 6.183131$

Compound interest $= 30.5(\$6.183131)$
$= \$188.59$

4. $\$20,000 \div \$100 = 200$

3 years $= 365(3) = 1,095$ days

Find the table value at the intersection of the 1,095-day row and the 5.25% column. Table value $= 17.056750$.

Compound interest $= 200(\$17.056750)$
$= \$3,411.35$

## 1

1. Present value $= \dfrac{\$15,000}{1 + 0.02} = \$14,705.88$

2. Present value $= \dfrac{\$15,000}{1 + 0.04} = \$14,423.08$

3. Present value $= \dfrac{\$30,000}{1 + 0.028} = \$29,182.88$

4. Present value $= \dfrac{\$148,000}{1 + 0.0346} = \$143,050.45$

## 2

1. Number of periods $= 4(1) = 4$ periods

   Period interest rate $= \dfrac{4\%}{1} = 4\%$

   Table value $= 0.85480$
   Present value $= \$35,000(0.8548)$
   $= \$29,918$

2. Number of periods $= 2(4) = 8$ periods

   Period interest rate $= \dfrac{4\%}{4} = 1\%$ per period

   Table value $= 0.92348$
   Present value $= \$15,000(0.92348)$
   $= \$13,852.20$

3. Number of periods $= 4(4) = 16$ periods

   Period interest rate $= \dfrac{4\%}{4} = 1\%$

   Table value $= 0.85282$
   Present value $= \$15,000(0.85282)$
   $= \$12,792.30$

4. Number of periods $= 6(4) = 24$ periods

   Period interest rate $= \dfrac{4\%}{4} = 1\%$

   Table value $= 0.78757$
   Present value $= \$15,000(0.78757)$
   $= \$11,813.55$

## 3

1. Number of interest periods $= 7(12) = 84$

   Period interest rate $= \dfrac{4.8\%}{12} = 0.4\% = 0.004$

   $PV = \dfrac{FV}{(1 + R)^{N}}$

   $PV = \dfrac{\$30,000}{(1 + 0.004)^{84}}$

   $PV = \dfrac{\$30,000}{(1.004)^{84}}$

   $PV = \$21,453.07$

   Calculator steps:
   30000 $\div$ ( 1.004 ) ^ 84 $\Rightarrow$ 21453.06649

3. Number of interest periods $= 2(12) = 24$

   Period interest rate $= \dfrac{12\%}{12} = 1\% = 0.01$

   $PV = \dfrac{FV}{(1 + R)^{N}}$

   $PV = \dfrac{\$800}{(1 + 0.01)^{24}}$

   $PV = \dfrac{\$800}{(1.01)^{24}}$

   $PV = \$630.05$

   $800 in two years is worth \$630.05 now. \$700 today is better.

2. Number of interest periods $= 4(1) = 4$

   Period interest rate $= \dfrac{10\%}{1} = 10\% = 0.1$

   $PV = \dfrac{FV}{(1 + R)^{N}}$

   $PV = \dfrac{\$7,000}{(1 + 0.1)^{4}}$

   $PV = \dfrac{\$7,000}{(1.1)^{4}}$

   $PV = \$4,781.09$

   Calculator steps:
   7000 $\div$ ( 1.1 ) ^ 4 $\Rightarrow$ 4781.094188

4. Number of interest periods $= 15(4) = 60$

   Period interest rate $= \dfrac{5.6\%}{4} = 1.4\% = 0.014$

   $PV = \dfrac{FV}{(1 + R)^{N}}$

   $PV = \dfrac{\$45,000}{(1 + 0.014)^{60}}$

   $PV = \dfrac{\$45,000}{(1.014)^{60}}$

   $PV = \$19,540.48$

# CHAPTER 14

## Section 14-1

# 1

1. Periodic interest rate = 2.9%. Number of periods = 4
   Annuity payment = $5,000
   End-of-year 1 = $5,000
   End-of-year 2 = $5,000(1.029) + $5,000
       = $5,145 + $5,000
       = $10,145
   End-of-year 3 = $10,145(1.029) + $5,000
       = $10,439.21 + $5,000
       = $15,439.21
   End-of-year 4 = $15,439.21(1.029) + $5,000
       = $15,886.95 + $5,000
       = $20,886.95 future value
   Total investment = $5,000(4) = $20,000
   Total interest = $20,886.95 − $20,000 = $886.95

2. Periodic interest rate = 3.42%. Number of periods = 3
   Annuity payment = $3,500
   End-of-year 1 = $3,500
   End-of-year 2 = $3,500(1.0342) + $3,500
       = $3,619.70 + $3,500
       = $7,119.70
   End-of-year 3 = $7,119.70(1.0342) + $3,500
       = $7,363.19 + $3,500
       = $10,863.19 future value
   Total investment = $3,500(3) = $10,500
   Total interest = $10,863.19 − $10,500 = $363.19

3. Periodic interest rate $= \dfrac{4\%}{2} = 2\%$
   Number of payments = 2(2) = 4 periods
   Annuity payment = $1,500
   End-of-period 1 = $1,500
   End-of-period 2 = $1,500(1.02) + $1,500
       = $1,530 + $1,500
       = $3,030
   End-of-period 3 = $3,030(1.02) + $1,500
       = $3,090.60 + $1,500
       = $4,590.60
   End-of-period 4 = $4,590.60(1.02) + $1,500
       = $4,682.41 + $1,500
       = $6,182.41

4. Periodic interest rate $= \dfrac{3\%}{2} = 1.5\%$
   Number of payments = 2(2) = 4 periods
   Annuity payment = $300
   End-of-period 1 = $300
   End-of-period 2 = $300(1.015) + $300
       = $304.50 + $300
       = $604.50
   End-of-period 3 = $604.50(1.015) + $300
       = $613.57 + $300
       = $913.57
   End-of-period 4 = $913.57(1.015) + $300
       = $927.27 + $300
       = $1,127.27

# 2

1. Number of periods = 8
   Period rate = 2%
   Table value at intersection of 8-periods row and 2% column = 8.583
   Future value = $4,000(8.583) = $34,332
   Total interest = $34,332 − ($4,000)(8)
       = $34,332 − $32,000
       = $2,332

2. Number of periods = 5(2) = 10
   Period rate $= \dfrac{4\%}{2} = 2\%$
   Table value at intersection of 10-periods row and 2% column
   = 10.950
   Future value = $6,000(10.950) = $65,700
   Total interest = $65,700 − ($6,000)(10)
       = $65,700 − $60,000
       = $5,700

3. Number of periods = 5(4) = 20
   Period rate $= \dfrac{8\%}{4} = 2\%$
   Table value at intersection of 20-periods row and 2% column
   = 24.297
   Future value = $1,200(24.297) = $29,156.40

4. Number of periods = 6(2) = 12
   Period rate $= \dfrac{6\%}{2} = 3\%$
   Table value at intersection of 12-periods row and 3% column
   = 14.192
   Future value = $2,500(14.192) = $35,480

# 3

1. Number of periods $= 4$
   Period rate $= 3.75\%$
   End-of-year 1 $= \$1,500(1 + 0.0375)$
   $\qquad\qquad\quad = \$1,500(1.0375)$
   $\qquad\qquad\quad = \$1,556.25$
   End-of-year 2 $= (\$1,556.25 + \$1,500)(1.0375)$
   $\qquad\qquad\quad = (\$3,056.25)(1.0375)$
   $\qquad\qquad\quad = \$3,170.86$
   End-of-year 3 $= (\$3,170.86 + \$1,500)(1.0375)$
   $\qquad\qquad\quad = (\$4,670.86)(1.0375)$
   $\qquad\qquad\quad = \$4,846.02$
   End-of-year 4 $= (\$4,846.02 + \$1,500)(1.0375)$
   $\qquad\qquad\quad = (\$6,346.02)(1.0375)$
   $\qquad\qquad\quad = \$6,584.00$
   Total paid in $= \$1,500(4) = \$6,000$
   Interest $= \$6,584 - \$6,000 = \$584$

3. Number of periods $= 2(2) = 4$
   Period rate $= \dfrac{3.8\%}{2} = 1.9\%$
   End-of-period 1 $= \$5,000(1.019)$
   $\qquad\qquad\quad = \$5,095$
   End-of-period 2 $= (\$5,095 + \$5,000)(1.019)$
   $\qquad\qquad\quad = \$10,095(1.019)$
   $\qquad\qquad\quad = \$10,286.81$
   End-of-period 3 $= (\$10,286.81 + \$5,000)(1.019)$
   $\qquad\qquad\quad = \$15,286.81(1.019)$
   $\qquad\qquad\quad = \$15,577.26$
   End-of-period 4 $= (\$15,577.26 + \$5,000)(1.019)$
   $\qquad\qquad\quad = \$20,577.26(1.019)$
   $\qquad\qquad\quad = \$20,968.23$

2. Number of periods $= 2$
   Period rate $= 4.25\%$
   End-of-year 1 $= \$4,000(1.0425)$
   $\qquad\qquad\quad = \$4,170$
   End-of-year 2 $= (\$4,170 + \$4,000)(1.0425)$
   $\qquad\qquad\quad = \$8,170(1.0425)$
   $\qquad\qquad\quad = \$8,517.23$

4. Number of periods $= 6$
   Period rate $= \dfrac{6\%}{12} = 0.5\%$
   End-of-period 1 value $= (\$50)(1.005)$
   $\qquad\qquad\qquad\quad = \$50.25$
   End-of-period 2 value $= (\$50.25 + \$50)(1.005)$
   $\qquad\qquad\qquad\quad = (\$100.25)(1.005)$
   $\qquad\qquad\qquad\quad = \$100.75$
   End-of-period 3 value $= (\$100.75 + \$50)(1.005)$
   $\qquad\qquad\qquad\quad = \$150.75(1.005)$
   $\qquad\qquad\qquad\quad = \$151.50$
   End-of-period 4 value $= (\$151.50 + \$50)(1.005)$
   $\qquad\qquad\qquad\quad = \$201.50(1.005)$
   $\qquad\qquad\qquad\quad = \$202.51$
   End-of-period 5 value $= (\$202.51 + \$50)(1.005)$
   $\qquad\qquad\qquad\quad = \$252.51(1.005)$
   $\qquad\qquad\qquad\quad = \$253.77$
   End-of-period 6 value $= (\$253.77 + \$50)(1.005)$
   $\qquad\qquad\qquad\quad = \$303.77(1.005)$
   $\qquad\qquad\qquad\quad = \$305.29$

# 4

1. Number of periods $= 10$
   Period rate $= 5\%$

   Table value for 10-periods row and 5% column $= 12.578$
   Future value $= \$3,000(12.578)(1.05)$
   $\qquad\qquad\quad = \$39,620.70$

3. Number of periods $= 5(4) = 20$
   Period rate $= \dfrac{8\%}{4} = 2\%$

   Table value for 20-periods row and 2% column $= 24.297$
   Future value $= \$500(24.297)(1.02)$
   $\qquad\qquad\quad = \$12,391.47$

2. Number of periods $= 5(2) = 10$
   Period rate $= \dfrac{6\%}{2} = 3\%$

   Table value for 10-periods row and 3% column $= 11.464$
   Future value $= \$1,000(11.464)1.03$
   $\qquad\qquad\quad = \$11,807.92$

4. Number of periods $= 5(2) = 10$
   Period rate $= \dfrac{8\%}{2} = 4\%$

   Table value for 10-periods row and 4% column $= 12.006$
   Future value $= \$1,000(12.006)(1.04)$
   $\qquad\qquad\quad = \$12,486.24$

   For both exercises, the amount paid is $10,000 over the term of the investment.

   Interest in #3 $= \$2,391.47$
   Interest in #4 $= \$2,486.24$

   The interest is slightly higher for payments of $1,000 because a larger amount earns interest from the very beginning.

# 5

1. $R = \dfrac{4.62\%}{12} = \dfrac{0.0462}{12} = 0.00385$ — Periodic interest rate

$N = 25(12) = 300$ — Number of payments

$PMT = \$250$

$FV_{\text{ordinary annuity}} = \$250\left(\dfrac{(1+0.00385)^{300}-1}{0.00385}\right)$

Mentally add within innermost parentheses.

$FV_{\text{ordinary annuity}} = \$250\left(\dfrac{(1.00385)^{300}-1}{0.00385}\right)$

Calculator sequence:

250 $\boxed{(}$ 1.00385 $\boxed{\wedge}$ 300 $\boxed{-}$ 1 $\boxed{)}$ $\boxed{\div}$ 0.00385 $\boxed{=}$ $\Rightarrow$ 140713.7814

The future value of the ordinary annuity is \$140,713.78.

2. $R = \dfrac{5.2\%}{52} = \dfrac{0.052}{52} = 0.001$ — Periodic interest rate

$N = 15(52) = 780$ — Number of payments

$PMT = \$30$

$FV_{\text{ordinary annuity}} = \$30\left(\dfrac{(1+0.001)^{780}-1}{0.001}\right)$

Mentally add within innermost parentheses.

$FV_{\text{ordinary annuity}} = \$30\left(\dfrac{(1.001)^{780}-1}{0.001}\right)$

Calculator sequence:

30 $\boxed{(}$ 1.001 $\boxed{\wedge}$ 780 $\boxed{-}$ 1 $\boxed{)}$ $\boxed{\div}$ 0.001 $\boxed{=}$ $\Rightarrow$ 35418.66671

The future value of the ordinary annuity is \$35,418.67.

3. $R = \dfrac{7.35\%}{12} = \dfrac{0.0735}{12} = 0.006125$ — Periodic interest rate

$N = 14(12) = 168$ — Number of payments

$PMT = \$200$

$FV_{\text{annuity due}} = \$200\left(\dfrac{(1+0.006125)^{168}-1}{0.006125}\right)(1+0.006125)$

Mentally add within parentheses.

$FV_{\text{annuity due}} = \$200\left(\dfrac{(1.006125)^{168}-1}{0.006125}\right)(1.006125)$

Calculator sequence:

200 $\boxed{(}$ 1.006125 $\boxed{\wedge}$ 168 $\boxed{-}$ 1 $\boxed{)}$ $\boxed{\div}$ 0.006125 $\boxed{=}$

$\boxed{\text{ANS}}$ $\boxed{(}$ 1.006125 $\boxed{)}$ $\boxed{=}$ $\Rightarrow$ 58790.47317

The future value of the annuity due is \$58,790.47.

4. $R = \dfrac{6\%}{26} = \dfrac{0.06}{26} = 0.0023076923$ — Periodic interest rate

$N = 35(26) = 910$ — Number of payments

$PMT = \$25$

$FV_{\text{annuity due}} = \$25\left(\dfrac{(1+0.0023076923)^{910}-1}{0.0023076923}\right)$

$\times\,(1+0.0023076923)$ — Mentally add within parentheses.

$FV_{\text{annuity due}} = \$25\left(\dfrac{(1.0023076923)^{910}-1}{0.0023076923}\right)(1.0023076923)$

Calculator sequence:

25 $\boxed{(}$ 1.0023076923 $\boxed{\wedge}$ 910 $\boxed{-}$ 1 $\boxed{)}$ $\boxed{\div}$ 0.0023076923 $\boxed{=}$

$\boxed{\text{ANS}}$ $\boxed{(}$ 1.0023076923 $\boxed{)}$ $\boxed{=}$ $\Rightarrow$ 77598.39391

The future value of the annuity due is \$77,598.39.

## Section 14-2

# 1

1. Number of periods $= 6$
   Period rate $= 4\%$
   Table value $= 0.1507619$
   Sinking fund payment $= \$12,000(0.1507619)$
   $\qquad\qquad = \$1,809.14$

2. Total paid $= \$1,809.14(6)$
   $\qquad\quad = \$10,854.84$
   Interest $= \$12,000 - \$10,854.84$
   $\qquad\quad = \$1,145.16$

3. Number of periods $= 10(4) = 40$
   Period rate $= \dfrac{4\%}{4} = 1\%$
   Table value $= 0.0204556$
   Sinking fund payment $= \$25,000(0.0204556)$
   $\qquad\qquad = \$511.39$

4. Total paid $= \$511.39(40)$
   $\qquad\quad = \$20,455.60$
   Interest $= \$25,000 - \$20,455.60$
   $\qquad\quad = \$4,544.40$

# 2

1. Number of periods $= 5$
   Period rate $= 4\%$
   Table 14-3 value $= 4.452$
   Present value $= \$5,000(4.452)$
   $\qquad\qquad = \$22,260$

2. Number of periods $= 20$
   Period rate $= 7\%$
   Table value $= 10.594$
   Present value $= \$20,000(10.594)$
   $\qquad\qquad = \$211,880$

3. Number of periods $= 10(4) = 40$
   Period rate $= \dfrac{8\%}{4} = 2\%$
   Table value $= 27.355$
   Present value $= \$7,000(27.355)$
   $\qquad\qquad = \$191,485$

4. Number of periods $= 20(2) = 40$
   Period rate $= \dfrac{6\%}{2} = 3\%$
   Table value $= 23.115$
   Present value $= \$10,000(23.115)$
   $\qquad\qquad = \$231,150$

# 3

1. $R = \dfrac{4.85\%}{12} = \dfrac{0.0485}{12} = 0.0040416667$    Periodic interest rate

   $N = 26(12) = 312$    Number of payments

   $FV = \$350,000$

   $\text{PMT}_{\text{ordinary annuity}} = \$350,000\left(\dfrac{0.0040416667}{(1 + 0.0040416667)^{312} - 1}\right)$

   $350000 \boxed{\times} 0.0040416667 \boxed{\div} \boxed{(} \boxed{(} 1.0040416667 \boxed{\wedge}$

   $312 \boxed{-} 1 \boxed{)} \boxed{=} \Rightarrow \text{PMT} = 561.3444827$ (round to nearest cent)

   Shameka should pay \$561.34 into the sinking fund each month.

2. $R = \dfrac{5.25\%}{12} = \dfrac{0.0525}{12} = 0.004375$    Periodic interest rate

   $N = 25(12) = 300$    Number of payments

   $P = \$2,000$

   $PV_{\text{ordinary annuity}} = \$2,000\left(\dfrac{(1 + 0.004375)^{300} - 1}{0.004375(1 + 0.004375)^{300}}\right)$

   $2,000 \boxed{(} \boxed{(} 1.004375 \boxed{\wedge} 300 \boxed{-} 1 \boxed{)} \boxed{\div}$

   $\boxed{(} 0.004375 \boxed{\times} 1.004375 \boxed{\wedge} 300 \boxed{)} \boxed{)} \boxed{=} \Rightarrow$

   $PV = 333751.794$    Round to nearest cent.

   **Mekisha** needs to have \$333,751.79 in the fund to receive an annuity payment of \$2,000 each month for 25 years.

# CHAPTER 15

## Section 15-1

# 1

1. $\$148,500(0.20) = \$29,700$

   Amount financed $= \$148,500 - \$29,700$
   $= \$118,800$

   Number of \$1,000 units $= \$118,800 \div 1,000$
   $= 118.8$

   Table 15-1 factor for 30 years and 5.75% interest rate $= \$5.84$
   Monthly payment $= 118.8(\$5.84)$
   $= \$693.79$

2. Number of \$1,000 units $= \$160,000 \div \$1,000 = 160$

   Table 15-1 factor for 20 years and 5.5% interest rate $= \$6.88$

   Monthly payment $= 160(\$6.88) = \$1,100.80$

3. Number of \$1,000 units $= \$160,000 \div \$1,000 = 160$

   Table 15-1 factor for 25 years and 5.5% interest rate $= \$6.14$

   Monthly payment $= 160(\$6.14) = \$982.40$

4. Number of units $= \$160,000 \div \$1,000 = 160$

   Table 15-1 factor for 30 years and 5.5% interest rate $= \$5.68$

   Monthly payment $= 160(\$5.68) = \$908.80$

# 2

1. Number of \$1,000 units $= \$195,000 \div \$1,000$
   $= 195$

   Table 15-1 value for 17 years and 6.25% interest rate $= \$7.97$

   Monthly payment $= 195(\$7.97)$
   $= \$1,554.15$

3. Monthly insurance payment $= \$1,080 \div 12$
   $= \$90$

   Monthly taxes payment $= \$1,252 \div 12$
   $= \$104.33$

   Adjusted monthly payment $= \$1,554.15 + \$90 + \$104.33$
   $= \$1,748.48$

2. Total paid $= \$1,554.15(17)(12)$
   $= \$317,046.60$

   Interest $= \$317,046.60 - \$195,000$
   $= \$122,046.60$

4. Monthly payment for loan of 15 years at 5.75%

   Interest $= 185.4(\$8.30)$
   $= \$1,538.82$

   Monthly payment for loan of 30 years at 6.25%

   Interest $= 185.4(\$6.16)$
   $= \$1,142.06$

   Marcella should finance for 30 years at 6.25%.

# 1

1. Month 1 interest = $118,800\left(\dfrac{0.0575}{12}\right)$

   $= \$569.25$

   Principal portion of 1st payment = $693.79 - \$569.25$
   $= \$124.54$

   End-of-month principal = $118,800 - \$124.54$
   $= \$118,675.46$

   Month 2 interest = $118,675.46\left(\dfrac{0.0575}{12}\right)$

   $= \$568.65$

   Principal portion of 2nd payment = $693.79 - \$568.65$
   $= \$125.14$

   End-of-month principal = $118,675.46 - \$125.14$
   $= \$118,550.32$

   | Month | Monthly payment | Interest | Principal | End-of-month principal |
   |---|---|---|---|---|
   | 1 | $693.79 | $569.25 | $124.54 | $118,675.46 |
   | 2 | $693.79 | $568.65 | $125.14 | $118,550.32 |

2. Month 1 interest = $160,000\left(\dfrac{0.055}{12}\right)$

   $= \$733.33$

   Principal portion of 1st payment = $1,100.80 - \$733.33$
   $= \$367.47$

   End-of-month principal = $160,000 - \$367.47$
   $= \$159,632.53$

   Month 2 interest = $159,632.53\left(\dfrac{0.055}{12}\right)$

   $= \$731.65$

   Principal portion of 2nd payment = $1,100.80 - \$731.65$
   $= \$369.15$

   End-of-month principal = $159,632.53 - \$369.15$
   $= \$159,263.38$

   | Month | Monthly payment | Interest | Principal | End-of-month principal |
   |---|---|---|---|---|
   | 1 | $1,100.80 | $733.33 | $367.47 | $159,632.53 |
   | 2 | $1,100.80 | $731.65 | $369.15 | $159,263.38 |

3. Month 1 interest = $160,000\left(\dfrac{0.055}{12}\right)$

   $= \$733.33$

   Principal portion of 1st payment = $982.40 - \$733.33$
   $= \$249.07$

   End-of-month principal = $160,000 - \$249.07$
   $= \$159,750.93$

   Month 2 interest = $159,750.93\left(\dfrac{0.055}{12}\right)$

   $= \$732.19$

   Principal portion of 2nd payment = $982.40 - \$732.19$
   $= \$250.21$

   End-of-month principal = $159,750.93 - \$250.21$
   $= \$159,500.72$

   Month 3 interest = $159,500.72\left(\dfrac{0.055}{12}\right)$

   $= \$731.04$

   Principal portion of 3rd payment = $982.40 - \$731.04$
   $= \$251.36$

   End-of-month principal = $159,500.72 - \$251.36$
   $= \$159,249.36$

   | Month | Monthly payment | Interest | Principal | End-of-month principal |
   |---|---|---|---|---|
   | 1 | $982.40 | $733.33 | $249.07 | $159,750.93 |
   | 2 | $982.40 | $732.19 | $250.21 | $159,500.72 |
   | 3 | $982.40 | $731.04 | $251.36 | $159,249.36 |

4. Month 4 interest = $159,471.18\left(\dfrac{0.055}{12}\right)$

   $= \$730.91$

   Principal portion of 4th payment = $908.80 - \$730.91$
   $= \$177.89$

   End-of-month principal = $159,471.18 - \$177.89$
   $= \$159,293.29$

   Month 5 interest = $159,293.29\left(\dfrac{0.055}{12}\right)$

   $= \$730.09$

   Principal portion = $908.80 - \$730.09$
   $= \$178.71$

   End-of-month principal = $159,293.29 - \$178.71$
   $= \$159,114.58$

   Month 6 interest = $159,144.58\left(\dfrac{0.055}{12}\right)$

   $= \$729.28$

   Principal portion = $908.80 - \$729.28$
   $= \$179.52$

   End-of-month principal = $159,114.58 - \$179.52$
   $= \$158,935.06$

   | Month | Monthly payment | Interest | Principal | End-of-month principal |
   |---|---|---|---|---|
   | 4 | $908.80 | $730.91 | $177.89 | $159,293.29 |
   | 5 | $908.80 | $730.09 | $178.71 | $159,114.58 |
   | 6 | $908.80 | $729.28 | $179.52 | $158,935.06 |

# 2

1. Amount mortgaged = $386,000 - \$84,000 = \$302,000$

   Loan-to-value ratio = $\dfrac{\text{Amount mortgaged}}{\text{Appraised value of property}}$

   Loan-to-value ratio = $\dfrac{\$302,000}{\$395,000}$

   Loan-to-value ratio = $0.764556962$ or 76%

2. Housing ratio = $\dfrac{\text{total mortgage payment (PITI)}}{\text{gross monthly income}}$

   Housing ratio = $\dfrac{\$1,482}{\$5,893}$

   Housing ratio = $0.2514848125$ or 25%, which is below the maximum percentage.

3. Debt to income ratio $= \dfrac{\text{total fixed monthly expenses}}{\text{gross monthly income}}$

Debt to income ratio $= \dfrac{\$1,675}{\$4,975}$

Debt to income ratio $= 0.3366834171$ or 34%

4. Housing ratio $= \dfrac{\text{total mortgage payment (PITI)}}{\text{gross monthly income}}$

PITI $= \$1,845 + \$74 + \$104 = \$2,023$

Housing ratio $= \dfrac{\$2,023}{\$5,798}$

Housing ratio $= 0.3489134184$ or 35%, which is above the maximum desired percentage, so her ratio is not favorable.

## CHAPTER 16

### Section 16-1

## 1

1. Depreciable value $= \$5,323 - \$500 = \$4,823$

2. Yearly depreciation $= \dfrac{\text{cost of equipment} - \text{salvage value}}{\text{years of expected life}}$
$= \dfrac{\$18,000 - \$3,000}{3} = \dfrac{\$15,000}{3}$
$= \$5,000$

3. Yearly depreciation $= \dfrac{\text{cost} - \text{salvage value}}{\text{years of expected life}}$
$= \dfrac{\$21,500 - \$4,000}{4}$
$= \dfrac{\$17,500}{4} = \$4,375$

4. Yearly depreciation $= \dfrac{\text{cost} - \text{salvage value}}{\text{years of expected life}}$
$= \dfrac{\$5,800 - \$1,500}{3}$
$= \dfrac{\$4,300}{3} = \$1,433.33$

## 2

1. Unit depreciation $= \dfrac{\$18,000 - \$3,000}{75,000} = \$0.20$ per mile

Depreciation after 56,000 miles $= \$0.20(56,000) = \$11,200$

2. Unit depreciation $= \dfrac{\$23,580 - \$2,300}{95,000} = \$0.224$ per mile

3. Unit depreciation $= \dfrac{\$28,700 - \$2,500}{300,000} = \$0.0873333$

Depreciation for 28,452 objects $= \$0.0873333(28,452) = \$2,484.81$

4. Unit depreciation $= \dfrac{\$7,500 - \$600}{60,000} = \dfrac{\$6,900}{60,000}$
$= \$0.115$ per hour
Year's depreciation $= \$0.115(8,500) = \$977.50$

## 3

1. (a) $\dfrac{8(8 + 1)}{2} = \dfrac{8(9)}{2} = 36$

(b) $\dfrac{12(12 + 1)}{2} = \dfrac{12(13)}{2} = 78$

2. Denominator of depreciation rate $= \dfrac{3(3 + 1)}{2} = 6$

Depreciation rate for each year: $\dfrac{3}{6}, \dfrac{2}{6}, \dfrac{1}{6}$

Original cost $-$ salvage value $= \$18,000 - \$3,000 = \$15,000$

Year 1 depreciation $= \$15,000\left(\dfrac{3}{6}\right) = \$7,500$

Year 2 depreciation $= \$15,000\left(\dfrac{2}{6}\right) = \$5,000$

Year 3 depreciation $= \$15,000\left(\dfrac{1}{6}\right) = \$2,500$

Accumulated Depreciation $= \$5,250 + \$1,500 = \$6,750$

End-of-Year 3 Book Value $= \$3,750 - \$1,500 = \$2,250$

Year 4 Depreciation $= \dfrac{1}{10}(\$7,500) = \$750$

Accumulated Depreciation $= \$6,750 + \$750 = \$7,500$

End-of-Year 4 Book Value $= \$2,250 - \$750 = \$1,500$

3. Year 1 Depreciation $= \dfrac{4}{10}(\$7,500) = \$3,000$

End-of-Year 1 Book Value $= \$9,000 - \$3,000 = \$6,000$

Year 2 Depreciation $= \dfrac{3}{10}(\$7,500) = \$2,250$

Accumulated Depreciation $= \$3,000 + \$2,250 = \$5,250$

End-of-Year 2 Book Value $= \$6,000 - \$2,250 = \$3,750$

Year 3 Depreciation $= \dfrac{2}{10}(\$7,500) = \$1,500$

| Total cost: $9,000 | Year | Depreciation rate | Depreciation | Accumulated depreciation | End-of-year book value |
|---|---|---|---|---|---|
| Depreciable value: $9,000 − $1,500 = $7,500 | 1 | $\frac{4}{10}$ | $3,000 | $3,000 | $6,000 |
| | 2 | $\frac{3}{10}$ | $2,250 | $5,250 | $3,750 |
| | 3 | $\frac{2}{10}$ | $1,500 | $6,750 | $2,250 |
| | 4 | $\frac{1}{10}$ | $750 | $7,500 | $1,500 |

**4.** Sum of the years' digits $= \dfrac{10(10 + 1)}{2} = \dfrac{10(11)}{2} = 55$

| Year | 1 | 2 | 3 | 4 | 5 | 6 | 7 | 8 | 9 | 10 |
|------|---|---|---|---|---|---|---|---|---|----|
| Rate | $\frac{10}{55}$, | $\frac{9}{55}$, | $\frac{8}{55}$, | $\frac{7}{55}$, | $\frac{6}{55}$, | $\frac{5}{55}$, | $\frac{4}{55}$, | $\frac{3}{55}$, | $\frac{2}{55}$, | $\frac{1}{55}$ |

| Total cost: $45,000 Depreciable value: $41,500 | Year | Depreciation rate | Depreciation | Accumulated depreciation | End-of-year book value |
|---|---|---|---|---|---|
| | 1 | $\frac{10}{55}$ | $7,545.45 | $ 7,545.45 | $37,454.55 |
| | 2 | $\frac{9}{55}$ | 6,790.91 | 14,336.36 | 30,663.64 |
| | 3 | $\frac{8}{55}$ | 6,036.36 | 20,372.72 | 24,627.28 |
| | 4 | $\frac{7}{55}$ | 5,281.82 | 25,654.54 | 19,345.46 |

## 4

**1.** (a) $\dfrac{1}{3} = 0.33333 = 33.33\%$

(b) $\dfrac{1}{3}(2) = \dfrac{2}{3} = 0.66667 = 66.67\%$

**2.** Double-declining rate $= \dfrac{1}{4}(2) = \dfrac{2}{4} = \dfrac{1}{2} = 0.5 = 50\%$

Year 1 depreciation $= \$18,000(0.5) = \$9,000$

End-of-year-1 book value $= \$18,000 - \$9,000 = \$9,000$

Year 2 depreciation $= \$9,000(0.5) = \$4,500$

End-of-year-2 book value $= \$9,000 - \$4,500 = \$4,500$

Year 3 depreciation $= \$4,500(0.5) = \$2,250$

End-of-year-3 book value $= \$4,500 - \$2,250 = \$2,250$

Year 4 depreciation $= \$2,250(0.5) = \$1,125$

End-of-year-4 book value $= \$2,250 - \$1,125 = \$1,125$

**3.** Double-declining rate $= \dfrac{1}{5}(2) = \dfrac{2}{5} = 0.4 = 40\%$

| Total cost: $4,500 | Year | Depreciation | Accumulated depreciation | End-of-year book value |
|---|---|---|---|---|
| | 1 | $1,800.00 | $1,800.00 | $2,700.00 |
| | 2 | 1,080.00 | 2,880.00 | 1,620.00 |
| | 3 | 648.00 | 3,528.00 | 972.00 |
| | 4 | 388.80 | 3,916.80 | 583.20 |
| | 5 | 233.28 | 4,150.08 | 349.92 |

**4.** 200%-declining rate $= \dfrac{1}{8}(2) = \dfrac{2}{8} = \dfrac{1}{4} = 0.25 = 25\%$

| Total cost: $25,000 | Year | Depreciation | Accumulated depreciation | End-of-year book value |
|---|---|---|---|---|
| | 1 | $6,250.00 | $ 6,250.00 | $18,750.00 |
| | 2 | 4,687.50 | 10,937.50 | 14,062.50 |
| | 3 | 3,515.63 | 14,453.13 | 10,546.87 |
| | 4 | 2,636.72 | 17,089.85 | 7,910.15 |
| | 5 | 1,977.54 | 19,067.39 | 5,932.61 |
| | 6 | 1,483.15 | 20,550.54 | 4,449.46 |
| | 7 | 1,112.37 | 21,662.91 | 3,337.09 |
| | 8 | 834.27 | 22,497.18 | 2,502.82 |

## Section 16-2

## 1

**1.** Year 9 depreciation $= 6.56\% \times$ total cost $= 0.0656(\$58,000) = \$3,804.80$

**2.** Year 8 depreciation $= 6.55\% \times$ total cost $= 0.0655(\$45,000) = \$2,947.50$

**3.** Year 14 depreciation $= 5.90\% \times$ total cost $= 0.059(\$83,500) = \$4,926.50$

**4.**

| Total cost: $58,000 | Year | MACRS rate | Depreciation | Accumulated depreciation | End-of-year book value |
|---|---|---|---|---|---|
| | 1 | 10.00 | $5,800 | $5,800 | $52,200 |
| | 2 | 18.00 | 10,440 | 16,240 | 41,760 |
| | 3 | 14.40 | 8,352 | 24,592 | 33,408 |
| | 4 | 11.52 | 6,681.60 | 31,273.60 | 26,726.40 |
| | 5 | 9.22 | 5,347.60 | 36,621.20 | 21,378.80 |
| | 6 | 7.37 | 4,274.60 | 40,895.80 | 17,104.20 |
| | 7 | 6.55 | 3,799 | 44,694.80 | 13,305.20 |
| | 8 | 6.55 | 3,799 | 48,493.80 | 9,506.20 |
| | 9 | 6.56 | 3,804.80 | 52,298.60 | 5,701.40 |
| | 10 | 6.55 | 3,799 | 56,097.60 | 1,902.40 |
| | 11 | 3.28 | 1,902.40 | 58,000 | 0 |

## 2

1. Year 3 depreciation $= (\$160{,}980 - \$112{,}000)(14.81\%)$
   $= \$48{,}980(0.1481)$
   $= \$7{,}253.94$

2. Year 8 depreciation $= (\$154{,}840 - \$112{,}000)(6.55\%)$
   $= \$42{,}840(0.0655)$
   $= \$2{,}806.02$

3. Year 2 depreciation $= (\$143{,}300 - \$112{,}000)(7.219\%)$
   (20-year property) $= \$31{,}300(0.07219)$
   $= \$2{,}259.55$

4. $2{,}800(\$50) = \$140{,}000$ (total cost)
   Year 1 depreciation $= (\$140{,}000 - \$112{,}000)(10.00\%)$
   (10-year property) $= \$28{,}000(0.10)$
   $= \$2{,}800$

# CHAPTER 17

## Section 17-1

## 1

1. Cost of ending inventory $= \$9(128) + \$8(79) + \$11(183) = \$3{,}797$

   Cost of goods available for sale $= \$9(314) + \$8(200) + \$11(300) = \$2{,}826 + \$1{,}600 + \$3{,}300 = \$7{,}726$
   Cost of good sold $= \$7{,}726 - \$3{,}797$
   $= \$3{,}929$

2. Cost of ending inventory $= \$2(317) + \$1.90(17) + \$2.10(123) + \$1.90(47) = \$634 + \$32.30 + \$258.30 + \$89.30 = \$1{,}013.90$

   Cost of goods available for sale $= \$2(538) + \$1.90(400) + \$2.10(200) + \$1.90(500) = \$1{,}076 + \$760 + \$420 + \$950 = \$3{,}206$

   Cost of goods sold $= \$3{,}206 - \$1{,}013.90 = \$2{,}192.10$

3. Cost of ending inventory $= \$7(117) + \$6(89) + \$9(36)$
   $= \$819 + \$534 + \$324$
   $= \$1{,}677$
   Cost of goods available for sale $= \$7(389) + \$6(400) + \$9(200)$
   $= \$2{,}723 + \$2{,}400 + \$1{,}800$
   $= \$6{,}923$
   Cost of goods sold $= \$6{,}923 - \$1{,}677 = \$5{,}246$

4. Cost of ending inventory $= \$0.86(115) + \$0.93(219) + \$0.95(28) + \$0.90(107)$
   $= \$98.90 + \$203.67 + \$26.60 + \$96.30$
   $= \$425.47$

   Cost of goods available for sale $= \$0.86(538) + \$0.93(576) + \$0.95(360) + \$0.90(624)$
   $= \$462.68 + \$535.68 + \$342 + \$561.60$
   $= \$1{,}901.96$

   Cost of goods sold $= \$1{,}901.96 - \$425.47 = \$1{,}476.49$

## 2

1. Units available for sale $= 314 + 200 + 300 = 814$

   Cost of goods available for sale $= 314(\$9) + 200(\$8) + 300(\$11)$
   $= \$2{,}826 + \$1{,}600 + \$3{,}300$
   $= \$7{,}726$

   Average unit cost $= \dfrac{\$7{,}726}{814} = \$9.49$

   Ending inventory $= 128 + 79 + 183 = 390$

   Cost of ending inventory $= 390(\$9.49) = \$3{,}701.10$

   Cost of goods sold $= \$7{,}726 - \$3{,}701.10 = \$4{,}024.90$

2. Units available for sale $= 538 + 400 + 200 + 500 = 1{,}638$
   Cost of goods available for sale $= 538(\$2) + 400(\$1.90) + 200(\$2.10) + 500(\$1.90)$
   $= \$1{,}076 + \$760 + \$420 + \$950$
   $= \$3{,}206$

   Average unit cost $= \dfrac{\$3{,}206}{1{,}638} = \$1.96$

   Ending inventory $= 317 + 17 + 123 + 47 = 504$

   Cost of ending inventory $= 504(\$1.96) = \$987.84$

   Cost of goods sold $= \$3{,}206 - \$987.84 = \$2{,}218.16$

3. Units available for sale $= 389 + 400 + 200 = 989$

Cost of goods available for sale $= 389(\$7) + 400(\$6) + 200(\$9)$
$$= \$2,723 + \$2,400 + \$1,800$$
$$= \$6,923$$

Average unit cost $= \dfrac{\$6,923}{989} = \$7$

Ending inventory $= 117 + 89 + 36 = 242$

Cost of ending inventory $= 242(\$7) = \$1,694$

Cost of goods sold $= \$6,923 - \$1,694 = \$5,229$

4. Units available for sale $= 538 + 576 + 360 + 624 = 2,098$

Cost of goods available for sale $= 538(\$0.86) + 576(\$0.93) + 360(\$0.95) + 624(\$0.90)$
$$= \$462.68 + \$535.68 + \$342 + \$561.60$$
$$= \$1,901.96$$

Average unit cost $= \dfrac{\$1,901.96}{2,098} = \$0.91$

Ending inventory $= 115 + 219 + 28 + 107 = 469$

Cost of ending inventory $= 469(\$0.91) = \$426.79$

Cost of goods sold $= \$1,901.96 - \$426.79 = \$1,475.17$

# 3

1. Ending inventory $= 128 + 79 + 183 = 390$

   Most recent units purchased March 1 $= 300$ units

   Units from February 1 purchase $= 390 - 300 = 90$

   Cost of ending inventory $= 300(\$11) + 90(\$8)$
   $$= \$3,300 + \$720$$
   $$= \$4,020$$

   Cost of goods available for sale $= 314(\$9) + 200(\$8) + 300(\$11)$
   $$= \$2,826 + \$1,600 + \$3,300$$
   $$= \$7,726$$

   Cost of goods sold $= \$7,726 - \$4,020 = \$3,706$

2. Ending inventory $= 317 + 17 + 123 + 47 = 504$ units

   Most recent units purchased October 1 $= 500$ units

   Units purchased on July 1 $= 504 - 500 = 4$ units

   Cost of ending inventory $= 500(\$1.90) + 4(\$2.10) = \$958.40$

   Cost of goods available for sale $= 538(\$2) + 400(\$1.90) + 200(\$2.10) + 500(\$1.90)$
   $$= \$1,076 + \$760 + \$420 + \$950$$
   $$= \$3,206$$

   Cost of goods sold $= \$3,206 - \$958.40 = \$2,247.60$

3. Ending inventory $= 117 + 89 + 36 = 242$

   Most recent units purchased February 25 $= 200$

   Units purchased on February 12 $= 242 - 200 = 42$

   Cost of ending inventory $= 200(\$9) + 42(\$6)$
   $$= \$1,800 + \$252$$
   $$= \$2,052$$

   Cost of goods available for sale $= 389(\$7) + 400(\$6) + 200(\$9)$
   $$= \$2,723 + \$2,400 + \$1,800$$
   $$= \$6,923$$

   Cost of goods sold $= \$6,923 - \$2,052 = \$4,871$

4. Ending inventory $= 115 + 219 + 28 + 107$
   $$= 469$$

   Most recent units purchased October 1 $= 469$

   Cost of ending inventory $= 469(\$0.90) = \$422.10$

   Cost of goods available for sale $= 538(\$0.86) + 576(\$0.93) + 360(\$0.95) + 624(\$0.90)$
   $$= \$462.68 + \$535.68 + \$342 + \$561.60$$
   $$= \$1,901.96$$

   Cost of goods sold $= \$1,901.96 - \$422.10 = \$1,479.86$

# 4

1. Ending inventory $= 128 + 79 + 183 = 390$

   Units in ending inventory from January 1 inventory $= 314$
   Units in ending inventory from February 1 purchase $= 390 - 314$
   $$= 76$$

   Cost of goods available for sale $= 314(\$9) + 200(\$8) + 300(\$11)$
   $$= \$2,826 + \$1,600 + \$3,300$$
   $$= \$7,726$$

   Cost of ending inventory $= \$9(314) + \$8(76)$
   $$= \$2,826 + \$608$$
   $$= \$3,434$$

   Cost of goods sold $= \$7,726 - \$3,434 = \$4,292$

2. Ending inventory $= 317 + 17 + 123 + 47 = 504$

   Units in ending inventory from January 1 inventory $= 504$

   Cost of goods available for sale $= 538(\$2) + 400(\$1.90) + 200(\$2.10) + 500(\$1.90)$
   $$= \$1,076 + \$760 + \$420 + \$950$$
   $$= \$3,206$$

   Cost of ending inventory $= 504(\$2) = \$1,008$

   Cost of goods sold $= \$3,206 - \$1,008 = \$2,198$

3. Ending inventory $= 117 + 89 + 36 = 242$

   Units in ending inventory from February 1 purchase $= 242$

   Cost of goods available for sale $= \$7(389) + \$6(400) + \$9(200)$
   $$= \$2,723 + \$2,400 + \$1,800$$
   $$= \$6,923$$

   Cost of ending inventory $= 242(\$7) = \$1,694$

   Cost of goods sold $= \$6,923 - \$1,694 = \$5,229$

4. Ending inventory $= 115 + 219 + 28 + 107 = 469$

   Units in ending inventory from January 1 $= 469$

   Cost of ending inventory $= 469(\$0.86) = \$403.34$

   Cost of goods available for sale $= 538(\$0.86) + 576(\$0.93) + 360(\$0.95) + 624(\$0.90)$
   $$= \$462.68 + \$535.68 + \$342 + \$561.60$$
   $$= \$1,901.96$$

   Cost of goods sold $= \$1,901.96 - \$403.34 = \$1,498.62$

# 5

1. Cost of goods available for sale $= 314(\$9) + 200(\$8) + 300(\$11)$
   $$= \$2,826 + \$1,600 + \$3,300$$
   $$= \$7,726$$

   Retail value of goods available for sale $= \$3,617.28 + \$2,048 + \$4,224$
   $$= \$9,889.28$$

   Cost ratio $= \dfrac{\$7,726}{\$9,889.28} = 0.78125$

   Ending inventory at retail $= \$9,889.28 - \$5,029.12$
   $$= \$4,860.16$$

   Ending inventory at cost $= \$4,860.16(0.78125)$
   $$= \$3,797$$

   Cost of goods sold $= \$5,029.12(0.78125) = \$3,929$ or $\$7,726 - \$3,797 = \$3,929$

2. Cost of goods available for sale $= \$1,076 + \$760 + \$420 + \$950$
   $$= \$3,206$$

   Retail value of goods available for sale $= \$1,554.37 + \$1,100 + \$608 + \$1,375 = \$4,637.37$

   Cost ratio $= \dfrac{\$3,206}{\$4,637.37} = 0.6913401346$

   Ending inventory at retail $= \$4,637.37 - \$3,171.32$
   $$= \$1,466.05$$

   Ending inventory at cost $= \$1,466.05(0.6913401346)$
   $$= \$1,013.54$$

Cost of goods sold $= \$3,171.32(0.6913401346)$
$$= \$2,192.46$$
$$\text{or } \$3,206 - \$1,013.54 = \$2,192.46$$

3. Cost of goods available for sale $= \$2,723 + \$2,400 + \$1,800$
$$= \$6,923$$

Retail value of goods available for sale $= \$3,948.35 + \$3,480 + \$2,610$
$$= \$10,038.35$$

Cost ratio $= \dfrac{\$6,923}{\$10,038.35} = 0.6896551724$

Ending inventory at retail $= \$10,038.35 - \$7,606.70$
$$= \$2,431.65$$

Ending inventory at cost $= \$2,431.65 \, (0.6896551724)$
$$= \$1,677.00$$

Cost of goods sold $= \$7,606.70(0.6896551724)$
$$= \$5,246 \text{ (rounded)}$$

4. Cost of goods available for sale $= \$462.68 + \$535.68 + \$342 + \$561.60$
$$= \$1,901.96$$

Retail value of goods available for sale $= \$763.42 + \$883.87 + \$564.30 + \$926.64$
$$= \$3,138.23$$

Cost ratio $= \dfrac{\$1,901.96}{\$3,138.23} = 0.6060613785$

Ending inventory at retail $= \$3,138.23 - \$2,436.22$
$$= \$702.01$$

Ending inventory at cost $= \$702.01(0.6060613785)$
$$= \$425.46$$

Cost of goods sold $= \$2,436.22 \, (0.6060613785)$
$$= \$1,476.50$$
$$\text{or}$$
$$\$1,901.96 - \$425.46 = \$1,476.50$$

# 6

1. Beginning inventory $= 314(\$9) = \$2,826$
   Net purchases $= 200(\$8) + 300(\$11)$
   $$= \$1,600 + \$3,300$$
   $$= \$4,900$$

   Cost of goods available for sale $= \$2,826 + \$4,900$
   $$= \$7,726$$

   Estimated cost of goods sold $= \$5,815(1 - 0.36)$
   $$= \$5,815(0.64)$$
   $$= \$3,721.60$$

   Estimated ending inventory $= \$7,726 - \$3,721.60$
   $$= \$4,004.40$$

2. Beginning inventory $= 538(\$2) = \$1,076$
   Net purchases $= 400(\$1.90) + 200(\$2.10) + 500(\$1.90)$
   $$= \$760 + \$420 + \$950$$
   $$= \$2,130$$

   Cost of goods available for sale $= \$1,076 + \$2,130$
   $$= \$3,206$$

   Estimated cost of goods sold $= \$2,058(1 - 0.42)$
   $$= \$2,058(0.58) = \$1,193.64$$

   Estimated ending inventory $= \$3,206 - \$1,193.64$
   $$= \$2,012.36$$

3. Beginning inventory $= 389(\$7) = \$2,723$
   Net purchases $= 400(\$6) + 200(\$9) = \$2,400 + \$1,800$
   $$= \$4,200$$

   Cost of goods available for sale $= \$2,723 + \$4,200$
   $$= \$6,923$$

   Estimated cost of goods sold $= \$4,283(1 - 0.4)$
   $$= \$4,283(0.6)$$
   $$= \$2,569.80$$

   Estimated ending inventory $= \$6,923 - \$2,569.80$
   $$= \$4,353.20$$

4. Beginning inventory $= 538(\$0.86) = \$462.68$
   Net purchases $= 576(\$0.93) + 360(\$0.95) + 624(\$0.90)$
   $$= \$535.68 + \$342 + \$561.60$$
   $$= \$1,439.28$$

   Cost of goods available for sale $= \$462.68 + \$1,439.28$
   $$= \$1,901.96$$

   Estimated cost of goods sold $= \$2,048(1 - 0.56)$
   $$= \$2,048(0.44)$$
   $$= \$901.12$$

   Estimated ending inventory $= \$1,901.96 - \$901.12$
   $$= \$1,000.84$$

# 1

1. Average inventory at cost $= \dfrac{\$13,217 + \$14,067}{2}$

    $= \dfrac{\$27,284}{2}$

    $= \$13,642$

    Turnover rate at cost $= \dfrac{\$71,817}{\$13,642}$

    $= 5.26$

2. Average inventory at cost $= \dfrac{\$8,915 + \$9,205}{2}$

    $= \dfrac{\$18,120}{2}$

    $= \$9,060$

    Turnover rate at cost $= \dfrac{\$48,206}{\$9,060}$

    $= 5.32$

3. Average inventory at retail $= \dfrac{\$5,972 + \$7,291}{2}$

    $= \$6,631.50$

    Turnover rate at retail $= \dfrac{\$74,508}{\$6,631.50}$

    $= 11.24$

4. Average inventory at retail $= \dfrac{\$35,169 + \$28,437}{2}$

    $= \dfrac{\$63,606}{2}$

    $= \$31,803$

    Turnover rate at retail $= \dfrac{\$107,582}{\$31,803}$

    $= 3.38$

# 2

1. Total sales $= \$3,816 + \$32,167 + \$67,015 + \$17,816$

    $= \$120,814$

    Overhead: Memorabilia $= \dfrac{\$3,816}{\$120,814}(\$12,516)$

    $= \$395.33$

    Brubaker's Restaurant $= \dfrac{\$32,167}{\$120,814}(\$12,516)$

    $= \$3,332.41$

    Engraving $= \dfrac{\$67,015}{\$120,814}(\$12,516)$

    $= \$6,942.57$

    Frame Shop $= \dfrac{\$17,816}{\$120,814}(\$12,516)$

    $= \$1,845.69$

2. Total sales $= \$17,815 + \$19,583 + \$58,982 + \$38,917 +$
    $\$27,895 + \$32,518 + \$62,906$

    $= \$258,616$

    Overhead: Paint $= \dfrac{\$17,815}{\$258,616}(\$25,116)$

    $= \$1,730.14$

    Lighting $= \dfrac{\$19,583}{\$258,616}(\$25,116)$

    $= \$1,901.84$

    Lumber $= \dfrac{\$58,982}{\$258,616}(\$25,116)$

    $= \$5,728.15$

    Plumbing $= \dfrac{\$38,917}{\$258,616}(\$25,116)$

    $= \$3,779.50$

    Tiles and Flooring $= \dfrac{\$27,895}{\$258,616}(\$25,116)$

    $= \$2,709.08$

    Chemicals $= \dfrac{\$32,518}{\$258,616}(\$25,116)$

    $= \$3,158.05$

    Home and Garden $= \dfrac{\$62,906}{\$258,616}(\$25,116)$

    $= \$6,109.24$

3.  Total floor space $= 100 \text{ ft}^2 + 120 \text{ ft}^2 + 80 \text{ ft}^2 + 130 \text{ ft}^2 +$
$140 \text{ ft}^2 + 300 \text{ ft}^2$
$= 870 \text{ ft}^2$

Overhead: text books $= \dfrac{100 \text{ ft}^2}{870 \text{ ft}^2} (\$12{,}196) = \$1{,}401.84$

Casebound books $= \dfrac{120 \text{ ft}^2}{870 \text{ ft}^2} (\$12{,}196) = \$1{,}682.21$

Paperbacks $= \dfrac{80 \text{ ft}^2}{870 \text{ ft}^2} (\$12{,}196) = \$1{,}121.47$

Children's books $= \dfrac{130 \text{ ft}^2}{870 \text{ ft}^2} (\$12{,}196) = \$1{,}822.39$

Electronic media $= \dfrac{140 \text{ ft}^2}{870 \text{ ft}^2} (\$12{,}196) = \$1{,}962.57$

Coffee shop $= \dfrac{300 \text{ ft}^2}{870 \text{ ft}^2} (\$12{,}196) = \$4{,}205.52$

4.  Total floor space $= 1{,}000 \text{ ft}^2 + 300 \text{ ft}^2 + 700 \text{ ft}^2 + 800 \text{ ft}^2$
$= 2{,}800 \text{ ft}^2$

Overhead: Fresh flowers $= \dfrac{1{,}000 \text{ ft}^2}{2{,}800 \text{ ft}^2} (\$7{,}815) = \$2{,}791.07$

Pottery $= \dfrac{300 \text{ ft}^2}{2{,}800 \text{ ft}^2} (\$7{,}815) = \$837.32$

Fine china $= \dfrac{700 \text{ ft}^2}{2{,}800 \text{ ft}^2} (\$7{,}815) = \$1{,}953.75$

Gifts $= \dfrac{800 \text{ ft}^2}{2{,}800 \text{ ft}^2} (\$7{,}815) = \$2{,}232.86$

# CHAPTER 18

## Section 18-1

# 1

1.  Estimated annual premium $= \left( \dfrac{\$200{,}000}{\$1{,}000} \right) (\$1.17)$
$= \$234$

2.  Estimated annual premium $= \left( \dfrac{\$500{,}000}{\$1{,}000} \right) (\$5.18)$
$= \$2{,}590$

   a.  Semiannual premium $= \$2{,}590(0.51)$
$= \$1{,}320.90$

   b.  Quarterly premium $= \$2{,}590(0.26)$
$= \$673.40$

   c.  Monthly premium $= \$2{,}590(0.0875)$
$= \$226.63$

3.  Estimated annual premium $= \left( \dfrac{\$300{,}000}{\$1{,}000} \right) (\$7.11)$
$= \$2{,}133$

Monthly premium $= \$2{,}133(0.0875)$
$= \$186.64$

4.  Estimated annual premium $= \left( \dfrac{\$600{,}000}{\$1{,}000} \right) (\$3.38)$
$= \$2{,}028$

Quarterly premium $= \$2{,}028(0.26)$
$= \$527.28$

# 2

1.  Estimated annual term premium $= \left( \dfrac{\$300{,}000}{\$1{,}000} \right) (\$3.51)$
$= \$1{,}053$

Years of term insurance $= \dfrac{\$12{,}594}{\$1{,}053} = 11.96$ years

2.  Estimated annual term premium $= \left( \dfrac{\$500{,}000}{\$1{,}000} \right) (\$4.72)$
$= \$2{,}360$

Years of term insurance $= \dfrac{\$13{,}512}{\$2{,}360}$
$= 5.73$ years

3.  Estimated annual term premium $= \left( \dfrac{\$250{,}000}{\$1{,}000} \right) (\$2.33)$
$= \$582.50$

Years of term insurance $= \dfrac{\$4{,}052}{\$582.50} = 6.96$ years

4.  Estimated annual term premium $= \left( \dfrac{\$300{,}000}{\$1{,}000} \right) (\$6.88)$
$= \$2{,}064$
$= \dfrac{\$12{,}892}{\$2{,}064} = 6.25$ years

# Section 18-2

## 1

1. Annual building premium $= \left(\dfrac{\$600,000}{\$100}\right)(\$0.62)$
   $= \$3,720$

   Annual contents premium $= \left(\dfrac{\$188,000}{\$100}\right)(\$0.67)$
   $= \$1,259.60$

   Total annual premium $= \$3,720 + \$1,259.60$
   $= \$4,979.60$

2. Annual building premium $= \left(\dfrac{\$350,000}{\$100}\right)(\$0.45)$
   $= \$1,575$

   Annual contents premium $= \left(\dfrac{\$200,000}{\$100}\right)(\$0.51)$
   $= \$1,020$

   Total annual premium $= \$1,575 + \$1,020$
   $= \$2,595$

3. Annual building premium $= \left(\dfrac{\$265,000}{\$100}\right)(\$0.54)$
   $= \$1,431$

   Annual contents premium $= \left(\dfrac{\$190,000}{\$100}\right)(\$0.62)$
   $= \$1,178$

   Total annual premium $= \$1,431 + \$1,178$
   $= \$2,609$

4. Annual building premium $= \left(\dfrac{\$328,000}{\$100}\right)(\$0.23)$
   $= \$754.40$

   Annual contents premium $= \left(\dfrac{\$185,000}{\$100}\right)(\$0.28)$
   $= \$518$

   Total annual premium $= \$754.40 + \$518$
   $= \$1,272.40$

## 2

1. Annual premium $= \$3,086$
   Time policy is in force $= 5$ months
   Short-rate percent $= 60\%$
   Short-rate premium $= \$3,086(0.60)$
   $= \$1,851.60$
   Refund $= \$3,086 - \$1,851.60$
   $= \$1,234.40$

2. Short-rate premium $= \$3,972(0.80)$
   $= \$3,177.60$
   Refund $= \$3,972 - \$3,177.60$
   $= \$794.40$

3. Short-rate premium $= \$2,805(0.18)$
   $= \$504.90$
   Refund $= \$2,805 - \$504.90$
   $= \$2,300.10$

4. Short-rate premium $= \$4,985(0.40)$
   $= \$1,994$
   Refund $= \$4,985 - \$1,994$
   $= \$2,991$

## 3

1. Full protection: $\$650,000(0.8) = \$520,000$
   Compensation $= \left(\dfrac{\$400,000}{\$520,000}\right)(\$82,000)$
   $= \$63,076.92$

2. Full protection $= \$492,000(0.8) = \$393,600$
   Compensation $= \left(\dfrac{\$350,000}{\$393,600}\right)(\$43,790)$
   $= \$38,939.28$

3. Full protection $= \$798,500(0.8) = \$638,800$
   Compensation $= \left(\dfrac{\$600,000}{\$638,800}\right)(\$590,000)$
   $= \$554,164.06$

4. Full protection $= \$690,000(0.8)$
   $= \$552,000$
   Compensation $= \left(\dfrac{\$550,000}{\$552,000}\right)(\$38,588)$
   $= \$38,448.19$

# Section 18-3

## 1

1. Bodily injury premium $= \$278$
   Property damage premium $= \$144$
   Comprehensive premium $= \$86$
   Collision premium $= \$167$
   Total premium $= \$278 + \$144 + \$86 + \$167 = \$675$

2. Bodily injury premium $= \$289$
   Property damage premium $= \$196$
   Comprehensive premium $= \$69$
   Collision premium $= \$104$
   Total premium $= \$289 + \$196 + \$69 + \$104 = \$658$

3. Bodily injury premium $= \$263$
   Property damage premium $= \$175$
   Comprehensive premium $= \$104$
   Collision premium $= \$188$
   Total premium $= \$263 + \$175 + \$104 + \$188 = \$730$

4. Bodily injury premium $= \$230$
   Property damage premium $= \$144$
   Comprehensive premium $= \$112$
   Collision premium $= \$168$
   Total premium $= \$230 + \$144 + \$112 + \$168 = \$654$

# CHAPTER 19

## Section 19-1

### 1

1. Sales tax = $19.95(0.0725) = $1.45
3. Sales tax = $49.99(0.0475) = $2.37

2. Sales tax = $298.99(0.029) = $8.67
4. Sales tax = $149.95(0.05) = $7.50

### 2

1. Marked price $= \dfrac{\$790}{1 + 0.07} = \dfrac{\$790}{1.07} = \$738.32$
   Sales tax = $790 − $738.32 = $51.68

2. Marked price $= \dfrac{\$5,852.25}{1 + 0.0625} = \dfrac{\$5,852.25}{1.0625} = \$5,508$
   Sales tax = $5,852.25 − $5,508 = $344.25

3. Marked price $= \dfrac{\$380,926}{1 + 0.0575} = \dfrac{\$380,926}{1.0575} = \$360,213.71$
   Sales tax = $380,926 − $360,213.71 = $20,712.29

4. Marked price $= \dfrac{\$12,583}{1 + 0.07} = \dfrac{\$12,583}{1.07} = \$11,759.81$
   Sales tax = $12,583 − $11,759.81 = $823.19

## Section 19-2

### 1

1. Assessed value = $338,500(0.25)
   = $84,625

2. Assessed value = $2,580,000(0.4)
   = $1,032,000

3. Assessed value = $2,839,800(0.5)
   = $1,419,900

4. Assessed value = $1,800,000(0.4)
   = $720,000

### 2

1. Property tax = $85,250(0.0958) = $8,166.95

2. Property tax $= \$720,000\left(\dfrac{\$3.45}{\$100}\right) = \$24,840$

3. Property tax $= \$125,300\left(\dfrac{\$78.45}{\$1,000}\right) = \$9,829.79$

4. Property tax $= \$72,520\left(\dfrac{72.5 \text{ mills}}{\$1,000}\right) = \$5,257.70$

### 3

1. Tax per $100 of assessed value $= \left(\dfrac{\$109,047,773}{\$4,098,530,000}\right)(\$100)$
   $= 0.02660655723(\$100)$
   $= \$2.660655723$
   $= \$2.67 \text{ per } \$100$

2. Tax per $1.00 of assessed value $= \left(\dfrac{\$5,347,364}{\$218,560,000}\right)(100\%)$
   $= 0.0244634334(100\%)$
   $= 0.03(100\%) = 3\%$

3. Tax in mills per $1.00 of assessed value $= \left(\dfrac{\$6,344,549.65}{\$544,029,090}\right)(\$1,000)$
   $= 11.6621515 \text{ mills}$
   $= 11.67 \text{ mills}$

4. Tax per $1,000 $= \left(\dfrac{\$68,914,808}{\$2,856,919,000}\right)(\$1,000)$
   $= \$24.1220728$
   $= \$24.13$

## Section 19-3

### 1

1. Taxable income = $62,596 − $10,109 − ($3,300)(3)
   = $62,596 − $10,109 − $9,900
   = $42,587

2. Taxable income = $105,896 − $12,057 − $3,300
   = $90,539

3. Taxable income = $115,993 − $18,930 − ($3,300)(5)
   = $115,993 − $18,930 − $16,500
   = $80,563

4. Taxable income = $68,929 − $5,150 − $3,300
   = $60,479

# 2

1. Locate range for $37,519 in Table 19-1. Range is $37,500–$37,550. Move across two columns to $4,874, the tax for "Married filing jointly" column.

3. Locate the range for $30,650 in Table 19-1. Range is $30,650–$30,700. Move three columns to the right to $4,226, the tax for "Married filing separately" column.

2. Locate the range for $31,795 in Table 19-1. Range is $31,750–$31,800. Move one column to the right to $4,501, the tax for "Single" column.

4. Locate the range for $38,456 in Table 19-1. Range is $38,450–$38,500. Move four columns to the right to $5,234, the tax for "Head of household" column.

# 3

1. Use Schedule Y-1 from Table 19-2. The range that includes $152,783 is $123,700–$188,450.
$152,783 - $123,700 = $29,083
$29,083(0.28) = $8,143.24
Total tax = $8,143.24 + $24,040
= $32,183.24

3. Use Schedule X from Table 19-2. The range that includes $117,832 is $74,200–$154,800.
$117,832 - $74,200 = $43,632
$43,632(0.28) = $12,216.96
Total tax = $12,216.96 + $15,107.50 = $27,324.46

2. Use Schedule Y-2 from Table 19-2. The range that includes $172,500 is $168,275 and over.
$172,500 - $168,275 = $4,225
$4,225(0.35) = $1,478.75
Total tax = $1,478.75 + $45,521.50
= $47,000.25

4. Use Schedule Z from Table 19-2. The range that includes $456,987 is $336,550 and up.
$456,987 - $336,550 = $120,437
$120,437(0.35) = $42,152.95
Total tax = $42,152.95 + $94,656.50 = $136,809.45

# CHAPTER 20

## Section 20-1

# 1

1. Total assets = $43,518 + $3,988 + $96,532 = $144,038

3. $105,095 + $6,503 + $190,014 = $301,612
$301,612 + $32,507 = $334,119
$6,007 + $4,761 = $10,768
$10,768 + $281,017 = $291,785
$291,785 + $42,334 = $334,119

2. Total liabilities and owner's equity = $15,817 + $9,892 + $418,250 + $45,986 = $489,945

4. $114,975 + $8,918 + $187,915 = $311,808
$311,808 + $29,719 = $341,527
$6,832 + $5,215 = $12,047
$12,047 + $279,409 = $291,456
$291,456 + $50,071 = $341,527

<table>
<tr><td colspan="2">Rayco, Inc.<br>Balance Sheet<br>December 31, 2007</td></tr>
<tr><td>Assets</td><td></td></tr>
<tr><td>Current assets</td><td></td></tr>
<tr><td>Cash</td><td>$105,095</td></tr>
<tr><td>Accounts receivable</td><td>6,503</td></tr>
<tr><td>Merchandise inventory</td><td>190,014</td></tr>
<tr><td>Total current assets</td><td>301,612</td></tr>
<tr><td>Plant and equipment</td><td></td></tr>
<tr><td>Equipment</td><td>32,507</td></tr>
<tr><td>Total plant and equipment</td><td>32,507</td></tr>
<tr><td>Total assets</td><td>$334,119</td></tr>
<tr><td>Liabilities</td><td></td></tr>
<tr><td>Current liabilities</td><td></td></tr>
<tr><td>Accounts payable</td><td>$6,007</td></tr>
<tr><td>Wages payable</td><td>4,761</td></tr>
<tr><td>Total current liabilities</td><td>10,768</td></tr>
<tr><td>Long-term liabilities</td><td></td></tr>
<tr><td>Mortgage note payable</td><td>281,017</td></tr>
<tr><td>Total long-term liabilities</td><td>281,017</td></tr>
<tr><td>Total liabilities</td><td>291,785</td></tr>
<tr><td>Owner's Equity</td><td></td></tr>
<tr><td>Frank Rayco, capital</td><td>42,334</td></tr>
<tr><td>Total liabilities and owner's equity</td><td>$334,119</td></tr>
</table>

<table>
<tr><td colspan="2">Rayco, Inc.<br>Balance Sheet<br>December 31, 2008</td></tr>
<tr><td>Assets</td><td></td></tr>
<tr><td>Current assets</td><td></td></tr>
<tr><td>Cash</td><td>$114,975</td></tr>
<tr><td>Accounts receivable</td><td>8,918</td></tr>
<tr><td>Merchandise inventory</td><td>187,915</td></tr>
<tr><td>Total current assets</td><td>311,808</td></tr>
<tr><td>Plant and equipment</td><td></td></tr>
<tr><td>Equipment</td><td>29,719</td></tr>
<tr><td>Total plant and equipment</td><td>29,719</td></tr>
<tr><td>Total assets</td><td>$341,527</td></tr>
<tr><td>Liabilities</td><td></td></tr>
<tr><td>Current liabilities</td><td></td></tr>
<tr><td>Accounts payable</td><td>$6,832</td></tr>
<tr><td>Wages payable</td><td>5,215</td></tr>
<tr><td>Total current liabilities</td><td>12,047</td></tr>
<tr><td>Long-term liabilities</td><td></td></tr>
<tr><td>Mortgage note payable</td><td>279,409</td></tr>
<tr><td>Total long-term liabilities</td><td>279,409</td></tr>
<tr><td>Total liabilities</td><td>291,456</td></tr>
<tr><td>Owner's Equity</td><td></td></tr>
<tr><td>Frank Rayco, capital</td><td>50,071</td></tr>
<tr><td>Total liabilities and owner's equity</td><td>$341,527</td></tr>
</table>

# 2

1. $105,095 ÷ \$334,119 = 0.315 = 31.5\%$
   $6,503 ÷ \$334,119 = 0.019 = 1.9\%$
   $190,014 ÷ \$334,119 = 0.569 = 56.9\%$
   $301,612 ÷ \$334,119 = 0.903 = 90.3\%$
   $32,507 ÷ \$334,119 = 0.097 = 9.7\%$
   $334,119 ÷ \$334,119 = 1 = 100\%$
   $6,007 ÷ \$334,119 = 0.018 = 1.8\%$
   $4,761 ÷ \$334,119 = 0.014 = 1.4\%$
   $10,768 ÷ \$334,119 = 0.032 = 3.2\%$
   $281,017 ÷ \$334,119 = 0.841 = 84.1\%$
   $291,785 ÷ \$334,119 = 0.873 = 87.3\%$
   $42,334 ÷ \$334,119 = 0.127 = 12.7\%$

**Rayco, Inc.**
**Balance Sheet**
**December 31, 2007**

|  | Amount | Percent |
|---|---|---|
| **Assets** | | |
| *Current assets* | | |
| Cash | $105,095 | 31.5% |
| Accounts receivable | 6,503 | 1.9% |
| Merchandise inventory | 190,014 | 56.9% |
| Total current assets | 301,612 | 90.3% |
| | | |
| *Plant and equipment* | | |
| Equipment | 32,507 | 9.7% |
| Total plant and equipment | 32,507 | 9.7% |
| Total assets | $334,119 | 100.0% |
| | | |
| **Liabilities** | | |
| *Current liabilities* | | |
| Accounts payable | $6,007 | 1.8% |
| Wages payable | 4,761 | 1.4% |
| Total current liabilities | 10,768 | 3.2% |
| | | |
| *Long-term liabilities* | | |
| Mortgage note payable | 281,017 | 84.1% |
| Total long-term liabilities | 281,017 | 84.1% |
| Total liabilities | 291,785 | 87.3% |
| | | |
| **Owner's Equity** | | |
| Frank Rayco, capital | 42,334 | 12.7% |
| Total liabilities and owner's equity | $334,119 | 100.0% |

2. $114,975 ÷ \$341,527 = 0.337 = 33.7\%$
   $8,918 ÷ \$341,527 = 0.026 = 2.6\%$
   $187,915 ÷ \$341,527 = 0.550 = 55.0\%$
   $311,808 ÷ \$341,527 = 0.913 = 91.3\%$
   $29,719 ÷ \$341,527 = 0.087 = 8.7\%$
   $341,527 ÷ \$341,527 = 1 = 100\%$
   $6,832 ÷ \$341,527 = 0.020 = 2.0\%$
   $5,215 ÷ \$341,527 = 0.015 = 1.5\%$
   $12,047 ÷ \$341,527 = 0.035 = 3.5\%$
   $279,409 ÷ \$341,527 = 0.818 = 81.8\%$
   $291,456 ÷ \$341,527 = 0.853 = 85.3\%$
   $50,071 ÷ \$341,527 = 0.147 = 14.7\%$

**Rayco, Inc.**
**Balance Sheet**
**December 31, 2008**

|  | Amount | Percent |
|---|---|---|
| **Assets** | | |
| *Current assets* | | |
| Cash | $114,975 | 33.7% |
| Accounts receivable | 8,918 | 2.6% |
| Merchandise inventory | 187,915 | 55.0% |
| Total current assets | 311,808 | 91.3% |
| | | |
| *Plant and equipment* | | |
| Equipment | 29,719 | 8.7% |
| Total plant and equipment | 29,719 | 8.7% |
| Total assets | $341,527 | 100.0% |
| | | |
| **Liabilities** | | |
| *Current liabilities* | | |
| Accounts payable | $6,832 | 2.0% |
| Wages payable | 5,215 | 1.5% |
| Total current liabilities | 12,047 | 3.5% |
| | | |
| *Long-term liabilities* | | |
| Mortgage note payable | 279,409 | 81.8% |
| Total long-term liabilities | 279,409 | 81.8% |
| Total liabilities | 291,456 | 85.3% |
| | | |
| **Owner's Equity** | | |
| Frank Rayco, capital | 50,071 | 14.7% |
| Total liabilities and owner's equity | $341,527 | 100.0% |

3. Show the vertical analysis for 2007 and 2008 on the same balance sheet. Use same calculations from Exercises 1 and 2.

4. In 2008 Rayco, Inc., had total assets of $341,527, which is more than the $334,119 reported as total assets for 2007.

**Rayco, Inc.**
**Comparative Balance Sheet**
**December 31, 2007, and December 31, 2008**

| | 2008 | Percent | 2007 | Percent |
|---|---|---|---|---|
| **Assets** | | | | |
| *Current assets* | | | | |
| Cash | $114,975 | 33.7% | $105,095 | 31.5% |
| Accounts receivable | 8,918 | 2.6% | 6,503 | 1.9% |
| Merchandise inventory | 187,915 | 55.0% | 190,014 | 56.9% |
| Total current assets | 311,808 | 91.3% | 301,612 | 90.3% |
| | | | | |
| *Plant and equipment* | | | | |
| Equipment | 29,719 | 8.7% | 32,507 | 9.7% |
| Total plant and equipment | 29,719 | 8.7% | 32,507 | 9.7% |
| Total assets | $341,527 | 100.0% | $334,119 | 100.0% |
| | | | | |
| **Liabilities** | | | | |
| *Current liabilities* | | | | |
| Accounts payable | $6,832 | 2.0% | $6,007 | 1.8% |
| Wages payable | 5,215 | 1.5% | 4,761 | 1.4% |
| Total current liabilities | 12,047 | 3.5% | 10,768 | 3.2% |
| | | | | |
| *Long-term liabilities* | | | | |
| Mortgage note payable | 279,409 | 81.8% | 281,017 | 84.1% |
| Total long-term liabilities | 279,409 | 81.8% | 281,017 | 84.1% |
| Total liabilities | 291,456 | 85.3% | 291,785 | 87.3% |
| | | | | |
| **Owner's Equity** | | | | |
| Frank Rayco, capital | 50,071 | 14.7% | 42,334 | 12.7% |
| Total liabilities and owner's equity | $341,527 | 100.0% | $334,119 | 100.0% |

# 3

1. Cash: $114,975 - $105,095 = $9,880
Accounts receivable: $8,918 - $6,503 = $2,415
Inventory: $187,915 - $190,014 = ($2,099)
Total current assets: $311,808 - $301,612 = $10,196
Equipment: $29,719 - $32,507 = ($2,788)
Total assets: $341,527 - $334,119 = $7,408
Accounts payable: $6,832 - $6,007 = $825
Wages payable: $5,215 - $4,761 = $454
Total current liabilities: $12,047 - $10,768 = $1,279
Mortgage note payable: $279,409 - $281,017 = ($1,608)
Total liabilities: $291,456 - $291,785 = ($329)
Rayco's capital: $50,071 - $42,334 = $7,737
Total liabilities and owner's equity = $341,527 - $334,119 = $7,408

2. Cash: $\frac{\$9,880}{\$105,095} (100\%) = 9.4\%$

Accounts receivable: $\frac{(\$2,415)}{\$6,503} (100\%) = 37.1\%$

Inventory: $\frac{(\$2,099)}{\$190,014} (100\%) = (1.1\%)$

Total current assets: $\frac{\$10,196}{\$301,612} (100\%) = 3.4\%$

Equipment: $\frac{(\$2,788)}{\$32,507} (100\%) = (8.6\%)$

Total assets: $\frac{\$7,408}{\$334,119} (100\%) = 2.2\%$

Accounts payable: $\frac{\$825}{\$6,007} (100\%) = 13.7\%$

Wages payable: $\frac{\$454}{\$4,761} (100\%) = 9.5\%$

Total current liabilities: $\frac{\$1,279}{\$10,768} (100\%) = 11.9\%$

Mortgage note payable: $\frac{(\$1,608)}{\$281,017} (100\%) = (0.6\%)$

Total liabilities: $\frac{(\$329)}{\$291,785} (100\%) = (0.1\%)$

Rayco's capital: $\frac{\$7,737}{\$42,334} (100\%) = 18.3\%$

Total liabilities and owner's equity: $\frac{\$7,408}{\$334,119} (100\%) = 2.2\%$

3.

| Rayco, Inc.<br>Horizontal Analysis of Comparative Balance Sheet<br>December 31, 2007, and December 31, 2008 | | | | |
| --- | --- | --- | --- | --- |
| | **2008** | **2007** | Increase or (Decrease) | Percent of increase or (Decrease) |
| **Assets** | | | | |
| *Current assets* | | | | |
| Cash | $114,975 | $105,095 | $9,880 | 9.4 |
| Accounts receivable | 8,918 | 6,503 | $2,415 | 37.1 |
| Merchandise inventory | 187,915 | 190,014 | ($2,099) | (1.1) |
| Total current assets | 311,808 | 301,612 | $10,196 | 3.4 |
| *Plant and equipment* | | | | |
| Equipment | 29,719 | 32,507 | ($2,788) | (8.6) |
| Total plant and equipment | 29,719 | 32,507 | ($2,788) | (8.6) |
| Total assets | $341,527 | $334,119 | $7,408 | 2.2 |
| **Liabilities** | | | | |
| *Current liabilities* | | | | |
| Accounts payable | $6,832 | $6,007 | $825 | 13.7 |
| Wages payable | 5,215 | 4,761 | $454 | 9.5 |
| Total current liabilities | 12,047 | 10,768 | $1,279 | 11.9 |
| *Long-term liabilities* | | | | |
| Mortgage note payable | 279,409 | 281,017 | ($1,608) | (0.6) |
| Total long-term liabilities | 279,409 | 281,017 | ($1,608) | (0.6) |
| Total liabilities | 291,456 | 291,785 | ($329) | (0.1) |
| **Owner's Equity** | | | | |
| Frank Rayco, capital | 50,071 | 42,334 | $7,737 | 18.3 |
| Total liabilities and owner's equity | $341,527 | $334,119 | $7,408 | 2.2 |

4. Read from the table formed in Exercise 3. The percentage of increase in total assets is 2.2%.

# Section 20-2

# 1

1. Gross profit = $5,385,920 − $2,073,587 = $3,312,333
   Net income = $3,312,333 − $498,507 = $2,813,826

2.

| Cedar Rapids Auto, Inc.<br>Income Statement for<br>December 31, 2008 | |
| --- | --- |
| Net sales | $5,385,920 |
| Cost of goods sold | 2,073,587 |
| Gross profit | $3,312,333 |
| | |
| Operating expenses | 498,507 |
| Net income | $2,813,826 |

3. Net sales = $597,341 − $10,514 = $586,827
   Cost of goods sold = $38,917 + $261,053 − $42,013 = $257,957
   Gross profit from sales = $586,827 − $257,957 = $328,870

4. Total operating expenses = $90,500 + $12,200 + $7,582 + $1,077 + $18,400 + $2,700 = $132,459
   Net income = $328,870 − $132,459 = $196,411

| Cassandra's DVD Shop<br>Income Statement for<br>December 31, 2008 | |
| --- | --- |
| Gross sales | $597,341 |
| Sales returns and allowances | 10,514 |
| **Net sales** | 586,827 |
| | |
| Beginning inventory cost | 38,917 |
| Cost of purchases | 261,053 |
| Ending inventory | 42,013 |
| Cost of goods sold | 257,957 |
| Gross profit from sales | $328,870 |
| | |
| Salary | 90,500 |
| Insurance | 12,200 |
| Utilities | 7,582 |
| Maintenance | 1,077 |
| Rent | 18,400 |
| Depreciation | 2,700 |
| Total operating expenses | 132,459 |
| Net income | $196,411 |

# 2

**1.**

| Cedar Rapids Auto, Inc. Income Statement for December 31, 2008 | | Percent of Net Sales |
|---|---|---|
| Net sales | $5,385,920 | 100.0 |
| Cost of goods sold | 2,073,587 | 38.5 |
| Gross profit | 3,312,333 | 61.5 |
| Operating expenses | 498,507 | 9.3 |
| Net income | $2,813,826 | 52.2 |

**2.**

| Cedar Rapids Auto, Inc. Comparative Income Statement for December 31, 2007 and December 31, 2008 | 2008 | Percent of Net Sales | 2007 | Percent of Net Sales |
|---|---|---|---|---|
| Net sales | $5,385,920 | 100.0 | $4,103,370 | 100.0 |
| Cost of goods sold | 2,073,587 | 38.5 | 1,992,500 | 48.6 |
| Gross profit | 3,312,333 | 61.5 | 2,110,870 | 51.4 |
| Operating expenses | 498,507 | 9.3 | 503,719 | 12.3 |
| Net income | $2,813,826 | 52.2 | $1,607,151 | 39.2 |

**3.**

| Cassandra's DVD Shop Income Statement for December 31, 2008 | | Percent of Net Sales |
|---|---|---|
| Gross sales | $597,341 | 101.8 |
| Sales returns and allowances | 10,514 | 1.8 |
| **Net sales** | 586,827 | 100.0 |
| Beginning inventory cost | 38,917 | 6.6 |
| Cost of purchases | 261,053 | 44.5 |
| Ending inventory | 42,013 | 7.2 |
| Cost of goods sold | 257,957 | 44.0 |
| Gross profit from sales | $328,870 | 56.0 |
| Salary | 90,500 | 15.4 |
| Insurance | 12,200 | 2.1 |
| Utilities | 7,582 | 1.3 |
| Maintenance | 1,077 | 0.2 |
| Rent | 18,400 | 3.1 |
| Depreciation | 2,700 | 0.5 |
| Total operating expenses | 132,459 | 22.6 |
| Net income | $196,411 | 33.5 |

**4.**

| Cassandra's DVD Shop Income Statement for December 31, 2008 | 2008 | Percent of Net Sales | 2007 | Percent of Net Sales |
|---|---|---|---|---|
| Gross sales | $597,341 | 101.8 | $435,913 | 101.9 |
| Sales returns and allowances | 10,514 | 1.8 | 8,019 | 1.9 |
| **Net sales** | 586,827 | 100.0 | 427,894 | 100.0 |
| Beginning inventory cost | 38,917 | 6.6 | 36,992 | 8.6 |
| Cost of purchases | 261,053 | 44.5 | 248,504 | 58.1 |
| Ending inventory | 42,013 | 7.2 | 41,007 | 9.6 |
| Cost of goods sold | 257,957 | 44.0 | 244,489 | 57.1 |
| Gross profit from sales | $328,870 | 56.0 | $183,405 | 42.9 |
| Salary | 90,500 | 15.4 | 82,450 | 19.3 |
| Insurance | 12,200 | 2.1 | 12,200 | 2.9 |
| Utilities | 7,582 | 1.3 | 6,097 | 1.4 |
| Maintenance | 1,077 | 0.2 | 817 | 0.2 |
| Rent | 18,400 | 3.1 | 17,800 | 4.2 |
| Depreciation | 2,700 | 0.5 | 2,300 | 0.5 |
| Total operating expenses | 132,459 | 22.6 | 121,664 | 28.4 |
| Net income | $196,411 | 33.5 | $61,741 | 14.4 |

# 3

**1.** Net sales increase = $5,385,920 − $4,103,370 = $1,282,550

$$\text{Percent increase} = \frac{\$1,282,550}{\$4,103,370}\,(100\%) = 31.3\%$$

Cost of goods sold increase = $2,073,587 − $1,992,500 = $81,087

$$\text{Percent increase} = \frac{\$81,087}{\$1,992,500}\,(100\%) = 4.1\%$$

Gross profit increase = $3,312,333 − $2,110,870 = $1,201,463

$$\text{Percent increase} = \frac{\$1,201,463}{\$2,110,870}\,(100\%) = 56.9\%$$

Operating expenses decrease = $498,507 − $503,719 = ($5,212)

$$\text{Percent decrease} = \frac{(\$5,212)}{\$503,719}\,(100\%) = (1.0)\%$$

Net income increase = $2,813,826 − $1,607,151 = $1,206,675

$$\text{Percent increase} = \frac{\$1,206,675}{\$1,607,151}\,(100\%) = 75.1\%$$

| Cedar Rapids Auto, Inc. Comparative Income Statement for December 31, 2007, and December 31, 2008 | 2008 | 2007 | Increase or (Decrease) | Percent of increase or (Decrease) |
|---|---|---|---|---|
| Net sales | $5,385,920 | $4,103,370 | $1,282,550 | 31.3 |
| Cost of goods sold | 2,073,587 | 1,992,500 | $81,087 | 4.1 |
| Gross profit | 3,312,333 | 2,110,870 | $1,201,463 | 56.9 |
| Operating expenses | 498,507 | 503,719 | ($5,212) | (1.0) |
| Net income | $2,813,826 | $1,607,151 | $1,206,675 | 75.1 |

2. Gross sales increase = $597,341 − $435,913 = $161,428

$$\text{Percent increase} = \frac{\$161,428}{\$435,913}(100\%) = 37.0\%$$

Sales returns and allowances increase = $10,514 − $8,019 = $2,495

$$\text{Percent increase} = \frac{\$2,495}{\$8,019}(100\%) = 31.1\%$$

Remaining increases and decreases and percents are calculated similarly.

| Cassandra's DVD Shop Income Statement for December 31, 2008 | | | | |
|---|---|---|---|---|
| | 2008 | 2007 | Increase or (Decrease) | Percent of increase or (Decrease) |
| Gross sales | $597,341 | $435,913 | $161,428 | 37.0 |
| Sales returns and allowances | 10,514 | 8,019 | 2,495 | 31.1 |
| **Net sales** | 586,827 | 427,894 | 158,933 | 37.1 |
| Beginning inventory cost | 38,917 | 36,992 | 1,925 | 5.2 |
| Cost of purchases | 261,053 | 248,504 | 12,549 | 5.0 |
| Ending inventory | 42,013 | 41,007 | 1,006 | 2.5 |
| Cost of goods sold | 257,957 | 244,489 | 13,468 | 5.5 |
| Gross profit from sales | $328,870 | $183,405 | 145,465 | 79.3 |
| Salary | 90,500 | 82,450 | 8,050 | 9.8 |
| Insurance | 12,200 | 12,200 | 0 | 0.0 |
| Utilities | 7,582 | 6,097 | 1,485 | 24.4 |
| Maintenance | 1,077 | 817 | 260 | 31.8 |
| Rent | 18,400 | 17,800 | 600 | 3.4 |
| Depreciation | 2,700 | 2,300 | 400 | 17.4 |
| Total operating expenses | 132,459 | 121,664 | 10,795 | 8.9 |
| Net income | $196,411 | $61,741 | 134,670 | 218.1 |

3. Net sales is the base when calculating percentages for a vertical analysis.

4. The dollar amount for the earliest year is used as the base.

# Section 20-3

## 1

1. Operating ratio $= \dfrac{\$2,073,587 + \$498,507}{\$5,385,920}$

$= \dfrac{\$2,572,094}{\$5,385,920}$

$= 0.478$ to 1

2. The ratio is desirable since it is less than 1.

3. Debt ratio $= \dfrac{\$291,456}{\$341,527} = 0.85$ to 1

4. This debt ratio is slightly high. The industry average for this ratio is generally from 0.05 to 0.75.

# CHAPTER 21

## Section 21-1

## 1

1. 12,735,676 shares

2. $26.49 − $25.30 = $1.19

3. A change of +$0.29 means the closing price the previous day (and the opening price today) was $0.29 less than today's closing price.
$26.38 − $0.29 = $26.09

4. Examine Column 15 to find AK Steel has a YTD% Chg of 80.4%.

5. Current price per share = $54
Net income per share = $4.32

$$\text{Price-earnings (P/E) ratio} = \frac{\text{current price per share}}{\text{net income per share (past 12 months)}}$$

$$\text{Price-earnings (P/E) ratio} = \frac{\$54}{\$4.32}$$

P/E ratio = 12.5 = 13

6. Current price per share = $25.38
Net income per share = $1.49

$$\text{Price-earnings (P/E) ratio} = \frac{\text{current price per share}}{\text{net income per share (past 12 months)}}$$

$$\text{Price-earnings (P/E) ratio} = \frac{\$25.38}{\$1.49}$$

P/E ratio = 17.03355705 = 17

# 2

1. $100,000(\$0.32) = \$32,000$

2. Dividends in arrears: $10,000(\$0.73) = \$7,300$

   Current dividends to preferred stockholders $= 10,000(\$0.73)$
   $$= \$7,300$$

   Remaining dividends $= \$2,800,000 - \$14,600$
   $$= \$2,785,400$$

3. Dividends paid to common stockholders $= \dfrac{\$2,785,400}{1,000,000}$
   $$= \$2.7854$$
   $$= \$2.79$$

4. $\$0.15(6,684,582) = \$1,002,687.30$

## Section 21-2

# 1

1. Column 3 shows $6\frac{3}{4}\%$ and a maturity date of 2025.

2. Column 5 shows a volume of 5 bonds sold for the week.

3. The net change (column 9) of $-0.38\%$ indicates a net change $=$ $(-0.0038)\,(\$1,000) = -\$3.80$

4. Column 4 is current yield. For JCPL the current yield is 6.8%.

# 2

1. $103.5\% = 1.035$

   $1.035(\$1,000) = \$1,035$

2. $130.13\% = 1.3013$

   $1.3013(\$1,000) = \$1,301.30$

3. $103.5\% + 0.75\% = 104.25\%$

   $104.25\% = 1.0425$

   $1.0425(\$1,000) = \$1,042.50$

4. $130.13\% + 0.38\% = 130.51\%$

   $130.51\% = 1.3051$

   $1.3051(\$1,000) = \$1,305.10$

# 3

1. Current price per share (NAV) $= \$11.17$

2. Yesterday's NAV $= \$11.17$ since there was no change.

3. Year-to-date % return $= 4\%$

   $$\text{NAV at beginning of year} = \frac{\$11.17}{100\% + 4\%}$$
   $$= \frac{\$11.17}{104\%}$$
   $$= \frac{\$11.17}{1.04}$$
   $$= \$10.74038462$$
   $$= \$10.74$$

4. Year-to-date % return $= 10.4\%$

   $$\text{NAV at beginning of year} = \frac{\$16.40}{100\% + 10.4\%} = \frac{\$16.40}{110.4\%}$$
   $$= \frac{\$16.40}{1.104} = \$14.85507246$$
   $$= \$14.86$$

# Answers to Odd-Numbered Exercises

## CHAPTER 1

### Section Exercises

## 1-1

1. Twenty-two million, three hundred fifty-six thousand, twenty-seven
3. Seven hundred thirty million, five hundred thirty-one thousand, nine hundred sixty-eight
5. Five hundred twenty-three billion, eight hundred million, seven thousand, one hundred ninety
7. 14,985
9. 17,000,803,075
11. 306,541
13. 480
15. 300,000
17. Three billion, five hundred eighty-five million dollars
19. 86,000,000

## 1-2

1. 1,600
3. 1,843
5. 33
7. 43,800
9. 89,445
11. 407

13.

| Region | W | Th | F | S | Su | Region Totals |
|---|---|---|---|---|---|---|
| Eastern | $ 72,492 | $ 81,948 | $ 32,307 | $ 24,301 | $32,589 | $243,637 |
| Southern | 81,897 | 59,421 | 48,598 | 61,025 | 21,897 | 272,838 |
| Central | 71,708 | 22,096 | 23,222 | 21,507 | 42,801 | 181,334 |
| Western | 61,723 | 71,687 | 52,196 | 41,737 | 22,186 | 249,529 |
| Daily Sales Total | $287,820 | $235,152 | $156,323 | $148,570 | $119,473 | $947,338 |

Difference = $436,662    Goal was not reached.

15. $923
17. Wages = $441 Gross profit = $399
19. 29 boxes
21. $199,500,000
23. $1,680,000

### EXERCISES SET A, P. 25
1. Four thousand, two hundred nine
3. $7,000,000,000
5. 400
7. 830
9. 300,000; 6,300,000
11. 5,000
13. 63,601
15. 22,000; 21,335
17. 240; 230 items
19. 4,000; 4,072
21. 50,000; 55,632
23. 244 fan belts
25. 782,878
27. 47,220,000
29. 1,550,000; 1,495,184
31. 336 radios per thousand
33. 7,777; (or 8,000 rounded); 8,805 R6
35. $12 per hour

### EXERCISES SET B, P. 27
1. ninety-seven thousand, one hundred sixty-eight
3. 26
5. 8,200
7. 30,000
9. 2,000 radios
11. 20,000,000,000
13. 59,882
15. 8,400; 8,759
17. 723 cards
19. 200,000; 182,902
21. 60,000; 74,385
23. 13 pounds
25. 6,840,462
27. 162,000
29. 200,000; 206,388
31. 88 R1 TVs per thousand people
33. 666; 505 R161
35. 77 coins

### PRACTICE TEST, P. 29
1. five hundred three
2. twelve million, fifty-six thousand, thirty-nine
3. 84,300
4. 59,000
5. 80,000
6. 600,000
7. 5,017,135,632
8. 17,500,608
9. 2,200; 2,117
10. 700; 641

**11.** 45,000; 41,032  **12.** 80; 75 R46  **13.** 1,153 items were counted  **14.** Only 15 boxes can be stacked  **15.** 249 packages

**16.** 20 pairs of shoes  **17.** $17 per hour  **18.** 280 pieces of fruit  **19.** 48 pages  **20.** 37 novels

# CHAPTER 2
## Section Exercises

## 2-1

**1.** proper  **3.** improper  **5.** proper  **7.** $1\frac{5}{7}$  **9.** 1

**11.** 2  **13.** $\frac{25}{4}$  **15.** $\frac{7}{3}$  **17.** $\frac{13}{8}$  **19.** $\frac{4}{5}$

**21.** $\frac{3}{4}$  **23.** $\frac{2}{3}$  **25.** $\frac{6}{16}$  **27.** $\frac{12}{32}$  **29.** $\frac{5}{15}$

## 2-2

**1.** $\frac{8}{9}$  **3.** $1\frac{3}{10}$  **5.** $12\frac{1}{3}$

**7.** $137\frac{47}{72}$  **9.** $9\frac{1}{6}$  **11.** $\frac{1}{2}$

**13.** $\frac{1}{28}$  **15.** $2\frac{2}{9}$  **17.** $8\frac{7}{60}$

**19.** $3\frac{1}{3}$  **21.** $42\frac{1}{8}$ yards  **23.** 89 feet

**25.** She can use the fabric.  **27.** $1\frac{5}{16}$ feet; $1\frac{1}{2}$ feet; $1\frac{3}{8}$ feet; $1\frac{3}{16}$ feet

## 2-3

**1.** $\frac{3}{10}$  **3.** $22\frac{13}{36}$  **5.** $\frac{12}{7}$  **7.** $\frac{1}{9}$

**9.** $\frac{7}{39}$  **11.** $\frac{5}{6}$  **13.** $2\frac{1}{10}$  **15.** $\frac{3}{20}$

**17.** $20\frac{20}{39}$ rooms  **19.** 6  **21.** $16\frac{1}{2}$ feet

### EXERCISES SET A, P. 63

**1.** $\frac{3}{5}, \frac{7}{9}, \frac{5}{8}, \frac{100}{301}, \frac{41}{53}$; proper fractions  **3.** $20\frac{2}{3}$  **5.** $8\frac{1}{2}$  **7.** $\frac{13}{3}$

**9.** $\frac{5}{6}$  **11.** $\frac{5}{8}$  **13.** $\frac{20}{32}$  **15.** $\frac{1}{7}$ of the employees

**17.** 168  **19.** $1\frac{2}{5}$  **21.** $11\frac{7}{8}$  **23.** 29 yards

**25.** $3\frac{3}{10}$  **27.** $1\frac{1}{2}$  **29.** $\frac{5}{18}$  **31.** 28

**33.** 4  **35.** 3  **37.** $\frac{4}{7}$  **39.** $1\frac{1}{4}$ inches

**41.** $192

# EXERCISES SET B, P. 65

**1.** $3\frac{7}{15}$  **3.** 7  **5.** $\frac{59}{8}$  **7.** $\frac{9}{10}$  **9.** $\frac{2}{7}$

**11.** $\frac{63}{81}$  **13.** $\frac{4}{15}$ of the class  **15.** 72  **17.** 1  **19.** $9\frac{5}{12}$

**21.** $\frac{1}{2}$  **23.** $7\frac{7}{8}$  **25.** Maxine Ford worked $2\frac{1}{2}$ hours more than George.  **27.** $3\frac{3}{7}$  **29.** 18

**31.** $\frac{3}{2}$  **33.** $\frac{8}{19}$  **35.** $6\frac{2}{3}$  **37.** $4\frac{1}{2}$  **39.** $5\frac{9}{20}$ feet

**41.** 13 feet

# PRACTICE TEST, P. 67

**1.** $\frac{1}{5}$  **2.** $\frac{5}{3}$  **3.** $\frac{5}{8}$  **4.** $\frac{4}{5}$  **5.** $\frac{3}{7}$

**6.** $\frac{7}{17}$  **7.** $\frac{21}{8}$  **8.** $\frac{37}{12}$  **9.** $2\frac{1}{3}$  **10.** $4\frac{4}{13}$

**11.** $\frac{1}{6}$  **12.** $1\frac{21}{40}$  **13.** $\frac{7}{16}$  **14.** $1\frac{1}{9}$  **15.** $1\frac{19}{23}$

**16.** 1,840  **17.** $5\frac{5}{6}$  **18.** $47\frac{1}{5}$  **19.** $\frac{1}{2}$ of the truckload remains to be unloaded  **20.** $\frac{3}{20}$

**21.** 100 sheets  **22.** $7\frac{3}{4}\%$

# CHAPTER 3

## Section Exercises

## 3-1

**1.** Five hundred eighty-two thousandths  **3.** One and nine ten-thousandths  **5.** Seven hundred eighty-two and seven hundredths

**7.** 0.312  **9.** 5.03  **11.** $785

**13.** $0.52  **15.** $32,048.87  **17.** 17.0

**19.** Nineteen dollars and eighty-nine cents

## 3-2

**1.** 933.935  **3.** $80.30  **5.** 109.57  **7.** $244.85  **9.** $7,270.48

**11.** 78.8  **13.** 1.474  **15.** 0.36719  **17.** 10.31  **19.** $\approx 0.02$

**21.** $85.81  **23.** $7.52 in change  **25.** $236.04  **27.** $1,470.00  **29.** Yes, each person will pay $6.18.

## 3-3

**1.** $\frac{3}{5}$  **3.** $\frac{5}{8}$  **5.** $7\frac{5}{16}$  **7.** 0.7  **9.** $\approx 0.58$  **11.** $\approx 2.13$

# EXERCISES SET A, P. 127

**1.** five-tenths  **3.** two hundred seventy-five hundred-thousandths  **5.** one hundred twenty-eight and twenty-three hundredths  **7.** 0.135  **9.** 1,700

**11.** 1.246  **13.** $28.82  **15.** 376.74  **17.** 135.6  **19.** 193.41

| | | | | | | | |
|---|---|---|---|---|---|---|---|
| **21.** 21.2352 | | **23.** ≈ 8.57 | | **25.** ≈ 1,559.79 | | **27.** $\frac{11}{20}$ | **29.** 0.85 |
| **31.** $20.93 | | **33.** $88.96 | | **35.** $19.20 | | | |

## EXERCISES SET B, P. 131

| | | | | |
|---|---|---|---|---|
| **1.** twenty-seven hundredths | **3.** one hundred twenty thousand seven hundred four millionths | **5.** three thousand and three thousandths | **7.** 384.7 | **9.** 33 |
| **11.** 41.233 | **13.** $34.93 | **15.** 479.41 | **17.** 277.59 | **19.** 1,347.84 |
| **21.** 1,101.15 | **23.** 13.52 | **25.** ≈ 1,706.45 | **27.** $\frac{3}{4}$ | **29.** 0.05 |
| **31.** 183.4 square meters | **33.** $555.00 | **35.** 212.14 inches | | |

## PRACTICE TEST, P. 135

| | | | | |
|---|---|---|---|---|
| **1.** 42.9 | **2.** 30 | **3.** twenty-four and one thousand seven ten-thousandths | **4.** 3.028 | **5.** 24.092 |
| **6.** 2,741.8 | **7.** 224.857 | **8.** 0.566 ≈ 0.57 | **9.** 447.12 | **10.** 0.0138 |
| **11.** 89.82 | **12.** 5.76875 | **13.** 34.366 | **14.** 7.3 | **15.** 179.24 |
| **16.** 37,417 | **17.** 1.7 degrees | **18.** $7,980.00 | **19.** $11,043.50 | **20.** $31.55 |

# CHAPTER 4

## Section Exercises

## 4-1

**1.**

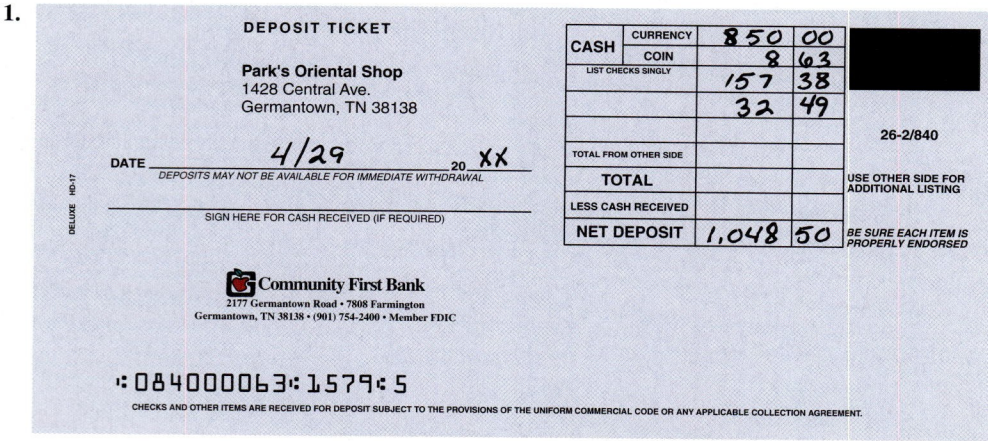

**3.** **5.**

**7.** $8,762.60;

| | | **RECORD ALL TRANSACTIONS THAT AFFECT YOUR ACCOUNT** | | | | | | BALANCE | |
|---|---|---|---|---|---|---|---|---|---|
| NUMBER | DATE | DESCRIPTION OF TRANSACTION | DEBIT | √ | FEE | CREDIT | | 7,869 | 40 |
| Dep | 4/29 | Deposit Payroll | $ | | | $ 1,048 | 50 | +1,048 | 50 |
| | | | | | | | | 8,917 | 90 |
| 456 | 4/29 | Green Harvest | 155 30 | | | | | −155 | 30 |
| | | | | | | | | 8,762 | 60 |
| | | | | | | | | | |

**9.** For Deposit to acct 26-8224021; Ronald H. Cox Realty; restricted endorsement

**11.** Answers will vary. Deposits can be made to checking or savings accounts. Withdrawals can be made from checking or savings accounts. Loan payments can be made on bank loans. Checking and savings account information can be accessed. Funds can be transferred from savings accounts to checking accounts and from checking accounts to savings accounts. All these transaction options must be arranged between the account holder and the bank and mutually agreed upon by both. Banks may charge from some or all of these transactions.

# 4-2

**1.** Leader Federal: $942.18; LG&W: $217.17

**3.** lowest: $2,403.55; highest: $4,804.87

**5.**

| | | RECORD ALL TRANSACTIONS THAT AFFECT YOUR ACCOUNT | | | | | BALANCE | |
|---|---|---|---|---|---|---|---|---|
| NUMBER | DATE | DESCRIPTION OF TRANSACTION | DEBIT (−) | √T | FEE (IF ANY) (−) | CREDIT (+) | 2472 | 86 |
| 1094 | 8/28 | K-mart | 42 37 | √ | | | −42 | 37 |
| | | | | | | | 2430 | 49 |
| 1095 | 8/28 | Walgreen's | 12 96 | √ | | | −12 | 96 |
| | | | | | | | 2417 | 53 |
| Deposit | 9/1 | Payroll Schering-Plough | | √ | | 2401 32 | +2401 | 32 |
| | | | | | | | 4,818 | 85 |
| AW | 9/1 | Leader Federal | 942 18 | √ | | | −942 | 18 |
| | | | | | | | 3,876 | 67 |
| AW | 9/1 | LG & W | 217 17 | √ | | | −217 | 17 |
| | | | | | | | 3,659 | 50 |
| 1096 | 9/1 | Kroger | 36 01 | √ | | | −36 | 01 |
| | | | | | | | 3,623 | 49 |
| 1097 | 9/1 | Texaco | 178 13 | √ | | | −178 | 13 |
| | | | | | | | 3,445 | 36 |
| 1098 | 9/1 | Univ. of Memphis | 458 60 | √ | | | −458 | 60 |
| | | | | | | | 2,986 | 76 |
| 1099 | 9/15 | GMAC Credit Corp | 583 21 | √ | | | −583 | 21 |
| | | | | | | | 2,403 | 55 |
| 1100 | 9/18 | VISA | 283 21 | √ | | | −283 | 21 |
| | | | | | | | 2,120 | 34 |
| 1101 | 9/10 | Radio Shack | 189 37 | | | | −189 | 37 |
| | | | | | | | 1,930 | 97 |
| 1102 | 9/10 | Auto Zone | 48 23 | √ | | | −48 | 23 |
| | | | | | | | 1,882 | 74 |
| Deposit | 9/15 | Payroll- Schering Plough | | √ | | 2401 32 | +2,401 | 32 |
| | | | | | | | 4,284 | 06 |

REMEMBER TO RECORD AUTOMATIC PAYMENTS/DEPOSITS ON DATE AUTHORIZED.

| | | RECORD ALL TRANSACTIONS THAT AFFECT YOUR ACCOUNT | | | | | BALANCE | |
|---|---|---|---|---|---|---|---|---|
| NUMBER | DATE | DESCRIPTION OF TRANSACTION | DEBIT (−) | √T | FEE (IF ANY) (−) | CREDIT (+) | 4,284 | 06 |
| 1103 | 9/15 | Geoffrey Beane | 71 16 | √ | | | −71 | 16 |
| | | | | | | | 4,212 | 90 |
| 1104 | 9/14 | Heaven Scent Flowers | 12 75 | √ | | | −12 | 75 |
| | | | | | | | 4,200 | 15 |
| 1105 | 9/20 | Kroger | 87 75 | | | | −87 | 75 |
| | | | | | | | 4,112 | 40 |
| ATM | 9/20 | Kirby Woods | 60 00 | √ | | | −60 | 00 |
| | | | | | | | 4,052 | 40 |
| 1106 | 9/21 | Travelers Insurance | 1,238 42 | √ | | | −1,238 | 42 |
| | | | | | | | 2,813 | 98 |
| 1107 | 9/23 | Nation's Bank-Savings | 500 00 | √ | | | −500 | 00 |
| | | | | | | | 2,313 | 98 |
| | 9/27 | Interest earned | | √ | | 9 48 | +9 | 48 |
| | | | | | | | 2,323 | 46 |
| | 9/29 | Statement reconciled | | | | | | |

| $ 6,982 68 | BALANCE AS SHOWN ON BANK STATEMENT |
|---|---|
| 0 | TOTAL OF OUTSTANDING DEPOSITS |
| 6,982 68 | NEW TOTAL |
| −717 21 | SUBTRACT TOTAL OF OUTSTANDING CHECKS |
| $6,265 47 | YOUR ADJUSTED STATEMENT BALANCE |

SHOULD EQUAL

| BALANCE AS SHOWN IN YOUR REGISTER | $ 6,284 42 |
|---|---|
| SUBTRACT AMOUNT OF SERVICE CHARGE | 0 |
| NEW TOTAL | 6,265 42 |
| ADJUSTMENTS IF ANY | −18 95 |
| YOUR ADJUSTED REGISTER BALANCE | $6,265 47 |

| Outstanding Deposits (Credits) | |
|---|---|
| Date | Amount |
| | $ 0 |
| Total | $ 0 |

| Outstanding Checks (Debits) | | |
|---|---|---|
| Check Number | Date | Amount |
| 3785 | 3/5 | $ 346 18 |
| 3789 | 3/15 | 72 83 |
| 3790 | 3/17 | 146 17 |
| 3791 | 3/17 | 152 03 |
| Total | | $ 717 21 |

| $ 2,600 58 | BALANCE AS SHOWN ON BANK STATEMENT |
|---|---|
| 0 | TOTAL OF OUTSTANDING DEPOSITS |
| 2,600 58 | NEW TOTAL |
| −277 12 | SUBTRACT TOTAL OF OUTSTANDING CHECKS |
| $2,323 46 | YOUR ADJUSTED STATEMENT BALANCE |

=

| BALANCE AS SHOWN IN YOUR REGISTER | $ 2,313 98 |
|---|---|
| SUBTRACT AMOUNT OF SERVICE CHARGE | 0 |
| NEW TOTAL | 2,313 98 |
| ADJUSTMENTS IF ANY  Interest | +9 48 |
| YOUR ADJUSTED REGISTER BALANCE | $2,323 46 |

| Outstanding Deposits (Credits) | |
|---|---|
| Date | Amount |
| | $ |
| Total | $ 0 |

| Outstanding Checks (Debits) | | |
|---|---|---|
| Check Number | Date | Amount |
| 1101 | 9/10 | $ 189 37 |
| 1105 | 9/20 | 87 75 |
| Total | | $ 277 12 |

**1.**

| 456 | | Date June 13 20 XX |
|---|---|---|
| Amount | $296.83 | |
| To | Byron Johnson | |
| For | Washing machine | |

| Balance Forward | $4,307 | 21 |
|---|---|---|
| Deposits | | |
| Total | 4,307 | 21 |
| Amount This Check | 296 | 83 |
| Balance | $4,010 | 38 |

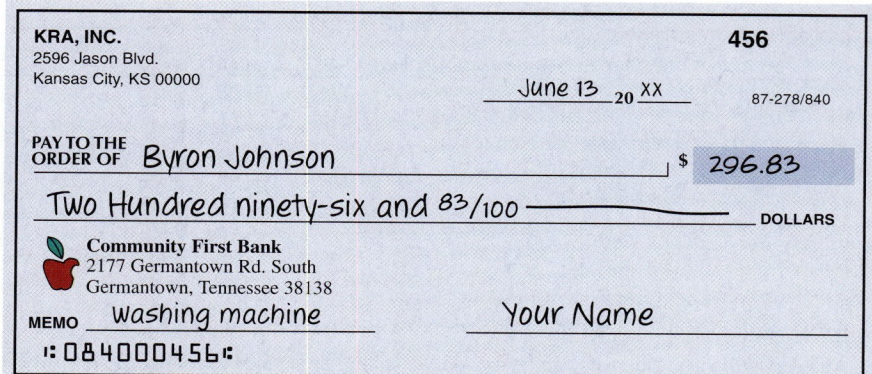

**KRA, INC.**
2596 Jason Blvd.
Kansas City, KS 00000

456

June 13 20 XX          87-278/840

PAY TO THE ORDER OF   Byron Johnson          $ 296.83

Two Hundred ninety-six and 83/100 ———————— DOLLARS

**Community First Bank**
2177 Germantown Rd. South
Germantown, Tennessee 38138

MEMO   Washing machine          Your Name

⑈084000456⑈

**3.**

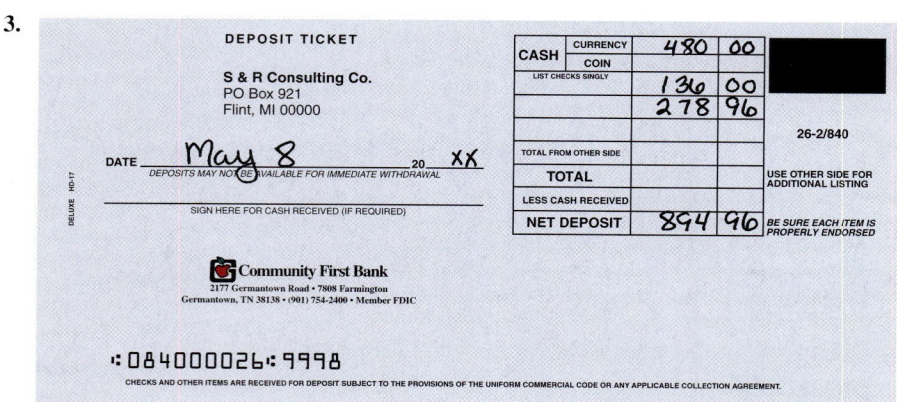

DEPOSIT TICKET

**S & R Consulting Co.**
PO Box 921
Flint, MI 00000

DATE  May 8  20  XX
DEPOSITS MAY NOT BE AVAILABLE FOR IMMEDIATE WITHDRAWAL

SIGN HERE FOR CASH RECEIVED (IF REQUIRED)

| CASH | CURRENCY | 480 | 00 | |
|---|---|---|---|---|
| | COIN | | | |
| LIST CHECKS SINGLY | | 136 | 00 | |
| | | 278 | 96 | 26-2/840 |
| TOTAL FROM OTHER SIDE | | | | USE OTHER SIDE FOR ADDITIONAL LISTING |
| TOTAL | | | | |
| LESS CASH RECEIVED | | | | |
| NET DEPOSIT | | 894 | 96 | BE SURE EACH ITEM IS PROPERLY ENDORSED |

**Community First Bank**
2177 Germantown Road • 7808 Farmington
Germantown, TN 38138 • (901) 754-2400 • Member FDIC

⑈084000026⑈ 9998

CHECKS AND OTHER ITEMS ARE RECEIVED FOR DEPOSIT SUBJECT TO THE PROVISIONS OF THE UNIFORM COMMERCIAL CODE OR ANY APPLICABLE COLLECTION AGREEMENT.

**5.** three          **7.** $238.00          **9.** $4,782.96          **11.** $29.36

**13.**

RECORD ALL TRANSACTIONS THAT AFFECT YOUR ACCOUNT

| NUMBER | DATE | DESCRIPTION OF TRANSACTION | DEBIT (−) | √ T | FEE (IF ANY) (−) | CREDIT (+) | BALANCE |
|---|---|---|---|---|---|---|---|
| | | | | | | | 4,782 96 |
| 716 | 7/1 | Dabney Nursery | 90 23 | ✓ | | | 4,692 73 |
| 717 | 7/1 | office Max | 42 78 | ✓ | | | 4,649 95 |
| Deposit | 7/3 | Louis Lechleiter | | ✓ | | 200 00 | 4,849 95 |
| Deposit | 7/5 | Tony Trim | | ✓ | | 175 00 | 5,024 95 |
| Deposit | 7/9 | Dale Crosby | | ✓ | | 50 00 | 5,074 95 |
| 718 | 7/10 | Texaco Gas | 29 36 | ✓ | | | 5,045 59 |
| 719 | 7/10 | Nation's Bank | 238 00 | ✓ | | | 4,807 59 |
| Deposit | 7/15 | Bobby Cornelius | | | | 300 00 | 5,107 59 |
| ATM | 7/20 | Withdrawal  Branch | 80 00 | ✓ | | | 5,027 59 |
| Debit card | 7/20 | A T & T | 30 92 | ✓ | | | 4,996 67 |
| 720 | 7/20 | Visa | 172 83 | | | | 4,823 84 |
| | 7/25 | Check Order | 21 17 | ✓ | | | 4,802 67 |
| | 8/2 | Statement Reconciled | | | | | — |

REMEMBER TO RECORD AUTOMATIC PAYMENTS/DEPOSITS ON DATE AUTHORIZED.

| $ 4,675 50 | BALANCE AS SHOWN ON BANK STATEMENT | | BALANCE AS SHOWN IN YOUR REGISTER | $ 4,823 84 |
|---|---|---|---|---|
| +300 00 | TOTAL OF OUTSTANDING DEPOSITS | | SUBTRACT AMOUNT OF SERVICE CHARGE | 0 |
| 4,975 50 | NEW TOTAL | | NEW TOTAL | 4,823 84 |
| −172 83 | SUBTRACT TOTAL OF OUTSTANDING CHECKS | SHOULD EQUAL | ADJUSTMENTS IF ANY Check Order | −21 17 |
| $4,802 67 | YOUR ADJUSTED STATEMENT BALANCE | ⟷ | YOUR ADJUSTED REGISTER BALANCE | $4,802 67 |

| Outstanding Deposits (Credits) | | | Outstanding Checks (Debits) | | |
|---|---|---|---|---|---|
| Date | Amount | | Check Number | Date | Amount |
| 7/15 | $ 300 00 | | 721 | | $ 172 83 |
| | | | | | |
| | | | | | |
| Total | $ 300 00 | | Total | | $ 172 83 |

**15.**

| $ 275.25 | BALANCE AS SHOWN ON BANK STATEMENT | | BALANCE AS SHOWN IN YOUR REGISTER | $ 587.63 |
|---|---|---|---|---|
| +745.99 | TOTAL OF OUTSTANDING DEPOSITS | | SUBTRACT AMOUNT OF SERVICE CHARGE | −7.50 |
| 1,021.24 | NEW TOTAL | | NEW TOTAL | 580.13 |
| −441.11 | SUBTRACT TOTAL OF OUTSTANDING CHECKS | | ADJUSTMENTS IF ANY | 0 |
| $580.13 | YOUR ADJUSTED STATEMENT BALANCE | SHOULD EQUAL | YOUR ADJUSTED REGISTER BALANCE | $580.13 |

| Outstanding Deposits (Credits) | |
|---|---|
| Date | Amount |
| | $ 120.43 |
| | 625.56 |
| | |
| | |
| | |
| Total | $ 745.99 |

| Outstanding Checks (Debits) | | |
|---|---|---|
| Check Number | Date | Amount |
| | | $ 144.24 |
| | | 154.48 |
| | | 24.17 |
| | | 18.22 |
| ATM | | 100.00 |
| Total | | $ 441.11 |

## EXERCISES SET B, P. 131

**1.**

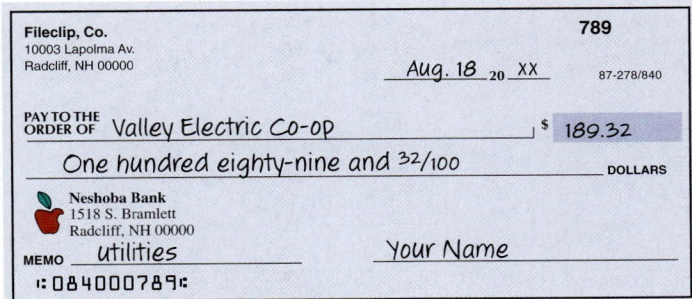

| 789 | Date Aug. 18 20 XX |
|---|---|
| Amount $189.32 | |
| To Valley Electric Co-op | |
| For Utilities | |

| Balance Forward | $1,037 | 15 |
|---|---|---|
| Deposits | — | |
| Total | 1,037 | 15 |
| Amount This Check | 189 | 32 |
| Balance | 847 | 83 |

Fileclip, Co.
10003 Lapolma Av.
Radcliff, NH 00000

789

Aug. 18 20 XX    87-278/840

PAY TO THE ORDER OF   Valley Electric Co-op    $ 189.32

One hundred eighty-nine and 32/100    DOLLARS

Neshoba Bank
1518 S. Bramlett
Radcliff, NH 00000

MEMO   Utilities         Your Name

⑆084000789⑆

**3.**

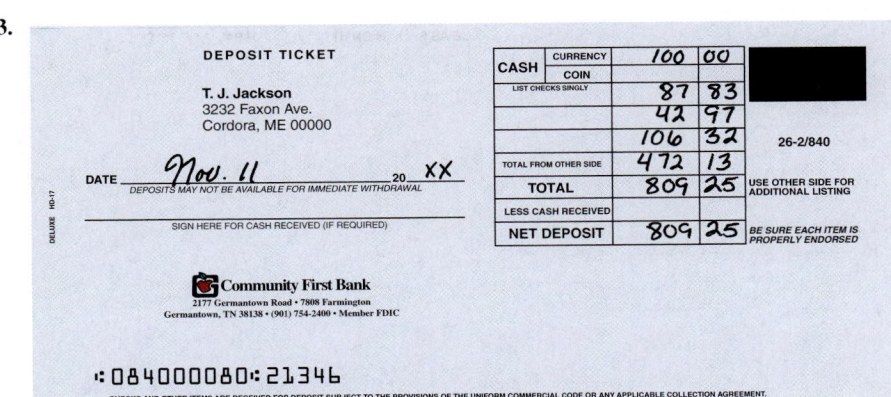

DEPOSIT TICKET

T. J. Jackson
3232 Faxon Ave.
Cordora, ME 00000

DATE   Nov. 11   20 XX
DEPOSITS MAY NOT BE AVAILABLE FOR IMMEDIATE WITHDRAWAL

SIGN HERE FOR CASH RECEIVED (IF REQUIRED)

DELUXE HD-17

| CASH | CURRENCY | 100 | 00 | |
|---|---|---|---|---|
| | COIN | | | |
| LIST CHECKS SINGLY | | 87 | 83 | |
| | | 42 | 97 | |
| | | 106 | 32 | 26-2/840 |
| TOTAL FROM OTHER SIDE | | 472 | 13 | |
| TOTAL | | 809 | 25 | USE OTHER SIDE FOR ADDITIONAL LISTING |
| LESS CASH RECEIVED | | | | |
| NET DEPOSIT | | 809 | 25 | BE SURE EACH ITEM IS PROPERLY ENDORSED |

Community First Bank
2177 Germantown Road • 7808 Farmington
Germantown, TN 38138 • (901) 754-2400 • Member FDIC

⑆084000080⑆21346

CHECKS AND OTHER ITEMS ARE RECEIVED FOR DEPOSIT SUBJECT TO THE PROVISIONS OF THE UNIFORM COMMERCIAL CODE OR ANY APPLICABLE COLLECTION AGREEMENT.

**5.** three    **7.** $82.75    **9.** $1,034.10    **11.** $82.75

**13.**

RECORD ALL TRANSACTIONS THAT AFFECT YOUR ACCOUNT

| NUMBER | DATE | DESCRIPTION OF TRANSACTION | DEBIT (−) | √T | FEE (IF ANY) (−) | CREDIT (+) | BALANCE |
|---|---|---|---|---|---|---|---|
| | | | | | | | 1,034 10 |
| Deposit | 4/1 | Payroll | | √ | | 850 00 | +850 00 |
| | | | | | | | 1,884 10 |
| Deposit | 4/3 | Payroll - Bonus | | √ | | 800 00 | +800 00 |
| | | | | | | | 2,684 10 |
| 5374 | 4/3 | First Union Mortgage Co. | 647 53 | √ | | | −647 53 |
| | | | | | | | 2,036 57 |
| 5375 | 4/3 | South Florida Utility | 82 75 | √ | | | −82 75 |
| | | | | | | | 1,953 82 |
| 5376 | 4/5 | First Federal Credit Union | 219 95 | √ | | | −219 95 |
| | | | | | | | 1,733 87 |
| 5377 | 4/15 | Banc Boston | 510 48 | | | | −510 48 |
| | | | | | | | 1,223 39 |
| Deposit | 4/15 | Payroll | | √ | | 850 00 | +850 00 |
| | | | | | | | 2,073 39 |
| 5378 | 4/20 | Northwest Air lines | 403 21 | | | | −403 21 |
| | | | | | | | 1,670 18 |
| 5379 | 4/26 | Auto Zone | 18 97 | | | | −18 97 |
| | | | | | | | 1,651 21 |
| ATM | 5/4 | Cordova Branch | 100 00 | | | | −100 00 |
| | | | | | | | 1,551 21 |
| | 4/30 | Service Fee | 12 50 | √ | | | −12 50 |
| | | | | | | | 1,538 71 |
| | 4/30 | Statement Reconciled | | | | | |

REMEMBER TO RECORD AUTOMATIC PAYMENTS/DEPOSITS ON DATE AUTHORIZED.

| $ 2,571 37 | BALANCE AS SHOWN ON BANK STATEMENT |
|---|---|
| 0 | TOTAL OF OUTSTANDING DEPOSITS |
| 2,571 37 | NEW TOTAL |
| −1,032 66 | SUBTRACT TOTAL OF OUTSTANDING CHECKS |
| $1,538 71 | YOUR ADJUSTED STATEMENT BALANCE |

SHOULD EQUAL

| BALANCE AS SHOWN IN YOUR REGISTER | $ 1,551 2 |
|---|---|
| SUBTRACT AMOUNT OF SERVICE CHARGE | −12 50 |
| NEW TOTAL | 1,538 7 |
| ADJUSTMENTS IF ANY | 0 |
| YOUR ADJUSTED REGISTER BALANCE | $1,538 7 |

Outstanding Deposits (Credits)

| Date | Amount |
|---|---|
| | $ |
| | |
| Total | $ 0 |

Outstanding Checks (Debits)

| Check Number | Date | Amount |
|---|---|---|
| 5377 | | $ 510 48 |
| 5378 | | 403 2 |
| 5379 | | 18 9 |
| ATM | | 100 00 |
| | Total | $ 1,032 66 |

**15.**

| $ 1,102 35 | BALANCE AS SHOWN ON BANK STATEMENT |
|---|---|
| +265 49 | TOTAL OF OUTSTANDING DEPOSITS |
| 1,367 84 | NEW TOTAL |
| −1,073 83 | SUBTRACT TOTAL OF OUTSTANDING CHECKS |
| $294 01 | YOUR ADJUSTED STATEMENT BALANCE |

SHOULD EQUAL

| BALANCE AS SHOWN IN YOUR REGISTER | $ 336 51 |
|---|---|
| SUBTRACT AMOUNT OF SERVICE CHARGE | −6 50 |
| NEW TOTAL | 330 01 |
| ADJUSTMENTS IF ANY | −36 00 |
| YOUR ADJUSTED REGISTER BALANCE | $294 01 |

Outstanding Deposits (Credits)

| Date | Amount |
|---|---|
| | $ 265 49 |
| | |
| Total | $ 265 49 |

Outstanding Checks (Debits)

| Check Number | Date | Amount |
|---|---|---|
| | | $ 617 23 |
| | | 456 60 |
| | Total | $ 1,073 83 |

## PRACTICE TEST, P. 135

**1.**

| 195 | | Date 5/25 20 XX |
|---|---|---|
| Amount $152.50 | | |
| To Lon Associates | | |
| For Supplies | | |

| Balance Forward | 2,301 | 42 |
|---|---|---|
| Deposits | 283 | 17 |
| Total | 2,584 | 59 |
| Amount This Check | 152 | 50 |
| Balance | 2,432 | 09 |

Khayat Cleaners
2438 Broad St.
Oklahoma City, OK 00000                    195

May 25 20 XX        87-278/840

PAY TO THE ORDER OF  Lon Associates        $ 152.50

One hundred fifty-two and 50/100 —————— DOLLARS

First State Bank
1543 S. Main
Oklahoma City, OK 00000

MEMO supplies              Lonnie Branch

⑈074200195⑈

**2.** $5,283.17    **3.** five    **4.** $0    **5.** $142.38    **6.** 3/15

**7.** $3,600    **8.** $6,982.68    **9.** $1,881.49

**10.**

| NUMBER | DATE | DESCRIPTION OF TRANSACTION | DEBIT (-) | √ T | FEE (IF ANY) (-) | CREDIT (+) | BALANCE |
|---|---|---|---|---|---|---|---|
| | | | | | | | 5,283 17 |
| 3784 | 2/27 | | 96 03 | √ | | | -96 03 |
| | | | | | | | 5,187 14 |
| 3785 | 3/5 | | 346 18 | | | | -346 18 |
| | | | | | | | 4,840 96 |
| 3786 | 3/5 | | 142 38 | √ | | | -142 38 |
| | | | | | | | 4,698 58 |
| 3787 | 3/11 | | 487 93 | √ | | | -487 93 |
| | | | | | | | 4,210 65 |
| 3788 | 3/11 | | 973 12 | √ | | | -973 12 |
| | | | | | | | 3,237 53 |
| 3789 | 3/15 | | 72 83 | | | | -72 83 |
| | | | | | | | 3,164 70 |
| Dep. | 3/15 | | | √ | | 1,600 00 | +1,600 00 |
| | | | | | | | 4,764 70 |
| 3790 | 3/17 | | 146 17 | | | | -146 17 |
| | | | | | | | 4,618 53 |
| 3791 | 3/20 | | 152 03 | | | | -152 03 |
| | | | | | | | 4,466 50 |
| 3792 | 3/31 | * | 182 08 | √ | | | -182 08 |
| | | | | | | | 4,284 42 |
| Deposit | 3/31 | | | √ | | 2000 00 | +2,000 00 |
| | | | | | | | 6,284 42 |
| | 3/31 | adjust for check # 3792 add 0.05 back | | √ | | .05 | +.05 / 6,284 47 |
| | 3/17 | Return check charge | 19 00 | √ | | | -19 00 |
| | 3/31 | Statement Reconciled | | | | | 6,265 47 |

| $ 6,982 68 | BALANCE AS SHOWN ON BANK STATEMENT | | BALANCE AS SHOWN IN YOUR REGISTER | $ 6,284 42 |
|---|---|---|---|---|
| 0 | TOTAL OF OUTSTANDING DEPOSITS | | SUBTRACT AMOUNT OF SERVICE CHARGE | 0 00 |
| 6,982 68 | NEW TOTAL | | NEW TOTAL | 6,284 42 |
| -717 21 | SUBTRACT TOTAL OF OUTSTANDING CHECKS | | ADJUSTMENTS IF ANY | -18 95 |
| $6,265 47 | YOUR ADJUSTED STATEMENT BALANCE | SHOULD EQUAL | YOUR ADJUSTED REGISTER BALANCE | $6,265 47 |

| Outstanding Deposits (Credits) | |
|---|---|
| Date | Amount |
| | $ 0 |
| | |
| | |
| | |
| | |
| Total | $ 0 |

| Outstanding Checks (Debits) | | |
|---|---|---|
| Check Number | Date | Amount |
| 3785 | 3/5 | $ 346 18 |
| 3789 | 3/15 | 72 83 |
| 3790 | 3/17 | 146 17 |
| 3791 | 3/17 | 152 03 |
| | | |
| | Total | $ 717 21 |

**11.**

| $ 860 21 | BALANCE AS SHOWN ON BANK STATEMENT | | BALANCE AS SHOWN IN YOUR REGISTER | $ 1,817 93 |
|---|---|---|---|---|
| +1,212 13 | TOTAL OF OUTSTANDING DEPOSITS | | SUBTRACT AMOUNT OF SERVICE CHARGE | -15 00 |
| 2,072 34 | NEW TOTAL | | NEW TOTAL | 1,802 93 |
| -483 24 | SUBTRACT TOTAL OF OUTSTANDING CHECKS | | ADJUSTMENTS IF ANY | -213 83 |
| $1,589 10 | YOUR ADJUSTED STATEMENT BALANCE | SHOULD EQUAL | YOUR ADJUSTED REGISTER BALANCE | $1,589 10 |

| Outstanding Deposits (Credits) | |
|---|---|
| Date | Amount |
| | $ 800 00 |
| | 412 13 |
| | |
| | |
| | |
| Total | $ 1,212 13 |

| Outstanding Checks (Debits) | | |
|---|---|---|
| Check Number | Date | Amount |
| | | $ 243 17 |
| | | 167 18 |
| | | 13 97 |
| | | 42 12 |
| | | 16 80 |
| | | |
| | Total | $ 483 24 |

## 5-1

| | | | | | |
|---|---|---|---|---|---|
| **1.** $A = 4$ | **3.** $C = 8$ | **5.** $R = 36$ | **7.** $B = 5$ | **9.** $R = 21$ | **11.** $X = 84$ |
| **13.** $A = 6$ | **15.** $B = 4$ | **17.** $K = 4$ | **19.** $C = 20$ | **21.** $A = 5$ | **23.** $K = 20$ |
| **25.** $J = 7$ | **27.** $B = 3$ | **29.** $X = 6$ | **31.** $B = 8$ | **33.** $N = 3$ | **35.** $N = 8$ |

## 5-2

**1.** The number of full-time hours is 9.

**3.** 132 tie-dyed shirts sold

**5.** 4 boxes of felt-tip pens and 8 boxes of ballpoint pens

**7.** 131,304,347.8 shares of stock

**9.** $\frac{5}{6}$ of a cup of milk

**11.** The seller pays $1,740.75 and the buyer pays $580.25.

**13.** Charris' salary is $17,155.20 and Chloe's is $11,436.80.

**15.** $N = 1,527.06$ Yuan

## 5-3

**1.** $S = \$39.99$

**3.** $C = \$33.87$

**5.** $C = T - S - I$

**7.** $V = LY$

### EXERCISES SET A, P. 171

**1.** $N = 7$

**3.** $N = 17$

**5.** $A = 24$

**7.** $x = 11$

**9.** $X = 7$

**11.** The number of cars sold is 9.

**13.** $96

**15.** $8.75 each hour

**17.** 280 headlights were purchased at a total cost of $3,906.
720 taillights were purchased at a total cost of $5,436.

**19.** $T = \$4,258.72$

**21.** $T = Np$

### EXERCISES SET B, P. 173

**1.** $N = 9$

**3.** $N = 12$

**5.** $A = 12$

**7.** $B = 5$

**9.** $X = 3$

**11.** 18 cookbooks

**13.** 27 hours

**15.** The purse sells for $43.49.

**17.** 1,897 imprints in 1 hour.

**19.** $C = \$137,509$

**21.** $A = LC$

### PRACTICE TEST, P. 175

**1.** $N = 11$

**2.** $A = 18$

**3.** $A = 5$

**4.** $N = 6$

**5.** $A = 12$

**6.** $R = 1$

**7.** $N = 9$

**8.** $B = 15$

**9.** $A = 5$

**10.** $A = 5$

**11.** The new salary is $285.

**12.** 130 containers are needed.

**13.** 116 ceramic cups and 284 plastic cups were sold. The value of the ceramic cups was $464. The value of the plastic cups was $994.

**14.** The cost of 200 suits is $27,200.

**15.** The cost of 2,000 pounds of chemicals is $1,940.

**16.** $N = 1,904.04$ EUR

**17.** $N = 28,982.147$ JPY

**18.** $I = \$27,346.38$

**19.** $D = \$3,173.50$

**20.** $D = I - T$

# CHAPTER 6

## Section Exercises

## 6-1

**1.** 39%  **3.** 75%  **5.** 292%  **7.** 39%  **9.** 340%  **11.** 225%

**13.** $\frac{2}{3}$%  **15.** 80%  **17.** 0.00125  **19.** 1.5  **21.** 0.004 (rounded)  **23.** $\frac{3}{5}$

**25.** $1\frac{4}{5}$  **27.** $\frac{1}{3}$

## 6-2

**1.** rate (%) = 48%
base (of) = 12
portion (is) = unknown
number

**3.** rate (%) = unknown number
base (of) = 158
portion (is) = 47.4

**5.** rate (%) = 15%
base (of) = unknown number
portion (is) = 80

**7.** $P = 75$

**9.** $P = 50$  **11.** $B = 54$  **13.** $P = 12$  **15.** $B = 70$

**17.** $R = 25\%$  **19.** $P = 86$  **21.** $R = 83.55\%$ (rounded)  **23.** $B = 4,285.71$ (rounded)

**25.** $51.66 saved  **27.** 74 gallons (rounded)  **29.** $6,373.91 original cost  **31.** 92%

**33.** 6% (rounded)

## 6-3

**1.** 2,309  **3.** $P = 108$  **5.** 33.75  **7.** 50%  **9.** 875

**11.** 7%  **13.** $1,752.75  **15.** $14.72  **17.** 12.5%

### EXERCISES SET A, P. 201

**1.** 23%  **3.** 3%  **5.** 60.1%  **7.** 300%  **9.** 20%  **11.** 17%

**13.** 52%  **15.** 125%  **17.** 0.0025  **19.** 2.56  **21.** 0.005  **23.** $\frac{1}{10}$

**25.** $\frac{89}{100}$  **27.** $2\frac{1}{4}$  **29.** 12.5%; $\frac{1}{8}$  **31.** $P = 81$  **33.** $B = \$12,000$  **35.** $R = 250\%$

**37.** $B = 30$  **39.** $169.26  **41.** 2,270 people  **43.** 26% (rounded) is *not* within the budgeted 25%  **45.** $145

### EXERCISES SET B, P. 203

**1.** 67.5%  **3.** 0.7%  **5.** 0.04%  **7.** 24.2%  **9.** 99%  **11.** 65%  **13.** 40%

**15.** 3.284  **17.** 0.52  **19.** 0.0002  **21.** $\frac{1}{5}$  **23.** $3\frac{61}{100}$  **25.** $\frac{1}{8}$  **27.** $\frac{1}{2}$; 0.5

**29.** 45%; $\frac{9}{20}$  **31.** $R = 200\%$  **33.** $R = 80\%$  **35.** $B = 305.88$  **37.** 115  **39.** $54  **41.** 540 fuses

**43.** $2,754.70  **45.** $56

### PRACTICE TEST, P. 205

**1.** 24%  **2.** 92.5%  **3.** 60%  **4.** 21%  **5.** 37.5%

**6.** $\frac{1}{400}$  **7.** $72  **8.** 250%  **9.** 87.5%, or $87\frac{1}{2}$%  **10.** $2.52

**11.** 22 rooms  **12.** 3%  **13.** 90 employees  **14.** $2.92 tip; Total bill = $22.39  **15.** 56,600 automobiles

**16.** 55%  **17.** $92,287.80  **18.** $140,790  **19.** $486  **20.** $271.19

## Section Exercises

## 7-1

**1.** 5,470

**3.** $15,679

**5.** 79.5

**7.** No score is reported more than once so there is no mode.

**9.** $14,978

**11.** a. $34,746
b. $34,991
c. There is no mode.

**13.** $29,840

**15.**

| Class Intervals | Tally | Class Frequency |
|---|---|---|
| 60–69 | // | 2 |
| 70–79 | /// | 3 |
| 89–89 | ℍℍ /// | 8 |
| 90–99 | ℍℍ // | 7 |

**17.**

| Class Intervals | Tally | Class Frequency |
|---|---|---|
| $0-$9.99 | ℍℍ ℍℍ | 10 |
| $10-$19.99 | ℍℍ //// | 9 |
| $20-$29.99 | ℍℍ | 5 |
| $30-$39.99 | /// | 3 |
| $40-$49.99 | /// | 3 |

**19.** 10%

## 7-2

**1.** Highest: Saturday ($611.77); lowest: Monday ($233.94)

**3.**

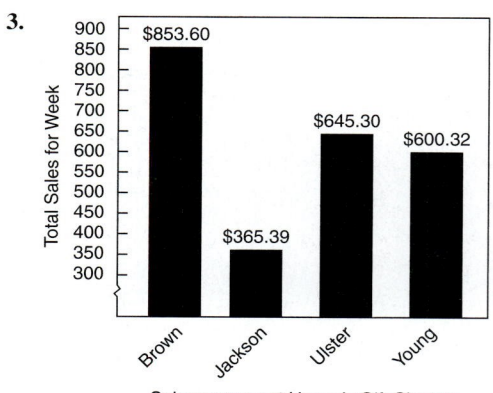

Salespersons at Happy's Gift Shoppe

**5.** April–June

**7.** 50%

**9.** 40 mph

**11.** 20 mph; compact car

**13.** Take-home pay $= $1,600$
Transportation percent $= 10\%$

**15.** Percent of take home pay allocated for food $= 25\%$.

**17.** 20%

**19.** $1000; 2.5%

**21.** Yes, the salary percent of increase was 13.9%, and it exceeded the rate of inflation.

## 7-3

**1.** 13

**3.** 1, 7, −6, −1, −1

**5.** 22

**7.** a. 15.87 scores (approximately 16 scores)
b. 97.72 scores (approximately 98 scores)

**9.** 12

**11.** 90

**13.** 4.242640687 or 4.24 (rounded)

## EXERCISES SET A, P. 245

**1.** Range = 14;
Mean = 22;
Median = 22, there is no mode

**3.** Range = $9.27;
Mean = $8.42;
Median = $5.53 (rounded);
Mode = $13.95

**5.**
1 = 291
2 = 624
3 = 799
4 = 790
5 = 801
6 = 640
7 = 639
8 = 584
9 = 293
10 = 123

**7.** Period 10

**9.** Early and late classes have lower enrollment than mid-morning classes.

**11.** 2006: $125,115; 2007: $137,340

**15.** September

**17.** 20%

**19.** $153

**21.** Mean = 87.1;
Median = 88;
Mode—no mode

**23.** 6.402256547 or 6.4

**13.** Sales for The Family Store, 2006–2007

|  | 2006 | 2007 |
|---|---|---|
| Girls' clothing | $ 74,675 | $ 81,534 |
| Boys' clothing | 65,153 | 68,324 |
| Women's clothing | 125,115 | 137,340 |
| Men's clothing | 83,895 | 96,315 |

## EXERCISES SET B, P. 249

**1.** Range = 32; Mean = 74.33; Median = 71; No mode

**3.** Range = 0.17; Mean = 1.145 kg;
Median = 1.125 kg; Mode = 1.1 kg

**5.** misc. expenses and general government

**7.** education costs

**9.** 90°

**11.**

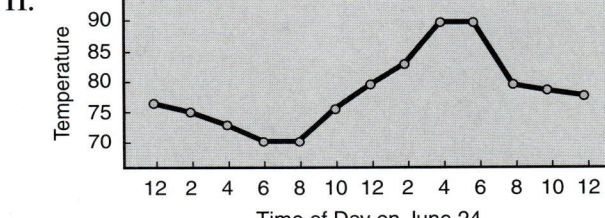

Time of Day on June 24

**13.** 15.1%

**15.** $69,000 cost of house with furnishings; 80.2%

**17.** 276°

**19.**

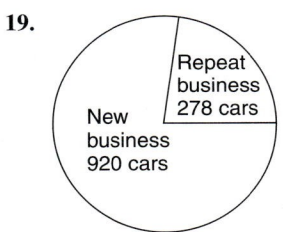

Automobile Dealership's New and Repeat Business

**21.** range = 13;
There are two modes: 89, 90

**23.** 79

## PRACTICE TEST, P. 253

**1.** a. 77; b. 41.8; c. 29.5; d. 15

**2.** $120

**3.** 37.5%

**4.** 33.3%

**5.** 29.2%

**6.** labor: 135°;
materials: 120°;
overhead: 105°

**7.**

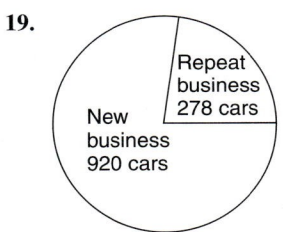

**8.** fresh flowers: $23,712; silk flowers: $17,892

**9.** fresh flowers: $10,380; silk flowers: $5,829

**10.** c. $5,000; other interval sizes would provide too many or too few intervals.

**11.**

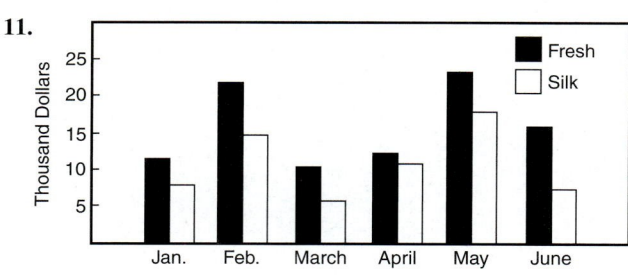

Sales for Katz Florist, January–June

**12.** smallest; 250; greatest; 1,117

**13.**

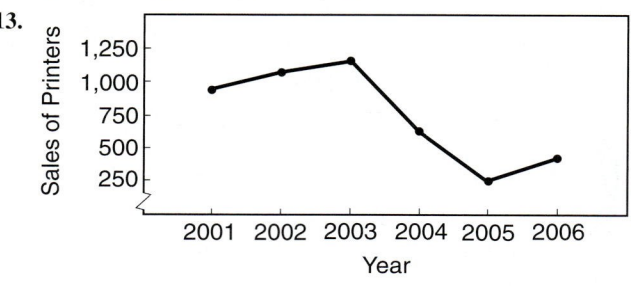

Sales of Laser Printers by Smart Brothers Computer Store

**14.** 11 bulbs (rounded)

# CHAPTER 8

## Section Exercises

## 8-1

**1.** $120

**3.** $58.68 trade discount

**5.** $234.72 net price

**7.** $234.72 net price

**9.** Answers will vary.

**11.** Notebooks: $22.50;
Loose leaf paper: $8.90;
Ballpoint pens: $23.70;
Total list price = $55.10;
40% trade discount = $22.04;
Net price = $33.06

**13.** Net price rate = 72%
Net price = $106,766.64

## 8-2

**1.** $17,095.73 total net price of TVs

**3.** $595.58

**5.** $72.90 trade discount; $196.10 net price

**7.** The better deal is $189.97 with discounts of 5/5/10.

**9.** The better deal is $1,899 with discounts of 5/10/10.

**11.** The better deal is $410 with a discount series of 10/10/5.

## 8-3

**1.** $10.80 cash discount

**3.** $432 net amount

**5.** No cash discount allowed. $450 is due.

**7.** $641.52 net amount

**9.** $667.44 total bill

**11.** $1,257.56 net amount

**13.** $1,225 net amount

**15.** $478.21 net amount

**17.** No cash discount allowed. $900 is due.

**19.** No cash discount allowed. $392.34 is due.

**21.** $2,061.86 amount credited to account; $1,920.62 outstanding balance

**23.** Better Bilt Bicycles paid the freight to the freight company.

**25.** The vendor pays the shipping company and adds the charge to Phyllis's invoice.

### EXERCISES SET A, P. 283

**1.** $45.00

**3.** $6.00

**5.** $307.23

**7.** Trade discount = $4.00;
Net price = $195.95

**9.** Net price rate = 96%;
Net price = $315.84

**11.** Net price rate = 89%;
Net price = $1,419.55

**13.** Decimal equivalents of complements =
0.9, 0.85, and 0.9;
Net decimal equivalent = 0.6885
Net price = $963.89

**15.** % form = 76.5%;
Single discount equivalent = 23.5%

**17.** % form = 74.34%;
Single discount equivalent = 25.66%

**19.** 16.21% single discount equivalent

**21.** $102.50

**23.** $94.50

**25.** $3.42 net price

**27.** $60 − $9.45 = $50.55; better deal

**29.** $5.40

**31.** $5,139.06

## EXERCISES SET B, P. 285

**1.** $4.80

**3.** $63.75

**5.** $0.77

**7.** Trade discount = $0.83;
Net price = $26.67

**9.** Complement = 95%;
Net price = $399.95

**11.** Complement = 92%;
Net price = $3,664.36

**13.** Decimal equivalents of complements:
0.8(0.85)(0.95);
Net decimal equivalent: 0.646
Net price: $22.61

**15.** Net decimal equivalent in percent
form: 82%;
Single discount equivalent in percent
form: 18%

**17.** Net decimal equivalent in percent form:
75.8%;
Single discount equivalent in percent
form: 24.2%

**19.** 23.05%

**21.** $0.375 or $0.38

**23.** $1,179

**25.** $513 net price

**27.** $190 less 10% or $171 = better deal

**29.** $0.50 cash discount

**31.** $515.46 amount credited;
$310.54 outstanding balance

## PRACTICE TEST, P. 287

**1.** $110 trade discount

**2.** $532.50 net price

**3.** $29.24 net price

**4.** $250 less 20% better deal

**5.** $47.88 net price

**6.** 42.4%

**7.** 0.684 net decimal equivalent

**8.** 85%

**9.** $42 trade discount

**10.** $1,080 net price

**11.** $2 cash discount

**12.** 3% discount if she pays on or before
September 11.

**13.** $392 net amount

**14.** $294.00 net amount

**15.** $400; no discount if not paid on or after
December 21.

**16.** $31 less 10%, 10%, 5% is the better deal.

**17.** $201.60 net price for dartboards;
$288 net price for bowling balls
$489.60 total net price

**18.** Manufacturer

# CHAPTER 9

## Section Exercises

## 9-1

**1.** $50

**3.** $24

**5.** a. $84.34
b. $154.34

**7.** a. $90
b. 150%

**9.** $4

**11.** $214

**13.** $8

**15.** $1.75

**17.** a. 80%
b. $318.40

**19.** 125%

**21.** 101.5%

**23.** $268.57

**25.** $15

## 9-2

**1.** 20%

**3.** 59.8%

**5.** $1,666.67

**7.** a. $18.46
b. $6.46

**9.** 42.8%

**11.** a. $333.33
b. $233.33

**13.** 150%

**15.** 49.6%

**17.** a. $935.94
b. $336.94

**19.** a. $7.80
b. $7.20

**21.** 170.3%

## 9-3

**1.** $M$ = $18; $M\%$ = 37.5%

**3.** $M$ = $350; $M\%$ = 41.2%

**5.** 49%

**7.** $0.38 (rounded)

**9.** $191.95 sale price

**11.** $101.25 first sale price;
$86.06 second sale price;
Final selling price = $33.75

**13.** $0.72

**15.** $4,632

## EXERCISES SET A, P. 331

**1.** $S = \$75$; $C\% = 100\%$; $S\% = 150\%$

**5.** $C = \$57$; $M\%_{cost} = 56.14\%$; $M\%_{selling\ price} = 35.96\%$

**9.** $C = \$16.11$; $M = \$2.84$; $M\%_{cost} = 17.63\%$

**13.** a. $24
 b. $36

**17.** 25%

**21.** a. $50
 b. $199.99

**3.** $S\% = 100\%$; $M\% = 58\%$; $S = \$90.48$; $M = \$52.48$

**7.** $C = \$68.45$; $S = \$95.83$; $M\%_{selling\ price} = \$28.57\%$

**11.** a. $36
 b. 25%

**15.** a. $18.50
 b. 31.62%

**19.** a. $38
 b. 10%

**23.** First markdown = $9.90;
 Sale price = $39.60;
 Second markdown = $11.88;
 Second sale price = $27.72

## EXERCISES SET B, P. 333

**1.** $C\% = 100\%$; $S = \$5$; $S\% = 125\%$

**5.** $C = \$486$; $M\%_{cost} = 42.86\%$; $M\%_{selling\ price} = 30\%$

**9.** $C = \$16.28$; $M = \$15.92$; $M\%_{cost} = 97.79\%$

**13.** a. $14.35
 b. $14.35

**17.** 525%

**21.** $M = \$12.00$; $N = \$27.99$

**3.** $S\% = 100\%$; $M\% = 50\%$; $S = \$172$; $M = \$86$

**7.** $S = \$48.08$; $M\%_{cost} = 92.32\%$; $M\%_{selling\ price} = 48.00\%$

**11.** a. $19.20
 b. 60%

**15.** 33.3%

**19.** $M = \$4.58$; $M\% = 15.3\%$

**23.** $M = \$200$; $M\% = 16.7\%$

## PRACTICE TEST, P. 335

**1.** $7.16   **2.** $73.80   **3.** $15.50   **4.** $173.25   **5.** $22.68   **6.** $91.65

**7.** $26.07   **8.** $60.83   **9.** $798.15   **10.** $489.99   **11.** 28.5%   **12.** 60%

**13.** $160   **14.** 40%   **15.** $331.31   **16.** $0.35   **17.** $1.67   **18.** 40%

**19.** $C = \$15.75$;   **20.** $C = \$127$;
 $M = \$29.25$   $M\% = 25.2\%$

# CHAPTER 10

## Section Exercises

# 10-1

**1.** $677.00   **3.** $4,415.00   **5.** $383.80   **7.** $802.95   **9.** $581.12   **11.** $538.32   **13.** $566.05

# 10-2

**1.** $14   **3.** $140   **5.** $62.34   **7.** Social Security
 tax = $160.15;
 Medicare tax = $37.45

**9.** Social Security tax for   **11.** $997.71
 December = $441.01;

 Medicare tax for
 December = $119.15

# 10-3

**1.** Employer's share of Social   **3.** Total withholding = $409;   **5.** $378.00   **7.** Payment of $122.64 must be
 Security and Medicare =   Total Social Security =   deposited by April 30.
 $595;   $305.91;
 Employer's tax deposit =   Total Medicare = $71.54   Payment of $45.36 must be
 $2,823   deposited by January 31 of
 Employer's tax deposit =   the next year since it does not
 $1,163.90   exceed $100.

# EXERCISES SET A, P. 369

**1.** $483.14

**3.** $452.80

**5.** $7,938

**7.** Her gross weekly earnings are still $425 since a salaried job does not normally pay overtime for hours worked over 40.

**9.** $722.10

**11.** $700

**13.** $1,191.20

**15.** $11

**17.** $15

**19.** $27.41

**21.** Social Security = $52.20; Medicare = $12.21

**23.** Social Security = $115.07; Medicare = $26.91

**25.** Social Security tax = $41.85; Medicare tax = $9.79; Net earnings = $523.16

**27.**

| Employee | Filing status/allowances | Gross earnings | Withholding | Social Security | Medicare |
|---|---|---|---|---|---|
| Guess, Marthe | Married/2 | $595 | $32 | $36.89 | $8.63 |
| Juarez, Abdul | Married/3 | $983 | $80.18 | $60.95 | $14.25 |
| Pounds, Clay | Single/1 | $2,840 | $653.08 | $176.08 | $41.18 |
| Totals | | | $765.26 | $273.92 | $64.06 |

# EXERCISES SET B, P. 371

**1.** $432.85

**3.** $318.40

**5.** $2,648

**7.** She earns $1,896 because salaried employees do not normally receive overtime pay.

**9.** $1,076.40

**11.** $763

**13.** $579.32

**15.** $51

**17.** $41

**19.** no withholding tax

**21.** Social Security = $217; Medicare = $50.75

**23.** Social Security = $76.01; Medicare = $17.78

**25.** Net pay = $1,426.38

**27.**

| Employee | Filing status/allowances | Gross earnings | Withholding | Social Security | Medicare |
|---|---|---|---|---|---|
| Chirinos, Chad | Married/4 | $845 | $49.67 | $52.39 | $12.25 |
| Claassen, Lars | Married/1 | $1,295 | $146.59 | $80.29 | $18.78 |
| Naramore, Lera | Single/3 | $4,240 | $1,054.11 | $262.88 | $61.48 |
| Totals | | | $1,250.37 | $395.56 | $92.51 |

# PRACTICE TEST, P. 373

**1.** $1,827

**2.** $371.91

**3.** $1,050

**4.** $1,374.75

**5.** $1,092

**6.** $875

**7.** $706.68

**8.** Social Security = $31.86; Medicare = $7.45

**9.** Social Security = $53.40; Medicare = $12.49

**10.** $20

**11.** $16

**12.** $1,138.90

**13.** Social Security = $45.57; Medicare = $10.66; Withholding = $72.00; Other deductions = $25.12; Net earnings = $581.65

**14.** Social Security = $41.78; Medicare = $9.77; Withholding tax = $54.00; Other deductions = $12.87; Net earnings = $555.38

**15.** Social Security = $30.51; Medicare = $7.14; Withholding = $21.00; Net earnings = $433.52

**16.** Social Security = $35.78; Medicare = $8.37; Withholding tax = $23.00; Other deductions = $4.88; Net earnings = $505.12

**17.** Social Security = $37.83; Medicare = $8.85; Withholding = $20.00; Net earnings = $543.45

**18.** $285.66

**19.** $378

**20.** 0.8%, or $56

**21.** $248.70

# CHAPTER 11

## Section Exercises

### 11-1

**1.** $I = \$264$ **3.** $I = \$989.52$ **5.** $MV = \$3,430$ **7.** 0.75 year

**9.** 1.5 years **11.** $MV = \$43,743$ **13.** $R = 0.185$, or 18.5% per year **15.** $T = \frac{1}{2}$ year, or 6 months

### 11-2

**1.** $213.04 **3.** $67.81 **5.** Non-leap year: 549 days Leap year: 550 days **7.** Exact time: 279 days

**9.** Exact time: September 16 **11.** $75.21 **13.** $10,463.97

### 11-3

**1.** $75 **3.** Discount = $149.50; Proceeds = $3,100.50 **5.** 8.9%

**7.** $5,138.59 **9.** Answers will vary. The payee may need quick cash and can sell the note to get the cash needed.

### EXERCISES SET A, P. 409

**1.** $120 **3.** (a) $1,539; (b) $5,814 **5.** 9%

**7.** 3.75 years **9.** $2,812.50 **11.** $\frac{7}{12}$ year

**13.** $5 **15.** $16 **17.** 117 days

**19.** Exact time: August 8 **21.** a. = $51.29 b. = $52 **23.** $10,040.56

**25.** 11.4%

### EXERCISES SET B, P. 411

**1.** $285 **3.** $19,252.80 (interest); $34,532.80 (MV) **5.** 8%

**7.** 3 years **9.** $800 **11.** $1\frac{1}{2}$ years

**13.** 10% **15.** $160.33 **17.** 217 days

**19.** 130 days **21.** September 11 **23.** $79.64 (discount); $1,900.36 (proceeds)

**25.** He will save $20.20 **27.** 9.2%

### PRACTICE TEST, P. 413

**1.** $60 **2.** $1,500 **3.** 12.5% annually **4.** 2 years

**5.** 287 days **6.** 168 days **7.** 159 days **8.** $4,100; $4,168.33

**9.** $210 **10.** $206.80 **11.** $3,450 **12.** $15.11

**13.** 13.0% **14.** 0.75 or $\frac{3}{4}$ year or 9 months **15.** 8.5% annually **16.** $350

**17.** $52 **18.** Yes, he saves $27. **19.** $122.26 **20.** $8.66

# CHAPTER 12

## Section Exercises

## 12-1

**1.** $749.20    **3.** $1,375.84    **5.** $760.48    **7.** $213.24    **9.** $69.08    **11.** $87.79    **13.** 11.25%    **15.** 11.00%

## 12-2

**1.** $\dfrac{171}{1,830}$ or 0.093    **3.** $190.34    **5.** $\dfrac{5}{28}$    **7.** $318.54

## 12-3

**1.** 1.15%    **3.** $37.33    **5.** Average daily balance = $2,138.51; Interest = $17.82

**7.** $2.19    **9.** $3.61    **11.** Finance charge = $18.21 New balance = $464.65

### EXERCISES SET A, P. 443
**1.** $1,585.96    **3.** $729    **5.** $30.51    **7.** $52.40    **9.** $390.25    **11.** $39.52
**13.** $3.98    **15.** $462.60    **17.** 13.75%    **19.** 21.5%    **21.** 14.25%

### EXERCISES SET B, P. 445
**1.** $711    **3.** $577    **5.** $132.14    **7.** $375.65    **9.** $126.35    **11.** $8.85
**13.** $5.19    **15.** $8.75 finance charge; $611.61 unpaid balance    **17.** 13%    **19.** 15.75%    **21.** 21.5%

### PRACTICE TEST, P. 447
**1.** $34    **2.** $690 installment price; Finance charge = $112    **3.** $336 installment price; Finance charge = $36    **4.** 21.5%

**5.** 16.25%    **6.** $2.89    **7.** 24%    **8.** $12.60
**9.** 11.5%    **10.** 10.75%    **11.** 21.5%    **12.** $875
**13.** $158.33    **14.** $654    **15.** $240.08    **16.** $393.93 average daily balance $6.89 finance charge $427.84 unpaid balance

**17.** Finance charge = $11.91 New balance = $746.39

# CHAPTER 13

## Section Exercises

## 13-1

**1.** Compound amount = $5,627.55; Compound interest = $627.55    **3.** Compound amount = $7,887.81; Compound interest = $887.81    **5.** Compound amount = $1,269.73; Compound interest = $269.73

**7.** $1,873.08 (third year) future value; Compound interest = $673.08; Simple interest = $576    **9.** Compound amount = $8,046.92; Compound interest = $1,746.92    **11.** $720.98

**13.** $15,373.05 compound amount; Interest = $4,873.05    **15.** $8\dfrac{1}{4}$% annually is the slightly better deal    **17.** Effective rate = 4.06%

**19.** Effective rate = 6.14%    **21.** Compound interest = $9.26    **23.** $27.99

# 13-2

**1.** $3,768.72  **3.** $7,880.30  **5.** $2,252.25  **7.** $19,462.47  **9.** $1,587.66  **11.** $6,736.20

## EXERCISES SET A, P. 477

**1.** Compound amount = $2,186.88
Compound interest = $186.88

**3.** Compound amount = $10,506.30
Compound interest = $506.30

**5.** $16,407

**7.** $7,718.19

**9.** $166.40 interest

**11.** $5,372.55 future value

**13.** Future value = $13,928.16

**15.** $1,052.87 compound amount;
$1,100 in one year would have a greater
yield than $900 invested today

**17.** $9.23 compound interest;
$2,009.23 compound amount

**19.** $1,126.97

**21.** $3,157.64

**23.** $1,597.41

## EXERCISES SET B, P. 479

**1.** Compound amount = $6,400.40;
Compound interest = $1,400.40

**3.** Compound amount = $8,541.33;
Compound interest = $1,541.33

**5.** $2,227.41

**7.** $13,396.51

**9.** $52.50

**11.** $41.22

**13.** 6.84848

**15.** $1,215.51 compound amount;
$215.51 compound interest

**17.** $134.50 compound interest;
$25,116.50 compound amount

**19.** $1,227.82

**21.** $3,334.80

**23.** $435.20

## PRACTICE TEST, P. 481

**1.** $450.09

**2.** $823.29

**3.** $3,979.30

**4.** $18,206.64

**5.** $1,893.72 compound amount;
$393.72 compound interest

**6.** $376.53 compound interest

**7.** 12.55%

**8.** $8.84

**9.** Compounding daily yields
slightly higher interest.

**10.** $2,499.10

**11.** $2,669.55

**12.** $2,053.44

**13.** $2,951.58

**14.** $5,476.68

**15.** $680 in one year is better.

**16.** $6,304.24

**17.** Option 2 yields the greater
return by $0.68

**18.** $2,536.48

**19.** $1,002.74

**20.** $13,586.96

# CHAPTER 14

## Section Exercises

# 14-1

**1.** $9,549

**3.** $26,824

**5.** $21,547.60

**7.** $945.90

**9.** $114

**11.** Harry will have $15,577.22 at the end of
three years.
Interest = $577.22

**13.** Amount invested = $91,000;
Interest = $20,059

**15.** The future value is $25,129. Latanya will
have invested 15($1,000) or $15,000
of her own money and will have received
$10,129 in interest.

**17.** The future value of the annuity is $11,734;
Your investment = $10,000;
Your interest = $1,734

**19.** The future value is $38,203.52;
Investment = $36,000;
Interest = $2,203.52

**21.** The future value is $17,546.58;
Investment = $15,600;
Interest = $1,946.58

**23.** Future value = $60,193.06;
Investment = $52,800;
Interest = $7,393.06

**25.** The semiannual annuity yields more
interest.

# 14-2

**1.** $2,050.02  **3.** $1,037.03  **5.** $839.55  **7.** $6,679.64  **9.** $21,072  **11.** $68,700

## EXERCISES SET A, P. 511

**1.** $7,432.60    **3.** $3,979.66    **5.** $10,311.07    **7.** $2,270.77    **9.** $135,900    **11.** $67,890

**13.** $5,359.69    **15.** (a) $39,620.70    **17.** $7,689.67
                          (b) $96,197.85

## EXERCISES SET B, P. 513

**1.** $25,482.80    **3.** $23,603.13    **5.** $893.18    **7.** $283.56

**9.** $156,772    **11.** $163,510    **13.** $3,641.14    **15.** $109,336.50

**17.** $17,708.46

## PRACTICE TEST, P. 515

**1.** $18,292.50    **2.** $8,851.12    **3.** $37,607.22    **4.** $5,591.70    **5.** $5,727.50    **6.** $11,477.22

**7.** $60,819.20    **8.** $65,076.54    **9.** $28,269.88    **10.** $48,417.60    **11.** $1,118.23    **12.** $25,938

**13.** $34,724.80    **14.** $3,327.06    **15.** $28,240    **16.** $21,884    **17.** $5,591.97    **18.** $3,584.07

**19.** $19,672.40    **20.** $10,822.50    **21.** $13,678.80    **22.** $3,861    **23.** $9,583.92    **24.** $136,775

**25.** $2,136.17 for payment starting at birth; $4,215.60 for payment starting at six years of age

# CHAPTER 15

## Section Exercises

# 15-1

| | Purchase price of home | Down payment | Mortgage amount | Annual interest rate | Years | Payment per $1,000 | Monthly mortgage payment | Total paid for mortgage | Interest paid |
|---|---|---|---|---|---|---|---|---|---|
| **1.** | $100,000 | $0 | $100,000 | 5.75% | 30 | $5.84 | $ 584 | $210,240 | $110,240 |
| **3.** | $ 95,000 | $8,000 | $ 87,000 | 5.75% | 25 | $6.29 | $ 547.23 | $164,169 | $ 77,169 |
| **5.** | $495,750 | 18% | $406,515 | 5.00% | 35 | $5.05 | $2,052.90 | $862,218 | $455,703 |

**7.** Down payment = $38,750;
Mortgage amount = $116,250;
Monthly payment = $697.50

**9.** $51,336

# 15-2

**1.**

| Month | Monthly payment | Interest | Principal | End-of-month principal |
|---|---|---|---|---|
| 1 | $584 | $479.17 | $104.83 | $99,895.17 |
| 2 | $584 | $478.66 | $105.34 | $99,789.83 |

**3.**

| Month | Monthly payment | Interest | Principal | End-of-month principal |
|---|---|---|---|---|
| 1 | $547.23 | $416.88 | $130.35 | $86,869.65 |
| 2 | $547.23 | $416.25 | $130.98 | $86,738.67 |

**5.**

| Month | Monthly payment | Interest | Principal | End-of-month principal |
|---|---|---|---|---|
| 1 | $2,052.90 | $1,693.81 | $359.09 | $406,155.91 |
| 2 | $2,052.90 | $1,692.32 | $360.58 | $405,795.33 |

**7.** Month 1 interest = $406.58;
Principal portion of 1st payment = $133.60;
End-of-month principal = $69,566.40;
Month 2 interest = $405.80;
Principal portion of 2nd payment = $134.38;
End-of-month principal = $69,432.02

**9.**

| Month | Monthly payment | Interest | Principal | End-of-month principal |
|---|---|---|---|---|
| 1 | $1,825.40 | $1,489.63 | $335.77 | $209,964.23 |
| 2 | $1,825.40 | $1,487.25 | $338.15 | $209,626.08 |

**11.** 29%

## EXERCISES SET A, P. 539

**1.** $2,018.25  **3.** $1,005.18  **5.** $196,880  **7.** $149,254

**9.**

| Month | Monthly payment | Interest | Principal | End-of-month principal |
|---|---|---|---|---|
| 1 | $2,926.20 | $2,438.50 | $487.70 | $487,212.30 |
| 2 | $2,926.20 | $2,436.06 | $490.14 | $486,722.16 |

**11.** $1,743.66  **13.** 28%

## EXERCISES SET B, P. 541

**1.** $2.926.20  **3.** $619.26  **5.** $565,732  **7.** $177,189.20

**9.**

| Month | Monthly payment | Interest | Principal | End-of-month principal |
|---|---|---|---|---|
| 1 | $1,005.18 | $793.23 | $211.95 | $152,088.05 |
| 2 | $1,005.18 | $792.13 | $213.05 | $151,875.00 |

**11.** $2,885.87  **13.** 35%

## PRACTICE TEST, P. 543

**1.** 6.44  **2.** $1,607.70  **3.** $348,772  **4.** 151.64%  **5.** $39,400

**6.** $157,600  **7.** $3,152  **8.** $1,416.82  **9.** $97,427.60

**10.** Monthly payment = $1,048.04; Interest = $219,694.40

**11.** $122,266.80  **12.** Interest = $919.33; Principal portion = $497.49

**13.** Portion of payment applied to:

| Month | Monthly payment | Interest | Principal | End-of-month principal |
|---|---|---|---|---|
| 1 | $1,416.82 | $919.33 | $497.49 | $157,102.51 |
| 2 | $1,416.82 | $916.43 | $500.39 | $156,602.12 |
| 3 | $1,416.82 | $913.51 | $503.31 | $156,098.81 |

**14.** Portion of payment applied to:

| Month | Monthly payment | Interest | Principal | End-of-month principal |
|---|---|---|---|---|
| 1 | $1,048.04 | $919.33 | $128.71 | $157,471.29 |
| 2 | $1,048.04 | $918.58 | $129.46 | $157,341.83 |
| 3 | $1,048.04 | $917.83 | $130.21 | $157,211.62 |

**15.** 37%

# CHAPTER 16

## Section Exercises

# 16-1

| Total cost $44,000 | Year | Annual depreciation | Accumulated depreciation | End-of-year book value |
|---|---|---|---|---|
| **1.** Depreciable | 1 | $6,000 | $6,000 | $38,000 |
| **2.** value = | 2 | $6,000 | $12,000 | $32,000 |
| **3.** $36,000 | 3 | $6,000 | $18,000 | $26,000 |
| **4.** | 4 | $6,000 | $24,000 | $20,000 |
| **5.** | 5 | $6,000 | $30,000 | $14,000 |
| **6.** | 6 | $6,000 | $36,000 | $8,000 |

| Total cost $38,000 | Year | Hours used | Annual depreciation | Accumulated depreciation | End-of-year book value |
|---|---|---|---|---|---|
| **7.** Depreciable | 1 | 24,848 | $1,789.06 | $1,789.06 | $36,210.94 |
| **8.** value = | 2 | 20,040 | $1,442.88 | $3,231.94 | $34,768.06 |
| **9.** $36,000 | 3 | 20,860 | $1,501.92 | $4,733.86 | $33,266.14 |

| Total cost $28,000 | Year | Depreciation rate | Annual depreciation | Accumulated depreciation | End-of-year book value |
|---|---|---|---|---|---|
| **11.** Depreciable value = $25,500 | 2 | $\frac{9}{55}$ | $4,172.73 | $8,809.09 | $19,190.91 |

| Total cost $285,900 | Year | Annual depreciation | Accumulated depreciation | End-of-year book value |
|---|---|---|---|---|
| **13.** | 1 | $21,442.50 | $21,442.50 | $264,457.50 |
| **15.** | 3 | $18,346.74 | $59,623.55 | $226,276.45 |

**17.**

| Total cost: $25,000 | Year | Depreciation | Accumulated depreciation | End-of-year book value |
|---|---|---|---|---|
| | 1 | $1,875 | $1,875 | $23,125 |
| | 2 | 1,875 | 3,750 | 21,250 |
| | 3 | 1,875 | 5,625 | 19,375 |

**19.** $1,140

**21.** Unit depreciation = $0.9066667 per hour; First year's depreciation = $3,493.39

**23.** Rate = 0.2857 (rounded to the nearest ten-thousandth); First year's depreciation = $10,653.75

# 16-2

**1.** $36,671.25

**3.** $12,790

**5.** $112,000 maximum

**7.** Year 1 depreciation = $5,999.40;
Year 2 depreciation = $8,001;
Year 3 depreciation = $2,665.80;
Year 4 depreciation = $1,333.80

**9.** Year 7 depreciation = $2,199.60

**11.** Depreciable amount = $70,000;
Year 1 depreciation = $10,003

**13.**

| Year | MACRS rate | Depreciation | Accumulated depreciation | End-of-year book value |
|---|---|---|---|---|
| 1 | 33.33% | $44,293.90 | $44,293.90 | $88,601.10 |
| 2 | 44.45% | $59,071.83 | $103,365.73 | $29,529.27 |
| 3 | 14.81% | $19,681.75 | $123,047.48 | $9,847.52 |
| 4 | 7.41% | $9,847.52 | $132,895.00 | $0 |

**15.**

| Year | MACRS rate | Depreciation | Accumulated depreciation | End-of-year book value |
|---|---|---|---|---|
| 1 | 20% | $57,200 | $57,200 | $228,800 |
| 2 | 32% | $91,520 | $148,720 | $137,280 |
| 3 | 19.2% | $54,912 | $203,632 | $82,368 |
| 4 | 11.52% | $32,947.20 | $236,579.20 | $49,420.80 |
| 5 | 11.52% | $32,947.20 | $269,526.40 | $16,473.60 |
| 6 | 5.76% | $16,473.60 | $286,000 | $0 |

## EXERCISES SET A, P. 573

**1.** $2,300

**3.** $4,500

**5.** $900

**7.** Unit depreciation = $0.50;
Yearly depreciation = $3,350

**9.** Unit depreciation = $0.25;
Yearly depreciation = $380

**11.** $0.18

**13.**

| Total cost: $4,200 | Year | Depreciation rate | Depreciation | Accumulated depreciation | End-of-year book value |
|---|---|---|---|---|---|
| Depreciable value: $4,200 − $750 = $3,450 | 1 | $\frac{5}{15}$ | $1,150 | $1,150 | $3,050 |
| | 2 | $\frac{4}{15}$ | $920 | $2,070 | $2,130 |

**15.** $949.03

**17.** Year 1: $1,160
Year 2: $1,856
Year 3: $1,113.60

**19.**

| Total cost: $3,270 | Year | MACRS rate | Depreciation | Accumulated depreciation | End-of-year book value |
|---|---|---|---|---|---|
| | 1 | 33.33% | $1,089.89 | $1,089.89 | $2,180.11 |
| | 2 | 44.45% | $1,453.52 | $2,543.41 | $726.59 |
| | 3 | 14.81% | $484.29 | $3,027.70 | $242.30 |
| | 4 | 7.41% | $242.30* | $3,270.00 | $0 |

*adjusted

## EXERCISES SET B, P. 575

**1.** $540.91

**3.** $5,875

**5.** $800

**7.** Unit depreciation = $0.25;
Yearly depreciation = $1,750

**9.** $2,080

**11.**

| Total cost: $15,000 | Year | Hours used | Depreciation | Accumulated depreciation | End-of-year book value |
|---|---|---|---|---|---|
| | 1 | 4,160 | $2,080 | $2,080 | $12,920 |
| | 2 | 3,140 | $1,570 | $3,650 | $11,350 |
| | 3 | 6,820 | $3,410 | $7,060 | $7,940 |

**13.** Unit depreciation = $0.20;
Year's depreciation = $516.80

**15.**

| Total cost: $6,000 | Year | Depreciation | Accumulated depreciation | End-of-year book value |
|---|---|---|---|---|
| | 1 | $4,000 | $4,000 | $2,000 |
| | 2 | $1,250 | $5,250 | $750 |
| | 3 | $0 | $5,250 | $750 |

**17.** Year 15: $6,736.45;
Year 16: $3,362.53

**19.**

| Total cost: $16,250 | Year | MACRS rate | Depreciation | Accumulated depreciation | End-of-year book value |
|---|---|---|---|---|---|
| | 1 | 20.00% | $3,250 | $3,250 | $13,000 |
| | 2 | 32.00% | $5,200 | $8,450 | $7,800 |
| | 3 | 19.20% | $3,120 | $11,570 | $4,680 |

## PRACTICE TEST, P. 577

**1.** 28

**2.** $33,690

**3.** Annual depreciation = $760
Accumulated depreciation:
year 1: $760; year 2: $1,520; year 3: $2,280;
year 4: $3,040; year 5: $3,800.
End-of-year book value:
year 1: $3,740; year 2: $2,980; year 3:
$2,220; year 4: $1,460; year 5: $700

**4.** $0.15264

**5.** 300

**6.**

| Total cost: $7,500 | Year | Depreciation rate | Depreciation | Accumulated depreciation | End-of-year book value |
|---|---|---|---|---|---|
| | 1 | $\frac{3}{6}$ | $3,000 | $3,000 | $4,500 |
| | 2 | $\frac{2}{6}$ | $2,000 | $5,000 | $2,500 |
| | 3 | $\frac{1}{6}$ | $1,000 | $6,000 | $1,500 |

**7.**

| Total cost: $2,780 | Year | Depreciation | Accumulated depreciation | End-of-year book value |
|---|---|---|---|---|
| | 1 | $1,390.00 | $1,390.00 | $1,390.00 |
| | 2 | $695.00 | $2,085.00 | $695.00 |
| | 3 | $347.50 | $2,432.50 | $347.50 |
| | 4 | $47.50 | $2,480.00 | $300.00 |

**8.**

| Total cost: $13,580 | Year | MACRS rate | Depreciation | Accumulated depreciation | End-of-year book value |
|---|---|---|---|---|---|
| | 1 | 33.33% | $4,526.21 | $4,526.21 | $9,053.79 |
| | 2 | 44.45% | $6,036.31 | $10,562.52 | $3,017.48 |
| | 3 | 14.81% | $2,011.20 | $12,573.72 | $1,006.28 |
| | 4 | 7.41% | $1,006.28 | $13,580.00 | $0 |

**9.** $2,859.71

**10.** $2,232.21

**11.** $3,160

**12.** $115,160

# CHAPTER 17

## Section Exercises

# 17-1

**1.**

| Date of purchase | Units purchased | Cost per unit | Total cost | Retail price per unit | Total retail value |
|---|---|---|---|---|---|
| Beginning inventory | 42 | $850 | $35,700 | $975 | $40,950 |
| February 5 | 21 | $1,760 | $36,960 | $2,115 | $44,415 |
| February 19 | 17 | $965 | $16,405 | $1,206 | $20,502 |
| March 3 | 28 | $480 | $13,440 | $600 | $16,800 |
| Goods available for sale | 108 | | $102,505 | | $122,667 |
| Units sold | 74 | | | | |
| Ending inventory | 34 | | | | |

**3.** $64,895

**5.**

| Cost per unit | Number of units on hand | Total cost |
|---|---|---|
| $12 | 43 | $516 |
| $9 | 11 | $99 |
| $11 | 7 | $77 |
| $15 | 21 | $315 |
| Ending inventory | 82 | $1,007 |

**7.** $949.12

**9.** $70,234.92

**11.** $997.12

**13.** 28 units @ $480 per unit;
6 units @ $965 per unit;
Cost of ending inventory = $19,230

**15.** June 2:    37 units @ $15 per unit
May 8:     15 units @ $11 per unit
April 12:    23 units @ $9 per unit
Beginning:   7 units @ $12 per unit
Total        82 items are in the
           ending inventory

**17.** 34 units @ $850 per unit

**19.** 82 units @ $12 per unit

**21.** $122,667

**23.** $66,028.95

**25.** 0.680

**27.** Estimated cost of goods sold = $80,808
Estimated ending inventory = $21,697

# 17-2

**1.** 2.42 times

**3.** 4.04 times

**5.**
| Toys | $789.47 |
|---|---|
| Appliances | $1,302.63 |
| Children's clothing | $1,342.11 |
| Books | $907.89 |
| Furniture | $1,657.89 |

**7.**
| China | $325.62 |
|---|---|
| Silver | $740.62 |
| Crystal | $243.36 |
| Linens | $159.61 |
| New gifts | $522.16 |
| Antiques | $740.62 |

**9.**
| Welding bay | $2,880.42 |
|---|---|
| Paint shop | $2,674.68 |
| Axles and steel storage | $1,069.87 |
| Flooring lumber | $521.22 |
| Office space | $685.81 |

## EXERCISES SET A, P. 611

**1.** $8,112

**3.** $4,291

**5.** Cost of ending inventory = $3,558.94;
Cost of goods sold = $4,553.06

**7.** Cost of goods sold = $3,804;
Cost of ending inventory = $4,308

**9.** 2.4 times

**11.** 5 times

**13.**
| Hardware | $3,066.67 |
|---|---|
| Plumbing | $2,300.00 |
| Tools | $1,533.33 |
| Supplies | $2,300.00 |

## EXERCISES SET B, P. 613

**1.** $1,374

**3.** Cost of goods available for sale = $788
Average unit cost = $11.76

**5.** Cost of ending inventory = $246.96;
Cost of goods sold = $541.04

**7.** Cost of ending inventory = $3,596;
Cost of goods sold = $8,673

**9.** 0.5 times

**11.**
| Nuts and bolts | $730.77 |
|---|---|
| Electrical | $1,948.72 |
| Paint | $1,120.51 |

## PRACTICE TEST, P. 615

**1.** $1,237

**2.** $761

**3.** $476

**4.** $11.04

**5.** Cost of ending inventory = $761.76;
Cost of goods sold = $475.24

**6.** Cost of ending inventory = $363

**7.** Cost of goods sold = $345;
Cost of ending inventory = $892

**8.**
| Cameras | $1,674.42 |
|---|---|
| Toys | $1,953.49 |
| Hardware | $1,883.72 |
| Garden supplies | $1,172.09 |
| Sporting goods | $1,325.58 |
| Clothing | $3,990.70 |

**9.**
| Furniture | $2,222.22 |
|---|---|
| Computer supplies | $1,777.78 |
| Consumable office supplies | $2,777.78 |
| Leather goods | $1,333.33 |
| Administrative services | $888.89 |

**10.** 4

**11.** 2.92

**12.** 2

**13.** Overhead expenses:
Purchasing = $132.06
Personnel = $468.02
Payroll = $493.02
Secretarial = $801.90
Total = $1,895

**14.**
| A | $2,827.59 |
|---|---|
| B | $1,413.79 |
| C | $2,431.72 |
| D | $1,526.90 |

# CHAPTER 18

## Section Exercises

## 18-1

**1.** $52.65      **3.** $90.74      **5.** The male pays a premium that is $3.75 higher.      **7.** 11.46 years

## 18-2

**1.** $1,246.50    **3.** $521.12    **5.** $238    **7.** $75,000    **9.** $316,000    **11.** $78,797.47    **13.** $5,820.36

## 18-3

**1.** $743    **3.** $733    **5.** $1,063    **7.** $709    **9.** $635    **11.** $57.92

### EXERCISES SET A, P. 639

**1.** Annual building premium = $2,306.40; Annual contents premium = $1,514.20; Total insurance premium = $3,820.60    **3.** Annual building premium = $1,029; Annual contents premium = $736.60; Total insurance premium = $1,765.60    **5.** $3,283.50

**7.** $737    **9.** $564    **11.** $650

**13.** $566    **15.** $676    **17.** Annual premium = $590.40; Monthly premium = $51.66; Quarterly premium = $153.50

**19.** $3.03    **21.** 14.79 years

### EXERCISES SET B, P. 641

**1.** $3,548.10    **3.** $3,677.10    **5.** $928.50    **7.** $562

**9.** $1,174    **11.** $705    **13.** $563    **15.** $501

**17.** Annual premium = $220; Monthly premium = $19.25; Quarterly premium = $57.20    **19.** $1,308.75    **21.** 1.61 years

### PRACTICE TEST, P. 643

**1.** $1,206    **2.** $767    **3.** $1,974.10    **4.** $554    **5.** $190.50

**6.** $732    **7.** $2,240.42    **8.** The straight-life policy is $220 more than the 20-year fixed-rate policy.    **9.** $73.94    **10.** $56.94

**11.** $53,448.28    **12.** $441    **13.** 4.18 years    **14.** $4,762.10

# CHAPTER 19

## Section Exercises

## 19-1

**1.** Sales tax = $30.36; Total sale = $622.72    **3.** Sales tax = $148.32; Total sale = $3,444.32    **5.** Marked price = $655.21; Sales tax = $26.21    **7.** Marked price = $371.05; Sales tax = $24.12

**9.** $15.87 (rounded)    **11.** $20.52    **13.** $172.06    **15.** Marked price = $788.86; Sales tax = $61.14

## 19-2

**1.** $4,537.90    **3.** $13,554.45    **5.** 8.12%    **7.** $26.76 per $1,000    **9.** $3.59 per $100

**11.** $52,500    **13.** $96,250    **15.** $3,982.50    **17.** $956.25    **19.** 2.7¢ per $1.00 assessed value

**21.** $31.26

# 19-3

**1.** $23,852 **3.** $123,379 **5.** $6,639 **7.** $4,171 **9.** $43,522.44

**11.** $14,491 **13.** $40,544 **15.** $2,744 **17.** Tax owed is *less* than tax paid so a refund is due. Amount of refund = $1,543 **19.** $39,669.36

## EXERCISES SET A, P. 671

**1.** $14.25 **3.** $33.80 **5.** $332.33 **7.** $13,750 **9.** $2,587,500 **11.** $250

**13.** $4,062.50 **15.** $527.25 **17.** $1,108.63 (nearest cent) **19.** $0.072 **21.** $1,840 **23.** $1 tax rate = $0.04; $100 tax rate = $3.26; $1,000 tax rate = $32.54;

**25.** $28,774 **27.** $6,476 **29.** $5,091 **31.** $46,992.55

## EXERCISES SET B, P. 673

**1.** $26.19 **3.** $134.95 **5.** $51.35 **7.** $94,000 **9.** $53,750 **11.** $10,350

**13.** $684.13 **15.** $2,325.00 **17.** $0.034 **19.** $812.50 **21.** $1 tax rate = $0.04; $100 tax rate = $3.40; $1,000 tax rate = $33.99 **23.** $31,755

**25.** $44,350 **27.** $6,439 **29.** $5,466 **31.** $37,313.50

## PRACTICE TEST, P. 675

**1.** $0.76 (rounded) **2.** $1.14 (rounded) **3.** $22.28 (rounded) **4.** $0.19 (rounded) **5.** $198.44

**6.** $4.47 **7.** $17.61 (rounded) **8.** $7.39 (rounded) **9.** $50.00 (rounded) **10.** $5.05 (rounded) sales tax

**11.** $89.20 **12.** $194,119.20 **13.** $13,328.05 (rounded) **14.** $1,071.77 (rounded) **15.** $2,966.40

**16.** $1,850.40 **17.** $3.02 (rounded up) **18.** $46,921.11 **19.** $5,226 **20.** $40,800

# CHAPTER 20

## Section Exercises

# 20-1

**Answers for 1, 5, 9**

Miss Muffins' Bakery
Comparative Balance Sheet
December 31

| | 2009 | Increase (decrease) | | Percent of total assets |
| --- | --- | --- | --- | --- |
| | | Amount | Percent | 2009 |
| **Assets** | | | | |
| *Current assets* | | | | |
| Cash | $1,985 | $223 | 12.7 | 22.8 |
| Accounts receivable | 4,219 | 434 | 11.5 | 48.4 |
| Merchandise inventory | 2,512 | 476 | 23.4 | 28.8 |
| Total assets | $8,716 | $1,133 | 14.9 | 100.0 |
| **Liabilities** | | | | |
| *Current liabilities* | | | | |
| Accounts payable | $3,483 | $(148) | (4.1) | 40.0 |
| Wages payable | 1,696 | 275 | 19.4 | 19.5 |
| Total liabilities | 5,179 | 127 | 2.5 | 59.4 |
| **Owner's Equity** | | | | |
| Mildred Galloway, capital | 3,537 | 1,006 | 39.7 | 40.6 |
| Total liabilities and owner's equity | $8,716 | $1,133 | 14.9 | 100.0 |

O'Dell's Nursery
Comparative Balance Sheet
December 31, 2009

| | 2009 | Percent of total assets 2009 |
|---|---|---|
| **Assets** | | |
| *Current assets* | | |
| Cash | $8,917 | 26.0 |
| Accounts receivable | 7,521 | 22.0 |
| Merchandise inventory | 17,826 | 52.0 |
| Total assets | $34,264 | 100.0 |
| **Liabilities** | | |
| *Current liabilities* | | |
| Accounts payable | $10,215 | 29.8 |
| Wages payable | 3,716 | 10.8 |
| Total liabilities | 13,931 | 40.7 |
| **Owner's Equity** | | |
| Janelle O'Dell, capital | 20,333 | 59.3 |
| Total liabilities and owner's equity | $34,264 | 100.0 |

**11.** 59.4%

# 20-2

**1.**

Sitha Ros's Oriental Groceries
Income Statement
for the Years Ending June 30, 2008, and 2009

| | 2009 | 2008 |
|---|---|---|
| Net sales | $97,384 | $92,196 |
| Cost of goods sold | 82,157 | 72,894 |
| Gross profit | 15,227 | 19,302 |
| Operating expenses | 4,783 | 3,951 |
| Net income | $10,444 | $15,351 |

Answers for 3, 5, 7

Miss Muffins' Bakery
Vertical Analysis of Income Statement for the Months Ending
July 31, 2007, and July 31, 2008

| | 2008 | Percent of net sales | 2007 | Percent of net sales | Increase (decrease) amount | Percent |
|---|---|---|---|---|---|---|
| Gross sales | $35,403 | 101.0 | $32,596 | 100.9 | $2,807 | 8.6 |
| Returns and allowances | 342 | 1.0 | 296 | 0.9 | 46 | 15.5 |
| Net sales | 35,061 | 100.0 | 32,300 | 100.0 | 2,761 | 8.5 |
| Cost of beginning inventory | 17,403 | 49.6 | 16,872 | 52.2 | 531 | 3.1 |
| Cost of purchases | 27,983 | 79.8 | 33,596 | 104.0 | (5,613) | (16.7) |
| Cost of ending inventory | 22,583 | 64.4 | 21,843 | 67.6 | 740 | 3.4 |
| Cost of goods sold | 22,803 | 65.0 | 28,625 | 88.6 | (5,822) | (20.3) |
| Gross profit | 12,258 | 35.0 | 3,675 | 11.4 | 8,583 | 233.6 |
| Total operating expenses | 3,053 | 8.7 | 1,894 | 5.9 | 1,159 | 61.2 |
| Net income | $ 9,205 | 26.3 | $ 1,781 | 5.5 | $7,424 | 416.8 |

# 20-3

**1.** 1.44 to 1

**3.** 0.542 to 1

**5.** George's current ratio = 4 or 4 to 1;
José's current ratio = 1.03 or 1.03 to 1

**7.** 71.0%

## EXERCISES SET A, P. 713

**1.** Total current assets = $11,271;
Total assets = $23,458

Total current liabilities = $3,098;
Total liabilities and owner's equity = $23,458

**5.** 1.57 to 1

**7.** 0.87 to 1

**9.** Operating ratio = 0.9 or 90%;
Gross profit margin = 0.25 or 25%

**11.** 20.1%

**3.**

Marten's Family Store
Income Statement
For Year Ending December 31, 2008

|  | | Percent of net sales |
|---|---:|---:|
| **Revenue** | | |
| Gross sales | $238,923 | 106.1 |
| Sales returns and allowances | 13,815 | 6.1 |
| Net sales | 225,108 | 100.0 |
| **Cost of goods sold** | | |
| Beginning inventory, January 1, 2008 | 25,814 | 11.5 |
| Purchases | 109,838 | 48.8 |
| Ending inventory, December 31, 2008 | 23,423 | 10.4 |
| Cost of goods sold | 112,229 | 49.9 |
| **Gross profit from sales** | $112,879 | 50.1 |
| **Operating expenses** | | |
| Salary | $ 42,523 | 18.9 |
| Rent | 8,640 | 3.8 |
| Utilities | 1,484 | 0.7 |
| Insurance | 2,842 | 1.3 |
| Fees | 860 | 0.4 |
| Depreciation | 1,920 | 0.9 |
| Miscellaneous | 3,420 | 1.5 |
| **Total operating expenses** | 61,689 | 27.4 |
| **Net income** | $51,190 | 22.7 |

## EXERCISES SET B, P. 717

**1.** Total current assets = $11,481;
Total assets = $22,856;
Total current liabilities = $3,570;
Total liabilities and owner's equity = $22,856

**3.**

Serpa's Gifts
Income Statement
For Year Ending December 31, 2007

|  | | Percent of net sales |
|---|---:|---:|
| **Revenue** | | |
| Gross sales | $148,645 | 106.4 |
| Sales returns and allowances | 8,892 | 6.4 |
| Net sales | 139,753 | 100.0 |
| **Cost of goods sold** | | |
| Beginning inventory, January 1, 2007 | 12,100 | 8.7 |
| Purchases | 47,800 | 34.2 |
| Ending inventory, December 31, 2007 | 11,950 | 8.6 |
| Cost of goods sold | 47,950 | 34.3 |
| **Gross profit from sales** | $91,803 | 65.7 |
| **Operating expenses** | | |
| Salary | 25,500 | 18.2 |
| Rent | 4,500 | 3.2 |
| Utilities | 1,445 | 1.0 |
| Insurance | 2,100 | 1.5 |
| Fees | 225 | 0.2 |
| Depreciation | 1,240 | 0.9 |
| Miscellaneous | 750 | 0.5 |
| **Total operating expenses** | 35,760 | 25.6 |
| **Net income** | $56,043 | 40.1 |

**5.** 0.83 to 1

**7.** 1.74 to 1

**9.** 0.8312766, or 83.1%

**1.**

**O'Toole's Hardware Store**
**Comparative Balance Sheet**
**December 31, 2008, and 2009**

| | 2009 | 2008 | Increase (decrease) Amount | Increase (decrease) Percent |
|---|---|---|---|---|
| **Assets** | | | | |
| *Current assets* | | | | |
| Cash | $7,318 | $5,283 | $2,035 | 38.5 |
| Accounts receivable | 3,147 | 3,008 | 139 | 4.6 |
| Merchandise inventory | 63,594 | 60,187 | 3,407 | 5.7 |
| Total current assets | 74,059 | 68,478 | 5,581 | 8.2 |
| *Plant and equipment* | | | | |
| Building | 36,561 | 37,531 | (970) | (2.6) |
| Equipment | 8,256 | 4,386 | 3,870 | 88.2 |
| Total plant and equipment | 44,817 | 41,917 | 2,900 | 6.9 |
| Total assets | $118,876 | $110,395 | $8,481 | 7.7 |
| **Liabilities** | | | | |
| *Current liabilities* | | | | |
| Accounts payable | $5,174 | $4,563 | $611 | 13.4 |
| Wages payable | 780 | 624 | 156 | 25.0 |
| Total current liabilities | 5,954 | 5,187 | 767 | 14.8 |
| *Long-term liabilities* | | | | |
| Mortgage note payable | 34,917 | 36,510 | (1,593) | (4.4) |
| Total long-term liabilities | 34,917 | 36,510 | (1,593) | (4.4) |
| Total liabilities | 40,871 | 41,697 | (826) | (2.0) |
| **Owner's equity** | | | | |
| James O'Toole, capital | 78,005 | 68,698 | 9,307 | 13.5 |
| Total liabilities and owner's equity | $118,876 | $110,395 | $8,481 | 7.7 |

**2.** 12.44 to 1          **3.** 1.76 to 1          **4.** 13.20 to 1          **5.** 1.60 to 1

**6.**

**Mile Wide Woolens, Inc.**
**Comparative Income Statement**
**For Years Ending December 31, 2007, and 2008**

| | 2008 | 2007 | Increase (decrease) Amount | Increase (decrease) Percent |
|---|---|---|---|---|
| **Revenue** | | | | |
| Gross sales | $219,827 | $205,852 | $13,975 | 6.8 |
| Sales returns and allowances | 8,512 | 7,983 | 529 | 6.6 |
| Net sales | 211,315 | 197,869 | 13,446 | 6.8 |
| **Cost of goods sold** | | | | |
| Beginning inventory, January 1 | 42,816 | 40,512 | 2,304 | 5.7 |
| Purchases | 97,523 | 94,812 | 2,711 | 2.9 |
| Ending inventory, December 31 | 43,182 | 42,521 | 661 | 1.6 |
| Cost of goods sold | 97,157 | 92,803 | 4,354 | 4.7 |
| **Gross profit from sales** | $114,158 | $105,066 | 9,092 | 8.7 |
| **Operating expenses** | | | | |
| Salary | 28,940 | 27,000 | 1,940 | 7.2 |
| Insurance | 800 | 750 | 50 | 6.7 |
| Utilities | 1,700 | 1,580 | 120 | 7.6 |
| Rent | 3,600 | 3,000 | 600 | 20.0 |
| Depreciation | 2,000 | 2,400 | (400) | (16.7) |
| **Total operating expenses** | 37,040 | 34,730 | 2,310 | 6.7 |
| **Net income** | $ 77,118 | $ 70,336 | $6,782 | 9.6 |

**7.** Operating ratio for 2007 = 0.645 or 64.5%;
Operating ratio for 2008 = 0.635 or 63.5%

**8.** Gross profit margin ratio for 2007 = 0.531 or 53.1%;
Gross profit margin ratio for 2008 = 0.540 or 54.0%

**9.** 1.56

**10.** 1.53

# CHAPTER 21

## Section Exercises

## 21-1

**1.** $30.48  **3.** $1.52  **5.** 5,626,775  **7.** $2,870,000  **9.** $10,000  **11.** $2.38  **13.** $1,394,000

## 21-2

**1.** $7\frac{3}{4}\%$ interest rate and a maturity date of 2013  **3.** 17

**5.** The one maturing in 2010 has a current yield of 8.5%, which is greater than the 2008 yield of 6.1%.  **7.** $1,000

**9.** 103.13%  **11.** $18.32

**13.** $16.82

### EXERCISES SET A, P. 745
**1.** 755,400 shares  **3.** $0.71  **5.** $0.70; $35.00; $70.00  **7.** $30,000  **9.** $440,000

**11.** 10  **13.** 2022  **15.** $1,003.80  **17.** $14.44

### EXERCISES SET B, P. 747
**1.** $1.42  **3.** 3.7%  **5.** AMB Property at $2.00 per share  **7.** $852,000  **9.** $2,546,000

**11.** 8%  **13.** GMAC dc6s11 is selling at a discount. GMAC $6\frac{1}{8}08$ is selling at a premium.  **15.** $1,460  **17.** $13.75

### PRACTICE TEST, P. 749
**1.** $0.81  **2.** 0.6%  **3.** $31.50 per share  **4.** $31.56 per share  **5.** 4,590,500 shares  **6.** $6,060

**7.** $3,780  **8.** $2,000  **9.** $2,000  **10.** $196,000  **11.** $2.61  **12.** 12

**13.** $210  **14.** 2009  **15.** $640 per bond  **16.** $723.75  **17.** Discount  **18.** $16.87

**19.** $14.57  **20.** $9.88

# Glossary/Index

**150%-declining rate:** a common declining-balance rate that is one-and-one-half times the straight-line rate, 557

**200%-declining-balance method:** *See* Double-declining-balance method, 557

**Accelerated cost-recovery system (ACRS):** a depreciation method implemented by the IRS for property placed in service after 1980 through 1986, 562

**Account register:** a separate form for recording all checking account transactions. It also shows the account balance, 107

**Accounts payable:** a current liability for merchandise or services that have not been paid for, 682

**Accounts receivable:** a current asset that is the money owed by customers, 682

**Accumulated depreciation:** the current year's depreciation plus all previous years' depreciation, 551

**Accumulation phase of an annuity:** the time when money is being paid into the fund and earnings are being added to the fund, 488

**Acid-test ratio or quick ratio:** the ratio of quick current assets to current liabilities, 702

**Addends:** numbers being added, 9

**Adjustable-rate mortgage:** the interest rate may change during the time of the loan, 524

**Adjusted balance due at maturity:** the remaining balance due at maturity after one or more partial payments have been made, 394

**Adjusted gross income:** the income that remains after allowable adjustments have been made, 349; total or gross income minus certain educator or moving expenses and specific deductions such as IRAs, student loan interest, tuition and fees, alimony paid, and so on, 659

**Adjusted principal:** the remaining principal after a partial payment has been properly credited, 394

**Adjustment:** amount that can be subtracted from the gross income, such as qualifying IRAs, tax-sheltered annuities, 401k's, or employer-sponsored child care or medical plans, 349

**Adjusted statement balance:** consists of the balance on the bank statement plus any outstanding deposits minus any outstanding checks, 115

**Allowances:** *See* Sales returns, 693

**Amortization:** the process for repaying a loan through equal payments at a specified rate for a specific length of time, 524

**Amortization schedule:** a table that shows the balance of principal and interest for each payment of the mortgage, 530

**Amount credited:** the sum of the partial payment and the partial discount, 274

**Amount financed:** the cash price minus the down payment, 422; the total amount that is to be paid in regular payments, 488

**Annual percentage rate (APR):** the true rate of an installment loan that is equivalent to an annual simple interest rate; effective rate of interest for a loan, 424, 461 tables, 425–427

**Annual percentage yield (APY):** effective rate of interest for an investment, 461

**Annuity:** a contract between a person (the annuitant) and an insurance company (the insurer) for receiving and disbursing money for the annuitant or the beneficiary of the annuitant, 488

**Annuity certain:** an annuity paid over a guaranteed number of periods, 488

**Annuity due:** an annuity for which payments are made at the beginning of each period, 488

**Annuity payment:** a series of equal periodic payments put into an interest-bearing account for a specific number of periods, 488
annuity due, 488
ordinary annuity future value tables, 488
simple interest basis of annuity future value, 488

**Approximate number:** a rounded amount, 7

**Assessed value:** a specified percent of the estimated market value of the property, 654

**Asset turnover ratio:** the ratio of the net sales to the average total assets, 683

**Assets:** properties owned by the business, including anything of monetary value and anything that can be exchanged for cash or other property, 550, 682

**Associative property of addition:** when more than two numbers are added, the addends can be grouped two at a time in any way, 9

**Automatic drafts:** periodic withdrawals that the owner of an account authorizes to be made electronically, 105

**Automatic teller machine (ATM):** an electronic banking station that accepts deposits and disburses cash when you use an authorized ATM card, a debit card, or some credit cards, 104, 114

**Average annual yield:** *See* Current bond yield, 737

**Average daily balance:** the average of the daily balances for each day of the billing cycle, 433

**Average daily balance method:** the daily balances of the account are determined, then the sum of these balances is divided by the number of days in the billing cycle. This is then multiplied by the monthly interest rate to find the finance charge for the month, 433

**Balance sheet:** financial statement that indicates the worth or financial condition of a business as of a certain date, 682
comparative, 687
horizontal analysis of, 688
preparing, 682
vertical analysis of, 685

**Bank discount:** the interest or fee on a discounted note that is subtracted from the amount borrowed at the time the loan is made, 396

**Bank draft:** *See* Check, 104

**Bank memo:** a notification of a transaction error, 104

**Bank reconciliation:** the process of making the account register agree with the bank statement, 114
bank statements, 114
checking account forms, 102

**Bank statement:** an account record periodically provided by the bank for matching your records with the bank's records, 114

**Banker's rule:** calculating interest on a loan based on ordinary interest—which yields a slightly higher amount of interest, 393

**Bar graph:** a graph that uses horizontal or vertical bars to show how values compare to each other, 224

**Base:** the original number or one entire quantity, 186

**Benchmarking:** comparing a company's performance, such as inventory turnover ratio, with industry standards or with a similar company's performance, 599

**Beneficiary:** the individual, organization, or business to whom the proceeds of an insurance policy are payable, 622

**Bill of lading:** shipping document that includes a description of the merchandise, number of pieces, weight, name of consignee (sender), destination, and method of payment of freight charges, 275

**Billing cycle:** the days that are included on a statement or bill, 433

**Biweekly:** every two weeks or 26 times a year, 342

**Biweekly mortgage:** payment made every two weeks for 26 payments per year, 524

**Bodily injury:** personal injury sustained in an accident, 632

**Bond:** a type of loan to the issuer to raise money for a company or municipality. The investor or bondholder will be paid a specified rate of interest each year and will be paid the entire value of the bond at maturity, 734
convertible, 734
corporate, 734
cost of buying, 736–737
coupon, 734
discount, 735
junk, 734
P/E ratio, 731
premium, 735
reading listings, 735
recallable, 734
registered, 734
treasury, 734
yield, 737

**Bond market:** the structure for buying and selling bonds, 735
Bond price, 736
Bond value, 734
Bond yield, 737

**Depreciation:** the amount an asset decreases in value from its original cost, 550
accelerated cost-recovery system, 562
declining-balance method of, 556–567
modified accelerated cost-recovery system, 562
section 179 deductions, 565
straight-line method of, 550
sum-of-the-years'-digits method of, 554
units-of-production method of, 552

**Depreciation schedule:** a table showing the year's depreciation, the accumulated depreciation, and the end-of-year book value, 551

**Deviation from the mean:** the difference between a value of a data set and the mean, 234

**Difference:** the answer or the result of subtraction, 12

**Differential piece rate (escalating piece rate):** piecework rate that increases as more items are produced, 344

**Digit:** one of the ten symbols used in the decimal-number system (0, 1, 2, 3, 4, 5, 6, 7, 8, 9), 4

**Discount:** an amount of money that is deducted from an original price, 260

**Discount bond:** a bond that sells for less than the face value, 735

**Discount period:** the amount of time that the third party owns the third-party discounted note, 398

**Discount rate:** a percent of the list price, 260

**Discounted note:** a promissory note for which the interest or fee is discounted or subtracted at the time the loan is made, 397

**Dividend:** the number being divided or the total quantity, 15; a portion of the profit of a company that is periodically distributed to the stockholders of a company, 728

**Dividends in arrears:** dividends that were not paid in a previous year and must be paid to cumulative preferred stockholders before dividends can be distributed to other stockholders, 732

**Divisor:** the number divided by, 15

**Double-declining-balance method (200%-declining-balance depreciation):** a method of declining-balance depreciation in which the rate of depreciation is twice the straight-line depreciation rate, 557

**Double-declining rate:** a declining-balance depreciation rate that is twice the straight-line depreciation rate, 557

**Down payment:** a partial payment that is paid at the time of the purchase, 422

**Driver class:** the class for the primary driver based on factors such as age, sex, marital status, and driving history, 632

**Effective interest rate for a simple discount note:** the actual interest rate based on the proceeds of the loan, 397

**Effective rate:** the simple interest rate that is equivalent to a compound rate, 461

**Efficiency ratio:** a financial ratio that measures a business's ability to effectively use its assets to generate sales, 703

**Electronic deposit:** a deposit that is made by an electronic transfer of funds, 104

**Electronic filing:** a paperless way to file income tax with the IRS. The tax forms are submitted electronically to the IRS, 665

**Electronic funds transfer (EFT):** a transaction that transfers funds electronically, 104
Employers payroll taxes, 358

**End-of-month (EOM) terms:** a discount is applied if the bill is paid within the specified days after the end of the month. An exception occurs when an invoice is dated on or after the 26th of a month, 272

**End-of-year book value:** total cost minus depreciation for the first year. Thereafter, it is the previous year's end-of-year book value minus the current year's depreciation, 551

**Ending inventory at cost:** the cost of the ending inventory, 591

**Ending inventory at retail:** the retail value of the ending inventory, 591

**Endorsement:** a signature, stamp, or electronic imprint on the back of a check that authorizes payment in cash or directs payment to a third party or account, 109

**Equation:** a mathematical statement in which two quantities are equal, 146
solving using addition or subtraction, 147
solving using more than one operation, 148–149
solving using multiplication or division, 146
solving with multiple unknowns, 150
solving with parentheses, 151–152
solving with proportions, 152–153
using to solve problems, 155

**Equity:** the difference between the expected selling price and the balance owed on property, 524

**Equity line of credit:** a revolving, open-end account that is secured by real property, 524

**Equivalent fractions:** fractions that indicate the same portion of the whole amount, 39

**Escalating piece rate:** *See* Differential piece rate, 344

**Escrow:** an account for holding the part of a monthly payment that is to be used to pay taxes and insurance. The amount accumulates and the lender pays the taxes and insurance from this account as they are due, 527

**Estimate:** to find a reasonable approximate answer for a calculation, 9

**Estimated life or useful life:** the number of years an asset is expected to be usable, 550

**Exact interest rate:** a rate per day that assumes 365 days per year, 392

**Exact time:** time that is based on counting the exact number of days in a time period, 389

**Excise tax:** a tax or duty levied on the sale or importation of goods for the purpose of raising revenue or discouraging a particular behavior, 650

**Exemption or allowance:** an amount of money that a taxpayer is allowed to subtract from the adjusted gross income for himself or herself, a spouse, and each dependent, 659

**Face value:** the amount borrowed; the maximum amount of insurance provided by a policy, 396, 622

**Face value (par value):** the value of one share of stock at the time the company first issued stock for sale, 728; the original value of a bond, usually $1,000, 734

**Factor:** each number involved in multiplication, 13

**Federal Housing Administration (FHA):** a governmental agency within the U.S. Department of Housing and Urban Development (HUD) that insures residential mortgage loans. To receive an FHA loan, specific construction standards must be met and the lender must be approved, 524

**Federal unemployment (FUTA) tax:** a federal tax required of most employers. The tax provides for payment of unemployment compensation to workers who have lost their jobs, 360

**Federal tax withholding:** the amount required to be withheld from a person's pay to be paid to the federal government, 347
rates and the percentage method, 352

**FIFO (first-in, first-out) inventory method:** an inventory valuation method in which items sold are assumed to be the oldest items in inventory and the most recently purchased goods are those remaining in the ending inventory, 588

**Filing status:** category of taxpayer; single, married filing jointly, married filing separately, or head of household, 660

**Finance charges (carrying charges):** the interest and any fee associated with an installment loan, 422

**Financial ratio:** an analysis of financial data to compare a business's performance with past performance or with other similar businesses, 700
acid-test ratio, 702
asset turnover ratio, 703
current ratio, 701
gross profit margin ratio, 702
operating ratio, 702
total debt to total assets ratio, 703
Financial statements:
balance sheets, 682
financial ratios, 700
income statement, 693

**Fire insurance:** an insurance that protects against fire losses or losses that may result directly from attempts to extinguish a fire, 626

**First mortgage:** the primary mortgage on a property, 524

**Fixed-rate mortgage:** the interest rate remains the same for the entire loan, 524

**Fixed-time endowment insurance:** a policy that is a combination insurance and savings plan that is paid for a fixed period of time, 624

**Fixed-time payment insurance:** a policy with a specified face value for the insured's entire life with payment made for a fixed period of time, 624

**FOB destination:** free on board at the destination point. The seller pays the shipping when the merchandise is shipped, 276

**FOB shipping point:** free on board at the shipping point. The buyer pays the shipping when the shipment is received, 275

**Formula:** a relationship among quantities expressed in words or numbers and letters, 186
writing to find an unknown value, 187–188

**Fraction line:** the line that separates the numerator and denominator. It is also the division symbol, 36

Fractions:
adding and subtracting, 52–57
decimal, 74
equivalent, 39
identifying types of, 36
multiplying and dividing, 50–54
proper and improper, 36–39
reducing, 39
refund, 430

**Freight collect:** the buyer pays the shipping when the shipment is received, 275

**Freight paid:** the seller pays the shipping when the merchandise is shipped, 276

Freight payment terms, 275

**Front-end load mutual fund:** a mutual fund for which the sales charge is included in the selling price of the shares, 738

**Fund family:** the mutual fund company that offers more than one type of fund, 738

**Future value, maturity value, compound amount:** the accumulated principal and interest after one or more interest periods, 454

**Good faith estimate:** an estimate of the mortgage closing costs that lenders are required to provide to the buyer in writing prior to the loan closing date, 527

**Graduated payments mortgage:** payments at the beginning of the loan are smaller and they increase during the loan, 524

**Graph:** a symbolic or pictorial display of numerical information, 224

**Greatest common divisor (GCD):** the greatest number by which both parts of a fraction can be evenly divided, 39

**Gross earnings (gross pay):** the amount earned before deductions, 342
based on commission, 345
based on hourly wage, 343
based on piecework wage, 344
based on salary, 342

**Gross income:** all income received in the form of money, goods, property, and services that is not exempt from tax, 659

**Gross margin:** *See* Gross profit, 592

Gross pay, 342

**Gross profit or gross margin:** net sales minus the cost of goods sold, 693; *See also* Markup, 296

**Gross profit (margin) inventory method:** a method for estimating the value of inventory that is based on a constant gross profit (margin) rate and net sales, 592

**Gross profit margin ratio:** the ratio of the gross profit from sales to the net sales, 702

**Grouped frequency distribution:** a compilation of class intervals, tallies, and class frequencies of a data set, 218

**Higher terms:** a fraction written in an equivalent value, determined by multiplying the numerator and denominator by the same number; the process is used in the addition and subtraction of fractions, 40

**Histogram:** a special type of bar graph that represents the data from a frequency distribution, 225

**Horizontal analysis of an income statement:** comparison of like entries for two years. The amount of increase or

decrease and the percent of increase or decrease are determined, 697

**Horizontal analysis of balance sheet:** a balance sheet analysis that compares the same item for two different years, 688

**Hourly rate (hourly wage):** the amount of pay per hour worked based on a standard 40-hour work week, 343

**Hourly wage:** *See* Hourly rate, 343

**Housing or front-end ratio:** monthly housing expenses (PITI) divided by the gross monthly income, 532

**Improper fraction:** a fraction with a value that is equal to or greater than 1. The numerator is the same as or greater than the denominator, 36

**Income shortfall:** the difference in the total living expenses of a family and the amount of income a family would have after the death of the insured. This shortfall can be used to project the amount of insurance needed by the family, 622

**Income statement:** a financial statement of the net income of a business over a period of time, 693
horizontal analysis of, 697
preparing, 693
vertical analysis of, 695

**Income tax:** local, state, or federal tax paid on one's income, 347, 659

**Income tax tables:** used to find the tax liability for taxable incomes of less than $100,000, 662–663

**Index numbers:** numbers that represent percent of change for several successive operating time periods (usually years) while keeping one selected year (base year) to represent the base or 100%, 705

**Installment loan:** a loan that is repaid in regular payments, 422

**Installment payment:** the amount that is paid (including interest) in regular payments, 422

**Installment price:** the total amount paid for a purchase, including all payments, the finance charges, and the down payment, 422

**Insurance:** a form of protection against unexpected financial loss, 622
fire, 626
life, 622
motor vehicle, 631

**Insured (policyholder):** the individual, organization, or business that carries the insurance or financial protection against loss, 622

**Insurer (underwriter):** the insurance company that assures payment for a specific loss according to contract provisions, 622

**Interest:** an amount paid or earned for the use of money, 382

**Interest period:** the amount of time after which interest is calculated and added to the principal, 454

Interpret financial ratios, 701

**Inventory:** merchandise available for sale or goods available for the production of products, 584
comparing methods for determining, 584
first-in, first-out (FIFO) method, 588
gross profit inventory method, 592

last-in, first-out (LIFO) method, 589
retail inventory method, 591
specific identification method, 585
turnover and overhead, 586, 587
weighted-average method, 586

**Inventory turnover:** the frequency with which the inventory is sold and replaced, 598

**Inventory turnover ratio:** another term for the inventory turnover rate, 598

**Isolate:** perform systematic operations to both sides of the equation so that the unknown or variable is alone on one side of the equation. Its value is identified on the other side of the equation, 146

**Issuer:** a company, state, or municipality that issues bonds to raise money, 734

**Itemized deductions:** a listing of deductions that can be used by certain taxpayers to reduce taxable income. Normally, taxpayers use itemized deductions when the total of their itemized deductions is greater than the standard deduction, 659

**Junk bonds:** high-risk bonds that are usually from companies in bankruptcy or in financial difficulty, 734

**Known amount (given amount):** the known amounts or numbers in an equation, 146

Knuckle method, 269

**Land:** value of the grounds or land owned by the business, 682

**Lapse:** the loss of insurance coverage due to nonpayment of premiums, 624

**Leading earnings:** a company's projected earnings-per-share for the upcoming 12-month period, 731

**Leading P/E ratio:** a company's P/E ratio calculated using the company's leading earnings per share as the net income per share, 731

**Least common denominator (LCD):** the smallest number that can be divided evenly by each original denominator, 43

**Leverage ratio:** a financial ratio that examines a business's indebtedness, 703

**Liabilities:** amounts that the business owes, 682

**Liability insurance:** protection for the owner of a vehicle if an accident causes personal injury or damage to someone else's property and is the fault of the driver of the insured vehicle, 631

**Life insurance:** an insurance policy that pays a specified amount to the beneficiary of the policy upon the death of the insured, 622

**LIFO (last-in, first-out) inventory method:** an inventory valuation method in which items sold are assumed to be from the newest items in inventory and the oldest goods are those remaining in the ending inventory, 589

**Line graph:** line segments that connect points on a graph to show the rising and falling trends of a data set, 227

**Line-of-credit accounts:** a type of open-end loan, 433

**Liquidation or payout phase of an annuity:** the time when the annuitant or beneficiary is receiving money from the fund, 488

**Liquidity ratio:** a financial that shows how well a business can be expected to meet its short-term financial obligations, 701

**List price:** suggested price at which merchandise is sold to consumers, 260

**Loan-to-value ratio :** the amount mortgaged divided by the appraised value of the property, 532

**Long-term liabilities:** liabilities that are paid over a long period of time, 682

**Lowest terms:** the form of a fraction when its numerator and denominator cannot be evenly divided by any whole number except 1, 39

**Maker:** the one who is authorizing the payment of the check; the person or business that borrows the money, 104, 396

**Margin:** markup or gross profit, 296

**Markdown:** amount the original selling price is reduced, 296, 316

**Marked price:** the purchase price before sales tax is added, 651

**Market value:** the expected selling price of a property, 524, 654

**Markup (gross profit or gross margin):** the difference between the selling price and the cost, 296

 comparing markup based on cost with markup based on selling price, 311

 finding final selling price for a series of markups, 318

 finding the selling price to achieve a desired profit, 320

 using cost as a base in markup applications, 296

 using selling price as a base in markup applications, 305

**Mathematical operations:** calculations with numbers. The four operations that are often called basic operations are addition, subtraction, multiplication, and division, 4

**Maturity date:** the date on which the loan is due to be repaid. 396; the date at which the face value of a bond is paid to the bondholder, 734

**Maturity value:** the total amount of money due at the end of a loan period—the amount of the loan and the interest, 383

**Mean:** the arithmetic average of a set of data or the sum of the values divided by the number of values, 214

**Measures of central tendency:** statistical measurements such as the mean, median, or mode that indicate how data group toward the center, 233

**Measures of variation or dispersion:** statistical measurements such as the range and standard deviation that indicate how data are dispersed or spread, 233

**Median:** the middle value of a data set when the values are arranged in order of size, 215

**Medicare tax:** a federal tax used to provide health-care benefits to retired and disabled workers, 354

**Merchandise inventory:** a current asset that is the value of merchandise on hand, 682

**Mill:** one-thousandth of a dollar, 654

**Minuend:** the beginning amount or the number that a second number is subtracted from, 12

**Mixed number:** an amount that is a combination of a whole number and a fraction, 37–39

 adding, 44

 multiplying and dividing, 50, 52–53

 subtracting, 46

**Mixed percents:** percents with mixed numbers, 182

**Mode:** the value or values that occur most frequently in a data set, 216

**Modified accelerated cost-recovery system (MACRS):** a modified depreciation method implemented by the IRS for property placed in service after 1986, 562

**Monthly:** once a month or 12 times a year, 342

**Monthly mortgage payment:** the amount of the equal monthly payment that includes interest and principal, 524

**Mortgage:** a loan in which real property is used to secure the debt, 524

 amortization schedule, 530–531

 monthly mortgage payment and total interest, 524

 *See also* individual types

**Mortgage closing costs:** fees charged for services that must be performed to process and close a home mortgage loan, 527

**Mortgage payable:** a long-term liability for the building and land the business owns, 682

**Motor vehicle insurance:** liability, comprehensive, and collision insurance for a motor vehicle, 631

**Multiple carriers:** two or more insurance companies that provide fire coverage on the same property at the same time. Each insurance company is responsible for paying its portion of a loss based on the total dollar amount of insurance coverage on the property, 629

**Multiplicand:** the number being multiplied, 13

**Multiplier:** the number multiplied by, 13

**Municipal bonds:** bonds issued by local and state governments, 734

**Mutual fund or investment trust:** a collection of stocks, bonds, and other securities that is managed by a mutual fund company, 738

**Net amount:** the amount you owe if a cash discount is applied, 271

**Net asset value:** the value of one share of a mutual fund, 738

**Net decimal equivalent:** the decimal equivalent of the net price rate for a series of trade discounts, 264

**Net earnings (net pay or take-home pay):** the amount of your paycheck, 342

**Net income or net profit:** gross profit or gross margin minus the operating expenses, 693

**Net pay:** *See* Net earnings, 342

**Net price:** the price the wholesaler or retailer pays, or the list price minus the trade discount, 260

 calculating using ordinary dating terms, 269

 calculating using receipt-of-goods terms, 273

 freight terms and, 275–276

 net decimal equivalent and, 264

 single discount equivalent and, 266

 trade discount series and, 264

**Net price rate:** the complement of the trade discount rate, 262

**Net profit:** difference between markup (gross profit or gross margin) and operating expenses and overhead, 296, 693

**Net sales:** total sales minus sales returns or allowances, 693

**Net worth:** *See* Owner's equity, 683

**New amount:** the ending amount after an amount has changed (increased or decreased), 192

**No-fault insurance:** protection for the owner of a vehicle for damage to the insured vehicle when the amount of damage is within the no-fault limits imposed by state law, 631

**No load mutual fund:** a mutual fund that does not charge a sales charge for buying and selling its shares, 738

**Nonforfeiture options:** the options that are available to a policyholder when payments are discontinued, 624

**Nonsufficient funds (NSF) fee:** a fee charged to the account holder when a check is written for which there are not sufficient funds, 114

**Nonterminating or repeating decimal:** a quotient that never comes out evenly. The digits will eventually start to repeat, 86

**Normal distribution:** a characteristic of many data sets that shows that data graphs into a bell-shaped curve around the mean, 236

**Note payable:** promissory notes that are owed, 682

**Notes receivable:** a current asset that is a promissory note owed to the business, 682

**Numerator:** the number of a fraction that shows how many parts are considered. It is also the dividend of the indicated division, 36

**Office furniture and equipment:** value of office furniture and equipment such as computers, printers, and copiers owned by the business, 682

**Office supplies:** supplies such as stationery, pens, file folders, and diskettes, 682

**Online banking services:** a variety of services and transaction options that can be made through Internet banking, 105

**Open-end credit:** a type of installment loan in which there is no fixed amount borrowed or fixed number of payments. Payments are made until the loan is paid off, 422

 average daily balance method, 433

**Operating expenses:** overhead or cost incurred in operating a business, 693

**Operating ratio:** the cost of goods sold plus the operating expenses divided by net sales, 702

**Opposites:** a positive and negative number that represent the same distance from 0 but in opposite directions, 235

**Order of Operations:** the specific order in which calculations must be performed to evaluate a series of calculations, 149

**Ordinary annuity:** an annuity for which payments are made at the end of each period, 488

Ordinary annuity future value table, 490

**Ordinary interest rate:** a rate per day that assumes 360 days per year, 392

**Ordinary life insurance:** *See* Straight-life insurance, 622

**Outstanding balance:** the invoice amount minus the amount credited, 274

**Outstanding checks:** checks that have been written and given to the payee but have not been processed at the bank, 114

**Outstanding deposits:** deposits that have been made but have not yet been posted to the maker's account, 114

**Overhead:** depreciation and expenses required for the operation of a business, such as salaries, rent or mortgages, utilities, office supplies, taxes, insurance, and maintenance of equipment, 600
based on floor space, 602
based on sales, 600

**Overtime pay:** earnings based on overtime rate of pay, 343

**Overtime rate:** rate of pay for hours worked that are more than 40 hours in a week, 343

**Owner's equity or stockholder's equity:** the difference between the company's assets and the liabilities, 683

**Paid-up insurance:** insurance that continues after premiums are no longer paid, 624

**Par value:** *See* Face value, 622

**Partial cash discount:** a cash discount applied only to the amount of the partial payment, 274

**Partial dividend:** the part of the dividend that is being considered at a given step of the process, 15

**Partial payment:** a payment that does not equal the full amount of the invoice less any cash discount, 274

**Partial product:** the product of one digit of the multiplier and the entire multiplicand, 13

**Partial quotient:** the quotient of the partial dividend and the divisor, 15

**Participating preferred stock:** a type of preferred stock that allows stockholders to receive additional dividends if the company decides to do so, 732

**Payee:** the one to whom the amount of money written on a check is paid; the person or business loaning the money, 104, 396

**Payor:** the bank or institution that pays the amount of the check to the payee, 104

Payroll:
employer's payroll taxes, 358
gross pay, 342

**Percent:** a standardized way of expressing quantities in relation to a standard unit of 100 (hundredth, per 100, out of 100, over 100), 182
mixed, 182
using the percentage formula, 187–188
writing as a number, 184
writing numbers as, 182

**Percent of change:** the percent by which a beginning amount has changed (increased or decreased), 193

**Percentage:** a part or portion of the base, 186

Percentage formula, 187–188

**Percentage method income:** the result of subtracting the appropriate withholding allowances when using the percentage method of withholding, 352

**Percentage method of withholding:** an alternative method to the tax tables for calculating employees' withholding taxes, 352

**Period:** a group of three place values in the decimal-number system, 4

**Period interest rate:** the rate for calculating interest for one interest period—the annual interest rate divided by the number of interest periods per year, 454

**Periodic or physical inventory:** a physical count of goods or merchandise made at a specific time, 584

**Perishable:** an item for sale that has a relatively short time during which the quality of the item is acceptable for sale, 316

**Perpetual inventory:** an inventory process that adjusts the inventory count after each sale or purchase of goods, 584

**Personal identification number (PIN):** a private code that is used to authorize a transaction on a debit card or ATM card, 105

**Piecework rate:** amount of pay for each acceptable item produced, 344

**PITI:** the adjusted monthly payment that includes the principal, interest, taxes, and insurance, 527

**Place-value system:** a number system in which a digit has a value according to its place, or position, in a number, 4

**Plant and equipment:** assets used in transacting business, 682

**Point-of-sale transaction:** electronic transfer of funds when a sale is made, 104

**Points:** a one-time payment to the lender made at closing that is a percentage of the total loan, 527

**Policy:** the contract between the insurer and the insured, 622

**Policyholder:** *See* Insured, 622

Policy premium, 622

**Portfolio:** a variety of types of investments, 738

**Portion:** another term for percentage, 186

**Preferred stock:** a type of stock that guarantees a specific dividend to the stockholder. The preferred stockholder does not have voting rights (*compare with* common stock), 728

**Premium:** the amount paid by the insured for the protection provided by the policy, 622

**Premium bond:** a bond that sells for more than the face value, 735

**Prepay and add:** the seller pays the shipping when the merchandise is shipped, but the shipping costs are added to the invoice for the buyer to pay, 276

**Present value:** the amount that must be invested now and compounded at a specified rate and time to reach a specified future value, 467
based on annual compounding for one year, 467
based on future value using a $1.00 present value table, 469

**Present value of an annuity:** the amount needed in a fund so that the fund can pay out a specified regular payment for a specified amount of time, 502

**Price-earnings (P/E) ratio:** the ratio of the closing price of a share of stock to the annual earnings per share, 731

**Prime interest rate (prime):** the lowest rate of interest charged by banks for short-term loans to their most creditworthy customers, 383

**Prime number:** a number greater than 1 that can be divided evenly only by itself and 1, 43

**Principal:** the amount of money borrowed or invested, 382

**Privately held corporation:** a company that is privately owned and does not meet the strict Security Exchange Commission filing required of publicly held corporations. Private corporations may issue stock and the owners are shareholders, 728

Problem solving:
using equations, 146
with decimals, 74
with fractions, 36
with percents, 182
with whole numbers, 4

**Product:** the answer or result of multiplication, 13

**Profitability ratio:** a ratio comparing profits and sales, 702

**Promissory note:** a legal document promising to repay a loan, 396
simple discount notes, 396
third-party discount notes, 398

**Proper fraction:** a fraction with a value that is less than 1. The numerator is smaller than the denominator, 36

**Property damage:** damage to the property of others in an accident, 632

**Property tax:** tax collected by county, municipality, or local governments from property owners. The tax is based on the type of property and the value of the property, 654

**Property tax rate:** the rate of tax that is paid for owning property, 654

**Proportion:** two fractions or ratios that are equal, 152

**Proprietorship:** *See* Owner's equity, 683

**Protractor:** a measuring device that measures angles, 229

**Publicly held corporation:** a company that has issued and sells shares of stock or securities through an initial public offering. These shares are traded through at least one stock exchange, 728

**Publicly traded:** a company's stock is said to be publicly traded if the company has issued securities through an initial public offering and these securities are traded on at least one stock exchange or over-the-counter market, 728

**Quick current assets:** assets that can be readily exchanged for cash, such as marketable securities, accounts receivable, or notes receivable, 702

**Quick ratio:** *See* Acid-test ratio, 702

**Quota:** a minimum amount of sales that is required before a commission is applicable, 345

**Quotient:** the answer or result of division, 15

**Range:** the difference between the highest and lowest values in a data set, 233

**Rate:** how the base and percentage are related expressed as a percent; the percent of the principal paid as interest per time period, 186, 382

**Ratio:** the comparison of two numbers through division. Ratios are most often written as fractions, 152

**Ratios to net sales:** ratios that make comparisons to net sales, 702

**Real estate or real property:** land plus any permanent improvements to the land, 524

**Recallable bonds:** bonds that can be repurchased by the company before the maturity date, 734

**Receipt-of-goods (ROG) terms:** a discount applied if the bill is paid within the specified days of the receipt of the goods, 273

**Reciprocals:** two numbers are reciprocals if their product is 1. 4/5 and 5/4 are reciprocals, 53

**Recovery period:** the length of time over which an item may be depreciated, 562

**Refund fraction:** the fractional part of the total interest that is refunded when a loan is paid early using the rule of 78, 430

**Registered bonds:** bonds for which investors receive interest automatically by being listed with the company, 734

**Regular pay:** earnings based on an hourly rate of pay, 343

**Relative frequency distribution:** the percent that each class interval of a frequency distribution relates to the whole, 219

**Remainder of quotient:** a number that is smaller than the divisor that remains after the division is complete, 15

**Repeating decimal:** *See* Nonterminating decimal, 86

**Restricted endorsement:** a type of endorsement that reassigns the check to a different payee or directs the check to be deposited to a specified account, 109

**Retail inventory method:** a method for estimating the value of inventory that is based on the cost ratio of the cost of goods available for sale and the retail value of goods available for sale, 591

**Returned check:** a deposited check that was returned because the maker's account did not have sufficient funds, 114

**Returned check fee:** a fee the bank charges the depositor for returned checks, 114

**Round, rounding, rounded:** a procedure to find an estimated or approximate answer, 7

**Rule of 78:** method for determining the amount of refund of the finance charge for an installment loan that is paid before it is due, 430

**Salary:** an agreed-upon amount of pay that is not based on the number of hours worked, 342

**Salary-plus-commission:** a set amount of pay plus an additional amount based on sales, 345

**Sales returns or allowances:** refunds or adjustments for unsatisfactory merchandise or services, 693

**Sales tax:** a tax that is based on the price of a purchase. The tax is collected at the time of purchase and the business periodically sends the collected tax to a governmental agency, 650

**Salvage value or scrap value or residual value:** an estimated dollar value of an asset at the end of the asset's estimated useful life, 550

**Scrap value:** *See* Salvage value, 550

**Second mortgage:** a mortgage in addition to the first mortgage that is secured by the real property, 524

**Section 179:** a tax deduction that can be taken on certain business property in the same tax year the property is purchased, 565

**Sector:** portion or wedge of a circle identified by two lines from the center to the outer edge of the circle, 229

**Self-employment (SE) tax:** the equivalent of both the employee's and the employer's tax for both Social Security and Medicare. It is two times the employee's rate, 355

**Selling price (retail price):** price at which a business sells merchandise, 296

**Semimonthly:** twice a month or 24 times a year, 342

**Service charge:** a fee the bank charges for maintaining the checking account or for other banking services, 114

**Share:** one unit of ownership of a corporation, 728

**Short-ratio premium:** the premium for a short-term policy, 627

**Short-term policy:** an insurance policy for less than one year, 627

**Signature card:** a document that a bank keeps on file to verify the signatures of persons authorized to write checks on an account, 105

**Signed numbers:** a combination of positive and negative numbers, 235

**Simple discount note:** a loan made by a bank at a simple interest with interest collected at the time the loan is made, 396

**Simple interest:** interest when a loan or investment is repaid in a lump sum, 382
finding the principal, rate, or time using the simple interest formula, 386
formula, 382
fractional parts of a year, 384
maturity value of a loan, 383
tables, 390

**Single discount equivalent:** the complement of the net decimal equivalent. It is the decimal equivalent of a single discount rate that is equal to the series of discount rates, 266

**Single discount rate:** a term used to indicate that only one discount rate is applied to the list price, 260
complements of, 261
finding the net price using, 261
finding the trade discount using, 260

**Sinking fund:** payment into an ordinary annuity to yield a desired future value, 500
payments, 501
present value of an ordinary annuity, 502

**Social Security tax:** a federal tax that goes into a fund that pays monthly benefits to retired and disabled workers, 354
calculating employee's contribution to, 342
employer's contribution to, 358–359

**Solve:** find the value of the unknown or variable that makes the equation true, 146

**Specific identification inventory method:** an inventory valuation method that is based on the actual cost of each item available for sale, 585

**Spread:** the variation or dispersion of a set of data, 233

**Standard bar graph:** bar graph with just one variable, 225

**Standard deduction:** a specified reduction of taxable income. The standard deduction amount is based on filing status and is adjusted yearly for inflation. Normally, taxpayers who do not use the standard deduction have eligible itemized deductions that exceed the standard deduction, 659

**Standard deviation:** a statistical measurement that shows how data are spread above and below the mean. The square root of the variance is the standard deviation, 235

**State unemployment (SUTA) tax:** a state tax required of most employers. The tax also provides payment of unemployment compensation to workers who have lost their jobs, 360

**Statistic:** a standardized, meaningful measure of a set of data that reveals a certain feature or characteristic of the data, 214
mean, 214
median, 215
mode, 216
range, 233
standard deviation, 235
variance, 235

**Stock:** the distribution of ownership of a corporation. Partial ownership can be purchased through various stock markets, 728
dividends, 728
price to earnings (P/E) ratio, 731
reading listings, 728

**Stock certificate:** a certificate of ownership of stock issued to the buyer, 728

**Stock listings:** Information about the price of a share of stock and some historical information that is published in newspapers and on the Internet, 728

**Stock market:** the structure for buying and selling stock, 728

**Stockbroker:** the person who handles the trading of stock. A stockbroker receives a commission for these services, 728

**Straight commission:** entire pay based on sales, 345

**Straight-life (ordinary life) insurance:** the insured pays premiums for his or her entire life. At the death of the insured, the beneficiary receives the face value of the policy. If the policy is cancelled, the insured is paid the cash value of the policy, 622

**Straight-line depreciation:** a method of depreciation in which the amount of depreciation of an asset is spread equally over the number of years of useful life of the asset, 550

**Straight-line rate:** when used with the declining-balance method of depreciation, the straight-line rate is a fraction with a numerator of 1 and a denominator equal to the number of useful years of an asset. This fraction is usually expressed as a decimal equivalent when making calculations and a percent equivalent when identifying the rate of depreciation, 557

**Straight piecework rate:** piecework rate where the pay is the same per item no matter how many items are produced, 344

**Subtrahend:** the number being subtracted, 12

**Suggested retail price, catalog price, list price:** three common terms for the price at which the manufacturer suggests an item should be sold to the consumer, 260

**Sum or total:** the answer or result of addition, 9

**Sum-of-the-years'-digits depreciation:** a depreciation method that allows the greatest depreciation the first year and a decreasing amount each year thereafter, 554

**Symmetrical:** a figure that if folded at a middle point, the two halves will match, 236

**Take-home pay:** *See* Net earnings (net pay), 342

**Tally:** a mark that is used to count data in class intervals, 218

**Tax:** money collected by a government for its support and for providing services to the populace, 650
income, 659–660
property tax, 654
sales tax, 650

**Tax credit:** an amount that is subtracted from the tax owed, in contrast to a deduction, which is subtracted from the gross income, 665

**Tax-filing status:** status based on whether the employee is married, single, or a head of household that determines the tax rate, 347, 660

**Tax owed:** the amount of income tax a taxpayer must pay when filing an income tax return. It is the difference in the total amount of tax that should be paid and the amount of tax already paid, 665

**Tax rate schedules:** directions for calculating the tax on taxable incomes of $100,000 or more, 664

**Tax Reform Act of 1986:** changed the tax rate; income is taxed at different rates depending on how much income falls into each of various income brackets, 664

**Tax refund:** the amount of income tax a taxpayer gets back when filing an income tax return. It is the difference in the amount of tax owed for a tax year and the amount of tax the taxpayer has paid during the year, 665

**Taxable income:** adjusted gross income minus exemptions and either the standard or the itemized deductions, 659

**Term:** the length of time for which the money is borrowed, 396

**Term insurance:** insurance purchased for a certain period of time. At the end of the time period, the policy has no cash value and the insurance ends, 622

**Terminating decimal:** a quotient that has no remainder, 86

**Territory:** the primary location where the vehicle is driven, 632

**Third party:** an investment group or individual that assumes a note that was made between two other parties, 398

**Third-party discount note:** a note that is sold to a third party (usually a bank) so that the original payee gets the proceeds immediately and the maker pays the third party the original amount at maturity, 398

**Time:** the number of days, months, or years that money is borrowed or invested, 382

**Time and a half:** standard overtime rate that is 1½ (or 1.5) times the hourly rate, 343

**Total:** *See* Sum, 9

**Total assessed value:** the total of all assessed values of property in a municipality or tax jurisdiction, 656

Total assets, 683

**Total cost:** the cost of an asset including shipping and installation charges, 550

**Total debt to total assets ratio:** the ratio of the total liabilities to the total assets, 703

**Total (or installment) price:** the total amount that must be paid when the purchase is paid for over a given period of time, 422

**Total price:** the marked price plus the sales tax, 651

**Total sales:** earnings from the sale of goods or the performance of services, 693

**Totaled:** when damages to a vehicle exceed the book value the insurance covers the damages up to the book value, 633

**Trade:** either the buying or the selling of a stock, 728

**Trade discount:** the amount of discount that the wholesaler or retailer receives off the list price, or the difference between the list price and the net price, 260

**Trade discount series (chain discount):** more than one discount deducted one after another from the list price, 264

**Trailing earnings:** a company's earnings-per-share for the past 12 months; found by dividing the company's after-tax profit by the number of outstanding shares, 731

**Trailing P/E ratio:** a company's P/E ratio calculated using the company's trailing earnings per share as the net income per share, 731

**Transaction:** a banking activity that changes the amount of money in a bank account, 102

**Treasury bonds:** bonds issued by the federal government, 734

**Trend analysis:** an analysis of business trends over an extended period of time, 705

Turnover. *See* Inventory turnover, 598

**Underwriter:** *See* Insurer, 622

**Undiscounted note:** another term for a simple interest note, 397

Unemployment taxes, 360

**Uninsured motorist coverage:** protection for the owner of a vehicle when damages are incurred in an accident that is not the owner's fault but the other driver has no insurance. This coverage only applies to the owner's vehicle, 631

**Unit depreciation:** the amount the asset depreciates with each unit produced or mile driven, 552

**Units-of-production depreciation:** a method of depreciation that is based on the expected number of units produced by an asset, 552

**Universal life insurance:** a policy with a flexible premium rate and death benefits, 624

**Unknown (variable):** the missing amount or amounts that are represented as letters in an equation, 146

**Updated check register balance:** consists of the checkbook balance minus any fees and minus any returned items, 107

**U.S. rule:** any partial loan payment first covers any interest that has accumulated. The remainder of the partial payment reduces the loan principal, 394

**Useful life:** *See* Estimated life, 550

**Variance:** a statistical measurement that is the average of the squared deviations of data from the mean, 235

**Vertical analysis of balance sheet:** the ratio of each item on the balance sheet to the total assets, 685

**Vertical analysis of an income statement:** comparison of each entry in an income statement to net sales, 695

**Veterans Administration (VA):** a governmental agency that guarantees the repayment of a loan made to an eligible veteran. The loans are also called GI loans, 524

**W-2 form:** a form an employer must provide each employee that shows the earned income, income tax withheld, and Social Security and Medicare taxes withheld, 660

**W-4 form:** form required to be held by the employer for determining the amount of federal tax to be withheld, 348

**Wages:** earnings based on an hourly rate of pay and the number of hours worked, 342

**Wages payable:** salaries a business owes its employees, 682

**Weekly:** once a week or 52 times a year, 342

**Weighted-average inventory method:** an inventory valuation method that is based on the average unit cost of the goods available for sale, 586

**Whole number:** a number from the set of numbers including zero and the counting or natural numbers (0, 1, 2, 3, 4, . . .), 4

**Whole-number part:** the digits to the left of the decimal point, 74

Whole numbers:
adding, 9
dividing, 15
multiplying, 13–14
reading and writing, 4, 6
rounding, 7
subtracting, 12

**Withdrawal:** a transaction that decreases an account balance; this transaction is also called a debit, 104

**Withholding allowance (exemption):** a portion of gross earnings that is not subject to tax, 347

**Working capital:** current assets minus current liabilities, 701

**Working capital ratio:** *See* Current ratio, 701

**Year's depreciation rate:** the depreciation rate for any given year of a depreciation schedule, 554

**Yield:** a measure of the profitability of the investment, 737